The Mahābhārata

Book 2 *The Book of the Assembly Hall*

Book 3 *The Book of the Forest*

Th

The University of Chicago Press *Chicago and London*

Mahābhārata

Translated and
Edited by
J. A. B. van Buitenen

2 *The Book of the Assembly Hall*

3 *The Book of the Forest*

The University of Chicago Press, Chicago 60637
The University of Chicago Press, Ltd., London

Phoenix edition 1981
Printed in the United States of America

09 08 07 06 05 04 03 02 01 00 6 7 8 9 10

Library of Congress Cataloging in Publication Data

Mahābhārata. English.
The Mahābhārata.
Includes bibliographical references.
CONTENTS: v. 1. The book of the beginning. v. 2. The book of the assembly hall. The book of the forest.
I. Buitenen, Johannes Adrianus Bernardus van, tr.
PK3633.A2B8 294.5′923 72–97802

ISBN 0–226–84648–2 (v.1, cloth); 0–226–84663–6 (v.1, paper)
0–226–84649–0 (v.2, cloth); 0–226–84664–4 (v.2, paper)

The relief sculpture on the title page, dating from the second half of the fifth century A.D., depicts Nara and Nārāyana in Visnu temple, Deogarh, U.P., Indiana, courtesy Pramod Chandra.

∞ The paper used in this publication meets the minimum requirements of the American National Standard for Information Sciences— Permanence of Paper for Printed Library Materials, ANSI Z39.48-1992.

For Nina

Contents

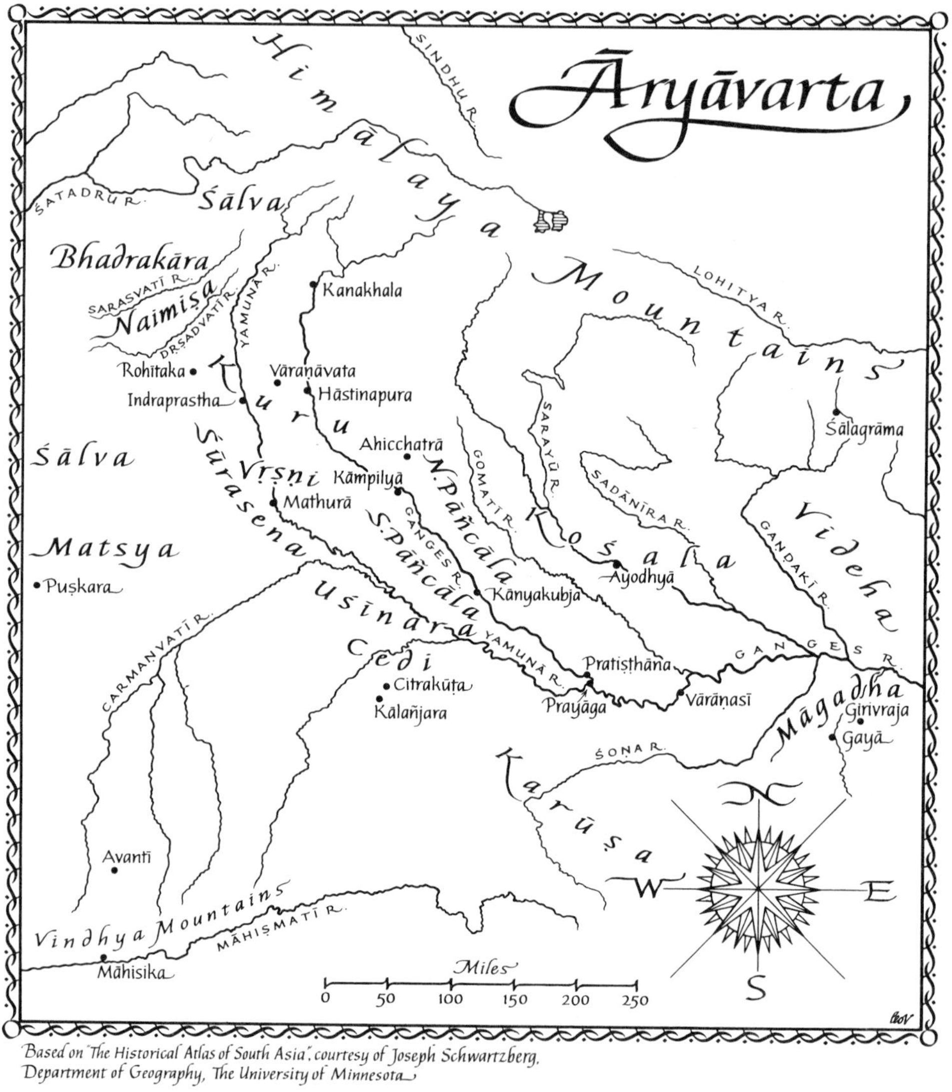

Based on "The Historical Atlas of South Asia", courtesy of Joseph Schwartzberg,
Department of Geography, The University of Minnesota

Preface

Since Book 2, *The Book of the Assembly Hall*, is considerably shorter than Book 1, *The Book of the Beginning*, it was decided to include in the second volume of my translation of *The Mahābhārata* not only Book 2 but Book 3, *The Book of the Forest*, in its entirety, even though this may seem to overbalance Volume I. It seemed wiser to do this than to divide Book 3 into two volumes. Although included in a single volume, the two Major Books, *The Book of the Assembly Hall* (*sabhāparvan*) and *The Book of the Forest* (*āraṇyakaparvan*), are treated as separate entities, each with its own Introduction. The annotations for both Major Books appear at the end of the volume, together with a consolidated index.

Most of the additional apparatus of Volume I is not repeated in Volume II. The reader is referred to Volume I for a general introduction to *The Mahābhārata* as a whole, including a summary, as well as a genealogical chart, a note on the spelling and pronunciation of Sanskrit, a list of names of important persons, and a concordance of the Critical Edition and the Bombay Edition. But it was considered useful to repeat the map (somewhat enlarged) and that much of the concordance that pertains to Major Books 2 and 3.

When this volume appears, it is hoped that the manuscript of Volume III will be ready for the press. Volume III will comprise Major Books 4 and 5, *The Book of Virāṭa* (*virāṭaparvan*) and *The Book of the Effort* (*udyogaparvan*), with which well over a third of the entire translation will have been completed.

This volume, and the enterprise as a whole, has been fortunate to find a patron in Haven O'More, director of The Institute for Traditional

Science, Cambridge, Massachusetts, who generously provided a substantial subsidy toward the publishing costs of this volume.

Once again I take pleasure in thanking Professor George V. Bobrinskoy for spending many hours with me in comparing my translation of *The Mahābhārata* with the Russian translation to which I allude in the introduction to Volume I. And it is a privilege to record here my thanks to my students. In the give and take of several seminars to which the publication of *The Book of the Beginning* gave rise, they afforded me many insights I would not have gained by myself.

A Correction

In my introduction to the first volume of *The Mahābhārata*, when reviewing English translations past and present, I had occasion to comment on the lack of apparatus to be found in the so-called Roy translation (Calcutta, 1883–96) and remarked that one looks in vain even for a table of contents. This criticism should have been applied to the *reprint* of the original translation that appeared in 1952–62. Since then it has been pointed out to me that the original, to which I now have access, does have a table of contents of sorts—each Major Book is normally preceded by a list in which a one-line description is given of each *adhyāya*. I often consult the "Roy" translation, and mean no slight to my predecessors. I should also like to amplify my observation that the translation appeared as if by P. C. Roy but was in fact executed by K. S. Ganguli. Ganguli himself adds an enlightening "Translator's Post-Script" at the end of the translation (p. 2). He writes:

> Before, however, the first fascicules could be issued, the question as to whether the authorship of the translation should be publicly owned, arose. Babu Pratapa Chandra Roy was against anonymity. I was for it. The reasons I adduced were chiefly founded upon the impossibility of one person translating the whole of the gigantic work. . . . I might not live to carry it out. . . . It could not be desirable to issue successive fascicules with the names of a succession of translators appearing on the title pages. These and other considerations convinced my friend that, after all, my view was correct. It was accordingly resolved to withhold the name of the translator.

Roy then acted as the publisher and general fund raiser for the enterprise, reaping no personal benefit from it, in fact incurring a considerable debt in furthering the translation and publication of the work, which was mostly distributed gratis.

Ganguli continues (p. 3):

> The entire translation is practically the work of one hand. In portions of the Ādi and Sabhā Parvas I was assisted by Professor Krishna Kamal Bhattacharya and about half a fasciculus, during my illness, was done by another hand.

It is clear that not only Kesari Mohan Ganguli but Pratapa Chandra Roy deserve our homage.

8 July 1974 J. A. B. van B.

The Mahābhārata

Translated

Book 2 *The Book of the Assembly Hall*

Introduction

The Place of the Book in the Main Epic

The Book of the Assembly Hall is the pivotal one of the eighteen Major Books of *The Mahābhārata*; it is also one of the more diversified and interesting ones.*

For all its length and variety, *The Book of the Beginning* has not done more than lay the groundwork of the epic as we now have it. We left it as a more or less closed whole: the ancestry of the protagonists and antagonists; their youth, early strife, and clouded claims on the succession; the attempts at assassination, and the safe deliverance of the Pāṇḍavas; their self-exile and glorious reappearance at Draupadī's Bridegroom Choice; their consequent marriage, alliance with Pāñcāla, and recognition by the senior Kauravas; and finally the acquisition of the kingdom of Indraprastha by the partition of the Field of the Kurus. Peace was restored in the end between the two branches of siblings through the wise guidance of their elders. One might well close *The Beginning* and never expect a sequel to it.

But *The Assembly Hall* makes all that went before just a beginning. Those were the pages of childhood and adolescence, in which the influence of the elders was strong and decisive. Now the heroes are on their own and begin to act in their own right; and their natures are willful. *The Assembly Hall* begins with establishing Yudhiṣṭhira and his brothers as prosperous princelings at Indraprastha. But this is not much: so far the Pāṇḍavas have simply acquired a new home base. Now, at the suggestion of a visiting messenger of the Gods—though

*This Introduction abbreviates and expands matter set forth in J. A. B. van Buitenen, "On the Structure of the Sabhāparvan of the Mahābhārata," in *India Maior* (Festschrift Gonda), Leyden, 1972, pp. 68–84.

not sent by the Gods—the seer Nārada, Yudhiṣṭhira conceives the desire to perform the ancient Vedic ritual of the *rājasūya*, the Royal Consecration. This, at first glance, appears as no more than the legitimization of his new, and so to say supernumerary, kingship by means of the old rite. It transpires, however, that there is much more to it than that; for through it Yudhiṣṭhira wishes to aspire to nothing less than universal sovereignty by becoming *samrāj*, an "all-king" or "emperor," to whom all other princes of the land will be submissive.

It is not at all clear on what personal accomplishments Yudhiṣṭhira could pretend to rest such a claim. After all, he has allowed himself to be ousted from the ancestral seat of Hāstinapura in return for a parcel of wilderness that still had to be cleared. True, he has won the alliance of Pāñcāla, but merely by marriage. The end of *The Beginning* has left us with the mild satisfaction that some attractive noble youths, after some bad luck and some good, in the end did not fare so ill. But imperial ambitions all of a sudden? Still, perhaps his ambition stood in need of no justification; for he is to embark on a grand Vedic ceremony, the *rājasūya*, and to qualify for it the performer's intention may suffice.

Once his desire has taken hold, Yudhiṣṭhira calls in Kṛṣṇa of the Vṛṣṇis for counsel. He had already pointed out the obvious: the performance requires the "unanimity of the baronage"[1] to be tributary to him. For the *rājasūya*,[2] as it is presented in this book is not just the installation of a new king, it is the glorification of a king of kings. There can only be one such suzerain at the time. So it requires not only the assent of the baronage, but also the removal of the present suzerain. The one *en titre* is Jarāsaṃdha, the king of the more eastern land of Magadha, a populous and prosperous realm. So Jarāsaṃdha is indeed removed, and the rest of the world, not excluding Rome and Antioch[3] and the "city of the Greeks," is made tributary. After the assassination of Jarāsaṃdha the performance takes place, but it is not concluded without resistance. While Yudhiṣṭhira's preeminence is never disputed, the high ranking of Kṛṣṇa is. The challenger, Śiśupāla, is eliminated by Kṛṣṇa, and Yudhiṣṭhira is suzerain indeed; but for a brief while. The title is wrested from him by the Hāstinapura Kauravas in a game at dice, when Yudhiṣṭhira loses on pain of an exile of thirteen years.

Most of the proceedings of this book take place in an assembly hall, a kind of longhouse for the men in which to hold council and

1. *Kṣatrasaṃpad:* 2.12.13.

2. On the Vedic *rājasūya* see J. C. Heesterman, *The Ancient Indian Royal Consecration* (Thesis Utrecht), The Hague, 1957.

3. See Franklin Edgerton, "Rome and (?) Antioch in the *Mahābhārata*" (J.A.O.S. 38: 262 ff.).

entertainment, and it is from such a hall that the book takes its title. There are two halls involved, the one at Indraprastha and that at Hāstinapura. It is the Indraprastha hall that becomes a bone of contention; it is in the Hāstinapura hall where it all ends.

The hall at Indraprastha was newly built by an Asura, Maya by name, who had been saved from the fire of the Khāṇḍava Forest,[4] which concluded *The Book of the Beginning*. So magnificent was that hall that it excited the envy of Kaurava's cousin Duryodhana, and this envy led to the game at dice on whose outcome the rest of *The Mahābhārata* hangs. When Yudhiṣṭhira has reached the pinnacle of temporal power as the acknowledged suzerain of all the world, he is challenged to the game. Why he felt he had to accept the challenge will be discussed later; here it suffices to note that there is a conspicuous thread in the book: the settlement at Indraprastha needs a hall—the hall needs validation as a royal court through the Royal Consecration—it evokes the others' envy—and brings about a game in another hall where Yudhiṣṭhira loses all.

Clearly therefore the structure of *The Assembly Hall* is much tighter than that of *The Beginning*, where the insertions and additions are quite obvious. The *Hall* too has its fuzzy edges: Nārada's long instruction in policy and administration is a clear instance. But otherwise the book hangs together remarkably well.

May we raise the question whether this structure is inherent or derivative? I think we may. *The Book of the Beginning* was so leisurely told, with so many digressions (until the very end when we are regaled with the story of the Śārngaka birds), that we are entitled to wonder why nothing is allowed to interfere with the orderly progression of *The Assembly Hall*.

The most fascinating, but puzzling, feature of the book is the question it inevitably raises: Why, when everything has been achieved, must it now be gambled away by the hero, in all of whose previous life there has not been so much as a hint of a compulsion to gamble, all of whose life has in fact been of exemplary rectitude and prudence? It is this disturbing contradiction in the character of Yudhiṣṭhira that demands the question whether this was indeed a contradiction, or whether the events in his life may not have been modeled on a preexisting structure. In my opinion there is such a model: the events of *The Assembly Hall* follow fairly closely the principal moments of the very *rājasūya* ritual that is central to the book.

In my view it cannot be coincidental that the Royal Consecration and Unction in *The Mahābhārata* are followed by a gambling match

4. *MBh.* 1 (19), I: 412 ff.

and that dicing is prescribed as mandatory after the Unction (*abhiṣeka*) in the *rājasūya* ritual.[5] There are other parallels between the book and the *rājasūya* sequence of events, to which we shall revert. Here at the outset I wish to submit that *The Assembly Hall* is structurally an epic dramatization of the Vedic ritual.

It has been said that this book is pivotal to *The Mahābhārata* as a whole. The remaining epic can almost be predicted in outline: there are to follow thirteen years of exile and the adventures thereof, described in *The Book of the Forest* and *The Book of Virāṭa*. Is it likely that the molestation of the Pāṇḍava's wife Draupadī at the hands of Duḥśāsana and Duryodhana will remain unavenged? Or that Duryodhana will surrender half the kingdom to Yudhiṣṭhira when he returns? We see looming *The Book of the Effort*, and the war books of *Bhīṣma*, *Droṇa*, *Karṇa*, *Śalya*, and the rest.

The Hall at Indraprastha: Builder and Building

In a way the Pāṇḍavas come by their hall at Indraprastha about as absentmindedly as by the Khāṇḍava Tract itself. So far—and this is where *The Beginning* ended—the Tract has been cleared by burning on a grand scale. This burning, ferociously fanned by Kṛṣṇa and Arjuna, has produced a few strange survivors: the disputatious Śārngaka fledglings, the Snake Aśvasena, and an Asura called Maya.

The oddest of them all is Maya, that is to say, the oddest in an Indian sense. Not only is it curious that an Asura with his divine powers finds himself in a forest at a critical time—a fact not surprising in the case of birds and snakes—but also he is completely *alone*, which in the Indian context is an astonishing feature. While we tend to think of demons of any sort as natural loners, in India personages of any kind, however demoniac, come in families. The other survivors from the Khāṇḍava fire, the birds and the snake, illustrate this point precisely. The birds are brothers, deserted by a philandering father, ineffectively protected by their mother, in the end saved by their wits and their father's forethought. The snake is rescued by its mother. But without any further explanation—which in the Indian epic style is itself inexplicable, because all circumstances must have preconditions—an Asura Maya turns up in the Khāṇḍava, entirely alone. He is odd.

Maya, in danger of being burned alive, darts forward from nowhere and seeks mercy from Arjuna. The Fire God was ready to pounce, Kṛṣṇa himself had his discus raised, yet Arjuna extends his safety

5. Heesterman, chap. 17.

without asking a question. This in spite of the fact that the Asuras are sworn enemies of the Gods, furtive, vindictive, treacherous creatures, an ever-lurking peril for humans. After having been spared Maya stays about, and at the beginning of *The Assembly Hall* he presses his gratitude on Arjuna. The hero however is noncommittal: "You have done everything,"[6] he replies, and of course Maya has done nothing, not even anything wicked, an oddity among the Asuras. Maya in other words comes through curiously alien, without the background of family and habitat, not of the race yet not inhuman, to rescue whom seems to be reward enough in itself.

The Asura patiently explains that he is a Viśvakarman, a "God Architect,"[7] of the Dānavas (in the context synonymous with Asuras), and a great artist (*kavi*). Arjuna again accepts his word without demanding amplification and replies, "Do something for Kṛṣṇa, that will be reward enough for me."[8] Kṛṣṇa in turn responds, "Build an assembly hall, Maya, where the designs of the Gods are laid out, and the designs of Asuras and men."[9] Maya is delighted. On a further occasion, when he is presented to King Yudhiṣṭhira, he speaks of the "feats of the ancient Gods."[10] Who are these Gods? The Asura announces that for his building materials he must go north, "where all the Dānavas (= Asuras) are to hold their sacrifices." There he has a cache of "precious stones," left there by King Vṛṣaparvan,[11] the ancient Asura king we have met in *The Story of Yayāti*, where he gave that king of hoary antiquity his daughter Śarmiṣṭhā—a rather human Asura. The northern location itself is described as an extremely ancient site where all the truly high Gods of the Vedic pantheon themselves go to worship "every one thousand eons." God Kṛṣṇa has donated to this center countless "sacrificial poles and most splendid altars."[12]

When Maya has built the hall, it is a wonder of the world, "ten thousand cubits in perimeter,"[13] or 62,500 square cubits, with golden pillars, "covering the sky like a mountain or monsoon cloud, long, wide, smooth, flawless and dispelling fatigue." Neither the fabled Sudharmā Hall of the Vṛṣṇis nor the palace of Brahmā himself matches it. And Maya built this hall in a full fourteen months,[14] a term not to be taken as short but extremely long. In building the hall he had an army of helpers and guards.

6. 2.1.3.
7. 2.1.5.
8. 2.1.7.
9. 2.1.10–11.
10. 2.1.15; *pūrvadevas*, "previous Gods," is a regular designation of Asuras.
11. 2.3.2–3.
12. 2.3.14–15.
13. 2.3.19.
14. *Māsaiḥ paricaturdaśaiḥ*, 2.3.34.

All these peculiarities surrounding the building of the hall and its builder have not failed to intrigue scholars. If we ignore a rather adventurous hypothesis,[15] we may state a generally acceptable theory as follows. Maya is an alien, but his credentials are not called into question. He is an Asura, but not inherently evil, in fact open-handed and grateful. He tells myths of the ancient Gods with whom Yudhiṣṭhira must have been vaguely acquainted; at least they are not outside the pale for him. He must return to a site in the remote north for his building materials, a site where ancient Indian Gods have been known to worship—if eons ago. The general theory that explains all this is that Maya hails from Īrān.[16]

Before they became synonymous with demons, the Asuras were a class of Gods common to the ancient Iranians and Indians. Ancient, but by no means forgotten. The Vedic Gods Varuṇa and Mitra, truly high Gods, are proudly styled Asuras.[17] For reasons not as transparent as one would wish, the word eventually took on in India the value of anti-God, i.e., anti-Deva, for a class of supernatural beings competitive with the *deva* Gods, disinherited, though never quite defeated and eradicated in the end. In Īrān, too, in the eventual Īrān of Zarathustra, the style of Ahura (= Asura) underwent a semantic transvaluation; it became the appellation of the God Mazdā, who champions the good against Ahrimān, who in turn represents the evil spirits—the Iranian anti-Gods, who are the *daēvas* (= *devas*). It seems very likely that our apparently dispossessed Asura Maya—alone, required to return to the north for his materials—is not a common or garden variety of Indian Asura who is now growing wild in Indian nature, but a follower of Ahura, deserving of rescue and respect. The phonetic change from *asura* to *ahura* is slight; already in Sanskrit the *s* and *ḥ* are allophones; in some Prākrits the change of intervocalic *s* to straight *h* is normal.[18]

This Asura, so responsive to the shelter Arjuna has vouchsafed him, works as an architect for the Pāṇḍavas and creates the wonder of this world. But wonders have predecessors: Maya must have built before.

15. Advanced by F. W. Thomas, "Dr. Spooner, *Asura Maya*, Mount Meru and *Karsā*" (J.R.A.S., 1916, pp. 262 ff.); he suggests that Asura is derived from the Ashur (Assur) of the Assyrians, whose might the Indo-Iranians supposedly had encountered. It would seem highly unlikely that the Indian bards retained the memory of the Assyrian palaces for more than a millennium before at last celebrating them.

16. The first scholar to raise the question was D. B. Spooner, "The Zoroastrian Period of Indian History" (J.R.A.S., 1915, pp. 68–89, 405–55), where he goes too far in asserting that Sanskrit *Maya* = Awestan *Mazdā*. Spooner's views were instantly reviewed by Vincent A. Smith (*ib.* pp. 800 ff.), A. B. Keith (J.R.A.S., 1916, pp. 138 ff.) and F. W. Thomas (above). A balanced judgment of the entire discussion is rendered by A. Foucher, *La vieille route de l'Inde* (Paris 1947): 330.

17. As are many other major gods in the *Ṛgveda*; cf. A. A. Macdonell, *Vedic Mythology*, reprint Varanasi, n.d.

18. For this reason there is little merit in A. B. Keith's objection to Spooner's assumption *asura* = *ahura*.

The theory that this Asura was Iranian finds support in the evidence that he was an architect. It is now accepted that early Indian stone architecture was an offshoot of that of the Achaemenid Empire of ancient Persia. After the Achaemenids were defeated by Alexander of Macedon and their empire was subsequently dismembered by the Seleucids—a goodly part of it going to King Candragupta Maurya of Magadha in exchange for five hundred war elephants—the old Zoroastrian dominion abandoned its artisans, artists, and architects to the outer world, notably to India.

At this time a new, India-based empire was growing out of Magadha, reaching to the borders of the Seleucid satrapies in Afghānistān. Magadha seems to have welcomed the architects warmly: the style of Persepolis, wantonly sacked by Alexander, has been convincingly recognized in the architecture of the Magadhan capital of Pāṭaliputra.[19]

There is nothing inherently improbable in the assumption that the description of Yudhiṣṭhira's great hall, built by an alien Asura from the north with his own myrmidons, who fetched his necessaries from the north, was patterned on the "sumptuous palaces" that Megasthenes, the ambassador of Seleukos I, observed in 302 B.C. in the Pāṭaliputra of Candragupta Maurya, the capital of a country that otherwise figures prominently in *The Assembly Hall*. For a brief while Indraprastha will be the capital of the entire world, as Pāṭaliputra was of a good part of India in the third century. Pāṭaliputra similarly displayed "the designs of Gods, Asuras, and men." If this view is correct, it throws light on the date of the present form of the book: it cannot have been composed at a date very far apart from the generation that saw Iranians helping to build up Pāṭaliputra and knew the source of the new imperial style.

The Hall Put in Its Place

No sooner has the hall been built than Nārada comes visiting, the divine seer who so often acts as a messenger of the Gods. After a long series of questions about political and administrative matters, to which we

19. Sir Mortimer Wheeler, *Civilizations of the Indus Valley and Beyond* (London, 1966), p. 118, quotes Megasthenes to the effect that in the palace of Pāṭaliputra much was "calculated to excite admiration, and with which Susa, with all its costly splendor, nor Ekbatana, with all its magnificence, can vie. In the parks tame peacocks are kept, and pheasants which have been domesticated; and cultivated plants . . . and shady groves and pastures planted with trees, and tree-branches which the art of the woodman has deftly interwoven . . . There are also tanks of great beauty in which they keep fish of enormous size but quite tame." Wheeler adds: "the whole description is significantly reminiscent of a Persian 'paradise,' and there can be no doubt as to whence the general character of Chandragupta's place was derived."

shall return, Nārada at Yudhiṣṭhira's request gives a description of the halls of the World Guardians and Brahmā. The World Guardians, *lokapālas*, are the Gods who are the regents of the four points of the compass: Indra of the East, Yama of the South—in India the region of death, Varuṇa of the West, and Kubera, the God of Riches, of the North. Nārada enumerates the kinds of people and spirits that populate these halls and lists the attributes of the Guardians: Indra's hall houses the sages, with one exception; Yama's, the warriors; Varuṇa's, an interesting assortment of groups of non-Gods, Snakes, and water denizens; and Kubera's, the Yakṣas, of whom he is the chief, as well as the God Śiva. At last the palace of Brahmā is described.

At first this episode looks extraneous to the main narrative of the present *Assembly Hall*, but it is not really so. It may of course have been composed and included after the main book was done, but extraneous it is not. The episode is meant to put Yudhiṣṭhira's hall in its proper place in cosmic space—hence the four points of the compass are significant—but this is a space that is visualized rather differently from the picture we have. Where are North, East, South, West, and what does this space look like?

For us, if we give the matter any thought at all, the four compass points are surface directions, and we represent them somewhere on the horizon. The ancient Indians structured their space differently. Space was shaped like two pyramids joined at their bases. The four corners of the joint base represent the four points of the compass, the top of the upper pyramid the zenith, the top of the inverted, lower pyramid the nadir. At the zenith is the World of Brahmā, "on the roof beam of heaven";[20] at the nadir, which is here on earth, is the hall of Yudhiṣṭhira. Each of these points is a *diś*, a direction, a word that therefore only in part corresponds with "points of the compass." Mention is frequently made of the "ten *diśas*," the four main points of the compass, the four intermediate ones, the zenith and nadir. These ten *diśas*, or the simple plural *diśas*, are synonymous with "space." Hence such usages as *dig-ambara*, the name of a sect of Jains who went naked: they were "robed in space."

Yudhiṣṭhira's hall is put in its place at the nadir of space thus structured, but not in a pejorative sense. Rather, by the precise indication of its position in the configuration of the cosmos—and this in my view is the intention of the descriptions of the "worlds" of the World Guardians and Brahmā—it is included in and made a structural component of cosmic space. Thus it epitomizes the entire mundane world. Like Rome, Delphi, or Jerusalem, it is "the center of the world,"

20. 2.11.12.

i.e., of earth placed at the nadir of space. It is no doubt at the opposite pole from Brahmā's world, but nevertheless equally contained within the structure of the universe.

This positioning of the hall in space has still another function. It prefigures the demand for a ceremony that is to validate the uniqueness of the king himself: "The title of suzerain partakes of everything."[21] For, if his place is comparable in its spot to those of the regents of the other *diśas* in theirs, he must be as much master of his world as the others are of theirs. He must be master of the earth universe, hence his need for the quest of universal sovereignty, which is the substance of *The Assembly Hall.*

Nārada adroitly suggests this need by mentioning that Hariścandra is the *only king* among a host of seers to inhabit Indra's world. Yudhiṣṭhira promptly questions him about this oddity, and the seer reveals that it is so because Hariścandra had offered up the sacrifice of the Royal Consecration. Here we should recall that on strictly Vedic terms the *rājasūya* does not really bestow universal sovereignty, or *sāmrājya*; this claim is reserved for another ritual. Our authors may or may not have known this fact, but that is irrelevant. In my view they wanted the *rājasūya* for the dramatic possibilities this rite offered.

The King Put in His Place

We have seen that as soon as Yudhiṣṭhira is installed in his hall at Indraprastha he receives a visit from the ubiquitous divine seer Nārada. The seer at once proceeds to interrogate the king with a string of rhetorical questions about his policies. A substantial part of this chapter, the *kaccid-adhyāya* or the "chapter of the perchances," also occurs in *The Rāmāyaṇa.*[22]

Nārada's questions take for granted the kind of political philosophy that is more precisely spelled out in *The Arthaśāstra,* "Manual of Policy," attributed to Kauṭilya, who was reputed to have been the prime minister and guiding spirit of Candragupta, the first of the Mauryas, on his rise to ascendancy in Magadha. The word that is used for "policy" is *artha,* the primary meaning of which is "the profit that one seeks out." It pictures the prince as a landowner who manages his estates for the primary purpose of turning a good profit. One is reminded that it is a frequent idiom that a king "enjoys" (the root *bhuj*) his realm.

21. 2.14.2.

22. Cf. E. Washburn Hopkins, "Parallel Features in the Two Sanskrit Epics" (J.A.O.S. 19: 138–51).

The text as we have it presents about a hundred questions, which seem to be reducible to about ten categories. More work on the compendium is in order, but it might be useful to present a rough breakdown of these rubrics.

There is first a general exhortation to practice Profit, but without neglecting the two other "Pursuits of man," Law and Pleasure: "You do not hurt the Law for Profit or the Profit for Law, or both for Pleasure? Do you always pursue Law, Profit, and Pleasure, distributing them over time?"[23] This admonition is followed by a more detailed investigation of guiding principles. Some of these come in numbers, presupposing a flourishing categorization of statecraft, so that a knowledge of the rubrics could be triggered by the numbers they carried. Stress is laid here on the importance of the king's alert and judicious use of council and councillors, and the necessity of his knowledge of ongoing affairs of state.

The third category deals with the king's immediate entourage: the qualities of his guru, minister, intelligence officer, house priest, and astrologer. We next descend to the level of government officials, army officers, and the king's troops. Insofar as they exercise real power and are the most clearly visible representatives of the king, the question arises, "Do your councillors govern the kingdom without oppressing the subjects too much with heavy punishment?" followed by, "People do not despise you as sacrificial priests despise one who has lost caste, and wives a loving but overbearing husband?"[24] Thus a fifth sequence of questions is in order, which emphasizes the importance of correct patronage and equitable treatment to all.

Since the state of the realm is contingent on the attitudes of neighbors, who at all times are regarded as potential marauders, the questioning now moves into the area of foreign relations and war: war is to be eschewed at all costs, or at least until other means have been exhausted; even then it is to be waged without interfering with the farmers, a practice also noted by Arrian: "Do you attack the enemies in battle without disrupting the harvesting and the sowing in their country?"[25] Success in war in turn depends on intelligence, and the question of espionage arises. Espionage, however, goes both ways, and questions concerning the king's personal safety are in order.

The neighbors being pacified, how well is the country faring? Are there sufficient checks on the king's extravagance: "Do they report to

23. 2.5.9–10.

24. 2.5.34–35.

25. Arrian, Indica XI, *ad finem*, transl. E. I. Robson (London: Loeb, 1933), p. 33: "If there is internal war among the Indians, they may not touch these workers [i.e., the farmers] and not even devastate the land itself, etc."; 2.5.54.

you in the morning your vice-induced outlays for drink, gambling, games, and loose women?"[26] Are income and expenditures properly reported? The appointment of greedy and corruptible officers is to be sharply avoided, for they are potentially expensive. "So that the harvest is not mothered by the rains alone," the king should also see that the irrigating tanks are plentiful.[27] If a farmer falls on hard times, he is to be given a loan to ensure that the seeding will be done in season.[28] On the local level the *pañcāyats* should be composed of men who are "upright and sensible" and who "bring security to the countryside in cooperation with one another."[29] The security of the rural areas is worth a further question or two.

The questions then move to the king's daily work routine. The king should comfort his women at night, but by no means tell them any of his secrets. He should secure that he sleep safely, and then rise early. In the morning he should show himself to the people hearty and well, but not without a proper bodyguard. At his morning audience he holds court and hears cases, to which he should attend with impartial justice. Then, in the afternoon one presumes, he should see to his physical fitness.

Of undeniable importance to the king's survival and the productivity of his estate is his personal popularity; he should inspire loyalty in all classes of his population—the townspeople by respectful treatment; the brahmins by feeding them properly and paying them stipends; the priests by performing the grand sacrifices. Homage should be paid to kinsmen as well as the deities and their sanctuaries. The king should be religiously just to all, and avoid the fourteen vices that are apt to beset him. Excise taxes should be equitable to traders, and the artisans should be shown due appreciation for their products.

Finally there is the continuing education of the king: he should acquire an expertise in horse, elephant, and chariot lore, in weaponry, archery, and even city engineering. And generally act, as according to the Books of the Law any king should act, to protect his people from fire, war, pestilence, and poison.

After none of his hundred-odd questions does Nārada pause for an answer. No doubt a sagacious nod on the part of Yudhiṣṭhira was sufficient reply. It is clear that Nārada's message is that there is more to being a king than building a hall that is the wonder of the world. Once the hall has been put in its place its ruler must be put in his.

26. 2.5.59.
27. 2.5.67.
28. 2.5.68.
29. 2.5.70.

Suzerainty: The Threat of Jarāsaṃdha of Magadha

The thought that Nārada has sown by extolling the *rājasūya* finds fertile soil in Yudhiṣṭhira's ambitions and rapidly grows into a desire himself to perform the Royal Consecration. Kṛṣṇa advises him that this is not a mere matter of personal volition but is dependent on the consent (*anumati*) of the entire baronage. Indeed, in a desire to become the king of kings the concurrence of the other kings must loom large as life. So at the opening stage of Yudhiṣṭhira's quest for suzerainty, the question of the consent is importantly raised; in the Vedic ritual of the *rājasūya*, too, the ceremony opens with a prayer for consent, which is concretized in an offering to the Goddess of Consent, Anumati.

Consent, though an agreement between two parties, goes both ways; in an interesting switch, it is not only the baronage that is to consent to Yudhiṣṭhira, but also Yudhiṣṭhira who has to consent to the baronage. Forever prudent, Yudhiṣṭhira is about as reluctant a candidate for suzerainty as he will be a candidate for being the loser at the dicing match that inexorably follows it.

Kṛṣṇa is sent for, though not as a matter of course, as we shall remark below. Yudhiṣṭhira "went out in his thoughts to Kṛṣṇa Vāsudeva, to seek a resolution regarding his task."[30] The Vṛṣṇi hero, now beginning to be elevated to close to divinity, arrives to make henceforth his presence felt at all important stages of the narrative except the dicing. The invitation was surely a matter of friendship, but not just that. The powerful, widespread, but oddly divided[31] Vṛṣṇi-Andhaka-Bhoja tribes, who seem to go under the general appellation of Yādavas, were southern neighbors of the Pāṇḍavas of Indraprastha on the same west bank of the River Yāmuna. Any new venture of the Indraprastha barons might well have required the support of Kṛṣṇa's people. We shall have to address ourselves later to the question of the role that this quasi-coalition of Vṛṣṇis play in this book.

When Kṛṣṇa's advice is sought, he at once goes into the history of the āryan baronage. We hear in passing of the hallowed Solar and Lunar dynasties of tradition; but we start really with the destruction of the "ancient baronage" by Paraśu-Rāma.[32] The baronial structure,

30. 5.12.25.

31. Śiśupāla, a cousin of Kṛṣṇa Vāsudeva's, is his fierce enemy; cf. below. The enmity of another cousin, Kaṃsa, is historic. When, in *The Book of the Effort*, it comes time to show allegiance, Kṛṣṇa sends his "cowherds" to Duryodhana, but pledges himself to the Pāṇḍavas as a noncombatant. His half-brother Rāma remains entirely neutral. Of Kṛṣṇa's cousins, Yuyudhāna Sātyaki sides with the Pāṇḍavas, and Kṛtavarman Hārdikya sends a grand army (*akṣauhiṇī*) to Duryodhana.

32. Which, according to tradition, spelled the end of the Tretā Yuga, just as the Mahābhārata war will spell the end of the Dvāpara Yuga, to usher in the present Kali Age. Kṛṣṇa's reference to the Solar and Lunar dynasts is rather skeptical: "the barons . . . have determined their lineage by the authority their words carry, that you know": in other words, their genealogical claims carried, if their authority could make them stick.

it transpires, has changed since this destruction. After it the barons had no single leader. There emerged a hundred and one baronial lines. Nevertheless, a number of incidental "suzerains" sprang up—as Kṛṣṇa here fails to say[33]—and in the present day a Caturyu Jarāsaṃdha has not quite achieved this dignity, but he is getting closer.

Kṛṣṇa makes no secret of his own resentment and vindictiveness toward Jarāsaṃdha. The Magadhan king has attacked the Vṛṣṇis of Mathurā and forced them to abandon their ancestral city[34] and fall back on Dvārakā in Gujarāt.[35] They regain Mathurā when Jarāsaṃdha withdraws, but obviously what balance of power there was has been out of order since. In the course of his wars, Jarāsaṃdha has captured the kings of 86 of the 101 lineages, and, being the 101st dynast himself, has been waiting for the remaining 14 to fall into his net. In one fell swoop, therefore, Yudhiṣṭhira can secure the allegiance of the 86 lineages by freeing the captive kings.

It is not clear how we should picture this wholesale imprisonment of hostile kings. Since Kṛṣṇa pictures the baronage as hopelessly riven into 101 competing lines, it seems likely that Jarāsaṃdha, erecting himself as *primus inter pares*, has been on the kind of "world conquest" that the Pāṇḍavas themselves will later institute, similarly one of the landslide type, in which the conquered follow the temporary banner of the conqueror.[36] Perhaps Jarāsaṃdha kept members of the ruling warlords as hostages to ensure tribute and future allegiance.

What is historically interesting is that at the time of the composition of *The Assembly Hall* the hegemony of Magadha clearly was accepted as a matter of fact (as it was in the fifth, fourth, and third centuries B.C.) to the extent that the audience of the epic would disbelieve any claim to actual suzerainty that did not include the reduction of Magadha. *The Assembly Hall* does not make this Magadha the Magadha of the Mauryan emperors, for their capital of Pāṭaliputra is not yet mentioned; nor for that matter is the even older capital of Rājagṛha. The seat is still Girivraja, a fastness in the hills, which has been excavated in recent years.[37] It was known to the authors of the book, for the hills that surround it are precisely identified.

At this point it might be useful to digress for a moment on what little is known of the historical importance of Magadha. This region emerges into full view with the coming of the great teachers Buddha and Mahāvīra, both born well to the east of the traditional heartland of Āryāvarta. The political center, which has been moving ever since

33. He mentions them 2.14.11.
34. 2.13.25 and 44.
35. 2.13.66.
36. Cf. *The Conquest of the World*.
37. See M. H. Kuraishī and A. Ghosh, *Rajgir* (Delhi, 1956⁴), with bibliography and maps, esp. pl. 10.

the first arrival of the Āryans in the subcontinent from the Northwest to the East and in the central story of *The Mahābhārata* is still arrested in the mesopotamia of the Yamunā and Ganges, by the fifth century B.C. has found a more durable lodging in Magadha. Kośala, its western neighbor, was under King Prasenajit (ca. 500 B.C.) still a force to be reckoned with, but internally weak. In Magadha ruled a King Bimbisāra, who characteristically sought conquest to the East, adding Anga, the "realm" of Karṇa,[38] to his dominions. Anga, with the city of Campā on the Ganges, controlled the lower area of the river, into the Bay of Bengal, and whatever overseas traffic there was at that time.

Bimbisāra's seat was Rājagṛha, down the hills from Girivraja. He had some control westward in the kingdom of the Kāśis, about the present Benares; his first queen was a sister of King Prasenajit of Kośala, who brought Kāśī (the city of the Kāśis, i.e., Benares) as a dowry. Close to the beginning of the fifth century B.C. Bimbisāra was dispossessed and assassinated by his son Ajātaśatru—we have met the name as one of Yudhiṣṭhira's—who warred on Prasenajit and conquered Kāśī. Next he turned north and vanquished the Vṛjjis on the northern bank of the Ganges from Rājagṛha.

Magadha prospers. The kingdom, now centered in Pāṭaliputra on the Ganges, has control of the Ganges basin and stretches toward the Pañjāb, having absorbed Āryāvarta. Alexander comes, goes, and dies. His empire is subdivided, the Seleucids reign in Īrān, and in Magadha the last king in the Nanda dynasty, which had ruled Magadha, is overthrown by Candragupta Maurya (ca. 321–297). The Maurya, "*Sandrokottos*," is visited by the Greek Megasthenes. Suddenly we are in the midst of history observed. Candragupta is eventually succeeded by Aśoka (ca. 279–236), who not only extended the boundaries of Magadhan suzerainty to most of India except the peninsular south, but also helped make Buddhism into a world religion.

There is little in *The Assembly Hall* that clearly reflects these important happenings. Ajātaśatru's *Drang nach Westen* perhaps might be read into Jarāsaṃdha's assaults on the Vṛṣṇis of Mathurā with the aid of Śiśupāla of Cedi, an expansion south of the Ganges that leaves Kurukṣetra and Pāñcāla untouched. How little it touches the epic is shown by the fact that Yudhiṣṭhira has to be alerted by Kṛṣṇa to the Magadhan peril, and that it is thereupon instantly removed by just a war party of three.

To return to *The Assembly Hall*. Jarāsaṃdha may be a peril; he is not a villain. Despite Kṛṣṇa's vindictive emphasis, it is hard to see where he got the notion that the emperor is going to slaughter all his

38. *MBh.* 1.127.15. 1: 281.

captive kings. Jarāsaṃdha's own reply to Kṛṣṇa's charges is that he has defeated them fairly and that he has "fetched them for the God," which means very little.[39] Otherwise Jarāsaṃdha appears as a generous and brahminic ruler. He has a quite laudable reverence for Snātakas, young brahmins who have completed, or perhaps are in the process of completing, their Vedic study with the final bath (*snātaka*= "the bathed one"). Possibly the meaning of *snātaka* might be extended to anyone under a studious vow of life, and to include the new mendicants who followed the Buddha or Jina, but that cannot be made out.[40] Yudhiṣṭhira too shows great consideration to Snātakas at his Royal Consecration, so this habit of Jarāsaṃdha's is by no means a despicable trait, or even a zealot's foible. The emperor wishes to welcome in person any new Snātakas that may arrive; if indeed these Snātakas are brahmins, that means that he personally encourages the immigration of the first of the twice-born. When he rides out on his elephant of state, brahmins perambulate the sacred fire around his person.[41]

Yet he is to die, as much to avenge the humiliation of the Vṛṣṇis as to ensure the success of Yudhiṣṭhira's claim to the suzerainty the Magadhan king in fact enjoys. Interestingly, in his plan of attack Kṛṣṇa counts on the honesty and generosity[42] of the enemy. He simply takes for granted that the old emperor will not be able to resist a personal duel if he is provoked or challenged. There is an intriguing parallel there with Yudhiṣṭhira's gambling attitude later on: Jarāsaṃdha too gambles, namely that he will win a duel after an accepted challenge, as Yudhiṣṭhira does at being challenged to the dicing match. Jarāsaṃdha did not have to rise to the challenge; he could simply have had his would-be assassins eliminated.

Not without misgivings, Yudhiṣṭhira allows a party of Kṛṣṇa, Bhīma, and Arjuna to set out on their mission. The three enter Girivraja surreptitiously, act arrogantly and provocatively, are dressed flamboyantly in spite of their supposedly austere life, and snatch garlands from the florists in the market. "Like Himālayan tigers who see a cowpen," they burst in on Jarāsaṃdha, rightly astonishing the well-fed Magadhans. Received by the emperor, they refuse his welcome.[43] Kṛṣṇa throws the challenge, accusing him of giving his "fellow barons the name of animals" by plotting to sacrifice them to Rudra. Jarāsaṃdha appeals to the Law of the baronage: "I take no

39. 2.20.27.
40. A. Holtzmann, Jr., *Das Mahābhārata und seine Theile* (Kiel, 1893), part 2, p. 48, wonders if Jarāsaṃdha was a Buddhist.
41. 2.19.20.
42. 2.18.8, though Kṛṣṇa calls it contemptuousness and pride.
43. 2.19.34.

king, unless I have defeated him!" and rises to Kṛṣṇa's bait: "Army against arrayed army shall I fight, or one against one, or one against two or three!"[44] Quite the old baron.

He never has a chance against Bhīma, though he lasts for thirteen days (his rival Yudhiṣṭhira will last for thirteen years, before triumphing). When Jarāsaṃdha is played out, Kṛṣṇa gives Bhīma a hint: "One should not lay hold of an enemy who is exhausted, for if he is brought down, he might give up the spirit entirely." Then he drives it home: "Show us the terrible force of the Wind God (= Bhīma's father) on Jarāsaṃdha today!"[45] Bhīma breaks Jarāsaṃdha's back.

There follows a curious glorification of Jarāsaṃdha's hereditary chariot on which the three drive off. I find this episode hard to separate from the chariot drive that the king in the Vedic *rājasūya* takes after removing a putative challenger. We must take up this point later.

Suzerainty: The Conquest of the World

While the elimination of Jarāsaṃdha and the release of the captive kings have in effect insured Yudhiṣṭhira's title to suzerainty, the entire known world still has to be formally subjugated and made tributary. One obviously is not *samrāj* unless all of earth acknowledges one as such.

The traditional term for world conquest in Sanskrit is *digvijaya*, the "conquest of the quarters," where we once more meet *diś* (which is pronounced *dig* in this collocation) in its plural sense of "all of space," here in the sense of all accessible space. The same world conquest is met with in the Vedic ritual of the *rājasūya*, where it is called *digvyavasthāpana*,[46] the "separate establishment of the quarters," which takes place when the king-to-be sets foot in each of the "five" quarters, i.e., the regular four and the one above. Accordingly the manuals prescribe that the king take a step in each of the five directions, so that he can be king on a cosmic scale. The five quarters sum up the entire universe: each one is associated with components of the Veda, the pantheon, the year—old symbol of the cycle of all natural life—and the people.

In the Vedic ritual the ceremony is reduced to a bare minimum. The totality of the Veda is simply represented by meters, the pantheon by five gods. Some manuals stop even shorter: the king is not required

44. 2.20.28.
45. 2.21.20; 2.22.4.
46. Heesterman, p. 103.

actually to take the steps, but to save himself that much exertion he may take them mentally. Evidently the manuals tell only part of the real story; yet, however reduced this rite may be, it still reflects the fact that, one way or the other, the king takes possession of space as the necessary precondition for his actual dominion. The king's declaration of his dominance by the very performance of the *rājasūya* must at some time have had substance to it. There must have been attending minor royalty, as at Yudhiṣṭhira's rite, and tribute-paying grandees of the land, if the kingdom had any size at all. For them the ritual expression of the king's dominion over them assuredly must have been more substantial than his taking five steps.

If in the ritual the story is reduced, in the epic it is no doubt expanded. The entire world is conquered, quarter by quarter, by the king's four brothers, "while Yudhiṣṭhira the King Dharma resided in the Khāṇḍava Tract."[47] If we put this statement in ritual terms we could say that by remaining in the center Yudhiṣṭhira takes the step to the zenith, the "world of Brahmā," which, as we have seen, is on exactly the opposite pole of where he sits, while his brothers as his alter egos take the steps to the quarters. Arjuna, the white knight, goes North. For eight days he battles Bhagadatta, king of Assam, who thereupon graciously complies. Then he presses into the Himālayas themselves, until he reaches the northern Kurus, the Ultima Thule of ancient India, where he is gently stopped by giant gatekeepers and turned away, though not without a gift. Bhīma takes the East, but his reduction of King Śiśupāla of Cedi, the marshal of the late Jarāsaṃdha, is wholly symbolic; he stays at the court of Kṛṣṇa's deadly enemy for thirty leisurely nights. Sahadeva goes South, where he encounters the Fire God, whom he pacifies. Nakula travels to the West, as far as the Persian Gulf.

In spite of the grandiose scale of the operations of the four brothers, the conquest remains a formality that demands recognition of Yudhiṣṭhira's claim to suzerainty; a recognition that, even if granted after battle, in no way changes the face of the earth.

Suzerainty: The Consecration

Two rulers did not pay tribute: Drupada, because of the marriage alliance, and Kṛṣṇa, because of friendship.[48] No tribute is sought from the Hāstinapura Kauravas, an important fact to which we shall return. Here suffice it to point out that Yudhiṣṭhira is not in competition with Hāstinapura. Nor as yet are the Kauravas in rivalry

47. 2.23.10.
48. 2.48.42.

with Indraprastha. When they have been invited they come readily enough. In view of the strained relations in the past, which necessitated the establishment of a junior branch at Indraprastha, one might have expected some comment from the Kauravas on the pretensions of the juniors. Yudhiṣṭhira seems to plead for a moratorium "at this sacrifice,"[49] but this hardly seems necessary, for they come in good faith. Not only that, the Kauravas are charged with responsibilities and "stride like masters." Yudhiṣṭhira's consecration therefore can only be described as a family affair: The family as a whole will be elevated to the level of the suzerain dynasty. That the Royal Consecration is indeed for the whole family is shown later on, when Duryodhana wishes to celebrate a *rājasūya* himself: It is pointed out that this is out of the question as long as Yudhiṣṭhira is there: apparently there can be only one *rājasūya* in the family.

When the entire world has been achieved, Kṛṣṇa arrives promptly with a large gift, and he gives Yudhiṣṭhira formal permission to proceed with the Consecration. It was noted above that this consent no doubt reflects the consent (*anumati*) prayed for at the beginning of the Vedic *rājasūya* by an oblation to Anumati. Why it should be Kṛṣṇa's to give is not clear. His baronial status is not all that high—he belongs to a dynasty of Bhojas rather than kings. Probably we should look to the reduction of Jarāsaṃdha for the answer. Kṛṣṇa was in charge of that war party, it was he who set the captive kings free and asked them for their consent to Yudhiṣṭhira's Consecration. In that sense the kings, as it were, had proxied their consent to Kṛṣṇa, and it is in their behalf that, now that the preliminaries are over, he gives the formal permission.

If suzerainty is a matter of straight power, what price kingship? Much has been written about the "divinity" of the ancient Indian king.[50] There is indeed some evidence of the sacral character of kingship, though it is very meager compared with the evidence for the sacred kings of the ancient Near East.[51] The historical conditions of ancient India did not lend themselves to the fostering of such ideas. Where such ideas are expressed, it is in connection with an abstract notion of "the king," rather than with regard to the specific individual king.[52] The complex of the "sacred king" seems to require the notion of the unique nation-king, and such unique kings are conspicuously rare in ancient India. The idea of the *cakravartin* is present in both

49. 2.32.2.

50. Cf. J. Gonda, *Ancient Kingship from the Religious Point of View* (Leiden 1957).

51. Cf. *La Regalità Sacra*, esp. G. Widengren's important contribution, "The Sacral Kingship of Iran" (Leiden, 1959), p. 242 ff.

52. A good summary of the spectrum is given by John W. Spellman, *Political Theory of Ancient India* (Oxford, 1964), p. 26 ff.

Hinduism and Buddhism, but is hardly built up on the Hindu side. The *cakravartins* or *samrāj's* that the epic mentions are no doubt heroic but by no means divine.

One may assume that the sacrality of a particular king is proportionate to the legitimacy, antiquity, and effectiveness of the dynasty to which he belongs. One may also assume that it is proportionate to the distance from which he is viewed. To the very humble he would appear as an exalted being with a divine effulgence; later on, in the temple worship of the great Gods, the God is provided with regal paraphernalia to express his high estate. On higher social levels where the person and the doings of the kings are more clearly visible, the king's sacrality would recede in proportion.

These desultory reflections are occasioned by the complete absence in *The Assembly Hall* of any mention of the sacredness of the king's person or his office. Would not one have reason to expect that just this book, whose concentrated purpose it is to treat of Yudhiṣṭhira's kingship, contain passages celebrating his sacrality if such a notion had been prevalent? But Yudhiṣṭhira is not at all a king by divine right or invested with divine dignities. He achieves his ambition by the mundane means of eliminating a rival, gaining the *kṣatrasaṃpad*, the unanimity of the baronage, and by the conquest of the world. Only then he is "consecrated" by the performance of the *rājasūya*, but this sacralization is of minimal interest to the authors of *The Assembly Hall*.

Nor can special importance be attached to the fact that Kṛṣṇa, as it were, invests him with royalty by voicing the consent that is obviously required as a remnant of the Vedic *rājasūya*. Despite the glorification of Kṛṣṇa in just this book, it cannot be said that he already acts as a God; on the contrary, his concerns are quite human, if not downright tribal. Nowhere is there any indication that he is bestowing divine dignity, even if it were his to bestow.

It is not different with the other kings. Jarāsaṃdha is surely a pious king, but by no means divine; in fact his zealous respects to any *snātaka* brahmin who enters his realm illustrates that he deems them more deserving of worship than himself. No divine grace touches Dhṛtaraṣṭra or Duryodhana, or even grandsire Bhīṣma himself.

The most therefore that can be said is that, if there were notions of the divinity of kingship at the time of the composition of *The Assembly Hall*, they were not sufficiently prevalent among the authors, and the audience for whom they composed, to merit even passing reference at points where they would indeed be most appropriate. For example, when Yudhiṣṭhira, after having gained full ascendancy over all the kings of earth is finally consecrated to the dignity of king of kings in the midst of his vassals and could have been glorified as King Divine, nothing of the sort is said. What is glorified again and again is the material aspect of his kingship, his stupefying wealth.

To return to Yudhiṣṭhira's installation, the principal rite of the Unction takes place amidst the happy disputations of the professional priests.[53] His anointing is followed by an episode whose function in the sequence of events becomes fully clear only if we once more refer to the Vedic *rājasūya*. The episode is that of the "taking of the guest gift."[54] The way it is represented in *The Assembly Hall*, this gift is the first one in a series of parting gifts to the kings who have been Yudhiṣṭhira's guests at the Consecration. This is, however, peculiar. Certainly guest gifts are very well known in ancient India; but they are invariably bestowed at the arrival of the guest, not at his departure. Also no mention is made of any other kings being presented with parting gifts by Yudhiṣṭhira. The conclusion therefore is that the story is concerned with this one gift made to one person immediately following the Unction.

Yudhiṣṭhira asks Bhīṣma's advice on whom the gift should be bestowed. Without hesitation Bhīṣma points to Kṛṣṇa Vāsudeva. At this point King Śiśupāla of Cedi, who earlier had been such an accommodating host to Bhīma on his world conquest,[55] interrupts the proceedings: "How can the Dāśārha [= Kṛṣṇa], who is not a king, merit precedence over all the kings on earth, so that he should be honored by you?"[56] He berates Bhīṣma and Yudhiṣṭhira, and finally Kṛṣṇa himself: "As a marriage is to a eunuch, as a show is to a blind man, so is this royal honor to you, Madhusūdana, who are not a king!"[57] He irately strides from the site of sacrifice with other kings.

The *rājasūya* rite suggests what in fact is going on here. In the Vedic ritual there occurs, following on the Unction, the rite of the bestowal of the remaining Unction water. This consecrated water is presented to the heir-apparent. Thus it establishes the successor of the king who has just been consecrated. It would seem that the "taking of the guest gift" parallels this event. The nature of the gift is nowhere described, and it may be assumed that it is the usual *arghya* (hospitality) water. The nature of the gift is indeed unimportant, for it is not the gift that matters, but the precedence it emphasizes.

Yudhiṣṭhira's *rājasūya*, it has been said, is a peculiar one, in that it does not so much legitimate a local king's dominion as validate one

53. 2.31.3 ff.
54. = *MBh.* 2 (25).
55. 2.26.11 ff.
56. 2.34.5.
57. 2.34.21.

king's claim to *sāmrājya*, suzerainty. Such suzerainty is not strictly an inheritable office, so, if the epic gift parallels the Vedic gift of the Unction water, the bestowal of it becomes the deliberate selection of the one who in the king's eyes is the most deserving of the honor after himself. Thus, if Kṛṣṇa stands first after Yudhiṣṭhira, the implication is that the purple might next well descend on the Vṛṣṇi chieftain. This bestowal is abhorrent to Śiśupāla, the erstwhile marshal of Jarāsaṃdha—he may well have such pretensions himself—for not only is Kṛṣṇa not a king, he is also the assassin of the previous *samrāj*. His protests are of no avail, and Kṛṣṇa is duly honored. Śiśupāla, "wrathfully, his eyes very red, addressed the kings: 'Am I still the commander of the army, or what do you think now? Do we stand ready to fight the assembled Vṛṣṇis and Pāṇḍavas?' When he had thus roused all the kings, the bull of the Cedis plotted with the kings to disrupt the sacrifice."[58] The last sentence is interesting because it shows that the taking of the guest gift was a component rite of the whole long sacrifice, and the sacrifice itself could still be disrupted—and brought to nought—if the bestowal were successfully challenged. The sacrifice is by no means over, for the kings are still in the *sadas*, the "sitting site" of the ceremonial, where indeed according to one branch of the Yajurveda the bestowal of the Unction water takes place.[59]

Śiśupāla throws his challenge. Addressing Bhīṣma, he denigrates that patriarch and belittles Kṛṣṇa's feats in no uncertain terms. Bhīṣma replies in kind, and the exchange continues. In the end Kṛṣṇa beheads the challenger with his discus.

It may be pointed out that the *rājasūya* too shows traces of a challenger who is defeated. The "chariot drive"[60] of the king, after the Unction, clearly refers to an original challenger. The newly anointed king mounts a chariot, drives it off, and attacks a baron who has taken up a position "somewhere to the east or north of the sacrificial compound."[61] The king shoots arrows at the baron, makes the chariot turn right, and returns to his starting point. Surely the new king can have no reason to attack a baron on his chariot, unless this baron is hostile; the context being that of the king's consecration, this hostility must have been expressed by some sort of challenge.

Ceremonies all over the world have a way of being abbreviated as well as expanded in the course of time. A neat parallel to our scene is

58. 2.36.15.

59. Heesterman, p. 124.

60. Heesterman, p. 127 ff.; this chariot drive takes place in the Vedic *rājasūya* immediately after the anointing and the disposal of the remaining unction water.

61. Heesterman, p. 129

offered by the coronation of the kings of Great Britain. There is a martial episode that was inserted in that ancient rite at an early date. After the coronation service in Westminster Abbey a banquet used to be held in Westminster Hall. During the first course a champion rode into the hall on horseback and provoked all dissenters, and therefore possible challengers of the king, by throwing down the gauntlet; this he did three times (inspired by the three banns before marriage?). The king thereupon drank to the champion from a silver-gilt goblet, which he handed to the other in reward. It was an elaborate and appropriate episode. Its later history is enlightening: it was last done so in 1821; the champion's claim was admitted as late as 1902, but at that time the banquet had fallen into desuetude. Henceforth the quondam champion was reduced to the office of bearing the standard of England. This function is even less revealing of its origin than the Vedic king's attack on a baron "somewhere to the north or east."

Where the Vedic rite according to the manuals has once more been reduced, the epic dramatization has again been expanded to an elaborate confrontation of the challenger with the kingmaker, and the threat of disruption of the consecration, and of war.

The Elevation of Kṛṣṇa Vāsudeva

Many of the foregoing events made Kṛṣṇa of the Vṛṣṇis quite impressive. Indeed, one of the striking features of this extraordinarily versatile book is the elevation of Kṛṣṇa to a level close to that of a deity. There has been little in *The Book of the Beginning* to prepare us for this. True, in the introductory portions he was hailed as the All-God, but the lateness of such additions made us discount it.

Kṛṣṇa was introduced in "Draupadī's Bridegroom Choice," as so often in the company of his older brother Balarāma.[62] He is the first one to recognize the Pāṇḍavas, who are disguised as brahmins, for what they are. When the wedding takes place, he sends a precious gift.[63] He is related to the Pāṇḍavas: their mother Kuntī was born Pṛthā, a sister of Kṛṣṇa's father, Vasudeva; so they are cousins. There is a further marriage alliance when Arjuna with Kṛṣṇa's connivance (he lends him his chariot) abducts his sister Subhadrā.[64] Once more he sends gifts. He is there at the founding of Indraprastha, and he joins with Arjuna in sating the Fire God at the conflagration of the Khāṇḍava Forest.[65] That Kṛṣṇa is a hero cannot be doubted; that he is a God remains to be seen.

62. *MBh.* 1.180.15, 1: 354 ff.
63. Ib., p. 377.
64. Ib., p. 406 ff.
65. Ib., p. 713 ff.

It still remains to be seen in *The Assembly Hall*, but with rather more expectation. Yudhiṣṭhira, as soon as he has conceived the desire to hold the *rājasūya*, sends for Kṛṣṇa. There is no cogent reason why Kṛṣṇa should be sent for. But once he is consulted, Kṛṣṇa takes matters firmly in hand: Yudhiṣṭhira can secure the allegiance of the baronage in one quick blow, by eliminating Jarāsaṃdha of Magadha. Jarāsaṃdha also happens to be an old enemy of the Vṛṣṇis, and Kṛṣṇa makes no bones about his desire to have him out of the way.

That very enmity shows that the hero is by no means omnipotent. Jarāsaṃdha had attacked the "Middle Country" and driven the Vṛṣṇis from Mathurā. They had to fall back on the town of Dvārakā. It is only after Jarāsaṃdha's withdrawal that the Vṛṣṇis can return to their ancestral home. In his attack on Mathurā, Jarāsaṃdha was aided by King Śiśupāla of Cedi. Since Śiśupāla was his army commander, it is likely that it was he who conquered Mathurā. This, incidentally, puts a different complexion on the conquest of Mathurā, for Śiśupāla was himself a Vṛṣṇi, who, in a process that is not made clear,[66] had become the king of adjacent Cedi. Was Śiśupāla simply out to add his mother country to his possessions under the patronage of his own powerful neighbor, Magadha? In any case, Kṛṣṇa lays the principal blame on Jarāsaṃdha, though Śiśupāla will not be forgotten.

It is Kṛṣṇa who is the leader of the would-be assassination party, crashing Jarāsaṃdha's gate and addressing him in the name of the others. He admonishes Bhīma (by saying the opposite) to kill the king, who in fact had already been defeated. Obviously the killing was unnecessary: I do not see how Jarāsaṃdha after his defeat could have survived as paramount king. Or is it intended as well-deserved punishment for his presumed immolation of the captive kings? But that intention on the part of the pious ruler might have been mere rumor, and no sacrifice has taken place as yet. However that may be, Jarāsaṃdha himself anticipated the possibility of death, for he had his son Sahadeva installed before the match.[67] It is Kṛṣṇa, too, who officially sets the captured kings free and rides the ancestral Chariot of State of the dethroned *samrāj*.[68]

It is Kṛṣṇa again who grants Yudhiṣṭhira formal consent to perform the Royal Consecration. At this ceremony Kṛṣṇa's near-apotheosis occurs. After the Unction the Gift is to be bestowed. Yudhiṣṭhira

66. We are reminded that according to the *Beginning* (p. 131) the progenitor Uparicara took Cedi and obtained Indra's chariot, which according to 2.22.16 is the selfsame state chariot of Magadha. It would appear that the state chariot therefore was originally Cedi's and that Magadha was later added to the expanded kingdom; it afterward became the realm's center, with old Cedi an important vassalage, where Śiśupāla was a kind of viceroy.

67. 2.20.29.

68. 2.22.20 ff.

consults Bhīṣma — it is the first time that he turns to the wise grandsire, who would have been a much more natural choice for Yudhiṣṭhira to consult when he was still thinking of the *rājasūya*. Bhīṣma gives preference to Kṛṣṇa, to the utter astonishment of Śiśupāla. The latter sums up the many facts that disqualify Kṛṣṇa for the honor, and belittles his feats — among which is the holding high of the hill Govardhana — and jeeringly points to Kṛṣṇa's marrying a second-hand bride.[69] By killing Śiśupāla, however, Kṛṣṇa has not answered all the questions.

One interesting question that remains is one raised by Kṛṣṇa himself: he has a rival who is also a Vāsudeva and pretends to Kṛṣṇa's title of *puruṣottama*, "Supreme Person." This Vāsudeva is a shadowy potentate from Puṇḍra, who is always spoken of in passing: he is also at Draupadī's Bridegroom Choice; he is also subdued by Bhīma as part of the world conquest; he is in fact also at Yudhiṣṭhira's *rājasūya*; and that is the end of his existence in *The Mahābhārata*. That he is shadowy is certainly due to the fact that Puṇḍra, and Anga and Vanga with which it is usually enumerated, are vague regions somewhere far out East, where brahmins turn away. But Kṛṣṇa's complaint that he is stealing his own honors is remarkable: do we here have one Kṛṣṇaite faction from Mathurā denouncing another faction from Puṇḍra?

The ubiquitous presence of Kṛṣṇa in *The Assembly Hall* makes his absence at the climax, the game at dice, the more conspicuous. Indeed he apologizes later.[70] He points out that he had important war business with Śaubha, who meanwhile had assaulted Dvārakā. That turned out to be a very difficult encounter, and we find Kṛṣṇa suddenly cut down a few rungs when we move from *The Assembly Hall* to *The Forest*, where again he is no more, and no less, than a Vṛṣṇi hero.

Whatever the original shape of *The Assembly Hall*, it is quite clear that the book has at least partially been reworked with a Kṛṣṇaite tendency. The *rājasūya* of Yudhiṣṭhira has been made an occasion to glorify Kṛṣṇa. He is not quite the God yet — at least not by *Bhagavadgītā* standards — but his incipient godhead already requires his absence from situations that he cannot dominate. Had he attended the dicing no doubt he would have interfered on behalf of the Pāṇḍavas, which would have meant the end of the game, and thus in effect the end of *The Mahābhārata*. And this the Kṛṣṇaites found, of course, impossible to arrange.

69. 2.42.15.
70. 3.14.2 ff.

Suzerainty Gambled Away

To some it might appear that I overstate the connection between incidents in the Vedic *rājasūya* and in *The Book of the Assembly Hall.* Yet it is not my cause I plead here, but that of the authors of this book. For we have not so far encountered wanton randomness in the main story of *The Mahābhārata,* while now we may seem to be on the edge of it. So far every single complication, however imaginatively presented or embroidered, was a real one that had some answer in Law.

There was the Bhārata line in danger of becoming extinct when Bhīṣma, to honor an infatuation of his father, vowed never to marry. There was the barren marriage of Vicitravīrya who left behind two wives capable of child-bearing; this problem was resolved by invoking the injunction of levirate. There was the inadequacy of the blind eldest son Dhṛtarāṣṭra, and the brief kingdom or regency of the younger Pāṇḍu, who then disqualified himself.

Consequently there is a real question of who held title to the throne of Hāstinapura, Dhṛtarāṣṭra's sons or Pāṇḍu's. Assassination of one party of claimants, an opprobrious but effective means of resolving the insoluble situation, proved unsuccessful. The intended victims went underground to emerge grandly allied with the Pāñcāla lineage. War was counseled at this point, but rejected because it would be lawless. Instead, the partition of Kurukṣetra between Hāstinapura and Indraprastha branches was advised and implemented.

Yudhiṣṭhira had acceded to partition and become ruler of the new domain of Khāṇḍava. But what manner of a king was he, what were his credentials? He had to legitimize his kingship through the ritual instrument of a *rājasūya,* which required him to demonstrate actual dominion. Given the framework of the Law, all these events followed not only as a matter of fact but as a matter of course. Now, is a neighboring kinsman's envy at Yudhiṣṭhira's good fortune sufficient reason for the new king, gloriously enthroned, the liege of tributaries, willingly to gamble it all away? At this point, events that were so far rational begin to make no sense at all, and at this point modern scholars have lost sight of the structure of *The Mahābhārata* as received and either decided that the whole story was twisted or just shrugged their shoulders and let the question drift.

The point of my cross-referencing the incidents of the Vedic *rājasūya* and the course of events in *The Assembly Hall,* whose entire import is the suzerainty celebrated and validated with the *rājasūya,* is to make intelligible the apparent anomaly of the dicing match. For according to the Vedic texts a dicing match *must* follow the installation of the new king.[71] The texts give no reason, just state the fact. But the fact is made quite innocuous: as in the incident of the "chariot drive," the new king cannot lose and simply goes through the motions. At the ancient realities behind the presence of a dicing game in the installation of a king one can only guess; one facile guess is that when claims of rivals within one ruling lineage were indeed as insolubly complex as here, the only answer was to decide by lot.[72]

We have pointed to the fact that there is no discord at all between Kauravas and Pāṇḍavas on the occasion of the consecration. They willingly participate, and for once Duryodhana's party does not plot war. In fact, Duryodhana acts as the receiver of the tributes. Here we have a family acting as one. Yudhiṣṭhira is not a unique individual acting in his own right; he is the representative of his family, and if he becomes suzerain, his family becomes the suzerain dynasty. Afterward, if trouble arose, it would be up to the House of Kuru to put order in its house.

Instrumental in enforcing this order is an ally by marriage, Prince Śakuni, brother of Duryodhana's mother Gāndhārī. He seems to have been at Hāstinapura ever since he married off his sister there. He is not Duryodhana's evil spirit; he is simply his maternal uncle and acts like it, always looking to the fortunes of his sister's issue. His nephew naturally looks to him: "When a man is in need, his mother's people are his only refuge. An intelligent man leaves his agnates alone, for they are his born enemies."[73] Witness the Kauravas and Pāṇḍavas.

On hearing of his nephew's envy of Yudhiṣṭhira's fortune, Śakuni laconically advises him to throw for it: "Yudhiṣṭhira is fond of gambling, but does not know how to play." In the context this is disingenuous, for Yudhiṣṭhira has not so far been at all fond of gambling—we have seen quite a bit of him now—and can hardly be regarded as under a private compulsion to rise to any game.[74] Nevertheless, he submits, though grudgingly: "Once challenged I cannot refuse."[75] He speaks in the same frame of mind as Dhṛtarāṣṭra, who allows the dicing because it is *diṣṭa*, "ordained."[76] And by what but the very structure of the Vedic *rājasūya* itself?

Once we accept the dicing as an integral part of the *rājasūya*, in *The Assembly Hall* as well as the ritual manuals, Yudhiṣṭhira is not at all the statue with the clay feet, the paragon of rectitude with the sudden tragic flaw. The text itself does not condemn Yudhiṣṭhira for

71. Heesterman, p. 140 ff.

72. Heesterman, p. 151 ff. sees in the dicing game features of birth and cosmogony.

73. *Bṛhatkathāślokasaṃgraha*, "The Travels of Sānudāsa," translated by J. A. B. van Buitenen in *Tales of Ancient India* (Chicago, 1959), p. 228.

74. Cf. his objections to the dicing 2.52.10 ff.

75. 2.52.13; 16.

76. 2.45.58.

his gaming.[77] Of course, if the gambling had been outside Yudhiṣṭhira's universe of Law, the authors could easily have dropped the game from their version of the *rājasūya*, but in a way this would have gone against the spirit of *The Mahābhārata* as a whole. We have remarked before that the epic is a series of precisely stated problems imprecisely and therefore inconclusively resolved, with every resolution raising a new problem, until the very end, when the question remains: whose is heaven and whose is hell? This point, counterpoint is typical of *The Assembly Hall* as well: suzerainty achieved, and then again gambled away.

Rather than dropping the dicing or treating it as perfunctorily as do the ritual manuals, the authors have seized upon the dicing rite of the Vedic ceremony as a ritually legitimate, even prescribed, way of swinging the doubt from Yudhiṣṭhira's apparently unassailable position to the claims of the Kauravas. With a masterly stroke of composition the dead letter of the Vedic game is dramatically revived. Meanwhile Yudhiṣṭhira remains the King Dharma: he had not been too happy before about his ambition to become *samrāj*,[78] he is now prepared to go to the bitter end.

And bitter it is. After an epical losing streak he finds himself obliged to stake his brothers, himself, and Draupadī—obliged, it seems, by the rules of this game, which unfortunately are never explained. Our knowledge of the rules of gaming in ancient India is extremely limited;[79] but the present dramatization in *The Assembly Hall* gives us at least some idea of this particular game's rules. Two parties, rather than two individuals, play, for Duryodhana's uncle Śakuni may play for him; it is Duryodhana who pays in the stake. The two parties pay in the first stake in the same amount. The loser adds to his stake, while the winner's presumably remains the same. It is not clear whether the entire stake stays in the game or the winner pockets the loser's last stake after each play.

Never stated but implicit is this game's rule that it will go through twenty plays, which are presented as two phases of ten each. In the first ten plays Yudhiṣṭhira forfeits most of his possessions, and after the tenth Vidura, the benevolent uncle of the Pāṇḍavas, makes an impassioned plea that the game be stopped.[80] To whom would one ordinarily expect such a plea to be directed? To the loser Yudhiṣṭhira, one fancies. But, on the contrary, Vidura urges Duryodhana's father to stop it and vilifies Duryodhana for persisting in it. This would make

77. Be it true that in *The Book of the Forest* there are disparaging remarks about Yudhiṣṭhira's dicing (this game only), and that the (late) *Book of Virāṭa* makes him a professional gambler.

78. Cf. the discussion in 2.14.

79. In a mimeographed article entitled "The Friendly Dicing Game," distributed to a class at Harvard, Daniel H. H. Ingalls offered an attempt at explanation.

80. 2.55–56.

no sense if Vidura considered Yudhiṣṭhira a free agent; it makes excellent sense if Yudhiṣṭhira is bound by the rules of his own *rājasūya* and must rise to the challenge.

The game is carried on for another session of ten plays. Yudhiṣṭhira first loses untold millions in the eleventh play, in the twelfth all his cattle, in the thirteenth all his land, in the fourteenth the sons of Draupadī by the five Pāṇḍavas, in the fifteenth Nakula, in the sixteenth Sahadeva, in the seventeenth Bhīma, in the eighteenth Arjuna, in the nineteenth himself. At the twentieth play, the final one of the game, Yudhiṣṭhira stakes Draupadī. The audience groans and protests, but does nothing to stop the play;[81] evidently the game is to be a complete one, with a total loser and a total winner. But our impish authors, masters of the doubt, have already planted one of their dubieties. The play for Draupadī is lost; she is subjected to indignities that shout for vengeance; she is disrobed but the power of her virtue replaces her skirt; she also poses the ultimate riddle.[82]

Had Yudhiṣṭhira staked and lost himself, she asks, before he staked me? If so, he had lost his freedom and, as a slave of the Kauravas, no longer owned her to stake. There is much argument, but it remains inconclusive.[83] In the end Dhṛtarāṣṭra rules that the last play was indecisive and that the game as a whole had been neither lost nor won. So the Pāṇḍavas depart free and still rich men.[84] It is clear that the undecided game is not over, only interrupted. At this point it becomes predictable that when the game goes on, it will be with a repeat of the twentieth play, which had been indecisive, and that there will be a single deciding play for an all-or-nothing stake between the two competing branches of the House of Kuru.

So promptly there follows the *anudyūta*, the follow-up game, in which Duryodhana, with his father's consent,[85] decides to stake Hāstinapura against Indraprastha.[86] It is the final moment of truth; this time not the slow attrition of possessions but an instant play for identity. Again Yudhiṣṭhira cannot refuse, for he is still under the same ritual obligation. However, our wily authors, bent upon keeping the story going, throw in one more of their artful dodges. It is not going to be *quite* an all-or-nothing play, but close enough. The parties stake victory against a twelve-year exile in the forest, to be followed by one year during which they must live in the open without being discovered. Yudhiṣṭhira loses this play too, and the next thirteen years will be two wholly different stories.

81. 2.58.38 ff.
82. 2.60.5 ff.
83. 2.60.40 ff.; 61.12 ff.; 62.14 ff.; 63–64.
84. 2.65.16 ff.
85. 2.66.24.
86. 2.67.9 ff.

Contents

2(20) *The Building of the Assembly Hall*

2.1–11 (B. 2.1–12; C. 1–513)
1 (1; 1). Maya, a Dānava who had been rescued by Arjuna from the Khāṇḍava fire, wishes to reciprocate. Arjuna declines and sends him to Kṛṣṇa, who suggests he build an assembly hall for the Pāṇḍavas (1–10). Maya is presented to Yudhiṣṭhira and begins the planning (10–15).
2 (2; 21). Kṛṣṇa wishes to return home and takes his leave (1–10). The Pāṇḍavas conduct him out (10–20).
3 (3; 58). Maya announces that near Lake Bindu he has a trove of treasure once held by the Asura king Vṛṣaparvan. He goes there. It is a favorite place of Viṣṇu (1–15). Maya brings a club for Bhīma and the conch Devadatta for Arjuna. Other treasures go into the building of the hall, which is described. During the building the hall is guarded by the Kiṃkara Rākṣasas (15–25). The idyllic palace is completed (25–30).
4 (4; 96). Yudhiṣṭhira takes possession, honors the brahmins, and receives seers and princes (1–30). Gandharvas and Apsarās play (30).
5–11. The Halls of the World Guardians.

Vaiśaṃpāyana said:
1.1 Then Maya, in the presence of Vāsudeva, spoke to the Pārtha,
folding his hands, with flattering speech and after many compliments:
"You have saved me from the angry Kṛṣṇa and the willing fire that
was ready to burn me, son of Kuntī. Tell me what I can do for you."
Arjuna said:
You have done everything. Farewell, depart, great Asura. Be
always friendly to us, and we shall be friendly to you.
Maya said:
5 My lord, that is spoken like you, bull among men! But I do wish to
do something in friendship, O Bhārata. For I am a great artist, a
Viśvakarman among the Dānavas, and I wish to make something for
you, Pāṇḍava.
Arjuna said:
You think that I saved you from deadly peril. Albeit so, I cannot
let you make anything. But neither do I wish to frustrate your design,
Dānava. Do something for Kṛṣṇa; that will be reward enough for me.
Vaiśaṃpāyana said:
Maya urged Vāsudeva, O bull of the Bharatas, and he pondered a
while on what he would demand. Then Kṛṣṇa commanded him,
"Build an assembly hall, Daitya, such as you deem worthy of the
King Dharma. Build a hall of such magnificence that people in the
entire world of men will be unable to imitate it, when they have
10 beheld it in wonderment. Build an assembly hall, Maya, where we
will see the designs of the Gods laid out by you, and the plans of
Asuras and men." On receiving this reply, Maya was delighted; and
he joyfully agreed to build an assembly hall for the Pāṇḍavas, which
would resemble a palatial chariot of the Gods.
Thereupon Kṛṣṇa and the Pārtha related all that had happened to
Yudhiṣṭhira the King Dharma and presented Maya to him. Yudhiṣṭhira
showed him appropriate honor, and Maya courteously accepted the
15 courtesies. The Daitya narrated then to the sons of Pāṇḍu the feats of
the ancient Gods in various places, O Bhārata, lord of the people.
After he had rested for some time, this Viśvakarman did the planning
and began the building of an assembly hall for the great-spirited sons
of Pāṇḍu. At the wishes of the Pārthas and the great-spirited Kṛṣṇa,
the august and mighty Asura performed the inauguration on an
auspicious day, fed eminent brahmins by the thousands rice boiled in
sugared milk, distributed many presents to them, and measured out
a terrain of ten thousand cubits, divinely beautiful, which possessed
the virtues of all seasons.

Vaiśaṃpāyana said:
2.1 After Janārdana had lived happily in the Khāṇḍava Tract, honored

to his deserts by the affectionate Pārthas, he became desirous of seeing his father and set his mind on going. The large-eyed hero bade the King Dharma and Pṛthā* farewell, and he who is worshipful to the world worshiped with his head the feet of his father's sister.* She kissed Keśava on the head and embraced him. Thereafter famous
5 Hṛṣīkeśa went to see his sister and shed a tear of affection. The blessed Lord gave the gentle and gentle-spoken Subhadrā meaningful, apt, helpful, brief, appropriate, and excellent advice, and she gave him messages for her family and honored and greeted him with many bows. After he had taken leave of the radiant Subhadrā and bid her good-bye, Janārdana went to see Kṛṣṇā and Dhaumya. Janārdana, greatest of men, saluted Dhaumya ceremonially, comforted Draupadī, and bade her farewell. Then the wise and strong hero, accompanied by the Pārtha, went up to the brothers; surrounded by the five
10 brothers, Kṛṣṇa stood like Indra surrounded by the Immortals. The bull of the Yadus worshiped the Gods and the brahmins with garlands, blessings, bows, and perfumes of many kinds.

After performing all his tasks, he, first of the steadfast, set out and distributed to those brahmins who were worthy of benedictions presents accompanied with bowls of curd and unhusked rice, and circumambulated them. He ascended his swift golden chariot, which bore the emblem of Garuḍa and carried his club, discus, sword, and other arms. The day, the stars, and the hour were propitious when the lotus-eyed hero drove out with his horses Sainya and Sugrīva. From affection King Yudhiṣṭhira ascended after him and, moving aside the driver Dāruka, ablest of charioteers, the lord of the Kurus himself
15 took the reins. Arjuna too mounted on the chariot and waved a large white yak-tail fan with a golden staff sunwise around Kṛṣṇa's head. The masterful Bhīmasena, too, and the twins followed Kṛṣṇa, surrounded by priests and townspeople. Keśava, killer of enemy heroes, as he was followed by the brethren shone like a guru amidst his beloved disciples. Govinda bade the sorrowful Pārtha farewell and embraced him, then saluted Yudhiṣṭhira, Bhīmasena, and the twins.
20 The twins clasped him hard with their arms in farewell. After making covenant with the Pāṇḍavas and turning them and their followers back, Kṛṣṇa departed for his own city like another Sacker of Cities.** They followed Kṛṣṇa with their eyes as far as the horizon, then followed him in their thoughts with love. While their hearts were still unsated of the sight of Keśava, the gracious Śauri soon disappeared from their eyes. Listlessly the Pārthas, whose thoughts had gone with Govinda, all turned back and the bull-like men returned to their city while Kṛṣṇa on his chariot in time reached Dvārakā.

* = Kuntī.
** = Indra.

Vaiśaṃpāyana said:

3.1 Then Maya said to Arjuna Pārtha, greatest of conquerors, "I say
good-bye, I must go, but I shall return soon. North of the Kailāsa
Plateau, by Mount Maināka, close to the delightful Lake Bindu, where
all the Dānavas are to hold their sacrifices, I have made a collection
of precious stones, which has remained in the assembly hall of
Vṛṣaparvan, who kept faith with his promises. I shall go and fetch it,
if it is still there, Bhārata. With it I shall build a hall for the famous
Pāṇḍava, a beautiful hall to delight all hearts, adorned with all manner
5 of gems. In Lake Bindu there is a superb club, O scion of Kuru, which
was placed there by King Yauvanāśva, after he had defeated his
enemies in war. It is heavy and embellished with golden eyes, hard
and able to withstand great weight and to kill all enemies; it is equal
to a hundred thousand. It would be a fitting weapon for Bhīmasena,
as the Gāṇḍīva bow is for you. There is also a large conch with an
excellent sound, which came from Varuṇa, Devadatta by name. I shall
give you all this, let there be no doubt."

After he had thus spoken to the Pārtha, the Asura departed in a
northeasterly direction. North of the Kailāsa, toward Mount Maināka,
there is a sacred mountain with great minerals, Hiraṇyaśṛnga, and
lovely Lake Bindu, where King Bhagīratha dwelled many years
10 watching the River Ganges, which is since known as Bhāgīrathī. It
was there that the great-spirited lord of all creatures offered up a
hundred great sacrifices, O best of the Bharatas, and gem-encrusted
sacrificial poles and golden altars have been set up there, for beauty's
sake, not to set an example. After offering there, the thousand-eyed
Consort of Śacī* attained to success. It is there that the eternal lord
of the creatures, after having created all the worlds, has been
worshiped in his fierce splendor amidst thousands of beings. There,
too, Nara and Nārāyaṇa, Brahmā, Yama, and Sthāṇu,** in the fifth
place, attend a sacrificial Session every one thousand eons. There
Vāsudeva always faithfully sacrifices with thousand-year sessions, for
15 the instruction of the learned. There Keśava donated thousands and
tens of thousands of golden-garlanded sacrificial pillars and most
splendid altars.

Arriving there, Maya took the club and the conch shell, Bhārata,
and the crystal building materials for the hall that were with
Vṛṣaparvan; he fetched all this with the aid of the Kiṃkara Rākṣasas.
The Asura brought everything back and built a peerless hall,
celestial, beautiful, studded with precious stones, which became
famous in the three worlds. He gave the superb club to Bhīmasena
and the matchless conch Devadatta to the Pārtha.

* = Indra.
** = Śiva.

The hall, which had solid golden pillars, great king, measured ten
20 thousand cubits in circumference. Radiant and divine, it had a superb
color like the fire, or the sun, or the moon. Challenging as it were
with its splendor the luminous splendor of the sun, it shone divinely
forth, as though on fire, with divine effulgence. It stood covering the
sky like a mountain or monsoon cloud, long, wide, smooth, faultless,
and dispelled fatigue. Made with the best materials, garlanded with
gem-encrusted walls, filled with precious stones and treasures, it was
built well by that Viśvakarman. Neither the Sudharmā hall of the
Dāśārhas,* nor the palace of Brahmā possessed the matchless beauty
that Maya imparted to it.

25 Eight thousand armed Rākṣasas, who were called Kiṃkaras, sky-
going, terrifying, gigantic, powerful, red-eyed and yellow-eyed, with
ears of mother-of-pearl, guarded and protected the hall at Maya's
behest. Inside the hall Maya built a peerless lotus pond, covered with
beryl leaves and lotuses with gem-studded stalks, filled with lilies and
water plants and inhabited by many flocks of fowl. Blossoming lotuses
embellished it, and turtles and fishes adorned it. Steps descended
gently into it; the water was not muddy and it was plentiful in all
seasons; and the pearl-drop flowers that covered it were stirred by a
30 breeze. Some kings who came there and saw it thick with precious
stones and gems did not recognize it for a pond and fell into it.
Around the hall stood tall trees that were always in bloom, lovely
trees of many kinds that were dark and threw cool shade. Everywhere
there were fragrant groves and lotus ponds made beautiful by wild
geese, ducks, and *cakra* birds. The wind carried the fragrance of
flowers on land or on water and fanned the Pāṇḍavas with it. Such
was the palace that Maya built in fourteen months, and when it was
finished, he informed the King Dharma.

Vaiśaṃpāyana said:

4.1 Thereupon King Yudhiṣṭhira made his entrance into the hall, and
the lord of men fed ten thousand brahmins with rice boiled in sugared
milk, clarified butter, delicious honey, roots and fruit, and gave them
new clothes and many kinds of garlands. The king gave each of them
a thousand cows, and the sounds of the Blessing of the Day seemed to
touch heaven, O Bhārata. When the chief of the Kurus had paid
worship to the deities with music, many songs, and various perfumes,
5 and had settled in, wrestlers, dancers, boxers, bards, and songsters
waited on the great-spirited Yudhiṣṭhira for seven nights. When he
had thus paid homage to the hall, the Pāṇḍava disported himself in
his lovely palace with his brothers, like Indra in his heaven.

* = Kṛṣṇa's people.

In that hall seers and princes from many countries sat with the Pāṇḍavas – Asita Devala, Satya, Sarpamālin, Mahāśiras, Arvāvasu, Sumitra, Maitreya, Śunaka, Bali, Baka Dālbhya, Sthūlaśiras, Kṛṣṇa Dvaipāyana, and we ourselves, Vyāsa's students: Śuka, Sumantu, and Jaimini. Then there were Tittira, Yājñavalkya, Lomaharṣaṇa and his son, Apsuhomya, Māṇḍavya-with-the-Stake, Kauśika, Dāmoṣṇīṣa, Traivaṇi, Parṇāda, Ghaṭajānuka, Mauñjāyana, Vāyubhakṣa, Pārāśarya, the two Sārikas, Balavāka, Śinīvāka, Sutyapāla, Kṛtaśrama, Jātukarṇa, Śikhāvat, Subala, Pārijātaka, the lordly Parvata and the hermit Mārkaṇḍeya, Pavitrapāṇi, Sāvarṇi, Bhāluki, Gālava, Janghabandhu, Raibhya, Kopavegaśravas, Bhṛgu, Haribabhru, Kauṇḍinya, Babhrumālin, Sanātana, Kakṣīvat, Auśija, Nāciketas, Gautama, Painga, Varāha, Śunaka, Śāṇḍilya the great ascetic, Karkara, Veṇujangha, Kalāpa, and Kaṭha – these and many other hermits, firm in Law, masters of soul and senses, learned in the Vedas and their branches, eminent seers, attended on the great-spirited king in his assembly hall, wise in the Law, pure and immaculate, and narrated auspicious tales.

Likewise the best of the barons attended on King Dharma, such as the majestic, great-spirited, law-spirited, prospering Muñjaketu, Saṃgrāmajit, Durmukha, the powerful Ugrasena, Kakṣasena, lord of his country, the unvanquished Kṣemaka, King Kamala of Kamboja, and the mighty Kampana, who by himself continued to terrify the Greeks, as the Thunderbolt-wielder terrifies the Kālakeya Asuras;

And Jaṭāsura, the king loved by the Madras,
Kunti and Kuṇinda king of Kirātas,
Anga and Vanga and king of Puṇḍra,
The Pāṇḍya, Udrāja, and Andhraka;

Sumanas, king of Kirātas, Cāṇūra, overlord of the Greeks, Devarāta, Bhoja and Bhīmaratha; Śrutāyudha of Kalinga, Jayatsena of Magadha, Suśarman, Cekitāna, and enemy-plougher Suratha, Ketumat and Kṛtakṣaṇa of Videha, Sudharman, Aniruddha, and powerful Śrutāyus, Anūparāja the unassailable, Kṣemajit of the rich stipends, Śiśupāla and his son, and the sovereign of the Karūṣas, and the godlike unassailable princes of the Vṛṣṇis – Āhuka, Viprṭhu, Gada, Sāraṇa, Akrūra, Kṛtavarman and Sātyaki son of Sini; Bhīṣmaka, Āhṛti, the mighty Dyumatsena; the great archers the Kekayas; Yājñasena of the Somakas; all the heroic princes who had chosen for Arjuna, learning from him the science of archery while clad in deer and antelope skins; and the scion of the Vṛṣṇis; and the princes who had been taught in the same school – Rukmiṇī's son, and Sāmba, and Yuyudhāna Sātyaki. These and many other princes, O king of the earth, were there. Dhanaṃjaya's perpetual friend Tumbura always sat there, and

Citrasena with his councillors, Gandharvas and Apsarās, clever in songs and music-making, skilled in the beat of cymbals, and Kimnaras, students of measures and rhythms—all these Gandharvas were exhorted by Tumbura and sang in unison. These experts sang to celestial tunes according to the rules of music and entertainingly waited on Pāṇḍu's sons, these seers, strict in their vows and true to their promises, and waited on Yudhiṣṭhira in his hall as the Gods wait on Brahmā in heaven.

2(20.a) The Halls of the World Guardians

5 (5; 136). The seer Nārada arrives with his pupils and is honored by Yudhiṣṭhira (1–5). He instructs his host by asking leading questions on policy (5–115).
6 (6; 269). Yudhiṣṭhira thanks Nārada (1–5), who praises the king's hall as the finest on earth. Nārada is asked about celestial halls (5–15).
7 (7; 291). Nārada describes Indra's hall and its familiars: divine seers and others, including King Hariścandra (1–25).
8 (8; 317). Yama's hall and the attendant kings, manes, and ascetics (1–35).
9 (9; 353). Varuṇa's hall with Ādityas, Snakes, Demons, oceans, rivers, Gandharvas, Apsarās, and mountains (1–25).
10 (10; 383). Kubera's hall with Gandharvas, Apsarās, Śiva, and the Goddess, and their familiars (1–20).
11 (11–12; 423). Brahmā's hall, to which Nārada was given privileged access, with the Prajāpatis, luminaries, planets, sciences, groups of Gods, etc. (1–40). Yudhiṣṭhira asks why Hariścandra sits with Indra (40–50). Nārada replies: because he performed the Royal Consecration; he reports that Pāṇḍu exhorts his son to do the same (50–70). Nārada leaves (70).

Vaiśaṃpāyana said:

5.1 While the great-spirited Pāṇḍavas were thus sitting in the hall, and the grand Gandharvas were also seated there, Bhārata, there came on a tour of all the worlds the exalted seer Nārada to the hall,

accompanied by other seers. The divine seer of boundless luster, who was traveling fast as thought with Pārijāta, the sagacious Raivata, Sumukha, and Saumya, had a wish to see the Pāṇḍavas in their assembly hall, O Indra of kings. Seeing the seer Nārada arrive, the first of the Pāṇḍavas, who knew all the Laws, instantly rose up with his brothers. With a courteous bow he welcomed him gratefully and
5 showed him in proper fashion a seat that was worthy of him; then the law-wise king honored him with gems and anything he might desire. Honored by all the Pāṇḍavas, the great seer, who was fully grounded in the *Vedas*, raised with Yudhiṣṭhira these questions compounded with Law, Profit, and Pleasure.

Nārada said:

Do your policies suffice? Does your mind delight in the Law? Do you enjoy pleasures and yet your mind does not suffer? Do you persist in the undiminished career that was followed by your grandfathers before you, a career accompanied with Law and Profit for your subjects, king of men? You do not hurt the Law for Profit or
10 Profit for Law, or both for Pleasure, of which joy is the soul? Do you always pursue, greatest of conquerors, Law, Profit, and Pleasure, distributing them over time, knowing their time, granter of boons?

Do you properly examine with the six royal virtues the seven means, your strengths and weaknesses, the fourteen factors? Do you examine yourself and your enemies, greatest of conquerors, before making peace, and pursue the eight trades? Your six officers are not corrupted perchance and, though rich, not addicted to vice and fully loyal to you, bull of the Bharatas? They are not left unprobed by reason or messengers? Are your counsels always kept secret by
15 yourself and your ministers? Do you pursue war and peace at their proper junctures, and follow the proper course with those who are neutral and in the middle? Are your councillors like yourself – pure in their thinking, capable of living, well-born and loyal, O hero? For the victory of kings, Bhārata, is rooted in their counsel, which is kept well hidden by ministers who are rich in advice and expert in the sciences. You do not succumb to the power of sleep but wake up in time? Do you in the later part of the night reflect on your policy, you who know policy? You do not take counsel alone, nor with too many? And the counsel you have taken does not make the rounds of the
20 kingdom? When you have decided on policies that have a short root but high developments, do you implement them at once and put no obstacles in their way? None of the affairs of state are unknown or half-known to you, or eschewed? For participation in them is essential. Do people know, king, those of your deeds that are done or mostly done, but not those that failed, hero? Do judicious teachers, all experts in the sciences, instruct the princes and the principal warriors

fully? Do you buy one wise man with thousands of fools? For it is a
25 wise man who can bring salvation when affairs are imperiled. Are all
your fortresses filled with treasure, grain, arms, water, tools,
craftsmen, and archers? A single minister who is intelligent, brave,
controlled, and shrewd brings great prosperity to a king or a prince.
Do you find out about the eighteen officers of the other side and the
fifteen of your own by means of groups of three spies unknown to one
another? Do you always carefully and unbeknownst to them keep
watch over all your enemies, always on your guard, slayer of your
foes?

Is your priest well-mannered, well-born, learned, is he a questioner
30 without jealousy, do you treat him properly? Is he in charge of your
fires, conversant with the ritual injunctions, intelligent and upright,
and does he always know the day when the oblations are to be made?
Is your astrologer skilled, educated in the Veda and its branches, a
propounder of the stars, one who knows what is fate in any upheaval?
Have you appointed great retainers to great offices, mediocre ones to
middling offices, and humble ones to lowly posts? Do you charge the
very best ministers, those who are above deceit, pure and bequeathed
by father and grandfather, with the very best tasks? Do your
councillors govern the kingdom without oppressing the subjects too
35 much with heavy punishment, bull of the Bharatas? People do not
despise you as sacrificial priests despise one who has lost caste, and
wives a loving but overbearing husband?

Is your commander bold, brave, shrewd, persevering, well-born,
loyal, and adroit? Are all the officers of your army experienced in
warfare, have they been known to accomplish great exploits and acts
of bravery, and do you honor them courteously? Do you give your
troops adequate food and pay, and on time, without postponements?
For arrears in food and pay turn retainers angry with their masters:
40 from their want great disasters are said to arise. Are all the sons of
good families, in the main, devoted to you, do they always risk their
lives in your cause? Is there not a single officer who for selfish
purposes exceeds his command and arbitrarily rules on the many
matters that relate to the army? If a person at his own initiative acts
beyond the call of duty, does he receive extra honors or more food
and pay? Do you recompense men who are trained in a science, and
experts in any branch of knowledge, according to their quality? Do
you support the wives of men who have died for you or have
45 otherwise come to grief, bull of the Bharatas? Do you grant
protection, as though to a son, to an enemy who bows down from
fear, or, losing heart, surrenders, or is defeated in battle, Pārtha? Are
you impartial and mild to all the world, lord of the world, like a
mother or father? When you hear that an enemy is in trouble, bull of

the Bharatas, do you inspect your threefold force and swiftly march
on him, knowing that resolution as well as defeat depends on the
rear guard, and paying your troops in advance, great king? Do you
distribute to the officers according to their rank the treasures that are
buried in enemy country, enemy-burner?

50 Do you plan to defeat enemies who are distracted and slaves of
their senses, after first having mastered yourself and your own senses?
When you are about to march on your enemies, do the diplomatic
means of persuasion, bribery, alienation, and punishment come first
and are they well applied? Do you fortify your base before you march
out, lord of the people, do you attack to win, and having won do you
spare them? Is your army with four kinds of troops and eight factors
well led by your officers to rout the enemy? Do you attack enemies in
battle without disrupting the harvesting and sowing in their country,
great king?

55 Do your many agents in your country and in enemy territory look
well after their tasks and protect one another? Are those that guard
your food, your ointments and perfumes, approved by yourself, great
king? Are your treasury, granary, stable, gate, arsenal and revenue
properly guarded by loyal servants of proven virtue?

Do you first protect yourself against your servants, inside or outside
your quarters, then them against your kinsmen and one another? Do
they report to you in the morning your vice-induced outlays for
60 drink, gambling, games, and loose women? Are your expenses cleared
with half the revenue, or a quarter, or three-fourths? Do you often
favor relatives, elders, the aged, merchants, artisans, and dependents
with goods and grains when they have fallen on bad times? Do all
the tellers and recorders of your income and outgo report to you on
both every morning? You do not dismiss officials who have many
years of service, wish you well and are loyal, from their post when
they have not been at fault before? When you have ascertained who
are good, middling, and bad, do you appoint them to the right job,
65 Bhārata? You do not entrust your affairs to greedy, thievish,
rancorous, or litigating persons? You do not oppress the kingdom
with greedy men, thieves, young princes, or a troop of women? Do
the farmers prosper? Are the reservoirs in your kingdom full and big
enough and properly distributed, so that the harvest is not bothered
by lack of rain? If seed and food are scarce, do you give a farmer a
charitable loan with an interest of one *pratika* a hundred? Are the
professions held by honest people? It is on the professions that this
70 world depends and by whom it prospers. Are the five officers who are
charged with the five duties upright and sensible, and do they bring
security to the countryside in cooperation with one another, prince?

To protect the city, are the villages guarded like towns and all the
hamlets depending on the villages guarded like villages? Are the old
robbers and their leaders on the run in your realm, pursued over the
rough and the smooth by your troops?

Do you comfort the women and keep them protected; but you do
not put your trust in them or tell them secrets, do you? After having
listened to your spies and reflected upon their tasks, and knowing
which people are inside, do you sleep securely and comfortably?
75 When you have slept for the first two watches of the night, O lord of
the people, do you rise in the last watch and reflect on Law and
Profit? After rising on time, knowing your times, do you show yourself
each morning to your people with proper adornment amidst your
councillors, Pāṇḍava? Do properly attired guards in red clothes attend
on you with sword in hand for your safety, slayer of enemies? Do you
examine the court cases fully and act like a Yama to those who must
be punished and those who must be honored, whether you like them
or not? Do you always cure bodily ailments with herbs and diet, and
80 mental ills by attending on the aged, Pārtha? Are the physicians in
charge of your body trained in eight-membered medicine and always
friendly and loyal? You do not, ever, from pride, confusion, or whim,
dismiss, O lord of the people, litigants who have come to you? And do
you ever, from greed or confusion, withhold a livelihood from those
who confidently or loyally seek shelter with you? Are townspeople
and those who inhabit your domain ever bought by your enemies,
and do they combine and rise against you? Is your weak enemy held
in check with force, your strong enemy with counsel, or with both,
Yudhiṣṭhira?

85 Are all the chief governors of the country loyal to you and ready to
risk their lives in your cause, if fetched by you? Do you pay a proper
respect, for your own good, to brahmins and good people according
to their quality in all branches of knowledge? Do you abide by the
Law, based upon the *Vedas*, which was observed by your predecessors,
to perform rites, and do you abide by the ritual? Do virtuous
brahmins eat tasty and good meals in your house before your eyes
and are they paid stipends? Do you, master of yourself, strive to
perform with a single mind all Vājapeya and Puṇḍarīka sacrifices and
90 complete them? Do you bow before your kinsmen, elders, deities,
ascetics, sanctuaries, holy trees, and brahmins? Do you have this
spirit and this conduct, prince sans blame, which bestows a long life
and fame, and insight into Law, Profit, and Pleasure? Of one who acts
with this spirit, the kingdom will not perish; and having conquered
the earth the king attains to supreme happiness. Is no pure-spirited
honorable man falsely jailed for theft by greedy persons who have

neither knowledge of the textbooks nor competence, and put to death?
Or is a thief, who has been questioned and apprehended and seen by
witnesses to commit a crime with his tools, set free for a bribe, bull
95 among men? Or do your ministers corrupted by bribes see matters
falsely if something arises between a wealthy man and a poor man,
Bhārata? Do you shun the fourteen kingly vices—heterodoxy,
untruthfulness, anger, carelessness, procrastination, avoidance of the
wise, sloth, absentmindedness, consultation with just one person,
consultation on policies with those ignorant of them, failure to act on
matters decided, failure to keep his counsel, failure to employ
auspicious rites, and attachment to sensations? Are the *Vedas*
fruitful, is your wife fruitful, is your learning fruitful?

Yudhiṣṭhira said:

100 How do the *Vedas* become fruitful, how does wealth become
fruitful, how does a wife become fruitful, how does learning become
fruitful?

Nārada said:

The *Vedas* become fruitful in the *agnihotra*, wealth in gifts and consumption, a wife in love play and sons, learning in good conduct and deportment.

Vaiśaṃpāyana said:

After having thus spoken, the great ascetic and hermit Nārada thereupon questioned the Law-spirited Yudhiṣṭhira as follows:

Nārada said:

Do those who live on customs duties take the agreed duties from
the merchants who come from afar in hope of gain? When they bring
their wares, are these people treated well in your city and domain
105 and not cheated with deceptions? Do you listen to the words on Law
and Profit of the aged, who always know Profit, my son, and have
insight into the Law? Do you give honey and butter to the brahmins
to help the crops, cattle, flowers, and fruit, and to increase the Law?
Do you always give all the artisans their materials and tools for up to
four months? Do you inspect the work and praise the maker and
honor him properly in the midst of good people, great king?

Do you learn all the textbooks, bull of the Bharatas, those on
110 horses and elephants and chariots, O lord? Are the textbooks of the
science of archery and of city engineering regularly studied in your
house, bull among Bharatas? Are all the weapons and Brahmā's Staff
known to you, prince sans blame, and all poison recipes that destroy
enemies? Do you protect your realm against danger from fire, snakes,
beasts of prey, disease, and demons? Do you, like a father, protect the
blind, the dumb, the crippled, the handicapped, the orphans, and
the vagrant ascetics, you who know the Law?

Vaiśaṃpāyana said:

The great-spirited bull of the Kurus heard
These words of that most eminent brahmin,
And joyously bowed and saluted his feet.
To celestial Nārada spoke the king:

115 "I shall act as thou hast commended to me,
For my insight now has grown even wiser."
And the king indeed did act on this wise
And obtained all of earth that is girt by the sea.

Nārada said:

A king who acts thus while protecting the society of the four classes disports himself on earth very happily and attains to the world of Indra.

Vaiśaṃpāyana said:

6.1 When the great seer had finished speaking, Yudhiṣṭhira the King Dharma paid homage and was given leave to speak. He answered his questions in sequence. "Blessed lord," he said, "you have pronounced decisions on the Law that are correct, and I carry out this injunction as is proper and within my power. The acts that kings of old performed and the manner in which they performed them fructified accordingly and they were both reasoned and meaningful. We wish, my lord, to walk the good path, but we are not able to walk it as they did who controlled themselves."

5 After he had spoken and paid homage, law-spirited Yudhiṣṭhira
paused a while; then, seeing that it was the right time and that the
world-traveling hermit Nārada was comfortably seated while he
himself sat below him, the wise Pāṇḍava questioned him amidst the
kings: "Sir, you always travel about, fast as thought, as a spectator
in all the many and various worlds that Brahmā of old has created.
Have you seen anywhere an assembly hall such as this one, or greater
still? Tell me at my bidding, brahmin!" Nārada, upon hearing the
10 King Dharma's request, smilingly replied in a gentle voice, "Among
men I have never seen nor heard, my son, of a hall like yours, built
of precious stones, King Bhārata. But I shall tell you of the halls of the
king of the Ancestors* and wise Varuṇa, of Indra and of the God who
dwells on Kailāsa; I shall tell you of the celestial hall of Brahmā,
where all fatigue is dispelled, if you have a mind to hear it, bull of the
Bharatas."

At these words of Nārada, Yudhiṣṭhira the King Dharma, in the company of his brothers and in the midst of all the kings, folded his

* = Yama.

hands and the great-spirited prince replied, "Tell of all those halls,
15 we wish to hear it! Of what are they built, brahmin, how wide are
they and how long? Who wait on the Grandsire in that hall, and who
on Indra, the king of the Gods, and on Yama Vaivasvata? Who attend
on Varuṇa and Kubera in their halls? All this we all wish to hear you
tell, divine seer, just as it is, for our curiosity is very great!"
Nārada replied to Yudhiṣṭhira's words, "Then hear of those
celestial halls one by one, O king!"

Nārada said:

7.1 Śakra's celestial and splendid hall, which he won with his feats,
was built by himself, Kaurava, with the resplendence of fire. It is a
hundred leagues wide and a hundred and fifty long, aerial, freely
moving, and five leagues high. Dispelling old age, grief, and fatigue,
free from diseases, benign, beautiful, filled with chambers and seats,
lovely and embellished with celestial trees is that hall where, O
Pārtha, the lord of the Gods sits with Śacī—the great Indrāṇī—and
5 with Śrī and Lakṣmī on his superb throne, Bhārata, wearing an
indescribable form, with diadem and upper-arm bracelets of copper,
spotless robes, bright-colored garlands, accompanied by Hrī, Kīrti, and
Dyuti. There wait upon him, the great-spirited God of the Hundred
Sacrifices, forever the Maruts, O king, all householders, and the
Siddhas and divine seers, the Sādhyas and the hosts of the Gods. With
their own retinues they all in their divine forms and beautiful
ornaments wait on the great-spirited king of the Gods, the tamer of
his foes. Likewise, Pārtha, all the divine seers attend on Śakra,
immaculate, sinless, and radiant like fire, splendid offerers of the Soma,
faultless and tireless—Parāśara, Parvata, Sāvarṇi, Gālava, Śankha,
10 Likhita, the hermit Gauraśiras, Durvāsas, Dīrghatapas, Yājñavalkya,
Bhāluki, Uddālaka, Śvetaketu, the masterful Śāṭyāyana, Haviṣmat,
Gaviṣṭha, King Hariścandra, Hṛdya, Udaraśāṇḍilya, Pārāśarya,
Kṛṣīhvala, Vātaskandha, Viśākha, Vidhātar, Kāla, Anantadanta,
Tvaṣṭar, Viśvakarman, Tumbura—these seers, born from wombs and
not born from wombs, living on the wind, maintaining the fires, all
wait upon the sovereign of the entire universe, the Thunderbolt-
wielder. So Sahadeva, Sunītha, the great ascetic Vālmīki, Samīka and
15 Satyavat and Pracetas true to his word, Medhātithi, Vāmadeva,
Pulastya, Pulaha, Kratu, Marutta, Marīci, Sthāṇu, the great ascetic
Atri, Kakṣīvat, Gautama, Tārkṣya, the hermit Vaiśvānara, the hermit
Kālakavṛkṣīya, Āśrāvya, Hiraṇyada, Saṃvarta, Devahavya, mighty
Viṣvaksena. All the divine Waters, the Herbs, Faith, Wisdom,
Sarasvatī, Law, Profit, and Pleasure, Lightning, O Pāṇḍava, the rain-
carrying clouds as well, and the Winds, Thunder, the Eastern Quarter,
the twenty-seven fires that carry the oblation, Agnīṣoma, Indrāgni,

Mitra, Savitar, Aryaman, Bhaga and all the Sādhyas, Śukra and
20 Manthin, O Bhārata, the Sacrifices, the Stipends, the Planets, all the
Stobhas, all the Mantras that carry the Sacrifices sit together there.
Likewise the Apsarās and the charming Gandharvas, O king, who
with dances, music, and songs and manifold entertainments amuse
the king of the Gods, Indra of the Hundred Sacrifices, O king of men,
praising with lauds and auspicious formulas and also with rites and
with feats of bravery the great-spirited Slayer of Vala and Vṛtra. All
brahmin seers and royal seers, and all divine seers, riding celestial
chariots of many kinds that blaze like fires, garlanded and adorned, go
25 in and out—Bṛhaspati and Śukra go there together—these and many
other ascetics of strict vows, beautiful looking like the moon on their
moonlike chariots, Bhṛgu and the Seven Seers go there at Brahmā's
behest. I myself have seen Indra's hall Puṣkaramālinī, great king.
Now hear from me about Yama's, prince sans blame!

Nārada said:
8.1 I shall tell you of that divine hall, Yudhiṣṭhira, listen, which
Viśvakarman built for Yama Vaivasvata. That glorious hall is over a
hundred leagues wide and long, King Pāṇḍava, bright like the sun,
resplendent, able to move anywhere. It is neither too cold nor too hot
inside; neither grief, old age, hunger, thirst, nor unpleasantness is
found there, nor misery, fatigue, or obstruction, unvanquished king!
5 All desires are satisfied there, human and divine, food and drink is
plentiful and tasty, tamer of foes. There are garlands of auspicious
fragrance, the trees are always in bloom and fruit. There is both hot
and cold water, tasty water.
In that hall holy royal seers and pure brahmins joyfully attend
upon Yama Vaivasvata, my son—Yayāti, Nahuṣa, Pūru, Māndhātar,
Somaka, Nṛga, Trasadasyu, Turaya, Kṛtavīrya, Śrutaśrava, Aripraṇud,
Susiṃha, Kṛtavega, Kṛti, Nimi, Pratardana, Śibi, Matsya, Pṛthvakṣa,
10 Bṛhadratha, Aiḍa, Marutta, Kuśika, Sāṃkāsya, Sāṃkṛtir, Bhava,
Caturaśva, Sadaśvormi, Kārtavīrya the king, Bharata, Suratha,
Sunītha, Nala of Niṣadha, Divodāsa, Sumanas, Ambarīṣa, Bhagīratha,
Vyaśva, Sadaśva, Vadhryaśva, Pañcahasta, Pṛthuśravas, Ruṣadgu,
Vṛṣasena, Kṣupa of very great strength, Ruṣadaśva, Vasumanas,
Purukutsa of the banner and chariot, Ārṣṭiṣeṇa, Dilīpa, and the
great-spirited Uśīnara, Auśīnara, Puṇḍarīka, Śaryāti, Śarabha, Śuci,
15 Anga, Ariṣṭa, Vena, Duḥṣanta, Saṃjaya, Jaya, Bhāngāsvari, Sunītha,
Niṣadha, Tviṣīratha, Karandhama, Bāhlika, Sudyumna, the powerful
Madhu, Kapotaroman, Tṛṇaka, Sahadeva and Arjuna, Rāma
Dāśarathi, Lakṣmaṇa, Pratardana, Alarka, Kakṣasena, Gaya, Gauraśva,
Rāma Jamadagnya, Nābhāga and Sagara, Bhūridyumna, Mahāśva,
Pṛthvaśva, Janaka, King Vainya, Vāriṣeṇa, Puraja, Janamejaya,

Brahmadatta, Trigarta, King Uparicara, Indradyumna, Bhīmajānu,
20 Gaya, Pṛṣṭha, Naya sans blame, Padma, Mucukunda, Bhūridyumna,
Prasenajit, Ariṣṭanemi, Pradyumna, Prthagaśva, Ajaka, the one
hundred Matsya kings, the one hundred Nīpas, the one hundred
Hayas, the one hundred Dhṛtarāṣṭras, the eighty Janamejayas, the
one hundred Brahmadattas, the one hundred feuding Īris, the royal
seer Śaṃtanu, and your father Pāṇḍu, Uśadgava, Śataratha,
Devarāja, Jayadratha, Vṛsādarbhi the royal seer, with Dhāman and
his ministers, and more thousands of Śaśabindus, who went after
25 having offered up many great Horse Sacrifices with rich stipends—
these holy royal seers of great fame and renown attend on Yama
Vaivasvata in his assembly hall. Likewise Agastya, Matanga, Time
and Death, sacrificers, Siddhas, and those who have a yogic body; the
Fathers are there as are the Fire-tasters, Froth-drinkers, Vapor-
drinkers, Oblation-takers, and Grass-sitters, and still others that have
bodies; the Wheel of Time and the blessed Lord Fire himself; men of
evil deeds and those who have died during the sun's southern course;
and those familiars of Yama who are charged with the conduction of
time; and the *śiṃśapā* and *palāśa* trees, *kāśa* and *kuśas* and other trees
and plants wait upon the king of the Law in bodily form, free from
30 diseases. There are many others who sit in the assembly hall of the
king of the Fathers, impossible to enumerate by name and deed; yet,
Pārtha, this fair hall, which can move at will, is never crowded—
Viśvakarman built it after accumulating over a long time the power
of austerities, and it is luminous as though on fire with its own
radiance, Bhārata. To it go ascetics of dread austerities, of good vows
and truthful words, who are tranquil, renouncing, successful, purified
by their holy acts, all wearing effulgent bodies and spotless robes, with
colorful upper-arm bracelets and garlands and bright earrings,
35 adorned by holy and good acts and by their paraphernalia; and so go
great-spirited Gandharvas and hosts of Apsarās by the hundreds.
Music, dance, song, frolic and mime, and auspicious perfumes and
sounds as well as celestial garlands crowd that hall all around,
Pārtha. A hundred hundred of thousands of law-abiding persons of
wisdom attend in bodily form on the lord of the creatures. Such is the
hall of the great-spirited king of the Fathers, O king. I shall now
describe to you the hall called Puṣkaramālinī of Varuṇa.

Nārada said:

9.1 Yudhiṣṭhira! Varuṇa's divine hall is lustrously white; in its
dimensions it is like Yama's with luminous walls and gate towers. It
was built by Viśvakarman in water and is surrounded by celestial
jeweled trees that yield flowers and fruit, covered with carpets of

flowers, blue, yellow, black, dark, white, and red, and with bowers
that bear clusters of blossoms. In the hall sweet-voiced birds of many
feathers fly about, indescribably beautiful, by the hundreds and
5 thousands. Every touch delights, it is neither too hot nor too cold
there, and the lovely white hall that is guarded by Varuṇa has many
chambers and seats. There Varuṇa sits with Vāruṇī, O Bhārata,
wearing celestial jewelry and attire, adorned with ornaments.
Garlanded and ornamented, trailing their flower garlands, the
Ādityas attend there on Varuṇa, lord of the waters; and so do
Vāsuki, Takṣaka, the Snake Airāvata, Kṛṣṇa, Lohita, Padma, the brave
Citra, the Snakes Kambala and Aśvatara, Dhṛtarāṣṭra and Balāhaka,
Maṇimat, Kuṇḍaladhara, Karkoṭaka and Dhanaṃjaya, Prahrāda,
10 Mūṣikāda, and Janamejaya, all marked with banners and circles and
spreading their hoods—these and many other Snakes wait on the
great-spirited Varuṇa in that hall, unwearied, Yudhiṣṭhira. King Bali
Vairocana and world conqueror Naraka, Prahrāda and Vipracitti, all
the Kalakhañjas, Suhanu, Durmukha, Śankha, Sumanas, Sumati,
Svana, Ghaṭodara, Mahāpārśva, Krathana, Piṭhara, Viśvarūpa,
15 Surūpa, Virūpa, Mahāśiras, Daśagrīva, Valin, Meghavāsas, Daśāvara,
Kaitabha, Viṭaṭūta, Saṃhrāda, Indratāpana, all the hosts of Daityas
and Dānavas with their bright earrings, all garlanded and diademed
and divinely garbed, all receivers of boons and champions, all beyond
death, all always held in the noose of the Law and observant of their
vows, attend on the great-spirited God Varuṇa in his hall.

Likewise the four oceans, and the River Ganges Bhāgīrathī, the
Kālindī, Vidiśā, Veṇṇā, Narmadā, Vegavāhinī, Vipaśā, Śatadru,
20 Candrabhāgā, Sarasvatī, Irāvatī, Vitastā, Sindhu, Devanada, Godāvarī,
Kṛṣṇaveṇṇā, Kāverī, best of rivers—these and other rivers and fords
and lakes, wells and springs in bodily form, Yudhiṣṭhira, and ponds
and tanks in bodily form, O Bhārata, the Quarters, Earth and all the
mountains and all water creatures wait upon the great-spirited God.
The hosts of Gandharvas and Apsarās with song and music all sit
together there praising Varuṇa. The mineral-rich mountains and the
25 herb juices found there all attend in bodily form on the lord. I myself
have flown to Varuṇa's hall, bull of the Bharatas, and have seen it.
Hear now of Kubera's hall.

Nārada said:

10.1 Kubera Vaiśravaṇa's lustrously white hall, O king, is one hundred leagues long and seventy wide. Vaiśravaṇa built it himself with the power of his austerities, prince. It is luminous like the moon, floating in the sky, like a peak of Mount Kailāsa. Carried by the Guhyakas, the celestial hall seems as though fastened to the sky, and tall trees of

gold adorn it. Irradiating rays, effulgent, redolent with divine
fragrances, charming and shaped like a white cloud or mountain peak,
it appears as though it is floating in space.
5 There sits enthroned the illustrious King Vaiśravaṇa in his colorful
ornaments and robes and sparkling earrings, surrounded by thousands
of women, seated on a superb throne, auspicious, resplendent like the
sun, covered with celestial cushions, and with a separate divine
footstool. A pure fragrant breeze carries the scents of noble coral
trees, redolent woods, and water lilies, of the lotus pond called Alakā
and of a forest of sandal trees, and, delighting mind and heart, waits
on the God. There the Gods and Gandharvas, surrounded by the hosts
10 of Apsarās, sing their divine songs with celestial melodies. There are
Miśrakeśī and Rambhā and the sweet-smiling Citrasenā, Cārunetrī,
Ghṛtācī, Menakā, Puñjikasthalā, Viśvācī, Sahajanyā, Pramlocā,
Urvaśī, Irā, Vargā and Saurabheyī, Samīcī, Budbudā, Latā—these
hosts of Apsarās and others by the thousands, all expert in song and
dance, attend upon the wealth-granting God, O Pāṇḍava. Never empty
of divine music, dances, and songs, the hall shines magnificently with
the hosts of Gandharvas and Apsarās. There are the Gandharvas
called Kiṃnaras and others called Naras—Maṇibhadra, Dhanada,
15 Śvetabhadra, Guhyaka, Kaśeraka, Gandhakaṇḍu, the mighty Pradyota,
Kustumbura, Piśāca, Gajakarṇa, Viśālaka, Varāhakarṇa, Sāndroṣṭha,
Phalabhakṣa, Phalodaka, Angacūḍa, Śikhāvarta, Hemanetra,
Vibhīṣaṇa, Puṣpānana, Pingalaka, Śoṇitoda, Pravālaka,
Vṛkṣavāsyaniketa, Citravāsas, O Bhārata, these and many other
Yakṣas, by the hundreds of thousands, are in attendance. So is also
the blessed mistress Śrī and Kubera's son Nalakūbara. I myself am
often there, and others of my rank; preceptors have been there and
20 divine seers. So is the blessed Lord, Paśupati, consort of Umā,
surrounded by his hundreds of thousands of creatures, he who wields
the trident and slew Bhaganetra, the Three-Eyed God, O tigerlike king,
with the unwearied goddess. Surrounded by his dwarfs, bloody-eyed
familiars, cripples, hunchbacks, fast as thought, who feast on flesh,
fat, and marrow and are horrible to hear or see, grimly brandishing
their many weapons, as though shaken by powerful gusts of wind.
He sits with his friend the wealth-granting God, O king. When
traveling in the sky I saw this hall of his. Now, O king, I shall tell of
the hall of the Grandfather, where all fatigue is dispelled.

Nārada said:

11.1 Of old, in the Eon of the Gods, O king, the blessed Lord Āditya came
down from heaven, unwearied, in order to see the world of men.
While he roamed about in human form, he told me truthfully of the

assembly hall of the self-existent Brahmā, as he had seen it, Pāṇḍava. When I heard of this celestial, incorporeal hall of measureless luster and indescribable majesty, bull of the Bharatas, which delights the thoughts of all creatures, I became curious to see its virtues myself, princely scion of Pāṇḍu, and I spoke to Āditya: "Lord, I wish to see the hall of the Grandfather. Through what austerities can it be seen, or through what acts, lord of cattle, or by applying what herbs or employing what wizardry? Tell me this, my lord—how can I set eyes on that hall?"

Thereupon the blessed and mighty lord Sun took me and went to that faultless hall of Brahmā, which knows of no fatigue. It is not possible to describe it as it really is, king of the people, for from instant to instant it has another indescribable appearance. I know neither its size nor its structure, Bhārata, and never before have I seen such beauty. The hall is very comfortable, king, neither too cold nor too hot; when one enters it, one no longer is hungry, thirsty, or weary. It is as though it is made up of many different shapes, all very colorful and luminous. No pillars support it. It is eternal and knows of no decay. It is self-luminous beyond the moon and the sun and the flame-crested fire; on the roof beam of heaven it blazes as though to light up the sun. In it sits the blessed lord, O king, the grandfather of the worlds who, alone, constantly creates the worlds with his divine wizardry.

The Lords of the Creatures attend on the lord, Dakṣa, Pracetas, Pulastya, Pulaha, Marīci, Kaśyapa, Bhṛgu, Atri, Vasiṣṭha, Gautama, Angiras; the Mind, Atmosphere, the Sciences, Wind, Fire, Water, Earth, Sound, Touch, Color, Taste, and Smell, O Bhārata, Source-stuff and Evolute and whatever else is cause of the world. Moon with the Asterisms, the Sun with its Rays, the Winds and Seasons, the ritual Intention and Breath, these and many others attend on the Self-existent One, and Law, Profit, and Pleasure, Joy, Hatred, Austerity, Self-control. The Gandharvas and Apsarās go there together, and the twenty-seven other World Guardians, Śukra, Bṛhaspati, Budha, Angāraka, Sanaiścara, Rāhu, all the Planets, Mantra, Rathaṃtara, Harimat, Vasumat, the Ādityas with their overlord, and those deities called by various double names; the Maruts, Viśvakarman, the Vasus, O Bhārata, all the hosts of the Fathers, all the Oblations, Ṛgveda, Sāmaveda, and Yajurveda, Pāṇḍava, the Atharvaveda and the Books, O lord of the people, Epics and subordinate Vedas, all the auxiliary Limbs of the Veda, the *soma* cups, Sacrifices, Soma, all the Deities, the Sāvitrī formula, savior from distress, the sevenfold Speech, Wisdom, Perseverance, Learning, Insight, Understanding, Fame, Forebearance, the Sāman chants, the Lauds, the Praises, the various Songs, the

Commentaries with their Arguments in an embodied form, O lord of
the people, the Instants, Moments, Hours, Day, Night, Fortnights,
Months, the six Seasons, Bhārata, the Years, the Lustrums, the four
kinds of Days and Nights, the divine, eternal, indestructible Wheel of
Time, Aditi, Diti, Dānu, Surasā, Vinatā, Irā, Kālakā, Devī, Surabhi,
30 Saramā, Gautamī, the Ādityas, Vasus, Rudras, Maruts and Aśvins, the
Viśve Devās, Sādhyas, Fathers, fast as thought, Rākṣasas, Piśācas,
Dānavas, Guhyakas, Birds, Snakes, and Cattle wait on the Grandfather.
There is the God Nārāyaṇa, there the divine seers, the Vālakhilya
seers, those born from wombs and those who are not. Whatever is
found in the three worlds, whether moving or standing, know that I
have seen it all in that hall, lord of men. The eighty thousand ascetics
who practice celibacy, the fifty thousand seers who have sons,
35 Pāṇḍava, they and all the other dwellers in heaven come to visit as
they please, bow their heads and return as they have come. And to
the lordly guests who come, Gods, Daityas, Snakes, hermits, Yakṣas,
Çaruḍas, Kāleyas, Gandharvas, and Apsarās, to them the
immeasurably wise Brahmā, Grandfather of the world, who has mercy
for all beings, acts as they deserve. Upon receiving their homage, the
all-soul, the self-existent One of boundless luster, bestows on them
joys intended to comfort, king of men. With all the visitors coming and
going, Bhārata, the divine, pleasure-giving hall is always busy, my
40 son. Dispelling all fatigue, the hall, built of all lights, frequented by
hosts of brahmin seers, shines radiantly with the plenty of Brahmā.
That rare hall is in all the world what yours is among men, O tigerlike
king! Those are the halls that I have seen among the Gods, Pāṇḍava.
Yours is the wholly most excellent hall in the world of men.

Yudhiṣṭhira said:

Almost the entire world of kings, as you have described it, eloquent
Lord, is in the hall of Yama Vaivaśvata. You say that the Snakes, the
lords of the Daityas, the rivers and oceans are mostly in Varuṇa's
45 hall. Likewise the Yakṣas, Guhyakas, Rākṣasas, Gandharvas, Apsarās,
and the bull-bannered Lord are in that of the God of Riches. And in
the hall of the Grandfather you say are the great seers, all the groups
of Gods and all the sciences. In the hall of the God of the Hundred
Sacrifices you have enumerated, hermit, distinctly, the Gods,
Gandharvas, and various great seers. Only one royal seer, Hariścandra,
you have mentioned as being inside the hall of the great-spirited king
of the Gods, great hermit. What feat did he accomplish, or to what
50 austerities was he strictly avowed, that this famous king rivals Indra?
And when you went to the world of the Fathers, you met my father,
the lordly Pāṇḍu, brahmin. What was the manner of your encounter?
What did he say, blessed lord? I wish to learn and hear all this from
you, for my curiosity is very great!

Nārada said:

As you ask me about Hariścandra, great king, I shall propound to
you the greatness of this wise king.

He was a mighty king, the sovereign of all the lords of earth, and
all the kings on earth always bowed to his behest. Standing upon his
single victorious chariot, which was embellished with gold, he
subjugated the seven continents with the might of his sword, lord of
55 men. After he had conquered the entire world with its mountains,
forests, and woods, he offered up, great king, the great Royal
Consecration Sacrifice. At his command all the kings brought riches
and at that sacrifice became waiters on the brahmins. The lord of
men was pleased to give wealth to the priests, what they demanded,
there and then, and that five times. He satisfied, when the ritual was
concluded, the brahmins who had come there from many countries
with manifold riches. And the brahmins, honored to their fill with
many kinds of food and delicacies, and gratified with piles of gems,
said contentedly that he was splendid and famous beyond all kings.
60 It is for this reason that Hariścandra outshines those thousands of
kings; Pārtha; understand this, bull of the Bharatas!

When the majestic Hariścandra had concluded his grand ceremony
and was consecrated, he was brilliant in universal sovereignty, O king
of men. Whichever kings offer up the great sacrifice of the
Consecration rejoice with the great Indra, Bhārata; and those who
find their deaths on the battlefield, without fleeing, they attain to
Indra's seat and rejoice, bull of the Bharatas; and those who shed
their bodies on earth by severe self-mortification attain to his abode
and are forever illustrious.

65 Upon seeing the glory of King Hariścandra, your father Pāṇḍu,
scion of Kuru, was astounded. "You can conquer the earth. Your
brothers obey you," he said, Bhārata, "offer up the great sacrifice of
the Consecration!" Do your father's wish, tigerlike Pāṇḍava! They
shall become of one world with the great Indra, along with their
ancestors. It is known that this great sacrifice is beset with many
obstacles, O king, for the brahmin Rākṣasas, who destroy rituals, seek
out its weak spots. War follows upon it, encompassing the destruction
of the earth, and there is some portent that brings on destruction.
70 Reflect on this, lord among kings, and do what is fitting. Always rise
watchfully to the protection of the society of the four classes, prosper,
rejoice, and satisfy the brahmins with gifts.

Thus I have described in detail what you have asked me. I now
take leave; I shall go to the city of the Daśārhas.*

Vaiśaṃpāyana said:

After he had thus spoken to the Pārtha, O Janamejaya, Nārada went

* = Dvāravatī.

in the midst of the seers with whom he had come, O king. And when Nārada had left, Yudhiṣṭhira and his brothers bethought themselves of the Royal Consecration, which is the highest of sacrifices, Bhārata Kaurava.

2(21) *The Council*

12–17 (B. 13–21; C. 514–853)
12 (13; 514). Yudhiṣṭhira thinks of performing the Royal Consecration (1–5) and calls a council. His advisers counsel him to undertake it (5–20). He decides to consult Kṛṣṇa and dispatches a messenger to Dvārakā (20–30). Kṛṣṇa arrives (30), and Yudhiṣṭhira puts the question to him (35–40).
13 (14; 565). Kṛṣṇa, replying, states that out of the original baronage 101 baronial lineages have been formed (1–5) and that one king, Jarāsaṃdha, has become universal sovereign, with the help of allies, including Śiśupāla. Few resist him (10–20), many have fled (25). Jarāsaṃdha, avenging his son-in-law Kaṃsa, who was killed by Kṛṣṇa and Balarāma, attacks their tribes with two warriors, Haṃsa and Ḍibhaka (25–35). Haṃsa and Ḍibhaka commit suicide after hearing it rumored that the other had died (40). Jarāsaṃdha reattacks, and the Vṛṣṇis flee from Mathurā to Dvārakā, which is heavily fortified (40–50). The warriors of the Vṛṣṇis (50–55). Jarāsaṃdha has jailed the defeated kings in Girivraja, meaning to sacrifice them to the Great God; setting them free would gain Yudhiṣṭhira the consent of the other lineages to seek universal sovereignty (60–65).
14 (15; 635). Yudhiṣṭhira still hesitates (1–5). Bhīma and Kṛṣṇa encourage him (5–20).
15 (16; 660). Yudhiṣṭhira remains uncertain (1–5). Arjuna urges him to conquest (5–15).
16 (17; 676). Kṛṣṇa advises a raid on the king's person (1–10). He describes Jarāsaṃdha's miraculous birth. To the sonless king Bṛhadratha of Magadha comes the hermit Caṇḍakauśika, who is welcomed with honor (10–25). Bṛhadratha refuses a boon, and laments that he has no son. A mango drops in the hermit's lap; he enchants it and gives it to Bṛhadratha (25–30). The king gives it to his two wives to eat, both get pregnant, and each gives

birth to half a child. Their midwives expose the half-children at a crossroads (30–35). The Rākṣasī Jarā takes them and joins them together; they become one man-child (35–40). The child cries out, and king Bṛhadratha and his wives come out. Jarā gives him the child, who is his son (45–50).

17 (18; 729). After suitable words Jarā disappears. The king calls his son Jarāsaṃdha and proclaims a festival in honor of Jarā (1–5). Caṇḍakuśika returns and predicts the child's great fortune; he will be a universal sovereign and behold Rudra (5–15). Bṛhadratha anoints Jarāsaṃdha and retires to the forest; he dies (20–25). His heir Jarāsaṃdha subjugates the kings (25).

Vaiśaṃpāyana said:

12.1 When Yudhiṣṭhira had heard this declaration of the seer, he sighed and, worrying over how to achieve the Consecration, he found no relief, Bhārata. For upon hearing of the grandeur of the great-spirited royal seers, and finding that sacrifices had won their worlds through their blessed acts, particularly Hariścandra in his felicity, the royal seer who had sacrificed, he wished to offer up the Royal Consecration. Yudhiṣṭhira paid homage to all who were sitting in his hall; and honored by all of them in return, he set his mind on the sacrifice.
5 And while pondering much, the bull of the Kurus made his mind intent upon performing the sacrifice of the Royal Consecration. Again the king, of wondrous power and majesty, guardian of the Law, thought upon that which would be beneficial to all the worlds. Yudhiṣṭhira, greatest of the students of all the Laws, favoring all his subjects, did what was beneficial for all without exception. As he thus went on, reassuring his people like a father; no one was found to hate him, and so he became known as Ajātaśatru.

Assembling his councillors and brothers, the eloquent king again
10 and again interrogated them about the Royal Consecration. And when they were questioned, the assembled councillors spoke this meaningful word to the wise Yudhiṣṭhira, who was anxious to sacrifice: "By means of this rite, through which the consecrated king attains to the stature of Varuṇa, he desires the full stature of a universal sovereign, even though he be already king. Your friends hold the opinion that the time has come for the Royal Consecration, as you are worthy of the stature of a universal sovereign, scion of Kuru. There is no set time for this sacrifice, since it depends on the consensus of the baronage—this ceremony of the Royal Consecration, in which priests of strict vows build six fires with Sāmaveda chants.

At the end of the sacrifice, when he has performed the ladle offerings
and has attained to all the rites and the anointing itself, he is declared
15 to be the conqueror of all. You are capable of it, strong-armed
warrior; we are all under your sway: set your mind without any
hesitation on the Royal Consecration, great king!"

So did all his friends speak, together and separately. When the Pāṇḍava, slayer of his enemies, heard their lawful word, bold, friendly, and distinguished, he accepted it. Listening to the words of his friends, and knowing himself to be capable of the rite, he often pondered on the Royal Consecration, Bhārata. The wise king repeatedly consulted with his brothers, great-spirited priests, and councillors like Dhaumya and Dvaipāyana.

Yudhiṣṭhira said:

How may this desire of mine, who speak in faith, for the great ceremonial of the Royal Consecration that is worthy of a sovereign be fulfilled?

Vaiśaṃpāyana said:

20 At these words of the king, O lotus-eyed king, they replied every
time to the law-spirited Yudhiṣṭhira, "You who know the Law are
worthy of the grand sacrifice of the Royal Consecration!"

When the priests and seers spoke thus to the king, his councillors
and brothers applauded their speech; and the wise king Pārtha, who
was master of himself, again reflected, for he wished well for the
worlds. A wise man who considers capability and implementation,
and weighs time and place, income and expenditure, and thus acts
with his whole mind will not perish. Realizing that a sacrifice is not
undertaken just to ruin oneself, and shouldering his task diligently,
25 he went out in his thoughts to Kṛṣṇa Janārdana, to seek a resolution
concerning his task—to Hari, whom he knew superior to all the world.
The Pāṇḍava bethought himself of the strong-armed hero,
immeasurable, unborn yet born among men out of his own desire;
and of his exploits that matched those of the Gods. Nothing was
unknown to him, there was nothing that did not spring from his
deeds, nothing that he failed to endure. It was thus that he thought
of Kṛṣṇa.

Once come to this final decision, Yudhiṣṭhira Pārtha as to a guru
quickly dispatched a messenger to the guru of all beings. The envoy,
swiftly reaching the Yādavas on his fast-running chariot, approached
30 Kṛṣṇa in his residence in Dvārakā. Acyuta, desirous of seeing the
Pārtha who desired to see him, went back to Indraprastha with
Indrasena. Swiftly traversing many countries on his fast chariot,
Janārdana traveled to the Pārtha who resided in Indraprastha. The
King Dharma, his brother, welcomed him as a brother to his house,
and so did Bhīma. Then Kṛṣṇa affectionately approached his father's

sister.* Joyously he enjoyed himself with his dear friend Arjuna, and received like a guru the homage of the twins.

When Acyuta had rested and was fit and at leisure, the King Dharma met with him in a pleasant spot and acquainted him with his intention.

Yudhiṣṭhira said:

35 I wish to perform the Royal Consecration. But you know full well
that it cannot be achieved by the mere wishing for it. That king finds
the Royal Consecration in whom everything is found, who is honored
everywhere and is the sovereign of all. My friends have said in
assembly that I should perform the Royal Consecration; my final
decision will be in accordance with your advice, Kṛṣṇa. For there are
those who out of friendship will not point out a mistake; there are
those who say pleasant things in hope of gain; there are those who
wish for matters that do at once please and benefit themselves: so is
40 generally people's advice on a proposition found to be. But you rise
above these motivations, and above anger and desire—pray tell what
is most fitting for us in the world.

Śrīkṛṣṇa said:

13.1 Because of all your qualities, great king, you are worthy of the
Royal Consecration. Yet, though you know everything, I shall tell you
something, Bhārata. That which is now called the baronage in this
world was born after the baronage that Rāma Jāmadagnya left as a
remnant. The barons on earth have determined their lineage by the
authority their words carry—that you know, bull of the Bharatas.
The kings, as well as the ranks of the other barons on earth, claim
5 descent from the lineages of Ila and Ikṣvāku. Know, king, bull of the
Bharatas, that the kings of Ila's dynasty and Ikṣvāku's form a hundred
and one different lineages. There is also a vast double dispersion of the
dynasties of Yayāti and the Bhojas, and this dispersion, great king,
extends to the four corners of the world. All the baronage honor
likewise their royalty.

However, after ruling the middle country, a certain king, Caturyu,
in whom the hundred and first lineage is vested, set his mind on
mutual dissension, and he, Jarāsaṃdha, has from birth attained to
universal sovereignty. Another king, the mighty Śiśupāla, has gone
over completely to his side and has, indeed, wise prince, become his
10 marshal. Vakra, the king of the Karūṣas, a powerful warrior who
fights with tricks, has joined him as a pupil joins his guru. Two more
great-spirited kings of great prowess have joined the mighty
Jarāsaṃdha, Haṃsa and Ḍibhaka. So have Dantavakra, Karūṣa,

* = Kuntī.

Kalabha, and Meghavāhana. The king who wears on his head the
divine stone that is known as the amulet of creation, who punished
the two Greek kings Mura and Naraka and rules in the West like
Varuṇa with limitless power—he, Bhagadatta, old friend of your
father's, great king Bhārata, bows for him in word and deed; but,
15 tied by his affections, he is in his heart loyal to you like a father. The
king who reigns in the southwestern end of the world, your heroic
maternal uncle Purujit, scion of the Kuntis, alone is loyal to you from
affection, that destroyer of his foes.

Likewise, that wicked king of the Cedis, whom I failed to kill before,
has gone over to Jarāsaṃdha, the one known as the Supreme Person,
who claims that he is the Supreme Person in this world and in his
folly always assumes my title—a king powerful among the Vangas,
Puṇḍras, and Kirātas, known in the worlds as the Vāsudeva of Puṇḍra.
20 And Caturu Bhīṣmaka, a Bhoja and a friend of Indra, O great king,
a powerful ruler who with the might of his knowledge defeated the
Pāṇḍya, Kratha, and Kaiśika, whose brother, the heroic Āhṛti, is like
a Rāma Jāmadagnya in battle, and who himself is a slayer of enemy
heroes, is loyal to the Magadhan king and holds no loyalty for us
who, as his relations, bow to him and loyally do him favors that he
returns with disfavor. Without recognition of his own lineage and
power he has chosen Jarāsaṃdha, just on seeing his blazing fame!
25 The Northern Bhojas and the eighteen tribes, my lord, have fled to
the West in fear of Jarāsaṃdha. So have the Śūrasenas, the
Bhadrakāras, the Bodhas, the Śālvas, the Paṭaccaras, the Sustharas,
the Sukuṭṭas, the Kuṇindas, and the Kuntis; and so have the kings
of the Śālveyas with their blood relatives and retainers, the Southern
Pāñcālas and the Eastern Kosalas in the Kunti country. Abandoning
the North in terror, the Matsyas and Saṃnyastapādas have fled
southward. Likewise, all the other Pāñcālas, haunted by their fear of
Jarāsaṃdha, have abandoned their kingdom and fled off in all
directions.

Some time before, Kaṃsa with his perverse mind harassed his
30 relatives and married two maidens to be his queens, the daughters of
Jarāsaṃdha Bārhadratha and Sahadeva's younger sisters, Asti and
Prāpti. With this power the perverse man offended his kinsmen and
got the upper hand over them, but it was an extremely poor policy of
him. When thereafter the evil man molested the elders of the Bhoja
barons, the latter concluded an accord with us; for they sought to
save their kin. After marrying off Sutanu, Āhuka's daughter, to
Akrūra, I, seconded by Saṃkarṣaṇa, did my duty by my family. Rāma
and I slew Kaṃsa and Sunāman.

However, with that danger discarded, Jarāsaṃdha rose in arms and
35 the eighteen junior branches held a council, king. Were we to kill

without resting with mighty weapons that kill a hundred at a time,
we would not be able to destroy him in three hundred years. For he
had two superb warriors, Haṃsa and Ḍibhaka, strong among the
strong, in power alike to the Immortals. These two champions
together, and the mighty Jarāsaṃdha, made three who, I believe, are
a match for the three worlds. And this is not only our belief, it is the
opinion of as many kings as there are, most judicious prince.
40 So there was a certain great king famed as Haṃsa, who met in
battle with the eighteen junior branches. Someone rumored that
Haṃsa had been killed, Bhārata, and hearing this, Ḍibhaka drowned
himself in the water of the river Yamunā, king. Deciding that he would
be unable to live in this world without Haṃsa, Ḍibhaka went to his
perdition. But when Haṃsa, sacker of enemy cities, heard the same
of Ḍibhaka, he too went to the Yamunā and drowned himself there.
When King Jarāsamdha heard that both had found their deaths in
the river, he went from Śūrasena to his own city, bull of the
Bharatas.

After the king's retreat, enemy-killer, all of us lived again happily
45 in Mathurā. Thereupon the lotus-eyed wife of Kaṃsa, Jarāsaṃdha's
daughter, came to her father the Magadhan king and, mourning the
misfortune of her husband, again and again urged him, O lord of
kings, enemy-tamer, to kill the killer of her husband. Then we
ourselves, remembering the counsel we had taken before, retreated
faintheartedly, O lord of men. Gathering up our great fortune, O king,
we ran separately and, with our treasures, kinsmen, and relations
fled in fear of him. After due reflection we all sought shelter in the
West, in a lovely town, Kuśasthalī*, which is adorned by Mount
50 Raivata. There we once more settled down, king, and such was the
setting of our fortress that it was unassailable even by the Gods. Even
women could fight there, let alone the bulls of the Vṛṣṇis! There we
are dwelling now, enemy-killer, without danger from anywhere; and
looking at that great mountain, the Mādhavītīrtha—the Mādhavas,
tiger among men, have found complete happiness!

Thus, under this perpetual harassment from Jarāsamdha, we, with
all our power, seek shelter with you, and with great insistence. Our
seat is three leagues deep, with a wall at each league. At every league
an army is posted, and in between there are fortifications with a
hundred gates and stepped defensive towers, manned by the barons of
55 the eighteen junior tribes, who are battle-drunk. In our lineage there
are eighteen thousand troops. Āhuka has a hundred sons, and each
has three hundred under him. Cārudeṣṇā and his brother,** Cakradeva,

* = Dvārakā.
** = Pradyuma.

Sātyaki, I myself, Rauhiṇeya, and Sāmba, the match of Śauri in bravery on the battlefield, we are the seven champions, king. Now hear about the others. Kṛtavarman, Anādhṛṣṭi, Samīka, Samitiṃjaya, Kahva, Śanku, and Nidānta are seven great warriors; the two sons of Andhakabhoja and the old king himself make ten. Destroyers of worlds, brave, heroic, and powerful, they live without care amidst the Vṛṣṇis, remembering the middle country.

60 You who possess at all times the qualities of a universal sovereign, best of the Bharatas, can make yourself the sovereign of the baronage. But, in my judgment, you cannot achieve the Royal Consecration as long as the mighty Jarāsaṃdha is alive. After he had defeated them all, he imprisoned the kings in his mountain corral, Girivraja, as a lion imprisons great elephants in a cave of the Himālaya. King Jarāsaṃdha wants to sacrifice the lords of the earth, for it was after he had worshiped the Great God that he defeated the kings on the battlefield. Whenever he defeated kings in battle, he took them in fetters to his own city and built a corral for men!

65 We too have had to abandon Mathurā, for fear of Jarāsaṃdha, great king, and leave for Dvārakā city. If, great king, you wish to achieve the sacrifice, then strive to set them free and to kill Jarāsaṃdha! For this can be the commencement, and this alone, scion of Kuru, to lead to the Royal Consecration in its completeness, most judicious king. This is my judgment, king, or do you think otherwise, prince sans blame? This being so, decide for yourself about my arguments and tell me.

Yudhiṣṭhira said:

14.1 You have said, wise friend, what no one else could have said, for
no one is found on earth who resolves doubts like you. In every house
there are kings who favor their own, and they have not achieved
Sovereignty, for the title of Sovereign partakes of everything. How can
one who knows the power of others praise his own? It is the one who
is praised in comparison with others who is really honored. Wide
and various is the earth and heaped with many gems: it is by
5 traveling far that one knows what is best, scion of the Vṛṣṇis. I deem
tranquillity highest, but no tranquillity will spring from their release.
If I undertake the rite, the highest goal cannot, I think, be attained.
This is what all wise men who are born in a lineage know: that some
time one of them will become the first of them, Janārdana.

Bhīma said:

A king without enterprise collapses like an anthill, and weak is the king who governs a strong one without policy. But a weak king who is enterprising can often defeat a strong enemy, if his policy is right, and win the goals that are of benefit to oneself. In Kṛṣṇa is policy, in

me strength, in Dhanaṃjaya victory: like the three fires we shall
accomplish the Magadhan king!

Kṛṣṇa said:

10 A fool, intent on his gain, will grasp but not look at the
consequences. Therefore they do not tolerate an enemy who is
foolishly out for gain. These five have become Sovereigns, so we have
heard: Yauvanāśva, by abolishing taxes; Bhagīratha, by protecting;
Kārtavīrya, by his discipline of austerities; the lord Bharata, by his
prowess; Marutta, by his riches. Jarāsaṃdha Bārhadratha has now
become the one to be chastised, by means that exemplify Law, Profit,
and Policy; recognize that, bull of the Bharatas. The hundred and one
lineages of kings will not comply with him, and therefore he now
exercises his Sovereignty by force. Indeed, kings who have their share
of riches wait on him, but even that does not satisfy a man who from
15 childhood has followed perverse policies. He plunders anointed kings
and eminent personages forcibly, and we have never seen him without
tribute from someone. On this wise he has brought under his power
all those kings, who now number close to a hundred. Now how,
Pārtha, can a weaker king march on him? What joy of life is left to
the kings who are sprinkled and cleansed in the house of Paśupati*
as sacrificial animals, bull of the Bharatas? When a baron dies by the
sword, he is honored—should we all then not beat back the Magadhan?
Eighty-six kings, king, have been led to their jail by Jarāsaṃdha;
20 king, fourteen are left, and then he will begin his atrocity! He who
frustrated him in this would achieve a blazing fame. And he who
defeats Jarāsaṃdha will certainly become Sovereign.

Yudhiṣṭhira said:

15.1 In desiring the stature of a Sovereign I am solely intent on my own
interest: how can I forcibly send all of you out? It would be cruelty!
Bhīma and Arjuna are my eyes, Janārdana I deem my mind: what
kind of life shall be left for me when I have lost my eyes and my
mind? For when you shall have met Jarāsaṃdha's invincible forces,
which are terrifyingly brave, exhaustion alone will defeat you. What is
the point of that? If the opposite is achieved of what is intended,
5 disaster results properly. Listen first to what I for one think: I should
like to abandon this task for good. My heart is now against it. The
Consecration is too hard to achieve.

Vaiśaṃpāyana said:

The Pārtha who had acquired the great bow, the two inexhaustible
quivers and the chariot, the banner and the assembly hall, now said
to Yudhiṣṭhira: "I have got bow, arrows, prowess, allies, land, fame,
power, O king, things to be wished for but hard to come by. Men of

* = Śiva.

great learning greatly praise a noble birth. Nothing equals power, but
bravery delights me. What use is a baron born in a heroic lineage
who does not show his prowess? A baron's living is always conquest.
10 For were he to lack all virtue, a man of prowess still routs his enemies;
were he to possess all virtues, what use is he without prowess? All
virtues indeed have their being in power. To be sure, determination
is the cause of victory; for one who, however well equipped with
troops, is careless is incapable of the exertion and the fate needed. It is
through this carelessness that an enemy with troops perishes before
his foes. As cowardice is in a king without troops, so is folly in one
with troops. A king who wants victory must abandon both destructive
courses. If we achieve by way of sacrifice the destruction of
Jarāsaṃdha and the release of the kings, what would surpass that?
15 If we fail to act, they will decide that we lack character—how can you
prefer to undoubted character the lack of it? Afterward the saffron
robe will be easily available for hermits who hanker for peace; but
hankering first for your Sovereignty we shall fight the enemy!"

Vāsudeva said:

16.1 Arjuna has shown the proper mentality of one born in the Bhārata
lineage and of a son of Kuntī! We do not know the time of our death,
whether at night or by day; but neither have we heard of one who
became immortal by shirking battle! This then is the heartwarming
task of a man who marches against the enemy with a policy that is
found in the rules. In an encounter the course of faultless policy
prevails; if the two sides are equal the issue is in doubt, but two sides
5 are never equal. If we adopt our policy and get near to the enemy's
person, how can we fail to finish him, as rivers in spate finish a tree?
When we jump on the enemy's weakness and cover up our own? It is
the policy of the prudent not to attack the stronger enemy with battle
ranks and rear guards, and this is my judgment too. We shall not
be blamed if without army formations we penetrate the seat of the
enemy, attack his person, and achieve our goal. For *he* alone bears
the eternal royal fortune, bull of the Bharatas, like the inner soul of
the creatures; if he perishes, his forces perish. Or if we are attacked by
his survivors in battle after we have killed him, we shall attain to
heaven for our endeavors to protect our kinsmen.

Yudhiṣṭhira said:

10 Kṛṣṇa, who is this Jarāsaṃdha? What are his exploits and feats
that he could touch you who are like a flame, and not burn up like a
moth?

Kṛṣṇa said:

Listen to the exploits and feats of Jarāsaṃdha, king, and hear why
we have ignored him, even though he had affronted us in many ways.

There was a king, Bṛhadratha by name, the overlord of Magadha,
the commander of three armies, and a proud warrior. He was a
handsome man of personal bravery, illustrious and incomparably
powerful; his body was always lean from his fasts at sacrificial
consecrations, and he had the appearance of a second Indra. In
splendor he resembled the sun, in patience the earth, in his anger
15 Yama the Finisher, in wealth Kubera. The entire world was pervaded
by the qualities proper to his high birth, best of the Bharatas, as it is
by the rays of the sun. The powerful lord married the twin daughters
of the king of the Kāśis, O bull of the Bharatas, who were prized for
their beauty and dowry. This bull among men made a compact with
his wives in their presence, that he would never offend them. This
king, O overlord of men, shone with his loving and suitable wives like
an elephant with its females. Between them the lord of the earth
glowed like the embodied Ocean between the Ganges and the Yamunā.
20 While he indulged in pleasure, his youth passed by, and no son
was born to him to be his heir. With many auspicious rites and
offerings, with oblations aimed at procuring desired sons, this eminent
king yet failed to obtain a son to prosper his line. Then he heard that
Caṇḍakauśika, the noble son of the great-spirited Gautama Kakṣīvat,
had chanced to come, exhausted by his austerities, and had sought
shelter beneath a tree. Together with his wives the king satisfied him
with all kinds of presents. Thereupon that eminent seer, who
persevered in the truth and always spoke the truth, spoke to the king:
25 "I am fully satisfied with you, king who are true to your vows. Choose
a boon!" Bṛhadratha and his wives bowed down, and he said in a
voice that was choked with the tears of his despair of ever setting eyes
upon a son—

Bṛhadratha said:

Blessed lord, what does a boon profit this unfortunate creature who
will give up his kingdom and depart for the forest of austerities?
What profits me the kingdom as I have no heirs?

Kṛṣṇa said:

Hearing this the hermit became disturbed and fell to thinking. He
was sitting in the shade of a tree that was a mango tree, and while
he was sitting there a mango dropped in his lap, whole, without holes
or parrot bites. The good hermit took it in his hand, silently cast a
spell on it, then gave the king the peerless fruit that could bestow
30 sons. And the great wise hermit said to the king, "Go, king, your wish
is done. Return, lord of men."

Remembering the compact he had made, the good king then
proffered the one mango to his two wives, bull of the Bharatas. The
beautiful princesses split the mango in two; and since the result was
sure to follow as the hermit had spoken the truth, they both became

with child from eating the fruit. And when he saw them the king became most happy.

When after due time their time came, wise king, they both gave birth to a child with half a body, each with one eye, arm, leg, and buttock, with half a face and belly. At the sight of these half-children they began to tremble wretchedly. Distressed, the two sisters took counsel together and miserably abandoned the two half-creatures who were yet alive. Their midwives swaddled the two child-pieces carefully and, departing from the gate of the women's quarters, exposed them and returned hastily.

Now a Rākṣasī named Jarā took the children who had been cast on a crossroads, tigerlike king, for she fed on flesh and blood. But, to make them easier to carry, the Rākṣasī, prompted by the power of fate, tied the two pieces together. As soon as the two halves were brought together, bull among men, they became one body and a male child appeared. The Rākṣasī, wide-eyed with amazement, was no longer able to carry the child, who was as hard as a diamond. The child balled its copper-red palm into a fist, put it in his mouth, and began to cry violently like a monsoon cloud before breaking. Upset by the sound, the people in the women's quarters rushed out together with the king, victorious tiger among kings. The two women, wan and despondent, their breasts full of milk, hurriedly came out to recover their child.

When Rākṣasī saw the women in that state, and saw the king who was so desirous of offspring, and the husky child, she thought to herself, "I must not carry off this little boy, as a strip of cloud carries off the sun, for I live in the domain of this king who yearns for a son." She assumed human form and spoke to the lord of men: "Bṛhadratha, this is your son; accept him as my gift. He was born from your two wives at the behest of that eminent brahmin, and abandoned by the midwives. I have saved him."

Thereupon, bull of the Bharatas, the beautiful daughters of the king of the Kāśis fell quickly upon the child and sprinkled him with their gushing milk. The happy king, upon witnessing all this, questioned the Rākṣasī who did not look like a Rākṣasī in her human form that shone like fresh gold. "Who are you, golden like the calyx of a lotus, who have given me my son? For the love of me, speak, beautiful damsel. Like a Goddess you appear to me!"

The Rākṣasī said:

17.1 I am Jarā, a Rākṣasī who can assume any form, be blest, O king! I dwell happily in your abode, lord among kings, honored by all. I have often wondered how to do you a favor in return, law-loving king. Then I saw the two halves of your son, and as luck would have it I united them and they became a man child. It was because of your own good luck, great king; I was only the instrument in this.

Kṛṣṇa said:

After she had said this, she vanished on the spot, sire. The king took the boy and entered into his own house. He performed thereupon the necessary rites for the boy and proclaimed a great festival in Magadha land in honor of the Rākṣasī. The father, the equal of Prajāpati, bestowed on him a name: since he had been joined together by Jarā he became Jarāsaṃdha. The son of the Magadhan king grew up with great luster, big and strong like a fire into which butter has been offered.

After some time had gone by, the blessed lord and great ascetic Caṇḍakauśika once more came to Magadha. Delighted at his arrival, Bṛhadratha came out with his ministers, retinue, and wives, and with his son. The king welcomed him with water to wash his feet, a guest gift, and water to rinse his mouth, then offered him his own son and his kingdom. The venerable seer accepted this homage and said with a happy heart to the Magadhan, "I knew it all by my divine insight, king. Now listen to what shall become of your son, Indra among kings. No king shall match the valor of this valiant prince. Even weapons cast by the Gods shall not cause him pain, no more than river currents hurt a mountain. On the heads of all those whose heads have been anointed he shall blaze forth, he shall outshine their light as the sun outshines the light of the stars. In attacking him kings of plentiful forces and mounts shall go to their perdition, as moths in a flame. Thus he shall seize the combined fortunes of all the kings, as the lord of the rivers and streams gathers up the rivers whose waters are swollen in the rainy season. He shall uphold correctly and with great force the society of the four classes, as the earth that bears all crops opulently supports both good and evil. All the lords of men shall submit to his sway, even as all embodied creatures submit to the Breath that is the soul of all beings. Transcending all the worlds with his might, the Magadhan shall with his own eyes behold Rudra, the Great God, the Destroyer of the Three Cities, he who is Hara."

With these words the hermit, contemplating his own tasks, dismissed King Bṛhadratha, O slayer of your foes. Amidst his kinsmen and relations the king of Magadha anointed Jarāsaṃdha and attained to the final serenity. After the unction of Jarāsaṃdha, King Bṛhadratha, who was followed by both his wives, rejoiced in the forest of austerities. While his father stayed in the forest of austerities with his two mothers, Jarāsaṃdha subjugated the kings with his own prowess.

After a long time King Bṛhadratha, who had withdrawn to the forest of austerities, having done austerities, went to heaven with his

25 wives. With Jarāsaṃdha were Haṃsa and Ḍibhika, who could never be killed with weapons. They were most sagacious in counsel, both experts in the science of war, these strong men about whom I talked to you before. These three, in my judgment, were a match for the three worlds.

This is the man, then, hero, whom the Kukuras, Andhakas, and Vṛṣṇis have ignored for reasons of policy, great king.

2(22) *The Killing of Jarāsaṃdha*

18–22 (B. 20–24; C. 768–952)
18 (20; 768). Kṛṣṇa suggests that he himself undertake a raid on Jarāsaṃdha with Bhīma and Arjuna (1–5). Yudhiṣṭhira praises Kṛṣṇa and agrees (5–20). Dressed as snātakas *they travel through Kosala and Mithilā and see the city of Magadha (20–30).*
19 (21; 798). Description of the five mountains and the environs (1–10). They enter the city by breaching the Caityaka ramparts (10–15). The opulence of the city (20). They enter Jarāsaṃdha's palace; he welcomes them (25–35). He berates them for their garments (35–40). Kṛṣṇa says that they are barons, come with hostile purpose (45–50).
20 (22; 854). Jarāsaṃdha pleads innocence (1–5). Kṛṣṇa points to his crime of imprisoning defeated kings, and challenges him (5–20). Jarāsaṃdha accepts the challenge (25) and has his son anointed (30).
21 (23; 890). Jarāsaṃdha chooses to fight with Bhīma (1–15). They engage in wrestling, for thirteen days (5–15). On the fourteenth day Jarāsaṃdha is exhausted, and Kṛṣṇa exhorts Bhīma (15–20).
22 (24; 925). At Kṛṣṇa's prompting Bhīma kills and tramples Jarāsaṃdha (1–5). Kṛṣṇa has Jarāsaṃdha's chariot yoked and the kings set free; he rides out (10–15). Description of the chariot and its flag mast (15–25). Kṛṣṇa is praised by the townsmen and the freed kings, who offer help (25–35). Kṛṣṇa tells them to support Yudhiṣṭhira's Royal Consecration; they so promise (35–40). Sahadeva is installed (40). The three return to Indraprastha with the freed kings, who are dismissed by Yudhiṣṭhira (45–50). Kṛṣṇa takes leave and departs on the chariot; the Pāṇḍavas prosper (50–55).

Vāsudeva said:

18.1 Haṃsa and Ḍibhika have fallen, Kaṃsa and his minister have been
felled. Now the time has come for the death of Jarāsaṃdha. Not even
Gods and Asuras can defeat him in battle, but, so we understand, he
can be defeated in a battle of breath. In me is vested policy, in Bhīma
power, and Arjuna is the guardian of the two of us. We shall
accomplish him, king, as the three fires accomplish the sacrifice!
When the king is set upon by the three of us, alone, there is no doubt
5 that he will engage one of us in a fight. The contempt in which he
holds the world, and his self-esteem, will, once he is cornered, surely
lead him to challenge Bhīmasena to fight. The mighty strong-armed
Bhīma is his match, as Death is of the world that is thrown to its
destruction. If your heart knows, if you have confidence in me, then
entrust Bhīmasena and Arjuna at once to me.

Vaiśaṃpāyana said:

To these words of the blessed lord Yudhiṣṭhira replied, looking at
Bhīma and the Pārtha* who stood there beaming: "Acyuta, Acyuta,**
do not speak to me like that, crusher of enemies! You are the
10 protector of the Pāṇḍavas, and we seek shelter with you. All that you
say, Govinda, is right, for you never guide those whom Fortune has
deserted. Jarāsaṃdha is dead, the kings are set free, I have achieved
the Royal Consecration, as I submit to your direction! You greatest of
men, you who act quickly, act so that the task that I have to
accomplish, this task for the world, may indeed befall. For without
the three of you I myself am unable to live, I am miserable like one
diseased, deprived of Law, Profit, and Pleasure. Without the Śauri* no
Pārtha, without the Pārtha no Śauri. There is nothing in the world,
15 methinks, that cannot be won by the two Kṛṣṇas. And this illustrious
Wolf-Belly, too, is the strongest of the strong. What would not this
famous hero accomplish if assisted by you two? A flood of forces that
are led well accomplishes the greatest task: a force must be led by the
skillful, they say, or it is blind and mindless. For as they lead the
water to the lowlands—so those who are rich in wisdom lead their
forces where there is a hole. Therefore, relying on Govinda, a man
famous in the world, who knows the rules of policy, we strive to
accomplish our task. In any task one should put first wisdom, policy,
and strength accompanied by working means, if one is to succeed
in it.

20 "Let Arjuna follow Kṛṣṇa, let Bhīma follow Dhanaṃjaya, and policy,
triumph, and strength will find success in prowess!"

When he had thus addressed them, all three brethren of plentiful
vigor, the Vṛṣṇi and the two Pāṇḍavas, set out for the Magadhan

* = Arjuna.
** = Kṛṣṇa.

king. Donning the garb of vigorous young brahmins returning home
from their studies, and bidden farewell with affectionate words by their
friends, they departed. And as they blazed with anger over the
humiliation of their kinsmen, their appearance in their fine raiment
and sunlike, moonlike, firelike forms became terrifying. Seeing the two
Kṛṣṇas, invincible in battle and yoked to the same task, led by Bhīma,
25 he thought Jarāsaṃdha already dead. For those two great-spirited
men were as much masters at dispatching any task as at suppressing
works that are to be done for Law, Profit, and Pleasure.

From the Land of the Kurus they traveled through the Jungle of the
Kurus, came to the beautiful Lotus Lake, passed beyond Kālakūṭa, and
crossed the rivers Gaṇḍakīyā, Śoṇa, Sadānīra successively, which
spring from the same mountain. After crossing the lovely river Sarayū
and espying the eastern Kosalas, they passed through their land to
Mithilā and crossed the rivers Mālā and Carmaṇvatī. Thereupon the
three heroes, continuing eastward, crossed the Ganges and the Śoṇa
and reached the Magadhan country, which is jacketed with *kurava*
30 trees. Upon reaching Mount Goratha, always teeming with wealth of
cattle, rich in water, and beautifully wooded, they set eyes on the city
of Magadha.

Vāsudeva said:

19.1 This, Pārtha, is the large and beautiful capital city of Magadha,
agreeable, cattle-rich, always flowing with water, healthy and wealthy
with fine houses. The five beautiful mountains, the wide Vaihāra,
Varāha, Vṛṣabha, Ṛṣigiri, and Caitya, my friend, with their high peaks
and cool trees, massing together, their interstices walled off, seem to
stand guard over Girivraja. They are as it were hidden under the
forests of *lodhra* trees so dear to trysting lovers, fragrant and charming,
5 with the tips of their branches wrapped in blossoms. It is there that
the great-spirited seer Gautama, strict in his vows, fathered on the serf
wench Auśīnarī such sons as Kakṣīvat. Because of his dwelling there
in his seat, Gautama loved the Magadhan dynasty for the favor its
kings showed him. The Angas and Vangas and other kings of very
great power came to Gautama's dwelling place where at one time they
found joy, Arjuna.

Look at the lovely rows of *priyālas*, the holy rows of *lodhras* that
grow close to the dwelling of Gautama, O Pārtha. The enemy-burning
Snakes Arbuda and Śakravāpin dwelled there, there was the lair of
10 Svastika, the supreme abode of the Snake Maṇi. Because of Maṇi this
Magadhan land shall never be avoided by the monsoon clouds.
Kauśika and Maṇimat indeed have increased their favors. Jarāsaṃdha
imagines that the success of his policies will never recede, yet we are
out to assail him, indeed today I shall strike down his pride!

Vaiśaṃpāyana said:

At these words all the brethren of plentiful prowess, the Vṛṣṇi and
the two Pāṇḍavas, started for the Magadhan city. They neared it, this
city filled with contented and well-fed people, teeming with the folk of
all four classes, with its extravagant festivals—unassailable Girivraja.
They avoided the lofty mountain that is the gate to the city, a place of
worship for Bṛhadratha's clan and the townspeople, where Bṛhadratha
once set upon the bean-eating Ṛṣabha and, after killing him, had three
15 beanstalks made into kettledrums. Stretching hides over them, he
placed them in his own city where at one time these drums sounded
forth under the drumsticks of divine blossoms.

They rushed on the Caityaka end, so beloved of the Magadhans, as
though as ready to conquer its peak as they were to kill Jarāsaṃdha.
It is a steadfast, quite wide tower, very big and ancient, worshiped
with garlands and wreaths and forever firmly rooted. The heroes broke
in and struck it with their many big arms, then they saw the city of
Magadha and made their entrance into it.
20 At this time Jarāsaṃdha's priests were worshiping the king, who
was seated on an elephant, by carrying around his person the sacred
fire. There the three made the entrance, disguised as avowed Snātakas,
with no other weapons than their arms, ready to do battle with
Jarāsaṃdha, O Bhārata. They saw the opulence of the bazaars that sold
food and garlands, a wealthy opulence that was adorned with all good
things and rich in all objects of pleasure.

Descrying those riches by the roadside, the great men, Kṛṣṇa,
Bhīma, and Dhanaṃjaya, strode along the royal road. The powerful
25 men forcibly took garlands from a garland maker. Thus, garbed in
their colorful robes, hung with garlands and fine earrings, they
entered the palace of the shrewd Jarāsaṃdha, as Himālayan lions who
see a cow pen. The arms of the big-armed warriors, pillars of rock,
scented with sandal and aloe, gleamed with light, great king. When
the Māgadhans saw them, bulky like elephants, tall like full-grown
śāla trees, and wide-chested, they fell to wondering. The bull-like men
passed through the three walls and enclosures that were filled with
people and, powerfully, arrogantly, made their way to the king.

Jarāsaṃdha rose and attended on them, who were worthy of water
to wash their feet and the honey mixture, and who deserved honors,
with due courtesy as they had come to be welcomed. And the lord the
30 king hailed them: "Be ye welcome!" For this was his life rule, O king,
which was celebrated on earth: whenever he learned that Snātaka
brahmins had arrived, the king-conqueror was wont to rise to meet
them, even though it were in the middle of the night. Observing them
in their exceptional guise, the good King Jarāsaṃdha approached
them and was astonished.

As soon as the bull-like men saw King Jarāsaṃdha, all three
enemy-killers spoke as follows, best of the Bharatas: "There shall be
prosperity and good health, sire!" They remained standing, casting
35 glances at the king, O tigerlike king, and at one another. Thereupon
Jarāsaṃdha said to the Yādava and the Pāṇḍavas who were disguised
as brahmins, Indra of kings: "Be ye seated!" All three bull-like men
took their seats, ablaze with good fortune as the three fires at a grand
sacrifice.

Then the king who was true to his promises said to them in a
censorious tone on account of their appearance, O Kauravya: "This
much I know that in the world of men brahmins who keep the
Snātaka vow do not wear outside either garlands or perfumes. You
here are wearing flowers and your arms are scarred by the bow string;
and while carrying the august aura of the baronage, you claim to be
40 brahmins. You with your colorful robes and your publicly worn
garlands and ointments, speak up, who are you? Truth shines among
kings! Why did you breach the Caitya tower and, without using the
gate, enter our domain, fearless of insulting its king? This act is out of
character—or what is your purpose now? Speak! The brahmin's
prowess lies mostly in his tongue! Now that you have approached me
in this manner, why then do you decline the honor that we have
courteously proffered? Why have you come to us?"

Upon his words the proud and eloquent Kṛṣṇa replied in a voice
that was both kindly and grave: "Brahmins, barons, and commoners
45 all have the right to the vow of a Snātaka. They have different rules as
well as common ones. The baron who always observes his particular
rule attains to good fortune; fortune is certain in those who wear
flowers, hence we wear them. A baron's might lies in his arms, his is
not the power of speech. Hence, Jarāsaṃdha Bārhadrathi, his word is
known not to be disdainful. The creator has put his own might in the
arms of the barons. If you wish to witness it, sire, then doubtless you
shall see. The strict never enter the house of their enemy by the door,
50 but the house of their friend always. So we avoided your doorstep.
Whenever we enter a house with a hostile purpose we never accept
the welcome. Know that this is our eternal vow."

Jarāsaṃdha said:

20.1 I do not recall that I have ever borne you malice, nor do I notice
upon reflection any hostile act toward you. And if there has been no
hostility, why then do you hold me who am innocent for your enemy?
Speak up, brahmins! For such is the compact among the strict. If one
lets go at an innocent man, even if one be a baron, his mind will
doubtless suffer from his breach of the Law. Therefore a man, however
wise in the Law and great in his vows, who acts perversely in this

5 world follows a wicked course and hurts himself in his welfare. Since
you know that I, foremost in the three worlds among the virtuous by
virtue of the Law of the baronage, am innocent, you must be prattling
in complete confusion!

Vāsudeva said:

There is a certain dynast, great king, who bears the burdensome
task his dynasty imposes. It is at his behest that we three have risen
up. You, king, have destroyed barons who live in this world: this
atrocious guilt you have incurred, and you think yourself innocent?
Greatest of rulers of men, how could a king molest honest kings? And
having imprisoned the kings you want to sacrifice them to Rudra! The
evil you have done, Bārhadrathi, might well affect us; for we follow
10 the Law and are capable of enforcing it. Never has there been witness
to human sacrifice: how then can you wish to sacrifice men to the
God-Who-Appeases? A baron yourself, you give fellow barons the
name of beasts! What other man has a mind as perverted as yours?
We who help the oppressed have come here to tame you who plot the
destruction of our kinsmen so that our kinsmen may prosper. If you
think that there is no man on earth among the barons to do this, you
are very greatly deceived, king! What baron who knows his own high
birth would not attain to eternal heaven beyond compare after dying
15 in battle? Setting their minds upon heaven, heroes are consecrated for
the rites that are battles, and thus worship the worlds; be aware of
that, overlord of Magadha! Victory, king, is the womb of heaven,
great fame is the womb of heaven, austerity is the womb of heaven,
and so is the straight road to battle. For that is the triumphant virtue
of Indra, forever attentive, by which the God of the Hundred Sacrifices
vanquished the Asuras and now protects the world. If one wants
heaven, what better man to fight than you, with your vast Magadhan
armies that pride themselves on their numbers and strength! Don't
20 despise others, king! Is there no might in any man? Only as long as
no glory is known equal to yours, lord of men, is it yours alone. But
we can match it, king, I tell you. Give up your pride and conceit when
you are among your equals, Magadhan! Don't tumble into Yama's
hell with your sons, your ministers, and your troops!

Dambhodbhava, Kārtavīrya, Uttara, and Bṛhadratha, kings as well
as troops, perished here, because they despised their betters. We who
want to rescue the kings from you are not self-styled brahmins. I am
Śauri Hṛṣīkeśa, and these champions are two Pāṇḍavas. We are
challenging you, king. Stand firm and fight us, Magadhan, or set free
all the kings, lest you tumble into Yama's hell!

Jarāsaṃdha said:

25 I take no king, unless I have defeated him. Defeated, who shall
stand against me? And whom have I failed to defeat? This they have

cited, Kṛṣṇa, as the lawful benefice of the baron, that he glories, vanquishes, and acts as he pleases. I have fetched these kings for the God. Should *I* now, Kṛṣṇa, let go of them, while remembering fully the life-rule of the baronage? Army against arrayed army shall I fight, or one against one, or one against two or three, at once or severally!

Vaiśaṃpāyana said:

Having spoken, the king at once ordered that Sahadeva be anointed,
30 for he stood ready to do battle with awesome feats. But, O bull of the
Bharatas, the king remembered when the hour of battle approached
his two commanders, Kauśika and Citrasena, whose names in the
world had been Haṃsa and Ḍibhika, names once renowned and
honored by people in the world of men. And, O king, the lordly Śauri
remembered that the king Jarāsaṃdha, of terrifying power in the
world, was the strongest of the strong, O tiger among men, with a
prowess that equaled a tiger's; this did the truthful Adeyuta remember,
and also that the lot of killing him had been assigned to another. Thus
Madhu's Slayer, younger brother of the Plough-armed Rāma, first of
those who have mastered themselves, did not aspire to kill him
himself, but heeded the behest of Brahmā.

Vaiśaṃpāyana said:

21.1 Then Adhokṣaja,* scion of Yadu, spoke eloquently to King
Jarāsaṃdha who had resolved to do battle: "With whom of us three,
king, do you wish to battle? Who must stand ready to fight?"

At this challenge from Kṛṣṇa the glorious Jarāsaṃdha of Magadha
chose battle with Bhīmasena, O king. His priest, holding the best
herbs, pain-killers, and restoratives, waited by the bellicose
5 Jarāsaṃdha. After a renowned brahmin had pronounced the
benediction, the shrewd Jarāsaṃdha, who was avowed to the Law of
the baronage, girded himself, took off his diadem, combed his hair,
then he rose like the ocean that rises beyond the tide line. Spoke the
clever king to Bhīma of terrible might, "Bhīma, I shall fight with you.
It is better to be defeated by a better man!" Then Jarāsaṃdha, the
glorious enemy-tamer, stormed at Bhīmasena as the Asura Bali once
stormed at Indra. Strong Bhīma, who had been blessed by Kṛṣṇa after
10 they had consulted, went at Jarāsaṃdha, eager to fight. The two
tigerlike heroes met with their bare arms, both in high spirits and out
to defeat the other. Their blows and holds and clutches resounded
terrifyingly with the noise of thunderbolts striking mountains. They
were both full of spirit, both extraordinarily strong, and tried for a hole
in the other's defense to bring him down. The duel in this contest of
two powerful fighters, which was close to the crowds—and indeed

* = Kṛṣṇa.

drove them off—was as terrifying as the battle of Indra and Vṛtra.
With forward pulls and clinches and holds and break-away clutches
15 they dragged each other along and brought up their knees. They
vilified each other in loud language and beat with blows that were
like rock upon rock. Wide-chested, long-armed, both expert fighters,
they rained body-blows with arms that were like iron bludgeons.

The match began on the first day of the month of Kārttika and
went on tirelessly, day and night, through the thirteenth when the
great-spirited fighters still were engaged. But on the fourteenth, at
20 night, the Magadhan disengaged from exhaustion. When Janārdana
saw that the king was exhausted, O king, he said to Bhīma of terrible
deeds, as though to advise him, "One should not lay hold of an enemy
who is exhausted and press him in a match, for if he is pressed he
might give up the spirit entirely. So don't press the king, Bhīma. Fight
him with your arms, bull of the Bharatas!"

From these words of Kṛṣṇa, Bhīma, slayer of enemy heroes, knew
that Jarāsaṃdha was open, and he decided to kill him. With a
grappling hold the Wolf-Belly, the scion of Kuru, strongest of the
strong, seized the undefeated Jarāsaṃdha in order to defeat him.

Vaiśaṃpāyana said:

22.1 Bhīmasena replied to Kṛṣṇa of the Yādavas with his mind fully
made up to kill Jarāsaṃdha, "Kṛṣṇa, this evil man does not deserve
from me the favor of his life now that I have girt my loincloth, tiger of
the Yadus!" Kṛṣṇa, tigerlike man, again said to the Wolf-Belly, to
hurry him, for he wanted Jarāsaṃdha dead, "Then quickly show us
the spirit you got from the Gods, show us the terrible force of the Wind
5 God on Jarāsaṃdha today!" Powerful Bhīma, enemy-tamer, lifted high
the mighty Jarāsaṃdha and hurled him around by his arms a hundred
times, king, bull of the Bharatas, then he threw him down on his
knee, broke his back, trampled his body, and roared out. When
Jarāsaṃdha was ground down and the Pāṇḍava roared, there was a
tumultuous din that terrified all creatures. All the Magadhans reeled
and their women aborted at the roars of Bhīmasena and Jarāsaṃdha.
"Has the Himālaya split open, has the earth been rent asunder?" So
the Magadhans thought at Bhīma's cries.

10 The enemy-tamers left the dead king, who seemed as though
asleep, at the palace gate and strode away in the night. Kṛṣṇa had the
bannered chariot of Jarāsaṃdha yoked, told the brothers to mount it,
and set his relatives free. The kings who were rescued from their great
danger came to Kṛṣṇa, worthy of riches, and bestowed riches upon
him. Unhurt, armed with his weapons, triumphant over his enemy, he
mounted the divine chariot and departed with the kings from
Girivraja. With its two warriors and Kṛṣṇa as charioteer the chariot

had indeed acquired blood brothers, and it appeared, killing repeatedly,
15 invincible to any king. With the warriors Arjuna and Bhīma riding in
it and Kṛṣṇa driving it, that superb chariot, invincible to any archer,
shone beautifully. It was on this chariot that Indra and Viṣṇu rode in
the battle for Tārakā; now Kṛṣṇa had mounted it and departed.
Glittering like refined gold, garlanded with circlets of tiny bells,
thunderous like the monsoon cloud, triumphal and enemy-slaying was
this chariot on which Indra destroyed the ninety-nine Dānavas; and
having won it now, the bull-like men rejoiced.

The Magadhans saw the strong-armed Kṛṣṇa with the two brothers
20 on the chariot and they were astounded. Yoked with divine steeds the
chariot, which matched the wind in speed, radiated light when Kṛṣṇa
had mounted it, O Bhārata. Over that superb chariot waved a flag,
free-floating, the handiwork of Gods, majestic and iridescent, which
could be seen at the distance of a league. Kṛṣṇa thought of his Garuḍa
and promptly it came. With him the flag mast rose tall like a temple
pillar. With other open-mouthed, screeching creatures on the banner,
Garuḍa, eater of Snakes, sat high on the superb chariot. Almost
blinding the creatures, he shone with a supernal splendor like the sun
25 at noon surrounded with its thousand rays. That most beautiful flag
never got entangled in trees, nor was it hurt by weapons, O king, for it
was celestial and visible to both Gods and men.

Having mounted the divine chariot, thunderous like the monsoon,
the tigerlike hero Acyuta departed together with the two Pāṇḍavas.
King Vasu had obtained it from Indra, Bṛhadratha from Vasu, and
thus in the course of time it had descended to King Jarāsaṃdha
Bārhadratha. The strong-armed, lotus-eyed Kṛṣṇa started out from
Girivraja and when he was outside it he stopped on the plain. There
all the townsfolk approached him, led by the brahmins, to pay homage
30 with the ceremonial that is found in the Rules, O king. The kings who
had been freed from their prison honored Madhusūdana with flattery:
"It is no great wonder, son of Devakī, that in you, seconded by the
power of Bhīma and Arjuna, the protection of the Law is vested. The
feat you have accomplished today, the rescue of kings who were
drowning in Jarāsaṃdha's loathsome morass with its mire of sorrow,
languishing in the dreadful mountain fortress, Viṣṇu, from this feat of
their fateful release you have reaped blazing fame, foremost of men!
What shall we do, tiger among men? Speak up, bull among men!
Know it for done, however hard even kings may find it!"

35 The great-minded Hṛṣīkeśa replied reassuringly, "Yudhiṣṭhira wishes
to offer up the sacrifice of the Royal Consecration. All of you must
render him aid for the sake of the sacrifice, since he who lives by the
Law aspires to sovereignty!" Thereon the kings all gave their spoken

promise in a spirit of confidence, bull of the Bharatas: "So shall it be!"
The lords of the earth then made the Dāśārha share in their riches,
and reluctantly Govinda took them, out of compassion for them.

Jarāsaṃdha's warlike son Sahadeva came out with his kin and
ministers in a procession that was headed by his house priest.
40 Sahadeva humbled himself before Vāsudeva, the God of men, and
approached him with many riches. Kṛṣṇa then granted safety to the
prince, who was possessed by fear, and he anointed Jarāsaṃdha's son
there and then. Having allied himself with Kṛṣṇa and being honored
by both the Pārthas, the wise king once more entered the city of
Bṛhadratha. But Kṛṣṇa of the lotus eyes, ablaze with supreme glory,
took the riches and departed with the Pārthas.
45 Acyuta and the Pāṇḍavas journeyed to Indraprastha and upon
meeting with the King Dharma spoke joyfully: "By our good fortune
Bhīma felled the mighty Jarāsaṃdha, and those kings have been set
free from their prison, best of kings! By our good fortune Bhīmasena
and Dhanaṃjaya, experienced fighters, have returned to their city
unharmed!" Yudhiṣṭhira paid honor to Kṛṣṇa, as he deserved, and
happily embraced Bhīmasena and Arjuna. Then King Ajātaśatru*
celebrated with all his brothers the victory the two brothers had
achieved in eradicating Jarāsaṃdha. Then the Pāṇḍava met with the
freed kings according to their age and, after showing them proper
50 hospitality and honors, dismissed them. On their dismissal by
Yudhiṣṭhira, the kings hastened in high spirits to their own countries
on their various mounts.

Thus that tiger among men, strong-armed Janārdana, with the aid
of the Pāṇḍavas killed the enemy Jarāsaṃdha; and after the deliberate
killing of Jarāsaṃdha the enemy-tamer took leave from King Dharma,
Pṛthā, and Kṛṣṇā, O Bhārata, of Sabhadrā and Bhīmasena, of Phalguna
and the twins, bade farewell to Dhaumya, and departed for his own
city. On that same grand chariot he stood, bright like the morning sun
and celestial, of which the King Dharma had made him a present,
55 thundering over the horizons. Led by Yudhiṣṭhira, the Pāṇḍavas
circumambulated Kṛṣṇa of unsullied deeds, bull of the Bharatas.

When the blessed lord Kṛṣṇa, son of Devakī, had left, the Pāṇḍavas, who had won a wide triumph and had granted security to the kings, saw their glory prosper the more for this feat, Bhārata, and they themselves occasioned the greatest joy in Draupadī, O king. At that time the king, renowned for the protection of his kingdom, did according to the Law all that was right and consistent with Law, Profit, and Pleasure.

* = Yudhiṣṭhira.

2(23) The Conquest of the World

23–29 (B. 25–33; C. 983–1202)
23 (25; 983). Arjuna announces that he will conquer the northern part of the world and sets out with Yudhiṣṭhira's permission. Simultaneously Bhīma departs to conquer the East, Sahadeva the South, and Nakula the West (1–10). Arjuna subdues many kings and proceeds to Prāgjyotiṣa where he battles with Bhagadatta for eight days; Bhagadatta gives in (10–25).
24 (27; 1011). Arjuna marches up the mountains, defeats many kings and chieftains, as well as Dasyus, conquers Kashmir, and subjugates the Bāhlikas. He collects unusual horses (1–25).
25 (28; 1038). Further north he reaches Lake Mānasa; he receives horses from the Gandharvas (1–5). On reaching Harivarṣa giant gatekeepers stop him; he cannot enter the Northern Kuru country; but they offer him divine gifts (10–15). He returns to Indraprastha.
26 (291; 1059). Bhīma sets out for the East, marches on Pāñcāla, Videha, and Dāśārṇa. The Dāśārṇa king Sudharman becomes his marshal (1–10). He proceeds to Cedi, where he is the guest of King Śiśupāla (10–15).
27 (30; 1075). He conquers Kosala, Ayodhyā, Malla, Kāśi, Matsya, Malaya, Vatsa, and Niṣāda (1–10). After defeating Janaka of Videha, he subjugates the Mountain Men (10). He goes on to Suhma and Magadha, defeats Karṇa, subdues Puṇḍra and Vanga; he returns with much booty (10–25).
28 (31; 1105). Sahadeva departs for the South, conquers Śūrasena, Matsya, and Paṭaccara. Kuntibhoja is won over (1–5). He proceeds to the river Narmadā and to Avanti, but is stopped in Mahiṣmatī, when his army mysteriously catches fire (10–15). The Fire God, apprehended as a paramour, had granted a boon to King Nīla of Mahiṣmatī that bellicose invaders would be set on fire (15–20). To the women of the country he gave the boon of being able to go as they please (20–25). Sahadeva supplicates the Fire. The Fire appears and gives in. King Nīla peacefully welcomes Sahadeva (25–35). Sahadeva conquers Āhṛti and Surāṣṭra and wins over Bhojakaṭa (35–40). He defeats mythical races, as well as Rome and Greece

(40–45). Vibhīṣaṇa of Lankā accedes to his requests. At last he returns to Indraprastha (45–55).
29 (32; 1183). Nakula goes West, conquers Rohītaka and many other countries, and sends envoys to Kṛṣṇa Vāsudeva (1–10). He marches on Madra and is welcomed by King Śalya, his mother's brother (10). He subjugates foreign races and returns with ten thousand camels carrying his booty (15).

Vaiśaṃpāyana said:
23.1 The Pārtha who had got the superb bow, the inexhaustible quivers, the chariot, the banner, and the hall said to Yudhiṣṭhira, "I have got bow, arms, arrows, allies, land, fame, and strength, whatever men desire and find hard to obtain. Now I think it is our task to swell our coffers—I shall levy tribute on all kings, great king! On a day, at an hour and under a star that are propitious, I shall set out to conquer the north, which is swayed by the God of Riches!"
5 Yudhiṣṭhira the King Dharma listened to Dhanaṃjaya's words and replied in a voice that was resonant with love and gravity, "Depart, bull of the Bharatas, with the blessings of worthy priests, to the grief of our enemies and the joy of our friends! Certain shall be your victory, Pārtha, win the joys you desire!"

Thus the Pārtha set out with a large army, riding on his celestial chariot of miraculous feats that the Fire God had given him. Likewise Bhīmasena set out, and the twins, bulls among men, with their own
10 armies, blessed by King Dharma. The son of Indra conquered the region that is beloved of the Lord of Riches, Bhīmasena the East, Sahadeva the South, and Nakula, expert in weaponry, conquered the West, O king, while Yudhiṣṭhira the King Dharma resided in the Khāṇḍava Tract.

Janamejaya said:
Pray describe to me at length, brahmin, their conquest of the world, for I never tire of listening to the great feats of my forebears!

Vaiśaṃpāyana said:
I shall tell you first of Dhanaṃjaya's conquest, for the Pārthas conquered the earth simultaneously.

First he conquered, the strong-armed Dhanaṃjaya, the kings in the land of Kuṇinda, with great severity. After conquering the Ānartas, the Kālakūṭas, and the Kuṇindas, he made Sumaṇḍala, vanquisher of
15 the evil, his rearguard. Together with him, O king, the left-handed archer, scourge of his enemies, conquered the island of Śakala and defeated King Prativindhya, the lords of the island of Śakala, and the princes of the Seven Islands—the battle between Arjuna and their

armies was a tumultuous one. After defeating them, bull of the Bharatas, the great archer stormed with all of them on Prāgjyotiṣa. There was a great king there, Bhagadatta, O lord of the people, and with him the great-spirited Pāṇḍava fought a great battle. Prāgjyotiṣa was surrounded by mountain men and Chinese and many other warriors who live close to the ocean beaches.

20 After having battled Dhanaṃjaya for eight days, the king said, laughing on the battlefield, still unwearied, "No less than proper, strong-armed scion of Pāṇḍu and heir of Indra, is this prowess in you that shines in battle! I am the friend of the Indra of the Gods and rival him in battle, yet you, my friend, I cannot face in war. What is it you want, Pāṇḍava? Tell me what I should do for you. Strong-armed champion, I shall do what you ask of me, son!"

Arjuna said:

The bull of the Kurus, Yudhiṣṭhira, son of Dharma, is king. I want
him to become the sovereign and demand that tribute be paid to him.
25 You are my father's friend and friendly disposed to me too; therefore
I am not ordering you—pay tribute graciously!

Bhagadatta said:

As you, who are Kuntī's son, are to me, so shall King Yudhiṣṭhira be. I shall do all that you ask. What else can I do for you?

Vaiśaṃpāyana said:

24.1 Having thus defeated him, the strong-armed son of Kuntī Dhanaṃjaya set out from there to the North, which is guarded by the God of Riches. Kaunteya, bull among men, vanquished the inner mountain, the outer mountain, and the upper mountain; and after vanquishing all the mountains and the kings who ruled there, he brought them under his sway and took all of their riches. With the riches he had taken he then pleasured those kings and marched with them on Bṛhanta who dwelled in Kulūta, quaking the earth with the sound of his excellent drums, the grinding of the fellies of his chariots, and the noise of his elephants.

Bṛhanta, a young man, sallied forth from his city with a four-
membered army and gave battle to the Pāṇḍava. It was a huge mêlée,
Dhanaṃjaya's and Bṛhanta's, but Bṛhanta was unable to hold out
against the Pāṇḍava's valor. Recognizing that the Kaunteya could not
at all be worn down, the king of the mountains, a man of little wit,
made common cause and brought out all his wealth. Arjuna
confirmed the kingdom, set out with Kulūta, and swiftly toppled
10 Senābindu from his kingdom, O king. He collected Modāpura,
Vāmadeva, Sudāman, who was greatly disturbed, and the Northern
Kulūtas and their kings. While he camped there at King Dharma's
orders, Dhanaṃjaya conquered the Five Countries with his troops.

Once he reached Divaḥprastha, the great citadel of Senābindu, the
lord made his camp there with his four-membered army.
In the midst of all of them the glorious bull of men marched upon
King Viṣvagaśva Paurava; and after vanquishing the warlike and
heroic mountaineers he conquered with his bannered army the city
15 ruled by the Paurava. After Paurava's defeat the Pāṇḍava subjugated
the seven Utsavasaṃketa tribes of Dasyus who live in the mountains.
Later the bull of the barons vanquished the Kashmirian barons and
Lohita with ten encircling armies, as well as the Trigartas, the Dārvas,
the Kokanādas, and many other barons who together attacked him,
king. The scion of Kuru went on to conquer the lovely town of
20 Abhisārī and to defeat in battle Rocamāna of Uraśā. Thereafter Indra's
son routed with his full might in a battle Siṃhapura where
Citrāyudhaśūra ruled; then the diademed bull of the Pāṇḍavas
crushed the Suhmas and Colas with his entire army. With supreme
gallantry the Kuru went on to subjugate the Bāhlīkas, always hard to
approach, in a huge holocaust. Taking their army and rejecting their
poor resources, the Pāṇḍava vanquished the Daradas with the
Kāmbojas. The lordly son of Indra defeated the Dasyus who live in the
northeast and those who dwell in the forest. Thereafter Arjuna
25 defeated the Lohas, the Upper Kāmbojas, and the Northern Ṛṣikas. The
battle in Ṛṣika country between the Upper Ṛṣikas and the Pārtha was
most terrifying, like that battle that was fought over Tārakā. After
laying low the Ṛṣikas in a pitched fight, O king, he collected eight
horses the color of a parrot's breast, others colored like peacocks, and
still others of both colors. Having conquered the Himālaya and the
Niṣkuṭa, the bull reached the White Mountain and camped there.

Vaiśaṃpāyana said:
25.1 When the hero had crossed over the White Mountain, O Bhārata,
he came to the country that is inhabited by the Kiṃpuruṣas and ruled
by Drumaputra. In a mighty mêlée in which many barons found their
death the best of the Pāṇḍavas conquered it and extracted tribute.
After taking the country called Hāṭaka, governed by the Guhyakas,
Arjuna single-mindedly occupied it with his army. Having won them
over with diplomacy, he set eyes on the superb Lake Mānasa and all
5 the rivulets of the seers. Upon reaching Lake Mānasa, the Lord
Pāṇḍava won the country adjacent to Hāṭaka, which is ruled by the
Gandharvas. There he received as ultimate tribute from the city of the
Gandharvas beautiful partridge-colored and flecked horses with the
bulging eyes of frogs. The scion of Indra and Pāṇḍu then reached the
northern region of Harivarṣa and aspired to conquer that too.
Gigantic, mighty, and powerful gatekeepers drew near to him and
genially said, "Pārtha, you are incapable of conquering this city in any

fashion. Turn back, good man, this should suffice you, invincible
10 champion! Any human who enters the city must die. We are pleased
with you, hero; your conquests should suffice. There is nothing left for
you to conquer, Arjuna. This is the land of the Northern Kurus, and
no war can happen here. And if you were to enter it, Kaunteya, you
would not be able to see anything, for no human eye can see what is
here. Yet, if there is something else that you wish to accomplish here,
tiger among men, then speak and we shall do it at your behest,
Bhārata."

Upon these words Arjuna Pākaśāsani spoke to them: "I wish to
15 assure the sovereignty of the wise King Dharma. I shall not enter your
domain if it is forbidden to humans, but let something be given as
tribute to Yudhiṣṭhira!" They then offered him divine textiles, divine
ornaments, and divine skins and hides as tribute.

Thus the tigerlike hero conquered the North, fighting a great many
battles with barons as well as Dasyus; and after he had conquered
those kings and made them pay tribute, he took from all of them
manifold riches and jewels as well as partridge-colored and flecked
horses colored like parrot feathers or peacocks, all as fast as the wind.
20 Amidst a huge, four-membered army the hero returned to the beautiful
city of Indraprastha.

Vaiśaṃpāyana said:

26.1 At the same time the mighty Bhīmasena, too, took his leave from
the King Dharma and set out to the East. At the head of a huge circle
of forces that routed enemy kingdoms the tiger of the Bharatas
marched out to increase the woes of his foes. The Pāṇḍava, tiger
among kings, marched first to the great city of the Pāñcālas and with
various means won over the Pāñcālas. Then the bull-like champion
vanquished Gaṇḍakī and the Videhas and shortly thereafter went on
5 to the Daśārṇas. There the Daśārṇa king Sudharman accomplished a
hair-raising feat: a great unarmed wrestling match with Bhīma
himself. And upon witnessing this feat, enemy-killer Bhīma made the
powerful Sudharman supreme commander of the army. Continuing to
the East, Bhīma of terrible prowess marched on with a large host, O
king, rocking the earth. The hero, strong among the strong, defeated
in battle Rocamāna, ruler of Aśvamedha, and his younger brother
with his strength. After laying him low with not too great severity, the
valiant Kaunteya, joy of the Kurus, conquered the eastern country.
10 Thereupon he marched south to the great city of the Pulindas and
overpowered Sukumāra and the overlord of men Sumitra. Later the
bull of the Bharatas, at the King Dharma's behest, marched upon the
mighty Śiśupāla, O Janamejaya.

He, the king of the Cedis, upon hearing of the Pāṇḍava's desire,
came out of his city and the enemy-burner welcomed Bhīma. When
the two met, great king, the bull of the Kurus and the bull of the
Cedis, they asked after the well-being of each other's lineages. The king
of the Cedis offered him his kingdom, lord of the people, and
laughingly said to Bhīma, "What is it you are doing, prince sans
15 blame?" Bhīma then told him of the desire of the King Dharma; and
after accepting it, the overlord of men acted accordingly. Bhīma spent
there thirty nights, king, as guest of Śiśupāla, then left with his hosts
and mounts.

Vaiśaṃpāyana said:

27.1 Then the enemy-tamer vanquished in the land of Kumāra Śreṇimat
and also the overlord of Kosala, Bṛhadbala. In Ayodhyā the Pāṇḍava
defeated the law-minded and powerful Dīrghaprajña with not too
great severity. Again the lord brought down Gopālakaccha and the
Northern Sottamas and the sovereign king of the Mallas. On the slope
of the Himālaya he encountered Jaradgava and powerfully brought the
5 whole country in his power after a short time. Then, after conquering
many different countries, the bull of men defeated Unnāṭa and took the
mountain Kukṣimat with his force, that the most powerful Pāṇḍava
did, strong among the strong. Great-armed Bhīma of terrible might
overpowered in battle the king of the Kāśis, the never-retreating
Subandhu. Then the bull of the Pāṇḍavas defeated Kratha, ruler of the
kings about Supārśva, whom he battled forcefully in an encounter.
Next the splendid warrior subjugated the Matsyas, the powerful
Malayas, the irreproachable Gayas, and all of Paśubhūmi. Strong-
armed Bhīma then withdrew and marched north, vanquishing Mount
10 Mardavīka with its footlands. The strong son of Kuntī forcefully
overthrew the land of the Vatsas, the overlord of the Bhargas, the
chief of the Niṣādas, and many landlords led by Maṇimat. Bhīma
Pāṇḍava then subjugated the Southern Mallas and Bhogavat, without
too much severity. The lord won over the Śarmakas and Varmakas
with diplomacy, and the sovereign of the earth, King Janaka of Videha,
also was defeated by the tigerlike hero, without too great a severity.
Tarrying in Videha, the son of Kuntī and Pāṇḍu vanquished, about
Mount Indra, the seven chieftains of the Mountain Men.
Thereafter the mighty Kaunteya defeated in battle the Suhmas and
the Eastern Suhmas, who witnessed it, and then marched on the
15 Magadhans. After defeating Daṇḍa and Daṇḍadhāra and the landlords,
he stormed Girivraja with all of them. He quieted Jarāsaṃdha's son
and made him tributary; and with all of them the mighty conqueror,
O king, hastened to his task. Shaking the earth with his four-

membered host, the best of the Pāṇḍavas battled with enemy-slaying
Karṇa. Having defeated Karṇa in battle and bringing him under his
power, Bhārata, he mightily laid low the chieftains who dwell in the
mountains. Afterward the Pāṇḍava, in a grand battle, defeated the
20 quite powerful King Modāgiri in a wrestling contest. Then, after
vanquishing in war the heroic and powerful Vāsudeva, overlord of the
Pauṇḍras, as well as the august king who dwells on the marshes of
the river Kauśikī, both champions of stern bravery and surrounded by
their troops, he marched on the king of Vanga, great king. He defeated
Samudrasena and King Candrasena as well as the ruler of Tāmralipti
and King Kaca of Vanga; and the chiefs of the Suhmas and those who
dwell on the ocean the bull of the Bharatas defeated, all the hordes of
Barbarians.

Then, after his triumph over many different lands and taking
treasure from them, the mighty son of the Wind went to the river
25 Lauhitya.* He had all the chiefs of the Barbarians who live on sea
islands bring tribute and treasures of all kinds, sandalwood and aloe
and textiles and priceless gems and pearls, gold, silver, diamonds, and
precious coral. With vast riches numbering in the hundreds of
millions, Bhīma of boundless spirit flooded the Pāṇḍava with a rain of
wealth. Having repaired to Indraprastha, Bhīma of terrible prowess
handed all that booty to the King Dharma.

Vaiśaṃpāyana said:

28.1 Likewise Sahadeva, too, after due honors from the King Dharma,
departed with a large host for the South. First the lord conquered in its
entirety the land of the Śūrasenas; and the mighty Kauravya forcibly
brought the king of the Matsyas into his power. In a grand battle he
defeated the sovereign of overlords Dantavakra, made him tributary,
and restored him to his kingdom. He overpowered Sukumāra and
5 Sumitra, the Western Matsyas and Paṭaccaras. Swiftly the illustrious
hero conquered the land of the Niṣādas and the great mountain
Gośṛnga as well as King Śreṇimat. After conquering the New Country,
he marched on Kuntibhoja, who diplomatically accepted his decree.

Thereupon he found the king, son of Jambhaka, on the bank of the
river Carmaṇvatī, the one who had been spared his life by his
quondam enemy Vāsudeva. He gave battle to the Bhoja on the spot,
O Bhārata; he defeated him in war and then turned south.

[The mighty warrior vanquished the Sekas and the Western Sekas,]
took tribute from them and manifold riches. Then, along with them,
10 he marched on the river Narmadā. The majestic son of the Aśvins

* = the Brahmaputra.

defeated in battle the two Avanti princes Vinda and Anuvinda, who
had a large host, took tribute from them, and continued to the city of
Māhiṣmatī. There the bull among men, majestic Sahadeva Pāṇḍava,
became embattled with Nīla and a grand battle ensued, such as to
strike the timid with terror, which destroyed his host and put his very
life at risk; for the blessed God Fire rendered aid to his enemy. Horses,
chariots, elephants, troops, and armor were seen to catch fire in
15 Sahadeva's army. The scion of Kuru became much perplexed in his
mind and was unable to give a rejoinder, Janamejaya.

Janamejaya said:

Why did the blessed Fire become Sahadeva's adversary in war, even
though the other was striving for the sake of a sacrifice, brahmin?

Vaiśaṃpāyana said:

It is related that the blessed Lord Fire who resides in Māhiṣmatī was
once caught as a paramour. He was led before King Nīla of the
Ancients after he had philandered at will in the guise of a brahmin.
When the law-observing king berated him according to the books, the
20 blessed Lord Fire blazed up with anger. On seeing this the king,
surprised, bowed his head before the Sage, and the Fire God showed
the king his grace. He who preeminently makes the offerings good
gratified the prince with a boon, and this lord of the earth chose as his
boon that his troops would ever be secure. Ever since, kings who in
their ignorance want to conquer that city are forcibly burned down on
the spot by fire, O king. It so happened at that time that the women in
the city of Māhiṣmatī, scion of Kuru, were not easily controlled, so
Fire gave the women the boon that they should not be kept
segregated; for the women there are their own masters and run about
25 as they please. Ever since, the kings have avoided that kingdom, O
best of men, great king, out of fear of the Fire.

The law-minded Sahadeva, now, on seeing his army panic-stricken,
encircled as it were by Fire, shook like a mountain, O king. After
having touched water and made himself pure, he thereupon addressed
the Fire.

"It is for thy sake that I have undertaken this task—homage to
thee, Black-Trailed Fire!"

"Thou art the mouth of the Gods, thou art the sacrifice, Purifier!
As thou makest pure, thou art the Purifier; as thou carriest the
oblation, thou art the Bearer of the Offering. For thy sake the Vedas
have sprung into being, and hence thou art Jātavedas.

"Pray, Bearer of the Offering, refrain from obstructing this
sacrifice!"

30 After this prayer the son of Mādrī spread *kuśa* grass on the ground
and then the tigerlike man sat down before the Fire in the ritual

fashion, in full sight of his entire army, which was terrified, Bhārata.
And the Fire did not pass beyond him, as the ocean does not pass
beyond the flood line. The Fire drew near to him and softly spoke to
Sahadeva, joy of the Kurus and god among men, this kindly word:
"Rise, rise up, Kauravya! I have acted thus in order to try you. I know
fully the intention of yourself and the son of Dharma. Yet I am
beholden to protect this city, best of the Bharatas, for as long as there
shall be heirs to carry on the lineage of this King Nīla. Still I shall do
what your heart desires, Pāṇḍava!"

35 Hereupon Mādrī's son stood up with joyful heart, and with bent
head and folded hands the bull-like man paid his homage to the Fire.
When Fire had withdrawn, King Nīla arrived, and he welcomed
Sahadeva, tiger among men, master of warriors. He accepted his
homage and made him tributary; then Mādrī's son marched
victoriously south.

He subjugated the king of Tripura, of boundless might, and the
strong-armed warrior swiftly subdued the lord of Potana. With a great
effort he then overpowered Āhṛti, the king of Surāṣṭra, whose
40 preceptor was Kauśika. While tarrying in the realm of Surāṣṭra, the
law-minded conqueror sent an envoy to King Rukmin Bhīṣmaka of
Bhojakaṭa, a wise man of great stature, who was befriended by Indra
himself. The strong-armed prince and his sons happily accepted his
decree, looking to Kṛṣṇa Vāsudeva, O king.

Thereupon the master of warriors, after taking much wealth,
progressed from thence to Śūrpāraka and the oligarchy named
Upakṛta, which the mighty and splendid victor vanquished along with
the Daṇḍakas. The kings who dwell on ocean islands, born from
barbarian wombs, the man-eating Niṣādas, and the folk who cover
themselves with their ears, and those who are called the Black-faced
Men, who spring from Rākṣasas, the entire mountain range of Killa
45 and the settlement of Muracī, the island called Tāmra and Mount
Rāmaka, and the King Timiṃgila—the wise warrior vanquished them
all. The one-footed folk who dwell solely in the bush, the town
Saṃjayantī, Picchaṇḍa, and Karahāṭaka, he subjected through envoys
and made them pay tribute. Likewise by means of envoys he
subjugated and made tributary the Pāṇḍyas and Tamils along with the
Coḍras and Keralas, the Āndhras and Talavanas, the Kalingas and
Uṣṭrakarṇikas, Antioch and Rome, and the city of the Greeks.

50 The wise son of Mādrī went on to Bharukaccha and, lordly king,
sent envoys to the great-spirited Vibhīṣaṇa Paulastya; here the law-
spirited enemy-tamer used diplomacy. The other happily accepted his
decree: the prudent king consented to it as an act of Time. Wealth of
many kinds did he send, sandalwood and aloes before all, with divine
jewelry, precious textiles, and costly gems.

Now the wise and majestic Sahadeva returned after having thus
conquered with dispatch, diplomacy, and conquest; and having made
55 the kings pay tribute the enemy-tamer retraced his steps. He handed
it all to the King Dharma, O bull of the Bharatas, and, his task
accomplished, dwelled there happily, O King Janamejaya.

Vaiśaṃpāyana said:
29.1 I shall now relate the feats and the conquest of Nakula, and how
this lord conquered the region that had been conquered by Kṛṣṇa
Vāsudeva. Departing from the Khāṇḍava Tract toward the west, the
wise warrior set out with a large host, shaking this earth with the
thunderous lion roars of his troops and the racket of the chariot
fellies.

First he marched upon wealthy and lovely Rohītaka, beloved of
5 Kārttikeya, rich in cattle, horses, prizes, and grain. There a grand
battle ensued with the Mattamayūraka champions; and the splendid
prince subjugated the Desert Country entirely as well as grain-rich
Śairīṣaka and Mahеccha, the lands of the Śibis, Trigartas, Ambaṣṭhas,
Mālavas, Five Karpaṭas, and the Madhyamikāya and Vāṭadhāna
brahmins. Circling around, the bull of men defeated the Utsavasaṃketa
oligarchies who dwell in the Puṣkara Forest, the mighty Grāmaṇeyas
who live on the banks of the Indus, the oligarchies of the Śūdras and
Ābhīras who dwell on the Sarasvatī river, the folk who live on fish
and those who live in the hills, all of the Land of the Five Rivers and
10 Western Paryaṭa, Northern Jyotika, the city of Vṛndāṭaka, and
Dvārapāla—the splendid prince defeated them all along with
Harahūṇas and all the princes of the West. While staying there, the
conqueror sent envoys to Vāsudeva, and he too accepted his decree
with his ten kingdoms.

Thereupon he marched to Śakala, capital city of the Madras, and
the powerful warrior aligned Śalya, his mother's brother, with
diplomacy. A deserving guest, he was received hospitably by the king,
O lord of the people; he took plentiful jewels and departed, a master of
15 warriors. He took into his power the highly dangerous Barbarians who
live by the Gulf, the Pahlavas, and the Barbaras, all of them. Having
extracted tribute and vanquished the kings, Nakula, best of men, who
knew rare paths, turned back. Ten thousand camels carried the rich
booty of the great-spirited prince, O great king, but with difficulty. The
illustrious son of Mādrī approached Yudhiṣṭhira, the hero in
Indraprastha, and handed the booty over to him.

Thus Nakula, bull of the Bharatas, conquered the West, under
Varuṇa's guardianship, which had been won by Vāsudeva.

2(24) The Royal Consecration

2.30–32 (B. 33–35; C. 1203–1306)
30 (33; 1203). Yudhiṣṭhira's kingdom thrives because of his virtue (1–5). While he is being pressed to perform the sacrifice, Kṛṣṇa arrives with rich gifts (10–15). Yudhiṣṭhira praises him and declares that he owes all to him; he asks permission to sacrifice (15–20). Kṛṣṇa approves (20–25). Dvaipāyana brings in the priests for the ritual. The sacrificial site is built up (30–35). Yudhiṣṭhira instructs Sahadeva to invite kings and brahmins; messengers are sent out (40). Yudhiṣṭhira is inaugurated, and the guests arrive and are housed and feasted (40–40). Yudhiṣṭhira sends Nakula to invite his Hāstinapura kinsmen (50).
31 (34; 1260). Nakula invites the Kauravas, and they accept (1). They arrive and are welcomed; many other princes arrive (1–20) and are sumptuously quartered (20–25).
32 (35; 1287). Yudhiṣṭhira asks for the affection of the Kauravas; he gives each an official function (1–5). Great gifts are made by the kings who have come (10–15). The sacrificial site is opulent (15).

Vaiśaṃpāyana said:

30.1 Because of the King Dharma's protection, his adherence to the
truth, and his subjugation of his foes, all the subjects were bent upon
their own tasks; because of the correct collection of revenues and his
law-abiding government, the monsoon rained abundantly and the
countryside was fattened. All affairs prospered, especially cattle-
tending, husbandry, and trade: all this was the doing of the king.
Neither from robbers or cheaters, nor from the king's favorites among
5 themselves, did one hear a false word about the king. Neither drought
nor floods, neither disease nor fires nor pestilence raged at all while
Yudhiṣṭhira was steadfast in the Law. Kings came to do favors, to pay
attendance, or to bring spontaneous offerings, and for no other
purposes. The accumulation of lawful income grew so large that it
could not be spent even in hundreds of years. Recognizing the size of
his treasury and granary, King Kaunteya, lord of the earth, set his
mind on sacrifice. All his friends said to him, severally and together,
"My lord, it is time for the sacrifice. Do what is fitting for it!"

10 As they were speaking in this fashion, Hari* arrived—He who is the ancient Seer, who encompasses the Veda and is visible to the enlightened, greatest of all who stand fast, origin and dissolution of the world, protector of what is, was, and shall be, Keśava, killer of Keśin, bulwark of all the Vṛṣṇis, the enemy-slayer who gives safety in distress. Having approached and placed Vasudeva Anakadundubhi in charge of his troops, and taking a manifold mass of wealth to the King Dharma, the Mādhava, tiger among men, arrived in the midst of a large force. Proclaiming his inexhaustible ocean of gems that soared to a flood of riches with the noise of his chariots, he made his entrance
15 into the great city. The city of the Bhāratas rejoiced in the coming of Kṛṣṇa as a sunless town in that of the sun, a windless town in that of the wind.

Yudhiṣṭhira joyously met him and received him with proper honors; and when they had exchanged inquiries regarding their health and Kṛṣṇa was comfortably seated, the tiger among men, in the company of Dhaumya, Dvaipāyana, and other priests, and of Bhīma, Arjuna, and the twins, said to him, "It is because of you, Kṛṣṇa, that all of earth is under my sway, and by your grace, Vārṣṇeya, that I have amassed great wealth. Now I myself wish to employ all this in the proper manner for the best of the brahmins and for the sacrificial fire,
20 Mādhava son of Devakī. I wish to sacrifice with you, strong-armed Daśārha, and with my brothers as companions: pray allow me! Undergo, strong-armed Govinda, your inauguration: for when you have solemnized the rite, I shall become guiltless, Daśārha. Or allow me with these brothers of mine to undergo it: with your consent, Kṛṣṇa, I may well attain to supreme ceremony."

To him Kṛṣṇa replied, after greatly praising the expanse of his virtues, "Thou, tiger of kings, are a worthy sovereign! Attain thou to the grand ceremony. When thou hast obtained it, we shall by that measure have achieved our task. Sacrifice the sacrifice thou fanciest, while I remain devoted to thy good. And charge me too in this task; I shall obey thy full decree."

Yudhiṣṭhira said:

25 My intention has fructified, Kṛṣṇa; success is assured to me, Hṛṣīkeśa, when you attend on me as you desire.

Vaiśaṃpāyana said:

So, with Kṛṣṇa's consent, the Pāṇḍava and his brothers began to arrange the means for the Royal Consecration. The Pāṇḍava, uprooter of his foes, commanded Sahadeva, master of warriors, and all his councillors: "Whatever appurtenances of the sacrifice the brahmins prescribe for this ceremony, likewise all the utensils and the auspicious

* = Kṛṣṇa.

paraphernalia and the sacrificial ingredients that Dhaumya mentions—
let the men quickly bring them according to the fitness of them for this
30 ceremony. Indrasena, Viśoka, and Pūru, Arjuna's charioteer, shall be
charged with procuring the foodstuffs in a spirit of kindness to me. Let
all manner of delicacies be fetched, of the right taste and fragrance,
such as please and delight the brahmins, you best of the Kurus!"

No sooner had he spoken than Sahadeva, best of the warriors,
announced it done to the great-spirited King Dharma. Thereupon, O
king, Dvaipāyana brought in the priests of the sacrifice, worthy
brahmins who seemed to embody the Vedas themselves. Satyavatī's
son himself did the office of the *brahmán*, while Susāman, the bull of
35 the Dhanaṃjayas, was the chanter of the *sāmans*. Yājñavalkya, most
profoundly grounded in the *brahman*, became the principal *adhvaryu*,
while Paila, son of Vasu, was the *hotar*, assisted by Dhaumya. The
flocks of their pupils and their sons, who, bull of the Bharatas, were
learned in the Vedas and their branches, all became acolytes. After
intoning the Blessing of the Day and arranging the ritual, they put
together the grand ceremony of the Gods as it is prescribed in the
texts. Carpenters, with precise instructions, built there the various
shelters, adorned with gems and spacious, like the houses of the
celestials.

40 Then the king, greatest of kings, best of the Kurus, instructed at
once his councillor Sahadeva, "Send out directly fast messengers to
carry the invitations!" When he heard the king's word, he dispatched
messengers: "Invite in the kingdoms the brahmins and landlords, and
bring in the commoners and serfs who deserve honor!" At the
Pāṇḍaveya's behest they brought the invitation to all the lords of the
land, and he dispatched still more envoys.

At this point, when the time was right, the priests inaugurated
45 Yudhiṣṭhira, son of Kuntī, for the Royal Consecration, Bhārata. After
this inauguration the law-spirited King Dharma Yudhiṣṭhira went to
the sacrificial terrain, surrounded by thousands of brahmins, his
brothers, his kinsmen, friends, ministers, and the barons who, lord of
men, had assembled from many countries, as well as his councillors—
he went, that best of kings, like the Law incarnate.

From every realm flocked in the brahmins, profound in all the
fields of knowledge, learned in the Vedas and their branches. At the
King Dharma's orders, carpenters by the thousands built cottages for
each of them and his party, filled with many foods and beds, cottages
with all the virtues of every season. There those brahmins dwelled,
grandly hosted, my king, telling many tales and watching dancers and
players. And when those priests were feasting and talking, a loud din
50 was incessantly heard from those great-spirited revelers. "Give, give!"
and "Feast, feast!" were the exchanges that were heard constantly.

Hundreds of thousands did the king give, Bhārata, in cows, beds, gold, and women to each of them.

Thus did the sacrifice begin of the great-spirited Pāṇḍava, the One Hero on earth, as of Śakra in heaven. Now King Yudhiṣṭhira sent Nakula Pāṇḍava off to Hāstinapura, O bull of the Bharatas, to invite Bhīṣma, Droṇa, Dhṛtarāṣṭra, Vidura, and Kṛpa, and whoever of all the brethren were attached to Yudhiṣṭhira.

Vaiśaṃpāyana said:

31.1 Nakula, victor in battle, went to Hāstinapura, and the Pāṇḍava
invited Bhīṣma and Dhṛtarāṣṭra. Out they set, happy of heart, preceded
by their brahmins, on hearing of the sacrifice of the King Dharma, for
they knew of sacrifices. And others came, bull among men, by the
hundreds, with contented hearts, desirous to see the assembly hall and
the King Dharma Pāṇḍava. From all horizons they foregathered there,
all the kings, O Bhārata, fetching along many and sizable riches.
5 All the princes, led by the Teacher*, Dhṛtarāṣṭra, Bhīṣma, the wise
Vidura, and all the brethren headed by Duryodhana were welcomed
and honored. So were Subala, king of the Gāndhāras, the powerful
Śakuni, Acala, Vṛṣaka, and that greatest of chariot warriors, Karṇa,
Ṛta, Śalya king of the Madras, and the great warrior Bāhlīka,
Somadatta Kauravya, Bhūri, Bhūriśravas, Śala, Asvatthāman, Kṛpa,
Droṇa, and Jayadratha Saindhava.
Yajñasena was there with his son, and so were the lord of the land
Śālva, the glorious Bhagadatta, king of Prāgjyotisa, with all his
10 Barbarians who live down by the ocean, the mountain kings and King
Bṛhadbala, Vāsudeva of Puṇḍra, the Vanga and the Kālinga, Ākarṣa,
the Vānāvasyas and Andhras, the Tamils and Singhalese, and the king
of Kashmir, Kuntibhoja of great splendor, and the powerful Suhma,
all the other Bāhlika champions and kings, Virāṭa with his sons, and
the great warrior Mācella—kings and sons of kings and the lords of
many countrysides.
Śiśupāla of great gallantry, and berserk in battle, came with his son,
15 O Bhārata, to the sacrifice of the Pāṇḍaveya. Rāma, Aniruddha,
Babhru, Sāraṇa, Gada, Pradyumna, Sāmba, and the valiant
Cārudeṣṇa, and Ulmuka, Niśatha, the heroic son of Pradyumna, and
all the other warlike Vṛṣṇis assembled in their sum. Still many other
princes, natives of the Middle Country, came to the grand ceremony of
the Royal Consecration of Pāṇḍu's son.
At the King Dharma's request, quarters were provided for them
with many chambers, O king, and beautified with ponds and trees.
20 The son of Dharma did them perfect honor, and upon their hospitable

* = Droṇa.

reception the princes went to their assigned quarters, towering like Kailāsa peaks, attractive and well-furnished, on all sides surrounded with high stuccoed walls that were sturdily built. The lattices were made of gold, the floors were paved with precious stones; the stairs rose gently, and the seats and appointments were large. The residences were decked with wreaths and garlands and redolent with superb aloes, white like goose feathers, quite visible from as far as a league, never too crowded, with doors equally wide, and adorned with a variety of features. Their elements were made of many metals, and thus they appeared like Himālayan summits.

When they had rested, their highnesses looked upon Yudhiṣṭhira the King Dharma, amidst his many *sadasyas*, generous with the
25 priestly stipends. His *sadas*, crowded by princes and great-spirited brahmins, shone like the vault of heaven peopled by the Immortals, O king.

Vaiśaṃpāyana said:

32.1 Yudhiṣṭhira rose to welcome his grandfather and his teacher, greeted them, and then spoke as follows to Bhīṣma, Droṇa, Kṛpa, Droṇa's son, Duryodhana, and Viviṃśati: "At this sacrifice all of you must show me your favor. All this wealth that is here is yours, and so am I. Be kindly disposed to me, as you please, without any constraints."

After having thus spoken to all of them, the eldest of the Pāṇḍavas, inaugurated for his sacrifice, immediately charged each with a function that was appropriate. He charged Duḥśāsana with the supervision of the comestibles and ordered Aśvatthāman to the reception of the
5 brahmins. Saṃjaya he assigned to the hospitality for the kings, and the wise Bhīṣma and Droṇa to the resolution of what should be done or left undone. The king charged Kṛpa with the watch over the gold and gems as well as the presentation of the stipends, and he likewise charged the other tigerlike men with this task or the other.

Bāhlīka, Dhṛtarāṣṭra, Somadatta, and Jayadratha, conducted by Nakula, enjoyed themselves there like masters. Vidura the Steward, who knew all the Laws, was the bursar, while Duryodhana received all the gifts of homage. All the world assembled, hoping for the ultimate reward and desirous of setting eyes on the assembly hall and
10 the King Dharma Pāṇḍava. No one brought a gift worth less than a thousand, and they prospered King Dharma with many gems. The kings, rivaling one another, gave riches, hoping "Will it be that the Kauravya attains to his sacrifice through my gift of gems?" With the residences, terraced and turreted and storied and surrounded by troops, with the palaces of the kings of the world and the bungalows of the brahmins, with the mansions made in the image of celestial

chariots, colorful, gem-studded, opulent with superb wealth, with the princes who had assembled, whose luster and affluence were all-surpassing, the *sadas* of the great-spirited Kaunteya shone richly.
15 Rivaling God Varuṇa in wealth, Yudhiṣṭhira brought worship with a sacrifice of six fires and ample stipends, and satisfied all the people plentifully in all of their desires.

Abounding with rice, rich in foods, crowded by well-fed folk, the assemblage was indeed a proper ground for the presentation of jewels. At this sacrifice, spread by the great seers with libations, butter offerings, Soma pourings, and oblations, accompanied by the erudition of spells, the Gods and the great seers waxed satisfied. And, like the Gods, so did the brahmins become satisfied at this sacrifice with the great shifts of stipends and food, and, with all the classes, they rejoiced.

2(25) *The Taking of the Guest Gift*

2.33–36 (B. 36–39; C. 1307–1412)
33 (36; 1307). On the day of the Unction brahmins and kings assemble at the altar; Nārada and the great seers appear (1–5). Nārada remembers that all these kings are partial incarnations of Gods and that Kṛṣṇa is Nārāyaṇa (10–20). Bhīṣma tells Yudhiṣṭhira to offer gifts to the guests. Yudhiṣṭhira asks his guidance in deciding precedence (20–25). Bhīṣma decides on Kṛṣṇa; Sahadeva offers the gift, and Kṛṣṇa accepts (25–30).
34 (37; 1337). Śiśupāla protests vehemently. Kṛṣṇa is not a king and is outranked by many present (1–10). The Pāṇḍavas show their lawlessness, Kṛṣṇa his unworthiness (15–20). He rises to leave with other kings (20).
35 (38; 1369). Yudhiṣṭhira urges Śiśupāla to consent (1–5). Bhīṣma extols the virtues and divinity of Kṛṣṇa (5–25).
36 (39; 1401). Sahadeva challenges any king who protests Kṛṣṇa's honor; no one accepts the challenge (1–5). Śiśupāla's party plots to disrupt the sacrifice (5–15).

Vaiśaṃpāyana said:

33.1 On the day of the Unction the brahmins and the kings made their entrance into the inner sacrificial enclosure. In order to pay their homage, the great seers, led by Nārada, seated themselves at the altar

of the great-spirited king and shone there with the royal seers: like Gods and divine seers assembled in the palace of Brahmā they attended one rite after the other and, boundlessly superior, discussed it: "This is right," "No, not that way!" "So, and in no other way!" Thus they
5 spoke in their multitude and argued with one another. Some made lean matters seem fat, others made fat ones lean with arguments that are definitively set forth in the textbooks. Some sagacious debaters tore apart conclusions completed by others, as vultures tear apart a piece of raw meat thrown into the air. Others, great in their vows and chief experts in all the Vedas, took pleasure in relating tales that were informed by Law and Profit. The sacrificial terrain, crowded by Gods, brahmins, and great seers, wise in the Veda, appeared like the unclouded sky with its asterisms. No *śūdra* nor anyone without vows was near the inner altar at Yudhisthira's habitation, O king.
10 Upon seeing the prosperity of the prosperous and wise King Dharma, which sprang from the performance of the sacrifice, Nārada became content. Then the hermit Nārada, O king, fell to thinking as he watched the assembly of the entire baronage; and he recalled the tale that long ago had been spun in the dwelling of Brahmā at the time of the partial incarnations. Knowing that this assembly was an assembly of Gods, O scion of Kuru, Nārada called to mind the lotus-eyed Hari. The lord Nārāyaṇa, slayer of the enemies of the Gods, conqueror of enemy cities, had himself been born in the baronage to keep his
15 promise—he, the creator, who of yore had himself commanded the Gods: "Ye shall regain your old worlds after killing one another." When he had thus ordered all the Gods, the propitious master of the world, the blessed Nārāyaṇa was born on earth in the house of Yadu, in the lineage of the Andhakas and Vṛṣṇis, as the foremost of those who uphold dynasties, and he shone with superb beauty as the moon among the stars. He, enemy-crushing Hari, the strength of whose arms Indra and all the Gods revere, had indeed become man. "O woe, the self-created God himself will once more carry off this powerful
20 baronage that has grown so great," such was the thought upon which Nārada reflected, wise in the Laws, for he knew that Hari Nārāyaṇa was the lord who is to be praised with sacrifices. The sage, greatest of those who are wise in the Law, remained at the grand ceremony of the wise King Dharma to honor him.

Thereupon Bhīṣma, O King Bhārata, spoke to King Yudhiṣṭhira: "Let presents of honor be made to the kings as each of them merits it. They declare that one's teacher, one's priest, one's relation, a *snātaka*, a friend, and the king are the six who deserve the guest gift, Yudhiṣṭhira. They also declare that when they have come and stayed for a year, they are worthy of it. These kings have come to us quite
25 some time ago: it is time now that the guest gift for each of them be

brought in. First bring in the gift for the one who is the most deserving of them!"

Yudhiṣṭhira said:

To which single person, scion of Kuru, do you hold that the gift be presented? Tell me, grandfather, what is proper!

Vaiśaṃpāyana said:

Bhīṣma Śāṃtanava then made the decision in his mind, O Bhārata, and decided that Kṛṣṇa Vārṣṇeya was the most worthy recipient on earth. "He is the one who in the midst of those who have assembled shines as though blazing with glory, strength, and prowess, as the sun shines among the stars! For this *sadas* of ours is brightened and gladdened by Kṛṣṇa, as a sunless place is by the sun and a windless one by the wind."

30 With Bhīṣma's assent the majestic Sahadeva offered in the ritual
manner the superb guest gift to the Vārṣṇeya. Kṛṣṇa accepted it
according to the rite that is found in the textbooks. Śiśupāla, however,
refused to consent to the honor paid to Vāsudeva. The powerful king
of the Cedis berated Bhīṣma and the King Dharma in the assembly and
went on to insult Vāsudeva.

Śiśupāla said:

34.1 This Vārṣṇeya does not deserve regal honor as though he were a
king, Kauravya, while great-spirited lords of the earth are present!
This is no way to behave for the great-spirited Pāṇḍavas, arbitrarily to
honor this Lotus-Eye, Pāṇḍava! You are children, you don't know!
For the Law is subtle, Pāṇḍavas! This short-sighted son of a river has
violated the Law: for if Bhīṣma like you acts out of favoritism while he
knows the Law, then he becomes the more despised in the world of
5 the honest. How can the Dāśārha, who is no king, merit precedence
over all the kings of the earth so that he should be honored by you?
If you consider Kṛṣṇa the elder, bull of the Bharatas, how can the son
merit it while the old Vasudeva, his father, stands by? Vasudeva may
favor you and be compliant, but how can a Mādhava merit the honor
when a Drupada is present? Or if you deem Kṛṣṇa your teacher, bull
of the Kurus, why do you honor the Vārṣṇeya while Droṇa stands by?
Or if you regard Kṛṣṇa as a priest, scion of Kuru, how can you honor
10 him when Dvaipāyana is present? This killer of Madhu is neither a
priest, nor a teacher, nor a king: is he not honored, best of the Kurus,
but out of favoritism? If you must honor Madhusūdana, why bring
these kings here—to insult them, Bhārata?

It was not out of fear for the great-spirited Kaunteya that we all offered him tribute, nor out of greed or to flatter him. He wanted the sovereignty and proceeded according to Law; so we gave him tribute and now he does not count us! What but contempt moves you, if in

an assembly of kings you honor Kṛṣṇa with the guest gift, while he
15 has not attained to the title? Suddenly the son of Dharma's reputation
for lawmindedness has vanished, for who could bring fitting honor in
this fashion to one who is apostate from the Law? Who, born in the
tribe of the Vṛṣṇis, once slew a *king*? Today law-mindedness has been
torn from Yudhiṣṭhira and replaced by meanness, for his granting the
gift to Kṛṣṇa! If the Kaunteyas are fearful and mean and wretched,
surely you could have enlightened them to what kind of honor you, a
Mādhava, deserve! Or if in their meanness they offered you honor of
which you are unworthy, Janārdana, why did you consent to it? No,
you prize this honor that does not befit you, like a dog that has found
20 the spillings of an oblation, to devour it in a lonely place! Not only is
there delivered an insult to these Indras of kings, the Kurus have also
shown you up for what you obviously are, Janārdana. As a marriage
is to a eunuch, as a show to a blind man, so is this royal honor to
you, Madhusūdana, who are no king! We have seen who King
Yudhiṣṭhira is, seen who Bhīṣma is, altogether and precisely!

And with these words Śiśupāla rose from his high seat and strode
out of the *sadas* with other kings.

Vaiśaṃpāyana said:
35.1 King Yudhiṣṭhira hastened to Śiśupāla and spoke to him this
friendly and courteous word: "It is not proper, king, the way you
have spoken. It is wholly lawless, king, and pointlessly rude. For
Bhīṣma Śāṃtanava would never misunderstand the ultimate Law;
prince, do not blame him wrongly! Look at these many kings older
than you are: they consented to the honor paid Kṛṣṇa, and you
5 should likewise forbear it. Bhīṣma really *knows* Kṛṣṇa, O lord of the
Cedis, and completely. You yourself do not know him as the Kaurava
does."

Bhīṣma said:
No courtesy be shown to one, nor does he deserve kindliness, who
refuses to condone honor paid to Kṛṣṇa who is the eldest of the world!
A baron who, the greatest of warriors, defeats a baron in war, and
having captured him sets him free, becomes that baron's guru. In this
meeting of kings I do not see one who was not defeated by the glory of
the Sātvatī's son. Not only to us is Acyuta supremely worthy of
10 honor, by all three worlds must Janārdana be honored. For Kṛṣṇa has
vanquished many bulls of the barons in battle, the entire world is
wholly founded on the Vārṣṇeya. Therefore, even in the presence of
elders, we honor Kṛṣṇa and no one else. You have no right to speak
as you did, get rid of the notion!

On many that are old in wisdom have I attended, king, and as they
recounted the virtues of virtue-rich Śauri in their assemblies, I heard

of those many virtues that are greatly esteemed by the honest. Often
and in many ways have I also heard people tell of the feats of this sage
man from the day he was born. It is not out of whimsy, king of the
Cedis, and not by putting our alliance first or because of any favors
15 from him, that we honor the one honored on earth by the honest, him
who brings all earthly happiness. It is in the full knowledge of his
fame, his bravery, and his triumph that we offer the honor. Not one,
however young, did we fail to examine; and passing over those who
have grown old in wisdom, we found Hari the most worthy of our
honor. Of brahmins he is the elder in knowledge, of barons the
superior in strength, and both these grounds to honor Govinda are
found firm. Knowledge of the Vedas and their branches, and boundless
might as well—who in the world of men possesses these so
distinguishedly if not Keśava?

Liberality, dexterity, learning, gallantry, modesty, fame, a supreme
resolve, humility, luster, pertinacity, contentment, and prosperity are
20 forever in Acyuta. All of you must agree that he, fully accomplished
teacher, father, and guru, is to be honored and worthy of honor!
Priest, teacher, eligible son-in-law, *snātaka*, friend, king—all this is
Hṛṣīkeśa, and therefore Acyuta stands honored. For Kṛṣṇa alone is the
origin of the worlds as well as their dissolution, for Kṛṣṇa's sake is all
that exists here offered. He is the Unmanifest Cause and the
Sempiternal Doer, higher than all creatures; it is thus that Acyuta is
the eldest. Spirit, mind, the Large One, wind, fire, water, ether and
25 earth, and the fourfold creation, all rest upon Kṛṣṇa. The sun, the
moon, the stars, the planets, the points of the compass and the
intermediate points—it all rests on Kṛṣṇa. This Śiśupāla is a fool who
does not know that Kṛṣṇa is everywhere and at all times—that is why
he speaks thus. For only a wise man who reflects upon the highest
Law will have an insight according to the Law, but not so this king of
Cedi.

Who among these great-spirited kings, young or old, does not deem
Kṛṣṇa worthy? Or *who* does not honor him? If Śiśupāla contends that
the honor was misplaced, let him act as he should about this
misplaced honor!

Vaiśaṃpāyana said:

36.1 Having spoken, famous Bhīṣma fell silent. In reply Sahadeva said
meaningfully, "If there is anyone, kings, who does not tolerate that I
honor Kṛṣṇa Keśava, the slayer of Keśin and of measureless prowess, I
put this foot of mine on the head of any strong prince! Let him reply
properly to my challenge! But let any sensible king agree that he is
the teacher, father, and guru, who is honored, to be honored, and
worthy of honor!"

Not one among these wise and good, proud and mighty kings spoke up when he pointed to his foot. Thereupon a shower of flowers fell on Sahadeva's head and disembodied voices exclaimed, "Good! Good!" Nārada flapped his black antelope skin, he who expounds the past and the future, the solver of all doubts, familiar with all the worlds.

All the hosts led by Sunītha who had come upon their invitation appeared wrathful and their faces paled. The kings spoke of Yudhiṣṭhira's unction and Vāsudeva's honor with disgust as they had decided they themselves deserved it. When they were being restrained by their friends, their appearance was like that of roaring lions that are dragged away from their raw meat. Kṛṣṇa then understood that the invincible sea of kings, surrounded by billowing troops, was making a covenant for war.

After having paid further honors to brahmins and baronage as they deserved it, Sahadeva, god among men, concluded the ceremony. When Kṛṣṇa had been honored, Sunītha, dragger of his enemies, wrathfully, his eyes very red, addressed the kings: "Am I still your commander of the army, or what do you think now? Do we stand ready to fight the assembled Vṛṣṇis and Pāṇḍavas?" When he had thus roused all the kings, the bull of the Cedis plotted with the kings to disrupt the sacrifice.

2(26) *The Slaying of Śiśupāla*

2.37–42 (B. 40–45; C. 1413–1627)
37 (40; 1413). When the kings stir angrily, Bhīṣma assures Yudhiṣṭhira that Śiśupāla is no match for Kṛṣṇa (1–15).
38 (41; 1433). Śiśupāla berates Bhīṣma, belittles Kṛṣṇa's feats, and accuses Bhīṣma of hypocrisy (15–25). The fable of the hypocritical goose who preaches Law and eats the eggs of the birds that protect him (25–40).
39 (42; 1472). Śiśupāla berates Kṛṣṇa and Bhīṣma (1–5). Bhīma is enraged but restrained by Bhīṣma (5–20).
40 (43; 1494). Bhīṣma describes Śiśupāla's birth; he is born four-armed and three-eyed, but it is predicted that two arms and the third eye will disappear when he is taken on the lap of his future killer (1–10). Once Rāma and Kṛṣṇa come to Cedi, and the queen, who is Kṛṣṇa's paternal aunt, puts Śiśupāla on Kṛṣṇa's lap; the arms and eye disappear (10–15). The mother asks a boon of Kṛṣṇa,

that he will pardon Śiśupāla; Kṛṣṇa promises that he will pardon him a hundred times (15–20).
41 (44; 1519). Bhīṣma assures Bhīma that Kṛṣṇa must want Śiśupāla's challenge (1). Śiśupāla indignantly invites Bhīṣma to praise other kings than Kṛṣṇa, who is a mere serf (5–15). Bhīṣma lives by the grace of other kings, as the bhūlinga *bird by the grace of the lion (15–20). Bhīṣma belittles the other kings who stir indignantly (25). Bhīṣma tells them to challenge Kṛṣṇa (30).*
42 (45; 1561). Śiśupāla challenges Kṛṣṇa (1). Kṛṣṇa describes the misdeeds of Śiśupāla, including his wooing of Rukminī (5–15). Śiśupāla jeers, and Kṛṣṇa cuts off his head (15–20). A divine radiance rises from the dead body and enters Kṛṣṇa's; the kings are divided (20–25). The Pāṇḍavas perform the funerary rites; the Consecration is concluded, and Yudhiṣṭhira is blessed by the kings (30–35). The kings take leave and are conducted to the border (35–40). Kṛṣṇa takes his leave (45–55). Yudhiṣṭhira follows on foot, then is dismissed with a blessing (50–60).

Vaiśaṃpāyana said:

37.1 Seeing the mass of kings who were angrily billowing like a sea, Yudhiṣṭhira said to the most wise Bhīṣma, the ancient grandsire of the Kurus, as the enemy-killing, widely invoked, most splendid Indra might say to Bṛhaspati, "This vast sea of kings is stormy with anger. Tell me, grandfather, how I should act in this. Tell me at once and in full, grandfather, how I should prevent the sacrifice from being disrupted and the subjects from being menaced."

5 At these words of the law-wise Yudhiṣṭhira the King Dharma, Bhīṣma, grandsire of the Kurus, said this word: "Have no fear, tiger of the Kurus. Can a dog kill a lion? There is a well-prepared and safe path that I have chosen before. These kings of the earth band together and bark like a pack of dogs around a sleeping lion. They stand before the sleeping lion of the Vṛṣṇis and bark furiously like dogs before a lion. And as long as Acyuta* does not wake up, that lionlike king, the
10 bull of the Cedis, makes lions out of them all. The dim-witted Śiśupāla, O best of kings, seems desirous of leading all the kings without exception to the seat of Yama, son! Surely Adhokṣaja* is ready to take away what glory Śiśupāla possesses, Bhārata. His senses have gone

* = Kṛṣṇa.

astray, good luck to you, most sensible prince, the Cedi kings's senses and those of all the other kings, Kaunteya. For whomever the tiger of men wants to take, his senses go mad like the Cedi king's. Of all the fourfold creation in the triple world, Mādhava* is the beginning and the end, Yudhiṣṭhira!"

15 When he had heard these words, the king of the Cedis gave Bhīṣma his harsh-spoken reply, O Bhārata.

Śiśupāla said:

38.1 How is it you are not ashamed of yourself, decrepit defiler of your family, while you frighten all these kings with your many threats? It surely befits you, most eminent Kuru, who live like a eunuch, to say things that run counter to Law! Like a boat adrift tied to another boat, like a blind man who follows the blind, so are the Kauravas, Bhīṣma, who have you for their guide. By proclaiming this man's feats of killing Pūtana and so forth you have made our minds collapse once more!

5 Supercilious fool, if you want to sing the praises of Keśava, why
doesn't that tongue of yours, Bhīṣma, splinter a hundredfold? You,
having grown old in wisdom, want to praise a cattle herd on whom
even the stupid may heap contempt? If he killed a vulture when he
was young, what is so wonderful about that? Aśva and Vṛṣabha were
no great fighters, Bhīṣma. If he kicked down with his foot an
inanimate wooden cart, what is the wonder of it, Bhīṣma? If he held
up the mountain Govardhana for seven days, that, I think, is hardly a
10 miracle, Bhīṣma; it is as big as an anthill! When we hear from you,
Bhīṣma, that he ate a lot of food while playing on a mountaintop, you
astound us the more. You who know the Law, is it not a great
wonder that he killed Kaṃsa, the mighty prince, whose food he had
eaten? Certainly you do not seem to have heard good people tell what
I shall now tell you, basest of Kuru's line who know of no Law. Strict,
honest, law-abiding people have always instructed us in the world not
to raise weapons against women, cows, brahmins, him whose food one
has eaten, and him who seeks mercy with you: all this is perverted
15 with you, Bhīṣma. You talk to me praising Kṛṣṇa as ancient in wisdom
and old and superior, as if I knew nothing? But how does a cow-
killer and woman-killer deserve praise, Bhīṣma?

Even though upon your word that "he is the wisest of all, he is the lord of the world," Janārdana believes that it is all true, surely it remains all a lie! No song lauds the singer, however often he sings it. Creatures follow their nature, like the *bhūlinga* bird. Your nature surely and undoubtedly is of the basest; and so the nature of the

* = Kṛṣṇa.

Pāṇḍavas must be quite evil, if they think Kṛṣṇa deserves the highest
honor and if you are their guide who speak of Law and do not honor
20 it, who have dropped from the path of the good. For what sage,
knowing himself to be law-abiding, would act as you did, Bhīṣma,
ignoring the Law? If you think yourself wise, knowing the Law, why
did you abduct Ambā who loved another? Your brother Vicitravīrya
followed the conduct of the good: the king did not seek the girl whom
you had abducted, Bhīṣma, he on whose wives another had to beget
offspring for you, and not according to the ways of the strict, while
you winked, thinking yourself wise! For you have no Law, Bhīṣma!
Your celibacy is a lie that you maintain either from stupidity or from
25 impotence, no doubt of that! I myself don't see you ever prosper; for
you have not served the old who say what the Law is; offerings, gifts,
learning, and sacrifices with large stipends are none worth a sixteenth
fraction of a son. Whatever is accomplished by means of many vows
and fasts, Bhīṣma, decidedly becomes all void if one has no son.
Childless and old you will, because of your false teaching of the Law,
now find your death at the hands of your kinsmen, as the goose did.
People wise in the lore used to tell a story that I am now going to
30 tell you precisely so, Bhīṣma, for you to hear. It happened an old
goose once lived by the ocean. Speaking of Law but failing in conduct
he preached to the birds, "Practice the Law, not lawlessness"; that is
what the birds constantly heard from the law-preacher, Bhīṣma. The
other birds, Bhīṣma, used to bring him food, fishes that live in the sea,
for the sake of his Law. Also, those birds would leave all their eggs
with him, Bhīṣma, and then frolic flying over the ocean water. The
brute ate the eggs of all the birds, that goose that was alert in his own
35 task while the others were negligent. When those eggs dwindled, some
other clever bird began to suspect him, then once saw him at it.
Having witnessed the crime of the goose, the bird, most unhappily,
told all the other birds. And the birds gathered, witnessed it
themselves, and killed the hypocritical goose, scion of Kuru.
So will these kings of the earth in their anger kill you too, Bhīṣma,
being of the same feather, just as the birds killed the goose. People
who know the Lore sing a song on this, Bhīṣma Bhārata, which I shall
40 precisely so repeat to you: "Thou, on the chariot of thy wings, thou
croakest a lie as thy soul turns the other way. Thy unholy crime of
eating the eggs passeth beyond thy preaching!"

Śiśupāla said:

39.1 Highly did I esteem him, the powerful King Jarāsaṃdha, who
refused to give battle to this one, saying he was no more than a serf.
Who shall give praise to the deed that was done by Keśava,
Bhīmasena, and Arjuna, the assassination of Jarāsaṃdha? By no gate

did Kṛṣṇa enter in his fraudulent brahmin's guise, and so set eyes on the majesty of the wise Jarāsaṃdha. Acknowledging his own brahminism, that law-spirited prince at first undertook to offer this cheat the unwanted foot water, and he invited Kṛṣṇa, Bhīma, and Dhanaṃjaya to a meal, Jarāsaṃdha did, Kaurava! Kṛṣṇa did wrong! If this is the maker of the world, as you, fool, imagine, why did he not *truthfully* know himself for a brahmin? What is a miracle to me is that the Pāṇḍavas, while dragged by you from the path of the strict, still think highly of you! Or mayhap it is not too strange that you, old and effeminate, are their guide in *all* matters!

Vaiśaṃpāyana said:

When he heard this long speech, harsh and harsh-spoken, majestic
10 Bhīmasena, strong of the strong, became enraged. His naturally long
and wide eyes, serene like lotuses, grew red and copper-cornered with
fury. All the kings saw him knitting his brow in three peaks, like the
three-coursed Ganges flowing over three peaks on his forehead. They
watched his face as he angrily gnashed his teeth, as of Time itself
when about to burn down all creatures at the end of the Eon. But as
the spirited man impetuously flew up, strong-armed Bhīṣma held him,
as the Lord might hold back Mahāsena. And while Bhīṣma restrained
15 Bhīma, Bhārata, the guru appeased his rage with various words. The
enemy-tamer did not transgress Bhīṣma's word, no more than the
ocean transgresses the flood line, however roused at the end of the
rains. Yet, Śiśupāla, with Bhīmasena berserk, O king, did not tremble
at all, but the hero remained steadfast in his manliness. As the enemy-
tamer again and again leaped up, he no more worried about him than
a lion about some small game. Bursting out laughing, the majestic
king of the Cedis spoke as he looked upon berserk Bhīma of terrible
prowess, "Let him go, Bhīṣma, so that these kings may watch him
burn in the fire of my majesty as a moth in a flame!"
20 Thereupon Bhīṣma, first of the Kurus, best of the wise, on hearing
the Cedi king's words, spoke as follows to Bhīmasena.

Bhīṣma said:

40.1 In the line of the king of the Cedis he was born with three eyes and
four arms, and shriek and bray he did like an ass! His mother and
father trembled before him, as did their relations; and seeing him so
monstrous they decided to cast him out. Then a disembodied voice
spoke to the king whose heart was befuddled with worry, and to his
wife, councillors, and house priest: "King, he is born your son,
illustrious and powerful, therefore be not afraid of him, but guard
5 your child anxiously. You are not to be his death, nor has his Time
yet come. His death, his slayer by the sword, has been born, lord of
men."

When they heard the hidden being speak this word, the mother, burned by her love for her son, spoke out: "I bow with folded hands to him who has spoken this word concerning my son. Now let him also speak further. I want to hear who shall be the death of this son!"

The hidden being thereupon spoke again: "He upon whose lap his
10 two extra arms will fall like five-headed snakes and that third eye in the middle of his forehead will sink away as he looks at him—he shall be his death."

When they heard that the child was three-eyed and four-armed, all the kings on the face of the earth arrived with a wish to see him. The king welcomed them as they arrived, in what way was seemly, and lifted his son on the lap of each of thousands of kings as they came; but the prediction did not come true.

Then the Yādavas Saṃkarṣaṇa and Janārdana* came to the city of
15 the Cedis to visit Yādavī who was their father's sister. Rāma and Keśava greeted him and all the kings in the proper order and according to seniority, inquired about their health, and sat down. Both heroes were welcomed, and with more than usual affection the queen herself put her son on Dāmodara's lap. No sooner was he placed on his lap than the two extra arms fell off and the eye in his forehead sank away.

Seeing this, the queen, in pain and trembling, prayed to Kṛṣṇa: "Give a boon to me, Kṛṣṇa, who am sick with fear, strong-armed one, for you are the relief of the oppressed and grant safety to those that are afeared!" "Do not fear," replied Janārdana to his father's sister,
20 "what boon must I give you, or what should I do, my aunt? Whether it can be done or not, I shall obey your word!"

At this she said to Kṛṣṇa, the joy of the Yadus, "Pray pardon, strong man, the derelictions of Śiśupāla!"

Kṛṣṇa said:

I shall forsooth forgive a hundred derelictions of your son, paternal aunt, even though they may be capital offenses. Do not sorrow.

Bhīṣma said:

That is how this evil king, this nitwit Śiśupāla, can challenge you, hero, emboldened by Govinda's boon.

Bhīṣma said:

41.1 It is not the Cedi king's own idea to challenge Acyuta. Surely it was the decision of Kṛṣṇa himself, the lord of the world. For what king on earth, Bhīmasena, would now dare berate me, like this defiler of his line, if not crazed by fate? He of a certainty is a particle of the

* = Rāma and Kṛṣṇa.

glory of Hari, strong-armed prince, and widely famous Hari wants to recover it. That is why this evil-minded king of Cedis roars fiercely like a tiger, tiger of the Kurus, without worrying about any of us.

Vaiśaṃpāyana said:

5 The Caidya did not suffer this discourse of Bhīsma and furiously gave Bhīṣma reply.

Śiśupāla said:

Let our enemies have the prowess that is Keśava's, Bhīṣma, whose praises you sing, forever on your feet like a songster! If your heart must always delight in the praising of others, Bhīṣma, then praise real kings bar Janārdana!

Praise Darada Bāhlīka here, the first of the kings, who rent this earth at his birth!

Praise Karṇa here, Bhīṣma, who draws the great bow, the peer of the Thousand-eyed God in might, the ruler of Anga and Vanga!

10 Praise well Droṇa and Drauṇi,* father and son, grand warriors, praise them, the admirable pair, ever-foremost of brahmins! Either of them, I am sure, if enraged could empty this earth of her swift and immovable creatures! For I fail to espy a ruler of men the equal of Droṇa in battle, or of Aśvatthāman, O Bhīṣma, and yet you refuse to praise them!

Why do you fail to praise such kings as Śalya and others, if as always your heart is set on praising, Bhīṣma?

But what indeed can I do, if you, king, fail to listen to the ancient ones who of yore spoke only of Law?

15 None of these four are done: censuring oneself, worshipping oneself, honoring a stranger, censuring a stranger: none of these are done by a noble!

If in your constant folly you must praise this man out of loyalty, this unlaudable Kṛṣṇa, no one else will agree with you, Bhīṣma!

How on this keeper of herds for a Bhoja, a criminal, can you lower the entire world out of utterly personal whimsy?

Or if your loyalty, Bhārata, does not come by nature—didn't I tell you before of the bird you resemble, the *bhūlinga*?

This *bhūlinga* bird lives on the farther side of the Himālaya, Bhīṣma;
20 the words that it speaks are always belied by the facts. "Do not act
recklessly," that's what this bird always advises, but she fails to
realize her own actions are foolhardy. For this foolish bird, Bhīṣma,
feeds on morsels of flesh that are stuck between the teeth of a feeding
lion! There is no doubt, Bhīṣma, that she lives at the lion's pleasure,
and you, like her, always speak words without knowing the right Law.

There is no doubt, Bhīṣma, that you live at these kings' pleasure; for there is no one like you whose acts are so hateful to people!

* = Aśvatthāman.

Vaiśampāyana said:
When he heard the bitter speech of the king of the Cedis, he replied
25 in his hearing, O king: "Indeed, I live at the pleasure of these kings! I
who do not count these kings any better than straw!" At this word of
Bhīṣma the kings were enraged. Some shuddered, others reviled
Bhīṣma. Other great archers cried upon hearing Bhīṣma's word, "This
evil, insolent, ancient Bhīṣma does not deserve our pardon! Let the
irate kings band together and kill this evil-minded Bhīṣma properly
like a beast of sacrifice, or burn him in a straw fire!"
30 Hearing their outcry, Bhīṣma, wise grandfather of the Kurus, spoke
to those lords of the earth: "I see no end here to all this talk. Listen to
what I shall say, kings, and that will be all. Kill me like a beast of
sacrifice, or burn me in a straw fire—I put this mere foot of mine on
your heads! Here stands Govinda Acyuta whom we have honored.
Whichever man's spirit hastens to death, let him now challenge Kṛṣṇa
the Mādhava, who wields bow and club, to a duel until he is felled
and enters the body of this God!"

Vaiśampāyana said:
42.1 Immediately upon hearing this from Bhīṣma, the Cedi king of vast
puissance, eager to battle Vāsudeva, challenged Vāsudeva: "I
challenge you, come and fight with me, Janārdana, until I have killed
you with all the Pāṇḍavas! For with you I must kill the Pāṇḍavas as
well, Kṛṣṇa, for they passed over kings and bestowed the honor on
you who are not a king. In their folly they honored you, a vicious
serf, not a king, as though you had earned the honor, Kṛṣṇa. Yes, I
hold I must kill them!" And having spoken the tigerlike king stood
there roaring and fuming.
5 Thereupon Kṛṣṇa spoke softly: "Princes, this son of a Sātvata
woman is a bitter enemy of us and with his cruel spirit wishes the
Sātvatas ill, though they have done him no wrong. Knowing that we
had gone to the city of Prāgjyotisa, this fiend, who is our cousin,
burned down Dvārakā, kings. While the barons of the Bhojas were at
play on Mount Raivataka, he slew and captured them, then returned
to his city. Malevolently, he stole the horse that was set free at the
Horse Sacrifice and surrounded by guards to disrupt my father's
10 sacrifice. When she was journeying to the country of the Sauvīras to
be given in marriage, the misguided fool abducted the unwilling
wife-to-be of the glorious Babhru. Hiding beneath his wizardry, the
fiendish offender of his uncle abducted Bhadrā of Viśāla, the intended
bride of the Karūṣa!

"For the sake of my father's sister I have endured very great
suffering; but fortunately now *this* is taking place in the presence of
all the kings. For you are now witnesses of the all-surpassing offense

against me; learn also now the offenses he has perpetrated against me in concealment. This present offense I can no longer forbear, and
15 his insolence amidst the full circle of kings deserves death. This fool, who must *want* to die, once proposed himself for Rukminī, but the fool no more obtained her than a *śūdra* a hearing of the Veda!"

All the assembled kings, upon hearing this and more from Vāsudeva, now began to revile the Cedi king. But when Śiśupāla heard it, the mighty man burst into loud laughter and jeeringly said, "Have you no shame at all, Kṛṣṇa, that you broadcast in assemblies, particularly before these kings, that your Rukminī was another man's first? For what self-respecting man but you would broadcast to the
20 strict that his wife had belonged to another, Madhusūdana?* Forgive me, if you have that much faith, or don't, Kṛṣṇa, what could possibly befall me from you, however angry or friendly?"

He was still speaking when the blessed Madhusūdana, scourge of his enemies, irately cut off his head with his discus. The strong-armed king fell like a tree that is struck by a thunderbolt.

Thereupon the kings watched a sublime radiance rise forth from the body of the king of the Cedis, which, great king, was like the sun rising up from the sky; and that radiance greeted lotus-eyed Kṛṣṇa, honored by the world, and entered him, O king. When they saw that, all the kings deemed it a miracle that that radiance entered the strong-
25 armed man, that greatest of men. In a cloudless sky heaven rained forth and blazing lightning struck and the earth trembled, when Kṛṣṇa slew the Caidya. There were kings there who did not say a word and at these indescribable times stared at Janārdana. Others indignantly kneaded their hands. Others bit their lips, swooning with fury. But other kings secretly applauded the Vārṣṇeya. Some were enraged, others undecided.

The great seers joyously went to Keśava, and so did great-spirited brahmins and powerful kings.

30 The Pāṇḍava told his brothers at once to perform the funerary rites for the great king who had been the son of Damaghoṣa. The brothers obeyed his command; and the Pārtha, along with the other kings, anointed his son king to the monarchy of the Cedis.

Thereafter, the sacrifice of the king of the Kurus, with all its opulence, shone forth with vast august power and brought joy to the youths, O king. Its disruptions appeased, its undertaking joyous, its properties and grains abounding, rich in food-stuffs, with plentiful eatables, it was well-guarded by Keśava. Janārdana of the strong arms brought the grand sacrifice of the Royal Consecration to its end: the blessed Śauri, who wields bow, discus, and club, stood guard over it.

* = Kṛṣṇa.

35 At last, when Yudhiṣṭhira the King Dharma had bathed at the
Removal Ceremony, the entire royal baronage approached him, and
they said, "By good fortune thou prosperest, Law-wise lord. Thou hast
attained to the Sovereignty! Ājamīḍha,* thou hast furthered the glory
of the Ājamīḍhas**; and with this rite thou hast accomplished, thou
Indra of kings, a very high Law. We bid thee farewell, tiger among
kings, we have been honored with all we desired. We shall return to
our kingdoms, pray give us leave."

On hearing these words of the kings, Yudhiṣṭhira the King Dharma
saluted the kings as they deserved; and he said to all his brothers,
"All these kings have come to us in a spirit of friendship. They have
bidden me farewell, and now these enemy-burners are departing for
their kingdoms. Pray conduct the good kings to the borders of our
40 realm. Good fortune to you!" The Pāṇḍavas, always following the
Law, obeyed their brother's order, and conducted each of the principal
kings as they deserved. The majestic Dhṛṣṭadyumna swiftly conducted
Virāṭa; the great warrior Arjuna the great-spirited Yajñasena; the
mighty Bhīmasena conducted Bhīṣma and Dhṛtarāṣṭra; the warlike
Sahadeva the heroic Droṇa and his sons; Nakula went with Subala
and his son; and the Draupadeyas and Abhimanyu with the mountain
kings. The bulls of the barons likewise accompanied the barons; and,
similarly honored, all the brahmins went their way.

45 When all the lordly princes had left, O bull of the Bharatas, the
majestic Vāsudeva said to Yudhiṣṭhira, "I must take leave of you. I
shall go to Dvāravatī, joy of the Kurus. By good fortune you have
attained to the greatest of rites, the Royal Consecration." The King
Dharma replied to Madhusūdana, "It is by your grace, Govinda, that
I have attained to the rite. By your grace that the entire royal
baronage came under my sway and attended on me, bringing rich
tribute. Without you, hero, we shall find no joy at all. Yet you must
go to your city Dvāravatī."

50 At these words, the law-spirited Hari of wide fame, accompanied by
Yudhiṣṭhira, went to Pṛthā and said with love, "Your sons have now
together attained to the sovereignty, successfully and affluently, aunt.
You must be pleased. Pray give me leave so that I can return to
Dvārakā." Keśava paid his compliments to Subhadrā and Draupadī,
then left the ladies' quarters in Yudhiṣṭhira's company. After he had
bathed and prayed and had brahmins bless him, Dāruka yoked the
well-wrought chariot, which looked like a beautiful cloud, and
55 approached Kṛṣṇa. When the latter saw that the chariot, crowned by
great Garuḍa, stood to, he circumambulated and ascended it; then the
lotus-eyed sage set out for the city of Dvāravatī.

* = descendant of Ajamīḍha; here: Yudhiṣṭhira.
** = the Bhāratas.

Illustrious Yudhiṣṭhira the King Dharma and his brothers followed the mighty Vāsudeva on foot. The lotus-eyed Hari stopped the great chariot awhile and spoke to Kuntī's son Yudhiṣṭhira: "Remain always alert in the protection of your subjects, lord of your people, as the Rain God does in the protection of the creatures, and the birds in that of their big tree. May your kinsmen live on you as the Immortals do on the Thousand-eyed God."

After making another engagement with each other, Kṛṣṇa and the
60 Pāṇḍava said farewell and each went to his own house. When Kṛṣṇa,
first of the Sātvatas, had left for Dvāravatī, O king, only Duryodhana
the prince and Śakuni Saubala still lodged in the divine hall, those
bulls among men.

2(27) The Dicing

2.43–65 (B. 47–73; C. 1662–2450)

43 (47; 1662). Duryodhana is tricked by the marvels in Yudhiṣṭhira's palace and is mocked. Resentful, he starts for home with Śakuni (1–15). At Śakuni's question he gives voice to his envy of Yudhiṣṭhira's wealth and threatens suicide (20–35).

44 (48; 1703). Śakuni extols the Pāṇḍavas: they are invincible (1–15), but Yudhiṣṭhira can be defeated at dicing by Śakuni, who is an expert gambler (15–20). Duryodhana asks Śakuni to bring up the matter before Dhṛtarāṣṭra (20).

45 (49; 1725). Śakuni conveys to Dhṛtarāṣṭra that Duryodhana is unhappy; Dhṛtarāṣṭra asks the latter for the reasons, since he enjoys all comforts (5–10). Duryodhana describes the tribute kings and brahmins brought (15–25). Yudhiṣṭhira feasts countless brahmins (25–30). Śakuni proposes to wager Yudhiṣṭhira for his wealth; Duryodhana concurs (35–40). Dhṛtarāṣṭra wants to consult Vidura, which displeases Duryodhana, and Dhṛtarāṣṭra orders built a thousand-pillared hall (45). He sends for Vidura, who demurs (50). Dhṛtarāṣṭra remains firm (50–55).

46 (50; 1766). Dhṛtarāṣṭra now cancels the dicing on Vidura's advice and tells Duryodhana to look to his blessings (1–15). Duryodhana protests and bitterly recounts at length Yudhiṣṭhira's magnificence, and how he himself was mocked (15–35).

47 (51; 1820). Continued description of the treasures brought to Yudhiṣṭhira from all over the world (1–30).
48 (52; 1857). Description continued; in spite of munificent gifts, many parties are refused admission (1–35). How Yudhiṣṭhira feasted his brahmin guests (35–40).
49 (53; 1908). Major kings provide Yudhiṣṭhira with the regalia for his Consecration (1–10). Kṛṣṇa anoints Yudhiṣṭhira with the ancient Vāruṇa conch; at the blowing of the conches, the kings fall prostrate except the Pāṇḍavas and three allies (10–20). The grandeur of the function (20–25).
50 (54; 1934). Dhṛtarāṣṭra warns Duryodhana against envy and counsels contentment (1–5). Duryodhana protests and argues that discontent fits a king, even if it means treachery (1–20). The Pāṇḍavas will overshadow the Kauravas (20–25).
51 (56; 1966). Śakuni again proposes to dice; Dhṛtarāṣṭra will seek Vidura's advice (1–5). Duryodhana protests that his father should make up his own mind (5). Dhṛtarāṣṭra is unwilling but gives in (10–15). He orders a hall built (15), and tells Vidura to invite the Pāṇḍavas; Vidura demurs, but Dhṛtarāṣṭra remains firm (20–25).
52 (58; 1992). Vidura goes to Indraprastha and is well received (1). Vidura conveys the invitation (5). Yudhiṣṭhira fears quarrels, and Vidura agrees (10). Yudhiṣṭhira accepts the challenge (10–15). They ride to Hāstinapura and are welcomed; they exercise and sleep (20–35).
53 (59–60; 2030). Śakuni challenges Yudhiṣṭhira, who accepts under protest (1–10). Duryodhana will stake and Śakuni dice; the elders enter (15–20). The stakes are made, and Śakuni wins the round (20–25).
54 (61; 2060). Yudhiṣṭhira stakes a hundred thousand gold pieces and loses (1): then his chariot (1–5), a thousand elephants (5–10), a hundred thousand slave girls (10), a hundred thousand male slaves (15), a hundred thousand chariots (20), Gāndharva horses (20), his army (20–25), and his treasury (25).
55 (62; 2095). Vidura interrupts the game, warning against Duryodhana and advising alliance with the Pāṇḍavas (1–15).
56 (63; 2111). He continues his admonitions (1–10).
57 (64; 2121). Duryodhana accuses Vidura of treason

(1–10); Vidura calls the other a fool and withdraws (10–20).

58 (65; 2141). Challenged anew by Śakuni, Yudhiṣṭhira stakes his wealth (1), cattle (5), city, country, and his people's property (5), the ornaments of the princes (10), Nakula (10), Sahadeva (10), Arjuna (15–20), Bhīma (20–25), and himself (25). Śakuni suggests he stake Draupadī; Yudhiṣṭhira describes her lovingly, stakes her, and loses (30–35). The elders are dismayed, Duryodhana's party is overjoyed (35–40).

59 (66; 2186). Duryodhana orders Vidura to fetch Draupadī; he refuses, with dark predictions (1–10).

60 (67; 2198). Duryodhana orders an usher to fetch her; he goes and tells Draupadī (1–5). Draupadī tells him to ask in the assembly if Yudhiṣṭhira lost himself before losing her; Yudhiṣṭhira gives no answer (5). Duryodhana orders the usher to bring Draupadī (10). Draupadī appears in the hall, clothed in one garment (15). Duryodhana tells Duḥśāsana to fetch Draupadī; he goes and drags her by the hair into the hall (15–20). She protests that she has her period (25–30). She appears; Duḥśāsana insults her (35). Bhīṣma fails to solve the problem whether she was Yudhiṣṭhira's to stake (40). Draupadī protests (40–45).

61 (68; 2255). Bhīma berates Yudhiṣṭhira (1–5), and Arjuna warns him (1–10). Vikarṇa urges the assembly to speak to the problem; he himself does not judge she was won (10–25). Karṇa berates him and judges her won (25–35). He orders the Pāṇḍavas and Draupadī to strip (35–40). Duḥśāsana tries to undress Draupadī; Bhīma swears he will drink his blood (40–45). Miraculously the stripped skirt is replaced; Duḥśāsana desists (45–50). Vidura urges the assembly to consider the question, which is their duty; he illustrates this with the story of the contest of Sudhanvan and Virocana, in which Virocana's father Prahlāda judges in favor of Sudhanvan after taking advice from Kaśyapa (55–75). The princes remain silent (80).

62 (69–70; 2340). Draupadī complains bitterly about the Kauravas' lawlessness in dragging her into the hall (1–10). Bhīṣma states that Yudhiṣṭhira should say whether Draupadī was lawfully won or not (10–20). Yudhiṣṭhira remains silent; Duryodhana presses the

question (20–25). Bhīma declares that Yudhiṣṭhira is the Pāṇḍavas' master (30–35).
63 (71; 2380). Karṇa declares that they all have been won (1–5). Bhīma speaks angrily (5). Duryodhana bares his thigh to Draupadī, and Bhīma swears to break it (5–15). Vidura warns once more (15). Duryodhana calls on Bhīma and Arjuna, but Arjuna brings the problem back to the assembly (20). The ominous portent of a jackal howl is heard, and Dhṛtarāṣṭra withdraws with his son (20–25). He grants Draupadī a boon; she chooses Yudhiṣṭhira's freedom (25–30). For a second boon she chooses the other Pāṇḍavas, but refuses a third boon (30–35).
64 (72; 2416). Karṇa taunts the Pāṇḍavas (10). Bhīma threatens battle, but is restrained (5–15).
65 (73; 2433). Yudhiṣṭhira asks Dhṛtarāṣṭra's wishes; the latter admonishes him not to heed insults (1–15). The Pāṇḍavas and Draupadī start back to Indraprastha (15).

Vaiśaṃpāyana said:

43.1 As he lodged in that hall, bull of the Bharatas, Duryodhana
gradually inspected the entire hall with Śakuni. In it the scion of Kuru
saw divine designs that he had never seen before in the City of the
Elephant. One time the princely Dhārtarāṣṭra came, in the middle of
the hall, upon a crystal slab, and thinking it was water, the flustered
prince raised his robe; then, bitter and shamefaced, he roamed about
5 the hall. Again, seeing a pond with crystalline water adorned with
crystalline lotuses, he thought it was land and fell into the water with
his clothes on. When they saw him fallen in the water, the servants
laughed merrily and gave him clean clothes at the king's behest.
Mighty Bhīmasena saw him that way, as did Arjuna and the twins,
and they burst out laughing. A choleric man, he did not suffer their
mockery; to save his face he did not look at them. Once more he
pulled up his robe, as though crossing a pool, to ascend firm land, and
10 again those people all laughed at him. He once tried a door, which
appeared to be open, and hurt his forehead; another time, thinking
the door was closed, he shrank from the doorway.

Having come there upon all these various tricks, O king of the people, Prince Duryodhana was excused by the Pāṇḍaveya*; and

* = Yudhiṣṭhira.

after having witnessed, with a far from happy mind, the incredible
opulence of the grand celebration of the Royal Consecration, he went
home to the City of the Elephant. Resentful of the fortune of the
Pāṇḍavas, Prince Duryodhana journeyed sunk in gloomy thought,
and his mind became evil.

Upon seeing the happiness of the Pārthas, the submission of the
kings, and the favor in which all the world held them, down to the
15 children, O scion of Kuru, and the sublime magnitude of the great-
spirited Pāṇḍavas, Duryodhana Dhārtarāṣṭra became pale. So he went,
distracted, recalling the assembly hall and the peerless opulence of
the wise King Dharma; and, absentmindedly, Dhṛtarāṣṭra's son
Duryodhana did not respond to Śakuni Saubala, who addressed him
again and again.

Seeing him so distracted Śakuni said to him, "Duryodhana, what
is the reason that you travel with so many sighs?"

Duryodhana said:

I saw the earth entire under Yudhiṣṭhira's sway, conquered by the
majesty of the weapons of the great-spirited white-horsed Arjuna.
20 I saw that grand sacrifice of the Pārtha, uncle, grand as that of Śakra
among the Immortals, prince of great splendor. Rancor has filled me,
and burning day and night I am drying up like a small pool in the
hot season. Look, Śiśupāla was felled by the Sātvata chieftain, yet
there was no man there who stood by him. They were burning, the
kings, with the fire that rose from the Pāṇḍava, and they pardoned
his dereliction. Yet who can forgive *him* that crime!

Vāsudeva did it, a great deed and a wrong one, and the feat was
25 made possible by the majesty of the great-spirited Pāṇḍaveyas. So, too,
the kings brought all kinds of riches and attended on the King
Kaunteya like commoners who pay taxes! When I saw all that blazing
fortune at the Pāṇḍava's, I fell prey to resentment and I am burning,
though that is not my way. I shall enter the fire, or drink poison, or
drown myself, for I shall not be able to live. For what man of mettle
in this world will have patience when he sees his rivals prosper and
himself decline? If I were to tolerate the fortune that has befallen
them, I would be neither a woman nor not a woman, neither a man
30 nor not a man! What man like me who sees their sovereignty over
earth, with such wealth and such a sacrifice, would not burn with
fever? All alone I am not capable of acquiring such a regal fortune;
nor do I see any allies, and therefore I think of death. Fate, methinks,
reigns supreme, and man's acts are meaningless, when I see such
bright fortune fetched to the Pāṇḍava. In the past I have made
attempts to kill him, Saubala, but he survived it all and grew like a
lotus in the water. Therefore, methinks, fate reigns supreme and man's
acts are meaningless, for the Dhārtarāṣṭras decline and the Pārthas

35 are always prospering. When I see their fortune and that splendid hall
and the mockery of the guards, I burn as if with fire. Allow that I
suffer bitterly now, uncle, and speak to Dhṛtarāṣṭra of the resentment
that pervades me.

Śakuni said:
44.1 You must harbor no resentment against Yudhiṣṭhira, for the
Pāṇḍavas have always enjoyed good luck. In the past you have often
made attempts on them with many wiles, and the tigerlike men
escaped because of their luck. They won Draupadī for their wife, and
Drupada with his sons for their ally, and the heroic Vāsudeva for their
helper in the winning of the earth. They won undiminished wealth as
their father's portion, king of the earth, and it grew through their
5 energy—why lament about that? Dhanaṃjaya, by sating the Fire,
won the bow Gāṇḍīva, the two inexhaustible quivers, and celestial
weapons. With that superb bow and the might of his own arms he
subjugated the kings—why lament about it? He freed the Dānava
Maya from the forest fire and had him build that hall—why lament
about that? At that same Maya's orders terrifying Rākṣasas called the
Kiṃkaras came to carry that hall—why lament about that?
You say you have no allies, King Bhārata; that is not true, for your
10 warlike brothers are your allies. So is the grand archer Droṇa and his
sagacious son, and the *sūta's* son Rādheya,* and the warrior
Gautama.** So am I with my brothers and the heroic Saumadatti***;
and together with all of us you must conquer the entire world!
Duryodhana said:
With you, king, and these other warriors I shall defeat them, if you
so approve! When they are defeated, the earth will be mine, and all
the kings, and that rich assembly hall!
Śakuni said:
Dhanaṃjaya, Vāsudeva, Bhīmasena, Yudhiṣṭhira, Nakula and
15 Sahadeva, and the august Drupada cannot be defeated in battle by
force, not even by the hosts of the Gods. They are great warriors and
archers, know their weapons, and are battle-crazy. But I know by
what means Yudhiṣṭhira himself can be defeated, king. Listen and
employ it.
Duryodhana said:
If they can be defeated without inconsiderateness to our friends and
other great-spirited allies, then tell me, uncle.
Śakuni said:
The Kaunteya loves to gamble but does not know how to play. If

* = Karṇa.
** = Kṛpa.
*** = Bhūriśravas.

the lordly king is challenged, he will not be able to resist. And I am a
shrewd gambler, I don't have my match on earth or in all three
20 worlds! Challenge the Kaunteya to a game of dice. With my skill with
the dice, king, I am certain to take from him his kingdom and his
radiant fortune, in your behalf, bull among men. Mention all this to
the king, Duryodhana, and if your father permits, I shall certainly
defeat him.

Duryodhana said:

No, you yourself must mention it in the right way to Dhṛtarāṣṭra,
the first of the Kurus, O Saubala. I shall not be able to bring up the
matter.

Vaiśaṃpāyana said:

45.1 After experiencing the great ceremonial of King Yudhiṣṭhira's Royal
Consecration in the company of Śakuni Saubala, the son of the
Gāndhāra king, the latter, having found out the mind of Duryodhana,
whom he wished well, and heard Duryodhana's words, approached
the seated wise King Dhṛtarāṣṭra, who had the eyesight of insight,
and said to him, "Duryodhana, great king, looks pale and yellow and
wan, he is wretched and prone to brooding, take notice, bull of the
5 Bharatas? Why do you not inquire and find out precisely the
unbearable grievance of your eldest son, which derives from the
enemy?"

Dhṛtarāṣṭra said:

Duryodhana, my son, what is the reason that you are so sorely
aggrieved? If I should hear of the matter, tell me, scion of Kuru!
Śakuni here told me that you looked pale and yellow and wan and
that you are brooding. I do not see a cause for your grief, for this
grand sovereignty entirely devolves on you, son, and your brothers
and friends do not do you ill. You wear fine clothes, you eat hash of
10 meat, purebred horses carry you—why are you yellow and wan?
Costly beds and charming women, well-appointed houses and all the
recreation you want—all this waits on your word, without a doubt,
as though on the words of Gods. You are unassailable, yet seem sad?
Why do you pine, my son?

Duryodhana said:

I eat and dress like any miserable man. I bear an awesome grudge
as I endure the passage of time. The intolerant man who suppresses
his own subjects if they obey his enemy and is willing to escape the
affliction that comes from his enemy, him they call a man.
Contentment and pride kill good fortune, Bhārata, as do compassion
and fear; if he is possessed by those, no man attains to greatness.
15 My pleasures no longer satisfy me, now that I have seen the radiant
fortune at Yudhiṣṭhira Kaunteya's, which causes my pallor. It is

because of perceiving the prosperity of one's rivals and the decline of
oneself, and watching the fortune at Kaunteya's, which, albeit
invisible, I seem to see readily before me, I have become pale, and
wretched, yellow, wan.

There are eighty-eight thousand *snātaka* householders whom
Yudhiṣṭhira supports, each of them with thirty slave girls. Ten
thousand more eat daily the best food at Yudhiṣṭhira's house from
golden platters. The Kāmboja sends him hides of the *kadalī* deer,
20 black, dark, and red, and costly blankets, chariots, women, cows,
horses by the hundreds and thousands, and three hundred times a
hundred camel mares wander about there. The kings brought all
manner of precious things to the son of Kuntī at his superb ritual, O
king, and in great plenty. Nowhere have I seen or heard of such an
inflow of wealth as at the sacrifice of the sagacious son of Pāṇḍu!
And as I have seen the limitless flood of wealth of my enemy, king, I
find no shelter and brood incessantly, my lord. Cattle-rich Vāṭadhāna
brahmins in parties of one hundred stood at his gate, bringing thirty
25 billions in voluntary tribute, but they were turned back. When they
brought beautiful golden water jars and thus fetched him their
tribute, they later gained entrance.

The Ocean bucket brought him a brass goblet containing the
Vāruṇa liquor, such as surpasses the mead that the women of the
Immortals fetch for Śakra; it was carried in a reticule of a thousand
gold pieces and adorned with many precious stones. When I saw it,
it became for me the visible form of a fever—they had got it by going
to the eastern and southern oceans, and likewise they went and
obtained it at the western one, bull of the Bharatas; but none go to
the northern shore, except for the birds.
30 And listen to me as I tell of a miracle there. Whenever a full one
hundred thousand of brahmins had been fed, a signal announcing it
would be given: the conch shell was blown continuously! I heard the
generous sound of the conch sounding forth all the time, Bhārata, and
it raised my hairs. The audience hall brimmed over with kings, who
had come to watch, and the kings came bringing all kinds of treasure,
lord of the people! At the sacrifice of the clever son of Pāṇḍu, great
king, the kings of this earth became the servitors of the brahmins, as
though they were commoners. Neither the king of the Gods, nor
Yama, nor Varuṇa, nor even the overlord of the Guhyakas has wealth
35 as is found at Yudhiṣṭhira's. And since I have seen the all-surpassing
wealth of the Pāṇḍava, I find no peace in my burning heart.

Śakuni said:

Now you whose prowess is your faith, hear the way in which you
can obtain the sublime fortune you have seen at the Pāṇḍava's. I am
an expert at dice, Bhārata, the greatest on earth; I know their heart,

I know the stake, I know the niceties of gaming. The Kaunteya loves to gamble but does not know how to play. If challenged, he will surely come. I shall challenge him to dice with me.

Vaiśaṃpāyana said:

At these words of Śakuni the Prince Duryodhana fell straight into
40 step and said to Dhṛtarāṣṭra, "This man knows the dice, king, and he is able to take the fortune of the Pāṇḍava in a game. Pray allow it."

Dhṛtarāṣṭra said:

It is my wise councillor the Steward on whose advice I wait. I shall confer with him and find out what to decide in this matter. For he is farsighted and will put first the Law and our ultimate benefit, and proclaim the truth of the case as it fits both parties.

Duryodhana said:

The Steward will turn you down, if he comes in on this! And when you are turned down, lordly king, I shall kill myself! Let there be no doubt! When I am dead, be happy with your Vidura, king. Surely, you shall have the pleasure of all earth: why bother about me?

Vaiśaṃpāyana said:

45 Dhṛtarāṣṭra heard the painful words that were spoken with affection; and, submitting to Duryodhana's demand, he spoke to his servants: "Let the carpenters build me a big hall of a thousand pillars and a hundred doors, heart-fetching and beautiful, and do it at once! And when they have splattered it with gems and thrown out the dice everywhere, report to me quietly that it is fully built and ready to be entered."

Thus the king decided, to appease Duryodhana; and the great King Dhṛtarāṣṭra sent for Vidura. For he never took any decision without asking Vidura; and though he knew the evils of dicing, he was drawn to it because of the love he bore his son.

50 When the sagacious Vidura heard that the Gate of Kali was upon them and the Maw of Destruction had opened, he hastened to Dhṛtarāṣṭra. Brother approached great-spirited elder brother, and bowing with his head to his feet, he spoke this word: "I do not welcome, my lord king, the decision you have taken. Act to avoid that a breach occur among your sons on account of dicing."

Dhṛtarāṣṭra said:

Steward, there shall be no quarrel among my sons with my other sons. The Gods in heaven will surely lend us their grace. Holy or unholy, beneficent or maleficent, the family game of dice shall
55 proceed, for certainly it is so destined. When I and the bull of the Bharatas Bhīṣma are near, no foul play ordained by fate can possibly occur. Go at once on your chariot, with steeds that match the wind in speed, to the Khāṇḍava Tract and bring Yudhiṣṭhira. My decision

shall not be circumvented, Vidura, I tell you! I deem it supreme destiny that makes this befall.

Thus spoken to, the sagacious Vidura thought, "It is not!" And, greatly disturbed, he went to the wise Bhīṣma, the son of the river.

Janamejaya said:

46.1 How came about that fateful dicing match of the brethren, where
my grandfathers the Pāṇḍavas incurred that calamity? Who were the
kings who were the gamesmasters at the assembly, most learned of
brahmins? Who cheered him on, and who were against him? I wish
to hear you tell this in detail, brahmin, for this was the root of the
destruction of the world, best of the twiceborn.

The Bard said:

Thus addressed by the king, Vyāsa's majestic student, who knew
everything, narrated it all as it had happened.

Vaiśaṃpāyana said:

5 Listen to me and hear the story once more in its detail, best of the
Bharatas, if you have a mind to listen.

Divining Vidura's mind, Dhṛtarāṣṭra, the son of Ambikā, spoke this
word to Duryodhana when they were alone: "Enough of the dicing,
son of Gāndhārī, Vidura does not approve of it. Nor would he, in his
very great sagacity, tell us aught that is in bad faith. For it is in good
faith that I think Vidura is speaking. Let it all be done that way, son!
10 I think that will be for your own good. Vidura, that great sage, knows
all, with its secrets, that the divine seer, the blessed lord Bṛhaspati of
profound wisdom, told to instruct his pupil, the sage lord of the Gods.
And I, my son, will always abide by his judgment. Vidura is
considered the first sage among the Kurus, just as the sagacious
Uddhava is acclaimed among the Vṛṣṇis, prince.

"Enough, therefore, of this dicing, son, for gambling is found to be
divisive. At a breach the kingdom perishes, therefore avoid it, son.
You have received what tradition says is the first obligation of a father
and a mother to their son—paternal and ancestral rank. You have
been taught and made sufficient in science; you have always been
cherished in the house, and you stand first among your brothers in
15 the kingdom. Do you find no virtue in this? You have better food and
clothing than ordinary folk can find; since you have got all this,
strong-armed prince, why do you grieve, my son? Commanding
always this great and prosperous kingdom bequeathed by father and
grandfather, you shine as the lord of the Gods shines in heaven! I
know that you are perceptive; then why has this source of grief, the
more dolorous, welled up for you? Pray tell me!"

Duryodhana said:

Evil is the man who looks to how he eats and dresses! Low is the
man, they say, who is incapable of indignation! A *common* fortune,
my lord king, does not delight me; and having seen the fortune that
20 seemed to blaze forth at the Kaunteya's, I suffer. I have seen all of
earth subject to Yudhiṣṭhira's sway, and still I stand steady here, still
alive! I speak to you in pain. Like prostrate serfs appear the Caitrikas
and Kaukuras, the Kāraskaras and Lohajanghas in Yudhiṣṭhira's
household. The Himālayas and oceans and marshes that produce all
the gems serve like the lowliest in Yudhiṣṭhira's household, lord of the
people! Yudhiṣṭhira deemed me the elder and his better, and paying
many compliments he charged me with the collection of the tributes.
Of the treasures that came in, superb and fetching any price, neither
25 the near end nor the far end could be seen there, Bhārata! As I
received the wealth, my hand did not hold out. I was still tired from
receiving the treasures fetched from distant parts, when the givers had
already departed.

Maya had built a lotus pond that seemed full of water but was
made out of crystal with jeweled water pools—I have seen it, Bhārata.
I pulled up my clothes and the Wolf-Belly laughed at me, as at one
who is destitute of treasure and confounded by the superior wealth of
his enemy. If I could have, I would have killed the Wolf-Belly! To be
derided by a rival burns me. Bhārata! Once again, when I saw a
similar pond full of lotuses, I thought it was likewise made out of
30 crystal and I fell in the water, king. Kṛṣṇa and the Pārtha laughed at
me aloud, and so did Draupadī and the women, offending my heart.
At the king's orders, servants gave me other clothes, because mine
were wet, which offended me more. Listen as I tell you of another
trick, king. When I went through what seemed a door but was not,
I hit a crystal slab with my forehead and got hurt. The twins saw me
from a distance and were amused! Mournfully they held me with their
arms, and Sahadeva said to me, almost smiling, "This is the door, go
35 this way, prince," and he said it again and again. I saw gems there
of which I had never even heard the names, and it burned my heart.

Duryodhana said:

47.1 Listen, Bhārata, what treasures I saw at the Pāṇḍava's, the choicest
treasures that kings had brought from everywhere. After seeing that
wealth of my enemy I no longer find myself steady: hear of the
tribute, either mined or grown. The Kāmboja gave as tribute fleeces
of *eḍa* sheep and feline furs embroidered with gold, and superb
deerskin jackets; horses, gray and dappled, three hundred of them,
with beaklike noses, and three hundred camel mares fed with dates,
5 *śamī*, and *inguda* nuts. The lordly Govāsana and Dāsamīya brahmins

had all come out of love for the great-spirited King Dharma, bringing three billion in tribute, and they stood at the gate, denied admission. When they brought beautiful golden jars and thus proffered their tribute, they gained entrance. The Śūdras of Bharukaccha brought as their full tribute a hundred thousand slave girls from Kārpāsika, dark, slender, and long-haired, decked with golden ornaments, as well as *ranku* deer hides, fully fit for brahmins; and they brought Afghan horses, great king. The folk who are born by the ocean bays and around rivers, and who live on crops that grow wild, and on river-mouth grain, the Vairāmas, Pāradas, Vangas, and Kitavas, brought as tribute all manner of gems, goats and sheep, cows and gold, donkeys and camels, arrack, all kinds of blankets, and they stood at the gate, denied admission.

The great warrior King Bhagadatta, gallant ruler of Prāgjyotiṣa, strong overlord of Barbarians, came with the Greeks with purebred horses, fast as the wind; and with all his tribute he was denied admission and stood at the gate. Bhagadatta of Prāgjyotiṣa went away after presenting a jade vase and swords with hilts of pure ivory. Other folk from different regions, with two eyes, three eyes, or one in their foreheads, turbaned and nomadic, Bāhukas, and Cannibals, and one-footed tribes I saw at the gate, denied admission, after they had arrived with large tributes in gold and silver. The One-Footers brought horses the color of fireflies, the color of parrots, fast as thought, or rainbow-colored, red like the morning sky at dawn, and of many shades, and also wild horses, fast as thought; and they presented him with priceless gold.

Chinese men I saw and Huns, Scythians, Orissans, the ones who live in the interior forest, Vārṣṇeyas, Robber Huns, Black Folk and Himālayans—I cannot get over the many who came and were denied admission, yet paid tribute to him, of so many shapes and so numerous. Black-throated, big-bodied asses, killers of hundreds, they brought by the tens of thousands, well-trained and famed all around, and textiles of ample size, rich in colors and good to the touch, that came from Bactria and China, wools, *ranku* hides, silk, jute, and cotton besides by the thousands of bales, of the color of red lotuses, and soft non-cotton cloth, tender fleeces and skins; sharp long swords, spears, lances and battle-axes, and a hundred sharp hatchets from the West; liquors, perfumes, and various gems by the thousands they brought as their full tribute and stood at the gate, denied admission.

Scythians, Tukhāras, Kankas, Romaśas and the Horned Men brought Mahāgama and Durāgama horses that numbered in the millions; and with their tribute of various kinds, of many crores, and with gold without count, they stood at the gate, denied admission. Costly seats, palanquins and beds, gem-studded chariots inlaid with

gold and mostly built of ivory, in many different shapes, with golden
decorations, which were harnessed with well-trained horses in
30 tigerskin housings, cushions of all kinds, thousands of gems, iron
arrows and half-iron shafts and various kinds of javelins were the
tribute that the king of the East paid when he entered the sacrificial
terrain of the great-spirited Pāṇḍava.

Duryodhana said:

48.1 Listen to me as I describe the manifold tribute that the kings paid
to the sacrifice, a mighty mass of riches. The kings who live by the
river Śailodā between Mount Meru and Mount Mandara and enjoy
the pleasing shade of bamboo and cane, the Khasas, Ekāśanas,
Jyohas, Pradaras, Dīrghaveṇus, Paśupas, Kuṇindas, Tanganas, and
Further Tanganas, they brought the gold called Pipīlaka, which is
granted as a boon by the *pipīlaka* ants, and they brought it by
5 bucketsful and piles. The mighty mountain men fetched as their
tribute yak-tail plumes, black and spotted and white, and still others
gleaming like the moon; also much sweet honey from Himālayan
flowers, and perfume with water that was brought down from the
Northern Kurus; besides powerful herbs from the northern Kailāsa,
and yet more; and they stood there bowing at the gate of King
Ajātaśatru, and they were denied admission. The mountain kings who
live beyond the Himālaya on Sunrise Mountain, on the bank of the
Vāriṣenā and by the Lohitya, eaters of fruits and roots and clad in
hides, brought loads of sandalwood and aloewood and agallochum,
10 piles of hides, gems, gold, and perfumes, and a myriad slave girls
from the mountains, exotic birds and animals that were to be kept as
pets, and many-splendored gold that had been collected from the
mountains—all this tribute they brought and stood at the gate, denied
admission.

Kāyavyas, Daradas, Dārvas, Śūras, Vaiyamakas, Audumbaras,
Durvibhāgas, Pāradas, Bāhlikas, Kāśmīras, Kundamānas, Paurakas,
Haṃsakāyanas, Śibis, Trigartas, Yaudheyas, Madra and Kekaya
barons, Ambaṣṭhas, Kaukuras, Tārkṣyas, Vastrapas, Pahlavas,
Vasātis, Mauleyas, Kṣudrakas, and Mālavas, Śauṇḍikas, Kukkuras,
15 Śakas, O lord of the people, Angas, Vangas, Puṇḍras, Śānavatyas,
Gayas, Sujātis, Śreṇimats, all grand and sword-wielding barons,
brought wealth by the hundreds for Ajātaśatru. The Vangas and the
Kalinga chieftains, the Tāmraliptas and Puṇḍrakas brought *dukūla*
raiment from the Kauśikī River, and silk and cloaks. Thereupon the
gatekeepers told them at the king's behest, "If you bring revenue and
good tribute, you will gain entrance." So they gave gold-caparisoned,
cloth-decked elephants with pole-long tusks, lotus-dotted, towering

like mountains, always rutting, which hailed from Lake Kāmyaka:
20 each gave a thousand tuskers covered with armor, patient and well-bred; then they entered through the gate.

These and many other hosts assembled from all the horizons; and other great-spirited princes offered precious things there. The Gandharva king Citraratha, a friend of Indra, gave four hundred wind-fast steeds. Tumbura the Gandharva happily gave a hundred horses the color of mango leaves, which were harnessed in gold. Kṛtin, the king of the Śukaras, O lord Kauravya, gave many hundred
25 prize elephants. Virāṭa the Matsya by way of tribute offered two thousand gold-caparisoned rutting elephants. King Vasudāna from the domain of Pāṃśu gave the Pāṇḍavas in full tribute twenty-six elephants and two thousand horses in golden harness, O king, of great speed and vigor, and the right age. Yajñasena presented fourteen thousand serving girls and ten thousand male slaves with wives, lord of the people, and twenty-six elephant-pulled chariots, great king; and he offered the Pārthas his entire kingdom for the
30 sacrifice. The Siṃhalas offered the choicest gifts of the sea, beryls and pearls and conches, and hundreds of elephant housings. Clad in robes embroidered with gems, swarthy, with copper-red eye corners, the men who brought the gifts stood at the gate and were denied admission.

Brahmins in a spirit of love, barons because they were defeated, commoners and serfs because they were obedient brought gifts, and out of affection and respect all the barbarians, of all classes, high, middle, and low-born, waited on Yudhiṣṭhira. At Yudhiṣṭhira's palace all the world seemed to be encompassed with the variety of races that had come from a variety of countries.

Now that I have seen all the many and manifold gifts that the kings sent to my enemies, my suffering makes me yearn for death.
35 Let me tell you of the Pāṇḍava's dependents, to whom Yudhiṣṭhira provides raw and cooked food. A myriad, a triple lotus count, number his elephant drivers and riders, a monstrous number of chariots and numerous foot soldiers! Here the food is measured out, there dressed, there cooked, there doled out, and elsewhere again rise the sounds of the Blessing of the Day. I have not seen one there who was not fed, not happy, not well-rewarded with alms among all the classes at Yudhiṣṭhira's establishment. There are eighty-eight thousand *snātaka* householders, each with thirty serving wenches, whom Yudhiṣṭhira supports. Happy, completely contented, they hope for the destruction
40 of his enemies. Another ten thousand celibate ascetics eat from golden platters at Yudhiṣṭhira's establishment. Yajñasena's daughter* does

* = Draupadī.

not eat until she has seen to it that every one, down to the hunchbacks and dwarfs, has eaten and is filled.

There are two who have not paid tribute to Kuntī's son, Bhārata, the Pāñcāla king because of the marriage alliance, the Andhaka-Vṛṣṇis because of friendship.

Duryodhana said:

49.1 The Āryan kings, true to their covenants, great in their vows,
sufficient in their knowledge, expounders of the *Veda*, cleansed in the
concluding bath of the *Upaniṣads*, imperturbable, restrained by their
modesty, law-spirited and famous, kings themselves whose heads have
been anointed, wait on him! I saw everywhere wild cows that had
been brought by the kings for the stipends of the priests, with brass
milking buckets, in many herds of thousands. The kings, with all due
honor and acting of their own accord, fetched religiously all manner
of treasure for his Unction, Bhārata.
5 It was Bāhlīka who fetched the chariot that was inlaid with gold,
and Sudakṣiṇa yoked it with white Afghan horses. Glorious Sunītha
brought the peerless axle tree; the king of the Cedis, acting of his own
accord, quickly fetched the ready standard pole. The ruler of the
Deccan brought the armor; the Magadhan the garland and the
turban; the great archer Vasudāna the state elephant of sixty years.
The Matsya fitted the axles, Ekalavya fitted on the sandals, the Avanti
king brought the various waters for the Unction. Cekitāna presented
the quiver, the king of the Kāśis the bow, Śalya the gold-hilted sword
10 and gold-threaded bandoleer. Dhaumya and Vyāsa of immense
austerities did the anointing, while giving precedence to Nārada and
Asita Devala, the hermit.
The great seers attended the Unction with pleasure. Others, steeped
in the *Veda*, came with Rāma Jāmadagnya, uttering spells, to the
great-spirited king of the generous stipends, as in heaven the Seven
Seers come to the great Indra, the king of the Gods. Sātyaki of proven
valor held up the king's umbrella, and Dhanaṃjaya and Bhīmasena
Pāṇḍava the two fans. The Vāruṇa conch shell, which, in a previous
age, Prajāpati had presented to Indra, the tublike Ocean now fetched
15 for him. The sling had been well made by Viśvakarman out of a
thousand gold pieces; and with this conch shell Kṛṣṇa anointed him.
At this my heart sank. They went to the eastern ocean and the
western one, and also to the southern one, but they do not go to the
northern ocean, father, except the birds. They blew conch shells by
the hundreds for good auspices, and as they were blown they roared
out, and my hairs bristled. The kings fell prostrate, deprived of their
vigor. Dhṛṣṭadyumna, the Pāṇḍavas, Sātyaki, and, in the eighth place,

Kṛṣṇa kept their mettle and, gifted with heroic might and mutually
friendly, laughed aloud when they saw the kings and me unconscious.
20 Thereupon the Terrifier, exhilarated, presented the principal brahmins
with five hundred bullocks with gold-plated horns.

Not Śambara's slayer, nor Yauvanāśva, nor Manu, nor King Pṛthu Vainya, nor Bhagīratha was ever so surpassingly endowed with superb fortune as the King Kaunteya, when he, like King Hariścandra, thus attained to the Royal Consecration. Having witnessed this fortune at the Pārtha's as at Hariścandra's, my lord, how can you see that it boots me to live, Bhārata? Like a yoke tied by a blind man all has come loose, O king: the junior branch prospers, the senior one decays, Bhārata!

25 And having seen this I find no shelter,
Wherever I look, most heroic of Kurus.
And thus my flesh has wasted away
And my body is pale and direly aggrieved.

Dhṛtarāṣṭra said:
50.1 You are the eldest, and the son of my eldest wife, son: do not hate
the Pāṇḍavas! A hater takes on as much grief as there is in death.
Why should one like you, bull of the Bharatas, envy a Yudhiṣṭhira, a
simple man who has the same goals as you, the same friends, and
does not hate you? Why do you, my son, a prince, a bull of the
Bharatas, his equal in birth and prowess, covet your brother's fortune
out of perplexity? Don't be that way! You must calm yourself! Or if
you covet that sacrificial glory, bull of the Bharatas, have your priests
5 spread a Sevenfold Session in a grand ceremony! Surely the kings will
bring you, too, vast wealth, gems, and ornaments, from affection as
well as respect. Son, coveting another's property leads to no good. Be
content with what you have, stay with your own Law—that way lies
happiness. An unconcern for the riches of others, a constant enterprise
in one's own tasks, an effort to protect one's own: that defines
ownership! If he refuses to grieve in times of trouble, the capable man
always on the rise, alert and self-disciplined, always finds the good
things. Giving riches at the altar, enjoying the joys you want, and
playing healthily with the women, be at peace, bull of the Bharatas!

Duryodhana said:
10 You know, yet you confuse me! Boat rigged to another boat! Have
you no attention for your own cause? Do you hate me? Do I own the
Dhārtarāṣṭras of whom *you* are the guide? You always say you have
some *future* matter to take care of! If a guide, seduced by his enemy,
gets confused about what path to take, how can his followers follow

his path? King, your wisdom is replete, you obey the Ancients, you
have mastered your senses, yet you utterly confuse us, who are intent
on our tasks.

Bṛhaspati has said that the way of kings differs from the way of the
world, and that therefore the king should endeavor always to think
15 of his own profit. The baron's way, great king, is to be devoted to
victory; let it be Law or Unlaw, bull of the Bharatas, as long as it is
his way! A driver drives out to all the horizons with his whip, bull of
the Bharatas, wishing to make an attempt on his adversary's fortune!
To those who know the sword, the sword means the entire enemy-
harassing enterprise, open and concealed, which reduces the enemy,
not just the sword that cuts.

Discontent is the root of fortune. That is why I want to be
discontented. Only he who reaches for the heights, king, is the
ultimate politician. Should we not pursue selfish ways when we have
power or are rich? Others take away what one had earned before!
20 For they know that that is the Law of the kings. Śakra made a
covenant not to fight; then he cut off Namuci's head. And that to him
was the hoary way with a foe. As a snake eats up mice, so earth
eats up these two: a king who does not contend, a brahmin who
does not travel. No one, lord of the people, is born anyone's enemy:
he is the enemy, and no one else, whose ways are the same as his
own. If one watches in his folly the rise of his enemy's side, the other
will cut his root, like a swelling disease. An enemy, however tiny,
whose might grows on and on destroys one as surely as an anthill
destroys the tree by whose foot it has grown.
25 Ājamīḍha! Bhārata! Don't let the enemy's luck please you! It is a
burden, this policy that the vigorous carry on their heads. If a man
expects that his riches will grow just as he himself has grown from
birth, does he prosper with his kin? Power means instant growth!
As long as I fail to recover the power from the Pāṇḍavas I shall be in
danger. For I shall get that fortune, or be killed on the battlefield: for
why should I now care to live, if I do not equal him? The Pāṇḍavas
improve day by day, but our fortunes stand still.

Śakuni said:

51.1 That fortune over which you have been grieving after you saw it
at Pāṇḍu's son Yudhiṣṭhira's, I shall take it from him, let the enemy
be challenged! I shall take no risk, nor fight a battle in front of
armies; I shall throw the dice and, whole of body and wise, defeat the
fools! Be sure, the dice are my bows and arrows, the heart of the dice
my string, the dicing rug my chariot!

Duryodhana said:

This expert gambler stands ready, king, to take their fortune from the sons of Pāṇḍu in a game. Father, it should please you!

Dhṛtarāṣṭra said:

I submit to my brother's behest, the behest of the great-spirited Vidura. I shall meet with him and find out the truth of the matter.

Duryodhana said:

Vidura will cut down your resolve, no doubt of that, Kaurava! He is less devoted to my cause than to that of the Pāṇḍavas. No man should undertake his own task on another's authority. No two people have the same mind on any point of duty, joy of Kuru! The fool who avoids risks and protects himself shrivels where he stands like a straw mat in the rainy season. Neither diseases nor death wait for recovery: try to recuperate as long as there is time!

Dhṛtarāṣṭra said:

10 Yet, son, I do not want to fight with people who are stronger. Enmity, as sure a weapon as though it were iron, makes matters worse.

A disaster you deem a profit, prince,
This horrible knotting together of feuds.
Once it starts, in whatsoever a fashion,
It will let loose the swords and the arrows.

Duryodhana said:

The Ancients bequeathed us the rules of the game,
There is no evil in it, nor blows.
Approve of Śakuni's plan today,
And order at once a hall to be built!

If we gamble, the heavenly gate will be nearer;
It is proper for us to engage in the game.
We two will stand on an equal footing:
Approve of our playing the Pāṇḍavas.

Dhṛtarāṣṭra said:

The word thou speakest I do not like,
But be done as it pleases thee, king of men.
Thou shalt suffer hereafter, recalling your word,
For no such word shall prosper the lawful.

15 'Twas Vidura who foresaw it all,
In days long past, with his wisdom and spirit.
The great danger that slays the seed of the barons,
It looms now for man, who is powerless.

Vaiśaṃpāyana said:

So he spoke, King Dhṛtarāṣṭra the wise,
As he deemed it high ineluctable fate.
His servants he ordered to obey his son,
And the king remained fate-smitten in mind.

"Of a thousand pillars with beryls and gold,
Of a hundred gates with crystalline arches,
Let them swiftly build a hall sublime
A cry-length deep and a cry-length wide!"

Having heard him the craftsmen tarried not
But artfully, cleverly built it fast,
And they fetched at his orders all manner of things
To the meeting hall, by the thousands of them.

Then, little time past, they announced to the king
With full confidence that the meeting hall stood,
Enticing and colorful, gem-encrusted,
And furnished with beautiful golden seats.

20 Thereupon did the wise king of men Dhṛtarāṣṭra
To Vidura, first of his councillors, speak:
"Pray, go to Yudhiṣṭhira, son of a king,
And at my behest bring him quickly here,

"Saying, 'Thou and thy brethren must come and see
The beautiful gem-studded hall I have built,
Appointed with precious stones, beds, and seats;
We shall have there a family dicing game.' "

Knowing his son's mind, the king of men Dhṛtarāṣṭra, deeming it high ineluctable fate, did as he desired. Vidura, first of the wise, at this improper address did not approve of his brother's word and said to him,

"I do not welcome this errand, king.
Do not do it! I fear for the ruin of our line!
When brothers are split, a quarrel is sure:
King, this I fear from the dicing game."

Dhṛtarāṣṭra said:

25 No quarrel bothers me, Steward, here,
For otherwise fate would run counter to dicing.
This world submits to the Placer's design,
And thus does the world run, not by itself.

Therefore, go today to the king at my command and bring Yudhiṣṭhira, Kuntī's unassailable son, swiftly here.

Vaiśaṃpāyana said:

52.1 Then Vidura started with noble horses,
Well-trained and strong, whose speed was great,
At King Dhṛtarāṣṭra's forceful command,
For the dwelling of Pāṇḍu's sagacious son.

He flew on the road to them, and upon reaching the king's city the wise Vidura entered it with the homage of the brahmins. He went to the king's palace that rivaled Kubera's, and the law-spirited envoy approached Yudhiṣṭhira, the son of Law.

The great-spirited king whose strength was his faith,
Ajātaśatru,* welcomed with honors
And courtesies Vidura; then Ājamīḍha*
Inquired about Dhṛtarāṣṭra and his sons.

Yudhiṣṭhira said:

5 I do not discern any joy in your heart—
May I hope thou, Steward, hast come in good health?
May I hope that the sons comply with their elder?
May I hope that the commoners follow his rule?

Vidura said:

The great-spirited king and his sons are healthy,
And he sits in the midst of his Indra-like kin,
Contented, O king, with his well-mannered sons,
Firm-spirited, worriless, pleased with himself.

But the king of the Kurus speaks to thee thus,
After asking thy health and prosperity,
"Pray come, my son, and see with thy brothers
This hall of mine that matches yours!

"Foregather there, Pārtha, with thy brethren
And play and enjoy a family game.
We should be pleased if thou camest to join us,
The Kurus are all assembled here."

The gamesters have been appointed there
By great-spirited King Dhṛtarāṣṭra.
Thou shalt find the gamblers collected there.
With this message I come; agree to it, king.

Yudhiṣṭhira said:

10 At a dicing, Steward, we surely shall quarrel.
Who, knowing this, will consent to a game?

* = Yudhiṣṭhira.

Or what does your worship think that is right?
We shall all of us abide by thy word.

Vidura said:
I know that the game will bring disaster.
I have made an effort to stop him from it.
But the king has sent me to your presence:
You have heard, you are wise, now do what is best.

Yudhiṣṭhira said:
What other gamesters will gamble there
Besides the sons of King Dhṛtarāṣṭra?
I ask thee, Vidura, tell us this,
With whom are we playing, amidst those hundreds?

Vidura said:
The king of Gāndhāra, Śakuni, lord,
Overplaying and dexterous knower of dice,
Viviṃśati and Citrasena the prince,
Purumitra and Jaya and Satyavrata.

Yudhiṣṭhira said:
Most dangerous gamblers have been collected,
Who are sure to play with wizard tricks.
But this world obeys the Placer's design—
I do not refuse now to play with those gamblers.

15 It is the King Dhṛtarāṣṭra's behest,
So I will not refuse, sage, to go to the game.
A son will always respect the father:
I shall, Vidura, do as thou tellest me.

I am not unwilling to play Śakuni;
If I were, he would recklessly challenge me
In that hall. . . . Once challenged I will not refuse,
For so I have sworn for eternity.

Vaiśaṃpāyana said:
Thus spoke King Dharma to Vidura,
And ordering quickly all gear for the journey
He set out on the morrow with troops and retainers,
With women and ranking Draupadī.

"Fate takes away our reason
As glare blinds the eye.
Man bound as with nooses
Obeys the Placer's sway,"

quoth King Yudhiṣṭhira, and set out with the Steward: the enemy-
taming Pārtha, intolerant of the challenge, set out.
20 Ascending the chariot that Bāhlīka had presented, the Pāṇḍava
Pārtha, decked with his regalia, went with his brothers. Preceded by
brahmins, he departed ablaze with the fortune of kings, as he was
summoned by Dhṛtarāṣṭra and the covenant of Time. He proceeded
to Hāstinapura and went to Dhṛtarāṣṭra's house; and the law-spirited
Pāṇḍava met with Dhṛtarāṣṭra. Likewise he met with Droṇa, Bhīṣma,
Karṇa, and Kṛpa, as was meet, and so did the lord with Droṇa's son.
The strong-armed and mighty king met with Somadatta, with
Duryodhana, Śalya, and Śakuni Saubala, and whatever other kings
25 had previously assembled there; and with Jayadratha and all the
Kurus. In the midst of all his brethren the strong-armed prince
entered the dwelling of wise King Dhṛtarāṣṭra. There he found Queen
Gāndhārī, avowed to her husband, who was surrounded by her
sisters-in-law as the asterism of Rohiṇī is by the stars. After greeting
Gāndhārī and having been welcomed by her in return, he saw the
aged father,* the lord, who had the eyesight of insight.

The king kissed the scions of the Kauravas on the head, the four
30 Pāṇḍavas that is, O king, beginning with Bhīma. Elation took hold of
the Kauravas, O lord of thy people, upon seeing the tigerlike men, the
Pāṇḍavas of pleasing aspect. Soon dismissed, they entered their
jeweled quarters, and the women led by Gāndhārī came and set eyes
on them. Seeing the superb wealth of the daughter of Yajñasena,**
which seemed to blaze, the daughters-in-law of Dhṛtarāṣṭra were none
too spirited.

Thereafter the tigerlike men went out, with their women's
foreknowledge, did their routines that began with exercise, and
groomed themselves; then, the daily rites done, they all, rubbed with
divine sandalwood and pure of mind, had the brahmins bless them,
35 ate a hearty meal, and returned to their quarters; and serenaded by
women, they slept, the joys of the Kurus. They enjoyed their love
play, and night went by for them blissfully; and lauded and relaxed
they shed their sleep in the morning. Happy sleepers during the night,
they did their daily rites in the morning and entered the lovely hall,
which was crowded by gamblers.

Śakuni said:

53.1 The carpet is rolled out in the hall, king, and these people have time to spare to enjoy themselves. When we sow out the dice, let there be a covenant to the game, Yudhiṣṭhira!

* = Dhṛtarāṣṭra.
** = Draupadī.

Yudhiṣṭhira said:

Gaming is trickery, an evil; there is no baronial prowess in it, nor steady policy, prince. Why do you praise dicing? For no one praises as proud a gambler's trickery: Śakuni, don't defeat us by crooked means and cruelly!

Śakuni said:

He who follows the numbers and spies the deceptions
And is tireless in moving the dice about
And is cunning enough to see through a gambit
Is a gambler who manages all in a game.

5 The handling of dice can defeat our foe;
That is why you say that it's Time that does it:
Shall we gamble, king? Do no longer tarry.
Set the stakes right now and wait no more!

Yudhiṣṭhira said:

Asita Devala, greatest of hermits who frequents at all times the
gates to the worlds, has said, "To game with gamblers who play
tricks is an evil, but victory in battle according to the Law is a good
game and superior to it." No Aryans speak in riddles nor work with
tricks: an honest fight, not crooked, is the vow of the strict. Within
our power we strive to endow the brahmins who deserve it. Don't
10 play us beyond those means, do not win beyond that, Śakuni! It is
not with tricks that I seek pleasures and treasures, for even without
the gambler's trickery gaming is not honored.

Śakuni said:

A scholar surpasses a nonscholar only through *his* trick, Yudhiṣṭhira, so does a wise man surpass a fool; but people don't call that a trick. You have come to me: if you think it is trickery, desist from the game if that is your fear!

Yudhiṣṭhira said:

Once challenged, I will not desist—that is the vow I have taken. The injunction is powerful, king. I am in the power of what has been decreed. Whom shall I have to play in this encounter? What is the counterstake? Then let the game begin!

Duryodhana said:

15 I shall stake my gems and my treasures, lord of the people! And this
Śakuni, my maternal uncle, shall play for me!

Yudhiṣṭhira said:

For one man to play in another's stead does not seem fair to me: you know this, so accept it. Now by all means, let the game begin!

Vaiśaṃpāyana said:

When the dicing game was laid out, all the kings, led by Dhṛtarāṣṭra, entered into that hall—Bhīṣma, Droṇa, Kṛpa, and the

sagacious Vidura, and the others, who were none too happy about it, followed, O Bhārata. They sat in couples, or alone, those lion-necked,
20 august barons, on their colorful and ample lion seats. That hall, O king, shone with the assembled kings as heaven shines with the lordly gathering of the Gods—with all these *Veda*-wise champions, like suns incarnate. Then, great king, the family game began at once.

Yudhiṣṭhira said:

Here is a costly prize, king, which has come from the whirlpool of oceans, a superb lace of pearls set in the best of gold. This is my stake, king, what is your counterstake? Let the order stand, friend, and I shall win this game!

Duryodhana said:

Have I no pearls too? And many kinds of treasure? I am not selfish with my possessions, I shall win this game!

Vaiśaṃpāyana said:

25 Then Śakuni grasped the dice, he who knew the facts of dice. And "Won!" cried Śakuni at Yudhiṣṭhira.

Yudhiṣṭhira said:

54.1 You have won this play from me by confusing me with a trick! All right, Śakuni! Let us now play and grasp the dice a thousand times! I have a hundred full jars with a thousand gold pieces each, my treasury holds inexhaustible gold ore and fine gold aplenty. That is my stake, king, I play you for it!

Vaiśaṃpāyana said:

And when he had spoken, Śakuni cried "Won!" at the king.

Yudhiṣṭhira said:

Here is my illustrious, thunderous regal chariot worth a thousand, beautifully wrought and hung with tiger skins, with fine wheels and appointments, adorned with a circlet of bells, the same chariot that
5 brought us here, blessed and victorious, thundering like the cloud and the sea, drawn by eight fine osprey-hued steeds that are admired in the kingdom, and not one of the creatures that walk the earth can escape from them! That is my stake, king, I play you for it!

Vaiśaṃpāyana said:

At these words Śakuni decided, tricked, and cried "Won!" at Yudhiṣṭhira.

Yudhiṣṭhira said:

I have a thousand *must* elephants, Saubala, with golden caparisons. They are crowned with chaplets, hung with garlands, and spotted with lotus dots. They are well-trained mounts, fit for a king, and deaf to any noise on the battlefield. Their tusks are as long as poles, and
10 each big-bodied bull has a herd of eight elephant cows. They are all bastion-battering tuskers, huge like mountains and monsoon clouds.

That is my stake, king, I play you for it!

Vaiśaṃpāyana said:

Śakuni Saubala laughed out loud at the Pārtha and cried "Won!" at Yudhiṣṭhira.

Yudhiṣṭhira said:

I have a hundred thousand slave girls, young and exceedingly pretty, with shell bracelets and upper-arm rings and necklaces of gold pieces, beautifully adorned. They are groomed with costly perfumes, well-robed, and sprinkled with sandalwood. They all wear gems and gold and sheer clothes. At my command these girls, skilled in song and dance, wait on *snātaka* brahmins, ministers, and kings. That is my stake, king, I play you for it!

Vaiśaṃpāyana said:

At these words Śakuni decided, tricked, and cried "Won!" at Yudhiṣṭhira.

Yudhiṣṭhira said:

15 I have as many thousands of male slaves, skilled and compliant, who are always wearing fine clothes, clever and sharp and dexterous youths with polished earrings, who day and night feed the guests with platters in their hands. That is my stake, king, I play you for it!

Vaiśaṃpāyana said:

At these words Śakuni decided, tricked, and cried "Won!" at Yudhiṣṭhira.

Yudhiṣṭhira said:

I have as many chariots with golden trappings and waving pennants, equipped with well-trained horses and drivers and marvelous fighters, who each earn wages of up to a thousand a month, whether fighting or not. That, king, is my stake, I play you for it!

Vaiśaṃpāyana said:

20 When Śakuni heard this, he decided, tricked, and cried "Won!" at Yudhiṣṭhira.

Yudhiṣṭhira said:

I have partridge-dappled Gandharva horses with golden harnesses, which Citraratha was pleased to give to the Gāṇḍīva bowman. That, king, is my stake, I play you for it.

Vaiśaṃpāyana said:

At these words Śakuni decided, tricked, and cried "Won!" at Yudhiṣṭhira.

Yudhiṣṭhira said:

Myriads of chariots, carts, and horses stand yoked for me,
surrounded by draught animals of many kinds; so stand sixty
25 thousand broad-chested men, who drink milk and feed on rice and
grain, and whom I have collected, thousand by thousand, from each
class. That is my stake, king, I play you for it!

Vaiśaṃpāyana said:

At these words Śakuni decided, tricked, and cried "Won!" at Yudhiṣṭhira.

Yudhiṣṭhira said:

I have four hundred coffers encased in copper and iron, each holding five buckets of beaten gold. That is my stake, king, I play you for it!

Vaiśaṃpāyana said:

At these words Śakuni decided, tricked, and cried "Won!" at Yudhiṣṭhira.

Vidura said:

55.1 Great king! Know and listen to what I shall tell you! Even though you may not be pleased with what you hear, no more than a dying man is pleased with his medicine!

> No sooner of yore was the evil-minded
> Duryodhana born than he cried out shrilly
> Like a jackal, the killer of Bharata's line.
> He shall be the fitting cause of our death!

Knowing that a jackal is living in your house, you are not alert to it, a jackal in Duryodhana's form! Hear from me Kāvya's word:

> The mead-drinker finds his mead
> And does not reckon that he'll fall:
> For having climbed, he must later drown
> Or come upon his deadly fall.

5 This man, drunk with playing dice, does not look about him, like the
mead-drinker, and in starting a feud with great warriors he does not
reckon his downfall. You know full well, great king, what is unnatural
for kings. The Andhakas, Yādavas, and Bhojas assembled, and
abandoned Kaṃsa; and when, at their behest, enemy-slaying Kṛṣṇa
slew him, all the kinsmen rejoiced for a hundred years. At your behest
let the left-handed archer* subdue Suyodhana** and let the Kurus
rejoice in happiness over the scoundrel's reduction. Buy peacocks with
this crow, tigers with this jackal, buy the Pāṇḍavas! Don't drown in a
10 sea of sorrow. "To save the family, abandon a man; to save the
village, abandon a family; to save the country, abandon a village; to
save the soul, abandon the earth," so spoke Kāvya, all-knowing, wise
in all matters and terror of all his enemies, to the great Asuras so
that they would abandon Jambha.

* = Arjuna.
** = Duryodhana.

They say that a man took wild birds, which spit gold, from the
forest into his house, king, and when they lived there he strangled
them out of greed. This man, O enemy-burner, blinded by greed for
gold, killed the birds on which he could have lived forever, and in
one blow destroyed what he had and could have had. Bull of the
Bharatas, don't betray the Pāṇḍavas for immediate gain! You will
15 later repent your folly, like the man who killed the birds. Like the
garland-maker, take the flowers from the Pāṇḍavas one by one as
they blossom, fostering them with constant care in the pleasure grove.
Don't burn them to the roots as the charcoal-burner burns his trees.
Don't go to your perdition, Bhārata, with your sons, ministers, and
troops. For who could battle the Pārthas when they stand arrayed,
were he Indra the Lord of the Maruts, king, together with the Maruts?

Vidura said:

56.1 The root of all quarrels, the dicing game,
Leads to mutual breach and to great war;
Dhṛtarāṣṭra's son now undertakes it,
Duryodhana starts an awesome feud.

The scions of Pratīpa, Śaṃtanu, and Bhīmasena, and the Bāhlīkas because of Duryodhana's sin will all come to grief. In sheer folly Duryodhana robs the kingdom of its safety, as in its folly a bull forcibly breaks its own horn.

Be he champion or sage, whoever complies
With another's mind, overruling his prudence,
Boards a boat that is steered by a child
And will surely drown in ugly vice.

5 Duryodhana games with the Pāṇḍava;
You are pleased for you think he is winning.
From this overdone pastime there grows a war,
From whence extinction comes to all men.

This misguided game brings downward fruit;
In advice-treader's heart absorption is deep.
With Yudhiṣṭhira friendship shall bear fruit,
From kindness Arjuna sheds his hatred.

Pratīpa's and Śaṃtanu's scions and kings,
Hear ye Kāvya's word, let him not overreach you:
This blazing and grisly fire that is mounting,
Extinguish it now before there is war!

If Ajātaśatru the Pāṇḍava,
Brow-beaten by dice, does not tame his fury,

Or Wolf-Belly, Arjuna, and the twins,
What haven is yours in the horror that comes?

Great king, you were a source of treasure
Before this game, of as much as you wished.
If you win great wealth from the Pāṇḍavas,
Who needs it? The Pāṇḍavas are your wealth!

10 We all know the game that Saubala plays,
The man from the mountains knows sleight-of-hand;
Let Śakuni go from whence he came,
For he fights with jugglery, Bhārata!

Duryodhana said:

57.1 You always boast, Steward, of the fame of the foe
And in secret revile Dhṛtarāṣṭra's sons.
We know whose friend you are, Vidura,
You despise us all, as though we were fools.

That man stands known whose love lies elsewhere,
For that way he bends both his praise and his blame.
Your tongue lays open your heart and mind!
Even more, he declares his contrariness!

Like a snake we took you into our embrace,
Like a cat you hurt the one who feeds you;
They say nothing is worse than fratricide—
Why, Steward, have you no fear of sin?

In defeating our foes we reap a rich harvest,
Don't, Steward, tell us off so harshly!
You welcome alliance with our haters,
And, foolish enough, go to feud with us!

5 By speaking impardonably, friend becomes foe,
And he hides his secret by praising the foe.
Why does not the shame of it stop his tongue?
You are telling us now what you really want!

Despise us not, for we know your mind!
Go, learn the mind of your elders and betters!
Protect the fame you have raised so far,
Don't meddle so much in another's affairs.

Don't, Vidura, taunt us that you are the doer,
Don't always berate us in such harsh words;
I never ask you for what you think;
Goodbye, you Steward, our patience is worn!

Only One is the Teacher, there is no other,
And that Teacher teaches a man in the womb,
And at His teaching, as water flows down,
I flow wherever He orders me!

He who splits a rock with his head or feeds a snake obeys His orders of what he must do. One who gives orders here by force finds thereby an enemy; the wise man looks to the one who behaves like a friend! If one has lit a blazing fire and does not run before it, he does not even find ashes left anywhere, Bhārata!

Never lodge a hater from the enemy's party,
Especially, Steward, if he wishes ill.
Now, Vidura, go wherever you wish;
A bad wife, though cajoled, will leave anyway!

Vidura said:

Tell him, king, that those who desert their friends
For this much alone see their friendships end.
For the minds of kings have a way of revolving,
After granting favors they slay with bludgeons!

You, son of a king, are no longer a child,
And, nitwit, you think that I am a fool!
Who once has made a man his friend
And then reviles him is only a child!

A stupid mind is led to no good,
Nor a corrupt wench to a scholar's house.
Of course it displeases this Bharata bull,
As a sexagenarian displeases a girl!

If all you would hear is what pleases you, prince,
In all that you do, be it good or bad,
Ask the women, prince, and the dumb and the halt,
Go ask those that are equally silly!

Surely for you, a scion of Pratīpa, it is easy to find here a man who flatters you; those that say and listen to unpleasant though apt advice are rare. Yet in him who relies on the Law and, forgetting what pleases or displeases his master, gives good advice, however unpleasant, in him does a king find a friend.

While healthy, yet pungent, and sharp and hot,
Inglorious, bitter, and reeking foully
Is the liquid the good drink and the evil refuse.
Great king, pray drink it and shed your wrath!

20 To Dhṛtarāṣṭra I wish all glory and wealth,
And I wish it his son, as I always have;
And this being so, I bid ye farewell,
And may the priests give me their blessing!

A wise man should never enrage those snakes whose venom gleams in their eyes: that is what I tell you, joy of the Kurus, I tell you solemnly!

Śakuni said:

58.1 You have lost vast wealth of the Pāṇḍavas, Yudhiṣṭhira. Tell me what wealth you have left, Kaunteya, what you have not yet lost!

Yudhiṣṭhira said:

I know of untold riches that I possess, Saubala. But, Śakuni, pray, why do you ask about my wealth? Myriad, ton, million, crore, a hundred million, a billion, a hundred thousand crores, an ocean count of drops I can stake! That is my stake, king, play me for it!

Vaiśaṃpāyana said:

At these words Śakuni decided, tricked, and cried "Won!" at Yudhiṣṭhira.

Yudhiṣṭhira said:

5 I have countless cattle and horses and milch cows and sheep and goats, whatever belongs to our color of people east of the Indus, Saubala. That is my stake, king, I play you for it!

Vaiśaṃpāyana said:

At these words Śakuni decided, tricked, and cried "Won!" at Yudhiṣṭhira.

Yudhiṣṭhira said:

My city, my country, the wealth of all my people, excepting brahmins, all my people themselves, excepting brahmins, are the wealth I have left, king. That is my stake, king, I play you for it!

Vaiśaṃpāyana said:

At these words Śakuni decided, tricked, and cried "Won!" at Yudhiṣṭhira.

Yudhiṣṭhira said:

Here are the ornaments with which the princes glitter, the earrings and breastplates and all the adornment of their bodies. That is my stake, king, I play you for it!

Vaiśaṃpāyana said:

10 At these words Śakuni decided, tricked, and cried "Won!" at Yudhiṣṭhira.

Yudhiṣṭhira said:

This dark youth with the bloodshot eyes and the lion shoulders and the large arms, this Nakula and all he owns shall be one throw.

Śakuni said:

But Prince Nakula is dear to you, King Yudhiṣṭhira! If we win this stake, what more do you have to gamble?

Vaiśaṃpāyana said:

Having said this, Śakuni addressed those dice and cried "Won!" at Yudhiṣṭhira.

Yudhiṣṭhira said:

This Sahadeva preaches the Laws,
And has in the world earned the name of a scholar:
For this loving prince who does not deserve it,
I play with you like an enemy!

Vaiśaṃpāyana said:

15 At these words Śakuni decided, tricked, and cried "Won!" at Yudhiṣṭhira.

Śakuni said:

I have now won, king, these two dear sons of Mādrī. Yet methinks Bhīmasena and Arjuna are dearer to you.

Yudhiṣṭhira said:

Surely this is an Unlaw that you are perpetrating, without looking to propriety! You want to pluck us like flowers!

Śakuni said:

A drunk falls into a hole, a distracted man walks into a tree trunk, you are our elder and better, king—farewell to you, bull of the Bharatas! When gamblers play, Yudhiṣṭhira, they prattle like madmen of things they have not seen asleep or awake!

Yudhiṣṭhira said:

20 Like a ferry he carried us over in battle,
Defeater of foes, a prince of vigor;
For this world hero who does not deserve it,
For Phalguna* I play you, Śakuni!

Vaiśaṃpāyana said:

At these words Śakuni decided, tricked, and cried "Won!" at Yudhiṣṭhira.

Śakuni said:

Here I have won the Pāṇḍavas' bowman,
The left-handed archer, of Pāṇḍu the son!
Now gamble, O king, your beloved Bhīma,
If that's what you, Pāṇḍava, have left to throw!

* = Arjuna.

Yudhiṣṭhira said:

Who led us, who guided us to the battle,
Like the Thunderbolt-wielder the Dānavas' foe,
Looking down, great-spirited, knitting his brow,
With a lion's shoulders and lasting wrath,

Whose equal in might is nowhere to be found,
The first of club warriors, enemy-killer—
For this good prince who does not deserve it
I play you, king, for Bhīmasena!

Vaiśaṃpāyana said:

25 At these words Śakuni decided, tricked, and cried "Won!" at Yudhiṣṭhira.

Śakuni said:

You have lost great wealth, you have lost your brothers, your horses and elephants. Now tell me, Kaunteya, if you have anything left to stake!

Yudhiṣṭhira said:

I myself am left, dearly loved by all my brothers. When won, we shall slave for you to our perdition.

Vaiśaṃpāyana said:

At these words Śakuni decided, tricked, and cried "Won!" at Yudhiṣṭhira.

Śakuni said:

This is the worst you could have done, losing yourself! If there is something left to stake, it is evil to stake oneself!

Vaiśaṃpāyana said:

30 Thus spoke the man so dexterous at dicing, who had won in the gaming all those brothers arrayed there, the champions of the world, each with one throw.

Śakuni said:

Yet there is your precious queen, and one throw is yet unwon. Stake Kṛṣṇā of Pāñcāla, and win yourself back with her!

Yudhiṣṭhira said:

She is not too short or too tall, not too black or too red, and her eyes are red with love—I play you for her! Eyes like the petals of autumn lotuses, a fragrance as of autumn lotuses, a beauty that waits on autumn lotuses—the peer of the Goddess of Fortune! Yes, for her lack of cruelty, for the fullness of her body, for the straightness of her
35 character does a man desire a woman. Last she lies down who was the first to wake up, who knows what was done or left undone, down to the cowherds and goatherds. Her sweaty lotuslike face shines like a lotus. Her waist shaped like an altar, hair long, eyes the color of

copper, not too much body hair . . . such is the woman, king, such is the slender-waisted Pāñcālī, for whom I now throw, the beautiful Draupadī! Come on, Saubala!

Vaiśaṃpāyana said:

When the King Dharma had spoken this word, Bhārata, the voices
that were raised by the elders spelled of "Woe! Woe!" The hall itself
shook, king, and talk started among the kings. Bhiṣma, Droṇa, Kṛpa,
40 and others broke out in sweat. Vidura buried his face in his hands and
looked as though he had fainted; he sat, head down, brooding,
wheezing like a snake. But Dhṛtarāṣṭra, exhilarated, kept asking, "Has
he won, has he won?" for he did not keep his composure. Karṇa,
Duḥśāsana, and their cronies were mightily pleased, but of others in
the hall the tears flowed freely. But Saubala, without hesitation, with
the glow of the winner and high with passion, again addressed the
dice and cried, "We have won!"

Duryodhana said:

59.1 All right, you Steward, bring Draupadī,
The beloved wife whom the Pāṇḍavas honor,
Let her sweep the house and run on our errands—
What a joy to watch!—with the serving wenches!

Vidura said:

The incredible happens through people like you,
You don't know it, nitwit, you are tied in a noose!
You hang over a chasm and do not grasp it,
You dumb deer to anger tigers!

You are carrying poisonous snakes on your head, their pouches full of venom! Don't infuriate them, fool, lest you go to Yama! Kṛṣṇā is not a slave yet, Bhārata! I think she was staked when the king was no longer his own master.

5 Dhṛtarāṣṭra's son the prince bears fruit,
Like the bamboo, only to kill himself:
He is ripe for death, but he fails to see
That dicing leads to a dangerous feud.

Be never hurtful or speak cruelly,
Nor extort the last from a penniless man,
Nor speak the wounding, hell-earning words
That when voiced hurt another man.

Those words beyond need fly from the mouth,
And the one they hurt grieves day and night:

Those words that strike where the other hurts
No wise man will loose on another man.

For this goat, they say, dug up a knife,
When a knife was missing, by pawing the ground.
It became a means to cut its own throat:
So dig up no feud with Pāṇḍu's sons!

They don't speak either good or ill
Of the forest-dweller or householder,
But of the ascetic of mature wisdom,
The same people bark like the curs they are.

10 This dreadful crooked door tilts toward hell—
You know it not, Dhṛtarāṣṭra's son;
There are many will follow you down that road,
Now the game has been won, with Duḥśasana!

The gourds will sink and the rocks will float,
And the ships will forever be lost on the seas.
Before the fool prince, Dhṛtarāṣṭra's son,
Will lend his ear to my apt words!

For this to be sure spells the end of the Kurus,
A grisly end, the perdition of all.
The words of the sage, so apt, and his friends
Are no longer heard, and greed just grows!

Vaiśampāyana said:
60.1 "A plague on the Steward," he said and rose,
Maddened with pride, Dhṛtarāṣṭra's son,
And he looked at his usher in the hall
And to him he spoke amidst those grandees,

"Go, usher, and bring me Draupadī here!
You have nothing to fear from the Pāṇḍavas.
The Steward is timid and speaks against it,
But never did he wish that *we* should prosper!"

The usher, a bard, at his master's word
Went quickly out upon hearing the king,
And he entered, a dog in a lion's den,
Crawling up to the Queen of the Pāṇḍavas.

The usher said:
Yudhiṣṭhira, crazed by the dicing game,
Has lost you to Duryodhana, Draupadī.

Come enter the house of Dhṛtarāṣṭra,
To your chores I must lead you, Yājñasenī!

Draupadī said:

How dare you speak so, an usher, to me?
What son of a king would hazard his wife?
The king is befooled and crazed by the game—
Was there nothing left for him to stake?

The usher said:

When nothing was left for him to stake,
Ajātaśatru wagered you.
Already the king had thrown for his brothers,
And then for himself—then, Princess, for you.

Draupadī said:

Then go to the game and, son of a bard, ask in the assembly, "Bhārata, whom did you lose first, yourself or me?" When you have found out, come and take me, son of a bard!

Vaiśaṃpāyana said:

He went to the hall and asked Draupadī's question. "As the owner of whom did you lose us?" so queries Draupadī. "Whom did you lose first, yourself or me?" But Yudhiṣṭhira did not stir, as though he had lost consciousness, and made no reply to the bard, whether good or ill.

Duryodhana said:

Let Kṛṣṇā of the Pāñcālas come here and ask the question herself. All the people here shall hear what she or he has to say.

Vaiśaṃpāyana said:

As he was in Duryodhana's service, the usher, who was the son of a bard, went to the king's lodgings and, as though shuddering, said to Draupadī,

The men in the hall are summoning, Princess!
Methinks that the fall of the Kurus has come.
That fool will not protect our fortunes
If *you* have to come to the hall, O Princess.

Draupadī said:

That is how he disposes, the All-Disposer,
Both touches touch the sage and the fool:
He said, "In this world only Law is supreme":
He shall bring us peace when the Law is obeyed!

Vaiśaṃpāyana said:

But Yudhiṣṭhira, on hearing what Duryodhana wanted to do, sent an acceptable messenger to Draupadī, O bull of the Bhāratas. In her one garment, knotted below, weeping and in her courses, she went to the hall, the Pāñcāla princess, and stood before her father-in-law.

Watching the courtiers' faces, the Prince
Duryodhana said gleefully to the bard,
"Bring her here, good usher, right here on this spot,
So the Kauravas may speak up to her face!"

So the *sūta* who was in Duryodhana's service,
But afraid of the wrath of the Drupada Princess,
Shed all his pride and asked the assembled,
"Who am I to speak to a Draupadī?"

Duryodhana said:
Duḥśāsana, he is a fool, this bard's son,
He is terrified of the Wolf-Belly!
Fetch and bring yourself Yajñasena's daughter,
How can our powerless rivals prevent you?

Vaiśaṃpāyana said:
Thereupon the son of the king rose up,
On hearing his brother, eyes reddened with wrath,
And entered the dwelling of those great warriors,
And he said to Draupadī, daughter of kings,

20 "All right now, come, Pāñcālī, you're won!
Look upon Duryodhana, without shame!
You shall now love the Kurus, long-lotus-eyed one,
You've been won under Law, come along to the hall!"

In bleak spirits did she rise,
And wiped with her hand her pallid face.
In despair she ran where the women sat
Of the aged king, the bull of the Kurus.

And quickly the angry Duḥśāsana
Came rushing to her with a thunderous roar;
By the long-tressed black and flowing hair
Duḥśāsana grabbed the wife of a king.

The hair that at the concluding bath
Of the king's consecration had been sprinkled
With pure-spelled water, Dhṛtarāṣṭra's son
Now caressed with force, unmanning the Pāṇḍus.

Duḥśāsana, stroking her, led her and brought her,
That Kṛṣṇā of deep black hair, to the hall,
As though unprotected amidst her protectors,
And tossed her as wind tosses a plantain tree.

25 And as she was dragged, she bent her body
And whispered softly, "It is now my month!
This is my sole garment, man of slow wit,
You cannot take me to the hall, you churl!"

But using his strength and holding her down,
By her deep black locks, he said to Kṛṣṇā,
"To Kṛṣṇa and Jiṣṇu, to Hari and Nara,
Cry out for help! I shall take you yet!

"Sure, you be in your month, Yajñasena's daughter,
Or wear a lone cloth, or go without one!
You've been won at the game and been made a slave,
And one lechers with slaves as the fancy befalls!"

Her hair disheveled, her half skirt drooping,
Shaken about by Duhśāsana,
Ashamed and burning with indignation,
She whispered again, and Kṛṣṇā said,

"In the hall are men who have studied the books,
All follow the rites and are like unto Indras.
They are all my *gurus* or act for them:
Before their eyes I cannot stand thus!

30 "You ignoble fool of cruel feats,
Don't render me nude, do not debase me!
These sons of kings will not condone you,
Were Indra and Gods to be your helpmates!

"The king, son of Dharma, abides by the Law,
And the Law is subtle, for the wise to find out:
But even at his behest I would not
Give the least offense and abandon my virtue.

"It is *base* that amidst the Kaurava heroes
You drag me inside while I am in my month;
There is no one here to honor you for it,
Though surely they do not mind your plan.

"Damnation! Lost to the Bhāratas
Is their Law and the ways of sagacious barons,
When all these Kauravas in their hall
Watch the Kuru Law's limits overstridden!

"There is no mettle in Droṇa and Bhīṣma,
Nor to be sure in this good man;

The chiefs of the elders amongst the Kurus
Ignore this dread Unlaw of this king."

35 As she piteously spoke the slim-waisted queen
Threw a scornful glance at her furious husbands
And inflamed with the fall of her sidelong glances,
The Pāṇḍavas, wrapped with wrath in their limbs.

Not the kingdom lost, nor the riches looted,
Nor the precious jewels plundered did hurt
As hurt that sidelong glance of Kṛṣṇā,
That glance of Kṛṣṇā sent in fury.

Duḥśāsana, though, watched only Kṛṣṇā
Who was looking down on her wretched lords,
And shaking her wildly—she was close to fainting—
Cried cruelly "Slave!" and laughed aloud.

And Karṇa applauded his word to the full
And heartily laughing acknowledged it,
And Subala's son, king of Gāndhāra,
Likewise cheered on Duḥśāsana.

Apart from these two and Duryodhana,
All other men who sat in the hall,
On seeing Kṛṣṇā dragged into the hall,
Were filled with misery beyond measure.

Bhīṣma said:

40 As the Law is subtle, my dear, I fail
To resolve your riddle the proper way:
A man without property cannot stake another's—
But given that wives are the husband's chattels?

Yudhiṣṭhira may give up all earth
With her riches, before he'd give up the truth.
The Pāṇḍava said, "I have been won,"
Therefore I cannot resolve this doubt.

No man is Śakuni's peer at the dice,
And he left Yudhiṣṭhira his own choice.
The great-spirited man does not think he was cheating,
Therefore I cannot speak to the riddle.

Draupadī said:

In the meeting hall he was challenged, the king,
By cunning, ignoble, and evil tricksters

Who love to game; he had never much tried it.
Why then do you say he was left a choice?

Pure, the best of Kurus and Pāṇḍavas,
He did not wake up to the playing of tricks,
He attended the session and when he'd lost all,
Only then he agreed to hazard me.

45 They stand here, the Kurus, they stand in their hall,
Proud owners of sons and daughters-in-law:
Examine ye all this word of mine,
And resolve my riddle the proper way!

Vaiśaṃpāyana said:

So she piteously spoke and flowing with tears
Kept looking at those who were her husbands;
Meanwhile Duḥśāsana said many words
That were bitter and mean and none that were gentle.

The Wolf-Belly looked and watched how she
Was dragged, in her courses, with upper cloth drooping,
Who so little deserved it, in desperate pain;
He looked at his brother and gave voice to his rage.

Bhīma said:

61.1 There are a lot of whores in the country of gamblers, Yudhiṣṭhira,
but they never throw for them, for they have pity even for women of
that stripe. The tribute that the king of the Kāśis brought and all our
vast wealth, the gems that the other kings of the earth brought in, the
mounts and prizes, the armor and weaponry, the kingdom, yourself
and we have all been staked and lost to others. This I didn't mind
much, for you are the master of all we possess. But you went too far,
5 I think, when you staked Draupadī. She did not deserve this! After she
had won Pāṇḍavas as a girl, she is now because of you plagued by
Kauravas, mean and cruel tricksters! It is because of her that I hurl
my fury at you! I shall burn off your arms! Sahadeva! Bring the fire!

Arjuna said:

Never before have you said words like these, Bhīmasena! Surely
your respect for the Law has been destroyed by our harsh enemies!
Don't fall in with the enemy's plans, obey your highest Law: no one
may overreach his eldest brother by Law. The king was challenged by
his foes, and, remembering the baronial Law, he played at the enemy's
wish. *That* is our great glory!

Bhīmasena said:

10 If I'd thought he'd done it for his own glorification, I'd have forced
his arms together and burned them in the blazing fire, Dhanaṃjaya!

Vaiśaṃpāyana said:

Hereupon, seeing the grief of the Pāṇḍavas and the torment of
Pāñcāli*, Vikarṇa, a son of Dhṛtarāṣṭra's, spoke out: "Ye kings!
Answer the question that Yajñasena's daughter has asked! We must
decide or we shall go to hell! Bhīṣma and Dhṛtarāṣṭra are the eldest of
the Kurus; they are here but say nought, nor does the sagacious
Vidura. Droṇa Bhāradvāja is here, the teacher of us all, and so is Kṛpa,
yet even they, most eminent of brahmins, do not speak to the
15 question! All the other kings, assembled here from every horizon,
should shed all partisan feelings and speak up as they think. Consider
the question that the beautiful Draupadī has raised repeatedly, kings,
and whatever your side, make your answer!"

Thus did he speak many times to all the men who were sitting in
the hall, but none of the kings said aught, whether good or bad.
Vikarṇa spoke again and again to all those kings, and sighing,
kneading his hands, he finally said, "Make your answer, kings, or do
not. But I shall tell you, Kaurava, what I think is right in this matter.
20 Ye best of men, they recount four vices that are the curse of a king:
hunting, drinking, dicing, and fornicating. A man with those
addictions abandons the Law, and the world does not condone his
immoderate deeds. The Pāṇḍava was under the sway of his vice when
the gamblers challenged him and he staked Draupadī. The innocent
woman is held in common by all the Pāṇḍavas, and the Pāṇḍava
staked her when he already had gambled away his own freedom. It
was Saubala who mentioned Kṛṣṇā when he wanted a stake.
Considering all this I do not think she has been won."

25 When they heard this, there was a loud outcry from the men in the
hall as they praised Vikarṇa and condemned Saubala. When the noise
died down, the son of Rādhā**, fairly fainting with fury, grasped his
shining arm and said, "Are there not many mockeries of the truth
found in Vikarṇa? As the fire burns the block from which it was
drilled, so the fire he generates will lead to his perdition! All these men
here have failed to reply despite Kṛṣṇā's urging. I hold that Draupadī
has been won, and so do they hold. You are torn to pieces by your
own folly, Dhārtarāṣṭra, for, still a child, you announce in the
30 assembly what should be said by your elders. A younger brother of
Duryodhana's, you do not know the true facts of the Law, if you
stupidly maintain that Kṛṣṇā, who has been won, has not in fact been
won. How, son of Dhṛarāṣṭra, can you hold that Kṛṣṇā has not been
won when the eldest Pāṇḍava staked all he owned in the assembly
hall? Draupadī is part of all he owns, bull of the Bharatas, then how
can you hold that Kṛṣṇā, won by Law, has not been won? Draupadī

* = Draupadī.
** = Karṇa.

was mentioned by name and the Pāṇḍavas allowed her to be staked—then by what reasoning do you hold that she has not been won?

"Or if you think that it was against the Law to bring her into the hall clad in one piece of clothing, listen to what I have to say in reply to that. The Gods have laid down that a woman shall have one husband, scion of Kuru. *She* submits to many men and assuredly is a whore! Thus there is, I think, nothing strange about taking her into the hall, or to have her in one piece of clothing, or for that matter naked! She, the Pāṇḍava's wealth, and the Pāṇḍavas themselves have all been won by Saubala here according to the Law.

"Duḥśāsana, this Vikarṇa is only a child, blabbing of wisdom! Strip the clothes from the Pāṇḍavas and Draupadī!"

Hearing this, all the Pāṇḍavas shed their upper clothes and sat down in the assembly hall. Then Duḥśāsana forcibly laid hold of Draupadī's robe, O king, and in the midst of the assembly began to undress her. But when her skirt was being stripped off, lord of the people, another similar skirt appeared every time. A terrible roar went up from all the kings, a shout of approval, as they watched that greatest wonder on earth. And in the midst of the kings Bhīma, lips trembling with rage, kneading hand in hand, pronounced a curse in a mighty voice: "Take to heart this word of mine, ye barons that live on this earth, a word such as never has been spoken before nor any one shall ever speak hereafter! May I forfeit my journey to all my ancestors, if I do not carry out what I say, if I not tear open in battle the chest of this misbegotten fiend, this outcaste of the Bharatas, and drink his blood!"

When they heard this curse, which exhilarated all the world, they offered him much homage and reviled Dhṛtarāṣṭra's son. A pile of clothes was heaped up in the middle of the hall, when Duḥśāsana, tired and ashamed, at last desisted and sat down. The gods among men in the hall raised the hair-raising cry of "Fie!" as they watched the sons of Kuntī. The people shouted, "The Kauravyas refuse to answer the question," and condemned Dhṛtarāṣṭra.

Thereupon, raising his arms and stopping the crowd in the hall, Vidura, who knew all the Laws, made his speech.

Vidura said:

Draupadī, having raised the question, now weeps piteously as though she has none left to protect her. If you do not resolve it, men in this hall, the Law will be offended. The man who comes to the hall with a grievance is like a blazing fire: the men in the hall must appease him with true Law. If a man comes with a grievance and raises a question of Law with the men in the hall, they must resolve the question and shed all partiality. Vikarṇa has answered the question according to his lights, kings of men; you too must speak to the

question according to yours. If a person sits in the hall and fails to
answer a question, although he sees the Law, he incurs half the guilt
that accrues if the answer is false. And he who has gone to the hall,
knows the Law, yet resolves it falsely, certainly incurs the full guilt of
the falsehood. On this they quote this ancient story, the exchange
between Prahlāda and the Hermit, Angiras' son.

Prahlāda, you know, was the king of the Daityas; his son was
60 Virocana, who ran into Sudhanvan Āngirasa over a girl. Their desire
for the girl made each aver that he was the better man, and, so we
have heard, they made a wager and staked their lives. They argued
the question and asked Prahlāda, "Which of us is the better man?
Resolve the question and do not speak falsely!" Frightened by the
quarrel, he looked at Sudhanvan, and Sudhanvan furiously said to
him, burning as Brahmā's staff, "If you speak falsely, Prahlāda, or if
you fail to speak, the Thunderbolt-wielder shall blow your head to a
hundred pieces with his bolt!" At Sudhanvan's words the Daitya
trembled like an *aśvattha* leaf, and he went to Kaśyapa to question that
most august sage.

65 *Prahlāda said:*

You are wise in the Law, both in that of the Gods and that of the
Asuras. Now listen, great sage, to a question of brahmin Law. Tell me
at my bidding what worlds hereafter may that man expect who fails
to decide a question of Law or gives the wrong answer?

Kaśyapa said:

He who knows the answer but either from love, anger, or fear fails
to resolve the question lets loose on himself a thousand of Varuṇa's
nooses; and for every noose to be loosened takes a year. Therefore say
the truth straightaway, if you know the truth! Where a Law comes to
the hall pierced by Unlaw and they do not pull out the thorn, there it
70 will pierce the men in the hall. The leader takes half, the culprit has a
quarter, and the last quarter goes to those in the hall who do not
condemn the culprit. The leader is guiltless, the men in the hall are
freed, and the blame goes to the culprit, if the culprit is condemned.
But they who explain the Law falsely, Prahlāda, to the one who brings
the question, kill their own offerings and oblations for seven
generations upward and downward. The grievance of the man whose
property has been stolen, of the man whose son has been killed, of a
man against a debtor, of one who has been mulcted by a king, of a
wife deserted by her husband, of a man dropped from a caravan, of a
75 bigamist's wife or a man beaten before witnesses, these grievances, so
the lords the Thirty Gods say, are equal. And all these grievances a man
incurs who judges falsely. As a witness is held to be the one who sees
or hears a misdeed in his presence, a witness who speaks the truth is
not hurt in his Law or his Profit.

Vidura said:

Having heard Kaśyapa's word, Prahlāda said to his son, "Sudhanvan is better than you, as Angiras is better than I. Sudhanvan's mother is better than yours, Virocana. Sudhanvan is now the master of your life."

Sudhanvan said:

You relinquish your love for your son to stand firm on the Law—set free your son, may he live for a hundred years!

Vidura said:

80 Thus you have heard the ultimate Law, ye all who are sitting in the
hall. Now ponder what should be done in response to Kṛṣṇā's
question!

Vaiśaṃpāyana said:

Even upon hearing Vidura's words the kings failed to speak. But Karṇa said to Duḥśāsana, "Take this slave wench Kṛṣṇā to the house!" Duḥśāsana, in the hall, dragged away the trembling and ashamed woman who miserably complained to the Pāṇḍavas.

Draupadī said:

62.1 I have a duty that is more pressing, which I could not perform
before, confused as I was by this strong man who dragged me about
forcibly. I must greet my betters in the assembly of the Kurus! Let it
not be my fault, if I did not do this before!

Vaiśaṃpāyana said:

He dragged her onward, and, wretched with misery, she fell to the ground. Unused to such treatment she lamented in the assembly——

Draupadī said:

I on whom the assembled kings set eye in the arena at my
Bridegroom Choice, but never before or after, I am now brought into
5 the hall! I whom neither wind nor sun have seen before in my house,
I am now seen in the middle of the hall in the assembly of the Kurus.
I whom the Pāṇḍavas did not suffer to be touched by the wind in my
house before, they now allow to be touched by this miscreant. The
Kurus allow—and methinks that Time is out of joint—their innocent
daughter and daughter-in-law to be molested! What greater
humiliation than that I, a woman of virtue and beauty, now must
invade the men's hall? What is left of the Law of the kings? From of
old, we have heard, they do *not* bring law-minded women into their
10 hall. This ancient eternal Law is lost among the Kauravas. How can I,
wife of the Pāṇḍus, sister of Dhṛṣṭadyumna Pārṣata, and friend of
Vāsudeva, enter the hall of the kings? Is the wife of the King Dharma
whose birth matches his a slave or free? Speak, Kauravas. I shall
abide by your answer. For this foul man, disgrace of the Kauravas, is
molesting me, and I cannot bear it any longer, Kauravas! Whatever

the kings think, whether I have been won or not, I want it answered, and I shall abide by the answer, Kauravas.

Bhīṣma said:

I have said, good woman, that the course of the Law is sovereign.
15 Great-spirited brahmins on earth fail to encompass it. What a
powerful man views as Law in the world, that do others call the Law
at a time when Law is in question. I cannot answer the question
decisively, because the matter is subtle and mysterious as well as
grave. Surely the end of this lineage is in sight, for all the Kurus have
become so enslaved by greed and folly. Those born in high lineages, do
not, good woman, stray from the path of the Law, however beset by
disaster, just as you who stand here as our bride. Such is the conduct
that you yourself practice, princess of the Pāñcālas, for though you
20 have come to grief, you still look to the Law. Droṇa and the other
elders who are wise in the Law sit bent over as though spiritless with
empty bodies. But Yudhiṣṭhira, I think, is the authority on this
question: let he himself speak out and say whether you have been
won or not.

Vaiśaṃpāyana said:

Upon witnessing all those many events
And Draupadī screeching, a winged osprey,
The kings said nought, neither good nor bad,
For they feared for Dhṛtarāṣṭra's son.

And seeing the sons and grandsons of kings
Keep silent, the son of Dhṛtarāṣṭra
Began to smile and said this word
To the daughter of the Pāñcāla king:

"Let the question now rest with the mettlesome Bhīma,
With Arjuna and with Sahadeva,
And your husband Nakula, Draupadī:
Let them speak the word that you have begotten.

25 "In the midst of these nobles they must declare
For thy sake that Yudhiṣṭhira's not thy master,
And thus they must make King Dharma a liar,
Pāñcālī, so you escape servitude!

"King Dharma, great-spirited, firm in the Law,
The peer of Indra, himself must declare
Whether he owns you or does not own you;
At his word you must choose, the one or the other.

"For all the Kauravas in the assembly
Are caught inside your misery:

They cannot resolve it, the noble-hearted,
And they look to your unfortunate masters."

The men in the hall all loudly approved
The word that the king of the Kurus had spoken;
There were those who cheeringly waved their clothes,
But also cries of "Woe!" were heard.
And all the kings in cheerful spirits
Applauded the Law of the first of the Kurus.

All the kings looked at Yudhiṣṭhira, their faces turned sideways: "What will the law-wise prince say? What will the Terrifier say, the Pāṇḍava undefeated in battle? And Bhīmasena and the twins?" thus they wondered, greatly curious. When the noise had died down, Bhīmasena spoke, grasping his broad, sandal-scented arm.

"Had Yudhiṣṭhira the King Dharma not been our own *guru* and lord of our family we should never have suffered this! He owns our merit and our austerities, he commands our lives. If he holds himself defeated, so are we defeated. No mortal who walks the earth would have escaped me with his life, for touching the hair of Pāñcālī! Look at my arms, long and round like iron-studded bludgeons: once caught in them not the God of the Hundred Sacrifices could escape from them! But now, like this, tied by the noose of the Law, constrained by his gravity and held back by Arjuna, I wreak no havoc! But if the King Dharma unleashes me, I shall crush the evil band of Dhṛtarāṣṭra with the swordlike flats of my hands, as a lion flattens small game!" And at once Bhīṣma and Droṇa and Vidura spoke: "Bear with it! With you anything is possible!"

Karṇa said:

63.1 There are three who own no property,
A student, a slave, a dependent woman:
The wife of a slave, you are *his* now, my dear;
A masterless slave wench, you are now slave wealth!

Come in and serve us with your attentions:
That is the chore you have left in this house.
Dhṛtarāṣṭra's men, and not the Pārthas,
Are now your masters, child of a king!

Now quickly choose you another husband
Who will not gamble your freedom away:
For license with masters is never censured:
That is the slave's rule, remember it!

Won have been Nakula, Bhīmasena,
Yudhiṣṭhira, Sahadeva, Arjuna!

Become a slave, come inside, Yājñasenī!
The ones who are won are no longer your men.

What use are now to the Pārtha himself,
His gallantry and his manliness?
In the midst of the hall he has gambled away
The daughter of Drupada, king of Pāñcāla!

Vaiśaṃpāyana said:

Hearing this, Bhīma bore it no longer;
A man tormented, he panted hard;
But avowed to the king and trapped by the Law,
Burning him down with wrath-shot eye,

Bhīma said:

I do not anger at a *sūta's* son,
For the Law of serfdom is surely upon us:
But could our enemies now have held me,
If you had not thrown for her, my liege?

Vaiśaṃpāyana said:

When he had heard the words of Rādheya*, Prince Duryodhana said to Yudhiṣṭhira, who was sitting silent and mindless, "Bhīma and Arjuna and the twins follow your orders, king. Answer the question, whether you think she has been won!" This he said to the Kaunteya, and crazed by his ascendancy, he took his cloth and looked invitingly at Pāñcālī. Then, smiling up at Rādheya, and taunting Bhīma, he exposed to Draupadī who was watching him his left thigh, soft like a banana tree and auspiciously marked—an elephant trunk and a thunderbolt in one. The Wolf-Belly saw it and, widening his bloodshot eyes, spoke up in the midst of the kings, willing the assembly to listen: "May the Wolf-Belly never share the world of his fathers, if I fail to break that thigh with my club in a great battle!" And as he raged, flames of fire burst forth from all the orifices of his body, as from the hollows of a tree that is on fire.

Vidura said:

Kings! Watch for the ultimate danger from Bhīma!
Kings! Watch it as if it were Varuṇa's noose!
For surely the hostile fate has emerged
That the Gods set of old for the Bhāratas.

This has been an overplay, Dhārtarāṣṭras,
Who fight over a woman in this hall!
Your security now seems much imperiled,
For evil counsels the Kurus now spell.

* = Karṇa.

Kurus, quickly decide on the Law of the case.
If it's wrongly perceived the assembly will suffer.
If this gamester here had staked her before,
He'd have been undefeated and still been her master.

Like a stake that is won in a dream is the stake,
If the stake is put up by one who does not own it!
You have listened to Gāndhārī's son*,
Now Kurus, don't run from the Law of the case!

Duryodhana said:
20 I stay with the word of Bhīmasena
And Arjuna's word and the word of the twins:
If they say Yudhiṣṭhira wasn't their master,
Then Yājñasenī, you won't be a slave!

Arjuna said:
The king was our master when first he played us,
Great-spirited Dharma, the son of Kuntī:
But whose master is he who has lost himself?
That you should decide, ye Kurus assembled!

Vaiśaṃpāyana said:
And there in the house of the King Dhṛtarāṣṭra
At the *agnihotra* a jackal barked,
The donkeys, they brayed in response, O king,
And so on all sides the grisly birds.

And Vidura, sage of all portents, listened
To the horrible sound, so did Saubala;
And Bhīṣma and Droṇa and wise Gautama
Made loud declarations of "Peace!" and "Peace!"

Thereupon Gāndhārī and Vidura the wise,
Who both had observed that ghastly omen,
At once unhappily told the king;
Whereupon the king gave voice to his word:

25 "You're lost, Duryodhana, shallow-brain,
Who in this hall of the bulls of the Kurus
Berated a woman most uncouthly,
And her a Draupadī, married by Law!"

Having spoken the wise Dhṛtarāṣṭra withdrew,
For he wished for the weal of his allies-in-law;
Kṛṣṇā Pāñcālī he pacified,
And thinking with insight, informed of the facts,

* = Duryodhana.

Dhṛtarāṣṭra said:

Choose a boon from me, Pāñcālī, whatever you wish; for you are to me the most distinguished of my daughters-in-law, bent as you are on the Law!

Draupadī said:

If you give me a boon, bull of the Bharatas, I choose this: the
illustrious Yudhiṣṭhira, observer of every Law, shall be no slave! Do
not let these little boys, who do not know my determined son, say of
Prativindhya* when he happens to come in, "Here comes the son of a
30 slave!" He has been a *king's* son, as no man has been anywhere.
Spoiled as he is, he shall die, Bhārata, when he finds out that he has
been a slave's son!

Dhṛtarāṣṭra said:

I give you a second boon, good woman, ask me! My heart has convinced me that you do not deserve only a single boon.

Draupadī said:

With their chariots and bows I choose Bhīmasena and Dhanaṃjaya, Nakula and Sahadeva, as my second boon!

Dhṛtarāṣṭra said:

Choose a third boon from us; two boons do not honor you enough. For of all of my daughters-in-law you are the best, for you walk in the Law.

Draupadī said:

Greed kills Law, Sir, I cannot make another wish. I am not worthy
35 to take a third boon from you, best of kings. As they say, the
commoner has one boon, the baron and his lady two, but three are
the king's, great king, and a hundred the brahmin's. They were laid
low, my husbands, but they have been saved: and they will find the
good things, king, with their own good acts!

Karṇa said:

64.1 Of all the women of mankind, famous for their beauty, of whom we
have heard, no one have we heard accomplished such a deed! While
the Pārthas and the Dhārtarāṣṭras are raging beyond measure, Kṛṣṇā
Draupadī has become the salvation of the Pāṇḍavas! When they were
sinking, boatless and drowning, in the plumbless ocean, the Pāñcālī
became the Pāṇḍavas' boat, to set them ashore!

Vaiśaṃpāyana said:

Hearing this amidst the Kurus, that a woman had become the
5 refuge of the sons of Pāṇḍu, resentful Bhīmasena said glumly, "Devala
has declared that there are three stars in man—offspring, deeds, and
knowledge; for creatures live on through them. When the body has
become impure, void of life, emptied, and cast off by the kinsmen, it is

* = Draupadī's son by Yudhiṣṭhira.

these three that survive of a man. Our light has been darkened, for our wife has been defiled, Dhanaṃjaya: how can offspring be born from one defiled?"

Arjuna said:

Bhāratas never babble of the insults, spoken or unspoken, from a lower man. The best people always remember only the good acts, not the hostilities they have been shown, acknowledging them because they have confidence in themselves.

Bhīma said:

10 I shall here and now kill all the enemies that have assembled! Or you go outside, Bhārata, lord among the kings, and cut them to their roots! What is the use for us to argue here, why suffer, Bhārata? I am going to kill them here and now, and you sway this world!

Vaiśaṃpāyana said:

When Bhīmasena had spoken, surrounded by his younger brothers like a lion amidst deer, he kept glancing at his club. While the Pārtha of unsullied deeds sought to appease and cool him off, the powerful strong-armed Bhīma began to sweat with his inner heat. From the ears and the other orifices of the raging man fire issued forth, smoking and sparking. His face became fierce to behold, with its folds of knitted brows, as the face of Yama himself when the end of the Eon has come. Yudhiṣṭhira restrained the strong-armed Bhīma with his arm, O Bhārata. "Don't!" he said. "Stay quiet!" And when he had restrained the strong-armed man, whose eyes were bloodshot with rage, Yudhiṣṭhira went up to his father Dhṛtarāṣṭra and folded his hands.

Yudhiṣṭhira said:

65.1 King, what should we do? Command us, you are our master. For we always wish to obey your behest, Bhārata.

Dhṛtarāṣṭra said:

Ajātaśatru, good luck to you! Go ye in peace and comfort. I give you my leave: rule your own kingdom with your own treasures. But keep in mind this admonition that I, an old man, utter; I have thought it through with my mind, as it is proper and beneficent above all.

Yudhiṣṭhira, my wise son, you know the subtle course of the Laws,
5 you are courteous and you attend to your elders. Where there is wisdom there is serenity: become serene, Bhārata. An ax does not sink in if it is not on wood, but on wood it cuts. The best among men do not remember hostilities; they see the virtues, not the faults, and they do not stoop to enmity. It is the lowliest that hurl insults in a quarrel, Yudhiṣṭhira; the middling ones return the insults, but the best and the steady ones never babble about hostile insults, spoken or unspoken. The good only remember the good that was done, not the hostile deeds, acknowledging it because they have confidence in themselves.

10 You have behaved nobly in this meeting of good people, therefore, my son, do not brood in your heart on Duryodhana's offensiveness. Look at your mother Gāndhārī, and at me, your old blind father before you, who longs for your virtues. It was from affection that I allowed this dicing game, as I wished to see my friends and find out the strengths and weaknesses of my sons. King, the Kurus whose ruler you are and whose councillor is the sagacious Vidura, expert in all the fields of knowledge, are they to be pitied? In you there is Law, in Arjuna prowess, in Bhīmasena might, in the twins, foremost among men, there is faith and obedience to their elders.

15 Ajātaśatru, good luck to you! Return to the Khāṇḍava Tract. May you have brotherly bonds with your brethren, and may your mind abide by the Law!

Vaiśaṃpāyana said:

At his words Yudhiṣṭhira the King Dharma, first of the Bharatas, having fulfilled the full covenant of the nobles, departed with his brothers. Riding their cloudlike chariots they started with Kṛṣṇā, and in cheerful spirits, for their good city Indraprastha.

2(28) The Sequel to the Dicing

2.66–72 (74–81; 2453 2709)

66 (74–75; 2453). At the Pāṇḍavas' dismissal, Duryodhana, Karṇa, and Śakuni plot. Duryodhana urges on Dhṛtarāṣṭra a continuation of the dicing (1–20). In spite of protests from the Kaurava elders and Gāndhārī, Dhṛtarāṣṭra agrees (25–35).

67 (76; 2491). Yudhiṣṭhira is recalled, and he returns. Śakuni proposes as stake twelve years in the forest and one in the open incognito (10–20). Yudhiṣṭhira loses (20).

68 (77; 2514). The Pāṇḍavas don deerskins (1). Duḥśāsana taunts them (1–10). Bhīma replies angrily (15–20). Duryodhana imitates Bhīma's gait (20), and the latter predicts he will kill Duryodhana, Arjuna will kill Karṇa, and Sahadeva Śakuni; both repeat that statement (20–40). Nakula too declares his warlike determination (40–45).

69 (78; 2560). Yudhiṣṭhira bids the Kauravas farewell (1). Vidura insists that Kuntī stay at his house, and pronounces blessings on the Pāṇḍavas (5–20).

70 (79; 2584). Kṛṣṇā takes her leave from Kuntī, who

laments her fate (1–10). Kuntī takes leave from her sons with much lamenting (10–20). The Pāṇḍavas depart (20).

71 (80; 2621). Vidura describes to Dhṛtarāṣṭra the manner of their going, and explains it (1–20). Menacing portents occur (25). Nārada appears and predicts the downfall of the Kauravas (25–30). The princes seek refuge with Droṇa, who grants it and predicts his own death (30–40). He urges Duryodhana to placate the Pāṇḍavas, and Dhṛtarāṣṭra supports him (45).

72 (81; 2672). Saṃjaya predicts to Dhṛtarāṣṭra that destruction is inevitable (1–5). Dhṛtarāṣṭra blames those who brought Draupadī into the hall and describes the portents (5–25) and his gift of boons to Draupadī (25). He avers he never wanted war with the Pāṇḍavas (30–35).

Janamejaya said:

66.1 When they found out that the Pāṇḍavas had been given leave to go
with their treasures of gems and riches, what was the mood of the
Dhārtarāṣṭras?

Vaiśaṃpāyana said:

When he found out that the wise Dhṛtarāṣṭra had given the
Pāṇḍavas leave to go, O king, Duḥśāsana immediately went to his
brother. On meeting Duryodhana and his councillors, O bull of the
Bharatas, he said in a pained voice, best of the Bharatas, "That old
man has made us lose everything we had collected with such great
trouble! He has made over the goods to the enemy! Take notice, great
warriors!"

5 Thereupon Duryodhana, Karṇa, and Śakuni Saubala in their pride
plotted together against the Pāṇḍavas; and they hastily went to the
wise king Dhṛtarāṣṭra Vaicitravīrya and spoke to him placatingly.

Duryodhana said:

Have you not heard, king, what the learned priest of the Gods,
Bṛhaspati, said when he propounded policy to Śakra? "Enemy-killer,
enemies must be cut down by any means before they, with war or
force, can do you evil!" We should pay homage to all the kings with
gifts obtained from the Pāṇḍavas' treasure; if we then attack them,
10 how can we fail? But if one puts furious and venomous snakes that
are ready to bite on his back and around his neck, how will he get rid
of them? Father, the Pāṇḍavas have grasped their swords, they have
mounted their chariots, and they are enraged. In their fury they will
annihilate us like poisonous snakes! Arjuna is going fully girt;

uncovering his two great quivers, he keeps picking up his Gāṇḍīva and looks about him, panting heavily. The Wolf-Belly swiftly raises his heavy club, we hear, and is fast riding out on the chariot he has teamed. Nakula has taken his sword and his shield with the eight moons, and Sahadeva and the king have made their attitude clear with gestures. Mounted on their chariots that are equipped with all weapon gear, and whipping the chariot teams, they are rushing out to raise their army. We have offended them, and they will never forgive us: who among them could forgive the molestation of Draupadī?

We must dice again with the Pāṇḍavas, bless you, to send them to the forest: so we shall be able to bring them in our power, bull of the Bharatas. They or we, whoever it be that is defeated at the dicing, must go into the forest clad in deerskins for twelve years. The thirteenth year they should live disguised among people, and if they are found out, again go into the forest for another twelve years. We or they shall live there: so let the game go on. Let the dice roll again, and let the Pāṇḍavas play the game. This, king, bull of the Bharatas, is our most pressing task—and Śakuni here knows the dice fully with all the lore of the game! We shall be firmly rooted in the kingdom as we embrace our allies and keep contented a vast, mettlesome, and invincible army. If they survive the vow after thirteen years, we shall vanquish them, king. Pray permit it, enemy-burner!

Dhṛtarāṣṭra said:

Bring them back at once, even if surely they are far on their way. The Pāṇḍavas must come back and play the game again!

Vaiśaṃpāyana said:

Then Droṇa, Somadatta, and the warrior Bāhlīka, Vidura and Droṇa's son, and the mighty son of the commoner's wench, and Śaṃtanu's son*, Bhūriśravas, and the warlike Vikarṇa, all of them said: "Don't dice!" and "Let there be peace!" But even though all the kinsmen who foresaw the outcome were unwilling, Dhṛtarāṣṭra made the challenge to the Pāṇḍavas, for he loved his son.

Thereupon Gāndhārī, tormented by grief because of her love for her son, yet yoked to the Law, O great king, spoke to Dhṛtarāṣṭra, the king of the people: "When Duryodhana was born, the wise Steward said, 'It is better to send this defiler of his race to the next world!' No sooner was he born than he howled like a jackal, Bhārata! Take notice, Kurus! He will be the end of this house! Do not prefer the opinion of children who are untaught, lord! Do not become the cause of the ghastly perdition of your line! Who would breach a dam that is closed, who would blow into a dying fire? Who, Bhārata, would anger the Pārthas, now that they are keeping the peace?

* = Bhīṣma.

"Ājamīḍha*, you surely remember, yet I shall remind you. Learning does not teach a fool, whether for good or ill. Nor will a simple-minded man in any way achieve maturity, king. You yourself should lead your sons lest, broken asunder, they abandon you.

35 By serenity, Law, and another's wisdom
Informed, thy wisdom be not contrary;
A cruelly built-up fortune vanishes,
But gently grown it descends with the line."

Whereupon the great king replied to Gāndhārī, who had seen the Law: "Surely, if our line must end, I shall not be able to avert it. Let it be as they wish, the Pāṇḍavas must return. Let my people resume the game with the Pāṇḍavas."

Vaiśaṃpāyana said:
67.1 At the behest of the wise king Dhṛtarāṣṭra, an usher spoke to Yudhiṣṭhira Pārtha, who had been far along on his way: "The hall has been spread with the carpet, king, and the dice have been strewn out, Yudhiṣṭhira! The father says to you, Bhārata, 'Come, Pāṇḍava, and play!' "

Yudhiṣṭhira said:
It is at the disposing of the Placer that creatures find good or ill. There is no averting of either, if we must play again. Although I may know that the challenge to the dicing at the old man's behest will bring ruin, I cannot disobey his word.

Vaiśaṃpāyana said:
5 Speaking thus, the Pāṇḍava turned back with his brothers, and knowing the wizardry of Śakuni, the Pārtha yet had to return to the game. Once more the great warriors entered that hall, and the bulls of the Bharatas pained the hearts of their friends. They sat down at their ease to resume the dicing, crushed down by fate, for the destruction of the entire world.

Śakuni said:
The old man released your wealth and I praise him for it. But there is one more throw, a great prize, listen to me, bull of the Bharatas! If
we are defeated by you at the dicing, we shall go into the great forest
10 for twelve years, clad in skins of the *ruru* deer, and live in disguise among people for a thirteenth year; but if found out, return to the forest for another twelve years. Or, if you are defeated by us, you must live in the forest for twelve years, together with Kṛṣṇā, clothed in deerskins. When the thirteenth year is full, either the ones or the others must have their kingdom back, as is proper. With this resolve,

* = Dhṛtarāṣṭra.

Yudhiṣṭhira, roll out the dice and play another game with us, Bhārata!

The men in the hall said:

Aho! Alas that his kinsmen cannot make him understand the great danger! Any mind can grasp it, but the bulls of the Bharatas themselves do not know it!

Vaiśaṃpāyana said:

15 The Pārtha, king of his people, heard the many speeches of the
people, but, compelled by his shame and his love for the Law, again
had to go to the game. Though he understood, wise as he was, he
returned to the game worrying, "Will it not spell the Kurus'
destruction?"

Yudhiṣṭhira said:

How indeed could a king like me, who guards his own Law, fail to return when summoned? I shall play with you, Śakuni!

Śakuni said:

Cattle, horses, milch cows, countless sheep and goats, elephants,
treasury, gold, male and female slaves, let them all be. This is now our
sole throw, Pāṇḍavas, for a stake of exile in the forest when you or we
20 lose; and with this resolve let us play, bull of the Bharatas! With one
roll of the dice, for a life in the forest, Bhāratas!

Vaiśaṃpāyana said:

The Pārtha accepted him, and Saubala grasped the dice. And Śakuni cried "Won!" at Yudhiṣṭhira.

Vaiśaṃpāyana said:

68.1 Defeated, the Pārthas set their minds on sojourning in the
wilderness, and one after the other they put on clothes made out of
deerskins. And seeing how the enemy-tamers, bereft of their kingdom,
donned the deerskins and were ready to depart for the forest,
Duḥśāsana cried, "Now the Wheel has begun of the great-spirited
king, the son of Dhṛtarāṣṭra! The sons of Pāṇḍu have been overcome
and they have come to the direct travails! Today the Gods have come
here by their smooth aerial pathways, for we are their elders in
5 virtues, their elders and more numerous than they! The Pārthas have
been thrown into hell, for a long time, an endless time, fallen from
happiness, bereft of their kingdom, for years without end. They, the
Pāṇḍavas who, power-mad, have been laughing at the Dhārtarāṣṭras,
now must go into the forest, defeated and robbed of their wealth!

"They must doff now their colorful coats of mail,
Their celestial garments and sparkling robes,
And they all must don now the *ruru* deerskins,
For they have agreed to Saubala's throw.

"Their spirits kept fattening on the thought
That there were no men like them in the worlds,
But the Pāṇḍavas now shall know themselves
In adversity, fruitless like barren seeds.

"Your sojourn in the forest, Kaurava,
Shall not be like that of high-minded hermits—
These are deerskins, lo! of the unconsecrated
As they are of the powerful Pāṇḍavas!

"The sagacious Somaka Yajñasena,
Gave Pāñcālī, his child, to the Pāṇḍavas:
That was ill done, for the Pārthas are eunuchs
And no longer men to Yājñasenī!

"Having seen the fine-clad reduced to deerskins,
And penniless, homeless, in the woods,
What joy shall you find, you Yājñasenī?
Now choose a husband who pleasures you!

"For all the Kurus are here assembled,
Forbearing and masterful and quite rich,
Choose one of them to be your husband,
This turn of the tide should not distress you.

"Fruitless like barren sesame seeds, like deer of which only the skin is left, so are the Pāṇḍavas now all, like barren barley!

"Why wait on the Pāṇḍavas? They have fallen!
It is useless to wait for barren seeds!"
And thus Dhṛtarāṣṭra's cruel son
Made the Pārthas hear his biting words.

And hearing them the intransigent Bhīma,
Reviling him loud and subduing his wrath,
Approached him with vehemence and spoke up,
A Himālayan lion to a jackal.

Bhīmasena said:
Insolent churl! You speak without weight, as is the wont of the evil! For you boast amidst kings by the grace of the expertness of Gāndhāra!* Just as you sorely hurt our weak spots with the arrows of your words, just so I shall make you remember them when I hurt yours in battle. And whoever, enslaved by desire and greed, will follow you as your guardians, I shall send them to Yama's world with their followers!

* = Śakuni.

Vaiśaṃpāyana said:

As Bhīma, so speaking, and clad in his deerskin,
Subdued by his grief, still kept to his Law,
The other, shameless, amidst the Kurus,
Pranced about him and challenged him, "Cow! You, cow!"

Bhīmasena said:

20 Abuse, rough and cruel, is possible with you, Duḥśāsana: for who else would dare to boast when he had won wealth with trickery? The Wolf-Belly son of Pṛthā shall not go to the happy worlds, if he does not rip open your chest and drink your blood in war! Only after I have killed the Dhārtarāṣṭras in battle before the eyes of all the bowmen shall I soon go to my peace, this I swear to you as the truth!

Vaiśaṃpāyana said:

As the Pāṇḍavas left the assembly hall,
Duryodhana stupidly imitated,
He a king, in a playful and frolicsome spirit,
Bhīma's lion-strides with his own gait.

"This won't win you the game," the Wolf-Belly said,
Half turning his body to Duryodhana.
"I'll remind you and make my reply to you, fool,
Soon enough, when you and your men lie dead!"

25 Having witnessed that insult to himself,
He, prideful and strong, yet restrained his wrath,
Obeying the king, in the Kauravas' meeting;
This merely said Bhīma as he strode out,

"I shall kill Duryodhana, Arjuna shall kill Karṇa, and Sahadeva shall kill Śakuni, crook with the dice. And this grave word I shall once more solemnly utter in the middle of the hall—the Gods shall make it true when there will be war between us: I shall kill this Suyodhana with my club in the fight, and I shall push his head into earth with my foot; and of this hero with words, this harsh and evil Duḥśāsana, I shall drink the blood like a lion!"

Arjuna said:

The strict Bhīma's resolution is not known merely by words. Thirteen years from now they shall see what is to be! Of Duryodhana, Karṇa, the evil Śakuni, and, fourth, of Duḥśāsana, the earth shall drink the blood. And at your command, Bhīmasena, I shall kill in battle this rabble-rousing praiser of the wicked, this Karṇa! Thus does Arjuna promise, as a favor to Bhīma: I shall kill with my feathered shafts both Karṇa and his men in war. And whatever other kings will fight me in their folly, I shall dispatch them all to Yama's domain with

35 my sharp arrows. Let the Himālayas move from their site, let the sun
dim its light, let the moon's coolness depart, if my truth should waver!
If thirteen years from now Duryodhana does not with all due honor
restore to us the kingdom, this shall come true!

Vaiśaṃpāyana said:

When the Pārtha had spoken, the illustrious son of Mādrī grasped
his own strong arm, and majestic Sahadeva spoke in his longing to
encompass Saubala's death, his eyes bloodshot with rage, hissing like
a snake: "What you thought were dice, fool, disgrace of the
Gāndhāras, are not dice but honed arrows that you have chosen for
40 war! I shall accomplish my task as Bhīma has declared it to be
concerning you and your kin, and by all means do yours! I shall kill
you in battle, overwhelming you and your kinsmen with alacrity!
That is, if you will stand up and fight by the Law of the baronage,
Saubala!"

After hearing Sahadeva's words, Nakula, too, O lord of your people,
he the most handsome looking of men, now spoke his: "This brood of
Dhṛtarāṣṭra, who have flung harsh insults at Yajñasena's daughter in
this game, in order to stay in Duryodhana's favor, this brood of
Dhārtarāṣṭras, moribund crooks who are beckoned by Time, I shall
45 in their plenty show the country of Yama! At the King Dharma's
command and walking in the footsteps of Draupadī, I shall soon empty
the earth of Dhārtarāṣṭras!"

Thus these tigerlike men all swore their oaths, with arms extended,
their many promises: then they went to Dhṛtarāṣṭra.

Yudhiṣṭhira said:

69.1 Farewell, I say! To the Bhāratas and the old grandfather, the king,
and to Somadatta and the great King Bāhlīka, farewell! To Droṇa,
Kṛpa, and the other princes, to Aśvatthāman, Vidura, and Dhṛtarāṣṭra
and all of Dhṛtarāṣṭra's sons, to Yuyutsu and Saṃjaya and all the
others who sit in this hall, I bid farewell before I go. I shall no doubt
see you when I come back!

Vaiśaṃpāyana said:

From shame those good men made no reply to Yudhiṣṭhira, as in
their thoughts they wished the wise prince well.

Vidura said:

5 The Lady Pṛthā, daughter of a king, must not go into the
wilderness: she is delicate and old, and always used to comforts. The
virtuous lady shall remain and live honorably in my house. Remember
this, Pārthas, and live in health in every way!

Yudhiṣṭhira, know this from me, bull of the Bharatas. No one who
has been defeated against the Law should suffer from his defeat. You

know the Laws: Dhanaṃjaya is wise in war, Bhīmasena is a killer of
foes, Nakula a collector of wealth, Sahadeva a subduer, while
Dhaumya is the most learned of those who know the Brahman. And
10 Draupadī walks in the Law and is wise both in Law and Profit. You
all love one another, and always speak kindly of the other. Being
contented you cannot be split by enemies. Then who does not envy
you in this world?

This, Bhārata, is your serenity of mind, good beyond anything: no
enemy, be he the peer of Śakra, can assail it, Acyuta. Long ago, when
you lived in the Himālayas, Sāvarṇin of Mount Meru instructed you.
So did, in the town of Vāraṇāvata, Kṛṣṇa Dvaipāyana, so Rāma on
Bhṛgu's Peak, and Śambhu by the river Dṛṣadvatī. Near Añjana you
have also listened to the great seer Asita, and your priest Dhaumya
has steadily seen Nārada lest you lose in the world-to-come this resolve
that the seers honor!

15 Pāṇḍava, with this resolve you surpass Purūravas Aila; with your
ability the other kings, with your obedience to the Law the seers. Set
your mind on the victory that is Indra's, on the restraint of your wrath
that is Yama's, on the liberality that is Kubera's, on the self-constraint
that is Varuṇa's.

In the gift of yourself you are like the moon. Get your sustenance
from water, forbearance from earth, all heat from the orb of the sun.
Know that your strength comes from the wind and your own origin
springs from the elements.

Let there be health for you, be blessed! I shall see you return: may
you at all times proceed, Yudhiṣṭhira, as is proper—in emergency
20 Laws, in dangers to Profit, in all your tasks, I bid you farewell,
Kaunteya: find, Bhārata, what is good for you. We shall see you
return, contented and blessed!

Vaiśaṃpāyana said:

At his address, the Pāṇḍava whose strength was his truth said, "So
shall it be!" And after bowing to Bhīṣma and Droṇa, Yudhiṣṭhira went
forth.

Vaiśaṃpāyana said:

70.1 When he was ready to start, Kṛṣṇā went up to the glorious Pṛthā,
and, bitterly grieving, she took her leave from her and from the other
women who were there. Having made her farewells and embraces as
each deserved, she made ready to go, and a loud lament arose in the
women's quarters of the Pāṇḍavas. Kuntī, sorely aggrieved, looked
upon Draupadī who was leaving; and she spoke with difficulty in a
voice that was blurred by pain: "My calf, do not worry in this grave
trouble that you have found. You know of the Laws of women and

5 you have character and manners. I have no need to preach to you, as
far as your husbands are concerned, sweet-smiling woman: two
families have been adorned by your combination of a good woman's
virtues. And these Kurus are lucky that you, irreproachable, have not
burned them to ashes. Strengthened by my thoughts of you, travel an
unthreatened path: for if a thing must be, good women are not
timorous. Guarded over by the Law of your elders, you will soon come
to better times. Always look to my son Sahadeva, when he lives in the
forest, so that in this trouble he has encountered his great mind does
not falter."

"So shall it be," said the queen, spotted by her flowing tears; and in
her sole garment, besmirched with blood, she went out, her hair
10 undone. As she walked away weeping, Pṛthā followed her wretchedly;
and she saw all her sons bereft of ornaments and robes, their bodies
covered with *ruru* deerskins, lowering their faces with shame amidst
their gleeful enemies, but mourned by their friends.

Lovingly she hastened to her sons, in the state they were in, and
with much lamentation she piteously said to them and their kinsmen,
"Why should you who were ever adorned by your fortitude in a
conduct that followed the Law, never lowly, always firmly loyal,
always bent on the worship of the Gods, why should you be overtaken
by misfortune? What is this contrary fate? Whose fault born from
15 envy has it been that I now must see you so? Well may it be my own
misfortune, for I gave birth to you, that you reap the anguish of a
grief beyond measure, however great you are in your virtues. . . .
How shall you, denied your wealth, dwell in the impassable wilderness,
lean of body though not of prowess, mettle, strength, enterprise, and
energy? If I had known that a life in the forest would be in store for
you, I would never have taken you down after Pāṇḍu's death from the
Hundred-Peak Mountains to the City of the Elephant. Yes, I think,
with his mind set on austerities and wisdom, your father was lucky,
for he set his mind on going to heaven before he had to suffer for his
sons. And now I think that Mādrī was lucky, who with unerring
foresight went the last journey, wise in the Law and virtuous in every
20 fashion. Love and thought and purpose decided me—a hanging-on to
Life: and a plague on it, for it has brought me misery."

When Kuntī lamented thus, the Pāṇḍavas solaced her, bade her
farewell, and joylessly went forth to the woods. Vidura and others
comforted the wretched Kuntī, citing reasons, and, suffering more
themselves, took her quietly into the Steward's house.

King Dhṛtarāṣṭra, whose mind was upset with grief, sent for the
Steward to come at once. So Vidura went to Dhṛtarāṣṭra's house and,
disturbed, he, the king of men, questioned him.

Dhṛtarāṣṭra said:
71.1 In what manner does the Kaunteya leave, Yudhiṣṭhira the King
Dharma? And Bhīmasena, the left-handed archer, and the twin sons
of Mādrī? How does Dhaumya depart, Steward, and poor Draupadī?
I want to hear everything, every movement they make.

Vidura said:
Kuntī's son Yudhiṣṭhira has covered his face with his shawl, and
Bhīma Pāṇḍava has spread his arms wide as he goes. The left-handed
archer follows the king, scattering sand, and Mādrī's son Sahadeva
5 goes with his face all streaked. Nakula is much distressed in his
thoughts and is walking with his whole body limned with dust, behind
his king, he the handsomest man on earth. Kṛṣṇā of the long eyes,
hiding her face in her hair, beautiful and crying much, follows the
king. Dhaumya is chanting the gruesome Chants of Death, lord of the
people, and as he walks the tracks he holds up *kuśa* grass in his hand.

Dhṛtarāṣṭra said:
The Pāṇḍavas are going in many different postures they have
assumed. Therefore tell me, Vidura, why are they traveling in these
strange ways?

Vidura said:
Even though with your deceitful connivance your sons took his
riches and kingdom, the mind of the wise King Dharma does not
10 stray from the Law. This king, forever compassionate to the
Dhārtarāṣṭras, Bhārata, although consumed by fury over the trickery,
refuses to cast his evil eye. That is why the Pāṇḍava king goes with
his eyes covered, "lest I burn these folk down to the ground if I look
at them with my evil eye."

Now listen to me as I tell why Bhīma goes in his way, bull of the
Bharatas. He knows that no one has as great strength in his arms as
he does. That is why he is going that way, with his arms extended
wide, showing his arms, proud of the bulk of his arms, ready to employ
them on his enemies in accordance with his arms' might.

Kuntī's son Arjuna, the left-handed archer, follows his king while
scattering about sand to forecast the number of enemies that will burn
15 with his arrows. Just as his grains of sand are separated from one
another, as severally shall he loose on his enemies the showers of his
arrows, Bhārata.

Lest anyone recognize his face today, Bhārata, Sahadeva has
streaked his face and thus is traveling with his king.

Lest on the road he should steal the hearts of the women, Nakula
has covered his whole body with dust and in this guise goes with him.

Dressed in her sole garment, disheveled and weeping in her courses,
her cloth wet and besmirched with blood, Draupadī has spoken this

word: "They because of whom I got this way, thirteen years from now
their wives will have their husbands dead, their sons dead, their
20 kinsmen and friends dead! Their bodies smeared with the blood of their
relatives, their hair loosened and themselves in their courses, the
women shall offer up the water to their dead, no less, as the Pāṇḍavas
enter the City of the Elephant!"

Dhaumya, their wise family priest, has fashioned the *kuśa* grass that
is dedicated to Nirṛti and leads their procession, chanting the Chants
that are devoted to Yama, Bhārata. Dhaumya is walking forth,
declaring: "When the Bhāratas have been killed in the war, the gurus
of the Kurus shall likewise sing these Chants!" On all sides the
anguished townspeople are crying, "O woe! Our protectors are leaving!
Look at this calamity!" With these guises and signs the spirited
Kaunteyas have given notice of the resolve that lodges in their hearts
as they go to the forest.

25 When these superior men in this fashion departed from the City of
the Elephant, lightning flashed on the cloudless sky and the earth
trembled, Rāhu swallowed the sun when no eclipse was due, lord of
your people. Meteors exploded widdershins around the city. Beasts of
prey roared forth with vultures, jackals, and crows around the temples
and sanctuaries of Gods and the watch towers of the palaces. Such were
the grave portents that occurred when the Pāṇḍavas departed for the
forest, to spell the Bhāratas' doom, king, at your ill counsel.

Vaiśaṃpāyana said:

Now Nārada appeared in the middle of the hall and stood before
30 the Kurus; and amidst great seers he spoke this ghastly word:
"Thirteen years from now the Kauravas who are here will perish,
through Duryodhana's guilt and Bhīma's and Arjuna's might." Having
spoken, the greatest of divine seers, wearing about his person the
ample fortune of the Brahman, strode up to the sky and soon
disappeared.

Hereupon Duryodhana, Karṇa, and Śakuni Saubala thought Droṇa
was their haven and offered the kingdom to him. Droṇa then
addressed the intransigent Duryodhana, Duḥśāsana, Karṇa, and all
the Bhāratas: "The twice-born have said that the Pāṇḍavas, who are
sons of Gods, cannot be killed. Yet I shall do whatever is in my power
35 for those who seek refuge with me. I cannot abandon the
Dhārtarāṣṭras and their king who with all their soul and devotion have
come to me for mercy—the rest is rooted in fate. In accordance with
the Law, the sons of Pāṇḍu, once they were defeated, have departed
for the forest; and they, Kauravas, shall live in the forest for twelve
years. Living as *brahmacārins*, possessed by anger and intolerance, the
Pāṇḍavas shall bring back their feud, to my own perdition. But I once

in a friendly contest unseated a king from his kingdom, King Drupada;
and in his rage he offered up a sacrifice for the sake of a son who
would kill me, Bhārata. Through the austerities of Yāja and Upayāja
he obtained a son from the fire, Dhṛṣṭadyumna, and also, from the
40 middle of the altar, the slim-waisted Draupadī. He was given by the
Gods, effulgent like fire, with bow, armor, and arrows; and since I am
subject to the Law of mortals, fear of him possesses me. This Pārṣata,
a bull among men, now has chosen their side; it is because of him
that I, already grievously dispossessed of life, shall give battle to your
enemies. All the world knows that he is meant to kill me, and he is
all-too-famous: 'Surely because of you has Time turned.'
"So hurry and do what is best; what you have done was not
enough. This respite of happiness is brief, like the shade of a palm tree
in winter. Offer up grand sacrifices, indulge in your pleasures, and
give. For thirteen years from now you will reap a great massacre.
45 Duryodhana, you have heard and understood it as it pleases you; now
rather placate the Pāṇḍaveyas, if so turns your fancy."

Vaiśaṃpāyana said:

After listening to Droṇa's words, Dhṛtarāṣṭra said this: "This
teacher says sooth—Steward, bring back the Pāṇḍavas! If they will not
return, may the Pāṇḍavas go with our blessings, with their little sons,
with their thousand chariots and footmen, with their joys."

Vaiśaṃpāyana said:

72.1 The Pārthas had gone to the forest, defeated in the dicing game,
when worry beset Dhṛtarāṣṭra, O great king. And as King Dhṛtarāṣṭra,
lord of his people, sat worrying, sighing, and greatly distracted,
Saṃjaya spoke: "You have now obtained all of the earth, lord of the
earth, filled with all of earth's wealth. The Pāṇḍavas have departed
from the kingdom, then why should you grieve, king?"

Dhṛtarāṣṭra said:

Is there nothing to worry for those who shall have a feud with the
Pāṇḍavas, berserkers in war, great warriors who have allies?

Saṃjaya said:

5 That has been your grand deed, king. A great feud will follow, and
the total destruction of everyone and his followers shall befall. Though
warned by Bhīṣma, Droṇa, and Vidura, your foolish and shameless
son Duryodhana sent the son of a *sūta* as his usher, to bring in
Draupadī, the Pāṇḍavas' beloved wife, who walked in the Law.

Dhṛtarāṣṭra said:

When the Gods deal defeat to a person, they first take his mind
away, so that he sees matters wrongly. When destruction is imminent
and his mind is beclouded, the wrong course appears as the right one

and cannot be dislodged from his heart. When his destruction is near, evil takes on the appearance of good, the good appears as evil, and thus they rise up before a man and he is content. Time does not raise a stick and clobber a man's head; the power of Time is just this upended view of things. This ghastly, hair-raising horror has been brought on by those who dragged the wretched Draupadī to the middle of the hall. Who but that crooked gambler would overpower and exhibit in the hall this effulgent and beautiful princess, not born of woman, issue of a great dynasty, glorious and conversant with all the Laws? The full-hipped Pāñcālī, ruled by the Law of women, clothed in her single garment, stained with blood, looked at the Pāṇḍavas, to find them robbed of their property, fading in spirit, robbed of their wife, robbed of their fortune, deprived of all pleasures, and reduced to slavery, as they were ensnared by the noose of the Law as if impotent of gallantry. Duryodhana and Karṇa in the assembly threw biting insults at the suffering Kṛṣṇā, angry and defiant. Earth herself would burn under her wretched eyes—would anything have been left of my sons, Saṃjaya?

All the women of the Bhāratas, who had gathered with Gāndhārī, cried out in anguish when they saw Kṛṣṇā brought to the hall. No *agnihotras* were offered up that evening, for the brahmins were enraged over the molestation of Draupadī. There was a grisly rumbling in the earth, and a fierce hurricane rose. Horrible meteors fell from the sky, and out of season Rāhu swallowed the sun, driving the people into a horrific panic. Fire appeared in the chariot stables and the flagmasts crumbled, spelling disaster for the Bhāratas. At Duryodhana's *agnihotra* the jackals howled fearsomely, and on all sides the donkeys brayed back at them. Bhīṣma then left with Droṇa, and so did Kṛpa, Somadatta, and the warlike Bāhlīka, O Saṃjaya.

At Vidura's urging I then said I shall give Kṛṣṇā a boon, whatever she pleases. Pāñcālī chose the Pāṇḍavas of boundless luster, and I permitted them to go with their chariots and bows. Thereupon the sagacious Vidura, who knows all the Law, said, "This signifies your end, Bhāratas, that Kṛṣṇā went into your hall. This daughter of the king of Pāñcāla is peerless Śrī, who was created by fate to marry the Pāṇḍavas. The furious Pārthas will not forgive her humiliation, nor will the great archers of the Vṛṣṇis, nor the powerful Pāñcālas. They are protected by Vāsudeva, who is true to his promises; and the Terrifier will come, protected by the Pāñcālas. Amongst them Bhīmasena will come, the mighty archer, brandishing his club as Death his staff. And when they hear the whirr of the great-spirited Pārtha's Gāṇḍīva and the whoosh of Bhīma's club, the kings will not be able to bear it. Therefore I have never wanted war with the

Pārthas, for I have always believed that the Pāṇḍavas are stronger
than the Kurus. The illustrious King Jarāsaṃdha was mighty, yet
35 Bhīma defeated him in a contest with a single blow of his arm. You
must make peace with the Pāṇḍavas, bull of the Bharatas, and do
without delay what is just to both parties."

Thus, Saṃjaya, did the Steward give his law-minded and apt advice; but I did not heed it, for I wanted to favor my son.

The Mahābhārata

Translated

Book 3 *The Book of the Forest*

Introduction

The Image of the Forest

áraṇyāny áraṇyāny asaú yā́ préva náśyasi /
kathā́ grā́maṃ ná pṛchasi ná tvā bhī́r iva vindatī́ṃ /
vṛṣarāvā́ya vádate yád upā́vati ciccikáḥ /
aghāṭíbhir iva dhāváyann araṇyānī́r mahīyate //
utá gā́va ivādanty utá véśmeva dṛśyate /
utó araṇyānī́ḥ sāyáṃ śakatī́r iva sarjati //
gā́m angaiṣá ā́ hvayati dā́rv angaiṣó ápāvadhīt /
vásann araṇyānyā́m sāyám ákrukṣad íti manyate //
ná vā́ aranyānir hanty anyáś cén nā́bhigáchati /
svādóḥ phálasya jagdhvā́ya yathākā́mam ní padyate //
ā́ñjanagandhiṃ surabhíṃ bahvannā́ṃ ákṛṣīvalām /
prāhám mṛgā́ṇām mātáram araṇyānī́m aśaṃsiṣam //
Ṛgveda 10.146

Lady Forest, Lady Forest! you there who seem to
disappear,
Why do you not ask for the village? Fear has not
found you yet?
When the grasshopper chirps its reply to the call
of the cricket,
Lady Forest exults like a king spreading terror with
drummers.[1]
Cows seem there to be grazing, a dwelling is seen
perhaps—

1. I follow here the interpretation of Paul Thieme, in "RV 10.146.2 āghātibhir iva dhāvayan," *Pratidānam* (Festschrift Kuiper), The Hague, 1968, p. 383–92.

Or is it the Forest Lady who seems to creak like
a cart?
Someone is surely there calling his cow, someone's
cutting up wood:
Spending the night at the Forest Lady's one thinks
that someone has screamed.
Lady Forest does not kill unless somebody attacks
her—
After eating the sweet fruit one later beds down
as he pleases.
Añjana-scented and fragrant and yielding much
fruit without ploughing—
She is the Lady Forest, the mother of game, whom
I now have praised.

The third Major Book of *The Mahābhārata, The Book of the Forest,* displays in a grand manner of what the Indian epic is capable. Its rich contents can be divided into two large blocks: the vicissitudes of the heroes and heroine in their forest exile and episodes relating to the main narrative on the one hand, and, on the other, the manifold narratives to which their sojourn in the forest gives occasion. Corresponding to these two interwoven parts the book has traditionally two names, the *vanaparvan, The Book of the Forest,* and *āraṇyakaparvan, The Book of the Forest Teachings.*[2] The critical edition found better testimony for the latter title, which it consequently adopted; in the translation I have chosen the briefer name, with the understanding that it implies the other.

In the first group, that of the "forest" proper, are included the Pāṇḍavas' encounter with the demon Kirmīra and his slaying;[3] Dhṛtarāṣṭra's worries and temporary breach with Vidura;[4] the arrival of Kṛṣṇa;[5] the admonitions addressed by Bhīma and Draupadī to Yudhiṣṭhira;[6] Arjuna's journey to the world of Indra;[7] Bhīma's search for the *saugandhika* flowers and his encounter with his half brother Hanūmān;[8] the cattle expedition of the Kauravas;[9] and the riddles of

2. *Āraṇyakaparvan* is also specifically the name of the first Minor Book (= 29) of the Major Book, and has thus lent the name to the entire Book 3, just as the *Virāṭaparvan* (= 75) lent its name to Book 4.
3. 3(29).12.
4. 3.5 ff.
5. 3(31.a).15 ff.
6. 3.28 ff.
7. 3(32).43 ff.
8. 3.146 ff.
9. 3(39).224 ff.

the crane.[10] The second group comprises the story of Nala;[11] the accounts of pilgrimages to the sacred places, and the many episodes that are inspired by the actual one;[12] the battle with the Nivātakavacas,[13] the Session with Mārkaṇḍeya,[14] and the story of Rāma related by Mārkaṇḍeya.[15]

Before we look at the two groups more closely, we do well for a moment to dwell on the ancient Indians' image of the forest. Be it first of all noted that the English word *forest* is misleading if it conjures up the image of a luxuriant rain forest, deep, steamy, tropical. The intention of the many Sanskrit words[16] for "forest" is wider: they denote in general any wild area of the countryside that has not been brought under cultivation, which is, in other words, outside the village, though not necessarily far away, and its acres. The contrast is of village and forest. The image of the "wilds outside" was not simply one of terror. There is that, no doubt, but it is muted as in the poem of the Ṛgvedic poet who finds himself surprised in the forest at night and invokes the Forest Lady in terms both placating and admiring—until in the end he beds down peacefully. No doubt, the forest is the haunt of barbarous tribes, of predatory animals, and of many kinds of stalking demons. This side of the image is quite nicely conveyed in the story of *Nala*, where Damayantī is deserted by her husband in the wilderness. But even there there is no escaping the impression that the forest, with its sudden dangers and miraculous deliverances, is a reaim of romance.

Insofar as the forest is the wilderness that has not been brought under cultivation, it may be described as *not yet* the village. But simultaneously it is also *no more* the village.[17] It is the place for those who, for various reasons, have said farewell to the village, either from necessity, as in the case of our heroes, or from personal choice.

The official *dharma* literature divides the life of a faithful Hindu into four *āśramas* or stages. There is in the first place the period of study that closes off childhood and begins with the boy's initiation (*upanayana*) into the ranks of the twiceborn, preparing him for the second life stage of householder (*gṛhastha*). As a householder the man marries, has children, performs the rituals, makes a living, and

10. 3(44).295 ff.
11. 3(32.a).50 ff.
12. 3(33).80 ff.
13. 3.165 ff.
14. 3(37).179.
15. 3(42.a).257 ff.
16. *Vana, araṇya, vipina, aṭavī, kānana, kāntāra, jangala*, etc.
17. I refer the reader to the description of the village-dweller who "turns his back" on the village in *The Latter Days of Yayāti* (1: 205).

generally conducts himself as the social creature he is. This stage is in particular the period of the village in his life.

When old age is nearing, his children have grown up, and his vigor is waning, he is enjoined to "depart for the forest" (*vanaprastha*). As Manu[18] decrees: "When the householder sees his wrinkles and gray hair, and his children's children, he should take refuge in the forest. Abandoning the food of the village and all his possessions, he should go to the forest, while entrusting his wife to his sons, or taking her with him. Taking along his *agnihotra*[19] and the necessaries for the domestic ritual, he should depart from the village for the forest and live there, mastering his senses." He retires to an *āśrama*, a "hermitage," a retreat outside the village, though not necessarily very far. While his wife may accompany him there, his contacts with, and especially his participation in, village life ceases and he devotes himself to a life of contemplation and study: "For the perfection of his self he should observe the various upaniṣadic scriptures."[20]

A further life stage is mentioned, that of *saṃnyāsa* or complete renunciation, when he cuts off all family and social bonds, ceases to be a social creature, and is to all intents and purposes dead to the world. Both the "forest-departed" and the ascetic are denizens of the forest.

Such a simple forest life, when one subsists on the fruit and roots that nature has to offer, had, or has, a great attraction for the Indian mind. It is the Indian, or at least the *brahmin* Arcadia: old men, hallowed by both their age and wisdom, will live in a retreat close by a river, tending the ancient fires of the rituals, contemplating matters supramundane, contented and wanting nothing. The "forest-departed" man will interrupt his sojourn in one place with occasional journeys to places of pilgrimage, and the even tenor of his existence will be enlivened by visits of other sages or passing guests.

The Book of the Forest shows this ambivalence of the wilderness: it is both demoniac and idyllic. To this is added another ambivalence, that of this specific stay of our heroes. For however meritorious life in the forest may be, it is not the place for them: they are there by accident. This awareness never leaves Bhīma and Draupadī; Yudhiṣṭhira is more stoic about it, and also avails himself of the consolations of the forest: he goes on a pilgrimage and allows himself to be comforted by the admonitions and narratives of passing Brahmins.

18. *Manusmṛti* 6.2–4.

19. While technically the name of a milk oblation at dawn and dusk, *agnihotra* in *The Mahābhārata* also stands for the sacred fire.

20. *Manusmṛti* 6.29.

The Function of the Book in The Mahābhārata

Though one can hardly imagine that in a more original form *The Book of the Forest* had the same size as in the present, it can also not be doubted that it always formed an important part of it. It is not in the Indian style to send heroes off to the forest and then to continue, "After twelve years they came back." The romance of the forest was too gripping and the theme of the prince exiled to the wilds too popular. In *The Mahābhārata* we have Arjuna's amorous self-exile in *The Beginning*, in *The Rāmāyaṇa* the exile of Rāma, in the story of *Nala* the tribulations of Damayantī, and so on. While it is unprofitable to speculate on the "original" contents of *The Book of the Forest*, I consider it likely that the romance of the wild, its danger and its peace, figured importantly in it. Even its present bulk has a nice propriety about it; twelve years is a long time, and as one goes on reading he does get a sense of the length of time that the Pāṇḍavas were exiled from their kingdom.

More than anything, *The Book of the Forest* serves to build up the character of Yudhiṣṭhira. It is taken for granted throughout that he lives in the forest as a result of deception[21] and that few would blame him if he assailed his deceivers before they could consolidate their power. It is the recurrent theme of Bhīma's recriminations. Draupadī's recurrent theme is that of vengeance for the wrongs done herself. Kṛṣṇa's people and the Pāñcālas, the family of Draupadī, are fully prepared to take on Hāstinapura in the cause of Yudhiṣṭhira.[22] Faced with all these temptations the King Dharma remains firm: he patiently points out that all that is very well, but that he had given his word and pledged to be gone for thirteen years; it is simply his fate. From this point of view *The Book of the Forest* is the celebration of the highest value in the moral code of the ancient Indians, truthfulness and faithfulness under all circumstances.

An important effect of Yudhiṣṭhira's firm faith is the solidarity of the family. There is never talk of splitting up. Yudhiṣṭhira had only pledged his own forest life, not that of his wife and brothers.[23] Draupadī might well have chosen to wait out the term in Ahicchatrā of Pāñcāla with her own family, just as Arjuna's other wife Subhadrā does in leaving for Dvārakā where her family lives.[24] Draupadī's brother Dhṛṣṭadyumna takes her sons to Pāñcāla;[25] she might well have considered that her place was with them rather than in the forest with her husbands, to whom she could only be a burden.

21. From 3.1.18 onward.
22. 3.19 ff.
23. Hence Dhṛtarāṣṭra's surprise at their solidarity.
24. 3.23.44.
25. 3.23.46.

The question of separation is never raised, though to others their solidarity is astonishing. The Pāṇḍavas act as one organism whose limbs it is impossible to amputate. However much of a strain the enforced idleness is for Bhīma, and however much it rankles with Draupadī that her honor remains unavenged,[26] they do not threaten to leave. Arjuna is a partial exception, for he is gone a good deal of the time. But whatever one may think of his journey to the world of Indra, where he stays on for five years, he did go after all in order to obtain the weapons that will make possible their eventual triumph.

It appears that these were popular themes. In *The Rāmāyaṇa* too Rāma's stay is the result of truthfulness. It is more complicated there: it was not his own word that brought his fate upon him, but his father Daśaratha's, who in a moment of weakness had promised one of his wives a boon; she chooses that her own son (once more a "Bharata") be Young King instead of Rāma. While Daśaratha is prepared to renege on his promise, Rāma will not have it and departs. He too is followed by his wife Sītā and his brother Lakṣmaṇa; neither one gives any thought to leaving Rāma.[27]

While *The Book of the Forest* celebrates the unshakable truthfulness of Yudhiṣṭhira, at the same time it points up the enormity of the Kauravas' wickedness. The latter not only have caused the exile but add to their infamy by even now plotting to raid the Pāṇḍavas and once and for all eliminate their possible threat. Their "cattle expedition," on the pretense of which they seek out the exiled brothers, fails ingloriously at the hands of the Gandharvas, from whom Yudhiṣṭhira has to rescue them. The magnanimity of the King Dharma illustrates another high value of the ancient Indians: generosity—which here is also paired with the respect so often shown to the baronial injunction that one should spare him who takes refuge with one.

It appears that one of the functions of *The Book of the Forest* is to establish these ideals and illustrate them in Yudhiṣṭhira's character. He has always been called the King Dharma, but we have not really seen many instances of his lawmindedness. It is by withstanding in the forest nearly irresistible temptations that he shows his character, and his brothers and wife theirs.

The Main Narrative

The narrative framework of *The Book of the Forest* is a relatively simple one. Essentially it is a period of simply waiting out the term, so it is a

26. *MBh.* 3.00.00.
27. *Rāmāyaṇa* (cr. ed.) 2.24 ff.; 28.

book of leisure, of visits paid and received, and an occasional battle with demons. The Pāṇḍavas, meanwhile, are not stationary; they travel from Kāmyaka to Dvaita to Kāmyaka, and eventually up the Snowy Mountains to Kubera's paradise, while Arjuna makes a solitary journey to Indra's heaven. The supernatural, entirely absent from *The Book of the Assembly Hall*, is very much in evidence, for indeed, the unpredictable is in the nature of the forest.

Promptly, on the threshold of the wilderness, the demon Kirmīra bars their way and is dispatched by Bhīma.[28] Reports of this battle travel to Hāsinapura, where they give Vidura, as always the patron of the Pāṇḍavas, occasion to expostulate with Dhṛtarāṣṭra about the course of the events. Vidura's advice is to call back the Pāṇḍavas. When Dhṛtarāṣṭra accuses Vidura of always siding with the sons of Pāṇḍu, the brothers fall out. Vidura thereupon joins the Pāṇḍavas in the forest.[29] Dhṛtarāṣṭra repents and sends his charioteer-herald Saṃjaya to fetch back Vidura. Meanwhile a plan of Duryodhana to pounce on the Pāṇḍavas and be done with them forever is thwarted by the personal intervention of Vyāsa, the Author, himself.[30] We have seen this ubiquitous recluse beget the dynasty[31] in *The Book of the Beginning*, guide the Pāṇḍavas to Draupadī's bridegroom choice,[32] and explain to King Drupada that there was no harm in Draupadī's marrying five husbands.[33] In *The Book of the Assembly Hall* he appears once, taciturn, at Yudhiṣṭhira's anointing.[34] Now he intervenes with Dhṛtarāṣṭra, steers the Pāṇḍavas to the Kāmyaka Forest,[35] and bestows on Yudhiṣṭhira a magic that will enable Arjuna to obtain weapons from Indra.

These intermittent incursions of Vyāsa are intriguing. He is not really a *deus ex machina*, and in fact not greatly needed. News of Draupadī's bridegroom choice could have come from any source, and *The Mahābhārata* counts enough saints to tell Drupada of the *Five Indras*. Of greater significance is his role in begetting posthumous children for Vicitravīrya: in that he acts as the older brother, and that could have been the end of his part. The question arises whether these appearances and interventions have become the source of the idea of Vyāsa's authorship of *The Mahābhārata* (and consequently of the eighteen *Purāṇas*). Or were they actual innovations in one received

28. 3(12).39 ff.
29. 3.6.
30. 3.9 ff.
31. 1.100 ff.
32. 1.157.
33. 1.188 ff.
34. 2.34, where he is the *brahmán* priest.
35. 3.37.20 ff.

Bhārata version by an author whose name has been preserved as Vyāsa?

With Vyāsa's magic Arjuna sets out for Indra's world, performing in the mountains the austerities that have been immortalized by the giant relief of Mahābalipuram.[36] On his journey he meets the God Śiva in his first major appearance in our text. The God wears the guise of a Kirāta, an aboriginal man from the mountains, a guise typical of the God who will remain the divine Outsider. The two become embattled over a boar they have shot simultaneously, with Śiva the inevitable but by no means easy victor.

This episode is interesting because, like *The Story of the Five Indras*,[37] it shows the ascendancy this God now has gained over the Vedic God-king Indra, for Śiva appears to have to give his consent to Arjuna's collection of Indra's weapons.

In Indra's heaven Arjuna is regally received and shares the God's throne, to the surprise of the seer Lomaśa, who later reports to Yudhiṣṭhira. Not the least curious part of the story is that Arjuna at Indra's bidding stays on for five years, learning how to sing and dance. The need for the latter accomplishments is no doubt inspired by Arjuna's disguise as a dance master at Virāṭa's court in *The Book of Virāṭa*.[38] In typical sanskritic fashion a reason must be provided to explain how this baron came to know how to dance; so why not in heaven where the Gandharvas and Apsarās play?

Eventually[39]—here the main narrative is taken up again after the long Tour of the Sacred Fords—the earth-bound Pāṇḍavas travel to Mount Gandhamādana where they are to meet with Arjuna. On the mountain Draupadī takes a fancy to a *saugandhika* flower that is floating down a river—we are reminded of the beginning of *The Story of the Five Indras*. Bhīma goes in search of the source of the flower and encounters on the road the monkey Hanūmān, his half brother, who, from extreme old age, is too frail to move out of Bhīma's way. Bhīma tries to raise the monkey's tail but fails.[40] Has this episode been the inspiration of the later retelling of *The Rāmāyaṇa* story? It is important to note that the author of the episode of Bhīma's encounter with Hanūmān attributes such antiquity to Hanūmān. This can only mean that at the time that this episode was received into *The Book of the Forest*, a *Rāmāyaṇa* had long been known. On a second search Bhīma reaches Kubera's paradise where he becomes embroiled with the Yakṣas who guard the pond with the celestial *saugandhika* flowers.

36. It is more popularly though erroneously known as the "Descent of the Ganges."
37. 1.189.
38. 4.1 ff.
39. 3.143.
40. 3.147.

He triumphs and thereby lifts a curse from Kubera.[41]

The Pāṇḍavas, reunited with Arjuna, dally in Kubera's park for four years, then they return to the Kāmyaka Forest, where Kṛṣṇa visits them.[42] Meanwhile, Duryodhana has been making plans to massacre the Pāṇḍavas. He arranges for an expedition to inspect and count the royal herds in the vicinity of the Pāṇḍavas, but the Kauravas are interdicted by Gandharvas, who claim that area. They capture Duryodhana after Karṇa infamously flees.[43] Yudhiṣṭhira has to rescue him.[44]

As though this were *de rigueur* for a woman temporarily alone in the forest, Draupadī like Sītā (and Damayantī almost) is also abducted, but unsuccessfully. A King Jayadratha and his cronies try to carry her off, but Bhīma and Arjuna rescue her and, inexplicably, spare the abductors.[45] This unlikely mercy is surely due to the fact that Jayadratha already had a later part to take in *The Mahābhārata*: he will bring one grand army to Duryodhana's forces.[46]

At this point, fairly abuptly, occurs the episode of Indra's begging Karṇa's armor. Among the Kauravas Yudhiṣṭhira fears no one more than Karṇa. Karṇa was the son of the Sun God by Kuntī (the story, already found in *The Book of the Beginning*, is retold in greater detail), and was born with a cuirass and earrings that were part of his body. Indra, in order to aid his son Arjuna, intends to rob Karṇa of his armor. The Sun warns Karṇa of Indra's intentions, but Karṇa replies that he cannot refuse a brahmin; whereupon Indra assumes the guise of a brahmin and persuades Karṇa to surrender his armor. Karṇa does so in exchange for a one-time miracle spear that will enable him to smite any enemy.[47]

The main narrative of *The Book of the Forest* ends with the chase of a deer, which had caught the fire-drilling woods of a brahmin in its antlers. They lose the deer and, tired, search for water. One after the other the brothers are struck down at a pond by a Yakṣa in the form of a crane who stops them from taking water. When finally Yudhiṣṭhira goes, the Yakṣa poses to him a series of riddles. Yudhiṣṭhira gives all the right answers. The Yakṣa thereupon reveals himself as the God Dharma and grants the Pāṇḍavas the boon that they will be unrecognized during their thirteenth year, when, according to the stipulation of the last dicing game of *The Book of the Assembly Hall*, they are to live in the open, but undiscovered.[48]

41. 3.158.
42. 3.180.
43. 3.230.
44. 3.235.
45. 3.255 f.
46. 5.152.
47. 3.294
48. The substance of *Mahābhārata* 4, *The Book of Virāṭa*.

The Episodes

More than half of *The Book of the Forest* is taken up by narratives that are extraneous to the main story. All of them have their own interest, which no doubt is the reason that they have been preserved in the library that is *The Mahābhārata*. Differently from the episodes inserted in *The Book of the Beginning*, those of *The Forest* have a pious intention – at least their setting is pious. An exception to this pattern is the first narrative, in which Kṛṣṇa recounts why he was unable to attend the dicing match and stop it.

The Razing of Saubha

Perhaps the easiest way of describing *The Razing of Saubha*[49] is as an early instance of science fiction. Kṛṣṇa becomes embattled with Saubha, which is at once the title of a demon king, Śālva, and his city, This city darts through the skies like a spaceship, spewing flames and missiles on the chariot-bound Kṛṣṇa. Saubha even resorts to the playing of illusions[50] that are dear to the hearts of psi-fi writers. On closer inspection the narrative appears to be the same, in structure and detail, as the tale of Arjuna and his battle with the Nivātakavaca demons, and fuller treatment may be postponed[51] till we can compare the two stories and remark on the implications of the fact that the same story is told of Arjuna as of Kṛṣṇa.

Nala

The prize of *The Book of the Forest* is surely the famous story of *Nala*,[52] with *The Bhagavadgītā* the best known episode of *The Mahābhārata* in the West, if not also in India. Its popularity in India is shown by the many versions it has inspired in Sanskrit and later dialects. As late as the twelfth century the highly esteemed Sanskrit poet Śrīharsa[53] wrote in a style that has little in common with that of his original:

> King Nala, having drunk whose story the wise have no regard even for the Elixir of Immortality, was a blazing mass of supernal glories, who had made the compass of his fame into his white umbrella. His remembered tale purifies the world in this Eon as with a bath of quintessences[54] – how will it fail to purify my speech, however uncouth, which honors it?

49. 3(31.a).15 ff.
50. 3.22.
51. Below, p. 202.
52. 3(32.a).50 ff.
53. Śrīharṣa, *Naiṣadhacarita* (Bombay, 1912), 1.1–2.
54. There is a pun on *rasa*, also "mood," here the erotic mood.

The original has a sweetness as well as a directness that makes it one of the finest examples of early Indian storytelling. Quite striking is the humanity of its characters, especially of the women, and Damayantī foremost, who are finely drawn. In spite of its pathos it has a curiously simple domesticity to it, which raises the question how far the story is a folktale that was sanskritized and adopted into *The Mahābhārata*.[55]

How far is the *Nala* story independent of *The Mahābhārata*? There are a number of similarities that cannot be coincidental. There is Damayantī's bridegroom choice; the envious grudge of Kali; Nala out of the blue is obsessed by an urge to dice; he dices with a kinsman; he loses his kingdom; he must dwell in the forest; his wife follows him; they rest in a traveler's lodge in the forest that is inexplicably called a *sabhā*,[56] an assembly hall; in this *sabhā* Damayantī loses half her skirt and is deserted; both Nala and the Pāṇḍavas assume incognito menial positions at a court; there is triumph in the end.

While it will not do to ignore these similarities, it will also not do to overstate them. Nala's dicing is not as organic to his story as Yudhiṣṭhira's is to his. He could have come to the same grief without the dicing. Nala hardly pauses in the forest; that Damayantī does is literarily inspired: it gives the author an opportunity to indulge in a favorite literary art form, the Lament. The emphasis of the *Nala* story, to be sure, is wholly different from that of *The Mahābhārata*.

The emphasis, it was pointed out to me, is on the theme of *viraha*, love in separation; and indeed the story seems to be one of the earliest examples of that theme so beloved of the later writers of *kāvya* poetry. Damayantī's almost demented search for Nala reminds one strongly of the ravings of Purūravas in the forest searching for Urvaśī in the controversial fourth act of Kālidāsa's *Vikramorvaśīya*, and Rāma's plaint in *The Rāmāyaṇa* (cr. ed.) 3.58.

We remarked on the domesticity of the *Nala* story; we might add the story's femininity. In spite of its traditional name it is much more the story of Damayantī than of Nala. The entire concatenation of events is treated strictly from a woman's point of view. From the beginning Damayantī is the center of attention. Her birth is interesting

55. Some of the ideas below were developed in a seminar on *The Mahābhārata* that I directed in the winter and spring of 1973.

56. 3.59.4: *sabhāṃ kāṃcid upeyatuḥ*; the word must be taken in a contextual meaning, "travelers' lodge," which seems to be unique to this locus. PW gives a similar meaning to *sabhā in MBh.* 13.24.17 (not urgent), *Manu* 9.264 (Bühler "assembly house"), *Mārkaṇḍeya Purāṇa* 14.65 (not likely, in context with *devālaya*), *Bhāgavata Purāṇa* 10.41.21 (Harvette-Besnault "salle de réunion"); the entry *Rāmāyaṇa* 1.5.13 cannot be traced, but in any case the context would be the description of Ayodhyā, where the regular meaning is more appropriate.

—the result of a boon—her four brothers are mentioned in passing, then *she* is eulogized encomiastically. He and she fall in love, but we hear more of Nala's pining than of hers. There is the romantic message of the wild geese, Nala's discomfiture at having to act as the Gods' go-between, Damayantī's composure when Nala appears in the *sérail*. Her bridegroom choice is the only free one we have so far encountered. The others were by parental arrangement,[57] tournament,[58] and abduction.[59] There are no less than five, identically appearing, suitors. Her trueness prevails upon the Gods to reveal themselves. He and she are happily married and have both a boy and a girl. As an additional womanly feature, Nala is given a talent to cook.

Disaster strikes! After many happy years Nala is obsessed. What to do? Safeguard the children! Nala loses all and is in the end denuded; Damayantī, unwittingly, helps to dress him. Damayanti is deserted, but reluctantly so, and all for her own good. She is a good wife, praising Nala in her misery, killing her male savior. Nala is quickly given a good home (where he never sets eye on another woman), Damayantī's hardships are protracted and pathetic. All initiative comes from her side: her father sends brahmins to spy her out: she is discovered, and behold, her mistress is her aunt! She conspires with her mother. Nala is found out through romantic poetry. To smoke him out she embarks on a plan of unheard-of boldness: a second bridegroom choice! The reunion is moving. Meanwhile, though in hiding, Nala has been a paragon of constancy.

It is profitless to speculate whether the story was written by a woman, but it is fair to assume that it was written for women. What would be the occasion for such a composition? The *Nala* story is not of the usual *pativratā* type; it is not simply in praise of the dutiful wife, it is in praise of womankind.

At this point in our reflections we might turn for some guidance to the folk versions of the story that are extant. The story is still alive in northern India, from where Nala himself hailed (in fact it is firmly believed that Nala was the founder of Narwār in Rājasthān, where he became king in A.D. 295).[60] There are versions from the Panjāb,[61] Chattisgaṛh,[62] and Narwār itself.[63] They differ, at times greatly, from

57. This seems to be the case with Kuntī (cf. 1.103.5; 105.2).

58. Draupadī's (1.178–79).

59. That of Ambā, Ambikā and Ambālikā (1.96). Ambā, however, had chosen for Śālva, and Bhīṣma released her.

60. Cf. Alexander Cunningham, *Report of the Archaeological Survey of India* 2 (Simla, 1871): 310.

61. Sohinder Singh Bedi, *Folklore of the Panjab* (Delhi, 1971), p. 121–22; R. C. Temple, *Legends of the Punjab* 2 (Patiala, 1963): 204–349.

62. Verrier Elwin, *Folksongs of Chhattisgarh* (Oxford, 1946), p. 371–401.

63. J. D. Beglar, *Reports of the Archaeological Survey of India* 7 (Calcutta, 1878): 95–101.

the Sanskrit version, though more in details than in structure. In the folk versions the story of *Nala* is extended with the story of his son Dholā.

It is facile to assume that the folk versions are bastardized descendants of the Sanskrit version. The well-documented existence of a variety of *Rāma* stories,[64] which are not direct descendants of Vālmīki's *Rāmāyaṇa*, should warn us from this easy course. It might be more prudent to hypothesize that the Sanskrit version of the *Nala* story is just as much based on preexisting oral literature as the present versions. The Sanskrit version has probably made additions as well as deletions. In view of the fact that the dicing episode is not an invariable part of the folk versions it might be argued that this could have been an innovation of *The Mahābhārata* version, where the story is introduced to console Yudhiṣṭhira with the misery of another king who had fallen on hard times, because of what else but gambling? On the other hand, a second-generation episode may have been cut out. On two occasions *The Mahābhārata* shows awareness of the existence of such a second-generation episode; here it is not the son, but the daughter. In 3.113.24 Indrasenā Nāḍāyanī, the daughter of Naḍa (= Nala) is extolled as an example of a good wife to Mudgala, while in 4.20.8 she is fabled to have followed her thousand-year-old husband. In both cases she is obviously proverbial, as proverbial as Damayantī's love for Nala (3.113.23 in the same context), and Sukanyā's love for Cyavana (4.20.7, same context). The stories of the others are well-known, Indrasenā's is not, clearly by accident.

The folk versions are women's stories, as I presume the Sanskrit version to be too. They celebrate that a good wife can overcome all obstacles and hardships, and for that reason they are sung appropriately to the woman at her wedding.[65]

The narrator of the *Nala* story is the sage Bṛhadaśva, and this is his sole contribution to *The Mahābhārata*. It is told in reply to Yudhiṣṭhira's plaintive question whether any man could be more miserable than he is, robbed as he is of his kingdom because of his fateful dicing. "Certainly," answers Bṛhadaśva, "there was Nala." The same device is also used to introduce the story of *Rāma*, after Yudhiṣṭhira laments over the abduction of Draupadī. In this simple fashion whole romances have been fitted into the leisurely hours of *The Forest*.

The Tour of the Sacred Fords

The contributions of two other sages, Lomaśa and Mārkaṇḍeya, are more numerous than Bṛhadaśva's. Lomaśa, who had been surprised

64. Dinesh Chandra Sen, *The Bengali Ramayanas* (Calcutta, 1920); W. F. Stutterheim, *Rāma-legenden und Rāma-reliefs in Indonesien* (Munich, 1927).
65. Charlotte Vaudeville, *Les Duha de Ḍhola-Maru* (Pondicherry, 1962).

to see Arjuna sitting next to his father on the throne of heaven,[66] is delegated by Indra himself to conduct Yudhiṣṭhira on a tour of the places of pilgrimage.[67] The Sanskrit word for such a place is *tīrtha*, a crossing, especially over water, a ford. While dry places, especially on mountains, can also be sacred, the Indian hierophany is typically seen in and by the rivers, so that the word *tīrtha* became the normal word for sacred place, even if the "ford" was found high and dry. The association of sacredness with water is, though not exclusively, at least characteristically Indian. Such places are found particularly on what are called "perennial rivers," and in this English expression too there are overtones of the eternally holy.

Yudhiṣṭhira had been prepared for a personal tour of the sacred fords by two successive counts of *tīrthas*, one by Pulastya as reported by Nārada, and one by the Pāṇḍavas' priest Dhaumya, who for once breaks his long silence. Both are catalogues. Pulastya's is particularly interesting in that the merits of visits to the places are ticked off in terms of the rewards that accrue to Vedic rituals: "This one is worth two horse sacrifices, that one is worth three Soma sacrifices." At present there is in Benares a *ghāṭ*, stairs descending into the water of the Ganges, which is called the *Daśāśvamedh ghaṭ*, proclaiming by its very name that to bathe there bestows the merit of ten horse sacrifices. This kind of equation shows two facts: that the Vedic ritual was obsolete enough for their complexity, difficulty, and cost[68] to be forgotten so that its ancient rites could become coinage of different denominations; and that in practical life the simple religious practice of visiting the sacred places was considered a highly meritorious act. The practice may well have antedated the Vedic sacrifices to begin with. In India there is a primordial aura about the perennial ford, and it is hard to believe that the people of the Indus Valley Civilization did not pay worship to the river system that supported them. One wishes that archaeologists would pay more attention to the sites of ancient places of pilgrimage; there is no telling what a dig at Pokkhar, celebrated in our accounts as Puṣkara, might bring to light.

It is of interest to note that Yudhiṣṭhira's pilgrimage is the first instance we have encountered of his being engaged in some form of religious practice, if we except his Royal Consecration, which is singularly lacking in religious spirit in the account of *The Book of the Assembly Hall*.

Not many of the places mentioned by Pulastya and Dhaumya can be identified. The text itself describes a number of them as hard to

66. 3.45.9 ff.
67. 3.45.30 ff.
68. Though in 3.80.35 it is said that they are out of the reach of the poor.

find, and suggests that one should go there "mentally."[69] The majority in Pulastya's account seem to lie in the Āryāvarta region where the main events of *The Mahābhārata* are played out. The most famous *tīrtha* of them all, Puṣkara or Puṣkarāraṇya, is the site of the only temple in India dedicated to the God Brahmā. Lest one might think that Brahmā is therefore neglected, it is pointed out that Puṣkara is so holy that no other temple is needed.[70]

Neither Pulastya nor Dhaumya expatiate on the question why the sacred fords they mention are so sacred. Many, as suggested, no doubt go back to prehistory. The seer Lomaśa, however, likes to recount legends that were connected with his places of pilgrimages, and some of his legends are classics.

Agastya

Agastya is one of the more famous seers of the *Ṛgveda*, and like Vasiṣṭha and Viśvāmitra, has a rich post-vedic life. His birth was miraculous. When the Gods Mitra and Varuṇa were sacrificing, they saw the nymph Urvaśī and promptly ejaculated.[71] Their seed fell in a jar, from which Agastya arose; hence his common nickname *kumbhayoni*: he whose womb was a jar. Agastya went on to become a culture hero, especially in the south of India. Supposedly he is still living there, for at one time the Vindhya mountains kept on growing in rivalry with Mount Meru, until Agastya appeared on his way to the South and told them to stop growing "until I come back." He has not returned yet, for the Vindhyas are no higher than they were.[72] Agastya went on to bring brahmin culture to the South, and eventually set sail for the East Indies, where he sometimes is regarded as a kind of Adam.

The present story contains most of the legendary material of Agastya in Hinduism. The most striking features are his enormous powers of ingestion and digestion, illustrated by his eating and digesting the demon Vātāpi and the ocean (he is hardly rivaled by the sage Jahnu who once, when the Ganges disturbed his meditations, irately drank up the river, but later released the river through his ear), and his marriage to Lopāmudrā, the daughter of a king.

The *Ṛgveda*, in 1.179, has preserved a dialogue in which Lopāmudrā seduces Agastya to lie with her: "Many autumns have I slaved early and late, all the aging mornings long. Age changes the beauty of bodies

69. 3.83.88.

70. Cf. Agehananda Bharati, "Pilgrimage sites and Indian Civilization," *Chapters in Indian Civilization* 1 (Dubuque, 1970): 83.

71. Cf. Emil Sieg, *Die Sagestoffe des Veda und der Itihasatradition* (Stuttgart, 1902).

72. 3.102.

—will the the males never come to their wives? For whoever in time gone before observed the ordinance and conversed with the Gods about the ordinances, they too have stopped, for they did not reach their goal—will the wives now be united with their men?" Agastya remonstrates, but Lopāmudrā is insistent: " 'I have lust for the reluctant reed, whether it arises from this or from that!' Thus Lopāmudrā seduced her husband, the foolish woman sucked empty the sage, until he gasped."

Some of this prolific background is still discernible in *The Mahābhārata* version of Agastya's and Lopāmudrā's union. A celibate, Agastya, like Jaratkāru in *Āstīka*, is ordered by his ancestors to beget offspring. He finds himself a wife, but orders her to "the same vows and way of life as her husband," and they perform austerities in the Himālayas. Lopāmudrā's seduction is muted to a demand for a fine bed, clothes, and jewelry; but these without doubt are meant for their first cohabitation.

The rambling story takes us to the demon Ilvala with his novel method for killing his enemies, the battle of Indra and Vṛtra, the escape of the surviving demons in the sea, and Agastya drinking up the ocean. Finally there is the descent of the Ganges to purify the ashes of the 60,000 sons of King Sagara and to fill up the dry ocean bed. It is hard to think up a more imaginative tale.

Ṛśyaśṛnga

This charming, and at first sight inconsequential, story of an ascetic's son, borne by a doe that had drunk water fertilized by that ascetic, has had an astonishing later history. It is a simple tale: the boy grows up in the forest completely innocent of woman and is seduced by a princess who brings him to her father's palace; her purpose was to bring the rains back to her father's kingdom.

It was a popular story in India itself. The ancient Indians were fascinated by the theme of the "erotic ascetic,"[73] and this tale had the additional charm of a youth discovering all by himself, and in the terms of his limited knowledge of humankind, his first woman. Apart from *The Mahābhārata* it is found in *The Rāmāyaṇa*, the *Padma* and *Skanda Purāṇas*, several *Jātakas* and other Buddhist texts, and the Tibetan *Kanjur*.[74] The abundant textual evidence has made it possible to reconstruct the original form of the story, in which it was indeed the Princess Śāntā (also known as Nalinī) who seduced the innocent youth.[75]

73. I refer to Wendy Doniger O'Flaherty, *The Erotic Ascetic* (Oxford University Press, 1974).
74. See Heinrich Lüders, "Die Saga von Ṛṣyaśṛnga," *Nachrichte Göttingen Academy*, Phil.-hist. class, 1897, for references.
75. Lüders, op. cit.

But its history does not end there. Already in some of the Sanskrit texts Ṛśyaśṛnga, who has a single antelope horn growing from his forehead, in memory of his mother, is given the name Ekaśṛnga "One-Horn." It transpires that in his later vicissitudes, which were so fatefully inaugurated by the seductive princess, this ancient youth, known since the *Jaiminīya-Upaniṣad-Brāhmaṇa* of ca. 800 B.C., is the ancestor of the unicorn of European lore.

According to the evidence so fetchingly marshaled by Odell Shepard,[76] two different strains have gone into the making of the unicorn legend. One is the series of reports starting with that of Ctesias, physician to Darius II and Artaxerxes, of a fabulous one-horned beast living in India whose horn has medicinal properties and which in all likelihood derives from the Indian rhinoceros, Aristotle is aware of its existence, and Aelian puts it firmly on the map for the Middle Ages by his descriptions in his *Historia Animalium* 3.31.[77]

Side by side with the real animal, an object for zoologists and pharmacologists, there is another unicorn that, merging with the first one, became a matter for mythographers, allegorists, and theologians. This first appears in the Greek Bestiary named *Physiologus*, apparently collected and composed in Egypt in the second century A.D. It describes a series of fabulous animals whose properties are related allegorically to biblical figures.

On the unicorn it speaks as follows:

> Physiologus says about the unicorn that it has this trait: it is a small animal like a goat and it is very gentle; it has a horn in the middle of its head. No hunter can capture it, since it is so strong. How do they catch it? They bring forth a chaste virgin; and when it sees her, it comes to her breast, and she caresses the animal and warms it, and thus it is captured and shown in the palace of the king.[78]

This is allegorized to signify the Virgin Mary who gives suck to her child Jesus, who subsequently is killed, a far-fetched interpretation that nevertheless made a deep impression on the pious minds of the Middle Ages. The allegorization of the virgin and the unicorn atrophied from now on a more obvious erotic treatment. That the images originally were erotic is shown by a Syriac version, which reads:

> There is an animal called *Dajja*, extremely gentle, which the hunters are unable to capture because of its great strength. It has in the middle of its brow a single horn. But observe the ruse by which the huntsmen take it. They lead forth a young virgin, pure and chaste,

76. Odell Shepard, *The Lore of the Unicorn* (New York, 1967).
77. Shepard, pp. 26 ff.
78. Quoted from Francis J. Carmody, *Physiologus; the Very Ancient Book of Beast, Plants and Stones*, limited edition (San Francisco, 1953).

> to whom, when the animal sees her, he approaches, throwing himself upon her. Then the girl offers him her breasts, and the animal begins to suck the breasts of the maiden and to conduct himself familiarly with her. Then the girl, while sitting quietly, reaches forth her hand and grasps the horn on the animal's brow, and at this point the huntsmen come up and take the beast and go away with him to the king.—Likewise the Lord Christ has raised up for us a horn of salvation in the midst of Jerusalem, in the house of God, by the intercession of the Mother of God, a virgin pure, chaste, full of mercy, immaculate, inviolate.[79]

Shepard, with the sharp sensitivity that characterizes his study, remarks on the

> emphasis upon sexual attraction as the source of the power exercised by the virgin over the unicorn. If the virgin-capture story had been deliberately composed as a symbol of Christ's incarnation —such a supposition implying, of course, that the virgin was always and from the start understood to represent the Virgin Mary—it would scarcely have been corrupted by Christians in this [i.e., Syriac] way. . . . The Syriac version seems to represent an idea about the right method of capturing unicorns which is older than the *Physiologus*; it suggests a possibility that the origin of the virgin-capture story, if it can be found, will turn out to be non-Christian and will rest more obviously upon sexual attraction than the Christianized form of the story usually does[80]

The same author also quotes from the Hayāt al-Hayawān al-Kubra of the fourteenth-century Arab encyclopedist al-Damīrī to the effect that a virgin or beautiful girl is put in the way of the unicorn. He leaps in her lap making signs for milk, of which he is naturally very fond. After he has been suckled he lies down drunk, as though with wine, and at that moment the huntsmen dash forth and tie up the unresisting beast.[81]

Pursuing his personal quest for the source of the unicorn legend, Shepard finally comes to rest with the account given by Fray Luis[82] of the capture of the African rhinoceros. Hunters take a trained she-monkey and bring it to the rhinoceros. She prances before the beast, which loves that. She jumps on its back and scratches it, then rubs its belly till the animal stretches ecstatically on the ground. Then the hunters kill it.

I think that a better source can be found. It is sad, and in view of his meticulous research not a little surprising, that Shepard was not

79. Quoted from Shepard's translation (p. 49) of the Latin translation of J. P. N. Land, *Anecdota Syriaca* 4 (Leyden, 1870): 146.

80. Shepard, pp. 49–50.

81. Shepard, p. 64.

82. Fray Luis de Urreta, *Historia de los Grandes y Remotos Reynos de la Etopia, Monarchia del Emperador llamado Preste Iuan* (Valencia, 1610), pp. 245 ff.

aware of an 1897 article by Heinrich Lüders, "Die Sage von Ṛṣyaśṛnga" (as he spells the name). In this article the brilliant German scholar had argued in passing that indeed the story of Ṛśyaśṛnga is the non-Christian source that Shepard suspects and comes close to postulating. Lüders foregoes much detail and points out that Samuel Beal had footnoted: "The connection of this myth with the mediaeval story of the Unicorn being capable of capture only by a chaste woman is too evident to require proof."[83]

The connection deserves more than a footnote; a few additional remarks may be allowed. It is not a complete rarity that Indian materials are, so to say, converted to Christianity. The signal example is the story of Barlaam and Josaphat, saints whose feast day was celebrated on 2 November and who were duly glorified in the *Golden Legend*[84] of the Middle Ages. They made their first appearance in Greek in *Barlaam and Iosaph*, a work long attributed to Saint John Damascene, but in fact composed by Saint Euthymius (d. 1028), who lived on Mount Athos. His book goes back to the Arabic *Kitāb Bilāwhar wa Yudasāph*,[85] which goes back to legends told in Sogdian about Bodisaf (the error of *y* for *b* is an easy one: the Arabic *y* has two subscript dots, the *b* one), who is the Indian Bodhisattva. And indeed *Barlaam and Iosaph* tells the tale of the Bodhisattva's encounters with the world of suffering and his consequent enlightenment as the Buddha.

We do not have, alas, so tidy a sequence for the unicorn story, but the internal correspondences with the Ṛśyaśrnga saga are convincing enough. First of all, of course, there is the fact that both are unicorns. There is a considerable Indian background to the "single horn." A section of the Buddhist canonical text the Suttanipāta (1.3), the *Khaggavisānasutta*, "sūtra of the rhinoceros horn," describes the life of the solitary ascetic; every line ends with the exhortation, "let him wander alone like the rhinocerous horn."[86] One of the elders in the Theragāthā, "songs of the elders," describes himself as having a rhinoceros horn.[87] We have met the irascible Śṛngin, "the horned one," an ascetic who cursed King Parikṣit; it is said he was born from a cow (1.46.2), apparently to explain his name.

The underlying notion is that of aloneness. Horns normally come in pairs; a single horn, doing duty for both, transcends duality and betokens the conquest of total self-sufficiency; this is not unlike the third eye of Śiva in his forehead, and the *uṣṇīṣa*, cranial protuberance,

83. Samuel Beal, *Romantic Legend of Śākya Buddhism* (London, 1875), p. 124, n. 2, quoted by Lüders, p. 115, n. 1, where the title is to be corrected.

84. Jacobus de Voragine, *The Golden Legend.*

85. *Kitāb Bilāwhar wa Budāsf*, ed. Daniel Gimaret (Beyrouth, n.d.).

86. *Khaggavisāna* also means "rhinoceros."

87. Theragāthā.

of the Buddha. Likewise the salient feature of the European unicorn is its solitude and the fact that it is no more conquerable by the "huntsmen" than the ascetic is by the lures of sensual life. It is also the symbol of sovereign power. It is said of a king that "he became the one horn of the entire wide earth."[88] Still another use of the antelope horn is in the Soma Sacrifice, when such a horn is among the paraphernalia with which the sacrificer is invested at his consecration.[89] Finally it may be pointed out that the change of an ascetic into a deer (and one of the European visualizations of the unicorn is as part-stag) is also recorded: the deer that curses Pāṇḍu when that king shoots it when it is mating is really a seer who has changed himself into a deer for the good reason that he preferred their company over that of humans.[90]

From Ctesias onward India has been considered the homeland of the unicorn as a one-horned animal, noted for its belligerence, solitary habits, and invincibility, which is most likely the rhinoceros. When the story of the one-horned ascetic migrated, the idea of the one-horned beast was already so firmly planted that the two were fused; both had in common, besides their horn, the qualities of solitariness and uncapturability. But while the rhinoceros is ferocious, Ṛśyaśṛnga was gentleness itself; part of the unicorn lore from the beginning was that the animal is *gentle*. The point of the Ṛśyaśṛnga story is that the ascetic youth could after all be seduced; this vulnerability was in turn transferred to the rhinoceros, as in the African account. Hence the curious construction that a horned animal is captivated by a human maiden. Since there apparently are no female unicorns, it is clear that the maiden originally was his mate, when he was a man.

Where did the notion that its captress should be a virgin come from? Again, this was likely to be an Indian trait. *The Mahābhārata* account of the story leaves the seducing to a courtesan. While Lüders appears to be right in showing that the princess originally was the seductress, our version keeps her implicitly virginal. Once the story of a fabulous, chaste, gentle, one-horned animal was received in Christian circles, its virgin-captress was inevitably identified with the Virgin Mary and the fabulous animal so innocently killed no less inevitably with Christ. And so Ṛśyaśṛnga, led by the maiden into the palace of the king, began his incredible European career. Who would have imagined that our gentle horned ascetic would end up in the British coat of arms?

With rather less assurance one last remark may be made. One of the powers of the unicorn is that it can make innocuous any mixture

88. Cf. 1.89.39.
89. W. Caland and Victor Henry, *L'agniṣṭoma* (Paris, 1906–7).
90. *MBh.* 1.109.27.

of poison;[91] for that reason unicorn horn was much prized at the courts of the Renaissance. In one Greek version of the *Bestiary* it is related that "when the animals assemble at evening beside the great water to drink they find that a serpent has left its venom floating on the surface. . . . They see or smell this venom and dare not drink, but wait for the unicorn. At last he comes, steps into the water, makes the sign of the cross over it with its horn and thereby renders the poison harmless."[92] This may perhaps be connected with the episode of the conception of the Indian unicorn. Ṛśyaśṛnga's father-to-be at the sight of an Apsarā involuntarily spills his semen, which is mixed with the water of the great lake in which he was bathing. A deer, herself a divine maiden under a curse, drinks the semen with the water and (conceptions through the mouth being not uncommon) becomes pregnant with Ṛśyaśṛnga. In a somewhat parallel fashion we have here two liquids, semen and water instead of poison and water, that combine and are made as one, and the aberrant liquid is ingested auspiciously. But it does not do to insist on this coincidence: the career of Ṛśyaśṛnga has already been marvelous enough.

Kārtavīrya

Kārtavīrya is really the story of Rāma, son of Jamadagni, known, not yet in the epic but in later literature, as Paraśurāma, Rāma-with-the-Axe, and then elevated to an incarnation of the God Viṣṇu. In the epic he is a brahmin, but a peculiar one, since he is a fighting brahmin. Our story tries to explain this switch in roles from a brahmin to a baron: his mother Reṇukā received a boon for herself and her own mother that both would conceive sons if Reṇukā would embrace an *udumbara* tree and her mother an *aśvattha*. They mix up the trees, and hence Reṇukā would have a son who, though a brahmin, would act as a baron, and her mother a baron who would act like a brahmin. The latter is the famous Viśvāmitra, the only one in the annals of Indian lore it seems who changed his class.[93] Upon hearing this prediction Reṇukā demurs and asks that her son Jamadagni's son act the baron, and this Rāma was destined to do.

It is interesting that the text feels the need for justification; it did not feel so in the case of the other fighting brahmins, Kṛpa and Droṇa. No doubt it was the scale of Rāma's martial exploits that inspired the need: he destroyed the baronage twenty-one times over. If one wonders how this is possible, *The Book of the Beginning* provides

91. This rises in part from the medicinal properties ascribed to rhinoceros horn.
92. Shepard, p. 60.
93. In *ŚatBr*, 11.6.2.10 King Janaka is called a brahmin by way of honorific, tantamount to the epic's *rājarṣi*.

the answer: the barons' wives survived their slain men, and every time begot a new generation of barons by brahmins.

It is not easy to decide exactly what to think of the wholesale slaughter of the baronage by a brahmin. It is out of the question to take this literally, as though some struggle over territorial power had taken place between the brahmin and the warrior classes. There are accounts of friction between the classes. It is of interest to note that Rāma is a Bhṛgu. According to the story of *Aurva*, the descendants of King Kṛtavīrya (*i.e.*, Kārtavīryas), envious of the riches amassed by the Bhṛgus who refused to surrender them, started massacring the Bhṛgus when they found a cache of wealth.[94] The Bhṛgu Aurva survives and threatens to destroy the world in revenge. In this story of Rāma we have the same structure: the son of Kṛtavīrya kills the Bhṛgu Jamadagni, and Rāma decides to kill off the baronage. What transpires from the two parallel accounts is a local conflict (Kārtavīrya was "king of the shorelands"[95]) between the heirs of this king and a group of Bhṛgus who had formerly been under the patronage of and enriched by the king.

But surely there is more to it. The exploits of Rāma (and the threatened disaster of Aurva) could hardly have assumed such a scale if there had been no sense that the old baronage had by and large disappeared. This seems to be the message of Kṛṣṇa in *The Book of the Assembly Hall*: "That which is *now* called the baronage was born *after* the baronage that *Rāma Jāmadagnya left as a remnant*. The barons on earth have determined their lineage *by the authority their words carry*" (emphasis mine). This seems to mean that the old baronage had disappeared (again as the result of Rāma's massacre), and that a new, *soi-disant* baronage had sprung up that was self-legitimizing. What may have happened therefore is that an old account of friction between Bhṛgus and barons, in which the latter were somehow worsted, was interpreted as the cause of the disappearance of the ancient baronage. For the brahmins survived as a class, while the barons did not.

In the epic as a whole Rāma is an ancient figure. Right at the beginning he has retired: he has given away everything he owns and has only his life and his weapons left; Droṇa receives the weapons.[96] Elsewhere his massacre is placed at the junction of the Tretā and Dvāpara ages,[97] just as the Bhārata battle takes place at the junction of the Dvāpara and Kali ages. In the present story he is an ancient seer, possibly dead, who makes an appearance on a mountain at the

94. 1(11.b.i).169 ff.
95. 3.118.19.
96. 1.121.16 ff.
97. 1.2.3.

junctions of the month. There are levels of antiquity that the epic recollection recognizes; a similar instance is the extreme old age of Hanūmān who declares that he belongs to a previous age.[98] The saga of Nara and Nārāyaṇa seems to be still older.

Rāma in *Kārtavīrya* appears as a dutiful son who blindly obeys his father even when he orders him to kill his own mother. It points up once more the total ascendancy that the father had over the mother: it was oracled to Duḥṣanta that "the mother is the father's water sack,"[99] in other words a convenient receptacle for his semen to beget a son. He has also complete dominion over his sons. Just as Yayāti curses his sons because they refuse to obey the unreasonable demand to assume their father's senility,[100] so Jamadagni curses his sons because they refuse to kill their mother. Like Yayāti's compliant son Pūru, Rāma is the fifth and youngest son.

Sukanyā

The story of how Cyavana, whom we saw being born in *Puloman*,[101] was rejuvenated in extreme old age by the Aśvins, to whom he in return granted the privilege of drinking the Soma at the sacrifice, is as old as *The Ṛgveda*.[102] *The Śatapatha Brāhmaṇa* (ca. 800 B.C.) has a full account,[103] which may be entered here for purposes of comparison. "When the Bhṛgus or the Angirases," reads this *Brāhmaṇa*, "attained to the world of heaven, Cyavana, the Bhārgava or Āngirasa was left here, worn out and witchlike. Śaryāta now wandered by with his tribe.[104] He settled down there neighboring him. His sons at play, holding the worn-out and witchlike man for worthless, pelted him with clods of earth. He got angry at the Śāryātas. He brought disharmony to them—father fought with son, brother with brother. Śaryāta thought, 'This has befallen because I have done something.' He had the cowherds and shepherds called together and said, 'Who has seen anything here today?' They said, 'There lies this worn-out and witchlike man. Your sons, holding him for worthless, have pelted him with clods of earth.' He knew he was Cyavana. Yoking his chariot and placing Sukanyā, daughter of Śaryāta, on it, he drove out. He went where that seer was. He said, 'Seer, homage to you. I gave hurt because I did not know. I tender this Sukanyā to atone to you. Let my tribe be in harmony.' Henceforth his tribe was in harmony. Thereupon

98. 3.148.5 ff.
99. 1.69.29.
100. 1.79.
101. 1.6.
102. *ṚV*. 1.116.10; 117.13; 118.6; 5.74.5; 7.68.6; 71.5; 10.39.4.
103. *ŚatBr*. 4.1.5.1. ff.
104. The word used is *grāma*, later "village," with original connotations of "cattle."

Śaryāta the Mādhava went off, thinking, 'Let me not harm him again.'

"The two Aśvins wandered about healing. They came up to Sukanyā and sought to lie with her. She did not consent. They said to her, 'Sukanyā, why do you lie with this worn-out and witchlike man? Obtain the two of us!' She said, 'I shall not desert while he lives the one to whom my father gave me.' The seer knew of this. He said, 'Sukanyā, what have those two said to you?' She told it to him. Informed, he said to her, 'If they talk to you again, you must tell them, "You yourselves are not all whole nor all perfect. Yet you despise my husband!" If they may say to you, "In what way are we not whole, in what way not perfect?" you tell them, "First make my husband young again, then I shall tell you." '

"They came to her again and talked the same. She said, 'You yourselves are not all whole nor all perfect, yet you despise my husband!' They said, 'In what way are we not whole and perfect?' She said, 'First make my husband young again, then I shall tell you.' They said, 'Bring him to this pond. He shall come out with the age which he covets.' She brought him to that pond, and he came out with the age he coveted. They said, 'Sukanyā, in what way are we not whole and perfect?' The seer replied to them, 'Yonder Gods are performing a sacrifice in Kurukṣetra. They exclude you from the sacrifice, therefore you are not whole and perfect.'

"Thereupon the Aśvins left and went to the Gods performing the sacrifice while the *bahiṣpavamāna sāman*[105] was sung. They said, 'Invite us in!' The Gods said, 'We shall not invite you in! You have been wandering much and closely among men healing them.' They said, 'You are sacrificing with a headless sacrifice!' 'How is it headless?'[106] 'First invite us in, then we shall tell.' Agreeing, they invited them. They drew for them the Aśvin draught."

It is instructive to note the changes that have been made, but it is more important to note how little has altered in the essentials of the story—and at least half a millenium must have passed between *The Śatapatha* version and *The Mahābhārata* one.

In *The Śatapatha* account the principal point of the story is to explain the presence at the Soma sacrifice of a *graha*, a Soma cup, dedicated to the Aśvins, and how the Aśvins, fairly lowly and easily polluted deities who "wander much and closely among men," came to be invited to partake of the Soma. This cup has been preserved in *The Mahābhārata* story, but no reader would suspect that this element is the entire point of the tale. Another ancient detail has been updated. *The Śatapatha Brāhmaṇa* can still speak of a nomad king and his tribe and herd finally settling down in a permanent location; for *The*

105. The chant sung at the first Soma pressing.
106. On this notion see J. A. B. van Buitenen, *The Pravargya* (Poona, 1968).

Mahābhārata's audience this surely would have been unintelligible, and the king and his nomads become four thousand women and an armed escort on an outing. It is not the king's sons who pester the sage Cyavana, but Sukanyā the princess herself. This rationalizes that Sukanyā is offered Cyavana by way of reparation. In *The Śatapatha* version the king offers her spontaneously; in *The Mahābhārata* version Cyavana asks for her, as he also does in another old version found in *The Jaiminīya Brāhmaṇa*;[107] in the latter the king declines a few times.

Why the king's people should have been stricken with constipation instead of internal dissension I am at a loss to explain. It is an odd form of punishment, to be sure.

Again, *The Mahābhārata* has in common with *The Jaiminīya* that the Aśvins and Cyavana appear identical and that Sukanyā must choose her husband; *The Jaiminīya* makes it easy for the woman, for Cyavana gives her a sign. The motif is of course the same as in the story of *Nala*, when the four gods assume the same form as Nala.

Māndhātar

There is little to be remarked about the story of *Māndhātar*, an ancient king and son of the Cakravartin Yuvanāśva. We note once more the ubiquitousness of the Bhṛgu brahmins in this series of tales of *The Forest*. It is as though we are not to be allowed to forget that *The Mahābhārata* is recounted in the Naimiṣa Forest to brahmins who are presided over by Śaunaka, himself a Bhṛgu. In general, if Lomaśa's stories have anything in common it is the celebration of the brahmin, his austerities, his rituals, and his power.

The old sacerdotal mentality comes through clearly in the "conception" of Māndhātar. When King Yuvanāśva by accident drinks the water consecrated with a *brahman* (*i.e.*, rite and incantation) to make the king's wife pregnant, biological law must make room for the superseding law of the rite, and the king himself becomes pregnant. We are still in the atmosphere of unbridled optimism of the *Brāhmaṇa* period in which anything whatever can be accomplished by the power of the brahmin and his *brahman*.

Jantu

The same spirit of confidence in the efficacy of ritual breathes in the story of *Jantu*, but at the same time a question of ethics is raised. When King Somaka has but one son by his one hundred wives he complains to his priest, who assures him that he can perform a rite that will produce a hundred sons, but it will require the immolation of

107. *JaimBr.* 3.121–28.

the one son. Somaka consents unhesitatingly, and the son is sacrificed amidst the wailing of his mothers. One hundred sons are duly born.

But the priest dies and is cast in a boiling hell for having sacrificed a human being. Somaka dies and is shocked to see his priest in hell. He insists with God Dharma that he himself burn in hell and the priest be set free, for the priest has been his agent. When that is impossible—"No one ever experiences another's fruit"—Somaka refuses to accept his own blessed worlds, and spends the same term in hell with his priest. The moral is clear: the ritual is all-powerful, but a line must be drawn against harmful magic. There was the same hesitation to produce a killer-son when Drupada went about searching for a priest who would help produce a son who would be able to kill Droṇa.[108]

The Hawk and the Dove

This story of King Sibi, already celebrated for his liberality in *The Latter Days of Yayāti*,[109] is a famous one in India. It has been suggested that since the Buddhists set so much store by generosity, the Śibi story is of Buddhist provenance. The conclusion is not urgent, for we find the same high value placed upon generous giving in Hinduism too, and it is more prudent to say that this value is all-Indian, irrespective of religious persuasion.

A comparable story of Śibi's generosity occurs in the Buddhist canon, *The Sivirājacariyam* ("The Feat of King Sivi [= Śibi]"),[110] found in *The Cariyāpiṭaka* ("Text of Feats"), which is part of *The Khuddakanikāya* ("Body of Short Portions") of *The Suttanipāta*, the first of the three divisions of the canon; it has been elaborated, among others, in the Pāli *Jātakas* (number 499) and in Āryaśūra's Sanskrit *Jātakamālā* (II).

I give here a translation of the canonical Buddhist Pāli version. The Bodhisattva is talking of past lives.

> In the city called Ariṭṭha I was a baron called Sivi. Sitting in my beautiful palace I thought, "There is no human gift that I have not given. If anyone asks for my eye, I shall give it cheerfully." Knowing my intention, Sakka [= Śakra or Indra], the lord of the Gods, who was sitting in the Gods' assembly, spoke this word: "Seated in his beautiful palace the very wealthy King Sivi, while reflecting on various gifts, does not see what cannot be given. Well, I shall investigate whether it is true or false. I shall go for a while, until I know his mind."

108. 1.155.
109. 1.88.17.
110. Ed. Bimala Churn Law (Poona, 1949).

He became a trembling, gray-headed, wrinkled, ailing, and blind-appearing man and approached the king. He stretched forth his left and right arms, and making the *añjali* gesture on his head he spoke this word: "Great king, law-abiding prosperer of the realm, I beg you. Your fame of devoted giver has risen among the Gods and men. Both my eyes have been stricken blind. Give me one eye, and live with one yourself."

Hearing his word I was happy and excited. I made the *añjali* and, delighted, spoke this word: "Having pondered today you have come here from your palace. Knowing my thought you have come to beg my eye. Aho! my intention has been accomplished, my desire fulfilled. Today I shall give the beggar a supreme gift never given before." [*Addressing his physician:*] "Come, Sīvaka, rise up! Do not tarry, do not tremble! Tear out both my eyes and give them to the beggar." Thus exhorted, Sīvaka did what I said. He pulled out my eyes like the pith of a palm and gave them to the beggar. When I gave the gift, my mood did not change—it was the cause of insight. My eyes were not hateful to me, my self was not hateful to me, but omniscience is dear to me, therefore I have given away my eyes.

Aṣṭāvakra

After the brief interruption of the story of the baron Śibi, brahmin power is once more the theme in the story of *Aṣṭāvakra*. It is a most interesting example of the *brahmodya*, a statement on the *brahman* or sacred erudition, which often takes the form of a contest. *The Brāhmaṇas* and *Upaniṣads* are quite full of such contests, quite frequently with a prize attached to them, as in *Śatapatha Brāhmaṇa* (11.6.2), where Yājñavalkya after such a contest walks off with a thousand cows, which King Janaka had put up as a prize.

In the story the same King Janaka, whom the *Brāhmaṇa* calls a brahmin (11.6.2.10), had at his court an expert riddler, Bandin, who defeated all brahmin contestants, but himself was of the *sūta*, charioteer-panegyrist, class. When he had defeated a rival, he drowned him in the sea. It turns out that his purpose is not cruel but helpful: his father Varuṇa, the God of the Ocean, is engaged in a sacrifice, and his son thus sends him his priests. One such, a defeated and drowned riddler, is Aṣṭāvakra's father Kahoḍa. When Aṣṭāvakra hears the truth about his father's death he goes to Janaka's court with his contemporary Śvetaketu, son of the famed Uddālaka who was Aṣṭāvakra's maternal grandfather. With some difficulty he gains entrance to challenge Bandin. King Janaka rather doubts the boy's erudition and engages him in some riddles of his own and is satisfied; he allows him to challenge Bandin. The contest in *brahmodyas*, or riddles on *brahman*, takes the form that each has to list entities that come in the same number. Bandin starts out with number one, Aṣṭāvakra follows suit with number two, Bandin replies with number three, and so on. Bandin makes it up to twelve, but falters when he reaches fourteen. Aṣṭāvakra accuses him of multiple brahmin-murder and orders him to be drowned. The previously drowned priests reemerge.

The series of entities are replete with ancient Vedic lore. It is a contest but in deadly earnest. One is reminded of the Upaniṣadic threat that a person's head shall burst if he does not know the answer to the enigma that is placed before him, or asks too much.[111]

Yavakrīta

The story of *Yavakrīta* is a different kind of contest but in the same realm of Vedic erudition. It is an intriguing account of the rivalry between Vedic brahmins and ascetics. Yavakrīta notices that his father Bharadvāja, being an ascetic and apparently not a brahmin, does not receive the honor that his brahmin friend Raibhya (known as an ancient teacher to *The Bṛhadāraṇyaka Upaniṣad*[112]) and his sons receive. Out of spite Yavakrīta performs austerities to acquire the *Vedas* by a shortcut, without spending many years with a guru. Indra makes several attempts to warn him off, but eventually gives in before the other's ascetic power and grants him the *Veda*. His father warns him not to fall prey to pride and insult brahmins like Raibhya who have acquired the *Veda* in the regular fashion.

Yavakrīta pays no heed and rapes Raibhya's daughter. Incensed, Raibhya creates a demon out of a strand of hair offered into the fire to kill Yavakrīta, as he does. In revenge his father curses Raibhya to be killed by his son.

The contest is a stand-off and has perhaps never been decided. The tension between *dharma* brahminism on the one hand and renunciatory asceticism on the other runs throughout the history of Indian civilization, the one maintaining the necessity of social order with all the regulations of the Law that governs it, the other maintaining the primacy of individual liberation and the relinquishment of all social duties. The stakes are hardly so high in the story of *Yavakrīta*, but the conflict has been engaged.

The Slaying of Jaṭāsura

The generally peaceable tenor of the Pāṇḍavas' forest life, with the visits of saints who tell their edifying tales and Yudhiṣṭhira's tour of sacred places, is interrupted by a more baronial tale of prowess and

111. E.g., *Bṛhad-āraṇyaka-upanniṣad* 3.7.1.
112. *BĀUp.* (Mādhyaṃdina) 2.5.20; 4.5.26.

violence, *The Slaying of Jaṭāsura*. It is a fairly routine Rākṣasa story, which serves to remind us that the forest is not only the tranquil domain of saints but the terrifying haunt of demons.

It has some interesting features. Usually when a Rākṣasa battle takes place, the demon is provoked by what he considers an outrageous intrusion into his territory;[113] after all, even demons must have a place to live. In the story of Jaṭāsura, however, the Rākṣasa has been living, disguised as a brahmin, with the Pāṇḍavas, his covetous eyes on their weapons. In this he has some affinity with Rāvaṇa of *The Rāmāyaṇa*, who also was disguised as a brahmin and bent on abduction.

Of interest is his name: the Asura with the ascetic braid. We see the beginning here of a tendency manifest in later narrative literature of attributing class to Rākṣasas, a particularly dangerous variety being the *brahmarākṣasa*, the brahmin-Rākṣasa. By now the Pāṇḍavas have shed all their fears of these ogres of the forest, witness Yudhiṣṭhira's cool and condescending scolding of Jaṭāsura. Bhīma had earlier recognized the demon for what he was, but had not bothered about him; now he dispatches him smoothly. There is something perfunctory about the appearances of Rākṣasas, as, it is true, there is about the comings and goings of saints. They both belong in the forest and can scarcely be avoided.

The War of the Yakṣas

If the grand Asuras, the anti-Gods of the Vedic period, in the course of history were reduced to bogey men, quite another fate was destined for the Asura Vṛṣaparvan. We have met him in the story of *Yayāti*[114] as the king of the Asuras, who were embattled in a deadly war with the Gods over the power of immortality. *The Assembly Hall* refers to him as an Asura king from the remote past, in whose palace, far north, the precious building materials are stored that Maya needs to build Yudhiṣṭhira's great hall.[115] Here Vṛṣaparvan, surely the same figure,[116] is provided with his own hermitage located at the northernmost point that humans can reach.

During the Pāṇḍavas' visit with him, Draupadī once more sends Bhīma off in quest of *saugandhika* flowers. In his first encounter he got embroiled with Rākṣasas; in the present one with Yakṣas, which is indeed more appropriate, for Kubera, whose playgrounds he violates, is the king of the Yakṣas, who are generally portrayed as genial leprechauns. One has the impression that the present story is a recast

113. Typical instances are Hiḍimba and Baka, *MBh.* 1(9) and (10) 1:294 ff.
114. *MBh.* 1(7.c) 1:171 ff.
115. *MBh.* 2(20), above p. 36.
116. Sörensen in his index distinguishes them.

of the first one: it corrects the "mistake" of introducing Rākṣasas where Yakṣas ought to roam and play—although Kubera does have genealogical connections with the Rākṣasas.[117] It also provides a rationalizing explanation of Kubera's inexplicable benevolence toward Bhīma, who in fact had been devastating his parks. The narrator of the second version felt that some reason was in order; he provides it with the usual power *ex machina*, a curse: by his killing of Maṇimat and harassing of the Yakṣas Bhīma unwittingly sets free the God of riches from a curse by Agastya.

Tucked away in *The War of the Yakṣas* is the important event of the return of Arjuna, who had been whiling away the last five years in Indra's heaven. One of Arjuna's adventures there was his battle with the demons called Nivātakavacas. As we noted before, the story of this battle is basically the same as that described in *The Razing of Saubha*.[118] Saubha was the aerial city of Śālva, which could move from Dvārakā on the Arabian Sea to Assam in the far northeast in hardly any time at all. In *Saubha* it was Kṛṣṇa who was mainly embattled with the demons. Kṛṣṇa finds the flying city by the sea, Arjuna does likewise. Both Kṛṣṇa and Arjuna first kill off many demons. Śālva causes Kṛṣṇa to hallucinate and have visions of his father; he panics but rallies; Arjuna too knows panic, but rallies soon. In both accounts there are rains of rock that threaten to bury the heroes alive, but they regain the initiative and finally each destroys the city.

I called the story of Saubha early science fiction and I find myself somewhat disappointed that Erich von Däniken has not made a more imaginative use of it in his *Erinnerungen an die Zukunft*,[119] which, under the English title *Chariots of the Gods?*, is at present enjoying a remarkable popularity in this country. What an opportunity to show that mankind did not always meekly obey, learn from, and pay homage to those ancient astronauts who brought reason, civilization, and whatnot to a primitive earth. Here we have an account of a hero who took these visiting astronauts for what they were: intruders and enemies. The aerial city is nothing but an armed camp with flame-throwers and thundering cannon, no doubt a spaceship. The name of the demons is also revealing: they were Nivātakavacas, "clad in airtight armor," which can hardly be anything but spacesuits. It is heartening to know that sometime in the hoary past a man stood up and destroyed the spaceship and aborted its mission with bow and arrow.

117. Cf. below 2.258 f.

118. *MBh.* (31.a), p. 253.

119. Econ-Verlag GmbH, 1968; Souvenir Press, London, 1969; the author quotes *The Mahābhārata*, to which he generously ascribes an antiquity of five thousand years.

The Fish

The earliest occurrence of the Indian version of the legend of the Flood is found in *The Śatapatha Brāhmaṇa* (1.8.1). It reads there: "In the morning they brought Manu water to wash up, just as nowadays they bring water for washing the hands. While he was washing thoroughly, a fish fell into his hands. It said to him: 'If you support me, I shall save you.' 'From what will you save me?' 'A flood shall wash away all these creatures. I shall save you from that.' 'How am I to support you?' It said, 'As long as we are little, there is much that can destroy us. Fish eats fish. You should keep me at first in a little jar. When I grow out of it, you should dig a hole and keep me in there. When I grow out of that, you should take me to the ocean. Then I shall be past destruction.' Eventually it became a sea monster, for that grows the largest. 'In such and such year the flood will come. Build a ship and wait for me. When that flood has risen, embark on that ship, then I shall rescue you.'

"Having kept it in this fashion, he took it to the ocean. In the year it had predicted, he built the ship and waited. When the flood rose, he embarked. The fish came swimming up, and he tied a noose from the ship to its horn. By means of this he coursed quickly to the Northern Mountain. It said, 'I have saved you. Moor the ship at a tree. The water must not cut you off while on the mountain. As the water recedes you may make your way down.' By and by he made his way down. Hence that side of the Northern Mountain is 'Manu's Descent.' That flood washed away all creatures.

"In a desire for offspring he practiced worship and austerity." Manu subsequently offers up a sacrifice, and from it a woman is born and creation begins anew.

In the treatments of the theme of the Flood it is always tacitly assumed that the Mesopotamian accounts are the source not only of the biblical legend but also of the Indian one. The reason is probably the immense antiquity we unconsciously attribute to the ancient Near East. But in fact these accounts are not really all that old. The Flood episode of the Gilgamesh epic, in Assyrian cuneiform, dates from the seventh century B.C. Other Mesopotamian versions are younger. Of the two versions that are fused in the Genesis account, the Yahweh version and the Priestly one, the former dates from the eighth century, the latter from the sixth.

The date of *The Śatapatha Brāhmaṇa* as a whole must antedate the sixth century, and there is of course no telling the real age of its component stories. There is, indeed, archaeological evidence for recurrent heavy floods in Mesopotamia between 4000 and 2800 B.C. and many see in those floods the occasion of the Flood legend. But there is also mounting evidence[120] that heavy flooding contributed to the downfall of the Indus Valley civilization, so that, by the same token, there is at least the possibility open that the legend originated in India. The matter cannot be decided definitely, and for the time being we should keep Manu in the distinguished company of Ut-Napishtim and Noah.

In the end it does not gravely matter what company Manu kept transculturally but what he left to his own culture. Compared with the Mesopotamian versions the Indian emphasis has not been on the man that survived the Flood, but on the agency that was indispensable for his survival. God in India was placed in the water that threatened the continuity of mankind. There are no birds that scout the earth for man, there is the fish that simply takes him home. While many cultures have the end of the world as either a fire or a flood, or both, India has both,[121] and as standard practice: worlds go continually through a redeath and rebirth. The man, Manu, was not important himself, as both Ut-Napishtim and Noah are; he is the flotsam of cosmic continuity. The continuity itself was vested elsewhere.

With its ritual sequel *The Śatapatha Brāhmaṇa* illustrates where this continuity was anchored: in the ritual, viz., the *Iḍā* offering, personified as Manu's Daughter; this continuity could easily have been generalized as the *brahman*, the trinity of rite, spell, and person, that was more and more seen as a God Brahmā, the ever-active creator; *The Mahābhārata* account of the Fish has no trouble whatever to call it Brahmā, and this Brahmā has no hesitation whatever to let Manu do his creating by means of ritual acts.

But *brahman* as Brahmā has lost some of his creativity. In a striking parallel with the Gilgamesh account, *The Mahābhārata* version has Manu take "the seeds of all creatures."[122] Could it be that those seeds were never lost, that they germinally survived in the being that has always led man from cosmos to cosmos? Here the eschatology that Mārkaṇḍeya narrates[123] comes into focus. After the ultimate conflagration, the Fire of Doomsday, the Ekpyrosis, which Mārkaṇḍeya like another Manu survives, the rains and floods come and render earth one vast ocean, and desolately he roams the vast desolation—a Manu without the need for an ark, but in search of his fish. He finds it in form of a child sitting in a banyan tree—the tree to which the fish piloted Manu?—the tree whose branches are roots. Inside the

120. R. C. Raikes, "The End of the Ancient Cities of the Indus," *American Anthropology*, 1964; "The Mohenjo Daro Floods," *Antiquity* 40, 1965.

121. Cf. Markaṇḍeya's account, below, p. 585 ff.

122. Tablet XI, line 27, translated in James B. Pritchard, ed., *Ancient Near Eastern Texts Relating to the Old Testament* (Princeton University Press, 1956): "Aboard the ship take thou the seed of all living things."

123. Below, p. 589 ff.

child[124] Mārkaṇḍeya explores the worlds in all their variety, and these "worlds" are of course nothing but their own seeds.

The ultimate celebration of this agency of renewal is the transmogrification—but how gradual—of the divine instrument of survival into the person of Nārāyaṇa, who sleeps in the ocean till a new dawn, tucked into the coils of the snake Ananta—the Serpent Eternal. From Nārāyaṇa's navel—the beginning of life—grows the lotus, symbol of the new, water-borne purity, in which the old Brahmā takes shape, and renewal has happened. Since Nārāyaṇa is the prototype of Kṛṣṇa, and Kṛṣṇa is Viṣṇu come to earth, and Viṣṇu has come to earth in his various *avatāras*, who is the fish in the end but an incarnation of Viṣṇu? And here, then, does the story of *The Fish* come to its close as the completed chronicle of the first of the God's ten *avatāras*.

Wherever the Flood legend came from, India has done well by it. The Fish in the end stands at the beginning of the redemptive renewals of the world by God's intervention that spells hope upon hope for all that lives.

Angiras

"The blessed lord God Guha is a complete mystery: he is said to be the son of Fire, or the Pleiads, or Rudra, or the Ganges,"[125] exclaims Duryodhana when the parentage of Karṇa is called into question. The story of *Angiras* offers sufficient illustration for the reasons of his puzzlement. Guha is a God of many names, and the name that Duryodhana aptly uses ("the mysterious one") is one of the less common ones. From the point of view of his sonhood he is Kumāra, the "Boy-child"; as son of Rudra he seems to be Skanda, the "Hopper"; as son of the Pleiads (*kṛttikāḥ*) he is Kārttikeya; he is also known as Subrahmaṇya, the "one of brahminic interests," as Ṣaṇmukha, the "six-faced one," and finally as Murugan, the name he bears in the South of India.

It has been argued, plausibly though not cogently, that this "God of war" indeed hails from the South; in any case he leaps suddenly into view, albeit that *The Mahābhārata* account, the oldest in Sanskrit, with all the various origins it attempts to combine, knows nothing of a southern one.

The most striking aspect of Kumāra's myth is the devious way in which he is born. The most persistent trait is that he is the son of Fire, and if fatherhood is claimed for Rudra-Śiva it is conceded that this God had assumed the guise of Fire. While his father is fairly well

124. This motif, also found in *The Bhagavadgītā* 11.7, has remained a popular part of the mythology of the child Kṛṣṇa.

125. *MBh.* 1.127.10, 1:281.

established, he has a surfeit of mothers. The first, "real" mother is Svāhā, the personification of a sacrificial call, *svāhā!*, cried at certain oblations. This word, though an interjection, can be interpreted as a feminine noun, and its exclusive association with the sacrificial fire apparently encouraged the idea of a romance between Svāhā and Fire. This Fire itself seems to be the primordial fire, fetched to earth by the primeval Seven Seers from the sun when it stood in conjunction with the moon at the Hour of Rudra.[126] Fire falls in love with the chaste wives of the Seven Seers, and the lovesick Svāhā assumes the shape of six of these wives—Arundhatī excepted—to coax out Fire's semen. She collects the spilling and takes it to the mountain Śveta in the shape of a Garuḍa bird; from the six portions of semen Kumāra takes shape, in effect without benefit of mother, and thus joins latterly the procession of great men who have assuredly fathers but hardly a mother.[127]

There are, however, quite a few candidates for honorary motherhood. Svāhā reveals herself eventually. The six wives of the Seven Seers, cursed by their husbands under suspicion of adultery, claim Kumāra as their son. And, most interestingly, for the first time there appears a band of demoniac Mothers, who beseech Kumāra to accept their motherhood. Obviously there were more stories: the motherhood of the Ganges, in which, according to parallel accounts of the myth, Śiva poured his seed, is not recorded in *The Mahābhārata*; nor is the reed bed that elsewhere figures in his conception-and-birth. Most notably absent from *The Mahābhārata* story is Pārvatī, the "daughter of the mountain" (surely the mountain Śveta where Fire's seed was collected), who in the end will be the only, official, mother of this motherless child of the many mothers.

The Mahābhārata, with all its interest in paternity, is largely indifferent to motherhood. Rare are the passages where the mother reveals herself as the loving nurse or makes any demands on her sons.[128] After having made herself useful as a wife by becoming a mother, the woman seems to recede from view. This feature makes the press of prospective mothers to Kumāra quite unusual and not easily explained. Whether or not Kumāra was an adaption of the Dravidian war god Murugan, his presence in the mythology of *The Mahābhārata* is an alien one. There is the strange notion that *a God is born*. Incarnations of Gods are legion, but the birth of a completely *new* God is unique. It is perhaps this uniqueness that made the myth

126. The Rudra is the first of the 30 "hours" (*muhūrta*) of 48 minutes in which the date is divided.

127. E.g., Droṇa, born from a trough; Kṛpa, from a reed stalk; Agastya, from a jar.

128. When Kuntī asks a favor of Bhīma, she is immediately reprimanded by Yudhiṣṭhira, *MBh.* 1.150.5 ff., 1:310.

clamor for a mother. *The Mahābhārata* version obviously has not sorted out who should be the right mother of this new God—it is at least a little clearer about his father. The mother candidates are, to say the least, odd. The six seer wives might be explained as inspired by the six faces of Kumāra. Inasmuch as their husbands, the Seven Seers, are also a constellation, their wives too might well have come to be considered a star cluster; Vasiṣṭha's uninvolved wife Arundhatī was already a star. Thus they become the Pleiads and replace the star Abhijit, which had dropped out of the firmament.

It is remarkable that as soon as there appears a procession of semidivine mothers the demoniac aspect of numinous motherhood manifests itself too. They are the Mothers, a kind of female counterpart to the Fathers, the Pitaras, the Deceased Ancestors, who are kept appeased by oblations and, of course, the begetting of sons. Here the Mothers with their Graspers are quite similar to the present village goddesses like Śitalā, Mārī, and so on, who are appeased to ward off children's diseases,[129] and to whom in South India offerings are brought at crossroads in very much the same manner as Cārudatta orders his buffoon to do in *The Little Clay Cart*.[130]

By the time of Kālidāsa Kumāra's parental parentage has been sorted out.[131] The "mother," that is really the woman whose love causes Śiva to spill his seed, is Pārvatī, the Daughter of the Mountain on which Śiva himself has his seat. And she will be the Goddess par excellence, benign but also destructive, under whom the Mothers can be subsumed.

Rāma

The relationship between the story of *Rāma* in *The Mahābhārata* and *The Rāmāyaṇa* of Vālmīki has over the years received a considerable amount of attention. Nevertheless, the question is still moot because the answers diverge widely.

Albrecht Weber, writing in 1870,[132] lists four ways in which the relationship between the two versions can be viewed: 1. the story of *Rāma* is the source of *The Rāmāyaṇa* (*Rām.*); 2. *Rāma* is an abridgement of an older, now lost, *Rām.*; 3. *Rāma* is an abridgement of *Rām.*; 4. both have developed out of a common, now lost, source. Weber himself could not bring himself to decide between the four choices.

129. It seems clear enough that "mother" is used euphemistically, expressing the hope that the demoness will act as a loving mother to the child.

130. J. A. B. van Buitenen, *Two Plays of Ancient India* (New York, 1968), p. 57.

131. See his *Kumārasaṃbhava*, "Birth of Kumara."

132. Albrecht Weber, "Ueber das Rāmāyaṇa," *Transactions Berlin Academy*, 1870.

Hermann Jacobi, writing in 1893,[133] mildly reproves Weber for his indecision. According to him the word "abridgment" is ill chosen and the problem really evaporates when we look upon *Rāma* as a *Nachdichtung of Rām.*; for by a number of literal or close quotations *Rāma* proves its dependence. While it may be true that in details *Rāma* shows variation from *Rām.*, such variation is, in his view, easily explained by the fact that the author of *Rāma* knew the *Rām.* by memory and might well be permitted to make changes on his own.

In 1901 E. Washburn Hopkins[134] was not persuaded by Jacobi's case (which, however, he does not refute in detail), but prefers to treat *The Mahābhārata* and *Rāmāyaṇa* texts such as we have them, as contemporaneous, so that at best we can arrive at chronological priorities of particular text *portions*. He considers *Rāma* to be prior to *Rām.* and, without saying so, considers by analogy *Rāma* to be the source of *Rām.*[135]

V. S. Sukthankar, who himself edited *The Rāmopākhyāna* for the critical edition of *The Book of the Forest*, aligned himself in 1941 with Jacobi,[136] stating contra Hopkins that a concordance of parallel passages between *Rāma* and *Rām.* indeed bears out the contention that *Rāma* is an abridgement of Vālmīki's *Rāmāyaṇa*. His arguments, however, do not seem to have convinced P. L. Vaidya, his successor as general editor of *The Mahābhārata*. Writing as a guest editor of *The Yuddhakāṇḍa* of the critical edition of *The Rāmāyaṇa* of Baroda,[137] he maintains that the variations between *Rāma* and *Rām.* simply do not allow us to derive *Rāma* from *Rām.*, and that *Rāma* is prior to, and the source of, *Rām.*

It is clear, considering the discussion over three quarters of a century, that there was a certain merit in the indecision of Albrecht Weber.

Let us consider Jacobi's case more closely. There is no gainsaying that the occurrence of many parallels between *Rāma* and *Rām.* is a potent argument. However, it works both ways, for Vālmīki could have borrowed them from *Rāma*. It is not all that easy to prove the originality of a line for one version over the other. Jacobi quotes with some zest the famous non-simile of the battle of Rāma and Rāvaṇa.[138]

133. Hermann Jacobi, *Das Rāmāyaṇa, Geschichte und Inhalt*, part three, para 2, pp. 69 ff.

134. E. Washburn Hopkins, *The Great Epic of India, Its Character and Origin* (New York), 1901), pp. 58 ff.

135. Pp. 63 ff., the analogy being that of *The Story of Nala* and *The Naiṣadhacarita*.

136. V. S. Sukthankar, "Epic Studies VIII: The Rāma Episode (Rāmopākhyāna) and the Rāmāyaṇa," in *A Volume of Indological Studies Presented to P. V. Kane* (Poona, 1941).

137. *The Vālmīki-Rāmāyaṇa*: vol. 6, *The Yuddhakāṇḍa*, critically edited by P. L. Vaidya (Baroda, 1971), Introduction, pp. xxl ff.

138. *Rāmāyaṇa* B. 6.107.52.

> *sāgaraṃ cāmbaraprākhyam ambaraṃ sāgaropamam /*
> *Rāma-Rāvaṇayor yuddhaṃ Rāma-Rāvaṇayor iva / /*

"The ocean compares with the sky, the sky is the simile for the ocean—the battle of Rāma and Rāvaṇa was like the battle of Rāma and Rāvaṇa." Compare with this line that of *Rāma*:[139]

> *Daśakandhararājasunvos tathā yuddham abhūn mahat /*
> *alabdhopamam anyatra tayor eva tathābhavat / /*

"There was such a great battle between Rāvana and the prince, such a one that no comparison for it can be found anywhere." Jacobi remarks: "This is, both in form and content, a piteous rewrite, which stands immediately betrayed as an imitation."[140] It is probably with this verse in view that Hopkins says, "Professor Jacobi is of the opinion that a verse of inferior form in the episode points to borrowing because it is inferior. But a great poet is more apt to take a weak verse and make it strong than a copyist to ruin a verse already excellent."[141] I agree; but it was necessary for Jacobi's case to assume, not a copyist, but a *Nachdichter*, in order to allow for the admitted variations; so the one verse *had* to be a poor recast of the other.

It is an important element in Jacobi's argument that *Rāma* betrays acquaintance with *The Uttarakāṇḍa*, the last canto of *Rām.* (which is generally agreed to be a late part of *Rām.*) so that *Rāma* presupposes *The Rāmāyaṇa* in its entirety. The parallel lines, however, occur in the preamble of the *Rāma*, and may not have formed part of the "original" *Rāma* at all. It describes the early history of Rāvaṇa and his ancestors, and is no more organically connected with the main story than the same episode is to *The Rāmāyaṇa* as such, or for that matter than the *Harivaṃśa* is to *The Mahābhārata*. It may well have been inserted in *Rāma* when the story gained currency with *The Uttarakāṇḍa*.

I agree with Jacobi that the transposition of events in the battle part of the story between *Rāma* and *Rām.* can be explained away as slips of the memory; the battle scenes are confusing enough because they are so similar. With more reluctance I might grant him that *The Rāmāyaṇa*'s repetitions of events might have been reduced in *Rāma*, which therefore is simpler only in appearance. But I will not grant that if a passage in *Rāma* is unintelligible without the aid of *Rām.*, it

139. *The Mahābhārata* (Bombay edition) 3.290.20, which is, however, not accepted in the critical edition *apud* 3.274.18, marked 1297* and 1298*. The fact that the critical edition has banished the verse to a footnote does not vindicate Jacobi; it merely indicates that it is a later interpolation in *Rāma* by a pedant who knew the "Rāmāyaṇa" line. The issue has been complicated (or simplified) to the absurd by the fact that the Baroda edition expunges the famous line (6.96 *apud* 19, appendix 3064* vs. 4–5), so it now becomes a chicken-or-the-egg question.

140. P. 74.

141. P. 63.

must therefore presuppose *Rām*. This deserves some attention, for it will lead into my own argument.

The passage is 3.266.15: "So that you will place trust in me," says Hanūmān to Rāma, "Jānakī told me the story of the reed cast at the crow on Mount Citrakūṭa, so that you should recognize it." The anecdote is detailed in *Rām.* 5.38. Sītā tells an intimate event in her life with Rāma, which he alone knows. Once on Mount Citrakūṭa Sītā was pestered by a crow. To get rid of the bird Sītā flings at it with her girdle. When she thereupon rises, her skirt slips down, much to Rāma's amusement and Sītā's embarrassment. Eventually she throws *kuśa* grass at the crow, and it turns into Brahmā's Staff to destroy the bird.

Surely we would not have ever guessed at this background of the *śloka* in *Rāma*, but is this as powerful an argument as at first sight it would appear to be? It is in the nature of abridgments to abbreviate most concisely those episodes that are best known. In the summary story of *Āstīka* it is said that the sage "softly wept his three words" (1.13.30). If we did not have the expanded story we would never surmise that this refers to his exclamation: "If there is a virgin of my name, and if she is given me as an alms, and if I need not support her, give me that virgin!" (1.42.15). Likewise in the summary of *The Latter Days of Yayāti* it is said that the king "dwelled in heaven joyously and blissfully, but after not too long a time he was again cast out of it by Indra" (1.81.1). The circumstances of this fall, irrecoverable from the statement itself, are detailed in the expanded story (1.83.1–5). On occasion there appear in the narrative itself enigmatic statements that look as though they have come out of a summary while the story behind them was forgotten. In the story of how snakes were set upon Bhīma it reads: "Waking, Bhīma ground all the snakes to death and struck his favorite charioteer with the back of his hand" (1.119.15). However enigmatic this reference, it was clearly part of the traditional lore about the assassination attempts on Bhīma, for it is repeated, again without explanation, in *The Book of the Forest* (3.13.77). The Mount Citrakūṭa episode, in my view, appears as a risqué story (not necessarily only told of Sītā), and the mere reference to "the reed cast at the crow" could bring instant recognition.

This, then, is how I should prefer to look upon the story of *Rāma*, not so much as an "abridgment" but as a "summary" of the type that we have met often, a brief, tersely stated compendium that the storyteller would know by heart and on the basis of which he could elaborate and improvise the full narrative. While in its origin such a "summary" might be an abridgment of the full story, it is not simply an abridgment; it will lead its own life and might become once more the source of a more expanded story. *Rāma* is not a *Nachdichtung*. The story is briskly, at times tersely, recapitulated without stylistic devices and literary pretenses.

We must agree with Vaidya that such a summary is likely to be more faithful to whatever original story it sums up than a fully worked up narrative would be. So if *Rāma* and *Rām*., show variations the probabilities are that *Rāma* is closer to its archetype than *Rām*. is to its own. *Rāma* cannot be a summary of *Rām*. as we have it now. Its variations cannot be explained as a simplification of *Rām*, for some major rearrangements would have to have taken place for which there is no reason in a summary of a well-known narrative. Let us look at the different story lines.

Rāma and *Rām*. are wholly parallel till the death of Jaṭāyu. Whilst *Rāma* carries on the story with Rāma and Lakṣmaṇa left in the forest, *Rām*. shifts the scene to Lankā where Rāvaṇa woos Sītā, is rejected and angrily gives her an ultimatum (3.51–52). This is not only a romantic intermezzo; it is a rationalization: it provides a reason why Rāvaṇa waited all those months before autumn (when Rāma will arrive) before importuning Sītā, by affording her a moratorium. Also in the story arrangement of *Rām*. the real confrontation of Rāvaṇa and Sītā takes place only after Hanūmān's jump to Lankā, and some kind of preconfrontation is needed. *Rāma* has no need of it.

Both versions flow parallel till Vālin has been killed by Rāma, Sugrīva is installed in the Kiṣkindhā forest, and Rāma and Lakṣmaṇa weather the rainy season. We note that *Rāma* is far more straightforward about Rāma's treacherous interference in the duel of Sugrīva and Vālin by shooting the latter. Clearly it was part of a compact: Sugrīva would assist Rāma in his search for Sītā if he in turn helped assassinate Vālin: "When great archer Rāma saw Sugrīva give the sign, he drew his fine bow and aimed at Vālin." (With the same uncomplicated directness Sugrīva is keeping his side of the bargain. When Lakṣmaṇa on behalf of Rāma inquires what has been done, Sugrīva says that he expects the search parties back within a month and goes to reassure Rāma. But that is a little later in both stories.)

While the rainy season goes on, Rāvaṇa woos Sītā, for the first time in *Rāma*, for the second in *Rām*. *Rāma* relates that Sītā was installed by Rāvaṇa in quarters near an *aśoka* grove and surrounded by female Rākṣasas. The parallel episode to *Rāma* (264.41 ff.) comes much later in *Rām*. (5.12 ff.). *Rāma*'s sequence is simple: Sītā installed, her sorry state, her retinue of Rākṣasīs, the friendly Rākṣasī Trijaṭā, the dream of Rāma's triumph, the visitation of Rāvaṇa, his wooing, his rejection, and his resignation. *The Rāmāyaṇa* sequence is more complex: Rāvaṇa's second visitation, his pleas, his rejection, repeated pleas, another moratorium, pleas and threads of the attendant Rākṣasīs, Sītā's laments. Trijaṭā's telling of the dream (5.12 ff.). It may be remarked that, in comparison, the *Rāma* sequence has a logic of its own; this is Rāvaṇa's first and only visit at Sītā's, which is preceded by the telling of the dream: the good fortune predicted by the dream might well have strengthened Sītā enough to reject Rāvaṇa. The ogre takes her refusal wryly enough: we have been told (264.55) that he had little choice; for he was under a curse that he would be impotent with an unwilling woman. Vālmīki on the other hand keeps up the suspense with moratorium after moratorium and has the dream in another place because it no doubt was nobler for Sītā to refuse Rāvaṇa without such oneiromantic encouragement.

There is a telling variation between *Rāma* and *Rām.* in the dream episode. In *Rām.* it is Trijaṭā's dream, but in *Rāma* it is not just the dream of some young and friendly demoness but the rather more official vision of a venerable Rākṣasa named Avindhya, who later comes in for a reward from Rāma. Vālmīki knows nothing of him. Now it is very difficult to understand why an abridger of *The Rāmāyaṇa* who, according to Jacobi, consistently simplifies his original, suddenly should invent a wholly new character. It is more likely that Vālmīki did not want any more friendly Rākṣasas than Vibhīṣaṇa.

Back now to the mainland and the search. As stated, Sugrīva has his search parties already on the way in *Rāma*; in *Rām.* he has been wallowing in women and done nothing, but then belatedly institutes a search. For that purpose he marshals vast armies in the *Rām.* version as though for a war instead of a search; this gathering of the monkey clans takes more appropriate place in *Rāma*, *after* Sītā has been found and the armies have a route to march. Whereas the south-bent party is captained by Angada in *Rām.*, in *Rāma* it is obviously Hanūmān who is the leader and he leads a far less ambitious expedition. The circumstances of the search are parallel, except that in *Rāma* the monkeys simply find light at the end of the tunnel, Maya's palace on the ocean, and an ascetic woman, Prabhāvatī, who is living there. In *Rām.* there is a whole city underground somewhere in the Vindhyas, from which a woman named Svayaṃprabhā translates the trapped monkeys to the ocean shore.

In both stories it is Hanūmān who tells the circumstances of the search that leads him to jump to Lankā, where he discovers Sītā, gives her a jewel of Rāma's to establish his good faith, receives in turn the story of the Mount Citrakūṭa incident, sets the city on fire, and returns to tell Rāma. The *Rām.* version seizes on this report to make it an eyewitness account of the second visitation of Rāvaṇa with Sītā, so that this episode in *Rām.* occurs only *after* the *Kiṣkindhākāṇḍa* and at the end of the *Sundarakāṇḍa*, justifying an earlier account of Rāvaṇa's first visit with Sītā; one could hardly expect to wait to hear what was going on in Lankā until three-quarters of the story was told.

As we saw, it is only at this point that *Rāma* raises the monkey armies that *Rām.* now merely regroups. The stories are largely parallel with some minor varieties in which structure is on *Rāma*'s side. In the Vibhīṣaṇa episode (*Rāma* 267.46; *Rām.* 6.11), *Rāma* has the demon defect after the causeway has been built, which makes better sense than to have him suddenly materialize on the other shore, offering advice where none is needed. In the episode of Angada's embassy, the attack on Lankā precedes this embassy in *Rām.* (6.31), while in *Rāma* (268) it more appropriately follows upon the failure of the embassy.

Finally the repudiation of Sītā. In *Rām.* (6.104) we have the well-known episode of Sītā entering, after her rejection, the fire, which, as the Fire God, returns her to Rāma, vindicated. Once more *Rām.* is much more dramatic than *Rāma*, but the latter (275.20 ff.) has a direct simplicity, even primitiveness, that has become familiar to us. "The wind of restless motion," swears Sītā, "which breathes in all creatures, shall leave my spirits, if I have done wrong! Fire, water, ether, earth and wind shall leave my spirit if I have done wrong!" Thereupon appear the Wind, the Fire, and Varuṇa, the God of water, to vouch for her. The three Gods make clear that they can speak with authority, for one of the manifestations of Wind is Sītā's breath, of Fire Sītā's digestive fire, of Varuṇa the juices in Sītā's body; it is as the deities of Sītā's bodily functions that they would have known if anything irregular had happened.

This resumé and comparison should show convincingly, after Vaidya, that *Rāma* cannot be considered an abridgement of *Rām.*, in spite of the parallel verses. *Rāma* tells the same story, but in a different arrangement and with telling variations from *Rām.* It is also exceedingly close to *Rām.* That may in part be due to feedback from *Rām.* into the *Rāma*, but that cannot have played a major role; for why then not rearrange *Rāma* entirely according to *Rām.*, let Hanūmān witness Rāvaṇa's visit to Sītā, and remove Avindhya?

The only conclusion that seems reasonable concerning the relationship between the story of *Rāma* and Vālmīki's *Rāmāyaṇa* is that the former is a summary of a fully expanded *Rāmacarita*, which, after its contents were fixed in the story of *Rāma*, underwent further development, acquired a new beginning and a new end, attracted subsidiary elements, and became known as the original poem (ādikāvya) of Vālmīki. The ones responsible for the inclusion of the story of *Rāma* in *The Book of the Forest* either did not know of Vālmīki's poem, or knew that the story of *Rāma* was different from it. Otherwise it is hard to explain why they should not simply have placed the narrative in Vālmīki's mouth; *The Book of the Forest* does not hesitate to recruit a sage out of the blue to tell a story, witness Bṛhadaśva and the story of *Nala*. *The Mahābhārata* does know Vālmīki as a sage.

Rather than viewing either one as the source of the other it is more profitable and also more interesting to see the story of *Rāma*, as preserved in *The Mahābhārata*, as the happy documentation of a stage in the development of *The Rāmāyaṇa* very close to the point in time when the main story of this text was given the form in which we now know it.

Sāvitrī

With the story of *Nala*, the glorification of the devoted wife in the story of *Sāvitrī* is one of the more celebrated episodes of *The Book of the Forest* in India itself and has found its way to the West in numerous translations. The appeal is easy to understand: a woman knowingly enters marriage with a man soon to die and by her perseverance gains her husband back from death.

In the Indian context the story carries a greater poignancy than that. To honour her decision Sāvitrī commits herself to widowhood, which for a woman is nothing less than living death. Now still a young woman, under no obligation but to herself, she will henceforth be known as the wife upon whose marriage her husband died. Having no more existence in her own family she will be a void in her husband's; and rather than face such a bleak half-life she might well prefer to choose death herself and become, or rather prove to be, a *satī*, a woman of virtue.

What gives the story additional charm is the way family life is sketched. In the concern of the parents for their son Satyavat, their judicious permission to let Sāvitrī accompany her husband into the forest, and Satyavat's worries about his parents' reaction to his tardiness there glows a domestic warmth that we do not normally encounter, probably because it was taken for granted. It is the same warmth as that of the brahmin household in the story of *Baka*.[142] Exile in the forest does not affect this warmth; perhaps it only adds to it: quite touching is the rallying to the worrying old father by his fellow recluses, who first comfort him and then, when Satyavat and

142. *MBh.* 1(10), 1:302 ff.

Sāvitrī happily return, gather with the parents and the couple around the fire to hear the story of Sāvitrī's vicissitudes.

The story illustrates that it is not so much love that triumphs over death, but wisdom. Yama, the God of Death, is reluctant enough to give up Satyavat and prepared to bestow the most extraordinary boons before releasing the one soul in his power. It is only Sāvitrī's demonstration of the wisdom of strictness and Law that prevails over him.

Contents

3(29) The Forest Teachings

1–11 (B. 1–10; C. 1–384)
1 (1; 1). Janamejaya asks how the Pāṇḍavas and Kṛṣṇā lived in the forest (1–5). When they leave town, the people criticize the Kauravas and wish to follow Yudhiṣṭhira, in order to consort with the good (5–30). Yudhiṣṭhira urges them to stay loyal to the Kauravas and to return, which they do (30–40). The Pāṇḍavas journey to the banyan tree Pramāṇa on the Ganges and sleep (40).
2 (2; 48). Yudhiṣṭhira seeks to dismiss the brahmins who had followed him: he will not be able to feed them; they decline (1–10). The brahmin Śaunaka consoles Yudhiṣṭhira: one should repress love and hatred (10–35); the life of a rich man is wretched (35–45). Yudhiṣṭhira protests that he must feed the brahmins (45–55). Śaunaka continues his admonitions (60–75).
3 (3; 131). Yudhiṣṭhira asks Dhaumya's advice (1). The latter points out that the sun is the source of all food; Yudhiṣṭhira worships the sun (1–10). The one hundred and eight names of the sun and their reward (10–30).
4 (3; 209). The Sun God appears and promises that Yudhiṣṭhira's food will never run out (1–5).
5 (4; 219). Dhṛtarāṣṭra consults Vidura (1). Vidura declares that the Kauravas have flouted the Law and should placate the Pāṇḍavas (1–15). Dhṛtarāṣṭra accuses

Vidura of partiality and disowns Vidura, who leaves for the Pāṇḍavas (15–20).
6 (5; 240). The Pāṇḍavas travel westward to the Ganges and visit the rivers Sarasvatī and Dṛṣadvatī, and come to the Kāmyaka Forest on the Sarasvatī, where they settle down (1). Vidura arrives and is welcomed (5–10). Vidura explains how he advised Dhṛtarāṣṭra and was rejected (10–20).
7 (6; 263). Dhṛtarāṣṭra regrets having sent away Vidura and tells Saṃjaya to fetch him back (1–5). Saṃjaya goes to the Pāṇḍavas and returns with Vidura (10–20). Vidura forgives Dhṛtarāṣṭra (20).
8 (7; 287). At Vidura's return Duryodhana worries that the Pāṇḍavas may be restored (1–5). Śakuni assures him they will not; Duḥśāsana and Karṇa agree (5–10). When Duryodhana pouts, Karṇa counsels to kill the Pāṇḍavas in the forest. Dvaipāyana appears (10–20).
9 (8; 311). He addresses Dhṛtarāṣṭra and warns against war with the Pāṇḍavas (1–10).
10 (9; 323). Dhṛtarāṣṭra agrees that the dicing was foolish (1). Dvaipāyana agrees that the love for a son transcends everything and tells the story of the cow Surabhi which cried before Indra over a bullock that was being beaten; Indra rains to stop the ploughing of the harassed bullock (5–15). He urges Dhṛtarāṣṭra to have Duryodhana make peace with the Pāṇḍavas (20).
11 (10; 346). The seer Maitreya arrives and is welcomed. Dhṛtarāṣṭra asks about the Pāṇḍavas (1–10). Maitreya berates the other for what has happened; Duryodhana should make peace with the Pāṇḍavas (10–25). Duryodhana ignores him, and Maitreya curses him: there will be war and Bhīma will smash his thighs. The curse will take no effect, if Duryodhana makes peace (25–35).

Janamejaya said:

3.1.1 When the Pārthas had thus been defeated at the dicing game and been incensed by the evil-minded Dhārtarāṣṭras and their councillors with their trickery, O best of the twiceborn, and harshly insulted by the others who effected the final feud, what did they do, the Kauravyas who were my forebears? How, fallen from their lordly power and suddenly come upon dire grief, did the Pārthas, who matched Śakra in might, pass the time in the forest? And who

followed them, when they had met that great misfortune? What did
they eat, how did they live? Where did the great-spirited men make
5 their dwelling? How, O best of the brahmins, did those twelve years
go by in the forest for those great-spirited enemy-killing heroes? And
how did the king's daughter,* choicest of women, stately and avowed
to her husbands, forever speaking the truth, live through that ghastly
sojourn in the wilderness, undeserving though she was of suffering?

Tell me all that in detail, you who are rich in austerities. I wish to hear you relate the geste of those men of great character and splendor, brahmin, for my curiosity is great!

Vaiśaṃpāyana said:

When the Pārthas had thus been defeated at the dicing and
incensed by the evil-minded Dhārtarāṣṭras and their councillors, they
departed from the City of the Elephant. They left the city through the
Vardhamāna Gate and went on with Kṛṣṇā to the north, carrying
10 their weapons. Their servants, Indrasena and the others, numbering
fourteen in all, followed with their wives on swift carts.

Upon learning that they were leaving, the townspeople, smarting
with grief, reviled Bhīṣma, Vidura, Droṇa, and Gautama** many times,
and without fear they banded together and said to one another, "This
dynasty is not secure, nor are we, nor are our houses, if the evil
Duryodhana, abetted by Saubala,*** Karṇa, and Duḥśāsana, aspires to
the kingdom! If there be no dynasty, no morality, no Law, how can
there be happiness, with that ruffian, abetted by ruffians, pretending
to the kingdom? Duryodhana hates his betters, he abandons both
morality and his kinsmen, he is greedy and arrogant, mean and by
15 nature cruel. This earth is not whole as long as Duryodhana is king!
We all better go where the Pāṇḍavas are going. They are
compassionate, of great spirit, masters of their senses as well as their
enemies, modest and famous, and bent upon the practice of the Law."

So they spoke, and all together they followed after the Pāṇḍavas.
With folded hands they all said to the sons of Kuntī and Mādrī,
"Where will you go—be blessed—deserting us who share your grief?
We too shall come along, wherever you are going. We have heard
that you have been defeated by pitiless enemies in a lawless way, and
we all are greatly anguished. Pray do not desert us who have always
20 been devoted to your happiness and well-being. Be friends and favor
those who are loyal to you, lest we all perish in a kingdom that is
ruled by a bad king! Listen, bulls among men, we shall declare how
consorting with good or evil effects virtues or vices. Just as perfume
makes a cloth, or water, or sesame seeds, and the ground fragrant

* = Draupadī.
** = Kṛpa.
*** = Śakuni.

with the scent of flowers, so too do virtues spring from association.
The source of the net of folly is the association with fools, while the
daily associations with the good is the source of Law.
"Therefore, those who seek serenity should consort with the wise,
25 the old, the upright, the austere, and the good. One should cultivate
those whose birth, knowledge, and action are all three pure. For
union with them is more important even than the Scriptures. Even if
we do not perform the rites, we may yet find merit with the good
whose habits are meritorious, just as we find evil by cultivating the
wicked. By seeing, touching, conversing, and sitting with the wicked,
law-abiding people lower themselves and do not succeed. By
consorting with the lowly a man's insight declines, by associating
with the middling it becomes middling, and it becomes best by
meeting with the best. The qualities that are hailed in the world as
sources of Law, Profit, and Pleasure, which result from proper practice
in the world and are set forth in the Veda and approved by the
30 educated, all those good qualities are found in all of you, together
and separately. We wish to dwell amidst the virtuous, as we wish for
our well-being."

Yudhiṣṭhira said:

Fortunate are we that the subjects led by the brahmins, being
moved by their love and compassion, speak of our qualities, although
we lack them. Therefore, I and my brothers request all of you: do not,
out of love and compassion for us, make matters worse. Bhīṣma the
grandfather, the king, Vidura, and my mother, as well as my friends
in general, live here in the City of the Elephant. If you have our
well-being at heart, you must, all of you, protect them with your best
effort, for they are anguished by grief and sorrow.
35 You have come far, pray return now; we swear that we shall meet
again. And turn your loving thoughts to my kinsmen, whom I entrust
to you. For that is the task that lies highest in my heart, and with
that you will content me fully and pay me homage.

Vaiśaṃpāyana said:

Thus admonished by the King Dharma, all the subjects in their
anguish cried out in fearful voices of sorrow: "O woe, our king!"
Dwelling with their thoughts on the virtues of the Pārtha, they
mournfully and unhappily and unwillingly turned back after their
encounter with the Pāṇḍavas.

When the townspeople had turned back, the Pāṇḍavas mounted
their chariots and traveled as far as the great banyan tree called
40 Pramāṇa on the bank of the Ganges. After journeying for the remainder
of the day to the banyan tree, the heroes spent the night, touching
the pure water. Wan with grief, they spent that night there,
partaking only of water.

Some brahmins had followed them that far out of love for them, some with their fires, others without, in the company of pupils and kinsmen; the king shone bright in the midst of these priests, who held forth on the Brahman. At the hour that is both lovely and fearful they brought out their fires, and a discussion began that was preceded by the sounds of the Brahman. Consoling the king, best of the Kurus, with voices sweet as the wild goose's, those eminent priests passed away the whole night.

Vaiśaṃpāyana said:

2.1 When the starry night had dawned, the brahmins, who lived on alms, stood before those men of unsullied deeds as they were ready to go into the forest. King Yudhiṣṭhira, son of Kuntī, said to them, "Robbed of all our wealth, robbed of our kingdom, robbed of our fortune, we shall now in our sorrow go into the forest and live on fruit, roots, and meat. The wilderness is full of danger and teeming with beasts of prey and snakes. There will certainly, I think, be great hardship for you there. The hardship of brahmins oppresses even the Gods, how much more then me! Turn back, brahmins, if you so please!"

The brahmins said:

5 Sire, we are ready to go the same journey as your lordships. Pray do not desert us who are loyal to you and see the good Law. For the Gods themselves have pity for their devotees, especially for brahmins who adhere to good conduct!

Yudhiṣṭhira said:

I too have always had the greatest devotion for the brahmins, ye twice-born, but the hardships of my companions seem to oppress me naturally. These brothers of mine, who now are to feed on fruit, roots, and deer, are perplexed by the sorrows that spring from their suffering, by the indignities done to Draupadī, and the plunder of our kingdom. I cannot burden them with more hardships, they are distressed enough!

The brahmins said:

10 Have no worry in your heart over having to feed us, king! We ourselves shall fetch our forest fare as we are following you. We shall bring you good luck with our meditation and prayers, and with suitable stories we shall amuse ourselves in the wilderness.

Yudhiṣṭhira said:

So be it, without a doubt. I shall enjoy the company of brahmins. Yet, because of the straits to which I have been reduced, I only seem to see my own shame. How shall I watch you fetch food for yourselves and suffer undeserved privations out of loyalty to me? A plague on the evil Dhārtarāṣṭras!

Vaiśaṃpāyana said:

Having thus spoken the grieving king sat down on the ground. A
certain wise brahmin, Śaunaka by name, who rejoiced in the Self and
was steeped in Sāṃkhya and Yoga, spoke as follows to the king:
15 "Thousands of occasions of sorrow and hundreds of occasions of
fear beset day after day the foolish, but not the wise. Men of
comprehension like yourself do not implicate themselves in acts that
run counter to knowledge, are full of error and destructive of well-
being. In you, king, rests the comprehension that is declared to be
eight-membered, which destroys all that is unholy, and is informed
by Revelation and Tradition. In adversities, in hardships, in the
misadventures of their kin, men like you do not collapse under the
sorrows of body and mind. Listen, I shall recite to you the verses that
the great-spirited Janaka once chanted for the steadying of the Self.
20 " 'This world is tyrannized by two kinds of sorrows that arise either
in the body or in the mind. Hear by what means they are alleviated,
separately and together. Disease, labor, meeting with the unloved,
and parting with the loved—these are the four causes from which
bodily grief arises. The pain of the body and the pain of the mind is
relieved by rapid countermeasures and by steadily ignoring it: these
are the two courses of action. For sensible physicians first relieve a
man's mental anguish by pleasing talk and delightful presents; for
mental ills affect the body, as a hot iron ball affects the water in a
25 pitcher. Thus one should appease the ailment of the mind with insight,
as one appeases fire with water; when the mental ailment is relieved,
the body quiets down. Love, it is known, is the root of mental pain,
for love makes a man attached, and thus he comes to grief. Grief
roots in love and fear springs from love. From love is born the
motivating passion that seeks out its object. Both passion and its
object run counter to well-being, but the former is held to be the
graver wrong. Just as a fire in the hollow of a tree will burn down the
tree to its roots, so even a small fault of passion destroys a man who
30 wishes for Law. One does not renounce by merely separating oneself:
the renouncer is he who sees the faults from close by; such a man
becomes dispassionate, uninimical, and detached from possessions.
Therefore one should by the means of insight turn back one's body-
born love, turn away from one's partisans, one's friends, one's
accumulated wealth. No love cleaves to the superior men who are
guided by insight, know their scriptures, and have made their souls—
no more than water cleaves to a lotus leaf.

" 'A man swayed by passion is dragged on by his desire; longing
rises in him, and from that longing springs Thirst. This Thirst indeed
is the greatest evil, forever deranging man, fearsome, pregnant of
35 Unlaw, and giving rise to evil. For the feeble of spirit it is hard to

relinquish, it does not age while man ages, it is a disease that saps his vigor. He who sheds this Thirst finds bliss. Beginningless and endless is this Thirst, canker of man's body; once it has arisen it destroys like a fire that has no origin. Just as kindling is destroyed by fire that sprang by itself, just so does a man who has not made his soul perish from his inborn greed.'

"The rich are no less afraid of the king, floods, fire, thieves, and their kinsmen than the living are of death. Birds devour a piece of meat in the air, predators do it on the ground, fish in the water, but all devour a rich man. To some men wealth will be a disaster; unless he detaches himself from the grandeur of wealth no man finds greatness. Therefore all the inflow of riches increases the follies of a mind: its poverty, vainglory, and pride, its fear and anxieties. The wise know the sorrows of the wealth of the embodied soul: the sorrows of earning it, preserving it, seeing it dwindle. Hard though it is when it perishes, hard though it is when it is spent, yet people murder for the sake of wealth. Riches are hard to renounce, but no less hard to conserve. Wealth that is so hard to come by a man should not mind losing: foolish are the discontented, content are the wise. There is no end to the Thirst, but contentment is the final happiness; therefore the wise see contentment as the only wealth in the world. Fugitive are youth and beauty, life and piled-up wealth, lordship, and the company of loved ones; no wise man should covet them. Therefore abandon your piles: who can endure the trouble they make! Not a man with a treasure is found without his worries! That is why men of Law praise the man indifferent to wealth—far better than wiping off the dirt is not having touched it!

"Yudhiṣṭhira, pray have no desire for riches: if you want to act in accord with the Law, stay clear of a longing for riches!"

Yudhiṣṭhira said:

I do not desire wealth out of a desire to enjoy it, but I wish for it in order to support the brahmins, not out of greed. For how, brahmin, can a man like me who is in the householder stage fail to support and preserve his followers? It is taught that one should share with all creatures; therefore, the householder must give to those who do not cook for themselves. In the houses of the good these four are never found lacking: straw, ground, water, and welcoming words. The sick deserve a bed, those tired of standing a seat, the thirsty water, the hungry food. One should lend one's eye and attention, speak the welcome, and rising to greet him meet the guest and honor him justly. The *agnihotra*, bullock, kinsmen, guests, relatives in marriage, son, wife, and servant burn down the one who does not pay just respect to them. One should not have food cooked for himself, nor wrongfully have cattle killed, nor eat it by himself, without offering in

the right way. Let him throw out food on the ground for the dogs,
the eater of dogs, and the birds, for this is the *vaiśvadeva*, which is
mandatory every evening and morning. It is for this reason that one
should daily eat the remnant of the offering and partake of the
Elixir: the remnant is the remainder from dependents, the Elixir is the
remnant of a sacrifice. To him who observes this practice as he
practices the householder life, the Law is sovereign, they say—or what
is your view, brahmin?

Śaunaka said:

60 Alas, great woe! This world has been overturned: the wicked
delight in what frightens off the good. For the sake of his penis and
his belly, the fool lays out a rich repast, being beset by confusion and
passion and swayed by the objects of the senses. Even the man who
is alert to them is seduced by his rapacious senses, as an unconscious
driver by vicious, bolting horses. When the six senses each get hold of
their objects, then the mind's plan, which has grown from a prior
intention, becomes clear though them. When a person's mind is
directed toward the objects of all the senses, desire springs up in him,
65 and he acts toward those objects. Then, pierced by desire—whose
strength is the intention—with the arrows of sense objects, he falls
into the fire of greed, as the moth falls because of its desire for light.
At last, crazed by his sports and meals, he drowns in the maw of
madness and does not know himself. Thus, in the runaround, he falls
here into womb after womb, spun around like a wheel by ignorance,
karman, and thirst. He rolls about in creatures, from Brahmā down
to a blade of grass, born over and over again, in water, on land, or in
the air.

That is the way of the ignorant; now hear from me also the way of
the wise, of those men who delight in the Law and their bliss and
70 rejoice in release. The precept of the *Veda* is this: "Do the rite and
renounce it": and by this precept one should never practice any Law
out of selfishness. There is an eightfold path of the Law taught, the
path of oblation, Vedic study, gifts, austerity, truthfulness, forbearance,
self-control, and greedlessness. Of these the first four travel the road
of the Ancestors' Journey; one should perform a task not out of
selfishness, but because it is to be done. The second four are the
Divine Journey, which is always traveled by the strict. And it is by
way of this eightfold path that a man of pure soul should journey: by
consistently correct intention, by correct subdual of the senses, by
75 correct and precise vows, by correct service to the elder, by correct
apportionment of food, by correct learning and transmission, by
correct renunciation of rites, by correct suspension of thoughts: thus
they perform their acts who wish to defeat transmigration. The deities
(the Rudras, Sādhyas, Ādityas, Vasus, and Aśvins) acquired their

power because they are free of love and hatred and, possessed of the power of Yoga, they sway these creatures. Likewise you too, Kaunteya Bhārata, must resort to a copious serenity and by means of austerities seek for success and success in Yoga. You have found the success one acquires by having a father and mother, and the success acquired by rites; now seek success by austerities, for the support of the twice-born. For once people have succeeded they do by the grace of their austerities whatever they wish: therefore undertake austerities and fulfill the desire of the soul.

Vaiśaṃpāyana said:
3.1 At this address by Śaunaka, Kuntī's son Yudhiṣṭhira went up to his
priest, and, in the midst of his brothers, he said, "These brahmins,
who are steeped in the *Veda*, have followed me when I departed; and
beset as I am with many worries I am unable to keep them. I can
neither abandon them nor provide for them. What is my duty in this?
The reverend must tell me."
Dhaumya, foremost of those who support the Law, reflected a little
while, searching for the course that was right by the Law, then spoke
5 to Yudhiṣṭhira as follows: "When the creatures were first created,
they suffered great hunger, and in his compassion for them the Sun
acted like a father. Going his northern course he absorbed with his
rays the saps of heat; then, on returning to his southern course, the
Sun impregnated the earth. Thereupon, when he had become the
fields, the Lord of the Herbs collected the heat from heaven, and, with
the water, engendered the herbs. Thus the Sun, having gone unto
earth, and ejaculated by the fervors of the moon, is born as the herbs
of the six flowers, which are sacrificial, and thus is he born as the
food of the living ones on earth.
"In this fashion, the food that sustains the life of the creatures is
made of the Sun, he is the father of all creatures; therefore go to Him
10 for refuge. For great-spirited kings, pure of womb and acts, rescue all
their people by turning to copious austerities. Bhīma, Kārtavīrya,
Vainya, and Nahuṣa pulled their people from disaster, as they abided
by austerity, Yoga, and concentration. Likewise you too, law-spirited
lord, made pure by your acts, must turn to austerity and support the
brahmins, Bhārata, according to the Law!"
Having thus been addressed by Dhaumya in words that were
appropriate to the occasion, the pure-spirited King Dharma undertook
the ultimate austerity. Law-spirited, living on wind, master of his
senses, he worshiped the Sun with offerings of flowers and fireless
oblations, turned to Yoga after touching the water of the Ganges, and
practiced the control of his breath.

Janamejaya said:
15 In what manner did that bull of the Kurus, the King Yudhiṣṭhira,
placate the Sun, of marvelous prowess, to support the brahmins?
Vaiśaṃpāyana said:
Listen attentively, king, after you have purified yourself, and attend
to my words: make time, Indra-like king, and I shall tell it all to you
exhaustively. Hear, wise liege, how Dhaumya proclaimed to that very
great-spirited Pārtha the holy one hundred and eight names of the
Sun.

Sūrya, Aryaman, Bhaga, Tvaṣṭar, Pūṣan, Arka, Savitar, Ravi,
Gabhastimat, Aja, Kāla, Mṛtyu, Dhātar, Prabhākara; Pṛthivī, Āpas,
Tejas; Kha, Vāyu; Parāyaṇa; Soma, Bṛhaspati, Śukra, Budha,
20 Angāraka; Indra, Vivasvat, Dīptāṃśu, Śuci, Sauri, Sanaiścara,
Brahmā, Viṣṇu, Rudra, Skanda, Vaiśravaṇa, Yama, Vaidyuta,
Jāṭhara, Aindhana, Tejasām-pati, Dharmadhvaja, Vedakartar,
Vedānga, Vedavāhana; Kṛta, Tretā, Dvāpara, Kali; Sarvāmarāśraya;
Kāla, Kāṣṭhā, Muhūrtas, Pakṣas, Māsas, Ṛtus, Saṃvatsarakāra;
Aśvattha, Kālacakra, Vibhāvasu, Puruṣa, Śāśvata, Yogin;
Vyaktāvyakta, Sanātana, Lokādhyakṣa, Prajādhyakṣo, Viśvakarman,
Tamonuda, Varuṇa, Sāgara, Aṃśu, Jīmūta, Jīvana, Arihan,
25 Bhūtāśraya, Bhūtapati, Sarvabhūtaniṣevita; Maṇi, Suvarṇa, Bhūtādi,
Kāmada, Sarvatomukha, Jaya, Viśāla, Varada, Śīghraga,
Prāṇadhāraṇa, Dhanvantari, Dhūmaketu, Ādideva, Āditya,
Dvādaśātman, Aravindākṣa, Pitar, Mātar, Pitāmaha, Svargadvāra,
Prajādvāra, Mokṣadvāra, Triviṣṭapa, Dehakartar, Praśāntātman,
Viśvātman, Viśvatomukha, Carācarātman, Sūkṣmātman,
Vapuṣānvita.

These are the auspicious one hundred and eight names of the
praiseworthy and great-spirited Sun that were recited by the great-
30 spirited Śakra. Nārada acquired them from Śakra, and Dhaumya
obtained them afterward. Yudhiṣṭhira obtained them from Dhaumya
and acquired all he desired.

Learn thou too to address the Giver of Light
Who is cherished by the hosts of the Gods and Fathers,
And honored by Asuras and Night-Stalkers;
He resembles the Fire and the choicest gold.

The one who at sunrise thoughtfully recites
This litany shall reap sons and riches
And obtain the gift of recalling past lives,
And find resemblance and final wisdom.

The man who proclaims with full attention
And pure of mind this laud of the best God

Is freed from the sea of the brushfire of grief
And obtains all the things that his mind may yearn for.

Vaiśaṃpāyana said:

4.1 Thereupon the Traveler of the Sky* was pleased and showed
himself to the Pāṇḍava, in his body and ablaze like a flaming fire.
"You shall attain to all that you aspire, king! I shall provide you with
food for twelve years. The four kinds of food—fruit, roots, viands, and
greens that are prepared in your kitchen—will be inexhaustible for
you; and so shall be all manner of riches." And having spoken He
disappeared.
The law-wise Kaunteya, on obtaining the boon, rose from the water
and took Dhaumya's feet and, undefeated, embraced his brothers.
5 He joined Draupadī; and while she watched, the Lord Pāṇḍava went
and prepared the food in the kitchen. The four kinds of forest fare,
once cooked, multiplied; the food grew to be inexhaustible, and with
it he fed the brahmins. While the brahmins were eating, Yudhiṣṭhira
fed his younger brothers, too, and afterward ate the remains, which
are known as the leftover. Pṛṣata's granddaughter** then first fed
Yudhiṣṭhira and ate the remnant herself. So it befell that the prince,
brilliant like the sun, obtained from the Sun this boon and gave to the
brahmins what their hearts desired.
At the proper days, stars, and moon phases they were led by their
priest and, intent upon those who were worthy of sacrifice, proceeded
10 according to the authority of the injunctions and spells. Then, their
journey blessed, the Pāṇḍavas traveled with Dhaumya; and
surrounded by hosts of twiceborn they journeyed to the Kāmyaka
Forest.

Vaiśaṃpāyana said:

5.1 To the woods had the Pāṇḍavas gone when the king
Whose eyesight was insight, Ambikā's son,***
Spoke to Law-minded Vidura, plumbless of spirit,
Dejected, these words while sitting at ease,

"Your thoughts are as pure as were Bhārgava's.****
You know the Law, both supreme and subtle.
Impartial you are acclaimed by the Kurus:
So declare what is right for them and for me.

"In this pass, tell, Vidura, what is our task?
How may the town folk be loyal to us

* = the sun.
** = Draupadī.
*** = Dhṛtarāṣṭra.
**** = Rāma.

Lest they uproot us with roots and all?
Nor do I wish them to perish instead!"

Vidura said:

King, rooted in Law is man's threefold goal,
And they say this kingdom is rooted in Law.
King, living by Law as much as you can,
Protect all your sons and the sons of Kuntī.

5 This Law was despoiled in the meeting hall
By those caitiffs by Śakuni Saubala led;
After challenging Kuntī's son to the dicing,
Your son defeated that truthful man.

King, as you were you were misguided,
Yet I see the means to save your remains,
So your son, O Kauravya, be rid of evil
And may in this world stand firm and good.

Let Pāṇḍu's sons regain it all
What you yourself took beyond your deserts.
For this is the sovereign Law: that a king
Be content with his own and not covet another's.

This now is your task—and no task is beyond it—
To gratify them and condemn Śakuni;
Lest no one remain from among your sons,
You, sire, should hurry and do this thing!

But if you fail to accomplish this, king,
The ruin of the Kurus shall surely befall.
For Bhīmasena and Arjuna angered
Shall leave no remains of their foes in a war.

10 They whose champion the left-handed archer is,
Whose bow is Gāṇḍīva unique in the world.
Whose champion the big-armed Bhīma is—
What is in the world beyond their reach?

I said, long ago, your son barely born,
What at that time would have been to your profit:
"Abandon your son, the scourge of his line!"
And yet, my king, you failed in the deed.
If this time, king, you again fail to follow
The same advice, you shall later repent!

If this son of yours will bind to agree
To hold one reign with the Pāṇḍavas,

You shan't regret your alliance with them—
Not when you take hold of your son and his helpers.
Lest the opposite happens, subdue your son
And install Pāṇḍu's son to be sovereign.

Let Ajātaśatru dispassionately
By the Law sway this earth, O king of the land.
Thenceforth, king, all of the lords of the land
Will at once obey us like commoners!

Duryodhana, Śakuni, the *sūta's* son,*
Should love sincerely the Pāṇḍavas, king;
Let Duḥśāsana plead with Bhīmasena,
In the midst of the hall, and with Draupadī.

15 You yourself, appease Yudhiṣṭhira:
Pay honor to him and install him as king.
You asked me; so what else could I have said:
Having done as I say, king, you'll have done your duty.

Dhṛtarāṣṭra said:

You have spoken your word in this assembly,
For me and the Pāṇḍavas, Vidura,
Beneficient to them and malefic to mine,
And my mind takes not to any of it!

For what reason now do you take the decision
In the cause of the Pāṇḍavas, as you declare it?
By which, methinks, you don't favor mine?
Can I pass my son for the Pāṇḍava?

Without misdoubting they** are my own sons,
Yet Duryodhana is my body's offspring.
And who if he wants to be equable says,
"I abandoned my body in another's cause"?

You have never, Vidura, told me wrong;
I shall endure your exceeding pique.
Now go where you want, or stay if you must:
A bad wife leaves, however much prayed!

Vaiśampāyana said:

20 Having heard this much Dhṛtarāṣṭra rose
On a sudden and stalked to his inner chambers,
And Vidura, murmuring, "It is not!"
Then hastened to where the Pāṇḍavas were.

* = Karṇa.
** = the Pāṇḍavas.

Vaiśaṃpāyana said:

6.1 The Pāṇḍavas, bulls of the Bharatas, with a view to sojourning in the woods, departed with their followers from the bank of the Ganges for the Field of the Kurus. They visited the Sarasvatī and Dṛṣadvatī rivers and the river Yamunā and traveled from forest to forest, always in a westerly direction. Then amidst the desert plains on the bank of the Sarasvatī they found the forest called Kāmyaka, which is loved by the hermits. There in that forest, which teemed with game and birds, the heroes settled down, accompanied and comforted by the hermits.

5 Then Vidura, longing to see the Pāṇḍus, arrived at the prosperous Kāmyaka Forest on a single chariot.

Upon reaching that wood on his chariot
Drawn by swift horses, Vidura
Saw King Dharma seated in a lonely spot,
With Draupadī, brothers, and the brahmins.

The truthful king then saw from the distance,
How Vidura quickly approached and drew closer;
And he spoke to his brother Bhīmasena:
"What will the Steward say when we meet?

"Might it be that he comes at Saubala's* word,
Once more to challenge me to a dicing?
Might it be that the mean-minded Śakuni
Wants to play us and win our weapons?

"If challenged by anyone with 'Come hither!'
I'm unable, Bhīma, to stay away.
Yet if somehow the Gāṇḍīva bow is risked,
We risk the reign of the kingdom itself."

10 The scions of Pāṇḍu all rose up
And welcomed Vidura, O king of men;
And after the honors the Ājamīḍha
Met with Pāṇḍu's sons in the usual way.

When their guest had rested, the bulls among men
Enquired for the reason behind his coming;
And he sat and at length explained to them
How Ambikā's son Dhṛtarāṣṭra had acted.

Vidura said:

Dhṛtarāṣṭra, who keeps me, Ajātaśatru,
After welcoming me and paying me honor,

* = Śakuni.

Said, "As matters stand now, without choosing sides,
Advise what is best for them and for me."

I told what was right for the Kauravas,
And proper and good for Dhṛtarāṣṭra;
But my advice did not reach his heart,
And I thought of nothing better to say.

I told what was best, O scions of Pāṇḍu,
But Ambikā's son did not listen to me;
When a man is ailing the proper diet
Is not to his taste—nor were my words.

He can be led to no good, Ajātaśatru,
Nor a corrupt wench to a scholar's house:
What I said displeased the Bharata bull,
As a sexagenarian displeases a girl.

Their ruin is assured of the Kauravas,
And Dhṛtarāṣṭra will not find peace;
As no water sticks to a lotus leaf,
So my good advice will not stick to him.

Enraged, Dhṛtarāṣṭra said to me,
"Go, Bhārata, where your confidence lies;
No more do I want you as my companion
To help me rule over city and land!"

I have been rejected by Dhṛtarāṣṭra,
And hastened here, king, to counsel you;
All the things that I said in his meeting hall,
Do bear them in mind, as I now repeat them.

The man who, sorely oppressed by his rivals,
Exerts his patience and bides his time,
Slowly feeding his means as he feeds a fire,
That self-possessed man rules the earth by himself!

If one shares one's wealth, king, with one's helpers,
One's helpers will also share in distress:
This is the means to retain one's helpers,
And to hold one's helpers is to win the world!

The truth be told best without complaints,
Food be equally shared with one's companions,
Oneself should not come before the others:
Such deportment prospers a king!

Yudhiṣṭhira said:

I shall do as you counsel me, Vidura,
And thoughtfully practice your great wisdom;
And what else you may say that fits time and place,
I shall act according to that advice!

Vaiśaṃpāyana said:

7.1 When Vidura had gone to the Pāṇḍavas in their hermitage, O king,
the wise Dhṛtarāṣṭra repented, Bhārata. He went to the door of the
assembly hall, and, bemused by his memories of Vidura, he fell in a
faint before the eyes of the kings. The king regained consciousness
and got up from the floor; and he said to Saṃjaya, who was at his
side, "My brother and friend is like the God of Law incarnate; as I
remember him now, my heart is torn apart. Quickly bring him back,
5 my law-wise brother!" This did he speak and lamented piteously.
Later, tormented by remorse and made sallow by his memories of
Vidura, he spoke again to Saṃjaya out of love for his brother: "Go,
Saṃjaya, and find out if my brother Vidura is still alive after the
onslaught of my evil rage. Never before has my brother, a wise man
and of boundless spirit, practiced any falsehood, however slight. Why
then should this sagacious man incur a falsehood from me? The sage
should not relinquish his life; go and bring him back, Saṃjaya!"
10 Upon hearing the king's words and agreeing with them, Saṃjaya
replied, "Surely!" and hurried to the Kāmyaka Forest. Shortly he
reached the forest where the Pāṇḍavas lived and saw Yudhiṣṭhira,
who was clothed in *ruru* deerskins, sitting with Vidura and thousands
of brahmins, surrounded by his brothers as the God of the Hundred
Sacrifices is by the Gods. Saṃjaya approached Yudhiṣṭhira and paid
his respects, then greeted Bhīma, Arjuna, and the twins as each
deserved. The king asked him about his health, and when Saṃjaya
was sitting at ease, he announced the reason for his coming and
15 said, "Steward, King Dhṛtarāṣṭra, the son of Ambikā, remembers you.
Go and see him at once, and revive our king! Seek the leave of the
Pāṇḍavas, scions of Kuru, best among men—you who bring honor
must return at the lionlike king's behest."
At these words the sagacious Vidura, who was fond of his kinsmen,
with Yudhiṣṭhira's leave returned to the City of the Elephant. Majestic
Dhṛtarāṣṭra said to the wise Steward, "By good fortune hast thou
returned, wise in the Law, by good fortune hast thou remembered me,
prince sans blame! Day and night, when I lay sleepless because of
thee, I looked upon my own body as a strange apparition!" He took
20 Vidura in his arms and kissed him on the head. "Forgive," he said,
"what I said to thee in anger."

Vidura said:

I have forgiven it, king. You are our highest guru. Indeed I returned at once solely to see you. For, O tiger among men, men who are law-minded hasten to the aid of the oppressed, king, and do not give it a second thought. Your sons are as dear to me as Pāṇḍu's. My only thought was that they were in distress, and my spirit went out to them.

Vaiśaṃpāyana said:

Having thus become reconciled, the two illustrious brothers Vidura and Dhṛtarāṣṭra found great happiness.

Vaiśaṃpāyana said:

8.1 When Dhṛtarāṣṭra's son, the evil-minded prince, heard that Vidura
had returned and that the king had humbly placated him, he burned
with rage. He had Saubala fetched and also Karṇa and Duḥśāsana,
and plunging in the darkness that sprang from his folly, the prince
said to them, "Vidura, the councillor so honored by Dhṛtarāṣṭra, has
come back, the wise friend of the Pāṇḍavas, to whose cause he is
devoted. Counsel me to my benefit so that Vidura does not reverse the
5 king's mind in order to bring the Pāṇḍavas back! If I see the Pārthas
somehow return here, I shall dry up, lifeless and penniless. I shall take
to poison, or the noose, or the sword, or the fire, for I cannot bear to
see them here rich again!"

Śakuni said:

Why do you, a king, a lord of your people, give in to these childish
thoughts? They made their covenant and went! They will not return.
All the Pāṇḍavas, bull of the Bharatas, abide by the truth of their
word, my son. They will never accept the king's invitation. If they
were to accept it and again returned to the city, they would have
10 violated the covenant, and we would play them again. We shall
remain uncommitted, following the king's* whim, and, ever on our
guard, wait for a weakness to develop in the Pāṇḍavas.

Duḥśāsana said:

It is indeed, wise prince uncle, as you declare it. Whenever you speak your mind it is pleasing to me.

Karṇa said:

All of us gladly look to your wishes, Duryodhana. There appears to be a consensus among us all.

Vaiśaṃpāyana said:

When Karṇa had so spoken, Prince Duryodhana, none too happy, at once turned away his face. Noticing this, Karṇa opened wide his

* = Duryodhana.

15 shining eyes and said in anger to Duḥśāsana and Saubala, furiously
rousing himself, "Aho, hear what my real thoughts are, ye princes!
We all want to do, with servants' hands, anything that pleases the
prince, but none of us can now remain in his favor without acting. Then
let us take up arms and in armor mount our chariots and together go
out to kill the Pāṇḍavas while they range in the forest! When they all
have been pacified and gone the unknown journey, the Dhārtarāṣṭras
and we shall be undisputed. As long as they are dejected, as long as
they wallow in their grief, as long as they remain friendless, we can
handle them—that is my view!"
20 When they heard him speak so, they cheered him again and again,
and all said "Yea!" to the *sūta's* son. Angrily they each mounted their
chariots and drove out in a body, resolved to kill the Pāṇḍavas.

Kṛṣṇa Dvaipāyana divined with his divine eye that they had set out and the pure-spirited sage appeared. The blessed lord, who is worshiped by all the world, halted them, then hastened to the king whose eyesight was insight, and spoke to him where he was sitting.

Vyāsa said:

9.1 Dhṛtarāṣṭra, man of wisdom, listen to my word. I shall speak to the
highest benefit of all the Kauravas. It does not please me, strong-
armed king, that the Pāṇḍavas have gone into the forest and that they
were defeated by Duryodhana's henchmen with trickery. When the
thirteenth year is full, they will angrily let loose their poison on the
Kauravas, remembering their hardships, Bhārata. Why does this
wicked and feeble-minded son of yours in his perpetual rage want to
5 kill off the Pāṇḍavas for the sake of the kingdom? The fool must be
stopped, once and for all; your son must calm down! If he wants to
kill them in the forest, he will lose his life. Do rightly what the wise
Vidura has said, and Bhīṣma and we and Kṛpa and Droṇa. War with
one's own kin is condemned, wise king: do not perpetrate lawless
infamy! Such is his obsession with the Pāṇḍavas, Bhārata, that if it is
disregarded it will skirt disaster. Rather, let your feeble-minded son go
to the forest, king, and live with the Pāṇḍavas, alone and without
10 his helpers. Then if from their association love were to spring up in
your son for the Pāṇḍavas, you would have succeeded, lord of men.
Still, the character that is inborn in a man at his birth, that, they say,
great king, does not leave him before he dies. What does Bhīṣma
think, what do Droṇa and Vidura? And you yourself? The right thing
must be done before the matter is out of hand.

Dhṛtarāṣṭra said:

10.1 My lord, neither did I like this talk of dicing. I think, hermit, fate
got the better of me and made me do it. Bhīṣma did not like it, nor

did Droṇa and Vidura. Gāndhārī did not want it. It was folly it got started. But I cannot abandon the mindless Duryodhana, because I love my son, my lord, even though I know, ascetic.

Vyāsa said:

King Vaicitravīrya, what you say is true. For surely, I know, a son
5 prevails, and nothing prevails over a son. Indra himself was awakened by the tears of Surabhi to the insight that no other property, however valuable, prevails over a son. On this I shall narrate a great and unexcelled story, the Colloquy of Indra and the cow Surabhi, O lord of your people.

They say, king, that Surabhi bellowed out in heaven, long ago, she who is the mother of the cows, my son; and Indra took pity on her.

Indra said:

Why do you cry like this, my pretty? I hope all is safe with the celestials, with men and kine? It cannot be a trifle!

Surabhi said:

No disaster whatever is looming for all of you, Lord of the Thirty. It is over a son of mine I grieve, and that is why I cry, Kauśika.*
10 Look at that dreadful peasant beating up with his goad that weak little son of mine who smarts under the plough! When I see one already so exhausted being beaten, I am seized with compassion, overlord of Gods, and my heart is aroused. There is the strong one who carries a heavier yoke, and there is the other of little strength and vigor, emaciated, held together by his veins. He is beaten with the goad and prodded again and again, but he can hardly pull the load; look at it, Vāsava! That is why I grievously and sorrowfully cry out and from compassion shed these tears from my eyes.

Indra said:

15 You have thousands of sons who are equally oppressed, my pretty. Why single out this one for your pity? He is only one of all those who are oppressed here!

Surabhi said:

I may have thousands of sons, and they are all equal to me; yet, Śakra, for the one who is suffering my pity is greater.

Vyāsa said:

Indra, having heard Surabhi, was greatly surprised, and he thought to himself, O Kauravya, that a son was even greater than life itself. And he rained down on that spot a torrential shower and stopped the peasant's ploughing—so acted our Lord the Chastiser of Pāka.

It is as Surabhi said: they may all be equal to you, but among all
20 your sons, my king, your pity is deepest for the one oppressed. You are my son as much as Pāṇḍu was, son, or the sagacious Vidura, and

* = Indra.

I speak now from love. You have a hundred and one sons to last you, king, but Pāṇḍu's appear to be only five, and they are simple and greatly unhappy. I ask myself, how will they live out the term, how will they prosper? And thus my heart is much disturbed over the dejected Pārthas. King, if you desire the Kauravyas to live, have your son Duryodhana go and make peace with the Pāṇḍavas!

Dhṛtarāṣṭra said:
11.1 It is as you say, wise hermit. I recognize this, as do all these kings.
Vidura, Bhīṣma, and Droṇa conveyed the same opinion as you
concerning what is properly helpful to the fortune of the Kurus,
hermit. If I am worthy of favor, if you have pity on the Kauravas,
then lecture Duryodhana, my wrong-minded son!
Vyāsa said:
Here comes the blessed seer Maitreya, king, to visit you after his
5 journey with the Pāṇḍava brothers. This great seer shall lecture your
son Duryodhana as it is fitting, king, to pacify this family of yours.
Whatever he may say, eminent king, carry it out regardlessly. For if
the task is not done, he shall in anger put a curse on your son.
Vaiśaṃpāyana said:
Having spoken Vyāsa went and there appeared Maitreya; and the
king and his sons welcomed him with honor. King Dhṛtarāṣṭra,
Ambikā's son, gave him the guest water and did all the other acts of
hospitality; and when the bull among hermits had rested, he said to
him courteously, "Has your journey in the Jungle of the Kurus been
comfortable, are the heroic five brothers, the Pāṇḍavas, in good
10 health? Do the bulls of men wish to abide by the covenant and will
the brotherliness of the Kurus remain unharmed?"
Maitreya said:
While on a tour of the places of pilgrimage I came to the Jungle of
the Kurus, and perchance I saw Yudhiṣṭhira and the King Dharma in
the Kāmyaka Forest. Crowds of hermits had arrived together to visit
the great-spirited man, who was garbed in deerskin and hairtuft,
while he lived in the wilderness of austerities, my lord. There I heard,
great king, of the frivolousness of your son and the wicked course of
action he had undertaken by way of a dicing match. Out of a concern
for the Kauravas I wended my way to you, for I have always had
15 particular love and affection for you, my lord. It does not answer,
king, that while you and Bhīṣma are alive, your sons should strive
with one another, lord of men! You yourself are the center pole, king,
for punishment as well as preferment: then why do you overlook this
dreadful wrongness that is springing up? That was like the behavior
of *dasyus*, what happened in your hall, scion of Kuru! It does not add
to your splendor, king, when ascetics meet!

Vaiśaṃpāyana said:
He turned to the intransigent King Duryodhana, and in a mild
voice the blessed seer Maitreya said, "Big-armed Duryodhana, listen,
20 you best of arguers, as I speak my word for your own good. Do not
offend the Pāṇḍavas, king. Do what is best for yourself, the Pāṇḍavas,
the Kurus, and the world, bull among men! All of them are men like
tigers, champions, valiant warriors, all of them have the vigor of a
myriad elephants and are as hard as diamonds. They are all avowed
to the truth, and they all pride themselves on their manhood. They
are killers of the foes of the Gods and of protean Rākṣasas like
Hiḍimba and Baka and others, and of the Rākṣasa Kirmīra, the one
who terrifyingly stood in the path of the great-spirited men like an
immovable mountain, when they trod, fallen, from here into the night.
Bhīma, boastful in battle, in brawn the best of the brawny, strangled
him like a beast at a sacrifice, as a tiger kills small game.

25 "Look, king, how at their conquest of the world Jarāsaṃdha, the
great archer who had the strength of ten thousand elephants, was
felled in battle by Bhīma. Vāsudeva is their friend, Drupada's son
Dhṛṣṭadyumna their brother-in-law: what man, subject to age and
death, would willingly encounter them in war? There must be peace
between you and the Pāṇḍavas, bull of the Bharatas! Follow my
advice, king, lest you succumb to death!"

Thus, O lord of the people, did Maitreya speak, and the other
slapped his thigh, which was shaped like an elephant's trunk.
Duryodhana pretended a smile and drew patterns in the dirt with his
foot. Saying nothing, the fool sat there with his head slightly bent.
30 When Maitreya saw that Duryodhana was not obeying and was
drawing patterns on the floor, anger seized hold of him, king.
Possessed by his anger, that best of hermits, pulled on by fate, decided
to put a curse on him. Eyes bloodshot from his rage, Maitreya
touched water and cursed the evil-minded son of Dhṛtarāṣṭra:

"Because you ignore me and refuse to obey my word, you shall soon
reap the reward of your insolence! Through your offense a great war
will flare up and during it the brawny Bhīma will smash your thigh
with the blows of his club."

35 When the curse had been pronounced, Dhṛtarāṣṭra, king of the
land, pleaded with the seer: "Don't let it happen!"
Maitreya said:
If your son seeks peace, king, then accordingly the curse shall not
take effect, my son. But if the contrary happens, it shall.
Vaiśaṃpāyana said:
Abashed, Duryodhana's father then queried Maitreya, O Indra
among kings: "How did Bhīma fell Kirmīra?"

Maitreya said:

I will not tell. You grumble, and your son is disobedient. Your Vidura will tell you all, when I have left.

Vaiśaṃpāyana said:

Having spoken Maitreya departed as he had come; and upset by the killing of Kirmīra, Duryodhana went outside.

3(30) The Slaying of Kirmīra

12 (B. 11; C. 385–460)

12 (11; 385). Vidura tells the adventure of the killing of Kirmīra. The Pāṇḍavas reach the Kāmyaka Forest at night. A Rākṣasa bars their way (1–5). Description (10–15). Dhaumya counters his wizardry (15–20). Yudhiṣṭhira questions Kirmīra, who states that he lives there and will kill them all, especially Bhīma who had killed his brother Baka and friend Hiḍimba (20–35). A tree fight follows between Bhīma and Kirmīra (40–60). Kirmīra falls (60–65).

Dhṛtarāṣṭra said:

12.1 Steward, I want to hear about the slaying of Kirmīra, tell me! How
went the encounter between Bhīmasena and the Rākṣasa?
Vidura said:
Then listen to this exploit of Bhīma, whose feats are superhuman, as
I have heard them tell it time and again in our conversations.
Defeated at the dicing, the Pāṇḍavas departed from here, O Indra
among kings, and journeyed for three days and three nights to the
forest called Kāmyaka. At night, at midnight, at the right time for
dacoits, when half the night has passed and the man-eaters roam, the
5 terrorizing Rākṣasas, it is the time when the ascetics and other forest
rangers always shun that forest from afar, so we hear, out of fear of
the man-eaters.

It was then that they entered the forest and saw a terrifying Rākṣasa with blazing eyes bar their way with a firebrand. Spreading wide his arms and making a terrible face, he stood there barring the path by which the scions of Kuru were going. There, behold! the demon, gnashing his eight fangs, eyes copper-red, the hair standing up on his head and aflame, like a monsoon cloud with its circle of sunbeams and lightning and its fellow-traveling cranes, setting loose his demoniac wizardry and giving forth loud screams, sending forth

the thunderous roar of a cloud carrying rain—behold, the demon!
10 Frightened by the noise, the birds fled in every direction, screeching,
and so did land animals and fish. Afoot with stampeding game,
elephant, buffalo, and bear, it was as though the entire forest was
ready to escape from his cry. Hit by the wind of his speeding thighs,
tall-grown creepers embraced their trees with arms of red blossoms.
The same instant a gusty wind began to blow, and the sky, overcast by
dust, lost its Bear.

Unbeknownst to Pāṇḍu's five sons, the great enemy was like the
15 insuperable impact of imminent grief upon the five senses. He detected
from afar the five Pāṇḍavas, clothed in their black deerskins, and
barred their way into the forest, like moving Mount Maināka. When
she came nearer, Kṛṣṇā of the lotus eyes trembled and fearfully closed
her eyes. With her hair disheveled and ruffled by Duḥśāsana's hand,
she looked like a river in spate that runs between five mountains. She
fell in a deep swoon, and the five Pāṇḍavas caught her, as the five
senses, attached to their object, catch their pleasure.

Meanwhile the powerful Dhaumya, before the Pāṇḍavas' eyes,
exorcised the ghastly apparitions of the demon with the various spells
that are designed to kill demons and that he employed accurately.
20 His wizardry destroyed, the brawny fiend, who could assume any
shape at will, appeared before them with eyes widened in fury, like
Time the Destroyer himself. Thereupon the far-sighted King
Yudhiṣṭhira said to him, "Who are you and whose? Tell us what we
should do for you!" The Rākṣasa replied to Yudhiṣṭhira the King
Dharma, "I am the brother of Baka, and renowned as Kirmīra. I dwell
in this empty forest of Kāmyaka without a worry, always feasting on
humans whom I have defeated in battle. Who are you who have come
to me as my meal? I shall defeat you all in battle and make my meal
of you, without a worry!"
25 When Yudhiṣṭhira heard these words of the evil Rākṣasa, he told
him the name of his lineage and so forth, O Bhārata: "I am Pāṇḍu's
son, the King Dharma; the name may have reached your ear.
Together with all my brothers, Bhīmasena, Arjuna, and the twins, I
have lost my kingdom and now am resolved to make my dwelling in
the forest. So I have come to this terrifying wood, which is your
domain." "It is my good fortune," said Kirmīra, "that the Gods after
such a long time have fulfilled my desire here today! For I have been
roaming the entire earth with my weapons ready to kill Bhīmasena,
30 but I did not find him. And now by good fortune I have come upon
him, the killer of my brother, as I have hoped for so long; for it was he
who, in the guise of a brahmin, killed my dear brother Baka in the
settlement of Vetrakīya, king, by resorting to some magic, for Bhīma
has no strength in his chest. This evil man once killed my good friend

Hiḍimba, who ranged in his forest, and abducted his sister. And now
the fool has come to my own dense wood, in the middle of the night,
35 the time when we stalk about. Today I shall wreak upon him the
grudge that I have harbored for so long and sate Baka with his
plentiful blood! Today I shall acquit myself of my debt to my brother
and my friend, and find everlasting peace by excising this thorn of the
Rākṣasas! Even if Bhīmasena once was let go by Baka, this very day I
shall devour him, before your own eyes, Yudhiṣṭhira. And after I have
killed the Wolf-Belly with all his brimming vigor, I shall eat and digest
him, as Agastya once did with the great Asura!"

At these words the law-spirited Yudhiṣṭhira, true to his promises,
said angrily, "You shall not!" and reviled the Rākṣasa. Thereupon the
strong-armed Bhīma quickly uprooted a tree ten armspans tall and
40 stripped it of its leaves. In hardly a twinkling of the eye Arjuna
Vijaya also strung his bow Gāṇḍīva, whose power had the impact of a
thunderbolt. Bhīma stopped Jiṣṇu, rushed upon the ugly Rākṣasa,
Bhārata, and shouted at him "Stay where you are!" The Pāṇḍava
tightened his girdle and, kneading furiously fist in palm, the powerful
man bit his lip. Armed with his tree, Bhīma ran to him nimbly.
Another Indra, he lowered his club like the staff of Yama with swift
force on the other's head, but the Rākṣasa appeared unconcerned in
45 their battle. He hurled at Bhīma his lighted firebrand like flaming
lightning, but that greatest of fighters kicked the cast-up torch back to
the Rākṣasa with his left foot. Kirmīra then forcefully pulled out a tree
and like the staff-wielding God* furiously engaged the Pāṇḍava in
battle; there began a tree fight that spared no tree, as of yore between
the brothers Vāli and Sugrīva, when they both wanted the fortune.
The trees that fell on their heads splintered in many pieces, as lotuses
that are hurled at the heads of rutting elephants. Withered like reeds,
the many trees there in the great forest looked like discarded tatters.

50 The tree fight went on for a long while, lord of your people, between
the chief of the Rākṣasas and that best of men. Then the raging
Rākṣasa lifted and threw a rock at Bhīma, who stood his ground in
battle, and Bhīmasena staggered. The Rākṣasa stormed on him while
he was numbed by the impact of the rock, as Svarbhānu,** with
scattering rays for arms, storms upon the sun. The two clasped each
other and dragged each other about—they appeared like bellicose bulls.
Their battle grew tumultuous and most dreadful as of proud tigers
55 armed with claws and fangs. Emboldened by the outrage of
Duryodhana and the prowess of his arms, the Wolf-Belly swelled
under Kṛṣṇā's eye. He fell upon him and grabbed hold of his arms

* = Yama.
** = Rāhu.

unforgivingly, as an elephant whose temple glands have burst falls
upon another.
In time the powerful Rākṣasa clutched him, and Bhīmasena, strong
among the strong, threw him off with his strength. As the two mighty
fighters sought to crush each other with their arms in that battle, a
ghastly whistle was heard like the whistle in reeds. Now the Wolf-Belly
threw him forcefully down and, holding him by the waist, shook him
60 mightily, as a fierce gale shakes a tree. In strong Bhīma's clutch the
weakening fiend throbbed and panted for breath, but kept dragging
the Pāṇḍava. Noticing that the other was exhausted, the Wolf-Belly
harnessed him with his arms, as a bullock is harnessed with thongs.
Roaring a mighty roar like a burst kettledrum, he spun him around
many times, convulsed and numbed. Knowing that he was fading, the
scion of Pāṇḍu quickly pulled the Rākṣasa up with his arms and
strangled him like a beast of sacrifice. The Wolf-Belly planted his knee
on his hips and pressed down with his hands on his throat; then,
65 when all the demon's body had gone limp and his wide-open eyes
became filmed, he cast him on the ground and said, "You will no
more rinse your eyes with tears over Hiḍimba and Baka, miscreant!
You are gone now to Yama's domain!"

> And having thus spoken, that hero of men,
> Eyes widened by rage, to that Rākṣasa,
> He let go of the quivering, lifeless corpse,
> Bared of clothes and adornment, empty of mind.
>
> When he had been slain in his bulk like a cloud's,
> Those sons of a king placed Kṛṣṇā first
> And, applauding Bhīma for numerous virtues,
> Went happy of heart to the Dvaita woods.

Thus it was, overlord of men, that Kirmīra was brought to his
70 downfall in battle at the word of King Dharma, O Kaurava. Having
rendered that forest thornless, the undefeated law-wise king went on
with Draupadī and made it his dwelling. The bulls of the Bharatas all
comforted Draupadī and, happy of heart, affectionately praised the
Wolf-Belly. The Rākṣasa slain, crushed down by the might of Bhīma's
arms, the heroes entered the safe and pestless forest. I myself, as I
traveled that way, saw the horrifying and evil-minded monster spread-
eagled on the road, killed by Bhīmasena's power in that large forest. It
was there that I heard of this exploit of Bhīma's, Bhārata, as the
brahmins who were assembled there told it.
75 And upon hearing that the great Rākṣasa Kirmīra had been slain
in battle, the king sank in thought and sighed as though in anguish.

3(31) The Mountain Man

13–42 (B. 12–41; C. 385–1713)
13 (12; 385). Kṛṣṇa and his people, Dhṛṣṭadyumna and the Pāñcālas, Dhṛṣṭaketu and the Cedis, and the Kaikeya brothers arrive to visit the Pāṇḍavas. Kṛṣṇa is enraged (1–5). Arjuna lauds the past exploits of Kṛṣṇa (10–35). Kṛṣṇa declares he is identical with Arjuna (35–40). Draupadī describes Kṛṣṇa's greatness, nevertheless he did not save her in Hāstinapura (40–55). She reviles the Pāṇḍavas who let her be molested (55–65). She lists the indignities the Pāṇḍavas have suffered from Duryodhana, in their youth, the lacquer house, in semi-exile where Bhīma kills Hiḍimba and Baka (65–95). How the Pāṇḍavas won Draupadī. Still they did not stand by her (95–110). Kṛṣṇa curses the Kauravas (110–115).
14 (13; 595). Kṛṣṇa explains that he was absent from Dvārakā when everything happened, so that he could not interfere with the dicing (1–15).
15–23 (B. 14–22; C. 614–902) The Razing of Saubha.
24 (23; 904). After Kṛṣṇa has departed the Pāṇḍavas continue to the forest (1). The people lament their departure, and follow him. Arjuna addresses them, and they leave (5–15).
25 (24; 919). They decide to live by Lake Dvaitavana (1–10). While numerous brahmins follow, they reach there and camp under a tree (10–25).
26 (25; 945). Mārkaṇḍeya arrives (1–5). He admonishes them to live out their forest exile (5–15).
27 (26; 964). The brahmin Baka Dālbhya discourses on the wisdom for a baron to live with brahmins (1–20).
28 (27; 989). Kṛṣṇā berates Yudhiṣṭhira for the hardships in which they are now finding themselves (1–20), and scolds him for not angering and imposing his authority on the enemy (20–35).
29 (28; 1029). Kṛṣṇā tells the story of the colloquy of Prahlāda and Vairocana on the merits of intransigence and forgiveness. Neither is always desirable (1–35).
30 (29; 1065). Yudhiṣṭhira's rejoinder, on the dangers of anger and the uses of patience (1–50).
31 (30; 1118). Kṛṣṇā replies that a man's fate is

decided by the Placer, whom she reviles (1–40).
32 (31; 1160). Yudhiṣṭhira accuses her of heresy and stresses the necessity of faith in the Law (1–40).
33 (32; 1202). Draupadī defends herself: she does not malign the Placer. He works through three factors that determine one's life: fate, chance, and one's own actions (1–45). It is no crime to fail if one acts (45–55).
34 (33; 1264). Bhīma joins the discussion: they should go to war; it does not do to be too prone to the Law, and there are precedents of justified deception; if it is against the Law, it can later be expiated (1–85).
35 (34; 1355). Yudhiṣṭhira reminds him that he himself has given his word (1–20).
36 (35; 1376). Bhīma continues his admonitions and expresses doubt that they will be successful in hiding during their thirteenth year (1–30).
37 (36; 1413). Yudhiṣṭhira replies that the Kauravas have the upper hand and cannot be defeated (1–15). Vyāsa arrives and tells Yudhiṣṭhira not to have fears (20). He will give him a magic knowledge to be passed on to Arjuna who must obtain divine weapons from Indra and Rudra; Arjuna is the ancient seer Nārāyaṇa. He teaches Yudhiṣṭhira the magic (25–35). Yudhiṣṭhira moves from Dvaitavana to Kāmyaka (35–40).
38 (37; 1456). Yudhiṣṭhira sends Arjuna to acquire divine weapons and teaches him the magic; Arjuna arms himself (1–15). Draupadī bids Arjuna farewell (15–25). Arjuna departs northward through the Himālaya and Gandhamādana, and is stopped at Indrakīla. An ascetic questions him and tells him to stay (25–30). When Arjuna declines, the ascetic reveals himself as Indra and gives him a boon. Arjuna chooses divine weapons. He will receive them after he has encountered Śiva (35–45).
39 (38; 1516). Arjuna performs austerities on a peak of the Himālaya (1–20). Fearful, the Gods approach Indra, who reassures them (25–30).
40 (39; 1550). Śiva takes on the form of a mountain man and carries his bow (1–5). A Daitya, Mūka, takes on the form of a boar to kill Arjuna, who takes aim. The mountain man shoots simultaneously (5–15). Arjuna protests and promises to kill the other hunter (15–20). Arjuna is unable to subdue him with his arrows, which run out (20–35). He attacks him with his bow and loses it to the other (35–40). Finally they fight with bare

hands; Arjuna is subdued (40–50). The mountain man reveals himself as Śiva; Arjuna has a vision of him and seeks mercy (50–60).
41 (40; 1632). Śiva praises Arjuna and gives him a boon. Arjuna desires the Pāśupata weapon (1–10). With due warning on its use, he receives it (10–20). Śiva disappears (20–25).
42 (41; 1665). The World Guardians appear and give him weapons: Yama his staff (1–20), Varuṇa his nooses (25–30), Kubera the disappearing weapon (30), while Indra invites him to heaven; his driver Mātali will come for him (35–40).

Vaiśaṃpāyana said:
13.1 The Bhojas, Vṛṣṇis, and Andhakas, on hearing that the Pāṇḍavas, dolorous, had renounced, came all together to the large forest. The heirs of the king of Pāñcāla, and Dhṛṣṭaketu, lord of the Cedis, and the puissant Kekaya brothers, renowned in the world, went to the Pārthas in the forest, filled with anger and indignation. Condemning the Dhārtarāṣṭras, they said, "What shall we do?" All those bulls of the barons, led by Kṛṣṇa Vāsudeva, surrounded Yudhiṣṭhira the King Dharma and sat around him.

Vāsudeva said:
5 Of Duryodhana, Karṇa, the evil-spirited Śakuni, and Duḥśāsana, the earth shall drink the blood! Thereafter we shall all consecrate Yudhiṣṭhira the King Dharma. One who serves with trickery deserves to be killed, that is the sempiternal Law!

Vaiśaṃpāyana said:
When Janārdana out of his partiality for the Pārthas had become so enraged, Arjuna appeased him, for he seemed prone to burn down the creatures. Seeing Keśava's rage, Phalguna* recited the feats of the previous lives of the great-spirited man, whose fame is true, the immeasurable, true, boundlessly lustrous lord of the Prajāpatis, the wise guardian of the world who is Viṣṇu.

Arjuna said:
10 For ten thousands of years you were of old a hermit, Kṛṣṇa, bedding down wherever night fell, wandering in the Gandhamādana mountain range.

For ten millennia and ten centuries you dwelled of old in the Puṣkara country, Kṛṣṇa, living on water.

For a hundred years did you, slayer of Madhu, stand on one foot with your arms raised in vast Badarī, living on the wind.

* = Arjuna.

Ripping off your upper cloth, lean, held together by your veins, you dwelled on the Sarasvatī River, Kṛṣṇa, at the Twelve-Year Session.

To Prabhāsa you came, that ford familiar to the good, and again for a divine millennium of years you stood there, Kṛṣṇa, on one foot in austerities, abiding in restraint.

15 You are the guide of all creatures, their beginning and end, Keśava, you are the storehouse of austerities, Kṛṣṇa, and the eternal sacrifice.

You slew the Hell-on-earth; taking two jeweled earrings, you set loose, when it was first engendered, O Kṛṣṇa, the sacrificial horse.

Having done this labor, a bull for the worlds, victor of all the world, you slew in a war all the gathered Daityas and Dānavas.

Thereupon, having entrusted the universal sovereignty that was yours to Śacī's spouse*, you became manifest, strong-armed Keśava, among mankind.

After having been Nārāyaṇa, you became Hari, enemy-burner, and
20 Brahmā, the Moon, the Sun, the Law, the Placer, Yama, the Fire, the
Wind, Vaiśravaṇa, Rudra, Time, Ether, Earth, the Directions; you are
the unborn Guru of all that moves and stands, the Creator, O Supreme
Person.

In the woods of Citraratha, O God Kṛṣṇa of great splendor, you offered up the Turāyaṇa sacrifice and others with rich stipends.

At each sacrifice, O Janārdana, there was gold portioned out, fully a hundred times a hundred thousand.

Having become the son of Aditi, O Joy of the Yādavas, you are renowned on earth as Viṣṇu, younger brother of Indra.

As a child you bestrode, enemy-burning Kṛṣṇa, heaven, atmosphere and earth with three strides by the grace of your majesty.

25 Having risen to the space of heaven and sitting in the seat of the sun, you outshone, O soul of the creatures, its orb with your own effulgence.

The Mauravas and Pāśas have been extirpated, Nisunda and Naraka slain, and thus the road to the city of Prāgjyotiṣa** has again been rendered safe.

Āhuti has been slain at Jārūthī, so have Kratha, Śiśupāla, and his people, Bhīmasena and the Śibi king, as well as Śatadhanvan.

On your chariot, thunderous like the monsoon and resplendent like the sun, you abducted your queen from the Bhojas after defeating Rukmin in battle.

Indradyumna has been killed in anger, and so has the Yāvana Kaśerumat; you have slain Śālva, lord of Saubha, and razed Saubha itself.

30 On the banks of the Irāvatī you killed the Bhoja, who was Kārtavīrya's peer in war, and also both Gopati and Talaketu.

* = Indra.
** = Assam.

After having made Dvārakā your own, joyous holy city beloved by the seers, O Janārdana, you shall bring it to the ocean.

There is no anger in you, no envy, no falsehood, Madhusūdana Dāśārha, no cruelty, much less dishonesty.

The seers came to you where you were sitting, radiant with your splendor, in the midst of their hearts, and all begged safety from you, Acyuta.

At the end of the Eon you dissolve all creatures, Madhusūdana, and having made the world your own within your very self, you remain thereafter, enemy-burner.

35 Neither the ancient nor the future shall match the exploits you
performed, most splendid God, while still a child.

You acted, lotus-eyed one, aided by Baladeva; and you lived in the palace of Vairāja with Brahmā.

Vaiśaṃpāyana said:

After the Pāṇḍava, who was the very self of Kṛṣṇa, had thus spoken
to himself, he fell silent and Janārdana said to the Pārtha, "You are
mine and I am yours, and my people are yours. He who hates you
hates me; who follows you follows me. You, invincible hero, are Nara
and I am Hari Nārāyaṇa. Nara and Nārāyaṇa, the seers, have come
40 from their world to this world. You are no other than I, Pārtha, I no
other than you, Bhārata, no difference can be found between the two
of us, bull of the Bharatas."

In this congregation of heroes all the kings became excited: Kṛṣṇā
of Pāñcāla, surrounded by her gallant brothers Dhṛṣṭadyumna and so
forth, went forward to the lotus-eyed one, who was seated with the
Yādavas, to her shelter seeking shelter; and she said, "They say that
you were the sole Prajāpati at the first creation of creatures. Asita
Devala says you are the creator of all beings. You, invincible, are
Viṣṇu, you are the sacrifice, Madhusūdana. You are the sacrificer and
45 the one to be sacrificed to, as Jāmadagnya has said. The seers have
said that you are the earth, O Supreme Person, and the truth. From
the truth you are born as the sacrifice, as Kaśyapa said. You are the
paramount sovereign of Sādhyas and Gods, O Prosperer of the world,
and lord of the world, as Nārada told us. You fill heaven with your
head, earth with your feet, ubiquitous lord; these worlds are your
belly, you are the eternal Man. You are the greatest seer of the seers
who burn with the austere heat of knowledge, who have regenerated
their souls with austerities, who have been perfected in the vision of
the soul, of the meritorious royal seers who never flee from their
battles, endowed with all the Laws—of them all you are the goal,
50 Supreme Person. You lord it first, you lord it wide, you are earth, you
are the soul, you are eternal. The World Guardians, the worlds, the

asterisms, the ten directions, sky, moon, and sun are all erected on you. The mortality of the creatures and the immortality of the Celestials, and all the business of the worlds are erected upon you, strong-armed one. And here am I, about to tell you of my grief, out of love—for are you not the lord of all creatures, whether human or divine, Madhusūdana?

"Then *how* was it that a woman like me, wife to the Pārthas, friend to you, Lord Kṛṣṇa, sister of Dhṛṣṭadyumna, came to be dragged into the hall? Subjected to the Law of women, stained with blood, shuddering in my sole piece of clothing, I was grievously dragged into the assembly of the Kurus. In the midst of the kings, inside the hall, overrun by my menses, they watched me, the Dhārtarāṣṭras, and burst out laughing, the foul-minded! Madhusūdana, they wanted to exploit me as a slave wench! While the sons of Pāṇḍu, the Pāñcālas, and the Vṛṣṇis were alive! Am I not Kṛṣṇā, by Law the daughter-in-law of Bhīṣma and Dhṛtarāṣṭra? And *I* was forcibly reduced to a slave!

"I *detest* the Pāṇḍavas, those grand strongmen in war, who looked on while their glorious consort in Law was molested! A plague on the strength of Bhīmasena! A plague on the bowmanship of the Pārtha*! Both stood by, Janārdana, when churls manhandled me! Is it not the ancient way of the Law, forever followed by the strict, that husbands, however feeble, protect their wives? When the wife is protected, the children are; when the children are protected, the soul is. For the man himself is born in his wife, and that makes her a wife. The wife protects her husband: 'Why! He must be born from my womb!' Have they ever refused supplicants who sought help? And have not the Pāṇḍavas ignored me who craved quarter? These five fathered on me these five sons of boundless luster, and for their sake, too, I should have been rescued, Janārdana. I had Prativindhya by Yudhiṣṭhira, Sutasoma by the Wolf-Belly, Śrutakīrti by Arjuna, Śatānīka by Nakula, and Śrutakarman by the youngest: with all of them the truth is their strength, Kṛṣṇa, they are great warriors like your Pradyumna, Kṛṣṇa.

"So aren't they the best with the bow, undefeatable in battle by their enemies? Then why did they suffer the jejune Dhārtarāṣṭras? It was an Unlaw that their kingdom was taken and they were all made slaves, and that I, in my month, was dragged around in their hall with my one piece of clothing! Even when corded with its string, the Gāṇḍīva bow cannot be handled by anyone save Arjuna, Bhīmasena, and yourself, Madhusūdana. But a plague on the strength of Bhīmasena and the Pārtha's Gāṇḍīva, Kṛṣṇa, if Duryodhana lives for another hour! It was he who threw them out of the kingdom with their mother, though they had done no wrong, long ago, when they

* = Arjuna.

were studious children and lived by the rules, Madhusūdana. The
scoundrel had poison dropped into Bhīmasena's food, freshly collected
from a cobra's pouch, virulent and hair-raising! He digested the
poison with his food, without any effects, Janārdana, for his time had
not come, strong-armed Supreme Person. At Pramāṇakoṭi the Wolf-
Belly was confidently asleep; Duryodhana tied him up, Kṛṣṇa, threw
75 him in the Ganges, and walked away. When the Kaunteya woke up,
he burst out of his fetters and stood up, the strong-armed mighty
Bhīmasena! He had him bitten by virulent cobras when he was
sleeping, in all the parts of his body, but the enemy-killer did not die.
When he woke up, the Kaunteya smashed them all and dealt his
favorite charioteer a blow with the back of his hand. Once more he
tried to burn them in Vāraṇāvata, when they slept with the lady, and
who could have done a thing like that!

"It was there that the lady, weeping and fearful, cried out to the
Pāṇḍavas, encircled by flames and fallen into great distress: "Ah, I am
80 lost! How shall we have peace from the fire? A widow, I must die with
my little sons!" Then big-armed Wolf-Belly Bhīma, whose valor is like
the impact of a gale, comforted the lady and his brothers: "Like
Garuḍa, son of Vinatā, of all birds the greatest, I shall fly up and you
shall be out of danger!" Without a moment's hesitation he took the
lady on his left hip, the king on his right, on his shoulders the twins,
and the Terrifier on his back. He flew up nimbly, the mighty man,
carrying them all, and powerfully he made good the escape of the lady
85 and his brothers from that fire. The glorious men all started out in the
night with their mother and went into the large wilderness close to
Hiḍimba's wood.

"Exhausted, they slept there wretchedly with their mother, and
while they slept a Rākṣasī named Hiḍimbā came upon them. She took
Bhīma's feet and put them firmly in her lap and the beautiful woman
carressed them happily with a gentle hand. Immense of soul, mighty
and valiantly true to his truth, Bhīma woke up to her and questioned
her: "What, blameless woman, is it that you want here?" Hearing
their conversation, Hiḍimba, lowliest of Rākṣasas, arrived, a terrifying
apparition of terrible mien, screeching loud: "With whom are you
90 talking? Bring him to me! Hiḍimbā, we shall have a feast, pray don't
be long!" But her heart was gripped by compassion; the strong-
minded and blameless woman had too deep a pity to betray him.
There he came, the man-eating Rākṣasa, making ghastly noises, and
indeed stormed at Bhīmasena. The powerful, furious Rākṣasa
impetuously rushed at Bhīma and grabbed hold of his hand with his,
95 a hard adamant hand whose touch was like Indra's thunderbolt. When
his hand was captured by the Rākṣasa's, strong-armed Wolf-Belly

Bhīmasena did not tolerate it and grew angry; there began an
alarming and dreadful fight between Bhīma and Hiḍimba, who both
knew of all weapons, as between Vṛtra and Vāsava.

Bhīma killed Hiḍimba and departed with his brothers, placing ahead
Hiḍimbā, who bore him Ghaṭotkaca. From thence the glorious group
hurried forth with their mother, heading for Ekacakrā in the company
of droves of brahmins. At their departure Vyāsa was their friendly
100 adviser, and the Pāṇḍavas of strict vows journeyed to Ekacakrā. There
too they encountered a man-eater of great strength, Baka by name, no
less formidable than Hiḍimba himself. Bhīma, greatest of fighters,
killed that dreadful Rākṣasa too, and with all his brothers went on to
the city of Drupada. I myself was won by the left-handed archer when
he lived there, just as you yourself, Kṛṣṇa, won Bhiṣmaka's daughter,
Madhusūdana, by achieving at my Bridegroom Choice a great feat
that others found most difficult.

"So, distressed by too many hardships and suffering greatly, we
105 have now settled down, without the lady but led by Dhaumya. They
are gallant like lions, Kṛṣṇa, in manliness the masters of their foes:
then why did they ignore me when I was molested by inferiors? Such
have been the indignities that they suffered at the hands of weaker,
evil, plebeian men, indignities that were kindled over a long time.

"I was born in a grand lineage, and by divine fate! I am the
favorite wife of the Pāṇḍavas, the daughter-in-law of the great-
spirited Pāṇḍu. And I was laid hold of by my hair, I who was the
choicest, while all the five who are like Indras looked on,
Madhusūdana!"

And with these words gentle-spoken Kṛṣṇā began to weep, covering
110 her face with her hands, which was tender as a lotus cup. Upon
unfallen breasts, hard, high-born, and well-favored, the Pāñcālī rained
the tears that welled up from her grief. She wiped her eyes and,
sighing again and again, spoke angrily from a tear-choked throat:
"I have got no husbands, no sons, Madhusūdana, not a brother nor a
father, nor you, nor friends, if you mercilessly ignored me when I was
plagued by the vulgar. For this grudge of mine shall never be
appeased: that a Karṇa laughed at me!"

Then in this gathering of heroes Kṛṣṇa said to her, "Weep shall the
115 women of those that have angered you, angry woman! Weep over
their men as they lie on the face of the earth, covered by the
Terrifier's arrows, showered by a rain of blood, cut down to relinquish
their lives! I shall do whatever the Pāṇḍavas can do; do not sorrow!
I make you a promise: you shall be a queen of kings! Let Sky fall
down, let Himālaya break, let Earth splinter, let Sea dry up, Kṛṣṇā—
my word shall not be false!"

Dhṛṣṭadyumna said:
I shall kill Droṇa, Śikhaṇḍin shall kill the grandsire, Bhīmasena shall kill Duryodhana, and Dhanaṃjaya shall kill Karṇa! If we rely on Rāma and Kṛṣṇa, we are invincible, sweet-smiling sister, were we to face the Slayer of Vṛtra himself in battle, so what of Dhṛtarāṣṭra's brood!"
Vaiśaṃpāyana said:
120 When all this was said, the heroes looked at Vāsudeva, and in the
midst of them the strong-armed Keśava spoke this word.

Vāsudeva said:
14.1 If I had been present in Dvārakā earlier, O king, you would not
have got into this trouble. I would have come to the dicing, even if the
Kauravas did not invite me, or if King Āmbikeya* and Duryodhana did
not, invincible lord! I would have stopped the gaming by pointing out
the many things that were wrong with it, and by bringing in Bhīṣma,
Droṇa, Kṛpa, and Bāhlīka. I would have told King Vaicitravīrya on
your behalf, "Be done with the dicing of your sons, Kaurava, lord
5 among kings!" and pointed out the deceptions by which you have
now become unseated and by which at one time Vīrasena's son was
deprived of his kingdom. I would have truthfully described how by
gaming a man loses what has not yet been eaten up, and how the
addiction to gambling lasts forever.
Women, dice, hunting, and drinking are the four vices that spring
from desire and make a man lose his fortune. Those who know the
texts believe that this can be said of any one of these vices, but the
experts find that this can be said of gambling in particular. In a single
day one may lose one's property, distress is certain, possessions are
10 lost without the enjoyment of them, and only insults are left. Of this
and other sources of bitterness I would have spoken before Ambikā's
son*, strong-armed lord. If at my words he had accepted my advice,
the Law of the Kurus would have been intact, scion of Kuru. If he had
not accepted my mild and apt advice, lord among kings, I would have
stopped him by force, best of the Bharatas. I would have shown up in
the same manner the other men in the hall, enemies pretending to be
friends, and I would have destroyed the gamblers. It was my absence
from Ānarta, O Kauravya, that has caused all of you to fall into the
15 distress that was brought about by the dicing. When I came to
Dvārakā, best of the Kurus, scion of Pāṇḍu, I heard from Yuyudhāna
exactly how you had come to distress. As soon as I heard it, I made
haste, greatly upset, here, desiring to visit you, lord of your people.
Aho! We have all come to grief, as we find you and your brothers in
this predicament!

* = Dhṛtarāṣṭra.

3(31.a) The Razing of Saubha

3.15–23 (B. 14–22; C. 614–902)
15 (14; 614). Kṛṣṇa relates that Śālva attacked Dvārakā in revenge of his killing Śiśupala and abused Kṛṣṇa (1–10). Enraged by his attack, Kṛṣṇa sets out to kill Śālva, as he does (15–20).
16 (15; 636). Yudhiṣṭhira asks for more details. Kṛṣṇa relates that Śālva besieged Dvārakā, which was heavily fortified and guarded (1–20).
17 (16; 659). Śālva attacks. Sāmba engages in a dual with General Kṣemavṛddhi, who flees, and is attacked by Vegavat whom he subdues (1–20). Cārudeṣṇa kills Vivindya (20–25). Śālva comes into action with his sky-going chariot. Pradyumna promises to defeat him (25–30).
18 (17; 695). Pradyumna attacks Śālva, who withstands him (1–15). Śālva is hit and collapses. He recovers and strikes down Pradyumna (15–20).
19 (18; 717). Pradyumna's charioteer drives him off. Pradyumna berates him and is answered that that is a charioteer's duty when the warrior is in danger (1–10). Pradyumna protests that that is not the Law of the Vṛṣṇis: all people will speak ill of him (10–30).
20 (19; 750). The charioteer defends himself and takes the chariot back to the battlefield; Śālva resumes his attack. Pradyumna is about to kill him when the Gods warn him that Kṛṣṇa is to be his killer (1–25).
21 (20; 777). On his return from Indraprastha Kṛṣṇa finds Dvārakā devastated and is told the cause. He promises to kill Śālva and departs for Mārtikavatī (1–15). He finds Śālva and his Saubha fortress by the ocean. He kills many demons (1–25). Śālva employs magic and pelts Kṛṣṇa with all kinds of weapons; Kṛṣṇa withstands him (30–35).
22 (21; 819). The battle continues. A messenger arrives from Dvārakā declaring Vasudeva's death (1–10). Kṛṣṇa is dispirited but concludes that it is wizardry (15–25).
23 (22; 849). Kṛṣṇa with chariot and horses is buried under rocks, but reappears (1–15). His charioteer urges him on. Kṛṣṇa razes Saubha with his discus and kills

Śālva (20–40). Kṛṣṇa returns to Dvārakā (40–45). Dhṛṣṭadyumna, Dhṛṣṭaketu, and the Kekayas leave Yudhiṣṭhira (45–50).

Yudhiṣṭhira said:

15.1 Why were you absent, Kṛṣṇa, scion of Vṛṣṇi? Where did you travel
and what did you do on your travels?

Kṛṣṇa said:

I went to Saubha, the city of Śālva, O bull of the Bharatas, in order
to destroy it, best of men: listen why. The august, strong-armed, and
famous King Śiśupāla, the heroic son of Dāmaghoṣa, had been killed
by me at your Royal Consecration, best of the Bharatas, over the gift
of honor, when that evil man under the sway of his anger did not
5 suffer me to receive it. When Śālva heard that I had killed him, he
stormed in a bitter rage on Dvārakā, which was empty, since I was
here with you. The young bulls of the Vṛṣṇis gave him battle, O king.
The cruel Śālva had come mounted on the Saubha chariot that can go
anywhere, and from it he killed many valiant Vṛṣṇi youths and evilly
devastated all the city parks. He cried, strong-armed lord, "Where has
that dregs of the Vṛṣṇi race Vāsudeva gone, that nitwit son of
Vasudeva's? I shall destroy in battle the pride of that man, who is so
10 eager for a fight! Ānartas, tell me truthfully: I shall go wherever he is.
When I have killed that murderer of Kaṃsa and Keśin, I shall return;
I shall not return before I have killed him, this I swear by my sword.
Where is he, where is he?" he cried as he darted from one place to
another, the king of Saubha, for he wanted to do battle with me!
"I shall send that evil, treacherous churl today to Yama's country, out
of rage over the death of Śiśupāla, for the evil-natured man has killed
my brother, King Śiśupāla; I shall slay him on the ground! My brother
was a youth and a king, and the hero was slain, not in a pitched
battle, but when he was distracted. I shall kill Janārdana!"

15 This and the like did he prattle; then after abusing me he took to
the sky on the Saubha, which can go anywhere, scion of Kuru. When
I came back, I heard how that evil-minded, evil-natured king of
Mārttikāvata had behaved toward me; with eyes red with rage I made
up my mind, King Kauravya, and decided to kill him as I learned of
his devastation of Ānarta, his abuse of myself, and the ripe insolence
of the miscreant.

So I departed to kill the Saubha, O king of the earth, and I found
20 him in a bay of the ocean while I was looking for him. I blew my
conch shell Pañcajanya, which was born from the ocean, and
challenged Śālva to battle, ready to fight. I had a long battle with the
Dānavas there. I overpowered them all and brought them down to the

ground. That was the business that kept me from coming as soon as I heard of Hāstinapura and the brutal gambling match.

Yudhiṣṭhira said:

16.1 Vāsudeva, strong-armed sage! Tell in detail of the killing of the
Saubha, for I never tire of listening to you!

Vāsudeva said:

When he heard, strong-armed king, that King Śrautaśrava had been
killed by me, Śālva marched on the city of Dvārakā, O best of the
Bharatas. That most wicked Śālva laid siege to the city on all sides and
from the air, with his battle ranks in position, son of Pāṇḍu. Having
taken his stand, the king attacked the city and started the war with a
total onslaught.

5 The city had prepared its defenses everywhere—there were flags,
gate towers, patrols, latrines, machines, sappers, mobile ramps,
avenues, eyries, turrets, towers, hair-catchers, catapults for firebrands
and torches, camels, O best of the Bharatas, kettledrums, cymbals,
drums, kindling, straw and *kuśa* grass, hundred-killers, plowshares,
flame-throwers, rock-pellets, arms, battle-axes, iron, leather, fire, and
nightsoil-hurlers—all the defenses provided for in the texts, Bhārata.
The city was outfitted with victuals of many kinds in ample stock, and
guarded by men like Gada, Sāmba, and Uddhava, quite capable of
hitting back, O tiger of the Kurus, heroes of famed families, whose
10 prowess had been proven in battle. Known for its solidity, it was
protected by high fortifications in the middle ramparts, and by horses
and foot soldiers. Such authorities as Ugrasena and Uddhava, who
were providing against negligence, passed orders throughout the city
that no liquor was to be drunk. Realizing that King Śālva might be
able to breach them if they were negligent, all the Vṛṣṇis and
Andhakas stayed sober. All the actors, dancers, and songsters of
15 Ānarta were expelled by the guardians of the treasuries. The bridges
were dismantled, all boat traffic stopped; the trenches were heavily
fortified with spikes, Kauravya, the wells destroyed, and the earth was
roughed up all around for a distance of two leagues. Our fortress is by
nature hard of access, by nature well-guarded, and by nature
exceptionally equipped with weapon gear, prince sans blame. Well
defended and guarded and outfitted with all kinds of arms, that city,
best of the Bharatas, was like Indra's fortress. No one without a stamp
could go out or be taken into the city of the Vṛṣṇis and Andhakas at
20 the time of the Saubha's advance, king. All over the roads and the
crossroad squares the army was out in force, King Kaurava, with
plenty of horses and elephants. The troops had been given their wages
and victuals, their armaments and armor, they were all paid up that
time, strong-armed king. No one had reason to anger at his pay, nor

was anyone overpaid, not one was specially treated, there was not a one whose courage had not been witnessed.

Thus Dvārakā was well-prepared, king, with well-paid troops and well defended by Āhuka the king, O lotus-eyed prince.

17.1 *Vāsudeva said:*
But, sire, Śālva marched on, the lord of Saubha, and laid siege with
an army that teemed with men and elephants. The troops under
Śālva's command, which were divided into the four divisions, settled in
on the plain, where the watershed was aplenty. The army settled in,
avoiding only burning grounds, sanctuaries of Gods, anthills, and
burial mounds. The way the ranks were spread out, all the roads were
properly taken care of, and the nine slopes were covered by Śālva's
5 camp. He deployed a mass of chariots, elephants, and horses, equipped
with and adept in all kinds of weaponry, Kauravya, bull among men,
with plentiful flags and footfolk, with a complement of contented and
well-fed people; this mass, marked by the marks of gallantry, with
colorful banners and armor, various kinds of chariots and bows, he
settled in about Dvārakā and then, Kauravya, like the king of birds
made his assault.
When they saw King Śālva's army attack, the young princes of the
Vṛṣṇis made a sally and gave battle, princes such as Cārudeṣṇa,
Sāmba, and the warlike Pradyumna, who refused to condone, O
10 Kaurava, the assault of King Śālva. With their beautiful banners and
ornaments, they all joined battle, harassed by the chariots and the
numerous bull-like warriors of King Śālva.
Grasping his bow, Sāmba, exhilarated, drew Śālva's councillor and
General Kṣemavṛddhi into battle. Jambāvatī's son let loose on him a
fierce shower of arrows, best of the Bharatas, as the Thousand-eyed
God lets loose his rain. General Kṣemavṛddhi survived that
alarming shower of arrows, great king, and stood immovable like the
Himālaya. Then Kṣemavṛddhi sent upon Sāmba a huger net of shafts
with his magic, but rending the magic with his own magic, Sāmba
rained a hundred thousand arrows on the other's chariot. Sāmba hit
General Kṣemavṛddhi, who ran off with swift horses, pressed by
Sāmba's arrows. Śālva's brutal general having fled, a powerful demon,
Vegavat by name, ran upon my son. Set upon, Sāmba, a scion of
Vṛṣṇi's line, stood fast and, O king, heroically endured the onslaught
of Vegavat.
Sāmba hurled at Vegavat his impacting club, O Kaunteya, and the
20 hero, whose strength was his truth, pierced him. Struck by the club,
Vegavat fell to the ground, as a giant of the forest with rotting roots
collapses when bruised by a wind gust. When the valiant great Asura
had fallen, dispatched by the club, my son invaded the mighty army
and made it give battle. A Dānava named Vivindhya, an acknowledged

warrior and great archer, joined battle with Cārudeṣṇa, and there
ensued a most terrifying fight between Cārudeṣṇa and Vivindhya,
as of yore between Vṛtra and Vāsava*, O king. They shot at each other
25 with arrows in a mutual rage, roaring like powerful lions. Rukmiṇī's**
son fixed an enchanted arrow to his bow, in power like the fire or the
sun, sure to kill the enemy. My warlike son angrily challenged
Vivindhya and shot him; and he fell dead.

Seeing Vivindhya dead and his army routed, Śālva returned on the
Saubha chariot, which could go anywhere. The entire Dvārakā-based
army now got into disorder, when they saw Śālva on his Saubha
earthbound. Then Pradyumna sallied out, O Kaunteya, regrouped the
30 army, and spoke to the Ānartas: "All of you hold your positions and
watch me in battle as I by sheer force halt the Saubha and its king in
the encounter! I shall destroy the army of the king of the Saubhas
with iron shafts as though with serpents, discharged from my bow by
my hand, and I shall do it this very day, Yādavas! Breathe again, have
no fear; today the king of Saubha is going to perish; the miscreant,
set upon by me, will perish with the Saubha!"

When Pradyumna called out so excitedly, brave scion of Pāṇḍu, his
army held their positions and gave battle happily.

Vāsudeva said:

18.1 After this address to the Yādavas, O bull of the Bharatas, Rukmiṇī's
son mounted his gilt chariot, which was yoked with armored bay
horses and over which a flag waved with the emblem of an
ornamented crocodile with a wide-open jaw. With his horses that
seemed to fly in the air, the powerful hero stormed at the enemies,
shooting and twanging his great bow, holding quiver and sword, with
wrist and finger guards tied on. He changed his bow with lightning
speed from palm to palm and sowed confusion among the Daityas and
5 all the settlers of Saubha. As he shot and reshafted the bow again and
again, no one could spy an interruption in the continuous flow of his
slaughter of the enemies in battle.

On his face the color did not change
Nor was there a tremor in his limbs;
The people heard the marvelous dominant
Leonine roar as he thundered his cry.

The crocodile flag on the golden mast
With its maw wide open, terror of fishes,
Waved brightly on the chariot, sowing fear
Before the army entire of Śālva.

* = Indra.
** = Pradyumna.

Pradyumna, plower of enemies, stormed with great speed onward and
fell upon Śālva, prepared to feud with him, O king. But the enraged
Śālva did not suffer being attacked by heroic Pradyumna, O prosperer
10 of Kuru's line. Drunk with fury, Śālva, winner of enemy cities,
dismounted from his ubiquitous chariot and engaged Pradyumna in
battle. People crowded together and watched that most terrifying duel
between Śālva and the champion of the Vṛṣṇis as between Bali and
Vāsava. His was a magic chariot that was decorated with gold, with a
mast and a flag, axle tree and quivers. The illustrious warrior
remounted that superb chariot, lord Kauravya, and powerfully shot
his arrows at Pradyumna. In that combat Pradyumna loosed a fast
shower of arrows with the speed of his arms, fairly bewildering Śālva.
15 The Saubha king could not bear being attacked by him in their
rencounter and sent arrows at my son, blazing like fire. When he was
struck by Śālva's shafts, Rukminī's son swiftly shot an arrow, which
sought out the other's weak spot; the shaft shot by my son pierced his
armor and cut into his heart. He fell and fainted. When their hero
King Śālva had fallen unconscious, the lordly Dānavas rushed near,
tearing the earth. The army of Śālva raised wails of woe, king of the
20 land, when the Saubha chief had fallen in a swoon. Then, regaining
his mind, Kauravya, he rose and nimbly and powerfully shot an arrow
at Pradyumna. Strong-armed Pradyumna was sorely hit, while he
stood his ground in the fight; it hit him in the breastbone, and the
hero sank down in the chariot. Upon hitting Rukminī's son, Śālva
roared a lion's roar, great king, filling the earth with his cry; and
while my son was lying unconscious, Bhārata, he quickly shot more
arrows, which could not be warded off. Struck by the many arrows
and rendered senseless, Pradyumna remained motionless on the
battlefield, best of the Kauravas.

Vāsudeva said:

19.1 When Pradyumna, strong of the strong, had been cut down by
Śālva's arrows, the Vṛṣṇis who had come to do battle lost purpose and
calm. The troops of the Vṛṣṇis and Andhakas all raised wails of woe
at Pradyumna's fall, while the enemies rejoiced, O king.

Seeing that he was unconscious, his skillful charioteer Dāruki
immediately carried him off from the battlefield with his swift horses.
The chariot had not gone very far when the halter of enemy chariots
regained consciousness and grasping his bow he said to the driver,
5 "What are you thinking of, son of a charioteer, that you turn your
chariot back? That is not what is called the Law of the Vṛṣṇis in war!
Were you driven out of your mind by the sight of Śālva in a battle
royal, or did you lose heart on witnessing war? Tell me the truth!"

The charioteer said:
I did not lose my mind, son of Janārdana, nor did I panic! But I
think that Śālva is too much for you, scion of Keśava. Therefore I
slowly withdrew, hero, for the fiend is powerful. A chariot champion
who is put out of action in an engagement should be saved by his
charioteer. Sir, I must always protect you, as you must protect me;
and thinking that the chariot warrior should always be safe, I
10 withdrew. You are by yourself, strong-armed warrior, and the
Dānavas are many—I withdrew upon deciding that the battle is
unequal, son of Rukmini!

Vāsudeva said:
While the charioteer was still speaking, Kauravya, the crocodile-
crested Pradyumna ordered him, "Turn the chariot around! Don't
ever do this again, son of Dāruka*, withdrawing from a battle while I
am still alive! No one born in the lineage of Vṛṣṇi ever forsakes his
given word or kills a fallen foe or one who surrenders. No one kills a
woman, child, or old man, one unseated from his chariot, one gone to
15 pieces, or one whose sword and weapons are broken. You were born
in a family of charioteers and trained in their craft, and you know full
well the Law of the Vṛṣṇis in war, Dāruki! And knowing the entire
conduct of the Vṛṣṇis in pitched battle, you shall never again, under
any condition, retreat!

If I retreat, am hit in the back, panic, or flee from a battle, what is
Mādhava**, the invincible senior of Gada, going to say to me? And
Keśava's drunken brother in his black robe, Baladeva, what will he say
when he returns? What will Śini's grandson*** say, the bowman, a lion
20 of a man, if I retreat from battle, or battle-winning Sāmba, invincible
Cārudeṣṇa, and Gada and Sāraṇa? What will the strong-armed
Akrūra tell me, charioteer, what the gathered women of the Vṛṣṇi
champions, me who am celebrated as a hero and have always prided
myself on my manliness? 'Pradyumna is frightened,' they will say, 'he
abandons the battle and retreats!' 'Fie on him!' they will say, and not
'Bravo!' To me or one like me ridicule with the cry of Fie! is worse
than death, son of a charioteer. Don't you ever withdraw again! Hari,
the slayer of Madhu, put his burden on me before he departed for the
25 sacrifice of the boundlessly lustrous Pārtha, the lion of the Bharatas. I
stopped the heroic Kṛtavarman, when he was about to make a sally,
saying, charioteer, 'Stay! I myself shall stop Śālva!' Hṛdika's son then
returned, for he respects me. If I now meet him after abandoning the
battle, what shall I say to the warrior? What shall I say to the

* = Dāruki.
** = Kṛṣṇa.
*** = Sātyaki.

invincible, lotus-eyed, big-armed man who wields conch, discus, and club, when he comes back? Sātyaki, Baladeva, and the other Vṛṣṇis and Andhakas who always vie with me, what am I going to tell them? If I must abandon the battle and be struck in the back by arrows while I am willy-nilly being carried off by you, I would not want to live, son of a charioteer! Turn the chariot immediately around again, son of Dāruka, and do not do it again, under any condition, were it a disaster! I won't think much of my life ever after I had fearfully shrunk from battle and been hit in the back by arrows! When, son of a charioteer, have you known me to be frightened? To run away from battle like a coward? You should not avoid battle, son of Dāruka, as long as I long to fight! Return to the battlefield!"

Vāsudeva said:

20.1 At these words, Kaunteya, the charioteer's son quickly replied to Pradyumna on that battlefield, in a gentle and placating voice: "I know no fear, son of Rukminī, when I drive the horses to combat. I know how the Vṛṣṇis fight, and it is precisely as you say. But, sir, there is this traditional instruction for those who live by charioteering that in all circumstances the chariot warrior must be protected. And you were greatly pressed! You were badly hit by Śālva's arrow, and you had lost consciousness, hero, that is why I retreated. Now that you happen to have regained consciousness, chief of the Sātvatas, watch my skill in the handling of the horses, son of Keśava! Dāruka fathered me and he taught me thoroughly! Fearlessly I drive into this mighty army of Śālva!"

With these words he goaded the horses onward, O hero, to the field of battle, steering them with the reins, and flew with great speed. Sped by the whip and guided by the reins, the horses carried out beautiful fanning in and out maneuvers, doubling back and around again, clever leftward and rightward turns, and the superb steeds seemed to be flying in the sky. Knowing Dāruki's deftness of hand, O king, they seemed to be on fire as they touched the earth with their hooves. With hardly any effort, he circled around Śālva's army leftward, bull of the Bharatas, and it was like a miracle!

Intolerant of Pradyumna, the king of Saubha violently shot three arrows at the charioteer when he was on his right, but Dāruki gave no thought to the impact of the arrows and pressed ever onward with his obedient horses, strong-armed king. Thereupon the Saubha king once more shot arrows of many kinds at my valiant son, the joy of Rukminī. Before they struck home the slayer of enemy champions deflected them with his own honed shafts, and he smiled as he displayed the deftness of his hands. Seeing his arrows deflected by Pradyumna, the Saubha king resorted to the dreadful wizardry of the Asuras when he shot his arrows; but realizing that Daitya missiles were being employed, Pradyumna powerfully deflected them halfway with his Brahmā missile and loosed more of his own shafts. The blood-drinking arrows drove the other's missiles off fast, and they pierced him in the head, chest, and face; and he fainted and fell.

When the lowly Śālva had fallen under the onslaught of the arrows, Rukmiṇī's son fixed another enemy-killing arrow to the bow string.

20 At the sight of this shaft being put to the string,
Which all the Dāśārha bulls used to worship
With blessings, alike to the fire and the sun,
The sky above began wailing with woe.

All the hosts of the Gods with Indra and the Lord of Riches sent off Nārada and the mighty Wind, and they went to Raukmiṇeya and told the words of the celestials: "Champion, you may not kill Śālva under any condition! Withdraw the arrow, for he is not to be slain by you. Not a man in battle is safe from this arrow, but, strong-armed warrior, the Placer has ordained that Devakī's son Kṛṣṇa is to be his death, and that may not be gainsaid!"

25 Supremely joyful, Pradyumna then withdrew that ultimate arrow from his great bow and replaced it in the quiver. In very bleak spirits Śālva stood up, great king, and quickly retreated with his troops, pressed by Pradyumna's arrows. Routed by the Vṛṣṇis, the cruel fiend abandoned Dvārakā, mounted his Saubha, and went up to the sky.

Vāsudeva said:

21.1 I returned to the Ānarta city, after he had abandoned it, when your great ceremonial of the Royal Consecration had been completed, king; and I saw Dvārakā lusterless, great king, its Vedic studies and sacrificial calls silenced, its beautiful women without ornaments. And noting that Dvārakā's parks were unrecognizable, I questioned Hṛdika's* son with great misgivings: "The men and the women of the city of the Vṛṣṇis look very much out of sorts. What is the matter, tiger among men? We want to hear it!"

5 At my bidding Hārdikya told me in full of the siege of the city by Śālva and its relief, O best of kings. When I had heard his full account, first of the Kauravas, I set my mind on the destruction of King Śālva. I set the people in the city at ease, best of the Bharatas, and, comforting King Āhuka and Anakadundubhi** as well as all the other champions of the Vṛṣṇis, I said, "Bulls of the Andhakas! Be always on your guard in the city! Now take note, I shall depart to destroy King Śālva, and I shall not return to the city of Dvāravatī until I have killed

* = Kṛtavarman.
** = Vasudeva.

him. I shall see you again after I have destroyed the Saubha city and
Śālva! Beat the kettledrum with its three tones, which terrifies the
enemy!"

10 Heartened by my speech, as they should have been, all the heroes,
O bull of the Bharatas, excitedly cried at me, "Start and cut down the
enemies!" The happy warriors bade me farewell with benedictions;
and after I had had the principal brahmins bless my way and had
bowed my head to Āhuka, I drove off on my chariot, which was
teamed with Sainya and Sugrīva, thundering to the horizons. Blowing
my superb conch Pañcajanya, I departed, tiger among men, in the
midst of a large force I had mustered, a four-membered army that
glowed with triumph.

I passed through many countries, over thickly wooded mountains,
15 lakes, and rivers, to his seat of Mārttikāvata. There I learned, tiger
among men, that Śālva had left the city, though he was still close by,
mounted on his Saubha, and I followed him in pursuit. I found him by
the ocean: Śālva, mounted on his Saubha, sat at a bay of the wavy
waters, at the navel of the seas, enemy-killer. He saw me coming from
afar, and with a ghost of a smile the miscreant again and again
challenged me to battle, enemy-killer Yudhiṣṭhira! The many arrows
I shot from my horn bow Śārnga, wonted to cut into weak spots,
failed to reach his stronghold, and it was then that rage seized me.
The evil-natured outcast of the Daityas rained, unassailably, showers
of arrows on me, by the thousands, O king; he showered my soldiers,
20 my charioteer, and my horses, but without minding the shots we
pushed on with the fight, Bhārata. The heroes that followed Śālva's
footsteps in war shot hundreds and thousands of smooth arrows at
me; the Asuras covered with weakness-spotting shafts my horses, my
chariot, and my Dāruka himself; neither horses, nor chariot, O hero,
nor my driver Dāruka could be seen under that blanket of arrows, nor
I or my troops.

Kauravya, I shot from my bow many myriads of arrows that were
25 enchanted with a divine spell; but I and my troops had no target,
Bhārata, for his Saubha clung to the sky at a league's length. All
spectators, as though standing at the fence of an arena, cheered me on
with lion roars and hand claps. The arrows that I shot from my bow
in that grand battle jumped into the bodies of the Dānavas like
bloodthirsty locusts. The wails of anguish increased in the middle of
Saubha as they were being killed by honed arrows and fell into the
vast ocean. Arms severed from their shoulders, the Dānavas, mere
trunks, kept falling down, screaming their ghastly screams.

30 I filled with my breath my ocean-born conch Pañcajanya, the color
of cow's milk, or jasmine, or the moon, or a lotus stalk, or silver.
Śālva, lord of Saubha, seeing them fall, engaged me in a great battle of

wizardry. He threw at me rockets, missiles, spears, spikes, battleaxes,
three-bladed javelins, flame-throwers, without pausing. But I got hold
of them with my own wizardry and destroyed them; and when his
wizardry was destroyed, he fought me with mountain peaks. One
moment it was night, the next it was morning, a foul day, a fair day,
a hot spell, or a cold spell, Bhārata.
35 Thus employing his wizardry the enemy fought me, but divining it
all I destroyed the apparitions with those of mine, and in time blew
them away into all directions with my arrows. The sky, great king,
seemed to hold a hundred suns, a hundred moons, Kaunteya, and a
hundred myriad stars. Neither day nor night could be made out, or the
points of compass; then I, close to complete confusion, fixed to my
bow the arrow of insight; and it blew away his arrows like cotton
tufts. There began a tumultuous and hair-raising battle as I once more
addressed the enemy when I saw light.

Vāsudeva said:
22.1 While that grand foe of the barons Śālva was embroiled with me,
O tiger among men, he again in our battle took to the sky.

He hurled hundred-killers and giant clubs
And flaming spikes and bludgeons and swords,
The feeble-brained foe threw them at me in fury,
This Śālva, hoping for victory, king.

I warded them off as they loomed toward me
With my swift-striking shafts, as they flashed through the sky,
And I cut them into two or three pieces with mine—
There was a great din in the sky above.

He scattered on Dāruka and my horses and chariot a hundred
5 thousand smooth arrows. Dāruka seemed to stagger and he said to me,
O hero, "I stay as I must under the pressure of Śālva's arrows." When
I heard the charioteer's piteous words, I looked at the man and saw
that he had been hit by arrows; not a spot did I see on his chest, head,
trunk, and arms that was not hit by an arrow, best of the Pāṇḍavas.
Under the impact of that rain of arrows, his blood flowed plentifully,
like a mountain with pink minerals that is showered by the monsoon
clouds. He still held the reins, my charioteer, but he was fading in the
battle; and when I saw that, I steadied my man who was giving away
under the pressure of Śālva's shots, strong-armed king.
10 Then a man from Dvārakā came running to my chariot, Bhārata, a
friend, and he gave a message from Āhuka whose servant he was; he
was desperate and breathless. Hear what he said, Yudhiṣṭhira:
"Āhuka, the overlord of Dvārakā, speaks to you this word, champion:

'Keśava, learn what your father's friend has to say: Today Śālva has attacked Dvārakā, O scion of the Vṛṣṇis, while you were being stopped, and he has killed Śūra's son Vasudeva with brute force! So enough of your fighting! Come back, Janārdana, rescue Dvārakā itself, that is your great task now!' "

15 When I heard his message I was totally depressed. I could reach
no decision on where my duty lay. In my heart I reviled Sātyaki,
Baladeva, and the warlike Pradyumna, O hero, when I heard that
hurtful message; for before I left to destroy Śālva, I had entrusted the
safety of Dvārakā and my father to them, scion of Kuru! Could the
strong-armed Baladeva be alive, that killer of enemies, and could
Sātyaki and Raukmiṇeya and the gallant Cārudeṣṇa, and the others
headed by Sāmba?—this thought depressed me greatly. For had they
been alive, tiger among men, the Thunderbolt-wielder himself would
20 not have been able to kill Śūra's son. It was clear, Vasudeva was dead;
therefore clearly they were too, Baladeva and all the others, so I had
to conclude.

In many a way I pondered on their total destruction, and, great king, I again attacked Śālva staggeringly. I saw Vasudeva falling from the Saubha, heroic king, and confusion seized me; it was the very likeness of my father tumbling down, lord of men, like Yayāti tumbling from heaven to earth when his merit was exhausted. His turban had come apart and was drooping, his clothes were awry, and his hair was disheveled, and so I saw him tumbling down, like a planet whose merit is exhausted.

25 My excellent bow Śārnga fell from my hand, and sinking in
confusion I sat down in the hollow of my chariot. On seeing me
unconscious my whole army raised wails of woe, as I nestled down in
the chariot as though I were dead, Bhārata. I saw the shape of my
father falling with flailing arms and legs, like a falling bird, saw him
fall and saw the demon heroes, armed with lances and three-bladed
spears, hit him sorely. They made my mind reel.

But in a moment I regained my wits,
So I did then, hero, in that great slaughter;
And I saw no more the Saubha and foes
Or Śālva nor saw my ancient father.

30 The conclusion dawned on my mind that it had been wizardry; and
I woke up and again sowed out my hundreds of arrows.

Vāsudeva said:

23.1 I took my glittering bow, best of the Bharatas, and cut with my
arrows the heads of the Gods' enemies on the Saubha. I shot well-
robed arrows, which looked like poisonous snakes, high-flying and

burning arrows, from my Śārnga at King Śālva. Then the Saubha
became invisible, O prosperer of Kuru's lineage, concealed by wizardry,
and I was astounded. The bands of the Dānavas, with grimacing faces
and disheveled heads, screeched out loud, as I held my ground, great
5 king. I quickly laid on an arrow, which killed by seeking out sound, to
kill them and the screeching subsided. All the Dānavas who had been
screeching lay dead, killed by the blazing sunlike arrows that were
triggered by sound.

When the noise had died down, a new noise arose in another
quarter, great king, and I shot my shafts there. In all ten directions
and sideways and upward the Asuras screamed, Bhārata, and I cut
them down. Suddenly the Saubha, which could go anywhere,
10 reappeared after a journey to Prāgjyotiṣa, blinding my eyes, O hero. A
Dānava in the shape of a monkey, a finisher of the world, covered me
on a sudden with a mighty shower of rocks. I was being bombarded
on all sides by a rain of mountains, and I became like an anthill
overlain by mountains. With horses, charioteer, and flag, I was buried
under the mountains, until I was completely invisible. The Vṛṣṇi heroes
who were my troops panicked and ran in all directions. Indeed, the
whole universe, lord of the people, gave voice to a wail of anguish,
sky, earth, and space, when I had thus become invisible. My friends
lost heart, king, and they cried and wept, filled with grief and sorrow.
15 Joy filled the enemies, grief the friends—as I heard afterward, when I
had won the day. Then I took my favourite weapon, which would cut
through any rock, and, raising my thunderbolt, shattered all the
mountains. My horses, pressed upon by the weight of the mountains,
had lost breath and motion and were shivering. Then my kinsmen
saw me reappear like the sun in the sky breaking through a mass of
clouds, and all recovered their good spirits.

20 Bowing and with folded hands, my charioteer said to me, "Look
sharp, Vārṣṇeya! There is the Saubha chief Śālva! Enough of
contemptuous treatment now, Kṛṣṇa, put out your best efforts!
Withdraw from Śālva your gentleness and feelings of friendship. Kill
Śālva, strong-armed Kṛṣṇa, don't let him live, slay the enemy with all
your gallantry, enemy-killing hero! No stronger man should despise
an enemy, however weak, even if he crawls at your footstool—let
alone one who stands firm in battle. Kill him, my lord, tiger among
men, with every effort, don't let the time pass you by, chief of Vṛṣṇi's
25 line! He cannot be won with gentleness; and he cannot be deemed a
friend, he who engaged you in war and devastated Dvārakā!"

Hearing this and more from my charioteer, Kaunteya, and knowing
that it was the truth, I set my mind on giving battle to encompass the
death of King Śālva and the downfall of the Saubha. I said to Dāruka,
"Stop a moment," then I took my favorite fire weapon, which could

finish anyone, divine, not to be halted or cut, tremendously powerful, splendiferous, great reducer to ashes of Yakṣas, Rākṣasas, Dānavas, and contrary kings, my honed-edged stainless discus, the like of Time, the Finisher, or Yama. I pronounced a spell on this peerless extirpator of foes: "Now smite with your prowess the Saubha and whoever are my enemies inside." Then I furiously hurled it at him with the strength of my arms. And the shape of Sudarśana as it flew in the sky was that of the haloed sun at the end of the Eon.

It approached the now lackluster Saubha city and aloft it cut it in
two as a saw cuts a log. Severed in twain at the impact of the force of
Sudarśana it fell down like the Three Cities razed by the Great God.
35 When Saubha had fallen, the discus returned to my hand. Whirling it
once more, I told it, "Now hurry to Śālva!" Just as Śālva was aiming
a heavy mace in that battle royal, the discus cut him in two, and it
blazed with its power.

The hero had fallen, and the Dānavas with trembling hearts took to the wailing skies, pressed by my arrows. I had my chariot stopped close to Saubha, and blowing my conch I brought great joy to the hearts of my friends. And on beholding the city, lofty like a peak of Mount Meru, on fire with its watch towers and gateways, the women fled away.

40 Thus I killed Śālva in battle and razed Saubha; then I returned to
the Ānarta country and brought joy to my friends. And this was the
reason, king, why I failed to come to the City of the Elephant. Had I
come, slayer of enemy heroes, Suyodhana would have been dead!

Vaiśaṃpāyana said:

When the strong-armed Supreme Person had finished speaking,
Madhusūdana took leave from the Pāṇḍavas and prepared to depart.
The strong-armed hero greeted Yudhiṣṭhira the King Dharma, and the
king and Bhīma kissed him on the head. Kṛṣṇa had Subhadrā and
Abhimanyu mount his golden chariot, then he himself mounted amidst
45 the homage of the Pāṇḍavas. On his chariot drawn by Sainya and
Sugrīva, which sparkled like the sun, Kṛṣṇa, having comforted
Yudhiṣṭhira, departed for Dvārakā.

At the Dāśārha's departure, Dhṛṣṭadyumna Pārṣata, too, went back to his own city, taking Draupadī's sons. Dhṛṣṭaketu, king of the Cedis, took his sister and, after his visit with the Pāṇḍavas, left for the lovely city of Śuktimatī. The Kekayas took their leave from the Kaunteya of boundless splendor and, bidding all the Pāṇḍavas farewell, also departed, O Bhārata.

The brahmins and commoners who lived in the area, though
50 insistently dismissed, refused to desert the Pāṇḍavas. This most
marvelous gathering, O Indra, of kings, remained in the Kāmyaka

Forest of those great-spirited men, bull of the Bharatas. Strong-minded Yudhiṣṭhira, after paying honor to the brahmins, in time ordered his men to yoke the chariots.

3(31) The Mountain Man (continued)

Vaiśaṃpāyana said:

24.1 When the chief of Dāśārha had departed,
Yudhiṣṭhira, Bhīma, and Arjuna
The twins and Kṛṣṇā and also their priest
Ascended their priceless and well-teamed chariots.

So the heroes, united, made out for the forest,
In countenance like unto the Lord of the Dead,
And they doled out to the *Veda*-wise brahmins
Many pieces of gold and cattle and clothes.

Armed servitors, twenty, went about before them;
And bows and shields and copper arrows
And bowstrings and arrows and implements
They gathered up, and brought up the rear.

Thereafter the charioteer Indrasena
Collected the clothes of the Princess, and
Her nurses and slave girls and ornaments;
He collected them quickly and brought up the rear.

5 The townspeople went to the chief of the Kurus
And, undejected, walked sun-wise around him;
The brahmins serenely saluted him,
And the chiefs of the people of Kuru's Jungle.

King Dharma serenely saluted them back
He himself and his four brothers as well;
And there he stood, the great-spirited monarch
And watched the flood of folk of the Jungle.

The great-spirited bull of the Kurus felt
For them as a father feels for his sons;
And to the grand chief of the Bharatas
They were as sons are to their father.

The people approached in large multitudes
The Kuru champion and stood around him,
Lamenting: "Ah, our protector, Ah, our Law!"
And bashful tears streamed down their faces.

"Of the Kurus the chief, of your people the lord,
As a father dost thou desert thy sons!
Abandoning townsmen and country folk all
Where wilt thou travel that art our King Dharma?

10 "On cruelest Dhārtarāṣṭra be shame,
With his Saubala and ill-minded Karṇa,
They wish for disaster, the evil ones, king,
Who threatened thee, who art steady in Law.

"Great-spirited, thou by thyself hast founded
This peerless great city, a city of Gods,
This Indraprastha, unfailing in deeds—
Where, leaving it, goest thou, our King Dharma?

"Great-spirited Maya built for thee
This matchless hall, like the halls of the Gods;
It is like the magic of Gods God-guarded—
Where, leaving it, goest thou, our King Dharma?"

And wise in Law, Profit, and Pleasure, the august
Bībhatsu* spoke loud to the gathered folk:
"As he makes his camp in the woods, our king
Shall wrest from his foes their claims to glory!

"Led by the brahmins, together and singly,
Approach ye us hermits, propitiate us,
And tell us, wise in Profit and Law,
How best we succeed in our policies!"

15 When this word was spoken by Arjuna,
The brahmins and all the classes, O king,
Rejoiced with joy and together they all
Walked round that best of the bearers of Law.

They bade farewell to the Pārtha and Wolf-Belly,
Dhanaṃjaya, Draupadī, and the twins;
With Yudhiṣṭhira's leave they then turned back
To the kingdom, wherever they dwelled, and despaired.

Vaiśaṃpāyana said:

25.1 When they had departed, Yudhiṣṭhira Kaunteya, ever true to his word and Law-minded, said to his brothers, "For these twelve years

* = Arjuna.

we must live in the empty wilderness, so let us look for a place in the great forest where deer and fowl abound, with plenty of flowers and fruit, which is beautiful, healthy, and frequented by virtuous folk: there we shall live out all these autumns in happiness." When he had spoken, Dhanaṃjaya paid honor to that strong-minded guru of men, as though to a guru, and said in reply,

Arjuna said:

5 You have sat at the feet of ancient seers and nought in the world of
men is unknown to you. You have always attended on the brahmins,
bull of the Bharatas, on Dvaipāyana and others, and the austere
Nārada, who, master of himself, forever visits the gates of all the
worlds, from the worlds of the Gods to that of Brahmā and those of
Gandharvas and Apsarās. Without misdoubting, you know all the
ways of the brahmins and you know the powers of all of them, king.
You yourself know well, sire, what will bring us weal: we shall make
our dwelling, great prince, where you desire.

10 There is this lake that is called Dvaitavana, frequented by virtuous
folk, lovely, with plenty of flowers and fruit, frequented by many kinds
of birds. Methinks we should while away our twelve years there, if you
agree, my king. Or do you think otherwise?

Yudhiṣṭhira said:

Pārtha, I agree with what you have said. Let us go to the renowned and auspicious great Lake Dvaitavana!

Vaiśaṃpāyana said:

Thereupon they departed, all the Pāṇḍavas who strode by the Law,
accompanied by numerous brahmins, for Lake Dvaitavana. There were
brahmins who had kept up the *agnihotra* and others who did not keep
the fires, others who studied the *Veda*, or begged for their food, or
15 recited prayers, or lived in the forest. The brahmins who accompanied
Yudhiṣṭhira were many, hundreds of ascetic brahmins avowed to
truth and strict in their vows. Thus, traveling with these many
brahmins, the Pāṇḍavas, bulls of the Bharatas, came to the lovely and
holy Lake Dvaitavana.

It was the summer's end and the lord of the kingdom
Saw the forest abundant with showers of flowers,
With *śāla* trees, mangoes and palms, arrac trees,
Kadambas, *sarjas*, *arjunas*, jasmine.

On the crowns of the giant trees there stood,
Giving voice to the loveliest sounds, the peacocks,
And gallinules, *cakoras* in flocks,
There in that wood, and forest cuckoos.

In the forest the lord of the kingdom saw
Great herds of grand elephants, leaders of herds,

That were flowing with rut and stood like mountains,
Together with herds of elephant cows.

20 He drew near to the lovely Bhogavatī
And he saw in that wood the many settlers
Of Siddhas and seers, Law-minded and poised,
Who wore bark clothes and matted hair tufts.

The king dismounted from his conveyance
And with his brethren and people entered
That wood, he first of the bearers of Law,
As boundlessly lustrous Śakra the sky.

To the truthful king came curiously down
The gathering crowds of Cāraṇas, Siddhas,
And wood-dwellers came to the lionlike king,
And they stood around the strong-minded man.

He made his greeting to all the Siddhas,
And he was returned, like a king or a God,
And with all his eminent brahmins he entered,
Hands folded, that best of the bearers of Law.

The great-spirited man of holy habits
As a father was greeted by Law-minded saints,
And the king sat down at the foot of a tree,
A mighty tree that stood in full blossom.

25 Dhanaṃjaya, Kṛṣṇā, Bhīma too,
The twins and the followers of the grand king,
All left their mounts and descended there
And joined him, those chiefs of the Bharatas.

That mighty tree with its canopy
Of lianas that bent it looked, with the five bowmen—
The great-spirited Pāṇḍavas coming to dwell—
Like a lofty mountain with elephant herds.

Vaiśaṃpāyana said:
26.1 When the Indra-like princes had reached the forest,
Once to comforts used, now fallen to grief,
They disported themselves in the holy groves
Of *śāla* trees on Sarasvatī's banks.

The majestic bull of the Kurus, the king,
With the choicest roots and fruits refreshed
The ascetics all in the woods and the hermits
And the eminent brahmins accompanying him.

While the Pāṇḍavas dwelled in the mighty forest,
Their chaplain Dhaumya, to the Kurus a father,
Of sovereign luster, performed the oblations,
The ancestral rites, and the first-fruit offerings.

While they lived there in exile from their kingdom,
The ancient seer Mārkaṇḍeya,
Of severe and abundant luster, arrived
As a guest of the illustrious Pāṇḍavas.

5 When the sage saw Kṛṣṇā Draupadī,
Yudhiṣṭhira, Bhīma, and Arjuna,
The great-spirited, boundlessly lustrous saint,
Remembering Rāma, smiled midst the ascetics.

Crestfallen it seemed, King Dharma said,
"These ascetics here are all abashed;
Why is it you smile as though amused,
While you look at me, as the others watch?"

Mārkaṇḍeya said:

I am not amused and I do not smile,
Nor has gleeful pride taken hold of me;
But seeing your sorrow today I recall
The truth-avowed Rāma, Daśaratha's son.

For that king, too, with Lakṣmaṇa,
At his father's behest sojourned in the woods,
And once while he roamed with his bow, O Pārtha,
I saw him on the peak of the Ṛśyamūka.

Great-spirited peer of the Thousand-eyed God,
Defeater of Maya and Namuci's slayer,
Though innocent made at his father's behest
His sojourn in the woods into his own Law.

10 In might the like of a Śakra, majestic,
Daśaratha's son, undefeated in battles,
Gave up his comforts and roamed in the woods—
So practice no Unlaw, thinking "Power is mine!"

Nābhāga, Bhagīratha and other kings
Had conquered this earth to her bounds of the seas,
And they won their worlds with their truth, my son—
So practice no Unlaw, thinking "Power is mine!"

The truthful king of the Kāśis and Kāruṣas,
A strict man, O best of men, they called a mad dog,

When he gave up his domains and his riches—
So practice no Unlaw, thinking "Power is mine!"

The ancient rule laid down by the Placer
Was honored, O best of men, by the strict
Seven Seers, and now they shine in the sky—
So practice no Unlaw, thinking "Power is mine!"

Behold the powerful tuskers, great king,
That stand tall as mountain peaks and yet
Abide by the rule that the Placer laid down—
So practice no Unlaw, thinking "Power is mine!"

15 Behold, O king, all the various creatures,
How all according to kind with force
Act out what the Ordainer ordained for them—
So practice no Unlaw, thinking "Power is mine!"

Surpassing all creatures in truth and Law,
In becoming conduct and modesty,
You too shall shine with glory and splendor,
O Pārtha, a glorious, light-making sun!

Live out this hardshipful term in the forest
As you have promised, majestic prince;
You shall then recoup from the Kauravas
With your own splendor your blazing fortune!

Vaiśaṃpāyana said:

And having thus spoken his word, the great seer,
Amidst the ascetics, to him and his brothers,
He bade farewell to Dhaumya and Pārthas
And departed from there on a northward course.

Vaiśaṃpāyana said:

27.1 While the Pāṇḍavas were living in Dvaitavana, the vast wilderness became filled with brahmins. The lake of Dvaitavana was continuously hallowed by the sound of the Brahman being recited on all sides, like the world of Brahmā itself. All around rose the lovely sounds of formulas, hymns and chants, and melodious prose, which were being intoned. The song of the bowstring and the sages' song of the Brahman made the baronage shine even brighter in unison with brahmindom.

5 Then, at twilight, Baka Dālbhya addressed Yudhiṣṭhira Kaunteya the King Dharma, as he was seated surrounded by brahmins: "Look, O Pārtha, best of the Kurus, in Dvaitavana the hour has come for the fire oblations of the ascetics and brahmins, when the fire is made to

blaze up. In this holy spot, under your protection, the vow observing Bhṛgus, Āngirasas, Vāṣisthas, and Kāśyapas, the lordly Āgastyas and the Ātreyas of great vows, practice the Law, all these eminent brahmins in all the world who have joined you. Now listen intently, O Pārtha, to this word of mine, you and your brothers, scion of Kuru and Kuntī, which I shall speak to you.

10 "Brahmindom joined by baronage and baronage joined by brahmindom elevate each other and burn down the enemies as fire and wind burn down the woods.

"Do not wish to remain without brahmins, son,
If you wish to win this world and the next;
With a brahmin learned in Profit and Law,
Who has shed his confusion, a king removes rivals.

"Living by the Law of supreme weal, achieved by his protection of his subjects, Bali had no other recourse than the brahmin.

"Virocana's Asura son never lacked
In comforts, his fortune was never wanting;
He gained all earth allied with the brahmins;
When he did them ill, he came to grief.

"This earth with her riches does not love the baron
For long, if he does not ally with the brahmin;
But the sea-girt earth will bow to him
Whom a brahmin teaches, learned in prudence.

15 "As of an elephant in battle that is out of its mahout's control the might of the baronage fades if it lack in brahmins. In brahminhood there is unequaled insight, in baronage matchless strength; when the two go together, the world is serene. As a great fire burns up the underwood fanned by the wind, so the baron burns down the enemy sided by the brahmin. To gain what he does not have and to prosper what he has gained, a wise man should seek out the advice of the brahmins.

"To gain the ungained, to prosper the gained,
And to obtain the recourse that is needed,
You must lodge a well-known *Veda*-wise brahmin,
A brahmin of wisdom and of great learning.

20 "Your conduct with brahmins, Yudhiṣṭhira, has always been the best, and therefore your fame shines wide in all the worlds!"

Hereupon all the brahmins applauded Baka Dālbhya, as he praised Yudhiṣṭhira, and they were again filled with joy. Dvaipāyana, Nārada, Jāmadagnya, Pṛthuśravas, Indradyumna, Bhāluki, Kṛtacetas,

Sahasrapād, Karṇaśravas, Muñja, Lavaṇāśva, Kaśyapa, Hārīta, Sthūnakarṇa, Agniveśya, Śaunaka, Ṛtavāk, Bṛhadaśva, Ṛtavasu, Urdhvaretas, Vṛṣāmitra, Suhotra, Hotravāhana, these and many other brahmins of strict vows spoke to Ajātaśatru as the seers speak to the Sacker of Cities.

Vaiśaṃpāyana said:

28.1 The forest-dwelling Pāṇḍavas were sitting in the evening with
Kṛṣṇā and exchanged conversation; they were mired in grief and
sorrow.
The beloved and lovely, wise and faithful Kṛṣṇā said to the King
Dharma, "He surely is not at all unhappy about us, that evil, cruel,
and vicious son of Dhṛtarāṣṭra! When you were banished to the
woods, with me, clad in deerskins, and with all your brothers, he did
not say anything, did he, and the ill-witted, evil-natured man had no
5 regrets, after dispatching us to the woods, did he? He must have a
heart of iron, that man of evil deeds, the rough things he said to you
who are the best of us, so prone to the Law! That crook with his gang
has brought all this suffering on a man like you, used to your
comforts and unworthy of hardships, and he rejoices, the fiend. There
were four crooks there who did not shed a tear, when you were
ousted to the woods, Bhārata, in your deerskin skirts! I counted
Duryodhana, Karṇa, the evil Śakuni, and that rotten brother, dreadful
Duḥśāsana! All the other kings, greatest of the Kurus, were
overwhelmed with grief and the water fell from their eyes!
10 "I remember your old bed and I pity you, great king, so unworthy
of hardship and so used to comfort! I remember your throne in the
hall; it was made of ivory and inlaid with jewels; and now I see your
kuśa cushion; ah, sorrow stifles me! I have seen you in the hall, with
your surrounding court of kings, and now I no longer see it—where
is the peace of my heart? I saw you, bright as a sun, well-oiled with
sandal paste, now I see you dirty and muddy, and do I not faint,
Bhārata? I who have seen you dressed in bright and costly silks, I
now, great king, must see you wearing bark!
15 "There was a time when cooked food was fetched from your house
on golden platters for thousands of brahmins, food to please every
taste; whether they were ascetics and homeless, or householders, the
very best food was doled out, lord. Now I no longer see it; where is
my peace of mind? Young cooks with polished earrings feasted your
brothers, great king, on delicious food superbly prepared; now I see
them all subsisting in the woods on forest fare. They have not
deserved discomfort, you Indra among men, and my heart finds no
20 peace. Bhīmasena I see, unhappy as he lives in the forest, sunk in
thought—doesn't your anger grow when the time is ripe? Seeing

Bhīmasena unhappy, him who used to accomplish his feats of his own
accord, why doesn't your anger grow? Wasn't he happily content
with his various wagons and manifold clothes, and now you see the
poor man in the forest—why doesn't your anger grow? The powerful
man could have killed *all* the Kurus, but the Wolf-Belly suffered it,
waiting for your grace.

"Now Arjuna, with his two arms the equal of many-armed Arjuna,
in the rapid volley of his arrows the match of Time, the Finisher, and
Yama, by the heat of whose weapons all the kings have been
humbled, the same kings who, at your sacrifice, great king, waited on
25 brahmins—this tiger among men who has been honored by Gods and
Dānavas, watch him sunk in thought—why doesn't your anger grow?
Seeing the Pārtha gone to the woods, so used to comfort, so unused
to hardship, your anger does not grow stronger, and it perplexes me,
Bhārata! On his single chariot he defeated Gods and men; now you
see him banished to the forest—why doesn't your anger flare up?
Did he not take much tribute from the kings, by force, in the midst of
marvelously shaped chariots, horses, and elephants, the enemy-
burner? Did he not shoot off in one shot five hundred arrows? Now
you see him banished to the forest; why didn't your anger rise? You
have seen the dark, tall Nakula in the forest, greatest of shield-bearers
30 in a war, so why didn't your anger increase? You have seen that
handsome warrior, Mādrī's son Sahadeva, in the forest, Yudhiṣṭhira,
and your anger has not grown?

"You have seen me gone to the forest, me who was born in the
lineage of Drupada, daughter-in-law of the great-spirited Pāṇḍu, so
why didn't your anger soar? Surely there is no anger left in you, you
the best of the Bharatas, if you can look at your brothers and at me,
and your heart feels no qualms! But there is no baron known in the
world without anger, without challenge; in you, a baron, I now see
35 the opposite. A baron who does not show his authority when the
moment comes all creatures will despise forever after, Pārtha! Don't
show patience to your enemies under any conditions, for with
authority alone you can cut them down, no doubt of that! Even so,
the baron who does not give in when it is time for forgiveness is hated
by all creatures and perishes here and hereafter."

Draupadī said:

29.1 On this they cite this old history, the Colloquy of Prahlāda and
Bali Vairocana.

Bali questioned his father's father Prahlāda, the great and wise
Asura, chief of the Daityas, to whom the knowledge of the Law had
been transmitted: "What is better, father, to forgive or to seek
revenge? I am uncertain about that, father, pray enlighten me at my

bidding. Tell me, you who know the Law, which of the two is
5 undoubtedly better, for I shall obey your instruction entirely." At his question his grandfather told it all, for he was wise and knew all the answers, to his grandson who was raising questions considering a problem.

Prahlāda said:

Revenge is not always better, but neither is forgiveness; learn to know them both, son, so that there be no problem. Son, a man who is always forgiving finds many things wrong; his servants despise him, and so do outsiders. No creatures ever bow to him, and that is why the learned criticize being always forgiving. For servants, despising him, will indulge in many vices, and the nitwits will seek to take his possessions away from him, his mount, clothes, ornaments,
10 bedding, seats, food and drink, and all his tools. When instructed that others should receive presents, his witless servants fail by their own whim to give the assigned gifts that according to their master's orders were to be presented. They never pay the master the proper respect he deserves, and in this world disrespect is condemned as worse than death. If he is such a forgiving man, my son, servants, sons, dependents, and even outsiders will say abusive things to him. Yes, they abuse the patient man and demand his wife; and the wife goes
15 her own way, bereft of sense. When the ever-rejoicing dependents deserve even the lightest punishment from their master, they rebel and, rebellious, wrong him. Those are the faults, and there are many others, of the forgiving man; but now learn, Vairocani, of the faults of the unforgiving.

If, rightly or wrongly, a man is constantly wrapped up in passion and wrathfully deals out punishment of various kinds on the strength of his authority, he will soon quarrel with his friends, wrapped in his authority, and he and his kin will receive the hatred of the world. On account of his contempt that man loses his wealth and reaps abuse,
20 disrespect, and remorse, and finds hatred, avarice, and enemies. A vindictive man who uses all kinds of punishment on people soon loses his power, his life, and even his kin. When a man bears down on benefactors and ill-wishers with the same authority, people shrink from him as from a snake that has got into the house. What kind of well-being is left to a man from whom people shrink? As soon as they see an opening, they are sure to hurt him. Therefore, one should neither always be domineering, nor always be gentle. He who is gentle at the right time and hard at the right time finds happiness in this world and the world hereafter.

Listen, I shall now declare to you in detail the times to be patient, and they should always be observed, even as the wise have
25 proclaimed them. A previous benefactor who may be involved in not

too great a wrong because of his earlier service should be forgiven, even if he did wrong. Wrong-doers who did not know what they did should be forgiven and seek mercy, for not everywhere is learning easily available to a man. Offenders who have acted with full knowledge and say they did not know, these hypocrites should be punished, even if the offence is quite small. Of any creature the first offence should be forgiven, but the second one should be punished, even if the wrong was small. If an offence is committed in ignorance, it should be forgiven, so they say, but only after careful examination.
30 With gentleness one defeats the gentle as well as the hard; there is nothing impossible to the gentle; therefore the gentle is the more severe. One should take action after considering the place and time and one's own strengths and weaknesses; at the wrong place and time it fails, therefore wait till both are right. Also an offender may be forgiven to appease the public. Thus have been declared the various occasions for forgiveness, and thus, too, have been said the occasions to use authority on the offenders.

Draupadī said:

Therefore, I think, king of men, that it has become time to use your authority on the greedy Dhārtarāṣṭras who are always offensive. There is no more time to ply the Kurus with forgiveness; and when
35 the time for authority has come, authority must be employed. The meek are despised, but people shrink from the severe: he is a king who knows both, when their time has come.

Yudhiṣṭhira said:

30.1 Anger kills men, anger prospers them: know, wise woman, that well-being and ill fortune are rooted in anger; for he who always controls anger reaps well-being, but, beautiful Kṛṣṇā, for a man who never controls his anger this terrifying anger leads to his downfall. Indeed, we find that the death of the creatures is rooted in anger; so how can a man like me indulge an anger that destroys the world? An angry man will do evil, an angry man may even kill his elders,
5 an angry man even abuses his betters with insults. For when angered, a man does not even distinguish between what may be said and what not; he is capable of doing and saying anything. In his rage he will hurt the innocent and honor the guilty, and he will even send himself to Yama's realm. With an insight into these views the wise control their anger, as they wish for the supreme good here and hereafter. Why should a man like me indulge an anger that the wise avoid? It is by reflecting on this, Draupadī, that my anger does not rise. A man who does not anger at an angry man saves both himself and the
10 other from grave danger and is the healer of both. If a weak person in his folly gets angry at stronger persons when he is harassed, he

loses his life in the end. For such a man, not master of himself, who
risks himself, the worlds hereafter perish. Therefore it is taught
Draupadī, that the powerless should restrain their anger. Likewise the
powerful man who does not anger, if he is wise, under harassment
will destroy his oppressor and rejoice in the next world. Thus both the
strong and the weak, they say, should always forgive, even in distress,
when they have this knowledge. For the good praise in this world the
suppression of anger, Kṛṣṇā, for to the forgiving and good is victory,
15 thus hold the strict. Truth prevails over falsehood, mildness over
cruelty; how can a man like me indulge in anger with its many vices
that the good avoid, were it to kill Suyodhana?* In him whom
farsighted men of learning call authoritative no anger is found, this is
certain. Him who checks his rising wrath with wisdom the wise, who
discern the truth, call authoritative. An angry man does not perceive
his task correctly, full-hipped woman; the raging man sees neither
task nor limit. In his anger he beats those who do not deserve it and
20 even insults his elders. Therefore, if authority is to be maintained,
anger must be kept far away. A man who is in the power of his anger
cannot easily attain to the competence, sternness, valor, and
promptness that are the attributes of authority. If he suppresses his
anger, a man can take proper hold of authority, while, wise woman,
the angry find it hard to endure authority when the occasion for it
arises. The ignorant always mistake anger for authority; but that
passion has been enjoined upon mankind for the destruction of the
world.

Therefore, a man who lives rightly should always avoid anger.
This much is certain that it is better that a man forsake his own Law
than that he fall a prey to anger. It is fools and nitwits who commit
25 all offences—how could a man like me offend, blameless woman? If
there were among men no persons as patient as the earth, there
would be no peace among men, for war roots in anger. If the
oppressed were to oppress, if one struck by his guru were to strike
back, it would mean the end of the creatures and Unlaw would be
abroad. Were every scolded person instantly to scold back, the hit to
hit back, the hurt to hurt back, were fathers to beat sons and sons
their fathers, the husbands to beat wives and the wives their
husbands, then in such an angry world there would be no more
birth, beautiful Kṛṣṇā, for know that the birth of creatures is rooted
30 in peace. In such a world all the creatures would soon perish,
Draupadī, and in this fashion anger leads to the destruction of
creatures and nonexistence. Since there are people found in the world
who are as patient as the earth, beings keep being born and existence
goes on. A man should be patient in all his troubles, my pretty, for

* = Duryodhana.

patience means the existence of the beings and is declared to be their
birth. If a man when insulted, beaten, and angered by a stronger
man forbears it, and always keeps his anger under control, he is a
sage and a superior person, as well as a man of dignity: his are the
sempiternal worlds, while the one of little knowledge, who is quick to
anger, perishes now and after death.

35 On this they always quote these verses of the patient man, Kṛṣṇā,
which were sung by the great-spirited and patient Kaśyapa:

"Patience is Law and rite, *Vedas* and learning,
He who knows patience thus can bear anything.
Patience is brahman, the truth, the past and the future,
Austerity and purity: patience upholds the world.
Beyond the worlds of the brahman-wise and ascetic,
Beyond those of the knowers of rites, go the patient to theirs.
The might of the mighty is patience, the brahman of hermits,
The truth of the truthful is patience, the gift and the glory."

40 How could a man like me abandon that kind of patience in which the
brahman, truth, sacrifices, and worlds are established? The sacrificers
enjoy their worlds, the forgiving enjoy other ones. A man of wisdom
should always forgive: for when he bears everything, he becomes
brahman. This world is of the patient, of the patient is the next; here
they come to be honored, hereafter they go the good journey. To
those men whose wrath is always governed by forgiveness belong the
highest worlds, hence forgiveness is deemed supreme.

45 Those were the verses that Kaśyapa used to sing of the patient
man, and now that you have heard them, Draupadī, be content to be
patient and do not anger. Grandfather Bhīṣma Śāṃtanava will honor
peace of mind, the Teacher* and Vidura the Steward will speak of it,
as will Kṛpa and Saṃjaya. Somadatta, Yuyutsu, the son of Droṇa, and
Vyāsa our grandfather are always speaking of peace. Under their
constant urging toward peace the king** is sure to return the
kingdom, I think; if not, he will perish by his greed.

A terrible time has come for the undoing of the Bhāratas; this has
been my conclusion, long before and since, angry Kṛṣṇā. Suyodhana
is not capable of patience, and therefore can find none; I am capable
50 of it, and therefore patience has found me. This is the way of those
who have mastered themselves, this their eternal Law, to be patient
and gentle, and thus I shall act!

Draupadī said:

31.1 Glory be the Placer and Ordainer who have befuddled you! While

* = Droṇa.
** = Duryodhana.

you should carry on in the way of your father and grandfather, your
mind has gone another way! In this world a man never obtains virtue
with Law and gentleness, or patience and uprightness, or tenderness,
if this insufferable disaster overtook you, Bhārata, which neither you
did deserve nor these august brothers of yours! Then as now they
knew that to you nothing was dearer than the Law, were it life itself.
5 Your kingdom was for the Law, your life was for the Law, and the
brahmins, elders, and Gods knew it well. You would, I think, abandon
Bhīmasena and Arjuna, the twin sons of Mādrī, and myself, before
you abandoned the Law.

The Law, when well protected, protects the king who guards the
Law, so I hear from the noble ones, but I find it does not protect *you*.
Never straying, your spirit always pursues the Law, tiger among men,
as his own shadow always pursues a man. You have never despised
your equals and inferiors, let alone your betters; and even after
10 winning all of earth your head did not grow! You always serve the
brahmins, the Gods, and the Ancestors with the *svāhā* calls, the
ancestral oblation and image worship, Pārtha. You always sate the
brahmins, ascetics, the householders, and the aspirants to release with
all that they desire, Bhārata. You offer the forest-dwellers copper
vessels, and there is nothing found in your house that may not be
given to the brahmins. Every morning and evening, at the end of the
vaiśvadeva, you first give the offerings to your guests and dependents
and you subsist on the remainder, king. Cake oblations, animal
sacrifices, desiderative and occasional rites, the cooked offerings and
15 other rituals go on continually. Even in this unpopulated vast forest,
infested by *dasyus*, where you live dethroned, your Law does not
falter. You have offered up the great rites of Horse Sacrifice, Royal
Consecration, the Lotus Ceremony, the Cow Ritual, with ample
stipends for the priests.

Then, king, your mind obsessed at your dishonest defeat in the
dicing, you lost your kingdom, riches, weapons, brothers, and me.
You were upright, gentle, bountiful, modest, truthful—how could the
spirit of gambling swoop down on you? My mind has become utterly
bewildered and burns with grief as I see this sorrow of yours and this
20 great distress. On this they quote this old story, how people are in the
power of the Lord and have none of their own.

It is the Lord Placer alone who sets down everything for the
creatures, happiness and unhappiness, pleasure and sorrow, before
even ejaculating the seed. These creatures, hero among men, are like
wooden puppets that are manipulated; he makes body and limbs
move. Pervading like ether all these creatures, Bhārata, the Lord
disposes here whatever is good or evil. Man, restrained like a bird
that is tied to a string, is not master of himself; remaining in the

25 Lord's power, he is master of neither himself nor others. Like a pearl
strung on a string, like a bull held by the nose rope, man follows the
command of the Placer, consisting in him, entrusted to him. At no
time whatever is man independent, like a tree that has fallen from
the bank into the middle of a river. Man knows nothing, he does not
control his own happiness or misery; pushed by the Lord he may
either go to heaven or to hell. As straw tops fall under the force of a
strong wind, so all creatures fall under the power of the Placer,
Bhārata. Yoking himself to deeds noble and evil, God roams through
30 the creatures and is not identified. This body they call "field" is
merely the Placer's tool by which the ubiquitous Lord impels us to
action that ends in either good or evil. Behold the power of wizardry
that the Lord displays: confusing them with his wizardry, he kills
creatures with creatures. Hermits with insight into the *Vedas* see
things one way, then they change course, like wind gusts. People see
things one way, and the Lord alters and changes them. As one breaks
wood with wood, stone with stone, iron with iron, the inert with the
35 insentient, so the blessed God, the self-existent great-grandfather, hurts
creatures with creatures, hiding behind a disguise, Yudhiṣṭhira.
Joining and unjoining them, the capricious blessed Lord plays with
the creatures like a child with its toys. The Placer does not act
toward his creatures like a father or mother, he seems to act out of
fury, like every other person! When I see noble, moral, and modest
people harassed in their way of life, and the ignoble happy, I seem to
stagger with wonder. Having witnessed your distress and the wealth
at Suyodhana's, I condemn the Placer, Pārtha, who allows such
outrages!
40 What does the Placer gain by giving the fortune to the Dhārtarāṣṭra
who offends against the noble scriptures, a cruel, avaricious diminisher
of the Law? If an act that has been done pursues its doer and no one
else, then surely God is tainted by the evil he has done! Or if the evil
that has been done does not pursue its doer, then mere power is the
cause of everything, and I bemoan powerless folk!

Yudhiṣṭhira said:

32.1 The words you have spoken and we have heard, Yājñasenī, are
beautiful, well-phrased and polished; but what you are saying is
heresy. I do not act in quest of the fruits of the Law; I give because
I must! I sacrifice because I must! Whether it bears fruit or not, I do,
buxom Draupadī, according to my ability, what a person who has a
household is beholden to do. I obey the Law, full-hipped woman, not
because of its rewards, but in order not to transgress the traditions and
to look to the conduct of the strict. By its nature my mind is beholden
5 to the Law. He who wants to milk the Law does not obtain its reward,

nor does the evil-minded man who after performing it has doubts out of a lack of faith. Don't doubt the Law, out of argumentativeness or mere folly, for the man who doubts the Law ends up an animal. The weak soul to whom the Law or the way of the seers is doubtful is as destitute of the undying and unaging world as a serf is of the *Veda*. If one studies the *Veda*, is dedicated to the Law, and is born high, glorious Kṛṣṇā, then kings who live by the Law must reckon him among the old. Worse than serfs, worse than thieves is the nitwit who transgresses the scriptures and casts doubt on the law.

10 You yourself have seen with your own eyes the great ascetic and seer Mārkaṇḍeya when he came here, a man of boundless soul and long-lived in the Law; Vyāsa, Vasiṣṭha, Maitreya, Nārada, Lomaśa, Śuka, and other seers of good thoughts have found perfection through Law alone. With your own eyes you have seen them, possessed of divine Yoga, equally capable of curse and grace, greater even than the Gods. They, the like of the Immortals, whose insight in the scriptures is evident, have from the first always told me that the Law alone is to be obeyed. Therefore, beautiful woman, you should not, with a passion-befuddled mind, revile the Placer and the Law, or cast doubt upon them.

15 He who doubts the Law finds in nothing else a standard and ends setting up himself as the standard, and insolently he despises his betters. The fool holds only the visible world that connects with the pleasuring of his senses for real and is confused about everything else. No expiation exists for one who doubts the Law; with all his reflecting, the wretched sinner attains to no worlds. Overstepping the standards, reviling the contents of *Vedas* and scriptures, pursued by desire and greed, the fool falls into hell. But he who always resolutely resorts to the Law alone, without questioning it, O beautiful woman, attains to infinitude hereafter. Transgressing the standard of the seers, not heeding the Laws, overstepping the scriptures, the fool finds no peace in his many births. Kṛṣṇā, do not cast doubt on the Law that is observed by the learned, the ancient Law proclaimed by the all-knowing, all-seeing seers. For those who travel to heaven, Draupadī, Law is the only ship: it is as a ship is for the merchant who sails for the farther shores of the ocean. Were the Law that is observed by the law-abiding to be fruitless, the whole world would sink into bottomless darkness, blameless woman; they would find no *nirvāṇa*, they would live like cattle, they would only meet with obstruction, they would
25 find nothing to their profit. If austerities, continence, sacrifice, Vedic study, liberality, and honesty were without their reward, the ancient and those before them and before them would not have observed it; it would be the ultimate deception, if acts were fruitless.

For what reason would the seers, the Gods, Gandharvas, Asuras,
Rākṣasas, all powerful creatures, so diligently obey the Law? No,
knowing that the Placer gives the rewards when the weal is assured,
they have always practiced the Law, Kṛṣṇā, for that is the eternal
Law. This Law bears fruit; Law is never said to be fruitless; for we see
30 that learning and austerity also bear fruit. So is it the case with
yourself: recall your own birth, Kṛṣṇā, as you have heard it described;
and you know also how the majestic Dhṛṣṭadyumna was born: this is
a sufficient analogy, sweet-smiling woman. Knowing that acts bear
fruits, the wise man is content even with little, while the ignorant
and foolish are discontented even with plenty; but after death they
have no shelter or acts that have sprung from Law. The fruition of
acts, both good and bad, their origin and disappearance, are the
mysteries of the Gods, my angry wife! Nobody knows them, these
creatures are in the dark about them, they are guarded by the Gods,
35 for the wizardry of the Gods is obscure. Those of the twice-born of
lean bodies and good vows, who have burned away their evil with
austerities and have serene thoughts, have an insight into them. The
Law should not be doubted, nor the Gods, just because the reward is
invisible; one should sacrifice, undistracted, and give without
demurring; this is the eternal Law: that acts yield fruit. Brahmā told
it to his son, as witnessed Kaśyapa. Therefore, let your doubts perish
like mist, Kṛṣṇā; and resolving that all this *is*, you must shed your
lack of faith. Do not revile the Lord of the beings, who is the Placer.
40 Learn of him, bow to him, do not harbor such notions! It is by the
grace of the supreme Deity that a devoted mortal becomes immortal
—do not censure him, Kṛṣṇā, in any way!

Draupadī said:

33.1 I do not revile or condemn the Law in any way, Pārtha; why
should I revile the Lord, the Father of creatures? Know me, Bhārata,
I am babbling from grief; listen with kindliness as I complain some
more.

Whatever is born, plougher of your enemies, surely must act; only
rocks and the like live without acting, not the other creatures. From
the suckling of their mother's breast till they lie on their deathbed
5 all moving creatures find their livelihood with acts, Yudhiṣṭhira, and,
among the quick, most of all the humans, bull of the Bharatas. They
want a living with their acts, here and hereafter. All beings know the
resurrection, Bhārata, and clearly, for all the world to see, they eat
up the fruit of their actions. As I see it, the creatures live off their
own resurrection, so do the Placer and Disposer, as does this crane
in the water. Do your thing! Do not falter! Be armed by your deeds!

For he who knows what his task is, is one in a thousand if that! Yet
he does have a task, to increase and to preserve; for if one eats up
without new sowing, one dwindles, as even the Himālaya dwindles.
10 Collapse would these creatures if they did not do their work! Do we
see people work and their work remain fruitless? We do not know of
anyone making a living in this world without work.

The man who believes that everything in the world is fate and the
one who professes that it is chance are both apostate; it is the spirit
to act that is extolled. He who obediently sits by fate and sleeps
happily without acting, that hedonist of malicious spirit will sink like
a jar in water. Likewise, the believer in chance, who, though capable
of acting, fails to act will not keep his seat too long and live as long
as a feeble man without a protector.

15 If a man unexpectedly achieves some purpose and people think,
"It was just chance," his efforts have been wasted. If a man obtains
anything labeling it fate, then, Pārtha, by divine ordinance they just
decide it *was* fate! But what a man himself, by his own acts, obtains
as the fruit of his acts, that is known, clearly for every eye to see, as
that man's *own* doing. A naturally active man may obtain things for
no visible reason—that, best of men, is the result that is natural.

So, what a man gets from chance and divine luck, from nature and
plain hard work, is the fruit of his previous acts. The Placer himself,
the Lord, ordains any one's acts, for whatever reason, and distributes
20 the fruits of what men have previously done. When a man does
anything, whether good or bad, know that it was ordained by the
Placer, arising as the fruit of acts done before. In any act this body is
but the tool of this Placer, and as he moves man, so man acts,
helplessly. The Great Lord, who enjoins us to this or that task, makes
all creatures act, Kaunteya, whether they want it or not.

One first decides with one's mind on one's goal, then achieves it
with acts: man himself, who has reason, is the cause of the result
following his resolve. To count the acts is impossible, bull among men;
25 the success of houses and towns is caused by man. In sesame is oil,
in cow milk, in wood finally is fire: with one's own intelligence one
should intelligently know the means to effect it; and it is on this
accomplishment of their acts that creatures live here. An act, capably
done, well planned by the doer, is clearly distinguished from another
act: "This was done by an incompetent!" There would be no fruit of
oblation or donation, there would be neither pupil nor teacher, if
man were not the cause of such results as are to be accomplished by
acts! It is because of his very doing of it that a man is praised at the
success of his doings, and blamed at their failure: how can one's
deeds disappear?

30 Yes, there are those who hold that everything is done by chance,
those who hold that it is fate, and those who hold that it springs from
man's efforts—it is called the triple answer. Others think *that* is not
enough to account for *task*. Of everything it is imperceptible whether
it is chance or fate that brought it about; for what is actually
perceived is the *chain* of the thing, whether it springs from chance or
fate. Some comes from chance, some from fate, some from one's own
doing; and it is thus that a man gets the fruit, there is no fourth
factor involved: so profess capable men, wise in the principles.

Even so, the Placer is the one who gives wanted or unwanted
results to the creatures. If he were not the one, none of the creatures
would go wanting: whatever thing a man wanted, he would perform
the act to bring it about. And would each of the acts fructify, unless
they were done before?

35 However, people who have no insight into the triple effectuation
of an intended result effect the wrong one, and they are as their
worlds are. Manu pronounces the decision, "The act has got to be
done!" for a man who does not try loses out completely. Generally,
Yudhiṣṭhira, if a man acts, his attempt works out, while the lazy man
nowhere finds things to succeed completely. If there is a good reason
for the result to be impossible, a rite of reparation is indicated; but as
long as the act is done, Indra among kings, one is acquitted. Bad luck
takes over the lazy, lying-down man; but a capable person, obtaining
40 indubitable results, achieves prosperity. Those who have shed all
doubt stop as useless the man whose condition is that of doubt, and so
does the poised and active man; but they do not stop the convinced.

At this time, of course, we have been rendered utterly useless. But
no, nothing is in doubt if you abide by action. If success does not
befall you, it is still your glory, and that of the Wolf-Belly, the
Terrifier, and the twin brothers. Others' acts may be rewarding, but so
may ours be; one who has done the work is the first to know what
its result is. The peasant cleaves the earth with his plow, then sows
45 the seed, then he sits by silently and the rain does the work. If the
monsoon does not favor him, the peasant is still without blame: "I
have done everything that the other man has!"

Suppose we fail, it will nowhere be held that it is our own fault;
this is what a wise man keeps in view, and he will not blame himself
for his failure. If the result is not achieved, Bhārata, even though you
have acted, there is no cause for despair; for there are two outcomes
to an act. There is success and there is failure; but failure to *act* is a
different thing. For it takes many factors together for an act to
succeed; in the absence of the proper quality, the fruit is defective or
nonexistent. Unless the act is undertaken, undefeated hero, neither

fruit nor quality can become visible. A sagacious man knots together time and place with his intelligence and according to his might and capacity, knots together the various means and the Godspeed for his
50 well-being. The diligent should act, and valor is the teacher: in the disciplines of action, valor is the principal force. A wise man sees another man who is superior in many virtues; so he tries to win him with conciliation and uses his acts upon him. One should hope for his removal and destruction, Yudhiṣṭhira, were he the Indus or as mountain, let alone one who is subject to the Law of the mortals.

A man, possessed of manhood, earns, by always watching for a weak spot in others, acquittance of his debt to the other as well as himself. No one should ever belittle himself; for no prosperity comes
55 to the one who has cowed himself, Bhārata. It is on this foundation, Bhārata, that the success of people rests; the actual ways to success are declared to be various, as they depend on various times and conditions.

My father once lodged a learned brahmin in our house; and he told my father of this matter, bull of the Bharatas. He taught this same policy, which was first propounded by Bṛhaspati, to my brothers at the time; and I listened to their conversations at home. He talked to me comfortingly, when I came in with an errand, or was sitting on my father's lap, listening eagerly, King Yudhiṣṭhira.

Vaiśaṃpāyana said:

34.1 After listening to Yājñasenī's words, the intransigent Bhīmasena approached the king with a sigh and angrily told him, "Travel the lawlike roadway of kingship, which is used by the strict! Why should we dwell in this wilderness of austerities and miss out on Law, Profit, and Pleasure? Duryodhana did not take our kingdom lawfully, or honestly, or gallantly, but by cheating at dice. Our kingdom was snatched away as a feeble scavenging jackal snatches a piece of raw
5 flesh from lions that are stronger. Why do you cover yourself with some tatters of Law, king, and throw away Profit, which is the source of Law and Pleasure, and mortify yourself in the wilderness? While we looked on in obedience to you, our kingdom was stolen, and even Śakra could not have taken it, protected as it was by Arjuna and his Gāṇḍīva. Our power was snatched away, even though we were alive and well, as *bilva* fruit are snatched away from the armless, and cattle from the crippled, and only because of you! It was to do you a favor, you so convinced of the pleasure of Law, that we landed ourselves in such a great calamity, Bhārata! We have plowed under our friends and delighted our enemies by controlling ourselves at your behest,
10 bull of the Bharatas. It was a mistake that we did not strike down the

Dhārtarāṣṭras but waited on your command, and the mistake is now hurting us.

Look at this animal's lair that you have made your home, king: it is a coward's haunt and not visited by the powerful. Kṛṣṇā does not welcome it, nor the Terrifier,* nor Abhimanyu, Sṛñjaya, I myself, or the twin sons of Mādrī. You are Law, and crying Law! you emaciate yourself always with your vows; but is it possible, king, that despair has prompted you to the life of a eunuch? For it is cowards who
embrace a futile, all-destructive despair when they are incapable of
15 recapturing their fortune. You have eyesight and capacity, in yourself
you see manliness, but, prone to gentility, you do not realize the trouble we are in, king!

Those Dhārtarāṣṭras regard us, who indeed have been patient enough, as plainly incompetent; and that is more galling than to die in battle! It would be better if we were to give battle there, straightforwardly, without turning away, even if we were all slaughtered: after the battle we would gain our worlds. And it surely would be better for us if we killed them off, bull of the Bharatas, and take back all of earth. If we are to observe our own Law, if we wish
to win plentiful fame, if we are to counter enmity, it is in war that
20 our task clearly lies. Others have stolen our kingdom: when the
renown of our feats becomes known as we fight for ourselves, we shall only reap glory and not blame. A Law that is a scourge for both ourselves and our allies is a vice, king; it is not Law, it is *wrong* Law! Law and Profit desert the man who always abides by the Law, just as they desert one who is weak in the Law, friend, as pleasure and misery desert the dead. He is not a wise man in whom Law produces anguish for the sake of Law; he does not know the purpose of Law, as a blind man does not know the light of the sun.

He who takes Profit to be for the sake of Profit is ignorant of
25 Profit: he is like a humble servant who watches over a forest. One
who seeks Profit beyond measure and ignores the other two goals ought to be slain by all creatures, despised like a brahmin's assassin. Likewise he who always seeks out Pleasure and ignores the other two will see his friendships perish and fall short of Law and Profit. The man who is lacking in Law and Profit is sure to die at the end of his Pleasure, like a fish that happily indulges its pleasure till its pond dries up. That is why the wise are never fooled about Law and Profit, for they are the preconditions of Pleasure, as the kindling block is of the fire. Profit is at any rate rooted in Law, while Law has Profit as its property. Know that both are each other's source, like the monsoon and the ocean.

* = Arjuna.

30 Love is the delight that springs up when one's touch impinges on
things of value; it is a configuration of the mind, there is no body to
it. The man who strives for Profit, king, seeks much Law; he who
strives for Pleasure seeks Profit, but from Pleasure he does not find
any other pleasure; for no other pleasure is produced by Pleasure as
its fruit, because it is used up like a fruit, just as a log is reduced to
ashes. Just as a fowler kills these little birds, O king, such is the nature
of the Unlaw of those who mean hurt for the creatures. He who from
desire and greed fails to discern the course of the Law deserves to be
killed by all creatures, and he is wrong-minded here and hereafter.
35 You clearly know, king, that Profit means the possession of property;
you also know its natural state and its many transformations. The
loss of it or its decay in old age and death is held to be a calamity,
and this is now upon us. The delight that arises when the five senses,
mind, and heart dwell upon their objects is Pleasure, I hold, the
highest fruit of one's acts. Thus discerning Law, Profit, and Pleasure
separately, a man must not be too prone to the Law, nor too prone
to Profit or Pleasure, but always cultivate all three. He should pursue
Law in the first, Profit in the second, and Pleasure in the last part of
the day, one after the other; that is the decree that is laid down in the
40 scriptures. One should pursue Pleasure in the first, Profit in the middle,
and Law in the last part of one's life, one after the other; that is the
decree that is laid down in the scriptures. Distributing Law, Profit,
and Pleasure correctly over time, O best of debaters, the scholar who
knows his times should cultivate them all. Whether renunciation or
success is a greater good for those who want happiness, scion of Kuru,
is a question on which you should decide with every means, and then
at once carry out the former, or proceed to success, king, for life is a
sick man's misery for the one who vacillates between the two.
You know the Law and you have always practiced it. Your friends
45 know and praise in you the injunction to action. Gifts, sacrifice, the
worship of the good, the retention of the *Veda*, and uprightness
constitute the highest Law, O king, that bears fruit here and hereafter.
But one who is destitute of wealth cannot practice it; yet these
virtues, tiger among men, should be kept entire, even though one may
have other ones. This world, O king, is rooted in Law; nothing is
greater than Law, and this Law can only be cultivated by means of
great wealth. Such wealth can never be obtained with begging or
timidity, only by one who is resolved to practice the Law. The
begging that gives the brahmin his success is forbidden to you,
therefore strive to satisfy your want of wealth by employing your
50 authority, bull among people. Begging is not enjoined on the baron,
nor is the livelihood of commoner and serf: for the baron the Law is
first of all the might of his chest. Wise people declare that the Law is

a noble Law, so strive for that which is noble and do not pause
below it.
Wake up, you know the eternal Laws, Indra among kings; you
have been born to savage deeds, from which other people shrink. The
reward you reap by protecting your subjects will not be condemned,
for it is the eternal Law, O king, that the Placer has enjoined upon
you. If you deviate from it, Pārtha, you will become the laughingstock
of the people, for people do not approve of deviation from one's own
55 Law. Make your heart a baron's heart, shed the weakness of your
mind, show bravery, Kaunteya, and carry the yoke like a beast of
burden. No king has ever conquered earth by being solely law-
minded, nor have they thus won prosperity and fortune. It is by using
a sweet tongue with the many lowly people whose minds are greedy
that one gains a kingdom with trickery as the fowler gains his meal.
The Asuras, elder brothers of the Gods, very prosperous in all respects,
were defeated by the Gods with trickery, bull of the Pāṇḍavas. In the
full knowledge that all spoils belong to the mighty, O king of the
earth, you must with your strong arms cut down the enemies by
resorting to trickery.
60 There is no bow-wielding warrior the equal of Arjuna in war, and
what man will equal me in wielding the club? Even a powerful man
fights with his own mettle, not with greater numbers or greater
enterprise; therefore be on your mettle, Pāṇḍava! Mettle is the root of
wealth, it is a lie to say otherwise. It is not superfluous like tree shade
in winter. If one wants greater wealth, he should give up some of his
present wealth by the simile of the seed that is sown, don't you doubt
it, Kaunteya. But where no gain is to be had equal to what has been
invested, or less than it, no outlay should be made, for that is like
scratching an itch.
65 In the same way, O king of men, by scrapping a lesser Law a man
obtains a greater Law, and he is judged to be wise. Sagacious men
alienate an enemy with allies from his allies; and when he is deserted
by his estranged allies and weakened, they overpower him. Even a
powerful man, king, fights mainly with his mettle; not just with effort
or by sweet talk are all subjects made one's own. When weak kings
band together, even a mighty adversary without allies can be beaten,
as bees kill a honey snatcher. Just as the sun protects and devours all
creatures with its rays, O king, so you must become equal to the sun.
70 For this is the ancient austerity of which we have heard, king, to
protect the land by decree, as our grandfathers did.

Seeing your sorrow the people have decided that the sun may well lose its light and the moon its beauty! When assemblies engage in discussions, jointly or severally, it is with praise for you and censure for the other. What is more, when brahmins and elders assemble,

king, they talk joyfully of the strength of your promises, how neither
confusion, baseness, greed, nor fear prompt you to lie, nor love or
75 selfishness. Whatever guilt a king incurs in winning his country he
wipes off later with richly paid-for sacrifices. By giving villages and
thousands of cows to the brahmins he is freed from all evil, as the
moon is freed from darkness. Townspeople and country folk all have
mostly praise for you, old and young included, Yudhiṣṭhira, scion of
Kuru. The kingdom fits Duryodhana as milk a dog's bladder, as the
brahman fits a serf, truthfulness a robber, and strength a woman: this
is the word that has long been broadcast over the earth, and even
women and children recite it as their *Veda*.

80 Mount your chariot with all its weapon gear, have eminent
brahmins give voice to lengthy recitations such as may contribute to
your purpose, this very day, and drive out today to the City of the
Elephant! Drive out amidst your weapon-wise brothers with their
hard bows, like venomous snakes, as the Slayer of Vṛtra drives out
in the midst of the Maruts. An Indra to Asuras, grind down the
enemies with your splendor and take the fortune away from the
Dhārtarāṣṭra, mighty Kaunteya! Not a mortal on earth can withstand
the impact of the arrows, robed in the feathers of vultures, which are
shot from bow Gāṇḍīva. There is not a hero, not an elephant, not a
noble steed, O Bhārata, that can withstand the swoop of my club as
85 I rage in battle. With the aid of the Sṛñjayas, the Kaikeyas, and the
bull of the Vṛṣṇis,* how could we fail to take the kingdom, Kaunteya?

Yudhiṣṭhira said:

35.1 They are doubtless true, O Bhārata,
Your biting words that hurt and destroy me.
I do not blame you for your bitterness,
For my wrong course brought this misery on you.

For I took the dice desirous to take
Duryodhana's kingship and kingdom away;
But Subala's son, the roguish gamester,
Thereupon played against me in Suyodhana's cause.

That trickster Śakuni, man from the mountains,
Sowed out the dice in the gaming hall
And played with tricks against me who knew none,
Then, Bhīmasena, I saw his guile.

On seeing the dice would always favor
The wishes of Śakuni, even and odd,
I'd still have been able to check myself,
But anger destroys a person's calm.

* = Kṛṣṇa.

5 One cannot restrain oneself if valor
And power and pride are girding one, brother.
I do not demur at your words, Bhīmasena,
But I think that it thus was fated to be.

The prince, Dhṛtarāṣṭra's son, was craving
For our realm and he cast us in misery,
And slavery was inflicted upon us
Till Draupadī became our sole refuge.

You know as well as Dhanaṃjaya knows
What the son of Dhṛtarāṣṭra told me
When we came to the hall to gamble again
And the Bhāratas listened, what one throw would stake.

"You will, son of a king, for a twelve-year spell
Live unconcealed as you please in the forest,
And another year you will live in concealment
And under disguise with all your brothers.

"If the spies of the Bhāratas hear of you
And discover, my friend, how you live that year,
You shall spend as many more years like that,
You must promise this, Pārtha, decidedly!

10 "If in all that time you are not found out
And you artfully fool my runners, O king,
Then I say as truth in the Kurus' assembly
You yourself shall have the Five Rivers back!

"If we are defeated by you, we too
And our brothers shall relinquish our comforts
And live out as long," said the king at the time;
In the midst of the Kurus I gave my word.

That most foul game began for us there,
We lost, and we all set out for the woods,
And ghastly-looking we on this wise
Roam over the earth and through ghastly woods.

Suyodhana had no truck with peace
And fell even worse a prey to his rage;
He goaded the Kurus who were there assembled
And those of the men who are in his control.

Having sworn to the treaty before honest men,
Who would want to break it, for the prize of a kingdom?
For a noble I think it is graver than death
To transgress the Law and hold sway over earth.

15 That time you'd have done a heroic deed
When during the game you fingered your club;
You'd have burned my hands had not Phalguna* checked you;
What misdeed, Bhīma, would that not have been!

Why did you not earlier, when we contracted,
Speak out like this, displaying your manhood?
Now you've found your time, but far too late,
You berate me now, and beyond your time!

But this pain burns me the fiercer, Bhīma,
Me who've tasted poison it burns more fiercely,
That we all watched Kṛṣṇā being molested,
And while watching condoned it, Bhīmasena!

We can do nothing at present, hero;
We must wait for the time that our luck reappears,
After filling the pledge we made to the Kurus,
As the sower waits for his crop to ripen.

When a man, brought down before by deceit
And aware that the feud shoots blossoms and fruit,
Bears many times more with the strength of his manhood,
He lives like a hero in the world of the living!

20 He obtains all the fortune there is in the world,
And methinks his enemies bow to him;
His friends will love him most passionately,
And live on him as the Gods live on Indra.

The promise I made is a true one, remember,
I choose, over life and eternity, Law.
Neither kingdom nor sons, neither glory nor wealth,
Can even come up to a fraction of Truth!

Bhīmasena said:
36.1 You have made a covenant with Time the winged Finisher, endless
and measureless, a torrent that carries off all—you, a mortal, bound
by Time, of the order of foam and the order of fruit, think Time is
present before you, great king! Why, Kaunteya, should Time wait for
one whose life diminishes every twinkling of the eye, as ground
mascara dwindles every time it is picked with a needle? Only one
whose life is without end or who knows its span can wait for Time, as
5 he can see it all clearly. While we are waiting about for thirteen years,
king, Time diminishes our life and leads us to death. For death is
sure to befall the bodies of all who have bodies: therefore, before we

* = Arjuna.

die, let us work for the kingdom! A king who does not acquit himself
and remains obscure without avenging feuds sinks like a cow in mire.
If a man of little mettle and energy does not avenge a feud, then I
think his life is useless, he is the son of a low-born woman. You have
arms made of gold, king, you'll have fame—once you kill your hater
in battle and enjoy the treasure won with your arms! Enemy-tamer,
10 king! If a man kills a cheater, were he to go to hell instantly hell
would be heaven to him!

The pain born from rancor burns hotter than fire; and burned by
it I find rest neither day nor night. The Pārtha here, the Terrifier,
champion archer, now sits grievously burning like a lion in its den.
He longs to take on all the bowmen on earth, and like a giant
elephant he represses the heat that is rising within him. Nakula and
Sahadeva and the old mother, bearer of man-children, who all wish
you well, sit stunned and dumb.

15 All your relations wish you well, so do the Sṛñjayas. I alone, with
Prativindhya's mother,* speak out in my anger; but what I may say
is all right by them too; they have all come to grief, they all welcome
war. No calamity can be worse, king, than this one that lower and
weaker men have stolen our kingdom and now enjoy it! Out of fear
to soil your character, gripped by warm feelings and moved by your
gentleness, enemy-burner, you endure your troubles, king—no one
praises you! Meek like a brahmin, how have you been born to the
baronage? Tough-minded men are usually born in baronial wombs.
20 You have heard of the baronial Laws as Manu has pronounced them
—tough ones, full of deceit, are enjoined, informed by no serenity.
There is work to be done, tiger among men; why sit there like a lazy
python? You have wit, courage, knowledge, and birth! You who want
to conceal us—do you want to conceal the Himālaya with a handful
of straw? You, renowned over all of earth, can no more live in
disguise and in hiding, Pārtha, than the sun in the sky! Like a huge
śāla tree, flowering and shooting near the water, like a white elephant,
25 how can Jiṣṇu** remained unrecognized? And these two young
brothers, looking like lions, Nakula and Sahadeva, how will they stay
hidden, Pārtha? Princess Draupadī, of sacred fame, mother of man-
children, Kṛṣṇā renowned all over, how will she remain unknown?
And me, king, all the subjects know me, down to the kids—I see me
incognito like Mount Meru!

Besides, we have exiled many kings and kings' sons from their
kingdoms, and they are now avowed to Dhṛtarāṣṭra. They, unseated,
have not recovered from their humiliations and undoubtedly will try
30 to humble us, to please him. They will employ on us many spies, they

* = Draupadī.
** = Arjuna.

will find us and inform on us, and that will be a very great risk for us. We have already lived in the woods for a full thirteen months—look upon them as as many years! A month may substitute for a year, say the wise, as *pūtīkas* may substitute for the Soma, so do it that way. Or you are absolved from this one sin by feeding to satiety a good bullock that pulls a good load, king! Therefore, king, resolve to kill off your enemies, for to any barons there is no Law but to fight!

Vaiśaṃpāyana said:
37.1 On hearing Bhīmasena's words Kuntī's son Yudhiṣṭhira, a tiger
among men and enemy-burner, sighed and brooded. And having
brooded a while he decided on his duty and immediately replied to
Bhīmasena: "It is as you say, Bhārata of the strong arms, but now
take to heart this other word of mine, you master of words. Evil deeds
that are undertaken out of sheer violence only bring hurt, Bhīmasena
5 Bhārata! When an act is well-counseled, well-wrought, well-done,
well-planned, it succeeds in its purpose and fate is right-handed. Now
you, stretching with the insolence of your strength, out of sheer
wantonness think on your own account that this is the thing to do,
but listen to me about that!
"Bhūriśravas, Śala, mighty Jalasandha, Bhīṣma, Droṇa, Karṇa,
Droṇa's powerful son, the unassailable Dhārtarāṣṭras led by
Duryodhana, all have their weapons ready and lie in ambush all the
time. The kings and the princes whom we chastised have taken the
10 Kauravas' side and love them now. They are now loyal to Duryodhana,
Bhārata, not to us. And with their coffers full and forces aplenty, they
will do their best to keep it so. All of them of the Kaurava army, with
their sons, ministers, and officers, have been apportioned riches and
privileges all around. Duryodhana has fawned on all those champions,
and I am sure they will risk their lives in battle. Even though Bhīṣma,
the strong-armed Droṇa, and the great-spirited Kṛpa feel the same to
us as to them, they will doubtless earn their royal rice-ball, I think.
15 That is why all those experts on divine weapons, all those followers
of the Law, will lay down their lives in battle, however precious to
them. I do not think they can be defeated, even by the Gods led by
Indra. Among them is the resentful warrior Karṇa, always excited,
expert on all weapons, unassailable, covered with impenetrable armor.
You cannot kill Duryodhana without allies, before you have defeated
all these notables in battle, too. Wolf-Belly, I cannot get to sleep from
worry over the deftness of the *sūta's* son, who surpasses all who
handle bows."

Bhīmasena, indignant though he was, understood the truth of what he was saying and became upset and alarmed; and he had no reply to make.

20 While the two sons of Pāṇḍu were thus arguing, the great yogin
Vyāsa arrived, Satyavatī's son. As he approached, the Pāṇḍavas
greeted him courteously; and the eloquent seer addressed Yudhiṣṭhira
as follows: "Yudhiṣṭhira of the strong arms, I know the thoughts of
your heart with my insight, hence I have hurried here, bull among
men. The fears that go around in your mind, of Bhīsma, Droṇa,
Kṛpa, Karṇa, and Droṇa's son, O Bhārata, slayer of your foes, I shall
dispel them with an argument that is found in the Rules. Hear it and
regain your composure; and bring it about with your deeds!"
25 Thereupon Parāśara's son took Yudhiṣṭhira aside, and, a master of
words, he spoke to him this word full of import: "The time shall come
of your fortune, best of the Bharatas, when Dhanaṃjaya the Pārtha
overpowers the enemies in battle. Receive from me this magic
knowledge I shall propound to you, which is called Conjuration and
is success personified. I shall tell it to you, for you seek my protection.
When strong-armed Arjuna has acquired it from you, he will make it
successful: he must go to both great Indra and Rudra, to obtain
weapons, and also to Varuṇa, and the God of Riches, and the king of
the Law, Pāṇḍava. For he will be capable, through his austerities and
gallantry, to set eye on Gods—he is the splendiferous seer, the ancient
sempiternal God whose companion is Nārāyaṇa, the eternal portion
of Viṣṇu!
30 "When he has obtained weapons from Indra, Rudra, and the World
Guardians, the strong-armed hero shall accomplish great exploits.
Now leave this forest, Kaunteya, and find another one that will be
suitable for you to live in, master of the earth. For a long sojourn in
the same place does not add to one's happiness and might disturb the
serene ascetics; the deer are eaten up, the plants and herbs dwindle,
for you are supporting many brahmins who are steeped in the *Vedas*
and their branches."
Having thus spoken to the pure man who had sought his protection,
35 the blessed lord, erudite in the principles of Yoga, pronounced to him
that incomparable magic lore; then he dismissed the Kaunteya and
disappeared then and there.
Law-spirited Yudhiṣṭhira trained his mind and retained that
brahman, wisely rehearsing it again and again. Pleased at Vyāsa's
words, he moved from the Dvaitavana Forest and went to the
Kāmyaka woods on the bank of the Sarasvatī. The austere brahmins,
masters of phonetics and syllables, followed him, great king, as the
seers follow the Indra of the Gods. When they got to Kāmyaka, the
great-spirited bulls of the Bharatas settled down there with councillors
40 and followers. The spirited champions lived there for some time, O
king, bent upon the art of archery and listening to the superb *Veda*.
They daily went hunting, seeking out deer with their purified arrows,

and made offerings to ancestors, Gods, and the brahmins as is
prescribed.

Vaiśaṃpāyana said:
38.1 After some time Yudhiṣṭhira the King Dharma, recalling the hermit's
message, spoke privately to Arjuna, bull of the Bharatas, of known
sagacity. Gently and smilingly he took him by the hand and after
musing for a moment, the enemy-tamer, the King Dharma, said to
Dhanaṃjaya in secret, "The entire art of archery is now vested in
5 Bhīsma, Droṇa, Kṛpa, and Droṇa's son, Bhārata. They fully know the
Brahmic, Divine, and Demoniac use of all types of arrows, along with
practices and cures. Dhṛtarāṣṭra's son has fawned on them, made
gifts to them, and satisfied them, and he behaves toward them as
toward a guru. His conduct with all the warriors is unexceptionable,
and, honored as they are, they will not be wanting in power when
the time comes. Presently the entire earth is subject to Duryodhana.
You are our last resort; on you rests our burden. I see a task for you,
and the time for it has now arrived, enemy-tamer!
"I have a secret knowledge that I acquired from Dvaipāyana, my
friend; if you employ it the entire universe will become visible to you.
10 Possessed of this *brahman*, you must most diligently seek the grace of
the Gods, brother. Yoke yourself to awesome austerities, bull of the
Bharatas, as a hermit of great mettle, armed with bow, armor, and
sword! Then journey to the North, allowing no one to pass you. For
with Indra are all the weapons of the Gods, Dhanaṃjaya; the Gods
gave Indra all their strength out of fear of Vṛtra. You will find all the
weapons assembled there in one place. Go to Śakra, and he shall give
you the weapons. Be consecrated and set out today to find the God
Sacker of Cities!"
After these words the lord King Dharma taught him that magic,
when he was ritually consecrated and controlled in word, body, and
thought; then the elder brother told his heroic brother to depart.
15 At the King Dharma's behest to find the God Sacker of Cities, he took
the bow Gāṇḍīva and the two inexhaustible quivers, and armored,
with wrist and finger guards tied on, the strong-armed warrior offered
into the fire, had brahmins bless his journey for gold coins, and
departed, holding the bow, for the destruction of the Dhārtarāṣṭras,
sighing deep and glancing at heaven.
When they saw the Kaunteya holding the bow, the brahmins,
Siddhas, and hidden creatures exclaimed, "You must soon obtain the
wish of your heart, Kaunteya!" Kṛṣṇā said to Arjuna, who strode like
a lion, with thighs like *śāla* trunks, taking with him the hearts of them
20 all, "Whatever Kuntī wished for you at your birth, strong-armed
Dhanaṃjaya, that must all come true and likewise all that you wish

for yourself. May we never be born in a lineage of barons again—I bow to the brahmins who never have to live on war! Surely all your brothers will enliven their waking hours by recounting your heroic feats, praising them again and again. Still, we shall find no joy in our comforts and possessions and even our lives, if you stay away long, Pārtha! On you now rest the happiness and misery of all of us, our life and death, kingdom and sovereignty. I bid you farewell, Kaunteya, be blessed, Pāṇḍava. Homage to the Placer and Disposer, go a safe
25 and healthy path. Be safe from the creatures of earth, sky, and heaven, and all others that may waylay you!"

The Pāṇḍava circumambulated his brothers and Dhaumya, then the strong-armed warrior departed, holding the bright bow. All the creatures left the road that he took with Indra's Yoga, mighty and ruttish. In just one day the spirited Pārtha reached the holy mountain, for with his Yoga he had become fast as thought, like the wind. He passed over the Himālaya, Mount Gandhamādana and its passes
30 unweariedly. When Dhanaṃjaya reached the Indrakīla, he stopped, for he heard in the sky the summons "Stay!" At the root of a tree the left-handed archer saw an ascetic blazing with the luster of *brahman*, yellowish, braided, and wan. The ascetic, seeing that he had stopped, said to Arjuna, "Who are you, son, arriving here in armor, with bow and arrows, with sword and wrist guards tied on, who follow the Laws of the baronage? Weapons are of no use here; this is the land of the serene, of ascetic brahmins who control their anger and joy. There is no use for bows here, nor for any fighting. Lay down your bow, you have reached the end of your journey."

35 Thus the brahmin repeatedly told Arjuna, hero of boundless puissance, as though he were any other man; but he could not move him from his resolve, for he was firmly decided. Then the brahmin began to laugh and said to him, pleased, "Choose a boon, bless you! I am Śakra, enemy-tamer!" With folded hands and bowing, Dhanaṃjaya, heroic scion of Kuru, replied to the Thousand-eyed God, "This is my desire, and grant it to me as a boon: I wish to learn from you, lord, all the weapons that exist!" With a laugh the Great Indra, much pleased, said to him, "What use will weapons be to you, now that you are here, Dhanaṃjaya? Choose wishes and worlds, you have
40 come to the end of your journey!" Replied Dhanaṃjaya to the Thousand-eyed God, "I do not want wishes or worlds, or divinity, still less happiness, nor the sovereignty over all the Gods, overlord of the Thirty! If I leave my brothers in the wilderness without avenging the feud, I shall find infamy in all the worlds for time without end."

The Slayer of Vṛtra replied to Pāṇḍu's son, coaxing him in a gentle voice, he who is honored in all worlds, "When you have seen the Lord of Beings, three-eyed, trident-bearing Śiva, then I shall give you

all the weapons of the Gods, son. Try hard to find the God who dwells
on high; by seeing him, Kaunteya, you will become successful and go
to heaven."
45 Having thus spoken to Phalguna, Śakra disappeared; and Arjuna
stayed there, wrapped in his Yoga.

Janamejaya said:
39.1 Sir, I wish to hear in detail the story of how the Pārtha of unsullied
deeds acquired the weapons. How did the long-armed and mighty
Dhanaṃjaya, tiger among men, enter the unpeopled and terrifying
forest? And what did he do when he lived there, O great scholar of
the *brahman*, and how did he satisfy the blessed Lord Sthāṇu? This I
want to hear by your grace, for you are omniscient and know matters
5 both human and divine. We have heard that Arjuna fought a
wondrous and hair-raising incomparable battle with Bhava,* O sage,
at that time, the greatest of fighters unvanquished in all his battles.
Upon hearing of it, the hearts of even the heroic Pārthas, lions among
men, trembled from despondency, joy, and utter amazement. Tell in
full whatever else the Pārtha accomplished, for I perceive not the
tiniest flaw in Jiṣṇu. Recite to me the entire geste of that champion!
Vaiśaṃpāyana said:
I shall narrate to you, son, the divine, great, and wondrous story
of that great-spirited man, O tiger among the Kauravas. Hear in full
the Pārtha's encounter, which involved bodily contact, with the
three-eyed God of Gods, prince sans blame.
10 At Yudhiṣṭhira's behest that most valiant man departed to set eyes
on Śakra, king of the Gods, and on Śaṃkara,* God of Gods. To ensure
success in his task, the powerful strong-armed Arjuna, bull among
men, took his divine bow and sword. The Kauravya, who was the son
of Indra, a great warrior in all the worlds, went in a northerly
direction toward the peak of Mount Himālaya, O king, with a steady
mind. With great speed, his mind set on austerities, he entered into a
ghastly, thorny forest, filled with all manner of flowers and fruit,
visited by all kinds of fowl, overrun by many sorts of game, and
frequented by Siddhas and Cāraṇas.
When the Kaunteya entered the forest, which was empty of people,
15 there arose in heaven the sound of conches and drums. A heavy rain
of flowers fell on the ground and massing clouds covered him
everywhere. After he had crossed through the impassable jungle at
the foot of the great mountain, Arjuna dwelled on the peak of the
Himālaya in all his splendor. He saw blossoming trees there, which
resounded with the sweet songs of birds, and streams full of whirlpools,
the color of blue beryl, resonant with geese and ducks, ringing with

* = Śiva.

the cries of cranes, echoing with the calls of the cuckoo, and loud
with curlews and peacocks. When that great warrior Arjuna saw
those streams with their lovely woods, filled with sacred, cool, and
20 pure water, he became joyous of spirit. Delighting in a beautiful spot
in the woods, the spirited man of awesome heat devoted himself to
awesome austerities. Dressed in grass and bark and carrying stick and
deerskin, he passed one month eating fruit every fourth night, a
second month he ate every eighth night, a third month only once a
fortnight, subsisting on a dead leaf that had fallen on the ground.
When the fourth month came and the moon was full, the strong-
armed scion of Pāṇḍu lived on wind alone, with arms raised, without
support, balanced on the tips of his toes. And because of his ceaseless
bathing the braided hair of the great-spirited hero of boundless might
took on the sheen of lightning and lotus.

25 Thereupon all the great seers went to the God who wields the
Pināka and prostrated themselves before the dark-throated Lord and
sought his grace. They all acquainted him with the doings of
Phalguna: "This mighty Pārtha has sought recourse to the peak of
the Himālaya and stands in awesome, impossible self-mortification,
casting smoke on the skies. None of us know, lord of the Gods, what
he wishes to achieve; he anguishes all of us—it were better he were
stopped!"

The Great Lord said:

Swiftly return in joyous spirit and unwearied whence you have come. I do know the intention that is lodged in his mind. He does not desire heaven, nor sovereignty, nor long life; this very day I shall accomplish what he desires.

Vaiśaṃpāyana said:

30 Having heard the words of the Hunter, the veracious seers returned
in happy spirit each to his own hermitage.

Vaiśaṃpāyana said:

40.1 When all the great-spirited ascetics had gone, the blessed Lord Hara,
who wields the Pināka, absolver of all evil, took on the guise of a
mountain man, which resembles the *kāñcana* tree, resplendent in his
beauty like another Mount Meru among the mountains. Taking up
his illustrious bow and arrows, which were like poisonous snakes, he
flew down in a blaze of flame, like a fire burning the underwood. The
lustrous God was accompanied by the Goddess Umā, in the same
guise and observing the same vow, and by excited creatures in all
5 kinds of shapes. Garbed in his mountain man guise, the God shone
surpassingly with his thousands of women, O King Bhārata.

Instantly the entire wood fell silent and the sounds of streams and birds ceased. As he approached the Pārtha of unsullied deeds, he saw

the wondrous-looking Mūka, a Daitya, who had taken on the form of a boar with the evil design of killing Arjuna. Phalguna said to the demon, taking up his bow Gāṇḍīva and arrows, which were like poisonous snakes, stringing his fine bow and twanging the bowstring,
10 "Since you seek to kill me who have come here innocently, I shall be the first to send you to Yama's realm!" But Śaṃkara in his mountain man guise, on seeing Phalguna taking aim with his heavy bow, suddenly stopped him: "I was the first to take aim at this dark cloud of a beast!" Ignoring his words, Phalguna shot at the animal. The resplendent mountain man simultaneously shot his arrow, like a flash
15 of lightning or a flame crest, at the same target. The two arrows shot by the two of them, struck simultaneously in the wide, mountain-solid body of Mūka. Both the arrows struck him with the impact of lightning and thunderbolt on a mountain. Hit by many arrows like snakes with blazing mouths, he died and once more assumed his terrible form of a Rākṣasa.

Jiṣṇu, enemy-slayer, looked at the golden-hued man who was garbed like a mountain man and surrounded by women; smilingly, for he was happy of heart, the Kaunteya said to him, "Who are you that are wandering in the empty wilderness with a host of women? Are you not frightened of this dreadful forest, golden man? Why did you shoot this beast that was mine? I was the first to catch this
20 Rākṣasa when he got here! Whether it was a whim or a slight, you will not escape from me with your life, for this is not the Law of the chase, what you have done to me today. For that I shall kill you, mountain man!"

At these words of his the mountain man laughed and said in a gentle voice to the left-handed archer Pāṇḍava, "I had taken aim at it first, so it was mine, and it was my arrow that killed it. Do not be so proud of your strength that you blame your own faults on another. You have insulted me, nitwit; you will not escape from me alive! Stand fast, I shall shoot you with arrows like thunderbolts; you shoot too and do as well as you can."

25 Shouting furiously again and again, they bored each other with arrows like poisonous snakes. Arjuna shot at the mountain man a shower of arrows and Śaṃkara received them with a tranquil mind. The Wielder of the Pināka received that downpour of arrows for a while and yet stood unhurt like a motionless mountain. When Dhanaṃjaya saw that his arrows were futile, he was astounded and exclaimed, "Good! Good! Aho, this man who lives on the top of the Himālaya with his delicate body receives undisturbed the iron arrows
30 that are shot from Gāṇḍīva! Who is he? A God, Rudra himself, a Yakṣa, the king of the Gods? For indeed, the Thirty Gods meet on this greatest of mountains. No one can withstand the impact of the

thousands of arrows that I have shot, except the God of the Pināka.
If it is a God or a Yakṣa, anyone but Rudra, who stands here, I shall
send him to Yama's realm with my sharp shafts!"
Arjuna then joyfully shot his iron arrows that cut into weak spots,
by the hundreds, as the sun shoots its rays. The blessed Lord, who
prospers the worlds and holds the trident, received the arrows
35 cheerfully, as a mountain a rain of rocks. In a while Phalguna
exhausted his arrows; and seeing that his arrows were gone, he began
to tremble. Jiṣṇu thought of the blessed Lord Fire, who had given him
the two quivers in the Khāṇḍava Forest. "Now what shall I shoot
with my bow? My arrows are gone. Who is this man who devours all
my arrows? I shall attack him with the nock of my bow, as one
attacks an elephant with the point of a spear, and send him to the
domain of staff-bearing Yama!"
The enemy-slaying Kaunteya began to assault him with the nock of
40 his bow, but the mountain man captured his divine bow, too. Bereft
of his bow, Arjuna stood his ground with sword in hand; and wishing
to put an end to the battle, he vigorously attacked him. With all the
might of his arms, Kuru's scion courageously hurled the sharp sword
that even mountains could not blunt at the other's head, but when it
hit his head it shattered. Phalguna went on to fight with trees and
rocks, and the giant lord in the mountain man guise withstood the
rocks as well as the trees. The powerful Pārtha, belching smoke from
his mouth, struck blows at the invincible mountain man with fists
that impacted like thunderbolts. The blessed Lord in his aspect of a
mountain man then struck Phalguna with fists that were like Śakra's
45 bolts, and a ghastly crackling sound rose from the fists of the
embattled Pāṇḍava and the mountain man. The hair-raising grand
battle went on for a while with hard striking arms, as that battle of
yore between Vṛtra and Indra. The powerful Jiṣṇu seized the mountain
man by the chest, and the other struck his wrestling foe with great
force. From the grinding press of their arms and the rubbing of their
chests a fire with embers and smoke blazed up in their limbs. Finally
the Great God got a good grip on Arjuna and assaulted him mightily
50 and furiously, stunning him out of his wits. And so, Phalguna, looking
like a ball of flesh with his limbs mangled by the God of Gods, O
Bhārata, lost control of his body. Subdued by the great-spirited God,
his breathing stopped and he fell down unconscious. And Bhava was
pleased.

The Blessed Lord said:

Bhoḥ, bhoḥ, Phalguna, I am pleased with your peerless deed, your
gallantry and endurance. There is no baron like you! Your splendor
and mine, and our might, have been matched today, prince sans
blame. I am pleased with you, strong-armed bull among men, set eyes

on me! I shall give you eyesight, wide-eyed hero! You have been a seer before, now you shall defeat all your enemies, may they be celestial!

Vaiśaṃpāyana said:

55 Thereupon Phalguna set eyes on the Great God who dwells in the mountains, trident in hand, in all his effulgence, and on the Goddess. He fell on his knees on the ground and made a prostration with his head; and the Pārtha, victor of enemy cities, propitiated Hara.

Arjuna said:

Wearer of shells, lord of all creatures, who took Bhaga's eyes, pray, Hail-bringer, forgive my offense. I have come to this great mountain desirous to see you, to this mountain that is your favorite, O lord of the Gods, the superb abode of ascetics. I beseech you, lord who are honored by all the creatures, let there be no guilt for me, Great God,
60 from my wanton violence. Śaṃkara, I throw myself on your mercy; forgive me for fighting you in ignorance!

Vaiśaṃpāyana said:

The resplendent God of the Bull-banner laughed and, taking the shining arm of Phalguna, now forgiven, he said to him,

The Blessed Lord said:

41.1 Nara you were in a previous body, with Nārāyaṇa your friend, and at Badarī you did awesome austerities for many myriads of years. In you there is great splendor as there is in Viṣṇu, the supreme person. The world is held up by the splendor of the two of you, who are the foremost of men. At the consecration of Indra you took the great bow that thundered like a monsoon cloud and with Kṛṣṇa chastised the Dānavas, lord. It was this same Gāṇḍīva, Pārtha, so used to your hands, which I just now wrested from you, best among men, by
5 employing my wizardry. You will have your two inexhaustible quivers once again, as you used to have them; I am indeed pleased with you, Pārtha, whose valor is your truth. Accept a boon from us, whatever you desire, bull among men. No mortal man is your equal, giver of honor, nor anyone in heaven. The baronage have their master in you, enemy-tamer!

Arjuna said:

If it pleases you to grant me my wish, Bull-bannered God, then I wish that divine weapon, the dreadful Pāśupata weapon, my lord, which is called Brahmā's Head, gruesome, of terrible power, which at the horrible end of the Eon will destroy the entire world. With it I may burn down in battle the Dānavas and the Rākṣasas, the evil spirits and
10 Piśācas, Gandharvas, and Snakes. From its mouth, when properly spelt, issue forth thousands of tridents, awful-looking clubs, and missiles like venomous snakes. With it I shall embattle Bhīṣma, Droṇa,

and Kṛpa, and the always rough-spoken son of the *sūta*.* This is my first wish, my lord, who took Bhaga's eyes, so that by your grace I may go forth competent!

The Blessed Lord said:

I shall give you the great Pāśupata weapon, which is my favorite, equally capable, Pāṇḍava, of maintaining, releasing, and destroying. Even great Indra does not know it, nor Yama, nor the king of the Yakṣas; neither Varuṇa nor the Wind God, how much less the
15 humans. However, Pārtha, you must never let it loose at any man in wanton violence, for if it hits a person of insufficient power, it might burn down the entire world. There is no one in all three worlds with their moving and standing creatures who is invulnerable to it, and it can be launched with a thought, a glance, a word, or a bow.

Vaiśaṃpāyana said:

Hearing this, the Pārtha hurriedly and attentively purified himself; and when he embraced the feet of the lord of the universe, the God said to him, "Now learn!" Then he taught the best of the Pāṇḍavas about this missile, along with the secrets of its return, this missile that is Death incarnate. Thenceforth it waited on the great-spirited hero as it does on Umā's three-eyed spouse, and Arjuna accepted it happily.
20 And earth with her mountains, forest, and trees, and oceans and odd spots of wilderness, with villages, cities, and mines, trembled. When the moment came there was an outcry of conches, drums, and kettledrums by the thousands, and a huge quake occurred. The Gods and the Dānavas witnessed how that fiercely burning dreadful missile stood bodily deployed at the side of the boundlessly lustrous Pāṇḍava. The Three-eyed God touched the boundlessly lustrous Phalguna, and whatever was ailing in his body, it all disappeared.

The Three-eyed God dismissed Arjuna, saying, "Now go to heaven." And, bowing his head, the Pārtha looked at the God with folded hands.

25 Whereupon the masterful lord of celestials,
Śiva, Umā's spouse, wise man of the mountains,
Gave unto that best of men Gāṇḍīva,
The killer of Piśācas and Dānavas.

And leaving with Umā the sacred mountain
With its white summits and banks and glens,
Frequented by fowl and by great seers,
He went up to heaven as Arjuna watched.

Vaiśaṃpāyana said:

42.1 The Bull-bannered God of the Pināka disappeared before his eyes, as the sun sets before the eyes of the world. Arjuna, killer of enemy

* = Karṇa.

heroes, was profoundly amazed, O Bhārata: "I have seen the Great
God in person! I am fortunate and greatly favored, for I have seen the
three-eyed, boon-granting Hara of the Pināka in his own form, and I
have touched his person with my hand. I know that I have completely
succeeded by myself; all the enemies are defeated and my purpose has
been accomplished."
5 Thereupon there appeared, in a hue of beryl, lighting up all the
horizons, the illustrious Lord of the Waters, surrounded by water
creatures, by Snakes and rivers male and female, Daityas, Sādhyas,
and godlings. Varuṇa, masterful lord of water creatures, came to that
region, and so did, in a hue of gold, riding a lustrous chariot, the Lord
Kubera, followed by the Yakṣas. The illustrious Lord of Riches had
come to visit Arjuna, setting all of space alight, and of most wondrous
aspect. Likewise the illustrious Yama arrived in person, the majestic
finisher of the world, with a retinue of Ancestors, embodied and
10 disembodied, prospering the world. With the staff in his hand he came,
the destroyer of all creatures, of inconceivable spirit, the king of the
Law, son of Vivasvat, brightening with his chariot the three worlds,
the Guhyakas, Gandharvas, and Snakes, like a second sun when the
end of the Eon has come. Drawing near to the colorful, effulgent peaks
of the great mountain, they saw there Arjuna devoted to austerities.
Soon after, the blessed Lord Śakra arrived on the head of Airāvata,
accompanied by Indrāṇī and the hosts of the Gods. With the white
umbrella that was held over his head he shone like the moon under
15 a white cloud. Hymned by Gandharvas, seers, and ascetics, he
approached the summit of the mountain and stood there like the
rising sun.

Thereupon, in a thunderous voice, the wise Yama, who knows the
Law entire, occupying the south, uttered this blissful word: "Arjuna,
Arjuna, behold us! The World Guardians have assembled. We bestow
on you eyesight, for you are worthy of seeing us. You are the mighty
ancient seer Nara, of measureless spirit. At Brahmā's behest you have
now become a mortal, son, born from Indra, of great might and
puissance. The baronage, hot to the touch like fire, which is protected
by Bharadvāja, and the powerful Dānavas who have been born men,
and the Nivātakavacas, are to be pacified by you, scion of Kuru!
20 Karṇa, who is a particle of my father, the God who sends heat to all
the worlds, the mighty Karṇa will be slain by you, Dhanaṃjaya. The
particles of Gods, Gandharvas, and Rākṣasas that have come to the
earth will, when you, enemy-plower, have slain them in battle, obtain
the destination they have won as the fruit of their own acts. Your
fame will remain everlasting in the world, Phalguna, for you have
satisfied the Great God himself in a grand battle; and with Viṣṇu you

will lighten the burden of the earth. Take my weapon, the irresistible
staff, strong-armed hero, for with this weapon you shall do great
deeds."

The Pārtha, scion of Kuru, accepted it in the proper manner, with
the spells, the correct mode of address, and instructions on unleashing
25 and returning it. Then mighty Varuṇa, black as a cloud, the lord of
water creatures, who occupied the west, uttered this word: "Pārtha,
you are the first of the barons and devoted to the Law of the baronage.
Behold me with your wide copper-red eyes; I am Varuṇa, lord of the
waters! Receive from me these inescapable Varuṇa nooses that I
present to you, Kaunteya, with their secrets and mode of return. With
these I subdued at the time thousands of great-spirited Daityas in the
battle over Tārakā. Take them from me, mettlesome warrior; they are
presented by my grace; for even Death cannot escape you when you
30 attack. When you go to war with this weapon, the earth shall
doubtless be emptied of barons."

After him spoke the Lord of Riches, who dwells on Mount Kailāsa,
when Varuṇa and Yama had given their divine weapons: "Strong-
armed, left-handed archer, ancient God everlasting, in eons gone by
you always labored at our side. Now accept from me too a gift, my
precious weapon of disappearance, which dissipates energy, vigor, and
splendor, and puts the foe to sleep, enemy-killer." Kuru's scion,
strong-armed and powerful Arjuna, accepted then also the divine
weapon of Kubera.

35 Now did the king of the Gods speak to the Pārtha of unsullied deeds,
coaxing him with gentle words, rumbling like a monsoon cloud or
kettledrum: "Strong-armed son of Kuntī, you are the ancient lord who
attained to the ultimate perfection and went in person the divine way.
For a very great task is yours to accomplish for the Gods, enemy-
tamer! You must ascend to heaven; be prepared, radiant man. My
chariot driven by Mātali shall come to earth for you, and in heaven I
shall give you the weapons of the Gods, Kaurava."

Having seen the World Guardians assembled on the mountain peak,
40 the wise son of Kuntī Dhanaṃjaya was amazed. Splendid Arjuna then
paid homage to the gathered World Guardians in the proper way, with
words as well as fruit. Honoring Dhanaṃjaya in return, all the Gods
returned as they had come, with the speed of thought at their beck
and call. Arjuna, bull among men, was very joyous that he had
received the weapons; and, his wishes fulfilled, he judged that he had
succeeded.

3(32) Arjuna's Journey to the World of Indra

43–79 (B. 42–80; C. 1714–4020)

43 (42; 1714). Mātali arrives on Indra's chariot and invites Arjuna to come along (1–15). Arjuna bathes and mounts; he bids Mount Mandara farewell (20–25). They ascend to heaven, pass the stars, and enter Nandana (25–35).

44 (43; 1756). Description of Nandana; Arjuna is greeted by the Gods (1–15). Indra welcomes and embraces him, and places him on his throne (15–20). Indra fondles Arjuna, while Gandharvas sing and Apsarās dance (25–30).

45 (44–47; 1788). Arjuna receives Indra's thunderbolt. At the latter's behest he stays five years (1–5). He learns celestial music and dance from Citrasena (5). The seer Lomaśa arrives and is amazed at seeing Arjuna on Indra's throne (5–10). Indra explains that Arjuna has to battle the Nivātakavacas on the Gods' behalf (15–25). Lomaśa should go to Kāmyaka and guide Yudhiṣṭhira on a pilgrimage (30–35).

46 (48–49; 1914). Dhṛtarāṣṭra complains to Saṃjaya that Duryodhana has alienated the Pāṇḍavas, especially Arjuna who is invincible (1–15). Saṃjaya agrees and describes Arjuna's prowess (20–25). Dhṛtarāṣṭra declares that Duryodhana and his councillors are fools (30–40).

47 (50; 1955). Vaiśaṃpāyana describes the Pāṇḍavas' food in the forest (1–10).

48 (51; 1970). Dhṛtarāṣṭra complains about the strength of the Pāṇḍavas and their allies (1–10). Saṃjaya agrees and recounts Kṛṣṇa's oath of assistance: he will restore the king forthwith, but Yudhiṣṭhira has him wait thirteen years (10–25). The Pāñcālas swear to avenge Draupadī (30–35). The Pāṇḍavas are sure to win (35–40).

49 (52; 2014). Bhīma berates Yudhiṣṭhira for sending off Arjuna and for bringing on all hardships (1–10). Yudhiṣṭhira should fight now (10–20). Yudhiṣṭhira bids him to wait thirteen years (25). The seer Bṛhadaśva arrives. Yudhiṣṭhira complains about his misfortune: has any man been as unhappy as he? (25–30). Bṛhadaśva quotes King Nala, and Yudhiṣṭhira asks for his story (35–40).

50–78 (B. 53–79; C. 2072–3088) Nala.
78 (79; 3063). Bṛhadaśva admonishes Yudhiṣṭhira and imparts to him the secret of the dice; he departs (5). News arrives of Arjuna's austerities (5–20).
79 (80; 3090). The Pāṇḍavas and Draupadī miss Arjuna in the Kāmyaka Forest, where they feed the brahmins (1–10). Draupadī laments over Arjuna (10–15), as do Bhīma (15–20), Nakula (20–25), and Sahadeva (25).

Vaiśaṃpāyana said:
43.1 When the World Guardians had left, the Pārtha, uprooter of his
foes, wondered, O Indra among kings, whether the chariot of the king
of the Gods would be coming. And as the sagacious Guḍākeśa was
wondering, the resplendent chariot arrived, driven by Mātali. Lifting
darkness from the sky and shredding the clouds, it filled all of space
with a roar like the thunder of the monsoon cloud. It held swords,
terrible spears, clubs of ghastly aspect, missiles of divine power, and
5 lustrous lightning flashes, as well as thunderbolts, wheeled battering
rams, bellows that raised gales, loud like peacock and thunder cloud;
Giant Snakes it carried, with fiery mouths, most terrifying, tall like
white clouds and hard like mountains; ten thousand bay horses, fast
as the wind, drew this eye-fetching, divine, magic chariot. On it he saw
the beautiful dark-blue flag Vaijayanta, dark like the blue lotus, and
the gold-ornamented flag mast.
Discerning on the chariot the charioteer, who was decked in twice-
10 melted gold, the strong-armed Pārtha thought him a God. And as he
was musing, Mātali approached Phalguna; with a bow he courteously
said to him, "*Bhoḥ bhoḥ*, son of Śakra! The illustrious Śakra desires to
see you! Quickly mount this honored chariot of Indra. That greatest
of the Gods, the God of the Hundred Sacrifices, your own father, has
told me, 'The Thirty Celestials must see Kuntī's son here on his
arrival!' Śakra himself, surrounded by Gods and the hosts of seers, and
by Gandharvas and Apsarās, is waiting anxiously to see you. Ascend
with me from this world to the world of the Gods at the behest of the
Chastiser of Pāka*; you will come back after you have obtained
weapons."
Arjuna said:
15 Mātali, hasten and mount the superb chariot, which can hardly be
obtained with even hundreds of Royal Consecrations and Horse
Sacrifices! Not the most lordly sacrificing kings, generous with
stipends, nor godlings nor Dānavas may ascend this superb chariot.
No one who has not done austerities is able even to set eyes on this
great divine chariot, or to touch it, much less to ride in it! As soon as

* = Indra.

you have taken your position, good man, and stand on the chariot
with the horses steady, I shall mount it, as a man of good deeds
ascends the path of the good.

Vaiśaṃpāyana said:

On hearing his word, Indra's charioteer Mātali quickly mounted the
20 chariot and steadied the horses with the reins. Arjuna bathed in the
Ganges, and, purified and in happy spirits, he muttered his prayers as
was proper. Then, after offering to the Gods, according to the rules and
precepts, he proceeded to bid the lordly Mount Mandara farewell:
"Mountain, thou art always the refuge of the good who practice the
Law, the hermits of holy deeds, who seek out the road that leads to
heaven. It is by thy grace, Mountain, that brahmins, barons, and
commoners attain to heaven and devoid of pain walk with the Gods.
King of mountains, great peak, refuge of hermits, treasury of sacred
25 places, I must go, farewell; I have happily lived on thee! Many are the
peaks of thine that I have seen, the valleys, rivers, and springs, and
thy very holy places."

Thus Arjuna, slayer of enemy heroes, having said farewell to the
mountain, ascended the divine chariot, brilliant like the sun. And on
this sunlike, divine, wonder-working chariot the wise scion of Kuru
flew joyously upward. While becoming invisible to the mortals who
walk on earth, he saw wondrous airborne chariots by the thousands.
No sun shone there, or moon, or fire, but they shone with a light of
their own acquired by their merits. Those lights that are seen as the
stars look tiny like oil flames because of the distance, but they are very
large. The Pāṇḍava saw them bright and beautiful, burning on their
own hearths with a fire of their own. There are the perfected royal
seers, the heroes cut down in war, who, having won heaven with
their austerities, gather in hundreds of groups. So do thousands of
Gandharvas with a glow like the sun's or the fire's, and of Guhyakas
and seers and the hosts of Apsarās.

Beholding those self-luminous worlds, Phalguna, astonished,
questioned Mātali in a friendly manner, and the other said to him,
35 "Those are men of saintly deeds, ablaze on their own hearths, whom
you saw there, my lord, looking like stars from earth below." Then he
saw standing at the gateway the victorious white elephant, four-
tusked Airāvata, towering like peaked Kailāsa. Driving on the roadway
of the Siddhas that most excellent Kuru Pāṇḍava shone forth as of old
the great king Māndhātar. The lotus-eyed prince passed by the worlds
of the kings, then looked upon Amarāvatī, the city of Indra.

Vaiśaṃpāyana said:

44.1 He looked upon the lovely city, which is frequented by Siddhas and
Cāraṇas, and adorned with sacred trees that flower in all seasons,

while a fragrant breeze, mixed with the perfumes of flowers and
redolent trees, fanned him. And he saw the divine park Nandana,
sought out by the hosts of Apsarās, with heavenly blossoming trees
that seemed to beckon to him. This world of those of saintly deeds
cannot be seen by one who has not done austerities or who has not
5 maintained the fires, nor by those averse to war, those who fail to
sacrifice, liars, persons devoid of the learning of the *Veda*, unbathed in
sacred fords, outside ritual and gifts. Those base men who disrupt
sacrifices and evil-doers who drink liquor, violate their teacher's bed,
or eat meat do not set eyes on it at all. And looking at that celestial
park, resonant with divine songs, the strong-armed hero entered
Indra's beloved city. He saw the Gods' chariots, which can go
everywhere, stationed by the thousands and moving by the myriads.

Gandharvas and Apsarās lauded the Pāṇḍava and pure and fragrant
10 breezes fanned him. The Gods, Gandharvas, Siddhas, and great seers
happily welcomed the Pārtha of unsullied deeds. Blessed with
benedictions and the music of divine instruments, the strong-armed
man set foot on the wide road of the stars, resounding with conches
and drums, which is renowned as the Path of the Gods. At Indra's
behest, he traveled by it and he was praised on all sides. There were
the Sādhyas, the All-the-Gods, the Maruts, the two Aśvins, Ādityas,
Vasus, and Rudras, the pure brahmin seers, numerous royal seers and
kings led by Dilīpa, and Tumbura, Nārada, and the Gandharvas Hāha
15 and Āhuhu. The scion of Kuru met with them all in the proper
manner, then he beheld the king of the Gods, the enemy-taming God
of the Hundred Sacrifices.

The strong-armed Pāṇḍava alighted from the superb chariot and
beheld in person his father Indra, the Chastiser of Pāka. A beautiful
white umbrella with a golden staff was held over him and a waving
fan, redolent with heavenly perfumes, cooled him. Viśvāvasu and the
other Gandharvas praised him with lauds and adoration, and eminent
brahmins blessed him with benedictions from the *Ṛg*, *Yajur*, and
Sāmavedas. The mighty Kaunteya drew near and bowed his head.
20 Śakra embraced him with his round arms and, taking him by the
hand, made him sit next to himself on Indra's throne, which is
worshiped by Gods and royal seers. God Indra, killer of enemy-heroes,
kissed him on the head and took him on his lap, while the other
humbly bowed. At the command of the Thousand-eyed God, the
Pārtha of measureless spirit bestrode the Indra throne like another
Indra.

Affectionately the foe of Vṛtra touched Arjuna's handsome face and
stroked it with his fragrant hand. Gently he caressed his long arms,
hardened by the lash of the bowstring, shining like golden columns.
25 The Slayer of Vala, the Thunderbolt-wielder, again and again squeezed

his arms with a hand that was scarred from holding the thunderbolt.
The thousand-eyed victor of Vṛtra kept looking at Guḍākeśa with a
semblance of a smile, his eyes blooming with joy, and was not sated.
Sitting together on one throne, they emblazoned the assembly hall as
the sun and the moon rising in the sky on the fourteenth.
The Gandharvas, led by Tumbura, sang verses with the sweetest
melody, being masters of melody and song. Ghṛtācī, Menakā, Rambhā,
30 Pūrvacitti, Svyaṃprabhā, Urvaśī, Miśrakeśī, Duṇḍu, Gaurī, Varūthinī,
Gopālī, Sahajanyā, Kumbhayoni, Prajāgarā, Citrasenā, Citralekhā,
Sahā, Madhurasvarā, these and other beautiful lotus-eyed nymphs
danced everywhere, bent upon enticing the hearts of the Siddhas, with
wide-flanked buttocks and bouncing breasts, stealing hearts and minds
with their quick glances, allurements, and sweetness.

Vaiśaṃpāyana said:
45.1 Then, divining the mind of Śakra, the Gods and Gandharvas quickly
fetched a superb guest gift and immediately welcomed Arjuna. They
offered the prince water to wash his feet, water to rinse his mouth,
and guided him into the palace of the Sacker of Cities. With such
honors Jiṣṇu dwelled in the house of his father, learning all the while
great weapons and the means to withdraw them. From Śakra's hand
he received his favorite weapon, the irresistible thunderbolt, and the
5 loud thunderclaps marked by clouds and peacocks. When he had
received the weapons, the Pāṇḍava Kaunteya bethought himself of his
brothers, yet at the behest of the Sacker of Cities he dwelled there
happily for five years.
When he had become skillful with the weapons, Śakra said to the
Pārtha at the right time, "Now learn how to dance and sing from
Citrasena, Kaunteya, the celestial music that is unknown in the world
of men. Acquire that art, Kaunteya, and it shall stand you in good
stead!" The Sacker of Cities gave him Citrasena for a friend, and
whenever they met the Pārtha enjoyed himself merrily with him.
One day the great seer Lomaśa in the course of his travels came to
10 Śakra's palace out of a desire to visit the Sacker of Cities. The great
hermit met and bowed to the lord of the Gods and saw the Pāṇḍava
occupying half of Śakra's throne. With Śakra's permission the eminent
brahmin, honored by the great seers, sat down on a stool that was
covered with *kuśa* grass. As he watched how the Pārtha sat on Indra's
throne, the thought occurred to him, "How is it that the Pārtha, a
baron, has risen to the throne of Śakra? What great merit has he
earned, or what worlds won, that he has thus attained to a place that
the Gods honor?"
Śakra, the Slayer of Vṛtra, divined his thought, and the Consort of
15 Śacī said to Lomaśa with a laugh, "Brahmin seer, listen to what you

want explained in your mind. This is not a mere mortal who was born
to baronhood. Great seer, this is my great-armed son, who was born
from Kuntī; because of a certain reason he has come here to obtain
weapons. Aho! is it possible that you do not know this eminent
ancient seer? Then listen to me, brahmin, while I tell you who he is
and what his purpose is. The two great ancient seers, Nara and
Nārāyaṇa, you should know, are now Hṛṣīkeśa and Dhanaṃjaya. That
sacred hermitage that is renowned as Badarī, which Gods and great-
20 spirited seers are unable to behold, was the dwelling place of Viṣṇu
and Jiṣṇu; from there springs the Ganges frequented by Siddhas and
Cāraṇas. At my injunction the lustrous pair have been born on earth;
these mighty two shall roll the burden off earth. For there are certain
Asuras, Nivātakavacas by name, who, driven mad by the gift of a
boon, are doing us disfavors. With the insolence of their strength they
have designs to slay the Gods, they do not heed the Gods, for such a
boon was given them: the terrible and powerful sons of Dānu are
living in Pātāla, and indeed, all the troops of the Gods are unable to
25 combat them. The illustrious Viṣṇu, the Slayer of Madhu, the blessed
Lord God, unvanquished Hari, who lived on earth under the name of
Kapila and who of yore with a mere glance destroyed the great-
spirited sons of Sagara who were digging toward the netherworld
Rasātala—he has to accomplish in a great battle this task for us,
eminent brahmin, together with the Pārtha, no doubt of that. He can
be a match for them all; after the champion has killed them, he will
return to men.

"You yourself must at my bidding now go to earth. You will find
30 Yudhiṣṭhira the hero living in the Kāmyaka Forest. The law-spirited
man, who is true to his promises, should be told on my orders, 'Do
not miss Phalguna too much; he will return as soon as he has finished
with the weapons. Without the purified prowess of his arms and
complete mastery of weapons, Bhīṣma, Droṇa, and the others cannot
be countered in battle. Strong-armed, spirited Guḍākeśa has received
the weapons and has gained a mastery of dance, music, and song. You
yourself, lord of men, enemy-tamer, should visit remote places of
pilgrimage together with all your other brothers. After bathing at
sacred fords you will become guiltless and feverless; and freed from
evil, O lord of kings, you will enjoy the kingdom.'

35 "You too, sir, best of the twice-born, should guard over him as he
wanders on earth with the power of your austerities. For in the straits
of the mountains and in rough country there always lurk ferocious
Rākṣasas—you must protect him from them."

The great ascetic Lomaśa promised, "So I shall." He went to earth
in the direction of the Kāmyaka Forest, and there he visited Kaunteya,
the enemy-taming King Dharma, in the company of all his brothers.

Janamejaya said:
46.1 Brahmin, what did the mighty Dhṛtarāṣṭra say when he heard
about that most wondrous feat of boundlessly lustrous Pārtha?
Vaiśaṃpāyana said:
Sire, when Ambikā's son the king heard from Dvaipāyana, greatest
of seers, that the Pārtha had gone to the world of Indra, he said to
Saṃjaya, "Do you too perchance know completely of the exploit of
the sagacious Pārtha, which I have heard in full detail, O bard? My
mad and evil-intentioned son, slow-witted in his rustic pursuits of the
5 Law, will in his folly massacre the earth. The great-spirited man*,
whose words are always true, even when spoken in jest, and who has
Dhanaṃjaya as his champion, shall win even the entire universe.
When Arjuna shoots his sharp-tipped, eared, iron arrows that have
been sharpened on a whetstone, who shall stand firm before him, even
if he may transcend death and old age? My evil-spirited sons have all
fallen into the power of death, for there looms for them a war with the
invincible Pāṇḍavas. Worry though I may incessantly, I do not see any
one who could stand up in battle to that Gāṇḍiva bowman. If Droṇa
and Karṇa were to counter him in battle, nay even Bhīṣma himself,
there would be a dangerous risk for the world itself; but I do not see
10 how we could win. Karṇa is compassionate and forgetful, the Teacher
who is his guru is old, the Pārtha is resentful, powerful, enraged, and of
steadfast valor. There will be a most terrifying war, with no one the
victor, for they are all experts on arms and champions, they have all
won great fame. None of them would even want total supremacy if
they had to gain it through defeat—surely peace will only come when
either they have been killed, or Phalguna. But there is no one who
will slay Arjuna, no one to defeat him. How can his fury be appeased
that has risen against fools?
"This hero, who matches the Lord of the Thirty, satisfied the Fire
in the Khāṇḍava Forest. He subdued all the kings at the grand
15 sacrifice of the Royal Consecration. A thunderbolt striking the head
of a mountain leaves a remainder, Saṃjaya, but the arrows shot by
the diademed warrior leave none, friend. For just as the rays of the
sun burn moving and standing creatures on earth, so the shafts shot
from Arjuna's hand will burn my sons. Surely, panic-stricken by the
sound of the left-handed archer's chariot, the whole army of the
Bharatas already appears shattered!

"Pouring out and pouring forth his shafts,
The diademed man will stand, bow drawn,
By the creator created our all-snatching death—
But what must be cannot be avoided."

* = Yudhiṣṭhira.

Saṃjaya said:
All that you have said, king, concerning Duryodhana is just as you
20 said it; it is no lie, king of the earth. For the Pāṇḍavas of boundless
luster have been possessed by fury ever since they saw Kṛṣṇā, their
glorious wife by the Law, brought into the assembly hall; and having
heard Duḥśāsana's words of dreadful consequences, and Karṇa's,
great king, I am sure they will not sleep.

I have indeed heard, king, how the Pārtha won in a battle the
satisfaction of Sthāṇu of the eleven bodies with his bow. Assuming the
guise of a mountain man, he engaged Phalguna in a fight, for the
blessed Lord, the shell-wearing lord of all the Gods, wished to find out
for himself. At the same time, the World Guardians appeared to
Arjuna, the bull of the Kauravas, who had been audacious in his
25 austerities for the sake of the weapons. No man could have dared to
obtain that but Phalguna, that vision of those lords in person on
earth. What man would dare wear out a hero whom the Great Lord
himself, in the form that he had assumed, could not wear out? By
molesting Draupadī and enraging the Pāṇḍavas, they brought this
dreadful quarrel and hair-raising danger on themselves, when Bhīma
with trembling lip spoke his mighty word at the sight of Duryodhana
showing Draupadī his thighs: "I shall break your thighs, miscreant,
with my adamant club, thirteen years from now, cheater at dice!"
30 They are all excellent fighters, all boundlessly lustrous, all expert on
any weapon, invincible even to the Gods. I hold that the Pārthas,
carried away by their rage, will put an end to your sons in a war, for
they are powerful and wrathful!

Dhṛtarāṣṭra said:
What has Karṇa wrought, bard, uttering those insults! It was
foolhardiness enough that Kṛṣṇā was brought into the assembly. Must
my sons not remain foolish, if their eldest brother and guru does not
behave himself? He did not even want to listen to my words, bard,
that man of misfortune, seeing that I lack eyesight, and therefore lack
35 energy and insight as well! And his councillors are fools, Karṇa,
Saubala, and the others, who mindlessly add to his many vices. Even
if the boundlessly lustrous Pārtha were to shoot his arrows in jest,
they would burn down my sons, let alone when they are shot in
anger. Unleashed with the force of Arjuna's arms, shot from a great
bow, exhilarated by the spells of divine weapons, they would strike
down even champions. What has he not won whose councillor,
protector, and friend is Janārdana Hari, the lord of the universe! This
is a very great miracle of Arjuna that he encountered the Great God
with his arms. All the world knows the feat that Phalguna* and

* = Arjuna.

Dāmodara* accomplished in the Khāṇḍava Forest to help the Fire. When the Pārtha and Bhīma and Vāsudeva Sātata are enraged, there is nothing left of my son with his councillors and kinsmen!

Janamejaya said:

47.1 All these complaints of King Dhṛtarāṣṭra were meaningless, hermit,
after he had driven the heroic Pāṇḍavas from their home. Why did
the king connive with his foolish son Duryodhana and thus enrage
those grand warriors, the sons of Pāṇḍu? Now tell me, what kind of
food did the Pāṇḍavas eat in the forest? Was it forest fare or
husbanded? Tell me that, sir.

Vaiśaṃpāyana said:

It was forest fare and game killed with purified weapons that those
5 bulls among men ate, after first providing the brahmins. When those
champions, mighty bowmen, dwelled in the forest, brahmins with
fire and without fire followed them there. There were another ten
thousand *snātaka* brahmins of great spirit and wise in the means of
release whom Yudhiṣṭhira also supported. With his arrows he laid
low *ruru* deer and black gazelles and other sacrificial forest game and
provided for the brahmins in ritual fashion. Among them not a man
was found ill-colored or diseased, thin or weakened, unhappy or
afraid. Like favorite sons or kinsmen or blood brothers he fed them,
10 Yudhiṣṭhira the King Dharma, best of the Kauravas. And like a
mother the glorious Draupadī served her husbands and all the twice-
born first, before she herself ate what remained.

The king hunted the east, Bhīmasena the south,
And the twins both hunted the west and the north
For the meat of deer, all wielding their bows,
And there they killed them, day after day.

Thus they lived in the Kāmyaka Forest
Without Arjuna, missing him sorely.
And all of five years did pass them by,
As they studied and prayed and sacrificed.

Vaiśaṃpāyana said:

48.1 Ambikā's son Dhṛtarāṣṭra heaved a deep hot sigh, and he summoned his bard Saṃjaya and said to him, O bull of the Bharatas, "Those two lordly sons of Gods, in splendor alike to the king of the Gods, the Pāṇḍavas Nakula and Sahadeva are berserkers in war, with hard weapons, shooting far, resolved on battle, deft of hand, firm in their anger, always concentrated, and vigorous. When they follow Bhīma and Arjuna into the thick of battle, they will stand fast with

* = Kṛṣṇa.

the valor of lions, unassailable like the Aśvins, and I do not see a remnant left of my troops, Saṃjaya. For those two warriors, unmatched by any warrior in war, the sons of Gods, are intransigent and will not forgive the molestation of Draupadī. The Vṛṣṇis, great archers too, and the august Pāñcālas, protected in battle by Vāsudeva, who is true to his word, and the Pārthas themselves will burn down the army of my sons in a war. Even mountains would not be able to withstand the onslaught of the Vṛṣṇis led by Rāma and Kṛṣṇa, if there is a war, son of the bard. The great bowman Bhīma, of terrible prowess, will stroll about in their midst with his iron-spiked, enemy-harassing club. The kings of men will not be able to endure the sound of the Gāṇḍīva like the roar of the thunderbolt and the impact of Bhīma's club. Then I shall remember the words that my friends spoke, words that I should have borne in mind, but that I did not follow before under Duryodhana's influence.

Saṃjaya said:

That is the great mistake you overlooked, king, that you, out of folly, failed to stop your son, though you could have. For when the unvanquished Madhusūdana heard that the Pāṇḍavas had been defeated at dice, he hurried to the Kāmyaka Forest and paid his respects to the Pārthas. Drupada's sons, led by Dhṛṣṭadyumna, did the same, and so did Virāṭa, Dhṛṣṭaketu, and the warlike Kaikeyas. I learned from a spy all that they talked about when they saw the Pārthas defeated, and I have told you. When they met, the Pāṇḍavas chose Madhusūdana as Phalguna's charioteer in case of war, and Hari agreed. Kṛṣṇa too was indignant when he saw the Pārthas in that condition, wearing black deerskins for upper garments, and he said to Yudhiṣṭhira, "The great fortune, beyond the grasp of other kings, that was the Pārthas' in Indraprastha at the Royal Consecration, where I saw all kings subdued by the fear of the might of your weapons—Vangas, Angas, Puṇḍras, Uḍras, Colas, Draviḍas, Andhrakas, those who live by the ocean and marshes and in settlements, Simhalese, Barbaras, Mlecchas, and other jungle folk, the western kingdoms by the hundreds from as far as the ocean, all the Pahlavas and Daradas, Kirātas, Yavanas, Śakas, Robber Huns, Chinese, Tokharians, Saindhavas, Jaguḍas, Ramathas, Muṇḍas, queen-ruled tribes, Tanganas, and all the many others who had come, bull of the Bharatas, as your servitors at the sacrifice—that same great fortune, fickle and making the rounds, I shall take with the lives of the ones who have taken it! With Rāma,* Bhīma, Arjuna, and the twins, O Kauravya, with Akrūra, Gada, Sāmba, Pradyumna, and Āhuka, the heroic Dhṛṣṭadyumna, and the son of Śiśupāla,** I shall kill

* = Bala-rāma.
** = Dhṛṣṭaketu.

Duryodhana this instant, O Bhārata, and Karṇa, Duḥśāsana, and Saubala and whoever fights back! Then, sitting as king in Hāstinapura with your brothers, in possession of Dhṛtarāṣṭra's fortune, you shall sway this world!"

Then the king spoke to him in that assembly of heroes, while all of them, headed by Dhṛṣṭadyumna, were listening: "I accept this word of yours as true, Janārdana. You shall kill my enemies, strong-armed hero, and their followers, but thirteen years from now: help me keep true, Keśava! For in the midst of kings I have given my promise that I would stay in the forest."

30 The assembled men led by Dhṛṣṭadyumna gave their promise at
this word of King Dharma and quickly pacified the furious Keśava
with gentle words such as suited the time. And they said to unsullied
Draupadī within Vāsudeva's hearing, "Queen, because of your anger
Duryodhana shall part with his life. This we promise as the truth. Do
not sorrow, beautiful princess. The same ones who saw you angered,
Kṛṣṇā, and laughed at you then, the beasts and the birds will eat their
flesh and laugh. The vultures and jackals will drink their blood,
dragging about the skulls of those who dragged you on the assembly
floor! Daughter of the Pāñcālas, you shall see their bodies lying on
the ground, dragged about and devoured without let by the
35 carnivores. The ones who molested you and the ones who ignored
you, earth shall drink their blood as they lie beheaded!"

Such were the words and others like them that those bulls among men spoke, all mighty champions, all of famous character. And when the thirteenth year is full, these great warriors who have been chosen by the King Dharma will march on us with Vāsudeva at their head.

Rāma and Kṛṣṇa, Dhanaṃjaya,
Pradyumna and Sāmba, the sons of Mādrī,
Yuyudhāna and Bhīma, the Kaikeya princes,
The sons of Pāñcāla with the King Dharma,

Against all these invincible champions,
Great-spirited, with their armies and troops,
Who shall stand up in battle, wanting to live,
Like angered lions of heavy mane?

Dhṛtarāṣṭra said:

40 At the time of the dicing Vidura told me,
"If you defeat the Pāṇḍavas, king,
It shall surely spell the end of the Kurus;
There shall be a horrible torrent of blood!"

I think that so it shall be, O bard,
As the Steward foretold me long ago.

There shall undoubtedly be a war,
When the time the Pāṇḍavas pledged runs out.

Janamejaya said:
49.1 When the great-spirited Pārtha had gone to the world of Śakra to
obtain the weapons, what did Yudhiṣṭhira and the other Pāṇḍavas do?
Vaiśaṃpāyana said:
When the great-spirited Pārtha had gone to the world of Śakra to
obtain the weapons, the bulls among men lived on with Kṛṣṇā in the
Kāmyaka Forest. One day those best of the Bharatas were sitting
unhappily with Kṛṣṇā in a desolate meadow. Missing Dhanaṃjaya,
tears caught in their throats and, quite miserable because of their
separation from him and the loss of their kingdom, they were all
flooded with grief.
5 Then Bhīma of the strong arms said to Yudhiṣṭhira, "It was on
your orders, great king, that that bull-like Arjuna went, he on whom
rest the lives of the sons of Pāṇḍu. If he dies, the Pāñcālas and their
sons, we ourselves and Sātyaki and Vāsudeva will perish without a
doubt. What can be more worrisome than that the mighty Terrifier,
not heeding the many troubles ahead, went at your command? All of
us have sought recourse to the arms of the great-spirited man,
thinking that now we had defeated our enemies in battle and gained
the earth. It was his influence, the archer's, that stopped me from
killing off the Dhārtarāṣṭras and Saubala in the midst of the assembly.
10 And here we are, strong in our arms, and endure our rage, which
sprang from you, protected only by Vāsudeva. For if we and Kṛṣṇa
had killed the enemies led by Karṇa, we would now sway all of earth,
reconquered with our own hands. It is thanks to your dicing that we
have all come to disaster, we who do not lack manhood, king, and
are stronger than the strong! Pray, great king, look to the baronial
Law! It is not, great king, the baron's law to sit in the forest!
Kingship alone, as the wise know, is the baron's supreme Law: you
who know the Laws of the baronage, do not destroy the lawlike
ways! King, let us strike down the Dhārtarāṣṭras, before the twelve
15 years are over, let us return from the woods, fetch the Pārtha and
Janārdana, and speedily strike them down with their ranks drawn up
in a grand war! I shall send the Dhārtarāṣṭras to the other world,
lord of your people; I shall slaughter all the Dhārtarāṣṭras, Saubala,
and Duryodhana and Karṇa and whoever else fights back! When I
have pacified them, you can later return from the woods, and if that
is the way it will be, no blame will attach to you, lord of the people.

"Brother, enemy-tamer, any evil can be appeased with one rite or the other: wipe it out, great king, and we shall go to the highest heavens! That is the way it should be, king, if our king weren't a

fool, weren't a procrastinator. But yes, you are prone to the Law.
20 A cheating mind, it is ruled, should be thwarted with deceit, for it is
not reckoned a sin when a cheater is killed by deceit. Also, Bhārata,
those wise in the Laws find it among the Laws, great king, that a day
and a night equal one year. Likewise, we hear constantly this text of
the *Veda*, my lord, that the year is over when there is an emergency,
great king. If the *Vedas* are your authority, unvanquished prince, then
know the thirteen years to be over after a day! Now is the time to kill
Duryodhana and his band, enemy-tamer, before he makes all of earth
loyal to him."

When Bhīma had said this, Yudhiṣṭhira the King Dharma kissed the Pāṇḍava on the head and said soothingly, "Without a doubt, strong-armed man, you shall kill Suyodhana, but thirteen years from now, you and the Gāṇḍīva bowman. What are you telling me, Pārtha, that 'the time has come,' my lord? I cannot tell a lie, for it is not in me. Kaunteya, without deceit, on which only the evil decide, you shall still kill off, unbreakable man, Suyodhana and his band!"

So did Yudhiṣṭhira the King Dharma speak to Bhīma, when there
30 arrived the lordly Bṛhadaśva, the great seer. When the Law-spirited
king saw him arrive, a man of Law, the King Dharma honored him
with the *madhuparka* according to Law and Scriptures. After the guest
had caught his breath and was sitting rested, Yudhiṣṭhira the King
Dharma faced him and lamented much. "Reverend sir," he said, "my
treasure and my kingdom have been stolen from me in a game at
dice, when I was challenged by gamblers who knew how to cheat and
were experts at dice. I did not know the dice, and evil-intentioned
persons cheated me and dragged my wife, who is dearer to me than
my life, into the hall. Now is there a king on earth more unlucky than
I, barring one you may have seen or heard of? There is no man, I
think, unhappier than I am."

Bṛhadaśva said:

35 Is that what you are saying, Pāṇḍava, great king, "There is no man
more unlucky than I was?" On this I can tell you a story, if it pleases
you to listen, prince sans blame, the story of a king, lord of the earth,
who was unhappier than you.

Vaiśaṃpāyana said:

The king told him, "Tell me, sir, I want to hear of the king who found himself in my situation."

Bṛhadaśva said:

Then listen to me attentively, unvanquished king, you and your brothers, about a king, O lord of the earth, who was unhappier than you.

In Niṣadha country there was a Prince Vīrasena. He had a son by
40 the name of Nala, who had insight in both Law and Profit. That king

was cheated and defeated, so we hear, by Puṣkara and undeservingly lived in the forest, sire. You on the other hand are surrounded by your brothers, heroes the likes of Gods, and by eminent twice-born, the likes of Brahmā—you have no reason to grieve!"

Yudhiṣṭhira said:

I want to hear in full the geste of that very great-spirited Nala. Pray, greatest of storytellers, tell me that story!

3(32.a) Nala

50–78 (B. 53–79; C. 2072–3088)

50 (53; 2072). Nala, handsome and talented, is king of Niṣadha (1). Bhīma, king of Vidarbha, is childless; the seer Damana bestows three sons on him, and a daughter Damayantī. She grows up beautiful (5–10). Nala hears her praises sung, she his; they fall in love (15). Nala catches a wild goose, which promises to speak to Damayantī. Damayantī catches it too and it speaks of Nala (20–30).

51 (54; 2103). Damayantī is out of sorts, as her friends report to her father Bhīma. He decides on a Bridegroom Choice, and princes gather (1–10). Nārada and Parvata visit Indra, who complains that no kings are falling in battle. Nārada explains that they are preoccupied with the Bridegroom Choice (10–20). The World Guardians and The Fire God decide to attend too, and see Nala, whom they wish to engage as a messenger to Damayantī (20–25).

52 (55; 2136). Nala agrees, under protest (1–10). He goes and enters Damayantī's chamber. He explains he is the God's envoy, and advises her to choose one of them (10–20).

53 (56; 2170). Damayantī insists on choosing Nala (1–10). He reports to the Gods (10–20).

54 (57; 2191). At the Bridegroom Choice the Gods all appear as Nala. Damayantī is bewildered and throws herself on the mercy of the Gods, swearing by her truth (1–20). The Gods assume their own forms, and Damayantī chooses Nala (20–25). The Gods give boons: Indra's appearance at sacrifices, and an unimpeded gait; immediate presence of fire anywhere and invulnerability to it; a taste for food and firmness in Law; the presence of

water anywhere, and a garland; also twin children (25–30). Nala marries Damayantī, and they live happily (30–35).
55 (58; 2236). Kali and Dvāpara meet the returning Gods. Kali is enraged that Nala has won Damayantī, and decides to possess him. Dvāpara is to enter the dice.
56 (59; 2254). Twelve years later Nala is polluted, and Kali enters him. Nala's brother Puṣkara challenges him to dicing. Nala loses consistently (1–10). The citizens protest, but Nala pays no heed (10–15).
57 (60; 2272). At Damayantī's suggestion the citizens reappear, but to no avail (1–5). Damayantī tells Nala's charioteer Vārṣṇeya to take the twin children to her parents (5–20).
58 (61; 2297). Nala loses all, except Damayantī. Clothed in one piece he leaves, followed by Damayantī. Nala stays outside the city for three nights (1–10). When golden-feathered birds come close, Nala casts his cloth over them to catch them; they fly away with it – they are the dice. Nala laments and hints that Damayantī go to her parents (10–20). Damayantī protests and declines: Nala should come along (20–30).
59 (62; 2333). Nala is too proud (1). They camp at a lodge; Nala decides to leave Damayantī for her own good (1–15). He does, but returns several times; at last Kali prevails, and he runs off (15–25).
60 (63; 2362). Damayantī finds Nala gone and laments piteously; she curses the cause of his suffering (1–20). A boa seizes her, but she is set free by a hunter, who leches after her (20–30). She curses him, and he dies (30–35).
61 (64; 2401). Damayantī wanders through the forest and laments (1–25). She questions a tiger and a mountain (30–55). After three days she finds a hermitage; the hermits promise reunion (55–90), and disappear (90–95). She questions an aśoka *tree (95–105). By a river she finds a caravan and joins it (105–20).*
62 (65; 2532). After many days the caravan is routed at night by elephants (1–10). Damayantī survives and wanders on to the city of the Cedis (10–20). The queen mother sees her and engages her as a chambermaid (20–35). Damayantī accepts under conditions (35–40).
63 (66; 2606). Nala rescues a snake from a forest fire. By way of a favor the snake changes him into a

hunchback, while poisoning Kali who possesses Nala (1–15). It advises Nala to seek employment with King Ṛtuparṇa of Ayodhyā (15–20).

64 (67; 2653). Ṛtuparṇa engages Nala under the name Bāhuka (1–5). Nala repeats an elegiac verse nightly; he explains it obliquely (5–15).

65 (68; 2653). Damayantī's father Bhīma dispatches brahmins to find Nala and his wife (1–5). The brahmin Sudeva comes to Cedi and discovers Damayantī (5–25) and greets her (25–30). The queen mother makes inquiries (30–35).

66 (69; 2694). Sudeva presents Damayantī (1–5). The queen mother recognizes her as her niece (5–15). Damayantī asks help to go home, where she arrives (15–25).

67 (70; 2721). At Damayantī's and her mother's urging Bhīma sends brahmins to search for Nala. Damayantī gives them verses to recite everywhere (1–15). The brahmins depart (20).

68 (70; 2744). The brahmin Parṇāda returns: he has been to Ayodhyā, where Bāhuka heard the verses and replied with his own, identifying himself obliquely (1–10). Leaving Bhīma in ignorance, Damayantī dispatches the brahmin Sudeva to Ayodhyā with the message of another Bridegroom Choice for Damayantī (1–20).

69 (71; 2772). Ṛtuparṇa orders Bāhuka to drive him to Vidarbha in one day for the Bridegroom Choice. He dejectedly picks horses (1–10). The king demurs at his choice but gives in. They almost fly on the way (10–20). Nala's old charioteer, Vārṣṇeya, now with Ṛtuparṇa, wonders if Bāhuka is Nala (20–30).

70 (72; 2808). Ṛtuparṇa's shawl falls, but it cannot be retrieved (1–5). The king sees a vibhīṭaka *tree and instantly counts its nuts. Bāhuka insists on checking the count (5–20). Bāhuka asks for the gift of that counting talent, which makes one an expert dice player, in return for his own talent with horses. The king does so, and Kali leaves Nala and enters the* vibhīṭaka *tree (20–35).*

71 (73; 2852). Damayantī hears the roar of the chariot and divines it is Nala driving (1–15). Bhīma is surprised at Ṛtuparṇa's arrival; there are no signs of a Bridegroom Choice (20–25). Damayantī remains in doubt (25–30).

72 (74; 2880), Damayantī sends her servant Keśinī to investigate Bāhuka (1–5). Keśinī questions Bāhuka,

reciting Damayantī's verses, and Bāhuka replies with Nala's (5–30). Keśinī reports this (30).
73 (75; 2922). Damayantī again sends Keśinī to find out about his divine gifts (1–5). Keśinī reports that the door lintel rises for Bāhuka, water and fire are immediately at hand, his garland never fades (5–15). Damayantī tells her to get some meat cooked by Bāhuka: it tastes like Nala's (20). Keśinī takes Nala's children to Bāhuka; he weeps aloud (20–25).
74 (76; 2951). Damayantī has Bāhuka brought to her and she laments (1–15). Nala replies that it was Kali's doing and complains about Damayantī's new Bridegroom Choice (15–20).
75 (76; 2976). Damayantī explains the subterfuge and protests her purity (1–10). The Wind confirms this (10–15). Nala now resumes his own body, and they embrace (15–20). They are reunited after three years (20–25).
76 (77; 3008). Bhīma receives Nala and they salute (1–5). Ṛtuparṇa congratulates Nala and asks his pardon (5–15). Nala grants him the gift of his talent with horses, and the other departs (15).
77 (78; 3030). Nala travels with an escort to Niṣadha and challenges Puṣkara to a game (1–10). Puṣkara accepts happily, hoping to win Damayantī (10–15). Nala beats Puṣkara but forgives him (15–20), and dispatches him (20–25). Nala enters his city (25).
78 (79; 3063). Nala lives out his life in happiness (1–5). Bṛhadaśva comforts Yudhiṣṭhira (5–10). The Story of Nala *spells happiness and wealth (10–15). Bṛhadaśva bestows on Yudhiṣṭhira the secret of the dice (15–20).*

Bṛhadaśva said:

50.1 There was a king by the name of Nala, the mighty son of Vīrasena, endowed with all good virtues, handsome and a connoisseur of horses, who like the lord of the Gods stood at the head of all the kings of men, rising like the sun far above them with his splendor. This hero, a friend to the brahmins and learned in the *Vedas*, was king of Niṣadha; he loved to gamble, spoke the truth, and was a great commander of armies. Beautiful women loved him, he was generous and master of his senses, a protector and excellent bowman, a Manu come to flesh.

So there also was in Vidarbha a King Bhīma, of terrible prowess, a hero endowed with all virtues, who longed for children; and he had none. Most diligently he strove very hard to have offspring. Then there came to him a brahmin seer by the name of Damana, O Bhārata; and Bhīma who knew the Law, and was desirous of offspring, gratified with his wife that lustrous guest with his hospitality, O Indra among kings. Graciously Damana bestowed a boon on the king and his wife—a jewellike daughter and three noble and renowned sons—Damayantī, Dama, Dānta, and the lustrous Damana, gifted with all virtues, terrifying, and of terrible prowess. Slim-waisted Damayantī won fame in all the worlds for comeliness, luster, and good name, beauty and lovableness.

Now when she attained to maturity, a hundred well-decked handmaidens and friends waited on her as on Śacī.* In the midst of her friends, Bhīma's daughter, adorned with all manner of ornaments and of flawless limbs, shone forth like garlanded lightning. She was exceedingly beautiful, like Śri, with long eyes; and not among Gods or Yakṣas or men had such a beautiful woman ever been seen or heard of before. The winsome girl stirred the hearts even of the Gods.

Nala, tiger among men, was peerless on earth in beauty, and in his appearance he was like Kandarpa** himself embodied. People praised Nala with great wonder in the presence of Damayantī, and they praised her in Nala's presence, again and again. And as they ceaselessly heard of each other's excellence, there rose in them a desire for the other unseen person, and love waxed in their hearts for each other, Kaunteya.

Unable to bear his desire in his heart, Nala once left secretly and sat in a woods by the women's quarters. There he saw wild geese decked in gold, and he captured one bird as they were stepping about in the woods. The fowl of the air then spoke out to Nala: "You must not kill me, king, for I shall do you a kindness. Within Damayantī's hearing I shall so speak of you, Niṣadhan, that she will never think of any other man but you." At these words the king let go of the wild goose, and the geese flew up and went to Vidarbha. When they reached the city of Vidarbha, they alighted close by Damayantī, and she saw the birds. Seeing the wondrously beautiful geese, she, surrounded by her bevy of friends, began chasing them excitedly. The girls each ran after her own bird.

But the bird that Damayantī was chasing from close by assumed human language and said to her, "Damayantī, there is a king in Niṣadha by the name of Nala, who rivals the Aśvins in beauty; no men are equal to him. If you were to become his wife, fair, slim-

* = Indra's wife.
** = the God of Love.

waisted girl, your life and your beauty would bear fruit. For we have
seen Gods, Gandharvas, men, Snakes, and Rākṣasas, but never before
have we seen his like. You too are a jewel among women, and Nala is
a prize among men: a union of one so distinguished with a man so
30 distinguished will surely be of great virtue!" At these words of the
goose, O lord of the people, Damayantī said to that goose, "Speak so
also to Nala!" The bird gave his promise to the daughter of the
Vidarbhas, O lord of your people, and, returning to Niṣadha,
mentioned everything to Nala.

Bṛhadaśva said:

51.1 After Damayantī had heard the words of the wild goose, O
Bhārata, she was no longer herself on account of Nala. She was prone
to brooding, dejected, pale and wan, and was given to much sighing.
She would raise her eyes to heaven, or sink in thought, looking like a
woman crazed, and she found no pleasure at all in lying, sitting, and
eating. Neither day nor night did she rest, often crying of woe. Her
friends knew from the signs that she was not well, when she looked
5 like that; and the flock of Damayantī's friends told the king of
Vidarbha, O lord among men, that his daughter was not well. When
he heard this from Damayantī's friends, he judged that he had a
grave task to perform on behalf of his daughter. The king reflected
that his daughter had reached womanhood, and he saw that it was
his task to hold a Bridegroom Choice for Damayantī.

He assembled the kings of the earth, O lord of the people, saying,
my lord, "Come and attend our Bridegroom Choice, heroes!" When
all the princes heard about Damayantī's Bridegroom Choice, they all
10 went there to Bhīma at Bhīma's behest. They thundered over earth
with the roar of elephants, horses, chariots, and their handsome
well-adorned troops with colorful garlands and ornaments.

At this same time two great ancient seers, the great-spirited
Parvata and Nārada of great vows, were wandering about and came
to the world of Indra. They entered Indra's palace and were well
received. After paying them his respects, the Thousand-eyed Lord
asked them about their unvarying good health that favored them
everywhere.

Nārada said:

My lord God, our health has been good everywhere, and on the
entire earth, lord Maghavat, the kings are also in good health.

Bṛhadaśva said:

15 When he heard Nārada's words, the Slayer of Vṛtra and Vala
asked, "Those law-wise kings of the earth who fight risking their lives
and at the appointed time go unflinchingly to their death by the
sword, theirs is this world forever, their cow of plenty, as it is mine!

But where are the heroic barons now? For I do not see any kings coming as my favorite guests!"

To this question of Śakra Nārada replied, "Listen to me, my lord,
why you do not see any kings. The king of Vidarbha has a daughter
20 who is known as Damayantī. In beauty she surpasses all women on
earth. Her Bridegroom Choice is to take place shortly, Śakra, and the
kings and princes are going there, all of them. The kings who are
seeking out this pearl of the earth desire her immensely, Slayer of
Vala and Vṛtra!"

While he was telling this, the World Guardians and the Fire God,
supreme Immortals all, came to join the king of the Gods. They all
heard Nārada's important words, and having heard them, they said
cheerfully, "Let us go too!" So it happened that they all, with retinue
25 and mounts, went to Vidarbha where the kings were. King Nala too
had learned of the gathering of the kings, O Kaunteya, and he betook
himself there in high spirits, avowed to Damayantī.

The Gods saw Nala on their way as he traveled on earth, like Manmatha* himself incarnate with the perfection of his beauty. When the World Guardians saw him, radiant like the sun, they stopped, forgetting their intentions, amazed by the perfection of his beauty. The celestials halted their chariots in the air, king, descended from the sky, and addressed the Niṣadhan: "*Bhoḥ, bhoḥ*, Nala of Niṣadha, Indra among kings! Nala, you are avowed to the truth—so lend us your help and become our envoy, best of men!"

Bṛhadaśva said:

52.1 "I will!" promised Nala, O Bhārata, then he questioned them,
folding his hands. "Who are you, and who is this one who wants me
for his envoy? What am I to do in this matter? Tell me precisely." To
these words of the Niṣadhan Maghavat** replied, "Know that we are
Immortals who have come for Damayantī. I am Indra, he is Agni,
this one is the Lord of the Waters, and he, king, is Yama, who puts
5 an end to the bodies of men. You tell Damayantī that we have come:
'The World Guardians and Indra are arriving with a wish to see you.
The Gods are wooing you, Śakra, Agni, Varuṇa, and Yama: choose
one of these Gods for your husband!' "

When Śakra had said this to Nala, he replied with folded hands, "Pray do not send me, as I have come for the same purpose!"

The Gods said:

"I will," you promised before all of us, Niṣadhan. Then why should you fail to do so? Go at once, Niṣadhan!

* = the God of Love.
** = Indra.

Bṛhadaśva said:

Nala replied to the words of the Gods, "The palace is well-guarded;
10 how can I dare enter?" "Enter you shall," answered Śakra. Saying,
"So shall it be," Nala went to Damayantī's dwelling, and he saw the
fair Vidarbha girl there surrounded by her flock of servants, ablaze
with her beauty and fortune. Most delicate she was in her limbs, of
tiny waist and pretty eyes, fairly eclipsing the light of the moon with
her radiance. As soon as he set eyes on the charmingly laughing girl,
his desire grew; yet wishing to abide by his promise, he mastered his
love.

When those beautiful girls saw the Niṣadhan, they were flustered;
15 assailed by his splendor, they flew up from their seats. Much pleased
and astonished, they gave praise to Nala, but without talking to him,
just thinking in their hearts, "*Aho*, what shape, *aho*, what beauty, *aho*,
the poise of the great-spirited man! Would he be a God, or a Yakṣa,
or a Gandharva?" None of them could utter a word—all the beautiful
girls, overcome by his splendor, were abashed. But Damayantī spoke;
and to the heroic Nala, who was smiling, she smilingly said in
wonder, "Who are you, of flawless beauty, feeding my heart's desire?
20 You have come like an Immortal—I wish to hear from you, hero sans
blame, how you came to enter here and how you did so unobserved.
For my house is well-guarded, and the king is severe in his
commands."

To these words of the princess of Vidarbha Nala replied, "Know
that I am Nala, my beautiful, come here as an envoy of the Gods.
Gods are wooing you, Śakra, Agni, Varuṇa, and Yama. Choose one of
these Gods for your husband, my pretty: it is by their power that I
have entered here unobserved. For when I entered, no one saw me
and stopped me. It is for this purpose that I have been sent, good
woman, by those best of the Gods. And having heard this, make up
your mind as it pleases you."

Bṛhadaśva said:

53.1 She bowed to the Gods and said to Nala with a laugh, "Show your
feelings in all good faith, king! What can I do for you? I myself and
whatever possessions I own are all yours—show your feelings with
confidence, my lord! The words that the wild geese spoke still
consume me, king; it is because of you, hero, that I have assembled
the kings. If you reject me, giver of honor, although I love you, I shall
on your account seek mercy from poison, fire, water, or the rope!"
5 Nala said in reply to these words of the princess of Vidarbha, "How
can you want a mortal man, when the World Guardians are here? I
am not worthy of the foot dust of these great-spirited sovereigns, the
makers of the world. Turn your mind to them! For a mortal who

displeases the Gods finds death. Save me, woman of flawless limbs, choose the great Gods!"

Thereupon sweet-smiling Damayantī gave tearful voice to her
answer and said softly to King Nala, "There is an infallible way that
10 I see, king, and that way no guilt whatever will attach to you. You
yourself, best of men, and the Gods led by Indra must all come
together to my Bridegroom Choice. Then, in the presence of the
World Guardians themselves, I shall choose you, tiger among men,
and so you will not be to blame."

When the princess of Vidarbha had spoken, King Nala, O lord of your people, returned to where the Gods were gathered. The World Guardians and the Lord saw him come; and when they saw him, they asked about all that had happened.

The Gods said:

Did you chance to see the sweet-smiling Damayantī, king? What does she say to all of us? Speak, king sans blame!

Nala said:

15 At your command I went to Damayantī's heavily walled house and
entered it, surrounded though it was by sturdy men with sticks. But
no one there saw me enter, by the grace of your power, except the
king's daughter. I saw her friends, and they saw me. They were all
astonished at seeing me, sovereigns of the Gods! I told the fair-faced
girl about you, but she had set her mind on me, and she will choose
me, good Gods: "Let the Gods come together with you, best of men,
20 to my Bridegroom Choice. I shall choose you in their presence, strong-
armed king, and then you will not be to blame." This is all that
happened, just as I have fully told you. But yours is the decision,
sovereigns of the Thirty!

Bṛhadaśva said:

54.1 Then, at the favorable instant on the right lunar day, when the
auspicious season had come, King Bhīma summoned the kings to the
Bridegroom Choice. When they heard the message, the herdsmen of
the earth, pressed by their love, all came hurrying, hoping to win
Damayantī. The kings entered the large arena, which was resplendent
with golden pillars and a splendid gateway, as lions enter a mountain.
There the princes took their seats on various kinds of thrones, wearing
5 fragrant garlands and shining earrings with precious stones. The regal
assembly filled with the tigerlike kings, as Bhogavatī with Snakes, or
a mountain cave with tigers. There one saw their sturdy arms like
clubs, well-shaped and very smooth, like five-headed snakes. The
handsome faces of the kings, with their fine locks and noses, shone
like stars in the sky.

Thereupon fair-faced Damayantī entered the arena, stealing with

her radiance the eyes and the hearts of the kings. And on whatever
limb the glances of the great-spirited princes happened to fall, there
10 they remained fixed without straying. While the names of the kings
were being proclaimed, O Bhārata, Bhīma's daughter saw five men of
identical aspect. When she saw them all stand there without any
difference in their appearance, she was so confused that she could not
make out who King Nala was; for any one of them she looked at she
thought was Nala. Worryingly the shining girl wondered in her
heart, "How am I to know who are the Gods, how am I to find out
who is King Nala?" As she was worrying most unhappily in this
fashion, the princess of Vidarbha bethought herself of the marks of
Gods she had heard of, Bhārata: "I have heard from the old people
about the marks that betoken Gods, but I do not perceive even one in
15 them while they are standing on the ground!" She thought this way
and that and hesitated again and again, until she decided the time
had come to throw herself on the mercy of the Gods. With voice and
thought she paid homage and honor to the Gods, and, with hands
folded, she said trembling, "If it be true that I chose the Niṣadhan to
be my husband, when I heard the words of the wild geese, then by
this truth the Gods must point him out to me! If it be true that I have
never strayed in speech and thought, then by this truth the Gods
must point him out to me! If it be true that the Gods themselves have
ordained for the king of Niṣadha to be my husband, then by this
20 truth the Gods must point him out to me! The World Guardians and
the Lord must display their own forms, so that I may recognize King
Puṇyaśloka!"

When they heard this piteous plaint of Damayantī, her complete
and true decision for the Niṣadhan, her love for him, the purity of her
heart, her spirit, devotion, and passion, O Bhārata, the Gods at her
summons displayed their ability to wear the marks of divinity. She
saw all the Gods without sweat, with unblinking eyes, with spruce
garlands, without dust, and standing without touching the ground.
And the Niṣadhan stood revealed by his shadow, his faded garland,
his dustiness and sweatiness, and the blinking of his eyes, while he
touched the ground.

25 Now that she could see the Gods and Puṇyaśloka of Niṣadha, O
Bhārata, the daughter of Bhīma chose him according to the Law.
Bashfully she touched the hem of his garment and threw over his
shoulders a most beautiful garland; and thus the fair woman chose
him for her husband. The assembled kings at once gave vent to their
woe, and the Gods and great seers voiced their applause in
wonderment, praising King Nala.

When Bhīma's daughter had chosen the Niṣadhan, the august
World Guardians, in joyful spirits, gave Nala all together eight boons.

Śakra, Śacī's pleased husband, gave the Niṣadhan the privilege of
seeing the God in person at his sacrifices, and an unimpeded course
30 wherever he walked. The oblation-carrying Fire God bestowed on
him his own presence wherever the Niṣadhan wanted it, and entrance
to places that were luminous with fire itself. Yama gave him a taste
for food and utter firmness in the Law. The Lord of the Waters
granted him the presence of water where the Niṣadhan wanted it,
and a most fragrant garland. All together they gave him twin
children. And after having so made their gifts, the Gods returned to
heaven.

After attending the wedding the kings, amazed but happy for
Damayantī, returned as they had come. King Puṇyaśloka, having
obtained this jewel among women, made love to her as the Slayer of
35 Vala and Vṛtra with Śacī. Extremely joyous and radiant like the sun,
the heroic king gladdened his people by protecting them according to
the Law. The wise prince offered up a Horse Sacrifice like Nahuṣa's
son Yayāti, and many other sacrifices of rich stipends. Like an
Immortal, Nala disported himself time and again with Damayantī in
lovely woods and parks. Thus, sacrificing and enjoying himself, the
ruler of men, lord of the earth, protected treasure-filled earth.

Bṛhadaśva said:

55.1 When the Niṣadhan had been chosen by the daughter of Bhīma, the
august World Guardians left and saw Dvāpara come with Kali. Said
Śakra, the Slayer of Vala and Vṛtra, to Kali when he saw him,
"Where are you going with Dvāpara, Kali? Tell me!" Kali told Śakra,
"To Damayantī's Bridegroom Choice. When I get there, I'll choose
her, for my heart has gone out to her!" Indra laughed and said to
him, "The Bridegroom Choice is over. She has chosen King Nala for
her husband, in our own presence."

5 When he heard Śakra's words, Kali was enraged. He addressed all
the Gods and said to them, "If she has found herself a human
husband in the midst of Gods, then for that she surely deserves a
severe punishment!" But the celestials replied to Kali, "We ourselves
permitted Damayantī to choose Nala. Who would not seek recourse
to King Nala? He is endowed with all virtues, he knows all the Laws
precisely, he observes vows. Truth, endurance, liberality, austerity,
cleanliness, self-control, and serenity are lodged firmly with him; that
10 tiger among men equals the World Guardians! The fool who would
want to curse Nala of such virtues would curse and kill himself by
his own hand. He would sink into a grievous hell, bottomless,
plumbless, and without crossing!"

After these words to Kali and Dvāpara, the Gods went on to
heaven. When the Gods had gone, Kali said to Dvāpara, "I cannot

control my anger! I shall take possession of Nala, Dvāpara, and unseat him from his kingdom; and he shall not have the pleasure of Bhīma's daughter! You must enter into the dice and give me assistance."

Bṛhadaśva said:

56.1 Having made this covenant with Dvāpara, Kali went to the place
where the king of Niṣadha sat. Constantly waiting for an opening, he
lived for a long time in Niṣadha; then, in the twelfth year, Kali saw
his chance. Once when the Niṣadhan had passed urine and touched
water, he attended to the twilight rites without washing his feet: it
was there that Kali entered into him.
When he had taken possession of Nala, he went to Puṣkara and
5 said: "Come and dice with Nala! With my help you will surely defeat
Nala at the dicing game. Defeat King Nala, prince, and win the
Niṣadha country!" Upon these words of Kali, Puṣkara went to Nala.
Kali again became the Bull-of-the-Cows and joined Puṣkara.
Puṣkara, slayer of enemy-heroes, approached heroic Nala, and
Nala's brother repeatedly urged, "Let us dice! With the Bull!" The
spirited king could not refuse the challenge and, although Damayantī
looked on, thought it was time to dice. Being possessed by Kali, Nala
lost in the game his stakes of raw and refined gold, wagons and teams
10 and clothes. He was crazed by the thrill of the dice, and none of his
friends were able to restrain him when he was mindlessly gambling.
All the townspeople came with the councillors to see the king, O
Bhārata, in order to stop the sick man. The bard came and said to
Damayantī, "All the townspeople are waiting at the gate with
business: the Niṣadhan should be told that all his subjects are
waiting for him and are impatient with the vice of their king, who
understands Law and Profit." In a tearful voice and wan with anxiety,
Damayantī said to the Niṣadhan, her mind ravaged with anguish,
15 "King, the townspeople are waiting at the gate to see you,
accompanied by all the councillors, and they pledge their loyalty to
their king. Pray see them!" she said over and over again. But the
king, possessed by Kali, gave no reply whatsoever to his plaintive,
slim-waisted wife of the shining eyes. Thereupon all the councillors
and city dwellers thought, "The man is lost!" and unhappily and
humbled returned home. In this fashion the dicing of Puṣkara and
Nala went on for many months, Yudhiṣṭhira. And Puṇyaśloka kept
losing.

Bṛhadaśva said:

57.1 When Damayantī saw that King Puṇyaśloka had lost his senses at
the game like a madman, she, herself far from mad, was overcome
with fear and grief, O king. And Bhīma's daughter thought that a very

grave task had to be done for the good of the king. Fearing for his
evil and wanting to do him a kindness, she said to her nurse, when
she saw that Nala had lost all, "Bṛhatsenā, go and bring the
councillors here on Nala's orders. Tell them what property we have
5 lost and what possessions remain." When all the councillors heard
Nala's summons, they said, "Has luck returned to us?" and came.
Bhīma's daughter told him that all the subjects had come for a
second time, and Nala did not welcome it. Seeing that her husband
did not welcome her words, Damayantī shamefacedly returned to her
house. When she learned that the dice kept being hostile to Puṇyaśloka
and that Nala had lost all, she said to her nurse, "Bṛhatsenā, go once
more and bring Vārṣṇeya the charioteer here on Nala's orders, good
10 woman. A grave task is pending." Bṛhatsenā heard Damayantī's
request and had the charioteer fetched by reliable servants. Bhīma's
blameless daughter said coaxingly to Vārṣṇeya in a gentle voice,
knowing that the time had come, as she knew of places and times,
"You know how correct the king always has been to you. Pray help
him now that he has come to grief; for the more the king loses to
15 Puṣkara, the more his passion for gambling grows. The dice are in
Puṣkara's power, and we see that disaster at the dice befalls the king
accordingly. He does not listen to the words of his friends and family
as he should, and surely, I think, the great-spirited Niṣadhan has
nothing left. Since the king in his folly does not welcome my
remonstrations, I have come to you for refuge. Charioteer, please do
as I ask; for my peace of mind is troubled—he may well end up
destroyed. Yoke Nala's favorite wind-fast horses to the chariot, take
the twins on it, and journey to Kuṇḍina. Leave the princes, the
horses, and chariot in trust with my kinsmen, and you yourself might
stay there too, or leave for another place."
Vārṣṇeya, Nala's charioteer, fully acquainted the principal
20 ministers of Nala with Damayantī's request. They met, reached their
decision, and gave him leave to go, O king of the earth. He took the
twins on the chariot and drove to Vidarbha. The charioteer left the
horses and superb chariot in trust there, and likewise the girl
Indrasenā and the boy Indrasena. Unhappily and sorrowfully he
informed King Bhīma about King Nala, then wandered about until he
came to the city of Ayodhyā. Mournfully he presented himself to King
Ṛtuparṇa and entered the king's service as his charioteer.

Bṛhadaśva said:

58.1 After Vārṣṇeya's departure Puṇyaśloka kept gambling; and Puṣkara
took his kingdom and all the property he possessed. Puṣkara laughed,
O king, and said to Nala when he had lost his kingdom, "Let the
game go on. What do you have left to stake? Only Damayantī remains

to you, I have taken everything else. Well, stake Damayantī if you
want to!" At those words of Puṣkara, Puṇyaśloka's heart was riven
5 with rage and he made no reply. Gripped by fury, Nala glanced at
Puṣkara, then the famous king threw down all the jewelry on his
body. And in a single robe, unclad, feeding the grief of his friends, the
king strode out, relinquishing his ample fortune; Damayantī, clad in
one skirt, followed behind him. The Niṣadhan camped outside the city
with her for three nights.

Puṣkara, however, great king, proclaimed in the city, "Anyone
who makes common cause with Nala I shall put to death!" And
because of Puṣkara's orders and the malice he bore Nala, the
10 townspeople showed no hospitality to him, Yudhiṣṭhira. So, close to
the city but not treated as a guest, much though he deserved it, the
king camped there for three nights, living only on water.

After many a day Nala, starving, saw some birds with feathers that
seemed made of gold. The mighty king of Niṣadha thought to himself,
"This will be my meal for today and it will be my treasure!" He threw
his robe over the birds, and they took hold of the robe and carried it
off to the sky. And as they flew up, those birds cried out to Nala,
seeing him standing naked on the ground, wretched, with his face
15 bent down, "We are the dice, fool, and we came to take your robe
too; for it did not please us to see that you still went clothed!" Seeing
the dice disappear and himself left naked, King Puṇyaśloka said to
Damayantī, "They through whose fury I was unseated from my
kingdom, blameless wife, and now find no livelihood but misery and
hunger, they for whose sake the Niṣadhans refused me hospitality,
they have now become birds and stolen even my robe! I have come
to great grief and sorrow, my mind is failing me. I am your husband,
20 listen to my words, which are for your own good. There are many
roads here that lead to the south, crossing Avanti and Mount
Ṛkṣavat. There is the mighty Vindhya range and the river Payoṣṇī
that leads to the ocean, and hermitages of great seers full of flowers
and fruits. This road goes to Vidarbha, this one to Kosala, and beyond
in the south is the country of Dakṣiṇāpatha. . . ."

In a tear-muted voice Damayantī, wan with anxiety, gave the
Niṣadhan her pitiful reply, "My heart trembles and my limbs all
25 weaken when I ponder and ponder on your intention, king. How
could I go and desert you in the empty forest, when you have lost
your realm, lost your wealth, unclothed, hungry, and tired? No, great
king, in the dreadful forest as you go tired and hungry, brooding on
your misery, I shall soothe your hurts. Physicians know of no
medicine in all sorrows that equals a wife—this I tell is the truth!"

Nala said:

It is right what you say, slim-waisted Damayantī, there is no friend
or a cure for a sick man like a wife. But I do not want to abandon

you; why do you fear, timid woman? I'd abandon myself before
abandoning you, innocent wife!

Damayantī said:

30 But if you did not want to leave me here, great king, why did you
point out to me the road to Vidarbha? I know, king, that you should
not desert me, but with your mind deranged you might. For you keep
telling me the way, best of men, and thereby you increase my
anxiety, Godlike husband. So, if it is your design that I should go to
Vidarbha, my king, let us go together, if you will. The king of
Vidarbha will honor you, giver of pride, and honored by him you will
live happily in our house, my king!"

Nala said:

59.1 Doubtless, even as the kingdom is your father's so it is mine. But I
will not go there as long as I am in this trouble. I went there once
prosperous and gladdening you—how could I go there now, wretched
and saddening you?

Bṛhadaśva said:

Thus King Nala spoke again and again to Damayantī, and he
soothed his wife covered by half her garment. The two, covered
between them with one robe, wandered hither and thither, until they,
5 hungry and thirsty and wearied, came upon a lodge. When they got
to the lodge, the overlord of Niṣadha sat down with the princess of
Vidarbha on the bare ground. Naked, dirty, balding, covered with
dust, he slept exhausted on the ground with Damayantī. The good
Damayantī too was overtaken by sleep, the delicate, piteous woman
who had suddenly found misery.

But, lord of the people, once Damayantī was asleep, King Nala
could not sleep as before, for his spirits were churned up by anguish.
He saw again the plunder of his kingdom, the desertion of all his
friends, and his languishing in the jungle; and he fell to brooding.
10 "What will happen if I do this, and what if I don't? What is better
for me, to die or leave this woman? For she has loved me and has
found misery because of me. But if she is free from me, she might one
day find her way back to her family. With me she is sure to find
more of this endless trouble. Yet, if I leave her there is a risk. Still she
might find happiness somewhere."

He turned it over many times in his mind and reached many
conclusions; then the king of men decided it would be better for
Damayantī if he left her. Reflecting that he had no clothes and she
15 only one, the king decided to tear hers in half. "But how do I tear her
cloth without my dear wife waking up?" and pondering this question
the king of Niṣadha paced the lodge. Nala paced back and forth,
Bhārata, then he found in a corner of the lodge a fine unsheathed
sword. He cut off half her skirt with it, and the enemy-burner wrapped

himself in it. Then he left the sleeping Damayantī and ran away mindlessly. But his heart held its string, and he went back to the lodge and looked upon Damayantī as she lay. The sovereign of Niṣadha wept.

"Neither sun nor wind has ever before seen my love, and here she
lies now, in the middle of a lodge, unprotected, on the bare ground.
20 Here she is clothed in a cut-up skirt, she of the happy laughter and
beautiful hips, as though she were crazed—how will she be when she
wakes up? All alone, beautiful, and deserted by me, how shall the
daughter of Bhīma fare in the ferocious jungle that is haunted by
game and beasts of prey?"

Nala went and went, but came back to the lodge every time, drawn
forth by Kali, drawn back by his love. The suffering man's heart was
cut in two; like a swing it kept going back and forth to the lodge.
Finally, drawn forth by Kali and bemused, Nala ran away, deserting
25 his sleeping wife, while he lamented piteously and much. Lost of soul,
touched by Kali, not reckoning this or that, the prince went in grief,
abandoning his wife in the empty jungle.

Bṛhadaśva said:

60.1 When Nala had run off, O king, callipygous Damayantī, refreshed
from her fatigue, woke up trembling in the unpeopled forest. She did
not see her husband and, panic-stricken, she cried out aloud in fear
for the Niṣadhan: "Mahārāja! Ah my protector, ah Mahārāja! Ah
master, why did you desert me? Ah I am lost and dead; I am afraid
in the empty forest! Haven't you always been true to your word, and
wise in the Law, great king? Then how could you speak such a lie
5 and go and desert me while I was asleep? How shall you fare after
deserting your submissive and obedient wife, you who were done no
wrong whatever, done wrong only by your enemy? Shall you be able
to make true those words that you once pronounced to me in the
presence of the World Guardians, king of men?

"Enough of this jest, it has gone far enough, bull among men! I am
frightened, tough warrior, show yourself, my lord! I see you, I see
you, king! There you are, Niṣadhan! You are hiding in the bushes;
why don't you reply to me? Ah cruelty, lord among kings, that you
know how I am crying here and yet do not comfort me in your arms,
10 my king! I do not lament over myself or anything else but you—how
will you fare by yourself? That is why I am weeping, my king! How
will you be when evening falls, king, thirsty, hungry, gaunt with
exhaustion, lying at the root of a tree, and not seeing me?"

Burning grief consumed her and rage inflamed her as she ran into every direction, weeping grievously. One moment the young woman started up, the next she collapsed confused, again she huddled

frightened and wept and wailed. Biting grief burned her, and she heaved hot sighs in her confusion; then the daughter of Bhīma strode out into the forest, true to her husband, and spoke in tears:
15 "Whatever creature it is by whose curse the suffering Niṣadhan finds more suffering, that creature shall reap even greater grief than his! The miscreant who has done such evil to the innocent-minded Nala will for that find greater grief and live a life of misery!"

Thus did the great-spirited king's wife lament as she went searching for her husband in the predator-infested wilderness. Like a crazed woman the daughter of Bhīma ran back and forth, hither and thither, wailing, "Oh, oh, my king!"

20 Drying out fast like a screeching osprey, lamenting much and piteously, and complaining again and again, Damayantī suddenly came upon a boa, and when she came closer, the giant grasper, which was hungry, laid hold of her. Yet, while she was being devoured by the reptile and was struck with anguish, it was not herself she mourned as much as the Niṣadhan: "Ah, my protector, here I am being devoured by this boa in the desolate jungle as though I had no protector—why don't you hurry? How will you feel after you have been delivered from your evil and have regained your spirit, mind, and possessions, and remember me? When you are tired and hungry and worn out, Niṣadhan, who will there be, giver of pride, to soothe your fatigue, tiger among men?"

25 As it happened, a hunter who was ranging in the deep forest heard her cries and ran quickly to her. When he saw the long-eyed woman being devoured by the snake, the hunter hastily came to her aid and cut off the snake's head with his sharp sword. The hunter cut up the snake until it lay motionless, then he freed her and cleansed her with water. He comforted her and gave her food to eat, then questioned her, O Bhārata: "Whose are you, doe-eyed woman; how have you wandered to this forest, and how have you landed in this great
30 danger, radiant woman?" At his urging Damayantī told him all, O lord of your people, in the way it had befallen, Bhārata.

The hunter had noticed that she was covered with only half a piece of cloth, that her hips and breasts were heavy, her limbs delicate and flawless, her face like the full moon, her eyes shaded by curved lashes, and her speech honeyed; and lust overwhelmed him. The huntsman coaxed her with a sweet and gentle voice, and the radiant woman saw that he wanted her.

When Damayantī, forever faithful to her husband, saw that he meant evil, a bitter rage took possession of her and she seemed to
35 flame up in fury. That evil-minded brute, sick with lust and ready to overpower her, thought that the unassailable woman had changed into a blazing flame crest. But Damayantī, miserable, without a

husband and kingdom, at this moment when the way of words was past, indeed cursed him in anger: "If even in my heart I have never thought of any man but Nala, so let this brute who lives off animals fall dead!" No sooner had she spoken than the hunter fell lifeless to the ground, like a tree caught in a fire.

Bṛhadaśva said:
61.1 When lotus-eyed Damayantī had struck down the animal hunter,
she struck out for another desolate and dangerous forest that hummed
with the chirps of crickets. The forest was infested by lions, tigers,
wild boar, bears, *ruru* deer, and elephants; flocks of all kinds of birds
crowded it, and it was prowled by Mlecchas and robbers. It was
wooded with *śāla* trees, cane, *dhavas*, fig trees, *tiṇḍukas*, *ingudas*,
kiṃśukas, *arjunas*, and soapberry trees, and sandalwood and cotton
trees; there were rose apples, mangoes, *lodhs*, catechus, teak trees,
bamboo, *kāśmarīs*, myrobalans, *plakṣas*, *kadambas*, *udumbaras*, jujube,
bilvas and banyans, *priyālas*, palms, *kharjūras*, *haritakas*, and
5 *vibhītakas*. She saw all kinds of hills that were girt with hundreds of
minerals, and groves resonant with birds, and wondrous-looking
caves, rivers, lakes, ponds, and all sorts of game and fowl, and many
Piśācas of terrible mien and Snakes and Rākṣasas, also pools and tanks
and hilltops all around, and streams and floods of wondrous aspect.
The daughter of the king of Vidarbha saw herds of buffalo, boar,
jackals, bears, monkeys, and snakes; and moving in splendor, glory,
steadfastness, and superb beauty, the princess of Vidarbha wandered
10 about alone, searching for Nala. King Bhīma's daughter was not
afraid of anything as she went about in the dangerous woods, thinned
by her husband's vice. The daughter of Vidarbha cried out in her bitter
grief, O king, her limbs pervaded by anguish over her husband,
seeking refuge on a stone slab.

Damayantī said:
Lion-chested, strong-armed ruler of the people of Niṣadha, where
may you have gone, O king, leaving me in the uninhabited wilderness?
You have offered up, hero, richly rewarded sacrifices like the Horse
Sacrifice, then how, tigerlike man, could you be false to me? Tiger
among men, of such great splendor, pray make true what you once
15 said, good man, in my presence, bull among men! Pray consider what
the birds said in front of you, king, and what they said in front of me!
They say that all the four *Vedas* with branches and subbranches and
all their prolixity, thoroughly committed to memory, on one scale are
balanced by truth alone on the other, O best of men. Therefore please
be true, enemy-killer, lord of men, and do what you once promised in
front of me, hero!

Ah, my hero, do you no longer want me, prince sans blame? Why don't you answer me in this grisly forest? This terrifying dreadful-looking king of the forest is threatening me with his open maw—why don't you deign to save me? That time you said, "No one is dearer to me than you, my love," so make good the word you have spoken, good king. If you love your crazed, wailing, panic-stricken, beloved wife, my love, my king and protector, why don't you answer me? I am thin, wretched, pale, dirty, O king of the earth, covered with half a skirt, alone and wailing without protection, a lonesome doe thrown out of her herd—why, my wide-eyed man, why don't you honor me, honorable plower of your enemies, as I here stand weeping? Great king, all alone in this vast forest your own wife is calling, why don't you answer me? I cannot find you today, you of high family and conduct, handsome in all your lovely limbs, I cannot find you today on this mountain, best of men! Are you sleeping in this dreadful forest that teems with lions and tigers, are you sitting or standing, prince of the Niṣadhas, or stealing away, best of men, feeding my grief? Whom shall I ask in my misery, wan with grief because of you, "Did you chance to meet and see King Nala in the forest?" Who is going to tell me today about Nala lost in the forest, the beautiful, great-spirited Nala, who kills the herds of his enemies? From whom shall I hear today the sweet message that King Nala of the lotuslike eyes whom I am seeking is here? Here comes the illustrious king of the forest, a four-tusked, broad-jowled tiger, to meet me, I am not afraid, I ask him, "Sir, sovereign of animals, you are the master of this jungle. Know that I am the daughter of the king of Vidarbha, Damayantī, wife of the lord of Niṣadha, the enemy-killing Nala! I am alone, miserable, thin from grief, searching for my husband—comfort me, king of beasts, have you seen Nala? Of if you will not speak of Nala, king of the forest, then eat me, great beast, and deliver this wretch from her misery!" The king of beasts hears my lament in the wilderness and goes off on his own to the clear waters of the river that flows to the ocean.

Here is a sacred rocky mountain with many lofty peaks, luminous, brushing the skies and lovely in all their colors; it is covered with many minerals, adorned with various stones, rising like the flagpole of this grand forest, visited by lions, tigers, elephants, boars, bears, and deer, and on all sides awarble with many-feathered fowl. It is adorned with *kiṃśuka, aśoka, bakula,* and *puṃnāga* trees, and with streams and hillocks aswarm with birds. So let me ask this king of mountains about my king: "Sir, greatest of mountains, divine of aspect and well-renowned, thou shelter of many beauties, I bow to thee, holder of the earth! I have come and bow to thee, know that I am the daughter of

a king, the daughter-in-law of a king, the wife of a king, the famous
Damayantī. The sovereign king of Vidarbha is my warlike father, he
the lord of the land Bhīma, protector of the society of the four classes.
He has offered up great sacrifices of rich stipends, the Royal
Consecration and Horse Sacrifice, that eminent prince, with eyes that
are wide, handsome, and curved. He is brahminic, virtuous in his
conduct, truthful in his speech, unprotesting, decorous, and strict,
widely famed, Law-wise, and pure. A perfect herdsman is he of the
Vidarbhas, a lord who has vanquished the band of his enemies, and
sir, know that I, his daughter, seek help from thee!
45 "The old king of the Niṣadhans is my father-in-law, great mountain,
famed as Vīrasena, and well taken is the name! This king has a
heroic son, illustrious and gallant in his truth, who now sways his
father's kingdom, to which he fell heir. Nala is his name, the enemy-
taming Puṇyaśloka, a brahminic, *Veda*-wise, eloquent and meritorious
keeper of the fires, who partakes of the *soma*. He sacrifices, he gives,
he wars, he rules perfectly, and know that I am his wife, best of
mountains, I who have come to thee, I who have lost my fortune,
lost my husband, lost my protector, beset by trouble, who am
50 searching for my husband, that very best of men. Thou with thy
hundreds of peaks that scrape the skies, hast thou perchance seen the
king, greatest of mountains, my Nala, in this grisly wood? He strides
like the king of elephants, he is wise, long-armed, and quick to anger,
valiant, true to his word, and poised, my famous husband. Did you
chance to see Nala, the overlord of Niṣadha!
"Why dost thou not comfort me, best of mountains, me who am
grievously lamenting in my solitude, with just a word, as though
wouldst comfort your own grieving daughter? Oh my hero, my
gallant, wise in the Law, true to your troth, lord of the earth—if you
are in this forest, king, then show yourself! When, when shall I hear
Nala's lovably rumbling voice, the voice like the thunder of the
55 monsoon, that equals the Elixir? Let it say, 'Woman of Vidarbha!'
that beautiful voice of the great-spirited king, which follows the *Veda*,
is full of all good things, and dispels my sorrows!"

Bṛhadaśva said:

So did the king's daughter address that good mountain; then
Damayantī once more departed, to the north. For three days and three
nights she walked, the loveliest of women, and beheld an
incomparable forest of ascetics that looked like a heavenly park.
Ascetics the likes of Vasiṣṭha, Bhṛgu, and Atri adorned it, self-
controlled, of lean diet, sober and pure, who lived on water or off the
wind, or fed on leaves, lordly masters of their senses, who longed to
60 see the road to heaven. The hermits, who had mastered their senses,
were clothed in bark shirts and deerskins, and it was their lovely

circle of hermitages that she saw. As soon as she saw the hermitage
hamlet, inhabited by all kinds of game and troops of monkeys as well
as the ascetics, the woman of the lovely brows, beautiful hair, well-
shaped hips, proud breasts, sparkling teeth and face, luminous, firm of
step, well-curved in her movements and eager, entered the hermitage
hamlet, the beloved of Vīrasena's son, pearl of womanhood, the lordly
and spirited Damayantī.

Bowing courteously she stood and greeted the wizened ascetics, and
65 they in turn pronounced their welcome. They, rich in austerities,
received her according to the rules and bade her sit and asked,
"Speak, what can we do?" The full-hipped woman said to them, "Do
the austerities, the fires, the Laws, and the deer and the birds of yours,
sirs, prosper well, and does your observance of the Law, my blameless
lords?" "They all prosper," they replied to the glorious woman. "But
speak, you that are flawless in all your limbs, who are you and what
do you seek to do? Beholding your sublime beauty and surpassing
radiance, we are greatly astonished. Be comforted, do not grieve! Are
you the great deity of this forest, this mountain? Or perhaps of this
river? Good and innocent woman, tell us the truth!"

70 "No, I am not the deity of this mountain," she said to the seers, "nor
of this forest, brahmins, nor am I the goddess of this river. All you
ascetics should know that I am a mortal, and if you all will listen, I
shall tell you in detail. In the country of Vidarbha there is a
resplendent king by the name of Bhīma. Know, all ye great brahmins,
that I am his daughter. The Niṣadhans had a great and wise and
glorious king, Nala by name, learned and a heroic victor in battle;
that king is my husband. He was given to worshiping the Gods, was
a friend to the twice-born, the lordly and splendid guardian of the
75 dynasty of Niṣadha. He spoke the truth, he knew the Law, he was
wise and true to his promises, he crushed his enemies. Brahminic
and a worshiper of the Gods, he was an illustrious conqueror of enemy
cities. Nala is his name, the greatest of kings, in luster the equal of
the king of the Gods, my large-eyed, moon-faced husband, slayer of
his enemies. Steeped in the *Vedas* and their branches, he offered up
great sacrifices and, resplendent like sun and moon, slew his rivals in
battle. Some persons of deceitful minds, lowly people up to no good,
challenged this herdsman of the earth, who was devoted to the Law
of truth, to a game at dice; and being skillful at gaming and crooked
they won his kingdom and possessions. Know ye that I am the wife
of this bull among kings, known by the name of Damayantī, and I
80 yearn to see my husband. Wretchedly I am wandering here through
forests and mountains, lakes and rivers, lovely meadow and
wilderness, all over earth, searching for my great-spirited husband,
Nala, the skillful warrior, past master of arms. Has a king by the name

of Nala, the ruler of Niṣadha, perchance come to your holy forest of austerities, sirs? It is because of him, brahmins, that I have gone to this terrifying, dangerous, and ghastly forest that is infested with tigers and game. If I do not find King Nala in a few days and nights, I shall yoke myself to a better world by abandoning my body. What does it profit me to live without that bull-like man? What shall become of me pressed down by grief over my husband?"

To this plaint of Bhīma's daughter Damayantī, alone in the forest, the true-spoken ascetics replied, "Your future, beautiful, shining woman, shall be beautiful. By the power of our austerities we discern that you will soon find the Niṣadhan, Nala, the king of Niṣadha, killer of his enemies. You will find that best of the upholders of Law, O daughter of Bhīma, rid of his fever, absolved from all his evil, and possessed of all riches, once more holding sway in his fine city and taming his foes. You shall find, good woman, that highborn king, sowing panic among his enemies and dispelling the sorrows of his friends." When they had thus spoken to Nala's beloved wife, the daughter of a king, the ascetics disappeared with their *agnihotras* and hermitages.

Damayantī of the flawless limbs, daughter-in-law of Vīrasena, saw that great marvel and was amazed. "Was it a dream I saw? What has happened here? Where is that holy river with its pure water resonant with all kinds of birds and those charming hillocks, pretty with fruit and flowers?" Bhīma's daughter, sweet-smiling Damayantī, was long lost in her thoughts; then, once more engrossed in her grief for her husband, the poor woman paled.

She went on to another region and, her eyes filled with tears, moaned in a voice that was muffled by sobs. Then she saw an *aśoka* tree. She approached that *aśoka*, best of trees, which stood in full blooms, bending under the weight of its shoots and echoing with the sounds of birds. "Ah, woe on me, here stands this beautiful tree in the deep of the forest, shining with its many chaplets of blossoms, like the illustrious king of Dramiḍa. Rid me swiftly of my grief, beautiful *aśoka*: have you chanced to see the king, free from sorrow and fear and torment? The enemy-tamer Nala is Damayantī's beloved husband —have you seen my darling, the sovereign of the Niṣadhas? Make it come about, *aśoka* tree, that I find without sorrow my hero, who is clothed in half a piece of cloth—he with his delicate body and skin and driven by his vice—make it come about that I find him come to this forest! Be true to your name, *aśoka*, by dispelling my sorrow!"

Thus the hurt woman spoke to the *aśoka* tree, circumambulating it three times; then the beautiful daughter of Bhīma went to an even grislier place. She saw many trees and many streams, many lovely hills and many animals and birds. As she was searching for her husband, Damayantī beheld forests and mountain slopes and wondrous rivers.

While she wandered on her way, sweet-smiling Damayanti came upon a long stretch of road, and she saw a large caravan with plenty of horses, elephants, and carts climbing up the bank of a lovely and clean river with clear water. The river was wide, with very cool water and ponds, overgrown with reeds, loud with cranes and ospreys and the cries of *cakravākas*; and it was inhabited by tortoises, dolphins, and crocodiles and adorned with sandbanks and islands. When Nala's glorious wife saw that large caravan, the fair-hipped woman ran
110 toward it and plunged in the midst of the people. She looked like a mad woman, full of hurts, covered with half a skirt, thin, pale, dirty, her hair overlain with dust. When they saw her, some of the people ran in fright, others stopped and started thinking, there were some who feared, some who sneered, and others who muttered. But there were also some who took pity on her, Bhārata, and asked questions: "Who are you, whose are you, good woman? What are you seeking in the woods? The sight of you disturbs us, for are you human? Tell the truth, are you the goddess of this forest, or mountain, or region,
115 good woman? We seek mercy from you! Are you a Yakṣī, a Rākṣasī, a noble woman? In any case, bring us luck, blameless woman, and protect us. Ordain, good woman, that this caravan safely depart from here, we seek your mercy!"

To these words of the caravan travelers, Princess Damayantī, virtuous woman who sorrowed over her husband's vice, replied to the caravan leader, the caravan, and the folk who were about, young and old and infants, and the guides of the caravan: "Know that I am a mortal, the daughter of a sovereign king, daughter-in-law to a ruler, the wife of a king, who is yearning to find her husband! The king of Vidarbha is my father, my husband is the king of Niṣadha, lordly Nala by name, and it is that undefeated king I am seeking.
120 If you know the king, then quickly tell me about my beloved Nala, tiger among kings, slayer of the host of his enemies!"

The leader of that large caravan, who bore the name of Śuci, said to the flawless woman, "Listen, good woman, to what I am going to say. I am the leader of this caravan, sweet-smiling and glorious wench, and I have not seen a man called Nala. I have seen elephants, leopards, buffaloes, tigers, bears, and deer in this dangerous forest, but no men live in it, so help us Maṇibhadra, the king of the Yakṣas!" She asked all the merchants and the caravan leader, "But where is this caravan going? Pray tell me!"

The caravan leader said:

125 This is the caravan of the true-spoken Subāhu, the king of the Cedis; it is traveling fast to that country for gain, princess!

Bṛhadaśva said:

62.1 When Damayantī of the flawless limbs heard the caravan leader's
words, she went with him, hoping to find her husband. Many days
later the merchants found in the vast and dangerous forest a large and
lovely pond, charming on all sides, fragrant with lotuses, with
abundant grass and firewood on its banks, and plenty of roots and
fruit, teeming with all kinds of birds. They saw that the water was
fresh and the pool itself heart-fetching and delightful; and since their
5 animals were very tired, they decided to camp there. With the caravan
leader's consent they went into the beautiful wood, and the large
caravan settled for the night at a late hour.

Half the night had passed and the tired caravan was sleeping
soundlessly and serenely when a herd of elephants came to drink at a
mountain stream that was muddied by their flowing ichor. The grand
caravan, soundly asleep, obstructed their way to the lotus pond, and
the herd trampled the sleeping people, who lay suddenly writhing on
the ground. Screaming, the merchants tried to find shelter and, still
blind from sleep, dived into the bushes to escape the grave danger.
Some were killed by tusks and trunks, others trampled underfoot. The
whole panic-stricken caravan with its many bullocks, donkeys,
camels, and horses mixed with travelers on foot took to flight,
10 crowding one another. Uttering fearful cries they fell on the ground,
clutched at trees with broken limbs, or stumbled into trenches; and so
that whole rich caravan camp was struck down.

When morning came, the survivors crawled out of the bushes,
bemoaning the slaughter that had taken place, and mourning
brother, father, son, or friend, O king. Damayantī grieved, "What evil
have I done that I found this sea of people in the empty forest and
now they are destroyed by a herd of elephants, surely because of my
own ill fortune! More suffering is doubtless in store for me for a long
time to come—as the old people say, no one dies before his time—if I
was not trampled to death in my misery by that elephant herd. For
15 nothing happens to men that is not brought about by fate. But I have
never done anything wrong, even as a child, in deed, thought, or
word, that could have brought on this disaster. I think it is because I
rejected the divine World Guardians who had assembled for the
Bridegroom Choice in favor of Nala. Surely it is through their powers
that I am now separated from him."

Giving plaintive voice to her miseries in this fashion, the beautiful
woman traveled on, tiger among men, plunged in sorrow and grief,
with surviving brahmins who were steeped in the *Vedas*. After a long
journey she came to a big town; and in the evening she entered,
covered by half a skirt, the good city of the strong-armed and true-
20 spoken king of the Cedis. When the city boys saw her enter the town

of the Cedi king, pale, wan, dejected, disheveled, unwashed, walking
like a crazed woman, the street urchins followed her curiously. They
surrounded her as she made her way to the royal palace, and the
king's mother saw her from the palace terrace, trailed by her train of
people. She stopped the crowd, had her ascend to the beautiful terrace,
O king, and questioned Damayantī wonderingly. "Even though visited
by misfortune, you carry a beautiful body and shine like lightning in
the clouds. Tell me, who are you and whose? For your appearance is
more than human, however bereft of ornaments, and, with the
splendor of an Immortal, you have no fear of these men, although you
are unaccompanied."

25 Damayantī replied to her words: "Know that I am a mortal woman
and devoted to my husband. I am a chambermaid of good birth, a
handmaiden who now lives where she wishes, subsisting on fruit and
roots, alone, bedding down wherever evening falls. My husband is a
man of countless virtues and has always been devoted to me, and I
have always followed my gallant husband like a shadow. By ill fate,
he has an unbounded addiction to gambling; and when he was
defeated at a game, he went alone into the forest. I followed the hero,
who had one piece of clothing left, and was disturbed like a madman.
30 I tried to comfort him. One day, when he was overcome with hunger
in some forest and looked desperate, he lost for some reason even that
one bit of clothing. I followed, in my own garment, the naked, crazed,
and mindless man, and did not sleep for many nights. After many a
day he deserted me somewhere while I was sleeping; he cut off half
my skirt and abandoned me who was guiltless. I have been looking
for my husband day and night, consumed by grief, but I cannot find
my beloved and Godlike master of my life and goods."

35 The king's mother said to the suffering princess of Vidarbha, after
she had spoken her plaint with tear-filled eyes, she herself suffering
with her, "Stay with me, good woman! I am pleased with you. My
men will search for your husband, my dear. Or he may come on his
own while he is wandering hither and thither. While you are living
here you will regain your husband, my dear." Damayantī replied to
the king's mother, "I can stay with you, but under certain conditions,
mother of heroes: I will not eat leftovers, nor wash people's feet, nor
converse at all with strange men. If a man importunes me, he must be
punished. But I will see brahmins in the cause of the search for my
40 husband. If this can be done, I shall certainly stay; if not, I cannot
find it in my heart to stay."

In happy spirits the king's mother said to her, "I shall do all this,
I commend you for such a life rule!" Then, O Bhārata, lord of your
people, the king's mother said to her daughter, who was called
Sunandā, "This woman who looks like a goddess will be your

chambermaid, recognize her, Sunandā. Enjoy yourself with her without a care!"

Bṛhadaśva said:

63.1 Now, when King Nala had deserted Damayantī, O lord of your
people, he saw a big forest fire in the deep of the woods. From the
midst of the fire he heard the loud cry of some creature, "Come here,
Nala," and "Come, Puṇyaśloka!" again and again. "Have no fear!"
Nala called out and, entering the center of the fire, he saw a king of
Snakes lying in coils. He folded his hands and said trembling to Nala,
"King, I am the Snake Karkoṭaka. I had captured an innocent
brahminic seer of very great austerities, and possessed by fury he
cursed me, king of men. Because of his curse I cannot move a step
from this place. If you will save me, I shall teach you what will profit
you. I shall be your friend, and there is no Snake who is my equal.
I shall become light to carry for you, pick me up quickly and go!"
When he had said this, the Snake dwindled to the size of a thumb, and
Nala picked him up and ran to a spot that was safe from the fire. He
came to a clearing that was beyond the black-trailed fire; and when
10 he was about to let the Snake go, Karkoṭaka said to him, "Walk on
some more and count your steps, Niṣadhan. I shall do you the greatest
favor while you are doing so, great king."
As he started counting, the Snake bit Nala at the tenth step; and
when he was bitten, his appearance changed instantly. Astonished,
Nala stopped, looked at himself, and saw that he was deformed; and
the king of the earth saw that the Snake had assumed his old shape.
Thereupon the Snake Karkoṭaka said soothingly to Nala, "I have
changed you, so that people will not know you. And he because of
whom you have been maimed with great sorrow, O Nala, he shall
15 henceforth dwell in you and hurt from my poison. As long as he does
not leave you, while hurting in all his limbs from my poison, so long
will he dwell in you in agonies of pain, great king! I have made you
immune to the one who out of anger and rancor cheated you, while
you were innocent and undeserving of it, king of the people. You will
have nothing to fear from tusked predators or enemies and the
knowers of spells, tigerlike king. You yourself shall suffer no pain from
the poison, king, and in battles you shall always be victorious. Depart
from here, king, to Ṛtuparṇa, saying that you are a charioteer, Bāhuka
by name, for he knows the tricks of the dice. Depart today, sovereign
20 of Niṣadha, for the lovely city of Ayodhyā. The king shall impart to
you his shrewdness with dice in return for your shrewdness with
horses; and the illustrious prince, a scion of the dynasty of Ikṣvāku,
shall be your friend. When you have become skilled with the dice, you
will be reunited with fortune and rejoin your wife—banish grief from

your heart!—and your kingdom and your two children; this I tell you is the truth. Whenever you want your own appearance back, king of men, think of me and don this garment. When you are clothed in this garment, you will regain your own appearance." With these words he gave him a pair of celestial clothes. And after these orders to Nala and after the gift of the clothes, O Kaurava, the king of the Snakes disappeared on the spot.

Bṛhadaśva said:

64.1 When the Snake had disappeared, Nala of Niṣadha set out and after ten days entered the city of Ṛtuparṇa. He approached the king, saying, "I am Bāhuka! No one in the world is my peer in driving horses. My advice may be sought in all matters of difficulty or requiring skill. And I know how to cook beyond all others. Whatever other skills there are in this world, or whatever is difficult to do, I shall strive to do it all, Ṛtuparṇa, retain me!"

5 *Ṛtuparṇa said:*

Stay, Bāhuka, bless you! You shall do all that. I have always had a special love for racing. Now you see to a yoke that will let my horses run fast! You shall be my equerry, your wages are a hundred hundreds. Vārṣṇeya and Jīvala shall henceforth work for you. Make merry with them and stay with me, Bāhuka!

Bṛhadaśva said:

At the king's request Nala settled down in an honorable position in Ṛtuparṇa's city with Vārṣṇeya and Jīvala. While he lived there the king kept thinking of the princess of Vidarbha, and evening after evening he always recited this couplet,

10 "Where may you, starving and thirsty,
Lie down to sleep, fatigued and wretched,
As you keep recalling that fool?
And who is it you have to serve now?"

When the king recited this at night, Jīvala said, "Who is that woman you always bemoan? I want to hear it, Bāhuka." Said King Nala, "Some nitwit had a woman he thought much of, and he was great things to her. For some reason the fool got separated from her, and while divorced our nitwit runs around pressed by misery, burning with great day and night without her. When night falls, he remembers her and sings his one couplet. He ran all over earth and got something
15 somewhere. There he lives now, without a right to, remembering endlessly his grief over her. That woman, you know, followed that man even into the dangerous forest. The bad one deserted her, it is unlikely she lives, she is alone, young, unfamiliar with the roads, unused to things, starving and thirsting—it is unlikely she lives. She

was left in a vast and fearful forest, always overrun by beasts of prey, deserted by that bad one, that nitwit, mate." That was the way the king of Niṣadha remembered Damayantī, while he lived in concealment in the king's compound.

Bṛhadaśva said:

65.1 When Nala had lost his kingdom and with his wife was reduced to
servitude, Bhīma dispatched brahmins to find Nala. Bhīma gave them
much wealth and instructed them, "Search for Nala and Damayantī
my daughter. When this task has been accomplished and the king of
Niṣadha has been discovered, I shall give a thousand head of cattle to
whoever of you brings them here. And I shall give him in freehold a
village the size of a town. And if Damayantī or Nala cannot be brought
here, I shall give a prize of a thousand head of cattle, if they are just
5 found!" The brahmins departed happily at his summons in every
direction, searching cities and countries for the Niṣadhan and his wife.

Now a brahmin named Sudeva came on his quest to the city of
Cedi and saw the princess of Vidarbha in the king's palace, at the time
of the king's Blessing of the Day, where she was accompanied by
Sunandā and only sparsely sparkled with her perfect beauty, like the
light of the sun that is girt by a mass of mist. When he saw the wide-
eyed princess, terribly dirty and thin, he concluded that she was
Bhīma's daughter, reasoning it out with arguments.

Sudeva said:

This woman is like the one I saw before. I have succeeded, now
that I have set eyes on this darling of the world who resembles Śrī.
10 Her face is like the full moon, she is dark, and her breasts are
beautifully round. She is a goddess who with her light undarkens all
the horizons, with beautiful eyes like lotus or *palāśa* petals, the image
of Love's Lust, beloved of all the world like the light of the full moon,
pulled from the lake of Vidarbha as by a flow of fate! Her limbs are
now besmeared with dust and mud like the very lotus stalk! She is the
night of full moon when the moon has been swallowed by Rāhu, and
wretched and bemused by her anguish for her husband, she is like a
river whose course ran dry. Or a lotus pond with withered flowers,
with its birds chased away, and with its mud stirred up and much
15 perturbed by elephant trunks. And she, so delicate, of such highbred
limbs, so accustomed to houses filled with jewels, fades in the heat like
a lotus that has been plucked too soon.

She has beauty and nobility, but no ornaments, though she is worthy of them, a sliver of the new moon in heaven but covered by dark clouds. Lost to her favorite pleasures and comforts, lost to her relatives, miserably supporting her body, so she may find her husband.

. . . Yes, a husband is a woman's finest ornament, even if she has none other; and without him she does not show, however showy. Nala must have great trouble without her—does he keep his body alive, does he not sink in grief? There she is, with the eyes like the hundred-petaled lotus, so deserving of happiness—and seeing her my mind flutters.

But when to be sure will the shining woman reach the further shore past unhappiness by meeting her husband, as Rohiṇī meets the moon? The Niṣadhan shall certainly rejoice when he regains her, the unseated king, and wins his kingdom back. She is as moral and young as he is, she has the same high birth—the Niṣadhan deserves the daughter of Vidarbha, and the black-eyed woman deserves him. It is my duty to comfort the wife of that immeasurable man of gallantry and mettle, who is yearning to find her husband. Here I shall comfort her, her with the face like the full moon, who has never before been a witness to sorrow but is now full of sorrow and given to brooding.

Bṛhadaśva said:

After he had come to his judgment with many arguments and by various signs, he approached Bhīma's daughter; and the brahmin Sudeva said, "I am Sudeva, princess of Vidarbha, your brother's favorite friend. I have come here on King Bhīma's orders to search for you. Your father is in good health, queen, so are your mother and brothers, and your long-lived children are with them, hale and healthy. But on your account the multitudes of your relatives are supine as though they were dead!"

Damayantī recognized Sudeva, and she asked him about all her relatives, O Yudhiṣṭhira, one after the other. The princess of Vidarbha, thin from grief, wept bitterly, king, when she so suddenly saw that good brahmin Sudeva, her brother's favorite brahmin. Sunandā saw her weep, wan with grief, O Bhārata, while she was talking alone with Sudeva; she sent word to her mother: "The chambermaid has been weeping bitterly since she met with a brahmin. Find out who she is, if you will." This brought the mother of the king of Cedi out of the king's dower house, and she betook herself to where that young woman was meeting with a brahmin. The king's mother had Sudeva fetched, lord of your people, and asked, "Whose wife is she, whose daughter is this radiant woman? How is it she is without relatives, and without a husband, this pretty-eyed woman? Do you know, brahmin, how she has come to this? I want to hear all of this from you and completely! Tell me the truth, for I ask about a woman who looks like a goddess!"

At her demand, O king, that good brahmin Sudeva sat himself down comfortably and told the true story of Damayantī.

Sudeva said:
66.1 The king of Vidarbha is the law-spirited Bhīma of terrible prowess.
This good woman is his daughter, renowned as Damayantī. The king
of Niṣadha is Nala by name, the son of Vīrasena, and the good woman
is his wife, the wife of the sagacious Puṇyaśloka. The king was
defeated by his brother playing dice and lost his kingdom. He went
with Damayantī nobody knows where. We have been roaming all over
earth to find Damayantī, and now the young princess has been found
in the house of your son! Not a mortal woman is found on earth her
5 equal in beauty. Between the eyebrows of the dark woman there is a
fine birthmark, shaped like a lotus, which I once noticed, but now it
seems to have disappeared. For the mole is covered with dust, as the
moon by light clouds; it was placed on her face by the creator as a
sign to betoken her good fortune. It does not shine forth clearly now,
like the sliver of the moon on a cloudy new-moon day. But her beauty
has not been lost, for her body may be caked with dirt and unadorned,
still it shines like gold for all to see! By this body and by that mole I
have recognized my queen, as fire that is covered by hot smoke.
Bṛhadaśva said:
When Sunandā heard these words of Sudeva, O lord of your people,
10 she cleaned off the dirt that covered her birthmark. And with the dirt
wiped off, Damayantī's mole shone forth like the moon in a cloudless
sky. Sunandā and the king's mother saw the mole, Bhārata, and,
weeping, they embraced her and held her a while. Shedding a tear,
the king's mother said softly, "You are my sister's daughter! Your
mole shows it! I and your mother are the daughters of a great-spirited
baron, beautiful girl, Sudāman, the overlord of Dāśārṇa! She was
married to King Bhīma, I to Vīrabāhu. I saw you when you were born,
in our father's house in Dāśārṇa. This house is as much yours as your
father's, radiant girl, and what I command is yours, Damayantī!"
15 With joyous heart, O lord of your people, Damayantī greeted her
mother's sister and said, "Even without being known I have lived here
happily, well served in all my wishes and always under your
protection. And my stay now would no doubt be even happier. But
pray, give me leave to go, mother. I have been long away from home.
Both my children have been taken there, and there the youngsters are
now living. They have been without a father, the poor dears, and
without me—how will they be doing? If you still want to do me a
kindness, I want to go to Vidarbha, order me a wagon at once!"
20 Her mother's sister said happily, "Yes, to be sure!" and with her
son's consent dispatched her on a majestic palanquin carried by men,
with plenty of food, drink, and baggage and guarded by a large escort,
O best of the Bharatas. Thus after a short time the radiant woman
arrived in Vidarbha, and her kinfolk all happily welcomed her. Finding

all her relatives and also her two children in good health, and likewise her mother and father and all her friends, the glorious and virtuous Damayantī paid homage to the deities and the brahmins, with the best
25 of rites. The pleased king gratified Sudeva at once with a thousand head of cattle, as soon as he saw his daughter Damayantī, and with a village and properties.

When the shining princess had slept the night in her father's house and woke up rested, O king, she spoke to her mother as follows.

Damayantī said:

67.1 If you want me to live, mother, then, I swear to you, see to it that that hero among men is brought here!

Bṛhadaśva said:

On these words of Damayantī the queen became very unhappy and, covered with tears, she had no answer to give, king. Seeing her in this state, the entire serail moaned beyond measure and wept most sorrowfully. Whereupon the queen said to Bhīma, O great king, "Your daughter Damayantī misses her husband. Abandoning all shame, she told me so herself, king. Have your messengers try to find Puṇyaśloka!" At her urging the king dispatched brahmins who were in his service to every country, saying, "Try and find Nala!" On the overlord of Vidarbha's orders those bulls among brahmins visited Damayantī and said, "We are starting." Bhīma's daughter said to them, "In all countries and at any meeting of people, keep asking this question:

"Gambler, where are you that cut up my dress and left,
Leaving, beloved, your loving wife asleep in a void?
10 Where you directed her, there she is sitting waiting for you,
Burning with grief, the fool woman, covered with half a skirt.
Constantly weeps she with that same sorrow, king of the earth,
Please show your grace and, hero, award her an answer!

"Speak so and likewise, so that he may take pity on me; for fire when driven by wind burns down a forest.

"Husband is always bound to protect and support his wife:
Both you neglect, but why, as you are so wise in the Law?
Famed as sagacious, of high birth, compassionate always,
Cruel you have now turned, I fear, when my luck disappeared.
15 Bull among men, have pity on me, you greatest of archers,
Gentleness is the greatest of Laws, as you often did preach me!

"If anyone responds to you when you say this, inquire closely who he is and where he works. And whatever response that man makes to you, bring his words here at once, good brahmins, and tell me them.

You must not be slow in returning here, so that he will not find out that you are abroad on an errand of Bhīma's. Whether he is rich or penniless or hungry for wealth, find out his plans."

20 Having heard her charge the brahmins fanned out to all the
horizons, O king, to hunt down the gambler Nala. To cities and
kingdoms they went, king, looking for Nala, those brahmins, to
villages and cattle stations and hermitages. And everywhere all those
brahmins sounded the exact message that Damayantī had given.

Bṛhadaśva said:

68.1 A long time later a brahmin by the name of Parṇāda returned to
the city and told Damayantī, "On my search for the Niṣadhan, day
and night, Damayantī, I came to the city of Ayodhyā and waited on
Ṛtuparṇa Bhāngasvari. Publicly I let the lordly Ṛtuparṇa hear the
words just as you had spoken them, fair-faced woman. King Ṛtuparṇa
heard them, but made no reply, nor did anyone in his retinue, though
5 I recited them to them often. Then Ṛtuparṇa let me go, and when I
was alone someone talked to me, a man of Ṛtuparṇa's, Bāhuka was
his name, a deformed man with short arms, the king's charioteer,
quite an expert at racing and an excellent cook.

"He heaved many sighs and often broke into tears. He asked about my health and later said to me,

" 'Women of family fend for themselves, though landed in trouble,
Fend for themselves by themselves, for surely they conquer heaven.
And though deserted by husbands, these women do not wax wroth.
If some foolish, unfortunate man who was fallen from joy
Might have deserted her, still there should be no cause for a grudge.
10 If in order to find a living he stole a cloth,
Suffering from his diseases, no beautiful woman would anger.
Honored or not so honored, she sees her husband reduced,
Without wealth, an unseated king—what beautiful woman would anger?'

"When I heard these words of his, I hurried back here. Now that you have heard them, the decision is yours; tell the king."

With eyes full of tears Damayantī listened to Parṇāda's words; she
went to her mother and said to her in private, "This matter should not
in any way come to King Bhīma's knowledge. In your presence I shall
15 give instructions to the grand brahmin Sudeva. You must see to it, if
you wish to do me a kindness, that King Bhīma does not learn of my

intentions. Let Sudeva start again at once for the city of Ayodhyā, so
that with the same good luck as he had before he may reunite me
soon with my relations by bringing Nala here."
Later, when Parṇāda had rested, the shining princess of Vidarbha
honored him with an excess of wealth, saying, "Brahmin, when Nala
comes here, I shall give you even greater riches. For you have done
more for me than anyone ever shall, if I am soon reunited with my
husband, eminent brahmin!" At these words of her he returned his
respects with auspicious benedictions, and the spirited brahmin went
20 home contentedly. Then Damayantī summoned the brahmin Sudeva
again, Yudhiṣṭhira, and in her mother's presence said to him
sorrowfully and mournfully, "Sudeva, go to the king who sits in
Ayodhyā and tell Ṛtuparṇa, 'Bhīma's daughter Damayantī wants
another husband and is again holding a Bridegroom Choice. All the
kings and sons of kings are going there, and as time is reckoned, it
will take place tomorrow morning. If you so fancy, go quickly, enemy-
tamer; at sunrise she will choose herself a second husband. For it is
not known whether that hero Nala is dead or alive."
And the brahmin Sudeva went, great king, and spoke to King
Ṛtuparṇa as she had told him.

Bṛhadaśva said:
69.1 When king of men Ṛtuparṇa heard Sudeva's words, he spoke
winningly to Bāhuka in a gentle voice, "I want to go to Vidarbha for
Damayantī's Bridegroom Choice—and in one day, horse expert, if you
think it can be done, Bāhuka!" At these words of the king, Nala's
heart was rent asunder from anguish, Kaunteya, and the spirited man
brooded: "If Damayantī would do a thing like that, she must be
demented with grief; or it might be a grand ruse she has thought up
5 for my sake. . . . Alas, the wretched woman of Vidarbha wants to
perpetrate a cruel act because I, a lowly, evil, irresolute man, deceived
her! A woman's nature is fickle in this world, and the wrong I did her
was fearsome. Let it be! But yet, will she, willy-nilly, forgetful of her
love, resentful of the grief I caused her, act so desperately, the slim-
waisted princess? No, she could not act like this ever, the less so since
she has the children. So we go, and I shall find out for certain what
the truth of the matter is. I shall do what Ṛtuparṇa desires and I
myself want!" Having made this decision in his heart, Bāhuka
dejectedly folded his hands and replied to King Ṛtuparṇa, "I give you
my word, king, you will get there in one day, tiger among men!"
10 Then this Bāhuka inspected the horses, O king, after he had left for
the stable on King Bhāngasvari's orders. Constantly harried by
Ṛtuparṇa, Bāhuka found himself four lean capable horses, durable on
the road, tough and strong, of fine breed and training, lacking inferior

marks, with wide nostrils and big jowls, perfect with all ten curls, horses that hailed from the Indus and were fast as the wind. When the king saw them, he said with a touch of anger, "What is this you intend to do? Surely you want to fool me! How can these nags of little strength and breath pull my chariot? How can horses like these cover that long stretch of road?"

Bāhuka said:

15 These horses will make Vidarbha without a doubt. But if you prefer
others, king, tell me which ones to yoke!

Ṛtuparṇa said:

You are the horse expert, Bāhuka, you are the master. If you think they can do it, then yoke them at once!

Bṛhadaśva said:

Expertly Nala put the four fast horses of fine breeding and training
to the chariot. The king quickly climbed on the ready chariot and
those fine steeds knelt on the ground. Then that best of men,
20 illustrious King Nala, eased the spirited mettlesome horses, controlled
them with his reins, and, lifting Vārṣṇeya the charioteer on the
chariot, he started. Bāhuka prodded those excellent steeds in the right
way, and they assumed their highest speed and seemed to fly in the
air, as though to bewitch the rider. When the sagacious king of
Ayodhyā saw the horses race with the speed of a gale, he was utterly
astounded. And when Vārṣṇeya heard the roar of the chariot and saw
the driver's control of the horses, he wondered about Bāhuka's
horsemanship. "Is this Mātali, the charioteer of the king of the Gods?
25 For I find the same great talent in this valiant Bāhuka. Or is he
Śālihotra, who knows the principles of horse breeding and has now
assumed this most ugly human form? Or could it possibly be King
Nala, victor of enemy cities? Might the king have come here?" he
thought. "Yes, Bāhuka knows the same tricks that Nala knew, for I
see that Bāhuka's horsemanship is equal to Nala's, and I think he and
Nala are the same age. This is not the mighty Nala, yet he has his
expertness—great-spirited men do roam on earth in disguise, when
they have been yoked by divine ordinance and scripture-spelt
30 disfigurements. Still I am divided in my mind about his change in
appearance, yet my doubts may be lacking foundation, I think. He is
the same age and size, but looks different. Yet, in the end I think
Bāhuka is Nala, with all his virtues." So Vārṣṇeya reflected with many
hesitations in his heart, Puṇyaśloka's old charioteer, O great king.
But King Ṛtuparṇa, who also thought on Bāhuka's horsemanship,
enjoyed himself as did Vārṣṇeya the charioteer. Watching Bāhuka's
strength, power, energy, and horse control, and his superb effort, he
was immensely pleased.

Bṛhadaśva said:

70.1 He crossed without stopping rivers and mountains, forests and
lakes, like a bird flying in the sky. Then, as the chariot sped on, King
Bhāngasvari, conqueror of enemy cities, saw that his shawl had been
swept off. When his shawl fell while he was racing on, the spirited
king said to Nala, "I'll fetch it! Halt these swift horses, clever man, so
5 that Vārṣṇeya can retrieve my shawl!" Nala replied, "Your shawl has
dropped a long way past, a league away, you cannot get it back." As
Nala was speaking, King Bhāngasvari came in the forest upon a
vibhītaka tree in full fruit, O king. Seeing it the speeding king said to
Bāhuka, "Now you too watch my great talent at counting! No one
knows everything, nobody is omniscient—knowledge is nowhere
lodged with any single person. In this tree, Bāhuka, the difference
between the leaves and the nuts still on the tree and those fallen on
the ground is a hundred and one: one more leaf and one hundred
10 more nuts, Bāhuka. Both those branches have five crores of leaves.
Take off the two branches and their twigs and you get from them
two thousand one hundred and ninety-five nuts."

Bāhuka jumped off the chariot and said to the king, "You boast of
something that seems beyond me, enemy-harassing king! So there be
nothing mysterious about your count, great king, I shall count the
leaves and nuts in the *vibhītaka* tree while you watch. For I do not
know whether your count is right or wrong. I shall count these nuts
in your full sight. Let Vārṣṇeya take over the reins of the horses for
the moment." The king replied to the charioteer, "We have no time to
tarry!" But Bāhuka said with the greatest insistence, "Wait just a
15 moment, or hurry on by yourself. The road is easy from here. Go on,
let Vārṣṇeya drive." Replied Ṛtuparṇa in a soothing voice, O scion of
Kuru, "You are the driver and no other on all of earth, Bāhuka. It is
because of you that I have hopes of reaching Vidarbha, horse expert!
I have counted on you, don't put obstacles in my way. I shall do what
you want, if only you tell me, Bāhuka, and if you drive at once to
Vidarbha and show me the sun rise there!" Bāhuka said, "I shall
20 count the *vibhītaka* nuts and then go on to Vidarbha. Do what I tell
you." Reluctantly the king said, "Go count them!" The other alighted
from the chariot and quickly cut down the tree. Then, totally
astonished, he arrived at exactly the same count as the king and said
to him. "This is a marvel of marvels, king. I have seen your forte! I
want to know the magic by which you knew their number, king!"
The king, who was in a hurry to go, replied, "Know that I know the
secret of the dice and am expert at counting." Bāhuka said, "Give me
the magic lore and in return take from me the secret of the horses,
bull among men!"

25 And so, because of the gravity of his pressing task, and because he
dearly wanted to acquire horsemanship, King Ṛtuparṇa said to
Bāhuka, "All right! If you wish, learn now the ultimate secret of the
dice; but you hold for me the secret of the horses for the nonce,
Bāhuka." And after these words Ṛtuparṇa imparted his knowledge to
Nala. Promptly Kali issued forth from his body when Nala had learned
the secret of the dice, incessantly vomiting from his mouth the bitter
venom of Karkoṭaka. The fire of Kali's curse came out of the king who
had been suffering from it; he had been worn thin from it and had for
a long time lost control of himself. Kali was now himself freed from the
poison and he took on his own body. Nala, sovereign of Niṣadha,
30 angrily wanted to curse him. Frightened, trembling, and folding his
hands, Kali said to him, "Restrain your anger, sire, I shall give you the
greatest fame. Once your wife, Indrasena's mother, cursed me in anger,
when you had deserted her, and I have been sorely pressed ever since.
I have lived inside you, undefeated Indra among kings, lived in great
pain, burning day and night with the poison of that king of the
Snakes. Whatsoever mortal shall glorify your fame tirelessly shall have
to fear no danger from me!"

At these words, King Nala restrained his rage and the cowardly
Kali quickly entered the *vibhītaka* tree; nobody had seen Kali converse
35 with the Niṣadhan. Cured of his fever the king of Niṣadha, killer of
enemy heroes, now that Kali was destroyed and he had counted the
nuts, was overcome with great joy and once more endowed with his
superb luster of old. And lustrously he ascended the chariot and drove
forth with the swift horses. Ever since the *vibhītaka* tree has stood in ill
repute, because Kali took possession of it.

Nala, in the highest of spirits, drove the sublime horses onward,
again and again, and they flew like birds. The spirited king continued
to Vidarbha; and when Nala was far past, Kali too went home. Rid of
his fever, King Nala, O king of the earth, was freed from Kali and only
left without his own body.

Bṛhadaśva said:

71.1 Ṛtuparṇa, whose word was his strength, arrived in Vidarbha in the
evening, and people informed King Bhīma of his arrival. With Bhīma's
approval he entered the city of Kuṇḍina, making the ten horizons echo
with the roar of his chariot.

Nala's horses heard the roar of the chariot there; and when they
heard it they got excited as before, whenever Nala had been with
them. So did Damayantī hear the roar of Nala's chariot, rumbling like
5 the monsoon cloud at the onset of the rainy season. And Bhīma's
daughter, like the horses, thought that the chariot thundered as
before, when Nala had driven Nala's horses. The peacocks on the

terrace, the elephants in the stable, and the horses heard the roar of
the king's chariot; and, hearing the chariot thunder, the peacocks and
elephants made sounds of yearning, as though they expected the
monsoon to break.

Damayantī said:

If the roar of the chariot that seems to fill the earth gladdens my
heart, it must be King Nala! If I do not see today that hero with the
moonlike face and countless virtues, I shall perish without a doubt.
10 If I am not held today in that hero's arms, of such delicious touch, I
shall perish without a doubt. If the Niṣadhan who roars like the
thunder of the monsoon, shining like gold, does not come to me today,
I shall perish without a doubt. If that Indra of kings, valiant as a lion,
who can stop a mad elephant, does not come, I shall perish without a
doubt. I remember no lies, I remember no wrongs, not a word that the
great-spirited man did not keep strictly, even in jest, my lord is patient
and gallant, gentle and controlled, the master of his senses. My
15 Niṣadhan has no vices, he has been like a eunuch to me. As I
remember his virtues, thinking of him day and night, my heart that is
separated from my love is rent asunder.

Bṛhadaśva said:

Moaning in this strain she went up the stairs of her great palace,
Bhārata, almost unconsciously, moved by her desire to see Puṇyaśloka.
She saw King Ṛtuparṇa standing in his chariot in the central court,
with Bāhuka and Vārṣṇeya. Thereupon Vārṣṇeya and Bāhuka
dismounted from the superb chariot, unharnessed the horses, and
secured the chariot. King Ṛtuparṇa descended from the pit of his
chariot and drew near to Bhīma of terrible prowess, O great king.
20 Bhīma received him with the greatest honor, when he so suddenly
and without clear reason arrived; for he did not know of the women's
conspiracy. "What may I do? Be welcome!" asked the king, O
Bhārata, for he did not know that the other had come for his daughter.
Sagacious King Ṛtuparṇa, however, whose strength was his word,
perceived no kings or princes, no talk of a Bridegroom Choice, nor an
assemblage of brahmins. And reflecting on this in his mind, the
sovereign king of Kosala said to him, "I have come to bring you my
greetings, sir." Bhīma smiled and thought to himself, "There is an
ulterior reason for his coming a hundred leagues, passing through
25 many villages, and he has not properly accomplished it. The reason he
gives for his coming is hardly sufficient. This is not it." The king
showed him hospitality and gave him leave to go, saying, "Pray rest!"
and "You are tired!" and saying it often.

Pleased with his reception by his pleased host, the king happily
enough settled in the guest house assigned to him, followed by the
king's servants. When Ṛtuparṇa had gone with Vārṣṇeya, O king,

Bāhuka took the chariot to the coach house. He freed the horses and tended to them according to the precepts, and when he himself had seen to their needs, he sat down in the pit of the chariot.

30 When Damayantī had seen King Bhāngasvari, and Vārṣṇeya, a charioteer's son, and Bāhuka in his disguise, she reflected unhappily, "Who made the chariot roar mightily like Nala's? I do not see the Niṣadhan! But surely, Vārṣṇeya must have learned the art, that is why the mighty roar of the chariot sounded like Nala's. Or is Ṛtuparṇa as able as Nala? Then the thunder of his chariot could be mistaken for Nala's." So Damayantī pondered the question, O king of your people; and she dispatched a woman as her messenger to find out the Niṣadhan.

Damayantī said:

72.1 Keśinī, go and find out who that equerry is, that deformed man with the short arms who is sitting in the chariot pit. Go to him, dear, and sweetly and thoughtfully inquire about his health. Find out exactly who he is, blameless woman. I have a deep suspicion that he is King Nala, for so contented is my mind and so tranquil my heart. You should in the course of your talk use Parṇāda's words, and mark his answer, buxom and blameless woman.

Bṛhadaśva said:

5 So she diligently went as a messenger and said to Bāhuka, while the good Damayantī looked on from the terrace.

Keśinī said:

Welcome, you Indra among mortals, I have come to ask you how you are doing! Damayantī asks a question and listen to it properly, bull among men: when did all of you start and why have you come here? Tell it truthfully, if it is in order—the princess of Vidarbha wants to know.

Bāhuka said:

The glorious king of Kosala heard today that Damayantī would hold a second Bridegroom Choice tomorrow, pretty girl. When he heard that, the king started out with superb wind-fast horses that would last a hundred leagues. I was his charioteer.

Keśinī said:

10 This third man in your party, where does he come from and whose is he? And whose are you, and how is it that the driving chore fell on you?

Bāhuka said:

He was the charioteer of Puṇyaśloka himself; he is known as Vārṣṇeya. When Nala ran off, Vārṣṇeya went to Bhāngasvari, good woman. I myself am a horse expert and an excellent cook, and Ṛtuparṇa himself retained my services as a driver and a cook.

Keśinī said:

Does Vārṣṇeya know where King Nala has gone? Has he said anything in your presence, Bāhuka?

Bāhuka said:

He left the two children of that unholy Nala here, and then went
15 off on his own. He does not know about the Niṣadhan. And there is
not a person who knows of Nala, good woman. He lives somewhere in hiding, the king has vanished. Nala alone knows who he is, and she who is closest to him. . . . For there are no outward signs that betray Nala.

Keśinī said:

That brahmin who came earlier to Ayodhyā constantly recited these words of some woman:

"Gambler, where are you who cut up my dress and left?
Leaving, beloved, your loving wife asleep in a void?
Where you directed her, there she is sitting waiting for you,
Burning with love, fool woman, covered with half a skirt.
20 Constantly weeps she with that same sorrow, king of the earth,
Please show your grace and, hero, award her an answer!"

Speak up, sagacious man, and tell her the story she loves. The blameless princess of Vidarbha wants to hear the same words. Ever since she heard the reply the brahmin says you gave him that time, the princess of Vidarbha has been waiting for you to repeat it.

Bṛhadaśva said:

When Keśinī said this to Nala, O scion of Kuru, his heart smarted and his eyes filled with tears. But although consumed with grief, the king suppressed his feelings and repeated in a tear-choked voice,

"Women of family fend for themselves, though landed in trouble.
Fend for themselves by themselves, for surely they conquer heaven.
And though deserted by husbands, these women never wax wroth;
Armored with goodness these good women preserve their lives.
'Twas in order to find a living, when birds took his robe—
Suffer he did from his illness, the beautiful one should forgive.
Honored or not so honored, she sees her husband reduced,
Without wealth, an unseated king, vice-ridden and starving."

As Nala in his bitter grief spoke these words, he could not restrain
30 his tears and fell to weeping, Bhārata. And Keśinī went and told
Damayantī everything that he had said, and the change that had come over him.

Bṛhadaśva said:

73.1 Damayantī listened most mournfully and, suspecting that he was

Nala, she said to Keśinī, "Go, Keśinī, and make more inquiries about
Bāhuka. Say nothing but stay near and notice what he does.
Whenever he does something that gives food for thought, my pretty,
observe closely what he does and when he does it. To thwart him you
should not even give him fire, my pretty; if he asks for water, do not
5 give it to him at all, or at your leisure, my pretty. Observe all he does
and come and tell me. And whatever else you happen to see, tell me
everything!"

At Damayantī's words, Keśinī went quickly; and after observing the
outward marks of the horseman, she returned and told Damayantī all
that had happened, and the divine and human features of Bāhuka she
had noticed.

Keśinī said:

Surely I have never in my life seen or heard of a mortal man who is
so exalted in his conduct, Damayantī! If he comes to a low
passageway, he does not lower his head, but on seeing him the lintel
rises, so that he may pass comfortably. A narrow opening opens very
10 wide for him. The king has sent all kinds of food for Ṛtuparṇa and a
goodly amount of beef; a tub has been provided to clean the meat. At
a mere glance from him it filled up with water! When Bāhuka had
cleaned the meat, he set himself to cooking it, took a handful of
straws, broke them, and made a little pile; and suddenly fire blazed up
in that pile! When I saw that miracle, I was amazed and came back
here. I noticed another great marvel there: when he chanced to touch
15 fire, it did not burn him, good woman. And water pours quickly forth
whenever he wants it. Still another surpassing marvel I saw: he took
flowers and gently ground them in his hands; and when they were
being ground they became once more fresh and fragrant. After seeing
these marvels, which were like miracles, I came quickly back here.

Bṛhadaśva said:

When Damayantī heard about Puṇyaśloka's deeds, she thought
that Nala had been discovered by his acts and gestures and was now
regained. Surmising that her husband Nala was wearing the
appearance of Bāhuka, she wept and again said to Keśinī in a gentle
20 voice, "Go once more, and when Bāhuka is distracted, take from the
kitchen some cooked meat that he has prepared, and come back here,
my pretty." Keśinī went, and when Bāhuka was preoccupied, she took
a very hot piece of meat as a favor to Damayantī and immediately
gave it to her, O scion of Kuru. She had been used before to meat of
Nala's cooking, and when she tasted it she knew that the cook was
Nala. She began to weep piteously, deeply moved; then she washed
her face and sent her two children with Keśinī, O Bhārata.

Bāhuka recognized Indrasenā and her brother, and the king ran to
25 them, embraced them, and took them on his lap. On finding once

more his own children, who were like the children of a god, he was wrapped in great grief and wept loudly. Thus the Niṣadhan showed his feelings, many times, then he suddenly let go of his children and said to Keśinī, "These two are very much like my own children; and when I saw them so suddenly, I had to shed a tear. You have been coming here too often, people will think ill of you. We are guests in this country: go, my dear, with my respects!"

Bṛhadaśva said:

74.1 When she had witnessed all the emotions of the wise Puṇyaśloka,
Keśinī returned quickly and told Damayantī. Thereupon Damayantī,
anxious and made eager by her surmise that he was Nala, sent Keśinī
again, now to her mother, with the message, "I have tried Bāhuka in
many ways, because I suspect that he is Nala. Doubt remains only
about his appearance. I want to find out for myself. Either let him be
brought in, or allow me to go to him, mother. It may be done with
father's knowledge or without."
5 At this message of the princess of Vidarbha, the queen spoke to
Bhīma; and the king approved his daughter's plan. With her father's
consent and her mother's, O bull of the Bharatas, she had Nala
brought to the room where she was staying. When Damayantī saw
Nala in that disguise, a bitter anguish seized the fair-faced woman.
Herself wearing an ocher robe, her hair matted, dirty, and muddy,
great king, Damayantī said to Bāhuka, "Have you ever seen anyone
who, supposedly law-minded, deserted his sleeping wife in the
10 wilderness and left her, Bāhuka? Who would leave his beloved and
innocent wife, overcome by fatigue, in the empty forest and go? Who
but Nala Puṇyaśloka? What a wrong must I not have done to the
king that he deserted me, fast asleep in the forest, and went away. He
whom I myself had once chosen, bypassing the Gods who were present
there, how could he desert his loving and faithful wife, the mother of
his children? The troth that he promised me, 'I shall support you,' me
whose hand he had taken in the presence of the fire in obedience to
the words of the wild geese—where has it gone?"
While Damayantī was saying all this, tears of grief welled up in her
15 eyes and flowed freely, O enemy-tamer. And when Nala saw those
streaming tears that flowed without let from her black-pupiled and
red-cornered eyes, he said pitifully, "It was not my own fault that I
lost my kingdom, it was Kali's doing, my timid, and also that I deserted
you. You yourself, most virtuous in the Law, had cursed him before,
when you were in the forest and sorrowfully suffered with me who
had lost my robe. Ever since, Kali, who dwelled in my body, has been
burning with your curse. Like kindling piled on a fire, he was always
ablaze with your curse. Now I have overcome him with resolve and

austerity, and there shall be an end indeed, beautiful woman, to our
20 misery. The evil spirit left me and went away; and thereafter I came
here, for your sake, woman of the curvesome hips, for I have no other
goal.

"But how could a woman ever abandon her loving and faithful husband, and, like you, timid woman, choose another husband? Messengers coursed all over earth at the king's command, saying, 'Bhīma's daughter will choose herself another husband, acting on her own, as it pleases her, a husband who is compatible with herself.' As soon as he heard it, Bhāngasvari hurried along!"

When Damayantī heard this plaint of Nala, she tremblingly folded her hands and fearfully spoke these words—

Damayantī said:

75.1 Pray, my good lord, do not suspect me of evil, for I sent Gods on
their way and chose you, king of Niṣadha! It was in order to prompt
you to come that brahmins went out all over and sang my words in
verse in all the ten regions. Thus a wise brahmin by the name of
Parṇāda found you, my king, in Kosala, in Ṛtuparṇa's compound.
When he brought back to me your answer to my words, precisely as
5 you had given it, I saw a way of bringing you here, Niṣadhan. For
besides you, lord of the land, there is no one on earth who is capable
of driving horses a hundred leagues in one day. Even as I hug these
feet of yours, even so I have not ever dishonored you even in my
thoughts! The ever-restless wind that courses through the world,
spying on all creatures, shall rid me of my life if I have done any
wrong. So the sting-rayed sun that forever travels over the world of
beings shall rid me of my life, if I have done any wrong. The moon
that moves through all creatures as a witness to their doings shall rid
10 me of my life, if I have done any wrong. These three Gods who
support all the three words shall pronounce the truth or relinquish me
on the spot!

Bṛhadaśva said:

No sooner had she spoken than the Wind spoke from the sky, "I
swear it is the truth, Nala, that she has done no wrong! King,
Damayantī has preserved her vast treasure of honor, we have been
her guardians for these three years. This stratagem that she devised
for your sake was unmatched, for no man on earth but you can go
one hundred leagues in a day. Bhīma's daughter has found you, king
of the earth, and you have found her. Harbor no suspicions in this
15 matter, rejoin your wife!" While the Wind spoke, a rain of flowers fell,
and the drums of the Gods sounded, and an auspicious breeze blew.

Upon seeing this great marvel, King Nala the enemy-tamer shed his suspicions about Damayantī, O Bhārata. The lord of the earth put on

that dustless robe, called to his mind the king of the Snakes—and
resumed his own body. When Bhīma's daughter saw her husband in
his own body, the blameless woman cried out aloud and embraced
Puṇyaśloka. And King Nala, too, shining as before, embraced
Damayantī and welcomed his two children back, as was just.
20 Damayantī of the beautiful face laid her face on his chest and,
overcome with emotion, the long-eyed woman heaved a sigh. Caked
with dirt as her body was, the sweet-smiling wife, streaming with
tears, kept embracing the tigerlike man for a very long time.
The mother of the princess of Vidarbha joyfully related to Bhīma all
that had happened to Damayantī and Nala. Quoth the great king,
"I shall see Nala with Damayantī tomorrow morning after he has
slept well and done his ablutions." Together the two talked that night
of all that wandering they had done in the forest and slept happily, O
25 king. Three years had passed before he was reunited with his wife,
and, his heart contented with all that he desired, he found complete
happiness. Damayantī too, on regaining her husband, was wholly
refreshed like an acre with half-grown crops on receiving rain.

Rejoined with her husband, her weariness gone,
Her fever appeased, heart swelling with joy,
Damayantī, in all her desires fulfilled,
Shone clear as the night with a rising moon.

Bṛhadaśva said:
76.1 After passing that night, King Nala in full ornaments visited in the
morning the king of the land with his wife. Nala humbly saluted his
father-in-law and after him the fair Damayantī greeted her father.
Bhīma welcomed him most joyously like a son; and the lord paid him
due respect and comforted the faithful Damayantī in Nala's presence.
When he had been paid honor in the proper manner, King Nala
5 brought him duly his own homage. There was a loud outcry of joy in
the city from the overjoyed people when they saw Nala returned in
this fashion. The city, emblazoned with flag masts, shone beautifully,
and the royal roads were sprinkled and raked and full of flowers. At
every door of the townfolk there was a display of cut flowers, and all
the sanctuaries of the Gods were worshiped.
When King Ṛtuparṇa heard that Bāhuka had been Nala in disguise
and that he had rejoined Damayantī, he was delighted. King Nala had
him fetched and begged the king's pardon; citing reasons, he who was
10 honored for his wisdom sought forgiveness. Responding to the
courtesy, the astonished king congratulated the Niṣadhan, "How
fortunate that you have rejoined your wife! Have I perchance slighted
you, Niṣadhan, when you were staying in concealment in my house,

king of Niṣadha? Or if I have wronged you in any way, knowingly or unknowingly, pray forgive me for it!"

Nala said:

You have not slighted me in the least, king! And if you had, I
would not mind, for I should surely forgive you. You have always
been my friend and relation, king, pray show me your affection
15 henceforth too. I have lived happily at yours, provided with all my
wants, more so in your house, king, than in my own! And the
knowledge of horses that I possess I shall willingly impart to you, if
you wish, king!

Bṛhadaśva said:

Having said this, the Niṣadhan gave Ṛtuparṇa his knowledge; and he accepted it with the rite that is found in the Rules. When he had received the secret of the horses, King Bhāngasvari engaged another charioteer and departed for his own city. After Ṛtuparṇa's departure King Nala, O lord of the people, stayed in the city of Kuṇḍina for not too long a time.

Bṛhadaśva said:

77.1 After a stay of a month, Kaunteya, the Niṣadhan took his leave
from Bhīma and with a small escort departed from the city for
Niṣadha, with a single sparkling chariot, a full sixteen tuskers, fifty
horses, and six hundred foot soldiers. Shaking the earth as he hastened
on, the spirited king entered the city swiftly and most wrathfully. Nala,
son of Vīrasena, went up to Puṣkara and said, "Let us play again, I
5 have acquired much wealth! Damayantī and whatever other riches I
have acquired shall be my stake, and you shall stake the kingdom,
Puṣkara. I have decided that the game must go on again, with a single
stake. Bless you, let us wager both our lives! When a party has won
and taken the other's property, be it a kingdom or treasure, a
counterstake should be offered; for this they call the last stake. If you
do not wish to gamble, the gamble of battle must begin, a chariot duel
until you find your peace or I, king! It is the decree of the elders that a
10 dynastic kingdom may be recovered by any means at all. Decide now
for one or the other, Puṣkara, either for a game at dice, or draw the
bow in battle!"

At this challenge of the Niṣadhan, Puṣkara began to laugh; thinking that he was sure to win, he replied to the king of the land, "How fortunate that you have acquired wealth for a counterstake, Niṣadhan, how fortunate that Damayantī's difficulties are past! How fortunate, king, uprooter of your enemies, that you and your wife are alive! Decked with this wealth, which I shall have won, the princess of Vidarbha will as clearly serve me as an Apsarā serves Śakra in heaven! I have thought of you constantly, Niṣadhan, and I have been

waiting for you. I do not enjoy gambling with parties who are not
15 family. And when today I have won the flawless callipygous
Damayantī, I shall have accomplished everything; for she has always
been in my heart!"
When he heard the words of the incoherent prattler, Nala was
angered enough to want to cut off his head with his sword. But
smilingly, his eyes copper-red with anger, the king said to him, "Let us
play, why talk? When you have won you can talk." So began the
game of Puṣkara and Nala, and, bless you, in one throw he was
beaten by Nala! He lost his whole pile of treasure and forfeited his life.
The king said laughingly to Puṣkara after he had lost, "All this
20 kingdom is mine, serene, without rivals. You cannot set eyes on the
princess of Vidarbha, degenerate king. Fool, you and your entourage
have been reduced to slaves! It was not your doing that I at the time
lost out; it was Kali's doing, but you did not know it, fool. I shall in no
wise blame on you the wrong done by another. Live as you please, I
return to you your life. Also I have affection for you, hero, let there be
no doubt. My brotherly feelings will never fail you. For you are my
brother, Puṣkara, live a hundred years!"
Thus Nala, whose strength was his truth, reassured his brother, and
25 with many embraces sent him off to his own city. After the Niṣadhan's
reassurances Puṣkara folded his hands, paid homage to Puṇyaśloka, O
king, and said in reply, "May your fame be undying, live in happiness
a myriad years, you who have spared my life and returned my seat, O
king!" Puṣkara then spent a month there as the king's guest and later
happily departed for his own city accompanied by his kin, with his
large host and well-mannered servants, shining like the sun with
beauty, O bull among men.
After the illustrious king had dispatched Puṣkara, rich and healthy,
he made his entrance into the city that was splendidly decorated. And
having made his entrance the king of Niṣadha reassured the citizenry.

Bṛhadaśva said:
78.1 When the excited city had calmed down and a great celebration had
begun, the king brought Damayantī in with a large army. Her father
of measureless soul, killer of enemy heroes, Bhīma of terrible prowess,
sent her off with full honors. After the arrival of the princess of
Vidarbha and her children, King Nala joyously passed his days like the
king of the Gods in the Nandana park. Having found renown among
the kings in Jambūdvīpa, the glorious monarch once more lived in the
5 kingdom he had regained. And he offered up, according to the
precepts, many sacrifices with plentiful stipends.

So you, too, O best of kings should live this out with your kinsmen
for not too long a time. To such misery did Nala, conqueror of enemy
cities, fall victim, O best of men, with his wife because of his gambling,
O bull of the Bharatas. Nala, who was all alone, found very great and
gruesome grief, O king of the earth, and then again his fortunes were
restored. You on the other hand are accompanied by your brothers
and by Kṛṣṇā, O Pāṇḍava, and enjoy yourself in the great forest while
observing the Law. You are daily attended on by lordly brahmins,
steeped in the *Vedas* and their branches, king—what have you to
complain about?
10 This history is said to spell the destruction of Kali; and when he has
heard it, a man like you can take courage, lord of the people.
Reflecting always on the impermanence of man's riches, be serene at
their coming and going, and do not worry. To him who narrates the
great story of Nala and listens to it ceaselessly, misfortune will never
befall. Riches will flow to him and he will become rich. After hearing
this ancient and eternal great story one shall find sons, grandsons,
cattle, and prominence among men, and without a doubt he will be
happy in health and love. The danger you foresee, that a skillful
15 gambler will once more challenge you, I shall obviate for you. I know
the whole secret of the dice, O Kaunteya, whose strength is your truth;
learn it from me. I am pleased and I shall tell you.

Vaiśaṃpāyana said:

Thereupon, happy of heart, the king said to Bṛhadaśva, "Sir, I wish
to hear the true secret of the dice!" Bṛhadaśva imparted to the great-spirited Pāṇḍava the secret of the dice; and, having done so, the great
ascetic went to Ford Aśvaśiras to bathe.

When Bṛhadaśva had gone, Yudhiṣṭhira, firm in his vows, heard
from brahmins and ascetics, who had gathered from hither and yon
and assembled from great mountains and places of pilgrimage, that the
wise Pārtha, the left-handed archer, was devoting himself to awesome
20 austerities, living on the wind. "The strong-armed Pārtha," they said,
"has undertaken impossible austerities, no one has ever seen anyone
with such powerful self-mortifications before." Also that Dhanaṃjaya
Pārtha was an ascetic of strict vows, a lone hermit, like the illustrious
Dharma embodied. Hearing that he was mortifying himself in the vast
forest, O king, the Pāṇḍava Kaunteya suffered for his dear brother
Jaya. And with burning heart, Yudhiṣṭhira, in order to seek solace in
the great forest, questioned brahmins of various eruditions.

3(32) *Arjuna's Journey to the World of Indra (continued)*

Janamejaya said:
79.1 Sir, after the Pārtha, my great-grandfather, had left the Kāmyaka
Forest, what did the Pāṇḍavas do without the left-handed archer? For
it appears to me that that great bowman, defeater of enemy armies,
was their refuge as Viṣṇu is the refuge of the Ādityas. Deprived of that
warrior, who matched Indra in prowess and never fled in battle, how
did my heroic forbears carry on in the forest?
Vaiśaṃpāyana said:
When the Pāṇḍava, the left-handed archer, had gone from the
forest, my friend, those Kauravas were immersed in grief and sorrow.
5 All the Pāṇḍavas were forlorn like pearls whose string has broken, or
birds whose wings have been clipped. The forest, which had lost that
man of unsullied deeds, had become like Citraratha's park when
Kubera is gone. Without that tigerlike man, Janamejaya, the Pāṇḍavas
lived in Kāmyaka joylessly. For the sake of the brahmins the warlike
and victorious men killed, O best of the Bharatas, many kinds of
sacrificial game animals with clean arrows. Day after day the tigerlike
men, tamers of their enemies, spread out and collected forest food and
10 offered it to the brahmins. So they dwelled there, when Dhanaṃjaya
was gone, cheerlessly, O king, and they all missed him, those bulls
among men.

The princess of Pāñcāla, remembering her middlemost husband, the
hero who no longer lived there, said to the eldest of the Pāṇḍavas,
"Without Arjuna who, two-handed, equaled the many-handed Arjuna,
without that best of the Pāṇḍavas, I have no joy in the forest. I look
upon this earth and find it empty everywhere. This wood with its
many marvels and flowering trees is no longer lovely to me without
the left-handed archer. This Kāmyaka Forest, dark like a rain cloud,
overrun by rutting elephants, I find no joy in it without that lotus-
15 eyed man. I remember the left-handed archer, whose bow sounded
with the roar of a thunderbolt, and I find no shelter, king."

When Bhīmasena, slayer of enemy heroes, heard this plaint of hers,
great king, he said to Draupadī, "Good woman of the slim waist, the
words that you speak are balm for the mind and they please my heart
like the taste of the Elixir. His arms were long and smooth and thick
like bludgeons, callused by the bowstring, and round, wielding sword
and weapon and club, squeezed by his golden rings and upper arm
bracelets—they were like five-headed snakes. Without that tigerlike
20 man the wood seems to have lost its sun. The Pāñcālas and Kurus had

recourse to the strong-armed hero, and he would not flinch were Gods arrayed against him in battle. We had recourse to the arms of that great-spirited man, all of us, and we thought our foes defeated in war and the earth regained. Without Phalguna the hero, I find no peace of mind in Kāmyaka; and I look upon this earth and find it empty everywhere."

Nakula said:

He went north and defeated powerful men in war, that son of Indra, and acquired the best Gandharva horses by the hundreds, the illustrious man, partridge-colored and dappled ones, O king, fast as the wind. And he affectionately and with love gave them to his brother at
25 the great sacrifice of the Royal Consecration. Without that man of the terrifying bow, the younger brother of Bhīma, a Godlike man, I no longer wish to live in the Kāmyaka Forest.

Sahadeva said:

Riches he won and girls, and defeated great warriors in battle, and then brought them all to the king at the grand celebration of the Royal Consecration. He, of measureless splendor, vanquished the assembled Yādavas on the battlefield and, with Vāsudeva's consent, abducted Subhadrā all alone. When I see Jiṣṇu's grass-roll empty in our hut, my heart never finds peace, great king. I think we should banish ourselves from this wood, enemy-tamer, for without that hero none of us like this wood.

3(33) *The Tour of the Sacred Fords*

80–153 (B. 81–155; C. 4021–11427)
80 (81–82; 4021). Nārada arrives and is welcomed. Yudhiṣṭhira asks about the rewards of a pilgrimage (1–10). Nārada relates that once on a pilgrimage Bhīṣma met Pulastya, to whom he paid honor (10–20). Pulastya then invites Bhīṣma to question him. Bhīṣma asks about the rewards of a pilgrimage (20–25). Pulastya exhorts to self-mastery (25–30). He adds that the Vedic rites are out of reach for the poor. They should visit the sacred fords, which match and outrank the great sacrifices (35–40). Puṣkara is extolled (40–55). Among many other places mention is made of Mahākāla and Bhadravaṭa (65), the rivers Narmadā and Carmaṇvatī, Prabhāsa, the mouth of the Sarasvatī (70–80), Dvāravatī, the mouth of the Indus (80–85). the River Pañcanada (100), Devikā (110–15), Sarasvatī's Vināśana (115), and Rudrakoṭi,

where Rudra created a crore of Rudras, one for each of a number of seers who were competing in honoring him (120–25), the confluence of the Sarasvatī (130).
81 (83; 6071). The greatness of Kurukṣetra (1–5), Viṣṇu's ford of Satata (5–10), the Lakes of Rāma filled with the blood of the baronage; Rāma's ancestors gave him a boon, and he asked for austerities and removal of his guilt for massacring the barons (20–30). Brahmāvarta (40), Mṛgadhūma, dedicated to Śiva (85), Naimiṣa (90), Saptasārasvata; here Mankanaka cut his finger, and vegetable juice flowed out of the wound. Transported with joy he began to dance and soon all the world danced with him (95–100). The Gods resort to Śiva to stop him. Śiva shows him that he has white ashes in his veins. The seer praises him (100–10). The place has remained sacred (110–15). Praise of Pṛthūdaka (125), Saṃnihitī (165–70), and Kurukṣetra (170–75).
82 (84; 7079). The Saugandhika Forest and the River Sarasvatī (1–5). Śākaṃbharī, where the Goddess long lived on greens (10–15). Suvarṇākṣa, where Viṣṇu placated Rudra (15). Praise of Naimiṣa (50–55). Benares, which is dedicated to Rudra (65). Gayā (80–85). Śālāgrāma, which is dedicated to Viṣṇu (105).
83 (85; 8143). The mouth of the Ganges and the island of the Ganges (5). Mount Ṛṣabha in the land of the Pāṇḍyas (15). The River Kāverī; praise of Gokarṇa (20–25). The rivers Veṇṇā and Kṛṣṇaveṇṇā (30–35). The Tungaka Forest where the Vedas are revived (40–50). Praise of Prayāga, the confluence of the Yamunā and Ganges (65–80). Bhīṣma is exhorted by Pulastya to go on a pilgrimage; Pulastya leaves (90–95). Nārada likewise exhorts Yudhiṣṭhira; many seers have gone before (95–105), Lomaśa will come and guide Yudhiṣṭhira, who will attain the fame of great kings (105).
84 (86; 8278). Yudhiṣṭhira dwells, before Dhaumya, on Arjuna's greatness (1–5). Arjuna shall slay Karṇa, after obtaining divine weapons (5–15). Yudhiṣṭhira will no longer live in the Kāmyaka Forest without Arjuna (15–20).
85 (87; 8297). Dhaumya, to comfort the Pāṇḍavas, describes the Sacred Fords, beginning with those of the East (1). The River Kauśikī and Viśvāmitra; Prayāga (5–10).

86 (88; 8329). The tīrthas *of the South. The River Payoṣṇī and King Nṛga (1–5). Agastya's hermitage (10–15). Surāṣṭra and Dvāravatī of Kṛṣṇa, who is praised (15–20).*
87 (89; 8356). The tīrthas *of the West, in Avanti (1–15).*
88 (90; 8372). The tīrthas *of the North. The Sarasvatī and Yamunā, an old sacrificial site of Sahadeva and Bharata (1–10). Praise of Nārāyaṇa (20–25).*
89 (91; 8407). The seer Lomaśa arrives and is welcomed (1). Lomaśa relates having seen Arjuna on Indra's throne; Arjuna has obtained a weapon from Rudra, and others from the World Guardians (5–10). Indra sends a message through Lomaśa: Yudhiṣṭhira should not be afraid of Karṇa, but go on a pilgrimage (15–20).
90 (92; 8432). Arjuna's message is that Yudhiṣṭhira visit the tīrthas *under Lomaśa's protection (1–5). Lomaśa promises Yudhiṣṭhira to be his guide (5–10). Yudhiṣṭhira is overjoyed; he dismisses the brahmins and citizens who had followed him (15–20). The latter leave for Hāstinapura where Dhṛtarāṣṭra receives them. Some brahmins remain with Yudhiṣṭhira (20).*
91 (93; 8458). The remaining brahmins ask permission to come along on the pilgrimage, which is granted (1–15). When the party is about to set out, Vyāsa, Nārada, and Parvata appear and exhort Yudhiṣṭhira; they bless his journey (15–20). They depart on fourteen chariots (20–25).
92 (94; 8487). Yudhiṣṭhira complains that while he, a virtuous man, suffers, his evil foes prosper (1). Lomaśa points out that lawlessness was the downfall of the Asuras (1–10). The Gods, however, went on pilgrimages; so did great kings (15–20). The Dhārtarāṣṭras will perish like the Asuras (20).
93 (95; 8509). The party reaches the Naimiṣa Forest, the River Gomatī, and Prayāga (1–5). They proceed to Gayā, where they sacrifice (10–15). A brahmin tells of King Gaya, who was a great and generous sacrificer (15–25).
94–108 Agastya.
109 (110; 9968). Yudhiṣṭhira proceeds to Mount Hemakūṭa, where landslides threaten continuously and rain falls constantly (1–5). Lomaśa explains that the

ascetic Ṛṣabha, irritated at talkative people, caused the landslide phenomenon to stop them from talking (5–10). The Gods, angered at the people who follow them around, reinforce the phenomenon with rain (10). They proceed to the River Kauśikī (15–20).
110–13 Ṛśyaśṛnga.
114 (114; 10095). Yudhiṣṭhira proceeds to the River Kauśikī and the country of Kalinga (1). Lomaśa explains that this is a sacrificial site of the Gods; here Rudra claimed his share of the sacrifices and took the animal; at the Gods' entreaties he released it (1–10). They bathe in the River Vaitaraṇī; by bathing Yudhiṣṭhira acquires far-distant hearing (10–15). In the local wood Svayaṃbhū Viśvakarman gave Earth to Kaśyapa; indignant, Earth threatened to repair to Rasātala and went under water; she reemerged, placated by Kaśyapa's austerities, in the form of an altar (15–20). At Lomaśa's advice Yudhiṣṭhira pronounces a benediction on the altar (20–25).
115–17 Kārtavīrya.
118 (118; 10214). Yudhiṣṭhira proceeds to the River Godāvarī, the Draviḍa country, and the Ford Śūrpāraka (1–10). He goes on to Prabhāsa. Kṛṣṇa and Rāma meet the Pāṇḍavas (15–20).
119 (119; 10237). At Janamejaya's bidding Vaiśaṃpāyana relates their conversation. Rāma comments on Yudhiṣṭhira's untoward fate and the Kauravas' good fortune. He predicts that the Pāṇḍavas will win out in the end (1–20).
120 (120; 10259). Sātyaki advocates that the Dāśārhas march on Hāstinapura and destroy the Kauravas; nothing is impossible for those warriors (1–15). Abhimanyu will govern, while Yudhiṣṭhira completes his vow (20). Kṛṣṇa replies that Yudhiṣṭhira will not agree (20–25). Yudhiṣṭhira promises to call on the Vṛṣṇis when the time is ripe (25). They part; Yudhiṣṭhira goes to the River Payoṣṇī (25–30).
121–25 Sukanyā.
126 Māndhātar.
127–28 Jantu.
129 (129; 10513). Lomaśa praises the Gate of Kurukṣetra on the Yamunā. By touching water there Yudhiṣṭhira sees all the worlds (1–15). They proceed to the Sarasvatī (20).
130 (130; 10536). Lomaśa points to the river's

vanishing point and its Cāmasa spring (1–5). They see Prabhāsa and go to Kaśmīr and Lake Mānasa (5–15). They visit Mount Bhṛgutunga (15–20).
131 The Hawk and the Dove.
132–34 Aṣṭāvakra.
135–37 Yavakrīta.
140 (139; 10820). The party presses north toward Badarī. Lomaśa betrays apprehension; he directs Bhīma to look especially well after Draupadī (1–15).
141 (140; 10839). Yudhiṣṭhira suggests that Bhīma return with Draupadī, Sahadeva, and the servants; he, Nakula, and Lomaśa will alone go on to Kailāsa (1–5). Bhīma declares that her desire to see Arjuna will sustain her. Bhīma will not turn back, nor will Sahadeva; if necessary he will carry Draupadī. Yudhiṣṭhira gives in (5–20). They meet King Subāhu in the Himālaya, who welcomes them. The party now proceeds on foot (20–30).
142 (141; 10870). Yudhiṣṭhira relates how he misses Arjuna, whose feats he describes (1–20). He wishes to carry on to Badarī and the Hermitage of Nara and Nārāyaṇa in the Gandhamādana range to find Arjuna (20–25).
143 (143; 10899). They start for the Gandhamādana (1–5). A gale rises, and they are blinded by the dust; they run for cover (5–15). The gale abates and heavy rains fall (15–20). Afterward they go on (20).
144 (144; 10986). Draupadī faints and is caught by Nakula. Yudhiṣṭhira blames himself (1–10). The brahmins utter blessings; Draupadī is comforted and comes to (10–20). Bhīma summons his Rākṣasa son Ghaṭotkaca (20–25).
145 (145; 11013). At Yudhiṣṭhira's behest, Bhīma orders Ghaṭotkaca to carry Draupadī; other Rākṣasas carry the Pāṇḍavas and brahmins; thus they fly to Mount Kailāsa (1–15). They behold the idyllic Hermitage of Nara and Nārāyaṇa and the jujube tree (1–20). They descend and see Vedic priests, who greet them joyously (20–35). The Pāṇḍavas dwell happily in the hermitage (35–40).
146 (146; 11058). They stay six days waiting for Arjuna (1–5). A northeasterly wind carries a saugandhika *flower. Delighted, Draupadī asks Bhīma to fetch her more flowers (5–10). Bhīma sets out; the scene is lovely (10–30). Bhīma worries how Yudhiṣṭhira will*

fare without Arjuna and himself, but presses on (35–40). He reaches a banana tree orchard, which he devastates; the animals flee (40–50). He sees flocks of water birds and follows them to a lake (50–55). The monkey Hanūmān, dozing, hears Bhīma's roar and responds by slapping his tail (55–60). Bhīma goes to investigate and finds Hanūmān, whom he tries to frighten. Hanūmān scolds him (60–80).

147 (147; 11166). *Bhīma bridles and identifies himself; Hanūmān refuses to make way, for he is too feeble (1–5). Bhīma states that if he did not believe that the Supreme dwelled in the monkey, he would jump over him as Hanūmān jumped the ocean. But he threatens to kill him unless he gives way (5–10). Hanūmān invites Bhīma to lift up his tail; he is incapable of it (15–20). Hanūmān identifies himself as Bhīma's half-brother and sketches the story of Rāma in outline (20–35). Hanūmān had asked Rāma the boon of surviving as long as the story of Rāma. Many thousands of years have passed since (35–40).*

148 (149; 11225). *Bhīma prostrates himself and asks to see the form Hanūmān assumed when he jumped the ocean. Hanūmān demurs: it is the wrong age for that (1–5). Description of the Kṛtayuga (10–20), the Tretā (20–25), the Dvāpara (25–30), and the Kali (30–35).*

149 (150; 11265). *Hanūmān assumes part of his old form, which is colossal. Bhīma says that Hanūmān alone could have taken on Rāvaṇa; he agrees, but he had wanted to leave Rāma the glory (1–15). He directs Bhīma to the* saugandhika *forest and praises the Law (15–35). The Law of the baron (35–50).*

150 (151–52; 11315). *The two embrace and part, after Hanūmān has promised to reinforce Bhīma's roar (1–15). Bhīma continues his journey and comes to a river pond (15–25).*

151 (153; 11352). *It is filled with* saugandhika *flowers and guarded by Rākṣasas, who question Bhīma (1–15).*

152 (154; 11367). *The Rākṣasas point out that this is Kubera's playground; he should give permission to pluck flowers (1–5). Bhīma challenges this (5–10). The Rākṣasas attack him and are defeated (5–20). They report to Kubera, who laughingly gives Bhīma permission (20–25).*

153 (155; 11395). *Bhīma gathers flowers. Meanwhile,*

when a gale rises, Yudhiṣṭhira notices Bhīma's absence (1–10). Draupadī explains his errand (10–15). Yudhiṣṭhira orders Ghaṭotkaca to take them to Bhīma, which he does (15–20). Yudhiṣṭhira berates Bhīma for his slaughter of the demons (20–25). All live happily in Kubera's park (25–30).

Vaiśaṃpāyana said:

80.1 Thus, missing Dhanaṃjaya, the lordly warlike Pāṇḍavas lived in the
forest with Draupadī. Then they saw Nārada, the great-spirited divine
seer, blazing with his brahminic luster, splendid like glowing fire. The
illustrious elder of the Kurus, surrounded by his brothers, shone wide
with an august effulgence like the God of the Hundred Sacrifices* in
the midst of the Gods. As the Sāvitrī does not desert the *Vedas*, nor the
light of the sun Mount Meru, so the good Yājñasenī did not according
to Law relinquish the Pārthas.
5 The blessed seer Nārada accepted their honors and reassured the
son of Dharma in proper terms, prince sans blame. And he said to
Yudhiṣṭhira the great-spirited King Dharma, "Speak, best of the
upholders of the Law, of what are you in need, what shall I give you?"
The king, son of Dharma, bowed with his brothers, and, folding his
hands, he said to the Godlike Nārada, "When you are content, great
lord, who are honored in all the worlds, methinks the throw is won by
your grace, saint of good vows! Yet if you have favor for me and my
brothers, great hermit sans blame, then prey resolve a doubt that has
10 lodged in my heart. If a man makes a sunwise tour of the earth to
visit the sacred fords, what reward accrues to him? Please propound
this entirely, brahmin!"

Nārada said:

Listen attentively, sire, to all that Bhīṣma heard from Pulastya, O Bhārata.

Once Bhīṣma, the best of the upholders of the Law, was living on the bank of the Ganges like a hermit, when he was observing a vow on behalf of his father, great king, at a holy spot, sacred and frequented by divine seers. The splendid man sat at the Gate-of-the-Ganges, visited by Gods and Gandharvas. Sublimely lustrous Bhīṣma offered to his ancestors and the Gods and satisfied the seers with the rite that is found in the Rules.

15 After some time, when the ascetic was praying, he saw Pulastya,
the great seer of wondrous appearance. Seeing the saint of awesome
austerities, fairly blazing with fortune, he was seized with unmatched
joy and overcome by the greatest amazement. He welcomed him on

* = Indra.

his arrival, great King Bhārata, did Bhīṣma, the best of the upholders
of the Law, with the rite that is found in the Rules. Holding the guest
gift on his head, the pure man, with thoughts intent, called out his
name to the great brahminic seer, "I am Bhīṣma, bless you, your
servitor, man of good vows. By merely looking at you I am freed from
20 all my sins!" Having said this, great king, Bhīṣma, best of the
upholders of Law, minded his speech and with folded hands he stood
and fell silent, Yudhiṣṭhira. And looking at Bhīṣma who had been worn
thin by his Vedic study and recitation, the hermit was pleased to
address the elder of the line of the Kurus.

Pulastya said:

I am completely satisfied, lordly scholar of the Law, with the
humility you show, and your control and veracity. It is because of this
Law of you, who are devoted to loyalty to your father, prince sans
blame, that you now see me and I have become pleased with you, son.
My vision is never troubled, Bhīṣma: tell me, what can I do for you?
I shall give you, prince sans blame, best of the Kurus, whatever you
ask.

Bhīṣma said:

25 When you are pleased, lordly sir, who are honored in all the worlds,
methinks the throw has been won, for I have set eyes upon you! Yet
if you have favor for me, best of the bearers of the Law, I shall speak
of a doubt in my heart; you, pray, resolve it. I have, blessed lord, a
doubt concerning the Law that derives from the sacred fords; and this
I should like to hear explained by you, with respect to every one of
them. A person who makes a sunwise tour of the earth, boundlessly
mighty brahmin seer, what reward does accrue to him, tell me that,
ascetic!

Pulastya said:

Aye, I shall propound to you the final goal of the seers: listen with
30 attentive mind to what reward accrues from the sacred fords. He who
has mastered his hands, feet, mind, knowledge, mortification, and
good repute attains to the reward of the fords. He who has retired
from possessions and is contented, restrained, pure, and without
selfishness, obtains the reward of the fords. He who is without deceit,
without designs, of lean diet, in control of his senses, and free from all
vices, he obtains the reward of the fords. The man without anger, O
Indra among princes, with the habit of truthfulness and firm in his
vows, who sees in the creatures the images of himself, obtains the
reward of the fords.

In the *Veda* the seers have expounded with precision the series of
35 the rituals and also the reward of all of them here and hereafter. A
poor man cannot rise to the sacrifices, for they require many
implements and a great variety of ingredients. Kings rise to them and

some rich folk, not those lacking in means and implements, who are
alone and without an establishment. But hear to what injunction even
the poor can rise, equaling the holy rewards of sacrifices. This is the
highest mystery of the seers—the holy visitation of sacred fords, which
even surpasses the sacrifices. Poor indeed becomes only he who has
never fasted for three nights and days, has never visited the fords, and
40 has not given away gold and cows. One may sacrifice with the Laud-of-the-Fire and other rites of rich stipends, yet not reap the reward that
visiting the fords brings.

A man of good fortune will visit in the world of men the famous
ford of the God of Gods, renowned in the three worlds, which is called
Puṣkara. At the three joints of the day ten thousand crores of sacred
places are present in Puṣkara. The Ādityas, Vasus, Rudras, Sādhyas,
and the band of the Maruts are always present there, lord, as well as
the Gandharvas and Apsarās. It is there that the Gods, Daityas, and
brahmin seers mortified themselves and, possessed of great merit,
45 achieved divine yoga. A man of spirit who, even if just in thought, has
a desire for Puṣkara is freed from all sins and honored on the rooftree
of heaven. In that same ford dwells forever and most joyously the
Grandfather esteemed by Gods and Dānavas. The Gods led by the seers
all together found perfection together in Puṣkara, possessing great
merit. The man who, devoted to the worship of Gods and ancestors,
does his ablutions there attains, the wise say, to ten Horse Sacrifices.
If he visits the Puṣkara wood and feeds but a single brahmin, he
50 rejoices because of his act both here and hereafter. If he himself just
lives on potherbs, roots, and fruit and gives that to a brahmin,
faithfully and without demurring, this wise man achieves by that very
act the fruit of a Horse Sacrifice. If great-spirited brahmins, barons,
commoners, or serfs bathe at this ford, they are not reborn in lower
forms. A person who goes to Puṣkara, especially on the full-moon
night of Kārttika, has the reward thereof grow inexhaustible. When
one with folded hands calls Puṣkara to mind in the morning and the
evening, it is the equivalent of bathing at all the fords; and in the seat
of Brahmā he earns worlds without end. Whatever evil a woman or a
man has done since birth is all destroyed by just a bath at Puṣkara.
55 Just as Madhusūdana* is the beginning of all the Gods, so is Puṣkara
said to be the beginning of the fords. A sojourn of twelve years in
Puṣkara makes a controlled and pure man achieve all the sacrifices
and reach the world of Brahmā. A man who offers the *agnihotra* for a
full hundred years and the man who stays in Puṣkara one full-moon
night of Kārttika are equal. Puṣkara is hard to reach, austerities in
Puṣkara are hard, gifts in Puṣkara are hard, to live there is very hard.

* = Kṛṣṇa.

After having stayed in Puṣkara for twelve nights, restrained and of meager diet, the pilgrim should circumambulate it and proceed to Jambūmārga. When one has entered Jambūmārga, which is frequented by the Gods, seers, and ancestors, he rises to the Horse Sacrifice and goes to Viṣṇu's world. A man who eats only every sixth meal and stays there for five nights will suffer no reverses and attain to ultimate fulfilment.

Departing from Jambūmārga, he should go on to Tāṇḍulikāśrama; he will suffer no reverses and be honored in the world of heaven. When he reaches Agastya's-Lake, a man, devoted to the worship of Gods and ancestors, who stays there for three nights, obtains the fruit of the Laud-of-the-Fire. Living on vegetables and fruits, he next finds the Step-of-Kumāra when he reaches Kaṇva's Hermitage, which is visited by good fortune and honored in the world. For that is the principal sacred forest of the Law, bull of the Bharatas, and as soon as one sets foot there he is freed from his evil. By worshiping ancestors and Gods, restrained and of meager diet, one obtains the fruit of a sacrifice that bestows all wishes. After circumambulating it he should go on to Yayāti's-Fall, and he obtains there the reward of a Horse Sacrifice.

From there he should go on, restrained and of meager diet, to Mahākalā and, by bathing at the Ten-Million-Ford, attain to the reward of a Horse Sacrifice. Thence proceed to the sacred place of Umā's Consort, Bhadravaṭa by name, which is famed in the three worlds. By going there to the Lord one can obtain the reward of a gift of a thousand cows and, by the grace of the Great God, attain to the rank of a Gaṇapati.

Traveling on to the River Narmadā, famous in the three worlds, and satisfying the ancestors and Gods with oblations, one obtains the reward of a Laud-of-the-Fire. Carrying on to the Southern River, while remaining chaste and the master of one's senses, one rises to the Laud-of-the-Fire and ascends a celestial chariot. Proceeding now to the Carmaṇvatī River, restrained and of meager diet, one obtains, with Rantideva's leave, the fruit of a Laud-of-the-Fire. Then one goes on to Arbuda, son of Himālaya, where at one time there was a chasm in the earth, Yudhiṣṭhira. Vasiṣṭha's hermitage was there, known in the three worlds, and by sleeping one night there one obtains the fruit of a thousand cattle. Chaste and master of one's senses, one should bathe at the Pinga Ford and thus obtain the fruit of a gift of a hundred red cows. From there one should go on to world-famous Prabhāsa, where the oblation-carrying fire is always present in person, the wind-driven fire, mouth of the Gods. When a man bathes at that eminent ford, pure and of humble mind, he obtains the fruit of both the Laud-of-the-Fire and the Overnight Sacrifice.

Continuing to the place where the Sarasvatī debouches in the
ocean, one obtains the reward of a gift of a thousand cows and
glories in the world of heaven, blazing forever with splendor like fire,
80 O bull of the Bharatas. Staying there for three nights, one should
offer to ancestors and Gods and shine like the moon, and rise to the
Horse Sacrifice. Thereafter, one should go on to the Gift-of-the-Boon,
where Durvāsas gave a boon to Viṣṇu, Yudhiṣṭhira; a bath there
brings the reward of a gift of a thousand cows. From there, one should
proceed to Dvāravatī, restrained and of meager diet, and by bathing
at Piṇḍāraka obtain the reward of a gift of much gold. In that ford,
until today, there are found seals marked with the stamp of the five
signs, a marvel indeed, and lotuses marked with the sign of the
Trident: the Great God is present here.
85 Going on to the confluence of the Indus and the ocean, one should
with a humble mind bathe at the ford of the king of water, offer to
ancestors, Gods, and seers, in order to obtain Varuṇa's world, while
blazing with one's own splendor. By worshiping the divine Lord of
the Conchlike Ears,* there is a tenfold Horse Sacrifice, so the wise say,
Yudhiṣṭhira. After circumambulating it, one should continue to a ford
that is famous in the three worlds, renowned under the name of
Dṛmi, which absolves all evil, where Brahmā and the other Gods pay
worship to the Great Lord. By bathing there and worshiping Rudra
in the midst of the hosts of Gods, a man pushes off all the evil he has
90 done since his birth. Dṛmi is praised by all the Gods; by bathing there
one rises to a Horse Sacrifice. It is here that majestic Viṣṇu once
cleansed himself after killing the rivals of the Gods.

From thence one should travel to the hymned Bearer-of-Treasure:
by just going there, one attains to a Horse Sacrifice. By bathing there
and offering to Gods and ancestors, a man of pious mind glories in
the world of Viṣṇu. There is a sublime and holy ford of the Vasus
there; by bathing and drinking there, one becomes the favorite of the
95 Vasus. Then there is a spot called Sindhūttama, which dispels all evil;
and by bathing there, one obtains much gold. Going on to
Brahmatunga while pure and of pious mind, a man of good deeds and
no passion attains to the world of Brahmā. On to the Ford-of-the-
Daughter-of-Indra, visited by the Siddhas; having bathed there a man
soon attains to the world of Indra. In the same area is the ford of
Reṇukā, which is frequented by the Gods; bathing there a brahmin
becomes pure like the moon.

Then one should go to Pañcanada, restrained and of meager diet,
and attain, one after the other, to the five sacrifices that are extolled.
100 From there one should travel to the prominent Site-of-Bhīma; by
bathing there, in the Womb, a man will become a Goddess's son,

* = Varuṇa.

wearing a body with earrings of refined gold, and obtain the great
reward of a gift of a hundred thousand cows. Proceeding to
Girimuñja, famed in the three worlds, and paying homage to the
Grandfather, one obtains the reward of a thousand cows. Then one
goes to the eminent ford called Vimala, where even today gold and
silver fish are seen; by bathing there, one rises to the Horse-Race
Sacrifice, and, one's soul cleansed of all evil, goes the best journey.
105 From there on one should go to Maladā, famed in the three worlds,
and at the western twilight do the ritual ablutions. One should
according to ability offer a *caru* oblation of rice boiled in milk and
butter to the seven-flamed fire; the wise say that this offering to the
ancestors becomes inexhaustible. This oblation in the fire surpasses a
hundred thousand cows, a hundred Royal Consecrations, and a
thousand Horse Sacrifices. Departing from there, one should proceed
to Vastrapāda and, by visiting the Great God* there, obtain the fruit
of a Horse Sacrifice. Going on to Maṇimat, chaste and diligent, and
staying there for one night, one obtains the reward of a Laud-of-the-
Fire.
110 Then one should proceed to world-famous Devikā, where, so it has
been revealed, the brahmins originated, the place—renowned in the
three worlds—of the Trident-wielder;* by bathing at Devikā and
worshiping the Great Lord, and, according to ability, offering a *caru*
oblation, a man obtains the reward of a sacrifice that bestows all
wishes. There is a ford of Rudra there, by the name of Kāma,
frequented by Gods and seers; when one bathes there, he soon
achieves success. Continuing to Yajana, Yājana, and Brahmavāluka
115 and bathing at Puṇyanyāsa, one will not worry over death. They say
that sacred Devikā, visited by Gods and seers, is five leagues long and
half a league wide.

Thereupon one should gradually go to Dīrghasattra, where the
Gods led by Brahmā, the Siddhas, and eminent seers attended a long
Session with stipends, strict in their vows. By going to Dīrghasattra
a man obtains the reward of a Royal Consecration and a Horse
Sacrifice. Then, restrained and of meager diet, one should go to
Vināśana, where the Sarasvatī disappears in the desert and reappears
at Camasodbheda, Śivodbheda, and Nāgodbheda. Having bathed at
Camasodbheda, one rises to a Horse Sacrifice, at Śivodbheda to a gift
of a thousand cows, and at Nāgodbheda to the World of the Snakes.
120 Continuing to Śaśāyana, a ford that is hard to find, where the lotuses
hide yearlong under the guise of rabbits and bathe in the Ganges
when the full moon in Kārttika comes around—by bathing there one
shines like the moon and obtains the reward of a gift of a thousand
cows.

* = Śiva.

Traveling onward to Kumārakoṭi, self-controlled, one should bathe there, devoted to the worship of Ancestors and Gods, and thus acquire the reward of a Gavāmayana. Then one should go diligently to Rudrakoṭi, where once a crore of seers came diligently and joyfully,
125 desirous of seeing the God. They approached, saying, "I shall be the first to see the bull-bannered God," and "I shall be the first to see him," as the story goes, O king. To prevent these seers of cultivated souls from becoming angry, the Lord of Yoga resorted to his yoga and created a crore of Rudras, one before each of the seers, so that each thought that he had seen him first. Pleased with the great devotion of these seers of awesome splendor, the Great God awarded them a boon: "Henceforth you shall increase in the Law!" A pure man who bathes at Rudrakoṭi obtains the reward of a Horse Sacrifice and saves his family.

130 From thence one should go to the world-famous and very holy confluence of the Sarasvatī, where the Gods led by Brahmā, the seers, Siddhas, and Cāraṇas go on the fourteenth of the bright fortnight and worship Janārdana. By bathing there one will find much gold and, his soul freed from all evil, go to the world of Brahmā. Proceeding to Sattravāsana, where the Sessions of the seers were accomplished, one will obtain the reward of a gift of a thousand cows.

Pulastya said:

81.1 Thence one should go on, great king, to much-lauded Kurukṣetra: all men who go there are freed from their evil. One who constantly says, "I shall go to Kurukṣetra, I shall live in Kurukṣetra," is freed from evil. One should dwell a month by the Sarasvatī, Yudhiṣṭhira, where the Gods led by Brahmā, the seers, Siddhas, Cāraṇas, Gandharvas, Apsarās, Yakṣas, and Snakes visit holy Brahmakṣetra.
5 If one desires to go to Kurukṣetra, even in thought, all his evil disappears and he goes to the World of Brahmā. For by going to Kurukṣetra in a spirit of faith a man obtains the fruit of a Royal Consecration and a Horse Sacrifice. When one has saluted there the Yakṣa Macakruka, the mighty gate-keeper, one will obtain the reward of a gift of a thousand cows.

One should then go on to Viṣṇu's incomparable place, of the name of Satata, where Hari is present. By bathing there and worshiping Hari, the source of the three worlds, one obtains the reward of a
10 Horse Sacrifice and attains to Viṣṇu's world. Thence one should proceed to the ford of Pariplava, renowned in the three worlds; one obtains the fruit of a Laud-of-the-Fire and an Overnight Sacrifice. Continuing to the ford of Pṛthivī, one will obtain the reward of a gift of a thousand cows; then going on to Śālūkinī, the pilgrim, by bathing at the Daśāśvamedhika, obtains that very reward. By visiting

Sarpadarvī, the greatest ford of the Snakes, one acquires the reward
of a Laud-of-the-Fire and finds the World of the Snakes. From there
one should go to the Gatekeeper Tarantuka and, by staying there one
night, obtain the fruit of a thousand cows.

Proceeding from there to Pañcanada, restrained and of meager diet,
one should bathe at the Koṭi Ford and acquire the reward of a Horse
Sacrifice; by going to the ford of the Aśvins one is reborn handsome.
15 Thence one goes to the eminent ford of the Boar, where at one time
Viṣṇu stayed in the form of a boar; when one bathes there one
obtains the fruit of a Laud-of-the-Fire. One should then approach the
ford of Soma at Jayantī; the man who bathes there has the reward of
a Royal Consecration; and by bathing at Ekahaṃsa the fruit of a
thousand cows.

The pilgrim who goes on to Kṛtaśauca, O scion of Kuru, obtains
the fruit of the Puṇḍarīka if he has cleansed himself. Then, continuing
to the Muñjavaṭa of the wise Great God and staying there for one
night, one attains to the rank of a Gaṇapati. In the same area there is
a world-famous Yakṣī; by attending on her one attains to blissful
20 worlds. This is known as the Gate of Kurukṣetra, O bull of the
Bharatas; after doing the circumambulation and bathing at that place
that equals the Puṣkaras and worshiping ancestors and Gods, at this
place that was set up by the great-spirited Jāmadagnya, the diligent
pilgrim becomes acquitted of his tasks, O king, and finds the reward
of a Horse Sacrifice.

From there the pilgrim should proceed to the lakes of Rāma, where
Rāma of blazing splendor, after his eradication of the baronage,
energetically and powerfully created five lakes, filling them, so we
have heard, with blood. Thus he satiated his fathers and grandfathers;
whereupon those pleased ascetics said to Rāma, "Rāma, lordly Rāma,
we are pleased, Bhārgava, with this your devotion to your ancestors
and with your bravery, O lord. Be blessed, choose a boon! What do
you wish, magnificent man?"

25 At these words of his ancestors, great king, Rāma, greatest of
fighters, spoke with folded hands this word to his ancestors who were
standing in the sky: "If you are pleased with me and if I am to be
favored, then by my ancestors' grace I wish for satiety in self-
mortification. And may I, by the grace of your splendor, be rid of the
evil I incurred by eradicating the baronage in my fury. And may my
lakes become sacred places, renowned on earth." When they heard
Rāma's auspicious words, the fathers were most pleased and rejoiced
greatly; and they said to Rāma, "Because of your superior devotion
30 to your forebears, your austerities shall grow ever greater. You are
free of any evil on account of your furious eradication of the
baronage: they were brought down by their own acts. Your lakes

will beyond doubt become places of sanctity. If one bathes in these lakes and offers to his ancestors, his pleased fathers will give him his heart's desire, however hard to attain on earth, and the everlasting world of heaven." After having thus given boons to Rāma, O king, his pleased ancestors bade the Bhārgava farewell and vanished on the spot.

So did the lakes of the great-spirited Rāma Bhārgava come to be. By bathing chastely in Rāma's lakes and worshiping Rāma, a man of good vows will obtain much gold.

Proceeding to Vaṃśamūlaka, O scion of Kuru, the pilgrim will rescue his own lineage by bathing there. Going on to the ford Kāyaśodhana, one obtains without doubt purity of body, if he bathes, and goes with his pure body to incomparable holy worlds. From there he should continue to the ford famous in the three worlds, where the puissant Viṣṇu once rescued the worlds: by visiting the Rescue-of-the-World, famed in the three worlds, and bathing there, one will rescue one's own worlds; and by going to the ford of Śrī he finds supreme fortune. Traveling to the ford of Kapilā, chastely and diligently, bathing there, and worshiping the deities and ancestors, a man finds the fruit of a gift of a thousand ruddy cows.

Approaching now the ford of the Sun, he should bathe there with restrained mind; by fasting and worshiping the ancestors and Gods he rises to a Laud-of-the-Fire, and goes to the world of the Sun. When the pilgrim next goes to the House-of-the-Cows and does his ablutions there, he will obtain the fruit of a thousand cows. Going on to the Śankhinī Ford there, the pilgrim, by bathing in the ford of the Goddess, will obtain a beautiful appearance. From there he should continue to the Gatekeeper Arantuka, to the ford of that mighty and great-spirited Yakṣa in the River Sarasvatī; by bathing there a man obtains the fruit of a Laud-of-the-Fire.

Thence he should go to Brahmāvarta, O law-wise king; a man who bathes at Brahmāvarta will attain to the world of Brahmā. He should then continue on to peerless Sutīrtha, where the ancestors and the deities are always present. He should do his ablutions there, intent upon the worship of ancestors and Gods; thus he rises to a Horse Sacrifice, and goes to the World of the Ancestors. Journeying next to Ambuvaśya: by bathing in the fords of the Lord of Treasures, one is freed from all diseases and glories in the world of Brahmā. There is also the Ford-of-the-Mother: when a man bathes there, his offspring increases and he attains to unending prosperity.

Thereupon he should go, restrained and of meager diet, to the Śītavana Ford: there is sanctity there unobtainable elsewhere, which alone purifies in one blow if one merely looks at it; by sprinkling one's hair one becomes pure. There is a spot there, Śvānalomāpaha,

where there are wise brahmins devoted to that ford. Superior
brahmins at this ford Śvānalomāpanayana pull out dog's-hairs with
breath exercises; and, of pure souls, they go the greatest journey.
Then there is the Daśāśvamedhika: by bathing at this ford one goes
the greatest journey. From there one should go on to the world-
famous Mānuṣa, where black antelopes, harassed by a hunter, once
plunged into the lake and became human. By bathing there a man
who is chaste and master of his senses is cleansed of all evil and
55 glories in the world of heaven. The distance of a cry east of Mānuṣa
there is a river called Apagā, visited by the Siddhas; when a man
offers there a meal of millet to Gods and ancestors, he will be richly
rewarded. When one brahmin is fed there, it is as though a crore of
them have been fed. By bathing there and worshiping deities and
ancestors, and staying overnight, one obtains the fruit of a Laud-of-
the-Fire.

From there one should proceed to Brahmā's greatest sanctuary,
which is noted on earth as Brahmā's *udumbara* tree. When one bathes
there in the Wells-of-the-Seven-Seers and at the Meadow-of-the-
60 Great-Spirited-Kapisthala, and draws near to Brahmā himself, pure
and of devoted mind, his soul is cleansed of all evil and he attains to
the world of Brahmā. When one has gone to the Meadow-of-
Kapisthala, which is hard to find, his sins are burned off and he
obtains the gift of disappearance. Thereupon one should go to world-
renowned Saraka and approach the Bull-bannered God on the
fourteenth of the dark fortnight; for thus one obtains all his desires
and goes to the world of heaven. In Saraka there are three crores of
holy places; a crore of Rudras are in the wells and the lakes. There
is also there the Abode-of-Ilā Ford: by bathing there and worshiping
the ancestors and Gods one suffers no misfortune and finds the
Horse-Race Festival.

65 By bathing at Kiṃdāna and Kiṃjapya a man finds the fruit of
countless gifts and prayers. By ablutions at Kalaśī a man of faith who
has mastered his senses attains to the reward of the sacrifice of the
Laud-of-the-Fire. East of Saraka there is the ford of the great-spirited
Nārada, known as Anājanma. When one has bathed there and
subsequently expires, he obtains, with Nārada's consent, worlds that
are hard of access. On the tenth of the bright fortnight one should go
to Puṇḍarīka: by bathing there a man will obtain the fruit of a
70 Puṇḍarīka sacrifice. From there he should go to Triviṣṭapa, well-
known in the three worlds, where flows the auspicious River
Vaitaraṇī, which releases from evil. By bathing there and worshiping
the Bull-bannered Trident-wielder, one's soul is cleansed of all evil
and one will go the greatest journey. Then one should proceed to
superb Phalakīvana, where the Gods always seek recourse and for

many thousands of years have performed many austerities. By bathing
in the Dṛṣadvatī and satisfying the deities, a man finds the reward of
a Laud-of-the-Fire and an Overnight Sacrifice. When one bathes at the
75 Ford-of-All-the-Gods, he obtains the fruit of a thousand cows. By
bathing at Pāṇikhātā and offering to the Gods, he rises to the Royal
Consecration and goes to the world of the seers.

From there one should continue to the great ford of Miśraka: there,
so we have heard, the great-spirited Vyāsa mixed all the fords for the
sake of the brahmins. He who bathes at Miśraka bathes at all
the fords. One should go there to the Grove-of-Vyāsa, restrained and
of meager diet, and by bathing at the Manojava attain the fruit of a
thousand cows. Proceeding to Madhuvatī, a ford of the Goddess, and
bathing there, and devoutly and purely worshiping Gods and
ancestors, one will obtain, with the Goddess's consent, the fruit of a
80 thousand cows. He who, keeping a meager diet, bathes at the
confluence of the Kauśikī and the Dṛṣadvatī is freed from all sins.
Then there is Vyāsasthalī, where the wise Vyāsa, consumed with grief
over his son, resolved to give up the body and was resurrected by the
Gods. By going to Sthalī one obtains the fruit of a thousand cows.
If one goes to the Kiṃdatta Well and proffers a measure of sesame
seeds, one finds supreme success and is released from his debts. Ahās
and Sudina are two fords that are hard to find; by bathing there one
goes to the world of the Sun.

85 Then one should proceed to Mṛgadhūma, famous in the three
worlds; by bathing there in the Gaṅgā Lake and worshiping the Great
God who wields the Trident, one obtains the fruit of a Horse Sacrifice.
By bathing at Devatīrtha one acquires the reward of a thousand cows.
Thereupon one should continue to Vāmanaka, renowned in the three
worlds; bathing there at the Step-of-Viṣṇu and worshiping the Dwarf,
one's soul is cleansed of all evil and one will attain to the world of
Viṣṇu. By bathing at Kulampuna one purifies his family. By going to
the Lake-of-the-Wind, the great ford of the Maruts, and bathing there
one glories in the world of the Wind. By bathing in the Lake of the
Immortals one glories with the power of the Immortals in the world
90 of heaven among the Immortals. Bathing religiously at Śālihotra's
Śāliśūrpa one obtains the fruit of one thousand cows. In the Sarasvatī
there is the Śrīkuñja Ford, O best of the Bharatas: bathing there one
acquires the reward of a Laud-of-the-Fire.

Then go on to the Arbor-of-Naimiṣa. The story goes that the
ascetics of Naimiṣa Forest once went on a pilgrimage to Kurukṣetra.
There they planted an arbor on the Sarasvatī, to provide a large
gratifying space for the seers. By bathing at that Arbor one will obtain
the fruit of a thousand cows. By bathing at the Maiden's-Ford one
95 acquires the reward of a Laud-of-the-Fire. From there one should go

on to the eminent sanctuary of Brahmā; bathing there a man of a
lower class becomes a brahmin, and a pure-spirited brahmin goes the
greatest journey. Thence proceeding to peerless Somatīrtha and
bathing there, one will go to the world of the Moon.

Then one should continue to the Saptasārasvata Ford, where
Mankanaka, famous in the world of the seers, found success. This
Mankanaka, so we have heard, once cut his hand with the tip of a
blade of *kuśa* grass, and from the wound flowed vegetable juice. When
he saw the vegetable juice, the ascetic was overjoyed and, with eyes
100 wide open with wonder, the brahmin seer began to dance. When he
was dancing, the animate and inanimate creatures, stunned by his
splendor, began to dance too. The Gods led by Brahmā, the seers, and
the ascetics told the Great God about the seer: "Pray, take measures,
God, so that he stop dancing!" The God, who had the well-being of
the Gods at heart, went in happy spirits to the seer and said to him,
"Aho, great seer who know the Law, why are you dancing? What,
bull among hermits, is the occasion of your present joy?"

The seer said:

Do you not see, God, that vegetable juice flows from my hand?
When I saw that, I was seized with great joy and began to dance!

Pulastya said:

105 The God said laughingly to the hermit, who was bemused by his
passion, "But I myself am not surprised, brahmin, for watch me."
With these words the wise Great God pricked his thumb with his
fingernail, and from the cut fell snow-white ashes. Seeing this, the
hermit became ashamed and fell at his feet: "No other God, I hold,"
he said, "is more supreme than Rudra! Thou art the goal, Trident-
wielder, of the worlds of God and Asura. Thou hast created this
universe of three worlds with its moving and standing creatures, and
110 into thee they return, blessed lord, at the end of the Eon. Even the
Gods cannot encompass thee, how much less I! In thee are seen
Brahmā and all the other Gods, blameless one. Thou art all, maker
and causer of the worlds. By thy grace all the Gods rejoice here in
complete security!" After having thus lauded the Great God, the seer
remained prostrate.

The seer said:

May by thy grace, Great God, my austerities never wane!

Pulastya said:

Thereupon the God spoke in joyous spirits as follows to the
brahmin seer: "Your austerities shall grow a thousandfold by my
grace, brahmin. And I shall dwell with you in this hermitage, great
115 hermit. They who will bathe and worship me at Saptasārasvata shall
find nothing beyond their grasp in this world and the next; and shall
without doubt go to the world of Sarasvatī."

From there one should go on to Auśanasa, where Brahmā, the
Gods, seers, and ascetics are present. Also, they say, the blessed Ford
Kārttikeya appears there at the three joints of the day, as a favor to
the Bhārgava. There is a ford Kapālamocana; by bathing thereat one
is freed from all sins. Thence one goes on to the Ford-of-the-Fire;
bathing there one attains to the world of the Fire and rescues one's
120 family. In the same area is the Ford-of-Viśvāmitra, O best of the
Bharatas; by bathing there one is born to brahminhood. Continuing,
pure and devout, to the Womb-of-Brahmā and bathing there, one
attains to the world of Brahmā and purifies his lineage to seven
generations, no doubt of that.

Then one should journey to Kārttikeya's Ford of Pṛthūdaka, famous
in the three worlds. One should do his ablutions there, intent upon
the worship of Gods and ancestors; whatever improper deed a man or
a woman has done in ignorance or knowingly with human resolve, it
vanishes all as soon as one bathes here; he rises to the fruit of a
125 Horse Sacrifice and goes to the world of heaven. They call Kurukṣetra
holy, but holier than Kurukṣetra is the Sarasvatī, holier than the
Sarasvatī are the fords, holier than the fords is Pṛthūdaka. He who,
while intent on prayer, gives up his body at Pṛthūdaka, this foremost
of all the fords, will not be tormented by fear of an imminent death.
It has been chanted by Sanatkumāra and the great-spirited Vyāsa,
and it is laid down in the *Veda*, king, that one should go to Pṛthūdaka.
No ford has greater sanctity than Pṛthūdaka: it is sacrificially pure,
purifying and lustrating. The wise say that even criminals go to
130 heaven if they bathe at Pṛthūdaka. There is also the ford Madhusrava;
a man who bathes there wins the fruit of a thousand cows.

Then one should continue next to the Goddess's-Ford, the world-
renowned confluence of the Sarasvatī and the Aruṇā. When one
bathes there after a three-night fast, he is absolved from brahmin
murder and finds the fruit of a Laud-of-the-Fire and Overnight
Sacrifice, and purifies his lineage to seven generations. There too is the
ford Avatīrṇa, which Darbhin created of old out of compassion for the
brahmins. A twice-born who practices vows, initiation, fasts, rites,
135 and spells no doubt is a brahmin; but by bathing there, even one
without rites and spells becomes a brahmin of accomplished vows;
that is found in the ancient lore. Darbhin has also collected here the
four oceans: by bathing in them one will suffer no reverses and find
the fruit of four thousand cows.

From there one should go to the Śatasāhasraka Ford where is also
the Sāhasraka, two famous places; for by bathing in them a man
obtains the fruit of a thousand cows and his gifts and fasts increase
a thousandfold. Then one should proceed to the great Reṇukā Ford,
do one's ablutions, and worship ancestors and Gods: one's soul will

be cleansed of all evil and one will attain to the fruit of a Laud-of-
140 the-Fire. Touching water at Vimocana, with temper and senses
controlled, one is freed from any errors committed in acquisition.
Then going to Pañcavaṭa, chaste and master of one's senses, one wins
great merit and glories in the world of the strict. Here the Lord of
Yoga, the Bull-bannered Sthāṇu is present in person; by merely going
there and worshiping the lord of Gods he succeeds.

Varuṇa's ford Aujasa blazes with its own splendor: it is here that
Brahmā, the Gods, the seers and ascetics anointed Guha* general of
the Gods. East of Aujasa is the Ford-of-the-Kurus; a man who bathes
there, chaste and master of his senses, is cleansed of all evil and goes
145 to the world of the Kurus. Thereafter one should journey, restrained
and of meager diet, to the Gate-of-Heaven: he goes to the world of
heaven and that of Brahmā. Thence the pilgrims should go on to the
Anaraka Ford: by bathing there a man suffers no reverses. Here
Brahmā himself is always present with the Gods, who, headed by
Nārāyaṇa, attend on him. Also present there is the wife of Rudra; if
one approaches the Goddess, one suffers no reverses. When, in the
same place, one approaches Umā's Consort, the Lord of the Universe,
150 the Great God, one is freed from all stains. Approaching Nārāyaṇa of
the lotus navel, the enemy-tamer, one attains shiningly to the world
of Viṣṇu. And when bathed at the Ford-of-All-the-Gods, one shines
like the moon, deserted by all sorrows.

Thereupon the pilgrim should continue to the City-of-Well-being
and in that purifying place satisfy the ancestors and Gods: a man thus
obtains the fruit of a Laud-of-the-Fire sacrifice. There is a Ganges lake
there and a well, bull of the Bharatas; in that well is the equivalent
of three crores of sacred places. By bathing in the Ganges and
worshiping the Great Lord, a man attains to the rank of a Gaṇapati
155 and rescues his family. Then one should go to Sthāṇuvaṭa, famed in
the three worlds; by bathing there and staying overnight, one will
attain to the world of Rudra. Next proceed to Badarīpācana,
Vasiṣṭha's hermitage; there one should fast three nights and then eat
jujube berries. One who would eat jujube berries for a full twelve
years and one who fasts there three nights are equal.

Coming upon Indra's-Pathway the pilgrim, by fasting a day and
night, glories in Śakra's world. If he goes to Ekarātra and fasts one
night, a restrained and true-spoken man glories in the world of
160 Brahmā. From there one should go to a ford famed in the three
worlds, where is found the Hermitage of the great-spirited Āditya,
the mass of splendor. Bathing at that ford and worshiping the sun,
a man goes to the world of Āditya and rescues his lineage. A pilgrim

* = Kārttikeya.

who bathes at the Ford-of-the-Moon attains, beyond a doubt, to the
world of the Moon. Thence one should continue to the Ford-of-the-
Great-spirited Dadhīca, which is very sacred, purifying, and world-
famous; here Angiras Sārasvata is present, vessel of austerities. By
bathing at that ford one obtains the fruit of a Horse Race Festival
and beyond doubt wins an entrance to the Sārasvatas.
165 From thence travel to the Maiden's-Hermitage, restrained and
chaste, stay for three nights observing a fast, and win a hundred
divine maids and go to the world of Brahmā. One should continue to
the ford of Saṃnihitī, where Brahmā, the Gods, the seers, and the
ascetics foregather every month, acquiring great sanctity. If one
touches water at Saṃnihitī when the sun has been swallowed by
Rāhu, one has eternally offered up a hundred Horse Sacrifices.
Whatever sacred fords exist on earth or in the sky, rivers male and
female, tanks and all the streams, wells, ponds, and holy sanctuaries,
they are all assembled every month at Saṃnihitī, that is certain.
170 Whatever wrong a man or a woman may have done, all that for a
certainty vanishes as soon as one bathes there: and he goes to the
world of Brahmā on a lotus-colored wagon. After saluting the
Gatekeeper Arantuka, one should touch water at Koṭirūpa and
acquire much gold. There is a Ganges lake there, which is the ford;
when one bathes there, chaste and attentive, one wins forever the
fruit of a Royal Consecration and a Horse Sacrifice.

On earth the Naimiṣa is sacred, in the sky the Puṣkara, but in all
three worlds Kurukṣetra stands out. Even the dust that is blown by
the wind in Kurukṣetra leads even the evildoer to the greatest
175 journey. They who dwell in Kurukṣetra south of the Sarasvatī and
north of the Dṛṣadvatī dwell in heaven. Even if one only utters the
sentence, "I shall go to Kurukṣetra, I shall live in Kurukṣetra," he is
released from all his sins. They who live in holy Kurukṣetra, the altar
of Brahmā, visited by brahmin seers, are in no wise to be pitied. That
country that lies between Tarantuka and Arantuka and between the
lakes of Rāma and Macakruka, that is Kurukṣetra-Samantapañcaka,
and it is called the Grandfather's-Main-Altar.

Pulastya said:

82.1 One should continue to the ancient Ford-of-Dharma: by bathing
there a law-abiding and attentive man purifies his lineage to seven
generations, without a doubt. Next he should travel to eminent
Kārāpatana: he obtains a Laud-of-the-Fire and goes to the world of
hermits. Afterward one should proceed to the Saugandhika Forest,
where Brahmā, the Gods, the seers, and ascetics are present, and the
Siddhas, Cāraṇas, Gandharvas, Kiṃnaras, and great Snakes. Entering
5 the forest, one is freed from all sins. Thereafter there is the best of

rivers, the stream that is the greatest of streams, the very auspicious Sarasvatī the Goddess, which flows from Plakṣa. When one bathes there in the water that flows from the anthill, and worships Gods and ancestors, he obtains the fruit of a Horse Sacrifice. There is a ford there, difficult to find, by the name of Īśānādhyuṣita, at a distance of six throws of a sacrificial peg from an anthill, it is declared. As is seen from the ancient lore, if one bathes there one finds the fruit of a gift of a thousand ruddy cows and a Horse Sacrifice.

If one goes to Sugandha, Śatakumbhā, and Pañcayajñā, one glories in the world of heaven. In the same area there is a ford called Triśūlakhāta; by going and doing ablutions there, intent on the worship of ancestors and Gods, one attains to the rank of a Gaṇapati after the body expires, no doubt of that. Next one should go to a rare sanctuary of the Goddess, which is famed as Śākaṃbharī and renowned in the three worlds. For a thousand divine years, it is told, she subsisted on vegetables from month to month. The seers, rich in austerities, came there out of devotion to the Goddess, and hospitality was shown them with vegetables. Hence her name became established as Śākaṃbharī. Going to Śākaṃbharī, chaste and attentive, one should stay there for three nights and eat vegetables, restrained and pure. The reward that is won by one who lives on vegetables for a full twelve years is won by the pilgrim at the Goddess's desire.

Now one should go on to Suvarṇākṣa, famous in the three worlds, where Viṣṇu once propitiated Rudra, to win his grace. He obtained very many boons such as are hard to find among the Gods; and, pleased, the Sacker of Tripura* said to him, "You will be more beloved even than we in the world, Kṛṣṇa. Your mouth shall be the entire universe, no doubting of it." By approaching and doing *pūjā* to the Bull-bannered God, one rises to a Horse Sacrifice and attains to the rank of a Gaṇapati. Further one should travel to Dhūmavatī; by staying there three nights one undoubtedly obtains all the desires of one's heart. On the southern side of this Goddess there is Rathāvarta, which one should climb with faith and controlled senses. By the grace of the great God one will go the greatest journey. After circumambulating it one should continue to Dhārā, which destroys all evil. By bathing there one does not suffer sorrow. From there one should go on, paying homage to the Great Mountain, to the Gate-of-the-Ganges, which doubtless equals the gate of heaven. By bathing there at the Koṭi Ford with full attention, one rises to a Puṇḍarīka and rescues one's lineage. By satisfying the Gods and ancestors at Saptaganga, Triganga, and Śakrāvarta in the regular fashion, one glories in the sacred worlds.

* = Śiva.

Then, after bathing at Kanakhala and staying three nights, one
obtains a Horse Sacrifice and goes to the world of heaven. The
pilgrim should proceed to Kapilāvaṭa, stay one night, and attain to the
fruit of a thousand cows. There is the Ford of the great-spirited
Kapila, the king of the Snakes, well known in all the worlds. One
should do ablutions at the Ford of the Snake: a man acquires the
30 fruit of a thousand ruddy cows. Thereupon one should continue to
the great ford of Śaṃtanu, Lalitikā; having bathed there a man will
suffer no reverses. He who bathes at the confluence of the Ganges and
the Saṃgamā rises to ten Horse Sacrifices and rescues his family.
From thence one travels to world-famous Sugandhā and, his soul
cleansed of all evil, he will glory in the world of Brahmā. Then going
to Rudrāvarta and bathing there, the pilgrim will glory in the world
of heaven. If bathed at the confluence of the Ganges and the
Sarasvatī, one obtains a Horse Sacrifice and goes to the world of
heaven.

35 Proceeding to Bhadrakarṇeśvara and worshiping the God in the
proper manner, one suffers no reverses and goes to the world of
heaven. Next the pilgrim should go to Kulyāmraka, where he obtains
the fruit of a thousand cows and heaven. Then, by touching the water
of the Sāmudraka at Arundhatīvaṭa and staying three nights, the
pilgrim finds the fruit of a thousand cows and rescues his lineage.
Going on to Brahmāvarta, continent and attentive, he obtains a
Horse Sacrifice and goes to the heavenly world. Then, having gone
to the Source of the Yamunā and having bathed in the river's water,
he acquires the reward of a Horse Sacrifice and glories in heaven.
40 Reaching now Darvīsaṃkramaṇa, a world-famous ford, he acquires
the reward of a Horse Sacrifice and goes to heaven. Journeying to the
Source of the Indus, visited by the Siddhas and Gandharvas, and
staying five nights, one will find much gold. By reaching the Altar,
which is most difficult of access, one obtains the Horse Sacrifice and
goes the journey of Uśanas.

Next one travels to Ṛṣikulyā and Vāsiṣṭha: by passing through
Vāsiṣṭha, all the classes become brahmins. Having bathed at Ṛṣikulyā
one attains to the world of seers, if one lives there for one month,
45 subsisting on greens. By going to Bhṛgu's-Peak one acquires the fruit
of a Horse Sacrifice; and by going to Vīrapramokṣa one is rid of all
sins. Now journeying to the ford of Kṛttikā and Magha the virtuous
man obtains the fruit of a Laud-of-the-Fire and an Overnight
Sacrifice. By going to the peerless Ford-of-Knowledge and bathing at
twilight, one becomes steeped in all fields of knowledge. One should
stay one night at the Great Hermitage, which frees from all sins, and
eat once a day: he enters auspicious worlds. Dwelling at Mahālaya

for a month and eating once every third day, one will find, his soul
cleansed of all evil, the reward of much gold.

50 Thereupon one should go to Vetasikā, which is favored by the
Grandfather: one rises to a Horse Sacrifice and will go the journey of
Uśanas. Afterward, on reaching ford Sundarikā, which is visited by
the Siddhas, he partakes of beauty: this is found in the ancient lore.
Coming on Brāhmaṇī next, chaste and master of his senses, he attains
to the world of Brahmā on a lotus-colored wagon. Then he should
proceed to auspicious Naimiṣa, which is visited by the Siddhas: there
dwells Brahmā always, in the midst of the hosts of the Gods. An
evildoer who desires to go to Naimiṣa loses half of his evil; by merely
55 entering into it he is freed from all his sins. The wise pilgrim should
dwell at Naimiṣa for a month, O Bhārata: by bathing there, restrained
and of meager diet, he obtains the fruit of a Gavāmayana sacrifice and
purifies his lineage to seven generations. He who, while given to
fasting, would abandon the spirits at Naimiṣa will rejoice in the
world of heaven, thus declare the wise. Naimiṣa is always auspicious
and sacrificially pure. Reaching Gangodbheda and fasting for three
nights, one attains to the fruit of a Horse Race Festival and becomes
Brahmā. Going on to the Sarasvatī, one should satisfy Gods and
ancestors: he rejoices without doubt in the worlds of Sarasvatī.

60 Thereupon one should go, chaste and attentive, to Bāhudā: thus a
man obtains the fruit of a Devasattra sacrifice. Traveling next to
Cīravatī, which is holy and inhabited by holy men, and devoting
himself to the worship of Gods and ancestors, he will rise to a Horse
Race Festival. By going to Vimalāśoka he shines like the moon; by
staying there overnight he glories in the world of heaven. Then he
should continue to Gopratāra, the greatest ford of the Sarayū River,
where Rāma went to heaven with retainers, troops, and mounts.
Abandoning the body there, one will go to heaven by the power of
this ford, and by the grace and resolve of Rāma. By bathing at this
ford of Gopratāra, he glories in the world of heaven, his soul cleansed
65 of all evil. By bathing at the Ford-of-Rāma in the River Gomatī, he
obtains a Horse Sacrifice and purifies his family. There is the
Śatasāhasrika Ford, best of the Bharatas: having done his ablutions
here, restrained and of meager diet, he obtains the holy reward of
a gift of a thousand cows.

Thence one should go to the peerless sanctuary of Bhartar; by
bathing at the Koṭi Ford and worshiping Guha, a man will find the
reward of a thousand cows and win splendor. Proceeding next to
Benares and worshiping the Bull-bannered God and bathing at the
70 Kapilāhrada, one obtains the reward of a Royal Consecration. After
traveling to the rare Ford-of-Mārkaṇḍeya at the world-famous

confluence of the Gomatī and the Ganges, he attains to a Horse
Sacrifice by merely visiting there. Then he should continue to Gayā,
chaste and master of his senses, and merely by going win a Horse
Sacrifice. There is the Akṣayavaṭa, famed in the three worlds; what is
given there to the ancestors becomes inexhaustible. If one bathes in
the River Mahānadī and satisfies ancestors and Gods, he attains to
inexhaustible worlds and rescues his family.

Next he should go to the Lake-of-Brahmā, which is adorned by the
Forest-of-Dharma: when the night has dawned, he obtains the reward
75 of a Puṇḍarīka. In this lake a sacrificial pole of Brahmā rises high: by
circumambulating the pole, one obtains the fruit of a Horse Race
Festival. From there one should go to world-renowned Dhenukā, stay
overnight and give away sesame and a milch cow: so one will
certainly reach the world of the Moon, his soul cleansed of all evil.
There is a sign there, even today, without a doubt; a ruddy cow used
to roam in the mountains with her calf, and even today her hoofprints
and the calf's can be seen there, Bhārata. At these hoofprints one
should touch water and whatever wrong has been committed will
vanish.

Thereafter one should continue to Gṛdhravaṭa, a sanctuary of the
80 wise God: he should approach the Bull-bannered God there and bathe
in ashes; if he is a brahmin it will be equal to accomplishing a
twelve-year vow; of the other classes all evil will disappear. One
should then go to Mount Udyanta, which is noisy with song: there
one may see the Footprint-of-Savitar. A brahmin of strict vows who
worships the dawn there is as good as though he had done so for
twelve years. There too is the famous Gate-of-the-Womb: by
approaching it a man is freed from any miscegenation. If one dwells
for both the dark and light fortnights at Gayā, he doubtlessly purifies
85 his lineage to seven generations. Many sons should be wished for, if
one goes to Gayā alone, or sacrifices with the Horse Sacrifice, or sets
free a dark bull.

Thereupon the pilgrim should go on to Phalgu: he rises to a Horse
Sacrifice and goes on to great success. From there he should diligently
continue to Dharmapṛṣṭha, where Dharma is always present,
Yudhiṣṭhira; by approaching it one obtains the reward of a Horse
Sacrifice. From there he should proceed to the eminent Ford-of-
Brahmā; and by worshiping Brahmā of boundless luster a man attains
to the fruit of a Royal Consecration and a Horse Sacrifice both. Then
the pilgrim should go to Rājagṛha; by touching water at the hot
90 springs he rejoices like Kakṣīvat. There a pure man should taste the
daily offering to the Yakṣiṇī; and by the Yakṣiṇī's favor he will be
absolved from aborticide. Next continuing to Maṇināga he will obtain
the fruit of a thousand cows, if he partakes of the daily offering to

Maṇināga. Poison will not touch him, even though bitten by a cobra; if he stays overnight, he is freed from all sins. Then he should go on to the grove of the brahmin seer Gautama; by bathing in the Lake-of-Ahalyā he will go the greatest journey; by approaching Śrī he finds the greatest fortune. There is a spring there that is renowned in the three worlds; doing his ablutions there, he rises to a Horse Sacrifice. Then there is the Well-of-the-Royal-Seer-Janaka, which is worshiped by the Thirty Gods; by bathing there one attains to Viṣṇu's world.

Next one should go to Vināśana, which frees one from all evil: he obtains a Horse Sacrifice and goes to the World of the Moon. By going to the River Gaṇḍakī, where springs the water of all the fords, one rises to a Horse Sacrifice and goes to the world of the Sun. If then he enters Adhivaṃśya, a forest of austerities, he undoubtedly rejoices among the Guhyakas. By continuing to the River Kampanā, visited by the Siddhas, he obtains a Puṇḍarīka and goes to the world of the Sun. Proceeding to the River Viśālā, which is famed in the three worlds, he obtains a Laud-of-the-Fire and goes to the world of heaven. Then, by going to the stream Maheśvarī, he attains to a Horse Sacrifice and rescues his family. A man who visits the Lotus-Pond-of-the-Celestials suffers no reverses and finds a Horse Race Sacrifice. Chaste and attentive, he should go to the Footprint-of-the-Great-Lord and by bathing there obtain the fruit of a Horse Sacrifice. A crore of sacred places are known to be there, which once were carried off by an evil Asura in the form of a tortoise and recovered by puissant Viṣṇu. By doing his ablutions at this Crore-of-Fords, Yudhiṣṭhira, he obtains a Puṇḍarīka and goes to the world of Viṣṇu.

From there he should go to the sanctuary of Nārāyaṇa, where Hari always dwells close by, called the Śālagrāma of miracle-worker Viṣṇu. By approaching the boon-granting eternal Viṣṇu, the Lord of the three worlds, he obtains a Horse Sacrifice and goes to the world of Viṣṇu. There is a well there that frees from all evil; the four oceans are always present there in that well. By touching water there he will suffer no reverses. Approaching the great God, the boon-granting eternal Viṣṇu, he shines like the moon, Yudhiṣṭhira, and he is freed from his debts. If one touches water at Jātismara, pure and devout of heart, one becomes after his ablutions capable of recalling former births, without a doubt. Continuing to Vaṭeśvarapura, worshiping Keśava and fasting, one no doubt wins what one desires. Going thence to Vāmana, which frees from all evil, and saluting the God Hari, he will suffer no reverses. Proceeding to the Hermitage-of-Bharata, which delivers from all evil, he should visit there the River Kauśikī, which destroys grave sins; one attains to the Royal Consecration.

Repairing thence to the great Campaka Forest, he should stay overnight and obtain the reward of a thousand cows. Visiting there

the highly esteemed ford Jyeṣṭhila and fasting one night one will
obtain the fruit of a Laud-of-the-Fire. Setting eyes there on the
resplendent Lord of the Universe and the Goddess, he attains to the
world of Mitra and Varuṇa. By going to Kanyāsaṃvedya, restrained
and of meager diet, one goes to the world of Manu Prajāpati. The
food and drink they offer at Kanyā becomes inexhaustible, thus declare
the seers of strict vows. Continuing to the River Niścīrā, famed in the
three worlds, one rises to a Horse Sacrifice and goes to the world of
120 Viṣṇu; people who make a gift at the confluence of the Niścīrā go to
the world of Brahmā, without a doubt. There is the Hermitage-of-
Vasiṣṭha, famous in the three worlds; by doing one's ablutions there
one will obtain a Horse Race Festival.

Proceeding next to Devakūṭa, cherished by the hosts of brahmin
seers, one attains to a Horse Sacrifice and rescues his family. Then
one should go to the lake of the hermit Kauśika;* he should stay a
month at the River Kauśikī, and gain the merit of a Horse Sacrifice in
125 a month. He who dwells at Mahāhrada, best of all fords, does not
suffer reverses and will find much gold. By approaching Kumāra,
who dwells in the Hermitage-of-the-Hero, a man undoubtedly obtains
the Horse Sacrifice. Going on to the River Agnidhārā, famous in the
three worlds, he attains to a Laud-of-the-Fire and does not return
from Heaven. If he goes to Grandfather's-Lake, which lies in the
Himālaya, and does his ablutions there, he will reap the reward of a
Laud-of-the-Fire. There is a stream there that flows from the Lake-of-
Grandfather, purifying the world, famed in the three worlds as the
130 River Kumāradhārā: when one bathes there one knows of oneself
that one has succeeded and by eating once every three days one is
absolved from brahmin murder.

After climbing the Peak-of-the-Great-Goddess-Gaurī, renowned in
the three worlds, a man of faith should enter the Wells-of-the-
Breasts: bathing there, intent on the worship of ancestors and Gods,
he obtains a Horse Sacrifice and goes to the world of Śakra. Going on
to Tāmrāruṇa, chaste and attentive, one obtains a Horse Sacrifice
and goes to the world of Śakra. Visiting at Nandinī the well that is
the favorite of the Thirty Gods he acquires the merit of a Human
135 Sacrifice, O scion of Kuru. At the Kālikā confluence of the Kauśikī and
Aruṇa a wise man, fasting three nights, is delivered from all evil. The
sage who proceeds to the Ford-of-Urvaśī and the Hermitage-of-the-
Moon, and bathes at the Hermitage-of-Kumbhakarṇa is honored upon
earth. That by bathing at holy Kokāmukha a chaste man of vows
gets the gift of recalling former births has been seen in the ancient
Lore. A brahmin who has once visited Mandā becomes perfect of
soul and, his soul cleansed of all evil, goes to the world of Śakra.

* = Viśvāmitra.

When he has gone to Bull-Island, which is worth visiting, the haunt
of curlews, and touched water in the Sarasvatī, he shines as though
140 mounted on a celestial chariot. Then there is the Ford-of-Uddālaka,
frequented by hermits: one should do his ablutions there and be rid
of all sins. Proceeding to the holy Ford-of-Dharma, which is visited by
brahmin seers, a man attains to a Horse Race Festival, beyond any
doubt. So, nearing Campā and taking the waters on the Bhāgīrathī,
he acquires, just by approaching Daṇḍārka, the reward of a gift of a
thousand cows. Next he should journey to Laveḍikā, holy and
frequented by the holy: he attains to a Horse Race Festival and is
honored, riding a celestial chariot.

Pulastya said:

83.1 Continuing thereupon to the great ford Saṃvedya, a man who
touches water there at twilight doubtlessly becomes wise. When he
goes to the River Lohitya, a ford that of yore was created by the grace
of Rāma, he will find much gold. Proceeding to the River Karatoyā
and fasting for three nights, he acquires the Horse Sacrifice, when the
rite of the Grandfather has been performed. The sages declare that
at the confluence of the Ganges and the ocean there is a tenfold
5 Horse Sacrifice. When he reaches the other island of the Ganges,
bathes there, and fasts for three nights, he will attain to all of his
desires. Going thereafter to the River Vaitaraṇī, which absolves from
evil, and visiting the ford Viraja, he shines like the moon. He is born
in a holy family and destroys all his evil; and obtaining the reward
of a thousand cows, he makes his family pure. By dwelling at the
confluence of the Śoṇa and Jyotirathyā a pure man receives the fruit
of a Laud-of-the-Fire after satisfying the Gods and ancestors. When
he touches water at Vaṃśagulma, the source of the Śoṇa and
Narmadā, he will obtain the reward of a Horse Sacrifice.

10 Traveling to the Ṛṣabha Ford at the River Kosalā and fasting three
nights, he obtains a Horse Sacrifice. While at the Kosalā he should
touch water at the Kāla Ford, and he obtains no doubt the fruit of
eleven bulls. By ablutions at Puṣpavati and a three-night fast he will
find the reward of a thousand cows, and rescue his family. Then,
bathing at the Badarikā Ford, with devout thoughts, he obtains a
long life and goes to the world of heaven. Proceeding next to Mount
Mahendra, which was frequented by Rāma Jāmadagnya, he will
obtain the reward of a Horse Sacrifice when he bathes at the Ford-
15 of-Rāma. There too is the Meadow-of-Matanga, scion of Kuru: by
bathing there one obtains the reward of a thousand cows. Going on
to Mount Śrī one should touch water at the river bank: he receives a
Horse Sacrifice and goes to the world of heaven. On Mount Śrī the
resplendent Great God lived very happily with the Goddess, and so did

Brahmā surrounded by the Thirty Gods. He should bathe there at
Devahrada, pure and with devout thoughts: thus he achieves a Horse
Sacrifice and supreme success. Going then to Mount Ṛṣabha in the
land of the Pāṇḍyas, which is honored by the Gods, he obtains the
20 Horse Race Festival and rejoices on the vault of heaven. Then
proceeding to the River Kāverī, which is crowded with hosts of
Apsarās, he should bathe there and obtain the reward of a thousand
cows. Thereafter he should bathe at the seashore, at the Ford-of-the-
Maiden, and having done so he is freed from all sins.

Continuing on to Gokarṇa, famed in the three worlds and honored
in all the worlds, which is situated in the midst of the ocean, where
Brahmā, the Gods, the seers and ascetics, Bhūtas, Yakṣas, Piśācas,
Kiṃnaras, great Snakes, Siddhas, Cāraṇas and Gandharvas, men and
25 Serpents, rivers and oceans wait upon the Consort of Umā, and
worshiping there the Lord with a three-night fast, he achieves ten
Horse Sacrifices and attains to the rank of a Gaṇapati. After staying
there twelve nights, a man becomes perfected of soul. From there to
the sanctuary of Gāyatrī, renowned in the three worlds; after a stay
of three nights, he obtains the reward of a thousand cows. There is a
sign in evidence there that is exceptional to brahmins: when a
brahmin of mixed parentage recites the Gāyatrī it sounds like a
non-Vedic verse or an ordinary song.

When he goes to the rare pond of the brahmin seer Saṃvarta, he
becomes beautiful of body and lucky in love. Proceeding to the River
Veṇṇā he should satisfy ancestors and Gods: he obtains a celestial
30 chariot drawn by peacocks and swans. Reaching then the Godāvarī
River, always frequented by the Siddhas, he attains to a Gavāmayana
and the world of Vāsuki. When he bathes at the confluence with the
Veṇṇā, he obtains the fruit of a Horse Race Festival; when at the
confluence with the Varadā, the reward of a thousand cows.
Journeying to the sanctuary of Brahmā and staying there three nights,
he will find the fruit of a thousand cows and go to heaven. At
Kuśaplavana he should stay three nights, chaste and attentive, and
thus receive the reward of a Horse Sacrifice. Then at lovely Devahrada,
the source of the Kṛṣṇaveṇṇā, and at Jātimātrahrada as well as the
35 Maiden's-Hermitage, where the king of the Gods went to heaven after
offering with hundreds of rituals, he finds a hundred Lauds-of-the-
Fire by merely going there. When bathed at the Pond-of-All-the-Gods,
he wins the reward of a thousand cows; when bathed at the
Jātimātrahrada, he will remember past lives.

Next, by journeying to the high auspicious Payoṣṇī, choicest of
rivers, intent on the worship of ancestors and Gods, one will obtain
the reward of a thousand cows. Repairing to the Daṇḍaka Forest and
touching water, there is the reward of a thousand cows from just

bathing. If one goes on to the Hermitages of Sarabhanga and the great-spirited Śukra, he suffers no reverses and purifies his family. Then he should go to Śūrpāraka, which was visited by Jāmadagnya, and bathe at Rāma's-Ford: he will find much gold. After bathing at the Saptagodāvara, restrained and of meager diet, he wins great merit and goes to the world of the Gods. From there he should, restrained and of meager diet, go on to the Pathway of the Gods: thus a man reaps the reward of a Devasattra.

Reaching the Tungaka Forest, chaste and master of his senses—there the seer Sārasvata taught of old the *Vedas*, the lost *Vedas* did the son of the hermit Angiras teach, seated on the upper garments of the great seers: when someone correctly enunciated the syllable OṂ according to the rules, the lore that he had previously rehearsed came back to him. The seers, the Gods, Varuṇa, Agni, Prajāpati, Hari, God Nārāyaṇa, and the Great God, the Grandfather, the resplendent blessed Lord with the Gods, enjoined upon the splendid Bhṛgu to officiate at a sacrifice. So the blessed lord once more performed properly the Laying of the Fire for all the seers, according to the ritual that is found in the Rules. Ritually satisfied by their share of clarified butter, the Gods went to the three worlds and the seers went where they wished. Now, when one enters that Tungaka Forest, man or woman, all one's evil disappears. A wise man will live there a month, restrained and of meager diet, and he will go to the world of Brahmā and purify his family.

Upon arriving at Medhāvika one should offer to ancestors and Gods: one obtains a Laud-of-the-Fire and wins memory and wisdom. Going on to Mount Kālaṃjara, famous in the world, he should bathe at the Devahrada and obtain the reward of a thousand cows. There he should perfect his soul, on Mount Kālaṃjara, and without a doubt he will glory in the world of heaven. Then, reaching the River Mandākinī* on that greatest of mountains Citrakūṭa, a river that delivers from evil, one should do ablutions, intent on the worship of ancestors and Gods, and he will achieve a Horse Sacrifice and go the greatest journey. Going thence to the peerless sanctuary of Bhartar, where the God Mahāsena is always present, a man succeeds by merely going. At the Koṭi Ford he wins, by bathing, the reward of a thousand cows. After circumambulating it, one should continue to Jyeṣṭhasthāna; and by approaching the Great God he shines like the moon. There is a famous well there, the four oceans reside in it, Yudhiṣṭhira; touching water there and doing the circumambulation, a pure and self-controlled man will go the greatest journey.

Now he should go to Śṛngaverapura, where Rāma Dāśarathi once crossed: a man who, chaste and attentive, bathes there in the Ganges

* = Yamunā.

becomes washed of evil and finds a Horse Race Festival. By
approaching the Great God and worshiping him and doing the
circumambulation he attains to the rank of a Gaṇapati.
65 Thence one should continue to Prayāga, hymned by the seers,
where Brahmā and the Gods, the quarters and the regents of the
quarters, the World Guardians, the Sādhyas, the Nairṛtas and the
Ancestors, the sublime seers led by Sanatkumāra, the other brahmin
seers led by Angiras, as well as the Snakes, Birds, Siddhas and
Cakracaras, the rivers and oceans, Gandharvas and Apsarās, and the
lord Hari placed first by Prajāpati, all reside. There are three
70 fire pits from between which the River Jāhnavī,* which precedes all
fords, courses out of Prayāga. There Tapana's daughter, the River
Yamunā, famed in the three worlds, flows together with the Ganges,
purifying the world. The land between the Ganges and the Yamunā
is known as the vagina of the earth; and Prayāga and Pratiṣṭhāna,
thus the seers know, form the end of the vagina, the vulva. Prayāga,
Pratiṣṭhāna, Kambala, Aśvatara, and the ford Bhogavatī are declared
to be the altars of Prajāpati. There the *Vedas* and Sacrifices take on
bodily form, Yudhiṣṭhira, and with the seers of great vows wait upon
Prajāpati; the Gods and Cakracaras worship him with sacrifices.
There is no place in the three worlds that is holier than Prayāga, O
75 Bhārata; Prayāga towers above all sacred fords. By hearing of this
ford, by reciting its name, or by taking some of its clay, one is freed
from sin. He who, strict in his vows, does his ablutions there at the
confluence attains to the holy merit of a Royal Consecration and a
Horse Sacrifice. For this is a sacrificial terrain which is honored even
by the Gods. What is given there, however little, grows big. Do not
let the declarations of the *Veda* and the statements of the world make
you abandon the resolve unto death in Prayāga. It is proclaimed,
scion of Kuru, that there are sixty crores and ten thousand fords
80 present there. The sanctity of a man schooled in the four *Vedas* or of
true-spoken persons one obtains by merely bathing at the confluence
of the Ganges and Yamunā. There is the great ford of Vāsuki,
Bhogavatī by name. He who does his ablutions there acquires a Horse
Sacrifice. There is that world famous ford, the Upflight-of-the-Swan,
and the Daśāśvamedhika, in the Ganges. The region where the
Ganges flows is a forest of austerities: the country adjacent to the
Ganges is known as the Field of the Siddhas.
This truth one should whisper into the ear of the twice-born, the
85 virtuous, one's son and friends and pupil and dependent. It is lawlike,
it is holy, it is sacrificially pure, it is felicitous, it is paradisiac, it is
lovely, it is supremely purifying. It is the mystery of the great seers,
delivering from all evil. When one has learned it amidst the twice-

* = Ganges.

born, one achieves immaculateness. He who may hear of the eternal
sanctity of the fords will be pure forever. He recalls many births and
rejoices on the vault of heaven. The fords have been stated to be
accessible as well as inaccessible: to the latter one should go in
thought, if he wishes to visit all the fords. Desirous of merit, the
Vasus, Sādhyas, Ādityas, Maruts, Aśvins, and the godlike seers have
visited them.

90 Likewise you too, Kauravya of good vows, must diligently journey
to the fords according to precept. And sanctity will increase with
sanctity. The strict, erudite, and insightful have had access before to
these fords through their perfected faculties, their orthodoxy, and
their vision of the *Veda*. No man of no vows, no man of unrefined
soul, no impure man nor a thief bathes at the fords, Kauravya, nor
a person of crooked mind. You, always of perfect conduct and insight
into Law and Profit, have carried across your ancestors and forebears
all. The Gods led by Grandfather, with the hosts of seers, have
95 always, O law-wise prince, been satisfied with your Law. Indralike
Bhīṣma, you shall attain to the very worlds of the Vasus, and obtain
on earth great and everlasting fame!

Nārada said:

Having thus spoken and taken his leave, the blessed Lord Pulastya
joyously, with joyful heart, disappeared then and there. Bhīṣma, tiger
of the Kurus, who sees the import of all the scriptures, roamed over
the world at Pulastya's words. He who will wander over the earth by
this precept shall after death enjoy the supreme reward of a hundred
Horse Sacrifices. You, Pārtha, will acquire a great eight-times-larger
merit of Law: for as you shall lead seers, your reward will be eight
100 times greater. These fords are overrun by bands of Rākṣasas,
Bhārata, and no one but you can go there, scion of Kuru!

He who upon arising in the morning will recite this geste of the
great seer, which incorporates the import of all the fords, is released
from all evil things.

The most eminent seers, Vālmīki, Kāśyapa, Ātreya, Kauṇḍinya,
Viśvāmitra, Gautama, Asita Devala, Mārkaṇḍeya, Gālava, Bharadvāja,
Vasiṣṭha, the hermit Uddālaka, Śaunaka and his son, and Vyāsa, first
of the mutterers of prayers, Durvāsas, best of the hermits, and the
105 great ascetic Jābāli, have all been waiting for you here, these great
seers and ascetics. In their company, great king, go and tour these
fords.

The divine seer Lomaśa, of boundless luster, shall meet with you,
and you must travel with him. Travel to the fords with me too,
Law-wise king, you shall earn great fame, like King Mahābhiṣa. Like
the great-spirited Yayāti, like King Purūravas, so you too, tiger of the
Kurus, will shine with your Law. Like King Bhagīratha, like famous

110 Rāma, so you too will shine as the sun above all kings. Like Manu,
like Ikṣvāku, like famed Pūru, like the glorious Vainya, so you too
shall be famous. Even as the Slayer of Vṛtra once burned down all his
rivals, so you shall destroy your enemies and protect your subjects.
Having obtained the earth, conquered with your Law, lotus-eyed
prince, you will rise by your Law to the glory of Arjuna Kārtavīrya!

Vaiśaṃpāyana said:

After he has thus encouraged the great-spirited king, the blessed Lord Nārada took his leave and disappeared on the spot. And Yudhiṣṭhira, inspirited with Law, reflected upon this matter and acquainted the seers with the sanctity that attaches to the tour of the sacred fords.

Vaiśaṃpāyana said:

84.1 King Yudhiṣṭhira, having probed the minds of his brothers and the
wise Nārada, now spoke to Dhaumya, who was like the Grandfather
himself: "I have sent into exile the tiger among men Jiṣṇu, whose
strength is his truth, the strong-armed hero of measureless soul, to
find weapons. For the champion is loyal and capable, O ascetic, a past
master of arms and a lord equal to Vāsudeva. Indeed I know,
brahmin, the two gallant enemy-killing Kṛṣṇas, and so does the
majestic Vyāsa know the lotus-eyed Vāsudeva and Dhanaṃjaya of
5 the three Eons. So does Nārada know them: he has always told me;
and so do I myself know them for who they are—the seers Nara and
Nārāyaṇa. Hence, knowing that he was capable of it, I sent out
Arjuna; not a lesser man than Indra, he, son of the God, is able to
set eyes on the lord of the Gods, and to take weapons from Indra:
that is why he was exiled. Bhīṣma and Droṇa are over-warriors, Kṛpa
is invincible, and so is Droṇa's son; these mighty men have been
elected by Dhṛtarāṣṭra's son for the war. They are all champions who
know their *Veda*, they are all experts on weapons.

"Then there is Karṇa, the powerful great warrior, the *sūta's* son
who has always wanted to fight the Pārtha and knows divine
weapons. He has the speed of a horse, the power of a gale, he roars
from the fire hearth that sparks his arrows, he is the dust cloud, the
10 anguish of weapons, raised by the wind of the Dhārtarāṣṭra.* He has
been set loose as the fire of Doomsday is set loose by Time; and
doubtlessly he shall set afire my chamber of troops. Only the breaking
monsoon-burst of Arjuna, driven by Kṛṣṇa's wind, mightily reinforced
by clouds of divine arms, wearing his white horses like cranes, and
ablaze with the rainbow of his Gāṇḍīva, shall ever quench the
burning fire of Karṇa in battle with the showers of his arrows.

* = Duryodhana.

"Surely the Terrifier, conqueror of enemy cities, shall acquire from
Indra himself the divine weapons. 'He is the match of them all,' I
keep thinking. 'No one can overmatch him in battle, there will be no
15 rematch for his enemies.' Yes, we shall all see Dhanaṃjaya Pāṇḍava
with the weapons he got, for the Terrifier has never sunk under a
burden he took on.

"Yet, bereft of that hero, in this same wood, O best of two-footed
men, we find no repose, nor does Kṛṣṇā with us, in this Kāmyaka
Forest. Sir, tell us of another good wood, one that has much food and
fruit, that is lovely and sought out by men of holy deeds, where we
might stay for some time, waiting for Arjuna the hero, whose bravery
is truth, as men who long for the rains wait for the cloud. Tell us of
various hermitages that have been noted by the brahmins, of lakes
20 and rivers and lovely mountains; for, brahmin, this stay without
Arjuna, this sojourn in the Kāmyaka Forest, no longer pleases us. Let
us go to another region!"

Vaiśaṃpāyana said:

85.1 When Dhaumya saw that all the Pāṇḍavas were depressed and
anxious to go, the Bṛhaspati-like priest said reassuringly, "Listen to
me describe, king, bull of the Bharatas, the sacred hermitages,
countries, fords, and mountains that are approved by the brahmins.
First I shall describe to you, as far as I remember, the lovely eastern
country, which is frequented by hosts of royal seers, Yudhiṣṭhira.

"In that region, which is sought out by Gods and seers, lies the
5 Naimiṣa, Bhārata. There are very holy fords that are sacred to
different Gods. There flows the lovely and holy River Gomatī, which is
visited by Gods and seers, the sacrificial terrain of the Gods, and the
slaughter site of Vivasvat. The great sacred mountain of Gaya is there,
which is honored by royal seers, the auspicious Lake of Brahmā,
which the Thirty Gods and the seers adore. It is for its sake, tiger
among men, that the ancient declare that one should wish for many
sons, if one may go to Gayā alone.

"There are also the rivers Mahānadī and Gayaśiras, prince sans
blame, and the brahmins celebrate the banyan tree Akṣayyakaraṇa,
where the food given to the ancestors becomes inexhaustible, O lord.
There flows a great river by the name of Phalgu, whose waters are
holy, Bhārata, and the Kauśikī River, which has plentiful fruit and
roots, bull of the Bharatas, where Viśvāmitra the ascetic became a
10 brahmin. Here is the sacred River Ganges on whose bank Bhagīratha
offered up many sacrifices of rich stipends, my son. They narrate that
in the Pāñcāla country there is the Lotus Cistern where Viśvāmitra
Kauśika sacrificed with Śakra. And upon seeing Viśvāmitra's

superhuman puissance the blessed Lord Jāmadagnya* sang there this
chronicle verse: 'In Kanyakubja, Kauśika drank Soma with Indra and
there he withdrew from the baronage, saying "I am a brahmin!"'
There is the world-famous confluence of the Ganges and the Yamunā,
lustrating, visited by the seers, holy and supremely purifying, where
the Grandfather, the soul of the creatures, sacrificed of yore: for that
reason it is called Prayāga, best of the Bharatas.
15 "Here, too, O Indra among kings, is the great Hermitage-of-
Agastya, and the Drop-of-Gold is described on Mount Kālaṃjara, king.
There is a mountain sacred beyond all other mountains, the holy
mountain of Mahendra of the great-spirited Bhārgava, O King
Kauravya, where, O son of Kuntī, the Grandfather once sacrificed,
and the sacred Bhāgīrathī** was in his *sadas*, Yudhiṣṭhira. Here is the
sacred river known as the Brahmaśālā, O lord of the people, crowded
by men whose evil has been washed off; its very sight is hallowing.
And, famous on earth, the purifying, auspicious, and eternal Meadow-
20 of-Matanga, a great and eminent hermitage; the lovely Mount
Kuṇḍoda, abounding in roots, fruit, and water, where the thirsty
Niṣadhan*** found water and shelter. In these parts are the lovely
Devavana, adorned by ascetics, and the rivers Bāhudā and Nandā on
the mountaintop.

"I have described to you, great king, the fords, rivers, mountains, and sacred sanctuaries of the eastern country. Now hear from me the holy fords in the other three regions, their rivers, mountains, and sacred sanctuaries."

Dhaumya said:

86.1 Now listen, Bhārata, as I describe in detail the sacred fords in the
south as far as I know them. In that region are enumerated the holy
River Godāvarī with many resting spots and abundant water,
auspicious and followed by ascetics, the Veṇṇā and Bhīmaratha, two
rivers that dispel the fear of sin, overrun by deer and birds and
adorned with hermitages. There is the river of the royal seer Nṛga,
O bull of the Bharatas, the Payoṣṇī with lovely fords and plentiful
5 water, visited by the twice-born. Here, too, the great yogin and
ascetic Mārkaṇḍeya chanted this chronicle verse of king of the earth
Nṛga: "We have heard this for certain of Nṛga when he sacrificed,
that Indra became drunk with Soma and the priests with their
stipends." On Mount Varuṇasrotasa there is the sacred Wood-of-
Māṭhara, auspicious and full of roots and fruit, and a sacrificial pole,
bull of the Bharatas. We hear that it is declared that to the north of

* = Rāma.
** = Ganges.
*** = Nala.

the Praveṇī and in the holy Hermitage-of-Kāṇva there are several
woods inhabited by ascetics.
In Śūrpāraka, my son, are the two Altars of the Great-spirited
Jamadagni, the lovely Ford-of-the-Stones and the Puraścandrā, O
10 Bhārata. In Martya country is the Ford-of-the-Aśokas with many
hermitages, son of Kuntī, in the land of the Pāṇḍyas the Fords-of-
Agastya-and-Varuṇa; there too are the Holy-Maidens said to be, bull
among men. I shall now mention the Tāmraparṇī, listen, Kaunteya,
where the Gods, longing for a great reward, did austerities. Gokarṇa
is celebrated in the three worlds, Bhārata, holy and auspicious, my
son, and the water is cool and abundant there. There is a lake of
extremely difficult access to people who have not perfected their souls.
There too is the holy hermitage of Agastya's pupil Tṛṇasomāgni
15 on Mount Devasabha, with plenty of fruit and roots. There is the
propitious and illustrious Mount Vaiḍūrya, which is made of precious
stones, and Agastya's-Hermitage with abundant roots, fruit, and
water. I shall also mention the sacred places in Surāṣṭra, hermitages,
rivers, mountains, and lakes, O king of men. The brahmins speak
there of Camasonmajjana and, on the sea, the ford Prabhāsa of the
Thirty Gods, Yudhiṣṭhira. There is holy Piṇḍāraka, visited by ascetics,
and great Mount Ujjayanta, which brings success quickly. The first of
the divine seers Nārada recited about it an ancient verse, listen,
20 Yudhiṣṭhira: "He who on the holy mountain of Surāṣṭra, Ujjayanta,
frequented by deer and fowl, mortifies the body glories on the vault of
heaven." There too is holy Dvāravatī, where the ancient God
Madhusūdana* dwells in person; he indeed is the sempiternal Law.
Brahmins who know the *Vedas* and men who know the higher soul
proclaim that the great-spirited Kṛṣṇa is the sempiternal Law. For
Govinda is said to be the greatest of all purifiers, holiest of the holy,
most auspicious of the auspicious. The eternal lotus-eyed God of Gods
is the universe, and Hari of inconceivable soul, the Slayer of Madhu,
dwells there.

Dhaumya said:
87.1 I shall now recite the purifying and holy places that are found in
the west, in Avanti. There is the River Narmadā, flowing westward,
abounding in *priyangu* creepers and mango groves, and bordered by
thickets of cane, a holy river, Bhārata. In that region lies the sacred
seat of the hermit Viśravas; the Lord of Riches Kubera, whose mount
is man, was born there. There is a holy and auspicious hill there by
the name of Vaiḍūryaśikhara, and trees of a green hue, with divine
5 blossoms and fruit. At the top of that hill lies the lake of a sage where
the lotuses blossom, king, visited by Gods and Gandharvas. A

* = Kṛṣṇa.

wonderful spot is found, great king, on that hill, that holy, heavenlike,
divine hill that is always visited by the Gods. There is also the lake-
rich, holy-forded River Pārā, the river of the royal seer Viśvāmitra,
O conqueror of enemy cities, on whose bank Nahuṣa's son Yayāti fell
in the midst of the honest. He fell but regained his Lawlike everlasting
worlds.

Here too is Holy-Lake, and the mountain Maināka, hero, and
10 Mount Asita full of fruit and roots. There is the holy Hermitage of
Kakṣasena, Yudhiṣṭhira Pāṇḍava, and the Hermitage-of-Cyavana,
which is famous everywhere. There men succeed with even a little
austerity, my lord. There is Jambūmārga, Rose-apple Row, best of
men, the hermitage of serene seers of cultivated souls, with flocks of
birds and deer. Also most holy Ketumālā, king, always crowded with
ascetics, and Medhyā, and the Wood-of-the-Ganges, O lord of the
earth. Famed is the Wood-of-the-Indus, holy and attended by the
twice-born; so is the Pond-of-the-Grandfather, Bhārata, holy Puṣkara,
the favorite hermitage of Vaikhānasas, Siddhas, and seers. In praise of
it Prajāpati chanted this verse about the Puṣkaras, O first of the
15 Kurus, best of the virtuous: "Of the spirited man who longs for the
Puṣkaras even in thought all evil falls away and he rejoices on the
vault of heaven."

Dhaumya said:

88.1 I shall now mention the holy fords and sacred places that are lying
in the north, tigerlike king. There are the Sarasvatī of holy currents,
full of lakes and embanked by woods, and the oceanward impetuous
Yamunā, O Pāṇḍava. There is that most holy ford, auspicious
Agniśiras, prince sans blame, where Sahadeva sacrificed after
5 measuring the terrain with a throw of a sacrificial peg. It is because
of that occasion that this verse, first chanted by Indra, goes around
the world repeated by the brahmins, Yudhiṣṭhira: "The fires that
Sahadeva built along the river Yamunā were a hundred hundred
thousands and the stipends were hundreds of thousands."

There also King Bharata, the glorious Turner of the Wheel, offered
up thirty-five Horse Sacrifices. The renowned hermitage of Sarakasta
is exceedingly holy, of him who, so I have heard, son, did the wishes
of the brahmins. The River Sarasvatī is always honored by the strict,
10 Pārtha: it is there that the Vālakhilyas offered, great king. In the same
quarter that most holy River Dṛṣadvatī is famous, Yudhiṣṭhira: here,
king of men, the very sacred Vaivarṇya and Varṇa, wise in the *Veda*,
both steeped in the sciences and the *Vedas*, always offered with holy
rituals, best of the Bharatas.

The Gods foregathered of yore in their multitudes, with Indra and
Varuṇa, and performed austerities at Viśākhayūpa; hence this spot is

very sacred. The great, lordly, glorious seer Jamadagni sacrificed
masterfully at the Palāśakas, which are both holy and lovely. All the
great rivers came in person to that best of seers, each bringing its own
water, and waited upon him, surrounding him. Here too, great king,
15 Viśvāvasu himself chanted this verse upon witnessing the puissance
of that great-spirited man: "When the great-spirited Jamadagni
worshiped the Gods, all the rivers came and satisfied him with honey."

That mountain, greatest of peaked mountains, made beautiful by
Gandharvas, Yakṣas, Rākṣasas, and Apsarās, dwelling place of
Mountain Men and Kiṃnaras, that mountain the Ganges cleft with
force at the Gate-of-the-Ganges, Yudhiṣṭhira; it is sacred, king, and
visited by hosts of brahmin seers. Here is Sanatkumāra, O Kauravya,
and holy Kanakhala, and the mountain called Puru, where
20 Purūravas was born. Bhṛgu did his austerities there, visited by hosts
of great seers: that is his hermitage, the great mountain known as
Bhṛgu's-Peak.

What is, or was, or shall be, bull among men, that is Nārāyaṇa,
the puissant, everlasting supreme person. Of this most glorious being
there is, along holy and wide Badarī, a sacred hermitage known,
which is renowned in the three worlds. The Ganges, which carries
warm water, is different along wide Badarī, carrying cool water and
gold sand. The seers and the Gods, lordly and august, always arrive
25 and pay homage to the omnipresent God Nārāyaṇa. Wherever God
Nārāyaṇa is, supreme soul and everlasting, there is the world entire,
Pārtha, and fords and sacred places. He is the holy, he is the supreme
Brahman, he is the ford, he is the forest of austerities. And with him
are the Gods, seers, Siddhas, and all the ascetics. Where the primeval
God, the great yogin Madhusūdana resides, that place is the holiest of
the holy: on that you shall harbor no doubt.

Thus, then, king, are the holy fords and sanctuaries of earth
described, best of men. They are visited by Vasus, Sādhyas, Ādityas,
Maruts, and Aśvins, by Brahmā-like seers of great spirit. If you go
30 there, Kaunteya, with the bulls of the brahmins and your lordly
brothers, you will shed your yearning.

Vaiśaṃpāyana said:

89.1 While Dhaumya was thus holding forth, O scion of the Kauravas,
the many-splendored seer Lomaśa arrived there. The king, eldest of
the Pāṇḍavas, his group, and the brahmins rose for the lordly man,
as the Immortals in the heaven rise for Śakra. Yudhiṣṭhira the King
Dharma greeted him courteously and asked him the reason for his
coming and the purpose of his wandering. At the Pāṇḍava's questions,
the great-minded seer was pleased and replied in a gentle voice,
5 gladdening the sons of Pāṇḍu: "While I was wandering through the

worlds at my whim, Kaunteya, I went to the seat of Indra and visited the lord of the Gods there. I also saw your heroic brother, the left-handed archer, who was sharing Śakra's throne. And it amazed me greatly to see the Pārtha thus seated, tiger among men! Then the lord of the Gods said to me there, 'Go to the sons of Pāṇḍu.' And here I have come at once to visit you and your brothers. At the behest of the much-lauded God and the great-spirited Pārtha, I shall tell you of matters that will please you greatly, joy of the Pāṇḍavas. Listen, king, with your brothers and Kṛṣṇā.

"You had told the strong-armed man to go out for weapons, bull
10 of the Pāṇḍavas; and indeed, the Pārtha has obtained from Rudra the great and incomparable weapon named Brahmā's-Head, which Rudra had acquired by self-mortification. That deadly weapon, which emerged from the Elixir, is now in the possession of the left-handed archer, with its spells and modes of withdrawal, expiation, and benediction. The boundlessly brave Pārtha also obtained the thunderbolt, staff, and other divine weapons from Yama, Kubera, Varuṇa, and Indra, O Yudhiṣṭhira, scion of Kuru. And from Viśvāvasu he has learned, according to all the rules, song and dance and melody and music. Thus he has succeeded with the weapons and learned the *Veda* of the Gandharvas. And now the Terrifier, your younger brother's junior, lives there happily.

15 "I shall now tell you the import of the message that the greatest of the Gods gave me, listen, Yudhiṣṭhira: 'You shall doubtless go to the world of men, and there at my behest you shall say to Yudhiṣṭhira, O best of the twice-born, "Your younger brother Arjuna shall soon return with the weapons after he has accomplished a great task for the Gods, a task of which the Celestials themselves are incapable. You and your brothers must endow yourselves with austerities: for austerities are the highest good, and one finds nothing that is greater than them. I know Karṇa well, bull of the Bharatas, and he is not
20 worth a sixteenth fraction of the Pārtha in battle. The fear you harbor of him in your heart, enemy-tamer, that fear I shall dispel when the left-handed archer has returned. The intention you entertain to visit the sacred fords, hero, to that Lomaśa shall no doubt speak fully. And you must give credence to what the great seer shall say concerning the rewards of austerities and of the fords, Bhārata!"' "

Lomaśa said:

90.1 Now listen to Dhanaṃjaya's message, Yudhiṣṭhira: "Bestow upon my brother Yudhiṣṭhira the fortune of Law, for you know the higher Laws and the austerities, ascetic, and you know the eternal Law of illustrious kings. And whatever else you know that is purifying for men, you should bestow on the Pāṇḍava with that sanctity of the sacred fords. Act with your whole heart in such a manner that the king visit the fords and make donations of cows," said Vijaya* to me. "Under your protection he should visit all the fords and he should be kept safe from the Rākṣasas in straits and perilous places. Protect the Kaunteya from the Rākṣasas, as Dadhīca protected Indra, and Angiras the Sun, O best of the twice-born. For there are many mountainous Rākṣasas who are warlocks; but if you protect the Kaunteya, they shall not besiege them."

So, at Indra's word and Arjuna's injunction, I shall journey with you, guarding you from dangers. I have visited the fords twice before, scion of Kuru; now I shall visit them with you for the third time. Virtuous royal seers like Manu and others have made the tour of the fords, Yudhiṣṭhira, great king, the tour that dispels all fears. No dishonest man, no man of unperfected soul, no man unlearned, no criminal, bathes at the fords, Kauravya, nor a man of crooked mind. But you have always been Law-minded, Law-wise, true to your promises: you shall be even more fully freed from all evil things. You shall become like King Bhagīratha, kings like Gaya and Yayāti, O son of Pāṇḍu and Kuntī!

Yudhiṣṭhira said:

My joy prevents me from finding an answer! For who is there that can be greater than he whom the king of the Gods remembers? Who is greater than he whom you visit, whose brother is Dhanaṃjaya, and whom Indra remembers? The mention you make of visiting the fords—I had made up my mind on that before, when Dhaumya spoke. Whenever you intend to go and visit the sacred fords, then I shall certainly set out, this is my total resolve!

Vaiśaṃpāyana said:

Quoth Lomaśa to the Pāṇḍava who was resolved to go: "Then travel light, great king, for unencumbered you will go more easily."

Yudhiṣṭhira said:

Let the brahmins and ascetics who live on alms go back, and also the citizens who have followed me out of loyalty for me, their king. Let them go to King Dhṛtarāṣṭra; he will in due time give them the pensions to which they have been accustomed. If the lord of men will not give you your accustomed pensions, the Pāñcāla king will give them to you as a favor to us.

Vaiśaṃpāyana said:

Thereupon the citizens, carrying heavy burdens, left for the greatest part for the City of the Elephant; and so did the brahmins and disciplined ascetics. Ambikā's son** the king received them all, and out of love for the King Dharma he satisfied them with appropriate

* = Arjuna.
** = Dhṛtarāṣṭra.

allowances. Kuntī's son the king contentedly stayed for three more nights in the Kāmyaka Forest, with Lomaśa and unencumbered brahmins.

Vaiśaṃpāyana said:
91.1 When the Kaunteya was starting out, the brahmins who had
remained in the forest came to him and said to him, O king, "Sire,
you are setting out for the sacred fords with your brothers and the
great-spirited divine seer Lomaśa. Pray take us too with you, great
King Pāṇḍava, for we are unable to go to them without you, Kaurava.
The straits and the perilous places are infested with beasts of prey,
and the fords cannot be reached by small companies of travelers, O
5 lord. You brothers are champions and masterful bowmen at all times;
under the protection of you heroes we too might reach them. By your
grace indeed we may attain to the holy rewards of fords and vows,
lord of the people, king of the land! Protected by your gallantry we
shall become pure by bathing at the fords and cleansed of evil by
visiting them, king. You too, Bhārata, will bathe at the fords and
surely attain to the rare worlds of King Kārtavīrya, of the royal seer
10 Aṣṭaka, of Lomapāda, and of the heroic sovereign Bharata. We want
to go with you and set eyes on fords like Prabhāsa, mountains like
Mount Mahendra, rivers like the Ganges, and trees like the Plakṣa! If
you have any love for the brahmins, king, then do now what we ask
of you, and you shall find fortune. The fords are infested with
Rākṣasas who always obstruct austerities, pray save us from them!
Make the tour of the fords that have been mentioned by Dhaumya
and the wise Nārada, and those of which the divine seer and ascetic
Lomaśa has spoken. Visit them all in the right way, shedding all evil,
accompanied by us and protected by Lomaśa!"
15 When he was thus prayed to by them and sprinkled with their
tears of joy, the bull of the Bharatas, standing in the midst of
Bhīmasena and his other brothers, said to the seers, "So be it then."
With Lomaśa's leave, and the priest Dhaumya's, the masterful eldest
of the Pāṇḍavas, his brothers, and the flawless Draupadī prepared to
start. Thereupon the sages, the lordly Vyāsa and Nārada and Parvata,
appeared to visit the Pāṇḍava in the Kāmyaka Forest. King Yudhiṣṭhira
paid his respects to them, and after the honors had been done the
lordly seers spoke to Yudhiṣṭhira: "Yudhiṣṭhira, twins and Bhīma,
practice uprightness in your hearts, be clean and pure, and go to the
20 fords! Controlling one's body, say the brahmins, is the human vow;
purifying the spirit with thought, say the twice-born, is the divine
vow. An unsoiled mind is a match for heroes, lord of men: adopt a
friendly spirit and, being pure, go to the fords. Purified by mental

vows of body control, and adopting the divine vow, you shall obtain
the reward that has been declared."
The Pāṇḍavas and Kṛṣṇā promised that they would do so. They all
had their journey blessed by hermits divine and human; they
embraced the feet of Lomaśa and Dvaipāyana, of the divine seer
25 Nārada and Parvata, great king; and, accompanied by Dhaumya and
the other forest-dwellers, the heroes set out from there on the day
when the moon of Mārgaśīrṣa had set under Puṣya. Wearing sturdy
bark and deerskins, hair braided, armored with impenetrable
cuirasses, they then went on their round of the sacred fords. With
Indrasena and the other retainers, with the full complement of
fourteen chariots, and with other servants busy at the mess carts,
taking their weapons, carrying quivers and arrows, their swords girt,
the Pāṇḍava heroes set out facing east.

Yudhiṣṭhira said:
92.1 I do not think of myself as without virtue, O best of divine seers,
yet I am set upon by sorrows as no other king on earth. My foes, I
think, have no virtue, nor are they devoted to the Law, yet they
prosper in this world, but for what reason, Lomaśa?
Lomaśa said:
You have no cause whatever, king, to feel sorry that people who
revel in lawlessness prosper outside the Law. A man prospers without
Law, sees good things, and defeats his rivals—but perishes with root
5 and all. For I have seen the Daityas and Dānavas prosper outside the
Law, and then they came to their downfall.
Of yore, in the Eon of the Gods, I witnessed it all, my lord, how the
Gods delighted in the Law and the Asuras abandoned it. The Gods
visited the fords, Bhārata, the Asuras did not. Springing from their
lack of Law, pride first invaded them; from pride grew vainglory,
vainglory begot anger, from anger came shamelessness, and
shamelessness destroyed their conduct. When they had become
shameless, profligate, corrupt, and debased, patience, fortune, and
Law left them soon. Fortune went to the Gods, and misfortune to the
10 Asuras. Thus pervaded by misfortune, their minds dominated by
pride, the Daityas and Dānavas were invaded by discord. Overwhelmed
by misfortune and discord, and overpowered by pride, Kaunteya,
lacking rites, driven mindless, and overcome with vainglory, their
destruction came to pass soon; and, defamed, the Daityas perished
totally.
The Gods, however, went to the oceans and rivers and lakes,
practicing the Law, and to sacred sanctuaries. By means of austerities,
rites, gifts, and blessings, Pāṇḍava, they shed all evil and found bliss.

15 Thus, fully observing gifts and rituals, the Gods went to the sacred fords and thereby attained to the highest prosperity. Likewise you too, great king, shall bathe with your brothers at the fords and find again your fortune: that is the eternal path. Just as King Nṛga and Śibi Auśīnara, as Bhagīratha and Vasumanas, Gaya, Pūru, and Purūravas, always observing austerity, were made pure and won sacred fame and treasure by touching water, going to the fords, and visiting with great-spirited men, O lord of the people, so you too, Indra among
20 kings, shall win ample fortune. Just as Ikṣvāku went with his sons, relations, and people, as Mucukunda, Māndhātar and King Marutta found sacred fame, as the Gods did by the power of austerities, and as the divine seers all did, so you too shall find it. But the Dhārtarāṣṭras, enslaved by their pride and ignorance, will no doubt soon perish like the Daityas.

Vaiśaṃpāyana said:
93.1 So the heroes and their company lodged here and there until they gradually reached the Naimiṣa Forest, O king. The Pāṇḍavas did their ablutions at the sacred fords of the River Gomatī, O king Bhārata, and gave away cows and wealth. The Kauravas satisfied there the Gods, ancestors, and brahmins again and again at the Ford-of-the-Maiden, the Ford-of-the-Horse, and the Ford-of-the-Cows. After staying the night at Vālakoṭi on Mount Vṛṣaprastha, the Pāṇḍavas all bathed
5 in the River Bāhudā, O king. They bathed their limbs and observed high austerity at Prayāga, king, and they stayed at the Offering-Place-of-the-Gods. At the confluence of the Ganges and Yamunā they bathed, keeping their vows, great-spirited and free from evil, and gave wealth to the brahmins. Then they went, the sons of Pāṇḍu, with the brahmins to the Altar-of-Prajāpati, which is frequented by ascetics, King Bhārata. The heroes stayed there, observing high austerity, always satisfying the twice-born with offerings of forest fare.

From there they proceeded to the mountain venerated by the Law-
10 wise, beneficient royal seer Gaya of peerless luster, where lies the Lake Gayaśiras, and where the holy Mahānadī flows; here too is the sublime Lake-of-Brahmā, very sacred and visited by the seers. It is here that the blessed Agastya went to Yama Vaivasvata and that the eternal Dharma himself lived, king. It is the well from which all rivers spring, lord of your people, and where the Great God-who-wields-the-Pināka* is always present. There the Pāṇḍava heroes offered up the Seasonal Sacrifices with the great rite of the seers at the great banyan tree Akṣayavaṭa. Ascetic brahmins gathered there by the hundreds; then they sacrificed with the Seasonal Sacrifice according to the rite
15 of the seers. Brahmins, steeped in the *Veda*, constant in knowledge

* = Śiva.

and austerities, expounded sacred tales of great-spirited men while they sat in the *sadas*.

It was there that a brahmin named Śamatha, versed in sciences
and vows, who kept the vow of virginity, told about Gaya
Āmūrtarayasa, O king. "Hear from me, Bhārata, the saintly deeds of
that most excellent of royal seers Gaya, the son of Amūrtarayas. He
held a sacrifice here of much food and rich stipends, where there
were mountains of rice by the hundreds and thousands, many streams
of *ghee* and rivers of curds, and torrents of delicious sauces by the
20 thousands. Day after day food was provided to all who asked, king,
and the brahmins ate other food that was specially cooked. At the
time of the distribution of the stipends the sound of the Brahman rose
to heaven, so that nothing could be heard but the sound of the
Brahman, Bhārata. Earth, space, sky, and heaven were filled with
that loud traveling sound, it was indeed a great marvel. Men sang
songs there, bull of the Bharatas, sated with the pure food and drink,
shining in all directions: 'What creatures are there who still want to
eat at Gaya's sacrifice? Where there are twenty-five mountains of
25 leftover food? No men before have done, nor shall men later do, what
Gaya, the royal seer of boundless luster, did at this sacrifice. How
shall the Gods, fully sated by Gaya with offerings, be able to partake
of anything more given by others?' Very many songs of this kind
were sung at the sacrifice of the great-spirited man, close to this lake,
scion of Kuru!"

3(33.a) Agastya

94–108 (B. 96–109; 8539–9967)
94 (96; 8539). The daitya Ilvala and his brother Vātāpi live in Maṇimatī. Ilvala has the power to revive the dead. He would change his brother Vātāpi into a goat, feed him to a brahmin, then call Vātāpi to life, thus killing his eater (1–10). Agastya sees his ancestors hanging in a cave. They demand offspring, which Agastya promises (10–15). Not finding a suitable woman, he creates one and gives her as daughter to the king of Vidarbha; she is called Lopāmudrā. She grows up lovely (15–25).
95 (97; 8569). Agastya goes to the Vidarbha king and demands Lopāmudrā; he reluctantly bestows her (1–5). Agastya has her forsake her finery; she becomes an ascetic. Finally he summons her to cohabitation (10–25).

She asks for fine adornment; Agastya pleads poverty, but promises to find some (20–25).
96 (98; 8595). Agastya asks a share of King Śrutārvan's wealth. The king shows that his income and expenses just balance (1–5). Agastya desists. With Śrutārvan he goes to King Vadhryaśva, where the same happens (5–10). Agastya, Śrutārvan, and Vadhryaśva go to King Trasadasyu; again the same happens (10–15). All now go to Ilvala (15–20).
97 (99; 8617). Ilvala receives them; he cooks his brother for a meal of mutton. Agastya eats and digests him before he can be revived (1–5). Agastya demands treasure, which Ilvala reluctantly bestows; he returns with it to Lopāmudrā (5–15). She asks for a superior son; after seven years Dṛḍhasyu is born (15–25).
98 (100; 8689). In the Kṛtayuga, the Dānavas banded with Vṛtra. The Gods resort to Brahmā, who tells them to beg the bones of the seer Dadhīca and to fashion a thunderbolt with them (1–10). Dadhīca's idyllic hermitage (10–15). Dadhīca complies and falls dead. Tvaṣṭar makes a thunderbolt out of his bones (15–20).
99 (101; 8714). The Gods attack Vṛtra and the demons; the Gods have to retreat, and Indra despairs. Viṣṇu's splendor enters the thunderbolt. Full of fear, Indra kills Vṛtra, then jumps in a lake. The demons retreat to the ocean (1–15). They decide to murder the ascetics and thereby the world (15–20).
100 (102; 8736). The Kāleya demons kill off ascetics in their hermitages, and the Gods are in distress. They resort to Nārāyaṇa, whom they praise (1–20).
101 (103; 8763). The Vindhya wanted the sun to circumambulate it too, as it does the Meru. Fate would not have it. The Vindhya then began to grow to obstruct the sun; even the Gods did not prevail. The Gods then went to Agastya (1–5). Agastya approached the mountain and told it to stop growing until he returned from a journey south. He has not yet returned (10). —— The Gods now ask Agastya to drink up the ocean; he agrees and goes to the ocean (15–20).
103 (105; 8805). Agastya drinks the ocean, and the Gods kill the Kāleyas (1–10). The Gods tell Agastya to restore the ocean, but it has already been digested. The Gods repair to Brahmā (10–15).
104 (106; 8825). Brahmā promises that eventually the

ocean will be restored on account of King Bhagīratha's kinsmen (1). King Sagara is sonless. After austerities, he sees Śiva whom he and his wives beg for a son. The God promises sixty thousand sons by one wife, and one by the other (1–15). The wife aborts of a pumpkin, the seeds of which are kept in incubators (15–20).
105 (107; 8849). Sixty thousand fierce sons are born, who oppress the earth; Brahmā predicts their downfall (1–5). King Sagara holds a Horse Sacrifice; the horse strays into the dry ocean bed. Sagara sends his sons to find it; they fail (5–15). They try again and dig up earth, at great cost of life. In the netherworld they see the sage Kapila (15–25).
106 (107; 8878). In their urgency they ignore Kapila, who irately burns all of them with a glance. Nārada tells Sagara (1–5). The king summons Aṃśumat, the son of Asamañjas, the king's one son by his second wife; he had banished this son since he molested the citizens (5–15). Sagara asks his grandson Aṃśumat to find and fetch the sacrificial horse (15). Aṃśumat placates Kapila, who releases the horse and promises the deliverance of the sixty thousand Sāgaras through Aṃśumat's grandson, Bhagīratha. Sagara concludes his sacrifice (15–30). Aṃśumat succeeds him, is succeeded himself by Dilīpa, who has a son Bhagīratha (35–40).
107 (108; 9921). Bhagīratha, a Cakravartin, turns to austerities and propitiates the Ganges (1–15). The Goddess appears. Bhagīratha explains about the unlaved ashes of his ancestors, the Sāgaras, and asks the river to come down and lave them. She agrees, if Hara catches her on his head. Bhagīratha so persuades Hara (15–25).*
108 (109; 9948). In response to Bhagīratha's prayers, the Ganges descends on Hara's brow (1–10). She asks Bhagīratha where to go; he guides her to the Sāgaras' ashes in the ocean bed. The river fills up the ocean (10–15).

Vaiśaṃpāyana said:

94.1 Thereupon King Kaunteya of the generous stipends departed, went to Agastya's-Hermitage, and stayed at Durjaya. There the king, best of interlocutors, questioned Lomaśa: "For what reason did Agastya here

*Page 561 of C. ends with 8,899, page 562 begins with 9,900, with a consequent error of 1,000 *ślokas* in the numbering.

immolate Vātāpi; and what was the power of the Daitya, that man-
killer? What roused the wrath of the Great-spirited Agastya?"

Lomaśa said:

There was once, scion of the Kauravas, a Daitya named Ilvala in
5 the city of Maṇimatī, and Vātāpi was his younger brother. The Daitya
said to a brahmin of ascetic power, "Blessed lord, grant me a son
equal to Indra!" The brahmin refused to give him a son of the
measure of Vāsava, and the Asura was exceedingly angry with the
brahmin because of that. Now, if Ilvala summoned with his voice one
who had gone to the realm of Yama Vaivasvata, that person would
resume his body and appear alive. He then changed the Asura Vātāpi
into a well-cooked goat, and after feeding him to the brahmin he
would summon the goat back. Then the great Asura Vātāpi broke
open the side of the brahmin and came out of him laughing, king,
10 lord of your people! In this fashion he fed brahmins again and again,
king, and brought them harm, this evil-minded Daitya Ilvala.

At this time the blessed Agastya saw his forebears hang in a cave
with their heads down. He asked his hanging fathers, "What is your
object, sirs?" "Offspring!" replied the scholars of the Brahman. They
said to him, "We are your own ancestors and have ended in this cave,
hanging down because we are wanting in progeny. If you, Agastya,
were to beget a sublime child, we would be released from this hell
15 and you, son, would attain to the goal!" That man of splendor, always
bent on the Law of truth, said to them, "I shall do your desire, fathers.
Let the fever of your minds depart."

As he reflected upon the matter of offspring, the blessed seer found
no woman equal to himself to bear his child. Then he collected from
different creatures such limbs as were matchless; and with those
limbs he fashioned a superb woman. Then the great ascetic and
hermit, when he had finished fashioning her, gave her to the king of
Vidarbha, who was pining for a child, to keep her safe for himself.
And there she was born, lovely like garland lightning, and she grew
20 up fair-faced, radiant with beauty. No sooner had she been born than
the king of Vidarbha announced her happily to the brahmins,
Bhārata. All the brahmins, O ruler of earth, welcomed her and the
twice-born gave her the name of Lopāmudrā. She grew up, great
king, wearing a superb beauty; she grew up quickly, like a lotus in
water, or the sacred crest of the fire.

When she was nubile, king, a hundred well-decked maidens and a
hundred slave girls waited on the beautiful damsel at her beck and
call. Surrounded by her hundred slaves and amidst her hundred
maidens, she sat resplendent as in the sky the asterism of Rohiṇī, my
25 lord. And although she was nubile and accomplished in manners and

conduct, no man chose her, out of fear of the great-spirited sage. Yet the true-spoken girl, who in beauty surpassed the Apsarās, contented her father and kinfolk with her manners. When he saw the princess of Vidarbha, so accomplished, become a woman, her father worried in his heart: "To whom may I give my daughter?"

Lomaśa said:

95.1 When Agastya thought she was ripe for householding, he
approached the king of Vidarbha and said, "Sire, I have resolved on
matrimony for the sake of a son. I elect you, herdsman of the earth:
give me Lopāmudrā!" At this address of the hermit, the king was split
in his mind, unable to refuse and unwilling to give. He went to his
wife. Said the king, "He is a powerful seer. If angered, he may burn
5 me with the fire of his curse!" Seeing the king and his wife so
distressed, Lopāmudrā went to them in time and said, "Please, sire,
do not because of me feel oppressed! Give me to Agastya and save
yourself by means of me, father."

At his daughter's word the king then bestowed, with the proper
rites, Lopāmudrā on the great-spirited Agastya, O lord of your people.
Having got himself a wife, Agastya said to Lopāmudrā, "Throw out
these fine clothes and ornaments!" They were beautiful and costly
and sheer, but the woman of plantain-tender thighs and long eyes
10 discarded the clothes. She put on tatters and bark skirts and
deerskins, and the long-eyed woman took on the vows and way of
life of her husband.

The blessed grand hermit went to the Gate-of-the-Ganges and together with his compliant wife undertook awesome austerities. She served her husband with love and respect, and the lordly Agastya found the greatest pleasure in his wife. Then, after many a day, the blessed seer, O king, glanced at his wife when she had bathed and was luminous with austerity. As he had been pleased by her attendance, her cleanliness and her discipline, her beauty and loveliness, he summoned her to intercourse.

15 With folded hands she stood there, blushing as though bashful,
and addressed the blessed lord with this love-pleading word: "No
doubt a husband finds himself a wife for the sake of children. But
pray return to me, seer, the pleasure that you find in me: please lie
with me on as fine a bed as the bed I had on the terrace of my
father's house, brahmin! And I'd like you to come to me garlanded
and decked with ornaments, while I am bejeweled with divine
ornaments to my taste."

Agastya said:

But Lopāmudrā, my pretty, no such treasures are found with me as are found with your father, woman of the pretty waist!

Lopāmudrā said:

20 With your austerities you are capable of fetching anything, great lord, anything at all that is found in the world of the living, and in an instant!

Agastya said:

It is as you say, but it would be a waste of my austerities. Order me so that my austerities do not dwindle!

Lopāmudrā said:

Little time is left of my season, ascetic, and I do not want to lie with you but so. Nor do I wish to waste your Law, ascetic, but please dispose as it pleases me.

Agastya said:

It is your desire, dear, your spirit has decided upon it. All right, I go, good woman, and do it. Stay here as you please.

Lomaśa said:

96.1 Thereupon, O Kauravya, Agastya went to beg treasure of King Śrutārvan, whom he knew to be richer than other kings. When the king heard that the jar-born sage had arrived, he and his ministers received him at the border of his realm with great honor. After he had tendered the guest gift in the proper fashion, the king of the land stood with folded hands and humbly asked for the purpose of his coming.

Agastya said:

Sire, know that I have come in search of wealth. Give me a share of it, if you can without depriving others.

Lomaśa said:

5 The king acquainted him with a full account of his income and expenditures. "Now that you know, take from it the wealth you want." Observing that income and expenses were equal, the equitably-minded brahmin judged that any taking would mean hardship for the subjects. He took Śrutārvan with him and went on to Vadhryaśva, who received them both at the border of his realm, as was proper. Vadhryaśva offered the guest gift and foot water, and begged leave to ask for the purpose of his coming.

Agastya said:

Know that we have come in quest of wealth, my lord of the land. Give us a share of it, if you can without depriving others.

Lomaśa said:

10 The king acquainted both with a full account of income and expenditures. "Now that you know, take what is left over." Observing that income and expenses were equal, the equitably minded brahmin judged that any taking would mean hardship for the subjects.

All three went to Trasadasyu Paurukutsa, who was rich—Agastya,
Śrutārvan, and King Vadhryaśva. And Trasadasyu received them all
at the border of his realm, as was proper, coming that far with his
mounts, great king. He greeted them in the right manner, that best
of kings Ikṣvāku; and when they were comfortable he asked for the
reason of their coming.

Agastya said:

15 Sire, we have come here wanting for riches. Give us a share, if you
can do so without depriving others.

Lomaśa said:

The king acquainted them with a full account of income and
expenditures. "Now that you know, take what is left over." Observing
that income and expenses were equal, the equitably minded brahmin
judged that any taking would mean hardship for the subjects. So all
those kings got together and looked at one another; and they said to
the great hermit, "There is this Dānava on earth, brahmin, the rich
20 Ilvala. Let us all go to him and ask him for wealth." They all thought
it right to go begging of Ilvala; and so they went off to Ilvala
together.

Lomaśa said:

97.1 When Ilvala learned that the kings had come with the great seer,
he and his ministers greeted them at the border of his realm. The
eminent Asura showed them hospitality and offered them his brother
Vātāpi cooked, Kauravya. The royal seers were all distressed and
rendered witless, when they saw the great Asura cooked as mutton.
Then the great seer Agastya said to the royal seers, "Do not despair,
5 I shall eat the great Asura." The great seer took the best seat and sat
down; and Ilvala, lord of the Daityas, served him with a semblance
of laughter. Agastya ate Vātāpi entire, and when he had finished
eating the Asura Ilvala summoned his brother. The great-spirited
seer gave vent to wind, and Ilvala despaired when he saw the great
Asura had been digested. With folded hands he and his ministers
said, "Why have you come? Speak, what can I do for you?"
Laughing, Agastya replied, "We all know that you are wealthy,
10 Asura, and a lord of riches. These kings are not too rich, and I have
a great need for wealth. Give us a share, if you can without depriving
others." With a gesture of salute Ilvala said to the seer, "If you know
what wealth I mean to give you, I will do so."

Agastya said:

You mean to give the kings ten thousand cows each, great Asura,
and as much gold. And to me you mean to give twice that, as well as
a golden chariot, great Asura, and two horses fast as thought.
Inspect the chariot at once: it is plainly made of gold.

Lomaśa said:

It was ascertained that the chariot was made of gold, Kaunteya,
15 and painfully the Daitya gave superior riches, and the horses Vivāja
and Suvāja yoked to the chariot. In a twinkling of the eye, O
Bhārata, the team hurried the treasure to Agastya's hermitage. Then
Agastya dismissed the royal seers, and they left. And the hermit did
everything that Lopāmudrā wanted.

Lopāmudrā said:

My lord, you have done my every desire. Now beget on me at once a child of the greatest power.

Agastya said:

I am pleased with your conduct, beautiful and radiant woman. I shall tell you the question I am deliberating concerning your offspring, listen. You shall have either a thousand sons, or a hundred who each match ten, or ten who equal a hundred each, or one son worth a thousand.

Lopāmudrā said:

20 Let me have one son who equals a thousand, ascetic; for one wise
and virtuous son is better than many of no virtue!

Lomaśa said:

"So shall it be," promised the hermit, and at the right time he faithfully lay with his faithful wife, who equaled him in virtue. And when he had planted the seed, he went to the forest.

While he lived in the forest, the embryo grew for seven autumns;
and when the seventh year was full, a glorious great sage issued
forth, fairly blazing with power, reciting the *Vedas* with their branches
and *Upaniṣads*, who bore the name of Dṛḍhasyu, O Bhārata. The great
and splendid seer became the seer's son. As a child this splendid son
used to fetch a load of kindling in his father's dwelling and hence
25 became known as Idhmavāha. Seeing his son so endowed the hermit
was happy; and his ancestors attained to the worlds they desired,
O king.

This is the famous Hermitage-of-Agastya, which flowers in all seasons; and thus was Vātāpi Prāhrādi killed by Agastya. His hermitage is lovely, king, and full of virtues; and here is the holy River Bhāgīrathī,* in which you should bathe to your liking.

Yudhiṣṭhira said:

98.1 I wish to hear more, to hear in full the exploits of the great-
spirited wise seer Agastya, O best of the twice-born!

Lomaśa said:

Then listen, great king, to the divine, wondrous, superhuman geste of Agastya and the power of the great-spirited seer.

* = Ganges.

In the Eon of the Winning Throw there were fearsome Dānavas, berserk in battle, very dangerous bands, who were notorious as the Kāleyas. They flocked to Vṛtra and, with their many weapons raised, stormed everywhere at the Gods led by Indra. The Thirty Gods then plotted the killing of Vṛtra, and placing the Sacker of Cities* at their head they approached Brahmā. He-Who-Dwells-on-High spoke to them all, while they folded their hands: "I know fully the task you wish to undertake, Gods. I shall propound to you the means by which you will kill Vṛtra. There is a great seer of profound mind who is known as Dadhīca. Go ye all together to him and beg a boon. The law-minded sage will grant it to you in very happy spirits. All of you, if you wish for victory, must say to him, for the well-being of the worlds, 'Give us your own bones!' He will abandon the body and give you his bones. With the bones you must fashion a hard and dreadful thunderbolt, large, sharp, six-cornered, of terrifying sound, which is capable of killing the foe. With this bolt the God of the Hundred Sacrifices will slay Vṛtra. All has been told you, so carry it out quickly."

When the Grandfather had thus spoken, the Gods took their leave and, placing Nārāyaṇa ahead, they went to Dadhīca's hermitage, on the other bank of the Sarasvatī. It was wooded with all kinds of trees and creepers, noisy with the humming sounds of bees like singers of Sāmans, mixed with the calls of the cuckoo, and alive with the whirring of insects. Buffalo grazed everywhere with swine, marsh deer, and yaks, without any fear of tigers. Elephants, their burst temples running with ichor, were playing with their females and plunged into ponds and thundered on all sides. The hermitage resounded with the mighty roars of lions and tigers and of other creatures that lie hidden in caves and hollows. It was to this very lovely hermitage of Dadhīca, adorned with all these features, like heaven in aspect, that the Gods went.

They found Dadhīca there, with a glow like the sun's, blazing bright with beauty as the Grandfather with Lakṣmī. The Gods bowed deep and greeted his feet, O king; and they all begged a boon, as Brahmā had told them.

Thereupon Dadhīca, greatly pleased,
Made this reply to the eminent Gods:
"I shall act today, Gods, toward your welfare,
And even abandon my body for you!"

Having spoken thus, that greatest of men,
Who controlled himself, gave up the ghost;

* = Indra.

And as he lay suddenly dead, the Gods
Took away his bones as they had been told.

In the highest of spirits and hope of triumph
The Gods repaired to Tvaṣṭar and spoke;
And on hearing their word the Carpenter worked
Devotedly, diligently, happy of heart.

He fashioned a thunderbolt, fearsome and hard,
And having made it spoke, pleased, to Śakra:
"With this most excellent thunderbolt, God,
Reduce to ashes the foul foe of the Gods!

"The enemy slain, sway at ease with your host
All of the third heaven, aloft in the sky!"
And at Tvaṣṭar's word the Sacker of Cities
Humbly and happily seized hold of the bolt.

Lomaśa said:

99.1 Then the Thunderbolt-wielder, protected by the powerful deities,
assailed Vṛtra, who kept covering heaven and earth, guarded all
around by the gigantic Kālakeyas like peaked mountains with
weapons raised. A battle instantly began between Gods and Dānavas,
best of the Bharatas, a mighty battle that caused great trembling. As
they grouped and raised their swords with their heroes' arms, the
5 sound of them thudding into bodies became terrifying. Heads tumbled
down from heaven onto earth and looked like cocoa nuts loosened
from their stalks. The golden-cuirassed Kāleyas, armed with bludgeons,
stormed at the Gods like mountains wrapped in fire.
The Thirty Gods were unable to withstand the onslaught of those
vehement, rushing ranks; they broke and ran in a panic. Seeing them
flee in fear, the Sacker of Cities of the Thousand Eyes became faint of
heart, while Vṛtra kept growing. But observing Śakra's faint-
heartedness, the eternal Viṣṇu placed his own splendor within him,
increasing his might. When the hosts of the Gods saw Śakra swollen
10 by Viṣṇu, they all placed their own splendor within him, and so did
the immaculate brahmin seers. Swollen mightily with the help of
Viṣṇu, the deities, and the lordly ones, Śakra waxed strong.

But knowing the band of the Thirty restored
To their power, the Coverer* roared great roars.
And his roar made earth and the quarters and sky
And heaven and mountains quake, all of them.

Upon hearing that roar, so gruesome and loud,
Great Indra himself was sorely beset

* = Vṛtra.

And, drowning in fear, led hastily loose
His powerful bolt to kill him, O king.

In his garland of *kāñcana* blossoms he fell,
Struck by Indra's bolt the great Asura fell,
As of olden times Mount Mandara,
Greatest of mountains, fell from Viṣṇu's hand.

15 The eminent Daitya was killed, but yet
Fear-stricken did Indra plunge in a lake;
In his fear he failed to believe in the bolt
That his hand had sped, or in Vṛtra's death.

All the Gods were delighted and full of joy,
The magnificent seers gave praise to Indra;
They fast engaged all the Daityas in battle
And killed those aggrieved at Vṛtra's death.

They were being slain by the Thirty Gods
And in panic they entered the waves of the ocean.
And down in the deep of the measureless sea
That is stirred by sharks and filled with pearls

They plotted together and made their plans
To destroy all the world with smiling faces.
Some there who were wise in deciding plans
Reflected upon the various ways.

And as they were thinking, this dreadful plan
In the course of Time became their resolve:
"The ones who are sages and ascetics
Shall be the first to be destroyed.

20 "For austerities hold up all the worlds,
So hasten to kill austerities!
Whatever ascetics there are on earth,
And those who know Law and grasp the Yon,
Of them a slaughter be made at once:
When they are gone the world will be gone!"

And having made it their decision and purpose,
Most gleefully, to destroy this world,
They made the pearl-rich, billowing ocean,
That realm of Varuṇa, their redoubt.

Lomaśa said:

100.1 When they had taken their refuge in Varuṇa's ocean, the Kāleyas made preparations to destroy the world. Every night the raging demons devoured whatever hermits they found in hermitages and sacred sanctuaries. In the Hermitage of Vasiṣṭha the miscreant band devoured a hundred and eighty-eight brahmins and nine other ascetics. They went to the holy Hermitage of Cyavana, which is visited by the twice-born, and ate one hundred of the hermits, who lived on fruit and roots. This they did in the nighttime; by day they vanished into the ocean. At the Hermitage of Bharadvāja they destroyed twenty restrained celibates who lived on wind and water. In this fashion the Kāleya Dānavas gradually invaded all the hermitages, maddened by their confidence in the strength of their arms, killing many hosts of twice-born, until Time crawled in upon them. The people did not know about the Daityas, best of men, even as they were oppressing the suffering ascetics. In the morning they would find the hermits, who were lean from their fasts, lying on the ground in lifeless bodies. The land was filled with unfleshed, bloodless, marrowless, disemboweled, and disjointed corpses like piles of conch shells. The earth was covered with shattered sacrificial jars, broken offering ladles, and scattered *agnihotras*. Under the oppression of the Kāleyas the study of the *Vedas* and the oblation calls had stopped, the practice of sacrificial festivals was lost, and thus the world was left without enterprise.

While men were wasting away in this manner, O lord of men, they ran from fear into all directions to save themselves. Some hid in caves, others behind waterfalls, others were so fearful of death that the fear killed them. There were also proud and heroic bowmen who did their utmost to hunt down the Dānavas; but they could not find them, for they were hidden in the ocean; and the bowmen succumbed to exhaustion and death. When the world neared perdition and the performance of sacrificial festivals had come to an end, the Thirty Gods became utterly distressed, O king. From fear they assembled and with Indra they took counsel together; and they sought recourse with the unvanquished Nārāyaṇa Vaikuṇṭha.

The assembled Gods spoke to Madhusūdana: "Thou art of us and the world creator, protector, and keeper, O lord! Thou hast created all this, whatever stirs or does not stir. When of yore the earth was lost, lotus-eyed God, thou didst rescue it from the ocean, assuming the form of a boar, for the sake of the world. The powerful, ancient Daitya Hiraṇyakaśipu was destroyed by thee, greatest of persons, in the form of a man-lion. The great Asura Bali, who was invulnerable to all beings, was thrown out of the three worlds by thee in the form of a dwarf. Thou hast caused the fall of the Asura archer famed as Jambha, the cruel wrecker of sacrifices. Countless indeed are thy feats such as these: Slayer of Madhu, thou art the refuge of us who are oppressed with fear! Therefore, O God, lord of Gods, we address thee for the good of the world: protect the creatures and the Gods and Śakra from this great ordeal!"

The Gods said:

101.1 It is on gifts from here that the four classes of creatures thrive; and
having been prospered, they prosper the celestials with their
oblations. Thus the different worlds have their being and rely on one
another; and it is thou who by thy grace keepst them safe and
undisturbed. Now this terrible peril has befallen the worlds, and we
do not know who kills the brahmins in the night. When the
5 brahmins have perished, the earth will fall to its perdition. When the
earth has perished, heaven will fall to perdition. May it please thy
grace, mighty-armed lord of the universe, that with thy protection all
the world survive!

Viṣṇu said:

I know fully, Gods, why the creatures are being destroyed, and I
shall tell you too; listen without fever. There is a very dangerous band
known as the Kāleyas. They joined Vṛtra and oppressed the entire
universe. When they saw Vṛtra killed by the wise Thousand-eyed
God, they saved their lives by entering Varuṇa's realm. They have
now plunged into the fearsome ocean, infested with crocodiles and
sharks, and by night they now kill the hermits on earth, to extirpate
10 the worlds. They cannot be killed, for they have shelter in the ocean.
You must set your minds on destroying the ocean, and who but
Agastya is capable of laying the ocean dry?

Lomaśa said:

Having heard this utterance of Viṣṇu, the Gods took their leave from Parameṣṭhin and went to Agastya's hermitage. There they found the great-spirited son of Varuṇa blazing with splendor, waited upon by seers as the Grandfather is by the Gods. They approached the great-spirited unvanquished son of Mitrāvaruṇa, a mass of austerities, in his hermitage and praised him for his acts.

The Gods said:

When of old the worlds suffered under Nahuṣa, you were their
refuge, and for the world's good this thorn of the creatures was
15 toppled from the sovereignty of the Gods. Out of anger with the sun,
the Vindhya, that best of mountains, began to grow suddenly, but it
could not trespass on your command, and the mountain stopped
growing. When the world was covered with darkness and the
creatures were beset by Death, they found you for their protector and
attained to complete safety. When we are afraid of danger, you,
blessed lord, always are our refuge—hence, we beg of you a boon in
our distress, for you are a granter of boons!

Yudhiṣṭhira said:

102.1 Why did the Vindhya suddenly begin to grow in a fit of anger? I wish to learn about this in full detail, great hermit.

Lomaśa said:

The Sun used to perform at his rising and setting a circumambulation of great Mount Meru, the golden mountain, the king of ranges. Upon seeing that, Mount Vindhya said to the Sun, "Perambulate me in the same fashion, Maker of Light, as you every day circumambulate Meru!" The Sun replied to that lord of mountains, "It is not by my own desire, mountain, that I circumambulate him: that is the path that was assigned to me by Him who created the world."

5 Upon hearing this answer the mountain became angry and began to grow suddenly, endeavoring to obstruct the paths of sun and moon, enemy-burner. All the Gods assembled and with Indra approached that great regal mountain. They tried with all means to make him desist, but he refused to do what they asked. Thereupon they went to the ascetic hermit Agastya, first of the upholders of the Law, in his hermitage, and together the Gods told him of the matter.

The Gods said:

This regal mountain the Vindhya is a prey to his anger and obstructs the paths of the sun and moon and stars. No one can halt him, best of the twice-born, except you, lordly seer: therefore make him desist!

Lomaśa said:

10 When the brahmin heard the words of the Gods, he went to the
mountain. Approaching it with his wife, he said to the Vindhya,
"Best of mountains, I demand you give me passage. I am going to the
south on some business. Wait until I return from there. When I have
come back you may grow all you want!" So he made a compact with
the Vindhya, and until today Varuṇa's son has not returned from the
south. Now I have told you at your bidding why the Vindhya stopped
15 growing, because of Agastya's power. Listen now as I tell you how
the Kāleyas were destroyed by all the Gods, when they had received
a boon from Agastya.

After hearing the prayer of the Thirty Gods, Mitrāvaruṇa's son said, "Why have you come, why do you want a boon from me?" The Gods replied to the hermit, "We wish you, great-spirited seer, to drink up the ocean. Then we shall kill those foes of the Gods, the Kāleyas, with their followers." The hermit assented to the request of the Thirty Gods: "I shall do your wish and show great favor to the creatures."

Having spoken, the seer of good vows went to the ocean, the husband of the rivers, together with the Gods and seers perfected in

20 austerities. Men, Snakes, Gandharvas, Yakṣas, and Kiṃpuruṣas
followed the great-spirited man, wishing to see his miracle. Together
they went to the sea of the terrible thunder, which seemed to dance
with its waves and to leap with the wind, to laugh with its foam
patches, and to stumble in its pits, teeming with all kinds of predator
fish and overflown by birds of all feathers. With Agastya, the Gods,
Gandharvas, great Snakes, and the lordly seers approached that great
vessel of water.

Lomaśa said:

103.1 When they had reached the ocean, the blessed seer Vāruṇi said to
the gathering Gods and seers, "Now, for the well-being of the world I
shall drink up Varuṇa's ocean. Quickly do what you have to do!"
With these few words the unvanquished Maitrāvaruṇi angrily drank
dry the ocean, while all the world looked on. When the Gods and
Indra watched the ocean being drunk, they were completely
5 astounded and honored him with praise: "Thou art our savior and
the disposer for the creatures, world prosperer! It is by thy grace that
the universe and the Immortals are saved from perdition!"

While he was being honored by the Gods, and the music of the
Gandharvas sounded on all sides, and divine blossoms were strewn
on him, the great-spirited man laid the ocean dry. When they saw
that the great ocean was empty of water, all the Gods rejoiced
greatly. They took the fine, divine weapons and with cheerful
gallantry killed off those Dānavas. The Dānavas were exterminated
by the great-spirited Thirty, who were mighty and impetuous and
noisy with roars; they could not withstand the impact of the
impetuous, great-spirited celestials. The Dānavas were being killed by
the Thirty, and roared terrifyingly, and at once put up a tumultuous
10 fight, O Bhārata. They had already been burned by the hermits of
perfect souls with the power of their mortifications; now, although
they strove their mightiest, they were destroyed by the Thirty. In their
ornaments of gold plates, earrings, and upper-arm bracelets, they
shone prettily as they lay dead like flowering *kiṃśukas*. Some of the
Kāleyas survived the rest, O best of men, and they cleaved Goddess
Earth and sought refuge in the netherworld.

Seeing the Dānavas slain the Thirty gave praise to that bull among
hermits with a variety of lauds, and they said to him, "It is by thy
grace, lordly seer, that the creatures have attained to great happiness,
and by thy splendor that the cruelly brave Kāleyas have been cut
15 down. Now, mighty-armed man, prosperer of the world, fill up the
ocean again: restore the water you have drunk." The blessed lord,
bull among hermits, replied, "I have already digested the water.
Think of another way to fill the ocean. Do your best!" When the

assembled Gods heard the reply of that great seer of perfected soul, they were amazed and distressed. They took leave of one another and bowed before the bull among hermits; then, O great king, all the creatures went their various ways. The Thirty Gods approached the Grandfather* with Viṣṇu, great king, after having again and again taken counsel with one another on how to fill the ocean. And, folding their hands, they all spoke concerning the filling of the ocean.

Lomaśa said:

104.1 Brahmā, the Grandfather of the world, spoke to the Gods who had
gathered: "Depart ye all, Gods, where and as you please. After a long
span of time the ocean will return to its natural state, and the
occasion will be the kinsmen of the great King Bhagīratha."

Yudhiṣṭhira said:

In what way were the kinsmen the occasion, brahmin, and what was the occasion, hermit? How was the ocean filled by the labors of Bhagīratha? This I want to hear in full, ascetic, as you recount the great gestes of the kings, priest.

Vaiśampāyana said:

5 At these words of the great-spirited King Dharma, the regal
brahmin told of the greatness of the great-spirited Sagara.

Lomaśa said:

There was a king by the name of Sagara, who was born in the
dynasty of Ikṣvāku, a majestic king of beauty, character, and strength.
He was sonless. He extirpated the Haihayas and the Tālajanghas,
Bhārata, he subjugated the other kings and swayed his own
kingdom. He had two wives who prided themselves on their beauty
and youth, one Vaidarbhī, a princess of Vidarbha, and one Śaibyā, a
daughter of the Śibis, O bull of the Bharatas. The king, who longed
for a son, performed very great austerities, having taken refuge at
10 Mount Kailāsa, O Indra among kings. While he was doing his very
great austerities and became possessed of *yoga*, he approached the
great-spirited Three-eyed God, the crusher of Tripura, the hail-
bringing Bhava the Lord, who wields the trident and the Pināka,
Śiva Tryambaka, the Dread Lord, the many-shaped Consort of Umā.

As soon as he saw the boon-granting God, the strong-armed king
and his two wives prostrated themselves, and he begged him for a
son. Kindly, Hara said to that good king and his wives, "As this is the
hour at which you have pleaded with me for a boon, king, sixty
thousand valiant sons shall be born to you by one of your wives, best
15 of men. They shall all perish together, king, but one hero shall be
born from the other wife and be the dynast." After these words
Rudra vanished on the spot. Thereupon King Sagara in the company
of his two wives returned to his dwelling place, exulting in his heart.

* = Brahmā.

Then his two lotus-eyed wives, O best of men, Vaidarbhī and
Śaibyā, got with child; and in time Vaidarbhī gave birth to a
pumpkin-gourd abortion. And the Śaibyā bore a man child of divine
beauty. The king decided to cast away the gourd, but then he heard
20 from the sky a rumbling voice: "Do not act rashly, do not reject your
sons! Take the seeds out of the pumpkin and let them be carefully
kept, each in a steaming pot filled with *ghee*. Then you will obtain
sixty thousand sons, O king. The Great God* has disposed the birth
of your sons in this manner, do not decide otherwise!"

Lomaśa said:
105.1 When he heard this from the sky, best of kings, the king trustingly
did as he was told, bull of the Bharatas, and sixty thousand sons of
unmatched splendor were born to the royal seer by the grace of
Rudra. They were ferocious, cruel of deeds, and crawled all over space;
and because of their number they despised all creatures, and even the
Immortals. The warlike champions pestered the Gods, Gandharvas,
Rākṣasas, and all other creatures.
5 While the worlds were being slaughtered by the slow-witted
Sāgaras, the creatures and all deities sought refuge with Brahmā. The
lordly Grandfather of all the worlds said to them, "Depart ye all,
Gods, with the creatures, the way you have come. After not too long
a time there will occur a very ghastly massacre of the Sāgaras,
brought on by their own deeds, ye Gods." Having been told this, the
Gods and creatures took leave from the Grandfather and went back as
they had come.

After many a day had passed, bull of the Bharatas, the mighty
King Sagara underwent the consecration for a Horse Sacrifice. His
10 horse roamed over the earth protected by his sons, and strayed to the
waterless ocean, which looked forbidding. There the horse disappeared,
well watched though it was. The Sāgaras, my son, thinking that their
fine stallion had been carried off, returned and told their father that
the horse had been stolen mysteriously. He ordered them, "Search all
the horizons for the horse!" At their father's command they searched
all the horizons for the horse, great king, and the entire surface of the
earth. Then they all gathered together again, but failed to find the
horse and the horse thief. They returned to their father, and, folding
15 their hands before them, they said to him, "Sire, at your behest we
have searched the earth entirely, with her seas and forests and islands,
her male and female rivers, her caves, mountains, and forested places,
but we have not found the horse, nor its thief."

When he heard their words, the king was insensate with rage, and
at divine prompting, king, he said to them all, "Go, never to return!
Search again for the horse, sons: you are not to return without the

* = Śiva.

sacrificial stallion!" Sagara's sons accepted the command and once
more began to search the entire earth. Then the heroes saw a gaping
chasm in the earth; they went into the hole and, digging down, dug
20 up the ocean bed with their hoes and spades. While it was being dug
into by the joint forces of the Sāgaras, Varuṇa's realm, rent on all
sides, suffered extreme pain. Asuras, Snakes, Rākṣasas, and all kinds
of creatures cried out in pain, when they were being killed by the
Sāgaras.

Once-alive creatures were now seen decapitated, trunkless, with
knees, bones, and skulls shattered—by the hundreds and thousands.
But although they dug up in this fashion the ocean, that haunt of
crocodiles, a long time passed and the horse was still unfound. Then,
in the northeastern corner of the ocean, O king of the earth, the
raging sons of Sagara dug down to the netherworld, and there they
saw the horse grazing on the ground; and they also saw the great-
25 spirited Kapila, a matchless mass of splendor, blazing with his
austerities as fire with its flames.

Lomaśa said:

106.1 Seeing the horse, king, they shivered with excitement and without paying heed to the great-spirited Kapila, since Time drove them on, they dashed furiously forward to recover the horse. This angered that great hermit Kapila, king, that great hermit Kapila whom they call Vāsudeva. He opened his eyes wide and shot his splendor at them. And the splendiferous seer burned down the slow-witted Sāgaras.

The great ascetic Nārada saw them reduced to ashes, and he went
5 to Sagara and told him. When the king heard this terrible news from
the hermit's lips, he stood for a moment mindless, then he recalled
Sthāṇu's* words. He consoled himself and thought about the horse.
He summoned his grandson, Aṃśumat, who was the son of
Asamañjas, O tiger of the Bharatas, and spoke to him thus: "Those
sixty thousand sons of boundless power have encountered the
splendor of Kapila and perished on my account. Your own father, too,
I have abandoned, blameless child, to safeguard the Law and to
benefit the citizens."

Yudhiṣṭhira said:

Why did Sagara, that tiger among kings, abandon his own heroic son, one so hard to abandon? Tell me, ascetic!

Lomaśa said:

10 Sagara had had a son by the name of Asamañjas, whom his wife Śaibyā had borne. This son used to grab the defenseless sons of the townspeople by their hooves and throw them screaming into the river. Flooded by fear and sorrow, the citizens assembled and, standing

* = Śiva.

with folded hands, all petitioned Sagara: "Great king, you are our protector from such dangers as the wheels of the enemy; therefore pray save us from the dreadful peril of Asamañjas!" When he heard this terrifying plea of his citizens, that best of kings stood mindless for a moment, then spoke to his ministers: "Let my son Asamañjas be banished from the city at once. If you want to do me a favor, do it at once!" At the king's speech the ministers hastened to do as their king had bidden them. This tells the whole story of how the Great-spirited Sagara, who had the welfare of his citizens at heart, banished his son.

Now I shall recount to you fully what Sagara said to the great archer Aṃśumat. Listen to me as I tell you.

Sagara said:

Son, I suffer under my rejection of your father, the death of my sons, the loss of my horse. Therefore rescue me, for I am suffering grievously and am senseless because of the disruption of my sacrifice, by bringing back the horse from the netherworld, grandson!

Lomaśa said:

At these words of the Great-spirited Sagara, Aṃśumat sorrowfully went to the place where the earth had been rent asunder. By the same way he entered the ocean and found the Great-spirited Kapila and the horse. Upon finding the ancient great seer, a mass of splendor, he bowed his head to the ground and told him his task. Splendid Kapila was pleased with Aṃśumat, and the Law-minded seer said to him, O Bhārata, "I am a granter of boons." The other chose first the horse for the good of the sacrifice, second he chose water to purify his fathers. Splendid Kapila, bull among hermits, said to him, "Bless you, I will give you whatever you seek, prince sans blame. On you are founded patience and Law and truth. Through you Sagara shall be fulfilled, and your father shall have sons. And by your power the Sāgaras shall go to heaven, and your grandson shall bring the River-of-the-Three-Courses* down from heaven, after he has satisfied the Great Lord, to purify the Sāgaras. Bless you, bring home the sacrificial horse, bull among men! The sacrifice of the Great-spirited Sagara must be concluded, my son!"

When the Great-spirited Kapila had spoken, Aṃśumat took the horse and went to the sacrificial grove of the Great-spirited Sagara. He greeted the feet of the Great-spirited Sagara, who kissed his head, and told him everything. He told him what he had seen and heard of the destruction of the Sāgaras and that the stallion had returned to the sacrificial grove. On hearing this King Sagara shed his grief over his sons and after honoring Aṃśumat concluded the ritual. His sacrifice concluded, Sagara was feasted by all the Gods, and he adopted the ocean, Varuṇa's realm, as his son. After reigning for a

* = Ganges.

long time over his kingdom, the lotus-eyed king placed his burden on
his grandson and went to heaven.
35 The Law-spirited Aṃśumat governed the sea-girt earth, O great
king, as his father had. He got a Law-wise son by the name of Dilīpa,
to whom he entrusted the kingdom; then he departed. But Dilīpa,
when he heard of the great massacre of his forebears, grieved with
sorrow and pondered upon their destiny. He made a very great effort
to bring down the Ganges, but though he acted to the fullness of his
power, he did not succeed. He in turn had a son, illustrious and
devoted to the Law, a son famed as Bhagīratha, true-spoken and
without demurrers. Dilīpa anointed him to the kingdom and sought
40 refuge in the forest; and, bull of the Bharatas, with the accumulation
of the perfection of his austerities, the king in time departed from the
forest for heaven.

Lomaśa said:

107.1 This warrior king,* a great bowman and a Turner-of-the-Wheel,
became the joy of the hearts and the eyes of all the world. The strong-
armed prince heard that the Great-spirited Kapila had brought about
that terrible end of his forebears, and that they had failed to go to
heaven. The king of men entrusted the kingdom to his minister and
with burning heart went to the slope of the Himālaya to do austerities
there, wishing to propitiate the Ganges.
His sins burned off by his self-mortifications, he set eyes, O best of
5 men, on the sublime Mount Himālaya, ornamented with many-shaped
and mineral-rich peaks, and on all sides embraced by clouds that
floated on the wind. Rivers and arbors and swells adorned it, it
abounded in water, and lions and tigers inhabited it, lying in caverns
and caves. The mountain was astir with all kinds of shapes of birds
that warbled their various tunes, with big bumble-bees, swans, moor
hens, moor cocks, peacocks, pheasants, cuckoos, woodpeckers, *cakoras*
with black-cornered eyes, and love-their-youngs down in its lovely
watery places, and it was abloom with lotus ponds. It was melodious
10 with the sweet cries of herons, and its rock plateaus were frequented
by Kiṃnaras and Apsarās. Everywhere the trees had been scratched
by the points of the tusks of the world elephants. The region, visited
by the Spirits of the Air, was covered with many kinds of precious
stones and infested with virulently poisonous snakes that had blazing
tongues.

Thus he approached the Himālaya, which here burned like gold, there shone like silver, there darkled like a mass of collyrium. It was there that the king engaged in dreadful austerities, living on fruit, roots, and water for a thousand years. When a divine millennium

* = Bhagīratha.

had gone, the great River Ganges showed herself in bodily form.

The Ganges said:

15 What do you wish from me, great king? What should I give you?
Speak, best of men, I shall carry out your word.

Lomaśa said:

At these words the king replied to the daughter of the Himālaya, "Boon-granting river, my grandfathers were sped to the realm of Yama by Kapila, when they were searching for their horse. The sixty thousand Great-spirited Sāgaras encountered Kapila's splendor and were instantly destroyed. As long as you do not wash their bodies, a sojourn in heaven will be denied to my dead ancestors. Lead the sons of Sagara, my forebears, to heaven, great lady, I beg you for their sake, mighty river!"

20 When she had heard the king's words, the Ganges, she who is
worshiped by the creatures, was greatly pleased and made to
Bhagīratha this reply: "I shall accomplish what you ask, great king,
beyond a doubt. But the impact of my fall from heaven will be most
difficult to endure. In all three worlds there is no one to sustain it but
the first of the Gods, the Blue-Throated Great Lord.* Placate the boon-
granting Hara with austerities, strong-armed king: the God shall
catch me on his head when I fall down. And he shall fulfill your
desire out of favor for your forebears."

On hearing her words, the great King Bhagīratha went to Mount
25 Kailāsa and placated the Hail-bringer. And after a span of time the
good man met with him and obtained from him the boon that he
would catch the Ganges, so that a sojourn in heaven would be
vouchsafed to his ancestors.

Lomaśa said:

108.1 After hearing Bhagīratha's plea, and to do a favor to the celestials,
the blessed Lord said to the king, "So shall it be! For your sake I shall
catch the auspicious, holy, and divine river of the Gods when she
falls from heaven, great king!" Having said this, O strong-armed king,
he went to the Himālaya surrounded by his terrifying familiars, who
brandished all kinds of weapons. He took his stand there and said to
Bhagīratha, best of men, "Now, strong-armed king, pray to the river,
the daughter of the Himālaya: I shall catch the greatest of rivers,
when she falls down from heaven."

5 When he heard this declaration of the Hunter, the king bowed
humbly and addressed his thoughts to the Ganges. And in response
to his thoughts, and seeing the Lord stand there, the lovely and holy
river mightily plunged from heaven. Seeing her plunge, the Gods and
great seers, the Gandharvas, Snakes, and Rākṣasas gathered to

* = Śiva.

witness the event. So the Ganges of the raging whirlpools, teeming with fish and crocodile, the daughter of the Himālaya, fell from heaven. And Hara caught the sky-girt Ganges when she fell on his brow, like a string of pearls.

10 Thus the Ganges became triple, meandering with water floods that were covered with patches of foam like rows of wild geese. Here tortuously coiling, there stumbling and tripping, she made her way like a drunken woman, wrapped in her robe of foam, but sometimes roaring a great roar with the thunder of her waves.

When she reached the surface of the earth, after showing a great many manifestations while she plunged from heaven, she said to Bhagīratha, "By what path should I go? Show me, great king. I have descended to earth for your sake, king of the earth!" Having heard her words, King Bhagīratha journeyed to the spot where the bodies lay of the great-spirited Sāgaras, O best of men, in order to purify
15 them with her holy water. —— After having caught the Ganges, Hara, who is worshiped by the creatures, went with the Thirty Gods to the great Mount Kailāsa. —— But the king went down to the ocean with the Ganges and with vigor filled up the ocean, which is the realm of Varuṇa. The king adopted the Ganges as his daughter and offered the water to his ancestors, and his desire was fulfilled.

So I have told you all that you asked me—how the Ganges-of-the-Three-Courses was made to descend to the earth to fill up the ocean, and how the brahmin-killer Vātāpi was led to his perdition by Agastya, my lord, great king.

3(33) The Tour of the Sacred Fords (continued)

Vaiśaṃpāyana said:

109.1 Thereupon Kuntī's son, O bull of the Bharatas, traveled in stages to the rivers Nandā and Aparanandā, which dispel the danger of evil. When the king reached the salubrious Mount Hemakūṭa, he saw very many marvelous and incomprehensible things. It is there that from the mere utterance of a word clouds arise and landslides of thousands of boulders fall, so that the despondent populace is unable to climb the mountain. The wind always blows there, and the God always
5 rains; and fire is visible in the morning and evening. Upon seeing such various things the Pāṇḍava again queried Lomaśa about the marvel.

Lomaśa said:
Listen attentively, enemy-plowing king, while I tell you as I have
once heard it related. On this peak of Mount Ṛṣabha there lived an
ascetic named Ṛṣabha. This man of austerities was many hundreds
of years of age, and very irascible. Now, when others kept talking to
him, he angrily said to the mountain, "If anyone says a word here,
you should throw rocks." The ascetic summoned the wind and said,
"Not a word!" And so a body that speaks out is stopped by a
10 raincloud. Thus that great seer in his anger accomplished certain
deeds and forbade others.
Once when the Gods came out to the River Nandā, so we hear,
king, people suddenly began following them around and watching
them. The Gods led by Śakra did not like being watched and rendered
the region inaccessible with mountainous obstacles. From then on,
Kaunteya, people have been unable to look at this mountain, let
alone ascend it. A man who has not done austerities cannot set eyes
on this great mountain, or climb it, Kaunteya: therefore control your
15 speech. Here all the Gods used to offer up grand sacrifices, and to this
day their traces can be found, Bhārata. This *durvā* grass has the
shape of *kuśa*, and the ground is covered with it. And, lord of your
people, these many trees are shaped like sacrificial poles. The Gods
and seers still live here today, Bhārata, and in the evenings and
mornings their fire of sacrifice can be seen.
The evil of those who bathe here is instantly destroyed, Kaunteya;
therefore, O best of the Kurus, perform here with your brothers the
proper ablutions. After you have bathed your limbs in the Nandā, you
will go to the River Kauśikī, where Viśvāmitra of yore practiced
austerities without equal.
Vaiśaṃpāyana said:
20 The king and his group bathed their limbs there and went on to
the holy and lovely River Kauśikī, whose waters are propitious.

3(33.b) Ṛśyaśṛnga

110–13 (B. 110–13; C. 9989–10094)
110 (110; 9989). On the bank of the Kauśikī lies the hermitage of Vibhāṇḍaka Kāśyapa, father of Ṛśyaśṛnga; the latter restored the crops to King Lomapāda of Anga and married his daughter Śāntā (1–5). At Yudhiṣṭhira's bidding (5–10) Lomaśa narrates. Vibhāṇḍaka engages in austerities by a great lake. On seeing the Apsarā

Urvaśī he spills his seed in the water (10). A thirsty doe drinks the water, becomes pregnant, and gives birth to Ṛśyaśṛnga, who wears an antelope horn; he never meets a human being but his father (15). King Lomapāda abuses the brahmins who thereupon leave; Indra stops raining. Lomapāda is advised that the brahmins are angry with him; he should seek their pardon and also fetch Ṛśyaśṛnga (15–25). Placated, the brahmins return. To lure Ṛśyaśṛnga, Lomapāda summons the courtesans, who consider it impossible. But one old bawd will try (25–35).
111 (111; 10077). The woman has a lovely hermitage built on a boat and moors close by Ṛśyaśṛnga's hermitage; she sends the daughter to the hermit (1–5). She greets him and is welcomed; she scorns his gift of fruit, instead offers him her own delicacies and fine raiment (5–10). She plays with a ball, plucks flowers, and sets out to seduce him, then retreats (10–15). Vibhāṇḍaka appears and questions his strange-looking son (15–20).
112 (112; 10051). Ṛśyaśṛnga describes his visitor's beauty, earrings, breasts, girdle, and anklets in hermit's terms (1–5). He recounts her ball-playing, embraces, offer of sweets and wine; he now feels lonely (10–15).
113 (113; 10070). Vibhāṇḍaka warns him that his visitor is from the demons, who should be shunned; he goes looking for her for three days (1–5). The courtesan returns, and Ṛśyaśṛnga follows her into the floating hermitage. They sail to the king's palace, and the king houses him in the serail. Indra starts raining, and Ṛśyaśṛnga marries the king's daughter Śāntā (5–10). The king stations herdsmen and cattle on Vibhāṇḍaka's road to his capital Campā. When Vibhāṇḍaka reaches them, they explain it is all his son's property. Vibhāṇḍaka is mollified; Ṛśyaśṛnga should return to the forest after the birth of a son. Ṛśyaśṛnga and Śāntā live happily (10–25).

Lomaśa said:

110.1 This is the Kauśikī, the holy river of the Gods, bull of the Bharatas; here shines forth the holy hermitage of Viśvāmitra. And so does the Hermitage, called Puṇya, of the great-spirited scion of Kaśyapa, the father of an ascetic son Ṛśyaśṛnga, who was the master of his senses: it was he who by the power of his austerities caused Vāsava to rain:

out of fear of him the Slayer of Vala and Vṛtra brought rain during a drought. This Kāśyapa's mighty and splendid son was born from a doe and performed a great miracle in the realm of Lomapāda. When the crops had been restored, King Lomapāda gave him his daughter Śāntā, as the sun gave Sāvitrī.

Yudhiṣṭhira said:

How was Ṛśyaśṛnga born from a doe as Kāśyapa's son, in forbidden miscegenation, and how did he acquire austerities? Why did Śakra, the Slayer of Vala and Vṛtra, rain forth when a drought was on, out of fear of the wise boy? What beauty did Princess Śāntā of strict vow possess that she seduced his heart when he lived like a deer? While it has been heard that Lomapāda was a law-abiding royal seer, how did it come about that the Chastiser of Pāka failed to rain in his realm? Pray, reverend lord, tell me, for I am curious to hear it, in full detail and truthfully, the geste of Ṛśyaśṛnga!

Lomaśa said:

Then listen how to the brahmin seer Vibhāṇḍaka, who had perfected his soul with austerities, whose virility was never-failing, and whose luster was as Prajāpati's, the majestic Ṛśyaśṛnga was born a son at a great lake, a most splendid boy, honored by the elders.

Kāśyapa had gone to this great lake, where he for a long time engaged in austerities, exhausting himself, and was honored by the Gods and seers. There he saw the Apsarā Urvaśī, and his seed spilled forth while he was bathing in the water, king. A thirsty doe drank it up with the water, and became with young, O lord; for the destiny laid down by fate unfailingly must be. From that doe a great seer was born a son, Ṛśyaśṛnga. The boy, always austere, grew up in that very forest. The great-spirited child wore an antelope horn on his head, king, and hence became famed as Ṛśyaśṛnga. Besides his father he had never seen a human being in his life, so that his mind was ever set on a life of chastity, my king.

At that time a friend of Daśaratha, Lomapāda by name, was the king of Anga. The story goes that he arbitrarily forced his whims on the brahmins, and the brahmins deserted the lord of the earth. So, because the king's priest had run away, the Thousand-eyed God spontaneously stopped raining and the subjects suffered. The king interrogated wise and austere brahmins, who were capable of making the lord of the Gods rain: "How will Parjanya rain forth? Find a means!" At his urging the sages spoke their own thoughts. But one eminent hermit among them said to the king, "Indra of kings, the brahmins are wroth with you—seek atonement! Fetch the hermit's son Ṛśyaśṛnga, king, he is a forest child, ignorant of women, and devoted to uprightness. If the great seer descends to your realm,

Parjanya will at once rain forth, I have no doubt of that."
Upon hearing this advice the king performed an expiation for
himself: he went away and returned when the brahmins had forgiven;
and seeing their king returned, the subjects received him back. Then
the king of Anga summoned his ministers, who were wise in their
counsels, and made an effort to decide on a counsel that would bring
Ṛśyaśṛnga. With the aid of his ministers, knowledgeable in the
sciences, proficient in profit, and well-versed in policy, the undefeated
30 king conceived of a plan. He had brought in the courtesans of the
first degree; and his majesty said to the women of the district, who
were skilled in everything, "Bring, with any means, the seer's son
Ṛśyaśṛnga to my realm, beautiful wenches, by seducing and
comforting him!"
The women, as fearful of the king's ire as of a curse, turned pale,
lost heart, and declared the task impossible. But one old woman
among them said to the king, "Mahārāja, I shall try to bring the
ascetic here. Pray allow for certain luxuries I have in mind. Then I
35 shall seduce the seer's son Ṛśyaśṛnga!" The king allowed for all the
woman's needs and gave her plentiful wealth and various gems. And,
king of the earth, she took several women, who were fully endowed
with beauty and youth, and went to the forest with alacrity.

Lomaśa said:

111.1 To further the success of the king's business, she designed a
hermitage mounted on a boat, Bhārata, both at the king's orders and
with her own ingenuity. It was prettily wooded with artificial trees of
various blossoms and fruit and landscaped with many kinds of
bowers that yielded sweet fruit of every taste. She designed it,
surpassing lovely and surpassing charming, this water-borne
hermitage, beautiful and of wondrous aspect. She made fast the boat
a short distance from Kāśyapa's hermitage and had some men scout
5 the grounds of the hermit. Then the courtesan, after reflecting on the
task in hand and perceiving an opportunity, sent off the daughter
who was renowned for her wit. The clever woman went to the
ascetic, approached the hermitage, and saw the seer's son.

The courtesan said:

Are the men of austerities in good health?
Are your fruit and roots, O hermit, abundant?
Do you take joy in this hermitage?
I have come to visit you here today!

The ascetics' austerities, do they grow?
Does your father maintain his wonted splendor,

And is he, O brahmin, pleased with you?
Have you done your lessons, Ṛśyaśṛnga?

Ṛśyaśṛnga said:

As an opulent light dost thou glimmer forth,
And I deem thy honor worth saluting.
I shall gladly give thee the foot water, sir,
And according to Law the roots and the fruit.

10 Pray sit at thy ease on this *kuśa* cushion,
Decked with a black deerskin and comfortable.
Where is thy hermitage, what is the name
Of this vow thou, brahmin, observeth like a God?

The courtesan said:

My lovely hermitage, Kāśyapa's son,
Is beyond these three leagues of mountain range.
There salutations are not of our Law,
Nor do we use water to wash our feet!

Ṛśyaśṛnga said:

I will give you fruit that have ripened, sir,
Like marking-nuts and myrobalans,
Parūṣaka, inguda, dhanvana berries,
And *priyāla* fruits for you to enjoy.

Lomaśa said:

But rejecting all that he offered, the woman
Presented him with the costliest viands,
Exquisite of taste and beautiful-looking,
Which gave Ṛśyaśṛnga pleasure aplenty.

She gave very fragrant garlands to him,
And colorful and flamboyant clothes,
And the finest liquors; and then she laughed
And happily played about, making merry.

15 She frolicked at his side with a ball,
Like a flowering creeper, loose and swirling;
And seductively touching his limbs with hers,
Embraced Ṛśyaśṛnga, embraced him often.

She bent the branches and plucked the flowers
Of *sarjas, aśokas,* and *tilaka* trees,
And shamelessly, overcome with liquor,
She began to seduce the seer's son.

Then seeing the change in Ṛśyaśṛnga,
She squeezed his body again and again,
And slowly retreated with many glances,
Pretending the *agnihotra* was due.

When she had gone, love crazed Ṛśyaśṛnga,
And the seer's son went out of his mind;
Left empty by feelings that followed her steps,
He heaved many sighs, a picture of grief.

In a while, with the tawny eyes of a lion,
Covered with hair as far down as his nails,
Possessed of learning, conduct, and insight,
Appeared Vibhāṇḍaka, Kaśyapa's scion,

20 Drew near and saw his son, who was seated,
Alone, and in thought, his mind disturbed,
The eyes raised to heaven, and often sighing—
Vibhāṇḍaka spoke to his wretched son,

"No kindling wood has been fetched yet, son?
Have you still not offered the *agnihotra*?
Are the offering ladles cleaned? Did you bring yet
The offering cow and her calf for the milk?

"You do not seem as you were, my son,
You are given to brooding and absentminded.
You look most troubled today, but why?
I ask you, who has been here today?"

Ṛśyaśṛnga said:

112.1 A student came, who had braided hair,
Full of spirit, not short, but neither too tall,
Of a golden color and long lotus-eyes,
As radiant as a son of the Gods.

His opulent body shone like the sun,
His eyes were white and black like *cakoras*,
His braids were blue-black, translucent, and fragrant,
Fastened with gold thread and very long.

At his throat he wore what looked like cups
That shone as the lightning shines in the sky,
And below the throat he had two globes,
Without a hair on them, most beguiling.

About the navel his waist was pinched,
But his hips again were very full;
And beneath his habit there glittered a girdle,
Like this belt of mine, but made of gold.

What is more, and a wonderful thing it was,
At his feet he seemed to have a tinkle;
To his hands likewise were tied some strings,
Like my prayer beads, but his made music.

Whenever he moved, these beads of his
Would sound like mad wild geese in a pond.
His habits were a marvelous sight,
They were not like mine, but prettily shaped.

And his face was no less wondrous a vision,
The words he spoke seemed to gladden the heart;
His voice was like the cuckoo's song,
That bothered my innermost soul as I listened.

Just as in the middle month of spring
The forest wafts fragrance stirred by the wind,
So he wafted a holy and beautiful fragrance,
Whenever, father, the wind would touch him.

His well-combed braids were so arranged
That they split on his brow in equal halves;
His ears were surrounded, it seemed, by circles,
Which were full of color and finely shaped.

With his right hand he bounced a round
And colorful object that looked like a fruit;
When it got to the ground again and again,
It would spring back and upward, wonderfully.

He would hit it and then swing himself around,
His body aquiver like a wind-tossed tree;
When I saw him, father, a child of the Gods,
Great joy and love were born in me.

He embraced my body time and again,
And pulling my hair he lowered my mouth;
He placed his mouth upon mine and sounded
A sound that begot great pleasure in me.

He held no truck with foot water either,
Nor by these fruit that I fetched for him.

"My life rule is this," he said to me,
And gave me other and novel fruit.

Those fruit of his, I ate them all,
Their taste was not like these at all,
Nor had they a skin like these ones have,
And, unlike ours, they did not have stones.

15 Magnanimously he gave me liquids
To imbibe of utterly flavorful taste:
As soon as I drank them, surpassing joy
Seized hold of me and the earth seemed to sway.

These are the beautiful fragrant garlands
That he himself knotted up with string.
He scattered the garlands and left for his own
Place of hermitage, bright with austerity.

His leaving left me out of my mind,
And my body feels exceedingly hot.
I want to go back to him straightaway,
And have him return here every day.

I am going, father, I'll go back to him,
Pray tell what the name of his life rule is,
I want to observe it together with him,
The awesome austerity practiced by him!

Vibhāṇḍaka said:

113.1 They are demons, son, who stalk the earth,
In all their wondrously beautiful shapes!
They are peerlessly lovely and very cruel,
And plot to prevent austerities.

Flaunting their beauteous bodies, my son,
They seek to seduce with various means;
And, dread in their deeds, they drop from their world,
And from their welfare, the forest hermits.

A self-controlled hermit must not frequent them
At all, if he seeks for the worlds of the strict.
They stop ascetics, and then they delight
In spoiling their penance, innocent son.

Those liquids were evil liquors, my son,
Forbidden, and cherished by wicked folk;

And garlands like these, fragrant and shining,
Are not described as fit for hermits.

Lomaśa said:

5 "They are demons!" Vibhāṇḍaka said to stop
His son, but then he went hunting for her;
Three days he searched, and when he failed
To find her, returned to his hermitage.

But meanwhile that Kāśyapa's scion had gone
To gather fruit in ascetical fashion,
That courtesan woman herself returned
To seduce the hermit Ṛśyaśṛnga.

No sooner did Ṛśyaśṛnga see her
Than he happily met her in great confusion.
And he said to her, "Quick, let us go to your
Retreat before my father returns!"

Thereupon they enticed him into the boat,
King, Kāśyapa's son, and sailed away,
While tempting him with all manner of lure,
Until they moored at the king of Anga's.

He had that exceedingly beautiful boat
Moored and anchored in view of a hermitage;
And likewise he built close to the bank
A lovely wood named the King's Retreat.

10 The king had Vibhāṇḍaka's only son
Brought to and kept in the women's quarters;
And suddenly saw the God raining forth,
And the earth being filled and flooded with water.

And Lomapāda, his wishes fulfilled,
Gave his daughter Śāntā to Ṛśyaśṛnga;
To counter Kāśyapa's wrath, he worked
With cattle and had the roads plowed up.

Wherever Vibhāṇḍaka had to pass,
The king ordered cattle and warlike herdsmen:
"When Vibhāṇḍaka comes in search of his son
And the eminent seer interrogates you,

"You must fold your hands and tell him thus:
'These cows are your son's and the crops are his.

Great seer, what may we do to please you?
We are all your slaves and wait on your word!' "

Then came the hermit, whose fury was fierce,
After gathering fruit and roots, back to his place;
And he looked for his son and did not find him,
And failing to find him, he waxed very wroth.

15 Then, split asunder by his own wrath,
Suspecting that this was the work of the king,
He went to Campā to set on fire
That king of the Angas and all his realm.

Exhausted and hungry, Kaśyapa's scion
Encountered prosperous cattle stations;
The herdsmen paid him courteous honors
As though he were king, and he spent the night there.

Receiving all honors from those his hosts,
He said, "Good men, whose tenants are you?"
Whereupon they humbly drew near and said,
"All this is the wealth that your son dispenses."

In place after place he was honored as guest,
And as he heard their flattering talk,
His anger was all but appeased, and happy
He approached in his city the king of Anga.

The bull among monarchs welcomed him,
And he saw his son, an Indra in heaven;
He saw Śāntā there, his daughter-in-law,
Running up to him like garland lightning.

20 On seeing the villages, herds, and his son,
And Śāntā, his towering rage subsided;
Vibhāṇḍaka now, O Indra of men,
Showed the greatest grace to the king of the land.

The great seer left his son there in trust,
And spoke to him shining like fire and sun,
"Once a son has been born, you shall come to the forest,
After granting this king all the favors he asks."

Ṛśyaśṛnga obeyed his father's behest
And returned to the spot where his father lived;
And Śāntā religiously waited on him,
As compliant Rohiṇī waits on the Moon,

As the lucky Arundhatī waits on Vasiṣṭha,
As Lopāmudrā attends on Agastya,
And as Damayantī did on Nala,
Or Śacī does on the Thunderbolt-wielder.

And as Indrasenā Nāḍāyanī
Obeyed Mudgala always, O Ājamīḍha—
So did Śāntā obey in the woods Ṛśyaśṛnga,
King, caring for him, possessed by love.

25 Here shines the holy retreat of that saint
Of holy renown, to Mahāhrada's luster:
Bathe here; and, your duty done and hallowed,
You shall, sire, proceed to other fords.

3(33) *The Tour of the Sacred Fords (continued)*

Vaiśaṃpāyana said:

114.1 Thereupon the Pāṇḍava set out for the river Kauśikī, O
Janamejaya, and visited one after the other all the sanctuaries. He
traveled to the ocean at the estuary of the Ganges and made his
ablutions in the middle of the five hundred rivers. Thereafter the
heroic overlord of the earth traveled with his brothers along the
shoreline, to the land of the Kalingas, Bhārata.

Lomaśa said:

This is Kalinga, Kaunteya, where the River Vaitaraṇī flows, where
5 even Dharma sought refuge with the Gods and did sacrifice. Here is
the northern bank, which the seers enjoy, a sacrificial terrain made
beautiful by the mountain, always sought after by the twice-born.
Here other seers, too, have of yore offered up the sacrifice and gone
to heaven by the even Route of the Gods. In this same place, O Indra
of kings, Rudra took the sacrificial animal at the sacrifice, lord of
men, and declared, "This is my share!" When the animal was stolen,
the Gods said to him, O bull of the Bharatas, "Do not threaten
another's property, do not destroy all the Laws!" Later they lauded
Rudra with eloquent words, satisfied him with an *iṣṭi*, and paid him
10 honor. Whereupon he let go of the animal and went by the Route of
the Gods. This is the chronicle verse of Rudra here, listen,
Yudhiṣṭhira: "Out of fear of Rudra, the Gods forever decided that the

best share of all that was not stale should be Rudra's." A man who touches the water while chanting this verse has the Route-of-the-Gods as his pathway and his eye shines forth.

Vaiśaṃpāyana said:

Then all the lordly Pāṇḍavas and Draupadī descended into the Vaitaraṇī and made offerings to the ancestors.

Yudhiṣṭhira said:

No sooner do I bathe in this river, blessed ascetic Lomaśa, than lo!
15 I transcend the human domain! By your grace, saint of good vows,
I have a full view of all the worlds—this is the sound of the great-
spirited Vaikhānasas as they pray!

Lomaśa said:

The place from which the sound you hear is coming is three hundred thousand leagues away, Yudhiṣṭhira! Sit silent, lord of the people.

The wood that appears here is the lovely wood of the Self-existent,
where, O King Kaunteya, the majestic Viśvakarman offered up his
sacrifice. At this sacrifice, in fact, the Self-existent gave earth with
her mountains and forested places as a fee to the great-spirited
Kaśyapa. No sooner given away than earth began to pine, Kaunteya,
and she angrily said to the lord sovereign of the worlds, "Lord, thou
20 mayest not give me away to any mortal! Thy gift has been in vain, I
shall go to Rasātala!" But when he saw earth despondent, the
blessed seer Kaśyapa appeased her, lord of the people. Pacified by his
austerities, O Pāṇḍava, earth once more emerged from the water and
appeared in the form of an altar, king, in the right configuration.
Ascend it, great king, and you shall be endowed with virility.

I myself shall pronounce the benediction
As soon as you have ascended the altar.
For when the altar is touched by a mortal,
It will enter the ocean, Ājamīḍha.

25 Now nimbly climb upon this altar,
While speaking this true word, O Pāṇḍava:
"Fire, Mitra, Womb, and Water Divine,
And Viṣṇu's seed thou art, navel of order!"

Vaiśaṃpāyana said:

When the blessing had been pronounced on him,
Great-spirited Yudhiṣṭhira went to the sea-altar,
And when he had done his entire behest,
He went to Mahendra and spent the night.

3(33.c) Kārtavīrya

115–17 (B. 115–17; C. 10123–10213)
115 (115; 10123). *Yudhiṣṭhira asks a hermit Akṛtavraṇa about the coming of Rāma Bhārgava; it will be on the morrow* (1–5). *He relates that King Gādhi of Kānyakubja retired to the forest; while he was there, a daughter Satyavatī was born to him. She is wooed by Ṛcīka Bhārgava. The father demands a thousand special horses as bride price; Ṛcīka promises them and in turn asks them from Varuṇa, who gives them at the Ford-of-the-Horses* (5–15). *Ṛcīka marries Satyavatī and is visited by Bhṛgu, who grants her a boon; she asks a son each for herself and her mother. Bhṛgu tells them to embrace certain trees after the* puṃsavana *rite; they mix up the trees. As a result Satyavatī will have a brahmin son who will behave like a baron and her mother a baron son who will act like a brahmin. Satyavatī asks that this be true not of her son but her grandson, which is granted* (15–25). *Jamadagni is born* (25–30).
116 (116; 10171). *Jamadagni marries King Prasenajit's daughter Reṇukā; they have five sons, Rāma being the fifth* (1). *Reṇukā sees King Citraratha at play and is moist with desire. Jamadagni reviles her; he orders his first four sons to kill their mother. When they refuse, he curses them* (5–10). *Jamadagni then tells Rāma to kill her; he cuts off her head. Jamadagni grants him a boon; he asks for his mother's life, obliviousness and guiltlessness for himself, and normality for his brothers* (10–15). *King Kārtavīrya arrives and ransacks Jamadagni's hermitage. When Rāma returns, he is enraged and battles Kārtavīrya and kills him; the king's heirs now kill Jamadagni, and Rāma finds him dead* (15–25).
117 (117; 10201). *Rāma blames himself and performs the funerary rites* (1–5). *He swears to kill off the baronage, which he does twenty-one times. He fills five lakes with their blood to offer to his ancestors* (5). *Ṛcīka stops him. Rāma sacrifices and gives the earth to the brahmins and the golden altar, which represents the earth, to Kaśyapa. The brahmins break up the altar into*

fragments (10–15). Rāma appears and is honored. Yudhiṣṭhira sojourns on Mount Mahendra, then goes south (15).

Vaiśaṃpāyana said:
115.1 After the king of the earth had spent one night there, he and his
brother showed the ascetics the greatest hospitality. Lomaśa called out
the names of the ascetics—Bhṛgus, Angirases, Vāsiṣṭhas, Kāśyapas.
On meeting them, the royal seer greeted them with folded hands; and
he questioned the hero Akṛtavraṇa, a follower of Rāma: "When will
Rāma Bhārgava appear to the ascetics? On that occasion I too wish
to see the Bhārgava."

Akṛtavraṇa said:
5 Rāma, who knows himself, knows of your coming. He bears you
love and will soon appear to you. The ascetics see Rāma on the
fourteenth and the eighth. When this night has passed, it will be the
fourteenth.

Yudhiṣṭhira said:
You are a follower of the powerful and heroic son of Jamadagni and have been a witness to all his old feats. Therefore tell, sir, how all the barons were defeated by Rāma in battle, in what manner and for what reason.

Akṛtavraṇa said:
There was a great king in Kānyakubja of very great puissance, who
was known in the world as Gādhi. He went to live in the forest.
10 While he lived in the forest, a daughter was born to him, comely as
an Apsarā. Ṛcīka Bhārgava wooed her, O Bhārata, and the king said
to the brahmin of sharp vows, "There is a custom in our lineage,
which began with our forefathers: know, best of the twice-born, that
we demand as bride price a thousand fast white horses, each with a
black ear. Yet you, sir, should not be told to pay, Bhārgava, for this
daughter of mine should be bestowed on a great-spirited man like
you."

Ṛcīka said:
I shall give a thousand fast white horses with one black ear, and your daughter shall be my wife.

Akṛtavraṇa said:
15 After making this promise, O king, he said to Varuṇa, "Give me for
a bride price a thousand fast white horses with one black ear!"
Varuṇa gave him the thousand horses, and the spot where the horses
emerged is famed as the Ford-of-the-Horses. Thereupon Gādhi gave
his daughter Satyavatī to him in Kanyakubja on the Ganges, and the

Gods were in the bridegroom party. Having obtained a thousand
horses and having seen the celestials and having married a wife
according to the Law, the eminent brahmin Ṛcīka enjoyed himself
with the slim-waisted woman to his heart's desire. After the wedding
the eldest of the Bhṛgus came to visit his son and the bride, and he
20 saw them and was delighted. Husband and wife paid their respects to
the elder, honored by the hosts of the Gods, when he was seated, and
waited on him with folded hands. Joyfully the blessed lord Bhṛgu said
to his daughter-in-law, "Choose a boon, lovely woman, for I shall
grant your desire." She pleaded with the elder for a son for herself
and her mother, and he showed his grace to her.

Bhṛgu said:

At the time of your season, when both of you have bathed for the
son-bearing-rite, you must each embrace a tree, she an *aśvattha*, you
an *udumbara*.

Akṛtavraṇa said:

But when they embraced the trees, they mixed them up. When
25 Bhṛgu one day came back he realized the mix-up. The puissant Bhṛgu
said to his daughter-in-law Satyavatī, "Your son shall be a brahmin
who will live like a baron; your mother's great son shall be a baron
with the conduct of a brahmin, a great hero who will travel the road
of the strict." But she beseeched her father-in-law again and again,
"Do not let my son be such, but rather my grandson!" He brought
her joy in return, O Pāṇḍava, saying, "So shall it be!" When the time
came she gave birth to her son Jamadagni, joy of the Bhārgavas,
endowed with splendor and brilliance. The splendid child grew up
30 surpassing many seers in Vedic learning, Pāṇḍaveya. The entire *Veda*
of archery came to him who in brilliance matched the sun, as well as
the fourfold weapon lore.

Akṛtavraṇa said:

116.1 This great ascetic, bent on Vedic learning, performed such great
austerities that he subjugated the Gods with his self-restraint. He
went to King Prasenajit, O king, and wooed Reṇukā; and the king
gave her to him. When he had obtained Reṇukā as his wife, the
scion of the Bhārgavas performed with his compliant wife even more
austerities in his hermitage. Four boys were born from her, and
Rāma was the fifth; but though born the last he was the first of
them all.

5 Once when all her sons had gone out to gather fruit, Reṇukā, who
kept to her vows, went to bathe. As she went, Reṇukā happened to
see King Citraratha of Mṛttikāvatī; and when she saw the wealthy,
lotus-garlanded king playing in the water with his wives, Reṇukā

coveted him. From this bad thought she wetted herself mindlessly in the water and returned trembling to the hermitage. Her husband found her out; and seeing that she had lapsed from constancy and had lost her brahminic beauty, the powerful and overbearing man
10 vilified her with *Fie*! Thereupon Jamadagni's eldest son, Rumaṇvat by name, came in, and so did Suṣena, Vasu, and Viśvāvasu. Their venerable father ordered them one after the other to kill their mother; but, being completely confounded and witless, they gave no reply. In his fury he cursed them, and upon his curse they lost their minds and began suddenly to behave like animals and birds, or inanimate things.

Afterward Rāma came into the hermitage, slayer of enemy heroes; and the great ascetic Jamadagni irately said to him, "Kill your wicked
15 mother, have no compunction, son!" Rāma took his ax and cut off his mother's head. The fury of the great-spirited Jamadagni soon subsided, great king, and he said serenely, "At my word you have done a difficult deed, child. Choose boons, Law-minded man, as many as you wish in your heart!" He chose that his mother would rise alive, that he forget the murder and be untouched by the crime, and that his brothers return to normality. The great ascetic Jamadagni granted him matchlessness in battle, O Bhārata, and longevity and all those things man wishes for.

Then one day, when his sons as before had gone out, O lord, the
20 heroic Kārtavīrya arrived, the king of the shorelands. The seer's wife welcomed him as he came to the hermitage, but the king, who was maddened by war craze, did not accept the welcome. He ransacked the hermitage, forcibly abducted the calf of the whining sacrificial cow, and broke down all the big trees. The father himself told it all to Rāma when he returned; and seeing the cow lowing miserably, Rāma was seized by fury. Overpowered by anger, he stormed at Kārtavīrya, and the Bhārgava, slayer of enemy heroes, bravely engaged him in battle. He grasped his shining bow and with his honed bear arrows cut off his arms, which numbered a thousand, sturdy like bludgeons.
25 Infuriated by Rāma, Arjuna's heirs thereupon rushed upon Jamadagni when he was in his hermitage without Rāma. They slew the powerful ascetic, who refused to fight, while he, unprotected, kept calling for Rāma.

After the enemy-taming sons of Kārtavīrya had murdered Jamadagni with their arrows, Yudhiṣṭhira, they went as they had come. They had gone, leaving Jamadagni as he was, when the scion of Bhṛgu returned to the hermitage carrying firewood. The hero saw his father worsted by death and most grievously mourned him who had not deserved this fate.

Rāma said:
117.1 It is my fault that Kārtavīrya's lowly and mindless heirs have killed
you with their arrows, father, like a deer in the forest! How did a
death like this befit you, father, always Law-minded and traveling the
path of the strict, without guilt to any creature? What evil have they
not wrought who with their hundreds of sharp arrows killed you, an
aged, unresisting man, abiding by your austerities? And what will
they not say to their companions and friends after shamelessly
murdering a lone Law-minded man who offered no resistance?
Akṛtavraṇa said:
5 Thus he lamented much, O king, piteously and variously; and the
ascetic performed all the obsequies for his father. He burned his father
in the fire, did Rāma, victor of enemy cities; and he swore to
massacre all of the baronage, Bhārata. The furious, puissant,
powerful hero grasped his weapon and, image of death, alone slew
the sons of Kārtavīrya. And the barons who were their followers, O
bull of the barons, Rāma, greatest of fighters, crushed them all.
Twenty-one times the lord emptied the earth of barons and built in
Samantapañcaka five lakes of blood. In them the bearer of Bhṛgu's
line offered up to his forebears.
10 Ṛcīka in person sought out Rāma and stopped him. Thereupon the
majestic son of Jamadagni satisfied the Indra of the Gods with a great
sacrifice and presented the earth to his priests. He gave the golden
altar to the great-spirited Kaśyapa, having built it ten fathoms long
and nine high, O lord of your people. With Kaśyapa's consent, the
brahmins broke it up in pieces, king, and therefore are known as the
Khāṇḍava-goers.
After giving the earth to this great-spirited Kaśyapa, Rāma of
15 boundless might has been living on this great mountain. And in this
manner he had a feud with the barons who lived in the world, and
thus was earth conquered by boundlessly puissant Rāma.
Vaiśaṃpāyana said:
On the fourteenth, according to the covenant, the great-minded Rāma appeared to those brahmins, and to the King Dharma and his brothers. Along with his brothers, the lord, who was an Indra among kings, worshiped him, and that strictest of princes paid supreme homage to the twice-born. Having worshiped Jāmadagnya and having been honored in return, the Overwhelmer spent the night on Mount Mahendra and then departed toward the south.

3(33) The Tour of the Sacred Fords (continued)

Vaiśampāyana said:

118.1 As that dread king made his royal progress,
He set eyes on holy and lovely fords
That were all adorned by a plenty of brahmins,
On the oceans, Bhārata, one after one.

The king bathed there, polite to them all,
So his brothers, the sons and grandsons of kings;
And, O son of Parikṣit, the son of Pāṇḍu
Went to the most blessed perennial river.

There that most awesome king had a bath
And offered up to fathers and Gods;
After giving largess to the best of brahmins,
He went on to sea-going Godāvarī.

Then, sinless in Draviḍa country, O king,
He approached the Sea, which is holy to people,
Agastya's-Ford, which is holy and pure,
And the hero visited all the stream's fords.

5 It was there he heard of the matchless deed
That Arjuna'd done, he the greatest of archers.
As the hosts of great seers paid homage to him
The scion of Pāṇḍu found joy sublime.

Having laved his limbs in all these fords,
Always followed by Kṛṣṇā, in his brothers' van,
And paying honor to Arjuna's bravery,
The leader of kings took pleasure in earth.

At those fords of the first of perennial rivers
He gave gifts of thousands of cattle away,
Delightedly, while with his brothers the king
Narrated of Arjuna's gift of cows.

So he went in stages, O king, to those fords
On the ocean and many others as well;
And when all his desires were fulfilled, he saw
That most holy of places, Śūrpāraka.

After crossing some tract on the ocean shore,
He drew near to a wood that is famous on earth:

Where the Gods once did their austerities,
A spot still beloved of the holiest kings.

10 There, long and thick in the arms, the virtuous
King saw the altar of that greatest of bowmen,
Ṛcīka's son, surrounded by hosts
Of ascetics, the altar worth adoration.

Thereupon at the holy sites of the Vasus,
Of the bands of the Maruts, and of the two Aśvins,
Vaivasvata, and Ādityas, Kubera,
And Indra, Viṣṇu, and the Lord Savitar,

Of Bhaga and Moon and the Maker of Day,
Of the Lord of the Waters and the hosts of the Sādhyas,
Of Dhātar and Fathers, the great-souled king,
And of Rudra with his assembly of Gaṇas,

Of Sarasvatī, and the Siddhas assembled,
And Pūṣan, and all the other Immortals—
On all their sites, on those beautiful sites,
That great-spirited king now set his eye.

And there he observed his various fasts
And gave away the costliest gems.
He bathed his limbs at all those fords,
And wended his way to Śūrpāraka.

15 Having traveled through this ford
At the sea, he departed with his brothers
And went to the site that on earth is proclaimed
By the first of the twice-born as Ford Prabhāsa.

It was there he bathed, with his wide red eyes,
And, with his brothers and Kṛṣṇā, brought
Up offering gifts to his fathers and Gods,
As did the brahmins with Lomaśa.

Twelve days he subsisted on water and wind,
And at dawn and at dusk he made his ablutions;
All around he set flame to numerous fires,
And bore the heat, that most Law-keeping man.

Rāma and Janārdana* got word
Of the awesome austerities he practiced;
The two principal Vṛṣṇis and their escorts
Made their way to Yudhiṣṭhira Ājamīḍha.

* = Bala-Rāma and Kṛṣṇa.

When the Vṛṣṇis set eye on the Pāṇḍavas,
Who lay on the ground, limbs covered with dirt,
Set eye on Draupadī, so undeserving,
They sadly complained with anxious voice.

20 They went up to Rāma and Janārdana,
To Kṛṣṇa's son Sāmba and Śini's grandson,
Went up to the other Vṛṣṇis and paid
With unbroken spirit the homage of Law.

They returned the homage to all the Pārthas
And were suitably guested by Pāṇḍu's sons;
Surrounding Yudhiṣṭhira, king, the guests
Sat down as the many Gods sit around Indra.

To them he told all the deeds of his foes,
Quite confidently, and their stay in the woods.
And how Pārtha, child of the king of Immortals,
Went to Indra for arms he related to Kṛṣṇa.

With relief they listened to his words,
And perceiving then their pitiful leanness,
Those men of Dāśārha, most powerful men,
Let stream from their eyes their dolorous tears.

Janamejaya said:

119.1 When the Vṛṣṇis and the Pāṇḍavas met at the Ford of Prabhāsa, what did they do, and what did they talk about, ascetic? For all these great-spirited masters of all arms, Vṛṣṇis and Pāṇḍavas alike, were friends together.

Vaiśaṃpāyana said:

When they encountered one another at the holy Ford of Prabhāsa on the ocean, the Vṛṣṇis surrounded the heroic Pāṇḍavas and paid them honor. Thereupon, dazzling white like cow's milk, jasmine, the moon, a lotus fiber, or silver, the plow-armed Rāma, wearing his garland of forest flowers, spoke to the lotus-eyed Kṛṣṇa,

5 "No, Kṛṣṇa, no life by the Law leads to good,
Nor does a lawless life to defeat,
If our forest-dwelling, hairtuft-wearing,
Bark-clad Yudhiṣṭhira has come to grief!

"Duryodhana is king of the earth,
And yet the earth does not swallow him up:
This may make a man of a shallow mind
Think Unlaw is better served than Law.

"As we find Duryodhana ever-increasing,
And lack-land Yudhiṣṭhira miserable,
A private doubt rises in men's mind:
What now should the creatures try to accomplish?

"For this was a king whose might was the Law,
Devoted to Law, a giving, a true man:
For though he lose kingdom and privilege, would
The Pārtha forsake his Law and thrive?

"How is it that Bhīṣma and Kṛpa the brahmin,
And Droṇa, the dynasty's eldest, the king,
Find joy after banishing Pārtha's sons?
A plague on those ill-minded Bhārata chiefs!

"Hereafter the chief of the earth will encounter
His fathers, but what is *he* going to say?
'I have done right by my sons'? When he
Had lowered his innocent sons from the throne?

"He did not see with the eye of his mind
What *he* had done to be born so blind
Among all the kings on this wide earth,
Banishing Kuntī's sons from his kingdom!

"Don't doubt it, Vicitravīrya's son*
And *his* sons see, after the havoc they wrought,
How the trees that rise from their father's death ground
Are blossoming now in the color of gold.

"One need not ask those tall and wide-shouldered,
Those red-eyed men to hear for sure
That he sped unsuspectingly to the forest,
Yudhiṣṭhira and brothers armed to the teeth.

"Unarmed, this Wolf Belly of long arms
Could slay that prosperous army of foes:
Merely hearing the Wolf-Belly's battle cry
The armies are scared out of piss and bowels!

"Lean from hunger and thirst and the journey, but well,
When he counters them, weapons and arrows in hand,
Remembering this vile stay in the forest,
He'll leave no survivors, I am sure of that.

"For upon this earth no equal of him
Shall be born to equal his prowess and valor.

* = Dhṛtarāṣṭra.

He is lean from the cold, heat, wind, and the sun,
And will leave no remnant of foes in the battle.

"The kings of the east he slew, on one chariot—
With their followers Wolf-Belly slew them in battle,
And welcomed he was, this great wild warrior,
Who now, bark-clad, must pine in the woods.

"Now look at this man, this man Sahadeva,
Who at Dantakūra defeated the lords,
The assembled kings of the southern countries—
An ascetic now, in ascetic garb!

"And the hero who, alone on his chariot,
War-drunk, defeated the kings of the west,
Now lives in the woods on roots and fruit,
With a dirt-caked body and wearing the hairtuft!

20 "The heroic king's daughter, who rose from the altar
At the opulent rite the king had spread,
How does she, so worthy of pleasure and good things,
Now bear this grievous stay in the forest?

"These sons of the Law and the God of the Wind
And the king of the Gods and both the Aśvins,
These children of Gods, how do they now range,
Deserving of joy, long-suffering the woods?

"When the son of Dharma lost out with his wife
And was cast out with his brothers and band,
When Duryodhana is now on the increase,
Why does not the earth collapse with her hills?"

Sātyaki said:

120.1 No, Rāma, this is not the time to lament:
It is later than that, and we must all act
According to now and not to the past,
Even if Yudhiṣṭhira fails to speak.

For those in the world who have protectors
Do not on their own undertake any task;
But in their tasks they have protectors,
As Yayāti had in Śaibya and others.

So those whose tasks in the world are assumed
By their protectors, who act on their own,
Those heroes of men are indeed protected
And fall to no grief as though unprotected.

Then *how* can it be said that he and his brothers
Must live in the woods when he has for protectors,
Protectors of all the three worlds, men as Rāma,
Janārdana, Sāmba, Pradyumna, myself?

5 Let the host of Dāśārhas march out today,
With their plentiful weapons and colorful armor,
Let the Dhārtarāṣṭra fall victim to Yama,
With his kin defeated by Vṛṣṇi power!

You alone in your fury could even surround
All of earth, not to speak of the Śārnga bowman:*
So slay Duryodhana and his gang,
As the Gods' king Indra destroyed the Vṛtra.

The Pārtha is a brother to me, a friend,
And a guru; he is Janārdana's soul—
Therefore our task looms at once before us,
Perform the great and impossible feat!

I shall counter his showers of arrows with my
Superior arms and defeat him in battle.
And with my venomous, flamelike shafts
I shall sever his head from the trunk, O Rāma!

With my sharp sword I shall in the battle
Cut off the head from its trunk with a might;
And then I shall kill his followers all,
Duryodhana and all the Kurus.

10 Let the earthlings joyfully watch me here
With my weapons ready to fight, thou Rāma,
When I alone kill the best Kuru fighters
As the doomsday fire burns down a dead wood!

Nor will Kṛpa, Droṇa, Vikarṇa, and Karṇa
Be able to bear Pradyumna's sharp arrows:
I know of the prowess of this, your boy,
Of how Kṛṣṇa's son stands fast in a war.

Let Sāmba punish Duḥśāsana,
With the strength of his arms routing chariot and driver;
There is nothing Jambāvatī's warrior son
Could find unendurable in a mêlée.

For he, when still a child, destroyed
On a sudden Śambara's demon army,

* = Kṛṣṇa.

And in the battle he slew Aśvacakra,
Of the rounded thighs and the long thick arms:
What man exists who once in the reach
Of Sāmba's arms could long hold out?

No man who has come within reach of Death
Will ever escape if his time has come:
And thus, once come within Sāmba's reach,
Who would escape in the war with his life?

15 Droṇa and Bhīṣma, great warriors both,
And Somadatta amidst his sons
With all their armies, our Vāsudeva
Shall burn down with the fire of his shafts!

And what is impossible either to Kṛṣṇa
In all the worlds with their deities?
When he holds his weapons and aims his great bow
And wields his discus, peerless in war?

Aniruddha, with sword and shield in hand,
Must deck this earth with Dhārtarāṣṭras,
Unconscious, killed, and their trunks beheaded,
An altar of sacrifice covered with grass!

Gada, Ulmuka, Bāhuka, Bhānu, and Nītha,
And the boyish Niśatha, hero in battles,
The warlike Sāraṇa and Cārudeṣṇa
Must display exploits befitting their line.

The assembled host of baronial champions,
Led by Vṛṣṇis, Bhojas, and Andhakas,
Must kill Dhṛtarāṣṭra's sons in a war
And reap in the world abundant fame.

20 Let Abhimanyu govern the earth
While the chief of the bearers of Law, great-of-spirit
Yudhiṣṭhira, first of the Kurus, fulfills
The vow that he swore at the dicing game.

His foes downed by the arrows we'll send,
The King Dharma then shall enjoy the earth
Rid of Dhārtarāṣṭras, with Karṇa dead—
It's our most glorious, gravest task!

Vāsudeva said:

This, Mādhava, is the undoubted truth:
We accept your word, man of unfailing courage.

But the bull of the Kurus will nohow desire
A land *not* won by his own arms.

For neither for lust, for fear, nor for greed
Will Yudhiṣṭhira ever forsake his Law,
And neither will Bhīma or Arjuna,
Nor the warlike twins and Drupada's Kṛṣṇā.

The Wolf-Belly and Dhanaṃjaya
Are both without peer in the world in war—
And why should he not rule all earth
Who receives the homage of Mādrī's sons?

25 But when the great-spirited king of Pāñcāla,
And the lord of Cedi, the Kekayas, we,
All march to battle and embattle our foes,
Suyodhana'll leave the world of the living!

Yudhiṣṭhira said:

Your speech, O Mādhava, does not surprise,
But my truth I must guard even over my kingdom.
It is Kṛṣṇa who knows me for what I am,
And Kṛṣṇa himself I do fully know.

As soon as this hero of men will know
That it's time for valor, O Mādhava,
Then you, Śini champion*, and Keśava
Will vanquish Suyodhana in that war.

Now let the heroic Dāśārhas depart;
I stand fast with protectors, protectors of men:
Attend to the Law, ye measureless men;
I shall see you again, when we happily meet!

Vaiśaṃpāyana said:

They made their greetings and said farewell,
Embracing the elders and all the young;
And the Yadu heroes went to their houses,
And the king went on to the sacred fords.

30 After Kṛṣṇa had left, King Dharma went
To the ford constructed by the king of Vidarbha,
And dwelt by the river Payoṣṇī, whose water
Was mixed with the Soma that had been pressed there.

* = Sātyaki.

3(33.d) Sukanyā

121–25 (B. 121–25; C. 10291–10423)

121 (121; 10291). On the river Payoṣṇī there is an old sacrificial site where King Gaya performed magnificent rituals (1–10). They bathe and proceed to Mount Vaiḍūrya and the river Narmadā, the joint of the Tretā and Dvāpara ages. Here Cyavana drank the Soma with the Aśvins and married Sukanyā (15–20).

122 (122; 10316). Bhṛgu's son Cyavana performs austerities by the Narmadā, sitting long in the same posture, until an anthill grows over him (1). King Śaryāti comes there with his daughter Sukanyā and many women. Sukanyā plays in front of the anthill, and Cyavana falls in love; he cannot make himself heard. Sukanyā sees his glittering eyes and pokes at them. Irately Cyavana constipates the king's escort (5–10). The king questions who has wronged Cyavana. Sukanyā admits she poked at a firefly in an anthill. King Śaryāti hastens to Cyavana and asks forgiveness (10–20). Cyavana demands Sukanyā in marriage and receives her. She waits on him hand and foot (20–25).

123 (123; 10344). The Aśvins see Sukanyā nude and desire her. She declares that she is Cyavana's wife. Laughing, the two ask why such a lovely young woman should wait on a decrepit man; she should choose them (1–5). They promise to rejuvenate Cyavana, then Sukanyā shall choose one of the three. Cyavana is to plunge in the river; all arise from the water young and identical; but Sukanyā, guided by her heart, chooses her husband (10–20). Cyavana promises to admit the Aśvins to the Soma (20).

124 (124; 10371). King Śaryāti visits; Cyavana will perform a sacrifice for him. At the rite Cyavana draws a Soma cup for the Aśvins, but Indra stops it, for the Aśvins are not worthy of it (1–5). Cyavana remonstrates, but Indra remains firm. Cyavana draws the cup; Indra threatens him with the thunderbolt, but Cyavana proceeds. When Indra is about to strike, he paralyzes his arm (10–15). Cyavana's wizardry becomes the Asura Mada, who rushes on Indra to devour him (15–20).

125 (125; 10397). Indra now admits the Aśvins, and Cyavana releases him; he portions Mada out over women, liquor, dice, and the hunt (1–5). Cyavana lives happily with Sukanyā (5–10).——Lomaśa and Yudhiṣṭhira visit other sacred places until they reach the Yamunā, where King Māndhātar worshipped (10–20).

Lomaśa said:
121.1 Nṛga once sacrificed here with the Soma, and Indra the Sacker of
Cities, so we hear, king, was satisfied till he was drunk. Here the Gods
and Indra, and also the Prajāpatis, offered up oblations with many
grand sacrifices of ample stipends. Here King Amūrtarayasa sated our
Lord the Thunderbolt-wielder with Soma at seven Horse Sacrifices. At
his seven sacrifices everything was made of gold that usually at a rite
5 is made of wood and clay. Seven rituals became famous at those
sacrifices of his. On every one of his sacrificial poles there were seven
rings mounted, Yudhiṣṭhira, and Indra and the Gods themselves
erected splendid golden posts at his sacrifices. At those magnificent
festivals of the lord of the land Gaya, Indra got drunk on Soma, and
the brahmins on their stipends! As countless as are the grains of sand
on earth and stars in the sky and drops in the rain, so countless was
the wealth, great king, that Gaya gave away to the *sadasyas* at his
10 sacrifices. And if the sand and the stars and the drops might still be
counted, beyond count would remain the stipends of that stipend-
giver! With cows wrought of gold by Viśvakarman he gratified the
brahmins, who had gathered from many countries. The land of the
great-spirited Gaya, who sacrificed everywhere, was so beset with
sanctuaries that there was little space left, O lord of your people. With
his deeds he won the worlds of Indra, Bhārata, and he who bathes in
the River Payoṣṇī will join him in his world. Therefore, king sans
blame, bathe here with your brothers and you shall be cleansed of
evil, guardian of the earth.
Vaiśaṃpāyana said:
15 That best of men* bathed with his brothers in the Payoṣṇī, and
together with them the faultless and splendid king went on to Mount
Vaiḍūrya and the great River Narmadā. The blessed seer Lomaśa
named for him all the lovely fords in their various spots, lord of the
people. In due order and as it pleased him, he made his progress,
repeatedly giving away largess to brahmins, by the thousands.
Lomaśa said:
Once a man has set eye on Mount Vaiḍūrya and descended into the
River Narmadā, O Kaunteya, he joins the worlds of Gods and kings.
This, best of men, is the joint of the Tretā and Dvāpara ages; once one
20 has come to it, he is released from all evil things. This is the site, my

* = Yudhiṣṭhira.

friend, of Śaryāti's sacrifice, where Kauśika* drank Soma with the Aśvins in person. The great Bhārgava ascetic Cyavana was wroth with Indra, and the lord paralyzed Vāsava; he also obtained the Princess Sukanyā for his wife.

Yudhiṣṭhira said:

How did the blessed lord paralyze the Chastiser of Pāka, and why was the great Bhārgava ascetic wroth with Indra? How, brahmin, were the Nāsatyas** made into drinkers of Soma? Tell me all this, sir, the way it happened.

Lomaśa said:

122.1 The great seer Bhṛgu had a son by the name of Cyavana Bhārgava,
and this glorious man performed austerities close to this lake. Rigid as
a post, the splendid ascetic maintained the *vīra* posture and stood in
the same spot for a very long time, Pāṇḍava, lord of your people. Over
a long span of time the seer turned into an anthill overgrown by
creepers, O king, and was covered by ants. Thus the sage became, so
to say, a pile of earth on all sides, king, while he continued his
austerities surrounded by the anthill.
5 Now after a long time a king named Śaryāti came to this supremely
lovely lake to amuse himself. There were four thousand women in his
retinue, Bhārata; one of them was the beautiful Sukanyā, his
daughter. She ran around there in the midst of her friends, adorned
with all her jewelry; and she found the anthill of Cyavana. There the
fine-toothed girl strolled around, surrounded by her friends, observing
and inspecting the beautiful trees. Comely, youthful, amorous, and
drunk, she broke off the most heavily flowering branches from the
10 forest trees. The wise Bhārgava saw her when her friends had left her
and she was by herself, wearing one piece of clothing and all her
finery, like a darting lightning flash. As he watched her in her solitude,
that most brilliant brahmin seer endowed with the power of his
austerities was enamored. He spoke out to the beautiful girl from his
dried-up throat, and she did not hear him. Then Sukanyā saw the eyes
of the Bhārgava in the anthill and, exclaiming, "Now what is this?"
she, confused in her judgment, curiously pricked the eyes with a thorn.
When she pricked his eyes, the very irascible sage waxed angry and
constipated the armed escort of Śaryāti. Observing that his escort
suffered from constipation, with bladders and bowels impeded, the king
15 began to question, "Who has done a wrong here today to the always
ascetic, old and great-spirited Bhārgava, who is particularly quick to
anger? Whether it was done knowingly or not, speak the truth at

* = Indra.
** = the Aśvins.

once!" The armsmen said, "None of us know of any wrongdoing. If
you please, find out, sire, by any means."
Thereupon the king himself, employing both flattery and threat,
interrogated the party of his friends, and they denied all knowledge.
Observing that the escort was most uncomfortable from constipation
and seeing her father distressed, Sukanyā said: "When I was
wandering around I saw some living creature in an anthill, which
gave out light. I thought it was something like a firefly and I pricked
it."
20 Upon hearing this, Śaryāti quickly sped to the anthill and there he
saw the Bhārgava, old both in age and austerities. Folding his hands,
the lord of the land beseeched him to spare his escort: "Pray forgive
what that little girl innocently did to you!" Cyavana Bhārgava then
replied to the king, "If I receive in marriage your daughter, so lovely
and noble yet a victim to greed and confusion, O king, I shall forgive;
this I swear to you, guardian of the earth." Upon hearing the seer's
word, Śaryāti unhesitatingly gave his daughter to the great-spirited
Cyavana.
25 After he had accepted the girl Cyavana became serene, and having
found forgiveness the king and his escort turned back. The innocent
Sukanyā, having found an ascetic for her husband, constantly waited
on him, with love, austerity, and restraints. Obedient without
demurring to the fires and the guests, the fair-faced woman quickly
ingratiated herself with Cyavana.

Lomaśa said:

123.1 After some time the two Aśvins from among the Gods saw Sukanyā,
O king, when she had bathed and was nude. When they saw the
lovely-limbed princess, like the daughter of the king of the Gods, the
Aśvins Nāsatyas hastened to her and said, "Whose are you, woman of
the shapely thighs, and what are you doing in the forest? We want to
know about you, pretty, do tell us, lovely!"
Sukanyā covered herself and told those best of the Gods that she
5 was Śaryāti's daughter and the property and wife of Cyavana. The
Aśvins laughed out aloud and again said to her, "How is it that your
father gave a beautiful girl like you to a man who had gone the road?
You radiate in the forest like garland lightning; even among celestials
we do not find a woman to equal you, blushing girl! In the full finery
of your jewels and clothed in a superb gown you would really glitter
with your faultless body, not like this, caked with dirt. Why does a
woman like you wait on a decrepit husband, my pretty, one long past
the joys of love? One incapable of protecting and nourishing you,
sweet-smiling maid? It were better you cast off Cyavana and chose

either one of us for your husband, you that are like the child of a God.
Do not spoil your best years!"
10 At these words Sukanyā addressed the Gods: "I am devoted to my
husband Cyavana, do not cast suspicion on me!" Again they resumed:
"We are the great divine healers. We shall make your husband young
and handsome, then choose yourself a husband from among the three
of us. Acquaint him with our covenant, fair-faced girl." At their behest
she approached the Bhārgava and repeated to the lord of the Bhṛgus
the words they had spoken.

When he heard this, Cyavana said to his wife, "Let it be done!"
And with her husband's consent she in turn said, "Let it be done!"
15 On hearing her declare that it should be done, the Aśvins said to the
princess, "Your husband must get into the water." Whereupon
Cyavana, who was desirous of beauty, rapidly plunged into the water,
and the Aśvins too jumped into the lake, my lord king. A little while
later they all climbed out of the lake, all young and divinely beautiful,
with shining earrings, wearing the same outward appearance. And
increasing the love of her heart, they all said to her, "Beautiful young
woman, choose one of us for your husband, whomever you desire."

When she saw them all stand there looking the same, the princess decided with heart and mind, and chose her very own husband. Cyavana, having acquired a bride and the youthful beauty he wanted, spoke joyfully this word to the Nāsatyas: "Now that you have endowed me, an old man, with beauty and youth, and I have acquired this woman for my bride, I am pleased and for that I shall entitle you to drink the Soma, before the very eyes of the king of the Gods—this I swear to you as the truth!"

After hearing his promise, the Aśvins went back to heaven in happy spirits; and Cyavana and Sukanyā cavorted together like Gods.

Lomaśa said:

124.1 Upon learning that youth had been restored to Cyavana, Śaryāti
joyously betook himself to the Bhārgava's hermitage with his escort.
King Śaryāti saw Cyavana and Sukanyā, beautiful like children of the
Gods, and he was as delighted as though he had won all of earth. The
king and his wife were hospitably received by the seer, and the wise
prince seated himself by his host and spoke of propitious matters.

Then the Bhārgava said to him in a soothing voice, O king, "I shall
5 celebrate a sacrifice for you, king. Procure the ingredients!" Most
joyfully King Śaryāti welcomed Cyavana's proposal, sire. On a blessed
day fit for the sacrifice Śaryāti had a splendid sacrificial terrain built
and filled it with a wealth of desirable objects of every kind. Then, sire,
Cyavana Bhārgava celebrated a sacrifice for him—hear from me of the
marvels that took place there. Cyavana drew a cup of Soma for the

divine Aśvins, and Indra stopped the cup that had been drawn for the Aśvins.

Indra said:

I hold that these two Nāsatyas are unworthy of the Soma. Since they are healers to the sons of Gods, their calling excludes them.

Cyavana said:

10 Do not despise these great-spirited Gods who are most rich in beauty
and possessions, Maghavat, for they have made me superior like an
ageless celestial. Why should they be unworthy of the libation next to
you and the other Gods? Indra of the Gods, Sacker of Cities, know that
the Aśvins too are Gods!

Indra said:

They are healers and servants, and, taking any form they please, they walk in the world of the mortals. So how could they deserve Soma here?

Lomaśa said:

When Vāsava kept repeating the same words, the Bhārgava drew
the cup without paying heed to Śakra. But seeing him about to pour
the excellent Soma for the Aśvins, the God Slayer of Vala said to him,
15 "If you of your own accord pour Soma for them, I shall hurl my
thunderbolt at you!" The Bhārgava smiled and looked at Indra; then
he ritually poured a sublime cup of Soma for the Aśvins. The Consort
of Śacī hurled his dreadful thunderbolt at him, and when he was doing
so the Bhārgava paralyzed his arm. Thereupon Cyavana offered into
the fire with the proper spells, and, intent upon sorcery, the splendid
seer stood ready to injure the God. By the power of his austerities the
seer's sorcery became a gigantic and powerful Asura by the name of
20 Mada, whom neither Gods nor Asuras could control. His mouth was
horrendous, gaping, with sharp-pointed tusks; one jowl lay on the
earth, the other reached heaven. His four fangs were a myriad leagues
long, his other teeth ten leagues, looking like castle towers and the
tips of spears. His arms were like mountains, each a myriad leagues'
long, his eyes like the sun and the moon, his maw like death.

Licking his lips with a tongue that darted and flashed like lightning, opening wide his ghastly-looking mouth, as though about to swallow all of the world forcibly, he furiously ran to the God of the Hundred Sacrifices to devour him, making the worlds echo his mighty, terrifying roar.

Lomaśa said:

125.1 When the God of the Hundred Sacrifices saw that ghoul-faced Mada
approach with his mouth agape like the maw of death, he kept licking
the corners of his mouth in fear—his arm was still paralyzed—and,
panicstricken, the king of the Gods said to Cyavana, "Henceforth the

Aśvins shall deserve Soma, Bhārgava. This word I speak to you as the
truth, brahmin! What you undertake is not without fruit, let this be
5 the abiding rule: I myself know, brahmin, that you do not act in vain.
Just as you today have rendered the Aśvins deserving of Soma, so
precisely was it laid down by me to happen, so that your power might
once more shine forth, and the fame of Sukanyā and her father might
spread in the world. Therefore have mercy on me: it shall be as you
wish."

At Śakra's words the wrath of the great-spirited Cyavana subsided,
and he quickly set free the Sacker of Cities. The powerful sage parceled
out Mada over liquor, women, dice, and the hunt, in which it had
previously been created over and over again, O king. Having thus laid
low Mada and sated Śakra with the drop, as well as the Gods who had
10 now been joined by the Aśvins, and having celebrated the sacrifice for
the king and broadcast his power in all the words, that most eloquent
speaker amused himself with his loving Sukanyā in the forest.

Here glistens his lake, king, noisy with birds. Bring here with your
brothers offerings to Gods and ancestors. After visiting this lake and
Sikatākṣa, O Bhārata, guardian of the earth, you should go on to the
Saindhava Forest, visit the canals and, great king, touch water at all
the Puṣkaras. There is Mount Arcīka, dwelling place of sages, always
in fruit, always with plenty of streams, the great abode of the Maruts.
Here are many hundreds of sanctuaries of the Gods, Yudhiṣṭhira: here
is the Ford-of-the-Moon, where the seers worship, as do the
Vaikhānasa seers and the Vālakhilyas.

15 Here are three holy peaks and three waterfalls: you should
circumambulate them all and bathe as you please. It is here, King
Kaunteya, that Śaṃtanu and Śunaka, and both Nara and Nārāyaṇa,
reached their everlasting rank. Here the Gods and the Fathers always
dwell with the seers, on Mount Arcīka, and here they have done their
austerities—worship them, Yudhiṣṭhira! There the seers eat the *caru*
oblations, lord of your people. This is the river Yamunā, which springs
eternal: here Kṛṣṇa engaged in austerities. The twins, Bhīmasena,
Kṛṣṇā, and we shall all go here as lean and good ascetics, plower of
your enemies!

20 This is the holy stream of Indra, overlord of men, where the Placer
and Ordainer and Varuṇa ascended: they dwell here, king, forgiving
and sublime in the Law; for this holy mountain is of the friendly and
the upright. This is the Yamunā, king, sought out by hosts of royal
seers, piled up with many sacrifices, holy and banishing the danger of
evil. It was here that the mighty archer king Māndhātar himself
worshiped, and the Somaka Sahadeva, greatest of givers, O Kaunteya.

3(33.e) Māndhātar

126 (B. 126; 10424–10469)
126 (126; 10424). Yudhiṣṭhira asks for Māndhātar's story (1). King Yuvanāśva is childless and retires to the forest. In the dead of night he visits the Hermitage of Bhṛgu, where a Bhārgava had prepared a potion for Yuvanāśva's wife and gone to sleep (5–10). Yuvanāśva drinks the potion thirstily in the dark and is berated for it the next morning: now he himself must become pregnant (10–20). After a hundred years the king's side opens and a son is born. Indra appears and puts his finger in the child's mouth, saying: "Māṃ dhātā, 'He shall suck me,'" hence he is known as Māndhātar. He becomes a great Cakravartin and sacrificer, who forces the rains down after a twelve-year drought (25–40).

Yudhiṣṭhira said:

126.1 Māndhātar was a tiger of a man renowned in the three worlds: how was that eminent king, the son of Yuvanāśva, born, great brahmin? And how did that man of measureless splendor reach the final goal-post? The three worlds were as subject to him as to the great-spirited Viṣṇu. This I wish to hear, the feats of that sage king: how he, in might the like of Śakra, whose prowess was unmatched, was born and received the name of Māndhātar, for you know how to tell it.

Lomaśa said:

Then listen attentively, king, how that great-spirited king's name of Māndhātar came to be celebrated in the worlds.

5 There was a king of the earth, Yuvanāśva, who was born in the lineage of Ikṣvāku, and that guardian of the world worshiped with sacrifices of ample stipends. This best of the bearers of the Law performed a thousand Horse Sacrifices and various other rituals at which the priests were richly recompensed. But the king, great of spirit and firm in his vows, was childless; and he entrusted his kingdom to his councillors and permanently lived in the forest. Alone he subjected himself to the Rules that are found in scripture; and, his heart dried up from thirst, he entered Bhṛgu's hermitage. That very night, great king, the great-spirited grand seer, the scion of Bhṛgu, had performed an *iṣṭi* to get a son for Yuvanāśva Saudyumni. A large jar

10 had been procured filled with water that was purified with spells. It
had earlier been set up and it stood there, Indra of kings, so that his
wife might sip the water and bear a son the like of Śakra.

The seers had placed the jar on the altar and, being tired from
waking through the night, gone to sleep. Saudyumni passed them; the
king, who was dry in his throat and athirst, badly in search of
something to drink, entered the hermitage wearily and asked for a
drink. But when the exhausted king cried out from a dry throat, no
one heard him; it was like the squeak of a bird. The prince saw the jar
full of water, ran quickly to it, drank from it, and threw the rest of the
15 water away. When the thirsty king had drunk the cool water, he
happily passed out; the sage slept very soundly.

Presently the seers awoke with the king, and they all found the jar
empty. They got together and asked, "Whose work is this?"
Yuvanāśva replied truthfully, "I did it." The blessed Bhārgava said:
"That was not right. This water was collected with austerity and kept
for your son! After bitter mortifications I had put a *brahman* on it, for
20 you to have a son, a royal seer of great valor and strength. A son of
great strength and power, possessed of the might of austerities, who
with his prowess might even send Śakra to Yama's realm. Such was
the rite by which I had prepared it, king. Your drinking the water this
very day was a deed ill done, king. But now we cannot change the
fact, for surely what you did was ordained by fate. As you thirstily
drank the water that was sanctified by spell and rite, great king, and
had been procured with the virility of my austerities, you yourself shall
by means of this water give birth to an equally virile son. We ourselves
shall perform this greatly miraculous *iṣṭi* for you, so that you, a virile
man, shall father a son the like of Śakra!"

25 A hundred years passed, then the great-spirited king's left side split
open and a son like another sun came out in great splendor; and King
Yuvanāśva did not die, which was miraculous. Most mighty Śakra
came to see him and put his forefinger into the child's mouth. The
Thunderbolt-wielder explained, "Me shall he suck!" and thus Indra
and the celestials named him Māndhātar. After he had tasted the
forefinger that Indra had offered him, the baby grew up to a height of
30 thirteen cubits, O guardian of the earth. The *Vedas* and the *Veda* of
weaponry and all the divine weapons appeared to this sovereign, great
king, when he merely thought of them. The bow named Ājagava,
arrows made of horn, and an impenetrable armor obeyed him.
instantly.

Maghavat Śakra himself anointed him, Bhārata, and with his Law
he conquered the three worlds, as Viṣṇu does with his strides.
Unimpeded, the Wheel of the great-spirited ruler rolled on, and tributes
flowed to the royal seer of their own accord. His, O lord of the earth,

was all of treasure-filled earth, and he offered up many and various
35 sacrifices with most decent stipends. Having piled up the altars and
acquired abundant Law, that splendid and boundlessly lustrous
sovereign, O king, partook of half of Indra's throne. In a single day
this wise and ever law-abiding sage subjugated by a mere command
all of earth with her jewel mines and settlements. Four-cornered earth
was pervaded by the fire altars he built for his richly paid sacrifices,
great king; not a spot was uncovered. They say that that great-
spirited king gave a myriad lotus counts of cows to the brahmins.
When there had been a twelve-year drought, the great-spirited man
made it rain for the growing of the crops, while the Thunderbolt-wielder
40 looked on. He like a roaring monsoon cloud routed and killed with his
shafts the grand overlord of Gāndhāra, who had been born in the
dynasty of the Moon. This great-spirited prince, O king, vanquished the
four kinds of creatures and with his own austerity and splendor lent
firmness to the worlds.

This is the terrain where he offered sacrifice to the Gods, radiant like the sun. Behold it in this most holy spot in the middle of the Field of the Kurus. Herewith has been fully related the grand geste of Māndhātar, O guardian of earth, and the marvelous birth concerning which you questioned me.

3(33.f) Jantu

127–28 (B. 127–28; C. 10470–512)
127 (127; 10470). King Somaka has a single son, Jantu, for whom the king's one hundred wives care excessively. Somaka complains that a single son is too great a worry. How can he obtain more sons? (1–15). A priest knows a rite; it requires sacrificing Jantu (15–20).
128 (128; 10491). Somaka agrees. Jantu is sacrificed, over the women's protests. All the women become pregnant; Jantu is reborn the eldest of a hundred (1–5). The priest dies, and Somaka soon follows. Somaka finds the priest boiling in hell for his evil rite. Somaka demands to take over the priest's guilt (5–10), but Law declares this impossible. Somaka then demands to live in hell for the same term; afterward he rejoins his happy worlds with his priest (10–20).

Yudhiṣṭhira said:
127.1 What power did King Somaka hold, most eloquent of men? I wish
to hear of his exploits and puissance such as they really were.
Lomaśa said:
Yudhiṣṭhira, there was a Law-abiding king named Somaka who had
a hundred wives of the same rank. This very king in spite of great
efforts failed to beget a son on them in however long a time.
Eventually, after he had grown old and was still trying hard, a son
5 named Jantu was born to him from those one hundred women. All the
mothers crowded together around him when he had been born, and
they waited on him, always carrying after him whatever might please
his taste, O lord of the people. Then one day an ant bit him in his
buttock, and the little child cried out in pain, king. They all clucked
around Jantu, and their wailing was terrific. The king heard this
sudden outcry of anguish while he was sitting with his priests in the
assembly of his councillors. The king sent out at once to discover what
had happened, and the steward reported to him what was the matter
10 with his son. Somaka and his councillors rose and hurriedly entered
the women's quarters; and the enemy-tamer soothed his son. Having
soothed his son, the king strode out of the women's house, sire, and
sat down with his ministers and priests.
Somaka said:
A plague on having a single son, 'twere better I had none! Since all
creatures are constantly sick, a single son is a worry! I inspected and
collected—he said, king—these hundred wives and married them to get
some sons, brahmin, and they bore none! Somehow this one son
Jantu got produced as I labored on them all—now what is more
15 painful than that! My and my wives' time is gone now, best of the
twice-born, and just as their lives depend on this lone little son, so does
mine. Won't there be some apposite rite that would get me a hundred?
However big or small or hard it might be?
A priest said:
Surely there is a rite by which you can get a hundred sons. If you
can do it, Somaka, I shall explain the rite.
Somaka said:
Permissible or not, if I can get a hundred sons, consider it done!
Explain it to me, reverend!
The priest said:
I'll lay out the rite, and you sacrifice your son Jantu, sire. Then in
20 no time at all you shall have a hundred illustrious sons. When his caul
is being offered, the mothers should inhale the smoke, and then they
will all give birth to very virile sons. Jantu shall be reborn your son
from the same woman; and his golden birthmark shall reappear on
his left side.

Somaka said:

128.1 Brahmin, whatever needs to be done, in whatever manner, let it be
done in that manner. Out of my desire for sons I shall follow your
words completely.

Lomaśa said:

Thereupon he sacrificed for Somaka with Jantu as the victim; but
his mothers, moved with compassion, forcibly pulled the child away.
Wailing, "O, we are lost!" and filled with bitter grief, the mothers
pulled him away, holding him by his right hand. But the priest held
him by his left hand and pulled him back. While the women screeched
like mournful ospreys, he dragged their son away from them; and he
5 immolated him according to the rite and offered up his caul. While the
caul was being offered, the anguished mothers inhaled the odor and
suddenly fell to the ground, O scion of Kuru. And all the king's women
became with child.

After ten months had passed, O Bhārata, lord of your people, a full
hundred sons were born by Somaka's wives. Jantu was born the eldest
of them, and by the same mother, Bhārata, and they all loved him
above their own. On his left side there was the golden birthmark.
Being endowed with fine qualities, he became the first among the
hundred sons.

Then Somaka's priest went to the world hereafter, and after some
10 time Somaka followed him. There he saw his priest boiling in a terrible
hell, and he asked, "Why are you boiling in hell, brahmin?" His guru,
being sorely boiled by the fire, said to him, "I sacrificed for you, king,
and this is the fruit of my work!" When he heard this, the royal seer
said to King Law, "I shall enter hell and set my sacrificial priest free.
For it is because of me that the lordly man is boiled by hellfire."

The Law said:

No one ever experiences another's fruit, king. These fruit that you
see are yours, most generous giver!

The king said:

Without this Vedic scholar I do not crave for the blessed worlds. I
only wish to live with him, be it in the realm of the Gods, or in hell,
15 King Law. My deed was the same as his: we should both share the
fruit, holy or unholy.

The Law said:

If such is your desire, king, then suffer with him his deserts for the same length of time. Thereafter you shall reach the course of the strict.

Lomaśa said:

The king of the lotus eyes did it all precisely so and in the end regained his proper blessed worlds, which he had won with his acts, together with his guru and priest, for he loved his guru.

This is his holy hermitage that shines before our eyes. A man who patiently spends six nights here goes the good way. We shall dwell here for six nights, Indra of kings, without feverishness, and self-restrained. Be prepared, scion of Kuru.

3(33) The Tour of the Sacred Fords (continued)

Lomaśa said:
129.1 It is here, they say, king, that Prajāpati himself of yore sacrificed
with a Session called Iṣṭikṛta, which lasted a thousand years. Ambarīṣa
Nābhāga sacrificed on the bank of the Yamunā, and through his
sacrifices and austerities he attained to complete success. This is the
most holy field of the sacrifices of Yayāti Nāhuṣa, where, after his
offering, he gave ten lotus counts away to his *sadasyas*. Look,
Kaunteya, on this sacrificial site of boundlessly lustrous Yayāti
5 Sārvabhauma, who rivaled Śakra. Look how the earth, piled up with
fire altars of many styles, seems to sink below Yayāti's many acts of
sacrifice! Here is the one-leafed *śamī* tree, and this is the superb Goblet;
behold the lakes of Rāma and the hermitage of Nārāyaṇa. This is the
Escape of Arcīka's son of boundless luster in the River Raupyā, of him
who roamed the earth with his *yogas*.
Listen, scion of Kuru, as I recite to you this chronicle verse that the
piśāca women, hung with mortars, once declaimed: "You eat curds in
Yugaṃdhara, spend the night in Acyutasthala, bathe at Bhūtilaya,
10 and you wish to stay here with your sons. If having stayed here one
night you stay one more, your deeds of the day and your deeds of the
night will be changed!" All right then, let us stay here tonight, best of
the Bharatas, for this, Kaunteya Bhārata, is the Gate to Kurukṣetra.
Here, sire, King Yayāti Nāhuṣa brought up a sacrifice with rituals
that abounded with many gems, in which Indra delighted. This ford of
the Yamunā they call Plakṣāvataraṇa, and the wise say that it is the
gate to the ridge of heaven. Here the great seers, after offering up the
sārasvata sacrifices, carrying poles and mortars, went to take the
15 terminal bath. In this same spot King Bharata repeatedly sent off his
black-dappled sacrificial horse, after he had obtained by Law all of
earth. In this very place, tiger among men, Marutta sat at the greatest
Session, protected by Saṃvarta, first of divine seers.

Bathe here, Indra of kings, and you will set eye upon all the worlds; having touched water, Bhārata, you will be cleansed of evil.

Vaiśaṃpāyana said:

After he had bathed there with his brothers amidst the lauds of the great seers, the eldest of the Pāṇḍavas addressed this word to Lomaśa:

"I gaze upon all the worlds by virtue of my austerity, O lord whose
valor is the truth; and while standing down here, I see that greatest of
Pāṇḍavas who has the white horses."*

Lomaśa said:

20 That is right, strong-armed warrior! And so do the eminent seers
see! Now look at this holy River Sarasvatī, crowded by those whose
only refuge she is! By bathing here, best of men, you shall be cleansed
of evil. Here the seers of the Gods sacrificed with the *sārasvata* rites,
and so, Kaunteya, did the brahmin seers as well as the royal seers.
This is Prajāpati's Altar, five leagues around, the Field of that great-
spirited sacrificer Kuru** itself.

Lomaśa said:

130.1 Here mortals do their austerities and go to heaven, Bhārata. People
who want to die come here by the thousands, king. For it was Dakṣa
who of old, when he sacrificed, pronounced this benediction: "They,
forsooth, who die here shall have won heaven!"

This is the holy and divine and billowing River Sarasvatī, and this is
the Vanishing-Point of the Sarasvatī, king of your people, the gate to
the land of the Niṣādas, out of hatred for whom the Sarasvatī entered
5 the earth, hero, lest the Niṣādas should know her. Now this is the
Cāmasa-Spring where the Sarasvatī can be seen, and here all the
ocean-going rivers converge into her.

And this, enemy-tamer, is the great Ford-of-the-Sindhu, where
Lopāmudrā met Agastya and chose him for her husband. Here too
shines forth the Ford-of-Prabhāsa, O you who shine as the sun shines,
which is Indra's favorite, holy, purifying, and cleansing of evil. Now
here we behold that prominent ford, the Footprint-of-Viṣṇu, and here
is this lovely and eminently purifying river, the Vipāśā. In this very
spot the blessed Lord Vasiṣṭha tied himself up out of grief over his sons
and threw himself down; and stood up unfettered.

10 This is the region of Kaśmīr, holy to all, O enemy-tamer, inhabited
by the great seers—look at it, you and your brothers! It was here that
all the northern seers, and Yayāti Nāhuṣa, and the Fire, and Kāśyapa
conferred together, Bhārata.

Now here appears, great king, the Gate-of-Lake-Mānasa; its rain-fed
area was created by the illustrious Rāma in the middle of the
mountains. This is the famous Vātikaṣaṇḍa, north of Videha, where
truth is might and whose gate is not breached. Here is the Seller-of-
Barley, called Ujjānaka, where the blessed seer Vasiṣṭha found peace
15 with his wife Arundhatī. This is the *kuśa*-rich lake where a lotus count
of priests bed down on *kuśa* grass. And the Hermitage-of-Rukmiṇī
where she found rest and shed her anger.

* = Arjuna.
** = Kurukṣetra.

You have heard, Pāṇḍaveya, of this compound of meditations—you will see it, great king, the great Mount Bhṛgutunga, and the rivers Jalā and Upajalā by the Yamunā, where Uśīnara, having sacrificed, excelled over Indra Vāsava.

In order to find out whether he was equal to the Gods, O lord of
your people, Vāsava approached him, as did the Fire God, Bhārata.
Desirous to try the great-spirited Uśīnara, and willing to grant a boon,
Indra became a hawk and the Fire a dove; and they went to his
20 sacrifice. From fear of the hawk the dove settled on the king's thigh,
and, seeking shelter, O king, the timid bird nestled there.

3(33.g) The Hawk and the Dove

131 (B. 131; C. 10560–10596)
131 (131; 10560). Indra, in the form of a hawk, and Fire, in the guise of a dove, test King Śibi. Śibi gives shelter to the dove. The hawk protests: the dove is his food (1). Śibi replies that he cannot surrender a refugee. The hawk argues that he and his family will die for want of food. Śibi offers him other food, but the hawk wants the dove; Śibi refuses (1–20). The hawk demands a piece of Śibi's flesh of equal weight as the dove's. Śibi agrees, but the dove is always heavier; in the end the king puts his entire body on the scale. Indra identifies himself and Fire, and praises Śibi's generosity (20–30).

The hawk said:

131.1 All the kings name you as one who is Law-minded: so why do you want to do a deed that runs counter to Law? Do not out of greed for Law begrudge me who am starving the food that has been ordained for me, king, or you will throw away the Law!

The king said:

Trembling and looking for shelter, and frightened of you, great fowl,
this bird has sought me out, praying for its life. Do you not see, hawk,
that if I did not give this refuge-seeking, safety-craving dove its safety,
5 it would be a heinous Unlaw? The dove looks ashiver and much upset,
hawk. It has come to me seeking life; abandoning it is condemned.

The hawk said:

Great lord, it is through food that all creatures find their being, by food that they thrive, by food that they live. Even after losing possessions that are hard to give up, a man can live for many a long night; but he could not abide long were he to give up eating. If I am deprived of my portion, lord of your people, my spirits will desert my body and go the way of no return. When I predecease them, Law-spirited king, son and wife will perish: so by protecting this dove you will kill many lives. A Law that spoils the Law is no Law but a bad Law; no, that Law is Law that runs counter to nothing, O king whose might is your truth! When matters are in conflict, guardian of earth, you should decide what is better and what is worse and observe that Law that does not oppress. After ascertaining the weightier and the less weighty in a decision on Law and Unlaw, you should decide on the Law where it does most good, king!

The king said:

Best of birds, your speech sounds very beautiful. Are you the Fair-winged Bird, king of the fowl? You are doubtless wise in the Law, for thus do you speak, lengthily and wondrously, concerning the Law. I see that nothing is obscure to you. Then how do you think it right to abandon a refugee? All this enterprise of yours, bird, is to get some food. But you can get your food in another, even better, way: I shall have a steer, a boar, a deer, or even a buffalo cooked for you, or whatever you want!

The hawk said:

I don't feed on boar or bullocks or any kind of deer, great king, so what use is their meat to me? Bull of the barons, let go of the staple that fate has ordained for me! Guardian of the earth, let that dove loose for me. Hawks eat doves, that is the everlasting rule. If you know the way, king, do not climb up a banana tree!

The king said:

You that are adored by the hosts of birds, reign over this rich kingdom of the Śibis. Or I shall give you whatever you want, hawk, but not, hawk, this bird that has sought shelter with me! Tell me what I should do, best of birds, so that you may desist, for I shall not give up this little dove.

The hawk said:

Uśīnara, if you love this dove, overlord of kings, cut off a piece of your flesh and weigh it against the dove. When your flesh balances the dove's, king, you will give it to me, and I shall be satisfied.

The king said:

Your request I deem a favor, hawk, so I shall give you at once as much of my flesh as balances the dove.

Lomaśa said:

Then the king, who knew the highest Law, cut his flesh and, Lord Kaunteya, weighed it against the dove. But on balance the dove was the heavier. Once more King Uśīnara cut from his flesh and gave it;

and when there was no more left of his flesh to balance the dove, he himself, all cut up, mounted the scale.

The hawk said:

I am Indra, Law-knowing king, and this dove is the sacrifice-carrying fire. We have come to you in your offering grove to test you in the Law. This shall be your shining glory, to master the worlds, lord of the people, that you cut the flesh from your limbs! As long as people in this world shall tell of you, king, so long shall your fame and your worlds last, eternally!

Lomaśa said:

So, son of Pāṇḍu, behold the seat of that great-spirited king, behold it with me, that holy and evil-releasing spot. It is here, king, that the Gods and the sempiternal hermits are witnessed by the brahmins and the great-spirited doers of good.

3(33.h) *Aṣṭāvakra*

132–34 (B. 132–34; C. 10597–10691)
132 (132; 10597). Aṣṭāvakra and Śvetaketu, nephew and uncle, are contemporaries who went to King Janaka to defeat Bandin (1–5).——Kahoḍa was Uddālaka's student, to whom he gave his daughter Sujātā in marriage. The child in Sujātā's womb belittles his father's scholarship and is cursed to be aṣṭāvakra, *"eightfold crooked" (5–10). Sujātā wants wealth, and Kahoḍa goes to King Janaka for patronage, but he is defeated by the* sūta *Bandin and drowned. Uddālaka tells his daughter to keep this fact from his grandson Aṣṭāvakra. After twelve years Aṣṭāvakra finds out and goes with Śvetaketu to King Janaka (10–20).*
133 (133; 10622). Aṣṭāvakra forces Janaka to make way for him; he gains entrance at the gate with difficulty (1–15). He asks Janaka's permission to challenge Bandin and wins it after displaying his riddling wit (15–25).
134 (134; 10651). Aṣṭāvakra challenges Bandin, who belittles him (1–5). Bandin starts off the contest by naming entities that are single, Aṣṭāvakra replies with entities coming in pairs, Bandin rejoins with groups of three, and so forth. When the contest reaches thirteen, Bandin falters and Aṣṭāvakra completes the list (5–20). Aṣṭāvakra orders Bandin killed; the latter identifies himself as the son of Varuṇa to whose twelve-year

sacrifice he has been sending the brahmins he defeated (20–30). The drowned priests, including Aṣṭāvakra's father Kahoḍa, reemerge. Aṣṭāvakra is honored (30–35).

Lomaśa said:

132.1 Behold the holy hermitage, king,
Of that knower of spells, the sublime sage
Śvetaketu, son of Uddālaka,
Where the earth-grown trees are always in fruit.

Here Śvetaketu saw in person
Sarasvatī wearing a human form;
And he said to the present Sarasvatī,
"Would that I knew the tongue divine!"

At that time, king, these two were the first
Of the knowers of *brahman*: Aṣṭāvakra,
The son of Kahoḍa, and Śvetaketu,
Uddālaka's son, who were uncle and nephew.

And these two priests, who were uncle and nephew,
Went to the earth-lord, the king of Videha,
And entered his sacrifice ground to debate
And together defeated the measureless Bandin.

Yudhiṣṭhira said:

5 Then of what prowess was that priest
Who defeated Bandin that was so gifted,
And why was he called an Aṣṭāvakra?
Relate to me, Lomaśa, all in truth.

Lomaśa said:

Uddālaka had one disciplined student
Who bore the name of Kahoḍa, O king.
An obedient student, subject to his teacher—
He pursued his studies for many years.

There were many brahmins around him as pupils,
But his guru knew that *he* had a priest's makings;
He gave him at once both all his learning
And his daughter Sujātā as a bride.

She got with child, a child like fire.
And that child now spoke to his studious father:
"All night you have been doing your studies,
And still you don't have it right yet, father!"

The sage, insulted amidst his own students,
Threw an angry curse at the child in the womb:
"Since you choose to speak while still in the womb,
You shall be crooked in all eight ways!"

10 And so exactly he was born, crooked,
The seer now famed as Aṣṭāvakra;
His maternal uncle was Śvetaketu,
And he was the other's equal in age.

Now, as her child grew up in her womb,
Sujātā meanwhile was greatly depressed,
For she wanted wealth, and said soothingly
To her lack-wealth husband in privacy,

"How shall we fare without wealth, great seer?
This month is the tenth I have been with child.
You have no riches with which, when delivered,
I could overcome the disaster that looms!"

At these words of his wife Kahoḍa went
And approached King Janaka for bounty;
But Bandin, astute in wrangling, defeated
The brahmin and drowned him in the sea.

Uddālaka got the news that Kahoḍa,
By a *sūta* defeated, had been drowned in the sea;
He spoke there then to his daughter Sujātā:
"This thing should be hid from Aṣṭāvakra."

15 She kept her counsel exceedingly well
And even when born the brahmin heard nothing.
He looked on Uddālaka as his father,
And as a brother on Śvetaketu.

Then, twelve years later, when Aṣṭāvakra
Was sitting on father's lap, Śvetaketu
Grabbed his hand and tore at the crying child
And said, "This is not *your* father's lap!"

The words that he said, ill-said, remained
In the other's heart and became a sore;
Going home to his mother, he wept and asked
This question of her: "Now where *is* my father?"

Sujātā herself was badly upset,
And, afraid of his curse, she told him all;

After hearing the truth entire from his mother,
The brahmin* spoke to Śvetaketu:

"Let us go to King Janaka's sacrifice,
His rite is said to be full of marvels!
We shall listen to brahmins engage in wrangling,
And eat there too his most excellent food!
Our learning too will surely increase,
For the sound of the *brahman* is holy and friendly."

20 So they, uncle and nephew, went
To that King Janaka's opulent rite—
They refused Aṣṭāvakra, but on the way
He encountered the king** and he spoke his piece.

Aṣṭāvakra said:

133.1 The road is a blind man's, the road is a deaf man's,
The road is a woman's, the road is a porter's,
The road is a king's, if he meets no brahmin;
If he does, to the brahmin goes the road!

The king said:

Then I now shall relinquish the road to you;
Wherever you wish, do travel at will.
Not a fire is found that is too little—
Even Indra bows to brahmindom!

Aṣṭāvakra said (to the gatekeeper):

We have come to see the sacrifice, friend,
For we could not be more curious, friend,
We have come as guests and seek entrance, friend!
We await, gatekeeper, your command.

On seeing the rite of Aindradyumni,**
We want to wrangle and visit the king!
Do not let our anger afflict you this instant
With incurable sickness, keeper of gates!

The gatekeeper said:

5 We here carry out the orders of Bandin:
"Observe the statement I issue here:
No brats who are brahmins may be admitted,
But the old, the wise, and the best of them enter!"

* = Aṣṭāvakra.
** = Janaka.

Aṣṭāvakra said:

If admission is open here to the aged,
I've a right to enter, keeper of gates.
For we have aged, and excel, in our vows:
By the power of knowledge entrance is ours!

Obedient we, we mastered our senses,
We have gone to the end in obtaining knowledge.
As they say, do not despise the young,
A young fire too will burn when you touch it!

The gatekeeper said:

Then recite the Vedic Sarasvatī,
One syllable long, but of many forms!
Come on, look at yourself, a child—
Why boast? It is hard to win in wrangling!

Aṣṭāvakra said:

Is it known that age means the age of the body?
Like cancerous growths on the *śālmali* tree?
No, short, small-bodied, and fruitful it ages;
The tree that is fruitless is not even old!

The gatekeeper said:

10 In this world the young receive their wisdom
From their elders only, till they too grow old.
No wisdom is possible in a short time,
Then why do you, child, expound as though aged?

Aṣṭāvakra said:

A gray head does not make an elder. The Gods know him to be an elder who *knows*, be he a child. Not by years, not by gray hairs, not by riches or many relations did the seers make the Law: "He is great to us who has learning." I have come to visit Bandin in the king's assembly. Announce me, gatekeeper, to the lotus-garlanded king!

Today you shall witness, warden of gates,
As goes on my wrangling with the learned,
How either I'll rise, or may be lowered,
While all the rest have fallen silent!

The gatekeeper said:

15 How could a ten-year-old boy like you
Get into a rite open only to wise
And disciplined men? I shall try my best
To let you in, but you must make an effort!

Aṣṭāvakra said:

Bhoḥ bhoḥ, king, best of the Janakas,
Praiseworthy thou art, all riches are with thee!
Art thou not a worker of sacrifices,
As before thee only was King Yayāti?

We have heard that Bandin the Wise defeats
Uncaring the *Veda*-wise in his wrangles;
And when broken, he has them all drowned in the sea,
By trustworthy men, king, sent by thee.

When I heard all this from the brahmins' lips,
I hastened here to recount some riddles:
Where is that Bandin so that I may find him
And obscure him, as sun obfuscates the stars?

The king said:

How can you hope to vanquish Bandin
Without knowing the other's power with words?
Dare others, of proven power, speak thus?
Experienced brahmin debaters have met him!

Aṣṭāvakra said:

20 They were not my likes, who wrangled with him;
That made him a lion, and now he roars.
After meeting me he'll be left here today
As a cart on the road that has broken its axle!

The king said:

The greatest sage is he who knows the meaning of that which has six naves, twelve axles, twenty-four joints, and three hundred and sixty spokes.

Aṣṭāvakra said:

May the ever-turning wheel of twenty-four joints, six naves, twelve fellies, and thrice eighty spokes protect thee!

The king said:

They are like two yoked mares, the downswoops of hawks: who of the celestials begets them? Whom do they bear?

Aṣṭāvakra said:

Let them stay away from your house, king, even your foes' house! The wind-driven one begets them, and they bear him.

The king said:

25 What does not close its eye when asleep? What does not stir when it is born? What has no heart? What does grow under pressure?

Aṣṭāvakra said:

A fish sleeps without closing its eyes. An egg when laid does not stir. A stone has no heart. A river waxes under pressure.

The king said:

Not a man I deem you, but the mettle of Gods;
You are not a child, I judge you ancient.
There is no equal to you in word use,
So I open the gate, and here is Bandin!

Aṣṭāvakra said:

134.1 Among these kings, king, with their dread armies,
Who have here foregathered, peerless all,
No room for escape should be found by debaters
Sounding forth like wild geese on wide-open water.

Thou that deemest thyself a great wrangler shall not
Carry off the stake like an onrush of rivers:
Stand firmly before me, Bandin, today,
Me who am like a fire ablaze on the kindling!

Bandin said:

Do not awaken a lying tiger,
Or a venomous snake that licks its mouth:
If you kick its head with your foot, you will
Not escape unbitten, be sure of that!

A man with a solid body, yet weak,
Who strikes a mountain in arrogance
Will lacerate only his own hand and nails,
And no wound at all is seen on the mountain.

5 To the king of Mithilā all these kings are as hills to Mount Maināka; the kings are below him as calves are below a bullock.

Lomaśa said:

Aṣṭāvakra, thundering in that contest,
Irately spoke to Bandin, O king:
"You give the reply to the riddle I ask,
And I give the answer to your riddle."

Bandin said:

There is only one fire,* which is variously kindled;
And one lone sun illumines all world;

* = Agni.

One king of the Gods,* a hero and slayer;
Yama alone is the King of the Fathers.

Aṣṭāvakra said:

Indra and Agni walk as a pair;
Nārada and Parvata are the two seers;
The Aśvins are two; two wheels to a cart;
The Ordainer made two into man and wife.

Bandin said:

This creature is thrice begotten by rite;
Three *Vedas* conjoint drive the Vājapeya;
The *adhvaryus* perform the pressing thrice;
The worlds, they say, and the lights, are three.

Aṣṭāvakra said:

10 The brahmin's stages of life are four,
And four altogether make sacrifice;
There are four regions, there are four classes,
And they always say the Cow is four-footed.

Bandin said:

The fires number five, the *pankti*'s five-footed,
The rites are five, and the senses are five;
In the *Veda* are five that are five-tufted;
On earth are renowned the five holy rivers.

Aṣṭāvakra said:

Six cows are the fee for Laying-the-Fire;
The wheel of Time is these six seasons;
The senses are six, the Pleiads are six;
And as found in all *Vedas*, there are six *sādyaskas*.

Bandin said:

There are seven kinds each of tame beasts and wild beasts,
The meters that carry the rite are seven;
There are seven seers and seven honors,
And the *vīṇā* is known to have seven strings.

Aṣṭāvakra said:

Eight *śānas* measure to count a hundred;
The lion-slaying *śarabha* has eight legs;
We hear among Gods of the group of eight Vasus;
The Sarvamedha has an eight-cornered pole.

* = Indra.

Bandin said:

15 Nine kindling-verses are said for the Fathers;
Creation they say goes through nine stages;
The *bṛhatī* meter had nine syllables;
There are always nine figures in calculation.

Aṣṭāvakra said:

Ten are the stages of men in the world;
A thousand they say is a full ten hundreds;
A woman with child bears for ten months;
The Irakas, Dāśas, and Arṇas are ten.

Bandin said:

Eleven the beasts of the eleven-day rite;
The poles at that rite are eleven too;
Eleven the changes of all that breathe;
Among Gods they count the eleven Rudras.

Aṣṭāvakra said:

They hold that the twelvemonth is the year;
A *jagatī* foot has twelve syllables;
A common rite lasts, they say, twelve days;
The brahmins relate there are twelve Ādityas.

Bandin said:

The thirteenth day of the fortnight is dread;
The earth has thirteen continents . . .

Lomaśa said:

20 Having said only this much, Bandin fell silent,
Aṣṭāvakra completed the rest of the verse:
"The Long-haired One ran for thirteen days,
The *aticchandas*'s start with thirteen."

A loud applause arose when they saw
That the son of the *sūta* had fallen silent,
Had lowered his head, and was lost in thought;
And that Aṣṭāvakra went on reciting.

While this excitement was going on
At King Janaka's opulent sacrifice,
All the priests, convinced, with folded hands
Approached to pay homage to Aṣṭāvakra.

Aṣṭāvakra said:

This man has drowned very learned brahmins,
I hear, when they had lost out in debate.
Let Bandin today obey the same Law,
Lay your hands on him and drown him too!

Bandin said:

I am the son of King Varuṇa!
A Twelve-year Session is taking place
For him concurrent with yours, Janaka:
So I sent the best brahmins to his rite!

25 Here they will all once more be returning
Who have gone to watch Varuṇa's sacrifice;
I honor the honorable Aṣṭāvakra
Because of whom I shall join my father.

Aṣṭāvakra said:

Brahmins you drowned in the ocean's water!
They lost, though learned, to word and wit!
With my wit I have rescued now the word:
So the strict may examine the words that are said.

As the blazing Fire Jātavedas spares
The homes of the strict and does not burn them—
So whenever small boys speak piteously,
The strict may examine the words that are said.

Has your strength been drained by *śleṣmātakī*,
Or perchance have flatteries made you drunk?
Like an elephant prodded, you, Janaka, hear
But listen not to this word of mine.

Janaka said:

Listen I do to your celestial speech
That is more than human; you too are divine:
In wrangling you have defeated Bandin,
Now Bandin is yours to dispose as you please.

Aṣṭāvakra said:

30 I have no use whatever for Bandin alive, king. If Varuṇa is his father, drown him in the sea.

Bandin said:

I am the son of Varuṇa, king,
I have nothing to fear from drowning in water!
Aṣṭāvakra soon will set eyes on his father
Kahoḍa who perished long ago.

Lomaśa said:

Thereupon all those priests, after having been properly honored by the great-spirited Varuṇa, emerged before Janaka.

Kahoḍa said:

It is for this, Janaka, that men desire sons with their deeds. My son has done what I was unable to do. To the weak has been born a strong son, to the foolish a learned son, to the ignorant a wise son, Janaka.

Bandin said:

35 With his honed axe the God of Death himself shall cut off in battle the heads of your foes—hail be to you!

The great *ukthya* was sung and the best of the *sāmans*,
At this Session the Soma was fully drunk;
At Janaka's rite the Gods themselves
Have happily taken their holy shares.

Lomaśa said:

When all the priests had emerged, O king—
And resplendent they were as never before—
Bandin, dismissed by King Janaka,
Entered the waters of the sea.

Aṣṭāvakra welcomed his father; and he,
Honored himself by the brahmins as due,
Returned to this hermitage with his uncle,
This fine hermitage, after Bandin's defeat.

So along with your brothers, O son of Kuntī,
Dwell confidently, happily, here with the brahmins;
Then with me you'll continue, pure of deeds and devoted,
To other fords, King Ājamīḍha!

3(33.i) Yavakrīta

135–39 (B. 135–39; C. 10692–820)
135 (135; 10692). Lomaśa relates that in the Hermitage of Raibhya the sage Yavakrīta found his death (1–5). Yavakrīta was the son of Bharadvāja, who had a friend Raibhya. Being an ascetic, Bharadvāja receives less honor than the brahmin Raibhya. Yavakrīta undertakes austerities to master the Veda *(5–15). Indra appears and advises Yavakrīta to learn from a guru, but he persists (15–20). Indra returns and repeats his advice, to no avail (20–25). To teach him Indra attempts damming the Ganges with handsful of sand; Yavakrīta's efforts are equally futile (25–35). In the end Indra grants Yavakrīta and his father the* Veda *(40).*
136 (135; 10734). Bharadvāja warns Yavakrīta against pride, citing the story of Vāladhi, who obtained a son

Medhāvin who would live as long as a mountain range stood. Medhāvin becomes insolent and insults the seer Dhanuṣākṣa, who curses him to die; when the curse is ineffective, the seer sunders the mountain range and Medhāvin falls dead (1–15). Yavakrīta gives his promise (15).

137 (136; 10752). Yavakrīta comes to Raibhya's hermitage, where he rapes the wife of Raibhya's son Parāvasu (1–5). Raibhya creates a bewitching woman and a Rākṣasa by offering two strands of hair into the fire, and he orders them to kill Yavakrīta. When the woman causes Yavakrīta to become polluted, the Rākṣasa kills him in Bharadvāja's hermitage (5–10).

138 (137; 10772). Bharadvāja notices that his fires are down and questions his guard who tells him of Yavakrīta's death. Bharadvāja bemoans his son and curses Raibhya to be killed by his eldest son (1–5). He cremates his son and dies himself (15).

139 (138; 10791). King Bṛhaddyuman holds a sacrifice with Raibhya's two sons, Parāvasu and Arvāvasu, as priests. At an interval, Parāvasu visits his father's hermitage and at night mistakes his father in the wood for an animal and kills him (1–5). After the funerary rites he tells his brother Arvāvasu to take over his guilt so that he can complete the sacrifice. When he has expiated the guilt, Arvāvasu returns to the sacrifice; Parāvasu has him thrown out as a brahmin-murderer (5–15). The Gods intervene and reinstate Arvāvasu, who asks as his boon that his father Raibhya, Bharadvāja, and Yavakrīta return to life and his brother be innocent and oblivious of his parricide (15). Yavakrīta asks the Gods how Raibhya could kill him who knew the Veda; *they explain that Raibhya had learned the* Veda *properly, while Yavakrīta had not (15–20).*

Lomaśa said:

135.1 This is the River Madhuvilā Samaṃgā, and here is the bathing place of Bharata, which is called Kardamila. After Śacī's Consort had killed Vṛtra, so we hear, he was afflicted by bad fortune; by bathing in the Samaṃgā he was released from all his evil. This is the place where Mount Maināka disappeared into the womb of the earth, bull among men, and where Aditi once cooked food in order to have sons. By ascending this king of mountains, bull among men, you will dispel all

5 inglorious and unspeakable ill fortune. These are the Kanakhala
mountains, king, favorites of the seers, and here, Yudhiṣṭhira, shines
the great River Gangā. In this spot the blessed Sanatkumāra attained
to supreme success; by bathing in this place, Ājamīḍha, you shall be
freed from all evil.

At this Lake-of-the-Waters named Puṇya, and the mountain named Bhṛgu's Peak, and the River Ganges, O Kaunteya, touch water silently, you and your household. Now appears within view the lovely Hermitage-of-Sthūlaśiras: shed pride and wrath here, Kaunteya. And here shines forth the illustrious Hermitage-of-Raibhya, where the sage Yavakrīta Bharadvāja found his death.

Yudhiṣṭhira said:

10 What discipline did the majestic seer Bharadvāja follow and why
did the seer's son Yavakrīta perish? I wish to hear it all as it happened,
Lomaśa, for I delight in hearing recited the feats of those who are like
the Gods!

Lomaśa said:

Bharadvāja and Raibhya were friends, and here, in the depth of the
woods, they lived together in the greatest friendship. Raibhya had two
sons, Arvāvasu and Parāvasu, and Bharadvāja had a son, Yavakrī, O
Bhārata. Raibhya and his sons were learned men; the other was an
ascetic, yet from boyhood their friendship had been unrivaled, Bhārata.
15 Yavakrī noticed that his father, being an ascetic, went unwelcomed,
while Raibhya and his brahmin sons did receive the welcome of
brahmins, prince sans blame. Thus this man of powers became vexed
and overcome with anger; and, Pāṇḍava, he performed dreadful
austerities in order to master the *Veda*. In a huge blazing fire the
mighty ascetic was burning his body, until he began to worry Indra.
So Indra came to Yavakrīta, O Yudhiṣṭhira, and he asked, "For what
purpose have you embarked on the ultimate self-torture?"

Yavakrī said:

I submit to this ultimate self-mortification, O thou that art
worshiped by the hosts of the Gods, so that those *Vedas* that are most
20 studied by the twice-born may become manifest to me. It is for the
sake of my own knowledge of the *Veda*, Chastiser of Pāka, that I have
undertaken this: I seek to learn all there is to know by means of
mortification, Kauśika. My lord, it takes a long time before the *Vedas*
can be had from a guru's lips: therefore I have undertaken this final
effort.

Indra said:

This is not the way you want to go, brahmin seer. What, brahmin, is the point of this self-destruction? Go and learn from a guru's mouth!

Lomaśa said:

With these words Śakra left, and so, Bhārata, did Yavakrī of measureless might leave too; and he once more tried self-mortification. As the mighty ascetic heated up with his awesome self-mortifications
25 O king, he sorely mortified the king of the Gods, we hear. Once more the God Slayer of Vala approached the great hermit, when he was heating up the hottest heat, and restrained him: "The goal you have undertaken is unfeasible, nor have you wisely planned how the *Vedas* should appear to you and your father."

Yavakrī said:

So, if I do not succeed in fulfilling my desire in this way, O king of the Gods, then with a greater discipline I shall mortify myself more awfully.

> In the blazing fire I shall offer up—
> Listen, Maghavat!—every limb of my body,
> If you refuse me here, king of the Gods,
> The thing that I desire entire!

Lomaśa said:

Realizing that such was the resolve of that great-spirited hermit, the
30 wise God in his vision pondered upon a means to prevent him. So Indra made himself the body of an ascetic brahmin, many hundred years old, feeble, and sick with consumption. At the ford where Yavakrīta was wont to go for his morning ablutions in the River Bhāgīrathī,* he began making a dam with scoops of river sand. When in spite of his admonitions that great brahmin had refused to obey his words, Śakra tried to fill the river with scoops of sand, and fistful after fistful of sand he let drift off in the River Bhāgīrathī, as he started his dam to teach Yavakrīta a lesson.

Yavakrīta saw his attempts to dam up the river, and that bull
35 among hermits laughed aloud and said, "What is going on, brahmin, what are you trying to do? For all this great effort you are making is to no purpose."

Indra said:

When I have damned up the Ganges, it will be easy to cross. For people who cross time and again have trouble doing so, friend.

Yavakrī said:

There is no way in which you can dam up this mighty torrent. Stop trying to do the impossible. Attempt something that is feasible!

Indra said:

I have burdened myself with this task, just as you have undertaken the impossible task of mortifying yourself to obtain the *Veda*.

* = Ganges.

Yavakrī said:

If you think that my attempt is as purposeless as yours, Chastiser of
40 Pāka, Lord of the Thirty, then vouchsafe to me what is possible for me, O leader of the hosts of the Gods: grant me boons by which I shall prevail over others.

Indra granted the boons for which the great ascetic asked: "The *Vedas* will become manifest to you and to your father as you wish; and you shall have whatever else you desire. Now go, Yavakrī!" And having obtained his wish, he went to his father and said——

Yavakrī said:

136.1 The *Vedas* have appeared to both of us, father, and we shall prevail over others: such are the boons I have obtained.

Bharadvāja said:

Son, you must be proud, now that you have received the boons you wanted. And, being filled with pride, you will soon perish wretchedly. On this they have quoted these verses that the Gods cited before:

Son, there once was a virile seer by the name of Vāladhi. Perturbed by grief over the death of his son, he did difficult austerities, so that he
5 might have a son who would be immortal. He got him: the Gods were gracious to him, but did not make him equal to the Immortals: "No mortal man is found to be immortal; his life shall be subject to definite cause."

Vāladhi said:

As surely as these mountains stand everlasting, best of the Gods, and indestructible, they shall be the portent of my son's lifespan!

Bharadvāja said:

Thereupon a son was born to him, the always irascible Medhāvin, and upon hearing of all his circumstances he became prideful and despised the seers. He wandered on earth hostile to the hermits, till he encountered the wise and powerful Dhanuṣākṣa. Medhāvin insulted him, and the potent seer cursed him: "Become ashes!" But he did not
10 turn into ashes at the other's word. Seeing Medhāvin unhurt, the powerful great seer Dhanuṣākṣa caused the other's portent to sunder. His portent destroyed, the child at once fell dead; and his father took him and lamented. And on seeing him loudly and grievously lamenting, the hermits of yore gave voice to this verse that was spoken in the *Veda*—hear it from me:

"No mortal is ever master enough to alter his fate:
With buffaloes did Dhanuṣākṣa cause the mountains to split."

Thus young people who have received boons and grow prideful
15 and rash soon come to perish, as you should not. This Raibhya is powerful, and his two sons are not less powerful; be wary that you not overreach him, son. For if he is angered, he is capable of crushing you with his wrath, son: the great seer commands knowledge, he has

austerity, and he is quick to anger.

Yavakrī said:

I shall do so, father, do not be harsh with me in any way. I honor Raibhya as my father, just as I must honor you.

Lomaśa said:

Thus did Yavakrī, who had nothing to fear, speak kindly to his father; and he greatly contented himself by offending other seers.

Lomaśa said:

137.1 On his wanderings Yavakrī, who had nothing to fear, came to the
hermitage of Raibhya in the month of Mādhava. There in the holy
hermitage that was adorned by flowering trees he saw the sage's
daughter-in-law sporting like a Kiṃnarī, O Bhārata. Yavakrī was
robbed of his senses by passion and shamelessly said to the bashful
woman, "Lie with me!" Knowing his character and fearful of his
curse as well as Raibhya's power, she said, "So be it," and went.
5 He led her to a lonely spot, Bhārata, and flooded her. Then Raibhya
returned to his hermitage, enemy-tamer, and when he found his
daughter-in-law, Parāvasu's wife, in tears and pain, he comforted her
with gentle words and questioned her, Yudhiṣṭhira. The good woman
told him all that Yavakrī had said, and what she herself had replied
with due deliberation.
When he heard of Yavakrīta's behavior, great anger seized
Raibhya, which seemed to burn his mind. Overcome by fury, the very
irascible ascetic plucked out a strand of hair from his head and offered
10 it into the well-prepared fire. Thereupon a woman arose who matched
the other in beauty. Once more he tore out a strand of hair and
offered it into the fire, and from it arose a Rākṣasa of evil eyes and
fearful aspect. They said to Raibhya, "What do we have to do?" The
seer said, "Kill Yavakrīta!" They promised so, and they went to kill
Yavakrīta.
The witch who had been created by the great-spirited sage
approached Yavakrīta; and she seduced him, Bhārata, and stole his
water bowl. When Yavakrīta, robbed of his bowl, had become unclean,
15 the Rākṣasa stormed at him with an uplifted pike. Yavakrī, seeing
him brandish the pike and fall on him with murderous intent, quickly
rose and ran to a pond. Finding the pond dry, Yavakrīta hurried to
all the rivers, but they too had all dried up. As the horrific Rākṣasa
pursued him with his pike, Yavakrīta ran in terror to the *agnihotra*
of his father. But when he entered he was forcibly halted by a blind
śūdra guard, king, and held at the door. While the *śūdra* held
Yavakrīta, the Rākṣasa beat him with the pike until his heart split
20 and he fell dead. After the killing of Yavakrīta, the Rākṣasa went back
to Raibhya. Raibhya dismissed him; and he went to roam with that
woman.

Lomaśa said:
138.1 Thereupon, O Kaunteya, Bharadvāja finished his daily studies and
entered his hermitage with a bundle of firewood. All the fires used to
rise to meet him when they saw him, but this day they did not,
because his son had died. Observing this change in the hermitage,
the great ascetic said to his watchman, the blind *śūdra*, who had
remained seated, "Why do the fires not welcome the sight of me,
śūdra, and why do you not either, as you have done before? Is all
5 safe in the hermitage? My slow-witted son has not perchance gone
to Raibhya? Tell me quickly, for my heart is not at ease."
The śūdra *said:*
Indeed your fool son went to Raibhya! And so he now lies dead,
slain by a powerful Rākṣasa. The Rākṣasa had pursued him with a
pike down to the fire hall, and I stopped your son at the door with
my arms. While he was searching for water, and being sorely polluted,
that fast Rākṣasa finished him with the pike he carried.
Lomaśa said:
Bharadvāja, upon hearing these hateful words of the *śūdra*, took
10 his dead son and lamented sorrowfully: "Had you not done
austerities for the sake, indeed, of the brahmins, so that the *Vedas*
that are unstudied by the twice-born might become manifest to you?
Thus your deportment toward the great-spirited brahmins was
impeccable; you had no guilt toward any creatures, yet you became
rude. I forbade you, son, to visit Raibhya's lodgings, yet you went to
that miscreant who is like Time, Death, and Yama. That prideful man
knew full-well that you were the only son of me, an aged man, yet,
utterly malicious, he flew into a rage. Now that I have come to
mourn you, my son, through Raibhya's deed, I shall in my
15 bereavement give up life, which is held most dear on earth. But just
as I shall sinfully abandon my body out of grief over my son, so
Raibhya shall innocently die by the hand of his eldest son. Blessed
indeed are the men to whom no sons have been born, for without
having to grieve over a son they then go as they please. And those
whose minds have been sorely perturbed by the grief brought on by
the death of a son and who curse their dearest friends—who could be
more evil than they? Dead did I find my son, and I have cursed my
dearest friend: who else is there who will suffer a like disaster?"
Having thus lamented much, Bharadvāja cremated his son and later
himself entered the well-kindled fire.

Lomaśa said:
139.1 It was at this same time that the lordly King Bṛhaddyumna, who
was Raibhya's sacrificial patron, held a Session. The wise Bṛhaddyumna
had elected Raibhya's two sons Arvāvasu and Parāvasu as priests for

the Session. With their father's leave they went there, Kaunteya,
and Raibhya and Parāvasu's wife remained behind in the hermitage.
Then Parāvasu came home alone to visit and saw his father in the
5 forest, wrapped in a black antelope skin. It was late in the night,
though not totally dark, and being blinded by sleep he mistook his
father walking in the dense forest for an animal. And under the
illusion that his father was an animal he killed him, not out of
wantonness, but to secure his own safety.

He performed all the rites of the dead, Bhārata, then returned to
that Session and said to his brother, "You are not at all able to carry
off this ritual by yourself. But I killed father, mistaking him for an
animal. So you must undertake the right vow for a brahmin killing
in my stead, hermit, for I can finish the ritual by myself."

Arvāvasu said:

10 Then you complete the Session of the wise Bṛhaddyumna, while I
expiate the brahmin killing on your behalf, mastering my senses.

Lomaśa said:

When he had concluded the brahmin-murder vow, Yudhiṣṭhira, the
hermit Arvāvasu returned to the Session. Parāvasu saw his brother
arrive and he said to Bṛhaddyumna who sat in assembly, "Don't let
this brahmin-killer enter to look at your sacrifice. By a mere glance
the brahmin-killer could doubtless injure you!" Arvāvasu then was
15 thrown out by the servants, O king. "I did not commit this brahmin-
murder," he kept repeating when the servants kept calling him a
brahmin-killer. He did not own that he had done the vow for himself:
"My brother did it, and I expiated it!"

The Gods were pleased with the deeds of Arvāvasu. They had him
elected the priest and Parāvasu dismissed. Thereupon the Gods led by
Agni granted him a boon; and he chose that his father stand up
alive, that his brother be guiltless and oblivious of his parricide, and
that Bharadvāja and Yavakrīta rise again. So all of them appeared
again, Yudhiṣṭhira.

Now Yavakrīta said to the Gods headed by Agni, "I had learned the
20 *brahman*, I had accomplished vows—then how could Raibhya strike
me down, me, a learned man and ascetic, by means of that rite, O
eminent celestials?"

The Gods said:

Do not act as you speak, hermit Yavakrīta. For you learned the Vedas in the easy way, without a guru, while he, after having painfully satisfied his gurus with his deeds, learned the ultimate *brahman* the hard way, and over a long time.

Lomaśa said:

Thus did the Gods headed by Agni speak to Yavakrīta; and, having revived all, they returned to heaven. This is his holy hermitage where the trees always stand in flower and fruit. Stay here overnight, tiger among kings, and you shall be freed from all evil.

3(33) The Tour of the Sacred Fords (continued)

Lomaśa said:

140.1 Bhārata, you have now passed beyond the mountains Uśīrabīja,
Maināka and Śveta, as well as Mount Kāla, King Kaunteya. Now here
shines forth the sevenfold Ganges, bull of the Bharatas, a lovely and
pure place, where the fire is always lit. Nowadays it cannot be seen
by a mortal, however; but if you collect yourselves without
distractions, you shall see these fords. We shall enter the Śveta range
and Mount Mandara, where dwell the Yakṣa Maṇicara and the Yakṣa
5 king, Kubera. Eight-eight thousand swift-traveling Gandharvas and
four times as many Kiṃpuruṣas and Yakṣas, in all their various forms
and guises and holding their manifold weapons, O best of men, attend
on that Indra of Yakṣas Maṇibhadra. Their wealth is tremendous, in
speed they equal the wind, and they surely could topple even the
king of the Gods from his seat. Watched by these powerful beings and
guarded by sorcerers, these mountains, O Pārtha my friend, are hard
of access, so concentrate thoroughly. There are other grisly ministers
of Kubera and his Rākṣasa friends: we shall encounter them, so be
on your mettle.
10 Mount Kailāsa stretches six hundred leagues, king: it is there that
the Gods assemble, and there lies Wide Badarī. Innumerable,
Kaunteya, are the Yakṣas, Kiṃnaras, Snakes, Suparṇas, and
Gandharvas by Kubera's abode. Plunge into them now, King Pārtha,
with authority and self-restraint, protected by myself and the strength
of Bhīmasena. May King Varuṇa bestow his blessing on you, and
Yama, triumphant in battle, and the Ganges, the Yamunā, and the
mountains!

O Goddess Ganges, I hear thy sound
On Indra's golden mountaintop:
Protect him, good lady, from these mountains,
This king whom all Ājamīḍhas* honor.
As the prince stands ready to enter these mountains,
Be his protectress, thou child of the mountains!

* = Kauravas.

Yudhiṣṭhira said:

15 Lomaśa's anxiousness is utterly new!
You all guard Kṛṣṇā and do not falter!
For he thinks this region is hardest to pass,
Therefore observe total cleanliness!

Vaiśaṃpāyana said:

Then he said to Bhīma of noble prowess,
"Watch carefully over Kṛṣṇā, Bhīma:
When Arjuna's gone or far away, brother,
It is you who love Kṛṣṇā in times of trouble."

The great-spirited man now joined the twins,
And he kissed their heads and touched their limbs.
With a tear-choked voice the king said to them,
"Go without fear, but go prudently!"

Yudhiṣṭhira said:

141.1 There are hidden creatures here and powerful Rākṣasas: with fire
and austerity we can pass them, Wolf-Belly. Drive off hunger and
thirst by a succession of feats of strength, Kaunteya, and resort to
your strength and dexterity, scion of Kuru! You heard the words of
the seer about Mount Kailāsa: reflect with your mind, Kaunteya, how
Kṛṣṇā will fare. Or else, overlord, turn back from here with Sahadeva
and Dhaumya, the cooks and the kitchen overseers, all the servants,
5 the chariots and the horses, and with all the brahmins who cannot
bear the travail of travel, long-eyed Bhīma, while we three, I, Nakula,
and the great ascetic Lomaśa, continue on our way, eating lightly
and observing our vows. Lodge at the Gate-of-the-Ganges, watch over
Draupadī until I return, and attentively await my coming.

Bhīma said:

The princess is weary and unhappy, Bhārata, yet she will surely
make the journey, the good woman, to see again the man of the
white horses.* You yourself too suffer ever more bitterly from not
seeing him: how much worse were you not to see also Sahadeva,
10 myself, and Kṛṣṇā, Bhārata. By all means let the chariots turn back
with all the servants, our cooks, and their overseers, if you think so.
I myself do not want ever to abandon you here, on this Rākṣasa-
infested mountain, and in hard and rough places! This lordly princess
who obeys her vows will no more be able to turn back without you,
tigerlike man; likewise Sahadeva, who is always avowed to you, will
never go back, for I know his mind. Besides, all of us are eager to set
eyes on the left-handed archer, great king; therefore we shall journey
15 together. If it is impossible to conquer this mountain of many chasms

* = Arjuna.

on our chariots, we shall go on foot, king, do not worry. I shall carry the princess of Pāñcāla wherever she cannot go by herself: so I have resolved, king, do not worry. The manly twins too, those joys of Mādrī who are very delicate, I shall ferry them over difficult places, if they cannot do it themselves.

Yudhiṣṭhira said:

And so may wax your strength, Bhīma, speaking like this, so that
you may be able to carry Draupadī on this long journey, as well as
the twins, bless you! No one else could do it! Your strength and
your fame, your Law and renown shall grow, if you are able to lead
20 your twin brothers and Kṛṣṇā: may you not grow weary, strong-
armed man, may you know no defeat!

Vaiśaṃpāyana said:

Then the lovely Kṛṣṇā laughed and said, "I will go, do not worry about me, Bhārata!"

Lomaśa said:

Mount Gandhamādana can be conquered with austerities. We shall all yoke ourselves with austerities, Kaunteya. Nakula, Sahadeva, Bhīmasena, I, and you, King Kaunteya, shall see the man of the white horses!

Vaiśaṃpāyana said:

While they were thus conversing, king, they joyously saw the
large realm of Subāhu, which is rich in horses and elephants, on the
25 Himālaya, a country overrun by Mountain Men and Tanganas,
inhabited by hundreds of Kuṇindas, a place full of marvels, which is
sought out by the Immortals. Subāhu too, the chieftain of the
Kuṇindas, was pleased to meet him at the border of his realm, and he
welcomed him with honors. They all lodged there happily and were
duly honored; and when the sun had cleared they departed for
Mount Himālaya. The great chariot warriors entrusted to the king,
the chieftain of the Kuṇindas, their servants headed by Indrasena, the
overseers, the cooks, and Draupadī's entire entourage, O king.
30 The powerful scions of the Kauravas, the Pāṇḍavas and Kṛṣṇā, then
proceeded slowly on foot from that country, but very joyfully, for
they wanted to see Dhanaṃjaya.

Yudhiṣṭhira said:

142.1 Bhīmasena, twins, and princess of Pāñcāla, listen. A fact does not disappear: look at ourselves ranging the wilderness. We may tell one another that we are feeble and hurt, yet we travel even through impossible country to set eyes on Arjuna. It burns my limbs, as fire burns a pile of cotton, that I do not see the heroic Dhanaṃjaya at my side! This, the desire to see him, and the insult done to Draupadī, burn me, O warrior, while I live in the wood, as much as they burn

5 my younger brothers. I do not see the boundlessly lustrous Pārtha, Nakula's elder, the invincible awesome archer, and it consumes me, Wolf-Belly! I have journeyed to the lovely fords and woods and lakes with you in the hope of finding him. For five years I have not seen the heroic Dhanaṃjaya the Terrifier, true to his word, and it consumes me, Wolf-Belly. I do not see the dark, strong-armed Guḍākeśa of the triumphant lion stride, and it consumes me, Wolf-Belly. I do not see that best of men, past master of arms, skilful in battle, the match of any archer, and it consumes me, Wolf-Belly.
10 He strides like Time, like angry Death for the bands of his foes; like a rutting elephant is the lion-shouldered Dhanaṃjaya! Great sorrow pervades me now that because of my own irreparable deed I do not see the invincible awesome archer Phalguna, him who is not the lesser of Śakra in might and mettle, the elder brother of the twins, the measurelessly powerful Pārtha of the white horses. His temper was patient, even when he was insulted by a lesser man. He gave shelter and safety to him who walked the straight path; but to one who was crooked, who sought to kill by trickery, were he the
15 Thunderbolt-wielder himself, he was a deadly poison. The mighty Terrifier of measureless soul and majesty was gentle even to an enemy, if he sought mercy and he granted him safety. Refuge of us all, he crushed the enemies in battle, took all their jewels, and brought us happiness. Through his prowess I once owned celestial gems aplenty of many kinds, which have now fallen to Suyodhana. Through the strength of his arms I once had an assembly hall, hero, a hall built of all manner of precious stones, famed in the three worlds, Pāṇḍava. I do not see the invincible, unvanquished Phalguna, Vāsudeva's equal
20 in might, Kārtavīrya's equal in war. The mighty enemy-slayer was born after the puissant Saṃkarṣaṇa,* after yourself, undefeated Bhīma, and after Vāsudeva. The Sacker of Cities does not match him in strength of arms and in dignity, nor does the wind match his speed, or the moon the beauty of his face, or everlasting Death his anger!

Now, desirous of seeing the tigerlike man, we shall all, O strong-armed warrior, enter Mount Gandhamādana, where lies Wide Badarī and the Hermitage-of-Nara-and-Nārāyaṇa. We shall see the sublime mountain, which is always peopled by Yakṣas, and the lovely lotus pond of Kubera guarded by Rākṣasas. We shall travel on foot,
25 observing great austerity. No one who has failed in austerities can reach that region, Wolf-Belly, nor can a cruel, greedy, or restless man, Bhārata. There we shall go, Bhīma, seeking Arjuna's footsteps, with our weapons and girt swords, accompanied by brahmins of great vows. The unprepared encounter flies, gnats, mosquitoes, tigers, lions,

* = Bala-Rāma.

and snakes, Pārtha; the prepared do not see them. So, having prepared our spirits and eating lightly, we shall enter Mount Gandhamādana to find Dhanaṃjaya.

Vaiśaṃpāyana said:

143.1 Thereupon the boundlessly lustrous heroes, the greatest of archers, who carried their tautened bows, quivers, and arrows, with their wrist and finger guards tied on, and held their swords, took the best of the twice-born and, followed by the princess of Pāñcāla, started toward the Gandhamādana, O king. They saw lakes and rivers, peaks and forests on the mountain's crest, and trees that threw ample shade; also places that always stood in fruit and flower, which were visited by the hosts of Gods and seers. Concentrating their spirits and living off roots and fruit, the heroes roamed through highland and lowland, craggy and rugged, espying many and various sorts of
5 beasts. The great-spirited men penetrated the mountain that was peopled by seers, Siddhas, and Immortals, beloved of Gandharvas and Apsarās, and overrun by Kiṃnaras.

While the heroes penetrated into Mount Gandhamādana, O lord of the people, there arose a fierce gale promising heavy rains. A huge dust storm blew up mixed with masses of leaves and completely covered earth and sky and heaven. Nothing could be made out when the sky was covered with dust, they could not even talk with one another. The darkness took their vision away, and they could not see one another while the rock and dust storm dragged them on,
10 Bhārata. A deafening roar rose up of trees and bushes that broke under the wind and crashed heavily on the ground. "Is the sky falling on earth, are the mountains splitting open?" they all wondered, confused by the wind. Frightened by the gale, they groped about with their hands for close-by trees or anthills or holes and threw themselves down. The mighty Bhīmasena raised his bow; he chanced to get hold of Kṛṣṇā and sought shelter by a tree. The King Dharma and Dhaumya lay down in a wood; and Sahadeva, who
15 carried the *agnihotras*, lay on a hill. Nakula, the great ascetic Lomaśa, and the other brahmins held trembling onto tree trunks, and lay scattered about.

Then the wind died down, and the dust began to settle; and a rainstorm arose at once with a torrential cloudburst. Rain and hail showers driven by fast wind gusts shot down ceaselessly, flooding the ground on all sides. Sea-going rivers gathered from right and left and burst forth muddy and foaming, O lord of the people. Driving their mighty torrents, aswim with foam and flotsam, they burst out,
20 thunderously crashing down trees. When the rain ceased, and the wind abated, and the water flowed off to the lowlands, and the sun

reappeared, they all came slowly out and regrouped, Bhārata; and
once more the heroes set out for Mount Gandhamādana.

Vaiśaṃpāyana said:

144.1 The great-spirited Pāṇḍavas had scarcely begun their journey
when Draupadī, who was not used to going on foot, sank down.
Exhausted and aching from the gale and the rain, the glorious
princess of Pāñcāla, so very delicate, fainted. When she was felled by
her faintness, the black-eyed woman clasped her thighs with her
round and comely arms. And thus, clasping her closed thighs that
tapered like elephant trunks, she fell on the ground, trembling like a
5 banana tree. Mighty Nakula saw the curvesome woman droop like a
clinging liana, and he hurried to her and caught her.

Nakula said:

King, the black-eyed daughter of the king of Pāñcāla has fallen to
the ground from fatigue, be considerate with her, Bhārata! This
tenderly moving woman, who deserves no grief, has found grief
beyond end: comfort her, great king, she is wasted away with
exhaustion!

Vaiśaṃpāyana said:

Upon his words the king became most upset, and Bhīma and
Sahadeva immediately ran to her. The Law-minded Kaunteya looked
at her, so thin and pale-faced. And, taking her on his lap, he lamented
10 sorrowfully: "She was accustomed to finely spread couches in well-
guarded houses—how is it that now, radiant and worthy of joy, she
has fallen on the ground? How is it that the very delicate feet and
the lotus-like face of her who is worthy of the choicest boons have
now because of me become darkened? What have I mindlessly
wrought in my passion for gambling, taking Kṛṣṇā with me as I
wander in an animal-infested wilderness? King Drupada, her father,
gave away the black-eyed bride, saying, "Now that she has found
the Pāṇḍavas for her husbands, Pāñcālī shall find happiness!" She
found nothing of the sort! Wasting away with fatigue and misery,
she has fallen on the ground because of my sinner's deeds!"

15 While Yudhiṣṭhira the King Dharma moaned in this fashion,
Dhaumya and the other good brahmins came to him. They calmed
him and blessed him with benedictions; and they muttered Rākṣasa-
slaying spells and performed rites. And while the eminent seers recited
the spells for appeasement, and the princess of Pāñcāla was again and
again touched by the Pāṇḍavas with cold hands and comforted by a
cool breeze that carried drops of water, she recovered and very
slowly regained consciousness. They laid the wretched Kṛṣṇā on
spread-out antelope skins and comforted her until she had regained
20 her senses. The twins gently massaged her red-soled, auspiciously

marked feet with their callused hands. Yudhiṣṭhira the King Dharma
soothed her; and the chief of the Kurus spoke this word to Bhīmasena,
"There are many mountains to come, strong-armed Bhīma, cragged
and impassable with snow—how will Kṛṣṇā be able to travel through
them?"

Bhīmasena said:

I myself shall guide you and the princess and the bull-like twins,
king; do not give in to despair, Indra among kings! Or better, at
your behest, prince sans blame, my son Ghaṭotkaca, whose strength
matches mine and who is able to fly, will carry us all.

Vaiśaṃpāyana said:

25 With the King Dharma's consent, Bhīma thought of his Rākṣasa
son; and no sooner had his father thought of him than the law-
minded Ghaṭotkaca appeared. The strong-armed Rākṣasa approached
with folded hands, greeted the Pāṇḍavas and the brahmins, and was
welcomed in return. And he whose valor was his truth said to his
father Bhīmasena, "You thought of me, and I obeyed and came
quickly. Give your orders, strong-armed hero, I shall surely do
anything!" And, hearing this, Bhīmasena embraced him.

Yudhiṣṭhira said:

145.1 Bhīma, let this Law-wise, powerful champion, this bull among
Rākṣasas, the son of your body and devoted to us, at once take his
mother! With the help of your strength, Bhīma of most terrifying
puissance, I shall journey unhurt to Gandhamādana with Pāñcālī.

Vaiśaṃpāyana said:

On hearing his brother's words, Bhīma, tiger among men, ordered
his enemy-plowing son Ghaṭotkaca: "Son of Hiḍimbā! Your undefeated
mother has become very tired: you can travel where you want, son,
5 and you are strong: carry her in the sky. Be blessed, lift her on your
shoulder, and accompany us from the sky, flying low so that it may
not upset her!"

Ghaṭotkaca said:

Even by myself I am able to carry the King Dharma, Dhaumya,
the princess, and the twins, and how more easily now that I have
company!

Vaiśaṃpāyana said:

And having spoken heroic Ghaṭotkaca carried Kṛṣṇā amidst the
Pāṇḍavas, and other Rākṣasas carried the Pāṇḍavas. Lomaśa of
peerless splendor went by the path of the Siddhas by virtue of his
own splendor of soul, like another sun. Tremendously powerful
Rākṣasas at the behest of their king took up all the brahmins and
10 went. Thus, while casting their glances at lovely woods and park
lands, they journeyed to Wide Badarī. Carried by those powerful and

fast Rākṣasas, the heroes swiftly covered a long distance shortly. They
saw countries inhabited by hordes of barbarians and covered by jewel
mines and foothills piled with various minerals. They passed over
many countries aswarm with Vidyādharas and abounding everywhere
with monkeys and Kiṃnaras as well as Kiṃpuruṣas and Gandharvas,
15 visited by all kinds of beasts, and made lovely by monkeys; they
passed even over the Northern Kurus, until they saw the great and
wondrous Mount Kailāsa.

In its environs they espied the Hermitage-of-Nara-and-Nārāyaṇa,
full of trees that always stood in flower and fruit. And they set eyes
on the beautiful, round-stemmed Jujube Tree, sleek, casting unbroken
shade, overspread by a superb luster, shining with a smooth and thick
foliage of soft leaves, wide, with heavy branches, boundlessly radiant,
piled up with plentiful sweet berries that dripped honey—forever
divine and sought out by the hosts of great seers. It was always
crowded by flocks of various fowl that cavorted madly, and grew
20 in a place without gnats and mosquitoes, and where water, roots,
and fruit were abundant, decked with blue grass, visited by Gods and
Gandharvas, its grounds perfectly level and naturally proportioned, a
lovely spot without thorns and gently touched by snow.

When they came near, the great-spirited men and the bulls of the
brahmins all descended slowly from the Rākṣasas' shoulders. The
Pāṇḍavas set eye on the holy hermitage to which Nara and Nārāyaṇa
had had refuge, as did the bulls of the twice-born, O king. This
blessed place was without darkness though untouched by the rays of
the sun, free from the afflictions of hunger and thirst, cold and heat,
25 and dispelling sorrow. It was crowded by hosts of great seers and
filled with Vedic luster, difficult of access, great king, to men outside
the Law. Thrown-offerings and fire oblations were made to the
sacred Hermitage, with very fine unguents; and it shone everywhere
with offerings of divine flowers. It was full of large fire halls and fine
bundles of ladles, and adorned with tall sturdy water jars—a divine
place of refuge for all creatures, resounding with the sound of the
30 *brahman*, a godly sanctuary that dispelled all weariness. Lordly
scholars of the *brahman* lived there, all become Brahmā, great seers
and ascetics who had regenerated their spirits and mastered their
senses in quest of release, who subsisted on fruit and roots, self-restrained, and wore clothes of bark and black deerskins, the equals
of the sun and the fire by the power of their austerities.

The wise and lustrous Yudhiṣṭhira, son of Dharma, approached with restraint and purity those seers in his brothers' company. When the great seers, who were endowed with divine knowledge, saw Yudhiṣṭhira come, they met him very joyously, and those devoted scholars of the *Veda* pronounced benedictions. Shining like fires, they

joyfully showed him their hospitality with the proper rite, and they
offered pure water, flowers, roots, and fruit. Yudhiṣṭhira, son of
Dharma, humbly and joyously accepted the welcome that the great
35 seers proffered. Happily, the unvanquished Pāṇḍava, together with
Kṛṣṇā and his brothers, entered into the divinely fragrant and lovely
holy hermitage, which resembled the seat of Śakra, nay heaven itself,
attended by beauty, O prince sans blame, in the company of brahmins
who were stepped in the *Vedas* and their branches.

Then the Law-spirited man set eye upon the site of Nara and
Nārāyaṇa, which is worshiped by Gods and divine seers and adorned
by the river Bhāgīrathī; the great-spirited brethren drew near to the
godly Jujube Tree of the honey-dripping berries that is visited by the
hosts of great seers, and they dwelled there with the brahmins. They
saw Mount Maināka, where various groups of twice-born live, and
40 the Golden Peak, holy Lake Bindu, and the well-forded sacred
Bhāgīrathī with her cool and pure water that was covered with
jeweled sprouts and adorned with trees. The great-spirited Pāṇḍavas
strolled about there, looking at the stream bestrewn with divine
blossoms that swelled the joy of their hearts; and thus the heroic
bulls among men dwelled there together with the brahmins, offering
time and again to the Gods and Ancestors. The God-like Pāṇḍavas,
tigers among men, delighted in watching the colorful frolics of Kṛṣṇā.

Vaiśaṃpāyana said:

146.1 The heroic, tigerlike Pāṇḍavas observed the most scrupulous
cleanliness there and stayed for six nights, hoping to see Dhanaṃjaya,
while they disported and amused themselves in that charming wood
that attracted the hearts of all creatures. As they looked at the
woodland made lovely by the trees that were blowing with flowers
and bowing under the burden of their fruit, lovely all around, and
astir with flocks of cuckoos—tender-leaved trees that stood in
unbroken rows, charming and casting sweet shade—and at colorful
lakes with tranquil water that on all sides glistened with lotuses and
lilies, as they watched all these beautiful sights the Pāṇḍavas
5 rejoiced. A fragrant breeze blew gentle to the touch, gladdening the
hearts of all the Pāṇḍavas, Kṛṣṇā, and the bull-like brahmins.

Then a pure northeasterly wind began to rise, and it carried with
it a sunlike celestial lotus of a thousand petals. The princess of
Pāñcāla saw that divinely redolent and lovely pure lotus carried by
the wind and fluttering to the ground. The beautiful woman hastened
to that incomparably beautiful *saugandhika* flower, O king, and most
joyously she said to Bhīmasena, "Look at this celestial and most
radiant flower beyond compare, Bhīma, with this perfect bouquet of
10 fragrance that delights my heart! This one, however, I must offer to

the King Dharma, enemy-tamer, if you will take it back to our Kāmyaka hermitage as a favor to me. But, if you love me, Pārtha, bring me many more, I want to bring them back to our Kāmyaka Forest!"

After having thus spoken to Bhīmasena, the flawless Pāñcāla went with the flower to the King Dharma; and having understood the queen's mind, Bhīma of terrifying might, bull among men, wishing to do a favor to his beloved, faced in the direction of the breeze from whence the flower had come. He took his gold-backed bow and his cobralike arrows and quickly went forth to fetch more flowers. Like an angry king of beasts, like a rutting wild elephant he went, the powerful hero. Relying on the strength of his arms and seeking the pleasure of Draupadī, he went up the mountain without fears or delusions. Over that holy mountain, which was trodden by Kiṃnaras, covered with thickets of trees and creepers, and surfaced with black slabs, the enemy-killer roamed. As though decked with all ornaments, it was colorful with minerals, trees, game, and fowl of many hues. Decked with all manner of gems, it stretched upward like earth's arm.

Both his eye and his will fastened upon the Gandhamādana peaks, lovely in all seasons, as he dwelled upon them in his heart. With ears, mind, and eyes tied to the heights that were aloud with cuckoos and the humming of bumblebees, he continued, boundless of might. Unbridled, the splendid man climbed, sniffing his way like a rutting elephant, following the trail of the bridleless fragrance that rose from the flowers of all seasons. His father, the chill wind that blows from the Gandhamādana, took away his fatigue and stood his hair on end. Thus, for the sake of the flowers, the enemy-tamer pranced through that region that is cherished by Yakṣas, Gandharvas, Gods, and brahmin seers.

With its cleanly exposed mineral patches, golden, black, and silver, which formed unequal patterns, it was as though the mountain had been painted with fingers. With the clouds that clung to its sides, it seemed to dance as with wings, and gushing, cascading streams piled it with pearl strings. Lovely were its rivers, groves, waterfalls, and hollow caverns where many peacocks danced to the tunes of the Apsarās's ankle rings. The elephants that guard the cardinal points rubbed the stone slabs with their trunk lips; and as the rivers irresistibly spurted forth and rushed down the mountain seemed to shed its skirt.

Healthy stags, chewing mouthfuls of cud, came close and, being ignorant of fear, watched him curiously. Shaking loose many tangles of creepers with the force of his thighs, the lustrous Kaunteya, son of the Wind, went on merrily; the bright-eyed youth of a lion's build,

tall as a golden fan palm, was determined to do his beloved's wish
and continued with the prowess of an elephant in rut, the vehemence
of an elephant in rut, the copper-red eyes of an elephant in rut, able
to ward off an elephant in rut, and was watched by the invisible
consorts of Yakṣas and Gandharvas, who were sitting at their lovers'
sides, gesturing expressively. The Pāṇḍava wandered along the lovely
ridges of Mount Gandhamādana as though holding up for sale a new
incarnation of beauty. Remembering the many afflictions Duryodhana
had inflicted, and eager to please Draupadī consigned to the forest,
35 it occurred to him to think, "Now that Arjuna has gone to heaven
and I have departed to find the flowers, how will Yudhiṣṭhira fare?
Surely both the love he bears the twins, and the distrust he bears the
forest, will not allow that best of men Yudhiṣṭhira to dispatch Nakula
and Sahadeva? How can I obtain the flowers swiftly?"

Worrying thus, Pāṇḍu's tigerlike, wind-fast son, the Wolf-Belly
traveled fast, speeding like the king of birds, shaking the earth with
his feet like the earthquake at the joints of time, frightening off herds
of elephants, crushing prides of lions and tigers, uprooting huge trees
40 and breasting them powerfully with his chest; trailing creepers and
lianas, he sped on, an elephant set to climb a mountainpeak, ever
higher and higher, thundering hugely like a lightning-streaked
monsoon cloud. His dreadful roar and the twang of his bow, O lord,
frightened herds of game, and they fled into all directions.

Thereupon the strong-armed man perceived on the ridge of Mount
Gandhamādana a very beautiful orchard of banana trees that
stretched for many a league. The powerful Bhīma quickly went for it,
for he wanted to shake them, and going there he trampled many trees
like an elephant with oozing temples. Strong among the strong,
Bhīma uprooted the banana tree trunks, which stood as tall as so
45 many fan palms, and smote them swiftly to all sides. Many large
creatures appeared, and herds of *ruru* deer, monkeys, buffalo, and
water animals. Angry lions and tigers assailed Bhīmasena with
threatening, gaping maws, roaring most frightfully. But Bhīma, son
of the Wind, relying on his strength, ferociously killed elephant with
elephant, lion with lion, and with the flat of his hand lordly,
powerful Bhīma struck others dead. In Bhīma's slaughter of lions,
tigers, and hyenas they all crawled away in fear, dropping piss and
dung. When the mighty, lustrous son of Pāṇḍu had driven them off,
50 he filled with his roar all the horizons of that wilderness; and that
awesome cry, that roar of Bhīmasena, terrified all the game and fowl
in the forest, and upon hearing the outcry of game and fowl, birds
flew up by the thousands with wet wings.

Observing those flocks of water birds, the bull of the Bharatas
followed their trail and found a beautiful and very wide lake, tranquil,

although it was fanned by golden banana tree clusters on its banks that were gently stirred by a breeze. He quickly plunged into the lake that teemed with red and blue lotuses, and that boundlessly lustrous, powerful man splashed vehemently like an unbridled, huge elephant
55 and, after a long time, having done playing, climbed out. Throwing himself forcefully into the densely wooded forest, the Pāṇḍava blew his sonorous conch with all his breath. The sound of the conch, the cry of Bhīmasena, and the fearsome slapping of his arms echoed from the mountain caves. The lions who were sleeping in the hollows heard the thunderous arms slapping, which had the impact of a thunderbolt, and they gave voice to a mighty roar; and the lion's roar frightened the elephants, Bhārata, and their loud trumpeting filled the mountain.

Now, a gigantic monkey by the name of Hanūmān, a bull among apes, heard that noise, and he started to yawn. He had been dozing in a clump of banana trees, this huge ape that was as tall as an Indra
60 pole; and as he yawned he slapped his tail against the ground with the thunder of Indra's bolt. Like a bellowing cow the mountain echoed on all sides the slapping of the tail from its caverns. The sound of his tail, out-thundering the trumpeting of drunk elephants, ranged over the colorful mountain peaks.

When Bhīmasena heard the noise, the hair on his body stood on end, and he wandered about the banana grove to seek out its source. Then the strong-armed man found the king of apes in the middle of
65 the plaintain grove sitting on a thick slab of stone, blinding like a lightning flash, yellow like a lightning flash, appearing like a lightning flash, nimble like a lightning flash. His thick, short neck lay on the cross of his arms; the waist over his hips looked slender below his towering shoulders; and he shone, as with a flag, with his erect, long-haired tail that was slightly bent at the end. His face, like the beaming moon, showed red lips, a mouth with copper-red tongue, pink ears, darting brows, and round-tipped protruding tusks. The brilliant white teeth inside his mouth shed luster on it, and a massive
70 mane crowned it like a mass of *aśoka* blossoms. Thus he sat, resplendent amidst the golden banana trees, ablaze with his beauty, like a blazing fire, staring fearlessly from honey-yellow eyes.

Bhīma of terrifying might quickly drew near to that brave and powerful giant monkey and roared a lion roar to warn him; and Bhīma's cry made beasts and birds tremble. The mettlesome Hanūmān opened his eyes a trifle and looked down at him contemptuously with honey-yellow pupils. Smiling, the ape addressed the Kaunteya and sat to the human, "Why did you wake me up from sweet sleep while I am sick? Should you not knowingly show compassion to all
75 creatures? We who come from animal wombs do not know the Law,

but men, being endowed with reason, have compassion for the
creatures. How can men like yourself, endowed with reason, stoop to
cruel deeds that sully body, speech, and mind and destroy the Law?
You don't know the Law, nor have you attended to the old, if you
stupidly uproot the animals of the forest! Speak up, who are you?
Why have you come to this forest, which is avoided by men? From
this point onward the mountain is inaccessible and insurmountable
80 but by the Siddhas—you have nowhere to go, hero! I am stopping
you, strong man, out of kindliness and friendliness. You cannot go
beyond here; relax, my lord. Eat these roots and fruit that taste like
Elixir, and turn back, if you will heed my words."

Vaiśaṃpāyana said:
147.1 Upon hearing these words of that sagacious monkey king, Bhīma,
enemy-plowing hero, said to him, "Who are you? Why have you
assumed the guise of an ape? The class next to the brahmin is
speaking, a *baron* is querying you, a Kaurava baron descended in the
Dynasty of the Moon, who was borne in the womb by Kuntī, the
son of Pāṇḍu begotten by the Wind who is famed as Bhīmasena!"
Hanūmān, son of the Wind, listened with a smile to Bhīmasena's
5 words and replied to the other son of the Wind, "I am a monkey, and
I shall not make way for you as you want. You had better turn back,
lest you meet your perdition!"

Bhīma said:
I am not asking you for perdition or anything else, monkey. Get up and make way for me, lest *you* meet your perdition!

Hanūmān said:
I do not have the strength to get up, I am ridden with sickness. If you really must go on, leap over me!

Bhīma said:
The Supreme Soul beyond all description pervades your body: Him who is to be known through insight I cannot humble, I cannot leap over. If I had not found Him who prospers the beings through my studies, I would have jumped over you and the mountain as Hanūmān jumped over the ocean!

Hanūmān said:
10 Who is that one named Hanūmān who leaped over the ocean? I
am asking you, best of the Kurus, tell me if you can.

Bhīma said:
He is my brother, celebrated for his virtues, endowed with reason, courage, and strength, a champion, a bull among monkeys, most renowned in *The Rāmāyaṇa*. For the sake of Rāma's wife, this Indra of the apes jumped the hundred-league ocean in a single leap. That great hero is my brother, and I equal him with my might in strength,

prowess, and battle: I can subdue you! Get up, make way for me, or
witness my manhood today: don't travel to Yama's domain by failing
to do my bidding!

Vaiśaṃpāyana said:

15 Realizing that the other was power-mad and carried away by the
strength of his arms, Hanūmān laughed at him in his heart and said,
"Have grace, I do not have the power to get up, I am too old, prince
sans blame! Have pity on me, lift my tail and pass!" With a
contemptuous smile Bhīma seized the great monkey's tail with his left
hand, but he could not move it. Then he pulled at the thing, which
stretched high like Indra's rainbow, with both his arms; and even
with both arms powerful Bhīma was unable to lift it. His eyebrows
were cocked, his eyes widened, his brow knit, his limbs sweated, but
20 Bhīma could not budge it. However he tried, there Bhīma stood at the
great monkey's side, exhausted from pulling up the tail, and he hung
his head in shame. The Kaunteya prostrated himself and with folded
hands spoke this word: "Forgive my insult, tigerlike ape, have mercy
on me! Whether you are a Siddha, a God, a Gandharva, or Guhyaka,
pray tell me at my bidding who you are that carry a monkey's
shape!"

Hanūmān said:

However great your curiosity, enemy-tamer, to know me fully, I
shall not tell you all; listen, joy of the Pāṇḍavas. I was begotten on
Kesarin's field by the Wind, who is the life breath of the world, O
thou of the lotus-petal eyes—I am the monkey named Hanūmān!
25 Great heroes waited on the two kings of all the apes, herdsmen of all
apes, on the Sun's son Sugrīva and Indra's son Vālin. I was friendly
with Sugrīva, enemy-plower, as the wind is with fire. Sugrīva was
tricked by his brother on some occasion, and he lived with me at
Ṛśyamūka for a long time. In those days, the strong hero named
Rāma Dāśarathi—Viṣṇu in human guise—walked this earth. Wishing
his father well, he, with wife and younger brother, took refuge in the
30 Daṇḍaka Forest, that greatest of bowmen. Rāvaṇa forcibly abducted
his wife from Janasthāna, after deceiving the sagacious Rāma by his
disguise as a deer. His wife abducted, Rāghava, searching with his
brother for his consort, saw Sugrīva, a bull among foes, on a
mountain-peak. The great-spirited Rāghava became friends with
Sugrīva and, after killing Vālin, elevated him to the kingdom.

Then he sent the monkeys to seek out Sītā. We ourselves were
dispatched with millions of monkeys to one place, where a vulture
communicated to us tidings of Sītā. Whereupon, in order to finish the
business for Rāma of unsullied deeds, I took a mighty jump across the
35 hundred-league-wide ocean. I did see the queen, in Rāvaṇa's palace;
I returned after proclaiming my name. Heroic Rāma then slew all the

Rākṣasas and recovered his wife, who had seemed lost like the sound
of the *Veda*. When Rāma had departed, I asked the hero, "Enemy-
killing champion, may I live as long as the tale of Rāma survives in
the worlds!" "So be it," he said.

Ten thousands of years and ten hundreds of years did Rāma reign
over his realm, then went to heaven. Now, my faultless friend,
Apsarās and Gandharvas amuse me here by singing of the feats of
40 that hero. And, joy of the Kurus, this road cannot be traveled by
mortals, that is the reason why I am stopping you from going on this
road, which is cherished by the Gods, lest anyone assail or curse you,
Bhārata. For this is a divine pathway, no humans travel it. But the
pond for the sake of which you came is close.

Vaiśaṃpāyana said:

148.1 At these words the majestic and strong-armed Bhīmasena
prostrated himself happily and lovingly before his brother and spoke
in a gentle voice to Hanūmān, lord of the apes: "Nothing is more
fortunate for me than setting eyes on your lordship. This is a great
favor for me; I am much pleased at this vision of you. Even so, I wish
you would do me this kindness, my lord: I wish to behold the
incomparable form you assumed, hero, when you leaped across the
ocean. Then I shall be fully contented and give credence to your
words."

5 The splendid monkey began to laugh and said, "Neither you nor
anyone can see that form, for that was in another age that is no
more. Time is different in the Eon of the Winning Throw, different in
the Trey and the Deuce: this is the age of deterioration, and I no
longer possess that form. Earth, rivers, trees, and mountains,
Siddhas, Gods, and great seers adjust to time from eon to eon, as do
the creatures; for strength, size, and capacity decrease and rise again.
Therefore enough of your seeing that form, scion of Kuru's line! I too
conform to the Eon, for Time is inescapable.

Bhīma said:

Tell me the number of Eons and the manner of each of them, the
state therein of Law, Profit, and Pleasure, of size, power, existence,
and death.

Hanūmān said:

10 That Eon is called the Winning Throw, my friend, in which the
sempiternal Law holds reign. In that age, that best of Eons, things are
done, not left to be done. There the Laws do not lapse nor do
creatures die; hence the name Kṛtayuga, which in time became
equivalent to virtue. In the Kṛtayuga there are no Gods, Dānavas,
Gandharvas, Yakṣas, Rākṣasas, or Snakes, my friend, there is neither
buying nor selling. The sounds of the Sāman, Yajus, and Ṛc do not

exist, nor is there human labor. Fruit appears when thought of, and the Law is relinquishment. At that junction of the Eons there are no diseases or diminishing of the faculties, no discontent, no tears, no pride, no libel, no strife, no lassitude, no hatred, no hostility, no fear, no suffering, no envy, and no jealousy. Then the supreme Brahman is the highest goal of the yogins, and the white Nārāyaṇa is the soul of the beings. Brahmins, barons, commoners, and serfs are well defined in the Kṛtayuga, and the creatures stick to their own tasks. The stages of life, conduct, knowledge, intelligence, and vigor are equally distributed, and the classes obtain their merit of Law by equally distributed activities. Being yoked to a single *Veda*, carrying out the prescribed rites with one and the same *mantra*, they are avowed to the same Law in their various Laws and single *Veda*. With their acts according to age conforming to the four stages of life and receiving the fruit without self-interest, they attain to the highest goal. The Law of the society of the four classes, conjoined with self-discipline, is well defined in the Kṛtayuga, complete in four quarters, and sempiternal.

This is called the Kṛtayuga, which transcends the conditions of the Three Constituents; now hear about the Trey, in which the Sacrifice appears. The Law now is diminished by one quarter, and Acyuta* becomes red. Men are bent upon truthfulness and devoted to the Law of rites. In the Tretā, sacrifices become current and all manner of Laws and rituals, now motivated by purposes and giving rise to fruit of acts and gifts. Given to austerities and donations, people do not stray from the Law in the Tretāyuga; they abide by their own Law and perform rituals.

In the Eon of the Deuce the Law survives only half. Viṣṇu becomes yellow, and the *Veda* fourfold. Some people know four *Vedas*, others three or two or one, while some have no hymns at all. While the Scriptures are thus broken up, the ritual becomes multitudinous; and, bent upon austerities and gifts, the creatures fall under the sway of the Constituent of Passion. Because the single *Veda* is no longer known, the *Vedas* multiply; and because there is now a collapse of truthfulness, few abide by truth. Many diseases strike those who have lapsed from truth, and lusts and disasters caused by fate arise, afflicted by which some men perform very severe austerities, while others, motivated by desires or the wish for heaven, hold sacrifices. Thus, having come to the Dvāparayuga, the creatures perish from lawlessness.

In the Eon of Discord, Kaunteya, only one quarter of the Law survives; and, having reached this age that is swayed by Darkness, Keśava becomes black. The Vedic life-rules, Law, sacrifice, and ritual

* = Kṛṣṇa.

come to an end. Crop failures, diseases, sloth, vices like anger and so
35 forth, calamities, sickness, and ailments prevail. As the Eons follow
one on the other, the Law deteriorates every time. And with the Law
the people deteriorate. With the degeneration of people, the forces that
prosper the world decline, and the Laws produced by the decline of
the world are perverted into prayers. Thus is described the Kaliyuga
that will be shortly at hand; those who live long conform to the
Eons they live in.

As to your curiosity to know me fully, enemy-tamer, what purpose
does a man of knowledge seek in meaningless matters? I have told
you all that you have asked me, the number of the Eons. Hail to thee,
strong-armed one. Now go!

Bhīma said:

149.1 I refuse to go without having seen your old form. If you find favor
in me, show yourself to me!

Vaiśaṃpāyana said:

At these words of Bhīma the monkey gave a smile and showed him
the form he assumed when he jumped the ocean. In order to do his
brother a favor he took on a very big shape, and his body grew in
stature and girth. Overshadowing the plantain grove, the boundlessly
5 lustrous ape stood as high as a mountain. Stretched to his full length
like another mountain, with copper-red eyes, sharp tusks, and
frowning eyes, and lashing his long tail, the monkey pervaded space.
Bhīma, the joy of the Kauravas, looked at the great shape of his
brother and was surprised and delighted time and again. Bhīma saw
him as a sun with its splendor, as a mountain of gold, as space on
fire, and he closed his eyes. With a faint smile Hanūmān said to
Bhīmasena, "This is as much of my body as you can stand seeing,
prince sans blame. I can grow bigger than this, as big as I want,
Bhīma, and in an encounter with my enemies my body grows
immense by my own power."

10 When he saw that wondrous, horrifying bulk of Hanūmān, which
equaled Mount Vindhya and Mount Mandara, the son of the Wind
was perplexed. Shuddering, but merry of heart, Bhīma folded his hands
and spoke to Hanūmān still in that form: "I have seen the huge
measure of your body, mighty hero; now contract yourself! I can no
more face you than the rising sun, you are an unmeasurable and
unassailable as Mount Maināka! I am greatly surprised in my mind,
hero, that Rāma himself attacked Rāvaṇa though he had *you* at his
15 side. With your puissance you were able, justly relying on the
strength of your arms, to devastate Lankā with its warriors and
mounts. For there is nothing impossible for you, son of the Wind, and
Rāvaṇa with all his hordes was no match for you alone!"

At these words of Bhīma the bull-like ape Hanūmān spoke in reply
these kindly words in a rumbling voice: "It is indeed as you say,
strong-armed Bhīmasena Bhārata; that degraded Rākṣasa was no
match for me. But had I slain Rāvaṇa, that thorn of the world, I
would have detracted from Rāghava's* glory; that is why I forewent
20 it. That hero, after slaying the Rākṣasa king and his hordes, conducted
Sītā to his own city and established his fame in the world. Now, my
sagacious brother, who are devoted to my well-being, go a safe and
secure way, under the Wind's protection. This path, best of the Kurus,
will lead you to the Saugandhika Forest, where you will find the
Garden of Kubera, which is guarded by Yakṣas and Rākṣasas. But you
must not impetuously pluck flowers yourself, for men must give special
honor to the deities.

"Bull of the Bharatas, when worshiped with thrown-offerings,
sacrifices, and spells, and with devotion, the deities bestow grace,
Bhārata. Do not perpetrate violence, my friend; guard your own
25 Law! Abiding by your own Law, you must learn and ascertain the
highest Law; for without knowing the Law and attending to the old,
even the likes of Bṛhaspati cannot understand the Law. One should
make sure in every case where lawlessness goes under the name of
Law, or Law is called lawlessness: that is where the ignorant become
confused. The Law springs from conduct, the *Vedas* rise from the Law,
the *Vedas* bring forth the sacrifices, the sacrifices establish the Gods.
The deities are sustained by the sacrifices that are promulgated by the
injunctions of Vedic life-rules, while men are sustained by the policies
pronounced by Bṛhaspati and Uśanas—marketing, mining, trading,
30 plowing, and cattle-breeding; all the world lives by a trade, by the
Laws, and by the twice-born. To the wise there are three fields of
knowledge: the triple *Veda*, a profession, and government; when these
three are properly applied, the commonweal is secured. Were there
no lawly activities, no Vedic Law, no government on earth, this
world would be unbridled. For without plying a trade and the Law
these creatures would perish, while with all three Laws well-pursued
the creatures survive. The one Law pertaining to one class is the
Elixir of the twice-born. Sacrificing, studying, and giving are known as
35 the three pursuits common to all; officiating and teaching are both
the sole property of the brahmins as protection is that of the baron
and food-providing that of the commoner. But obedience to the twice-
born is declared to be the Law of the serfs, as it is of those who study
with a guru, though the former are denied the mendicancy, oblations,
and vows of the latter.

"Yours, Kaunteya, is the baron's Law: protection by the Law.
Attend to your own Law, restrained in conduct and passions. He

* = Rāma.

who is well established after having consulted with the elders, the
strict, the wise, and the learned rules with his staff; the vicious lose
out. When a king correctly proceeds with repression and benevolence,
40 the boundaries of the people are well laid out. Therefore, it is
necessary continuously to find out, through spies, the state of affairs
in the country, the fort, the capabilities of enemy and ally, and their
growth and decline. Kings have four aids: wise counsel, valor,
repression-benevolence, and the dexterity to see to success. Diplomacy,
bribery, alienation, repression, and deliberate disregard suffice to
accomplish affairs when applied to the whole or the part. All policies
are rooted in counsel, and so are the spies, bull of the Bharatas; well-
counseled policies lead to success, and one should consult with those
45 who know how to counsel. On secret matters one should not consult
a woman, a fool, a greedy man, a child, a trifler, or those who are
touched by madness. One should consult sagacious men, have the
actions taken by capable men, and the policies worked out by loyal
men; fools should be avoided in all cases. One should assign Law-
minded men to matters of Law, learned men to matters of Profit,
eunuchs to women, and vile men to vile tasks. The mentality of
action, as it arises from things done and not done, and the relative
strengths of one's enemies should be ascertained from one's own
people as well as the foe's. One should rightly admit to one's circle
men whom one has got to know thoroughly in one's mind, and have
the untrained and unbridled repressed. When a king correctly
proceeds with repression and preferment, then the boundaries of the
people are well laid out.
50 "This is the harsh and difficult Law that is enjoined for you,
Pārtha; guard it humbly in accordance with the disposition of your
own Law. Just as the brahmin attains to heaven through austerities,
Law, self-control, and oblations, and the commoner goes the good
journey through gifts, hospitality, and rites, so the baronage goes to
heaven on earth through repression and protection; for by using
their staff correctly, devoid of love and hatred, without greed and
innocent of anger, they share the world of the strict."

Vaiśaṃpāyana said:

150.1 Thereupon the monkey contracted his body, which he had swollen
at his will, and again embraced Bhīmasena with his paws. And while
his brother embraced him, Bhārata, Bhīma's fatigue disappeared and
everything was comfortable.

With tears in his eyes, the monkey once more said to Bhīma,
speaking in a voice that was choked with affection, "Go to your own
dwelling place, hero; you must remember me in your conversations.
5 Do not tell anyone that I am here, best of the Kurus. This is the time

and the place, strong man, for the women of the Gods and Gandharvas to come, when they are dismissed from the abode of Kubera. My own eyes have found profit; and by touching in you another human body I have been reminded of Rāghava. Now, let your vision of me prove beneficial for you, too, hero: looking to our brotherhood, choose a boon, Bhārata. If I should go to the City of the Elephant and destroy the lowly Dhārtarāṣṭras, I shall do it; or if I should raze the town with a rock, I shall at once carry out your wish, mighty man!"

10 Upon hearing these words of the great-spirited Hanūmān, Bhīma replied with a happy heart, "All this you have already done for me, bull among apes! Hail to thee, strong-armed friend, I beg forgiveness —have grace for me. With you so puissant a protector all the Pāṇḍavas have found protection! With your splendor we shall vanquish all our enemies!"

Hearing this, Hanūmān said to Bhīmasena, "Out of brotherly love and friendship I shall do you a kindness. When, after plunging into the enemy's army bristling with arrows and spears, you shall raise
15 your lion's cry, mighty hero, I shall reinforce your cry with mine. Perching on the flagstaff of Vijaya,* I shall utter fearful roars that will rob your enemies of their lives," and so speaking he disappeared.

When the best of monkeys had gone, Bhīma, first among the strong, continued along that road to vast Gandhamādana. Reflecting on the other's body and incomparable luster on earth, and dwelling on the greatness and majesty of Rāma Dāśarathi, he went his way. He convulsed the lovely woods and parks as he journeyed eagerly to the Saugandhika Forest. He saw flowering woods colorful with blooming lotuses, and herds of mad elephants that were moist with
20 mud, Bhārata, like masses of pouring monsoon clouds. Bucks with darting eyes and their does, chewing mouthfulls of grass, watched the illustrious man, who went on swiftly. Then, fearless like the champion he was, Bhīmasena threw himself on the mountain infested with buffalo, boar, and tiger, as though he had been invited by the trees in the forest that were stirred by the wind, their branches bowing under the blossoms and tender with reddish shoots. Passing on his way by lotus ponds, with pleasing bushes and fords, visited by crazy bumblebees, which with their lotuses seemed to hold up folded hands, Bhīma's eyes and mind were fixed on the flowery mountain peaks, and with Draupadī's words as his provender he moved very fast.

25 When the day had turned around, he saw in the deer-crowded forest a wide river with spotless golden lotuses; it was full of excited *kāraṇḍava* ducks and pretty with *cakravāka* birds, and it was as though it were fashioned as a garland of spotless lotuses for that mountain.

* = Arjuna.

In the curve of the river the mettlesome Bhīma beheld the large Saugandhika Forest, which stirred his joy, resplendent like the morning sun. Seeing this, the son of Pāṇḍu knew in his mind that he had gained his desire; and in his thoughts he went out to his beloved, who was pining in the forest.

Vaiśaṃpāyana said:

151.1 He went and saw on the beautiful wooded crest of Kailāsa that
lovely pond, guarded by Rākṣasas, which sprang from mountain falls
close to Kubera's dwelling, very lovely, of ample shade, and
surrounded with all kinds of trees, covered with yellow lilies and
divinely floating with golden lotuses—enough to purify the world,
holy, and of wondrous aspect. The Pāṇḍava, who was Kuntī's son,
saw there the cool, light, holy, and clear water, tasting like Elixir,
5 salubrious and plentiful. The beautiful pond stood full of *saugandhika*
lotuses and was covered with fragrant golden water flowers, with fine
beryl stems, many-colored and heart-fetching, which, shaken by wild
geese and ducks, emitted a white pollen. This was the play-garden of
Kubera, the great-spirited king of the Yakṣas, and held in great honor
by Gods, Gandharvas, and Apsarās; the celestial pond was visited by
seers, Yakṣas, Kiṃpuruṣas, Rākṣasas, and Kiṃnaras, and protected
by Vaiśravaṇa.*

No sooner did the mighty Kaunteya set eyes on that divine lake
10 than he was filled with extreme joy at the sight. Hundreds and
thousands of Rākṣasas by the name of Krodhavaśas stood guard over
it with marvelous weapons and accoutrements at the king's command.
As soon as they saw the enemy-taming Kaunteya, that heroic Bhīma
of terrible strength, fearlessly draw near, clothed in deerskins, with
golden upper-arm bracelets, armed, with sword girt, who had now
come to pluck the flowers, they shouted at one another, "This
tigerlike man with weapons and deerskin garb—ask him for what
purpose he has come here!" Then they all approached the strong-
15 armed Wolf-Belly and asked the glorious man, "Who are you, pray
tell! You are wearing the hermit's garb and appear to be dressed in
bark. Why have you come? Tell us, lustrous one."

Bhīma said:

152.1 I am Bhīmasena Pāṇḍava, younger brother of the son of Dharma; I had come with my brothers to Wide Badarī, Rākṣasas. There the princess of Pāñcāla saw a peerless *saugandhika* lotus carried to her by the wind, and at once she wanted many of them. Know, Stalkers of the Night, that I have come to gather flowers as a favor for my flawless wife by the Law.

* = Kubera.

The Rākṣasas said:
5 This is the favorite play-garden of Kubera, bull among men. A
mortal man cannot disport himself here! Divine seers, Yakṣas, and
Gods ask the permission of the chief of the Yakṣas to drink and play
here, Wolf-Belly Pāṇḍava, and so do Gandharvas and Apsarās play
here. Whoever wishes to amuse himself here unlawfully, disregarding
the Lord of Riches, that miscreant must inevitably perish. You wish
to ignore him and forcibly take lotuses from here: then how is it that
you call yourself the brother of King Dharma?

Bhīma said:
Rākṣasas, I do not see the Lord of Riches anywhere near, and even
if I saw him I would not trouble to beg the great king. For kings do
not beg, that is the eternal Law; and I do not want to abandon in
10 any measure the Law of the baron. This lovely lotus pond has sprung
from mountain falls, it is not part of the domain of the great-spirited
Kubera, for it belongs equally to all creatures as well as Vaiśravaṇa.
As matters lie thus, who should beg whom?

Vaiśaṃpāyana said:
After having said this to all the Rākṣasas, majestic Bhīmasena plunged in, while the Rākṣasas warned him, "Don't! Stop!" and angrily abused him on all sides. Ignoring the Rākṣasas, the illustrious Bhīma of terrible might plunged on, as all tried to stop him.

"Seize hold of him, tie him, hack him!
We shall cook and feed on Bhīmasena!"
They angrily said, and quickly pursued him,
Lifting their arms and distending their eyes.

15 Then he seized his heavy and massive club
That was plated with gold, like the staff of Death;
And the violent man threw himself upon them
And shouted at them, "Stand fast, stand fast!"

The Krodhavaśas, most terrifying,
Then wildly attacked him with all their weapons,
With battle-axes and spears and the like,
And fearfully circled around him to kill him.

The mighty, impetuous champion son
Of the Wind by Kuntī, killer of foes,
Forever devoted to truth and the Law,
In prowess invincible by his foes,

Great-spirited, cut their many passes
And bludgeoned down his enemies' weapons;
From their leaders down the hero slew them,
Slew over a hundred of them by the pond.

Perceiving his power and bravery,
The strength of his knowledge, the strength of his arms,
Unable to fight him with all their numbers,
With their leaders slain, they retreated in haste.

20 Utterly devastated they quickly
Took to the sky, their senses benumbed,
Those Bhīma-crushed, shattered Krodhavaśas,
And ran up to the Kailāsa peaks.

Having downed the Daityas and Dānavas
Like Indra, and vanquished their many hordes,
The victor dived in the lotus pond,
And plucked the lotuses at his whim.

Then, drinking that Elixir-like water,
He regained superbly his vigor and splendor;
He pulled out and gathered the water-grown
Saugandhikas, fragrant beyond compare.

Thereupon the Krodhavaśas, abashed
By Bhīma's force, met the Lord of Riches
And, extremely dejected, they told him the truth
Of Bhīma's power and prowess in battle.

Having heard the Rākṣasas' words, the God
Began to laugh and spoke to them:
"Bhīma shall take all the flowers he wants,
The purpose of Kṛṣṇā is known to me."

25 Thereupon the Lord of Riches dismissed them,
And unangry they went to the chief of the Kurus,
And watched in that selfsame lotus pond Bhīma
Happily playing, all by himself.

Vaiśaṃpāyana said:
153.1 The Bhārata bull gathered those precious, celestial, dustless flowers
of many colors in plenty. Then a big gale, blowing up the gravel,
slowly began to rise, gritty to the touch, predicting battle. A huge,
fiercely blazing meteor fell down in a whirlwind; the sun lost luster,
its rays were obscured, and it was covered with darkness. A ferocious
whirlwind gathered while Bhīma persisted in his bravery. The earth
5 shook, and a dust storm fell. The skies were red. Game and fowl
screeched shrilly. All was covered by darkness. Nothing could be
made out.

Observing this strange happening, Dharma's son Yudhiṣṭhira, greatest of speakers, spoke out: "Who is about to overwhelm us?

Good luck, war-crazed Pāṇḍavas, be prepared: from what I see by the signs our dominance will be restored!" Having spoken, the king looked around, and Dharma's son Yudhiṣṭhira did not see Bhīma. The enemy-tamer queried Kṛṣṇā and the twins, all close to his person,
10 about his brother Bhīma, of terrible feats in time of war: "Pāñcālī, did Bhīma want something to do, or has the hero perpetrated some violence already, prone to violence as he is? For all of a sudden all these portents, which foresee a great battle and forecast severe danger, are occuring on every side."

Spirited Kṛṣṇā replied to his words, his beloved, sweet-smiling queen, who wanted to please him: "Today I felt in a loving mood and had Bhīmasena bring me *saugandhika* flowers, for the wind had blown us one earlier, king. Also I told the hero that if he should find many
15 more, to take the flowers and return at once. Surely to do me that favor the strong-armed Pāṇḍava must have gone up to the northeast to fetch them, king." When he had heard her words, the king said to the twins, "In that case we shall immediately together go where the Wolf-Belly has gone. The Rākṣasas shall carry the brahmins to the degree that they are tired and feeble, and you, Ghaṭotkaca, who resemble an Immortal, must carry Kṛṣṇā. Surely, I think, Bhīma has got far from here: he has been gone long and in speed he matches the wind. He is as fast as Garuḍa in crossing distances on land; he
20 will leap up into the air and alight as he pleases. With the aid of your puissance we shall go after him, Stalkers of the Night, before he trespasses upon the *brahman*-learned Siddhas."

They all assented. Led by Hiḍimbā's son and being familiar with the region of Kubera's pond, O bull of the Bharatas, they took the Pāṇḍavas and numerous brahmins, and departed with Lomaśa, happy of heart. They journeyed together until they all saw the lotus pond with flowering lotuses in that woods. They saw the great-spirited Bhīma standing on its bank, and the wide-eyed Yakṣas he had slain.
25 He stood on the bank raising his club with his arms, like Death wielding his staff at the time of the annihilation of the creatures. The King Dharma embraced him again and again, when he had found him, and he said in a gentle voice, "Woe, Kaunteya, what is this violence you have perpetrated, displeasing the Gods? Good luck to thee! If you wish to do me a kindness, never act like that again!"

After he had thus admonished the Kaunteya, they gathered lotuses,
30 and amused themselves like Immortals in that lotus pond. At that same time big-bodied guards of the garden, armed with rocks, made their appearance. When they saw the King Dharma, the divine seer Lomaśa, Nakula, and Sahadeva, and the other bull-like brahmins, they all prostrated themselves and bent down with humility, Bhārata. The King Dharma appeased the Stalkers of the Night, and they grew calm.

Then the bulls among men, scions of Kuru, lived there for a brief while with Kubera's knowledge and enjoyed themselves.

3(34) The Slaying of Jaṭāsura

154 (B. 157; C. 11428–526)
154 (157; 11428). The Rākṣasa Jaṭāsura, desirous of the Pāṇḍavas' weapons, abducts the brothers and Draupadī, except Bhīma, who is absent, and Sahadeva, who escapes (1–5). Yudhiṣṭhira berates the demon (5–15) and grows heavy on him (15–20). Sahadeva challenges Jaṭāsura (20–25). Bhīma arrives and challenges (25–35). Jaṭāsura abandons the others and attacks; they wrestle (35–55). Bhīma breaks Jaṭāsura (55–60).

Vaiśaṃpāyana said:
154.1 While the Pāṇḍavas were peacably staying there, after the
Rākṣasas as well as Bhīmasena's son* had departed, they happened
one day to be without Bhīmasena, and a Rākṣasa abducted the King
Dharma, the twins, and Kṛṣṇā. He had attended on them daily, saying
that he was a brahmin expert in spells and most knowledgeable about
all weaponry. His name was Jaṭāsura, and he coveted the quivers and
5 the bows of the Pārthas, waiting for his opportunity. So, when
enemy-taming Bhīmasena had gone out hunting, that evil Rākṣasa
took on his other huge, deformed, and terrifying form, took all the
weapons, seized Draupadī and three Pāṇḍavas, and departed. But
Sahadeva Pāṇḍava had a chance to run off and shout for Bhīmasena
in the direction he had gone.
As he was being abducted, Yudhiṣṭhira the King Dharma said to
the ogre, "Your merit of Law is dwindling, fool, and you do not mind.
Anyone belonging to humankind, and the brute creation, the
Gandharvas, Yakṣas, and Rākṣasas, birds and cattle, all live off men,
10 and so do you. Your world prospers by the prosperity of ours; if our
world suffers, the deities suffer along, but they grow when ritually
worshiped with oblations and ancestor offerings. We are the herdsmen
of the kingdom and its protectors, Rākṣasa; if the kingdom goes
unprotected, whence can there be prosperity, whence happiness? A
Rākṣasa must never despise a king if he is guiltless, and we have not
committed the slightest offense, man-eater. One should never threaten

* = Ghaṭotkaca.

friends and trusting people, those whose food one has eaten and with whom one has found shelter. You had shelter with us, we honored you, and you lived comfortably; having eaten our food, how can you want to abduct us, nitwit? You were false in your conduct, false in your age, false in your mind—you should deserve a false death, but it shall not be false today! If you must be evil-minded and destitute of all Laws, return our weapons and take Draupadī after a fair fight with us; but if you foolishly persist in this outrage, you will reap nothing but lawlessness and infamy in the world. Today you have laid hands on this human woman, Rākṣasa: you have stirred up poison and drunk it from a jug!"

Thereupon Yudhiṣṭhira grew heavy on him; and, pressed by his weight, the ogre could not go as fast. Yudhiṣṭhira said to Draupadī and Nakula, "Have no fear of fool Rākṣasas. I have slowed his pace. The strong-armed son of the Wind cannot be too far away. When he comes after a while, the Rākṣasa will be no more."

Now, Sahadeva, after seeing that befuddled Rākṣasa, spoke to Kuntī's son Yudhiṣṭhira: "O king, what can give a baron greater contentment than to face his foe in battle and die, or defeat his enemies? In a fight, strong-armed enemy-burner, he may finish us, or we him: this is the time and the place, king. The time has arrived for the Law of the baronage, prince whose valor is the truth. Whether we win or fall, we shall have earned the good journey. If that Rākṣasa still lives when the sun goes down, I shall never call myself a baron again, Bhārata! *Bhoḥ bhoḥ* Rākṣasa, stop! I am Sahadeva Pāṇḍava, either kill me and take them, or fall and sleep!"

When he was saying this, strong-armed Bhīmasena chanced to appear like Indra with his thunderbolt. He saw his two brothers, the glorious Draupadī, Sahadeva on the ground challenging the Rākṣasa, and the Rākṣasa himself, whose brains had been smitten by Time and who, having lost his way, was wandering hither and thither, stopped by fate. On seeing his brothers and Draupadī being abducted, the strong Bhīma flew into a rage, and he said to the Rākṣasa, "I found you out before, when you were trying to inspect our weapons, but I did not care about you, so I did not kill you. Hiding beneath your brahmin disguise you never said anything unpleasant to us. Why should I have killed you—you were doing us favors, never giving offense, a guest who appeared to be an innocent brahmin. Anyone who had killed you, even though knowing you for a Rākṣasa, would have gone to hell. The time was not ripe for killing you, but now that this is your design, this design wished upon you by miracle-mongering Time, to abduct Kṛṣṇā, you have surely ripened! You have swallowed the hook that dangled from the string of Time, like a fish in the water whose mouth has been hooked! How will you escape from me now? That place for which you have started, and which you had already reached in your mind, you shall not reach, you shall go the road of Baka and Hiḍimba!"

At these words of Bhīma, the Rākṣasa, prompted by Time, fearfully threw them all down, and approached to give battle. He replied to Bhīma with his lower lip trembling with anger, "I did not lose the way, I tarried to get you. I have heard of each of the Rākṣasas you killed in combat, and today I shall offer them the funerary water with your blood!" Bhīma licked the corners of his mouth, and with a faint smile he, like Time and Death personified, ferociously stormed at the Rākṣasa to begin a wrestling match. The Rākṣasa too impetuously rushed to Bhīma, who stood ready to fight, like Vala who rushed on the Thunderbolt-wielder.

Then, as the terrible wrestling bout of the two began, both the sons of Mādrī angrily rushed in; but Kuntī's son the Wolf-Belly laughingly stopped them. "I am up to this Rākṣasa, you just watch," he said. "By myself, by my brothers, by the law which I have observed well, and by my oblations I swear I shall finish this Rākṣasa off, king!" The two heroes who were challenging each other, the Rākṣasa and the Wolf-Belly, clashed ruthlessly in battle as a God and a Dānava. They uprooted tree after tree and hurled them at each other; and the powerful pair roared like two clouds at the end of the hot season. Immensely strong, they broke down tree trunks with their thighs, as they set on each other, each holding out for victory. A tree fight went on that destroyed many trees, as of old in the battle between the brothers Vālin and Sugrīva, lions among apes; they hurled tree after tree at each other for a while, and thrashed away with roar after roar. When in the whole region all the trees had been felled, and the two in their murderous lust had reduced them to a heap by hundreds, the strong men took for a while to rocks, Bhārata, and fought, as powerful mountains fight with clouds; with those ugly, awesome, huge rocks which flew apace, they pelted each other mercilessly as with flying thunderbolts. Then, after this stoning, swollen with pride of strength, they grabbed each other again with their arms and dragged away like elephants. They buffeted each other with mean fists, until the great-spirited wrestlers made crackling noises.

Bhīma now clenched his fist, like a five-headed snake, and struck the Rākṣasa's neck. Bhīmasena saw that the Rākṣasa, already tiring, was reeling under his blow and attacked him. The strong-armed, God-like Bhīma lifted him up high and powerfully crashed him to the ground. The Pāṇḍava fractured all his limbs and with a blow of his elbow snapped the head off the trunk. Jaṭāsura's head, severed by Bhīmasena's force, fell with clamped lips, bulging eyes, and clenched teeth to the ground smeared with blood.

After the kill the great bowman walked up to Yudhiṣṭhira and the great brahmins praised him even as the Maruts praise Vāsava.

3(35) *The War of the Yakṣas*

155–72 (B. 158–75; C. 11527–2315)
155 (158; 11527). The Pāṇḍavas and Draupadī live in the Hermitage of Nārāyaṇa, awaiting Arjuna who is to meet them on Mount Śveta, to which they depart (1–15). On Mount Gandhamādana they visit the hermit Vṛṣaparvan (15–20). They continue northward and reach Mount Śveta and Mount Mālyavat (25–35). Description of the landscape (35–85). They visit the hermit Ārṣṭiṣeṇa (85–90).
156 (159; 11628). The hermit welcomes them, preaches to them, and relates that the mountain is the abode of divine beings (1–20). It is impossible to go farther: they should stay with him (20–30).
157 (160; 11661). Janamejaya asks about the Pāṇḍavas' life there (1–5). They spend the remainder of the year (5–10). A breeze carries celestial flowers; Draupadī sends Bhīma to fetch more (15–20). He sets out (25–30) and reaches Kubera's domain, where Yakṣas and Rākṣasas attack him (35–40). Bhīma slaughters them (40–50). The demon Maṇimat rallies the Rākṣasas and counterattacks (50–65). Bhīma slays him (65–70).
158 (161; 11739). Missing Bhīma, the Pāṇḍavas go in search of him and find him amidst the carnage (1–5). Yudhiṣṭhira berates him (5–10). The Rākṣasas report the slaughter to Kubera, who is enraged and orders the army yoked (10–25). Kubera meets the Pāṇḍavas and turns benevolent (25–35). He forgives Bhīma, explaining that his feat has freed him from a curse by Agastya (35–45). Once, when Kubera was on his way to Kuśavatī, his friend Maṇimat spat on Agastya's head; for which the seer cursed Maṇimat to be killed and Kubera to come to grief; upon seeing the killer of Maṇimat's killer Kubera's curse is lifted (50–55).
159 (162; 11803). Kubera preaches to them and sends them back to Ārṣṭiṣeṇa's hermitage, where they will live under his protection (1–15). He relates that Arjuna is in

heaven, from whence Śaṃtanu sends greetings (15–20). Arjuna will soon join them (25). Kubera departs (25–35).

160 (163; 11841). Dhaumya shows Yudhiṣṭhira the sacred mountains, especially Mount Meru (1–20). Sun and moon circle around Meru (20–35).

161 (163; 11883). The Pāṇḍavas await Arjuna on the mountain, which is described (1–15). Then, on Indra's chariot driven by Mātali, Arjuna arrives; he greets everyone and is joyfully received (15–20). Mātali returns, and Arjuna relates how he has received the celestial weapons, then sleeps (10–15).

163 (167; 11935). Yudhiṣṭhira questions Arjuna (1–5). The latter relates that on Bhṛgu's Peak he encountered a brahmin, who exhorted him to asceticism (5–10). He practices austerities; then a demon in the shape of a boar appears, pursued by a Mountain Man, who is accompanied by many women (10–15). They shoot the boar simultaneously, whereupon the man challenges Arjuna, while assuming many forms and swallowing up the other's weapons (20–35). Finally Arjuna is wrestled down, the man assumes his form of the Great God and returns to him his bow and arrows, bestowing a boon (35–45). Arjuna asks for the pāśupata *weapon, which thereupon in bodily form comes to his side (45–50).*

164 (168; 11992). The next day Arjuna meets the same brahmin, to whom he tells all; he predicts that Arjuna will meet the World Guardians and Indra (1–5). The Gods appear and bestow their weapons; Indra warns him on their use and disappears (5–25). Indra's chariot arrives with Mātali, who takes him to Indra's world, which is described (25–50). Arjuna studies weaponry and the arts of the Gandharvas (50–55).

165 (168; 12054). Indra tells Arjuna to perform a task; the latter promises to; he is to destroy the demoniac Nivātakavacas (1–10). On Indra's chariot he departs with the blessings of the Gods, who give him the conch Devadatta (10–20).

166 (169; 12079). The demons' city lies at the ocean; at Arjuna's arrival they close the city gates, and Arjuna blows his conch (1–10). The demons come out and clash with him (10–20).

167 (170; 12103). They engage. Arjuna kills many

(1–10). He employs his Mādhava missile and slaughters the demons, who now resort to magic (10–25).
168 (171; 12131). He counters a rain of rocks, a torrential downpour, and a fire storm (1–10). Then he is plunged into total darkness; Mātali panics (10–15). Arjuna reassures him and destroys the illusion; the demons go into hiding (15–30).
169 (172; 12162). Arjuna routs the demons, and they flee to their city (1). The demons attack him from the sky, halt his chariot, and pile mountains on him (1–10). He breaks out with the thunderbolt missile (10–15). Arjuna enters the demons' city, which is magnificent (10–25). Mātali explains that it is an old city of the Gods, which the demons have conquered; Arjuna was to come to destroy the demons (25–30). Arjuna starts to return to Indra (35).
170 (173; 12197). On his way he sees a grand city. Mātali relates that the demon couple Kālaka and Pulomā after austerities received the boon that their descendants, who now inhabit the city, would be invincible to the Gods; the city, Hiraṇyapura, was created for them by Brahmā (1–10). Arjuna decides to destroy the demons, and slaughters them (10–20). The city becomes airborne; Arjuna shoots it down, battles the demons, and finally lays on the Raudra missile, which produces countless apparitions that kill the demons (20–45). The battle won, Mātali praises Arjuna (50). The grief of the demons' women (55). Arjuna returns to Indra and is much praised (60–65).
171 (174; 12274). After five years Indra tells Arjuna to return to his brothers, with whom he now finds himself reunited (1–10). Yudhiṣṭhira pronounces blessings (10–15).
172 (175; 12291). Arjuna shows them the weapons. Nature protests, celestials appear, and Nārada warns Arjuna not to use them (1–20).

Vaiśaṃpāyana said:

155.1 When the Rākṣasa had been slain, the lordly King Kaunteya returned to the Hermitage of Nārāyaṇa and made his dwelling there. One day he assembled all his brothers and Draupadī and, remembering his brother Vijaya,* spoke to them as follows: "Four years have gone by, while we lived piously in the forest. Bibhatsu promised that in the

* = Arjuna.

fifth year he would come to that king of mountains, Mount Śveta, greatest of peaks. We too, looking forward to our reunion, should keep the appointment. The Pāṇḍava of boundless luster has made a covenant with me: 'I shall live five years as a student.' We shall see the enemy-taming Gāṇḍīva bowman return to this world from the world of the Gods with the weapons he has obtained." Having spoken, the Pāṇḍava consulted all the brahmins and informed the ascetics concerning the matter. The Pārtha circumambulated the brahmins of awesome austerities, and, pleased, they approved it as being propitious and conducive to well-being, and, bull of the Bharatas, said that his anguish would soon result in happiness: "After having made the crossing according to the Law of the baronage, Law-wise king, you shall govern the earth."

The king accepted these words of the ascetics, and the enemy-tamer departed with his brothers and the brahmins; the illustrious prince was accompanied by Draupadī, followed by Hiḍimbā's son* and other Rākṣasas, and protected by Lomaśa. Some stretches he did on foot, elsewhere the resplendent man of good vows was carried with his brothers by the Rākṣasas. Reflecting on his many troubles, King Yudhiṣṭhira turned to the northern region, which is haunted by lions, tigers, and elephants. He beheld Mount Kailāsa and Mount Maināka, the foothills of the Gandhamādana, and the mighty rock pile of Meru, and, ever higher in the mountains, many auspicious streams, until, on the seventeenth day, he came to the plateau of the Himālaya. Close to the Gandhamādana, O king, the Pāṇḍavas saw on the holy crest of the Himālaya, wooded with all kinds of trees, that most holy hermitage of Vṛṣaparvan, which was surrounded with flowering trees that grew by whirling streams.

The enemy-taming Pāṇḍavas approached the Law-spirited royal seer Vṛṣaparvan, and when they greeted him they shed all fatigue. The royal seer welcomed the Bharata bulls like sons, and the enemy-tamers stayed there with full honors for seven nights. On the morning of the eighth day they consulted the world-renowned seer Vṛṣaparvan and decided to depart. They presented the brahmins one by one to Vṛṣaparvan to be held in his trust for the time being, well-treated like kinsmen. Then the Pāṇḍavas entrusted to the hermitage of Vṛṣaparvan their fine robes and beautiful ornaments. The Law-wise seer, who knew the past and the future, proficient and informed of all Laws, instructed the Bharata bulls like sons. With his leave the great-spirited heroes started with Draupadī and great-spirited brahmins for the north. King Vṛṣaparvan followed them when they departed, then, after entrusting the Pāṇḍavas to the care of the brahmins, and blessing them with benedictions, the glorious Vṛṣaparvan made his

* = Ghaṭotkaca.

farewell and, having told them the way, turned back. Yudhiṣṭhira,
Kaunteya, whose valor was his truth, went with his brothers on foot
through the wilderness, which teemed with all kinds of game.

The Pāṇḍavas, camping on mountain ridges that were enclosed by
many kinds of trees, reached Mount Śveta on the fourth day, a
beautiful mountain with abundant water, which appeared like a huge
cloud, lovely with minerals and gold and many-peaked. They followed
the path that Vṛṣaparvan had told them, and, seeing many mountains,
30 they passed, ever higher on the mountain, over impassable caverns
and many inaccessible places with complete ease. Dhaumya, Kṛṣṇā,
the Pārthas, and the great seer Lomaśa all went together and none of
them failed. The courageous party made its way to the great
mountain Mālyavat, noisy with game and fowl, astir with all kinds of
birds, sought out by packs of monkeys, very lovely and holy, with
lotus lakes, pools, and vast woods. Then they beheld the habitation
of Kiṃpuruṣas, visited by Siddhas and Cāraṇas, Mount Gandhamādana,
35 and their hair stood on end. Vidyādharas roamed through it, and the
women of the Kiṃnaras; it was overrun by elephants and lions, and
full of excited *śarabhas*; many other animals, whose cries were sweet,
filled this Gandhamādana Forest, which resembled the paradise of
Nandana.

Joyfully, Pāṇḍu's heroic sons entered in slow stages this beautifully
forested wilderness that delighted both mind and heart. The heroes,
accompanied by Draupadī and the great-spirited brahmins, listened
to the delightful, sweet and melodious, pure, ear-filling, and charming
warblings of the birds, looked at the trees bowing under the burden
of their fruit, abounding in plenty of fruit in all seasons, ablaze with
40 bloom in all seasons—flowering mangoes, hog plums, palms,
tindukas, *ajātakas*, *jīras*, pomegranates, citrons, breadfruit, *likucas*,
mocas, *kharjūras*, mango cane, *pārāvatas*, *campakas* and lovely
cadambas, *bilvas*, *kapitthas*, rose apples, *kāśmarīs*, jujubes, figs,
udumbaras, *aśvatthas*, milky trees, cashew nuts, myrobalans, yellow
myrobalans, *vibhītakas*, *ingudas*, oleanders, and big-fruited *tindukas*,
these and many other trees they saw on the ridges of the
Gandhamādana, laden with sweet fruit as tasty as Elixir; likewise
45 *campakas*, *aśokas*, jasmines, *bakulas*, *puṃnāgas* and *saptaparṇas*,
karṇikāras and jasmine, bignonia, lovely *kuṭajas*, corals, blue lotuses,
śālas, palms, *tamālas*, *parijātakas*, *kovidāsas* and pines, *priyālas*,
bakulas, *śāmalīs*, *kiṃśukas*, *aśokas*, sissoos and thorn apples, which
were filled with *cakoras*, woodpeckers, shrikes, parrots, cuckoos,
sparrows, pigeons, pheasants, *priyavratas*, *cātakas*, and many other
birds, which sang sweet songs lovely to the ears. Also colorful lakes
with clear water filled with night-blooming lotuses, white lotuses, red
waterlilies, blue lotuses, white lilies, and red lotuses on all sides.

50 Gray-winged geese, *cakravākas*, ospreys, water cockerels, *kāraṇḍava*
ducks, *plavas*, geese, herons, divers, and other water birds abounded
everywhere. Lovely red lotus ponds were sweetly humming with
excited bumblebees made lazily tipsy by the liqueur of day-blooming
lotuses and red-dusted with the pollen and filaments that had escaped
from the chalices of lotuses—they saw them all on the ridges of the
Gandhamādana. In beautiful lily clusters and little liana bowers
everywhere they noticed peacocks with their hens, excited by the
frenzied lust that the drums of the clouds brought about, which
uttered their musical and melodious calls; spreading their colorful
tail plumes, playfully, lustfully, lazily, the wood-loving birds danced
55 about. Others played happily with their loves in valleys that were
overgrown with vines and creepers. In the clearings of the woods
they watched on the treetops certain species of beautiful birds with
spreading plumage like colorful diadems. Luxuriant *sindhuvāra*
plants, like arrows of the God of love, covered with golden flowers
were growing on the mountain peaks, as well as *karṇikāras*, which
were fashioned like choice earrings, and *kurubakas* flowered in the
mountain ranges like a volley of Kāma's* arrows which bring longing
to those in love. They saw *tilakas* that shone as though they had been
60 made into noble beauty marks of the woodlands, and lovely mango
trees, shaped like the arrows of the Bodiless God, humming with bees,
which glistened with blossom clusters. Trees with blossoms golden or
fiery like a forest fire, red and mascara-black, or the color of beryl—
śālas, *tamālas*, begonias, and *bakulas*—clung to the mountaintop like
garlands. And thus feasting their eyes at every step they penetrated
the dense jungle, provender of elephants and haunt of lions and tigers,
which echoed with the roars of *śarabhas* and resounded with all kinds
of animal cries, abounding with fruit and blossoms in all seasons, on
65 the ridges of the Gandhamādana. The forest ranges were yellow-
colored like the sun, there were no thorny plants there or trees
without flowers; the trees were smooth of leaf and fruit on the ridges
of the Gandhamādana. The Pāṇḍavas also saw lakes and rivers on the
mountain ridges, like transparent crystal, peopled with white-
feathered geese and noisy with cranes, colorful waterlilies, and blue
lotuses, and fragrant garlands, and juicy fruit. The trees on the
mountain ridges stood effulgently in bloom, and many other forest-
grown arbors and many kinds of creepers were laden with leaves,
blossoms, and fruit.

Yudhiṣṭhira, casting his glance on the trees upon that greatest of
70 mountains, spoke these words to Bhīmasena in sweet tones: "Look
at the beautiful spots all around us, Bhīma, playgrounds of the Gods.
Walking this path no human has trod we have become perfected,

* = God of Love.

Wolf-Belly. The grand flowering trees, embraced by many vines,
glitter on the ridges of the Gandhamādana, Pārtha. Listen to the
sound of the calling peacocks with their hens on the mountain ridges,
Bhīma. *Cakoras, śatapattras,* drunk cuckoos, and mynah birds perch
75 on the tall, flowering, foliate trees. Red, yellow, and roseate birds in
the treetops and flocks of pheasants keep staring at one another,
Pārtha. All about the green and reddish grasslands and on the slopes
of the mountain cranes can be made out. Bee-kings and ducks and
redbacked birds sing their sweet songs, which charm the hearts of all
creatures. Four-tusked, lotus-colored elephants and their cows shake
this beryl-hued lake. From the height of many palm lengths yonder
cascades splash down from the mountain's peaks and its many slopes.
Various silver veins, glittering like the sun, white like the clouds of
80 autumn, lend beauty to the mountain. Some minerals are colored
mascara-black, others are golden, or pigeon-hued, or the color of
inguda nuts. There are caves of realgar, red as the massing clouds of
dusk, minerals reddish like a hare, or white as mustard, reflecting
the colors of black and white clouds or the light of the morning sun
—in all their many forms they resplendently impart loveliness to the
mountain. As Vṛṣaparvan said, one can see Gandharvas on the
85 mountaintops, Pārtha, with their mistresses, and Kiṃpuruṣas. The
sounds of songs and rhythms and melodies are heard aplenty, Bhīma,
charming the hearts of all creatures. Look at the holy and beautiful
river of the Gods, the great Ganges, visited by flocks of geese and
cherished by the seers and Kiṃnaras. And look at this king of
mountains, Kaunteya, enemy-tamer, filled with minerals, rivers,
Kiṃnaras, game and fowl, Gandharvas, Apsarās and charming woods
and beasts of prey, and its hundreds of variously shaped peaks."

Traveling that superb path, the enemy-burning heroes of happy
hearts were not sated looking at that king among mountains. Then
they saw the hermitage of the royal seer Ārṣṭiṣeṇa, which stood full
90 of flowers and fruit-laden trees, and they approached the seer of
severe austerities, who was so lean he was held together by his veins,
a sage steeped in all the Laws.

Vaiśaṃpāyana said:

156.1 Yudhiṣṭhira came up to the sage, who had burned away all stains
with his austerities, and happily greeted him with his head bowed,
citing his name. After him Kṛṣṇā, Bhīma, and the glorious twins
came with their heads bowed and waited on the royal seer,
surrounding him. Likewise Dhaumya, the Pāṇḍavas' Law-wise priest,
punctiliously came up to that seer of strict vows. With his divine eye
the Law-wise hermit had already recognized the Kuru chiefs, Pāṇḍu's
sons, and he told them to sit.

5 The ascetic paid honor to the sagacious bull of the Kurus and,
when he was sitting with his brothers, questioned him regarding his
health: "You do not perchance set your mind on untruth, but abide
by the Law? Your conduct with father and mother does not sag?
You do honor all your gurus, your elders, the learned? You do not
perchance set your mind on evil deeds, Pārtha? You do know, chief
of the Kurus, how to requite a favor and ignore a disfavor properly,
and do not boast? You pay honor to the good as they deserve, so
that they rejoice? Although living in the forests, you still follow the
10 Law? Has Dhaumya had occasion to deplore your actions in
austerities, purity, uprightness, and forebearance? Do you observe the
conduct of father and grandfather, Pāṇḍava, do you walk the path
trodden by the royal seers? For, as they say, when a son or grandson
is born in their lineage, the ancestors in their ancestral world grieve
or laugh: 'What will happen to us, if he acts wickedly? Or shall we
gain prosperity from his virtue?' He who honors father, mother, fire,
guru, and self has conquered both worlds, Pārtha.
15 "On the moon-phase days the seers who live on water and the
wind come to visit this greatest of mountains, flying through the air.
Also loving Kiṃpuruṣas and their beloved, devoted to each other,
become visible on the mountain peaks, O king. Many throngs of
Gandharvas and Apsarās are to be seen, Pārtha, wearing dustless and
silken raiment; and multitudes of garlanded, handsome Vidyādharas,
and great Snakes, Garuḍas, and serpents. Upon the mountain the
sound of kettledrums, cymbals, conches, and drums is heard on the
20 moon-phase days. You can hear it all while remaining here, bulls of
the Bharatas, you should on no wise resolve to come closer: from
here onward it is impossible to go, bulls of the Bharatas, for here is
the play garden of the Gods, beyond the course of humans. All the
creatures here hate a human who errs in the slightest, and the
Rākṣasas kick him, Bhārata. Beyond the peak of this mountain,
Yudhiṣṭhira, lies the course of the fully perfected divine seers. If one
continues the journey through fickleness beyond this point, O Pārtha,
enemy-killer, the Rākṣasas beat him with iron spikes and the like.
25 Naravāhana Vaiśravaṇa can be seen in all his wealth on the moon-
phase days, surrounded by Apsarās, and all the creatures behold the
sovereign of all the Rākṣasas, sitting on the mountain peak, like
the rising sun. This peak, best of the Bharatas, is the garden of the
Gods, Dānavas, and Siddhas as well as Vaiśravaṇa. When Tumburu
on the moon-phase days entertains the Giver of Wealth, the sound
of his songs and melodies are heard on the Gandhamādana, my son.
All the creatures in their multitudes behold this marvel here on the
moon-phase days, Yudhiṣṭhira.
30 "Dwell here, best of the Pāṇḍavas, while feasting on all kinds of

dishes and juicy fruit, until you see Arjuna. Now that you have come here, my son, you must not be fickle. After dwelling here pleasantly and sporting confidently, best of swordsmen, you shall govern the earth."

Janamejaya said:
157.1 "For how long a time did the great-spirited sons of Pāṇḍu, all of
divine prowess, dwell on Mount Gandhamādana? What comestibles
did the great-spirited heroes of the world find as they lived there?
Tell me, good sir. Tell me in detail of the prowess of Bhīmasena,
whatever the strong-armed man accomplished on Mount Himālaya.
Surely he did not again war on the Yakṣas, O best of brahmins? Did
they perchance meet with Vaiśravaṇa?* For the Giver of Riches does
5 come there, as Ārṣṭiṣeṇa said, I wish to hear this in all detail, ascetic,
for I am not sated hearing of their feats."
Vaiśaṃpāyana said:
After they had heard the beneficial advice of that peerlessly
splendid sage, the bulls of the Bharatas always acted accordingly.
Living on hermit fare and juicy fruit and the meats of game that had
been shot with unpoisoned arrows, pure viands, and many honey
dishes, the Pāṇḍavas, bulls of the Bharatas, dwelt on the ridge of the
Himālaya. And while they lived on this wise and listened to the
10 manifold sayings of Lomaśa, the fifth year went by. Ghaṭotkaca had
left well before with all the other Rākṣasas, saying that he would
come whenever he was needed. Many months went by as the great-
spirited brothers lived in Ārṣṭiṣeṇa's hermitage and saw great marvels.
While the Pāṇḍavas amused themselves there and played, lordly
hermits and Cāraṇas affectionately came to visit them, with souls
perfected and strict in their vows, and the best of the Bharatas held
pious conversations.
After some days the Fair-winged Bird forcibly abducted a
15 prosperous big Snake that had been living by a lake. The huge
mountain began to tremble, tall trees collapsed, and all the creatures
and the Pāṇḍavas stared at that marvel. Then a breeze carried from
the top of that greatest of mountains beautiful and most fragrant
flowers of all kinds toward the Pāṇḍavas. The Pāṇḍavas and their
friends saw those celestial, five-colored flowers, and so did the
glorious Draupadī. At this time Kṛṣṇā said to Bhīmasena, when that
strong-armed man was sitting happily in a lonely spot on the
mountain, "Flowers of five colors were suddenly dropped by a gust in
the wake of the Fair-winged Bird and the wind, bull of the Bharatas,
20 close by the river Aśvarathā, as all creatures watched. Your brother,**

* = Kubera.
** = Arjuna.

who was true to his promises, once stopped Gandharvas, Snakes, and Rākṣasas, nay Indra himself, in the Khāṇḍava Forest and, after killing wizardly ogres, obtained the bow Gāṇḍīva, O lord of men. You too possess great splendor, you too great power of arms, such as is irresistible and unassailable, a match for the God of the Hundred Sacrifices.* All the Rākṣasas, terrified of the impact of the power of your arms, shall abandon the mountain and flee in all ten directions, Bhīmasena, so that all your friends can visit the top of this great mountain, auspicious and wearing colorful flowers, when they have shed fear and confusion. For a long time my heart has been set on seeing the mountaintop, Bhīma, sheltered by the power of your arms."

25 Feeling as though goaded by Draupadī, the strong-armed enemy-burner would no more stand it than a fine bullock a blow. The illustrious, noble, golden, spirited, powerful, proud, highminded Pāṇḍava, the champion who moved like a lion or a bull, with red eyes, wide shoulders, the prowess of a maddened elephant, and the tusks of a lion, big-shouldered and tall like a young *śāla* tree, great-spirited, handsomely built, with lined neck and big arms, took his gold-backed bow, sword, and quivers and, like a haughty lion, like a rutting elephant, the strong man threw himself upon the mountain without fear or confusion.

30 All the creatures saw him loom with his bow, arrows, and sword, like a lion or a rutting elephant. To further Draupadī's happiness, the Pāṇḍava, armed with his club, shedding all fear and confusion, penetrated that king of mountains. Neither fatigue, nor fear, nor cowardice, nor envy ever bothered the Pārtha, who was the son of the Wind. He came upon an ugly-looking rough path, just wide enough, and by it the powerful man climbed to the peak, which was many palm lengths high. Exciting the Kiṃnaras, great Snakes, hermits, Gandharvas, and Rākṣasas, the powerful man reached the mountaintop.

35 There the Bharata bull saw Vaiśravaṇa's domain, which was adorned with golden and crystalline houses. A very pleasant breeze blew there, which rose from the Gandhamādana, carrying all good scents and gladdening all the creatures. The most beautiful trees of all kinds stood there, beyond imagining, marvelous and colorful, laden with wondrous blossoms. The bull of the Bharatas beheld the palace of the overlord of Rākṣasas, surrounded by jeweled lattices, sporting marvelous flowers, and auspicious. Then strong-armed Bhīmasena stood unmovable like a mountain, with club, sword, and
40 bow in hand, ready to risk his life. He blew his conch, which brought shudders to his enemies, and he panicked the creatures with the

* = Indra.

twanging of his bowstring and the slapping of his hands. With their hair on end, the Yakṣas, Rākṣasas, and Gandharvas rushed to the sound and the Pāṇḍava. The clubs, bludgeons, swords, spears, spikes, and battle-axes that the Yakṣas and Gandharvas had taken up glistened, and a battle began between them and him, Bhārata. Bhīma cut with his terrible and very fast arrows the spears, spikes, and battle-axes employed by the giants. The powerful man pierced the limbs of the roaring Rākṣasas, in the sky and on earth, with his shafts. A cloudburst of blood rained down on the mighty man, showers that fell on all sides from the bodies of the Rākṣasas. Numerous bodies and heads of Yakṣas and Rākṣasas were seen cut up by the discharge from Bhīma's powerful arms. All the creatures saw the handsome Pāṇḍava obfuscated by the Rākṣasas as the sun is by massing clouds. Just as the sun penetrates everything with its rays, so the powerful, strong-armed man, whose valor was his truth, penetrated them all with his arrows. They threatened and roared loud roars, but none of the Rākṣasas saw any confusion in Bhīmasena. All their limbs wounded by his arrows and panicking before Bhīmasena, they yelled in anguish at him and threw their weapons away. Abandoning their clubs, spikes, swords, spears, and battle-axes, they fled to the south, terrified of that man with the hard bow.

Then, wide-chested, strong-armed, brandishing spike and club, there remained a Rākṣasa named Maṇimat, Vaiśravaṇa's friend, and he mightily displayed his authority and manly prowess. On seeing them flee he said with the semblance of a smile, "Defeated with all your numbers in battle by a single human, what will you say to the Lord of Riches when you get to Vaiśravaṇa's dwelling?" With such words the Rākṣasa stopped them all, then, brandishing spear, spike, and club, stormed at the Pāṇḍava. When he violently fell on him like a rutting elephant, Bhīmasena shot him in the side with three calf-toothed arrows. Furiously the mighty Maṇimat grasped a huge club and hurled it spinning at Bhīmasena. Bhīma shot the huge and dreadful club that flashed like lightning in the sky with many arrows that had been wetted on stone, but all the shafts were blunted on the club and with all their impact could not halt its fast course. Then, knowing the maneuvers of club fighting, the mighty Bhīma of terrible prowess warded off his strike. The sagacious Rākṣasa now grasped an awesome javelin with a golden shaft and struck him when he saw an opening. The fearfully whistling missile pierced Bhīma's right arm and then fell grimly and vehemently on the ground, wrapped in flames. Sorely wounded by the javelin, the boundlessly valiant great archer Kauravya, who was expert at club fighting, grasped his club; and, brandishing his club, which was entirely made of damasked steel, Bhīma ran with great speed to Maṇimat. Maṇimat, too,

flourishing a huge blazing spike and yelling his battle cry, threw it
roaring at Bhīmasena. Breaking the spike with the end of his club,
the expert club fighter flew at him, as Garutmat at a snake. Shaking
his club violently, the strong-armed man jumped up in the air and
threw it, roaring in the battle. Like the thunderbolt hurled by Indra,
it struck the Rākṣasa with the speed of the wind, then, hitting the
ground, fell down like a witch. All the creatures witnessed how the
Rākṣasa of terrible strength was felled by Bhīmasena, as a bull by
70 a lion; and upon seeing him dead on the ground, the surviving
Stalkers of the Night yelled in anguish at Bhīma and fled to the east.

Vaiśaṃpāyana said:
158.1 Hearing the caverns on the mountain resound with all manner of
noise, Ajātaśatru Kaunteya,* the two sons of Mādrī, Dhaumya, Kṛṣṇā,
the brahmins, and all their friends saw that Bhīmasena was gone,
and they all became worried. The warriors left Draupadī in
Ārṣṭiṣeṇa's charge and the champions, in arms, went together up the
mountain. When they reached the mountaintop, the great warriors
5 and archers looked around and saw enemy-tamer Bhīmasena, as well
as the writhing and dead giant Rākṣasas, powerful and dreadful, which
Bhīmasena had killed. The strong-armed man, who carried club,
sword, and bow, glowed like Maghavat** after slaying all the Dānavas
in battle. The Pārthas, who had gone their incomparable way,
stepped over them, embraced the Wolf-Belly, and sat down there.
With those four great bowmen the mountain peak shone as heaven
with the lordly Guardians of the World, best of the Gods.
When he saw the palace of Kubera and the slain Rākṣasas,
10 brother said to his seated brother Pāṇḍava, "Whether you have
committed this outrage out of foolhardiness or confusion, it is no
more worthy of you, hero, than a lie is of a hermit. Those who know
the Law know that one should not act against the wishes of the king,
and this deed you have done, Bhīmasena, is hateful to the Thirty
Gods. He who sets his mind on evil, without heeding Law and Profit,
Pārtha, shall surely find the fruit of his evil deeds. Don't act like this
again, if you want to please me!" Thus spoke Law-minded brother
to unvanquished brother; and Kuntī's splendid son Yudhiṣṭhira, who
knew the divisions of the facts conducive to profit, ceased speaking
while he pondered the matter.
Meanwhile all the Rākṣasas who had survived Bhīmasena's
15 massacre repaired to Kubera's seat. They hastened and soon reached
Vaiśravaṇa's palace, screaming fearfully, terror-stricken by

* = Yudhiṣṭhira.
** = Indra.

Bhīmasena. Having lost their weapons, exhausted, their accoutrements
soaked with blood, their hair disheveled, they said to the overlord of
the Yakṣas, O king, "All your leading Rākṣasas, armed with clubs,
bludgeons, swords, javelins, and missiles, have been slain, sire. A
single human has violated the mountain recklessly, Lord of Riches,
and has killed multitudes of Krodhavaśas in battle. The foremost of
Rākṣasa lords and Yakṣas, O God of wealth, lie slain, their lives and
20 spirits gone. He took the mountain, we escaped, your friend Maṇimat
is dead—a human did it, now see to the sequel!"

The overlord of all the multitudes of Yakṣas was enraged when he
heard this, and with eyes red with fury he exclaimed, "How can it
be!" Hearing of this second offense of Bhīma, the Yakṣa king, Lord of
Riches, said wrathfully, "Yoke the horses!" They yoked his beautiful
chariot, massive like a cloud and as high as a mountain, with
Gāndharva horses; his superior steeds had all the good qualities, were
clear of eye, resplendent, strong, and fast, and their harness was
25 studded with gems. The shining horses, when yoked and ready to fly
like arrows, excited one another with ripplings that presaged victory.
The blessed and lustrous king of kings took his stand on the grand
chariot and started amidst the praises of the Gods and Gandharvas.
And as the great-spirited Lord of Riches and all the Yakṣas proceeded,
red-eyed, golden-hued, gigantic, and powerful Yakṣas, armed and
girt with swords, counting ten hundred myriad, all very impetuous
heroes, surrounded and waited on their king.

The Pāṇḍavas saw the great and benign-looking Lord of Riches
30 draw near, and they quivered with excitement. Kubera too grew
pleased when he saw Pāṇḍu's mettlesome and warlike sons with their
bows and swords in their hands. Like birds the nimble Yakṣas flew
up to the mountain peak and, with the Lord of Riches at their head,
stood around them. Then the Yakṣas and Gandharvas saw that he
was kindly disposed towards the Pāṇḍavas, O Bhārata, and they stood
about without anger. The great-spirited Pāṇḍavas, Nakula, Sahadeva,
and the Law-wise son of Dharma, bowed before the masterful Lord of
Riches. Deeming themselves guilty, the warriors stood around the
35 Lord of Riches with folded hands. The God sat upon his regal throne
Puṣpaka, which had been wrought by Viśvakarman, with colorful
borders. The giant Yakṣas and Rākṣasas with pointed ears sat below
their seated king by the thousands. Hundreds of Gandharvas and
throngs of Apsarās surrounded and waited on him, as the Gods on
the God of the Hundred Sacrifices. Bhīmasena, who wore on his head
a beautiful golden chaplet and held bow, arrows, and sword in his
hands, looked up to the Lord of Riches. He knew no fear or fatigue,
though he had been wounded by the Rākṣasas, even as in this pass
he looked at Kubera.

40 Upon seeing Bhīma standing there belligerently and holding sharp
arrows, Naravāhana said to the son of Dharma, "All creatures know,
Pārtha, that you have their well-being at heart, so live without fear
on the mountaintop with your kinsmen. You must not be angry with
Bhīmasena, Pāṇḍava, they had already been killed by Time, and
your younger brother was but the instrument. You need not be
ashamed if violence has been perpetrated: the Gods have foreseen the
destruction of the Yakṣas and Rākṣasas, and I have no anger for
Bhīmasena, I am pleased, bull of the Bharatas! I have long been at
45 peace with this deed of Bhīma." Having spoken to the king he
addressed Bhīmasena, "It shall not weigh on your mind, son, best of
the Kurus, if you have indulged this rashness for Kṛṣṇā's sake, Bhīma,
this slaughter of Yakṣas and Rākṣasas, heeding neither me nor the
Gods, relying on the strength of your arms—I am pleased with you
for it, for I have now been set free from a dreadful curse, Wolf-Belly.
I was once cursed by the eminent seer Agastya because of some
misstep, and now it has been expiated. As I have foreseen this grief,
joy of the Pāṇḍavas, killer of your enemies, no guilt attaches to you."

Yudhiṣṭhira said:

Why were you cursed by the great-spirited Agastya, blessed Lord?
I wish to hear, God, the reason for your curse. It is a matter of
50 surprise to me that the anger of that sage did not at the time
annihilate you with your troops and footmen!

Vaiśravaṇa said:

There was a council of the Gods in Kuśavatī, lord of men, and I
went there amidst three hundred lotus counts of grisly Yakṣas, who
bore all kinds of arms. On the way I saw that greatest of seers,
Agastya, performing awesome austerities on the bank of the Yamunā,
which teemed with flocks of birds and was bedecked with flowering
trees. My illustrious friend Maṇimat, the overlord of the Rākṣasas, saw
him standing with his arms raised, facing the sun, a mass of splendor
like a well-kindled, blazing fire, and out of folly, ignorance, insolence,
and stupidity, Bhārata, he spat on the great seer's head from the sky.
55 In anger he said to me, as though setting fire to all of space, "For the
outrage this miscreant has committed out of contempt for me while
you looked on, Lord of Riches, he shall with all these armies find his
death at the hands of a human. You too, evil-minded one, shall find
grief with these troops. But when you see that human, you shall be
freed from your sin. But the forceful sons and grandsons of these
troops will not be touched by this dreadful curse. Go, he shall carry
out your orders."

This was the curse that I once earned from that best of seers, and
your brother Bhīma, great king, has set me free from it.

Vaiśravaṇa said:

159.1 Yudhiṣṭhira, perseverance, skill, place, time, and valor make up
the fivefold rule for the affairs of the business of this world. In the
Kṛtayuga people were persevering and skillful in their professions,
Bhārata, and they knew the rule of valor. The persevering hero who
knows time and place and is informed of the rules of all the Laws, he,
best of barons, governs the earth. The man who thus proceeds in all
his affairs, heroic Pārtha, wins fame in this world and a good journey
5 after death. Śakra* displayed his valor when he had sought out his
opportunity in time and place, and thus the Slayer of Vṛtra attained
with the Vasus to kingship in heaven. The evil-spirited, evil-minded
man who pursues nothing but evil, without knowing the boundaries
of acts, perishes here and hereafter. The utter fool who does not
know his times, nor the differences between acts, has all his
enterprises fail and perishes here and hereafter. Wicked is the resolve
of those ill-spirited and deceptive men who act violently and want to
be capable of anything. Bull of the Bharatas, your fearless Bhīmasena
knows of no Law, he is violent, feeble-minded, and intransigent:
instruct him, bull among men.

10 When you have returned to the hermitage of the royal seer
Ārṣṭiṣeṇa, dwell there without fear of grief for the first dark
fortnight. The Alakas, joining forces with Gandharvas, Yakṣas, and
Rākṣasas and all those who live in the mountains, shall at my orders
protect you, strong-armed Indra of men, you and those good
brahmins. Your Wolf-Belly, who has been indulging in foolhardy acts
on this mountain, you should keep thoroughly in check, king who
are the first of the upholders of the Law. From here on the forest
creatures shall look after you, wait on you, and always protect you
anywhere, Indra of the kings. My familiars will wait on you with
15 many tasty viands and liquors, bull among men. Just as Jiṣṇu** is
under the great Indra's protection, the Wolf-Belly under the Wind's,
you yourself under Dharma's, whose natural son you are, born in
Yoga, and both the twins under the Aśvins's, the sons of whose
bodies they are, so all of you are under my protection here too,
Yudhiṣṭhira.

Phalguna,** Bhīmasena's junior, knows the divisions of the facts
of profit, he knows the distinctive features of all the Laws, he has
become an expert in heaven. Every one of the perfections that rank
highest in the worlds have been vested since birth in Dhanaṃjaya,
my son. Self-restraint, bounty, strength, spirit, modesty, perseverance,
and utter authority, these virtues are vested in that mettlesome,

* = Indra.

** = Arjuna.

20 boundlessly splendid man. Jiṣṇu never does foolishly an act that is
condemned, Pāṇḍava, nor do people recount to others any false
sayings of his. Honored by Gods, Ancestors, and Gandharvas, this
prosperer of the fame of the Kurus is studying weapons in Indra's
abode, Bhārata. Your own father's grandfather, that most august
Śaṃtanu, who once brought all the kings of this earth under his rule
by the Law, is pleased in heaven with the Pārtha of the Gāṇḍīva bow,
Pārtha. That heroic king, glorious beast of burden of his dynasty,
who always properly paid honor to Ancestors, Gods, and brahmins,
performed the seven principal sacrifices by the River Yamunā: he the
sovereign, your great-grandfather Śaṃtanu, O king, who won heaven
and now dwells in Śakra's world, asks about your health!

Vaiśaṃpāyana said:

25 Thereupon, bull of the Bharatas, did the Wolf-Belly put aside his
spear, his club, his sword, his bow, and bowed to Kubera. And the
Overseer of Riches, a shelter, spoke to him who sought shelter: "Be
the breaker of the pride of your enemies, and the magnifier of the
joy of your friends. Torturer of your foes, dwell in these lovely
houses; the Yakṣas shall accommodate your wishes, bulls of the
Bharatas! Quite soon that bull-like man Guḍākeśa Dhanamjaya shall
join you, dismissed by Maghavat* himself, a master of arms."

Having thus instructed Yudhiṣṭhira of the virtuous deeds, the
overlord of the Guhyakas went home to that greatest of mountains.
The Yakṣas and Rākṣasas followed him by the thousands on their
30 wagons, which were covered with pillows and studded with many
kinds of gems. The grand horses whinnied as they went like birds
along the path of Airāvata to the seat of Kubera. Those steeds of the
Lord of Riches swiftly cleft the firmament and seemed to trail clouds
and to gorge on the wind. The corpses of the Rākṣasas were removed
from the mountaintop at the orders of the God of Wealth; for it had
been the hour of the curse set for them by the sage Agastya, and
35 therefore they and Maṇimat had all been slain. And the great-
spirited Pāṇḍavas stayed that night in those houses, unalarmed and
honored by all the Rākṣasas.

Vaiśaṃpāyana said:

160.1 Then, O enemy-tamer, when the sun rose and he had done the
daily rites, Dhaumya came with Ārṣṭiṣeṇa to the Pāṇḍavas. They all
greeted the feet of Ārṣṭiṣeṇa and Dhaumya, then paid honor to the
brahmins with folded hands. Dhaumya took Yudhiṣṭhira by the right
hand, and looking eastward the great seer said, "Yonder king of
mountains Mandara covers the earth to its ocean borders in all its

* = Indra.

magnificence, great king. Indra and Vaiśravaṇa* guard this region, Pāṇḍava, which is bedecked with mountains, woods, and forests. Wise seers, who knew all the Laws, have said that it is the seat of the great Indra and King Vaiśravaṇa, my son. The creatures worship the sun as it rises from there, as do the Law-wise seers, the Siddhas, Sādhyas, and deities. Law-spirited King Yama, master of all living beings, governs the south, which is the course of the dead. This is holy Saṃyamana of most wondrous aspect, the abode of the King of the Dead, which is endowed with superior prosperity. This king of mountains the wise call Sunset Peak, king, where the sun abides by the truth, when it has set there. King Varuṇa, who dwells on this king of mountains and in this vast ocean, protects the creatures. Brightening the north there rises the famous great Mount Meru, my lord, the propitious course of the knowers of the Brahman. On it lies the *sadas* of Brahmā, where Prajāpati, soul of the creatures, dwells, creating everything that exists, whether standing or moving. The great Meru is also the domain, auspicious and without diseases, of the willborn sons of Brahmā, the seventh of whom is Dakṣa. Here too the seven divine seers daily rise and set, my son, led by Vasiṣṭha.

"Behold the pure land, the superb peak of the Meru, where the Grandfather dwells with the Gods, who are content with their souls. Beyond the seat of Brahmā shines the supreme abode of the lord Nārāyaṇa, God without beginning and end, whom they call the lasting cause of the causes of all creatures; even the Gods can only with difficulty look at that divine and auspicious place, which is made of light. That abode of the great-spirited Viṣṇu, which is brighter than sun and fire, is difficult to see for the Gods and Dānavas because of its splendor. When they reach there, even the celestial luminaries no longer shine, for the Lord of undaunted spirit outshines them by himself. Ascetics go there to Nārāyaṇa Hari through their devotion, yoked with the utmost austerity and perfected by their holy deeds. Great-spirited, perfected by Yoga, devoid of darkness and delusion, they go there and no more return to this world, Bhārata. This, lordly Yudhiṣṭhira, is the lasting, indestructible, and imperishable place of the Lord: always bow to it!

"The blessed Lord the Sun, who dispels darkness, circumambulates it, pulling all the stars. The shining sun, on reaching Sunset Peak and passing through dusk, then takes the northern course. Having circled the Meru the God Savitar** reappears in the east, bent upon the well-being of all creatures. Likewise the blessed Lord the Moon goes this course with the constellations, dividing the month in many parts on the moon-phase days. After circling the great Meru untiringly,

* = Kubera.
** = Sun.

the sun returns to the Mandara to prosper all creatures. Thus the
Sun God, who dispels darkness with his rays, prospering the world,
30 circles by the same uncrowded route. When he wishes to produce
the cool seasons, he takes the southern course, then wintertime comes
upon the creatures. When the sun returns, he saps with his own
vigor the vigor of standing and moving creation. Sweat, weariness,
lassitude, and exhaustion affects men, and all living creatures
constantly seek sleep. Thus the sun covers this road that cannot be
described, and the blessed lord, prospering creatures, creates rain.
After increasing all standing and moving beings with pleasant rain,
35 wind, and heat, that most splendid God once more turns. Unweariedly
circling the wheel of time, Pārtha, and pulling all creatures, the sun
revolves, and its course is constant, it never stands still, Pāṇḍava, it
takes the creatures' vigor and restores it again. Measuring out the life
and work of all creatures, Bhārata, the ubiquitous lord constantly
creates days and nights, the measures of the moon, and the moments
of time."

Vaiśaṃpāyana said:

161.1 As they all dwelled on that Indra of mountains,
Great-spirited and much given to vows,
They took delight and enjoyed themselves
As they waited to see Arjuna.

Many throngs of Gandharvas and great seers
Affectionately came to visit them,
Those valiant men of the purest mettle,
Resplendent, abounding in truth and poise.

Having reached that greatest of mountains, bedecked
With flowering trees, those warriors
Attained to superior quiet of mind,
As the Maruts did on attaining to heaven.

Setting eyes on the peaks and the ridges of that
Great mountain, resounding with peafowl and geese,
And all bestrewn with flowers aplenty,
They all indulged in the greatest joy.

5 By Kubera himself entertained, they saw
On that finest of mountains mountain streams
With wooded banks; and lotus lakes
With *kādambas*, geese, and *kāraṇḍavas*,

And grounds for playing, of opulent colors,
With beauty grown from the colorful borders,

And choicest gems, such as tempted their hearts,
As are found with the king who is Lord of Riches.

While they constantly, most austerely, roamed
Upon that peak that was covered with fragrant
Many-colored trees and wreathed with clouds,
They failed to grasp that mountaintop.

Because of the splendor of that great mountain
And the power of its phosphorescent herbs,
Not the slightest bit of difference appeared
Between day and night, O champion of men.

The boundlessly lustrous sun dwells there
And prospers the standing and moving creatures;
And as they stayed there, those lions of men
Kept watching the sun's rise and its decline.

10 The heroes saw how darkness fled
At the rise of the sun, and returned when it set,
And they watched how all the horizons were wrapped
In the spreading nets of the rays of the sun.

They learned their lessons, did the daily duties,
Were bent on the Law, and pure in their vows,
And abode by the truth, as they awaited
The coming of that truth-sworn great warrior.

"In this very spot shall we soon have the joy
Of meeting Dhanaṃjaya, master of arms!"
The Pārthas said with superior blessings,
And devoted themselves to Yoga and penance.

They looked at the colorful mountain forests,
And always thought of the diademed man;
And day and night became for them
Quite equal to a whole year's span.

The moment that Jiṣṇu* with Dhaumya's permission
Had matted his hair and started out,
That moment happiness had left them—
What joy could they find whose hearts went with him?

15 They had been grief-stricken, ever since Jiṣṇu
Of the elephant stride had followed his brother
Yudhiṣṭhira's orders and had departed
From the wilderness of the Kāmyaka woods.

* = Arjuna.

While they thought of the man who drove the white horses,
Who had gone to Indra in quest of arms,
The Bhāratas, Bhārata, painfully passed
The span of a month on that self-same mountain.

Then one day the warriors suddenly saw
Indra's bay horses pull up his chariot
That flashed like lightning, while they were thinking
Of Arjuna; and they all rejoiced.

The flickering chariot, suddenly, lighting
The skies, which was driven by Mātali,
Shone forth like a meteor amidst the welkin,
Like the smokeless crest of a flaming fire.

Upon it the diademed man could be seen,
Garlanded and wearing the choicest arms;
Matching the Thunderer's power, Dhanaṃjaya
Came to the mountain, ablaze with beauty.

20 When he came to the mountain, diadem-crowned,
The hero descended from Indra's chariot,
And first he saluted Dhaumya's feet,
And after that those of Ajātaśatru.*

He also greeted the Wolf-Belly's feet,
And then was greeted by Mādrī's two sons;
He met with Kṛṣṇā and comforted her,
Then, bowing, he stood below his brother.

It was joy superb that touched them all
On uniting with that immeasurable man;
And he, diadem-crowned, on beholding them
Rejoiced as he voiced his praise of the king.

The Pārthas approached the Indra chariot,
The one on which Namuci's Slayer had slain
The seven bands of the sons of Diti,
And went around it with happy hearts.

Exceedingly pleased, they showed Mātali
Hospitality worthy of the king of the Gods,
And the sons of the kings of the Kurus inquired
Of the health of the Gods, as was proper, from him.

25 Mātali in his turn saluted them too
And instructed them as a father his sons,

* = Yudhiṣṭhira.

Then he went on the peerlessly splendid chariot
Back to the presence of heaven's lord.

The chariot of the great God having left,
The son of Śakra, scourge of all foes,
Great-spiritedly presented the gifts,
Most precious, beautiful, that Indra had given,
The ornaments sparkling like the light of the sun,
Loving to loving Sutasoma's mother.*

Then he took his seat amidst the bulls
Of the Bharatas, glowing like sun and fire,
Amidst the bull-like brahmins he sat,
And related to them all that had occurred.

"Thus have I learned these magical weapons
From Śakra, the Wind God, and Śiva himself,
And the Gods with Indra all were pleased
By the way I acted and concentrated."

Having briefly narrated his entrance in heaven
To them, the diademed man of pure deeds
Bedded down for the night and trustingly slept
That night together with Mādrī's sons.

Vaiśaṃpāyana said:

162.1 At this time there was the tumultuous sound of all the musical
instruments of the celestials in the sky, the noise of chariot fellies,
and the tolling of bells, Bhārata, the cries of beasts of prey, small
game and all kinds of fowl erupted everywhere, and Gandharvas and
Apsarās followed on all sides the enemy-taming king of the Gods on
their sun-like wagons. Then he swiftly drove up to the Pārthas on
5 his thunderous, gold-decked, bay-drawn chariot, the king of the Gods,
the Sacker of Cities, ablaze with superb luster; and having arrived the
Thousand-eyed God descended.
As soon as he saw the great-spirited king of the Gods, the
illustrious Yudhiṣṭhira the King Dharma approached him with his
brothers, and that prince of the amply rewarded sacrifices paid honor
to the immeasurably spirited God with the correct rite that is found
in the Rules. And splendid Dhanaṃjaya threw himself in the dust and
stood crouched like a servant before the king of the Gods, the Sacker
10 of Cities. When he saw Dhanaṃjaya standing humbly nearby, Kuntī's
majestic son Yudhiṣṭhira kissed the spotless, austere hairtuft of the
king of the Gods as so great a joy at seeing Phalguna pervaded him.
The Sacker of Cities, the sage king of the Gods, spoke this word to the

* = Draupadī.

joyous king, who was bathed in bliss: "King Pāṇḍava, thou shalt reign this earth. Hail, Kaunteya, repair again to the Kāmyaka Hermitage!

The Pāṇḍava has with much diligence
Got all the weapons from me, O king.
Dhanaṃjaya's brought me great happiness:
All these worlds cannot defeat him."

Having thus spoken to Kuntī's son Yudhiṣṭhira, the Thousand-eyed
God went joyfully to heaven, praised by the great seers.
15 The wise man who attentively studies for a year this meeting of
the Pāṇḍavas with Śakra at the house of the Lord of Riches will, if
chaste, restrained, and strict in his vows, live an unimpeded and most
happy life for a hundred autumns.

Vaiśaṃpāyana said:
163.1 When Śakra had gone as he had come, the Terrifier joined by his
brothers and Kṛṣṇā paid his respects to the son of Dharma. As Arjuna
was greeting him, Yudhiṣṭhira kissed him on the head and joyously
said to him in a voice that stammered from delight, "How did you
pass the time in heaven, Arjuna? How did you satisfy the king of the
Gods and obtain the weapons? Have you learned the weapons
correctly, Bhārata? Was the overlord of the Gods pleased and did
Rudra give you arms? I wish to hear how you saw Śakra and the
5 blessed Lord who wields the Pināka, how you obtained the weapons,
how you propitiated him, why the God of the Hundred Sacrifices said
to you enemy-tamer, 'You have given me pleasure'—what had you
done to please him? I wish to hear it all with full particulars, lustrous
man! Tell me all, and completely, how you satisfied the Great God
and the king of the Gods, Dhanaṃjaya, prince sans blame, and how
you pleased the Thunderbolt-wielder."

Arjuna said:
Then listen, great king, and hear the manner in which I set eyes
on the God of the Hundred Sacrifices and the blessed Lord Śaṅkara
and learned the science as you had told me, enemy-plowing king.
At your behest I departed to the forest to mortify myself. I went
10 from the Kāmyaka Forest on to Bhṛgu's Peak and undertook
austerities. When I had passed one night there, I saw a brahmin on
the road, Kaunteya, and he questioned me, "Where are you going?
Tell me!" I told him the whole truth, joy of the Kurus, and when he
had heard the truth from me, best of kings, he paid honor to me and
was pleased with me. He said to me joyously, "Undertake austerities,
Bhārata! If you do, you shall soon see the overlord of the Gods."
At his advice I ascended the Cold Mountain and observed austerities,

great king. One month I lived on roots and fruit, a month passed while I lived on water, the third I abstained from all food, joy of the Pāṇḍavas, and the fourth I stood with both arms raised. Yet I did not lose my vigor, it was like a miracle. When the fourth month had gone by and the first night had passed, a demon in the form of a boar came up to me, pounding the ground with its snout, scratching it with its hooves, rubbing it with its belly, and rolling over repeatedly. Behind him there was another large creature wearing the guise of a mountain man; he carried bow, arrows, and sword and was surrounded by throngs of women.

I took my bow and the inexhaustible quivers and shot that terrifying demon with an arrow. The mountain man too had drawn his powerful bow and simultaneously with me shot it very hard, so that my mind seemed to reel. He said to me, "It was my catch first! Why did you abandon the Law of the chase and shoot it? I'll break your pride with my honed arrows, stand firm!" The towering giant stormed at me and covered me with arrows while I stood like a mountain. I countered him with feathered arrows with blazing tips that had been enchanted, as a mountain with thunderbolts. Then he changed into a hundred, a thousand forms, and I shot at these bodies with my shafts. The bodies became one again when I dispersed them. He became tiny with a big head, and big with a tiny head, and then, in one body again, rushed at me for battle, King Bhārata. When I could not master him with my arrows in combat, I took my *vāyavya* shaft, bull of the Bharatas, but, the wonder of it, I could not hit him. When that shaft had been worsted, I was greatly surprised, and once more I carefully showered the creature with a massive volley of arrows. I laid on the *sthūṇākarṇa, ayojāla, śaravarṣa, śarolbana, śaila,* and *aśmavarṣa* arrows and went at him. Laughingly he swallowed up all my arrows, prince sans blame, and when he had pacified all of them, I laid on the Brahmā weapon. He was all covered with blazing arrows, and while I piled on him my great missile, he grew in bulk. The world was set afire by the blaze I had discharged, and for a moment all of space was alight. But instantly that splendid creature knocked out that weapon too.

After the Brahmā weapon had been defeated, panic seized me, king. With bow and inexhaustible quivers I hit the creature violently, but these weapons too he swallowed up. When my arrows had been struck down and my weapons devoured, I and the creature engaged in a wrestling fight. We battled each other with fists and slapped each other with the flat of the hand, then the creature felled me, and I fell motionless on the ground. Then with a loud laugh, great king, the being disappeared then and there with his women, before my eyes, and I thought it a miracle.

40 After his feat the blessed Lord, abandoning his mountain man
guise, took on another body, great king, a divine one that wore a
wondrous robe, and there he stood, the blessed lord of the Gods, the
Great Lord, in his own celestial form. The blessed lord, who has the
bull in his banner, appeared in person to me accompanied by Umā,
yellow-eyed, many-shaped, holding the Pināka. And while I likewise
faced him, after my encounter in battle, O enemy-burner, the
Trident-bearer said to me, "I am pleased with you." Then the blessed
Lord took the bow and the quivers that never run out of arrows and
45 gave them to me. "Choose a boon," he said, "I am pleased with you,
Kaunteya. Speak, what can I do for you? Speak the desire of your
heart, I shall grant it. Excepting immortality, say what you desire."

I folded my hands, and, my mind dwelling on weapons, I bowed
my head to the Hunter and addressed him: "If the blessed Lord is
pleased, this is the boon I crave: I wish to learn all the weapons that
the Gods possess." "I shall give," the blessed lord Tryambaka replied
to me. "My Rudra weapon shall wait on you, Pāṇḍava." Pleased,
the lord gave me his *pāsupata* weapon, and as he gave me that
everlasting weapon, the Great God said, "It should in no wise be used
50 on humans. Only if you are severely pressed, you may use it,
Dhanaṃjaya, and you should employ it for no other purpose than to
counter other missiles." The divine, irresistible weapon that defeats all
others stood in bodily form beside me by the grace of the Bull-
bannered God, bane of all enemies, destroyer of enemy armies,
unassailable, impossible to endure even for Gods, Dānavas, and
Rākṣasas. With his permission I sat down, and as I looked on, the
God disappeared.

Arjuna said:

164.1 By the grace of the God of Gods, the great-spirited Tryambaka,
O Bhārata, I happily spent the night there. Having passed the night
and completed the morning rites, I saw that good brahmin whom I
had seen before. I told him all that had occurred, Bhārata, saying
that I had met the blessed Great God. The good brahmin said to me
in a pleased manner, Indra of kings, "You have beheld the Great God
5 as no one else has. You shall meet Vaivasvata* and all the other
World Guardians; then, prince sans blame, you shall see the Indra of
the Gods, and he shall give you weapons." After these words he
embraced me again and again, O king; thereupon that brahmin, who
shone like the sun, went where he listed.

In the afternoon of that day a pure wind began to blow, killer of
your rivals, which seemed to make the world new again. Close by me
at the foot of the Cold Mountain fresh, fragrant, divine flowers

* = Manu.

appeared. Celestial, melodious instruments were heard on all sides
10 and lovely litanies in praise of Indra. Throngs of Apsarās and
Gandharvas all sang songs before the God of Gods. Bands of Maruts
arrived on divine wagons, as well as great Indra's followers, who live
in the seat of the God. Then Marutvān* accompanied by Śacī came
on well-decked chariots that were yoked with bay horses, along with
all the Immortals. At the same time, surrounded by great wealth,
Kubera Naravāhana appeared before me, king. I saw Yama
established in the southern quarter, and Varuṇa and the king of the
Gods each on their station.

15 Then the bull-like Gods spoke to me comfortingly, great king:
"Left-handed archer, behold the World Guardians arrayed. Thou hast
seen Śankara in order to accomplish a task for the Gods. From us too
thou shalt take weapons." I purified and prostrated myself before
those bulls among Gods, and I received in the proper fashion the
grand weapons, my lord. After receiving the weapons I was dismissed
by the Gods, enemy-taming Bhārata, and all the Gods went as they
had come. Maghavat,* the lord of the Gods, also mounted his
resplendent chariot, and with a faint smile the blessed slayer of the
20 Gods' foes said, "I knew you well before you came here, Dhanaṃjaya:
I have appeared to you earlier, bull of the Bharatas. You have bathed
often in the sacred fords and performed austerities: for that you shall
go to heaven, Pāṇḍava. You shall again perform the most awesome
austerities." Then the blessed lord related the complete performance of
austerities. "At my behest Mātali will bring you to heaven, for you
are well-known to the Gods and great-spirited seers."

I said to Śakra, "Blessed lord, have grace for me. I choose you for
my teacher, lord of the Thirty, so that I may learn the weapons!"

Indra said:

25 Once you know the weapons, my son, you will accomplish cruel
feats. Then obtain the desire, enemy-burning Pāṇḍava, for which you
seek to gain the weapons.

Arjuna said:

Then I said, "I shall never, enemy-killer, employ the weapons on humans, except when my other arms have been countered. Bestow on me the celestial weapons, overlord of the Gods. Afterward, bull among Gods, I shall attain to the worlds the weapons have won."

Indra said:

I spoke as I did in order to test you, Dhanaṃjaya. Your words are
fitting for one begotten by my own body. When you come to my
house, you shall learn all the weapons, Bhārata, from Wind, Fire, the
Vasus, Varuṇa, the bands of the Maruts, those of the Sādhyas,
30 Grandfather, Gandharvas, Snakes and Rākṣasas, all those of Viṣṇu as

* = Indra.

well as Nirṛti, and all that I myself have, scion of Kuru.

Arjuna said:

After these words Śakra disappeared. Then I saw Indra's chariot, yoked with his bays, arrive, celestial and magical, which was driven by Mātali, O king. When the World Guardians had left, Mātali said to me, "Śakra, the king of the Gods, wishes to see you, lustrous man. Carry out your unparalleled task successfully, strong-armed hero! While still in your body, set eyes on the worlds of the meritorious—come to heaven." At Mātali's words I bade the Cold Mountain farewell; then I mounted that great chariot after having
35 circumambulated it. The generous Mātali, an expert in the science of horses, started the steeds, which sped like thought and the wind, in the proper fashion. The charioteer looked at my face as I stood on the swinging chariot, king, and he said in surprise, "This appears to me most marvelous and wonderful today that you have not moved a foot while riding on this celestial chariot! Even the king of the Gods I have always found to stagger at the first upward start of the horses, bull of the Bhāratas. But you stand right there on the swinging chariot, scion of Kuru, and methinks your mettle surpasses Śakra's!"

40 Then Mātali, as he traversed the sky, showed me the domain of the Gods and their palaces, King Bhārata. Śakra's charioteer Mātali showed me affectionately Nandana and the many other parks of the Gods, and I saw Śakra's city of Amarāvatī, bedecked with celestial trees that fructified any whim, and with precious stones. The sun does not illumine it, neither cold nor heat is felt there, nor fatigue; there is no dust, mud, or darkness, nor old age, O king. No grief or misery or pallor is ever observed with the celestials, great king, tamer
45 of your enemies, nor lassitude. Neither anger nor greed exists there, or anything unholy, lord of your people, and in the dwellings of the Gods the creatures are always contented and happy. The green-leafed trees are always in blossom and fruit, there are all sorts of ponds full of lotuses and *saugandhikas*. A cool, fragrant, pure, and refreshing breeze blows there, and the ground, decked with flowers, is colorful with precious ores. Many sweet-voiced deer and birds sparkle, and numerous Immortals can be seen, riding their chariots. I saw the Vasus, Rudras, Sādhyas, the bands of the Maruts, the Ādityas, and
50 Aśvins, and I paid honor to them all. They hailed me with blessings for valor, fame, splendor, strength, weapons, and victory in war.

Then I entered the lovely city that is cherished by the Gods and Gandharvas; and with folded hands I approached the thousand-eyed king of the Gods. Śakra, most generous giver, was pleased to give me half his throne; the Vāsava* touched my limbs with great honor. Together with the Gods and Gandharvas, O Bhārata, bountiful

* = Indra.

sacrificer, I dwelled there in heaven for the sake of the weapons and
studied them. Viśvāvasu's son Citrasena became my friend, and he
55 taught me the entire Lore of the Gandharvas. Thereafter, having
mastered the arms, I lived happily and honorably in the house of
Śakra, provided with all I desired, while I listened to the sound of
songs and much music, and watched the finest Apsarās dance, enemy-
killer. Without neglecting anything and finding out the truth, I
concentrated diligently on the weapons, Bhārata. The thousand-eyed
lord waxed content with my desire, and as I lived in this manner in
heaven, O king, all this time went by.

Arjuna said:
165.1 When I had mastered the arms and become quite confident, the
God who drives the bay horses touched my hand with both his hands
and said: "Now even the multitudes of the Gods cannot vanquish you
in battle—not to speak of humans in their world, who have not made
their souls—for you are beyond measure, unassailable, and matchless
in war." Again, with a shudder that stood his hair on end, the God
said, "No one, hero, shall equal you in arrow combat. You are never
distracted, clever, true-spoken, master of your senses, brahminic,
5 and a weapon-wise champion, O scion of Kuru. You have acquired
the missiles, the ten and the five; in all five ways, Pārtha, you have
no peer. You know how to employ, cancel, return, placate, and
counteract them all, Dhanaṃjaya.

"Now the time has come, enemy-burner, for your guru's fee:
promise to carry it out, then I shall know the sequel." Thereupon,
O king, I said, to the king of the Gods, "If I am able to do it, tell me
the deed!" The Slayer of Vala and Vṛtra laughed and said, "Now
10 nothing in the three worlds is impossible for you. I have enemies, the
Dānavas who are called the Nivātakavacas; they live in an
inaccessible spot by the ocean bay, they number thirty million, and
all are the same in shape, strength, and sheen. Kill them right there,
Kaunteya; that shall be your guru's fee."

He gave me his celestial, shining chariot driven by Mātali, which
was yoked with steeds that had fur like peacock feathers. He tied to
the crown of my head this magnificent diadem and presented me
with body ornaments that were similar to those he himself wore, with
this impenetrable coat of mail, beautiful and fine both to the touch
and the eye, and fastened this unaging bowstring to my Gāṇḍiva.
15 Thereupon I set out on that sparkling chariot, on which the lord of
the Gods once vanquished Bali Vairocani. All the Gods, alerted by its
sound, thought I was Indra and assembled, O lord of your people,
and seeing me they asked, "What are you to do, Phalguna?" In
accordance to the facts I told them, "This I shall accomplish in battle:

know that I am departing to see to the slaughter of the Nivātakavacas.
Bless me holy, blameless lords!" They praised me graciously as the
city-sacking God: "On that chariot Maghavat fought and vanquished
Śambara, Namuci, Vala, Vṛtra, Prahlāda, and Naraka; over many
thousands and millions and tens of millions of Daityas did Maghavat
20 win victory on this same chariot. On it you, too, Kaunteya, shall
vanquish the Nivātakavacas in your war, striding across them as
once the masterful Maghavat did. And this is the mighty conch with
which you shall defeat the Dānavas: with the same conch the great-
spirited Śakra too conquered the worlds!"

I accepted the Devadatta, gift of the waters, which the Gods
proffered to me, while the Immortals praised me to strengthen me for
victory. With conch, armor, arrows, and bow firmly held, I started
for that most fearful Dānava domain to seek war.

Arjuna said:

166.1 Everywhere I went I was praised by great seers, then I beheld the
fearful ocean, the ageless lord of the waters. Towering waves can be
seen there, like moving mountains, foaming, scattering, and colliding,
ships by the thousands everywhere laden with gems, and tortoises,
whales, and swallowers of whales, and crocodiles like hills sunk in
the water. Thousands of conches are on all sides visible below the
5 waters, like stars at night covered by thin clouds. Clusters of pearls
were floating about by the thousands, and a violent wind whipped
the waves—it was a marvel. I crossed that great and impetuous
gathering place of all waters and saw from close by the city of the
Daityas, which was teeming with Dānavas.

Mātali swiftly descended to dry land and drove to the city, filling
it with the roar of his chariot. When the Dānavas heard the roar of
the chariot, which was like a thunderclap in the sky, they thought
I was the king of the Gods, and they became quite upset. With
turbulent hearts they stood there, holding bows and arrows, spikes,
10 swords, axes, clubs, and pestles in their hands. Their hearts atremble,
the Dānavas closed the gates and brought the city into readiness for
the defense; not a one could be seen about. I took the conch
Devadatta of the great sound and blew it gently while I circled the
Asura city. The sound froze the sky and engendered echoes, and even
the largest creatures trembled and lay low.

Thereupon Diti's sons the Nivātakavacas all began to appear in
their thousands, armored with all kinds of mail, brandishing all sorts
of weapons, armed with large iron spikes, clubs, pestles, three-bladed
15 spears, scimitars, and cartwheels, O Bhārata, with hundred-killers,
catapults, and swords all brilliantly ornamented. Mātali reflected
thoroughly on the various chariot courses, then drove the horses to

level ground, O bull of the Bhāratas. So fast did the swift steeds go
under his prodding that I could make out nothing—it was a marvel.
The Dānavas in their multitudes exhorted all the warrior gangs, who
had changed their natures. That loud sound made hundreds of
thousands of fish, as big as mountains, float up on the sea, giving up
20 the ghost. Very impetuously the Dānavas now stormed toward me,
letting loose arrows by the hundreds and thousands. They and I
clashed fearsomely and dreadfully, Bhārata, for the doom of the
Nivātakavacas. Divine seers, throngs of Dānava seers, brahmin seers,
and Siddhas assembled on the battlefield, and the hermits hoping for
victory praised me with suitable and melodious words, as once they
praised Indra at the battle for Tārakā.

Arjuna said:

167.1 The Nivātakavacas all stormed at me impetuously, Bhārata,
grasping their weapons to do battle. The warriors cut off the path
of my chariot, and, yelling, they surrounded me and showered me with
rains of arrows. Other braves of the Dānavas, wielding spikes and
three-bladed spears, loosened on me spikes and catapults. Powerful
showers of spikes mixed with clubs and javelins were incessantly let
5 loose by them and fell on my chariot. Other Nivātakavacas rushed
at me to give battle with sharp missiles, gruesome fighters in the
shape of Time. Them I cut down on the battlefield with various swift
and straight-traveling arrows from my Gāṇḍīva bow, ten arrows
each, and my stone-whetted shafts turned them all back. Mātali
quickly prodded the horses and they accomplished many chariot
maneuvers fast as the wind, and, well-guided by Mātali, they
trampled the Daityas. A hundred hundreds of bay horses were yoked
to that great chariot, but under Mātali's hands they maneuvered like
few. Under their trampling feet, the rattling chariot fellies, and the
10 onslaught of my arrows, the Asuras fell by the hundreds. Others,
both the dead and the bow-wielding warriors who had lost their
charioteers, were carried off by their horses. The fighters covered all
points of space and hit with all sorts of weapons, and my heart began
to sink. But then I saw Mātali's superbly marvelous mastery as he
effortlessly controlled his impetuous horses. With manifold light shafts
I cut down the arms-bearing Asuras in that battle, by the hundreds
and the thousands, king.

15 While I thus carried on with all my effort, enemy-killer, Śakra's
brave charioteer was delighted. Being set upon by the horses and the
chariot, some met their perdition, others ceased fighting. As though
to rival us in battle the Nivātakavacas warded me off on all sides with
mighty showers of arrows. With manifold nimble shafts, enchanted
with the Brahmā weapon, I blew them asunder by the hundreds and

thousands. While they were so being pressed, the great Asuras,
enraged, in turn pressed me, all together, with cloudbursts of arrows,
spikes, and swords. Thereupon I laid on the ultimate fiery missile,
favorite of the king of the Gods, which was named Mādhava, O
20 Bhārata. With the power of the missile I cut swords, tridents, and
javelins, which they let loose by the thousands, into a hundred pieces.
Having first broken their weapons I furiously pierced them with ten
arrows each. On that battlefield the shafts fell from the Gāṇḍīva like
swarms of bees, and Mātali applauded. They too covered me with
their arrows, numerous as locusts, but I powerfully scattered them
with mine. Under this onslaught the Nivātakavacas once more
25 surrounded me on all sides with showers of arrows. I parried the
impact of them with ultimate, blazing, arrow-destroying missiles and
shot them by the thousands. Their cut-up limbs spouted blood like
cloudburst-hit mountain peaks in the rainy season. The Dānavas,
beaten by my swift, straight-traveling shafts that impacted like
Indra's lightning, became desperate. Their bodies and guts pierced in
hundreds of places, and their weapons having lost this power, the
Nivātakavacas began to battle me with wizardry.

Arjuna said:

168.1 On all sides there appeared a shower of rocks, which sorely
pressed me with terrifying stones as big as mountains, but with my
swift lightning-like arrows shot from Indra's weapon I shattered each
into a hundred pieces. When the rocks had been pulverized, a fire
broke out, and the powdered rocks fell into it like sparks. With the
rock shower abated, a powerful rain of water descended upon me
5 with jets as wide as cart axles. The jets poured from the sky by the
thousands with fiery force and covered all of heaven and space
entirely. The downpour of the rains, the whistling of the wind, and
the roaring of the Daityas blocked out everything. All space between
heaven and earth was one sheet of water, and the jets that
incessantly poured on the earth disconcerted me; I hurled the divine
desiccating missile that Indra had taught me, and the fearful blazing
thing dried up the water.

With the rock shower abated and the water dried up, O bestower
10 of honor, the Dānavas set loose their wizardry, fire, and wind. I blew
out all the fire with the water missile, and halted the impact of the
wind with the great rock missile. That magic too encountered, the
war-crazed Dānavas employed simultaneously various delusions,
Bhārata. A powerful, hair-raising rain burst loose of ghastly missiles,
fire, gale, and rocks. The magic rain pressed me down in my battle,
15 then a fearful intense darkness fell all around. As the world was
completely covered with terrifying dense darkness, the horses reared

and Mātali tumbled forward. The golden goad dropped from his hand
to the ground, bull of the Bharatas, and he kept asking me, "Where
are you, where are you?" When he lost his wits, a terrible fear
seized me. His mind wandering, he said, shaking, "There once was a
mighty war between the Gods and the Asuras in the cause of the
Elixir, Pārtha, and I witnessed it, prince sans blame. At the killing of
Śambara there was a fierce battle, and I drove the chariot for the
king of the God then too. Likewise I drove the horses at the killing of
20 Vṛtra, and I saw the grisly battle of Vairocani.* All these gruesome
wars I have witnessed, but never before did I lose my wits, Pāṇḍava.
Surely the Grandfather had ordained the annihilation of all creatures,
for this battle can only betoken the destruction of the world!"

When I heard his words, I took a grip on myself, and ready to
delude the delusive power of the Dānavas, I said to the fearful Mātali,
"Behold the power of my arms, and the might of my missiles and the
bow Gāṇḍīva! With the wizardry of my weapon I shall now defeat
their grisly wizardry and this awesome darkness. Have no fear,
25 charioteer, hold your ground!" I set loose the magic of my weapon,
overlord of men, which bewilders all enemies, for the benefit of the
celestials. With those various delusions baffled, the august Asura
lords again threw many hexes. Now it became light, then it was
swallowed again by darkness, now the world would become invisible,
then sink in the ocean. When it was light, Mātali drove the chariot
with the well-led horses on the hair-raising battlefield. Then the
dreadful Nivātakavacas fell upon me, and wherever I saw an opening
30 I sent them to Yama's domain. And while the battle raged for the
doom of the Nivātakavacas, I suddenly no longer could see any of
the Dānavas: they had hidden themselves with their wizardry.

Arjuna said:

169.1 Invisible, the Daityas combatted me with magic, and I carried on
the fight with the power of missiles. The shafts discharged from the
Gāṇḍīva, precisely propelled by charms, cut off heads wherever they
might be. The Nivātakavacas, battered by me in the battle, suddenly
withdrew the magic and streamed into their city.

When the Daityas had gone off and visibility was restored, I saw
the Dānavas there slaughtered by the hundreds of thousands.
5 Their shattered weapons, ornaments, bodies, armor lay stacked, and
there was no room for the horses to move a foot. With a jolt they
flew up and became airborne. Then the Dānavas too covered the
whole sky and, invisible, attacked, hurling massive rocks. Others of
them, who had gone underground, halted the feet of the horses and
the wheels of the chariot, Bhārata. Having halted the bay horses and

* = Bali.

the chariot, while I kept fighting, they piled mountains on me and
10 the chariot, surrounding me on all sides, and with the mountains
piling up and more falling down, the place where we were became
like a cave. Completely covered with mountains, and the horses
brought to a standstill, I became extremely worried. Mātali noticed
that I was frightened, and he said, "Arjuna, Arjuna, have no fear!
Now throw the thunderbolt missile!" When I heard him, I unleashed
the thunderbolt, the favorite missile of the king of the Gods, O overlord
of men. I spoke charms over Gāṇḍīva and turning to the immovable
wall around me began shooting sharp iron arrows that had the
15 impact of thunderbolts. The arrows propelled by the thunderbolt
became thunderbolts themselves, and they penetrated all those hexes
of the Nivātakavacas. Smitten by the impact of the thunderbolts, the
mountainous Dānavas fell upon the flat of the earth, embracing one
another. The Dānavas who underground had laid hold of the chariot
horses were sought out by the arrows and sent to Yama's domain.
The place was covered with the scattered corpses of mountainous
Nivātakavacas as with scattered mountain ranges. Neither the horses,
nor the chariot, nor Mātali, nor I had suffered any hurt—it was like
a miracle.

20 Mātali began to laugh and he said to me, king, "Not even the
Gods have the prowess that is found in you!" When the multitudes
of Asuras had been slain, all their wives began to wail in the city,
as herons in autumn. Together with Mātali I went into the city,
terrifying the Nivātakavaca women with the thunder of my chariot.
On seeing the ten thousand peacock-colored horses and the chariot,
which blazed like the sun, the women fled in droves. The noise that
the terrified women made with their ornaments was that of stone
25 slabs falling in the mountains. Trembling, the Daitya women went
into their dwellings, which sparkled with many precious stones and
were built of gold.

When I saw that beautiful city of miraculous structure, which surpassed the city of the Gods, I asked Mātali, "Why do not the Gods inhabit this wondrous place, for methinks it surpasses the city of the Sacker of Cities!"

Mātali said:

This was of old the city of our king of Gods, but the celestials were
driven out of it by the Nivātakavacas. They had performed many
severe austerities and won the grace of Grandfather. The boon they
30 chose was to live here and be secure from the Gods in war. Thereupon
the self-existent God was besought by Śakra: "May the blessed lord
dispose in this matter with his own interest at heart!" The blessed
lord told Vāsava what was fated in this matter: "You yourself shall
be their end, but in another body, Slayer of Vṛtra." So Śakra gave

you the weapons to destroy them, for the Gods were unable to slay
those whom you have slain. When the time had ripened, you arrived
here, Bhārata, to put an end to them, and you have done so. The
great Indra taught you the great ultimate power of the great weapons
in order to annihilate the Dānavas, Indra among men.

Arjuna said:

35 After entering the city and killing those Dānavas, I returned once
more with Mātali to the seat of the Gods.

Arjuna said:

170.1 As I was returning, I saw another great city, divine and
resplendent like fire and sun, which moved freely, abode of colorfully
jeweled trees and sparkling birds, and of Paulomas and Kālakeyas,
who were eternally happy, a city impregnable with gate towers,
watchtowers, and four gates, filled with all precious stones, celestial
and of wondrous aspect. Trees made of divine gems, which stood in
blossom and fruit, surrounded it, and lovely celestial birds nestled
there. It was filled everywhere with always joyous, garlanded Asuras
armed with spikes, spears, and clubs, and carrying bows and
5 hammers. On seeing this marvelous city of the Daityas, O king, I
asked Mātali, "What is this I see?"

Mātali said:

There once were a Daitya woman called Pulomā and a great
Asurī Kālakā, who observed extreme austerities for a milennium of
years of the Gods. At the end of their mortifications the self-existent
God gave them a boon. They chose as their boon that their progeny
should suffer little, Indra of kings, and be inviolable by Gods,
Rākṣasas, and Snakes. This lovely airborne city, with the splendor of
good works, piled with all precious stones and impregnable even to
the Immortals, the bands of Yakṣas and Gandharvas, and Snakes,
Asuras, and Rākṣasas, filled with all desires and virtues, free from
sorrow and disease, was created for the Kālakeyas by Brahmā, O best
10 of the Bharatas. The Immortals shun this celestial, sky-going city,
O hero, which is peopled by the Pauloma and Kālakeya Asuras. This
great city is called Hiraṇyapura, the City-of-Gold, and it is defended
by the grand Pauloma and Kālakeya Asuras. They are always happy
and cannot be slain by any of the deities, O Indra of kings, and they
live here unworried, with nothing left to desire. But Brahmā has of
old decreed that a human would be their death.

Arjuna said:

Having learned that they were inviolable to Gods and Asuras, my
lord, I said happily to Mātali, "Go quickly to the city, so that I may
dispatch with my weapons to their perdition these enemies of the
king of the Gods! For surely these evil God-haters are in no wise

15 inviolable to me!" Mātali drove me fast to the environs of Hiraṇyapura
on the celestial chariot that was pulled by the bay horses. When the
Daityas in their colorful robes and ornaments noticed me, they
gathered with great speed and, in armor, took to their chariots.
Furiously the Dānava lords, whose bravery was fierce, attacked me
with spears, iron arrows, javelins, lances, darts, bolts, and three-
bladed pikes. I warded off the thick rain of weapons with a dense
shower of arrows, O king, relying on the strength of my knowledge.
I bewildered them all as I maneuvered on the battlefield with my
chariot. Utterly confounded, the Dānavas began to fell one another;
20 and as they foolishly attacked one another, I cut their heads off by
the hundreds with blazing shafts.

When the Daityas were being slaughtered, they again took to their
city and employing their Dānava wizardry flew up to the sky, city
and all. I stopped them with a mighty volley of arrows, and blocking
their road I halted the Daityas in their course. But because of the
boon given them the Daityas easily held their celestial, divinely
effulgent, airborne city, which could move about at will. Now it
would go underground, then hover high in the sky, go diagonally
25 with speed, or submerge in the ocean. I assaulted the mobile city,
which resembled Amarāvatī, with many kinds of missiles, overlord
of men. Then I subdued both city and Daityas with a mass of arrows,
which were sped by divine missiles. Wounded by the iron, straight-
traveling arrows I shot off, the Asura city fell broken on the earth,
O king. The Asuras, struck by my lightning-fast iron shafts, milled
around, king, prompted by Time. Mātali swiftly descended to earth,
as in a headlong fall, on our divinely effulgent chariot.

30 The sixty thousand chariots of those intransigent warriors
encircled me, Bhārata, and I blew them asunder in the battle with
arrows that were plumed with vulture feathers, and they fell back
like waves in the ocean. Thinking that no human could vanquish
them in battle, I laid on all my missiles one after the other. Those
thousands of chariots of the skillful warriors and my divine missiles
canceled each other out gradually. The warriors could be seen by
the hundreds and thousands making intricate maneuvers with their
35 chariots on the battlefield. With their sparkling diadems and chaplets,
sparkling armor and banners, and sparkling ornaments they brought
joy to my heart. But with all my showers of arrows sped by missiles
I could not overcome them, rather did they overcome me. As I was
being pressed closely by the many masters of arms who were
experienced at warring, I began to feel pain in the great battle, and
great fear seized me. Then I bowed down on the battlefield to the
God of Gods Rudra, and saying, "Hail to the creatures!" laid on the
grand missile that is famed as the Raudra and destroys all enemies.

Thereupon I beheld a three-headed, nine-eyed man with three faces
and six arms, blazing flames for hair, and his head surrounded with
tongue-flashing serpents, O enemy-killer.

40 On seeing that terrifying sempiternal Raudra weapon, I lost fear and
laid it on my Gāṇḍīva, bull of the Bharatas; I bowed to the
boundlessly lustrous, three-eyed Hunter and shot, Bhārata, to defeat
the Dānava lords. Scarcely had I shot it before thousands of shapes
appeared on the battlefield, of deer, lions, and tigers, O lord of your
people, of bears, buffalo, snakes, cattle, elephants, marsh deer,
śarabhas, bulls, boar, apes, hyenas, ghosts, *bhuruṇḍas*, vultures,
45 Garuḍas, crocodiles, ghouls, Yakṣas, God-haters, Guhyakas and
Nairṛtas, elephant-faced fish, owls, shoals of fish and turtles, and,
brandishing all kinds of weapons and swords, warlocks who carried
clubs and hammers—these and many other creatures in all sorts of
shapes filled up all the universe when that weapon was launched.
The apparitions—three-headed, four-tusked, four-faced, four-armed, in
all kinds of shapes—devouring flesh, fat, and marrow—incessantly
killed off the Dānavas that had come together there. And with my
other enemy-destroying arrows, resplendent like sun and fire,
flashing like lightning and hard as rock, I struck down the Dānavas
in a short time, Bhārata.

50 When I saw them hit by the Gāṇḍīva arrows, lifeless, fallen from
the sky, I again bowed to the God who destroyed the Three Cities.*
Perceiving that the demons in all their divine jewelry had been
shattered by the Raudra missile, the charioteer of the Gods was
overjoyed. Having seen the impossible deed done that was
unattainable even for the Gods, Śakra's charioteer Mātali paid honor
to me. He folded his hands and said in a pleased voice, "The feat
that you have accomplished was impossible for Gods and Asuras!
Not even the lord of the Gods could achieve this in battle. For this
great airborne city, which was invincible to the Gods, you have
sacked, hero, by the power of your bravery, weaponry, and
austerities."

55 After the city had been destroyed and the Dānavas slain, all the
women came out of the city wailing. With disheveled hair, mourning
and wretched like ospreys, they fell on the ground grieving over
their sons, fathers, and husbands and wept loud from painful throats
over their dead masters, beating their breasts with their hands and
throwing off garlands and ornaments. The grieving lusterless Dānava
city, struck by sorrow and misery, bereft of its splendor, bereft of its
masters, no longer glittered. Like a City of Gandharvas, like a pond
deserted by elephants, like a forest of dead trees, the city vanished.

* = Śiva.

60 Mātali then took me, rejoicing after I had done the deed, quickly
from the battlefield to the dwelling of the king of the Gods, and I
returned to Śakra after breaking Hiraṇyapura and slaying the great
Asuras and Nivātakavacas. Mātali related my deed fully to the Indra
of the Gods, just as it had happened, O lustrous one, the sack of
Hiraṇyapura, the thwarting of the delusion, and the slaughter in
battle of the august Nivātakavacas. And on hearing it the blessed
lord, the illustrious Sacker of Cities, was pleased amidst the Maruts,
65 and he said, "Well done!" Again and again the king of the Gods
encouraged me and along with the other Gods spoke these very
pleasing words: "You have accomplished in battle a feat that was
beyond the Gods and Asuras. Slaying my enemies, you have brought
me a great guru's gift, Pārtha! You shall always remain as steadfast
in conflict, Dhanaṃjaya, and, unconfused, achieve an understanding
of weapons. Neither Gods nor Dānavas nor Rākṣasas shall withstand
you in battle, nor Yakṣas, Asuras, or Gandharvas, birds or snakes.
And Kuntī's law-spirited son Yudhiṣṭhira shall reign over the earth
that you have won with the power of your arms."

Arjuna said:
171.1 Then one time, when the arrow wounds had healed and I was at
ease, the king of the Gods favored me with these words: "All the
divine weapons are with you now, Bhārata. Not a man on earth can
overcome you. Bhīṣma, Droṇa, Kṛpa, Karṇa, Śakuni, and all the
kings are not worth a fraction of you when you stand on the
battlefield." The lord Maghavat bestowed on me this divine,
5 unbreachable coat of mail and a golden garland; the God gave me
the conch Devadatta of the mighty sound, and Indra himself placed
this divine diadem on my head. Śakra gave me also these celestial
robes and ornaments, beautiful and abundant. Thus honored, O king,
I dwelled happily in Indra's holy abode with the children of
Gandharvas. Then Śakra and the Immortals said to me graciously,
"It is time for you to go, Arjuna, for your brothers are thinking of
you."
Thus, King Bhārata, did I spend five years in the dwelling of Indra,
10 remembering the discord that sprang from the dicing; then I saw you
and your brothers on the top of this mountain, when you had come
to the Gandhamādana.

Yudhiṣṭhira said:
By good fortune, Dhanaṃjaya Bhārata, have you obtained the
weapons, by good fortune have you propitiated our mighty lord, the
king of the Gods. By good fortune have you set eyes on the person
of the blessed Lord Sthāṇu* himself and on the Goddess and satisfied

* = Śiva.

him with a good fight, prince sans blame. By good fortune did you encounter the Guardians of the World, bull of the Bharatas, by good fortune have we thriven, by good fortune have you returned. Now I think we have won all of Goddess Earth with her garland of cities
15 and subjugated Dhṛtarāṣṭra's sons. But I wish to see your divine weapons, Bhārata, with which you slew the heroic Nivātakavacas.

Arjuna said:

Tomorrow when it dawns you shall see all the celestial weapons, with the help of which I felled the dreadful Nivātakavacas.

Vaiśaṃpāyana said:

And after Dhanaṃjaya had thus related the circumstances of his arrival, he spent the night with his brothers.

Vaiśaṃpāyana said:

172.1 When the day had dawned, Yudhiṣṭhira the King Dharma and his brothers rose and did the necessaries. Then he prompted Arjuna, the joy of his brothers: "Show us the weapons, Kaunteya, with which you vanquished the Dānavas!" The illustrious Dhanaṃjaya Pāṇḍava showed the celestial arms that the Gods had given him, King Bhārata, in proper order, after first observing meticulous purity. Shiningly Dhanaṃjaya took his place on the earth chariot, whose pole are the mountains, whose axle the trees, whose pole joint
5 beautiful bamboo; clad in that bright armor he took the bow Gāṇḍīva and sea-born Devadatta. Bathed in light, the strong-armed Kaunteya began to demonstrate those divine weapons one after the other.

But while he was about to employ the divine weapons, earth with its trees started to tremble under his feet. The rivers and the great ocean itself shook and the mountains were rent asunder. No wind blew, no sun shone, no fire blazed, no *Vedas* came to mind at all to
10 the twice-born. The creatures that lived underground felt oppressed, Janamejaya, came out, and surrounded the Pāṇḍava. Trembling, they all folded their hands and covered their faces. Burning with those weapons they prayed to Dhanaṃjaya.

The brahmin seers, Siddhas, and divine seers, and all moving creatures, took their stands; so did the eminent royal seers, the celestials, Yakṣas, Rākṣasas, Gandharvas, and birds. Grandfather himself arrived and all the World Guardians, and the blessed Great
15 God with his familiars. The Wind faced the Pāṇḍavas on all sides, great king, carrying pretty fragrant celestial flowers; the Gandharvas, prompted by the Gods, sang various chants, and the throngs of Apsarās danced in their multitudes, O king. At this tumultuous time Nārada came prompted by the Gods, my lord, and spoke to the Pārtha these words worth hearing: "Arjuna, Arjuna, do not employ

the divine weapons! They are never to be used on an unfit target,
20 Bhārata, nor should one use them ever on a fit target, when not pressed; for in the use of these weapons lies very great evil, joy of the Kurus! If you guard them as you have learned, Dhanaṃjaya, these mighty weapons shall doubtless bring happiness, but if not so guarded they will lead to the destruction of the universe, Pāṇḍava: never do it again! Ajātaśatru,* you shall see the weapons when the Pārtha uses them in battle for the extirpation of the enemies."

All the Gods, after having stopped the Pārtha, and all the others who had foregathered there, went as they had come, bull among men. And when they all had gone home, Kauravya, the Pāṇḍavas camped in that forest with Kṛṣṇā.

3(36) The Boa

173–78 (B. 176–81; C. 12316–58)
173 (176; 12316). The Pāṇḍavas spend four years on the mountain for a total of ten (1–5). Bhīma exorts the king to fight Duryodhana (5–15). Yudhiṣṭhira says farewell to the mountain (15). Ghaṭotkaca carries them down (20).
174 (177; 12339). The Pāṇḍavas travel down to Vṛṣaparvan's hermitage (1–5) and carry on to Badarī (5–10). They visit King Subāhu, who receives them; their charioteers rejoin them there and Ghaṭotkaca leaves (10–15). They spend the twelfth year near Mount Yāmuna, then proceed to Lake Dvaita (20).
175 (178; 12363). Bhīma wanders through the lovely woods (1–10) and sees a huge boa. The serpent seizes him by virtue of a boon (10–20).
176 (179; 12395). Bhīma asks who the snake is; it is King Nahuṣa, who has been cursed by Agastya (1–15). The curse will end when someone answers his questions correctly (15–20). Bhīma pleads with the snake for his brother's sake (25–35). Yudhiṣṭhira sees ominous signs and follows Bhīma's trail; he finds him captive (40–50).
177 (180; 12449). Yudhiṣṭhira addresses the boa, which identifies itself; he will let Bhīma go if his questions are answered (1–10). He queries Yudhiṣṭhira about what makes a brahmin; the reply is conduct (15–20), not just birth (20–30). The boa sets Bhīma free (30).

* = Yudhiṣṭhira.

178 (181; 12489). Yudhiṣṭhira queries the boa about moral qualities, karman, *and the manner in which knowledge is acquired (1–20), and mind and awareness (20–25). Asked about Nahuṣa's fall, he relates how he oppressed the brahmins and was cursed by Agastya (25–40). Freed from his curse, Nahuṣa returns to heaven, and Yudhiṣṭhira tells the brahmins everything (45–50).*

Janamejaya said:

173.1 When that master of arms and great chariot warrior
Had returned from the dwelling of Vṛtra's Slayer,
What did the Pārtha's further accomplish,
Rejoined by heroic Dhanaṃjaya?

Vaiśaṃpāyana said:

In the selfsame woods those Indras of men,
Those heroes, disported themselves on that finest
Of mountains with Indra-like Arjuna,
In the lovely grounds of the God of Riches.

Casting his glance at the peerless mansions,
The playgrounds wooded with various trees,
The bowman, Indra of men, ranged much,
Engrossed in his weapons, forever crowned.

Having found a lodge by the graces of Lord
Vaiśravaṇa, all those sons of a king
No longer yearned for creature comforts,
And the time they spent was peace for them.

5 Rejoined with the Pārtha, they spent four years,
And the years they dwelled there were like one night.
With the earlier six it was ten years now
That the Pāṇḍavas peaceably camped in the woods.

Then the violent son of the Wind raised his voice—
And Jiṣṇu did, as they sat by the king,
And the valiant twins did, the matches of Indra—
In private, his voice both good and kind:

"Your promise it was, O king of the Kurus—
And to keep it true, and do you a kindness,
We followed you to the woods and postponed
Killing Suyodhana and his ilk.

"It is the eleventh year now we are camping out,
And Suyodhana's grasped the joys that are ours.
We should trick that lowest of fools now, and start
A comfortable stay where no one will know us.

"At your behest, king, we fearlessly shed
Our pride and waited here in the woods:
Beguiled by the years that we lived close by,
They will not know us if we move abroad.

"Having spent away our year in hiding,
We'll uproot with ease that vilest of men
And avenge our feud with blossom and fruit,
O Indra of kings, on that foulest of men,

"On Suyodhana, courted by all his gang—
Then take the earth for yourself, King Dharma:
We that roam this mountain like paradise
Can, God among men, kill off this grief.

"Your fragrant renown, O Bhārata,
Might die in the world of the firm and the fast:
By regaining the realm of the bulls of the Kurus
Great deeds can be done, great sacrifices.

"Whatever you now obtain from Kubera
You can get anytime, you Indra of men:
Set your mind on the death of your haters now
And their punishment, Bhārata, *for they wronged you.*

"Not the Thunderbolt-wielder himself could stand,
Were he to meet you, your awesome might;
For even encountering Gods, King Dharma,
If working to help you gain your goal,

"The Bird-bannered God* and the grandson of Śini**
Will never, those two, find any grief;
No more than Kṛṣṇa, the Śini champion,
Has found his match in the world, O king.

"If working to help you gain your goal,
The heroic twins will succeed in the cause,
Our twins, O best of the kings of men,
No less than Kṛṣṇa and Yādava;**
And excelling in might if your goal is at stake,
We shall do the same when we meet the foes!"

* = Kṛṣṇa.
** = Bala-Rāma.

Thus learning their mind the great-spirited
Most eminent son of the Dharma went,
And knowing of Profit and Law, most august,
He made the rounds of Vaiśravaṇa's seat.

Farewell he said, the King Dharma, to houses,
To streams and ponds and the Rākṣasas all,
And looked down the way by which he had come
And looked up again to the mountain peak.

And he made his resolve, "When my deeds are done,
When I and my friends have regained the realm
And rid it of rivals, then, steady of soul,
Great mountain, I'll come to see you for penance!"

20 Amidst the brahmins and followers
The lord of the Kurus was once more carried,
With them and his folk, across hill and fall,
By Ghaṭotkaca as he had done it before.

And seeing them leave that eminent seer
Lomaśa like a father instructed
Them all and with lightened heart went off
To the holiest house of the heaven-dwellers.

Instructed by him, and by Ārṣṭiṣeṇa,
The tiger-like men paid visits to grand
And lovely fords and hermits' forests
And other ponds, as they made their progress.

Vaiśaṃpāyana said:
174.1 The bulls of the Bharatas found no joy
In leaving that most pleasant abode,
That lovely mountain with cascading streams
And cardinal elephants, Kiṃnaras, fowl.

But once more their joy soared mightily
When the Bharata bulls set eyes again
On Kubera's favorite Mount Kailāsa,
The mountain that looked like a sea of clouds.

The heroes saw the mountain passes
And steep inclines, the cowpens, craggy
Ridges, and many deep precipices,
And flatlands here, and lowlands there.

Espying other large forests, the haunts
Of elephant, game, and fowl, they went

With confidence farther, those best of men,
Armed with their bows and holding their swords.

5 The bulls of men night after night
Found places to camp in lovely woods,
By rivers and ponds, and up in the mountains
In mountain caverns and deep defiles.

Having spent many nights in impassable spots
And crossed Kailāsa, incredible mountain,
They made their way to Vṛṣaparvan's
Superbly beautiful hermitage.

Vṛṣaparvan the king, on meeting them,
Received them warmly, and unconfused
They told Vṛṣaparvan in full detail
About their safe and propitious journey.

They spent one night quite comfortably
At his holy cell, which seers and Gods seek,
Then went on to the jujube tree Viśāla,
Where the heroes again made their pleasant camp.

Those foremost of men, whose power was great,
Dwelled there when they reached Nārāyaṇa's place,
And gazed on Kubera's beloved pond,
That Siddhas and Gods seek, and shed their grief.

10 They gazed at that pond, did Pāṇḍu's sons,
Most heroic of men, and shed their grief,
And enjoyed it as brahmin seers enjoy
Without fear their sight of Nandana.

In Badarī they spent a pleasant month,
Then went to the realm of the mountaineer king
Subāhu in stages, and followed the road
By which all the heroes had earlier gone.

They passed the Chinese, Dard and Tukhāra,
Kuṇinda and Dārva lands rich in gems,
And crossed the hard Himālaya pass
Till the heroes reached Subāhu's town.

When he heard that these sons and grandsons of kings
Had all arrived in his kingdom, Subāhu
Came happily out to receive them, the king,
And the bulls of the Kurus saluted him.

They met with King Subāhu, and with
All the charioteers whom Viśoka headed,
With Indrasena, and their old servants,
Their overseers, and the kitchen men.

15 They stayed overnight there a pleasant night,
Dismissed Ghaṭotkaca and his troop,
Engaged the drivers and chariots all,
And continued their way to Mount Yāmuna.

Upon this mountain of cascading streams,
Whose pale-red ridges were robed in snow,
The champions of men reached the sacrifice pole
Viśākha and they there made their dwelling.

The great wood, like the park of Citraratha,
Which teemed with boar, much game, and birds,
They safely roamed as they went out hunting,
And they spent in that wood another year.

It was there that the Wolf-Belly came upon a snake
That was starving and looked like Death itself,
Somewhere in the crevice of a mountain,
And his inner soul was perturbed with despair.

An isle was there where Yudhiṣṭhira,
The first of the lawful, of boundless splendor,
Secured the release of Wolf-Belly Bhīma,
All whose limbs had been caught in the grasper's grip.

20 The trusting Kurus whiled in the woods
The twelfth year away, as it rolled along;
Ablaze with luck and austere, they left
The wood that matched Citraratha's park.

Thereafter they went to the desert's edge,
Those men devoted to archery;
And, coming to the River Sarasvatī,
Sought out Lake Dvaita, to settle there.

On seeing them come to Dvaitavana
And settling there, the ascetics arrived,
Subdued, behaved, contemplative folk,
With water, straw, vessels, food, grinding stones.

Fig trees, nut trees, *rohītakas*, cane,
And spurges and jujubes, *khadiras*, *śirīṣas*,

Bilvas, ingudas, pīlus, śamīs, and thorns
Covered the River Sarasvatī's banks.

Those sons of a king lived joyfully
While they pleasantly ranged the Sarasvatī,
Beloved of seers, Gandharvas, and Yakṣas,
The sacrifice ground of the Gods themselves.

Janamejaya said:
175.1 How can it be that the powerful Bhīmasena, who had the vigor of
a myriad elephants, took such a bad fright of that boa, hermit? He
who prideful of his strength challenged Pulastya's son, the God of
Riches, to a battle, after massacring the best of the Yakṣas and
Rākṣasas at the lake? You said that that enemy-plower had come to
grief and was panic-stricken. I wish to hear it, for I am most curious.
Vaiśaṃpāyana said:
While the awesome archers were living in the forest of many
wonders, king, having come there from the hermitage of King
Vṛṣaparvan, the Wolf-Belly happened to inspect the lovely woods,
which were visited by Gods and Gandharvas, with bow in hand and
5 sword girt. He saw the beautiful landscapes of Mount Himālaya,
where Gods, seers, and Siddhas roam and which the throngs of the
Apsarās visit. It was loud everywhere with partridges, *cakravākas,*
pheasants, cuckoos, and bumblebees, and wooded with always
blossoming and fruit-bearing trees, soft with a touch of snow, which
threw ample shade and delighted both the heart and the eyes. As he
gazed at the mountain streams the color of beryl, with water touched
by the snow and astir with myriads of geese and *kāraṇḍava* ducks, and
10 the pine forests, which seemed to trap the clouds, mixed with yellow
sandalwood and tall turmeric trees, he went hunting on the desert
flats, and the powerful man roamed about shooting deer with
unpoisoned arrows.
Thereupon he saw a huge snake to make one shudder, which had
crawled into a mountain crevice and filled the cavern up with its
bulk. Its coils were as high as a hill, its body brightened with coiling
colorful skin that was dotted with moon-like and sun-like circles,
overall yellow as turmeric. It kept licking the corners of its mouth
from a glistening cavernous maw with four fangs, and its fiery eyes
15 were deep copper-red: the reptile struck terror in the hearts of all
creatures, like Time the Finisher and Yama, as it threatened all with
the moist hiss of its breath. The starving boa suddenly attacked Bhīma,
and the goat-eating grasper seized him powerfully by both arms. No
sooner was Bhīmasena caught than he lost his senses, for such was
the boon the snake had received. Bhīma might have the strength of

ten thousand elephants in his arms, unmatched by others, but the
splendid man was so overpowered by the snake that he could not
20 move, only stir slightly. Vigorous as a myriad elephants, lion-
shouldered, strong-armed he was, but when he was caught he lost
his mettle, confounded by the other's boon; for while he made a
bitter attempt to free himself, the hero could not match the snake
at all.

Vaiśampāyana said:

176.1 Splendid Bhīmasena, overpowered by the snake, worried about its
miraculous strength, and he said to the snake, "If it pleases you,
snake, who are you, greatest of serpents, what will you do with me?
I am Bhīmasena Pāṇḍava, younger brother of the King Dharma: how
can it be that I who possess the vigor of a myriad elephants have
been mastered by you? I have faced many lions, tigers, buffalo, and
5 elephants in battle and killed them; Dānavas, Piśācas, and mighty
Rākṣasas were unable to withstand the impact of my arms, best of
serpents! Is it the power of some knowledge, or the gift of a boon,
that you have overpowered me in spite of my efforts? This I know
for certain: the valor of man is as nothing, if you, a serpent, can
thwart my great strength!" As the heroic Bhīma of unsullied deeds
was speaking, the snake wrapped him in one mighty coil. When it
had subdued the strong-armed man, leaving only his thick arms free,
10 it spoke these words: "How fortunate that the Gods have sent you
with the big arms as fodder when I was starving, how fortunate after
all this time, for life is dear to creatures with bodies! But I must
surely tell you now how it befell that I became a snake; listen, good
enemy-tamer. It was the anger of sages that brought me to this state.
I shall tell you the fate of this snake, hoping to put an end to the
curse.

"Surely you have heard of the royal seer, Nahuṣa, ancestor of
yourself and your forebears, the dynast-heir of Āyu. I am he, and
because of a curse of Agastya and my contempt for brahmins I have
15 fallen to this estate; behold this fate of mine! Although you, my
benign heir, are inviolate, yet I shall devour you now, behold how
fate disposes! For once I have grasped a prey at the sixth time of the
day, it never gets free from me, be it elephant or buffalo, O best of
men. You have not been caught by a mere snake that behaves like
any animal, best of the Kauravas: I have received a boon. For when
I fell fast from the great chariot on which Śakra sits, I asked the
blessed lord, greatest of hermits, 'Set an end to my curse!' And the
splendid sage, flooded with compassion, said to me, 'You shall be
20 freed after some time has lapsed, O king.' Then I fell down on earth,
but I did not lose my memory. From ancient times it has been fixed

in my mind what I then learned: 'He who replies precisely to the
questions you ask him will set you free from the curse,' thus spoke
the seer to me. And I heard brahmins say, who were compassionate
and friendly to me, 'When you have caught any creature, king, be it
stronger than you and superior, it shall instantly lose its mettle'; then
they disappeared. Now here I live in this filthy hell, born a snake,
doing most evil deeds while I bide my time, O lustrous one."
25 Strong-armed Bhīmasena then said to the snake, "I am not angry
with you, great spirit, nor do I blame myself. Since a man may be
capable or incapable of happiness or unhappiness at their coming
and going, he should not worry his mind about them. Who can
avert fate with his own deeds? I deem fate supreme, human purpose
is meaningless: for look, because of a contrary fate I who rely on the
power of my arms have here and now without cause been reduced to
this state. But I do not mourn so much that I have met my doom
as I mourn that my brothers have fallen from the kingdom and been
30 banished to the forest. The Himālaya haunted by Yakṣas and Rākṣasas
is extremely dangerous: when they see me thus they will be so
distracted that they will tumble down, or when they know me dead
they will lose all energy, for they live by the Law, and it is I who in
my greed for the kingdom drive them. Or the sagacious Arjuna, who
knows all the weapons and is invincible to Gods, Gandharvas, and
Rākṣasas, will fall prey to despair. The strong-armed, powerful man
is capable with his strength of toppling even the king of the Gods
from his throne, let alone Dhṛtarāṣṭra's false-playing son, hated by all
35 the world and bent on greed and deceit. And I grieve for my poor
mother, yearning for her sons, who has always wished us to be
greater than any. How idle will all the desires she had for me
become when I am dead and she is left helpless! The twins Nakula
and Sahadeva, who followed their elder and were always supported
by the strength of my arms so that they deemed themselves men,
will lose their energy and fail in power and bravery, when they are
orphaned by my death. . . . Such are my thoughts." Thus the
Wolf-Belly lamented much, as he was held in the snake's grip and
could not move.
40 Now Yudhiṣṭhira Kaunteya saw omens that upset his mind and he
thought about the evil portents. For a frightened she-jackal made a
dreadful and unholy noise south of the hermitage where the sky
was reddening. A one-winged, one-eyed, one-footed quail of evil
aspect was seen to spit blood, screeching harshly in the direction of
the sun. A rough, hot, gravel-laden wind began to blow. All game
and fowl cried out in the south, and from behind a black crow cawed,
45 "Go! Go!" His right arm kept throbbing, his heart trembled, his left
foot twitched, and there was an ill-boding throb in his left eye.

Sensing great danger, O Bhārata, the sage King Dharma asked Draupadī, "Where is Bhīma?" The Pāñcāla princess said that the Wolf-Belly had been long gone. Thereupon the strong-armed king, after telling Dhanaṃjaya to guard Draupadī and ordering Nakula and Sahadeva to the brahmins, set out in the company of Dhaumya. The king followed Bhīma's footprints from the hermitage and saw the
50 ground marked with the signs of his passing. He saw trees twisted and broken by the wind of his thighs where that wind-fast hero had rushed by on his hunt. Going by these signs he found his younger brother in the mountain cave, held motionless in the grip of that king of snakes.

Vaiśaṃpāyana said:

177.1 Yudhiṣṭhira came closer to his beloved brother, who was circled by the snake's coils, and he said to the hero, "How have you come to this misfortune, son of Kuntī, and who is this great snake that matches the mass of a mountain?" When Bhīma saw his brother the King Dharma, he told him all that had happened, from his being being caught onward.

Yudhiṣṭhira said:

5 Snake, say truly whether you are a God, a Daitya, or a Serpent. Yudhiṣṭhira himself is asking you! What must be fetched for you or taught to you that will satisfy you, snake? What food should I bring? How will you set him free?

The Snake said:

I was formerly a king by the name of Nahuṣa, your ancestor, prince sans blame, the famous son of Āyu and the fifth from the moon, overlord of men. Through my sacrifices, austerities, *Veda* study, self-control, and prowess I obtained the undisputed sovereignty of the three worlds. When I had become sovereign, pride took possession of me, and a thousand brahmins carried my litter. Then, when I was crazed by my dominion and insulted the brahmins, Agastya reduced
10 me to this state, O king of the earth; but by the grace of the great-spirited Agastya my reason has not left me until now, King Pāṇḍava. At the sixth time of the day your younger brother became my fodder. I shall not set him free, nor do I want any other food. But if you answer the questions I put to you, you will thereafter free the Wolf-Belly, your brother.

Yudhiṣṭhira said:

Ask what you please, Snake, and I shall give the answers if I can, so that I may win your pleasure. You know fully what a brahmin may know here, O king of the Snakes. When I have heard you I shall make my reply.

The Snake said:

15 Now, who is a brahmin, king, and what may he know, Yudhiṣṭhira? Speak up, for from your words we gather that you are very wise!

Yudhiṣṭhira said:

He is known as a brahmin, king of Snakes, in whom truthfulness, liberality, patience, deportment, mildness, self-control, and compassion are found. And he may gain knowledge of the supreme Brahman, beyond happiness and unhappiness, Snake, on reaching which they grieve no more. What more do you wish to say?

The Snake said:

Authority, truth, and the Brahman extend to all four classes: even *śūdras* may be truthful, liberal, tolerant, mild, nonviolent, and compassionate, Yudhiṣṭhira. The object of knowledge, you say, king of men, is beyond happiness and unhappiness; but not a thing is free from either, and I do not think it exists.

Yudhiṣṭhira said:

20 The marks of the *śūdra* are not found in a brahmin; but a *śūdra* is not necessarily a *śūdra*, nor a brahmin a brahmin. In whomever the brahmin's marks are found, Snake, he is known as a brahmin; and in whom they are not found, him they designate as a *śūdra*. However, if you proclaim that this object of knowledge does not exist, since there is not a thing here that is free from either happiness or unhappiness, that is your opinion, Snake, that there is nothing free from either. Just as in between cold and heat there is neither cold nor heat, so there can be some thing somewhere in which there is neither happiness nor unhappiness: this is my view, Snake, or what do you think?

The Snake said:

25 If you judge a brahmin by his conduct, king, then birth has no meaning, my dear sir, as long as no conduct is evident.

Yudhiṣṭhira said:

I think, great and wise Serpent, that birth is hard to ascertain among humankind, because of the confusion of all classes when any man begets children on any woman: language, intercourse, birth, and death are the common lot of all men. The standard of the seers is expressed in the formula *ye yajāmahe*, "We, such as we are, give worship." Therefore those see the truth of it who know that conduct is the chief postulate. It is enjoined that the birth rite take place before the navel string is cut; the Sāvitrī formula is called the mother there, and the teacher the father. One is reckoned the same as a
30 *śūdra* by conduct as long as one is not reborn in the *Veda*. In the difference of opinion on this Manu Svāyaṃbhuva has said decisively, "Class is determined by observance of tasks. If no conduct is observed, there is judged to be overwhelming class mixture," O Indra of Snakes.

But him, now, in whom cultured conduct is postulated, him I have earlier called a brahmin, best of Snakes.

The Snake said:

I have heard your answer, Yudhiṣṭhira, who know what there is to be known. Now how could I devour your brother the Wolf-Belly?

Yudhiṣṭhira said:

178.1 You are such a scholar of the *Veda* and its branches in this world —tell me, by doing what acts does one go the highest course?

The Snake said:

By giving to a worthy person, saying kind words, and telling the truth, and by being devoted to noninjurious behavior, one goes to heaven, that is my view, Bhārata.

Yudhiṣṭhira said:

Which is found to be the more important, Snake, gift-giving or truthfulness? Tell the importance, or lack of it, of noninjuriousness and kindness.

The Snake said:

The relative importance of devotion to gift-giving, truthfulness,
noninjuriousness, and kindliness appears from the greater or lesser
5 importance of their effects. For truthfulness may at times surpass
some form of charity, O Indra of kings, and again some charity may
surpass true speech. Likewise, great archer, king of the earth,
noninjuriousness is found to be superior to kindness of words, at
other times kindliness prevails. Thus it all depends completely on the
effect, king. If you have something else on your mind, tell me, so I
can explain.

Yudhiṣṭhira said:

How should one perceive ascension to heaven and the lasting results of the acts of the embodied soul, Snake? Explain these matters to me.

The Snake said:

There are three ways one can go as a result of one's own acts,
O king, and these three are human birth, sojourn in heaven, and
10 animal birth. From the world of men one attains to heaven by
unwearied acts of charity, et cetera, and by actions informed by
noninjurious intentions. By contrary actions, O Indra of kings, a man
will be born an animal. I shall tell you the distinctive features, my
son. A man controlled by desire and anger, given to injury and greed,
falls from human estate and is born an animal, while one born an
animal, so it has been laid down, may become human. Cows, horses,
are found to become deities. A creature who does acts goes all these
three courses, and makes himself firm in the daily and principal
15 rite. In birth after birth the substantial and embodied soul seeks out

the fruit and experiences it, my son, though it be separate from the
body, and brings about the particular features of the creatures.

Yudhiṣṭhira said:

O Snake, tell me truly how this soul comes to dwell undistracted by sound, touch, color, taste, and odor. Why do you not perceive the objects of the senses indiscriminately, sage? Best of Snakes, answer all that I ask!

The Snake said:

When the soul substance has taken possession of a body and
controls its faculties, long-lived sir, it enjoys the experience of those
faculties according to the nature of each of them, good sir.
Perception, awareness, and mind, so learn from me, bull of the
Bharatas, are the faculties in the body that govern the soul's
20 experience. By means of the mind, which focuses on a representative
of any of the sense objects, the embodied soul, leaving its particular
field, explores the sense objects one after the other. The creature's
mind is fixed on any one at a time, and cannot perceive all of them
indiscriminately. The soul, which dwells between the eyebrows,
launches its awareness in varying degrees on the various substances.
After the operation of its awareness follows, according to the view of
the wise, the actual experience; this, tiger among kings, is the order
that brings about the functioning of the soul as an *embodied* soul.

Yudhiṣṭhira said:

Tell me what precisely defines mind and awareness; that insight is declared to be the chief task of those who should know the nature of the soul.

The Snake said:

25 As a result of the shock awareness is declared to follow the
dictates of the soul, my son. This consciousness derives from the soul,
yet becomes the governor of it in its search for action. Awareness is
not subject to the constituents, the mind is. Thus I have declared,
my son, how awareness and mind are distinguished. You too are
enlightened in this matter: what view do you hold?

Yudhiṣṭhira said:

Aho, this spirit of yours is beautiful, greatest of spirits! You know what there is to know, so why ask for my view? How could confusion blind you, who are omniscient, while you dwelt in heaven you whose works are miraculous? I am in great uncertainty there.

The Snake said:

30 Be he ever so wise and strong, wealth confounds a man. In my
view, anyone living in bliss fails to reason. Power-bred confusion
inebriated me, Yudhiṣṭhira, and I fell, fully enlightened, to enlighten
you now. You have done your task by me, enemy-burner, great king,
my grievous curse has been lifted by my talking with your good self.

For before, when I rode around heaven in a celestial chariot, I was
so drunk with self-grandeur that I did not think of anyone else.
Brahmin seers, Gods, Gandharvas, Yakṣas, Rākṣasas, and Kiṃnaras,
35 all denizens of the universe, paid taxes to me. On whatever creature
my eye might fall, lord of the earth, I robbed him of his splendor, for
such was the power of my glance. A thousand brahmin seers carried
my litter, and this misconduct brought about my fall from fortune,
king, for while the hermit Agastya was busy carrying me, I kicked
him with my foot. An unseen being then called out angrily, "Perish,
you Snake!"

My ornaments fell off, and I fell from that finest of chariots, and
while I was tumbling down headlong, I realized that I had become a
predatory reptile. I asked that brahmin, "Let there be an end to this
curse, blessed lord, pray forgive one who acted from ignorance!"
40 And as I was falling he said to me compassionately, "Yudhiṣṭhira,
the King Dharma, shall free you from your curse. When the fruits of
your dreadful arrogance and strength have dwindled, great king, you
shall attain to your good fruits." Upon seeing the power of austerity
I was amazed, and therefore I questioned you about Brahman and
brahminhood.

Truthfulness, self-control, austerity, discipline, noninjuriousness,
and continual charity are people's means to greatness, and not birth
or family, king. Your strong-armed brother Bhīma here is unhurt and
free. Hail to you, great king, I shall return to heaven.

Vaiśaṃpāyana said:

45 With these words King Nahuṣa shed his boa body and, assuming a
celestial form, went up to heaven; and Yudhiṣṭhira, illustrious and
Law-spirited, went back to the hermitage, joined by his brother Bhīma
and accompanied by Dhaumya. Thereupon Yudhiṣṭhira the King
Dharma told everything that had occurred to all the assembled
brahmins. And having heard it all those brahmins, the other three
brothers, and the glorious Draupadī were much impressed, O king.
All the good brahmins, who had the well-being of the Pāṇḍavas at
50 heart, censured Bhīma's rashness and told him to desist; and the
Pāṇḍavas, seeing the powerful Bhīmasena escaped from danger,
showed their happiness and enjoyed themselves joyously.

3(37) The Session with Mārkaṇḍeya

179–221 (B. 182–231; C. 12539–4649)
179 (182; 12539). The rainy season passes and autumn comes (1–10). They live by the River Sarasvatī,

then return to Kāmyaka (10–15).
180 (183; 12557). Kṛṣṇa comes to visit with his wife Satyabhāmā (1–10). Arjuna tells him his adventures; Kṛṣṇa praises Yudhiṣṭhira (10–20). He reports to Draupadī on her family's health (20–25). Arjuna's son Abhimanyu too is doing well (25). Kṛṣṇa's people is ready to come to Yudhiṣṭhira's aid; the king thanks him (30–35). The sage Mārkaṇḍeya arrives and is welcomed; so does Nārada (35–45).
181 (183; 12609). Yudhiṣṭhira asks about the workings of karman *(1–5). Mārkaṇḍeya relates how originally men were holy (10–15), then degenerated (15–20).* Karman *dictates man's life after death (20–30). The reward of living by the Law (35–40).*
182 (184; 12653). On the greatness of brahmins, Mārkandeya recounts how a Haihaya prince killed a brahmin by accident; his tribe is dejected (1–5). They search out his father and find Tārkṣya; when they look for the dead brahmin's body, it is gone: he has resurrected himself by the power of his brahminhood (5–20).
183 (185; 12678). Atri decides to retire to the forest; his wife suggests he first collect wealth from King Vainya and divide it among his dependents (1–5). Atri has enemies at the king's court, but goes nonetheless (5–10). When Atri praises the king as supreme, Gautama abuses him and they argue; they go to Sanatkumāra for a decision (10–20). Sanatkumāra upholds the greatness of kings, whereupon Vainya rewards Atri lavishly (20–30).
184 (186; 12715). Tārkṣya questions Sarasvatī about man's best course; she extols the brahman-knower, who goes to heaven (1–10). Asked about the agnihotra, *she replies that a* śrotriya *priest should perform it. She herself has arisen from the* agnihotra *(10–15). Praise of oblations (15–25).*
185 The Fish.
186 (188; 12809). Yudhiṣṭhira questions Mārkaṇḍeya about the end of the world (1–10). Mārkaṇḍeya states that Kṛṣṇa is the supreme being (10–15). In the beginning is the Kṛta age, which lasts 4,800 years, followed by Tretā (3,600 years), Dvāpara (2,400), and Kali (1,200); together the ages comprise one Eon of twelve thousand years, and a thousand such Eons is one Day of Brahmā (15–20). At the end of an Eon people

and life degenerate (20–30), the population increases, and morality declines (35–55). There is a drought of many years, seven suns desiccate the earth, and a fire storm devastates the land (55–60). Clouds gather and flood the earth with rain until all is one ocean (65–75). Mārkaṇḍeya roams in the desolation with great fear, till he comes upon a banyan tree, in which a child is sitting —Kṛṣṇa, who tells him to enter his mouth (75–85). In it he sees the entire universe, which he explores for a hundred years (85–110). Then he is exhaled and sees just the child; Mārkaṇḍeya questions him about this mystery (110–25).

187 (189; 12950). The God reveals himself as Nārāyaṇa and the universal soul (1–20). He is the ultimate goal and reward; he creates himself whenever the Law languishes (20–25). In the end he destroys the world (25–35). During the Dissolution he sleeps for a thousand Eons, having absorbed the universe that Mārkaṇḍeya saw within him (35–45). Mārkaṇḍeya praises Kṛṣṇa to Yudhiṣṭhira (45–55).

188 (190; 13008). The Pāṇḍavas honor Kṛṣṇa (1). Yudhiṣṭhira asks Mārkaṇḍeya about life at the end of the Eon (1–5). The four ages and the deterioration of society (10–80). When the Eon has closed it is regenerated (85). The brahmin Kalki is born and brings tranquillity back to the world (85–90).

189 (191; 13107). Kalki extirpates the dasyus *and restores the Law (1–10). Concluding admonitions: Yudhiṣṭhira should heed the Law; he promises to do so (20–30).*

190 (192; 13143). The Frog.

191 (199; 13331). Indradyumna.

192–95 (201–4; 13483). Dhundhumāra.

196–97 (205–6; 13628). The Devoted Wife.

198–206 (207–16; 13701). The Colloquy of the Brahmin and the Hunter.

207–21 (217–31; 14100). Angiras.

Vaiśaṃpāyana said:

179.1 While they were living there, the rains came, the season that puts an end to the summer heat and brings solace to all creatures. The thunderous rain clouds obfuscated space and skies and darkly poured down day and night, ceaselessly, signaling the end of the heat in their

hundreds and thousands, obscuring the net of the sun's rays and
shining bright with lightning. Grass burst from the ground, gnats and
snakes went drunk, earth, sprinkled with water, saw her smoke, dust,
5 and dawn appeased. When everything was blanketed with water,
nothing could be made out, level ground or pitfalls, rivers or dry land.
Roaring rivers in spate that were whistling like arrows lent beauty
to the forest when the rains began. In the wooded tracts the manifold
cries were heard of boar, deer, and fowl as they were battered by the
rains. *Stokaka* birds, peafowl, and flocks of cuckoos madly flew about,
while the frogs gloried.

Thus did the rainy season in its many apparitions and with the
echoes of the thundering clouds go safely by while they roamed the
10 wilderness; and autumn took its turn, overspread with curlews and
geese, building new enclosures and forest tracts, and making tranquil
the waters that flowed to the lowlands. Safe was autumn to them,
with heaven and stars washed clean, and crowded it was with game
and birds for the great-spirited Pāṇḍavas. They watched the nights,
cooled by the clouds, when all the dust had settled; they were
brightened by the light of planets, stars, and the moon. The safe
rivers, which carried cool water, were bedecked everywhere with
night-lotuses, day-lotuses, and beds of waterlilies.

They ranged the River Sarasvatī of the holy fords, with banks as
wide as the empyrean and bowers of cadambas and wild rice.
15 The heroes of the hard bows took pleasure in gazing at the safe,
brimming Sarasvatī of the tranquil waters. Most holy was the autumn
night to them on the moon-phase days, and while they were
dwelling there the full moon rose in the Pleiads, Janamejaya. The
Pāṇḍavas, those chiefs of the Bharatas, spent that most excellent
conjunction entirely in the company of holy, mettlesome ascetics;
and when darkness appeared the Pāṇḍavas continued with Dhaumya,
the chariots, and the kitchen men their journey to the Kāmyaka
Forest.

Vaiśaṃpāyana said:

180.1 When the Kaunteyas, led by Yudhiṣṭhira, arrived at Kāmyaka, they
were welcomed by throngs of hermits, and they settled down with
Kṛṣṇā. The joys of Pāṇḍu lived there trustingly while many brahmins
from all around waited on them. One brahmin said, "Arjuna's good
friend is about to come here, the strong-armed Prince Śauri* of noble
mind. For it is known to Hari* that you, the scions of Kuru, have
come; all this time Hari has been waiting to see you, wishing you
5 well. And the great ascetic Mārkaṇḍeya, who has lived a life of many
years yoked to *Veda* study and self-mortification, will visit you soon."

* = Kṛṣṇa.

He was still speaking when Kṛṣṇa appeared, greatest of chariot
warriors, on his chariot, which was drawn by Sainya and Sugrīva,
and he was accompanied by Satyabhāmā as Maghavat* is by Paulomī;
Devakī's son had come to visit the chiefs of the Kurus. Kṛṣṇa alighted
from his chariot, and the sagacious man joyfully greeted the King
Dharma and Bhīma, strong of the strong, paid his respects to
Dhaumya, and was himself saluted by the twins. He embraced
10 Guḍākeśa** and spoke comforting words to Draupadī. Seeing the
beloved hero Phalguna,** who had returned at last, the Dāśārha***
embraced the enemy-tamer again and again. Likewise Satyabhāmā,
the beloved chief queen of Kṛṣṇa, embraced Draupadī, the dear wife
of the Pāṇḍavas. Thereafter all the Pāṇḍavas, their wife, and their
priest paid homage to their lotus-eyed guest, and they all sat down
around him.

And Kṛṣṇa the sage, rejoined by the Pārtha
Dhanaṃjaya, bane of the Asuras,
Shone like the great-spirited Lord of Creatures,
The blessed lord, reunited with Guha.

The diademed hero related all
Their forest adventures to Gada's senior,***
Just as they had happened, then asked of him
How Subhadrā was faring and Abhimanyu.

15 The Slayer of Madhu*** brought proper honor
To the Pārthas and Kṛṣṇā and their priest,
And he said to the king, in order to praise him,
To Yudhiṣṭhira when he was seated with them,

"The Law is higher than a kingdom won;
They say that austerity leads to it, king.
While you lived by the Law, uprightly and truly,
You have won this world and the world beyond.

"At first you studied, obeying vows,
Then acquired entire all the lore of war,
Obtained your wealth by baronial Law,
And regained all ancient sacrifices.

"You found no joy in the Laws of the rustics,
Nor, Indra of men, pursued your desires,
Nor abandoned the Law out of greed for Profit,
And thus by nature you *are* King Dharma.

* = Indra.
** = Arjuna.
*** = Kṛṣṇa.

"Liberality, truth, austerities, sire,
And faith and peace and endurance and patience
Were always your greatest joy, O Pārtha,
After winning kingdoms, riches, and comforts.

20 "Who else but you could endure, son of Pāṇḍu,
That spectacle robbed of all Law and manners,
When the gathering folk of the Kuru jungles
Saw Kṛṣṇā afraid and reduced to a slave?

"No doubt you shall soon once more protect
Your people, restored to all your claims,
And we here shall act to repress the Kurus,
When once your promise has been fulfilled!"

To Dhaumya, Kṛṣṇā, Yudhiṣṭhira,
To the twins and to Bhīma, the Daśārha lion
Said, "Lucky indeed, and good fortune to you,
That the diademed man has come back with the arms!"

The lord of Daśārha and his friends
Then spoke unto Kṛṣṇā Yājñasenī:
"Your little ones, Kṛṣṇā, are vowed to the truth,
Well-mannered, and bent on mastering arms.
They consort with the strict, your sons, Yājñasenī,
And they practice the art of strict concentration.

"Your father, Kṛṣṇā, your brothers too,
Have plied them with kingdom and domains,
But no joy do the children find in the houses
Of Yajñasena, or their uncles'.

25 "They journeyed safely toward Ānarta,
Fully devoted to the arts of war,
Your sons, and they entered the fort of the Vṛṣṇis,
And have no envy, Kṛṣṇā, of Gods!

"As you yourself would have guided their way
Of life, or as Lady Kuntī would have,
So and more even does Subhadrā
Always guide them without distraction.

"And Rukminī's son* himself is your sons'
Pathfinder and guide, no less than he is
Of Aniruddha and Abhimanyu,
Or of Sunītha and of Bhānu.

* = Pradyumna.

"Prince Abhimanyu, unwearied and thorough,
Has been training the champions in battles with clubs,
Sword duels, shield wielding, in shooting projectiles,
In skills in riding and charioteering.

"And Rukminī's son like a guru has given
Them excellent training and numerous weapons,
And now he is well content with the prowess
Both of your sons and of Abhimanyu.

30 "Whenever your sons go out, Yājñasenī,
In order to watch some sport outside,
They are each of them followed by an entourage
Of chariots, wagons, and elephants."

Then Kṛṣṇa further addressed King Dharma:
"The Daśārha, Kukura, and Andhaka warriors
Stand ready to execute your command,
And hold their ground wherever you wish, sire.

"Let the hosts of the Madhus, who blow up a gale
With their bows and are led by the plow-armed hero,*
Now fully prepared, king, turn to your business,
With foot, horse, chariot, and elephant!

"Let, Pāṇḍava, now Dhṛtarāṣṭra's son
Suyodhana, who is the vilest of sinners,
With his following and the bands of his friends
Go the way of Saubha and Saubha's king!**

"You are free to stand by the promise you made,
O Indra of kings, in the hall of assembly:
But let the Elephant City await you
With a garrison of Dāśārha warriors!

35 "When you have done roaming wherever you please,
And shed your anger, and cleansed your evil,
You shall without grief forthwith return
To prosperous Elephant City and realm."

Upon hearing the view that that best of men
Had set forth precisely, great-souled King Dharma
Approved it. He folded his hands at his forehead
And looked and said to Keśava,

"There is no doubt, that you, Keśava, are
Our recourse, for the Pārthas take refuge with you.

* = Bala-Rāma.
** = Śālva.

When the time has come, you shall again
Accomplish your feat, no doubt of that.

"After whiling away the promised time,
The full twelve years, in the wilderness,
And properly spending our year of hiding,
The Pāṇḍavas, Kṛṣṇa, will come to you!"

Vaiśaṃpāyana said:

While the Vārṣṇeya and the King Dharma were speaking thus,
O Bhārata, there appeared the Law-spirited ascetic Mārkaṇḍeya, who
wore many thousand of years and had grown old in self-mortification.
40 All the brahmins, Kṛṣṇa, and the Pāṇḍavas paid honor to the age-old
seer upon his arrival. When the great seer had been welcomed,
refreshed, and seated, Keśava, with the consent of the brahmins and
the Pāṇḍavas, addressed him: "The Pāṇḍavas and the assembled
brahmins, Draupadī, Satyabhāmā, and I myself are eager to hear your
matchless words. Tell us the holy tales of the past, informed by good
conduct, which are everlasting, of good kings and women and seers,
Mārkaṇḍeya!"
While they were sitting there, the divine and pure-spirited seer
45 Nārada too arrived to visit the Pāṇḍavas. That great-spirited sage all
the bulls among men also welcomed in proper fashion with foot
water and guest gift. Knowing that they were waiting for Mārkaṇḍeya
to begin speaking, the divine seer Nārada assented. Smilingly, Nārada,
who was a good judge of time, said to him, "Tell the Pāṇḍavas what
you wish to tell them, brahmin seer!" Mārkaṇḍeya the ascetic replied,
"Then be at leisure, for there is much to be narrated." At his words
the Pāṇḍavas took their ease and looked at the great hermit, who
shone like the sun at noon.

Vaiśaṃpāyana said:

181.1 The Pāṇḍava, king of the Kurus, observing that the great hermit
was willing to speak, urged him so that he might begin the tales:
"Sir, forever have you known the exploits of all the deities, Daityas,
great-spirited seers, and wise kings. We hold you worthy of our
service and attendance, and long have we wished for you; and right
now Devakī's son here has come to visit us too.
"When I look at myself fallen from happiness, and at all the evil
5 Dhārtarāṣṭras prospering, the thought occurs to me that man is the
agent of all acts, for good or for evil, and that he reaps his reward—
so how does God act? Is it true, greatest of Brahman scholars, that
the acts of men, for good or ill, follow him in this life or in another
birth? How, best of the twice-born, is the embodied soul on shedding
his body hunted by his good or bad deeds and joined with them,

hereafter or here? Is an act confined to this world, or does it pursue one to the next? And where do the acts stay, Bhārgava, when a man is dead?"

Mārkaṇḍeya said:

This question is worthy of you, most eloquent man: you know what
10 there is to know, and you ask to establish the doctrine. I shall instruct
you in this matter, therefore listen now with a single mind, how here
and beyond a man finds happiness and unhappiness.

The Lord of the Creatures in the beginning created immaculately
pure bodies, obedient to the Law, for the souls to be embodied in.
Those ancient men were never frustrated in strength and resolve,
they observed good vows, they spoke the truth, they were holy and
as Brahmā, O joy of the Kurus. They all foregathered in heaven with
the Gods as it pleased them, then went back to earth again as the
fancy took them. Those men died when they wanted, and lived when
they wished, they were unoppressed, free from pain, fulfilled, and
15 unobstructed. They saw clearly before themselves the throngs of the
Gods, the great-spirited seers, and all the Laws, they had self-control
and knew no envy. They lived for thousands of years and had
thousands of sons.

Then in the course of time men became confined to walking on
earth alone, were beset by lusts and angers, and lived off tricks and
deceit; and these men, enslaved to greed and confusion, were
deserted by the Gods. They wickedly perpetrated evil, became animals
or went to hell, and were again and again roasted in all kinds of
transmigrations. Their wishes were vain, their plans vain, their
knowledge vain, and witlessly they fell prey to fear of anything; and
they reaped their share of misery, marked as they gradually were by
20 their unholy deeds. Ill-born, disease-ridden, evil-spirited, lacklustered,
the wicked became short-lived and reaped a harvest of grisly deeds,
hankered for any gratification, lost faith, and burned their bridges.

Kaunteya, a dead man's course here is governed by his own acts
done here. Your thought was, where does the treasure of acts stay of
both the wise and the foolish, and from whence does he recover his
good or ill-done deeds? Now hear the answer. Man in his original,
God-created body piles up a great lot of good and bad acts. At the end
of his life he abandons his mostly deteriorated carcass and is instantly
25 reborn in a womb; there is no intermission. His acts, which had
followed him like a shadow, fructify, and he is born deserving a good
or a bad lot. They who lack the eye of insight believe that this
creature is governed by the rule of death and is unaffected by either
good or bad markings; but this has been declared to be the course of
the stupid, Yudhiṣṭhira, now learn the superior course of the wise
beyond that.

Those men who have practical austerities, are steeped in all the
scriptures, firm in their vows, given to speaking the truth, obedient to
their gurus, of good habits, of clean birth, forgiving, self-controlled,
self-respecting, are normally reborn from noble wombs and nobly
30 marked. Being masters of their senses, they are in control; being pure,
they suffer little illness; having little fear of repression, they find no
obstacles. Whether born prematurely or maturely or still in the
womb, they all know with the eye of knowledge their own soul and
the Supreme: after having come to this earth because of past deeds
they again regain heaven.

Some comes from fate, some from chance, some from their acts, what men acquire, king; do not think more about it. There is a parable concerning this; listen to it, you best of debaters. This I hold, Yudhiṣṭhira, that what is the greatest good in this world one man will find here and not beyond, another beyond and not here, a third both here and beyond, the last neither here nor there.

35 The ones of great wealth enjoy themselves
From day to day and adorn their bodies;
They, slayer of enemies, own this world,
But not the next, being body-happy.

But of those who, yoked to Yoga, austerely
And while studying the *Veda* age their bodies,
Controlling their senses and helping the creatures,
Of them is *that* world, O victor, not this.

Who first and last abide by the Law
And in time by the Law obtain their riches,
Acquire a wife, and offer with rites,
Theirs is this world and theirs is the next,

And those who toil not on knowledge and gifts
And mortify not and beget no children,
Those unfortunate men find no happiness,
This world is not theirs, and no more is the next.

But ye all of transcending vigor and mettle,
Of power divine, and of healthy bodies,
Who have come to the earth from the world beyond,
Having learned your lessons, on the business of Gods—

40 When as champions you will have done great deeds,
Always wonted to penance and self-control,
And contented the Gods, the seers, and Fathers
In all their numbers with excellent rites,

Then as time passes by, you shall by your acts
Win highest heaven where good men dwell:
Don't ever doubt it, Kaurava lord
Who deserve your joys, when you look at your troubles!

Vaiśaṃpāyana said:

182.1 The sons of Pāṇḍu then said to the great-spirited Mārkaṇḍeya,
"We wish to hear of the greatness of the brahmins, who are the first
of the twice-born. Tell us!" At their words the great ascetic, blessed
Lord Mārkaṇḍeya, of superb splendor and scholarship in all branches
of knowledge, lifted his voice.
"There was a prince, a city-sacking dynast of the Haihayas, a
handsome and powerful nobleman, who once went out to hunt.
While he was stalking in the forest, which was overgrown with grass
and bushes, he saw close up a hermit who wore a black antelope skin
as an upper cloth. He mistook him for a deer and shot him in the
5 forest. Mournful and conscience-stricken, he appeared before the
Haihayas of famous spirits, and the lotus-eyed prince told those nobles
what had happened, king of the earth. When they heard and saw
that the root- and fruit-eating hermit was hurt, my son, their spirits
fell. Inquiring everywhere whose son he was, they soon came to the
hermitage of Tārkṣya Ariṣṭanemi.
"They saluted the great-spirited hermit of strict vows, and then
10 they all stood there while the hermit returned the honor. Then they
said to their great-spirited host, 'We are unworthy of your
hospitality, hermit, for we have done wrong, we have hurt a
brahmin.' The brahmin seer replied, 'How did you kill a brahmin,
speak up you all, where is he? Behold the power of my austerities!'
They told him everything that had happened, but all of them
together could not find the dead seer there, however much they
searched, and they felt embarrassed and foolish as though they had
been dreaming it all.
"Then the heroic Tārkṣya, sacker of enemy cities, said to them,
'Could this be the brahmin, the one that you killed? This is my son,
nobles, who possesses the power of austerities!' They looked at that
seer, and, astounded, they exclaimed, 'A miracle!' O lord of the
15 earth. 'For we have seen him dead. How could he come back alive?
Is this the power of austerities, that he lives again? We wish to hear
it, brahmin seer, if it be for us to hear.' He replied, 'Death holds no
power over us, nobles. I shall expound to you in brief the cause and
reason thereof. We recognize nothing but truth, we do not think of
falsity; we observe our own Law, and therefore we have no fear of
death. We speak to the well-being of the brahmins, and not of their

misdeeds, and therefore we have no fear of death. We feed and lave
our guests, we overfeed our dependents, we live in a country of
powerful men, and therefore we have no fear of death.'
20 " 'So you have been told it in a nutshell. Now be without envy
and go away together. Do not fear that you have sinned.' 'So be it,'
they said, and saluted the great hermit; and those nobles, bull of the
Bharatas, returned to their own land."

Mārkaṇḍeya said:
183.1 Hear further from me of the greatness of the brahmins!
A wise king by the name of Vainya was consecrated for a Horse
Sacrifice. We have been told that Atri wanted to go to him for a fee,
but then he did not agree with himself, for he saw what his specific
Law was. The splendid man thought upon it and decided to go to the
forest.
He called his lawful wife and sons and said, "If we are to reap an
immensely fruitful and unthreatened harvest quickly, you should all
agree that for our greater virtue we at once move to the forest."
Said his wife, who approved of the Law, "Go to the great-spirited
Vainya and seek a lot of wealth from him. Being a patron at a
5 sacrifice, the wise king will give you wealth! Take it, brahmin seer,
accept the wealth, divide it among your dependents and sons, then
go where you please! That is the foremost Law, which those wise in
the Law quote!"
Atri said:
The great-spirited Gautama told me, lordly lady, that Vainya is
seized of the meaning of the Law and avowed to Truth. However,
there are brahmins living there who hate me, so Gautama tells me,
so I have decided not to go. Any beautiful speech I make informed by
Law, Profit, and Pleasure they are going to call meaningless. But let
me go then, wise woman, I like what you say. Vainya will give me
cows and a large lot of wealth.
Mārkaṇḍeya said:
10 Having spoken, the great ascetic sped to Vainya's sacrifice, and
upon reaching the ritual site Atri lauded the king: "Sire, Vainya,
master art thou, thou art prime among kings on earth: the hosts of
hermits praise thee, but for thee no one knows the Law!" Angrily
an ascetic brahmin said, "Never speak so again, Atri! Your mind is
wandering! For us great Indra himself stands first, the Lord of
Creatures." Quoth Atri to Gautama, "He is as much a provider as is
Indra the Lord of Creatures! You are utterly confounded, you have
no wits at all!"
Gautama said:
I know, I am not confused! It is you who are so ready to talk who

is confused. The only reason you praise him is for profit, relying on
15 your visit with him. You have no knowledge of the highest Law, nor
do you grasp its meaning. You are a foolish child, how did you get
old?

Mārkaṇḍeya said:

While they stood arguing in full view of the hermits, who had
arrived for the king's sacrifice, they asked, "What are these two up
to? Who allowed them this entrance into Vainya's congregation?
For what purpose are they standing shouting like that?" Kāśyapa,
that most Law-spirited, most Law-wise king, pointed his finger at the
pair who had arrived arguing. Whereupon Gautama spoke to those
good hermits who were *sadasyas*: "Now hear the question that has
been raised between the two of us, ye bulls among brahmins. Atri
says Vainya is the Provider, and I greatly doubt that!"

20 No sooner did they hear this than the great-spirited hermits hurried
to Sanatkumāra to resolve the doubt, for he knew the Law. Having
heard their statement, which was true to the facts, the great ascetic
made this reply informed by Law and Profit:

Sanatkumāra said:

Brahmindom is allied with the baronage, baronage with
brahmindom; the king is the supreme Law, and the master of his
subjects. He is Śakra and Śukra, the Creator, Bṛhaspati, Prajāpati,
ruler, sovereign, baron, earth lord, guardian of men: who is not
worthy of respect who is praised by these titles? The king is called
the Ancient Womb, Triumphant in Battle, Attacker, Joyous,
25 Prosperous, Guide to Heaven, Joint Victor and Wide Ruler, True in
Wrath, Survivor in War, Furtherer of Truth and Law. Out of fear of
Lawlessness the seers have entrusted power to the baronage. The sun
in heaven dispels with its splendor darkness among the Gods:
likewise on earth the king mightily dispels Lawlessness. Hence the
supremacy of the king is shown by the authority of the scriptures and
that side prevails that spoke for the king.

Mārkaṇḍeya said:

Thereupon the great-minded king, delighted that his side had won,
spoke happily to Atri who had praised him: "You said that I was
supreme among all men, brahmin seer, equal to any of the Gods, and
30 preeminent, therefore I shall give you manifold and abundant riches: a
thousand young slave girls dressed in fine clothes and ornaments,
a hundred million worth of gold, and ten loads of golden ornaments:
all this I must give you, for I think you are omniscient!" The great-spirited Atri accepted it all in the right manner, and the splendid
ascetic returned to his house. Pleased, the self-controlled brahmin
gave this wealth to his sons, resolved on austerity, and departed for
the woods.

Mārkaṇḍeya said:

184.1 Listen, heroic victor of enemy cities, to the verses that Sarasvatī chanted when she was questioned by the wise seer Tārkṣya in this matter.

Tārkṣya said:

What, good lady, is best for a man here on earth?
What way should he act lest he stray from his Law?
Pray tell me, woman of beautiful limbs:
Instructed by you I won't stray from my Law.

How should one make offerings into the fire,
How worship and when, lest his Law be impaired?
Propound all this to me, fair woman,
So that I may roam the worlds without passions.

Mārkaṇḍeya said:

Thus questioned by the loving sage
And judging him willing and brilliant of mind,
Sarasvatī spoke to the brahmin Tārkṣya
This benevolent word conjoint with Law:

Sarasvatī said:

He who knows the Brahman in every locus,
Is constant in study, undistracted and pure,
Shall go to the cities of God's city
And find delight amidst the Immortals.

There are lovely and vast and sorrow-free
And holy flowering lotus lakes,
Unmuddied, rich in fish and fords,
That are covered with golden lotuses.

On the banks the man of holy deeds
Sits blissfully down and is glorified
By fragrant and well-decked Apsarās—
And the sheen of their skin is the color of gold.

The givers of cows reach highest heaven,
Those who give an ox gain the world of the sun;
Giving lodging, he goes to the world of the moon,
Giving gold, he attains immortality.

If one gives a dependable milch cow that yields
Much milk, does not stray, and has fine calves,
He'll enjoy in heaven as many years
As the number of hairs on his body are counted.

10 He who gives a reliable bullock of burden,
Which draws the plow and has strength unending,
Young, vigorous, trained to carry the yoke,
Gains ten of the worlds of the giver of a cow.

If one virtuously offers into the fire
For seven years, Tārksya, and keeps one's vows,
One purifies seven generations,
Up and down, by one's own acts.

Tārkṣya said:
The ancient vow of the *agnihotra*,
Explain it to me at my bidding, O fair one;
Instructed by you I shall henceforth know
The ancient vow of the *agnihotra*.

Sarasvatī said:
An impure man, one with unwashed hands,
Not knowing the *Veda*, nor wise, may not offer;
For the Gods when they hunger demand one be clean,
And take no food from the unbeliever.

A *śrotriya* priest be engaged for the rite,
Any other will throw the oblation away:
None but an accomplished *śrotriya*, Tārkṣya,
I say, may offer the *agnihotra*.

15 They who faithfully offer into the fire
And devoutly eat the leftover food
Will go to the fragrant world of the cows
And behold the God who is highest and true.

Tārkṣya said:
I think of you, who are my guide
In matters celestial, piercingly wise
Of the outcome of rites, as an insightful Goddess,
And ask you, beautiful lady, who are you?

Sarasvatī said:
I have risen myself from the *agnihotra*
To resolve the doubts of the bulls among priests.
Encountering you I felt kindly disposed
And so spoke of these matters precisely and truly.

Tārkṣya said:
There is no woman the equal of you,
For you shine as radiantly as Śrī;

Your celestial body is surpassingly lovely,
You display, fair lady, the wisdom of Gods.

Sarasvatī said:

I have grown on the choicest of gifts, O sage,
Most eminent man, which the offerers bring
When they make their oblations at their rites;
They filled me and made me beautiful, priest.

20 Whatever is used as an offering gift,
Be it wooden or iron or made of clay,
Know, sage, that a man by that gift prevails
In celestial beauty as well as wisdom.

Tārkṣya said:

Considering this the greatest good,
The hermits strive fully confident:
Propound to me the superior bliss
Of final release, which the wise secure.

Sarasvatī said:

The *Veda*-wise are devoted to that
Famed Ancient Spirit, supreme above all;
And with study, gifts, vows, and holy Yoga
The ascetics find freedom beyond all grief.

In the middle of it, a fragrant cane tree
Of a thousand branches stands pure and effulgent:
From its roots well up and flow the rivers,
The lovely streams of the honeyed water.

The great rivers flow from branch to branch like falling sand, those
rivers of grain and cakes, meat and potherbs, with the mud of milk
25 and rice. In the ritual the Gods with Indra and Maruts, whose mouth
is the fire, are worshiped with the finest acts: that, hermit, is the
highest point.

3(37.a) The Fish

185 (B. 187; C. 12746–802)
185 (187; 12746). Manu, son of Vivasvat, practices austerities at Badarī (1–5). A fish in the River Vīriṇī asks his protection, and he places it in a water jar (5–10). When it outgrows the jar he places it in a pond,

then in the Ganges, at last in the ocean (10–20). The fish predicts a flood and tells Manu to build an ark and fill it with the seeds of all creatures; a cable should be fastened to it (25–30). Manu will recognize the fish by its horn (30). Manu survives the flood on his ship. The fish appears, and Manu ties the ship to its horn; the fish pulls the ship for many years (30–40). The fish brings the ship to the highest peak of the Himālaya where Manu moors it (40–45). The fish is Brahmā, who tells Manu to create the creatures (45–50).

Vaiśaṃpāyana said:

185.1 Thereupon the Pāṇḍava again said to Mārkaṇḍeya, "Relate to me the deeds of Manu Vaivasvata."

Mārkaṇḍeya said:

There was a son of Vivasvat, king, tiger among men, a great seer
of high puissance, who had the radiance of Prajāpati. In augustness,
splendor, fortune, and especially austerity this Manu surpassed his
own father and grandfather. This lord of men practiced severe and
great self-mortification at the jujube tree Viśālā, while he stood on one
5 foot with his arms raised. With bent head and eyes unblinking, he
performed awesome austerities for ten thousand years.

Once when he was thus engaged, wearing a wet bark shirt and
matted hair, a fish came swimming to the bank of the River Vīriṇī,
and spoke to him: "My lord, I am but a tiny fish, and I am afraid of
the big fish. Pray, sage of great vows, save me from the fish. For the
stronger fish always eat the weaker ones, as our immemorial way has
ordained it to be. Therefore, please save me from the tide of fear in
which I am drowning. If you do so, I shall return the deed."

10 On hearing the words of the fish Manu Vaivasvata was filled with
compassion and took the fish in his hand. He took it away from the
river and threw the fish, which glistened like moonbeams, into a
small water jar. There the fish, which was very well cared for, grew
up, O king, and Manu loved it as a son. After a great while the fish
grew so big that it no longer fitted in the water jar. When the fish
saw Manu, it again spoke up: "Sir, please take me now to another
15 place!" The blessed hermit Manu pulled it from the jar, brought it to
a large pond, and threw it in, O victor of enemy cities. And the fish
kept growing for many years; that pond had the length of two
leagues and the girth of one, and when the fish no longer fitted in the
pond, lotus-eyed lord of the people, and could not move, it said to
Manu, "Please, sir, take me to the Ganges, the chief queen of the
rivers, and I shall live there, father, if you think so too."

At its words, Manu, who was a powerful man, took the fish to the
20 River Ganges and, undaunted, threw it in himself. There for a while
the fish kept growing, enemy-tamer, and when it saw Manu, it said
again, "I cannot move any more in the Ganges because of my size,
sir. Bring me quickly to the ocean, take pity on me, my lord!" Manu
pulled the fish out of the water of the Ganges, took it to the ocean,
and set it free there, Pārtha. Although the fish was huge, to Manu's
mind it was easy to carry and pleasant to touch and smell.
25 When the fish had been thrown into the ocean by Manu, it said to
him with a seeming smile, "My lord, you have given me every
protection. Now listen to what you should do when the time comes.
Soon, my lord, everything on earth, standing or moving, will be
destroyed, for the time is near for the cleansing of the world.
Therefore learn now what shall be of the greatest profit to you. The
horrors of doomsday are at hand for all that moves and stands and
stirs or does not stir. You must have an ark built, a sturdy one, with
a cable tied to it. You will embark on it with the seven seers, great
30 hermit. All the seeds of creatures I have enumerated before you should
place in the ark and then wait for me, O favorite of the hermits. I
shall come and you shall know me by my horn, ascetic. Thus should
you act; farewell, I shall go. Do not doubt my words too much, my
lord!" "I shall do so," he replied to the fish, and after taking leave of
each other, both went their way.
Thereupon, great king, Manu, as he had been told by the fish,
collected all the seeds, and floated in that beautiful ship on the
35 billowing ocean, enemy-taming hero. And Manu thought of the fish,
king, and knowing his thought the fish came, victor of enemy cities,
wearing a horn; and it soon arrived, bull of the Bharatas. When
Manu saw that fish in the ocean, Indra of kings, wearing a horn in
the way it had said, and as tall as a mountain, he made a loop in the
cable and made fast to the horn on the fish's head. Held fast by the
loop the fish began to pull the ark with great speed into the ocean,
victor of enemy cities. It crossed the ocean with the ark, which
40 danced in its billows and roared with its water, O king. The ship,
battered by hurricanes, staggered on the ocean like a drunken whore,
conqueror of enemy cities. There was no more earth to be made out,
no points of space at all, everything was covered with water, space,
and firmament, bull among men.
While all the world was overcome by this turbulence, bull of the
Bharatas, only the seven seers, Manu, and the fish could be seen. And
for many a year that fish pulled the ark untiringly, O king, on the
expanse of the water. Then the fish pulled the ark to the highest peak
45 of the Himālaya, bull among men, joy of the Kurus. And, gently
laughing, it said to the seers, "Moor the ship quickly to this Himālaya

peak." And upon hearing the words of the fish they quickly moored the ship to the peak of the Himālaya. Know, Kaunteya, bull of the Bharatas, that till this very day the highest peak of the Himālaya is still called "the Mooring."

The unblinking creature said to the assembled seers, "I am Brahmā, the Lord of the Creatures. Nothing is found that is superior to me. In the form of a fish I have set you free from danger. Manu is now to create all the creatures, Gods, Asuras, and men, all the worlds,
50 whatever stirs and does not stir. By virtue of his very severe self-mortifications the manner shall be manifest to him and by my grace he shall make no mistake in creating the creatures." Having spoken these words, the fish instantly vanished; and Manu Vaisvata became desirous himself to bring forth the creatures. He was unsure about the manner of creating and performed many austerities; then, aided by his great asceticism, Manu himself proceeded to create all the creatures rightly, bull of the Bharatas.

Thus have I narrated to you the Lore that is famous as the Purāṇa of the Fish, which cleanses all evil. He who daily listens to the deeds of Manu from the beginning will be happy and successful in all his designs, and go to the world of heaven.

3(37) The Session with Mārkaṇḍeya (continued)

Vaiśaṃpāyana said:

186.1 Thereupon Yudhiṣṭhira the King Dharma courteously questioned the glorious Mārkaṇḍeya: "You have witnessed, great hermit, the end of many thousands of eons; no one in the world has lived as long as you have, except the great-spirited Brahmā Parameṣṭhin. At the time of dissolution, when earth is skyless and empty of Gods and Dānavas, you attend on Brahmā, brahmin. When the dissolution is complete and Grandfather waxes again, you watch the creatures
5 being created by Parameṣṭhin, in the right four orders of beings, after he has filled space with air and moved off the waters, O brahmin seer. You, best of the twice-born, propitiate the guru of the world himself, the Grandfather of all the worlds, with meditation that is focused on him. Therefore death, which finishes all, and old age, which destroys the body, do not invade you, brahmin, by the grace of Parameṣṭhin. When there is no more sun, nor fire, nor wind, nor moon, and nothing at all remains of heaven and earth, when the world of the firm and the quick is reduced to one vast ocean, when

the orders of Gods and Asuras are destroyed and the great Snakes devastated, then you alone remain to worship Brahmā, lord of all beings, while the God of boundless soul, enthroned on the lotus, is sleeping in the lotus.

"All that went on before has been manifest to you, best of brahmins, therefore we wish to hear your account with the causes of everything. For you alone have experienced it many times, good brahmin, and there is nothing in any of the worlds that is unknown to you."

Mārkaṇḍeya said:

Yea, I shall tell you, after bowing to the Self-existent, the Ancient Person, everlasting and imperishable. It is Janārdana* of the long, wide eyes, and the yellow cloak, the maker of the elements that brings forth the universe: he is the unimaginable wonder, the supreme means of purification without beginning and end, the all-being, indestructible and imperishable. This maker is not made, but the cause of all agency; even the Gods do not know who knows him, the Person.

In the beginning, after the destruction of the entire universe, O tiger among men, there is the Kṛta age, which, they say, lasts four thousand years, preceded by a dawn and followed by a dusk of four hundred. The Tretā age is said to last for three thousand years, preceded by a dawn and followed by a dusk of three hundred each. The Dvāpara lasts two thousand years, with a dawn and dusk of two hundred each. The Kali age is taught to be one thousand years long, with a hundred years each of dawn and dusk: note that dawns and dusks are equal in length. When the Kali age has been spent the Kṛta comes around again. This total period of twelve thousand years is called an Eon. The unit of a thousand such eons is cited as a Day of Brahmā. When the entire universe reverts to its home in Brahmā, O tiger among men, the wise know this as the reabsorption of the worlds.

At the end of the Eon, bull of the Bharatas, when little time remains of the last thousand years, all men in general become speakers of untruth. Substitute persons perform the sacrifices, Pārtha, substitutes give the gifts, substitutes observe the vows in that age. Brahmins do the work of serfs, as the Eon expires, serfs become gatherers of wealth or practice the Law of the baronage. In the Kali age brahmins will cease sacrificing and studying, neglect the offerings to the fathers, and fall to eating any food. Brahmins will be prayerless, my son, and the serfs prayerful. When the world is upside down, it is the portent of destruction. Many barbarian kings, O overlord of men, will rule the earth with false policies, being given to

* = Kṛṣṇa, Viṣṇu.

30 evil and lies. Āndhras will be kings then, Scythians, Pulindas, Greeks,
Kambojas, Aurṇikas, serfs, and Ābhīras, best of men. Not a brahmin
then lives by his own Law, and likewise the barons and commoners
work at the wrong tasks, O king. People are short-lived, enfeebled, of
little vigor and valor, weak-bodied, short on substance, and rarely
speaking the truth. The countrysides are largely empty, the land is
overrun by game and predators, when the end of the Eon comes, and
the students of the Brahman are false. The serfs will say "Hey you!",
the brahmins will say "Pray, sir!"

At the end of the Eon the population increases, tiger among men,
35 and odor becomes stench, and flavors putrid. When the Eon perishes,
women will have too many children, O king, be short of stature, cast
off all morals, and have intercourse through the mouth. At the end
of the Eon the countryside will bristle with towers, the crossroads
with jackals, the women with hair, O king. The cows will yield little
milk, and the trees, teeming with crows, will yield few flowers and
fruits. Brahmins will accept the gifts of kings who are tainted with
brahmin-murder and accuse falsely, O king. Brahmins, wrapped up in
greed and folly, falsely flaunting their Law, will plunder the land bare
40 for alms. Householders, out of fear of the burden of taxes, will become
thieves, and others hiding under the guise of hermits will live off
trade; and men will let their hair and nails grow under false pretenses.
Vedic students will be false, because of their greed for possessions,
tiger among men, misbehave in the hermitages, drink liquor, swive
their teachers' wives, pursue the goals of this world, and pander to
their flesh and blood. Overrun by many imposters and discussing the
virtues of great meals, there will be no hermitages left at the end of
the Eon, tiger among men.

The blessed lord, the Punisher of Pāka,* will no more rain in the
right season; none of the seeds that are sown will grow right,
Bhārata, and the harvest of lawlessness will be rich, prince sans
45 blame. The one who observes the Law can be reckoned to live but
briefly, for no Law survives then, king. People trade their wares
mostly with false measures, and the merchants abound with tricks.
The Law-minded dwindle, the evil prosper, the Law loses strength,
and lawlessness gains it. The Law-minded become short-lived and
impoverished, and the lawless long-lived and rich, at the close of the
Eon. Creatures carry on their affairs with means that fall wholly short
50 of the Law, and with even small capital the arrogant grow rich. Men
are widely resolved to plunder the funds that had been placed
confidently in their trust, king, as they plot their deceitful procedures.
Man-eating creatures, birds, and game lurk in the cities' parks and
their very sanctuaries. Girls get pregnant at the age of seven and

* = Indra.

eight, king, and boys of ten and twelve become fathers. Men turn
gray in their sixteenth year, and quickly live out their lives. When the
Eon is spent, great king, the young have the habits of the old, and
55 the aged behave like children. The women are corrupt and, secretly
deceiving their husbands, lasciviously fornicate with slaves and even
cattle.

When the close of the thousand Eons has come and life has been
spent, there befalls a drought of many years that drives most of the
creatures, of dwindling reserves and starving, to their death on the
face of the earth, O lord of the land. Seven scorching suns drink up
all the water in the oceans and rivers; whether wood or straw, dry or
60 wet, bull of the Bharatas, all is turned into ashes. The Fire of
Annihilation then invades, with the force of a gale, a world that had
already been desiccated by the suns. The Fire splits the earth, spreads
to the underworld, and strikes terror in Gods, Dānavas, and Yakṣas. It
burns down the world of the Snakes and all that is found on earth,
and instantly destroys everything that is underneath. The ill wind and
the Fire of Annihilation burn down hundreds and thousands of
twenty-league stretches—the lord of the world blazes up and sears
the entire universe with Gods, Asuras, and Gandharvas, with Yakṣas,
Snakes, and Rākṣasas.

65 Wondrous-looking huge clouds rise up in the sky, like herds of
elephants, in the finery of garlands of lightning, some darkling like
blue lotuses, others like white lotuses or fibers, others yellow or
turmeric-ochre, the color of spiders and of red lotus petals, and
vermilion; some are shaped like grand cities, others like elephant
herds, still others black as collyrium, others in crocodile shapes—clad
in garlands of lightning, the clouds rise up. In their terrifying shapes,
with their horrible echoing blasts, the clouds cover the entire expanse
70 of the sky, great king, they fill up all of earth and her mountains,
mines and forests, and flood her with rains. At the command of
Parameṣṭhin, the terrible thundering clouds inundate everything.
Showering their masses of water and filling up the earth, they douse
the evil, gruesome, panic-spreading fire that had been raging.

For twelve years during that upheaval the clouds, at the impulse
of the Large Spirit, fill earth with their showers, till the ocean rises
above its tide line, Bhārata, mountains are sapped and collapse, and
75 earth itself collapses. Then sudden winds whirl around the skies and
under their hurricane gusts the clouds are torn to shreds. And the
self-existent God, O Bhārata, overlord of men, drinks up these winds
and lies sleeping on the Lotus of the Beginning.

In this desolate mass of nothing but ocean, with all standing and
moving creatures dead, with the hosts of Gods and Asuras dead,

empty of Yakṣas and Rākṣasas, without men, without beasts and
trees, in this world without sky, king, I alone wander about with
grave concern. And as I roam on this desolate total ocean, without
80 seeing a single creature, I become terribly afraid. I go to all lengths
and swim, king, and despite my fatigue find nowhere a resting place
as I keep going. Then one day I see in the flood of the waters a tall,
wide banyan tree. I see a child sitting on a spreading branch of that
tree, in a cradle made up with divine coverlets, Bhārata, great king,
a child with a face like the full moon and eyes as wide as a blooming
lotus. I am greatly amazed: "How can this babe lie here, when all the
85 world has come to an end?" I may meditate with all the strength of
my austerities, I may know the past, present, and future, yet I do
not understand this child. His skin the color of cornflowers, his chest
marked with the Śrīvatsa curl, he appears to me like the abode of
Lakṣmī herself.

The lotus-eyed and radiant child, who wears the Śrīvatsa, says to
me these words, which gladden my ears: "I know that you are very
tired, friend, and desirous of rest: sit here, Mārkaṇḍeya Bhārgava,
for as long as you wish. Enter my body, good hermit, and rest here,
90 sir, I shall make room for you as a favor." When the child says this
to me I become tired of my long life and my human estate, Bhārata.
On a sudden the child opens its mouth wide, and powerlessly I am
translated into it by an act of fate. And when I so suddenly enter
the hollow of his mouth, O king, I behold all of earth overspread with
kingdoms and cities, the rivers Ganges, Śatadru, Sītā, Yamunā,
Kauśikī, Carmaṇvatī, Vetravatī, Candrabhāgā, Sarasvatī, Sindhu,
95 Vipāśā, Godāvarī, Vasvokasāra, Nalinī, Narmadā, Tāmrā, Veṇṇā of
holy and luck-bringing waters, Suveṇā, Kṛṣṇaveṇā, Irāmā, Mahānadī,
Śoṇa, Viśalyā, and Kampunā, tiger among men. These and whatever
other rivers there flow on earth, best of men, I see there as I wander
about inside the Large Spirit.

I see the ocean, teeming with fish, a mine of pearls, vast resting
place of water. I see the heavens illumined by sun and moon and
blazing with lights that are like sun and fire; I see the earth, king,
adorned with forests. The brahmins are giving worship with many
soma pressings, the barons are at work to make friends of all the
100 classes, the commoners carry out in proper fashion their plowing,
O king, and the serfs are bent upon obedience to the twice-born.
While I roam about inside the Large Spirit, O king, I see the Himālaya
and Mount Hemakūṭa, I see the Niṣadha and the silver-decked Śveta.
I see Mount Gandhamādana, O king, tiger among men, Mount
Mandara, and the great mountain Nīla. I see, great prince, the golden
mountain Meru, the Mahendra, and the superb Vindhya range. I see
105 the Malaya and Mount Pāriyātra, and whatever other mountains there

are, I see them all in his belly, decked with all their gems. I wander around while I see tigers, lions, boar, snakes, and all other species of creatures that dwell on earth, O lord of the earth.

Having entered into his belly, and roaming all the quarters, I see all the hosts of the Gods headed by Śakra, the Gandharvas and Apsarās, Yakṣas, seers, Daityas and Dānavas, king, and the Kāleya ogres and the sons of Siṃhikā and all other foes of the Gods. Whatever creature, either moving or standing, which I had seen before in the world I see again in the belly of the Large Spirit. Living off fruits I
110 explore this entire universe inside his body for more than a hundred years, and nowhere do I see an end to his body, however far I roam while I am thinking, lord of the people.

Finding no end to the Large Spirit, O king, I throw myself in the proper fashion on the mercy of this covetable boon-granting God with both my mind and my deeds. Suddenly a wind gust expels me from the wide open mouth of the Large Spirit, O best of men, and he sits on the branch of that same banyan tree, O tiger among men, holding
115 the entire universe, where I see him of boundless luster, marked with the Śrīvatsa, while he sits in the guise of a child. With the beginning of a laugh, O hero, that radiant, Śrīvatsa-wearing, yellow-clothed child says to me, "Have you dwelled restfully today in this body of mine, good hermit Mārkaṇḍeya? Tell me!" Instantly a new eyesight becomes evident in me by which I see the liberated soul that has
120 gained consciousness. I take his red-soled, firmly planted feet, which are delicate and adorned with soft red toes, humbly in my hands and salute them with my head.

Having witnessed the limitless power of the boundlessly august God I humbly fold my hands and approach him eagerly. I see the lotus-eyed God as the soul that has become elemental, and folding my hands and doing homage I say to him, "God, I wish to know yourself and this supernal wizardry! I entered into your body through your mouth, O lord, and saw all the worlds together in your body. In your body, O God, dwell the Gods, Dānavas and Rākṣasas, the Yakṣas, Gandharvas and Snakes, the world of standing and moving creatures.
125 And by your grace, O God, my memory did not fail me while I, always running, quickly explored the inside of your body. Faultless, lotus-eyed one, I wish to know of you why you stay here in your own person as a child. You drank up the entire universe, therefore pray tell, for what purpose does the universe survive entire within your body, blameless one? How long a time are you to bide here, enemy-tamer, this I wish to hear, Lord of Gods, for I seek instruction in the *brahman* from you in full detail as it really is, lotus-eyed God. For what I have seen, my lord, is greatly beyond my understanding."

At my words the radiant and resplendent God of Gods most
eloquently speaks to me comfortingly.

The God said:

187.1 Surely, not even the Gods know me as I really am, brahmin, but
out of love for you I shall declare the manner in which I create this
world. You are devoted to your ancestors, brahmin seer, you have
taken refuge with me, hence you have seen me in person; and your
brahman practice is great.

The waters are called *nāras*: I gave them the name; therefore I
am called Nārāyaṇa, for the waters are my course. I am the creator
5 of all creatures as well as their destroyer, best of brahmins. I am
Viṣṇu, I am Brahmā, and Indra the lord of the Gods. I am King
Vaiśravaṇa, and Yama the lord of the dead, I am Śiva, Soma, and
Kaśyapa Prajāpati. I am the Placer and Disposer, I am the Sacrifice,
great brahmin. Fire is my mouth, earth my feet, sun and moon my
eyes, the sky and the cardinal points are my body, and the wind
dwells in my nose. I am in the sacrificial terrain, where the *Veda*-wise
worship me with many hundreds of rites of ample stipends, which I
had performed first. On earth the lords of the barons, the kings,
worship me desirous of heaven, and thus also do the commoners
who wish to win the world of heaven.

10 As Śeṣa I support this treasure-filled earth that is girt by the four
oceans and adorned with the Meru and Mandara. Assuming the form
of a boar I once with my might pulled out this earth, when it had
sunk in the water. As the mare-headed fire I drink up the turbulent
waters, good brahmin, and discharge them again. Brahmindom is my
mouth, baronage my arms, the commoners cling to my thigh, and
the serfs share my feet, because of my puissance and stride. Ṛgveda,
Sāmaveda, Yajurveda, and the Atharvans have come forth from me,
15 and to me they return. The ascetics devoted to serenity, aspiring to
release, who have subdued themselves and are free from lust, ire,
and hatred, detached and without evil, living in a state of purity
beyond self-assertion, and always knowledgeable about matters of the
soul—these brahmins ever contemplate me and wait on me.

I am the Light of Annihilation, I am the Yama of Annihilation, I
am the Sun of Annihilation, I am the Wind of Annihilation. The
stellar forms that are seen in the sky, know, best of the twice-born,
that they are forms of me. The jewel mines are my clothing, the
20 oceans my bed, all of space my dwelling. Know, good brahmin, that
lust, ire, joy, fear, and confusion are all forms of mine, and so is what
men obtain by doing meritorious acts, speaking the truth, making
gifts, performing severe austerities, and harming no creatures. My

injunction is enjoined on all who live in bodies; they act, not by their
own volition, but with their minds controlled by me.

That great reward that the brahmins obtain by learning the *Veda*
perfectly, offering up various sacrifices, mastering themselves, and
conquering their wrath—which, sage, cannot be gained by ill-acting
men who are in the power of their anger, wretched, ignoble, and of
25 unmade souls—know that I am that high reward, the goal of the
man of good deeds, the road chosen by the yogins but closed to the
befuddled. Whenever, sage, the Law languishes and Unlaw rears up,
I create myself. When Daityas bent on harm spring up in this world
invincible to the chiefs of the Gods, and terrifying Rākṣasas, then I
take on birth in the dwellings of the virtuous and, entering a human
body, I appease it all.

After I have created Gods, men, Gandharvas, Snakes and Rākṣasas,
and the unmoving creatures, I destroy them with my own wizardry.
30 When it is time to act, I once more think of a body and, entering
into a human form, create myself to hold the boundaries firm. White
is my color in the Kṛta age, yellow in the Tretā, red when I reach the
Dvāpara, black in the Kali age. At the end of time lawlessness reigns
for three-fourths; and when the age ends, I become most terrifying
Time and by myself destroy the entire universe with moving and
standing creatures. I am the One of the Three Strides, the soul of all,
bringer of happiness to all the worlds, sovereign, omnipresent, the
wide-striding Hṛṣīkesā. I alone set in motion the wheel of Time,
brahmin, I am the formless, the pacification of all creatures, who do
what is best for all the worlds.

35 Thus I have insinuated myself completely into all creatures, good
hermit, Indra of brahmins, yet no one knows me. Whatever hurt you
have felt while within me, brahmin, is all for your greater happiness
and well-being, faultless one. And whatever you have seen of the
moving and standing creation was in every way but myself set up
there, good hermit. The grandfather of all the worlds is half of my
body, I am the one called Nārāyaṇa, who carries the conch, discus,
and club. As the soul of the universe I sleep, the Grandfather of all
40 the worlds, for a full revolution of a thousand Eons. All that time I
stay here, good hermit, not a child though disguised as one, until
Brahmā wakes up. I have often been pleased with you, who are
adored by the hosts of brahmin seers, and in my form of Brahmā I
gave you a boon, brahmin. After seeing all of the universe flooded to
a single ocean, with all the firm and the quick gone, you became
alarmed. I knew it, so I showed you the universe. You entered inside
my body, and, seeing all the world together there, you were amazed
and did not understand; hence I translated you quickly from my
mouth, brahmin seer, and declared myself to you, however difficult I
am to know for Gods and Asuras.

45 Wander happily and confidently here, brahmin seer, until the
austere lord Brahmā awakes. When he has wakened, the Grandfather
of all worlds, good brahmin, I shall as one create from this my body
space, earth, light, wind, and water, and whatever else there be in
the world, firm or quick.

Mārkaṇḍeya said:

After he has spoken thus, my son, that most wondrous God
vanishes and I foresee these creatures, of many kinds and of many
makes.

This I witness, king, when the end of the Eon comes, this wonder,
50 O best of the Bharatas, first of the upholders of the Law. The God
whom I have seen before, of the lotus-like eyes, he, tiger among men,
is your ally Janārdana. Because of boons he bestowed upon me my
memory has not deserted me, and I have title to a long life and to
death at my choosing, Kaunteya. That primeval person, the
ubiquitous lord, is Kṛṣṇa Vārṣṇeya, the strong-armed Hari of
unimaginable soul, who sits here as though at play. This Sātvata is
the Placer and Disposer and Destroyer, this Govinda of the Śrīvatsa
curl is the sovereign master of the Prajāpatis. When I saw the tigerlike Vṛṣṇi, this memory returned to me: that he is the unborn God of
55 the beginning, Viṣṇu, the Person of the yellow robe. The Mādhava is
the father and the mother of all the creatures: bulls of the Bharatas,
go to him for refuge, he shall grant it!

Vaiśaṃpāyana said:

188.1 After this address the Pārthas and the bull-like twins, together with
Kṛṣṇā Draupadī, bowed to Janārdana; he, in turn, O tiger among
men, with the sweetest grace comforted them in the correct fashion,
for he deemed them worthy of high honor. Yudhiṣṭhira Kaunteya
questioned the great hermit Mārkaṇḍeya again about the future
course of the world under his sovereignty.

"We have heard from you, eloquent Bhārgava seer, the wondrous
5 origin and destruction that occur at the turn of the Eon. Now, I am
curious about the Kali age too: what will be left when all the Laws
are confused? What vigor will men possess, what diets and pleasures
will they have, how long will they live, what dress will they wear at
the end of the Eon? After what end mark will the Kṛta age rise again?
Tell it fully, hermit: you tell here all manner of tales!"

At his words that best of hermits once more spoke in order to
please the tiger-like Vṛṣṇi and the Pāṇḍavas.

Mārkaṇḍeya said:

Listen to me, bull of the Bharatas, as I tell of the future of all the
world when it comes upon its time of troubles.

10 Of yore, in the Kṛta age, the Law was potent among men, intact
in all its four quarters, without guile and devoid of obstruction. In the

Tretā age the Law lost one quarter, but was still established; in the
Dvāpara age the Law, it is said, was mixed half and half. Now
lawlessness has overrun the world, three-quarters rampant, but a
quarter of the Law has stayed with men. Learn this from me: age
after age in man's lifetime virility, wisdom, strength, and influence
shrink by one-fourth, Pāṇḍava. Kings, brahmins, commoners, and
15 serfs will only pretend at their Law and be hypocrites. People who
think of themselves as learned will abbreviate the truth, others will
kill the truth; hence their lifetime will be shortened. Their shorter
lives will not allow them to teach knowledge in full, and those who
fall short in knowledge will be beset by greed because of their
ignorance. A prey to greed and ire, confused, addicted to pleasures,
men will be locked in rivalry and wish each other dead.

Brahmins, barons, and commoners will mix marriages and become
like serfs, without austerity or truth. The lowest will rise to the middle
ranks, the middle ones will end up at the bottom; that is to be the
20 way of the world when the end of the Eon is at hand. Hemp will be
the best of textiles, poor man's grain the best of crops, and men shall
be the enemies of their wives at the end of the Eon. People will live
on fish, bad meat, and milk goats and ewes, for the cows will have
perished at the end of the Eon. Men will rob and harm one another,
they will be prayerless, creedless, and thievish at the close of the
Eon. They will have the river banks dug up with spades and sown
with herbs, and the herbs shall yield little fruit at the end of the Eon.
Men who had always been firm in their vows at a *śrāddha* or sacrifice
25 will be harnessed with greed and exploit one another. Father shall
exploit son, and the son his father, and proper uses shall be
transgressed at the end of the Eon. The brahmins shall find fault with
the *Veda* and abandon their vows; seduced by argumentations, they
will offer neither worship nor sacrifices. People will plow in the
lowlands, put milch cows to the yoke, and drive calves of one year
old. Son may kill father, father may kill son, but, undisturbed and
talking big, neither will be blamed. The entire world will be
barbarized, without rites and sacrifices, without joy, without feasts.
30 As a rule, people will rob the possessions of the poor, and even of
kinsmen and widows. Enfeebled, puffed up, enslaved to greed and
folly, they will be delighted with gifts in name only even from the
wicked and take possession, while possessed by their own evil ways.
Ill-intentioned kings will hire assassins, Kaunteya, and foolishly,
though thinking themselves wise, prepare for reciprocal murder—
the barons at the end of the Eon will be the thorns of the earth;
giving no protection, greedy, prideful, and egotistic, they will only
rejoice in punishment at the end of the Eon. Mercilessly, Bhārata,
they will time and again violate and enjoy the wives and the property

35 of the good, weep though they may. No one proposes for a maiden,
no one gives one away: they will all grab for themselves, when the
end of the Eon is at hand. The kings, too, being befuddled in their
minds, will by any and all means steal the property of others, when
the end of the Eon is at hand. All the world will be barbarized,
Bhārata, and one hand will rob the other, when the end of the Eon
is at hand. Men who think they are learned will abbreviate the truth,
the aged will think as children and children as the old. The timid
pretending to be brave and the brave collapsing timorously will not
inspire confidence in each other, when the end of the Eon is at hand.
40 The entire world will eat the same food, in a frenzy of greed and
folly; lawlessness looms large, no Law prevails.

No brahmins, barons, or commoners will be left, overlord of men:
the world will all be one class at the end of the Eon. No father will
condone his son, no son his father, and not a wife will be obedient to
her husband. People will migrate to barley- and wheat-eating
countries, when the end of the Eon is at hand. Eating whatever they
please, lord of your people, men and women will not tolerate each
45 other, when the end of the Eon is at hand. Yudhiṣṭhira, the entire
world will have become barbarous, for people won't even satisfy their
ancestors with *śrāddhas*. No one will be anyone's student or anyone's
guru, the world will be swallowed by the darkness of ignorance, lord
of men. Life will at most last sixteen years, then they will give up the
breath, when the end of the Eon is at hand. Girls will give birth in
their fifth or sixth year, and boys will be fathers at seven and eight.
Husband and wife will find no satisfaction in each other, O tiger
50 among men, at the end of the Eon. People will be poor and wear false
emblems, harmfulness will prevail, and no one will be anyone's
benefactor at the end of the Eon. The countrysides will bristle with
towers, the crossroads with jackals, and the women with hair, at the
end of the Eon.

At the end of time all men—there is no doubt—will be omnivorous
barbarians, cruel in all their deeds. When it is time to buy or sell,
best of Bharatas, everyone will cheat the other out of greed for a
livelihood at the end of the Eon. Without having the right knowledge
they will perform the rites and carry on with their own whimsy,
55 when the end of the Eon is at hand. All people will be naturally cruel
in their deeds and suspicious of one another, when the end of the
Eon comes. Without concern they will destroy parks and trees, and
the life of the living will be ruined in the world. Slaves of greed, they
will roam this earth, become brahmins, and exploit the possessions
of brahmindom. Crying fie, the twice-born, fearful and oppressed by
the serfs, will wander upon this earth without finding a savior. When
men become gruesome and cruel murderers and harmers of living

60 beings, then the Eon will be brought to an end. The terrified twice-
born will run and seek refuge, scion of Kuru's line, by rivers, in
mountains and rough terrain. The brahmins will become like crows,
king, as they are oppressed by the Dasyus and are constantly
oppressed by evil kings with the burden of taxes; and giving up their
poise, O prince, at the dreadful collapse of the Eon, they will perform
the wrong rites as servitors of serfs. Serfs will propound the Laws;
and the brahmins, their servants, will become their pupils and abide
by their authority.

This world will be totally upside down: people will abandon the
Gods and worship charnel houses, and the serfs will refuse to serve
65 the twice-born at the collapse of the Eon. In the hermitages of the
great seers, in the settlements of brahmins, at the temples and
sanctuaries, in the lairs of the Snakes, the earth will be marked by
charnel houses, not adorned by the houses of the Gods, when the
Eon expires, and that shall be the sign of the end of the Eon. When
men become for good gruesome and lawless meat eaters and liquor
drinkers, the Eon will collapse. When flower procreates in flower,
and fruit in fruit, then, great king, the Eon will collapse. When the
Eon goes, the Rain God will not rain in season, men's rites will be
70 out of step, and serfs will feud with brahmins. The earth will soon be
overrun by barbarians, while the brahmins, out of fear of the tax
burden, flee in all ten directions. All countries will equally suffer from
drought, and the people, living on fruit and roots, will fall upon the
hermitages. In this turbulent time there will be no limits, pupils will
not abide by their instructions, but act disagreeably; thereafter the
teacher will live without charges, friends; kinsmen and relatives will
depart for the sake of gain; and all the creatures will come to
nothing at the end of the Eon. All of space will blaze up, the
constellations will move, the stars will bode evil, the winds will be
turbulent, and there will be many showers, betokening great danger.
75 The sun will burn with six others, everywhere there will be terrifying
thunder and conflagrations, twilight clouds will obscure the sun at
dawn and dusk. The thousand-eyed God will not rain in season, and
the crops will not grow, when the end of the Eon is at hand.

The women will at all times be harsh and rough-spoken and quick
to cry, and they will fail to obey their husbands. Sons will kill their
fathers and mothers at the end of the Eon, women will kill their
husbands and rely on their sons. Rāhu will eclipse the sun at the
wrong time, great king, and at the end of the Eon fire will blaze up
80 everywhere. Travelers may ask but will receive no water, food, or
shelter and, cast out, sleep on the road. Crows of ill omen, snakes,
birds, game, and fowl will screech awfully, when the end of the Eon
is at hand. Friends and relations will abandon their folk and

surroundings, when the end of the Eon is at hand. They will gradually
seek refuge in other countries, regions, settlements, and towns.
People will wander over earth, piteously crying out to one another,
"Ah, father, ah, son!"
85 Then, when the Eon is closing amidst terrifying destruction, the
world begins gradually to regenerate from the brahmins onward. At
this time fate once more turns favorable in order to prosper the world
again. When sun, moon, Tiṣya, and Jupiter are in conjunction in the
same sign of the zodiac, the Kṛta age will begin again. Parjanya rains
in season, the stars are favorable, and the planets, making their orbit,
are propitious. There will be safety, plenty of food, and health without
sickness. A brahmin by the name of Kalki Viṣṇuyaśas will arise,
prodded by Time, of great prowess, wisdom, and might. He will be
90 born in the village Sambhala, in a pious brahmin dwelling, and at his
mere thought all vehicles, weapons, warriors, arms, and coats of mail
will wait on him. He will be king, a Turner of the Wheel, triumphant
by the Law, and he will bring this turbulent world to tranquillity.
That rising brahmin, blazing, ending the destruction, noble-minded,
will be the destruction of all and the revolver of the Eon. Surrounded
by brahmins, that brahmin will extirpate all the lowly barbarians,
wherever they are.

Mārkaṇḍeya said:

189.1 After destroying the robbers he will ritually make over this earth
to the twice-born at a grand celebration of the Horse Sacrifice. He will
reestablish the sacred limits that the Self-existent one has ordained,
and, when he has grown old in works of holy fame, he will retire to
the forest. People who live in the world will follow his habit, and,
with the robbers destroyed by the brahmins, safety will prevail.
Establishing the black antelope skins, the spears, the tridents, and the
emblematic arms in the conquered territories, that tiger-like brahmin,
5 Kalki, praised by the chief brahmins and honoring their leaders, shall
walk the earth, forever bent upon the slaughter of the Dasyus. Now
the Dasyus are wailing piteously, "Ah, father, ah, son!" as he leads
them to their perdition.

Lawlessness will decline and Law increase, Bhārata, and the people
will observe the rites when the Kṛta age arrives. Resting-places,
sanctuaries, temple tanks, wells, and the many ceremonies reappear
in the Kṛta age. The brahmins will be strict, the hermits will be
ascetic, the hermitages, heretical of late, will abide by the truth, the
10 people will be subjects. When sown all seeds will grow, and in all
seasons, O Indra among kings, all crops will wax. Men will be ready
to give, to make vows, and follow observances, the brahmins will be
prone to prayer and sacrifice, always desire the Law, and rejoice;

and the princes will guard this treasure-filled earth according to the Law. The commoners will be devoted to their affairs in the Kṛta age, the brahmins devoted to their six tasks, the barons to giving protection, the serfs to obedience to the three classes.

Such is the Law in the Kṛta age, the Tretā, the Dvāpara, and the last phase of the Eon, which I have proclaimed to you. The numbers of the Eon are known to all the world, Pāṇḍava: I have declared to you all that is past and future, as I remember the Lore, lauded by the
15 seers, that was promulgated by the Wind God. Long-lived as I am, I have often witnessed and experienced the pathways of transmigration, and I have told them to you.

Now listen to these other words of mine, you and your brothers, unvanquished one, which will set you free from doubts concerning the Law. Always embrace the Law, chief upholder of the Law, for a Law-spirited king enjoys happiness, here and hereafter. Listen to the sacred message that I shall declare to you, prince sans blame: never oppress a brahmin, for an offended brahmin will destroy the worlds by his mere promise!

Vaiśaṃpāyana said:

His superbly lustrous majesty, the most eminent of the Kurus,
20 heard the words of Mārkaṇḍeya and made this important reply: "If I am to protect my subjects, hermit, what Law should I observe? How must I behave lest I be apostate from my own Law?"

Mārkaṇḍeya said:

Have compassion and profit all creatures lovingly, contentedly, and devote yourself to your subjects as though they were your children. Heed the Law, shun Unlaw, honor the fathers and the Gods, and repair what you neglected to do with an appropriate gift. Be done with pride, be humble. And this sums up the Law that was and shall be.

You know all that is past and future on earth, so, my son, do not
25 worry so much in your heart. This time is Time for all the celestials too—the creatures are confused, my son, they are being urged on by Time. Do not hesitate too much about the matters I speak to you, prince sans blame: you will lose Law by too great a doubt of my words.

Bull of the Bharatas, you have been born in the famous dynasty of the Kurus, now practice it all in deed, in thought, and in speech.

Yudhiṣṭhira said:

I shall try my best to carry out your teaching, my lord, just as you have told it in words that fetch both ear and heart, best of brahmins! I have no greed, great brahmin, no fear, no envy—I shall do all that you have told me, my lord.

Vaiśaṃpāyana said:

30 Hearing the reply of the great-spirited Pāṇḍava, all the Pāṇḍavas and the Śārnga bowman* rejoiced, O king. Having heard the sacred discourses of the sage Mārkaṇḍeya, they were greatly astonished upon learning the Lore.

3(37.b) The Frog

190 (B. 192; C. 13143–211)
190 (192; 13143). The Ikṣvāku king Parikṣit finds a lovely pond in the woods; he bathes and explores the bank (1–5). He hears a song and finds a maiden; the king desires her (5–10). He may have her, if he never shows her water; he takes her home and is absorbed in her (15–20). The king's minister builds a waterless park for the couple, where they play (20–25). There is a water pool camouflaged with a layer of stucco; when the woman descends into the water she disappears; only a frog is found (25–30). The king orders all frogs killed (30). The king of the frogs pleads with him; the king will not desist, for the frogs have killed his beloved (30–35). The frog king identifies the maiden as his daughter; she has played a trick on the king, but he still wants her; the frog gives her up (35–45). The king has Śala and two other sons. Śala, out hunting, borrows the horses of the sage Vāmadeva and refuses to return them (40–55). Vāmadeva appears before the king and they argue; Vāmadeva has Śala cut down by Rākṣasas (60–65). His brother Dala is anointed; when he tries to shoot Vāmadeva, he kills his own son; when about to shoot a second time, Vāmadeva stifles him (65–75). Vāmadeva grants Dala's wife a boon; she chooses that Dala be free from guilt (75–80).

Vaiśaṃpāyana said:

190.1 Once more the Pāṇḍava said to Mārkaṇḍeya, "Pray tell of the lordliness of the brahmin!" So Mārkaṇḍeya narrated.

* = Kṛṣṇa.

A king born in the line of Ikṣvāku at Ayodhyā, Parikṣit by name, went hunting. He had one horse as he pursued a deer, and the deer took him far. He became tired on the way, and hungry and thirsty, then he spied somewhere a shady cluster of trees. He entered it. In the middle of the grove of trees he saw a surpassingly lovely pond, and he and his horse dipped in the water. Refreshed, the king placed lotus fibers before his horse, then explored the bank of the lotus lake. He lay down there and heard a lovely song. The hearing of it set him a-wondering: "I do not see any man's track here. Now who is singing?"

Then he saw a maiden of exceedingly beautiful shape who was plucking flowers and singing. She progressed to the king's presence. Said the king, "Whose are you, my lovely?" She replied, "I am a virgin." Quoth the king, "I want you." The maiden replied, "You can have me on only one condition." The king asked for the condition, so the maiden said, "Never show me water." The king said, "Never!" and won her and sat with her. While the king was sitting there, his escort came up behind. They had followed his footsteps and stood by the king and waited. Fully rested, the king departed with her in a litter; she was still intact. Upon reaching his town he lived with her in secret and looked at nothing else.

The chief minister interrogated the women of the king's retinue: "What is the meaning of this?" Said the women, "We saw something new: no water gets brought here." So the minister had a park without water built, nobly wooded, with plenty of roots, blossoms, and fruit, then he came to the king privately and said, "Here is a noble, waterless park. Do enjoy yourself here happily." So, at his bidding, in he went, into the park with the queen. One day he strolled with her in that lovely park. He got hungry, thirsty, and tired, and he saw an extraordinary grove of *atimuktas*. He entered it, the king, with his beloved, and he saw a pond full of pure water, but covered with a layer of stucco. No sooner did the king see it than he descended into it with his beloved down the pond's rim. Quoth king to queen, "Come, descend into the water of the pond!"

She heard his words, descended, and plunged into the pond. She did not come up again. The king searched for her, but did not find her. He emptied the pond and found a frog in the mouth of a chasm. He passed out stern orders, "Kill all the frogs! Whoever wants something from me better attend with a gift of dead frogs."

As the grisly massacre of frogs went on, fear invaded the frogs everywhere. The frightened animals conveyed to the frog king what was happening. Thereupon the frog king put on an ascetic's garb and went to the king. He approached and said, "Sire, do not fall prey to wrath! Have mercy, you must not massacre the frogs, which are innocent. There are two couplets on this:

"Do not wish to kill the frogs,
Hold your wrath, victorious king!
Dwindle will their plentiful wealth
If men wish to be ignorant.

"Pledge that when you happen to meet them
You will withhold your anger from them.
Stop the lawlessness perpetrated,
What good are slaughtered frogs to you?"

The king, whose soul was encompassed by grief over his beloved, replied to the frog, "I cannot forgive it. I shall kill them! These wicked creatures have devoured my beloved. I have doomed the frogs in any case, pray do not obstruct me, sage!" Hearing his word, the frog replied with perturbed heart and senses: "Have mercy, sire! I am the frog king called Āyu. She is my daughter Suśobhanā. She has this bad streak: many are the kings she has deceived before." Said the king, "I want her, give her to me!" The father gave her to the king and said to her, "Obey the king!" And he also said to his daughter, "Since you have deceived kings, your children shall be unbrahminic because of your mendacity."

And having obtained her, the king in his heart fastened on the excellence of his love making with her, and feeling as though he had won the sovereignty of the three worlds, prostrated himself and honored the frog king, saying in a voice choked with tears of joy, "I have been favored!" The frog king took his leave from his son-in-law, and went as he had come.

After a while that king had three boys by her, Śala, Dala, and Bala. The father consecrated Śala, the eldest of them, and, as his soul was bent on austerity, he departed to the forest. This Śala once went hunting. He found himself a stag and pursued it on his chariot. He said to his driver, "Drive me faster!" The driver replied to the king, "Do not insist. You could not catch this stag even if you had the Vāmya horses yoked to your chariot." Said the king to his charioteer, "Tell me about the Vāmya horses, or I'll kill you." At these words he said to the king, equally afraid of the king's danger as of Vāmadeva's curse, "The Vāmyas are Vāmadeva's horses, and fast as thought."

Thereupon the king said to him, "Go to Vāmadeva's hermitage." He went to Vāmadeva's hermitage and said to the seer, "Reverend, a stag I hit ran off. I must recover it. Pray give me your Vāmyas." The seer said, "I will give you the Vāmyas. When you are done, return them to me at once." He took both the horses, took his leave of the seer, and started out after the stag on his chariot, which was now yoked with the Vāmyas. As he went he said to his charioteer, "These horses are jewels! They do not become a brahmin. I am not going to return them to Vāmadeva." He spoke, caught the stag, returned to his city, and stabled both horses by the women's quarters.

Now the seer thought, "This young prince has got himself fine
55 horseflesh and enjoys it. He won't return them to me. Ah, the bother
of it!" Having thought upon it, he told his pupil when the month was
full, "Go there, Ātreya. Tell the king: 'If you are done, return my
teacher's Vāmyas.'" He went and told the king. The king replied,
"This is royal horseflesh. Brahmins do not rate such gems. What
would brahmins do with horses? You'd better go back." He went and
told his teacher. Hearing this unpleasant message, Vāmadeva was
deeply angry. He went himself to the king and demanded his horses.
The king refused.

Vāmadeva said:

60 Return, my king, my horses to me—
You have done what others cannot do—
Lest Varuṇa kill you with terrible nooses:
You are splitting brahmin from baronage.

The king said:

A brahmin's proper mount, Vāmadeva,
Are these two well-trained and docile bullocks.
Drive them wherever you wish, great seer,
The *Vedas* carry a man like you.

Vāmadeva said:

The *Vedas* carry a man like me,
But they are in the world hereafter, king.
In the present world these are my mounts,
And those of others like me, my liege.

The king said:

Then let four donkeys drive you, sir,
Or excellent mules, or bay-colored horses.
Drive those, but the Vāmyas deserve a baron
Like me, for, look, they cannot be yours!

Vāmadeva said:

They say that a brahmin's vow is awesome:
If I have lived by such a vow here, king,
Then terrible giants with iron bodies
And sharpened pikes will quarter you!

The king said:

65 Those who know that you, Vāmadeva, a brahmin,
Are ready to kill with deed, word, and thought,
Let them cut you down and your pupil too,
At my behest, with their sharpened spikes.

Vāmadeva said:

A brahmin is not to be questioned, king,
In either deed, or word, or thought.
But the sage who has reached the Brahman with penance
Can humble the pride of even the best!

Mārkaṇḍeya said:

When Vāmadeva had spoken thus,
Terrible Rākṣasas rose, O king,
And the king, being struck by the spike-armed ogres,
Declared this word then, loud of voice:

"If all the Ikṣvākus, brahmin, and Dala
And the commoners are to be ruled by me,
I cannot release, Vāmadeva, the Vāmyas,
For they are by no means law-abiding men."

He was still speaking when the Rākṣasas
Struck his royal person and he fell on the ground.
And learning their king had been cut down
The Ikṣvākus anointed Dala king.

70 The brahmin went to the kingdom then,
And Vāmadeva declared this word
To Dala the king: "That the brahmins be gifted,
That, king, is taught among all the Laws.

"If you fear to transgress the Law, O king,
I now demand the Vāmyas back!"
On hearing the words of Vāmadeva
The king spoke angrily to his driver:

"Go fetch me one of the colorful arrows
I keep, and dip it in poison, man.
Pierced by it Vāmadeva shall lie
And be painfully torn apart by the dogs!"

Vāmadeva said:

You have a son who is ten years old,
Born by your queen, king, Śyenajit:
At the goad of my word you shall kill him now,
Your beloved son, with your terrible arrows.

Mārkaṇḍeya said:
As commanded by Vāmadeva, O king,
That arrow of fiery force shot down
The son of the king in the women's quarters
When Dala released it; and learning this

75 The king said: "Ikṣvākus, I do you a favor,
I destroy this brahmin and kill him off.
Go fetch me another fiery arrow
And watch my bravery, lords of the earth!"

Vāmadeva said:
This terrible arrow, dipped in poison
You have put on the bow and now aim at me,
This masterful arrow you shall be unable
To shoot or even to aim, king of men!

The king said:
Ikṣvākus, behold, I am caught! I stand
Unable to shoot this arrow at all!
I cannot attempt the killing of him.
Let the long-lived Vāmadeva live!

Vāmadeva said:
Now touch your queen with this arrow, king,
Thereupon you shall be free from your guilt.

Mārkaṇḍeya said:
The king then did as he was bidden to do;
And the princess spoke these words to the hermit:

"If, Vāmadeva, I have praised my husband,
And day after day have lain with him,
And have sought the favors of brahmins, brahmin,
So may I obtain the world of the pious!"

Vāmadeva said:
80 You have saved the race of the king, fair-eyed one!
Choose a matchless boon, I shall give it to you.
Rule, faultless princess, your relatives
And all the vast kingdom of the Ikṣvākus.

The princess said:
This single boon I choose, my lord,
That my husband now be free from his guilt,
And that you think well of him and his kin,
For this is the boon I choose, great brahmin.

Mārkaṇḍeya said:

On hearing the princess's word the hermit
Said "So shall it be!" O bravest of Kurus.
And the king became joyous, and with a bow
Returned to him the Vāmya horses.

3(37.c) Indradyumna

191 (B. 199; C. 13331–48)
191 (199; 13331). The ancient King Indradyumna falls from heaven, because no one remembers his renown. He asks Mārkaṇḍeya whether he recognizes him. Mārkaṇḍeya refers him to an owl in the Himālaya. Changing into a horse, Indradyumna takes Mārkaṇḍeya there (1–5). The owl refers him to a crane in Lake Indradyumna; they all go to the crane, which refers them to a tortoise in the same lake (5–10). The tortoise recognizes the king, and a divine chariot appears to take Indradyumna back to heaven (15–25).

Vaiśaṃpāyana said:

191.1 The seers and the Pāṇḍavas questioned Mārkaṇḍeya, "Is there anyone longer-lived than you?" He said to them:

Well, there is the royal seer Indradyumna. When his merit was exhausted, he fell from heaven. "Thy fame has become extinct," they said. He came to me: "Do you recognize me, sir?" I told him, "We are not alchemists, we pursue our goals by suppressing our body. But there is an owl in the Himālaya by the name of Prākārakarṇa. Mayhap he will know you. The Himālaya is quite a ways, but there he lives."

5 He became a horse and carried me to where that owl was. The royal seer interrogated it: "Do you recognize me, sir?" It thought a while, then replied, "No, I do not recognize you." At this reply the royal seer Indradyumna again said to the owl, "Is there anyone longer-lived than you?" Replied the owl, "Well, there is a lake called Indradyumna's lake. A crane lives there, by the name of Naḍījangha. He is older than we. Ask him."

10 Indradyumna took me and the owl and went to that lake where that crane called Naḍījangha lived. It was questioned by us: "Sir, do

you recognize King Indradyumna?" It thought a while. "No, I don't recognize King Indradyumna." We asked of him, "Is there anyone older than you?" It replied, "Well, here in this lake lives a tortoise by the name of Akūpāra; he is my senior." Said we, "Mayhap he will recognize the king, let us ask that Akūpāra."

15 The crane then addressed the tortoise Akūpāra. "There is some
matter we wish to ask you about. Be good enough to come." The
tortoise heard, emerged from the lake, and arrived where we were
standing on the bank of the lake. When it had come we asked it,
"Sir, do you recognize King Indradyumna?" It thought a while, then
its eyes filled with tears. With a fluttering heart, trembling and almost
fainting, it said, folding its limbs, "How could I fail to recognize him?
For a thousand times of yore he piled upon me his fire altars! This
very lake was created by the trod of the cattle he gave away as
stipend. And now I still live in it."

No sooner did we hear the utterance of the tortoise than a divine
20 chariot appeared from the world of the Gods, and words were heard
regarding Indradyumna: "Heaven has begun for thee! Return to the
place to which thou art wonted. Thou hast fame. Go unconcerned.

"The sound of good deeds echoes to heaven and earth—
As long as the sound lasts, so long lasts man.
Whatever creature's infamy is known on earth
He falls to the nethermost world as long as it is bruited.
So a man on earth should do good till the end,
Shun criminal acts, and work by the Law."

On hearing this the king said, "Wait until I have returned these
25 elders to their sites." He returned me and the owl Prākārakarṇa to
our accustomed place and himself returned on that same chariot
successfully to his wonted place. That is what I witnessed, long-lived
as I am.

This was what Mārkaṇḍeya narrated to the Pāṇḍavas. And the Pāṇḍavas said happily, "Good! You did well to restore King Indradyumna to his proper place when he had fallen from the world of heaven!" He replied to them, "But did Devakī's son Kṛṣṇa not also rescue the royal seer Nṛga, when he was sinking in hell, and returned him again from his distress to heaven?"

3(37.d) Dhundhumāra

192–95 (B. 201–4; C. 13483–628)
192 (2011; 13483). Yudhiṣṭhira asks about Kuvalāśva's

change of name to Dhundhumāra (1–5). The seer Utanka propitiates Viṣṇu, who appears before him and is lauded (5–20). Viṣṇu gives him a boon; he asks for high morality. Viṣṇu also gives him a Yoga by which King Kuvalāśva will kill the demon Dhundhu (20–25).
193 (202; 13516). The genealogy of Kuvalāśva, whose father Bṛhadaśva wishes to retire (1–5). Utanka tries to prevent his retirement by pointing to his duties: in the desert Ujjānaka lives the Dānava Dhundhu, who causes earthquakes and disturbs Utanka; Bṛhadaśva should kill him (5–25).
194 (203; 13546). Bṛhadaśva assigns this task to Kuvalāśva (1–5). At the end of the Eon Viṣṇu sleeps on Śeṣa in the ocean; a lotus sprouts from his navel, in which Brahmā is born. The demons Madhu and Kaitabha see Brahmā and intimidate him. Viṣṇu wakes up and grants the two a boon, but they would rather give him a boon (5–20). Viṣṇu chooses that he kill them; they agree on the condition that the site of the killing be covered; the only such place is his own covered loins, and he kills them with his discus (20–30).
195 (204; 13583). Madhu's and Kaitabha's son Dhundhu practices austerities. Brahmā gives him a boon; he chooses invincibility—except by humans (1). He assaults Viṣṇu in revenge for his parents' death. He lives underground in the desert Ujjānaka and puts pressure on Utanka's hermitage (5). King Kuvalāśva rides out to kill him. His sons dig up the desert and find Dhundhu, who sets them on fire (10–25). Kuvalāśva oozes water that douses Dhundhu's fire and burns him: hence he is known as Dhundhumāra (25). The Gods grant him a boon; he chooses Viṣṇu's friendship (30–35).

Vaiśaṃpāyana said:
192.1 Yudhiṣṭhira the King Dharma, O bull of the Bharatas, put a
question to the long-lived and sinless Mārkaṇḍeya, who had grown
old in austerities: "You know, Law-wise sage, the Gods, Dānavas,
and Rākṣasas, the various royal dynasties, and the eternal lineages of
the seers. There is nothing in this world that is unknown to you, best
of the twice-born. You know, hermit, the divine story of men, Snakes,
and Rākṣasas. Now, I wish to hear you tell truthfully, brahmin, why
the unvanquished Ikṣvāku called Kuvalāśva by a change of name
5 became Dhundhumāra. This I wish to hear, best of the Bhṛgus, why
in truth the wise Kuvalāśva's name was changed.

Mārkaṇḍeya said:

Aye, I shall tell you that most lawly story of Dhundhumāra, listen, King Yudhiṣṭhira, how the Ikṣvāku king Kuvalāśva became Dhundhumāra.

There was a famous seer by the name of Utanka, O Bhārata my son, and his hermitage was in the lovely desert sands, Kaurava. This Utanka, great king, performed the most difficult austerities for many periods of years, as he wished to propitiate Viṣṇu. Pleased with him the adorable God appeared to him in person; and on seeing him the seer, prostrate, praised him with various lauds: "By thee, O God, have been created all the creatures, with Gods, Asuras, and men, the beings that stand still and those that move about, Brahman, the *Vedas* and all that is knowable, lustrous deity. Heaven is thy head, God, sun and moon thine eyes, the wind thy breath, and fire thy glow, Acyuta; the four regions are thine arms, the great ocean thy belly, the mountains thy thighs, God, the sky thy navel, Madhusūdana, Goddess Earth thy feet, the herbs thy body hair. Indra, Soma, Agni, and Varuṇa, the Gods, Asuras, and great Snakes attend on thee prostrate, as they praise thee with various lauds. Thou pervadest all creatures, lord of the universe; the most powerful yogins and great seers praise thee. When thou art contented, all the world is breathing; but in great danger, when thou art angered: thou alone art the remover of dangers, supreme Person. Thou bringst happiness to Gods, men, and all beings. With thy three strides, O God, thou hast fetched the three worlds and spelled the perdition of the prosperous Asuras. Through thy strides the Gods have gone to supreme bliss, the Daitya chiefs to defeat at your wrath, lustrous God. For thou art the maker and divider of all creatures here. By placating thee all Gods aspire to happiness."

Having been thus praised by the great-spirited Utanka, Viṣṇu Hṛṣīkeśa said to him, "I am pleased with you, choose a boon!"

Utanka said:

Sufficient boon is it to me that I have seen Hari, the everlasting Person, divine creator of the world, the lord!

Viṣṇu said:

"I am pleased with your constancy and loyalty, best of brahmins. But you certainly must take a boon from me, brahmin!" Plied with a boon by Hari, Utanka folded his hands and chose a boon, best of Bharatas: "Adorable God of the lotus-like eyes, if thou art pleased with me, then let my resolve be fixed on the Law, truth, and self-control for ever and ever, and my habits be those of eternal devotion to you, great lord."

Viṣṇu said:
25 All this shall befall by my grace, brahmin. A Yoga shall become
manifest, yoked with which you shall accomplish a great task for the
celestials and all three worlds. A great Asura named Dhundhu is
performing terrifying austerities in order to extirpate the worlds, and
you shall kill him. Listen. There shall be a king famed as Bṛhadaśva
who shall have an obedient and pure son known as Kuvalāśva. This
excellent prince shall resort to my yoga power and at your command
become Dhundhumāra, the Slayer of Dhundhu.
Mārkaṇḍeya said:
And having spoken thus to Utanka, Viṣṇu disappeared.

Mārkaṇḍeya said:
193.1 After Ikṣvāku's funeral, Śaśāda inherited the land, O king, and,
being supremely Law-spirited, became king at Ayodhyā. Kakutstha
was Śaśāda's heir and a powerful prince. Anenas succeeded
Kakutstha, and Anenas's son was Pṛthu. Pṛthu's scion was
Viṣvagaśva, from whom descended the wise Ārdra, who had
Yuvanāśva, whose son was Śrāvasta, the king who built Śrāvasti.
Śrāvasta's heir was the mighty Bṛhadaśva, and Kuvalāśva is
5 remembered as Bṛhadaśva's son. Kuvalāśva had twenty-one thousand
sons, all steeped in knowledge, powerful, and unassailable.

Now, Kuvalāśva surpassed his father in talents, and Bṛhadaśva anointed this heroic, greatly Law-loving Kuvalāśva to the kingdom at the appointed time, great king. King Bṛhadaśva, having transferred the fortune to his son, went wisely to the wilderness of austerities for mortification, this killer of his enemies.

Utanka, that great brahmin, heard that the royal seer Bṛhadaśva had departed for the forest, King Yudhiṣṭhira; and the splendid Utanka of measureless soul approached the great man, who was first among the experts of all weaponry, and restrained him.

Utanka said:
10 Your task is to protect, therefore, pray, do that first of all. By your
grace, king, we may live without fear. As long as you great-spiritedly
protect the earth, king, it will remain fearless—do not go to the
forest! For the main Law is found to lie here in the protection of the
subjects, it is not equally found in the forest: therefore abandon such
a resolution. No greater Law is found anywhere, Indra of kings, than
that which the royal seers have always observed by protecting their
subjects. Deign to protect those subjects who deserve protection from
their king.

Indeed, I myself am no longer able to observe my austerities
15 unobstructed, king: close by my hermitage in the desert flats there is

a sea of sand known as Ujjānaka, many leagues in length and width.
There lives a terrible and dangerous Dānava lord of great bravery
and prowess, a son of Madhu and Kaitabha, Dhundu by name. He
lives under the ground, and his puissance is boundless. Slay him,
great king; later repair to the forest. He lies there performing gruesome
austerities to ruin the world and to destroy the Thirty and the worlds.
He cannot be killed by Gods, Daityas, and Rākṣasas, or any of the
Snakes, Yakṣas, and Gandharvas, as he has obtained that boon from
20 the Grandfather of all the worlds, O king. Destroy him, hail to thee,
do not resolve otherwise, and you shall win great everlasting fame,
firm and never to fade. When at the end of the year that ogre, who
sleeps under the sands, heaves a sigh, the entire earth, with
mountains, forest, and wilderness, trembles. The wind of his sigh
raises a huge dust cloud that covers the path of the sun, and the
earthquake lasts for seven days, with sparks and flames and smoke—
most terrifying.

That is the reason why I cannot remain in my own hermitage.
Destroy him, Indra of kings, for the good of the world: let the worlds
be healthy again when that Asura has been slain; for I deem you
sufficient to the slaying of him. Viṣṇu shall replenish your fiery force
25 with his own. Viṣṇu once gave me his boon for his destruction: that
whichever king would slay that great grisly Asura would be pervaded
by Viṣṇu's own unassailable force. Take that fiery force, king, which
is unsupportable on earth, kill the evil Daitya of gruesome prowess:
for not even in hundreds of years can the mighty Dhundhu be
burned up with but a little fiery force.

Mārkaṇḍeya said:

194.1 At these words of Utanka, the unvanquished royal seer folded his
hands and replied, O best of the Kauravas, "Your coming shall not
remain fruitless, brahmin. I have a son, reverend sir, who is known
as Kuvalāśva, persevering and quick to act, whose bravery has no
match in the world. He shall accomplish this entire desire of yours,
no doubt of that, amidst all his heroic sons, who are armed with
5 clubs. Dismiss me, brahmin, for now I have laid down my weapons."
The boundlessly lustrous hermit said, "So be it then." And after
directing his son to the great-spirited Utanka, saying, "Carry it out,"
the royal seer went to a fine forest.

Yudhiṣṭhira said:

Who was this powerful Daitya, O reverend ascetic, whose son was
he, whose grandson? This I wish to learn. I have not heard of this
mighty Daitya, reverend ascetic, and I wish to hear it all in full
detail the way it was, wise ascetic.

Mārkaṇḍeya said:
Listen, king, to all that happened.
When there was but a single, dreadful ocean, and the moving and standing creation had perished, and all the creatures had come to an end, bull of the Bharatas, the blessed Viṣṇu, the everlasting source of all creatures, the eternal Person, slept solitarily on his ocean bed in
10 the vast coil of the boundlessly puissant snake Śeṣa. The maker of the world, the blessed lord Acyuta Hari slept, my lord, while encompassing the girth of this earth with the vast coil of the snake. While the God was sleeping, a lotus of the luster of the sun sprouted from his navel; and there, in that sun-like and moon-like lotus, Grandfather himself was born, Brahmā, the guru of the world, the One of the four Vedas, the four forms, the four faces, unassailable because of his own puissance, and of mighty strength and prowess.
Madhu and Kaitabha saw the lord Hari of great splendor as he lay in his divine lair, the coil of the snake, which was many leagues wide and many leagues long. He wore his diadem, the Kaustubha jewel,
15 and a yellow robe of silk; and he blazed with fortune, splendor, and beauty, O king, with the light of a thousand suns, of the most wondrous aspect. Madhu and Kaitabha were greatly astonished, when they saw the lotus-eyed Grandfather in the lotus. Thereupon those two began to intimidate boundlessly mighty Brahmā; and, repeatedly terrified by the pair, glorious Brahmā shook the lotus stalk and Keśava woke up. Govinda then saw the powerful Dānavas; and upon seeing them the God said, "Be welcome, mighty ones. I shall give you a superb boon, for I am pleased with you."
The powerful Asuras began to laugh at Hṛṣīkeśa, great king, and
20 both replied to Madhusūdana, "Ask *us* for a boon, God, we are your benefactors, best of celestials; we shall surely give you a boon, ask without hesitation!"
The blessed lord said:
I accept your boon, heroes, there is a boon I desire; for you are both of great prowess, and there is no man who is your equal. Now, for the good of the world, I wish to fulfill this desire: that the two of you, who are strong in the truth, may be killed by my hand!
Madhu and Kaitabha said:
Not even in jest have we ever spoken a lie before, let alone in fact. Know, best of persons, that we are devoted to truth and Law. No one is our equal in strength, beauty, bravery, serenity, Law,
25 austerity, generosity, and in character, mettle, and self-control. A great calamity looms before us, Keśava. But carry out your word, for Time is unavoidable. Yet we wish you to do one thing, God our lord, that you, greatest of celestials, do the killing where space is uncovered

and we shall become your sons, fair-eyed one. Know that this, O God
who are the first of the Gods, is our boon.

The blessed lord said:

I shall certainly do so; thus shall it all be,

Mārkaṇḍeya said:

Thereupon Govinda reflected; but Madhusūdana saw no place on
30 earth or in heaven that was uncovered. Then the great God looked
at his own uncovered thighs; and glorious Madhusūdana cut off the
heads of Madhu and Kaitabha with the sharp edge of his discus,
O king.

Mārkaṇḍeya said:

195.1 The splendid and radiant Dhundhu was the son of that pair. He
performed great austerities, being mighty and imperious. He stood on
one foot, while he was so emaciated that he was held together by his
veins. Pleased, Brahmā gave him a boon, and the lord chose a boon:
"May I be invincible to Gods, Dānavas, Yakṣas, Snakes, Gandharvas,
and Rākṣasas—this is the boon I choose." "So shall it be. Go!" quoth
Grandfather. At these words he touched the God's feet with his head,
and went.

5 Having obtained the boon, Dhundhu, who was mighty and
imperious, remembered his parents' killing, and he rushed to Viṣṇu.
Intransigently, Dhundhu defeated Gods and Gandharvas and
repeatedly pressed all the Gods and Viṣṇu sorely. There is a sea of
sand known as Ujjānaka, and the demon went to that place, bull of
the Bharatas, and put all the pressure of his power on the hermitage
of Utanka, my lord. He went underground and hid in the sands, this
Dhundhu, the fiercely imperious son of Madhu and Kaitabha. In
order to devastate the worlds, he drew on the power of his austerities
and lay there close to Utanka's hermitage, breathing flames of fire.

10 At this time enemy-crushing King Kuvalāśva rode out with
soldiery and ordnance, amidst his twenty-one thousand sons, to the
dwelling of this Dhundhu, in Utanka's company. The blessed Viṣṇu
entered him with his fiery force at the behest of Utanka, for the good
of the worlds. As he started out, invincible, a loud voice spoke from
heaven: "This majestic prince shall become Dhundhumāra, the
Slayer of Dhundhu." The Gods strewed celestial flowers all around,
15 and the kettledrums of the Gods sounded of their own accord. And a
cool breeze blew over the journey of the wise king, and the king of
the Gods rained, rendering earth dustless. In the sky above the spot
where the great Asura Dhundhu lived the chariots of the Gods
appeared, Yudhiṣṭhira. In the company of Gods and Gandharvas, the
great seers watched curiously to witness the battle of Kuvalāśva and
Dhundhu.

Swollen with the fiery force of Nārāyaṇa, O Kauravya, the king and
his sons swarmed quickly in all directions. King Kuvalāśva had that
sea of sand dug up, and after his sons had dug into that sea for seven
20 days, they found the mighty Dhundhu. There was his huge, loathsome
body that blazed with a fiery force like that of the sun, bull of the
Bharatas! Dhundhu was asleep, tiger among kings, covering the
western horizon with a glow like that of the fire of doomsday. All
surrounded by his sons, Kuvalāśva stormed at him with sharp arrows,
clubs, hammers, three-bladed spears, bludgeons, projectiles, and
spotlessly honed swords. As he was being battered, the mighty demon
rose wrathfully and angrily devoured all the manifold weapons.
Vomiting fire from his maw, fire like the Fire of Annihilation, he set
25 with his fiery force all the king's sons ablaze, irately, with the fire of
his mouth, as though to bring perdition to the worlds, in an instant,
O tiger-like king, just as the lord Kapila had done before, when he
furiously burned the sons of Sagara—it was like that same miracle.

When they had been burned by the fire of his fury, best of
Bharatas, the fiery king Kuvalāśva approached the awakened great-
spirited ogre, who was like another Kumbhakarṇa. Much water
flowed from his body, great king, and the other's fiery force was
drunk up; the king doused the fire, which consisted of water, with
his water, O king, as a yogin does with his yoga. Thereupon the king
burned down the cruelly imperious Daitya with his Brahmā weapon,
best of Bharatas, for the security of the worlds. And because he
burned down with his weapon that great Asura, enemy of the Gods,
like another lord of the three worlds, the enemy-killing royal seer
Kuvalāśva became famed as Dhundhumāra.

30 Happily all the Thirty Gods and the great seers said to him,
"Choose a boon!" And he folded his hands and bowed; and greatly
delighted, O king, he spoke these words: "Invincible to my enemies,
may I give wealth to the chief brahmins, may I enjoy the friendship
of Viṣṇu, be no threat to any creature, always devoted to the Law,
and forever dwell in heaven!" "So shall it be!" said the pleased Gods,
the seers, and the Gandharvas as well as the sage Utanka in reply to
the king. After regaling the king with various blessings, Gods and
great seers repaired to their dwellings.

Three sons were left to him, Yudhiṣṭhira Bhārata, by the names of
Dhṛḍhāśva, Kapilāśva, and Candrāśva; from them stems the
35 succession of the great-spirited Ikṣvākus, king. So, then, did
Kuvalāśva kill that mighty Daitya Dhundhu, the son of Madhu and
Kaitabha, my good friend, and ever since the talented King Kuvalāśva
has been known by the style of Dhundhumāra.

Thus I have told you entirely what you asked me, the story anent
Dhundhumāra, by whose feat it has become famed. He who hears this

holy tale, which is a narrative laud of Viṣṇu, will become Law-spirited and the father of sons. Listening to it on the moon-phase days he becomes long-lived and persevering, he will suffer no disease and be beyond danger.

3(37.e) The Devoted Wife

196–97 (B. 205–6; C. 13628–700)
196 (206; 13268). Yudhiṣṭhira asks about the glory of faithful wives (1–10). Mārkaṇḍeya affirms that sons are the glory of a woman, and so is obedience to her husband (10–20).
197 (206; 13652). A crane drops dung on the brahmin Kauśika; he kills it with a glance, then feels remorse (1–5). He begs food at a house where the mistress tells him to wait: she first is to serve her husband (5–15). The brahmin protests; the woman explains that her husband is her greatest God and discourses on brahminhood (25–40). A hunter in Mithilā will tell the brahmin the Law (40).

Vaiśaṃpāyana said:
196.1 Then King Yudhiṣṭhira, the best of the Bharatas, questioned the lustrous Mārkaṇḍeya concerning a difficult matter of Law: "Sir, I wish to hear you tell of the greatness of women and the subtleties of the Law, O brahmin. For, best of brahmin seers, the sun and the moon, the wind, the earth, the fire, father and mother, and the cows, and whatever has been ordained, are the deities that are visible to us, scion of Bhṛgu. I regard them all as gurus, and likewise do I regard
5 faithful wives. The obedience of women who are devoted to their husbands seems to me very difficult. Pray, my lord, tell of the greatness of devoted wives who continuously think of their husbands as Gods, while restraining their senses and controlling their minds. This appears to me quite difficult, my lord, a woman's obedience to her father, mother, and husband. I do not see anything harder than the terrible Law of the women. Alas, fathers and mothers aggravate the tasks that virtuous women always perform assiduously. What is more marvelous than to be born a woman who is devoted to her husband, speaks the truth, and carries a child for ten months in the
10 womb? After exposing themselves to great danger and suffering immense pain, women give birth to sons with great hardship, and rear them with great love, best of brahmins.

"I also think that men who are engaged in cruel tasks and are loathed for that, yet continue to perform those tasks, have a difficult life. Tell me truly of the observance of the baronial Law, brahmin; the Law is hard to carry out for a cruel man of evil spirit. I wish to hear from you, sir, who are most knowledgeable about questions, about this question, O chief of the lineage of Bhṛgu, keeper of good vows."

Mārkaṇḍeya said:

Aye, I shall answer entirely this difficult question of yours, best of
15 Bharatas, listen to me as I speak truthfully. Some hold the mother for
higher, my son, others the father; but the mother who rears her
children does a difficult thing. Fathers wish for sons by means of
austerities, worship of the Gods, adoration, forbearance, and magic
aids. Having thus, after much toil, obtained a son, who is not easy to
obtain, a man always worries how he will turn out. A father and a
mother hope for glory for their sons, for fame, wealth, progeny, and
Law. A Law-minded son who fulfils their hopes, O Indra among kings,
and at all times earns their contentment, reaps fame and Law here
20 and hereafter forever. For a woman no sacrifice, *śrāddha*, or fast is of
any avail: she attains to heaven by the obedience she brings to her
husband. On this subject, King Yudhiṣṭhira, listen attentively to the
fixed Law of devoted wives.

Mārkaṇḍeya said:

197.1 Bhārata, there was an eminent brahmin, scholar of the *Veda*,
austere, ascetic, making a habit of the Law, who went by the name
of Kauśika. This good brahmin studied all the *Vedas*, with branches
and upaniṣads. He once stood under a tree while he was reciting the
Vedas. On top of the tree a female heron was perched and dropped
dung on the brahmin. Angrily the brahmin looked up, sent the heron
5 an injurious thought, and he stared at it balefully. Hit by the ill
thought of the brahmin, the heron fell to the ground.

When the brahmin saw the heron lying dead and inanimate,
compassion overwhelmed him, and he grew sorrowful. "I have done
wrong because passion and hatred possessed me," he said again and
again; then the sage went to the village to beg food. Making the
rounds of pure households in the village, he entered a house that he
had visited before. "Give!" he demanded, and the housewife said,
"Wait!" until she could clean the bowl. Meanwhile her husband
suddenly came home, he was very hungry, best of the Bharatas.
10 When the good woman saw her husband, she forgot about the
brahmin. She gave her man water to wash his feet, water to rinse his
mouth, and a stool, and the dark-eyed woman humbly waited on her
husband with food, delicacies, and sweet words. She always ate the
leftovers of her husband, Yudhiṣṭhira, and thought of her lord as a
God, guessing at his wishes. Neither in fact nor in thought did she

eat or drink ahead of him; she was filled with all thoughtful affections and took pleasure in obeying her master. Virtuous of conduct, pure, clever, and concerned with the well-being of the
15 family, she always acted in the husband's interest. She always was in command of her senses, and obedient to the Gods, guests, dependents, and parents-in-law.

Then the pretty-eyed woman noticed the mendicant brahmin who had been waiting while she attended her husband, and remembered about him. The good woman became embarrassed, best of the Bharatas, and the reputable wife took an alms and went out to the brahmin.

The brahmin said:

What is the meaning of this? You told me to wait, fair woman, and delayed me without dismissing me!

Mārkaṇḍeya said:

Seeing that the irate brahmin was fairly blazing with fieriness, O
20 Indra of men, she said soothingly, "Pray forgive me, brahmin. My husband is my greatest God, and he came home hungry and tired, and I saw to his wants."

The brahmin said:

Brahmins are not more important? You make your husband superior! While living by the householder's Law you belittled the brahmin! Indra himself bows to him, let alone a man on earth. Insolent female, don't you know, have you not heard from the elders? Brahmins like fire can burn up even all of earth!

The woman said:

I do not belittle the brahmins, they are spirited and equal to Gods. Please forgive my error, blameless sir! I know of the fieriness and greatness of the wise brahmins. In their wrath they made the ocean
25 salty and undrinkable. I know the power of the hermits of perfected soul, whose austerities blaze up: the fire of their fury is still not extinguished in the Daṇḍaka Forest. Because of his oppression of brahmins, the wicked Vātāpi, a great and cruel Asura, came upon the seer Agastya, and was digested.

Surely I have heard of the plentiful powers of the scholars of the Brahman: great is the wrath of those great-spirited beings, and so is their favor, brahmin. Now do excuse me for this transgression, blameless sage. The Law that I must obey one husband is a pleasing one to me. Among all deities my husband is my paramount God. I must obey my Law by him without discrimination, best of brahmins.
30 Just look at the result of my obedience to him: through it I know that you irately burned a female heron; but ire, good brahmin, is the enemy that lives in a man's body, and the Gods know him for a brahmin who abandons both ire and folly. Him the Gods also know

for a brahmin who speaks truths, satisfies his teacher, and, when hurt,
does not hurt in return. Him the Gods know for a brahmin who is
master of his senses, prone to the Law, devoted to *Veda* study, pure,
and in control of passion and anger. Him the Gods know for a
brahmin who, being Law-wise and spirited, regards all the world as
himself and has love for all the Laws. Him the Gods know for a
brahmin who teaches and learns, sacrifices and has others sacrifice,
35 and makes gifts where he can. Him the Gods know for a brahmin
who, as the chief of the twice-born, chastely studies the *Vedas* and
is undistracted in his daily study.

A brahmin will proclaim to us people what is good for brahmins,
and so, while speaking the utter truth, their minds do not rejoice in
lies. They say that a brahmin's property is his study, self-control,
uprightness, and constant restraint of his senses, my good brahmin.
Law-wise people quote truthfulness and uprightness as the highest
Law. The sempiternal Law is hard to know, but it is founded on
truthfulness; the elders teach that the Law should be authorized by
Revelation. Many a time the Law has been seen as subtle, great
40 brahmin, and you too are aware of the Law, devoted to study, and
pious; yet, sir, I do not think you know the Law really.

A hunter who lives in Mithilā, one obedient to his father and mother, true-spoken, in command of his senses, shall explain the Laws to you. Good luck to thee, go there, if you please, best of brahmins. If I have talked too much, please forgive it all, blameless sir, for women are inviolate to all folk who know of the Law.

The brahmin said:

I am pleased with you, good luck to you. My ire has gone, beautiful woman, for the reprimands you voiced are my salvation. Luck be with you; I shall go and be a better man, beautiful woman!

Mārkaṇḍeya said:

She gave him leave, and he left and went back to his dwelling, that good brahmin Kauśika, blaming himself, O best of men.

3(37.f) The Colloquy of the Brahmin and the Hunter

198–206; (B. 207–16; C. 13701–4099)
198 (207; 13701). The brahmin departs for Mithilā (1–5) and asks for the hunter, whom he finds in the slaughterhouse (5–10). The hunter greets him and takes him home (10–15). The brahmin asks why he follows

his vile occupation; the hunter explains that it is his family occupation, on which he discourses (15–25). On class Law and virtue (25–55). The conduct of the strict (55–90).
199 (208; 13802). The killing of cattle and the eating of meat (1–10), karman, *and the inevitability of killing (10–35).*
200 (209; 13842). Law and karman, *which governs all (1–20), the eternality of the soul (25), and how the soul is reborn (25–50).*
201 (210; 13898). Vice (1–10), the elements and their properties, the manas, buddhi, *and* sahaṃkāra, *the* guṇas, *and* avyakta *(10–20).*
202 (211; 13920). The elements and their properties (1–10). The manifest, the unmanifest, and the soul (10–15). Self-control (15–25).
203 (213; 13946). The three guṇas *(1–10). The* Prāṇas *(10–30). The contemplation of the soul (30–35). The moral virtues (35–50).*
204 (214; 14000). At the hunter's invitation the brahmin visits the hunter's parents and is welcomed (1–10). The proper treatment of parents (15–25).
205 (215; 14031). The hunter admonishes the brahmin to honor his parents (1–15). The brahmin gives his promise. He asks how the hunter became what he is (15–20). In a previous life the hunter had been a brahmin and once shot a hermit by mistake and was cursed to become a hunter (20–25).
206 (216; 14063). But he would retain his wisdom (1–5). Final admonitions (5–25). The brahmin and the hunter part (25–30).

Mārkaṇḍeya said:

198.1 The brahmin reflected fully upon the curious matter that the woman had set forth to him, blamed himself, and showed a guilty appearance. Pondering on the subtle course of the Law, he said, "I must have faith. I shall myself go to Mithilā. There, she said, dwells a Law-knowing hunter who has perfected his soul. This very day I shall go to that man so rich in austerity and query him about the Law." Thus he reflected in his mind, and he had faith in the woman's words, because of her convincing mention of the heron, and her Law-like and virtuous discourse.

5 Filled with curiosity, he departed for Mithilā. He passed through forests, villages, and towns and at length came to Mithilā, which was well governed by Janaka. It was a city demarcated by the boundaries of the Law, rich in sacrifices and festivals, holy, defended by gates and watch towers, and adorned with houses and walls. He entered the lovely town, which was surrounded by many palaces, filled with many wares, with the main streets well laid out, crowded with many horses, chariots, elephants, and wagons, teeming with happy, well-fed people, and bristling with constant festivals.

10 As he passed through, the brahmin saw its many happenings; he inquired after the pious hunter, and was told about him by the brahmins. He went there and found the sage established in the center of the slaughterhouse, selling venison and buffalo meat. Because of the press of the customers the brahmin waited on the side. But the other sensed that a brahmin had come and on a sudden he rose nervously and came where the brahmin was sitting on the side.

The hunter said:

I greet you, reverend sir, be welcome, great brahmin. Hail to thee, I am but a hunter: what can I do? Command me! A faithful wife has told you to come to Mithilā; I know the full reason why you have come here.

Mārkaṇḍeya said:

On hearing his words the brahmin was much impressed, and he
15 thought, "This is the second marvel." Said the hunter to the brahmin, "You are standing where you should not stand. Let us go home, if you please, faultless sir." Happily the brahmin responded, "By all means!" and the other placed him before himself and went to his house. The brahmin entered the lovely dwelling, was favored with a seat, accepted the foot water and rinsing water, and when he was sitting comfortably, he addressed the hunter: "It appears to me that your occupation is not a fitting one for you. I am very sorry, my son, that you do these wicked things."

The hunter said:

It is my family occupation, which has come down to me from
20 father and grandfather. Be not angry, brahmin, if I do my own job. I just carry out the task that the Ordainer has ordained; I do my best to obey my old parents, I speak the truth, good brahmin, do not grumble, give what I can, and live on what my Gods, guests, and dependents leave me. I despise nothing and hold no one more powerful than I in contempt; for one's previous deeds follow the doer, good brahmin.

A man's living in this world is plowing, cattle tending, trade, government, and the three *Vedas*; that is what people live on. Service

is for the serf, plowing for the commoner, fighting for the baron, as
they say, and the pursuit of learning, austerity, spells, and
25 truthfulness is for the brahmin. A king sways by the law his subjects
who do their own jobs, and yokes those who do the wrong job to
their own tasks. Kings are always to be feared, for they lord it over
their subjects, and they kill off the one who does the wrong job, as
the hunter kills off a deer with his arrows. Janaka here has no one
doing the wrong job, brahmin; no, all four classes are devoted to their
own tasks. If our King Janaka had a bad son who was a jailbird he
would throw him in the dungeon; but he does not bother a Law-
abiding man. Our king, who uses his runners well, sees everyone
with the eye of the Law. Fortune, kingship, and the staff belong to the
baron, brahmin.

30 Kings, now, hope for greater fortune by observing their own Law,
and the king is the protector of all the classes. I myself sell hogs and
buffalo killed by other people; I don't kill them myself, but I do sell,
always. Nor do I eat meat, I lie with my wife only when I should, I
fast every day and eat at night. A man might be born without culture,
yet he may become cultured; while a Law-type person may grow to
like hurting living creatures. The great Law becomes confused by the
35 errors of kings, lawlessness rises up, the subjects intermarry. People
are born stunted, dwarfish, hunchbacked, large-headed, impotent,
blind, deaf, drooping, and stammering because of the lawlessness of
kings, and the subjects diminish continuously.

Our King Janaka sees everything according to the Law and always
favors all those subjects who are devoted to their own Law. I myself
gratify all people with accomplished deeds, whether they praise me or
abuse me. Kings who live and take their pleasure according to the
Law and do not live at the expense of anyone or anything are
competent and always in the ascendant. Such virtues of mortals as
generosity with food according to capacity, constant patience,
fortitude in the Law, reciprocity according to a person's worth, and
compassion for all creatures root in a man out of no other aspiration
40 than relinquishment. One should avoid lies, do good unsolicited, and
not cast off the Law out of lust, rashness, or hatred. One should not
rejoice too much in happiness, go feverish in unhappiness, or get
befuddled enough to abandon the Law in a failure of affairs.

If some action was wrong, one should not repeat it but apply
himself to what he considers right. Be no criminal to a criminal, but
always a man of virtue. A criminal who wants to commit crime only
hurts himself. The acts of the wicked and deceitful are unholy. Those
who mock the pure, thinking that there is no Law, and who give no
45 credence to the Law, perish without doubt. The criminal always
swells up like a wind bag; the arrogant fools' prattle is stupid and

shows up their inmost soul, as the sun shows up shapes. An idiot does not make his mark in the world by mere self-praise, but a learned man does, even though he be not too clean, if he does not abuse anyone and does not applaud himself. Virtue is not a matter of appearance alone in this world.

When one rues his misdeeds, he is freed from the sin of them, and freed from repeating them by repenting "I will not do it again," freed from any evil by whatever act, O foremost of brahmins: this is the revelation that is found in the Laws.

50 Unknowing of sins committed before
The man of Law destroys them thereafter.
The Law, O brahmin, dispels the guilt
One incurred, forgetfully, here before.

Having done ill, a man should think that it was not he; he should have faith and not protest, and seek to do what is right. If one, so to say, covers up the holes in good folks' garments, he will come to good, even though he had done wrong; he is freed from all evils, as the moon from big clouds. Just as the sun upon rising dispels all darkness, so a man who does good is freed from all evil. Know, good brahmin, that greed is the locus of evil. Men who are greedy and, being not too wise, resolve on evil, are lawless though disguised by
55 Law, like wells that are covered by grass. Surely they have self-control, purifiers, conversations informed by the Law, they have it all —still the deportment of the strict is hard to acquire.

Mārkaṇḍeya said:

Then the sagacious brahmin questioned the pious hunter: "How should I understand the deportment of the strict, best of men? Declare it truly, wise hunter!"

The hunter said:

Sacrifice, gifts, austerities, the *Vedas*, and truthfulness, my good brahmin, are the five purifying means for those whose deportment is informed, and they are always effective. After mastering lust and anger, arrogance, greed, and insincerity, the strict are contented with the Law and are applauded by the strict. They who practice sacrifice and *Veda* study will not lack in livelihood; they guard proper
60 deportment, which is the second characteristic of the strict. Obedience to the guru, truthfulness, lack of anger, liberality are all four always present in the deportment of the strict, brahmin. When one has set his mind on strict deportment and always keeps at it, he earns a satisfaction that cannot be gained by anything else. The secret of the *Veda* is truthfulness, the secret of truthfulness is self-control, the secret of self-control is at all times relinquishment, in the deportment of the strict. The follower of those who, in the folly of their spirits,

protest against the Law and travel by the wrong road is equally oppressed. But the strict, well-regulated, given to learning and relinquishment, ascend the path of the Law, while devoted to truth and Law. Men who practice strict deportment control the highest spirit; they are obedient to their teachers and by their perseverance learn to perceive the purpose of the Law. Resort to knowledge, cherish the Law-abiding, and shun the heterodox; those who transgress the boundaries are cruel and evil-intentioned. Build the ship of steadfastness and cross the river awash with the five senses and filled with the crocodiles of lust and greed, and pass beyond the straits of existence. Law, which is gradually accumulated and consists of a discipline of the spirit, grows large and becomes the ornament of strict deportment, like red dye on a white cloth. Nonviolence and true speech betoken the highest well-being of all creatures; nonviolence is the highest Law, and it is founded on truth; activities prosper when founded on truth. But the truthfulness that is cherished in strict deportment is weightier; the Law is the conduct of the good, and the good are defined by their conduct. Each creature follows his own nature, whatever it is. The ill-spirited man who has no hold over himself acquires such vices as truculence, passionateness, and so on. An enterprise informed by good rules is called Law, while it is the teaching of the strict that misconduct is Unlaw.

The unangry, unprotesting, unselfish, unenvious, sincere and serene have the deportment of the strict. Those who have become elders in the three *Vedas* are pure, have livelihood, and are mindful, obedient to their gurus, and self-controlled, have the deportment of the strict. Whatever is ugly dies in those who are resilient, accomplish hard feats of deportment, and are hallowed by their own acts. When wise men perceive according to the Law that this rare strict deportment, which is ancient, sempiternal, and fixed, is the Law, they go to heaven. The strict who are orthodox, prideless bringers of honor to the brahmins, and conduct themselves according to the scriptures go to heaven.

The higher Law is stated in the *Veda*, the other Law in the Books of the Law, and is also acted out by the strict: this is the threefold definition of the Law. Strict deportment is exemplified by complete knowledge of the *Vedas*, the bathing in sacred fords, forbearance, truthfulness, sincerity, and purity. The strict, who are dear to the brahmins, are always compassionate to all creatures and devoted to nonviolence, never speak scathingly. The strict who are accepted by the strict recognize what is true fruition in the accumulation of good and evil acts. Possessed of sound rules, possessed of virtues, wishing the whole world well, the strict who are pure win heaven and are firmly footed on the good path. Givers and sharers and benefactors of the poor and compassionate to all creatures are the strict who are accepted by the strict. Worshipful to all, possessing faith as well as austerities, and always liberal, they attain to the blissful worlds, and to fortune here.

85 When the strict meet with the strict, they give over and beyond
their means, thoughtfully, even at the detriment of wife and
dependents. The strict act while looking to their livelihood, Law, and
self-interests and prosper for years without end. Nonviolence, true
speech, mildness, sincerity, abstention from threats, lack of too great
a pride, modesty, forbearance, self-control, serenity; wise, poised,
compassionate to the creatures, devoid of lust and hatred, the strict
are honored by the world.

These three, they say, are the marks of good men and tantamount
to matchless conduct: he shall not menace, he shall give, he shall
90 always speak the truth. The strict, who have compassion for
everything and always feel pity, walk most contentedly in this world
the supreme road of the Law. Great-spirited men of strict conduct are
those who have fully decided on the Law, and are complacent, patient,
serene, contented, pleasant-spoken, free from lust and ire, and
practicing the conduct of the strict. Men who are always tireless in
the Laws cherish the strict conduct, the high road of the good
informed by deed and learning, as they ascend to the terrace of
insight and watch the great public in its confusion and observe the
manifold occupations of the world, and the great good deeds as well
as the bad ones, O greatest of brahmins.

And this, brahmin, bull of the twice-born, tells you all that I can grasp and have learned, if you put first the conduct of the strict.

Mārkaṇḍeya said:

199.1 Said the lawlike hunter to the brahmin, Yudhiṣṭhira, "No doubt,
my living is loathsome, but the Ordinance of our previous deeds is
powerful and hard to pass by, brahmin. This is the resultant evil of
the evil I did before, and I do my best, brahmin, to kill it off. When
Ordinance has so ordained before, the killer is but the instrument,
and so are we but the instrument of previous *karman*, good brahmin.
It was their Law for those that are killed and whose meat we sell to
be eaten and enjoyed, and to regale the deities, guests, dependents,
5 and ancestors. Herbs, garden greens, cattle, game, and fowl, so
Revelation reveals, are the foodstuffs of the world. King Śibi
Auśīnara won a difficult heaven by proffering his own flesh, good
brahmin. In old King Rantideva's kitchen two thousand cows were
butchered every day. Rantideva served meat dishes daily, and the
king's fame is peerless, good brahmin: he always slaughtered cattle
at the seasonal sacrifices. Revelation reveals that the fires are hungry

for meat, and at his sacrifices the brahmin always kills animals, which,
being sacramentalized by the incantations, then go to heaven, as we
hear.
10 "Now, brahmin, if the old fires had not been so hungry for meat,
no one would eat it now. Even now the hermits rule in the matter of
eating meat: 'He who always eats only after having offered to deities
and ancestors according to the Ordinance and with faith does not
incur guilt by eating the remainder.' Revelation reveals that one
thus equals a meat abstainer: a scholar of the *Veda* who goes to his
wife at her season remains a brahmin. Even now the rule that judges
truth and lie is propounded: old King Saudāsa ate men, O brahmin,
when he was under the heavy influence of a curse—what do you
think of that?

"I know this is *my* Law, and I will not give it up, good brahmin.
15 I know it is due to my old acts, and I live by this job. It is considered
lawless here, brahmin, if a man abandons his own work. If he does
what is his task, it is decided to be the Law. For the previously
committed acts do not leave the embodied man alone. The Placer
viewed this Ordinance in manifold ways, when he decided on
anyone's work. A man who is toiling at a loathsome task has to find
out how he can make his job a good thing, brahmin, how to avoid
being brought down by it. The final judgment of this loathsome job
will be varied. I myself have always been bent upon the giving of
gifts, the speaking of truth, obedience to my betters, honoring the
brahmins, and observing the Law. I refrain from speaking too much
and minding too much, best of brahmins.

"They hold that plowing is good, but it is well enough known what
injuries it inflicts. Men who furrow with plowshares kill many
creatures that lie in the ground, as well as plenty of other living
20 things, what do you think? Those seeds of grains they call rice and so
forth, they are all alive, good brahmin, what do you think of that?
Man strides upon, kills, and eats animals, he cuts trees and herbs,
brahmin. There are many living creatures in trees and fruit, and
many in water, what do you think of that? Everything is filled with
living, breathing things, brahmin: fish swallow fish, what do you
think of that? Creatures live off other creatures, good brahmin: the
25 living are cannibals, what do you think of that? Just by walking
about men trample many living things that cling to the ground,
brahmin, what do you think of that? Untold living things that squat
or lie and have consciousness and knowledge are crushed, what do
you think of that? They hurt all this air, this earth, both filled with
living things, in their ignorance: what do you think of that?

"Surely those men of yore said in astonishment, 'Nonviolence!'
But who in this world does not hurt something alive, good brahmin?

Come to think of it, no one fails here to hurt. Those same ascetics so
devoted to nonviolence still give hurt, good brahmin, although their
30 efforts do decrease it. Quite visible people, of great virtue, born in a
ranking family, may still do ghastly acts, and still are not ashamed.
Friends do not welcome friends, nor enemies their enemies, nor
people who look to correctness other correct men. Kinfolk even do not
welcome rich relatives; fools, thinking themselves scholars, criticize
teachers.

"Much in this world can be viewed as upside down, good brahmin,
35 lawly or lawless—what do you think of that? Much can be said about
deeds lawly and lawless; yet he who is devoted to his own task wins
great renown."

Mārkaṇḍeya said:

200.1 The pious hunter, best of the upholders of all the Laws, once more
sagely addressed that bull among brahmins, O Yudhiṣṭhira, and said,
"As the elders say, 'What is Law depends on whether Revelation
authorizes it.' For the course of the Law is subtle, greatly ramified,
and without end. One may voice a lie when about to expire, or when
about to marry: then the lie becomes truth and the truth a lie. It is
generally held that that word that is entirely beneficial is the truth,
and that the opposite creates an Unlaw: notice the subtlety of the
Law!

5 "Whether a man does good deeds or bad deeds, good brahmin, he
inevitably and indubitably reaps the result. The unschooled person,
upon incurring misfortune, blames the Gods severely, for he does not
know where his acts were at fault. The fool, the cheat, and the freak
possess neither the well-guided wisdom nor the manly courage to
save themselves when their good luck or bad luck reverses itself.
Whatever object one may desire, he will find it, as long as man's
activity depends on no other. But controlled, capable, intelligent men
are yet found to be frustrated and deprived of their successes; while
10 another who is forever ready to inflict hurt on creatures and to cheat
people lives happily. Luck can wait on someone who sits down doing
nothing, while an active man may never get to his goal. Wretched
men who want sons may worship the Gods and perform austerities;
and when the sons have been born after having been carried in the
womb for ten months, they turn out to be spoilers of the family;
while others, equally obtained by auspicious means, lay claim by
birth to all the wealth and grain and pleasure their fathers piled up.

15 "The diseases of men stem no doubt from their previous deeds;
they are plagued by ailments as small game by hunters. Capable and
competent physicians who have collected herbs chase the ailments as
hunters chase game. Those who have the wherewithal to eat fine

foods are then afflicted with indigestion, you see, pillar of Law, and cannot enjoy their meals, while many others with powerful arms are badly off and have trouble finding a meal, good brahmin. Thus the world, flooded with folly and sorrow, is helpless and battered and washed away every time by the powerful current. None would die, none would age, all would have their desires, none would see hateful
20 things, were they but masters of their fate. Everyone wants to excel over others and strives as best he can, and still it does not work. We find many that were born under the same stars and on the same lucky days, yet how dissimilar are their rewards in the junctures of their previous deeds! No one, great brahmin, is master of his own lot; what we behold here is the maturity of the deeds that were peculiarly his. It is as Revelation has it, brahmin: The soul is indeed eternal, and the body of any living being in this world is transient. When the flesh is being killed, the body perishes, and the soul migrates to another one, bound by the fetters of his deeds."

The brahmin said:

25 In what way, eloquent upholder of the Law, is the soul eternal? This I wish to know truthfully.

The hunter said:

The soul does not die when the body is severed,
But fools hold falsely the soul can die.
The soul moves on that was hid in the body;
The body's demise is return to the Five.

None other inherits the deeds that were done;
The doer alone shares the luck and the ill luck;
For whatever deeds the man has done
He alone inherits, his deeds survive.

The erstwhile polluted will now become pure;
The greatest of men may become new sinners.
A man in this world is chased by his deeds;
They prepare his existence, and then he is born.

The brahmin said:

How does he take shape in the womb, how does it come about that the good are born good and the wicked wicked? How does he go, good man?

The hunter said:

30 It appears that the *karman* is linked up with conception; but I shall explain to you briefly and rapidly, good brahmin, how one is born again when the ingredients have been brought together, the good in good wombs, the bad in bad ones.

As a result of good acts one becomes a God, because of mixed ones
a man, because of befooled ones one is born from animals, because of
criminal ones one goes below. It is his own old vices that cook a man
in transmigration, where he is forever attacked by the miseries of
birth, old age, and death. Bound by the bonds of their deeds, the souls
wander about to thousands of animal species, and to hell.
35 A creature dies, suffers the deserts of whatever deeds he has done,
and falls heir to an impure womb, to remedy his previous
wretchedness. Thereupon he collects once more a pile of new deeds,
and is cooked all over again, like a sick man who has eaten what
does not agree with him. Thus being in a state of constant suffering,
yet unsuffering and called happy, he keeps transmigrating, because
his bonds have not been cut and his deeds once more prevail—keeps
transmigrating around a wheel of lives, living in much pain. When
the bondage has been terminated and he is freed from it, he attains
to the worlds of merit, where, once he has reached them, he will no
more suffer. Therefore one should strive to do good and avoid doing
40 what lowers him. If unprotestingly, gratefully, a man seeks out only
things of beauty, a man attains to happiness, Law, profit, and heaven.
A sanctified, self-controlled, disciplined, self-collected, wise man has
an incomparable existence both here and hereafter.

One should act according to the Law of the good, perform rites like
the strict, and, brahmin, desire the way of life that does not offend
others. There are strict men to whom the knowledge has come down,
educated and wise in the scriptures: in this world the rite is to be
performed by one's own Law, this is the true meaning of the act. The
wise man rejoices in the Law, he lives on the Law, and when he has
gained possessions by the Law, good brahmin, he waters the root of
45 that Law, wherever he sees virtues. So he becomes Law-spirited, and
his mind grows tranquil; he is contented with his friends, and he
rejoices here and hereafter. He gains the sound, the touch, the shape,
the smell he loves, good man, and ascends to lordship. This they
know as the fruit of the Law.

Having obtained the fruit of the Law, he is not satisfied, great
brahmin; and, being dissatisfied, he accepts his distaste with the
vision of insight. A man endowed with the eyesight of wisdom refuses
to condone the wrong. If it pleases him, he renounces; but he does
not cast off the Law. Observing that the world is by its nature
transient, he strives to renounce everything, then strives for release,
50 not by the wrong means, but by the right. Thus he accepts the
distaste, relinquishes evil deeds, becomes a man of the Law, and
attains to final release. Austerity is a creature's greatest good, and its
roots are serenity and self-control; by it he obtains all the desires he

desires in his heart. By repressing the senses, by truthfulness and self-control, he attains to the place of Brahman, which is the yonder, good brahmin.

The brahmin said:

What are these faculties they call senses, man of strict vows? How can they be subdued, and what is the reward if they are subdued? And how does one get their reward, first pillar of Law? This, the Law, I wish to learn truly, good man of the Law!

Mārkaṇḍeya said:

201.1 At these words of the brahmin, O Yudhiṣṭhira, the pious hunter
made his reply. Listen how, my prince.

The hunter said:

The mind first operates in men, for the sake of cognition. Having
acquired a mind, one partakes of desire and anger, good brahmin. In
order to satisfy both, one acts and undertakes great deeds and
accustoms oneself to pleasing shapes and smells. Thereupon passion
for these objects begins to prevail, and this passion is at once followed
5 by hatred. Then greed prevails, at once followed by folly. So man is
ruled by greed and battered by love and hatred; his spirit is not
pointed to the Law, but he pretends to observe the Law. He pretends
to follow the Law, but, in his dissembling, enjoys Unlaw. His spirit
delights in the riches to which he succeeded while he dissembled,
good brahmin, and then turns to evil. His friends and the learned may
restrain him, good brahmin, and the reply he offers them will be
consonant with Revelation and be informed by it. Yet, under the
influence of the vice of his passion, his lawlessness flourishes triply:
he thinks evil, speaks evil, does evil. The good qualities of this
lawlessness-prone person vanish, and only the like-minded stay
10 friends with this man of evil deeds. All he reaps is misery, and
hereafter he perishes.

This is what becomes of the evil-minded man. Now hear the profit of the Law. He who in his wisdom foresees these faults and is familiar with what is happy and unhappy, cultivates good men. By undertaking good acts, his spirit turns to the Laws.

The brahmin said:

You proclaim the gladsome Law, which finds no proclaimer. I think of you as a very great seer, of divine puissance!

The hunter said:

Like the Ancestors, the lordly brahmins are always fed first; in this world a wise man, with all his heart, should carry out what is pleasing to them. I shall tell you, good brahmin, what is pleasing to them. After I have bowed to the brahmins, hear from me the brahmin's wisdom.

15 This entire universe, not conquerable by any means, consists in
the five elements, brahmin; and beyond them there is nought. These
five elements are ether, wind, fire, water, and earth. Their properties
are sound, touch, shape, taste, and smell. All have properties, but
there is a succession of properties: each in the series has all the
properties that are found in the three elements before it.

The sixth element is consciousness, which is called the mind, the
seventh is the spirit, and beyond that the ego-formulation. Then
there are the five senses, and *sattva, rajas,* and *tamas.* The seventeenth
constitutes the mass known as the Unmanifest. The property
consisting in both the Unmanifest and the Manifest, well concealed
20 here by all the sense objects, both manifest and unmanifest, is called
the Twenty-fourth. —— This tells you all; what else do you wish to
know?

Mārkaṇḍeya said:

202.1 At this address by the pious hunter, O Bhārata, the brahmin once
more pursued their colloquy, which increased his pleasure.

The brahmin said:

O best of those who are wise in the Law, they say that there are five elements. Tell me precisely what the properties of each of the five are.

The hunter said:

There is earth, water, fire, wind, and ether; I shall tell you all their
respective properties. Earth has five properties, brahmin, water has
four, fire three, and there are three between wind and ether.
5 Audibility, touchability, visibility, sapidity, and redolence are the five
properties of earth, which has more properties than all others. The
properties enumerated of water, O brahmin of good vows, are
audibility, touchability, visibility, and sapidity. Fire has these three
properties: audibility, touchability, and visibility; wind has audibility
and touchability; ether has only sound.

These fifteen properties subsist in all five elements together,
brahmin, and operate in all creatures on which the worlds rest; they
do not encroach on one another, they form a whole, brahmin. But
when the standing and moving creatures become imbalanced, then
10 the soul in time wanders away to another body. The elements perish
in sequence and regenerate in sequence; and in every instance the
layers of the five elements are perceived. They cover this entire world
of moving and standing creatures.

That which is created with the senses is known as the manifest; that component which is above the senses, and to be known as the Mark, is called the unmanifest part. When the individual holds that the senses that make him perceive the sense-objects of sound are his possessions, he is in trouble here. If he sees the soul stretched out in the world, and the world stretched out in the soul, then, having knowledge of the higher and the lower, yet still attached, he sees all the elements. As he sees at all times all the elements in all their conditions, and thus becomes Brahmā; he will no longer be paired with the evil.

15 For anyone who has passed the folly-born hindrance that ultimately
is rooted in knowledge, the world becomes visible by the illumination
of the spirit as the road to the object of wisdom. The wise teacher
has declared that man is without beginning and end, self-born,
forever eternal, beyond compare, disembodied, says the wise lord.
Whatever you query me about is all rooted in austerity. Heaven and
hell, it is all the senses; if they are tamed, they lead to heaven; if
unbridled, they lead to hell.

The entire method of Yoga comes down to the control of the
senses. The senses are the basis of all austerity, as well as hell. By
clinging to the senses a person without a doubt reaps evil; but by
20 taming them one earns success. If one succeeds in mastering these six
constants in himself, he is not visited by evil, let alone disaster, for
he is the master of his senses.

> They see a man's body is his chariot,
> And the soul is the driver of the horselike senses;
> With these good steeds tamed, the undistracted
> Soul, steady charioteer, will see happiness.

If one steadily holds the reins of the always present and disturbing
senses within the soul, he is the complete charioteer. He who holds
the released senses steady as horses on the road will surely triumph
over them by the steadiness of his driving. For if the mind always
obeys the helter-skelter senses, it carries off the spirit as the wind
25 carries off a boat in the water. He who concentrates resolutely on the
six senses, over which others foolishly quarrel regarding the outcome
of fruit, finds the fruit, which is born from his meditation.

Mārkaṇḍeya said:

203.1 After the pious hunter had explained this subtle point, the
attentive brahmin once more inquired about a subtle matter.

The brahmin said:

Explain at my bidding precisely what the properties are of *sattva*, *rajas*, and *tamas*.

The hunter said:

Aye, I shall expound to you what you ask. Listen as I explain their properties at your bidding. The *tamas* among them is characterized by ignorance, the *rajas* by motivation, while the *sattva* is declared to be the highest of them because of its great illuminating power. Governed by *tamas* is one who is largely ignorant, stupid, habitually drowsy, witless, ill-looking, darkling, resentful, and lazy. Governed by *rajas* is one of ready speech and good advice, friendly, argumentative, eager to learn, arrogant, and proud, O brahmin seer. Governed by *sattva* is one who is illumined, steady, aloof, unprotesting, free from anger, wise, and self-controlled. Enlightenment, the mark of *sattva*, is troubled by the ways of the world; when one has learned that which is to be learned, he loathes the way of the world. Once this character of dispassion prevails, his self-pride mellows and his sincerity becomes serene. Thereupon all the pairs of opposites are mutually appeased, and he does not exert himself at all in any cause. A man who observes the virtues of this good estate, if born a serf, will become a commoner, O brahmin, or a baron. When he abides by uprightness, he lays claim to brahminhood.

Thus I have described to you all the *guṇas*. What else do you wish to hear?

The brahmin said:

What happens to the body fire when it reaches the element earth, and how does the wind by its particular location actuate a person?

Mārkaṇḍeya said:

When the great-spirited brahmin had given voice to this question, Yudhiṣṭhira, the hunter, explained it to him.

The hunter said:

The fire that resides in the head while it guards the body is the *prāṇa*, which operates both in the head and the fire and is active. Past, present, and future all depend on the *prāṇa*. We reverently hold that this brahman-fire is the highest of all elements. The being that ensouls all existing things is the sempiternal Person; he is made up by the mind, the spirit, and the ego, and the focus of the elements. While he does reside in all parts of the body, he is protected by the *prāṇa* and goes his various ways, backed by the *samāna*.

The fire that lies at the bottom of the bladder and in the intestines is the *apāna*, which carries off excrement and urine. The breath that alone inspires energy, activity, and vigor is called *udāna* by the experts on the human person. The breath that resides in all the various joints of the human body is declared to be the *vyāna*. The fire that pervades the elements of the body is called the wind, which rushes about activating the juices, the organs, and the humors. By the combination of the *prāṇas* that combination is produced that is known as the digestive fire, which digests a person's food. *Prāṇa* and *vyāna* insert themselves between *apāna* and *udāna*, and the resulting fire completely digests its substratum. It governs the organ called the intestinal tract, which terminates at the anus. From this fire spring

25 the various channels among all the *prāṇas* of the person. Impelled by
the impact of fire, the *prāṇa* goes down as far as the belly, then,
coming up again, exhales the fire. Below the navel is the area of
digested food, above it the area of undigested food, while the central
area of the navel is the base of all the *prāṇas*. Ten channels, which
radiate from the heart upward, downward, and horizontally, all
activated by the *prāṇas*, carry the food juices. This is the path by
which the yogins go to the supreme; having mastered fatigue and
posture, and having become imperturbable, they placed their soul on
the head.

It is in this way that *prāṇa* and *apāna* are stretched out in all
persons. The person undergoes eleven transformations, and is a
composite of fractional components; know that it is embodied and
30 always subject to the influence of previous deeds. Know that the
eternal fire within it, like a fire piled in a brazier, is the soul, always
subject to the influence of Yoga. Know that the God contained within
it, like a drop contained within a lotus, is the knower-of-the-field,
always subject to renunciation. Know that *sattva*, *rajas*, and *tamas*
consist in vitality, and that vitality is a property of the soul, and that
the soul consists in the supreme.

> They say that sentience is the mark of life,
> It acts, and activates all creatures;
> The knowers-of-the-field know beyond it the supreme,
> Who has created the seven worlds.

The elemental soul, which is thus in all creatures, is not manifest;
35 those who have insight perceive it with a superior, subtle spirit. By
means of the serenity of his spirit the sage destroys the good and bad
consequences of previous deeds, and, when he serenely abides in his
soul, attains to infinite bliss. The sign of serenity is that one always
sleeps comfortably and contentedly; lighted up with good health, one
gives off light, like a lamp in a windless spot. If one yokes the mind
in the early and late night, eats lightly, and is pure of soul, he sees
the soul within himself. As though with a lighted lamp he sees, with
the lamp of his mind, that the soul is separate from himself, and then
he is released. Greed and anger must be tamed by any means; this is
the purifying agent of sacrifice, and this self-mortification is regarded
as the bridge.

40 One should always guard one's austerity from anger, one's wealth
from an envious man, one's knowledge from esteem and disdain,
one's self from distraction. Kindliness is the highest Law, forbearance
the greatest strength, self-knowledge the highest knowledge, the vow
of truthfulness the highest vow. A spoken truth may be good, a
known truth beneficial, but the truth that is in all respects beneficial

to the creatures is regarded as the highest. He whose actions are always devoid of self-interest and who has sacrificed everything to renunciation is a wise renouncer. This is the Yoga of the Brahman, from which even one's guru cannot shake one as he prepares one, the Relinquishment that is called the Union.

45 One must never harm any creatures, but go the road of
benevolence; once embarked upon his life he should never feud with
anyone. Self-unimportance, profound contentment, selflessness, and
perseverance lead to high knowledge, and the knowledge of the self
is always the highest knowledge of all. Give up your possessions and
be strict in your vows with your spirit: thus you reach the sorrowless
place that is unshakable here and hereafter. Be always austere, self-
controlled, ascetic, master of yourself, desirous of winning the unwon,
detached from attachments. Marked by no properties, detached, of
single purpose, uninterrupted—that, brahmin, is your conduct, which
50 they call, in one word, *bliss*. If a man renounces both happiness and
unhappiness, he attains to Brahman; by detachment he passes
beyond the end.

Here I have related it all to you in summary, grand brahmin, just as I myself have heard it. What else do you wish to hear?

Mārkaṇḍeya said:

204.1 When this entire Law of release had been propounded, O Yudhiṣṭhira, the brahmin, greatly joyous of heart, spoke to the pious hunter: "You have expounded all this with complete arguments. Nothing is found in the world that is unknown to you!"

The hunter said:

See with your own eyes, best of the twice-born, the Law that is mine, by virtue of which I have attained to success, bull among brahmins. Rise, your reverence. Quickly enter my house, and deign to visit my father and mother, sage of the Law.

Mārkaṇḍeya said:

5 At his invitation the brahmin entered and set eyes on a much cherished, lovely, and very charming stuccoed house of four halls, which resembled the house of a God, and was indeed much honored by the deities; it was crowded with couches and stools, and redolent with superb perfumes. His honored, white-robed parents were sitting there on fine seats, relaxing contentedly after their meal. When the pious hunter saw them, he fell with his head at their feet.

The old ones said:

Arise, arise, sage of the Law, the Law shall defend you. We are pleased with your purity, live a long life! You have been a good son, child, you have honored us for a long time; even among the deities you have known no other deity. Because of your piety you have

10 become endowed with the self-control of the brahmins. Your father's
grandfathers and great-grandfathers are continuously pleased with
your discipline in honoring us. You have never lacked obedience in
either thought, deed, or word, nor has your spirit strayed wrongly,
that we have seen. Son, you have done all, and more, that Rāma
Jāmadagnya did in honoring your parents!

Mārkaṇḍeya said:

Thereupon the pious hunter presented the brahmin to them, and
the elders received him with welcome. The brahmin accepted their
homage and questioned the old couple: "Are you, with son and
retainers, in good health at home? Are your bodies still healthy?"

The old ones said:

15 We are all in good health at our home and among our servants.
We hope you yourself have come here unhindered by ailments,
reverend sir?

Mārkaṇḍeya said:

"Indeed, I have," replied the brahmin happily. Then the pious
hunter spoke this meaningful word to the brahmin: "These two, my
father and mother, reverend, are my highest divinity. I do for them
what is done for the Gods. These parents are as worshipful to me as all
the thirty-three Gods led by Indra are to the world. Just as the twice-
born act with respect to the deities, bringing them offerings, so I
20 untiringly act with respect to these two. My father and my mother
are my highest divinity, brahmin, and I continually satisfy them with
flowers, fruit, and gems. They are to me like the fires of which the
sages speak, or like sacrifice and the four *Vedas*—they are all to me,
brahmin. My life, wife, sons, and friends are in their service; with
wife and sons I always show obedience to them.

"I bathe them myself and wash their feet. I myself bring them
their meal, good brahmin. I tell them pleasant stories, and avoid the
unpleasant ones; I do things for them even if it means breaking the
25 Law, as long as they are pleased. Knowing that the Law is my guru
I always obey them tirelessly, best of the twice-born. A man who
wishes to prosper must have five gurus: his father, his mother, his
fire, himself, and his guru, O best of the twice-born. If he treats them
properly, they become for him forever his well-kept fires; for one
in the householder stage of life this is the eternal Law."

Mārkaṇḍeya said:

205.1 Having presented his father and mother to the brahmin as his
gurus, the piously inspired hunter again said to the brahmin, "I have
become foresighted, behold the power of my austerities! It was
because of this that that self-controlled, truthful and faithful wife told

you, 'Go to Mithilā! A hunter who lives there shall explain the Laws to you.' "

The brahmin said:

Sage of the Law, strict in your vows, when I recall the words of that faithful, truthful, well-mannered wife, I know that you indeed have virtue!

The hunter said:

The things you say about me, best of the twice-born, were indeed perfectly foreseen by that faithful wife, no doubt of that. Yet, in a spirit of grace for you, brahmin, I have shown you what I have shown you. Now, brahmin, my son, listen to the words I shall speak to you. You have slighted your parents, good brahmin, you left the house without their dismissal, faultless sir. What you did was not consonant with the statement, injunction, and meaning of the *Veda*. Your poor parents have been blinded with grief over you. Go and comfort them, lest the great Law overtake you. You are austere, great-spirited, and always bent upon the Law; all this may prove meaningless, unless you placate your parents. Have faith in me, brahmin, please do not act differently. Go at once, brahmin seer, I am telling you for your own good!

The brahmin said:

All you have said is the truth, without a doubt. I am pleased with you, sage of the Law, who have the virtues and the conduct of the strict.

The hunter said:

You who are equal to the deity, so avowed to the ancient, divine, eternal Law, hard to find for those of unmade souls: go quickly and pay honor tirelessly to your parents; beyond that I see no more Law for you to pursue.

The brahmin said:

I came here by good fortune, and by good fortune I found you. Men like you, who vividly show the Law, are difficult to find in this world. Among a thousand people one may find one Law-wise man—or one may not. I am pleased with your truthfulness, good luck to you, best of men! I was falling to hell, and you saved me! It was fated to be that I found you, man without fault. King Yayāti fell and was rescued by his daughter's good sons: so, tiger among men, have I been rescued here by you. I shall follow your word and show obedience to my parents; for no one of unmade soul knows how to decide between Law and Unlaw.

The eternal Law is obscure to one who has been born a serf. I do not think you are a serf: it was surely fate that caused you, as your previous deeds matured, to come to this estate of serfdom. I wish to find out what the truth in this matter is, sage, and, if you so please, do tell me how it really is, for you are the master of your soul.

The hunter said:

Surely, no brahmin must be ignored, good brahmin! So hear all that happened to me in my previous body, faultless sir. Yes, I was a brahmin before, O son of an eminent brahmin; I studied the *Veda*, was very clever, finished the branches of the *Veda*, and by my own mistake fell to my present state, brahmin.

A certain king, who was adept at archery, was my friend, and
through this association I, too, became a master with the bow,
brahmin. At that time the king went out hunting one day,
accompanied by his best warriors and surrounded by his counselors.
25 He shot a good many deer close to a hermitage. I too shot a wicked
straight arrow, good brahmin, and it hit a hermit. He fell to the
ground and spoke in a resounding voice, "I was innocent of any sin! Who has done this wicked thing?" Still thinking he was a deer I ran to him and then saw that seer pierced by my straight arrow, that awesomely austere brahmin, who was now breathing his last on the ground. My heart trembled at my vile deed, and I cried out, "I did not know what I was doing! Pray forgive me!" So I spoke to the hermit, but faint with anger the seer replied to me, "Thou shalt be a hunter, cruel man, born from a serf, brahmin!"

The hunter said:

206.1 When I had so been cursed by that seer, O best of brahmins, I tried to placate the eloquent saint with these words: "I did not know that I was doing this vile deed, hermit! Pray forgive it all, be appeased, my lord!"

The seer said:

The curse will not be changed; it will doubtless befall as I have
said. But my natural kindliness prompts me to do you a favor now.
Although born from a serf womb, you shall be a sage of the Law and
5 undoubtedly pay obedience to your father and mother. Through this
obedience you shall attain great success. You shall have the memories of your previous birth, and go to heaven. And, when the curse has expired, you shall again be a brahmin.

The hunter said:

In this manner was I of yore cursed by that seer of awesome heat, but was shown grace by him too, O best of men. I pulled the arrow out of him, brought him to the hermitage, and he failed to die. This tells you all that befell me before. I shall go to heaven, best of brahmins.

The brahmin said:

These are the vicissitudes, happy as well as unhappy, that man incurs, good sage. Pray have no regrets, for you have accomplished

a difficult task, son, as you know your real birth. Your present vile
10 profession is due only to your caste, sage. Suffer it for the time being,
then you shall be a brahmin! Even now I doubt not that you are a brahmin; while a brahmin, living in crime that is sure to hasten his fall, and arrogant and wallowing in misdeeds, is equal to a serf. Any serf who always rises to self-control, truthfulness, and Law, I judge him a brahmin; for one becomes a brahmin through one's conduct, while one will go a ghastly wrong course by the evil of one's doing. But with regard to you, I think the guilt is gone, best of men. Please have no regrets, for the likes of you never give up: they know how to conduct themselves in the adventures of the world, and always uphold the Law.

The hunter said:

15 Kill mental pain with wisdom, as you kill bodily pain with herbs.
This capacity for wisdom shall not come equally to fools. Men of little spirit suffer pains of the mind when they are visited by the unpleasant and divorced from the pleasant. All creatures are gifted with some good things, and some bad; there is no reason for grief if it occurs to a single person. When people see something unpleasant, they quickly withdraw; they take measures when they see it coming. Nothing becomes of the surprised complainer: he can only suffer.

Those men who relinquish both the pleasant and unpleasant
increase their happiness, for they are wise and contented with their
20 knowledge. Discontented are the fools, contented the wise: to
discontent there is no end, but contentment is the greatest happiness: those who have gone the way do not complain, for they see their ultimate goal. Do not set your mind on despair; despair is a deadly poison, which kills the silly fool like an angry cobra. If despair overcomes a man when he gets into trouble, he is deprived of inner strength and finds no human purpose. We see that the deeds that have been done inevitably bear fruit, but nothing good comes to him who has succumbed to despair. Rather should one look for a means to get rid of all suffering entirely, and uncomplainingly begin again, and be yoked and without vice.

25 If one reflects upon the misfortunes that happen to the creatures,
one reaches the high limit of one's spirit; and once they have seen the final goal, the enlightened do not complain. I myself do not complain, sage, I am eagerly waiting for my Time. With these showings before me, good brahmin, I do not lose hope.

The brahmin said:

You are enlightened and wise, and your insight is ample. I do not complain of you, for you are contented with your knowledge and you know the Law. I take my leave of you, good luck to you, the Law shall guard you all around. Let there be no negligence in the matter of Law, first of the upholders of Law!

Mārkaṇḍeya said:

"Surely!" replied the hunter with folded hands, and the good
30 brahmin circumambulated the other, and departed. The brahmin went, and was thereafter completely obedient to his father and mother, and to his elders, according to the rules, for he was now firmly resolved.

So have I fully related to you, Yudhiṣṭhira, the Law about which you asked me, my son, first of the upholders of the Law: the greatness of the faithful wife, and of the brahmin; while obedience to father and mother has been celebrated in the person of the hunter.

Yudhiṣṭhira said:

Yes, this account of the Law was close to incredible, brahmin, first of all upholders of the Law, the way in which you told it, best of the twice-born. I have listened happily, sage, so it seemed only a brief span. Yet I am still not sated of listening to the highest Law.

3(37.g) Angiras

207–21 (B. 217–31; C. 14100–649)

207 (217; 14100). Yudhiṣṭhira asks Mārkaṇḍeya about the origin of Skanda (1–5). Agni is jealous of Angiras, who asks to be his son (5–15). Angiras himself has a son, Bṛhaspati (15).

208 (218; 14122). Genealogy of various fires (1–5).

209 (219; 14130). Origin and names of sacrificial fires (1–25).

210 (220; 14156). Five ascetics beget a son Pāñcajanya, who has five colors (1–5). As Tapas he creates the Gods, five dynasties, and five hindrances of the ritual (1–15).

211 (221; 14175). Bhānu is Tapas's son and has offspring who are fires (1–30).

212 (222; 14207). The fire Gṛhapati (1). Agni hides in the ocean and tells the atharvan *Angiras to become the sacrificial fire. The fish betray Agni and are cursed (5–10). Agni enters earth and creates the ores (10). Roused by the* tapas *of great ascetics, Agni hides in the ocean. Angiras churns the ocean and the sacrificial fire reappears (10–15). It creates rivers (20). All fires are really one (25–30).*

213 (223–24; 14241). Gods and Asuras are embattled,

the latter are victorious (1–5). Indra goes looking for a champion; by Lake Mānasa he finds a crying woman and the Asura Keśin, whom he berates and defeats (1–15). She is Devasenā; her husband will be a great champion (15–20). There is a portentous conjunction of sun and moon at the Rudra hour (20–30). Brahmā predicts a great child (35). The seven seers led by Vasiṣṭha sacrifice and summon the Fire God from the sun (35–40). Fire is aroused by the seers' wives (40–45). Svāhā, in love with Fire, assumes the shapes of the seers' wives (50).

214 (225; 14298). Fire lies with Svāhā in the shape of Angiras' wife Śivā (1–5). She takes the semen and flies away in the shape of Garuḍa to Mount Śveta, where she deposits it (5–10). She assumes the shapes of the other seers' wives except Vasiṣṭha's wife Arundhatī (10–15). From the six portions of semen Skanda is born with six heads; he takes form in four days and frolics (15–25). He is joined by his Companions; he cleaves Mount Krauñca and Mount Śveta; the mountains fly away and earth trembles (25–35).

215 (226; 14339). People accuse Garuḍa of producing Skanda; the bird declares it is his mother. The seers divorce their wives except Arundhatī; Svāhā declares herself the mother (1–5). Viśvāmitra performs the sacraments for the child (5–10). The Gods order Indra to kill Skanda; he says that only the Mothers are able to do that. The Mothers declare he is their son (10–15). Fire plays with Skanda (20).

216 (227; 14370). Indra marches out to attack Skanda, who burns his army (1–10). From the thunderbolt's impact on Skanda, Viśākha is born (10).

217 (228; 14388). Lesser Kumāras arise (1–15). The Mothers have sons by Skanda (5–10).

218 (229; 14401). Śrī honors Skanda (1–5). The seers declare he should be Indra; Indra supports this, but Skanda declines (5–15); instead he will be the army commander (20). Rudra appears and is claimed to be the Fire that is Skanda's father (20–30). Skanda is anointed commander (35–40). Indra marries off Devasenā to Skanda (40–45).

219 (230; 11454). The six wives of the seers appear and want Skanda as son; they become the Kṛttikā constellation (1–10). The Mothers demand the offspring

of mothers (10–20); they may afflict children until age sixteen, and they send out Graspers of various kinds (20–40). Other types of Graspers (40–55).
220 (231; 14514). Svāhā claims motherhood; she will dwell with Fire (1–5). Brahmā explains Skanda's multiple origin (10). Skanda's emblems (15–20). The scene on Mount Śvetā (20–25).
221 (231; 14541). Procession of Rudra and the Gods (1–25). An army of Dānavas appears to attack the Gods; they do battle (25–45). The Gods flee before Mahiṣa who attacks Rudra (35–60). Skanda kills Mahiṣa and destroys the demons; Indra praises him (60–80).

Vaiśaṃpāyana said:

207.1 When the King Dharma had heard this holy narrative informed by Law, he once more questioned the ascetic seer Mārkaṇḍeya.

Yudhiṣṭhira said:

What was the reason that the Fire once departed for the forest, and that the great seer Angiras, in the absence of the Fire God, became fire and carried the oblations? Though the Fire God is one, fires are found to be many in the various rites, reverend sir. I wish to know all this—how Kumāra was born, how he became the son of the Fire God, how he was born from Rudra by the Ganges and the
5 Pleiades. This I wish to learn from you, O joy of the Bhārgavas, just as it befell, great hermit, for I am filled with curiosity.

Mārkaṇḍeya said:

On this they quote this ancient tale, of how the Fire God angrily went to the forest in order to perform austerities, and how the venerable Angiras became himself the God of Fire, warming with his own glow and dispelling the darkness, surpassing the old Fire, while the lordly sage dwelt in his hermitage, having become like the Fire and illuminating all the world.

The Fire God practiced austerities, and he became greatly vexed with the splendor of the other ascetic, and the resplendent God did not know what to think. The venerable Carrier of the Oblation therefore
10 mused, "Brahmā has let loose on the worlds another Fire God, for my fieriness has vanished while I was practicing austerities. How shall I become the Fire God again?" While he was thus thinking, he beheld the great hermit, who was glowing like fire itself. He approached slowly and fearfully, and Angiras said to him, "Now quickly regain your old being of the Fire God, and prosper the worlds once more. In the three worlds you are well-known to the moving and standing creatures. You were the first to be created by Brahmā, in order to

dispel the darkness. Regain your old position at once, Remover of the Night!"

The Fire God said:

My renown in the world has gone—you have become the Fire God.
15 People will know you, not me, for the God of Fire. I renounce my fieriness, you be the premier Fire, and I shall be the secondary Fire, the Prājāpatyaka.

Angiras said:

Bestow the benefits that lead creatures to heaven! Be the Fire that Dispels the Darkness! And make me at once your first-born son, O God Fire!

Mārkaṇḍeya said:

Upon hearing these words of Angiras, Jātavedas* did as he had said, O king, and Angiras had a son by the name of Bṛhaspati. Knowing that Angiras' son was the first-born son of the Fire, the Gods approached, O Bhārata, and inquired concerning the cause thereof. At the Gods' questions he told them the reason, and the Gods accepted Angiras' reply.
20 I shall tell you of the various luminous fires that are known for all the many rites, and of their variety as declared in the *Brāhmaṇas.*

Mārkaṇḍeya said:

208.1 This third son of Brahmā, O scion of the lineage of the Kurus, wed the daughter of Āpava. I shall mention his children; listen, king: Bṛhajjyotis, Bṛhatkīrti, Bṛhadbrahman, Bṛhanmanas, Bṛhanmantra, Bṛhadbhāsa, and Bṛhaspati. Angiras' first daughter, Goddess Bhānumatī by name, was without peer among his children. Angiras' second daughter, whom all creatures loved, was because of this love
5 called Rāgā. Of Angiras' third daughter, Śinīvalī, the creatures said that she was like Kapardin's daughter, so thin that she was no sooner seen than she vanished. Arciṣmatī was seen with her luminousness, Haviṣmatī with her oblations, while they named Angiras' sixth blessed girl Mahiṣmatī. The seventh Angiras girl, being well-honored at the great fiery sacrifices, was renowned as Mahāmatī. And that venerable daughter of Angiras at whose sight people exclaimed in surprise that she was one and indivisible they named Kuhū.

Mārkaṇḍeya said:

209.1 Bṛhaspati's wife was the glorious Cāndramasī, who gave birth to the six fires and to one daughter. The fire for which the butter offering is enjoined at the oblations is Śaṃyu, the luminous son of Bṛhaspati; he is the fire to whom the first-born animal is offered at the Seasonal Sacrifices, the Oblation, and the Horse Sacrifice; this

* = Fire.

mighty fire is one, though ablaze with many-splendored flames.
Śaṃyu's matchless wife was Satyā, who was a daughter of Dharma;
5 he had the blazing Agni as son, and three avowed daughters. The fire that is honored at the sacrifice with the first butter portion, the fire Bharadvāja, is said to be his first son. The fire named Bharata, to which butter is offered with the *sruva* ladle at all the Full-Moon Sacrifices, is the second son who was born to Śamyu. There were three daughters, who were wed by Bharata. He had a son Bharata and one daughter, Bharatā. The Bharata fire is the son of the fire Prajāpati; when it is high it is extremely fierce, O best of the Bharatas.

Bharadvāja's wife was Vīrā, his heir was Vīra. The brahmins declare that he gets the same worship as Soma, but in a soft voice.
10 The fire that joins the Soma in the second oblation is called Rathaprabhu, Rathadhvāna, and Kumbharetas. He begot Siddhi on Sarayū, and obfuscated the sun with his splendors; it was he who fetched the Fire Hymn, and is always mentioned in the invocations. The fire named Niścyavana—because it never declines, whether in fame, power, or fortune—always lauds the earth. The fire Vipāpā—without evil, free from taint, pure, blazing with flames—is his son, true in the acts of the covenant. The fire named Niṣkṛti—who accomplishes the restoration of creatures that are crying out—
15 beautifies when assiduously cultivated. His son is the fire called Svana, by means of which people who suffer from pains continue to groan; it inflicts pain.

The fire that keeps striding upon the resolve of the entire universe, this fire is called the Viśvajit fire by those who know of the matters of the soul. And the intestinal fire, which, lying within, digests the food that people have eaten, is everywhere at the sacrifice called Viśavabhuj, O Bhārata. The brahmins pay worship, at their oblations of cooked food, to the brahminic and self-restrained fire, at all times abounding in vows, which is known as Gopati; it loved a river; with
20 this fire all rites are performed by those who perform rites. The upward-sharing fire, that most terrifying Mare's Head fire, which drinks water, is called Ūrdhvabhāj; this sage is vested in the breath. That most excellent fire from which the butter rises as well-offered when the daily northern-door oblation is offered at home is known as the Sviṣṭakṛt.

Now his daughter—a fire that becomes wrath in placid beings—was born Mañyātī, the very sap of anger, and abides, under the name *svāhā!*, cruelly and fearfully among all creatures. The fire Kāma, whom no one in heaven matches in beauty, was so named by the Gods because of his matchlessness. And the fire that destroys enemies

in battle—holding his anger from sheer excitement, armed with the
bow, decked with garlands, erect on his chariot—is the fire Amogha.
25 And, lordly sir, the Uktha lauded with three *ukthas*, which
generates a large voice, that they know as the Sakāmāśva.

Mārkaṇḍeya said:

210.1 Kāśyapa, Vāsiṣṭha, Prāṇa, the Son of Prāṇa, Agni Āngirasa, and
Cyavana Triṣuvarcaka performed severe austerities for many years
in the cause of a son: "May we obtain a most lawly son, in fame the
peer of Brahmā!" Having been contemplated upon with the aid of
the five Great Utterances, a blazing light made up of splendor issued
forth, majestic and of five colors. A well-kindled fire was his head, his
arms were like unto the sun, skin and eyes like the hue of gold, his
5 shins darkling, O Bhārata. As he had been made in five colors by
these five men with the aid of their austerities, he is known in the
Veda as Pāñcajanya; and he became the founder of five dynasties.

As an ascetic he performed austerities for ten thousand years and,
creating offspring, begot the dreadful Fire of the Fathers: and he
created the *bṛhat* and *rathantara* melodies—those fast thieves—from
his head and mouth, Śiva from his navel, Indra from his strength,
Wind and Fire from his breath, and from his arms the two accents,
the All-Gods and the creatures. Having created those, he created the
five sons of the Fathers: Praṇidhi, son of Bṛhadūrjas, Bṛhattara of
Kāśyapa, Bhānu the male child of Angiras, Saubhara the son of
10 Varca, Anudātta of Prāṇa; thus are explained the five dynasts. He
created the Gods, the Sacrifice, Dawn, and the western fifteen. Tapas
created Abhima, Atibhīma, Bhīmabalābala, Sacrifice, and Dawn—
these five Gods. This Tapas brought forth the Gods named Sumitra,
Mitravat, Mitrajña, Mitravardhana, and Mitradharman. The same
Tapas produced the following five: Surapravīra, Vīra, Sukeśa,
Suvarcas, and Surahantar. These three classes of five each are
stationed here on earth. Now, the sacrificers that sacrifice for the sake
15 of heaven, of them they steal the offering, and kill it big on earth.
Out of spite for the sacrificial fires they kill and steal. But, when the
fire has been put in its proper place, they do not creep up to the
oblation on the altar, or to the gift thereof begun by the competent.
The piled-up fire that carries up the sacrifice frustrates them on both
sides; for when appeased by the spells, they do not steal the sacral
offering.

The son of the heat of Bṛhaduktha lives on earth, and on earth
the strict worship him when the *agnihotra* is offered. The *rathantara*
is a fire declared to be a son of this heat; the *adhvaryus* know that
his oblation is destined for Mitravinda.

The glorious man rejoiced, being most pleased with his sons.

Mārkaṇḍeya said:

211.1 The fire called Bharata is subject to severe restrictions; the fire
named Puṣṭimati provides prosperity when it is gratified. As it
supports all creatures, it is called Bharata. The fire called Śiva is bent
upon the worship of Śakti, and it is always *śiva* because it gives
succor to all that are inflicted with suffering.
To Tapas, after he had seen the great and augmented fruit of
austerity, a wise son was born, Purandara, in order to rescue the
fruit. Uṣman was born from Tapas, and this fire is observed in all
creatures. Also the fire named Manu, who officiated as Prajāpati.
5 Brahmins who are expert in the *Veda* also mention the fire Śaṃbhu,
and the twice-born make another mention of the blazing fire
Āvasathya. Thus the fire Tapas engendered five sacrificial fires,
bestowing vigor, carrying the oblation, and like gold in their splendor.
The fire Gavāṃpati begot the terrible Asuras, and the mortals of
various sorts, my lord, when it was exhausted at its setting. Angiras
created Tapas' son Manu, as well as Bhānu; but brahmins who are
expert in the *Veda* call him Bṛhadhānu.
Bhānu's wife was Suprajā, as well as Bṛhadbhāsā and Somajā.
They begot five sons—hear of the women's manner of offspring.
10 They name the fire Balada the first son of Bhānu; it bestows a body
on weak creatures. Bhānu's second son was the fire called Manyumat,
which becomes a terrible grudge in tranquil creatures. Then the fire
that is called Viṣṇu, and named Dhṛtimat Angiras; to this fire the
oblation at the New Moon and Full Moon ritual is said to be offered
on earth. The Āgrayaṇa fire is a son of Bhānu to which, along with
Indra, the *āgrayaṇa* oblation is offered. Niragraha, which does not
fail to seize the regular oblations at the Seasonal Sacrifices, is a son
of Bhānu along with the previous four.
15 Bhānu begot a daughter Niśā, and the Agnīṣomas; she became
Manu's wife and gave birth to the five *pāvaka* fires. The one who,
along with Parjanya, is honored at the Seasonal Sacrifices with the
first oblation is the lustrous fire Vaiśvānara. The fire Viśvapati, which
is declared to be the lord of this world, is Manu's second son.
Sviṣṭakṛt is considered the chief. Through it the butter is well-
offered. There was a girl Rohiṇī, the daughter of Hiraṇyakaśipu;
because of her deeds she appeared as his wife; she is a Prajāpati fire.
The fire that, residing in the breath, sets in motion the bodies of the
20 embodied is called Saṃnihita; it brings about word and form. The
deity whose course is white and black and who carries the oblation
is seated in anger; this is the Akalmaṣa fire and effects stained deeds.
The Kapila fire is the great seer whom the ascetics call Kapila, the

founder of Sāṃkhya and Yoga. The fire through which the *agra*
oblation comes to the deceased at all the various rites here is called
the Agraṇī fire.

He engendered the following *pāvaka* fires, copious and famed on
earth, which are meant for reparations of what goes wrong at the
agnihotra. If because of wind the fires somehow touch one another,
25 an oblation on eight sherds must be made for the Śuci fire. If the
Southern Fire gets mixed with the other two, an oblation on eight
sherds must be made for the Vīti fire. If the fires come in touch with a
conflagration in the house, an oblation on eight sherds must be made
to the Śuci fire. When a woman in her menses touches the
agnihotra, an oblation on eight sherds must be made for the Dasyumat
fire. If one hears that a living being has died or if cattle die, an
oblation of eight sherds must be made for the Abhimat fire. A sick
brahmin who has not offered into the fire for three nights should
30 make an oblation on eight sherds for the Northern Fire. He for whom
the New Moon and Full Moon rites remain waiting must do an
oblation on eight sherds to the Pathikṛt fire. If the confinement fire
touches the *agnihotra* fire, an oblation on eight sherds must be made
for the Agnimat fire.

Mārkaṇḍeya said:

212.1 Muditā was the beloved wife of Saha Āpa; and the lord of Bhūḥ
and Bhuvaḥ begot an eminent fire. This fire is called the lord of
earth. This blessed and very glorious fire goes about continuously as
the lord on earth of all great beings. This fire, named Gṛhapati, is
worshiped daily at the sacrifices; it carries the oblation offered by the
5 world. The wondrous and lordly Apāṃgarbha with his son is called
lord of Bhūḥ, lord of Bhuvaḥ, and lord of Mahat. His son was the
Bharata fire that burns dead creatures. At the *agniṣṭoma* the Niyata
is the greatest rite of the multitude. When he saw the Niyata come,
he hid from fear in the ocean; the Gods did not get it and looked in
all directions. Upon seeing Atharvan* the fire said, "Carry the
oblation to the Gods, hero, I am too feeble. Atharvan, become the
honey-eyed one—do this favor to me!" And having sent Atharvan,
he went to a different country. The fishes reported on him, and in
10 anger he said to them, "You shall be the food of creatures in your
various modes of being." And the Carrier of the Oblation spoke again
to Atharvan.

Though Atharvan coaxed him greatly at the behest of the Gods,
he refused to carry the oblation and abandoned his entire body.
Having relinquished his body he entered into earth, and as he
touched the earth he created the ores one by one. From his mouth

* = Angiras.

sulfur and gold, from his bones the *deodar* pines, from his phlegm quartz, from his bile emeralds, from his liver black iron: with the latter three glitter the creatures. His nails became mica, his arteries coral: thus, O king, the various elements arose from his body.

15 Having thus abandoned his body, and remaining in the greatest austerity, he was roused by the mortifications of Bhṛgu, Angiras, and others. Swollen with the power of austerity, the crested fire blazed forth mightily; but on seeing the seers he hid from fear in the great ocean. At his disappearance the world, frightened, turned to Atharvan, and Gods and seers worshiped him. When Atharvan espied the fire, he himself created the worlds and, while all the creatures looked on, churned up the great ocean. Thus the lost fire was of yore called back by the blessed Atharvan, and ever since it has carried the oblations of all creatures.

20 Thus he created the hearths mentioned in the *Vedas*, and the many Gods, as he roamed and wandered through different countries. The Five Rivers except the Indus, the Devikā, Sarasvatī, Ganges, Śatakumbhā, Sarayū, Gaṇḍakī, Carmaṇvatī, Mahī, Medhyā, Medhātithi, the three rivers Tāmravatī, Vetravatī, and Kauśikī, Tamasā, Narmadā, Godāvarī, Veṇṇā, Praveṇī, Bhīmā, and Medratha, O Bhārata, the Bhāratī, Suprayogā, Kāverī, Murmurā, Kṛṣṇā, Kṛṣṇaveṇṇā, Kapilā, and Śoṇā—these rivers are famed as the mothers of hearths.

25 Adbhuta had a wife Pryiā; her son was Viḍūratha.

There are as many Soma rites as there are fires. They were born in the lineage of Atri as the will-born sons of Brahmā. Wishing to beget sons, Atri bore them in himself, then the fires issued from Brahmā's body.

Thus I have related to you the great-spirited and boundless fires
that dispel darkness, and how they originated. Know that they all
have the greatness, proclaimed in the *Vedas*, of Adbhuta, for there is
only one fire. The blessed first Angiras was the only one; it issued
30 from the body in various ways, like the *jyotiṣṭoma* rite. So, then, I
have celebrated the grand genealogy of the fires; when purified with
various spells it carries the creatures' oblations.

Mārkaṇḍeya said:

213.1 I have related to you, prince sans blame, the various genealogy of the fires; now hear, O Kauravya, of the birth of the sagacious Kārtikeya. I shall tell you how that wondrous, boundlessly mighty son of Adbhuta, brahminic and prospering fame, was born by the wives of the seven seers.

In the olden days the Gods and the Asuras strove to destroy one another, and in their battles the dreadful-shaped Dānavas always

vanquished the Gods. Seeing his army many times massacred by
them, the Sacker of Cities* became greatly concerned over finding a
5 commander of his forces: "I must find a man who, when he sees the
army of the Gods broken by the Dānavas, will be brave enough to rescue it." Much musing on this matter he went to Mount Mānasa, and he heard a terrible cry of anguish voiced by a woman. "Hurry to me, anyone, and save me! Let him show me a husband, or himself be mine!"

The Sacker of Cities said to her, "Have no fear, you are in no
danger." Having said this he saw Keśin standing before him, wielding
10 a club and wearing a crown, like a mineral-rich mountain. Vāsava*
took the maiden by the hand and said to him, "Why do you ignobly seek to rape this maiden? Know that I am the Thunderbolt-wielder—cease molesting her!"

Keśin said:

Let go of her, Śakra, I want this girl. You better go back to your city with your life, Chastiser of Pāka!

Mārkaṇḍeya said:

As he said this, Keśin hurled his club at Indra to destroy him, but Vāsava hacked it in two with his thunderbolt while it came flying at him. Thereupon Keśin, enraged, flung a mountain peak, and the God of the Hundred Sacrifices, seeing it fly at him, splintered it with his
bolt, O king, and it fell to the ground. Keśin was hurt by the falling
15 peak, and he abandoned the maiden and fled in great pain. The Asura
gone, Vāsava said to the maiden, "Who are you, whose are you? What are you doing here, pretty girl?"

The maiden said:

I am the daughter of Prajāpati, known as Devasenā. My sister is Daityasenā, she was raped by Keśin before. Together we sisters used to come to Mount Mānasa with our friends for pleasure when Prajāpati allowed us, and this great Asura Keśin always sought to abduct us. Daityasenā liked him, and I did not, Chastiser of Pāka; so she was abducted by him, my lord, and I was set free by your might.

Indra said:

20 You are the daughter of my mother's sister: Dākṣāyaṇī is my
mother. I want you to tell me of your strength.

The maiden said:

I am a weak woman, strong-armed God, but my husband will be strong. By the gift of a boon from my father he shall be honored by Gods and Asuras.

Indra said:

What will be the strength of your husband, Goddess? That I wish to hear from your lips, blameless woman.

* = Indra.

The maiden said:
He shall be found the mighty and powerful conqueror of Gods,
Dānavas, Yakṣas, Kiṃnaras, Snakes, and Rākṣasas. He shall vanquish
all beings together with you—such shall my husband be, brahminic
and prospering fame.

Mārkaṇḍeya said:
25 Upon hearing her words, Indra thought sorrowfully, "There is no
such husband of whom this Goddess speaks." Then the God of
luminous splendor saw the sun on Sunrise Mountain, and he saw the
lordly moon entering the sun. The hour of Rudra set in on the New
Moon Day, and he saw God and Asura embattled on Sunrise Peak.
The God of the Hundred Sacrifices saw the dawn covered with
blood-red clouds, and the lord observed that Varuṇa's ocean was
bloody. The fire was taking the oblation that had been offered with
30 manifold spells and was entering the sun. The twenty-four moon-
phase days gathered about the sun, and the law-coursing moon of the
Rudra hour was conjoint with the sun.

Watching the uniting of the moon and sun, and observing their
conjunction at the Rudra hour, Śakra thought, "This conjunction is
fearful and great and full of splendor, this concourse of the moon
with sun and fire is miraculous. If the moon begets a son, he will be
the husband of this Goddess. The fire too is endowed with all the
virtues, fire too is a God. If fire were to beget a son, he would be this
Goddess's husband." With such thoughts the lord went to the world
of Brahmā, taking Devasenā, and he saluted Grandfather and said:
"Pray assign a gallant husband to this Goddess!"

Brahmā said:
35 The matter shall be as you thought about it, Slayer of Dānavas:
there shall be an embryo of great strength and vast puissance. He
shall be captain of your host, together with you, God of the Hundred
Sacrifices, and he shall be the gallant husband of this Goddess.

Mārkaṇḍeya said:
When the Indra of the Gods heard this, he paid homage and went
with the maiden where the divine seers were—these eminent Indras
of the brahmins, great in their vows, who were headed by Vasiṣṭha.
Preceded by the God of the Hundred Sacrifices, the Gods went to their
sacrifice for their share, desirous of imbibing the soma that had been
obtained through their mortification. After having performed,
according to the rules, an *iṣṭi* oblation into the well-kindled fire, the
40 great-spirited priests offered the oblation to all the Celestials. The
Adbhuta fire was summoned from the orb of the sun, and the
sovereign Fire came out and appeared, restraining its speech, according
to the rules. Entering the *āhavanīya* hearth, into which the priests had
offered with the requisite spells, the Carrier of the Oblation accepted

the manifold offering from the seers, O best of the Bharatas, and proffered it to the Celestials.

As the Fire came out, he saw the wives of the great-spirited priests
—who sat in their own hermitages—while they were bathing
themselves at leisure, radiant like golden altars, spotless like a digit
of the moon, glowing with the glow of fire, all marvelous like stars.
Watching the wives of these Indras of priests, Fire became excited in
his senses, and, his heart lost to them, fell under the power of lust.
45 But he thought further: "It is not proper for me to be excited, for I
am lusting after the good wives of eminent brahmins, and they are
without passion. I cannot watch and touch them without cause—
therefore I shall enter the household fire and look at them
perpetually." Touching all these golden women, as it were, with his
flames, and watching them too, Fire rejoiced in the household hearth,
while he lived there and entrusted his heart to the beautiful women
under whose spell he was. But then, when he did not obtain these
brahmin wives, Fire's heart was sick with love, and he set his mind
on abandoning his life, and left for the forest.

50 Now Svāhā, the daughter of Dakṣa, had been in love with Fire
before, and for long the radiant girl had been looking for an opening,
but yet the blameless woman had found none in the ever-vigilant
God. When she learned that Fire had truly departed for the forest,
and was indeed sick with lust, the radiant girl thought, "I shall
assume the shapes of the wives of the seven seers, and when he has
been deluded by their shapes, I shall make love to lust-plagued Fire.
This done, he will be pleased, and my love will be satisfied."

Mārkaṇḍeya said:

214.1 Now Śivā was the wife of Angiras, and endowed with a fine
character, beauty, and virtue. It was her body the Goddess assumed
first, my lord of the people, and the beautiful woman went to Fire
and said, "Make love to me, Fire, I am ablaze with lust. If you will
not, be sure that I shall die. I am Śivā, O Eater of the Oblation, the
wife of Angiras. I have come only after deliberating this decision with
my friends."

Fire said:

How did you know that I was sick with love, how did all the others you mention, the beloved wives of the seven seers?

Śivā said:

5 You were always dear to us, but we were afraid of you. When we
came to know your heart by your gestures, they sent me to you. I
have come to lie with you here, now quickly make the love we want:
the mothers are waiting for me to return, O Fire.

Mārkaṇḍeya said:

Thereupon Fire most happily and joyfully lay with this Śivā; and
overcome by pleasure the Goddess took his seed in her hand. She
thought, "If people see this body in the forest, they will tell of the
brahmin wives' faithlessness with Fire. Therefore, in order to prevent
this, I'll become a Garuḍa bird, so I'll escape easily from the woods."
10 She became a fair-winged bird and left the vast forest, and she saw
Mount Śveta, all covered with reed stalks. The mountain was guarded
by wondrous poison-eyed and seven-headed serpents, and peopled by
Rākṣasas, Piśācas, and terrifying bands of ghosts, and by Rākṣasīs
and countless game and fowl.

She went to the inaccessible mountain ridge and hurredly threw
the seed into a golden basin. She assumed the guises of the other
wives of the great-spirited seven seers, and then made love to Fire.
But she was not able to assume the shape of Arundhatī, because of
15 the power of her austerities and her faithfulness to her husband. Six
times did she cast down the seed of Fire, O best of the Kurus, did the
loving Svāhā, into the mountain basin, on the first day of the
lunation. The spilled seed, gathered together in heat, engendered a
son who was worshiped by the seers; and the spilled seed became
Skanda.*

This child, this Kumāra, had six heads, twice as many ears, twelve
eyes, arms, and feet, one neck and one trunk. Guha took form on the
second day, was a babe on the third, and grew his major and lesser
limbs on the fourth. Enveloped by blood-red clouds with their
20 lightning, he shone like the sun rising on a vast cloud. He held an
immense and hair-raising bow, cleaver of the enemies of the Gods,
which had been placed there by the Slayer of Tripura.** Holding that
greatest of bows, he roared powerfully, enough to stun the three
worlds with their moving and standing creatures.

When they heard his roar, which sounded like masses of monsoon
clouds, the great Nāgas Citra and Airāvata jumped up; and seeing
them falling on him the heir of Fire, with the glow of the morning
sun, seized them with two of his hands, grasped with another hand
a spear, and embraced with yet another arm a red-combed cock, a
huge wild cock, foremost of the strong. Holding these he roared out
terrifyingly and frolicked mightily. With two of his hands the powerful
God took a conch shell and blew on it to strike terror even in mighty
25 creatures. With another pair of hands he pounded the air again and
again, and as he frolicked, Mahāsena was drinking up the three
worlds with his mouths; and on that mountain peak the boundlessly
spirited child was as the sun on Sunrise Peak.

* = Kumāra.
** = Rudra.

Wondrous of prowess and measureless of spirit he sat on the
mountaintop and regarded the horizons with his numerous faces.
Descrying all manner of beings he bellowed his roar again, and
hearing his cry, many creatures collapsed; and frightened and panic-
stricken they sought refuge with him. Those many-colored creatures
that attached themselves to the God the brahmins call his most
30 puissant Companions. He arose strong-armed and comforted the
creatures; then he displayed the bow and shot arrows at great Mount
Śveta. He cleaved Mount Krauñca, son of the Himālaya, and through
that breach the geese and vultures travel to Mount Meru. The
shattered mountain fell down, groaning loudly in pain, and when it
had crashed, the other mountains groaned greatly in fear. Although
the strong child heard the groans of the sorely afflicted, he did not
waver and in boundless spirits raised his spear and bellowed. The
great-spirited warrior threw his huge javelin and violently cleft the
35 awesome top of Mount Śveta. At his stroke Mount Śveta, quite upset,
flew up with other mountains, leaving the earth from fear of that
great spirit. This caused the earth to tremble and she was rent on all
sides; in pain she sought refuge with Skanda and appeared strong
again. And the mountains paid homage to him and came back to
the earth. Now the people worship Skanda on the fifth day of the
bright fortnight.

Mārkaṇḍeya said:

215.1 The seers, however, upon witnessing terrifying portents of many
kinds, were upset, and, being prosperers of the worlds, performed
rites of appeasement for the worlds. The people who lived in the
forest of Citraratha declared: "This great calamity has been fetched to
us by Fire, when he lay with the six wives of the seven seers."
Others, who had seen the Goddess at the time go about in that guise,
said of the Garuḍa bird: "You have brought on this disaster!" Not a
person knew that it had been the doing of Svāhā. When the Garuḍa
bird heard it said that Skanda was its son, it went up to him quietly
5 and said: "I am your mother." And upon hearing that a mighty son
had been born the seven seers divorced the six wives, excepting the
divine Arundhatī. The forest dwellers called him the son of the six,
but Svāhā told the seven seers that he was her son. "I know it, the
rest is not true!" she said again and again, O king.

The great hermit Viśvāmitra, after concluding the oblation of the seven seers, had followed Fire from behind unseen, when the God was sick with love. In that manner he had discovered the entire truth, and thus Viśvāmitra was the first to seek refuge with Kumāra, and he composed a divine hymn of praise for Mahāsena. All the thirteen sacraments pertaining to childhood the great hermit performed for

10 him, from the sacrament of birth onward. He sang of the glory of the
Six-faced God, and the efficacy of the cock, the Goddess Śakti, and the
Companions, and he performed rituals for the good of the world.
And thus the seer Viśvāmitra came to be held dear by Kumāra. The
great hermit discovered Svāhā's changes of form and told all the
hermits that their women had not erred; but although they learned
the truth from him they divorced their wives all the same.
When the Gods heard about Skanda, they all said to Vāsava,
"Skanda's power is unsupportable. Kill him at once, Śakra, do not
delay! If you do not smite him he shall now become Indra and with
15 his strength oppress the three worlds, ourselves, and you." Trembling
he said to them, "This child has very great prowess. He would
overcome the creator of the three worlds himself in battle and
annihilate him. But let all the Mothers of the world attack Skanda
this time, for they have the power and the will to slay him." The
Mothers agreed and went. Seeing that he was without peer in
puissance, their faces fell; and reflecting that he was invincible they
sought refuge with him. They said: "You are our son. We hold the
world. Welcome us all, we are yielding milk, overcome with love."
After he had honored them and done their wishes, Mahāsena,
20 strong of the strong, saw his father Fire arrive. Fire received his
homage, along with the band of the Mothers, and remained about the
steadfast Mahāsena protecting him. The one woman among all the
Mothers who had been born from Fury guarded Skanda with a spike
in her hand, as a nursing mother guards her son. The cruel daughter
of the blood sea, who feasts on blood, embraced Mahāsena and
guarded him like her son. Fire became a goat-faced trader with many
children and amused the child on the mountain as with toys.

Mārkaṇḍeya said:

216.1 The planets and comets, the seers and the Mothers, all ablaze and
led by the Fire, the bands of the Companions and many others of the
terrifying celestials remained about the person of Mahāsena with
the group of Mothers. The Lord of the Gods, wishing for victory but
finding it doubtful, mounted the shoulders of Airāvata and marched
out with the deities; and in hope of victory over Mahāsena, Indra
journeyed fast.
The ranks of the Gods were awe-inspiring and full of vigor, rich in
luster, colorful with flags and accoutrements, diverse in their mounts
and bows, decked in choice apparel, waited on and adorned by
5 Fortune; but Kumāra marched out on Śakra, who was intent on
killing him. Mighty Śakra roaring down the path approached swiftly,
heartening the hosts of the Gods who were out to slay the son of the
Fire. Amidst the praises of the Thirty Gods and the supreme seers

Vāsava came close upon Kārtikeya. The lord of the Gods roared his lion's roar along with the Gods, and Guha too, hearing the cry, roared out like the ocean. And his mighty roar shook the Gods' army, splendid like the gale-swept ocean, out of their wits.

The son of Fire, upon seeing the Gods encroach on him in the hope
of a killing, angrily belched from his mouth huge bolts of flames. The
flames burned the Gods' hosts that lay writhing on the ground. Heads
and bodies on fire, weapons and mounts ablaze, they suddenly
10 appeared as colorful clusters of stars that had fallen. As the Gods
burned, they sought refuge with the son of Fire, deserting the
Thunderbolt-wielder, and found peace again. Deserted by the Gods,
Śakra loosed his thunderbolt at Skanda's right side and split open the
side of the great-spirited God, great king. From the impact of the bolt
on Skanda, another person was born, a youth accoutred in gold,
wielding a spear, and wearing divine earrings; and because he was
born from the entering of the thunderbolt he became Viśākha. Seeing
still another one arise, with the glow of the doomsday fire, Indra
15 folded his hands in fear and sought refuge. Skanda afforded him as
well as his army safety, best of men, and thereupon the Thirty Gods
merrily sounded their instruments.

Mārkaṇḍeya said:

217.1 Now hear of the awesome and wondrously shaped Companions of
Skanda, the lesser Kumāras, who were born from the thunderbolt's
impact on Skanda, and who cruelly rob babies, both newborn and
still in the womb. From the impact of the thunderbolt powerful
maidens were born of him. The Kumāras made Viśākha their father.
The blessed lord, having become goat-faced, stands guard in battle
surrounded by the multitudes of the maidens and all his own sons,
and as Bhadraśākha gives help while the Mothers look on. So people
5 on earth call Skanda the father of boys: people who want sons or have
sons always worship in different regions Rudra, Agni, and the
powerful Umā as Svāhā.

The maidens, whom the Fire called Tapas begot, came to Skanda,
and he asked: "What shall I do?"

The Mothers said:

May we by your grace be the ultimate Mothers of all the world,
and worshipful to it: do us this favor.

Mārkaṇḍeya said:

He replied: "Surely!" and repeated noble-mindedly: "Ye shall be of
different kinds, propitious and unpropitious." After making Skanda
their son the band of Mothers went. Kākī, Halimā, Rudrā, and Bṛhalī,
Āryā, Palālā, and Mitrā became the seven mothers of newborn sons;
10 they had each a most terrifying, red-eyed, and frightening son by the

grace of Skanda, named the Newborn; the Eight Heroes are called they who were born from the band of the Mothers of Skanda; and are called the Nine together with the Goat-face—know that the sixth face of Skanda from among the six heads is a goat's face, king, and it is worshiped by the band of the Mothers. The foremost among his six heads is the one called Bhadraśākha, through which he created the divine Śakti.

Thus these various events occurred the fifth day of the bright fortnight; fierce war occurred on the sixth, O lord of the people.

Mārkaṇḍeya said:

218.1 To this Skanda, who was sitting in his golden coat of mail, with a
golden crest jewel and diadem, golden eyes and great luster, dressed
in red clothes, sharp of tusk, and charming, endowed with all the
marks of excellence, and held dear by all three worlds—to this boon-
bestowing heroic youth of the polished earrings Śrī herself, in a bodily
form shaped as a lotus, paid homage. The creatures saw the widely
famed chief Kumāra sitting as he was being cherished by Śrī like the
5 moon of full-moon night. The great-spirited brahmins honored the
mighty youth, and this is what the great seers said to Skanda:
"Golden-colored One, hail to thee! Become thou the savior of the
worlds. By thee who wert born in six nights all the worlds have been
subdued, and thou hast restored to them freedom from fear, greatest
of Gods. Therefore thou shouldst become Indra, freeing the three
worlds from fear."

Skanda said:

What does the Indra of all the worlds do, ascetics? How does the
lord of all the Gods always protect the hosts of the Gods?

The seers said:

Indra assigns to the creatures their strength, splendor, offspring,
and happiness. When satisfied, the lord of the Gods bestows all the
10 shares—from evil-doers he withdraws them, to the good he renders
them. The Slayer of Vala enjoins upon the creatures their tasks—
were there no sun he would become sun, were there no moon he
would become moon. He becomes fire, wind, earth, and water with
their causes. This is Indra's task, for great strength resides in Indra:
you, hero, are the greatest in strength—therefore be you our Indra.

Śakra said:

Be you, strong-armed bringer of happiness, the Indra of us all. You shall be anointed at present, for you are fit for the task, great one.

Skanda said:

You yourself shall reign over the three worlds, single-mindedly bent upon victory. I am your servitor, Śakra, I do not aspire to Indrahood.

Śakra said:

15 Your might is a marvel, hero—smite the foes of the Gods! Amazed by your prowess the worlds will despise me, though I am incumbent as Indra, since I am of lesser strength and vanquished, champion. And, unwearied, they will strive to bring about a split between us. When you have been split off, O lord, people will separate into two parties, and when the people have broken apart in their decisions about the two of us, there will result strife in consequence of the splitting of the people, powerful one. Then you will defeat me in battle, believe me, my son, therefore you must now become Indra, do not hesitate!

Skanda said:

You are the king—hail to thee—of the three worlds and of me. What can I do for you, Śakra? State your command of me!

Śakra said:

20 If you have spoken the truth by your own decision, and if you wish to obey my command, Skanda, then listen to me: be anointed to the captaincy of the Gods, powerful champion, and at your behest I shall be Indra.

Skanda said:

Then, for the destruction of the Dānavas, for the advancement of the cause of the Gods, for the protection of cows and brahmins, anoint me to the captaincy!

Mārkaṇḍeya said:

So he was anointed by Maghavat* and all the hosts of the Gods,
and while the great seers worshiped him he shone beyond measure.
The golden umbrella he held sparkled like the nimbus of a well-
25 kindled fire. The Slayer of Tripura** himself, glorious God, fastened
upon him a divine golden garland that had been created by
Viśvakarman—the blessed lord had come with the Goddess, O enemy-
burning tiger among men, and the bull-crested God quite joyously
paid him homage. The brahmins call the Fire Rudra, hence he is
Rudra's son. The seed secreted by Rudra had become Mount Śveta,
and it was on Mount Śveta that the manhood of Fire was placed by
the Kṛttikās. Upon seeing Guha, first of the virtuous, honored by
Rudra, all the celestials called him thereafter the son of Rudra; for
the child had been born after Rudra had permeated Fire: it was thus
30 that he became Rudra's son. Skanda, best of the Gods, was born by
the power of Rudra, Fire, Svāhā, and the six women, hence he
became Rudra's son.

The son of Fire was clothed in a pair of dustless red clothes, and with his fiery body shone majestically like the sun clothed in two red clouds. The cock given him by Fire, which was his ornamental crest,

* = Indra.
** = Śiva.

sparkled as it perched high over his chariot, red like the fire of
doomsday. His body was stuck in the coat of mail with which he was
born and that was always visible when the God was at war. Spear,
armor, splendor, beauty, truthfulness, invulnerability, brahminic faith,
35 lack of confusion, protection of devotees, eradication of enemies, and
defense of all the worlds were all born with Skanda, O lord of the
people.

Having thus been anointed by all the hosts of the Gods, the God in
his finery, confident and joyous, glowed and his visage was like the
moon at its fullest. As though at play Pāvaki was anointed by all the
various Gods, happy, contented, and ornamented, with the requisite
sounds of Vedic portions, the music of the Gods, the songs of Gods
and Gandharvas, and all the hosts of Apsarās. And the celestials
looked upon the anointed Mahāsena as the sun that rises after slaying
40 the darkness. Thereupon all the armies of the Gods came to him by
the thousands, saying on all sides, "Thou art our master!" Surrounded
by all the races of creatures the blessed lord received them and, when
he had been worshiped and praised, gave comfort to them.

After the anointing of Skanda to the captaincy, the God of the
Hundred Sacrifices bethought himself of Devasenā, the one whom he
had rescued; and with the thought that Brahmā himself had surely
ordained Skanda to be her husband, he brought Devasenā in, decked
with ornaments. And the Slayer of Vala said to Skanda, "This maiden,
O best of Gods, was destined by the Self-existent to be your wife, even
45 before you were born. Therefore take with your hand the right hand,
blushing as a lotus, of this Goddess with the proper spells and in the
ritual fashion." At these words he ritually grasped her hand, while
Bṛhaspati recited the spells and made the oblation. Thus the Gods
knew Devasenā as the chief queen of Skanda, her whom the brahmins
call Ṣaṣṭhī, Lakṣmī, Āśā, Sukhapradā, Sinīvalī, Kuhū, Sadvṛtti, and
Aparājitā. When Devasenā received Skanda as her perpetual husband,
the Goddess Lakṣmī herself attended on him in bodily form. Skanda
was joined by Śrī on the fifth, hence the day is known as Śrīpañcamī.
And his success fructified on the sixth, hence the sixth is a great
lunar day.

Mārkaṇḍeya said:

219.1 When Mahāsena had been joined by Śrī and was made the
husband of Devasenā, the six Goddesses, the wives of the seven seers,
came to him. The virtuous women of the great vows, who had been
divorced by the seers, went quickly and said to the lord the husband
of Devasenā, "Son, our god-like husbands have divorced us in anger
without cause, and now, dear son, we have fallen from our pure

estate. Someone had cited that we, so they say, had borne you.
5 Agree that that is an untruth and pray save us from it. May heaven be ours without end by your grace, O lord! We wish you for our son; and when you have done so, be free from any debt."

Skanda said:

Indeed you are my mothers, and I am your son, ladies without reproach. And all shall be for you just as you desire it.

Mārkaṇḍeya said:

When this had been said he spoke to Śakra: "What is there to be done?" And Vāsava, told to speak, said to Skanda, "The Goddess Abhijit, the younger sister of Rohiṇī and her rival, has gone to the forest to mortify herself, for she wishes to be the eldest. I am bewildered over it—hail to thee—for now a constellation has dropped from heaven. Ponder with Brahmā the important time that
10 constellation measured. Brahmā has measured out time from Dhaniṣṭha onward. Rohiṇī was the first, so the number used to be full." At Śakra's words the Kṛttikās went to heaven and now twinkle as a constellation, in the form of a cart, with Fire as their regent.

And Vinatā said to Skanda, "You are my son to offer the funerary oblation. I wish to stay with you forever."

Skanda said:

So be it, homage to thee! Command me with motherly love. You shall dwell here forever, honored by your daughter-in-law.

Mārkaṇḍeya said:

Then the entire band of the Mothers spoke to him: "The poets recall that we are the Mothers of all the world. We wish to be mothers to you, honor us!"

Skanda said:

15 You are my mothers and I am your son. Tell me what I should do that pleases you.

The Mothers said:

Let ours be the estate of those who before had been fabricated as the Mothers of this world, and it shall be no more theirs. Let us be worshipful to the world, and let *them* be not so, bull among Gods. They have robbed our progeny on your account, restore it to us!

Skanda said

You cannot cherish progeny that have been given away. I'll bestow on you what other offspring you may desire.

The Mothers said:

We want to devour the offspring of those Mothers—give them to us, them and their Gods who are different from yourself.

Skanda said:

20 I give you the offspring, but you have spoken a dire thing. Hail to ye—spare the offspring when they honor ye well.

The Mothers said:

Hail to thee—we shall spare the offspring, Skanda, if you wish so. We wish to make our abode with you for good, Lord Skanda!

Skanda said:

Afflict the young children of men in your various forms until they are sixteen years old. I shall give you a Rudra-like immortal soul, and you shall dwell with it in complete happiness, being much worshiped.

Mārkaṇḍeya said:

Thereupon a powerful, golden-hued spirit flew out of Skanda's body
25 to devour the offspring of the mortals. It fell on the ground, senseless
and starving, and with Skanda's leave it became a Grasper in a
Rudra-like form. Eminent brahmins call that Grasper Skandāpasmāra
—Skanda's forgetfulness. Vinatā is said to be the horrible Bird Grasper.
They call Pūtanā a Rākṣasī—one should know that she is the Pūtanā
Grasper: she is an awful Stalker of the Night, evil in her ghastly shape.
One horrifying Piśācī is called Śītapūtanā; this terrible-shaped specter
aborts the foetus of women. They say that Aditi is Revatī; her Grasper
is Raivata; this horrible big Grasper afflicts small children. Diti, the
mother of the Daityas, is said to be Mukhamaṇḍikā; this
30 unapproachable demoness feasts gluttonously on children's flesh. The
Kumāras and Kumārīs that sprang from Skanda are also all foetus-
eaters and very dangerous Graspers, Kauravya; the Kumāras are
known as the husbands of the Kumārīs, and these Rudra-like acting
demons snatch small children, while they remain unknown. The
informed call Surabhi the mother of the cows; a bird perches on her
and swallows children on earth, O king. The divine Saramā is the
mother of the dogs, lord of the people—she too snatches the foetus of
men at all times. The mother of the trees lives in the *karañja* tree;
people who want sons therefore pay homage to her in the *karañja*.
35 These eighteen Graspers, and others as well, like flesh and strong
liquor; they always stay in the confinement chamber for ten nights.
When Kadrū in a subtle form enters a pregnant woman, she eats the
foetus inside her and the mother gives birth to a snake. The mother
of the Gandharvas takes away the foetus and goes; thus that woman
therefore is found on earth to be one whose foetus has vanished. The
progenitrix of the Apsarās takes the foetus and sits, therefore the wise
call that foetus a sitting one. The daughter of the blood sea is known
as the nurse of Skanda; she is worshiped as Lohitāyanī in the
40 *kadamba* tree. Just as Rudra dwells in men, so does Āryā dwell in
women. Āryā, a mother of Skanda, is worshiped separately to obtain
wishes.

Herewith I have proclaimed the great Graspers of the Kumāras who are malign for sixteen years, then turn benevolent. The enumerated bands of Mothers and the male Graspers are all always to be known by embodied creatures as the Skanda Graspers. To propitiate them one should use oblations, incense, collyrium, thrown-offerings, and gifts, and especially the rite of Skanda. When thus propitiated they all bestow well-being on people, and long life and virility, O Indra of kings, if properly honored with a *pūjā*.

45 Now after an obeisance to Maheśvara, I shall proclaim the Graspers
that afflict men after their sixteenth year. The man who sees Gods,
whether awake or asleep, goes quickly mad; they know him for
God-Grasped. He who, sitting or lying, sees the Fathers goes quickly
mad, he is known as Father-Grasped. He who despises the Siddhas
and whom they thereupon irately curse goes quickly mad; he is to
be known as Siddha-Grasped. He who smells scents and tastes flavors
that are different goes quickly mad; he is to be known as Rākṣasa-
Grasped. The man whom the divine Gandharvas touch on earth goes
50 quickly mad; they call him a Gandharva-Grasped. The man whom the
Yakṣas enter in the course of time goes quickly mad; he is to be
known as Yakṣa-Grasped. The man whom Piśācas bestride anywhere
goes quickly mad; they know him for Piśāca-Grasped. A man whose
mind is enraged by the humors and becomes confused goes quickly
mad; his cure is according to the texts. He who goes mad quickly
because of perplexity, fear, and the sight of ghastly things is cured by
tranquillity.

55 Graspers are of three kinds: playful, gluttonous, and lustful; they afflict men until they are seventy years old; beyond that age the fever becomes the equal of a Grasper for people. Graspers always avoid the faithful and right-thinking man whose senses are not scattered, who is controlled, pure, and always alert. This is the description of the Graspers of people; no Graspers touch those who are devoted to God Maheśvara.

Mārkaṇḍeya said:

220.1 When Skanda had fulfilled the wishes of the Mothers, Svāhā said to him, "You are the child of my womb. I wish to obtain from you a bliss that is very hard to obtain." Skanda said to her, "What bliss do you wish?"

Svāhā said:

I am the beloved daughter of Dakṣa, Svāhā by name, O strong-armed one. From childhood on I have always been in love with the sacrificial Fire. Fire does not fully know how I love him, my son. I wish to dwell forever with Fire.

Skanda said:

5 Whatever oblations to the Gods and Ancestors the twice-born who act well and follow the right path shall from this day onward offer into the fire with the appropriate spells shall henceforth always be

presented, O Goddess, with the cry *svāhā!* Thus you shall always dwell with Fire, beautiful woman.

Mārkaṇḍeya said:

At these words Svāhā, honored by Skanda, grew contented and, conjoined with her husband Fire, she pays homage to Skanda.

Thereupon Brahmā Prajāpati said to Mahāsena, "Go to Mahādeva,* the Slayer of Tripura: he is your father. You have been begotten, invincible, for the good of all worlds, by Rudra permeating Fire and Umā permeating Svāhā. The great-spirited Rudra poured his seed into the womb of Umā; and it spilled and lay on the mountain; from it sprang Miñjika and Miñjikā. The remaining seed flowed into the blood river, and flew into the rays of the sun, and fell upon earth, while some stuck to the trees: thus it spilled in five ways. Your ghastly flesh-eating Companions in their various guises are known to the wise as the Gaṇas."

"So be it," said Mahāsena, and the measureless spirit paid worship to his father Maheśvara, who loved his son. They who are desirous of wealth should worship the five Gaṇas with *arka* blossoms and do *pūjā* to them if diseases are to be cured. The Miñjika and Miñjikā twins who sprang from Rudra should always be honored by one who wishes for the well-being of the young. People desirous of sons should honor the man-eating divine women called Vṛddhikās, who were born from trees. Thus are known the countless bands of the Piśācas.

Now learn from me the origins of the bell and the pennant, O king. Airāvata wore two bells known as the Vaijayantīs, and the sagacious Śakra himself brought and gave them to Guha. One bell went to Viśākha, the other to Skanda. The pennants of Kārtikeya and Viśākha are blood-red. The powerful God Mahāsena frolicked with the toys that the Gods had given him.

Surrounded by the bands of the Piśācas and the hosts of the Gods, he shone forth on the golden mountain, ablaze in Śrī's company. The mountain of pure gold shone with that hero as Mount Mandara of the lovely caves shines with the rays of the sun. Mount Śveta was bright with blossoming *saṃtānaka* woods and *karavīra* groves, with *pārijāta* plantations and *japā* and *aśoka* woods, with clusters of *kadamba* trees and celestial herds of game and celestial flocks of birds. All the hosts of the Gods were there, and all the great seers, and the drum sounds of the clouds were thundered like the wind-swept ocean. The celestial Gandharvas danced there, so did the Apsarās, and the grand jubilation was heard there of joyous creatures. Thus all the world and Indra gathered on Mount Śveta, joyfully gazed upon Skanda, and did not tire of looking.

* = Śiva.

Mārkaṇḍeya said:
221.1 When the blessed lord had been anointed to the captaincy, the
lustrous Hara* happily departed for Bhadravaṭa on a sun-colored
chariot, and the God journeyed with Pārvatī. A thousand lions were
yoked to that excellent chariot, and it flew to the bright heaven
goaded by Time. Drinking up space as it were, and causing the
moving and standing creatures to tremble, the lions with their
handsome mane went roaring in the sky. Standing on the chariot the
Lord of Cattle** shone with Umā as the sun with lightning on a
5 rainbow-colored cloud. Ahead of him the blessed Lord of Riches who
rides a Man*** went with the Guhyakas on his splendid Puṣpaka
chariot. Śakra on Airāvata followed the bull-crested Granter of Boons
as he went along with the Gods. The great Yakṣa Amogha, adorned
with Jambhakas, Yakṣas, and Rākṣasas wearing garlands, went on
his right side and to his right went the Marut Gods of the varied
weapons, accompanied by the Vasus and Rudras. Yama, along with
Death in a gruesome shape, went surrounded on all sides by hundreds
10 of grisly diseases. Behind Yama followed Rudra's dreadful three-
pointed spike Vijaya, which was beautifully decorated. Encircling it,
surrounded by various sea monsters, came slowly Lord Varuṇa, king
of the ocean. After Vijaya again came Rudra's three-bladed spear
amidst clubs, pestles, javelins, and so forth, and superb thrusting
weapons. Rudra's umbrella, of great splendor, followed the spear,
O king, and after it came the gourd amidst crowds of great seers. To
the right of it shone the staff as it went by, accompanied by Śrī and
15 honored by the Bhṛgus and Angiras, along with the Gods. Hard upon
them in his stainless chariot came Rudra, gladdening all celestials
with his luster. The seers, Gods, Gandharvas, and Snakes, male and
female rivers, trees and bevies of Apsarās, constellations, planets, and
the children of the Gods and women of various shapes followed Rudra
in the rear. Shapely women scattered showers of flowers and
Parjanya followed paying homage to the Pināka bowman.* The moon
held a white umbrella over his head, and the Wind and Fire on either
side held the chowries. Śakra came behind them, O king, in the
company of Śrī and all the royal seers, praising the bull-crested God.
20 Gaurī, Vidyā, Gāndhārī, Keśinī, and Sumitrā all followed behind
Pārvatī with Sāvitrī. All the many sciences that have been created by
the wise and of which the Gods with Indra are the speakers went in
the vanguard of the army. Ahead went the Rākṣasa Graha holding
the standard, and Rudra's friend Pingala, chief among the Yakṣas,
always busy in the burning field, who gives bliss to the world.

* = Śiva.
** = Paśupati Śiva.
*** = Kubera.

In their company the God went as it pleased him, in front or in the rear, for his course was not steady. The mortals on earth worship the God Rudra with good rites under the name of Śiva, him whom they
25 call Lord Rudra the Pināka bowman. They worship Maheśvara*
with all manner of things. Thus the husband of Devasenā, amidst the armies of the Gods, the brahminic son of the Kṛttikās, followed the lord of the Gods.

Then the Great God spoke to Mahāsena this weighty word: "Always protect the seventh division of the Maruts carefully."

Skanda said:

My lord, I shall guard the seventh division of the Maruts. Tell me quickly what else I should do, God.

Rudra said:

You must always look at me in your affairs, son. From looking at me and from devotion for me you shall attain the supreme good.

Mārkaṇḍeya said:

Having spoken Maheśvara embraced and dismissed him; and when
30 Skanda had been dismissed, there appeared on a sudden a great
portent, great king, which bewildered all the Gods. Heaven and the stars caught fire, the world was profoundly stunned, earth shook and groaned, and the world was covered with darkness, O lord. Seeing the terrifying portent, Śaṃkara* was shaken, and so were the lordly Umā and the Gods and great seers. While they stood about bewildered, a great army appeared, awesome, with all sorts of arms, like a mountain or monsoon cloud. This awesome countless force, uttering various cries, stormed at the Gods and Lord Śaṃkara to do battle. They let loose on their ranks masses of arrows, mountains, hundred-
35 killers, missiles, clubs, and maces. As they were being pelted by these
terrible big weapons, the ranks of the Gods dispersed instantly and all appeared to be crestfallen. Crestfallen seemed the army of the Gods, hurt by the Dānavas, its warriors, elephants, and horses cut down, their arms and chariots splintered; battered by the Asuras, as a forest by as many fires, it fell, mostly burned down like a wood of tall trees. The celestials slumped down, beheaded, and found no savior as they were being slaughtered in the great battle.

Then, seeing his mighty army in flight, the God Sacker of Cities, Slayer of Vala, spoke encouragingly to the Dānava-pressed troops:
40 "Shed your fear, hail to ye, pick up your weapons, heroes! Set your
minds on gallantry, do not worry about anything! Vanquish those rascal Dānavas with their ugly shapes! Let us now all, you and I, storm those grand Asuras, hail!"

Hearing Śakra's word the celestials were solaced and fought the Dānavas, relying on Śakra. All the Thirty Gods and the powerful Maruts reversed with great impact, as did the Sādhyas and the Vasus.

* = Śiva.

The weapons they furiously hurled into the ranks in that battle and
45 the arrows hitting the Daityas' bodies drank plenty of blood. Their
honed arrows cleft their bodies and plunged out again like snakes
from anthills. The Daitya corpses severed by the arrows fell to the
ground, king, like shredded clouds, everywhere. Then the Dānava
army, terrified of all the hosts of Gods with their many kinds of
arrows, made a turnabout. There was a loud crying out of the
jubilant Gods, who brandished their weapons, and all their many
instruments were sounded.

Thus went on that grisly battle, soiled with flesh and blood, of the
50 Gods and the Dānavas. Suddenly the discipline of the Gods broke
down, and the Dānavas massacred the celestials in like manner.
There were the ringings of instruments, the deep sounds of kettledrums,
and the dreadful lion roars of the Dānava chiefs. From the dread army
of the Daityas there emerged a powerful Dānava, Mahiṣa by name,
who had grabbed a great mountain; and the celestials seeing him
hold high a mountain—like the sun that is completely decked with
clouds—ran, king, ran. Mahiṣa fell on the Gods and hurled his
mountain; and the grim-looking stone mass in its fall felled a myriad
55 God soldiers and crushed them on the earth, O lord. Along with the
other Dānavas this Mahiṣa, panicking the Gods, stormed nimbly into
the mêlée as a lion pounces on small game. Indra and the celestials
saw Mahiṣa fall upon them and fearfully fled from the battlefield, arms
broken and crests fallen.

Angrily Mahiṣa then at once attacked Rudra's chariot, and he ran
to and grabbed hold of Rudra's chariot pole; and when the furious
Mahiṣa vehemently made for the chariot of Rudra, heaven and earth
groaned deeply, and the great seers fainted. The big-bodied Daityas,
the likes of rain clouds, roared and they were sure that victory was
60 theirs. But even in this pass the blessed lord declined to kill off
Mahiṣa in battle, for he remembered that Skanda was to be the death
of the miscreant. But Mahiṣa, recognizing Rudra's chariot, bellowed
evilly, striking fear in the Gods and delighting the Dānavas.

And when this grisly danger beset the Gods, out came Mahāsena,
furiously blazing sun, girt in his blood-red robe, sporting blood-red
garlands and jewelry, blood-mouthed, the strong-armed, gold-armored
lord riding his sun-like, gold-sparkling chariot; and on seeing him the
65 Daitya army suddenly vanished from the field. And, great king,
puissant Mahāsena threw his blazing, shattering spear at Mahiṣa,
and, once thrown, the spear hit the big head of Mahiṣa; and Mahiṣa's
head was split, and he fell down relinquishing his life. Throw after
throw the spear smote the foes in their thousands and then, as
witnessed the Gods and the Dānavas, it returned again to Skanda's
hand. Mostly killed off by the cunning Mahāsena with his missiles,
the remnant of the gory Daitya troops, frightened and panicked by

Skanda's unstoppable Companions, fell and were eaten by the
hundreds. They feasted on the Dānavas and gulped their blood; and
in no time they cleaned the world of Dānavas and made very merry.
70 Thus did Skanda destroy the enemies, famously, by his own
strength as sun destroys darkness, fire trees, mountain clouds; and
much honored by the Thirty Gods he saluted Maheśvara, and he, the
son of the Kṛttikās, shone as the sun at its full scattering of rays.
When Skanda had destroyed the foe and had approached Maheśvara,*
the Sacker of Cities** embraced Mahāsena and said to him, "Skanda,
thou hast killed Mahiṣa to whom Brahmā had given a boon, him for
whom the Gods were but straw, greatest of victors. Thou, strong-
armed chieftain of victors, hast slaughtered that rival of the Gods.
Thou hast slain a hundred Dānavas, the peers of Mahiṣa, enemies of
75 the Gods, who heretofore had us humbled. Other Dānavas by the
hundreds have been eaten by thy bands. Invincible art thou in battle
to any foe, like the lord who is Umā's husband. This deed shall be
thy first claim to fame and thy glory shall be imperishable in the
three worlds—the Gods shall be in thy power, son of a God,
Mahāsena!" Thus spoke Śacī's husband with the deities and ceased;
and he was dismissed by the Lord Tryambaka.
Rudra went on to Bhadravaṭa and the celestials returned. The
Gods had been told by Rudra to look upon Skanda as himself. Having
slain the bands of the Dānavas, he, son of the Fire, subdued within a
day the three worlds while the great seers paid homage to him.
80 He who reads aloud attentively this birth of Skanda attains to
prosperity here, and to the world of Skanda hereafter.

3(38) The Colloquy of Draupadī and Satyabhāmā

222–24 (B. 233–34; 14650–721)
222 (233; 14650). Kṛṣṇa's wife Satyabhāmā asks Draupadī how she keeps the Pāṇḍavas happy (1–5). Draupadī condemns spells and drugs (5–15). The virtues of a good wife (15–35). Yudhiṣṭhira's erstwhile wealth (40–55), and her present misery (55).
223 (2341; 14710). The duties of a wife and her secret (1–10).

---

* = Śiva.
** = Indra.

Vaiśaṃpāyana said:

222.1 When the brahmins and the great spirited Pāṇḍavas were seated, Draupadī and Satyabhāmā went inside together; and laughing merrily they sat there at ease. They were seeing each other after a long time, great king, so the sweet-spoken women told each other remarkable stories of the Kuru and Yadu kings. Then the slender-waisted Satyabhāmā Sātrajiti, who was Kṛṣṇa's chief queen, said to Yājñasenī in private, "How do you conduct yourself, Draupadī, when you attend on the Pāṇḍavas? These young men are gallant like the World Guardians and highly regarded—how then have they come under
5 your ban, why are they never angry at you, beautiful woman? The Pāṇḍavas are always amenable to you with your pretty face, and I tell you, they always watch your face. Have you followed a vow, done austerities? Is there a special ablution, spells, herbs? A powerful knowledge of roots? Some prayer, or fire oblation, or drug? Tell me the glorious secret of your sexual power, Kṛṣṇā,* so that Kṛṣṇa will always be amenable to me too."

The renowned Satyabhāmā stopped speaking; and Draupadī, stately and avowed to her husbands, replied, "What you are asking, Satyā, is how wanton women behave! Why should there be praise
10 for the path traveled by the wicked? Such questions and uncertainties do not become you. You, the beloved queen of Kṛṣṇa, have sense enough yourself. When a husband finds out that his woman uses spells or drugs on him, he gets as frightened of her as of a snake that has got into the house. What peace does a frightened man have, and what happiness without peacefulness? No husband has ever been made uxorious with a spell! It is murderous men who under the name of herbs use poison or the dreadful diseases that have been sent by his ill-wishers. The powders a man takes on the tongue or the skin will
15 kill him shortly, no doubt of that. Women make their men dropsical that way, or leprous, gray-haired, impotent, dumb, blind, or deaf. Those evil women with their wicked ways in effect kill their husbands, and a woman should never in any way do anything displeasing to her husband. Listen, I shall tell you the whole truth of how I behave to the Pāṇḍavas, glorious Satyabhāmā.

"I serve the Pāṇḍavas and their wives always religiously without selfishness, likes, and dislikes. In return for their affection I place my soul in theirs, obey them without self-seeking, and guard the hearts
20 of my husband without fear of a wrong word, wrong stand, wrong glance, wrong seat, wrong walk, or misinterpretation of a gesture; that is the way I serve the Pārthas, men like sun, fire, and moon, great warriors who kill with a glance, awesomely sharp and mighty. No other man could please me, be he a God, man, Gandharva, a

* = Draupadī.

well-groomed youth, rich, or handsome. I do not eat or lie down until
my husband has eaten or lain down or bathed, ever, even when
there are servants. When my husband comes home from the field, the
wood, or the village, I get up to meet him and make him feel welcome
with a seat and a drink of water. My storerooms are scrubbed, my
25 food is good. I serve the meal in time, I am at it, the rice is well
stored, the house is spotless. I talk directly, and do not seek out bad
women for company, and I am always agreeable and never lazy. I
avoid laughing when there is no joke, only briefly tarry at a door, am
not long in the privy or the gardens. I avoid laughing too much or
carping too much and give no cause for anger. I am always devoted
to truly serving my husbands, and never in any way do I wish them
ill. When my husband sleeps out on some family business, I go
30 without flowers and make-up, and follow a vow. What my husband
does not drink, what my husband does not chew, what my husband
does not eat, I avoid it all. Well-trained according to the prescriptions,
well-adorned and most eager, beautiful woman, I am bent on what is
good for my husband.

"The laws that forever operate in households, I have heard them
all from my mother-in-law; the begging, the thrown-offering, the
śrāddha, the milk dish at new and full moon, and whatever other
matters the mindful mind, I know them. Don't I follow them all, day
and night, untiringly, forever, and with all my soul concerned with
my duties and constraints? I wait on my meek enough, truthful
enough, virtuous enough husbands as though they were furious
venomous snakes.

35 "My Law rests on my husband, as, I think, it eternally does with
women. He is the God, he is the path, nothing else: what woman
could displease him? I don't outsleep my men, nor out-eat or out-talk
them, and never complain about my mother-in-law, however
aggravated I am. And by this constant attention, my lovely, by this
daily up-and-about, and by obedience to my elders I got the upper
hand of my husbands. There is no day that I do not wait on the lady
Kuntī, mother of heroes, speaker of truth, all by myself, bathing her,
dressing her, feeding her. Would I ever contradict her, in matters of
clothes, jewelry, or food? No, I never complain about our Pṛthā,* who
equals earth herself.

40 "At one time eight thousand brahmins ate daily from golden dishes
in Yudhiṣṭhira's mansion. Yudhiṣṭhira supported eighty-eight
thousand Snātaka householders with thirty slave girls each. There
were another ten thousand highly continent ascetics who took their
well-cooked food on golden plates. I honored all the *brahman-*

* = Kuntī.

disputing brahmins with the first serving according to rank, and with
drink, clothing, and food. The great-spirited Kaunteya had a hundred
thousand slave girls, with shell necklaces and bracelets, coins around
45 their necks, much jewelry, precious garlands and ornaments and
gold pieces, sprinkled with sandalwood, parading their beads and
gold, all clever at dancing and singing—and I knew the name, and
the figure, and the meals, and the dresses of every one of them, as
well as their work, what they did and did not do. The sagacious son
of Kuntī had a hundred thousand serving wenches, and they fed the
guests day and night, plates in hand. A hundred thousand horses, ten
myriad elephants Yudhiṣṭhira owned, all stabled in Indraprastha.

"He had it made, the king, as long as he ruled the earth and I laid
down the number and chores of the servants and listened to them—
50 all the chores done and undone by all the women and retainers, down
to the cowherds and shepherds, all the income of the king's revenues
and the outgo, I alone knew it, pretty woman, of all the glorious
Pāṇḍavas. The Bhārata bulls piled all the household on me, pretty
woman, and they surely made up to me. It was I who tackled the
whole burden, unassailable by scoundrels, and I forewent all pleasure
day and night. The treasury, an ocean that even Varuṇa couldn't
manage, this treasury of my so very virtuous husbands, I alone knew
55 how full it was. Day and night I endure hunger and thirst, and, as I
wait on the Kaunteyas, day and night are the same to me. I am the
first to wake up, the last to bed down—that, Satyā, is my charm, all
the time. Yes, I know how to put a charm on my husbands, and no,
I do not practice the ways of bad women, nor do I want to."

Having heard this account, informed by Law, from Kṛṣṇā, Satyā paid honor to the Pāñcālī woman of the lawlike habits: "I am with you, Pāñcālī Yājnasenī, forgive me; for is it not the way with women friends to speak freely in jest?"

Draupadī said:

223.1 Let me talk of the way, unopprobious way,
For a woman to hold the heart of her husband:
You walk that way, friend, the proper way,
And you'll cut your man from his mistresses.

There is no such deity, Satyā, here
In all worlds with all their divinities
Like a husband: you're rich in every wish
If you please him right; if he's angry you're dead.

You get children and all kinds of comforts,
A place to sleep and to sit and marvelous sights,

And clothes and flowers and certainly perfumes
And the world of heaven and steady repute.

No bliss is easily found on earth,
A good woman finds happiness through hardship;
So worship Kṛṣṇa with happy heart
With love and always the acts of affection.

When from tasty dishes and beautiful garlands,
From domestic adeptness and various perfumes
He reasons that he must be dear to you,
He himself will embrace you with all his love.

When you hear the sound of your man at the door,
Rise up and stand in the middle of the house;
When you see he has entered make haste with a seat
And receive him with water to wash his feet.

And send your serving woman away,
Get up and do all the chores yourself;
Then Kṛṣṇa will surely know your heart:
She loves me completely, Satyā, he'll think.

Whatever your lord may say in your presence,
Even though no secret, keep it a secret:
A co-wife of yours will surely report you
To Vāsudeva and he'll turn away.

Invite for a meal, by hook or by crook,
Your husband's favorites, faithfuls, and friends,
And cut forever his foes and opponents,
His ill-wishers, blackguards, and the insolent rude.

If you find your man either drunk or distracted,
Control your temper and hold your tongue;
Though Pradyumna and Sāmba are your sons,
Don't ever attend to them secretly.

Strike up a friendship with highborn ladies
And women of virtue and without vice;
The bellicose, bibulous, gluttonous ones,
The bad, thievish, fickle you must avoid.

This is the glorious secret of sex
That leads to heaven and uproots the foes;
Worship your husband while wearing your costly
Flowers and jewels and make-up and scents.

3(39) The Cattle Expedition

224–43 (B. 235–57; C. 14722–15350)
224 (235; 14722). Satyabhāmā comforts Draupadī and departs with Kṛṣṇa (1–15).
225 (236; 14741). A brahmin brings news of the Pāṇḍavas to Dhṛtarāṣṭra, who mourns their fate and praises their rectitude (1–2). He foresees disaster (20–30).
226 (237; 14772). Karṇa urges Duryodhana to flaunt his power and gloat over the Pāṇḍavas' misfortune (1–20).
227 (239; 14820). A cowherd arrives and suggests a cattle count (1–5). Dhṛtarāṣṭra has misgivings: they may encounter the Pāṇḍavas (5–15). Śakuni persuades him (15–20). The Kauravas ride out (20–25).
229 (240; 14850). Duryodhana inspects cattle, plays, and hunts (1–10). He reaches Dvaitavana, where they camp. The Gandharvas stop him: the lake is their playground (10–20). Duryodhana's men report to him (20–25).
230 (241; 14881). Duryodhana orders the attack (1–10). The Gandharva Citrasena irately orders a counterattack (5–10). Only Karṇa holds his ground and rallies the Kauravas (10–20). Many flee to Yudhiṣṭhira (20–25). Karṇa, Duryodhana, and Śakuni fight on (25–30). Karṇa is dismounted and flees (30).
231 (242; 14913). Duryodhana is dismounted and captured with his brothers; the rest take refuge with Yudhiṣṭhira (1–10). Bhīma berates the Kauravas (10–20).
232 (244; 14957). They arm themselves and engage the Gandharvas, gently at first, demanding the others' freedom, then in force (1–20).
234 (245; 1479). Arjuna employs his celestial weapons (1–5). The Gandharvas take the Kauravas to the sky, but Arjuna covers them with a net of arrows and checks them (1–15). Citrasena joins and after a fight appears as Arjuna's old friend (15–25).
235 (246; 15009). Citrasena discloses Duryodhana's mocking intentions (1–5). Arjuna tells him to free him;

they report to Yudhiṣṭhira, who orders Duryodhana freed and dismisses the Gandharvas (5–15). Yudhiṣṭhira admonishes Duryodhana and releases him (15–25).
236 (247; 15038). At Janamejaya's bidding, Vaiśaṃpāyana relates Duryodhana's shame. Karṇa ignorantly compliments him on his victory (1–15).
237 (248; 15053). Duryodhana admits to his defeat and capture by the Gandharvas, and Arjuna's triumph over them (1–15).
238 (249–50; 15070). Duryodhana relates how Yudhiṣṭhira set him free, to his shame (1–5). He decides to fast unto death (10–20). He wishes to consecrate Duḥśāsana, who protests and begs his brother to reconsider (20–30). Karṇa urges him likewise (30–45).
239 (251; 15125). Śakuni adds his voice and counsels gratitude and reconciliation (1–5). Duryodhana is adamant and prepares himself (5–15). The Dānavas learn of his resolve and send a witch, Kṛtyā, to fetch him; she does so (15–25).
240 (252; 15155). The Dānavas remonstrate with Duryodhana: he is a deity; the other Kauravas will be possessed by demons and fight; Karṇa has been created to kill Arjuna (1–20). Indra will rob Karṇa's armor (20). Kṛtyā takes him back and he wakes up; he tells no one (25–35). Karṇa admonishes him on the morrow, and he returns in state to Hāstinapura (35–45).
241 (253–55; 15209). Bhīṣma rebukes Duryodhana, who leaves him brusquely and mockingly (1–10). He takes counsel and confesses his desire to have a Royal Consecration; priests are summoned (10–20). They advise that the Royal Consecration is impossible as long as Yudhiṣṭhira lives, but he should melt his tributaries' gold into a plowshare and perform the Vaiṣṇava sacrifice (25–30). Duryodhana consents (30–35).
242 (256; 15298). The Kauravas are elated and kings are invited (1–5). So is Yudhiṣṭhira, who declines, while Bhīma adds threats (5–15). The ceremony is held with great pomp (15–20).
243 (257; 15324). Duryodhana enters Hāstinapura (1–10) and is congratulated by Karṇa, who vows to kill Arjuna (1–15). Yudhiṣṭhira, on hearing the news, is worried (15–20). Duryodhana rules the land (20).

Vaiśaṃpāyana said:

224.1 Janārdana Madhusūdana, after having sat with Mārkaṇḍeya, the
other brahmins, and the great-spirited Pāndavas in appropriate
conversation, now excused himself from them properly; then Keśava,
who was ready to mount his chariot, called Satyā. Satyabhāmā
thereupon embraced the daughter of Drupada and spoke these cordial
words in tune with her affectionate mood: "Do not fret, Kṛṣṇā, do not
worry, do not lie awake. You will win the earth, when your God-like
5 husbands have regained it. No woman as good and as propitiously
featured as you will find trouble for long, my black-eyed friend.
Inevitably, so I have heard, you will enjoy the earth with your
husbands, their rivals destroyed, and set free from discord. When the
Dhārtarāṣṭras have been killed off and the feuds avenged, I shall,
daughter of Drupada, see the earth rest on Yudhiṣṭhira. The arrogant
ladies who laughed at you when you were in exile you shall soon see
bereft of their self-pride. Those people who did you ill when you were
a prey of grief, know, Kṛṣṇā, that they all will depart for Yama's
10 domain. Your son Prativindhya and Prince Sutasoma, Śrutakarman
of Arjuna, Śatānīka of Nakula, and Ṣrutasena who was born the son
of Sahadeva are all cunning champions and masters of arms; and
like Abhimanyu they are all happy and very fond of Dvāravatī city.
Subhadrā loves them like you with her whole soul, without any
conflict of emotions, and is free from any fever about them.
Pradyumna's mother* dotes on them completely, and Keśava is
instructing them along with Bhānu and the others. My father-in-law
always watches over their food and shelter, and the Andhakas and
Vṛṣṇis from Rāma onward all love them, for they like them as much
as Pradyumna, beaming woman."
15 Having said these kind, heartwarming, and charming words
affectionately, she prepared to mount Kṛṣṇa's chariot. Beautiful
Satyabhāmā, the chief queen of Kṛṣṇa, circumambulated Kṛṣṇā and
ascended the chariot of Śauri;** and after he had smilingly comforted
Draupadī, the enemy-burning Yadu chief turned and departed with
his swift steeds.

Janamejaya said:

225.1 When these eminent men lived in the forest,
Lean from cold and heat and wind and glare,
And came to the lake and the blessed wood,
What did they thereafter do, the Pārthas?

* = Kṛṣṇa's wife Rukminī.
** = Kṛṣṇa.

Vaiśaṃpāyana said:

The sons of Pāṇḍu came to the lake,
Dismissed their people, and gave them orders.
Then through the lovely forests and hills
They wandered, and spots along the river.

So while those champions dwelled in the forest
And did their studies and austerities,
There arrived the ancient knowers of the *Veda*;
And those eminent men paid honor to them.

And then one day a brahmin came by,
One versed in the stories, to visit the Kurus.
Having visited onward he went by chance
To visit the king, son of Vicitravīrya.*

5 He was seated and treated in return
By the aged king the chief of the Kurus;
And upon his urging he started his tales
How the sons of Dharma, Wind, Indra, and the twins—

Coarse, lean from the wind and the heat,
Prostrate on their faces in awful grief—
And the hero-protected, yet unprotected
Kṛṣṇā of troubled virtue were faring.

And having heard that brahmin's tale,
Vicitravīrya's son was filled with pity,
And learning his royal grandsons and sons
Lived in the woods in a river of sorrow,

His inner soul was beset with compassion
And stricken with sighs and tears for the Pārthas;
Somehow he collected himself and said,
Reflecting on how he had caused it all,

"Why, the truthful, pure, and nobly behaved
King Dharma, the first of my sons, must now,
He Ajātaśatru, sleep on the ground
Who formerly slept on *ranku* deer wool?

10 "There were bands of minstrels and bards who daily
Awakened the Indra-like prince with praises:
Now before dawn there are flocks of birds
That surely awake him from his lair on the earth.

* = Dhṛtarāṣṭra.

"Why, his limbs grown lean from sunshine and wind,
The Wolf-Belly, body engulfed with fury,
Lies on mother Earth, however unwonted,
Just there on the floor, before Kṛṣṇā's eyes.

"And the delicate, spirited Arjuna,
Subject to the king the son of Dharma,
Will hardly spend the nights without ire,
With all the limbs of his body aching.

"The twins he sees, and Kṛṣṇā, and Bhīma,
And Yudhiṣṭhira too, bereft of comforts—
He will hiss like an awfully powerful snake,
And hardly sleep through the nights without ire.

"The twins so deserving of comfort are wretched,
Whose bodies were rich like the Gods in the sky;
They are surely awake now and come to no peace,
And only checked by their Law and their truth.

15 "That very strong son of the Wind himself,
Who matches the Wind God himself in strength,
Whose awful might is trapped by the Law,
Must sigh now and suffer it all in a rage.

"As he tosses and turns on the ground he must
Contemplate the massacre of my sons,
Restrained but by his truth and his Law,
But biding his time, for he beats them in warring.

"When Ajātaśatru was tricked into losing,
Duḥśāsana spoke his scathing words;
They must have pierced the Wolf-Belly's body
And burned his guts as fire burns the sticks.

"The son of Dharma won't think of misdeeds,
And Dhanaṃjaya surely follows his course;
But in his forest-exile there is growing
In Bhīma a wrath as fire in the wind.

"That hero driven by that great fury
And beating his fist in the palm of his hand
Does heave a most gruesome, searing sigh
And he puts my sons and grandsons on fire.

20 "Wolf-Belly and the Gāṇḍīva bowman,
Berserk like the fire at the end of time,
Will leave no remains of the enemy army
As they scatter their arrows like thunderbolts.

"Duryodhana, Śakuni, the son of the *sūta*,*
Duḥśāsana of the most foolish wits,
Foresee only honey and not the big crash,
Nor the Wolf-Belly, nor Dhanaṃjaya.

"Having done his right or wrong, any man
Awaits the fruit of the thing he has done;
The fruit is yoking him willy-nilly,
For how can a man escape from that?

"When the acre is plowed and the seed is sown
And the God has rained while the season was right,
Will the fruit not grow? Who has ever seen that,
Unless methinks some fate interfered?

"One who knew the dice did not play fair
With the always proper Pāṇḍava;
But neither did I who was swayed by bad sons,
And became for the Kurus this doomsday fire.

25 "For surely the wind will blow unbidden,
And surely the carrying woman will bear,
And surely the dawn spells the death of night,
As evening twilight the end of day.

"Why labor if others fail to labor
And do not make gifts of what they earned?
Comes the time of profit, where is the profit?
It's done on the ground of why do it at all.

"We guard our wealth lest it be split off,
Run off, or erode in little driblets—
If we did not it'd split into hundreds of pieces,
But surely no act gets lost in the world.

"Dhanaṃjaya went to the world of Śakra
From his forest—behold his hero's exploit;
Celestial weapons of four kinds
He knew when he came and re-entered this world.

"Having gone to heaven, in his own body,
What human would want yet to come back here?
Unless he saw that countless Kurus
Were about to die, overtaken by Time.

30 "The bow-seizing Arjuna, left-handed archer,
His Gāṇḍīva bow, the essence of all,

* = Karṇa.

And all those celestial weapons of his—
Who can overcome the might of those three?"

Duryodhana and Saubala secretly
Overheard the words that the king had spoken;
They went up to Karṇa and told him all,
And left him unhappy and low of spirits.

Vaiśaṃpāyana said:

226.1 When Karṇa in Saubala's company heard these words of
Dhṛtarāṣṭra, he said to Duryodhana at that time, "Now that you have
exiled the heroic Pāṇḍavas with your might, Bhārata, enjoy this
earth alone as the Slayer of Śambara* enjoys heaven! The eastern,
southern, western, and northern kings have all been made tributary
to you, king of the people. The shining fortune that once loved the
5 Pāṇḍavas, you have now won, king, with your brothers. The shining
good luck that we, lean from grief, saw briefly at Yudhiṣṭhira's in
Indraprastha, that you have wrested from that King Yudhiṣṭhira,
strong-armed hero, with the force of your cunning. Likewise, Indra
among kings, slayer of enemy heroes, all the kings now abide by your
decree, and they ask for your orders. Yours, O king, is the entire
divine, ocean-clad earth now, with her mountains and forests,
villages, towns, and mines, with her many woods and landscapes, and
adorned with settlements. Saluted by the brahmins, king, and honored
by the kings for your gallantry, you shine among the princes as the
10 sun among the Gods in heaven. As King Yama amidst the Rudras,
Vāsava* amidst the Maruts, you radiate in the midst of the Kurus,
king, like the moon itself. We now see how the Pāṇḍavas, who did not
heed you and never worried, are bereft of their fortune and live in the
forest. For it is said, great king, that the Pāṇḍavas are living with
forest-dwelling brahmins by the Lake Dvaitavana. Therefore march
out, great prince, decked with your superb fortune, and burn the sons
of Pāṇḍu like the sun with the heat of your splendor! Look you,
possessed of the kingdom, bathing in glory and wealthy, on the sons
of the Pāṇḍu who have fallen from the kingdom, been robbed of their
15 fortune and are poor! And let the Pāṇḍavas stare at you as at Yayāti
Nāhuṣa, invested with high nobility and assured of great fortune!
Potent indeed is the luck, O lord of the people, that friends and foes see
shine in a man. What greater happiness is there than to stand on the
plain and see your enemies in the rough, to stand on a mountain and
see them below on earth? Not the birth of a son, or the winning of
wealth, or a kingdom, brings so great a bliss, tiger among kings, as the
sight of the plight of one's enemies. What pleasure won't be his who,

* = Indra.

himself successful in his affairs, watches Dhanaṃjaya in a hermitage,
20 dressed in bark and deerskin? Let your well-dressed wives stare at the
wretched Kṛṣṇā in her bark skirt and deerskin, and add to her misery!
Let her curse herself and her life, as she has been left without riches,
and the grief she felt in the middle of the assembly hall cannot match
that of seeing your wives in their finery!"
Thus Karṇa and Śakuni spoke to the kings; then they both fell
silent at the end of their speech, Janamejaya.

227.1 *Vaiśaṃpāyana said:*
When Prince Duryodhana heard this speech of Karṇa, he was
delighted at first, but then grew sad again; and he said: "All that you
say, Karṇa, has occurred to me too, but I shall never get permission to
go where the Pāṇḍavas are. King Dhṛtarāṣṭra mourns the heroes, and
now thinks the more of the Pāṇḍavas because of their austerities. If
the king learns of our plans, he will, in order to protect the future, not
5 allow us to go, for there is no other purpose in going to Dvaitavana
than to eradicate my enemies in the forest. You know what words
the steward used to me and you and Saubala, and his other
complaints. When I think of those old words and the later grieving, I
cannot decide whether to go or not. For me too it would indeed be a
great joy to see Bhīma and Phalguna* miserable in the forest with
Kṛṣṇā. Were I to win the earth I could not find greater pleasure than
to see the Pāṇḍavas in their bark and deerskin clothes. What could
surpass the sight, Karṇa, of Drupada's daughter Draupadī in her ochre
robe in the forest? If the King Dharma and Bhīmasena Pāṇḍava could
see me decked with a superb fortune, that would be living! But I do
not see any means by which we could go to that forest or how the
king would permit me to go. You with Saubala and Duḥśāsana must
find me a clever stratagem by which we could go to that forest. I too,
after I have decided whether to go or not, will go to the king tomorrow
15 morning; and when I am sitting with Bhīṣma, the chief of the Kurus,
you and Saubala must tell the stratagem that you may have found.
After hearing what Bhīṣma and the king have to say about my going,
I'll make up my mind and beg Grandfather." The others agreed and
went back to their quarters.
When morning dawned, Karṇa went to Prince Duryodhana and
said laughingly, "I have found a way, listen, my prince. All the
cowherd stations in Dvaitavana are still waiting for you, lord of the
people, and we can surely go there on the pretext of a cattle
20 expedition, for it is always proper to go on a cattle expedition, and
thus your father should give his permission, my lord Prince." While
they were discussing the cattle expedition, the Gāndhāra prince Śakuni

* = Arjuna.

said, laughing in his turn, "I find this stratagem for going flawless: the king will not only allow us, but urge us! Indeed, the cowherd stations in Dvaitavana are still waiting for you, lord of the people, and surely we can go on the pretext of a cattle expedition!" Laughing heartily all three offered their palms, and having decided on it, they went to see the chief of the Kurus.

228.1 *Vaiśaṃpāyana said:*
Thereupon they all visited Dhṛtarāṣṭra, O Janamejaya, and inquired
about the king's health, and the king returned the inquiries. Then a
cowherd by the name of Samaṅga, whom they had instructed earlier,
informed Dhṛtarāṣṭra about the cattle in the vicinity; and immediately,
O lord of your people, Rādheya* and Śakuni said to King Dhṛtarāṣṭra
best of kings, "Kaurava, at this time the cowherd stations are lovely
spots. The time for the count has come, and for the branding of the
5 calves. This is also a good time for your son to go hunting, king. Pray
give Duryodhana leave to go."
Dhṛtarāṣṭra said:
The hunt is a good thing, son, and so is the inspection of cattle.
I recall that the cowherds are not to be trusted. But I hear that those
tiger-like men are in that vicinity, therefore I do not approve that all
of you go there yourselves. They were defeated with a trick and now
are living frugally in the great forest, the capable warriors, constant in
their austerities, Rādheya. The King Dharma won't get angry, but
Bhīmasena is intransigent, and the daughter of Yajñasena is one
10 fierce fire. You are arrogant and sure to offend them, and they will
burn you down with the power of austerities they possess, or else the
heroes, overcome with fury, will, with arms and sword girt, together
burn you with the fire of their weapons. Or if you somehow slaughter
them, because you are many, that would be the ultimate disgrace, but
I think it is impossible, for the strong-armed Dhanaṃjaya has dwelt in
the world of Indra and returned to the forest after he had obtained
celestial weapons.
"Of yore the Terrifier conquered the earth without such weapons—
15 why should the warrior not kill you now that he has got them? Or if
you obey my words and are careful there, it will be an anxious
sojourn, and unhappiness will result from their mistrust. Or else, if
some soldiers were to offend Yudhiṣṭhira, the act, however unintended,
will be blamed on you. Therefore let some trusted men go there for the
count; I do not approve of your going there yourself, Bhārata."
Śakuni said:
The eldest Pāṇḍava knows the Law and remembers the promise he
made in the assembly that he would live in the forest for twelve

* = Karṇa.

years, Bhārata. All the Pāṇḍavas follow the Law and his example.
20 Yudhiṣṭhira Kaunteya will not quarrel with us, and we very much
desire to go hunting. We want to do the count, not to visit the
Pāṇḍavas. There will be no ignoble behavior, and we will not venture
where they are camping.

Vaiśaṃpāyana said:

At these words of Śakuni, King Dhṛtarāṣṭra gave Duryodhana and
his councillors permission, but reluctantly. When he had obtained his
permission, Gāndhārī's son, chief of the Bharatas, accompanied by
Karṇa, rode out amidst a large force with Duḥśāsana and the gambler
25 Śakuni, his other brothers, and thousands of women. All the
townsmen and their wives followed the strong-armed prince to the
forest when he rode out to visit Lake Dvaitavana. There were eight
thousand chariots, thirty thousand elephants, many thousands of foot
soldiers, and nine thousand horses; and carts, vending wagons, and
whores, traders and bards, and expert hunters by the hundreds and
thousands. And the prince's progress was noisy with the roar of raging
gales in the rainy season, O lord of your people. At the distance of two
cries Duryodhana set up camp with all of his mounts ajourneying to
Lake Dvaitavana.

229.1 *Vaiśaṃpāyana said:*

While camping from place to place in the forest, Prince Duryodhana
then arrived at the cowherd stations and settled down there. The men
made him quarters in a lovely open and wooded spot with plenty of
water that served all their needs, and likewise made separate quarters
close by for Karṇa, Śakuni, and all his brothers. The prince inspected
cows by the hundreds and thousands, and marked them all with signs
5 and figures. He had the calves branded, he learned which heifers had
been crossed, and had the cows with young calves tallied.

When he had completed the count and marked the three-year-olds,
the scion of Kuru began to play merrily amidst the cowherds. All the
townspeople and thousands of soldiers played about like Immortals in
the forest as it pleased them. The cowherds, great singers and clever at
dance and music, and their lasses in full ornaments waited on the son
of Dhṛtarāṣṭra. The prince, surrounded by his women, happily
distributed largess to them according to their worth, and food and
10 drinks of all kinds. They all chased hyena, buffalo, deer, gayal, bear,
and swine on all sides. Shooting game with his arrows and catching
elephants in the forest, he had the animals driven to pleasant spots.
He drank cow's milk and ate delicacies, Bhārata, and feasted his eyes
on lovely flowering woods that were buzzing with crazy bees and noisy
with the cries of peacocks.

Gradually he made his way to auspicious Lake Dvaitavana, covered
with great opulence like great Indra himself, the Thunderbolt-wielder.
It so happened that that same day Yudhiṣṭhira the King Dharma
offered with the *sadyaska* sacrifice of the royal seers, O lord of your
people, and the king, chief of the Kurus, did the divine rite with forest
15 fare. Having done it, the wise Kaurava king went with Draupadī, his
wife-by-the-Law, to his camp by the lake.

Then Duryodhana and his younger brothers, O Bhārata, gave orders
to the servants: "Quickly set up the game tents!" The servants told
the Kauravya they would and they went to Lake Dvaitavana to set up
the game tents. Meanwhile the vanguard of the son of Dhṛtarāṣṭra's
army arrived at Lake Dvaitavana, and the Gandharvas stopped the
entering troops at the gate of the wood; in fact, lord of the people, the
king of the Gandharvas had earlier come from Kubera's palace
20 surrounded by his host. As he was in the habit of sporting with groups
of Apsarās and the children of the Thirty Gods he had closed off the
lake in order to play there. When the servants of the king found the
lake closed by him, O king, they went back to the spot where Prince
Duryodhana was. Upon hearing their report, the Kauravya sent his
war-crazed troops and told them to drive the others away. At these
orders of the prince soldiers of the vanguard went to Lake Dvaitavana
and said to the Gandharvas, "A mighty king named Duryodhana, the
25 son of Dhṛtarāṣṭra, has come here to amuse himself, so run off!" The
Gandharvas began to laugh, lord of your people, and replied harshly
enough to the men, "Your slow-witted King Suyodhana does not use
his mind if he orders us celestials in this manner as though we were
his subjects! You are doomed to die, nitwits, no doubt of that, if you
mindlessly speak to us at his orders. Hurry back, all of you, to the
Kaurava king, lest you depart right now to the hateful domain of the
King of Law!" Upon these words of the Gandharvas the king's
vanguard soldiers all fled back to the prince, the son of Dhṛtarāṣṭra.

Vaiśaṃpāyana said:

230.1 All together, they thereupon went to Duryodhana, O great king,
and told him what they had said about the Kaurava. The majestic
Dhārtarāṣṭra was filled with indignation that his army should have
been sent away by the Gandharvas, Bhārata, and he told the troops,
"Punish those churls, ignorant of the Law, who offend me, if it were
the God of the Hundred Sacrifices himself at play with all the Gods!"
Having heard Duryodhana's words the powerful Dhārtarāṣṭras and
5 thousands of warriors all armored themselves. They routed the
Gandharvas and forced their way into the wood, filling the ten
directions with a mighty lion's roar. The Kaurava troops were being

checked by other Gandharvas, king of the earth, and the Gandharvas
tried to stop them gently, but they paid no heed to them and entered
the vast wood.

When the Dhārtaraṣṭras and their king did not halt at their bidding,
they all became airborne and reported to Citrasena. The king of the
Gandharvas said to them all concerning the Kauravas: "Punish those
ignoble men!" quoth Citrasena very indignantly. Citrasena dismissed
the Gandharvas, and they seized their weapons and stormed at the
10 Dhārtarāṣṭras, Bhārata. When they saw the swift-flying Gandharvas
attack them with weapons raised, they all fled from the battle before
the eyes of the son of Dhṛtarāṣṭra. Upon seeing all the Dhārtarāṣṭras
run away from the battle, the gallant Vaikartana* did not. At the
sight of the onslaught of the Gandharvas' vast army Rādheya*
countered them with a huge shower of arrows, and the *sūta*'s son
with his razor-edged shafts and his bear-tipped calf's-tooth and iron
arrows slew Gandharvas by the hundreds due to his agility. Felling the
heads of the Gandharvas, the great warrior shortly blew apart the
15 whole host of Citrasena. The Gandharvas that were slain by the *sūta*'s
sagacious son returned once more by the hundreds and thousands. In
an instant the earth became one vast stretch of Gandharvas with the
impetuous troops of Citrasena attacking.

Thereupon Prince Duryodhana, Śakuni Saubala, Duḥśāsana,
Vikarṇa, and the other sons of Dhṛtarāṣṭra cut down the army on
their chariots that screeched like Garuḍas. Once more they gave
battle, placing Karṇa at their head, with the loud clatter of their
chariots and the stamping of horses, and, supporting Vaikartana, they
halted the Gandharvas. All the Gandharvas fell upon the Kauravas,
and a frightful battle ensued, which was hair-raising.

20 Pressed by the arrows, the Gandharvas softened and the Kauravas
yelled out loud when they saw the Gandharvas harassed. Seeing the
Gandharvas frightened, the intransigent Citrasena flew angrily up
from his seat, intent on killing them all. Cunning in marvelous ways,
he did battle with the aid of his wizardry missile, and Citrasena's
wizardry bewildered the Kauravyas. One by one the warriors of
Dhṛtarāṣṭra's son were turned about by ten Gandharvas each,
Bhārata. Hard pressed by the vast army, they ran in fear from the
25 battle to where King Yudhiṣṭhira was standing. The ranks of the
Dhārtarāṣṭras were being hacked everywhere, but Karṇa Vaikartana,
O king, stood immobile like a mountain. Although sorely wounded,
Duryodhana, Karṇa, and Śakuni Saubala kept fighting the Gandharvas
on the battlefield. All the hundreds and thousands of Gandharvas
together stormed toward Karṇa in the mêlée to finish him off. With
their swords, three-bladed javelins, spikes, and maces, the powerful

* = Karṇa.

fighters countered the *sūta's* son on all sides, seeking to slay him.
Some broke the yoke, others lowered the flagpole, others brought
30 down the shafts, horses, and driver. Still others attacked the umbrella
and the bumping ledge, and the driver's box: thus the Gandharvas
in their many thousands broke the chariot into pieces. Holding sword
and shield the son of the *sūta* leaped from the chariot, mounted
Vikarṇa's, and whipped the horses to escape.

Vaiśaṃpāyana said:

231.1 With the great warrior Karṇa broken by the Gandharvas, O great
king, the whole army took flight before the Dhārtarāṣṭra's eyes.
Seeing all the Dhārtarāṣṭras flee away, Duryodhana still held his
ground, great king. When he saw that the grand host of the
Gandharvas was attacking him, the enemy-tamer showered them
with a mighty rain of arrows. Without heeding the arrow shower,
the Gandharvas, seeking Duryodhana's death, surrounded his chariot
5 on all sides. They cut down its yoke, shafts, armor, flag, charioteer,
horses, *triveṇu*, and seat to pieces the size of sesame seeds. When
Duryodhana was unseated from his chariot and had fallen to the
ground, strong-armed Citrasena ran to him and captured him alive.
With him captive, O Indra among kings, the Gandharvas surrounded
Duḥśāsana, who was still on his chariot, and took him prisoner.
Others, taking Citrasena along, stormed at Viviṃśati; others again at
Vinda and Anuvinda and all the princes' wives. Dhārtarāṣṭra's
soldiers, driven off by the Gandharvas and bringing along those who
10 had been wounded before, went to the Pāṇḍavas. Carts, vending
wagons, and whores, carriages and vehicles all sought refuge with the
Pāṇḍavas when their king had been captured. The strong-armed and
powerful Prince Priyadarśana Dhārtarāṣṭra was taken by the
Gandharvas, and the Pārthas went after him. Duḥśāsana, Durviṣaha,
Durmukha, and Durjaya were caught and tied by the Gandharvas,
and so were all the princes' wives. Likewise Duryodhana's councillors,
yearning for their prince, all wretchedly approached Yudhiṣṭhira,
weeping with sobs of misery.

Thereupon Bhīmasena spoke to the old, suffering, and wretched
15 councillors of Duryodhana, who were begging Yudhiṣṭhira: "The
matter has gone wrong for those who did wrong, if the Gandharvas
now have accomplished what we should have done! Ill-advised,
friends, was that deed of the false-playing prince; as we have heard
it said, 'Others will bring down the enemy of a coward.' We have
been witnesses to this feat of the Gandharva, which was beyond mere
humans—we are lucky that there still is a man in this world who
wishes us well and has made us happy by lifting our burden, while
we were sitting by! That evil-minded man, being comfortable himself,

wanted to see us live in discomfort, suffering the cold, wind, and heat,
and lean from austerities. Those who imitate the habits of that
20 lawless, ill-spirited Kaurava will soon see their undoing. For it is
because of his lawlessness that this lesson has been taught, cruel
Kauravyas, and I call you the witnesses of it!" And to the intransigent
Bhīmasena Kaunteya who spoke in this fashion, the king said, "This
is not the time to be harsh."

Yudhiṣṭhira said:

232.1 Why must you speak like this, my friend, to the Kauravas, now
that they have come to grief and fearfully have resorted to us seeking
shelter? Breaches and quarrels do occur between kinsmen, Wolf-
Belly, feuds drag on, but the family Law does not thereby perish.
When, however, an outsider attacks the family of kinsmen, the strict
do not tolerate the stranger's importunity. This ill-minded Gandharva
knows that we have been dwelling here for a long time, yet he has
5 ignored us and done this displeasing thing. Because of the Gandharvas'
forcibly capturing Duryodhana in battle, and this stranger's molestation
of the women, our family has been robbed. For the refuge of shelter-
seekers and to rescue our family arise ye, tiger-like men, and ready
yourselves forthwith!

Arjuna, the twins, and you yourself, invincible Bhīma, must set
Suyodhana Dhārtarāṣṭra free from captivity. Here are the chariots,
tiger-like man, equipped with all weapons and sporting golden flag
staffs, which are driven by Indrasena and the other charioteers:
mount them, brothers, to give battle to the Gandharvas, and
10 unwearyingly strive for the freedom of Suyodhana. Any baron with
all his might would protect one who had come to him for refuge, let
alone a man like you, Wolf-Belly! Who here would be different if
urged to rush to rescue, even if he might be an old enemy seeking
shelter with folded hands? The bestowal of a boon, kingship, the
birth of a son, and the freeing of an enemy from trouble, of these the
last is equal to the three before, Pāṇḍava. What is more satisfying
than this that Suyodhana has come for help and hopes for his life by
relying on the strength of your arms? I myself would have rushed
forward, Wolf-Belly, no doubt of that, if this sacrifice were not still
15 going on. Endeavor with any means to set Suyodhana free peaceably,
Bhima, joy of the Kurus; and if that Gandharva will not return him
peacefully, then free Suyodhana in mild combat. But if he will not
free the Kauravas after mild combat, Bhīma, then subdue the enemies
with any means, for set free they must be. This much can I give of
orders, Wolf-Belly, as long as my sacrifice goes on, Bhārata!

Vaiśaṃpāyana said:

When Dhanaṃjaya heard these words of Ajātaśatru, he complied
with the elder's command to liberate the Kauravas.

Arjuna said:
20 If the Gandharvas do not free the sons of Dhṛtarāṣṭra peacefully,
then earth today shall drink the blood of their king!
Vaiśaṃpāyana said:
And on hearing the promise of the true-spoken Arjuna, the spirits of the Kauravas once more returned to them, O king.

Vaiśaṃpāyana said:
233.1 After hearing Yudhiṣṭhira's words, the bulls among men led by
Bhīmasena all arose with joyous mien. All the warriors tied on their
impenetrable armor, O Bhārata, their coats of mail that sparkled with
gold. Armed with chariots, showing their pennants, and brandishing
their bows, the Pāṇḍavas appeared like blazing fires. Mounted on their
chariots, which were well-equipped and yoked with swift horses,
5 those chariot tigers quickly rode out. Loud jubilation broke out among
the Kaurava soldiers at the sight of the warrior sons of Pāṇḍu
together coming forward. Flushed like conquerors the sky-rangers and
the warriors quickly, within an instant, encountered one another
unafraid in that forest.
On seeing the four heroic Pāṇḍavas on their chariots, the
Gandharvas, flushed with victory, fell back. While the Gandhamādana
dwellers watched the radiant men, prepared like the World Guardians
themselves, they arrayed their ranks and took their stand. At King
10 Dharma's behest, they first engaged in battle only gently, but the
Gandharva king's slow-witted soldiers could not be made to see how
gentleness would profit them. Thereupon the left-handed archer,
unassailable enemy-burner, addressed the sky-rangers peaceably on
the battlefield: "This despicable act is not worthy of the king of the
Gandharvas, molesting other men's wives and consorting with
humans! Release these great champions, the sons of Dhṛtarāṣṭra, set
free their wives at the King Dharma's behest!"
At these words of the famous Pāṇḍava the Gandharvas smiled,
15 and they replied to the Pārtha, "Friend, we take the orders of only
one on earth, and when we know his commands, we act without a
care. We do what he alone orders us to do, Bhārata, and beyond that
lord of the Gods we recognize no commander." Kuntī's son
Dhanaṃjaya replied to the Gandharvas' words: "Gandharvas, if you
will not release the son of Dhṛtarāṣṭra peacefully, I shall show my
might and set Suyodhana free myself!" With these words Dhanaṃjaya
Pārtha, left-handed archer, shot his honed, sky-ranging arrows at the
20 rangers of the sky. Proud of their strength, the Gandharvas likewise
showered the Pāṇḍavas with a rain of arrows, and the Pāṇḍavas
showered the celestials. And thus began the frightful battle of the
swift Gandharvas, terrifyingly nimble, and the Pāṇḍavas, O Bhārata.

Vaiśaṃpāyana said:

234.1 Thereupon the Gandharvas, equipped with celestial weapons and
adorned with golden garlands, surrounded them on all sides shooting
fiery arrows. The four Pāṇḍava champions and the Gandharvas by
the thousands fell upon one another in that battle, king, and it was
like a marvel. Just as the Gandharvas had broken the chariots of both
Karṇa and Dhārtarāṣṭra into a hundred pieces, so they now tried to
do it to theirs. While the Gandharvas attacked by the hundreds on the
battlefield, the tiger-like men repulsed them with countless showers of
5 arrows. Spattered by the arrow rains on all sides, the sky-rangers
could not even come close to the sons of Pāṇḍu. Arjuna, noticing
that the Gandharvas were enraged, then employed his grand celestial
weapons.

Proud of his prowess, Arjuna dispatched with his *āgneya* weapon
a thousand thousands of Gandharvas to Yama's realm in that war.
Bhīma, great bowman, first of the strong in a fight, slew Gandharvas
by the hundreds, king, with sharpened arrows. Mādrī's two sons,
fierce fighters, tied them up in front and killed hundreds of the
10 enemy. When the Gandharvas were being killed off by the great-
spirited men with celestial weapons, they took Dhṛtarāṣṭra's sons and
flew up to the sky; but when Kuntī's son Dhanaṃjaya saw them
about to fly up, he enveloped them all around with a net of arrows.
They got caught in the arrow net like birds in a cage, and angrily
showered Arjuna with rains of maces and spears, but Dhanaṃjaya hit
the Gandharvas' bodies with bear arrows. With heads and feet and
arms flying, it was like a rain of rocks, and the others took fright.

15 While the Gandharvas were being butchered by the great-spirited
Pāṇḍava, they spattered him down on earth from the sky with rains
of arrows, but the left-handed archer, enemy-burner, warded off those
flights of arrows with his own missiles, and the splendid man pierced
the Gandharvas in return. Arjuna, joy of the Kurus, released the
sthūṇakarṇa, the *indrajāla*, *saura*, *āgneya*, and *saumya* missiles, and
under the impact of Kuntī's son's projectiles the Gandharvas caught
fire and fell to total despair like the Daityas assailed by Śakra. When
they tried to escape upward, they were checked by the arrow net and,
when they crawled away, stopped by the left-handed archer with his
bear arrows.

20 At the sight of his Gandharvas being frightened by Kuntī's
sagacious son, Citrasena grasped his mace and rushed toward him
with his mace in his hand to do battle. The Pārtha split the solid iron
mace into seven pieces with his arrows when the other stormed at
him. On seeing his mace shattered to pieces by the swift warrior's
arrows, he concealed himself with his magic and battled the Pāṇḍava,
and, standing in the sky, fought off the other's celestial weapons. The

powerful Gandharva king hid in his wizardry, and when Arjuna saw he was hiding and still striking, he pelted him with sky-going celestial missiles on which spells had been put. Angrily Arjuna Dhanaṃjaya of the many shapes dissipated the other's disappearance by resorting to sound-aiming.

25 When he was crowded by the great-spirited Arjuna with those
missiles, the Gandharva thereupon showed himself as Arjuna's good
friend; and on beholding his dear friend Citrasena, of mean strength
in war, the bull of the Pāṇḍavas withdrew the missile he had
launched. When the other Pāṇḍavas noticed that Dhanaṃjaya had
withdrawn his projectiles, they reined in their galloping horses,
arrows, and bows. And Citrasena, Bhīma, the left-handed archer, and
the twins asked about one another's health while they stood on their
chariots.

Vaiśaṃpāyana said:

235.1 Thereupon the great and illustrious archer Arjuna said with a
laugh to Citrasena amidst the Gandharva troops, "Why did you
resolve, hero, to punish the Kauravas? Why did you take Suyodhana
and his wives captive?"

Citrasena said:

The great-spirited God who is sitting there knows the purpose of
the evil Duryodhana and Karṇa, Dhanaṃjaya. These people, knowing
that you were living in the forest and were suffering undeservedly,
5 came here to mock you and the glorious Draupadī. On learning their
intention the lord of the Gods told me, "Go and fetter Duryodhana
with his councillors and bring him here. And you must watch over
Dhanaṃjaya and his brothers in the battle, for the Pāṇḍava is your
good friend and pupil." At the behest of the king of the Gods I came
quickly here; and after I had fettered that wicked soul, I'll go to the
realm of the Gods.

Arjuna said:

Set him free, Citrasena! Suyodhana is our brother. Do it at the King Dharma's behest, if you wish to do me a favor."

Citrasena said:

He is a forever corrupted crook and does not deserve his freedom—
10 he cheated the King Dharma and Kṛṣṇā, Dhanaṃjaya! Kuntī's son,
the King Dharma of the great vows, does not know what he set out
to do, surely. Now that you have heard it, act as you please.

Vaiśaṃpāyana said:

They all went to King Yudhiṣṭhira and told him of Duryodhana's misdeed. When Ajātaśatru* heard the Gandharva's words, he had all the Gandharvas set free, and he declared, "It is fortunate that despite

* = Yudhiṣṭhira.

your strength and might none of you has harmed the wicked
Dhārtarāṣṭra and his councillors, kinsmen, and relatives. You have
done me a great favor, good rangers of the sky: by setting that evil
15 soul free you have not violated my family. Tell me your wishes, for
we are pleased with your visit; and when you have satisfied your
demands, depart swiftly."

The Gandharvas, when they were dismissed by the sagacious son
of Pāṇḍu, went happily, led by Citrasena, away with their Apsarās.
The king of the Gods revived the Gandharvas who had died in the
battle at the hands of the Kauravas with a divine rain of Elixir. The
Pāṇḍavas set all their kinsmen and the princes' wives free, and,
having done this difficult deed, remained quite pleased. Paid honor by
the Kurus and their women and children, the great-spirited warriors
20 shone like fires amidst the Kurus. Yudhiṣṭhira, after having freed
Duryodhana and his brothers, said affectionately, "Never again
commit such violence, friend, for those who do violence do not come
to a good end, Bhārata. Scion of Kuru, go safely home with all your
brothers as you please, and do not be downcast." Prince Duryodhana,
having been dismissed by the Pāṇḍava, went back to his city, riven
with shame. And with the Kauraveya gone, Kuntī's heroic son
Yudhiṣṭhira and his brothers received the homage of the brahmins;
25 and in the midst of all the ascetics, as Śakra amidst the Immortals, he
disported himself joyously in the Dvaitavana woods.

Janamejaya said:

236.1 It seems to me that when the haughty and evil-spirited Duryodhana
a boastful man, arrogant and conceited as he always was, forever
praising himself and despising the Pāṇḍavas for their manliness and
generosity, later returned to Hāstinapura when he had been defeated
and captured by his enemies, and set free by the great-spirited and
heroic Pāṇḍavas, his entrance into the city must have been a difficult
one. Relate to me fully, Vaiśampāyana, how he made his entrance,
shamefaced, and grief-stricken in his heart.

Vaiśaṃpāyana said:

5 Suyodhana Dhārtarāṣṭra, after having been dismissed by the King
Dharma, hung his head in shame and made his way back slowly,
despondent and greatly troubled. The prince, who was followed by his
four kinds of troops, went back to his city, while his mournful mind
dwelled on his defeat. On the way, in a region with fine grass and
water, he dismissed his wagons, camped in a pleasant and lovely spot
as the fancy took him, and had his elephants, horses, chariots, and
foot soldiers bivouac according to their rankings. When the prince
had seated himself on a palanquin, brilliant as fire, he himself
eclipsed like the moon that has been grasped by Rāhu at the waning

of the night. Karṇa came up to him in the early morning and said to Duryodhana, "How fortunate that you are alive, Gāndhāri! How
10 fortunate that we have met again! How fortunate that you have defeated the Gandharvas of the many shapes! It is fortunate that I see all your brothers, joy of the Kurus, those great warriors who came victoriously away from the battle after vanquishing the enemies. I myself was put to flight by all those Gandharvas, before your very eyes; I could not stop my own troops when they were routed; and sorely wounded by arrows and pressed, I fled. I deem it a great marvel, Bhārata, that I now see you here unhurt, unwounded, with wives, possessions, and mounts intact, having escaped from that superhuman battle. Not a man can be found in this world, Bhārata, who can do what you have done in the battle with your brothers, great prince!"

15 At these words of Karṇa Prince Duryodhana lowered his head, king, and said in a tear-choked voice,

Duryodhana said:

237.1 I do not resent your words, Rādheya, for you do not know. You think that I defeated the Gandharva foes with my own splendor. Surely, my brothers and I were embattled with the Gandharvas for a long time, strong-armed hero, and there was slaughter on both sides. But when those champions employed their wizardry and took to the sky, our battle with the sky-rangers became unequal. We were defeated in the fight and taken captive with our retainers, councillors, wives, possessions, and mounts. Miserable, we were taken high
5 through the sky. Then some soldiers and councillors went to the warlike Pāṇḍavas, who gave them shelter, and they told them, "Prince Duryodhana Dhārtarāṣṭra and his younger brothers have with their councillors and wives been taken to the sky by the Gandharvas. Hail to thee! Set the prince and his wives free, lest all the Kuru wives be violated!"

At these words the Law-minded eldest son of Pāṇḍu appeased his brothers and ordered them to free us. The Pāṇḍavas, bulls among men, went to that place, and those warriors, capable though they
10 were, first asked them in a conciliatory way. When the Gandharvas, in spite of their tactfulness, did not release us, Arjuna, Bhīma and the twins, wallowing in their strength, shot off many showers of arrows at the Gandharvas. Thereupon they all abandoned the battle and fled to the sky, happily dragging us along in our misery. Then I saw Dhanaṃjaya, wrapped on all sides in a mass of arrows, employ his superhuman weapons. When space was covered with sharp arrows by the Pāṇḍavas, Citrasena, a friend of Dhanaṃjaya, showed himself. The enemy-burning Gandharva and the Pāṇḍava embraced and

15 asked each other's good health. On meeting each other they shed
their armor, and the heroic Gandharvas mingled with the Pāṇḍavas,
while Citrasena and Dhanaṃjaya paid honor to each other.

Duryodhana said:

238.1 When he met with Citrasena, Arjuna began to laugh, and the
slayer of enemy champions spoke this far from cowardly word:
"Pray set free our brethren, hero, chief of the Gandharvas! As long
as the Pāṇḍavas are alive, they do not deserve to be harassed!" At
the words of the great-spirited Pāṇḍava the Gandharva told him with
what plans we had come out, Karṇa—to see the Pāṇḍavas with their
wife deprived of comforts. And when that Gandharva made his
speech, I was covered with shame, and I hoped for the earth to split
5 so that I could enter. The Gandharvas then went with the Pāṇḍavas
to Yudhiṣṭhira and told him of our evil design; and they presented us
to him in fetters. There stood I, before the eyes of my women, a
wretched, fettered prisoner of the enemy, and now offered to
Yudhiṣṭhira—what could be more grievous! The very men whom I
had chased away and whose enemy I had always been now set me
free, me the villain, and I owe them my life! It would have been
better, hero, had I met my death in that grand battle than to live out
such a life. My fame at having been killed by Gandharvas would have
been broadcast on earth, and I would have earned the blissful,
everlasting worlds in the realm of Indra.

10 Bulls among men, hear what I have now resolved to do. I shall
sit down here and fast to death. But you must go home: all my
brothers must now return to the city, and so must my friends and
relations, headed by Karṇa, now return to the city, and place
Duḥśāsana first. As I have been humbled by the enemy, I shall not
return to the city. I who robbed the enemy of his pride and added to
the pride of my friends, but now have come to inflict sorrow on my
friends and to raise the spirits of the enemy—what shall I have to say
to the king on returning to the City of the Elephant? Bhīṣma, Droṇa,
Kṛpa, Aśvatthāman Drauṇi, Vidura, Saṃjaya, Bāhlīka, Somadatta,
15 and the others who are well honored by the elders, the brahmins, the
guild provosts and those of independent means—what will they say
to me and what shall I reply to them? After I have stood on my
enemies' head and paraded on their chest, what shall I tell them now
that I have fallen by my own fault? Ill-reared men who find a fortune
or learning or power do not long keep it, madly proud just like me.
O woe that I did a base crime in my folly, miscreant that I am, so
that now I have fallen into peril!

Therefore I shall fast unto death, for I can no longer live. What
man of spirit would want to live after his enemy has saved him from

20 danger? A proud man, I have been mocked by my enemies and
robbed of my manhood—the richly puissant Pāṇḍavas have looked
down upon me with contempt!

Vaiśaṃpāyana said:

Thus overcome by sorrow he spoke to Duḥśāsana: "Duḥśāsana
Bhārata, listen to my word! Receive the consecration that I bestow
upon you, and henceforth be king. Rule the abundant earth protected
by Karṇa and Saubala. Watch over your brothers as confidently as
the Slayer of Vṛtra watches over the Maruts. Your relatives shall live
off you as the Gods live off the God of the Hundred Sacrifices. Always
live by the brahmins, without distraction, and always be the recourse
25 of your friends and relations. Look after your kinsmen as Viṣṇu looks
after the throngs of Gods. Protect the elders. Now go and rule the
earth, gladdening all your friends and threatening the enemies!" And
he embraced him and said, "Go!"

Miserably Duḥśāsana folded his hands and prostrated himself. And
a prey to great sorrow, with tears in his throat, he said these
stammered words to his eldest brother: "Have pity!" and he fell to
the ground, with burning heart, fell at the other's feet shedding tears.
Said the tiger-like man, "This shall not be! Let earth with her
mountains be riven, and heaven be splintered, let the sun lose its
30 light and the moon its coolness, let the wind lose its speed and the
Himālaya walk, let the oceans dry up and the fire shed its heat, I shall
not rule the earth without you, king!" And again and again he said,
"Have pity! In our lineage," he said, "you alone shall be king for a
hundred years."

Speaking thus, Indra among kings, Duḥśāsana wept aloud, and
grasped the honor-deserving feet of his oldest brother, O Bhārata. And
seeing Duḥśāsana and Duryodhana in their sorrow, Karṇa, himself
grief-stricken, drew near and said in turn, "Why, Kauravyas, do you
despair in your folly like two commoners? No one's grief is stopped by
35 grieving! And if grief does not remove the plight of the grieving,
what power do you detect in the grief you are indulging? Take
command of yourselves and do not gladden the enemies with your
miseries! For the Pāṇḍavas had no choice but to set you free, king:
the people of a king's realm must always be amenable to him, for they
live without a care under your protection. So pray do not give way
to resentment like a commoner! Your brothers are despondent over
your resolve on death. Rise, stride, hail to thee, and solace your
brothers!

"King, I do not understand your frivolousness here today. What is
so strange, hero, that the Pāṇḍavas set you free, when you had just
fallen into enemy hands, plower of your foes? The people of a realm
who live by the sword must do what is pleasing to their king,

40 whether they are known for it or not. Oftentimes leaders who shake
up the enemy army are captured on the battlefield and rescued by
their own soldiers. Men who join and live by the sword and dwell in
the realms of kings must properly strive for the cause of their king.
What cause of complaint is there, king, if the Pāṇḍavas, who live in
your realm, chanced to set you free? What was wrong is that the
Pāṇḍavas did not follow you, greatest of kings, when you marched
out with your army! Those champions and strongmen, who did not
follow you into battle, had before been rendered your slaves in your
45 assembly hall. Today you enjoy the Pāṇḍavas' riches! But look at the
Pāṇḍavas: they have mettle and do *not* fast unto death! Rise, king,
hail to thee, and have no worry. Inevitably the people of a king's
realm must do favors for him—what is there to complain in that?
Indra among kings, if you do not act on my words I shall stay right
here and obey your feet, enemy-crusher! Deprived of you, bull among
men, I cannot endure to live. If you fast unto death, you shall be the
laughing stock of the kings!"

Vaiśaṃpāyana said:

At these words of Karṇa King Duryodhana did not intend to rise, being resolved upon heaven.

Vaiśaṃpāyana said:

239.1 To the intransigent King Duryodhana, who was set to starve to
death, now spoke soothingly Śakuni Saubala, O king. "Surely what
Karṇa said is right, you have heard it, Kaurava! Why should you
foolishly relinquish the plentiful riches that I took, and, best of kings,
foolishly forsake your life? And it occurs to me today that you have
not frequented your elders. If one does not control sudden joy or
depression, he perishes with his fortune like an unbaked clay pot in
water. Fortunes do not take to a king either too timid or cowardly,
woolgathering or absent-minded, or beset with the vices of the senses.
5 How can you mind having been treated well when you were down?
Don't destroy the Pārthas' fine act by feeling sorry! You should be
happy and give the Pāṇḍavas their due. Instead you are moping,
Indra of kings, about this setback. Please, do not kill yourself,
remember a good turn with gratitude! Return the Pārthas their
kingdom, and you will earn fame and Law. Recognize the deed, don't
be an ingrate. Act the brother to the Pāṇḍavas, reestablish them, and
return to them their ancestral kingdom: then you can have
happiness!"

When he heard Śakuni speak, Duryodhana looked with brotherly
love at Duḥśāsana who had fallen at his feet, a hero turned timid;
10 and with his well-formed arms he raised up enemy-taming Duḥśāsana,
embraced him, and kissed him affectionately on his head. Thinking

on Karṇa's and Saubala's words, King Duryodhana, already wholly desperate and overcome with shame, fell to utter despondency. And having listened to his friends he angrily said, "I set no store anymore by Law, wealth, comfort, power, authority, or pleasures. Do not be frustrated, but go! My mind is made up: I shall starve myself to death. All of you, go to the city and honor my elders!"

But they replied to the enemy-crushing king, "We go where you
go, Bhārata, Indra of kings. How could we enter the city without
15 you?" His friends, councillors, brothers, and kinfolk talked to him in
many ways, but he did not change his mind. And in this resolve Dhṛtarāṣṭra's son spread *darbha* grass on the ground, touched water and cleansed himself, and he sat down on the ground. Clothed in a skirt of *kuśa* grass and rags, observing the ultimate restraint and keeping silence, that tiger among kings out of yearning for heaven piled up his thoughts and ignored the outer world.

Thereupon the Daityas and Dānavas, hearing of his decision, the gruesome denizens of the nether world who had been defeated by the Gods, now, in the knowledge that Duryodhana would wreck their party, performed a sacrificial rite in order to summon him. Wise in
the spells, they executed with spells and prayers certain rituals that
20 are found in the *Upaniṣad*, and with spells spoken by Bṛhaspati and
Uśanas and found in the *Atharvaveda*. Most attentively brahmins, who possessed spells and prayers and were expert in the *Vedas* and their branches and held firm vows, poured an oblation of milk into the fire with the requisite spells.

At the conclusion of the rite, Kṛtyā, a wondrous woman with gaping mouth, arose from the fire, O king, and she said, "What must I do?" The Daityas told her with well-pleased hearts, "Bring King Dhārtarāṣṭra here, he is fasting unto death." Kṛtyā gave her promise
and went forth and in a twinkling of the eye went to King Suyodhana.
25 She took the king and entered the nether world and a little while
after handed him over to the Dānavas. When they saw that the king had been fetched, the Dānavas foregathered at night, and all were in high spirits and their eyes were blooming a little. And they spoke this prideful word to Duryodhana.

The Dānavas said:

240.1 Lord Suyodhana, Indra among kings, scion of the Bhāratas, as
always surrounded by champions as well as great-spirited men, why have you perpetrated this violent deed, starvation unto death? For he who kills himself goes down and incurs notorious ill-repute. Indeed, wise men like you do not indulge in acts that are contrary to their interests, beset with calamities and striking at the root. Suppress this intention of yours, king, which is destructive of Law, Profit, and

Pleasure, kills off fame, majesty, and steadfastness, and brings joy to
5 your enemies! Hear, my Lord, the truth about your own divinity,
king, and about the creation of your body. Then find fortitude.

Long ago we obtained you with our austerities from the Great
God.* The whole upper part of your body was fashioned from piles
of diamonds, impenetrable to arrows and swords. Your lower body,
prince sans blame, was made by the Goddess out of flowers and is
seductive to women for its beauty. Thus your body, best of kings, is
imbued both with the Lord and with the Goddess, tiger among kings.
You are divine, not human! Puissant barons led by Bhagadatta,
champions who know divine weaponry, will lead your enemies to
10 their doom. Enough therefore of your despair! You are in no danger,
for the Dānavas have become heroes on earth in order to assist you.
Other Asuras will take possession of Bhīṣma, Droṇa, Kṛpa, and the
others; and possessed by them they will fight your enemies ruthlessly.
When they engage in battle, best of the Kurus, they will give no
quarter to either sons or brothers, parents or relatives, students or
kinsmen, the young or the old. Pitiless, possessed by the Dānavas,
their inner souls overwhelmed, they will battle their relations and
cast all love far off. Gleefully, their minds darkened, the tiger-like
men, befuddled with ignorance by a fate set by the Ordainer, will say
to one another, "You shall not escape from me with your life!"
15 Standing firm on their manly might in the unleashing of manifold
weapons, best of the Kurus, they will boastfully perpetrate a holocaust.
The great-spirited Pāṇḍavas will capably strike back, and the
powerful men, spurred by fate, will slaughter them. Bands of Daityas
and Rākṣasas will take on lives in the wombs of the baronage and
fight mightily with your enemies, O king, with maces, clubs, swords,
and various striking weapons. Whatever fear arises in you from
Arjuna here, for that too we have devised a means: the soul of the
slain Naraka that has assumed the body of Karṇa in order to kill
Arjuna. Remembering their feud, O hero, he will fight Keśava and
20 Arjuna; and proud of his puissance the warrior Karna, greatest of
swordsmen, will vanquish the Pārtha in battle, and all the enemies.
Knowing this the Thunderbolt-wielder, in order to protect the left-handed archer, will rob the armor and earrings of Karṇa with a ruse.
Therefore the hundreds and thousands of Daityas with us, and the
Rākṣasas who are styled the Sworn Warriors, will strike down heroic
Arjuna. Do not grieve! This earth will be yours to enjoy without
rivals, O king! Do not lead us into despair, for that is not fitting to
you. If you perish, our party will diminish, Kaurava. Go, hero, have
no other purpose whatever: you are always our recourse, as the
Pāṇḍavas are of the Gods.

* = Śiva.

Vaiśaṃpāyana said:
25 When they had thus spoken, the Daityas embraced that elephant
among kings, and the Dānava bulls comforted the unassailable
warrior like a son. Having steadied his resolve, and spoken kind
words, they dismissed him, Bhārata, saying, "Go now!" and "Find
victory!" The same Kṛtyā brought the strong-armed man back when
he was dismissed, to the very spot where he had been fasting unto
death. Kṛtyā put the hero down, saluted him, and when the king had
dismissed her, vanished then and there.
After she was gone, King Duryodhana thought that it all had been
a dream, Bhārata, and he was left with this thought: "I shall vanquish
30 the Pāṇḍus in battle." Suyodhana thought that Karṇa and the Sworn
Warriors were charged with the slaying of enemy-killing Pārtha, and
that they were capable of it.
Thus the hope of defeating the Pāṇḍavas was strengthened in
Dhārtarāṣṭra's evil mind. Karṇa too, with the inner soul of Naraka
possessing his mind and spirit, set his cruel mind on killing Arjuna.
The Sworn Heroes, whose minds had been possessed by the Rākṣasas
and were overcome with Passion and Darkness, sought the death of
Phalguna.* And Bhīṣma, Droṇa, Kṛpa, and the others were no longer
so friendly toward the sons of Pāṇḍu, now that their minds had been
taken over by the Dānavas; King Suyodhana did not tell anyone
about it.
35 The next morning Karṇa Vaikartana said to King Duryodhana
smilingly and with folded hands these reasoned words: "No dead man
conquers his enemies, only a live one sees fortune. Whence would a
dead man get fortune, Kauraveya, whence victory? This is not the
time for despair, for fear, or for dying!" The strong-armed man
clasped the other in his arms and said, "Rise up, king! Why lie down,
why grieve, enemy-killer? How can you want to die when you have
set the enemy on fire with your splendor? Or if fear has beset you on
witnessing Arjuna's prowess, I promise you in truth that I shall kill
Arjuna in battle! When the thirteenth year is full, I swear by my
sword that I myself shall bring the Pārthas under your yoke, king of
the people!"
40 Having thus been addressed by Karṇa, Suyodhana, prompted by
the words of the Dānavas and the prostrations of the others, arose. He
made a firm resolve in his heart after having heard the words of the
Daityas, and the tiger-like man ordered his army yoked, with its many
chariots, elephants, and horses, and teeming with foot troops. The
grand army marched out, king, like the flooding Ganges, with white
umbrellas and pennants, and white yak-tail plumes. Astir with
chariots, elephants, and foot soldiers, it shone beyond measure, as the

* = Arjuna.

sky shines at the season when the massing clouds have gone and
autumn has not yet come. Brahmins lauded King Dhārtarāṣṭra with
blessings for triumph as though he were emperor, and he accepted
45 the homage of garlands of folded hands. Suyodhana rode ahead ablaze
with good fortune, together with Karṇa, O Indra among kings, and
the gambler Saubala.* All his brothers were there, from Duḥśāsana
onward, and Bhūriśravas, Somadatta, and great King Bāhlīka. On
chariots of manifold aspects, horses, and the finest elephants the
scions of Kuru followed the lion-like king on his march, and after a
short time, sire, they entered their city.

Janamejaya said:

241.1 What, good man, did the great archers the Dhārtarāṣṭras do while
the great-spirited Pārthas were living in the forest, Karṇa Vaikartana,
mighty Śakuni, Bhīṣma, Droṇa, Kṛpa, and the others? Pray relate it
to me.

Vaiśaṃpāyana said:

When the Pārthas had gone in this fashion and Suyodhana had
been dismissed and, freed by the Pāṇḍavas, had returned to
Hāstinapura, great king, Bhīṣma spoke to Dhārtarāṣṭra as follows:
"Son, I told you before, when you went to the forest of ascetics, that
5 I did not approve of your going, but you did not obey me. So you
were taken forcibly captive by enemies and set free by the Law-wise
Pāṇḍavas. Have you no shame? Before your very eyes, Gāndhāri,**
and that of the army, lord of the people, the son of the *sūta* was
frightened of the Gandharvas and fled from the battle. While you, so
great a king and the son of a king, and your troops were whining,
you witnessed the gallantry of the great-spirited Pāṇḍavas and that of
the evil-minded son of the *sūta* Karṇa, O strong-armed prince. Karṇa
is not worth a fraction of the Pāṇḍava, good king, whether in archery,
bravery, or Law, lover of Law! Peace with the great-spirited Pāṇḍavas
now is best for you, first of the sages of peace, for the furtherance of
the dynasty."
10 Upon these words of Bhīṣma the king the son of Dhṛtarāṣṭra burst
out laughing, sire, and departed brusquely with Saubala. And
noticing him leaving, Karṇa, Duḥśāsana, and the other great bowmen
followed the mighty Dhārtarāṣṭra. When he saw that they had left,
Bhīṣma, grandsire of the Kurus, was humbled with shame, king, and
he went to his own quarters. With Bhīṣma gone, great king, the
princely Dhārtarāṣṭra returned to the same place and counseled with
his councillors: "What will be the best course for us? What remains
to be done? How to act right now?" And he took counsel, Bhārata.

* = Śakuni.
** = son of Gāndhārī-Duryodhana.

Karṇa said:
15 Hear, Duryodhana Kaurava, what I have to say to you; and having
heard it carry it all out, enemy-tamer. Yours is the earth now, hero,
greatest of kings, without a rival. Watch over her like Śakra, great-
minded, with your enemies slain!

Vaiśaṃpāyana said:
The king replied to Karṇa, "Nothing is out of reach for him who
has you, Karṇa, bull among men! You are ready to serve me as my
faithful companion. I have a plan in mind; hear how it goes. When
I watched the grand celebration of the Royal Consecration of the
Pāṇḍavas, I was seized by a desire: fulfil it for me, son of the *sūta*!"
20 At these words Karṇa said to the king, "All the kings of the world
are subject to you now, greatest of kings. Let the brahmins be
summoned and the ritual ingredients be collected according to the
injunction, chief of the Kurus, and the necessities for the sacrifice.
The summoned priests, all experts in the *Vedas*, shall perform the rite
for you according to the letter of the text, enemy-tamer! Let your
grand sacrifice proceed, bull of the Bharatas, with plenty of food and
drink, and full of the richest virtue!"

Upon Karṇa's words, O lord of your people, Dhārtarāṣṭra had his
25 house priest brought in and he said to him, "Offer up the Royal
Consecration, that best of sacrifices, complete with choice stipends,
on my behalf according to the rules and sequences." That bull among
brahmins then replied to the king, "The greatest of sacrifices cannot
be performed in your family as long as Yudhiṣṭhira is alive, great
Kaurava, best of kings. Also Dhṛtarāṣṭra, your long-lived father, is
still alive. Therefore the rite is forbidden to you, great king. But there
is another great session, Sire, equal to the Royal Consecration.
Sacrifice with that one, Indra among kings, and hear what I have to
say. All the rulers of earth that are tributary to you, prince, must
30 bring their tribute and gold, both wrought and unwrought. With
that you must fashion a plowshare, best of kings, and with it you
must plow the ground of your sacrificial enclosure, Bhārata. Let a
sacrifice, very well prepared and with plenty of food, commence there
according to the rules, and unobstructed on every side, the sacrifice
called Vaiṣṇava, which is familiar to good people. No one has offered
with that one except ancient Viṣṇu. This great rite rivals that best of
sacrifices, the Royal Consecration. This would be pleasing to us and
augur your good fortune, Bhārata. May it befall without hindrance,
and may your desire bear fruit!"

Thus addressed by the priests King Dhārtarāṣṭra spoke to Karṇa,
35 Saubala, and his brothers: "All that the brahmins have said pleases
me, no doubt of that. If it is pleasing to you too, tell me so at once."
All conveyed their consent to the king of men. Thereupon the king

gave orders to those engaged in the enterprise, one after the other, and assigned all the artisans to the manufacture of the plow. And everything, O best of kings, was carried out step by step as ordered.

Vaiśaṃpāyana said:

242.1 Thereupon all the artisans and the chief councillors as well as the
sagacious Vidura made known to Dhārtarāṣṭra: "The great ritual is
ready, sire, and the time for it has come, Bhārata. The divine and
very costly golden plow has been fashioned." Upon hearing this, O
lord of your people, that greatest of kings Dhārtarāṣṭra gave orders
to proceed with that king of rites. The sacrifice of plentiful and well-
prepared food commenced, and the son of Gāndhārī was consecrated
5 according to the texts and in the proper sequence. Dhṛtarāṣṭra was
filled with joy, and so were famed Vidura, Bhīṣma, Droṇa, Kṛpa,
Karṇa, and the glorious Gāndhārī. He dispatched swift envoys to
invite the kings, O Indra among kings, as well as the brahmins. They
went out as ordered on fast mounts; and Duḥśāsana said to one
messenger who was starting, "Go quickly to Dvaitavana, and invite
the evil Pāṇḍavas according to the rules, and the brahmins in that
great forest."

He went to the dwelling place of the Pāṇḍavas, and bowed down
before them; and he said, "Great king! Duryodhana, scion of Kuru,
best of kings, is sacrificing with the mass of wealth he has won with
his own bravery. Kings and brahmins are going there from everywhere,
10 and I have been sent, king, by the great-spirited Kaurava, with the
message: 'King Dhārtarāṣṭra, lord of the people, invites you to be
pleased to witness the king's sacrifice, which he holds dear.' " On
hearing the messenger's message King Yudhiṣṭhira, tiger among
kings, replied, "It is indeed fortunate that King Suyodhana sacrifices
with that eminent rite and increases the fame of his forebears. We
too shall come, but not as yet. We have to keep our covenant until
the thirteenth year has passed."

When Bhīma heard the King Dharma say this, he said, "*Then*
indeed Yudhiṣṭhira the King Dharma shall go! When he tumbles him
in the Fire that has been lit with swords and spears at the Session of
15 war after the thirteenth year, when the Pāṇḍava gives vent to the
Oblation of his wrath upon the Dhārtarāṣṭras, *then* we shall have
come! Tell that to Suyodhana!" The other Pāṇḍavas too spoke words
of abuse, and the messenger reported to Dhārtarāṣṭra what had
happened.

Princes arrived from many a countryside, and lordly brahmins
came to the city of Dhārtarāṣṭra. They were welcomed according to
the texts and their class and rank, and rejoiced with great happiness
and affection, lord of men. Dhṛtarāṣṭra, in the midst of all the

Kauravas, was filled with great joy and he said to Vidura, great king,
20 "Take measures at once, Steward, that all the people are happy and
contented, and provided with food on the site of the sacrifice." At his
command sagacious and Law-wise Vidura honored all the classes
according to rank, O enemy-tamer, and happily provided them with
food, eatables and drink, and with fragrant garlands and manifold
garments.

When the hero had completed the final ceremony according to the texts and in proper sequence, he comforted his guests; and that Indra among kings bestowed much largess. Then he dismissed the thousands of kings and brahmins. And after dismissing the kings he entered Hāstinapura with Karṇa and Saubala, surrounded by his brothers.

Vaiśaṃpāyana said:

243.1 Bards praised the unfailing prince, great king, and the people sang
the praises of the archer who was the first of kings. Scattering fried
rice grains and sandalwood powder over him, the people said, "By
good fortune, O king, has your rite been completed without
hindrance." But other garrulous men told the king, "Your rite does
not match the sacrifice of Yudhiṣṭhira! It does not equal a sixteenth
fraction of his rite!" So did some talkative men speak to their king.
5 His friends, however, said, "Your rite excells all others! Yayāti,
Nahuṣa, Māndhātar, and Bharata have all gone to heaven when they
were sanctified by offering up this rite!"

While listening to these auspicious words of his friends, O bull of
the Bharatas, the king joyously entered his city and his house. He
saluted the feet of his father and mother, lord of your people, and the
feet of Bhīṣma, Droṇa, Kṛpa, and the sagacious Vidura. He himself
was saluted by his younger brothers, whom he held dear, and in their
midst sat down in the seat of honor. The son of the *sūta* rose, great
king, and said to him, "It is by my good fortune, best of the Bharatas,
10 that your grand rite has been completed! I shall congratulate you
again, greatest of men, when the Pārthas have been slain in battle
and you have offered up the Royal Consecration." The great king,
glorious Dhārtarāṣṭra, replied, "You speak the truth, hero: when the
evil-spirited Pāṇḍavas have been killed, best of men, and the great
rite of the Royal Consecration has been obtained, then you shall
congratulate me again!" With these words the sagacious Kaurava
embraced Karṇa, O Bhārata, and he thought on that greatest of rites,
the Royal Consecration. Then the good king said to his friends at his
side, "Kauravas, when shall I offer up the great and costly rite of the
15 Royal Consecration after killing all the Pāṇḍavas?" Karṇa then said
to him, "Listen to me, elephant among kings! I shall not wash my
feet until Arjuna is dead!" The warrior sons of Dhṛtarāṣṭra, great

archers, roared in approval when Karṇa vowed to kill Phalguna in battle, and they thought the Pāṇḍavas were already vanquished.

Duryodhana then dismissed those bulls among men, O Indra of
kings, and the illustrious prince entered his house like the Park of
Citraratha; and all the great archers went to their own dwellings. But
the Pāṇḍavas, those great archers, spurred by the message of the
envoy, worried about the matter and found no pleasure anywhere.
Also, runners brought them the news of the vow of the *sūta's* son to
20 kill Vijaya.* When he heard this, the son of Dharma was greatly
troubled, O king, and deeming Karṇa of the impenetrable armor to be
marvelously valiant, and remembering his hardships, he found no
repose. Then the great-spirited man, beset as he was with worries,
decided to leave the Dvaitavana Forest, which teemed with deer and
beasts of prey.

King Dhārtarāṣṭra now began to rule the earth with his heroic brothers and Bhīṣma, Droṇa, and Kṛpa. Duryodhana paired off with Karṇa, the *sūta's* son, who shone in battle, and the king remained all the time set on the others' pleasure. The enemy-burner honored the eminent brahmins with rites of plentiful stipends, and worked to please his brothers, O king, for the hero had decided that the fruits of wealth are to give and enjoy.

3(40) The Deer in the Dream

244 (B. 258; C. 15353–68)

244 (258; 15353). Deer appear to Yudhiṣṭhira in a dream at Dvaitavana and complain that their numbers are dwindling because of the Pāṇḍavas' incessant hunting (1–5). Yudhiṣṭhira is sorry and promises to leave (5–10). The brothers depart for Kāmyaka (10–15).

Janamejaya said:

244.1 What did Pāṇḍu's mighty sons do in that forest after they had set
free Duryodhana?

Vaiśaṃpāyana said:

When Yudhiṣṭhira Kaunteya was sleeping that night in Dvaitavana,
there appeared to him in his dream some deer with tears in their
throats. They folded their hoofs and stood trembling. The great king
said to them, "Say what you have to say! Who are you and what is
your wish?" At these words of the famed Pāṇḍava Kaunteya, the
5 deer, the remnant of many killed, replied to Yudhiṣṭhira, "We are the

* = Arjuna.

deer that survive in Dvaitavana, Bhārata. Change your abode, great
king, lest we all be killed off. All you brothers are heroes and expert
armsmen, and you have reduced the herds of forest game to but few.
We have been left as the seed of the future, O sage, may we prosper
by your grace, Yudhiṣṭhira, Indra among kings!" Upon seeing the
trembling and frightened deer that survived as mere seed, Yudhiṣṭhira
the King Dharma felt very sorry; and the king, who was intent on
the well-being of all creatures, agreed: "You are speaking the truth,
and I shall do as you say."

10 At dawn the good king woke, and filled with compassion he said to
his brothers concerning the deer, "Deer talked to me in a dream last
night, survivors of their herds. 'We have dwindled,' they said, 'hail
to thee. Take pity on us.' They spoke the truth, we should show the
forest game compassion. It has been a year and eight months now
that we have lived off them. There is still the lovely wood of Kāmyaka
with its plentiful game at the edge of the desert by famed Lake
Tṛṇabindu. Let us spend our remaining days there happily."

Thereupon the Law-wise Pāṇḍavas quickly departed, O king, with
the brahmins who lived with them and followed by Indrasena and
15 their other servants. Traveling by established roads with good food
and pure water, they saw the holy retreat of Kāmyaka, peopled by
ascetics. Surrounded by the bull-like brahmins, the Kauraveyas, O
best of the Bharatas, entered it as the virtuous enter heaven.

3(41) The Measure of Rice

245–47 (B. 259–61; C. 15369–570)
245 (259; 15369). The Pāṇḍavas' unhappy condition (1–5). Vyāsa arrives and comforts Yudhiṣṭhira, pointing to the rewards of virtue (5–25). Yudhiṣṭhira asks about the relative importance of giving and asceticism; Vyāsa upholds giving and refers to the story of Mudgala (25–30).
246 (260; 15405). Mudgala subsists on gleaning rice, yet is generous with his hospitality (1–10). The naked hermit Durvāsas comes to test him, demands food, and eats up everything. He comes back and repeats this for six more times; in spite of his hunger Mudgala remains equable (10–20). Durvāsas praises him (20–25). The Envoy of the Gods arrives and invites Mudgala to heaven; the latter insists on a description of celestial bliss (25–35).

247 (261; 15441). Praise of heaven (1–15). Beyond it are the worlds of Indra, Brahmā and the Ṛbhus (15–25). But karman *persists and causes those in heaven to fall (25–35). Mudgala refuses heaven in favor of a state from which there is no more falling away (35–40). He devotes himself to meditation (40–45).*

Vaiśaṃpāyana said:
245.1 While the great-spirited Pāṇḍavas lived in the forest, eleven years
went by full of hardship, O bull of the Bharatas. Though deserving of
happiness the great men endured misery, eating fruit and roots, as
they pondered their opportunity. The strong-armed royal seer
Yudhiṣṭhira, who considered the great suffering of his brothers the
consequence of his own sinful deed, did not sleep well, as though
pierced in his heart with thorns, and reflected on the wickedness of
5 what arose from the dicing game at the time. The Pāṇḍava
remembered the harsh words of the sons of the *sūta* and sighed
bitterly, carrying the strong poison of his wrath. Arjuna, the twins,
the glorious Draupadī, and the powerful Bhīma, strongest of them all,
suffered incomparable grief as they watched Yudhiṣṭhira. Believing
that but a short time remained the bull-like men were so agitated by
vigor and rage that their very appearance seemed to change.
After a while Satyavatī's son Vyāsa, the great yogin, came to visit
the Pāṇḍavas. When Kuntī's son Yudhiṣṭhira saw him arrive, he
arose to receive the great-spirited sage and welcomed him properly.
10 Obedient and self-controlled, the joy of the Pāṇḍavas sat down below
him and gratified him with a prostration. When he saw his grandsons
so gaunt from living on forest fare, the great seer said compassionately
in a tear-choked voice, "Listen, strong-armed Yudhiṣṭhira, best of the
bearers of the Law, one does not find great happiness without having
suffered, son, for men experience happiness and sorrow in turns. No
one finds nothing but sorrow, bull among men. But the man of
wisdom who is endowed with superior vision, knowing that luck
15 rises and sets, does not rejoice, nor does he mourn. Enjoy the good
luck when it befalls, endure the ill luck when it befalls, and bide your
time as the plowman does with his crops. For nothing is higher than
austerity, through austerity one obtains great things: know, Bhārata,
that nothing is out of reach for austerity. Truthfulness, honesty,
patience, willingness to share, self-control, serenity, unenviousness,
nonviolence, purity, and sense control are the means of the virtuous
men, great king. People who revel in lawlessness, who are confused
and given to the ways of beasts, go to a grievous womb and find no
happiness. Whatever deed is done here will fructify in the next world,

therefore one should yoke one's body with austerity and self-restraint.
20 One should give gifts according to ability, joyfully, to the right person
at the right time, without begrudging, but with honor and homage
shown, O king. He who speaks the truth and is honest will find an
untroubled life, and the man without anger and malice obtains
supreme peace. One who is master of himself and given to serenity
does not find adversity all the time, nor does a self-controlled man
feel hurt when he sees fortune go to another. The sharer and the
giver reap joy and happiness, and the nonviolent man attains to
perfect health. If one honors those who deserve it he will attain to
birth in a great house, and when he has mastered his senses he will
25 not be visited by misfortune. For if a man's spirit is amenable to good
deeds, then when the Law of Time befalls him he reappears with a
righteous mind because of that."

Yudhiṣṭhira said:

Lord, which of the two weighs more heavily hereafter, the merits of gifts or austerities, and which is held to be the more difficult?

Vyāsa said:

Nothing on earth is more difficult than giving, for the thirst for
wealth is great, and wealth is acquired with hardship. Brave men
enter into battle to gain wealth, risking their dear life, or enter into
ocean and wilderness. For the sake of wealth some men go farming
and cattle-tending, while others become servants. To give up what
has been so laborious to come by is very difficult. Nothing is harder
30 than to give, therefore I prize giving. But the important feature is that
wealth that has been honestly acquired should be bestowed on the
good, on the right person, and at the right time and place. But if one
practices giving with wealth that has not been acquired honestly, it
does not save the giver from great danger. A gift, however small, that
is given to the right person at the right time in a pure spirit,
Yudhiṣṭhira, is known to yield endless fruit hereafter. On this they
cite the ancient story of how Mudgala reaped great reward by
relinquishing a measure of rice.

Yudhiṣṭhira said:

246.1 Why did the great-spirited man give up a measure of rice? To whom did he give it, blessed lord, and in what fashion? Tell me. For that law-abiding man's birth has borne fruit, I think, whose deeds satisfy the Lord whose Law is manifest.

Vyāsa said:

King, there was once a law-minded man in Kurukṣetra, an observer of strict vows, truthful and without malice, who subsisted on gleaning rice. While living like a pigeon he still received guests and performed rites. So the great ascetic observed the sacrificial session called Iṣṭikṛta. The hermit used to eat for a fortnight with wife and sons, and the next fortnight he would glean a measure of rice in the fashion of pigeons. He would perform the Full and New Moon Sacrifices unstintingly, and feed his body on the leftovers of the deities and guests. Indra himself, the lord of the three worlds, accepted his share with the other Gods every full and new moon, great king. Living as a hermit he gave with a happy heart food to his guests on those days. The leftovers of the food the great-spirited man liberally gave that day for his measure of rice would multiply when a guest visited. Hundreds of wise brahmins ate the food, but the food kept multiplying because of the purity of the hermit's generosity.

Now the air-clad Durvāsas heard about that most Law-like Mudgala of the strict vows, king, and the hermit went to him, wearing the unruly aspect of a madman, Pāṇḍava, his head shaven bald, and flinging about abuse. When the hermit arrived he said to the brahmin, "Remark that I have arrived in want of food, good hermit." "Be welcome!" replied Mudgala to the hermit. He provided water to wash the feet and rinse the mouth and being an avowed host and firm in his vows gave the excellent food he had earned with mortifications to his hungry guest, the madman whom he trusted completely.

The hungry madman ate up all the food, which was tasty, and Mudgala kept giving him more. When he had eaten all the food, he smeared his body with the leftovers and went the way he had come. The next time the sage observed the Moon Day, Durvāsas came back and ate up all the food of the gleaner. The hermit went without food and had to go gleaning again, but his hunger could not change Mudgala's temper. No anger, or envy, or contempt, or puzzlement invaded the gleaning brahmin or his sons and wife.

In the same way, six times over, that determined hermit Durvāsas visited the habitual gleaner; and the hermit saw no change whatsoever in the other's heart. What he saw in the pure-hearted man was his pure and unstained mind. Thereupon the hermit said, pleased, to this Mudgala, "There is no host on earth the like of you, without any begrudging. Hunger drives off the very name of Law and takes away self-possession, the tongue, which obeys the senses, chases after the juices. Life rises from food, the volatile heart is hard to restrain: this concentration of mind and senses is definitely a self-mortification. Even a pure spirit finds it difficult to give up what has been acquired by hard labor, yet you, good man, have accomplished it all precisely. We are pleased, indeed favored, to have met you. Mastery of the senses, fortitude, sharing, self-control, serenity, compassion, truthfulness, and the Law are all vested in you. Your deeds have won you the worlds, you have gone the ultimate way.

Aho! the celestials proclaim your superb giving. Grand observer of
thy vow, thou shall go to heaven in thy body!"
30 The hermit Durvāsas was still speaking when the Envoy of the
Gods approached Mudgala on a celestial chariot, which was harnessed
with swans and cranes and sported a circlet of tiny bells; the chariot
could go where it wished and it was colorful and fragrant with divine
perfumes. He said to the brahmin seer, "Mount this chariot that you
have earned with your deeds, for you have attained to the ultimate
course, hermit." The seer replied to the Envoy of the Gods, "I want the
virtues described by you of those who dwell in heaven: what are the
virtues like of those who live there? What is their austerity, what
their resolve? What is the celestials' happiness in heaven, what are
35 their wants, good Envoy of the Gods? Strict men used to family ways
say that the friendship of the strict is that of the seven steps. I now
presuppose such friendship on your part, and I query you, ubiquitous
lord. Do not hesitate to tell me what is true and proper, and when I
have heard you, I shall do as you say."

The Envoy of the Gods said:

247.1 Great seer, is your mind not made up yet, do you still deliberate
about the infinite pleasure of the heaven you have attained and
which is highly esteemed? Are you out of your wits? That world up
there is called "heaven." It is way up, with fine roads, and always
traveled with divine conveyances, hermit. No humans without
mortifications, no offerers of small sacrifices, no liars or deniers go
there, Mudgala. The Law-minded, the masters of self, the serene and
5 controlled and unenvious, those accustomed to the Law of giving, and
champions with the scars showing—they go there, having achieved
the best in acts of serenity and self-control, to those worlds of the
meritorious that are treasured by strict men, O brahmin. The Gods,
Sādhyas, the All-Gods, the Maruts, and the great seers, the Yāma
deities and the Dhāman deities, O scion of Mudgala, the Gandharvas
and the Apsarās dwell there. Multitudinous, one after the other, are
the luminous, wish-fulfilling, splendiferous, and beautiful worlds of
these hosts of Gods. It is there that the golden Meru sits, king of the
mountains, thirty-three leagues high, where the gardens of the Gods
are situated, Mudgala! The holy park of Nandana and the other ones
are the pleasure grounds of the blessed of deeds! There is no hunger
10 or thirst, no fatigue, no concern about cold or heat, no atrocity or
unholiness. No diseases rage there. All the smells are attractive, no
touch is repugnant. Sounds come there from everywhere, hermit,
appealing to the ear and the heart. There is no sorrow, no old age,
no effort or complaint. Such, hermit, is the world that is won by the
fruits of a man's own deeds, and by virtue of their own good deeds

men come to share in it. The bodies of those who partake of it are
luminous; they are born from one's deeds, Maudgalya, not from a
father and mother. There is no sweat or foul smell, neither feces nor
15 urine, and not a speck of dust spoils their garments, hermit. Their
garlands, of heavenly fragrance and beautiful, never fade, and the
blessed inhabitants are driven about in celestial chariots, brahmin.
And they are without jealousy, sorrow, and fatigue, devoid of
confusion and envy, they who have won heaven and live there
happily.

But beyond these blissful worlds, bull among hermits, far, far above
them, are the worlds of Indra endowed with divine virtues; and
beyond those the holy and luminous worlds of Brahmā, where the
seers go, brahmin, who have been made pure by all their pious acts.
There are the Ṛbhus, who are the Gods of the Gods, their worlds are
20 the highest and the Gods worship them. They are self-luminous and
radiant worlds, supreme cows of plenty. They suffer no slights from
women, no one is envious of overlordship, they do not practice
oblations, they do not even feed on Elixir. Their bodies are divine, but
not corporeal. They have no desire for happiness, those sempiternal
Gods of the Gods; and they do not revolve with the revolutions of the
Eons. Whence would there be old age and death for them, whence
joy, pleasure, and happiness? Neither happiness nor suffering exists
there, so whence love and hatred, hermit? That is the highest course,
Maudgalya, which even the Gods covet, but this highest attainment
is hard to attain, and it is inaccessible to those who still have desires.

25 There are thirty-three worlds. The wise reach the remaining worlds
by the greatest restraints, or by ritual gifts. And this blissful dawn,
created by your gifts, you have now attained. You have attained it
with your deeds—enjoy it with your radiance kindled with austerities.

Such is the bliss of heaven, brahmin, and such are those worlds. I
have described to you the virtues of heaven, now also hear of its
faults. The fruit of acts done, which is enjoyed in heaven, cannot be
undone and must be consumed, down to the last of its roots. This I
deem a fault, as also the fall at the end of it, the fall of those whose
30 minds had been permeated with bliss, Mudgala. The discontent and
resentment after having seen the most brilliant beauties, as are felt
by those who dwell in a lower region, are hard to endure. The
confusion of consciousness, the harassment by passion, the fear of the
one about to fall when his garlands begin to fade are awful faults,
Maudgalya; they are present as far as the abode of Brahmā—though
not in the eyes of men of good deeds who count their blessings by the
myriad. Another great feature of those who have fallen from heaven
is that in the aftermath of their good deeds they are born among men.
There one is born very high and partakes of happiness. But when one

35 does not gain insight there, he goes to a lower rank. The acts that
have been done in this world are enjoyed hereafter. This is the world
of the act, brahmin, the other is held to be the world of the fruit. So
I have explained everything you have asked me, Mudgala. By your
favor let us go now our happy way without delay!

Vyāsa said:

When Maudgalya had heard him out, he reflected in his mind; and
having reflected the eminent hermit spoke to the Envoy of the Gods:
"Envoy of the Gods, I salute you. Now go, friend, as you wish. I set
no store by heaven or bliss, if they are so faulty. That fall is a great
tribulation, the resentment most horrifying. Those who have shared in
heaven again fall back down here, therefore I do not covet heaven.
40 I shall search only for that infinite place where they do not grieve, do
not suffer, do not chance to fall once they have gone there."

Having thus spoken the hermit dismissed the Envoy of the Gods.
He gave up his life of gleaning and took to complete serenity. He
became indifferent to praise and blame; a piece of clay, a rock, and
gold were all the same to him; and he was forever immersed in
meditation with the pure yoke of insight. Through the yoke of
meditation he gained strength, and having acquired an incomparable
fortune he attained to the eternal and supreme perfection that is
marked by Extinction.

Therefore, son of Kuntī, you too must not harbor grief. You have
fallen from your opulent kingship, and you shall regain it, through
45 austerity. Suffering follows happiness, happiness follows suffering,
they revolve in circles around man, like spokes around an axle. A
man of boundless prowess, you shall regain your paternal and
ancestral kingdom when the thirteenth year is full. The fear in your
mind must go.

Vaiśaṃpāyana said:

Having thus spoken to the joy of the Pāṇḍavas the venerable and
wise Vyāsa went back to his hermitage for austerities.

3(42) The Abduction of Draupadī

248–83 (B. 264–99; C. 15571–6917)
248 (264; 15571). The Pāṇḍavas go hunting, leaving Draupadī with Dhaumya at a hermitage (1–5). Jayadratha of Sindhu passes by with his retinue and is stunned by Draupadī's beauty. He asks his companion Koṭikāśya to inquire (5–15).

249 (265; 15589). Koṭikāśya addresses Draupadī in polished language, introducing Jayadratha and his companions (1–10).
250 (266; 15602). Reluctantly Draupadī identifies herself and explains that her husbands are out hunting; Jayadratha should await their return (1–5).
251 (267; 15611). Jayadratha enters the hermitage and Draupadī receives him (1–10). He proposes she come with him (10–20).
252 (268; 15639). She refuses indignantly (1–5). Jayadratha insists and Draupadī warns of reprisals; he pulls her up into his chariot (5–20). Dhaumya protests and follows the party (25).
253 (269; 15668). Yudhiṣṭhira perceives portents and the Pāṇḍavas return; they meet Draupadī's distraught maid (1–5). Questioned by Indrasena she entreats the Pāṇḍavas to rescue Draupadī (5–20). They follow the trail (20–25).
254 (270; 15695). Draupadī identifies the Pāṇḍavas to Jayadratha (1–20).
255 (271; 15716). The Pāṇḍavas attack (1–20) and drive Jayadratha to flight (20–35). Yudhiṣṭhira forgives him (40). At Draupadī's protests Bhīma and Arjuna go looking for him (40–45). They dismount him and he flees on foot (45–55).
256 (272; 15777). Bhīma catches and thrashes him but is stopped by Arjuna (1–5). Bhīma shaves Jayadratha's head and shows him to Yudhiṣṭhira; Draupadī tells Bhīma to let him go (5–15). Yudhiṣṭhira admonishes and dismisses him (15–20). Jayadratha placates Śiva, who gives him a boon: he will stay all the Pāṇḍavas in battle, except Arjuna (20–30).
257–75. Rāma.
276 (292; 16603). Mārkaṇḍeya points out that Yudhiṣṭhira, unlike Rāma, has powerful brothers and admonishes him not to grieve (1–10).
277–83. Sāvitrī.

Vaiśaṃpāyana said:

248.1 The great warriors, the first of the Bharatas, amused themselves like Immortals in Kāmyaka, playing in the game-rich forest. They gazed upon numerous wooded spots all around, and on flowering forest tracts that showed the loveliness the season imparted. And the

Pāṇḍavas roamed hunting through the vast wilderness, the peers of
Indra, and enjoyed themselves for the time being.
Then all of them at the same time went out hunting in all four
directions, the tiger-like enemy-burners, to have food to feed the
5 brahmins, leaving Draupadī behind in a hermitage of Tṛṇabindu, with
the consent of that great seer of blazing austerities and of their priest
Dhaumya. Meanwhile the famed king of the Sindhus, the son of
Vṛddhakṣatra, was proceeding to the land of the Śālvas, being in a
marrying mood. Surrounded by a large retinue as befitting a king
and accompanied by many princes, he arrived at Kāmyaka. There he
saw the glorious Draupadī, beloved wife of the Pāṇḍavas, standing at
the hermitage gate in the empty forest, radiating superb beauty with
her person, and illuminating the wooded spot as lightning a dark
cloud. They all stared at the blameless woman who had folded her
10 hands: "Is she an Apsarā, or the daughter of a God, or an illusion
created by the Gods?"
The king of the Sindhus Jayadratha Vārddhakṣatri was astounded
and happy of heart at the sight of her flawless limbs. Love-smitten, he
said to Prince Koṭikāśya, "Whose is this woman of flawless limbs, if
she is human at all? There is no point for me to marry now that I
have seen this superbly beautiful lady! It is she I shall take and return
to my kingdom! Go and find out, my friend, whose she is, who she is,
and from where. Why has this woman of the lovely brow come to the
15 thorny forest? Will this gem of the world with the comely curves, the
perfect teeth, the long eyes, the slender waist, share my love today?
Shall my desires be fulfilled by my obtaining this choicest of women?
Go and find out who her protector is, Koṭika!"
Hearing this, Koṭika, who was wearing earrings, jumped from the
chariot and approached her as a jackal approaches a tigress; and he
asked,

Koṭikāśya said:

249.1 Who are you that bend a *kadamba* branch,
Alone in the hermitage, lighting it up,
Ablaze like the flame of a fire in the night,
With your lovely brow, that is fanned by the wind?

An exquisite loveliness adorns you—
How is it you have no fear in the woods?
A Goddess, a Yakṣī, a Dānavī,
An Apsarā, or a Daitya nymph?

Or are you a beautiful Serpent maiden,
Or a night-stalking sprite who roams the woods?

Perchance the wife of King Varuṇa,
Or of Yama or Soma or the Lord of Riches?

Have you come from the mansion of Dhātar, Vidhātar,
Lord Savitar, or from the palace of Śakra?
For you do not question us who we might be—
Nor do we know who is your protector.

For we, to heighten your pride in yourself,
Good woman, ask for your father and source.
Name us your relations, husband, and house,
And tell us in truth your business here.

I myself am the son of the king Suratha,
And people know me as Koṭikāśya;
And yonder upon his golden chariot,
Standing like fire that is poured on an altar,
Is the king of Trigarta with lotus-leaf eyes,
A hero whose name is Kṣemaṃkara.

Behind him, holding that giant bow,
Is the excellent son of the king of Kuṇinda,
Wide-shouldered, who stands there staring at you
In amazement—he's always at home in the mountains.

And there, standing close by that lotus pond,
That handsome youth with the swarthy complexion,
Is the son of Subala, king of Ikṣvāku,
A slayer of foes he, graceful woman.

And he in whose train march, waving their flags,
The twelve Sauvīraka princes all,
On chariots yoked with blood-red horses,
Like fires that are blazing at sacrifice sites—

Aṅgāraka, Kuñjara, Guptaka,
Śatruṃjaya, Saṃjaya, Supravṛddha,
Prabhaṃkara, Ravi, and Bhramara,
Kuhara, Pratāpa, and Śūra by name—

Who is followed by six thousand chariot warriors
And elephants, horses, and soldiers on foot:
If you've heard the name of Jayadratha,
King of Suvīra, this is he, lucky woman!

His brothers, all of undaunted mettle,
Balāhaka, Anīkavidāraṇa,
And the other heroic Suvīra youths
Are behind the king in all their strength.

The king is ajourneying with these companions,
As Indra amidst his Marut guards.
Now you of the lovely looks pray inform us
Whose wife you are and of whom the daughter.

Vaiśaṃpāyana said:

250.1 Spoke the daughter of King Drupada
To the question of the chief of the Śibis,
With a languid glance, letting go of the branch,
And gathering in her *kuśa* grass skirt,

"I know in my heart, O son of a king,
That a woman like me should not reply.
But no one else is here to respond
To your query, be it a man or a woman.

"I am here alone now and therefore I shall
Myself reply, friend, so listen well.
For how shall I, alone in the forest,
Converse with you, if I love my Law?

"I know that you are Suratha's son,
Whom people know as Koṭikāśya:
Therefore I shall likewise speak to you
Of my relations, O man from Śibi.

5 "The child am I of King Drupada,
Whom, Śaibya, the people know as Kṛṣṇā;
I have chosen five men to be my husbands,
Of whom you have heard: they're from Khāṇḍavaprastha.

"Yudhiṣṭhira, Bhīma, and Arjuna,
And the two heroic sons of Mādrī;
The Pārthas have settled me here while they
Spread out to the four directions to hunt.

"The king went north, Bhīmasena south,
Eastward went Jaya,* the twins to the west:
Methinks the time is now at hand
For those great warriors here to return.

"Proceed where you wish after they have paid homage:
Unyoke your mounts and descend for the nonce.
The great-spirited son of Dharma loves guests
And is sure to be pleased when he finds you here."

* = Arjuna.

This much did Drupada's daughter speak
With her moon-like face and trusting to Śaibya,
And she entered the holy cottage of leaves
As she thought on her Law in receiving these guests.

Vaiśaṃpāyana said:

251.1 Thereupon, while all the kings were seated, Bhārata, the king of Suvīra, having listened to Koṭikāśya's report, spoke to the Śaibya: "How could you come back when my heart delights in this finest of women who made her reply? Now that I have seen her, strong-armed friend, all other women look like monkeys to me, I tell you the truth. With her mere glance at me she stole my mind completely. Now tell me, Śaibya, whether that beautiful woman is a human."

Koṭikāśya said:

5 She is the famous Princess Kṛṣṇā Draupadī, the highly held queen of the five sons of Pāṇḍu. She is very beloved and greatly esteemed by all five Pārthas. Now that you have encountered her, king of Suvīra, go happily back to the land of Suvīra!

Vaiśaṃpāyana said:

He replied, "Let us visit Draupadī!" quoth the lord of Suvīra and Sindhu, wicked Jayadratha. He entered the empty hermitage, like a wolf in a den of lions, in a party of seven; and he said to Draupadī, "I salute you, curvaceous woman! Are your husbands in good health, and are they whom you wish well in good health?"

Draupadī said:

10 King Yudhiṣṭhira Kauravya, son of Kuntī, is keeping well, and so am I, his brothers, and the others you ask about. Accept this water to wash your feet and this seat, son of a king. Let me give you a breakfast of fifty deer! Kuntī's son Yudhiṣṭhira himself will give you black antelope, spotted antelope, venison, fawn, *śarabha*, rabbit, white-footed antelope, *ruru*, *śambara*, gayal, many deer, boar, buffalo, and other kinds of game.

Jayadratha said:

You have already done me fully all the honors of a breakfast.
Come, mount my chariot and find complete happiness. Now don't be
so amenable to the wretched forest-haunting Pārthas: their fortunes
are down, and they have lost their kingdom and their wits. No
intelligent woman enjoys a husband whose luck is down. She should
15 ride when he is riding high, not stay when his fortune is gone. They
have lost their wealth, they have been driven from their kingdom,
for all eternity. Be there an end of your waiting on trouble, just out of
love for Pāṇḍu's sons! Be my wife, woman of the beautiful hips,
desert them, and enjoy yourself! With me you get all the land of
Sindhu and Suvīra!

Vaiśaṃpāyana said:

At these heart-shattering words of the king of Sindhu, Kṛṣṇā strode
20 away, knitting her brow. Contemptuously the slender-waisted Kṛṣṇā
ignored his words and said, "Don't speak like that!" to the Saindhava,
and "Shame on you!" Expecting her husbands to return presently,
the blameless lady spun out words in order to distract the other.

Vaiśaṃpāyana said:

252.1 With her lovely face now crimsoned with anger,
Her eyes blood-red, her brows raised and knit,
She snorted at the king of Suvīra,
And Draupadī's daughter said to him,

"You insult famed warriors like venomous snakes,
You fool, why do you not feel ashamed?
The likes of great Indra, intent on their tasks,
Who have stood in battle with Yakṣas and demons!

"People never speak anything ill of a hermit,
Whose wisdom is full, who deserves all praise,
Whether a householder or forest dweller—
The swinish, Suvīra, alone speak like this!

"I myself think none here in this grand
Assemblage of barons would lift a finger
And seize your hand to prevent you from falling
Into this abyss that has opened before you.

5 "You are like a man with a stick who tries
To chase off from his herd in the foothills a rutting
Mountainous Himālayan elephant,
If you hope to vanquish and kill King Dharma.

"Having kicked in your folly a sleeping lion
And plucked the eyelashes from the face
Of the powerful beast, you will hasten to flee
When you see my furious Bhīmasena!

"Like a man who with his foot kicks a lion,
Ferocious, powerful, fully grown,
Turned yellow, and sleeping in mountain caverns,
You wish to confine our irate Jiṣṇu!*

"Like a madman who stomps with his feet on the tails
Of two black, fork-tongued, venomous cobras,

* = Arjuna.

You are if you'll battle with both the gallant
Youngest of all the Pāṇḍava brothers.

"As the bamboo, reed, and banana trees
Give fruit then to die but not to prosper,
As a crab bears to die, so you too wish to take
Me, a woman, under their full protection!"

Jayadratha said:

10 I know fully well and am quite aware
What manner of men those princes are;
But, Kṛṣṇā, this is insufficient threat
For you to be able to frighten us off.

We too have all been born, my Kṛṣṇā,
In the seventeen high dynasties;
We are surely not lacking in those six virtues
We think the Pāṇḍus lack, Draupadī.

Now quickly mount chariot or elephant,
We cannot be stopped by words alone!
Or rather speak piteously and hope
For the possible grace of the king of Suvīra!

Draupadī said:

I am strong, but now the king of Suvīra
Believes I'm a weakling, he thinks that I
Who am sure of myself would panic and plead
In piteous tones to the king of Suvīra!

For both the Kṛṣṇas* will follow my trail,
The war companions, riding one chariot:
Not Indra would manage to carry me off,
Then how would a mere and miserable mortal?

15 When the diademed** slayer of enemy heroes,
Who shatters the hearts of his foes on his chariot,
On my account invades your army,
He'll rage like a summer fire in deadwood!

Janārdana's*** band of Vṛṣṇi heroes,
And all the great Kekaya archers as well,
And all the princes will gleefully
Assemble and follow hot on my trail.

* = Kṛṣṇa and Arjuna.
** = Arjuna.
*** = Kṛṣṇa.

The arrows released with a thunderous roar
From the string of Gāṇḍīva, shrieking with speed,
Which have been dispatched by Dhanaṃjaya's hand,
Will fearfully whine with a terrible wail.

When Gāṇḍīva's wielder again and again
Spits forth from his bow mighty masses of arrows
That speed through the skies like flocks of birds,
With the noise of conches and snapping wrist guards,
And fixes his arrows right there on your chest,
What thoughts may then well be crossing your mind?

Seeing Bhīma attack with his club in his fist
And Mādrī's sons rage every way,
Spitting out the virulent venom of fury,
You will come to rue it a very long time!

20 And if it be true that I've nohow and never
Done wrong in my thoughts to my honorable husbands,
By that truth I shall watch you be taken captive
And dragged about by the sons of Pṛthā.*

However harshly molested by you
I cannot be brought to a state of terror,
For I shall meet the heroic Kurus
And again return to the Kāmyaka Forest!"

Vaiśaṃpāyana said:

With wide open eyes she watched them now
Attempting to seize her, upbraiding them;
And in fear, she cried out, "Don't touch, don't touch me!"
And she screamed for the help of Dhaumya the priest.

Jayadratha held her by her skirt,
But with all her strength she pushed him away;
And, his body repulsed by her, that miscreant
Fell down like a tree whose roots have been cut.

But, once more seized with great vehemence,
The princess began to pant heavily.
She was dragged along up on to the chariot
And Kṛṣṇā saluted Dhaumya's feet.

Dhaumya said:

25 You cannot abduct her without having vanquished the warriors! Look to the ancient Law of the baronage, Jayadratha! By committing

* = Kuntī.

this meanness you shall reap evil undoubtedly, when you encounter the Pāṇḍava heroes led by the King Dharma!

Vaiśaṃpāyana said:

And Dhaumya followed the glorious princess when she was being carried off, and walked with the troops of foot soldiers.

Vaiśaṃpāyana said:

253.1 Having wandered all over the four directions
And laid low deer, boar, and buffalo,
The Pārthas, greatest of archers on earth,
Who had roamed by themselves now came together,

To the mighty forest resounding with birds,
That teemed with game and birds of prey;
And Yudhiṣṭhira, hearing the cries that the deer
Sounded forth, thereupon addressed his brothers.

"The birds and the animals flee to the side
That is lit by the sun, and they make harsh noises,
Revealing they are in terrible anguish—
Or the loud invasion by enemies.

"Let's return at once and be done with the deer,
For my mind is consumed by a blazing fire;
In my body the lord of my life is afire
And covers my spirit with its rage.

5 "Like a lake whose snakes have been caught by Suparṇa,*
Like a realm without king and bereft of his fortune,
So Kāmyaka now appears to me,
Or a jar of liquor drunk up by drunkards."

They returned thereupon to that hermitage,
The heroes, riding on chariots high
And yoked with the nimblest of Saindhava steeds,
Which sped with the speed of the wind or a flood.

As they were returning a jackal appeared
On their left, and it sounded a piercing howl.
The king perceiving it uttered a cry
And spoke to Bhīma and Dhanaṃjaya.

"The way this low-born animal speaks,
This jackal appearing here on our left,
It is fully clear that the wicked Kurus
Have contemptuously mounted a brutal attack!"

* = Garuḍa.

After the chase in the wilderness vast
They entered that other wood, and they saw
A young woman who was the foster-sister
And serving maid of their wife. She was weeping.

10 And Indrasena hurried to her
And jumped from the chariot, ran to her,
And spoke this word, O Indra of kings,
To the foster-sister, himself in anguish.

"Why are you crying prostrate on the ground?
Why is your face so pale and dry?
Have not perchance cruel evildoers
Molested the Princess Draupadī
Of the flawless limbs and the wide-open eyes,
Whose body matches the bulls of the Kurus?

"Even if the queen has entered the earth,
Ascended to heaven or plunged in the sea,
The sons of Pṛthā will follow her trail,
For so sorely tortured is the King Dharma.

"For who in his folly would wish to abduct
The woman as dear as their lives to such
Enemy-crushers enduring their troubles
Unvanquished, their priceless ornament?
He knows not she has protectors now?
She's the walking heart of the Pāṇḍavas!

"Whose body today will their sharpened arrows
Horribly pierce and pin to the ground?
Don't be sorry about her, you're timid,
Know that Kṛṣṇā shall be back today,
For the Pārthas will kill all those who hate them,
And then gather in their Yājñasenī!"

15 And wiping her comely face she said,
To chariot driver Indrasena,
"Jayadratha routed the place and abducted,
Disregarding Indra's peers, their Kṛṣṇā.

"Their trails remain and are still quite fresh;
Though broken, the branches have not yet withered:
Turn round then, pursue them with all due speed,
For the princess could not be far gone.

"Now gird yourselves, all you equals of Indra
With your bulky and handsome coats of mail,

Take hold of your very precious bows
And arrows, and take to the road at once,

"Before she, maddened by threats and sticks
And her wits out of joint, with hot flushed face,
Starts burning an unworthy's body to death,
Like a butter-filled offering spoon in hot ashes.

"Before an oblation is poured in a chaff fire,
Or the wreath is cast on the burning field,
And before the altar-bound *soma* is licked
By the dog as the priest folk stand by flustered,
Before, having gone to hunt in the forest,
The jackal invades the lotus pond!

20 "Lest your loved one's face, of fine nose and eyes,
That was tranquil before and clear as moonlight
And blessed, is touched by some useless man,
As a dog might eat up the offering cake,
You must follow those tracks and do so at once
Lest time too quickly pass you by!"

Yudhiṣṭhira said:
My dear, be quiet and hold your tongue
Lest you speak too rudely while we are here:
Whether kings or princes, they'll be deceived
If they pridefully trust in the strength of their arms.

Vaiśaṃpāyana said:
Having said this much they quickly departed,
And they followed hard on those selfsame tracks,
Again and again as predators panting,
And twanging the strings on their powerful bows.

But then they discerned the dust of the troop,
Which was cast up by the hoofs of its steeds,
And Dhaumya who walked in the midst of the footmen
And shouted at Bhīma, "Attack! Attack!"

Feeling wretched at heart they quieted Dhaumya,
"Sir, be you at ease," said the sons of the king,
And like vultures drawn by the sight of the raw meat,
They pounced with a will on that army of his.

25 In prowess the equals of mighty Indra,
Enraged by the threat imposed on Kṛṣṇā,
Their fury flared forth as they saw Jayadratha
And their loved Yājñasenī upon his chariot.

They bellowed their cry at the king of Sindhu,
The Wolf-Belly bellowed, Dhanaṃjaya,
The twins, and the king, great archers all;
And the enemies then all lost their senses.

Vaiśaṃpāyana said:
254.1 An ugly noise arose in the forest from the intolerant barons on seeing Bhīmasena and Arjuna.

Having spied the crests of the flags of the bulls
Among Kurus, the king, who was innately wicked,
Jayadratha, spoke to Yājñasenī
Who was held on the chariot, himself crestfallen,

"They're coming now, five huge warriors,
I am sure they must be your husbands, Kṛṣṇā.
You know them, my fair one, enlighten us
Who is which of the Pāṇḍavas chariot-borne?

Draupadī said:
Would it help you to know those archers, fool,
After doing your ugly and deadly deed?
For here have my champion husbands come
And none of you will be spared in this war!

5 But, let all be told to the man who must die!
I must, for you ask me, and so is the Law.
I feel no pain, no fear, from you,
When I see King Dharma and his younger brothers.

At the crest of whose flag there sound his two drums,
The sweet and well-used Upananda and Nanda,
Him follow the folks that have tasks at all times,
He who knows to decide on the meaning of Law.

That one who is pure and fair like gold,
With aquiline nose, lean, wide of eyes,
They call him the foremost chief of Kurus,
Yudhiṣṭhira, Dharma's son, and my husband!

To even a foe who had come for shelter
He'd give his life, my law-walking hero.
Fool, run to him fast, run for your own good,
For your own, down your weapons and fold your hands!

Do you see now that other one on his chariot,
Strong-armed, like a full-grown *śāla* tree?

He has clasped his lips, his brow is furrowed,
He's a husband of mine, named Wolf-Belly.

10 Powerful well-trained thoroughbreds
That have great strength carry him, my hero!
The feats he has done are more than human
And the cry of him on this earth is: He's Bhīma!

No quarter from him will the guilty receive,
Nor will his enmity be forgotten;
Having put an end to the feud he will come
To serenity afterward but not too quickly.

Gentle, generous, famous, and grave,
In control of his senses, paying heed to the old,
Yudhiṣṭhira's brother as well as his pupil—
Such is my husband Dhanaṃjaya.

Neither lust nor fear nor greed would cause him
To abandon the Law, or act cruelly;
In splendor the match of the Fire God, he churns
His enemies fiercely, this son of Kuntī.

The sage who knows of all the Laws
The import, who takes the fear from the fearful,
Whose body they say is the fairest on earth,
Him the Pāṇḍavas all shall guard;

15 That hero is Nakula, my husband,
More dear than my life and true to his vows,
And the other, a swordsman of swift cunning hand,
Is the mighty, sagacious Sahadeva.

His handiwork, fool, you will witness today,
As of Indra himself in the war of the Daityas,
A champion fighter both shrewd and wise,
Who pleases the regal son of God Dharma.

In splendor the peer of the moon and the fire,
The youngest and dearest of Pāṇḍavas,
Whose mind to match not a man is found,
Decisive speaker among the strict,

An always intransigent hero is he,
My man Sahadeva, sagacious, wise;
He'd sooner abandon and burn his body
Than ever do aught that is outside the Law,
High-minded and firm in the Law of the barons,
A hero held dearer than life by Kuntī.

Like a pearl-filled ship at the edge of the ocean
That founders and breaks on the spine of a whale,
You shall see your army destroyed by the Pāṇḍus
With all its warriors extirpated!

20 Thus I have named you the sons of Pāṇḍu
Whom you in your folly have shown contempt;
If you escape them with unscathed body
You'll have been reborn while still being alive!

Vaiśaṃpāyana said:
The Pāṇḍavas five like unto five Indras,
Ignoring the trembling and pleading footfolk,
In fury attacked from all sides, and they cast
A darkness of reeds on the chariot army.

255.1 *Vaiśaṃpāyana said:*

"Stand firm! Strike! Surround them!" urged the Saindhava king on the princes. Thereupon the ugliest clamor arose from the embattled armies when they saw Bhīma, Arjuna, and the twins with Yudhiṣṭhira. Śibi, Sindhu, and Trigarta lost heart when they saw those tigers among men, proud of their strength like tigers. Bhīma seized his club, its bulge sparkling with gold, the loop wrought of solid iron, and he
5 stormed at the Saindhava who now was summoned by time. Covering a gap in the other's defenses, Koṭikāśya attacked and warded off the Wolf-Belly with a large string of chariots. Despite the many spears, javelins, and iron arrows propelled by heroes' arms that rained upon him, Bhīma did not stagger, but clubbed, in the vanguard of the Saindhava's army, an elephant with its mahout and fourteen footmen. In the vanguard the Pārtha slew five hundred champions from the mountains, great warriors all, as he held out for Sauvīra.* The king himself** killed in a twinkling of the eye a hundred Suvīra chieftains
10 who attacked him on the battlefield. Nakula was seen leaping from his chariot, brandishing his sword, and he scattered like seeds the heads of the men who guarded the elephants' legs. Sahadeva engaged the elephant warriors on his chariot and toppled them with iron spikes like peacocks from trees.

Thereupon Trigarta alighted from his large chariot with his bow and, being dextrous with his club, bludgeoned the king's mounts. The King Dharma, joy of Kuntī, shot the nearby foot fighter in the chest with a crescent-topped arrow. His heart rent asunder, spitting blood from his mouth, the hero fell before the Pārtha like a tree whose roots
15 have been cut. Seconded by Indrasena the King Dharma leaped from

* = Jayadratha.
** = Yudhiṣṭhira.

his chariot, since his own horses had been killed, and got on to
Sahadeva's big chariot. Meanwhile Kṣemaṃkara and Mahāmukha
targeted on Nakula and pelted him from two sides with showers of
sharp arrows; but while they were raining arrows on him like two
clouds in the rainy season, the son of Mādrī killed them with a large
arrow each. The Trigarta prince Suratha took his stand on the pole of
his chariot and had Nakula's chariot shattered by an elephant, being
cunning in elephant fighting. But fearlessly Nakula came down from
his chariot, wielding sword and shield, and whirling his sword took
20 his stand, immovable like a mountain. Suratha then sent his elephant
to kill Nakula, a furious beast that raised up its trunk, but Nakula
closed in on the animal and hacked off its trunk and tusks at the root.
With a loud wail the elephant, which wore rings on its feet, fell with
lowered head to the ground, shattering its mahouts. Having
accomplished his great feat, Mādrī's champion son got to Bhīmasena's
chariot where the warrior found shelter.

Bhīma now, locked in combat with the attacking Prince Koṭikāśya,
shaved off with a razor-sharp blade the head of the other's charioteer,
25 who was prodding the horses. The prince did not realize that his
driver had been killed by strong-armed Bhīma, and his driverless
horses ran wild all over the battlefield. Thereupon Bhīma Pāṇḍava,
strongest of strikers, killed off the steedless, driverless prince with a
handled javelin. Dhanaṃjaya cut off with honed bear arrows the bows
and heads of all twelve Suvira princes. The superior warrior slew
Śibis, Ikṣvāku chiefs, Trigartas, and Saindhavas in the battle as soon
as they came within range of his arrows. Many were the ones who
were seen felled by the left-handed archer, elephants with their flags,
30 and warriors with their standards. And headless trunks and trunkless
heads lay covering the ground all over the battlefield. Dogs, vultures,
herons, crows, ravens, kites, jackals, and birds feasted on the flesh and
blood of the fallen heroes.

With his heroes fallen, King Jayadratha of Sindhu tremblingly let go
of Kṛṣṇā and was minded to flee. With his army in disarray that vilest
of men helped Draupadī down and fled to the woods to save his life.
The King Dharma saw Draupadī being led by Dhaumya, and he had
35 the heroic son of Mādrī take her up in the chariot. When Jayadratha
had deserted, the Wolf-Belly attacked the routed ranks, aiming at them
with iron arrows; but the left-handed archer, observing that
Jayadratha was in full flight, stopped Bhīma from killing off the
Saindhava's soldiers.

Arjuna said:

Jayadratha, because of whose misconduct we have got into this endless trouble, is nowhere to be seen on the battlefield. Seek him out, hail to thee! Why kill off these fighters? There is no meat in this, what do you think?

Vaiśaṃpāyana said:

At these words of the sagacious Guḍākeśa, Bhīmasena looked at
40 Yudhiṣṭhira and said eloquently, "The enemies have lost their
champions and have largely been driven off. Take Draupadī, king, and
withdraw from here. Take Draupadī to the hermitage, king, with the
twins and great-spirited Dhaumya, and comfort her, Indra of princes!
For this nitwit Saindhava king will not escape alive from me were he
to flee to hell or were Indra to drive his chariot!"

Yudhiṣṭhira said:

The Saindhava does not deserve to die, strong-armed Bhīma, evil though he is, as long as we care for Duḥśalā and the glorious Gāndhārī.

Vaiśaṃpāyana said:

But when Draupadī heard that, she furiously told Bhīma, in a rage,
45 shamed and cunning—told her husbands Bhīma and Arjuna, "If you
want to do me a kindness, kill off that wretched abortion of the
Saindhavas, the evil, ill-minded defiler of his race! A wife-snatcher
without a cause and a foe who steals a kingdom do not deserve to
live, even if they beg you in battle!" And at her words the two tigerlike men went to look for the Saindhava, while the king returned with
Kṛṣṇā and his priest.

When he entered the hermitage, he saw that the pillows and
pitchers were overthrown, and Mārkaṇḍeya and the other brahmins
scattered. Then, accompanied by his wife and between his brothers,
the wise king met with the assembling brahmins who had been
50 grieving over Draupadī. At the sight of the king returning and
Draupadī being brought back after the defeat of the Sauvīras of Sindhu
they all rejoiced. The king seated himself right there, surrounded by
the others, and the beaming Kṛṣṇā entered the hermitage with the
twins.

Bhīma and Arjuna, meanwhile, hearing that the enemy was a mere
cry distant, goaded their horses and pursued him swiftly. And this
wondrous feat did this manly Arjuna accomplish that he shot the
Saindhava's horses from the distance of a cry; for this possessor of
celestial weapons, unperturbed even in this time of stress, accomplished
55 this difficult deed with arrows that were enchanted. Thereupon the
two champions Bhīma and Dhanaṃjaya stormed at the horseless,
solitary, frightened man from Sindhu who had lost his wits. And the
Saindhava, seeing his own horses dead and Dhanaṃjaya
accomplishing his gallant exploits, was greatly troubled, set his mind
on flight, and ran to the woods. Strong-armed Phalguna saw that the
Saindhava was now in full flight, chased him, and said, "Why did you
forcibly woo a woman with all this bravery? Turn around, you son of
a king, flight does not befit you! Why do you run and desert your
followers in the midst of the enemy?"

But the Saindhava did not turn around at the Pārtha's word, and mighty Bhīma rushed at him: "Stop you, stop!" "But don't kill him!" said the compassionate Pārtha.

Vaiśaṃpāyana said:
256.1 Jayadratha, on seeing the two brothers raise their weapons, ran off
quickly, deeply troubled but bent on saving his life. Mighty Bhīmasena
dismounted from the chariot, pursued the running man, and
indignantly seized him by the hair. In anger he raised him up in the
air, crashed him on the ground, grabbed him by the throat, and
thrashed him. When the other came to his senses, tried to get up, and
5 started to whine, strong-armed Bhīma kicked him in the head. He
kneed him and hit him with his fist until the king succumbed to the
blows and lost consciousness. But Phalguna stopped the irate
Bhīmasena: "For Duḥśalā's sake, do what the king said, Kaurava!"
Bhīmasena said:
"This evil man, this despicable molester of the innocent Draupadī,
does not deserve his life from me! How can I do what our always
compassionate king says? You too always bother me with your child's
brain!" Then the Wolf-Belly shaved the other's head with a crescent
10 arrow till there were five tufts of hair left. Jayadratha said nothing. The
Wolf-Belly said to the king, giving him the choice: "Listen to what I
am going to say if you want to survive, fool! You shall say at
assemblies and courts that you are our slave, then I will spare your
life. This is your victor's command!" King Jayadratha, in danger of his
life, replied, "So shall it be," to the tiger-like Bhīma who was brilliant
in battle. Wolf-Belly Pārtha, obedient to the Pārtha, then tied him till
he could not move, hoisted the senseless, dust-covered man on the
chariot, and went off to Yudhiṣṭhira, who was in the center of the
hermitage.
15 Bhīma showed Jayadratha in the state he was in, and at the sight of
him the king began to laugh. "Let him go," he said. Bhīma replied to
the king, "Tell Draupadī that the evil-minded wretch has become the
slave of the Pāṇḍus!" Gently the eldest brother said, "Let the wretch
go, if you mind my words." With a look at Yudhiṣṭhira Draupadī told
Bhīma, "Set the king's slave free, you have shaved his head down to
five tufts."
The king was set free, and he went up to King Yudhiṣṭhira, saluted
20 him, and bowed in confusion to all the hermits; and the compassionate
king, Yudhiṣṭhira son of God Dharma, spoke to Jayadratha, who, he
saw, was being held upright by the left-handed archer: "Go a free
man! You are free, but do not ever do it again. A curse on you, lecher,
you are vile, and your companions are vile. What lowest of men but
you would act like that?" At the sight of the close to lifeless man

whom he knew to be the perpetrator of wickedness, the king of men, chief of the Bharatas, felt compassion: "Your spirit shall increase in Law, do not set your mind on lawlessness! Go in peace, Jayadratha, with your horses, chariots, and footmen."

Embarrassed, taciturn, his face slightly downcast, the king went to Gaṅgādvāra, grieving much, O Bhārata. There he sought shelter with the Three-Eyed God,* Consort of Umā, and did much austerity. The Bull-bannered God* was pleased with him; and the Three-Eyed One contentedly accepted his offering, in person. The God gave him a boon. He accepted it—listen: "May I vanquish all five Pāṇḍavas on their chariots!" Thus spoke the king to the God, and the God told him, "Nay! But, invincible and unslayable though they be, you will be able to stay them in battle, except the strong-armed Arjuna whom even the Gods find it hard to assail. For he, the first of the knowers of arms, is protected by the Kṛṣṇa of the conch, discus, and mace, whom they call the Unvanquished God."

30 And having been told this, the king went to his own place, and the Pāṇḍavas went on living in the Kāmyaka Forest.

3(42.a) Rāma

257–75 (B. 273–91; C. 15850–6602)
257 (273; 15850). Yudhiṣṭhira complains to Mārkaṇḍeya about Draupadī's abduction. Was any man more unfortunate? (1–10).
258 (274; 15872). Mārkaṇḍeya mentions Rāma (1–5). Rāma's and Sītā's descent (50). Rāvaṇa's grandfather is Prajāpati who begot Pulastya, who begot Vaiśravaṇa. The latter deserts his father Pulastya for Prajāpati. In anger Pulastya begets Viśravas. Prajāpti heaps favors on Vaiśravaṇa, who reigns in Lankā (5–15).
259 (275; 15888). Viśravas begets Rāvaṇa and Kumbhakarṇa on Puspotkaṭā, Vibhīṣaṇa on Mālinī, and Khara and Śūrpanakhā on Rākā; they live on the Gandhamādana (1–10). They perform austerities until Brahmā plies them with boons (10–20). Rāvaṇa asks for invincibility—except by humans; Kumbhakarṇa for sleep (25); Vibhīṣaṇa for moral virtue; he is granted immortality (30). Rāvaṇa ousts Kubera Vaiśravaṇa from Lankā and is cursed; Vibhīṣaṇa follows Kubera (30–35). Rāvaṇa terrorizes the Gods (40).

* = Śiva.

260 (276; 15929). The Gods complain to Brahmā, who states that Viṣṇu has already descended to kill Rāvaṇa; the Gods must father sons on the apes to help him; Dundubhī becomes Mantharā (1–15).

261 (277; 15945). Daśaratha's eldest son is Rāma (1–5); his virtues (5–10). Daśaratha announces his elevation to Young King (10–15). Mantharā tells Daśaratha's wife Kaikeyī, who goes to the king and reminds him of his promise to her of one boon (15–20). She demands that her son Bharata be Young King and Rāma and Lakṣmaṇa be exiled (25). Rāma, his brother Lakṣmaṇa, and his wife Sītā go to the forest (25). Daśaratha dies; but Bharata refuses the kingdom, and is regent from Nandigrāma (25–35). Rāma lives in the Daṇḍaka Forest; there he mutilates Śūrpanakhā's face; she runs to her brother Rāvaṇa (35–45). Rāvaṇa goes to his old minister Marīca (45–55).

262 (278; 16000). Marīca scents danger; Rāvana tells of Rāma's treatment of Śūrpanakhā and vows revenge (1–5). Marīca warns him but reluctantly promises to help: he is to change himself into a golden deer (5–10). The two repair to Rāma's hermitage. At Sītā's request Rāma gives chase to the deer. After a long hunt he kills it; when Marīca dies, he cries out in Rāma's voice (10–20). Sītā sends Lakṣmaṇa to succor Rāma, but he laughs it off; Sītā scolds him severely and he goes (20–30). Rāvaṇa appears before Sītā in a hermit's guise and seeks to tempt her (30). She scorns him, and he abducts her; he is seen by the vulture Jaṭāyu (35–40).

263 (279; 16042). Jaṭāyu berates Rāvaṇa and attacks him; Rāvaṇa shears off its wings (1–5). Sītā drops a trail of ornaments; on a mountain plain with five apes she drops her robe (5). Rāma and Lakṣmaṇa return to the hermitage; Rāma is worried, then finds Sītā gone (10). On his search he finds Jaṭāyu, who tells him of Rāvaṇa's misdeed; he has gone south; the vulture dies (15–20). Rāma and Lakṣmaṇa encounter the demon Kabandha; he captures Lakṣmaṇa, who laments (20–30). Together they dismember and kill Kabandha; a celestial spirit rises from the carcass: it is a Gandharva freed from a curse. He tells them to seek the help of the ape Sugrīva, who will find Rāvaṇa's Lankā (30–40).

264 (280; 16092). Rāma, pining for Sītā, is admonished by Lakṣmaṇa (1–5). They find Sugrīva on Mount

Ṛśyamūka; the ape shows them Sītā's robe. They compact that Rāma kill Sugrīva's rival Vālin and Sugrīva help find Sītā (5–10). In the Kiṣkindhā Forest Sugrīva challenges Vālin, whose wife Tārā warns him; he suspects her of infidelity (15–25). Sugrīva and Vālin argue and engage; at Sugrīva's sign Rāma shoots Vālin; Sugrīva appropriates Kiṣkindhā and Tārā (25–35). Rāma lives for four months on Mount Mālyavat (40). Rāvaṇa houses Sītā and has her guarded by demonesses, who threaten to eat her; Sītā insists on her love for Rāma (40–50). The demoness Trijaṭā tells Sītā of a dream vision of the Rākṣasa Avindhya: Rāvaṇa, who is impotent because of a curse, will be slain with his followers; Vibhīṣaṇa will survive and reign on Mount Śveta. Portents of Rāma's victory and reunion with Sītā (50–70).

265 (281; 16166). Rāvaṇa visits Sītā in all his finery and tempts her (1–15). She scorns him (15–20). Though spurned, Rāvaṇa remains chivalrous (20–30).

266 (282; 16197). Rāma and Lakṣmaṇa see autumn appear; Rāma thinks Sugrīva is laggard and sends Lakṣmaṇa to remind the ape of their compact (1–10). Sugrīva receives Lakṣmaṇa well and reports that monkey search parties are out and expected back presently; Lakṣmaṇa and Sugrīva go to tell Rāma (10–20). All parties return unsuccessfully, except the one gone south: two months pass till Hanūmān and his party are sighted merrily ravaging a nearby wood; Rāma is encouraged (20–30). At Rāma's bidding Hanūmān tells that he has found Sītā: his party entered a cave where they found a celestial palace inhabited by an ascetic woman, Prabhāvatī, who fed them; she directed them to the ocean shore (30–40). At the ocean the monkeys are desperate and prepare to fast unto death; while they talk about the vulture Jaṭāyu, the latter's brother Sāṃpati appears and is told of Jaṭāyu's death and Rāma's sorrow (40–50). Sāṃpati's knowledge of the whereabouts of Lankā encourages them. Hanūmān jumps the ocean (55), and sees Sītā, whom he tells of Rāma's good health and alliance with the monkeys. She gives him tokens of recognition (55–65).

267 (283; 16267). Armies of monkeys rally to Rāma (1–10). Rāma marches out with Hanūmān in the vanguard; they reach the ocean (15–20). Rāma rejects several proposals on crossing the ocean; he presses the

ocean and it appears personified in a dream; Rāma threatens the ocean, which suggests that he have the monkey Nala build a causeway; this is done (20–45). Vibhīṣaṇa visits Rāma, who anoints him king of the Rākṣasas (45). For a month the army crosses over (50).
268 (284; 16323). Rāvaṇa fortifies Lankā (1–5). Angada approaches him as envoy with the ultimatum that he free Sītā; Rāvaṇa is enraged, but Angada escapes (5–20). Rāma attacks Lankā and in the end destroys the city (20–40).
269 (285; 16365). Rāvaṇa engages Rāma; other Rākṣasas fight with Lakṣmaṇa and the chief monkeys (1–10).
270 (286; 16379). Prahasta is felled by Vibhīṣaṇa (1). Dhūmrākṣa routs the monkeys and is killed by Hanūmān (5–10). Rāvaṇa orders Kumbhakarṇa to fight (15–25).
271 (287; 16408). Kumbhakarṇa slaughters the monkeys and captures Sugrīva; Lakṣmaṇa kills the demon (1–15). He and Hanūmān kill Vajravega and Pramāthin (15–25).
272 (288; 16438). Rāvaṇa orders his son Indrajit to fight (1–5). Lakṣmaṇa, Angada, and later Rāma fight Indrajit, who fells the brothers (5–25).
273 (289; 16465). Rāma and Lakṣmaṇa are trapped in a net of arrows; Vibhīṣaṇa revives them and introduces a Yakṣa messenger from Kubera with water that helps them see invisible demons (1–10). Lakṣmaṇa fights Indrajit and kills him; Rāvaṇa sees his son's empty chariot (15–25). Rāvaṇa wants to kill Sītā in revenge, but is dissuaded by Avindhya: he should kill Rāma (25–30).
274 (290; 16498). The monkeys maul Rāvaṇa's army. Rāvaṇa resorts to magic (1–10). Indra's charioteer Mātali appears and instructs Rāma to kill Rāvaṇa (10–15). The two engage, and Rāma kills Rāvaṇa with an enchanted arrow; the demon evaporates (15–30).
275 (291; 16529). The Gods honor Rāma (1). He gives Lankā to Vibhīṣaṇa (5). Avindhya brings Sītā, but Rāma rejects her: he has only done his duty, but he cannot take her back (5–10). Sītā and the others are stunned (15). Brahmā, Fire, Wind, and the World Guardians appear; so does Daśaratha; Sītā calls on the Wind and the elements to vindicate her (15–25). The Wind, Fire, and Varuṇa do so (25). Brahmā and Daśaratha reassure Rāma: he

should rule Ayodhyā (25–35). Rāma relents; he rewards Avindhya and Trijaṭā (35). From Brahmā he receives the boon of Law, victory, and the revival of the fallen monkeys. Sītā bestows on Hanūmān longevity for as long as Rāma's fame will last (40–45). Rāma returns to the mainland on the chariot Puṣpaka and rewards the monkeys (50–55). He consecrates Angada Young King (55). Rāma and Lakṣmaṇa rejoin their brothers Bharata and Śatrughna (60). Vasiṣṭha and Vāmadeva consecrate Rāma; he dismisses Sugrīva and Vibhīṣaṇa and returns the chariot Puṣpaka to Kubera; he performs ten Horse Sacrifices (65).

Janamejaya said:

257.1 What did these tigers of men the Pāṇḍavas do after they had incurred incomparable trouble because of Kṛṣṇā's abduction?

Vaiśaṃpāyana said:

After having freed Kṛṣṇā and defeated Jayadratha, Yudhiṣṭhira the King Dharma sat with the throngs of hermits. From among the listening and commiserating great seers it was to Mārkaṇḍeya that the scion of Pāṇḍu addressed himself.

"Methinks, Time is mighty, and so are the divine workings wrought by fate and the predestination of creatures, which brooks no
5 infringement. For else, how could such a happening befall our Law-wise and Law-abiding wife, as a false charge of theft might fall on a pure man? Not a sin had Draupadī committed, not a blameworthy deed anywhere; indeed, among the brahmins themselves she had perfectly carried out the great Law. King Jayadratha of the muddled mind abducted her by force; and because of his abduction of her he had his head shaved. With his companions he suffered defeat in battle. We may have recovered her by killing the Saindhava army, but we did have our own wife abducted absent-mindedly.

"Life in the forest is miserable; we live by hunting, which means forest-dwellers injure forest-dwelling game. And this exile has been
10 brought about by kinsmen who were resolved on falsehood. Is there indeed a man more unfortunate than I, have you even seen or heard of one before?"

Mārkaṇḍeya said:

258.1 Rāma, O bull of the Bharatas, suffered incomparable misery: his wife, Janaka's daughter, was abducted by a powerful Rākṣasa, King Rāvaṇa, from their hermitage by way of the sky, after swiftly killing the vulture Jaṭāyus by resorting to his wizardry. Relying on the army of Sugrīva, Rāma recovered her by bridging the ocean and burning down Laṅkā with honed arrows.

Yudhiṣṭhira said:

In which lineage was Rāma born, how brave was he, how gallant?
5 And whose son was Rāvaṇa, and what was his feud with him? Pray
tell me all this completely, my lord, I wish to hear the geste of Rāma of unsullied deeds.

Mārkaṇḍeya said:

There was a great king by the name of Aja, who was born in the lineage of Ikṣvāku. His son was Daśaratha, who was always devoted to learning and pure. Four sons he had who were expert in the import of the Law, Rāma, Lakṣmaṇa, Śatrughna, and the mighty Bharata. Rāma's mother was Kausalyā, Bharata's Kaikeyī, while the enemy-burners Lakṣmaṇa and Śatrughna were the sons of Sumitrā. Janaka was the king of Videha, and his daughter was Sītā, O king, whom the Maker himself had destined to be Rāma's beloved queen.

10 Thus have I related the provenance of Rāma and Sītā; I shall now
also explain that of Rāvaṇa, lord of your people.

Rāvaṇa's[1] grandfather was the God Prajāpati himself, the Self-existent, the ascetic lord creator of all the worlds. He had a beloved son named Pulastya, who had been born from his mind, and this lord begot a son Vaiśravaṇa on a cow. He[2] deserted his father and joined his grandfather. Angry with him over this, the father created a new self by himself, and, having been thus born twice, he angrily begot the twice-born Viśravas with half of himself, in order to counter
15 Vaiśravaṇa. But Grandfather happily bestowed on Vaiśravaṇa
immortality, lordship of the riches, and guardianship of one quarter, the friendship of Īśāna, a son Nalakūbara, and as his capital seat Lankā, which was peopled with multitudes of Rākṣasas.

Mārkaṇḍeya said:

259.1 The hermit Viśravas, the son who was born from half of Pulastya
out of anger, began to look upon Vaiśravaṇa with anger. But Kubera, king of the Rākṣasas, knew that his father was angry and always strove to placate him, O king. The kings of kings, whose mount is a man, while living in Lankā gave three Rākṣasa women to his father for servants. They were eager to gratify the great-spirited seer, and slender of waist, O tiger among Bharatas, and expert dancers and
5 singers. Puṣpotkaṭā, Rakā, and Mālinī were their names, lord of your
people, and wanting the best they rivaled one another, O king. And

1. 7.2. 2. Cf. 7.2.

contentedly the great-spirited lord gave them boons, sons the likes of the World Guardians, as each of them desired.

Puṣpotaṭā gave birth to two sons, Rākṣasa princes: Kumbhakarṇa and Ten-headed Rāvaṇa, who was unequaled on earth in strength. Mālinī bore one son, Vibhīṣaṇa. And from Rākā twins were born, Khara and Śūrpanakhā. Vibhīṣaṇa now was superior to all in beauty; the lordly prince was a protector of the Law, and he delighted in ritual. Ten-headed Rāvaṇa was the eldest Rākṣasa bull of them all, of mighty energy, mighty prowess, and mighty mettle and valor. Kumbhakarṇa surpassed all in strength, he was a wizard and berserker in battle, a terror-inspiring Stalker of the Night. Khara was gallant with the bow, hated brahmins, and guzzled raw meat; while Śūrpanakhā was terrifying and obstructed ascetics. All were *Veda*-wise champions, all observed their vows well, and they lived happily with their father on Mount Gandhamādana.

Then they saw Vaiśravaṇa there, him who rides a man; he was seated with his father amidst extreme opulence. Inspired by rivalry, they resolved on austerity, and gratified Brahmā with their awesome feats of austerity. Ten-headed Rāvaṇa stood on one foot for a thousand years, lived on the wind, amidst five fires, with full concentration. Kumbhakarṇa lay on the ground and was strict in diet and vows. The sagacious Vibhīṣaṇa made his meal of one withered leaf, was given to fasting and the muttering of prayers; the noble-minded prince observed severe self-mortifications all the time. And Khara and Śūrpanakha, with happy hearts, waited on and guarded them, as they were performing austerities.

When a full thousand years had passed, invincible Ten-headed Rāvaṇa cut off a head and offered it into the fire; and the lord of the world was pleased by this. Brahmā thereupon himself came and stopped them from mortifying themselves by tempting each of them with the gift of a boon.

Brahmā said:

I am pleased with you, my sons; now cease, and choose boons. Excepting immortality, whatever you desire shall be yours. The head that you have offered into the fire out of desire for great fruits shall again be joined to your body. Your body shall know no ugliness. You shall be able to assume any form you desire, and be victorious in battle, no doubt of that.

Rāvaṇa said:

May I never suffer defeat at the hands of Gandharvas, Gods, Asuras, Snakes, Kiṃnaras, and Ghosts!

Brahmā said:

You shall be in no danger from those you have mentioned, except from man. Hail to thee, I have so ordained!

Mārkaṇḍeya said:

At these words Ten-headed Rāvaṇa was satisfied, for the foolish man-eater despised humans.

Kumbhakarṇa was then addressed by the Great-grandfather, and he chose a long sleep, for his mind was seized by darkness. "So shall it be," he said; and he spoke to Vibhīṣaṇa, "Choose a boon, my son, I am pleased," repeating it often.

Vibhīṣaṇa said:

30 May lawlessness never occur to me, even when I am in the final
straits; and, O lord, may the untaught Brahmā weapon be manifest
to me.

Brahmā said:

Inasmuch as your mind does not delight in lawlessness, plower of your enemies, although you are born from a Rākṣasa womb, I grant you immortality!

Mārkaṇḍeya said:

The Ten-headed Rākṣasa, O lord of your people, once he had
received his boon, vanquished the God of Riches in battle and toppled
him from Lankā. The lord left Lankā, and, followed by Gandharvas
and Yakṣas as well as Rākṣasas and Kiṃpurusas, went to
Gandhamādana. Rāvaṇa battled for, and took, his celestial chariot
35 Puṣpaka. Vaiśravaṇa cursed him, "You shall never ride on it! He who
shall kill you in battle shall ride on it. And as you have shown me,
your elder, contempt, you shall soon cease to be." The Law-minded
Vibhīṣaṇa, mindful of the Law of the strict, followed him, O king, in
superb splendour. The God of Riches, his brother, was pleased and
wisely conferred on him the marshalship of the armies of both the
Yakṣas and the Rākṣasas.

The man-eating Rākṣasas and powerful Piśācas all assembled and
consecrated Ten-headed Rāvaṇa king; and he of the ten faces, drunk
with power, marched and took the jewels of Daityas and Gods, for he
40 could assume any form and travel the skies. He was called Rāvaṇa,
because he made the worlds cry out: Ten-headed Rāvaṇa of wilful
might brought terror to the Gods.

Mārkaṇḍeya said:

260.1 Thereupon the brahmin seers, Siddhas, Gods, and royal seers,
placing the Fire at their head, sought shelter with Brahmā.

Fire said:

Viśravas' ten-headed and powerful son has been made invincible by you, our lord, with the gift of a boon. Now the mighty Rākṣasa oppresses all creatures with hostile acts. Lord, save us from him, for there is no other savior!

Brahmā said:
Splendid Fire, he cannot be defeated by Gods and Asuras. Still it has
5 been ordained in his case what is to be done to subdue him. For that
purpose Four-armed Viṣṇu has descended to earth at my behest, the
greatest of strikers. He shall carry out the deed.
Mārkaṇḍeya said:
In their presence Grandfather uttered this word: "Take ye on form
on earth with all the hosts of the Gods. Beget ye all on bears and
monkeys heroic sons, mighty and able to assume any shape, to be
Viṣṇu's helpers." Thereupon the Gods, Gandharvas, and Dānavas all
took pleasure in descending to earth with varying portions of
themselves. Before their eyes the boon-granting God ordered a
Gandharvī by the name of Dundubhī to make successful the mission of
10 the Gods; and having heard Grandfather's words the Gandharvī
took form in the world of men as the hunch-backed woman Mantharā.
All the great Gods led by Śakra begot sons on monkeys and bears; and
they all equaled their fathers in fame and strength. Cleavers of
mountain peaks they all were, armed with *śāla* and palm trees and
rocks, hard as diamond, all were strong as a river in spate, all as
gallant as they wished to be and proficient in fighting, with the vigor
of a myriad elephants and the speed of the wind. Some of them dwelled
where they pleased, some lived in the forest.
Having thus disposed it all, the blessed Lord who prospers the
world enlightened Mantharā about her tasks and the manner thereof.
15 She acknowledged his words and carried them out swift as thought,
darting hither and thither, bent on fomenting a feud.

Yudhiṣṭhira said:
261.1 My lord, you have detailed the births of Rāma and each of the
others. Now I wish to hear the reason of their exile, pray tell, brahmin.
Why were Daśaratha's two heroic sons Rāma and Lakṣmaṇa and the
glorious Mithilā princess banished to the forest, brahmin?
Mārkaṇḍeya said:
King Daśaratha, who delighted in ritual, was devoted to the Law,
and always heeded his elders, rejoiced in the birth of his male
children. In the course of time his sons grew up very vigorous, and
became fully fledged in the *Vedas* and their mysteries and in the art of
5 archery. They completed their student years, and took wives, O king,
and at all times Daśaratha was pleased and happy. Rāma was the
eldest, and he was a Rāma because he enchanted the subjects; he was
sagacious and made content his father's heart with his charm.
The[1] wise king, deeming himself advanced in age, sought the

1. 2.1–6.

counsel of his ministers and Law-wise priests. They all held the view, these good councillors, that the time had come for Rāma to be consecrated Young King, O Bhārata. His eyes were red, his arms strong, his gait was that of an elephant in rut; he had long arms, a wide chest, dark, curly hair, and the hero, not the lesser of Śakra in strength, shone with splendor; he knew completely all the Laws, and was Bṛhaspati's peer in mind. All the subjects were devoted to him, and he was expert in all sciences, the master of his senses, and pleasing to the eye of even his enemies. The evil he tamed, the law-abiding he protected, and he was an imperturbable and unassailable and never defeated conqueror. Upon such a son, who increased the joy of Kausalyā, did the king gaze, and he was utterly contented, O joy of the Kurus.

Reflecting on the virtues of Rāma, the puissant and heroic king was pleased to salute his priest: "Hail to thee! Tonight the stars of Puṣya are in an auspicious conjunction. Let the ingredients be collected, and Rāma invited!"

When[1] Mantharā heard this word of the king, she went to Kaikeyī, and said to her in time, "Today the king has proclaimed your great misfortune, Kaikeyī! A fierce and furiously poisonous snake is biting you, unfortunate woman. Indeed, Kausalyā is the fortunate one, for now *her* son will be consecrated. Where will you find good fortune, if your son has no part of the kingdom?" On hearing this Kaikeyī put on all her jewelry, and, displaying a superb beauty, this woman of the waist that was indented like an altar approached her husband in private. Smiling sweetly, almost laughing as if to show her love, she said charmingly, "You who are true to your promises, once you promised me you would grant me one desire. Now fulfil your promise, O king, and free yourself from the burden!"

The king said:

I shall grant you the boon, speak! You shall receive what you wish. What innocent man must be killed? What guilty man set free? Whom shall I give wealth? Or from whom take it away? Mine is all wealth on earth, except the brahmins'!

Mārkaṇḍeya said:

When Kaikeyī heard this, she embraced the king. Realizing her power, she said to him, "Bharata is to receive the consecration you disposed for Rāma, and the Rāghava is to go to the forest." The king heard this bitter word, source of misery, and he was overcome with grief, O chief of the Bharatas; and he made no reply. But when Rāma heard that his father had said what he had said, the Law-minded hero departed for the forest: "The king shall be true!" Lakṣmaṇa, the

1. 2.7–35.

glorious bowman, followed him, and so did Sītā, his wife—hail to thee—the daughter of Janaka of Videha.

After[1] Rāma had gone to the forest, King Daśaratha succumbed to the body's Law of the passing of Time. Queen[2] Kaikeyī, knowing that Rāma was gone and the king had passed away, had Bharata brought in and she said to him, "Daśaratha has gone to heaven. Rāma and Lakṣmaṇa are in the forest. So take the vast kingdom safely, and without rivals." Said the Law-minded prince, "Fie! Out of greed for riches you have committed cruelty, killing your husband and uprooting the house. So fulfil your desire by heaping disgrace on my head, mother, you defiler of the family!" and he began to weep.

He[3] absolved himself from guilt before all his subjects and journeyed after his brother Rāma, hoping to return him. Hoping to bring Rāma back, sorrowfully he placed Kausalyā, Kaikeyī, and Sumitrā on wagons in the vanguard and came himself with Śatrughna, accompanied by Vasiṣṭha and Vāmadeva, and thousands of brahmins as well as townsfolk and countrymen. He[4] found Rāma with Lakṣmaṇa on Mount Citrakūṭa, carrying his bow and wearing the scant adornment of ascetics. Rāma,[5] who was implementing his father's promise, dismissed Bharata; and[6] the latter ruled his kingdom in Nandigrāma, but kept his brother's sandals in front of himself.

Rāma,[7] however, fearing that the townsfolk and countrymen would return, entered the great forest by the hermitage of Śarabhaṅga. He paid homage to Śarabhanga, went on to the Daṇḍaka Forest, and settled down by the lovely River Godāvarī. While[8] Rāma was dwelling there, he had a great quarrel with King Khara of Janasthāna, which was occasioned by Śūrpanakhā. In[9] order to protect the ascetics, the Rāghava, who loved the Law, slew fourteen thousand Rākṣasas on earth; and by killing the powerful Dūṣaṇa and Khara, the sagacious Rāghava made the Forest of the Law safe again. After[10] those Rākṣasas had been slain, Śūrpanakhā, her nose and lip cut off, went to Lankā, which was her brother's seat. Then the Rākṣasī, faint with grief, went to Rāvaṇa and fell at her brother's feet with the blood dried on her face.

When[11] Rāvaṇa saw her so mutilated, he nigh swooned from fury. Grinding his teeth he jumped angrily from his throne, dismissed his councillors, and asked her in private, "Who forgot and despised me, my dear, to do this to you? Who has found himself a sharp spike and uses it on all his body? Who started a fire by his head and has gone confidently to sleep? Who is kicking a gruesome poisonous snake? Who has grabbed the maned lion by its tusks?" And while he was

1. 2.58. 2. 2.66–67. 3. 2.73; 76. 4. 2.92. 5. 2.97. 6. 2.107. 7. 3.4; 1. 8. 3.16–19. 9. 3.24–28. 10. 3.30. 11. 3.32.

speaking, flames burst forth from the apertures of his body as from inside a hollow tree at night.

His sister related to him all the gallantry of Rāma and the defeat of Khara, Dūṣaṇa, and the other Rākṣasas. Rāvaṇa[1] resolved on his task. He comforted his sister, and after taking measures for his city, the king strode through the sky. He passed Mount Trikūṭa and Mount Kāla, and gazed upon the deep ocean where the crocodiles dwell. Ten-
headed Rāvaṇa passed over it, and went to Gokarṇa, the safe and
55 beloved city of the great-spirited Trident-wielder. Ten-headed Rāvaṇa
went to Mārīca, his previous minister, who, out of fear of Rāma, had become an ascetic.

Mārkaṇḍeya said:

262.1 When[2] Mārīca saw Rāvaṇa come, he was flustered and welcomed him hospitably with fruit, roots, and the like. The Rākṣasa was sitting along with his guest who was seated and rested, and spoke to him this courteous word, one eloquent man to another: "You have not your normal color. Is your city secure? Do your subjects love you as
before? What task has brought you here, lord of the Rākṣasas?
5 Consider it done, however difficult it may be!" Rāvaṇa told him of
Rāma's whole exploit, and[3] Mārīca listened and said briefly to Rāvaṇa, "Cease harassing Rāma, for I know his bravery. Who indeed is able to withstand the impact of the arrows of the great-spirited man? That bull among men is indeed the reason that I have become an ascetic. What malicious creature has shown you this course, which is the beginning of your destruction?" Rāvaṇa[4] berated him angrily: "If you do not carry out my order, you will be sure to die!" Mārīca thought, "Better to die at the hand of a superior man. As death is inevitable I
shall do what he wants." Then Mārīca replied to the lord of the
10 Rākṣasas, "What help can I give you? I shall willynilly do it." Ten-
headed[5] Rāvaṇa told him, "Go and tempt Sītā. Become a deer with jeweled antlers and gem-encrusted hide. Surely, when Sītā sees you, she shall send Rāma. With Kākutstha gone, Sītā shall be in my power. I shall abduct her, and then the evil-minded man will be no more because of his separation from his wife. Render me this help!"

Thus having been told Mārīca performed the water offering for
15 himself and sorrowfully followed Rāvaṇa, who went ahead. They went
to the hermitage of Rāma of unsullied deeds, and there the two did everything they had plotted before. Rāvaṇa became a shaven ascetic, carrying bowl and triple staff, Mārīca became a deer, and so they went to that place. Mārīca showed himself to the princess of Videha in the guise of a deer, and, prompted by fate, she sent Rāma after him.

1. 3.32. 2. 3.34. 3. 3.35. 4. 3.38. 5. 3.40.

To[1] do her pleasure Rāma quickly took his bow, entrusted her to
Lakṣmaṇa's protection, and went off to catch the deer. Carrying his
bow, the quiver tied on, with his sword and arm and finger guards,
20 Rāma pursued the deer, as Rudra the stellar deer. Now the Rākṣasa
disappeared, then came into view again, and so drew him out a long
way. Then[2] Rāma recognized him; and knowing he was a Stalker of
the Night, the enlightened Rāghava took an unfailing arrow and killed
the other in his guise of a deer. Hit[3] by the arrow he imitated Rāma's
voice and cried out in a tone of hurt, "Ah Sītā, Lakṣmaṇa!" She
hurried to where his voice came from, but Lakṣmaṇa said to her,
"Stop those fears, timid woman, who will resist Rāma? In a little while
25 you will see Rāma return, sweet-smiling one." At these words the
weeping woman, afflicted by her female nature, became suspicious of
her brother-in-law, whose gem-like conduct was pure, and the virtuous
and devoted wife began speaking harshly: "This is not the time you
have been waiting for in your heart, fool! I'd rather take a sword and
kill myself, or throw myself off a mountain peak, or enter into the fire
than ever desert my husband Rāma and wait on you, wretch, like a
tigress on a jackal." When he heard this, Lakṣmaṇa, who loved
Rāghava and was strictly behaved, stopped his ears and left to go
where Rāghava was and, carrying his bow, followed Rāma's trail.
30 Meanwhile[4] the Rākṣasa Rāvaṇa appeared, ungentle though in
gentle guise, like a fire covered with ashes, in the guise of a hermit, for
he wished to abduct the blameless woman. When she saw him appear,
Janaka's Law-wise daughter invited him to a meal of fruit, roots,
and the like. He[5] scorned it all, and assuming his own form, the bull
of the Rākṣasas tried to appease Vaidehī: "Sītā, I am Rāvaṇa, the
famous king of the Rākṣasas. My lovely city called Lankā lies across
the vast ocean. There you shall shine with me amidst choice women.
Become my wife, woman with the beautiful hips, desert Rāghava the
hermit!"
35 When[6] Sītā Jānakī heard these and suchlike words, the fair-hipped
woman stopped her ears, and said, "Be silent! The sky may fall with
its stars, the earth may splinter, fire become cold, before I desert the
scion of Raghu! For how could an elephant cow, after serving her
forest-ranging spotted bull with ichor flowing, touch a swine? What
woman who has drunk mead and honey brew will have a taste for
jujube juice?" With these words she entered the hermitage.
40 Rāvaṇa[7] followed the fair-hipped woman and stopped her. Abusing
her in a rough voice, he grasped the swooning Sītā by the hair and
strode up to the sky. The vulture Jaṭāyu, who lived on a mountain,
saw the poor woman being abducted, who wept "Rāma, Rāma!"

1. 3.41. 2. 3.42. 3. 3.43. 4. 3.44. 5. 3.45. 6. 3.46. 7. 3.47.

Mārkaṇḍeya said:

263.1 The[1] mighty king of vultures Jaṭāyu, son of Aruṇa and brother of
Saṃpāti, was a friend of Daśaratha. There the bird saw then the
latter's daughter-in-law Sītā in Rāvaṇa's arms, and he angrily stormed
at the lord of the Rākṣasas. And he said to him, "Let go of Maithilī, let
go! How shall you carry her off, Stalker of the Night, while I am still
alive? You shall not be rid of me alive, if you don't give up that wife!"
So[2] he spoke to the Indra of the Rākṣasas and tore at him powerfully
with his talons; and sorely lacerated by blows from the bird's wings
and beak, Rāvaṇa shed much blood, like a mountain with its mineral-
5 colored streams. When he was being assailed by the vulture, who
wished to do Rāma a kindness, he took his sword and cut off the
bird's wings. Having[3] felled the vulture king, like a mountain with
shredded clouds, the Rākṣasa strode skyward with Sītā in his arms.
Whenever Vaidehī saw a circle of hermitages, or a lake, or a river, she
dropped her ornaments. On a mountain plateau she saw five bull-like
apes, and there the mindful woman let go of her wide, celestial robe.
The bright yellow cloth fluttered in the wind and fell in the midst of
the five kingly apes, like lightning within a cloud.
10 While[4] Vaidehī was being abducted, sagacious Rāma, after killing
that great deer, on his return met his brother Lakṣmaṇa. When he
saw his brother, he scolded him: "Why did you leave Vaidehī alone in
this demon-infested wilderness and come here?" Reflecting on his own
being drawn away by the Rākṣasa in the guise of a deer, and on the
arrival of his brother, he became worried. Scolding the other, Rāma
quickly went up to him: "Is Sītā alive? I don't see her, Lakṣmaṇa!"
Lakṣmaṇa repeated all that Sītā had said, and her last untoward
15 words. With[5] a burning heart Rāma ran to the hermitage and
encountered the fallen vulture, which rose like a mountain. Suspecting
a Rākṣasa, Kākutstha drew his mighty bow and ran to him with
Lakṣmaṇa. Said the powerful bird to Rāma and Lakṣmaṇa, "I am the
king of the vultures, hail to ye, a friend of Daśaratha's." When they
heard that, they relaxed their bright bows: "Who is this? He mentions
our father by name," they said. The bird told them how Rāvaṇa had
20 smitten him in Sītā's cause, and Rāghava asked, "What way did
Rāvaṇa go?" The vulture told them with motions of his head, and
died. Rāma understanding his gesturing cried: "South!" and
performed the last rites in honor of his father's friend.

He found the hermitage empty, the pillows and pots in disorder, the jars toppled, and the place was filled with an army of jackals. Invaded by sorrow and grief, pained by the abduction of Vaidehī, the enemy-burners went south in the Daṇḍaka Forest. In that vast forest Rāma and Sumitrā's son saw herds of deer running in all directions,

1. 3.48. 2. 3.49. 3. 3.50. 4. 3.55. 5. 3.63.

and heard the horrible noise of the creatures, which roared like a
25 forest fire. Soon[1] thereafter they saw the hideous Rākṣasa Kabandha,
huge like a cloud or a mountain, with a trunk like a *śāla* tree, big
arms, one wide eye in his chest, and a large belly and mouth. He
happened to catch Lakṣmaṇa by the hand, and Sumitrā's son at once
fell prey to despair, O Bhārata. He looked at Rāma as the ogre pulled
him to his maw, and said despairingly to Rāma, "See my condition,
the abduction of Vaidehī, this calamity of mine, your own fall from the
kingdom, and the death of father. I shall no more witness your return
with Vaidehī to Kosala and your reestablishment in the ancestral
30 kingdom of earth. Fortunate are those who will see your head
consecrated with *kuśa* grass, parched rice, and *śamī* logs, like a moon
with bits of cloud!"

Thus did the sagacious Lakṣmaṇa lament in many ways, but,
undisturbed amidst these disturbances, Kākutstha said to him, "Do not
lose heart, tiger among men, he is nothing when I am here. Cut off his
right arm while I sever his left." As he was speaking, Rāma cut off his
35 arm, like a joint of sesame, with his very sharp sword. When he saw
his brother holding his ground, Sumitrā's powerful son hit the demon's
right arm with his sword. And Lakṣmaṇa hit the Rākṣasa hard on the
other side, and the huge Kabandha fell lifeless to the ground. From the
body escaped a person of divine aspect and was seen to ascend to the
sky, blazing in the sky like a sun. Rāma[2] asked him eloquently, "Who
are you? Speak freely to my question. What is this strange happening?
It seems to me like a miracle!" He replied, "I am the Gandharva
Viśvāvasu, king. Through a curse of Brahmā I was born from a
Rākṣasa womb. Sītā has been abducted by King Rāvaṇa, who dwells in
40 Lankā. Go to Sugrīva, he will render you help. Close by Mount
Ṛśyamūka there is Lake Pampā with salubrious water and frequented
by wild geese and ducks. Sugrīva lives there with four councillors; he
is the brother of the monkey king Vālin, of the golden garlands. This
much I can tell you: you shall see Jānakī. The monkey king surely
knows Rāvaṇa's seat." Having spoken, that resplendent divine person
disappeared to the amazement of the two heroes Rāma and Lakṣmaṇa.

Mārkaṇḍeya said:

264.1 Grieving[3] over the abduction of Sītā, Rāma made his way, not too
far, to Lake Pampā, which abounded in day-blooming and night-
blooming lotuses. While cherished by a pleasant cold breeze redolent
with the elixir of immortality in that wood, he went with his thoughts
to his beloved. And remembering his loved one the Indra of kings
lamented, struck by the arrow of love. Sumitrā's son said to him,
"May such a feeling never again touch you, giver of pride, as a disease

1. 3.65–66. 2. 3.67–69. 3. 3.71–4.1.

touches a man in control of himself and with the habits of the old. You have received tidings of Vaidehī and Rāvaṇa—now recover her with manliness and cunning. Let us go to Sugrīva in the mountains, that bull among apes; take courage as long as I am your pupil, servant, and companion!" At these various words of Lakṣmaṇa, Rāghava returned to normalcy, and became engrossed in his task. They used the water of Pampā, and after making a libation to the ancestors they both started, the heroic brothers Rāma and Lakṣmaṇa.

They went to Mount Ṛśyamūka, abounding in fruit and roots, and on top of the mountain the heroes saw five apes. Sugrīva[1] sent to them his wise ape councillor Hanūmān, who stood as tall as a mountain. After talking with him first, they went to Sugrīva, O king, and Rāma contracted friendship with the monkey king. When[2] the apes were told of his task, they showed both of them the robe that Sītā had dropped by the apes while she was being abducted. Having[3] found the monkey king Sugrīva worthy of his trust, Rāma himself consecrated him to the overlordship of all the monkeys on earth; and Kākutstha promised to kill his brother Vālin in battle, and Sugrīva promised to bring Vaidehī back, O king.

After[4] thus having concluded a covenant and given each other their trust, they all went to the Kiṣkindhā Forest, where they stayed, hoping for battle. On[5] reaching Kiṣkindhā, Sugrīva gave forth a cry with the roar of a flood, which Vālin could not bear. Tārā[6] stopped him: "The way that mighty ape Sugrīva roars, he must have found a protector, I think. Please do not go out." Golden-garlanded Vālin, her husband and lord of the apes, said this eloquent word to Tārā of the moon-like face: "You know the cries of all creatures, and are endowed with cunning: look with whom this mock brother of mine has found protection." Tārā of the moon-like luster thought a while, then she sagely spoke to her husband: "Hear it all, lord of the apes. Daśaratha's mettlesome son Rāma has been bereaved of his wife, and the great archer has contracted an alliance of friendship and common enemies with Sugrīva. His wise and strong-armed brother, Sumitrā's unvanquished son Lakṣmaṇa, stands ready to bring the task to completion. Mainda, Dvivida, Hanūmān the son of the Wind, and the king of bears Jāmbavat stand by Sugrīva as his councillors. They are all great-spirited, powerful, and sagacious, and suffice for your destruction with the shelter of Rāma's bravery."

The[7] lord of the apes rejected her words, which she had spoken for his own good, jealously suspecting her of being in love with Sugrīva. Speaking harshly to Tāra, he went out of his cave and said to Sugrīva, who was standing near Mount Mālyavat, "Fool, I have defeated you

1. 4.2–5. 2. 4.6. 3. Cf. 4.25. 4. 4.12. 5. 4.14. 6. 4.15, with variants. 7. 4.16, with variants and omissions.

numerous times, you who are as dear to me as life. Why hurry once more to your death, thinking that a brother will be set free?" At these words, enemy-killer Sugrīva spoke to his brother reasonably, as though to alert Rāma that the time had come: "Know that the capacities for life of Rāma, who has lost his wife, and of myself, who have lost the kingdom to you, have joined forces!" Vālin and Sugrīva argued in many ways, then fell upon each other in battle, armed with *śāla* trees, palms, and rocks. They hit each other, fell on the ground together, jumped about wonderfully, and beat each other with their fists. Dripping with blood, lacerated by nails and teeth, the heroes appeared like flowering *kiṃśuka* trees. Neither showed superiority in the fighting. Then Hanūmān hung a garland around Sugrīva's neck, and with the garland around his neck the hero shone as majestic Mount Malaya with a garland of clouds. When great archer Rāma saw Sugrīva give the sign, he drew his fine bow and aimed at Vālin. The twang of the bow was like that of a mill; Vālin, shot in the heart, tumbled. Hit in his weak spot, which was severed, and spitting blood from his mouth, he saw Rāma in position close by with Sumitrā's son. Reviling[1] Kākutstha, he fell swooning on the ground. Tārā[2] saw him on the ground, like a fallen moon. With Vālin[3] dead Sugrīva appropriated Kiṣkindhā and Tārā of the moon-like face, whose lord had fallen. Rāma lived for four months on the beautiful crest of Mālyavat, and, waited upon by Sugrīva, the wise warrior made his dwelling there.

Rāvaṇa,[4] after arriving in Lankā, was driven by lust; he installed Sītā in his palace, which was like the Nandana paradise, near an *aśoka* grove, which was like the hermitage of an ascetic. Thin[5] from thinking of her husband, wearing the garb of an ascetic, much given to fasting and mortification, the wide-eyed woman dwelled out her wretched nights there, living on fruit and roots. The[6] king of the Rākṣasas consigned to her guard Rākṣasīs who carried spears, swords, spikes, axes, clubs, and firebrands; one had two eyes, another three, or an eye in the forehead, with a long tongue or no tongue, with three breasts and one foot, three crowns and one eye. These and others with eyes blazing and hair shiny as a young elephant's sat by Sītā day and night, unwearyingly. Piśācīs[7] with awful voices and gruesome mien abused the woman of the long eyes in harshly articulated words: "Let us eat her, tear her up in pieces the size of sesame seeds, for she lives here in contempt of our master!"

Thus[8] did they revile her again and again; and, thoroughly frightened, she sighed from grief for her husband and said to them, "Gentle women, eat me soon, I have no more lust for life without my lotus-eyed man with the black curly hair. Will I not go without food,

1. 4.17. 2. 4.19. 3. 4.25. 4. Cf. 3.52–53, 5.12; 18. 5. 5.19. 6. Cf. 3.54; 5.20. 7. 5.21–22. 8. 5.23.

deprived of him whom I love as my life, and dry out my limbs like a snake in a palm tree? But I shall not go to any man but Rāghava—know that this is the truth, and do to me what is next." When[1] they heard these words of her, the rough-spoken Rākṣasīs went and told the Indra of the Rākṣasas everything from the beginning.

While they were gone, a Rākṣasī named Trijaṭā, who knew the Law
and was gentle-spoken, consoled Vaidehī: "Sītā,[2] I shall tell you
something, put your trust in me, friend. Let your fears disappear, fair-
thighed one, and listen to my words. There is a wise old bull-like
55 Rākṣasa by the name of Avindhya. Having the good of Rāma at heart,
he told me for your sake, "Let Sītā be told at my behest, after she has
been comforted and appeased, that her husband, the mighty Rāma, as
well as Lakṣmaṇa, is in good health. The illustrious Rāghava has made
an alliance with the king of the apes whose might matches Śakra's
and stands ready in your cause. Have no fear, timorous woman, of
Rāvaṇa, who is execrated by the world, for you are protected by the
curse of Nalakūbara, blameless woman. For of yore the evildoer has
been cursed, when he sought Rambhā for his wife, that he would be
impotent with the woman at his mercy and out of control of his
60 senses. Your husband will soon be here, under Sugrīva's protection
and in the company of Lakṣmaṇa, and he shall cleverly set you free
from here. For[3] I have had dream visions, most awesome and of
ghastly aspect, presaging the destruction of that evil-minded killer of
the family of Pulastya. For that wicked Stalker of the Night of the
ignoble deeds is terrifying and raises the fear of all by his nature and
his vicious character. In my dreams I have seen the portents of the
destruction of him who, his mind overcome by Time, rivals all the
Gods. Ten-headed Rāvaṇa, soaked with oil and shiny, often appeared
standing on a donkey cart and made as if to dance, while he was
65 sinking in the mud. Kumbhakarṇa and the others, naked and
disheveled, with red garlands and ointments, were dragged toward the
south. Only Vibhīṣaṇa remained, with a white umbrella, turbaned,
wearing bright garlands and ornaments, and ascended Mount Śveta.
His four councillors, decked with bright garlands and unguents, will
escape from the great danger and ascend Mount Śveta. Earth with her
oceans will be encircled by Rāma's missile, and your husband shall
fill all of earth with glory. I saw Lakṣmaṇa standing on a pile of bones,
70 eating honey and rice boiled in milk, and looking in all directions. I
have seen you often, weeping, your body wet with blood, protected by
a tiger and going toward the north. You shall find joy, Vaidehī, and
soon be rejoined by your husband and with his brother, the scion of
Raghu, O Sītā."

1. 5.25. 2. Omission until vs. 61. 3. 5.25.

When the young woman with the eyes of a tender doe heard these words of Trijaṭā she regained hope of a reunion with her husband; and when the gruesome, terrifying Piśācīs came back, they saw her as before seated with Trijaṭā.

Mārkaṇḍeya said:
265.1 Then[1] Rāvaṇa visited her, as she grieved for her husband, wretched,
wearing soiled clothes and the remnant of her jewels, weeping as a
devoted wife, while she was waited upon by the Rākṣasīs; she was
sitting on a slab of stone when he approached her. Dazed by Kandarpa,
the demon who was unvanquished in battle by Gods, Dānavas,
Gandharvas, Yakṣas, and Kiṃpuruṣas, went into the *aśoka* grove
5 smitten with the arrows of love. Dressed in divine robes, lustrous, with
polished jeweled earrings, and crowned with celestial flowers, he was
like spring embodied. Carefully adorned, he looked like a tree of wishes,
but in spite of his finery he was terrifying like an *aśvattha* tree in a
cremation field.
In the presence of the slender-waisted woman the Night Stalker
appeared as the planet Saturn in conjunction with Rohiṇī. Struck by
the arrow of the flower-crested God, he addressed the beautiful-hipped
young woman, who was like a frightened doe, and said, "Sītā, you
have sufficiently shown your husband your favor, now have grace for
me, my slender one, you must now be adorned. Love me in costly
ornaments and robes, woman of the beautiful hips, be my choicest
10 bride of all, fair one. I have daughters of the Gods, women of the royal
seers; I have daughters of the Dānavas, and women of the Daityas.
Fourteen crores of Piśācas wait on my word, twice that number again
of man-eating Rākṣasas of dreadful deeds, and three times as many
Yakṣas carry out my demands, while some of them have joined my
brother, the God of Riches. When I am in my drinking hall,
Gandharvas and Apsarās wait on me as they do on my brother, good
woman of the shapely thighs.
"I am the son of the brahmin seer and hermit Viśravas himself, and
the glorious tiding has been broadcast that I am the fifth of the World
15 Guardians. I have celestial foodstuffs and viands and many choices of
liqueurs. Let the ills brought on by your life in the forest be deleted—
become my life, fair-hipped one, a queen like Mandodarī."
At[2] these words the lovely-faced Vaidehī turned away from him,
and counting him no more than a straw in her heart, she said to the
lowly Night Stalker, showering her most beautiful thighs and
unsagging breasts with unpropitious tears, as she held her husband
for a God, "So often have I, by my misfortune, heard these desperate

1. 5.18. 2. 5.19.

20 words of yours, lord of the Rākṣasas! Hail to thee who enjoy your
pleasures—turn away these thoughts. I am another man's wife and
unattainable. Forever shall I be devoted to my husband. A wretched
human, I am not a suitable wife for you. If you violate a helpless
woman, what pleasure will you find? Your father is a brahmin, the
equal of Prajāpati, and born from Brahmā: how is it that you, who
equal a World Guardian, do not protect the Law? Your regal brother,
the King of Kings, the lord of riches, the friend of the Great Lord—have
you no shame in naming him?"
25 As she said this she began to weep, bouncing her breasts, and
covered her throat and face with her cloth. The long and well-knit
braid on the indignantly weeping woman's head, deep dark and
smooth, looked like a black snake. Upon hearing these very harsh
words uttered by Sītā, the witless Rākṣasa, though spurned, said
again, "The[1] crocodile-crested God may burn my limbs at will, Sītā,
but I will not, woman of the lovely hips and charming smile,
importune you, if you are unwilling. What indeed can I do, when even
now you are devoted to Rāma alone, a human and our staple?"
Having thus spoken to the woman of the flawless limbs, the lord of
the hosts of the Rākṣasas disappeared then and there, and went where
30 he listed. Thin from grief, Vaidehī, surrounded by the Rākṣasīs,
dwelled there while she was waited upon by Trijaṭā.

Mārkaṇḍeya said:

266.1 Rāghava[2] and Sumitrā's son, meanwhile, lived under Sugrīva's
protection on the peak of the Mālyavat and stared at the cloudless sky.
In the clear sky the enemy-killer saw the spotless moon followed by
the planets, constellations, and stars. Then he smelled the fragrance of
lotuses and water lilies on a cool breeze, and the mountain-dweller
was suddenly alerted. Downhearted, the Law-minded Rāma said in the
morning to the gallant Lakṣmaṇa, as he thought of Sītā captive in the
5 Rākṣasa's dwelling, "Go, Lakṣmaṇa, I know that the monkey king is
in the Kiṣkindhā, distracted by vulgar ways, ungrateful and keen on
his own profit. This fool, the lowest of his race, I have had consecrated
to be king of all the apes; cow-tailed monkeys and bears love him, for
I have slain Vālin, together with you, strong-armed scion of Raghu, in
the Kiṣkindhā Forest. I consider that monkey outcast an ingrate on
earth; for, Lakṣmaṇa, that fool, situated as he is, no more thinks of
me. I think he does not know how to keep a covenant, and in his
10 petty mind he surely holds me, his benefactor, in contempt. If he lazily
lies there indulging in pleasure, you must send him by Vālin's path to
the final destination of all creatures. But if that bull among apes acts in
our cause, then bring him here, Kākutstha, hurry and do not delay!"

1. 5.20 with variants. 2. 4.29.

At[1] his brother's words, Lakṣmaṇa, bent on the well-being and
behest of his betters, took his bright bow with arrows and string and
started, reached the entrance of the Kiṣkindhā, and entered without
being halted. The monkey king, thinking that he was angry, went out
to meet him. With his wife the courteous Sugrīva, king of apes, kindly
received him with the honor due to him. Sumitrā's son, afraid of
nothing, bowed, folded his hands, and told Rāma's entire message.
15 King[2] Sugrīva of the apes, with wife and retainers, was pleased, O
great king, and he said to Lakṣmaṇa, elephant among men, "I am not
a fool, Lakṣmaṇa, nor an ingrate or without mercy. Listen[3] what
efforts I have made to find Sītā. I have dispatched trained monkeys to
all the quarters, and set for all a date to return within a month. They
are to search the entire sea-girt earth with forest, mountains, and
cities, villages, towns, and mines. The month will be full in another
five nights, then you shall hear with Rāma what great service I have
20 rendered." At[4] these words of the sagacious monkey king, Lakṣmaṇa
shed his ire and with happy spirits honored Sugrīva in return.
Accompanied[5] by Sugrīva he went to Rāma on Mount Mālyavat and
informed him of the development of their task.

As[6] promised, the monkey chiefs by the thousands returned after
searching the three quarters, but those who had gone south did not.
They told Rāma that they had searched the sea-girt earth, but had not
found Sītā and Rāvaṇa. Kākutstha, putting his hopes in the bull-like
25 apes who had gone south, kept up his sorrowful spirits. When[7] a
period of two months had passed, some monkeys came in haste to
Sugrīva and told him, "That opulent big wood Madhuvana, which
Vālin always guarded and now you, chief of the monkeys, is now
being enjoyed by the son of the Wind, and by Vālin's son Angada and
other bulls among apes, king, whom you had sent out to search the
south."

When[8] he heard of their conduct, he thought that they had been
successful, for such is the behavior of servants who have done their
duty. The wise ape told Rāma, and Rāma too inferred that Sītā had
30 been found. Led by Hanūmān, the monkeys, now rested, came to their
king in Rāma's and Lakṣmaṇa's presence; and when Rāma saw
Hanūmān's walk and complexion, he was the more convinced that
Sītā had been found, O Bhārata. Headed by Hanūmān the self-
contented apes bowed properly to Rāma, Sugrīva, and Lakṣmaṇa.

Picking[9] up the bow and arrows, Rāma said to the newcomers,
"Will you bring me back to life? Have you been successful? Shall I
once more rule the kingdom of Ayodhyā, after slaying the enemies in
35 battle and recovering Janaka's daughter? I cannot bear to live without

1. 4.30; 33. 2. Cf. 4.34. 3. Cf. 4.36 ff. 4. Cf. 4.35. 5. Cf. 4.37. 6. 4.46. 7. 5.61. 8. 5.62. 9. 5.63.

freeing and killing foes in a war, bereft of my wife and exiled!"
To this word of Rāma the son of the Wind replied, "My message is
pleasing, Rāma: I have found Jānakī! After[1] searching the south with
its mountains, forests, and mines, we were tired, but[2] after some time
we saw a big cave. We entered it; it was many leagues long, dark, full
of thickets, and deep, and infested with worms. We went a long way
40 to sunlight, and there we saw close by a celestial palace. It[3] was, they
say, the dwelling of the Daitya Maya, Rāghava. A[4] female ascetic by
the name of Prabhāvatī was performing austerities there. She[5] gave
us all kinds of food and drink, and when we had eaten and regained
our strength, we went by the path she had pointed out away from
that place and on the ocean shore we saw Mounts Sahya and Malaya,
and saw Varuṇa's realm. And[6] we became dejected, distressed,
fatigued, and without any hope for life. We thought about the vast
ocean, many hundreds of miles wide, the domain of whales, crocodiles,
45 and large fish. Deciding to fast unto death, we sat there, and[7] as we
were talking, the story of the vulture Jaṭāyu came up. Thereupon[8] we
saw an ugly-looking and terrifying bird as big as a mountain peak,
another Garuḍa. He planned to eat us, came closer, and said, '*Bhoḥ*,
who is this that is telling the story of my brother Jaṭāyu? I am his
older brother Saṃpāti, king of the birds. In a contest with one another
we ascended to the assembly hall of the sun, and these wings of mine
burned off, but not those of Jaṭāyu. Then my long-seen brother became
the beloved king of the vultures, while I fell with burned wings on this
mountain.'

50 "When[9] he had spoken, we told him that his brother had been
killed, and in brief told him of your misfortune. And on hearing this
very bad news, O king, Saṃpāti dispiritedly asked us again, enemy-
tamer, 'Who is this Rāma, how was Sītā abducted, and how did
Jaṭāyu die? I wish to hear it all, best of monkeys.' I told him fully
about all the misfortune that had befallen you, and the reason of our
own fast unto death. Then[10] the king of the birds made us rise with
55 this word: 'I know Rāvaṇa and his great city Lankā. I have seen it on
the ocean shore in the valley of Mount Trikūṭa. Vaidehī will be there,
of that I have no doubt.' When[11] we heard his words, we all quickly
rose and took counsel together, enemy-burner, on how to jump the
ocean. Nobody resolved to cross the ocean, so[12] I myself entered my
father and jumped across the big sea, which measures the width of a
hundred leagues, after killing a marine Rākṣasī.

"There[13] I saw Sītā; she was in the women's quarters of Rāvana,
fasting and performing austerities, yearning to see her husband,

1. 4.48. 2. 4.49. 3. 4.50. 4. 4.49. 5. 4.50 with variants and omissions. 6. 4.52; 55. 7. Omitted, cf. 4.55. 8. 4.55. 9. 4.56. 10. 4.57. 11. 4.63. 12. 5.1. 13. 5.13 with variants.

wearing[1] her hair in a tuft, her body dirty and soiled, lean, wretched,
and miserable. Having recognized Sītā by these various marks on her,
60 I approached and told the lady in secret, 'Sītā,[2] I am the monkey who
is the son of the Wind, the envoy of Rāma! I have come here through
the sky, hoping to catch sight of you. The two princes, Rāma and
Sumitrā's son Lakṣmaṇa, are in good health and under the protection
of Sugrīva, the king of the monkeys. They ask about your health, and
so out of friendship does Sugrīva. Your husband will come with the
monkeys, have confidence in me, queen, I am a monkey, not a
Rākṣasa.' Sītā[3] thought for a while, then she replied to me, 'From
65 Avindhya's words I know that you are Hanūmān: Avindhya is a
strong-armed Rākṣasa, respected by the elders, and he told me about
Sugrīva surrounded by councillors like you. Go[4] now,' said Sītā to me,
and gave me this jewel by which the blameless woman had been
sustained all this time. So that you will place trust in all this, Jānakī
told me the story of the reed cast at the crow on Mount Citrakūṭa, so
that you should recognize it, tiger among men. I made myself listen to
it, then[5] set the city on fire and came back." Rāma[6] paid honor to the
bringer of good news.

Mārkaṇḍeya said:

267.1 As[7] Rāma was sitting there with them, the chiefs of the monkeys
came to him at Sugrīva's behest. Surrounded by a thousand crores of
agile monkeys, the illustrious Suṣeṇa, Vālin's father-in-law, came to
Rāma. The powerful monkey kings Gaja and Gavaya appeared
separately in the midst of a hundred crores. Leading sixty thousand
crores, Gavākṣa of frightening aspect made his appearance, the cow-
5 tailed monkey, O great king. Renowned Gandhamādana, who dwelled
on the Gandhamādana, brought a thousand crores of awesome tawny
monkeys. The wise ape named Panasa, of very great strength, led ten,
twelve, and thirty-five crores. The illustrious and mighty monkey elder,
Dadhimukha by name, brought a large army of tawny monkeys of
terrible might. Jāmbavat appeared with a hundred thousand crores
of black, streaked-faced bears. These and many other leaders of
10 monkey herds, innumerable, assembled in the cause of Rāma. There
arose a tumultuous noise, as of roaring lions, as the *śirīṣa*-flower-like
creatures ran hither and thither. Some stood as tall as mountain peaks,
others were the size of buffalo, or like autumn clouds and with faces
red as ground vermilion. Flying up, falling down, leaping, and raising
the dust, the monkeys foregathered from all directions. With Sugrīva's
approval, they set up camp there, this vast world of monkeys like
the ocean at high tide.

1. 5.17. 2. 5.29 ff. 3. Omitted. 4. 5.36. 5. 5.38; 39. 6. 6.1. 7. 4.39.

15 When[1] all those monkey kings had assembled, the illustrious Rāma
marched out with Sugrīva, his army arrayed in ranks, as though to
beat the worlds to pieces; it was on an auspicious day under a
favorable star and at an honored hour. The vanguard was Hanūmān,
the son of the Wind, while Sumitrā's son, afraid of nothing, brought
up the rear. The two scions of Raghu, with their wrist and finger
guards tied on, shone amidst these monkey worthies like sun and
moon amidst the planets. The monkey army, armed with *śāla* trees,
palms, and rocks, appeared like a very vast rice field at sunrise.
Guarded by Nala, Nīla, Angada, Krātha, Mainda, and Dvivida, the
very huge army marched in order to accomplish Rāma's purpose.
20 Passing through duly blessed countries, which abounded in roots and
fruit, were abundant with honey and meat, rich in water, and
salubrious, and camping unopposed on mountain ridges, the monkey
army came upon the salty ocean. The troops with their many
pennants, which looked like another ocean, went into the coastal
forest and set up camp there.

Thereupon[2] the illustrious son of Daśaratha said to Sugrīva, amidst
the chiefs of the apes, this timely word: "Do ye know by what means
to jump the ocean? This army is huge and the ocean hard to cross."
25 Some apes, of keen mind, said, "The monkeys are unable to jump the
entire distance of the sea." Others decided on boats, others on various
ways of jumping. But Rāma said, gentling them, "No, all these
monkeys are not able to jump the hundred-league-wide ocean, heroes.
This is not your final view. There are not enough boats to ferry over
this massive army, and why should people like us do damage to the
merchants? Besides, the enemy might strike this vast army, if it is
broken up. Crossing either by jumping or by rafts does not look right
30 to me. No,[3] I shall attack the ocean with a ruse and press it back; and
the One who dwells underneath will show himself to me. And if he
does not show a way, I shall set it afire with mighty and irresistible
missiles that blaze fiercely with fire and wind."

Having[4] spoken, Rāma and Sumitrā's son touched water ritually on
spread *kuśa* grass and pressed back the ocean. The Ocean appeared in
a dream to Rāghava, the illustrious God who is the husband of rivers
and streams; he was surrounded by water monsters. "Son of
Kausalyā," he addressed him, and, in the midst of hundreds of mines
35 of pearls, went on to say gently, "Tell me what I can do to help you,
bull among men." Rāma replied, "I am an Ikṣvāku, your kinsman.
I want you to make a path for my army, lord of the rivers, by which
I can go and kill ten-headed Rāvaṇa, defiler of the Paulastyas. If you
will not make way at my bidding, I shall dry you up with arrows that
have been enchanted with divine spells." Having heard Rāma's word,

1. 6.4. 2. 6.13. 3. 6.14 with variants. 4. 6.15 with variants.

the Ocean folded his hands and said, pained, "I do not wish to obstruct you. I am not putting obstacles in your way. Listen to what I say,
40 Rāma, and do the needful. If I make way for your marching army at your behest, others will order me likewise under the threat of their bows. But there is a monkey here called Nala, who is respected by the artisans, the powerful son of Viśvakarman, the God Carpenter. If he throws wood, straw, and rock into me, I will endure it all, and it will become a causeway." Having spoken he disappeared.

Rāma said to Nala, "Make a causeway in the ocean. You are capable of it, I think." By this means Kākutstha had a causeway built,
45 ten leagues wide and a hundred long, which even now is famous on earth as Nala's Bridge and exists by Rāma's orders, tall as a mountain.

The[1] law-spirited Vibhīṣaṇa, the brother of the chief of the Rākṣasas, met Rāma there with his four councillors, and great-minded Rāma welcomed him. Sugrīva feared that he might be a spy. When[2] Rāghava had satisfied himself about the truth from the other's movements, gestures, and deportment, he paid honor to him. He consecrated Vibhīṣaṇa king of all the Rākṣasas, and made him the
50 friend and councillor of Lakṣmaṇa. And[3] at Vibhīṣaṇa's advice he crossed with his army the ocean by way of that causeway for the space of a month, O lord of men. When he got there and came to the gardens of Laṅkā, which were many and large, he had them all laid waste by the monkeys. There[4] were two Rākṣasas, Śuka and Sāraṇa, ministers of Rāvaṇa, who were spies in the guise of monkeys, and Vibhīṣaṇa caught them. When the Night Stalkers assumed their own Rākṣasa forms, Rāma showed them to the army, and later let them go. After[5] encamping his army in a park, the hero sent the wise ape Angada as his envoy to Rāvaṇa.

Mārkaṇḍeya said:

268.1 When[6] he had bivouacked the army in this forest, with plentiful water and food and abounding in fruit and roots, Kākutstha guarded it properly. Rāvaṇa fortified Lankā as prescribed by the science; the city was naturally impregnable, with heavy walls and watch towers, the moat being bottomless and teeming with fish and crocodiles; seven moats there were, impassable, reinforced with spikes of *khadira* wood, hard to storm because of catapults, war towers, and rocks, guarded by soldiers with jars filled with poisonous snakes and resin powder,
5 attended with clubs, firebrands, iron spikes, spears, swords, and battle axes, hundred-killers, and cudgels dipped in beeswax. At all the city gates there were battle stations, stationary and movable, filled with foot soldiers and many elephants and horses.

1. 6.11. 2. 6.12. 3. Cf. 6.12. 4. 6.16. 5. 6.31. 6. 6.28.

Angada[1] approached the gate area of Lankā, was announced to the lord of the Rākṣasas, and entered without a care. In the midst of many crores of Rākṣasas the powerful ape shone like the sun surrounded by garlands of clouds. He approached Paulastya, who was accompanied by his ministers, addressed him, and eloquently began to voice the message of Rāma: "Sire, Rāghava, the glorious king of Kosala, sends you this timely word: accept it and carry it out! Countries and cities that incur a king of unmade soul who is bent on bad policy are themselves the victims of such a policy, and destroyed. It is you alone who have committed a crime by abducting Sītā forcibly. But this will lead to the slaughter of others who are innocent. Before this you have, possessed by pride and strength, done injury to forest-dwelling seers and shown even the Gods your contempt. You have killed royal seers and taken their weeping wives. Now the fruit of your wrongdoing has matured. I shall kill you with your ministers. Be a man and give battle! Behold the power of this bow of mine, a human Stalker of the Night. Set Sītā Jānakī free! If you fail to do so, I shall rid the world of Rākṣasas with sharp arrows."

When he heard the harsh words spoken by the messenger, King Rāvaṇa could not bear them and was insensate with rage. Thereupon four Night Stalkers, who understood the signs of their master, seized him by his four limbs, as birds attack a tiger. Angada leapt upward to a terrace with the Rākṣasas hanging on to his limbs, and the speed of his jump caused the Night Stalkers to fall on the ground, with broken hearts, reeling under the blow. He left and jumped down again from the palace roof and, after crossing the city of Lankā, returned to his troops. Angada went to the Kosala king and reported everything, and then the splendid ape took rest, complimented by Rāghava.

Thereupon[2] the scion of Raghu had the wall of Lankā breached by the total attack of wind-fast monkeys. Lakṣmaṇa, assigning the lead to Vibhīṣaṇa and the king of the bears, tore down the southern city gate that was close to impregnable. He fell upon Lankā with a thousand crores of vermilion-red, war-seasoned monkeys. With the monkeys jumping up, flying about, and leaping down, the sun became invisible and its light was darkened by the dust. Astounded, the Rākṣasas everywhere with their women and elders, O king, saw their wall turn orange with these monkeys that looked like rice shoots, with the color of *śirīṣa* flowers, hued like the morning sun, and white as reeds. They broke the bejeweled pillars and the catapult towers and scattered the machines whose powers were broken and destroyed. They took the hundred-killers, the wheels, war towers, and rocks and scattered them with the speed of their arms in the center of Lankā. The hordes of Rākṣasas that manned the wall took flight by the hundreds when

1. 6.31, midway. 2. 6.31, beginning.

assailed by the monkeys. Then, on the orders of their king, fierce-
looking Rākṣasas who could change their forms came out by the
hundreds of thousands, and, raining showers of weapons, they put the
forest-dwellers to flight, clearing the wall with a show of extreme
bravery. The wall was once more made clear of monkeys by the
35 terrible looking Night Stalkers, who resembled piles of beans. Many
bulls of the monkeys fell, their bodies pierced by spikes, and so did
Rākṣasas fall, broken, off the pillars and the gate ramparts. It became
a hair-to-hair battle between the Rākṣasas and the monkeys as the
warriors ate one another with nail and tooth. They gasped their last
on both sides as they were hit and fell on the ground, but they did not
let go of one another. Rāma rained masses of arrows on Lankā like a
cloud, and they killed Rākṣasas. Sumitrā's son, too, indefatigable, shot
iron arrows from his sturdy bow at the Rākṣasas on the fortifications
40 and felled them. Then, on Rāghava's orders, the armies withdrew now
that Lankā was destroyed and Rāma had the upper hand, finding aim
everywhere.

Mārkaṇḍeya said:

269.1 Then,[1] while the soldiers were camping, some groups of Rākṣasa
and Piśāca followers of Rāvaṇa attacked them, Parvaṇa, Pūtana,
Jambha, Khara, Krodhavaśa, Hari, Praruja, Aruja, Praghāsa, and
others. The evil ones attacked invisible, but Vibhīṣaṇa put an end to
their invisibility; and once they were sighted the powerful and far-
jumping monkeys killed them all, O king, and they fell lifeless on the
5 ground. Unable to bear this, Rāvaṇa marched out with his army,
which he arrayed in the order of Uśanas, and had them take on the
monkeys. Rāghava, however, marched out against ten-faced Rāvaṇa
with his arrayed army and opposed the Rākṣasa with the battle
formation of Bṛhaspati. Rāvaṇa and Rāma engaged and gave battle,
and so Lakṣmaṇa likewise fought with Indrajit, Sugrīva with
Virūpākṣa, Nikharvaṭa with Tāra, Nala with Tuṇḍa, Paṭuśa with
Panasa. Whomever one considered his match he engaged and fought
10 him in the hour of battle, relying on the strength of his arms. And the
engagement, raising the fears of the fearful, grew and grew, hair-
raising and frightful, as of yore between the Gods and the Asuras.
Rāvaṇa got to Rāma with spears, spikes, and swords raining down,
and Rāma to Rāvaṇa with sharp iron arrows. Likewise Lakṣmaṇa to
cautious Indrajit with arrows that cut into weak spots, while Indrajit
too pierced Sumitrā's son with many arrows. Vibhīṣaṇa pelted
Prahasta, and Prahasta Vibhīṣaṇa, with bird-feathered honed arrows,
without a care. There was a clash of powerful grand weapons, which
distressed all three worlds, both moving and standing.

1. 6.32–33.

Mārkaṇḍeya said:
270.1 Then[1] Prahasta suddenly came at Vibhīṣaṇa and, roaring, the
rough fighter beat him with his club; but the sagacious and strong-
armed champion did not stagger under the terrible impact of the club
and stood firm. Vibhīṣaṇa took his big spear Śataghaṇṭā, enchanted it,
and threw it at his head. The fast-flying weapon, which whirred as a
shaft of lightning, cut off the Rākṣasa's head and he was seen to be
5 falling to the ground, like a tree broken by the wind. When
Dhūmrākṣa saw that the Night Stalker Prahasta had fallen in battle,
he stormed at great speed at the monkeys. His terrifying army, which
resembled a monsoon cloud, attacked, and as soon as they saw that,
the bulls of the monkeys were suddenly scattered. When he saw them
suddenly scatter, Hanūmān, tiger among monkeys, attacked, standing
his ground. And upon seeing the son of the Wind holding his ground
in the battle, all the monkeys returned again with great speed, O king.
There arose a tumultuous and hair-raising noise from the armies of
10 Rāma and Rāvaṇa that were storming at each other. As the ghastly,
blood-smeared battle went on, Dhūmrākṣa drove the monkey army to
flight with his arrows. Hanūmān, son of the Wind, vanquisher of his
rivals, quickly intercepted the mighty Rākṣasa. A frightful fight
developed between the monkey and Rākṣasa heroes who sought to
vanquish each other, as between Indra and Prahlāda. The Rākṣasa
beat the monkey with maces and clubs, and the monkey struck back
with trees, trunk and branches and all. Thanks to his greater size, the
sagacious Hanūmān, son of the Wind, killed Dhūmrākṣa, with horses,
chariot, and charioteer.
15 When the monkeys saw the great Rākṣasa Dhūmrākṣa killed, their
confidence returned and they attacked and killed the soldiers. Being
slaughtered by the strong monkeys, who were flushed with victory, the
Rākṣasas lost heart and in fear fell back on Lankā. Broken, sole
survivors, the Night Stalkers fell back on the city, and they all related
to King Rāvaṇa what had happened. On learning from them that
Prahasta and the great archer Dhūmrākṣa with his army had been
killed in battle by the bull-like monkeys, he sighed very deeply, and
jumped from his fine seat. And[2] he said, "The time has come for
Kumbhakarṇa to go to work." After saying this, he awakened with all
kinds of loud musical instruments the somnolent Kumbhakarṇa, who
was sleeping; and when he had woken him up with great trouble and
the mighty Kumbhakarṇa was sitting happily and idly, but no longer
asleep, the ten-headed King of the Rākṣasas said to him, "You are
lucky that you can sleep so well, Kumbhakarṇa, and do not know what
a frightful and dangerous time it is! This Rāma has crossed the ocean
with his monkeys by way of a causeway, and in utter contempt for us

1. 6.41–42. 2. 6.48–55.

all is perpetrating a great slaughter. For I abducted his wife Sītā
Jānakī, and he bridged the vast ocean with a causeway and has now
25 come to set her free. He has killed the great Prahasta and others, our
kinsmen. No one but you can slay him, enemy-plower! He is armored
—march out now, strong of the strong, and kill Rāma and all the
others in battle, enemy-tamer! Dūṣana's two younger brothers,
Vajravega and Pramāthin, will follow you with a large force."

Having thus spoken to the puissant Kumbhakarṇa, the king of the
Rākṣasas ordered Vajravega and Pramāthin to the task. The heroes
submitted to Rāvaṇa, and Dūṣaṇa's brothers placed Kumbhakarṇa in
the lead and marched quickly out of the city.

Mārkaṇḍeya said:

271.1 When Kumbhakarṇa marched out of the city with his followers, he
saw before him in position the army of the monkeys, flushed with
victory. The monkeys ran to him, surrounded him on all sides, and
beat him with many huge trees, while others lacerated him with their
nails, ignoring their acute danger. The monkeys, embattled on the
pathways of the battlefield, struck the terrible chief of the Rākṣasas
with all kinds of weapons. But while he was being beaten, he laughed
out loud and devoured the apes, such as Panasa, Gavākṣa, and the
5 ape Vajrabāhu. And on seeing the harrowing deeds of the Rākṣasa
Kumbhakarṇa, Tāra, and the others screeched out in terror. Sugrīva
ran to the screeching Tāra and the other monkey herds, fearless before
Kumbhakarṇa. The great-minded elephant among monkeys
vehemently fell on Kumbhakarṇa, and beat him powerfully on the
head with a *śāla* tree; great-spirited and nimble Sugrīva splintered the
śāla on Kumbhakarṇa's head, but he failed to as much as stagger.
Kumbhakarṇa roared and laughed and, fully awakened by the blow of
the *śāla*, he took Sugrīva by the arms and pulled him away forcibly.
10 But Lakṣmaṇa, the joy of his friends, saw Sugrīva being abducted by
Kumbhakarṇa, and the hero hastened to him. Lakṣmaṇa, killer of
enemy heroes, attacked and shot at Kumbhakarṇa a tall swift arrow
with a golden nock. The arrow penetrated his body cover and body
and came out in back, smeared with blood, and split open the ground.
His rib case pierced, the great archer Kumbhakarṇa let go of the
monkey king, took a slab of rock for his weapon, and stormed at
Sumitrā's son, raising the large slab. As he came storming at him,
15 Lakṣmaṇa sliced off his upraised arms with two honed razors. The
other became four armed. Sumitrā's son cut off all of the other rock-
bearing arms with honed razors, displaying his deft weapon. He now
became a giant with many legs, heads, and arms, and Lakṣmaṇa
burned him, who resembled a mass of mountains, with the Brahmā
spell. Felled by the divine weapon, the great hero fell in the battle like

a tree in full shoot that is burned down by a shaft of lightning.
When the Rākṣasas saw the impetuous Kumbhakarṇa, the like of
Vṛtra, fallen dead on the ground, they fled in terror. Upon seeing the
warriors flee, Dūṣaṇa's younger brothers stopped them and furiously
20 attacked Lakṣmaṇa. Sumitrā's son received the furiously attacking
pair, Vajravega and Pramāthin, with his winged arrows. A terrifying
battle developed, hair-raising, between Dūṣaṇa's younger brothers and
the sagacious Lakṣmaṇa, O son of Pṛthā. He showered the Rākṣasas
with a vast rain of arrows, and the two furious heroes too showered
him. The battle between the two, Vajravega and Pramāthin, and the
strong-armed son of Sumitrā lasted a while; then Hanūmān, son of
the Wind, took a mountain peak, attacked, and took the life of
25 Vajravega. Nīla attacked Dūṣaṇa's younger brother Pramāthin with a
big stone, and the powerful ape crushed him. Thereafter the ferocious
battle of the armies of Rāma and Rāvaṇa, which assailed each other,
continued once more. The forest-dwellers slew the Rākṣasas by the
thousands, and the Rākṣasas the monkeys—but more Rākṣasas fell
than monkeys.

Mārkaṇḍeya said:

272.1 Upon hearing that Kumbhakarṇa and his followers had been killed
in battle, as had the great archer Prahasta and the fierce Dhūmrākṣa,
Rāvaṇa said to his gallant son Indrajit, "Slayer of enemies, kill Rāma,
Sugrīva, and Lakṣmaṇa! For you, my good son, have earned blazing
fame by vanquishing the Thunderbolt-wielder in battle, the thousand-
eyed Consort of Śacī. Invisible or in the open, slay my enemies,
enemy-killer, with celestial weapons presented as boons—you are the
5 greatest of warriors. Rāma, Lakṣmaṇa, and Sugrīva are unable to
withstand the onslaught of your arrows, let alone their followers,
prince sans blame. The avenging of Khara, which Prahasta and
Kumbhakarṇa have left unfinished, strong-armed prince sans blame,
you yourself must achieve in battle! Delight me today by killing the
enemies and their soldiers with honed arrows, my son, as of yore by
fettering Vāsava!"

At[1] these words Indrajit consented, O king. He mounted his chariot
in full armor and drove quickly out to the battlefield. There the bull of
the Rākṣasas clearly shouted his name and challenged the luck-marked
10 Lakṣmaṇa to a fight. Lakṣmaṇa grasped his bow and arrows and ran
there, sowing terror with the clapping of his hands, as a lion frightens
small game. A grand and fierce battle began between the two, who
were both thirsty for victory, proficient in divine weaponry, and rivals
of each other. When Rāvaṇa's son did not get the better of him with
his arrows, that first warrior among the strong made an even greater

1. 6.35.

effort. He pressed him with fast-flying javelins, but Sumitrā's son
parried them as they came with sharp arrows and, cut down by the
sharp shafts, they fell down on the flat of the earth. Vālin's[1] illustrious
son Angada lifted a tree, ran to him with great speed, and hit him on
15 the head. Unperturbed, the heroic Indrajit aimed a missile at his chest,
but Lakṣmaṇa cut it down. Rāvaṇa's son hit the gallant Angada, who
had come close, with a club on the left side, but Vālin's powerful son,
bull among apes, did not heed the blow—the enemy-victor let angrily
go of a *śāla* trunk at Indrajit. The tree, which Angada hurled in a rage
to kill Indrajit, instead destroyed his chariot, with horses and
charioteer, O Pārtha. With his horses and charioteer dead, Rāvaṇa's
son leaped from his chariot and disappeared then and there through
20 his wizardry. Noticing[2] that the wizard Rākṣasa had disappeared,
Rāma went to that spot and watched over his army. The enemy took
aim and hit Rāma and the great warrior Lakṣmaṇa in all limbs with
arrows obtained through a boon; whereupon the champions Rāma
and Lakṣmaṇa both fought off Rāvaṇa's invisible son, who had
vanished by magic, with their arrows. Angrily he aimed arrows by the
hundreds and thousands at all the limbs of these lion-like men.
Searching for the invisible fiend, who shot arrows incessantly, the
25 monkeys took to the sky, grasping big rocks, and the invisible
Rākṣasa pierced them with his shafts, and, enveloped by his magic,
Rāvaṇa's heroic son thrashed them sorely. Covered with arrows, the
two gallant brothers Rāma and Lakṣmaṇa fell from the sky to the
ground, like the sun and the moon.

Mārkaṇḍeya said:

273.1 When[3] he saw the boundlessly puissant brothers felled, Rāvaṇa's
son trapped them with missiles obtained from a boon. And the two
heroic tigers among men, trapped by Indrajit on the battlefield with a
net of arrows, appeared as two birds trapped in a cage. Seeing them
fallen on the ground, covered with hundreds of arrows, the king of
apes Sugrīva stood all around him with his monkeys, Suṣena, Mainda,
5 Dvivida, Kumuda, Angada, Hanūmān, Nīla, Tāra, and Nala. Then
Vibhīṣaṇa[4] capable in his deeds, came to that spot and brought the
heroes back to consciousness with the spell of awakening. Sugrīva[5] rid
them instantly of the arrows by means of the thorn-rinsing herb over
which a divine spell had been cast. Returning to consciousness, the
great men arose, freed from the arrows, and soon the warriors'
sluggishness and fatigue were gone. Seeing Rāma cured of his fever,
Vibhīṣaṇa folded his hands, O Pārtha, and said to Rāma, scion of
Ikṣvāku, "This[6] Guhyaka has come to you from Mount Śveta, at the
10 behest of the king of kings, carrying this water. The great King Kubera

1. 6.34. 2. 6.35. 3. 6.35–36. 4. 6.39. 5. 6.40. 6. Omitted.

presents this water to you to enable you to see invisible creatures, enemy-burner. When this water has touched your eyes, you and whoever you will give it to will see the hiding creatures." "So be it," said Rāma, accepting the consecrated water, and he washed his eyes with it. So did the great-minded Lakṣmaṇa, as well as Sugrīva, Jāmbavat, Hanūmān, Angada, Mainda, Dvivida, Nīla, and most of the monkey chiefs. And it befell as Vibhīṣaṇa had said: their eyes at once became clairvoyant, Yudhiṣṭhira!

Indrajit,[1] having finished his task, told his father of his deeds, and they hastened to return to the main battlefield. Sumitrā's son, following Vibhīṣaṇa's advice, stormed at the furious enemy, who had returned with a lust for battle. Lakṣmaṇa, now that his consciousness had returned, wanted to kill off the enemy, who was flushed with victory, before he had done the daily rites, and hit him ferociously with arrows. Then began a battle between both who sought to vanquish the other, a strange and wondrous battle, as between Śakra and Prahlāda. Indrajit cut Sumitrā's son to the quick with sharp arrows that hit weak spots and were fire to the touch, and Lakṣmaṇa hit Rāvaṇa's son. Faint with rage from the strikes of Lakṣmaṇa's arrows, he shot eight arrows like venomous snakes at Lakṣmaṇa. Listen to me as I tell you how Sumitrā's heroic son took the other's life with three feathered arrows that were fire to the touch. With one he severed the bow-wielding arm from his body, with the second he dropped the arm that held the iron arrows on the ground, with the third arrow, luminous and with a wide blade, he took his handsome, fair-nosed head with the sparkling earrings. The trunk, severed at the arms and the shoulders, was a fearful sight. After killing him, the strong man also killed his charioteer with his arrows. The horses carried the chariot into Lankā, and Rāvaṇa saw the chariot empty of his son.

When[2] Rāvaṇa saw that his son had been slain, his eyes rolled from fear and, stricken with sorrow and confusion, he made ready to kill Vaidehī. With sword in hand the wicked fiend hurried to her where she sat in the *aśoka* grove, yearning to see Rāma. But Avindhya, upon seeing the evil intention of the evil-minded Rāvaṇa, appeased his rage—listen with what argument. "You who have the splendid position of Great King must not kill a woman. Killed is a woman already when she is captive in your house, even if she is not separated from her body, so I think. Kill her husband! When he is dead, she is dead. Even the God of the Hundred Sacrifices is not your equal in bravery, for repeatedly you have caused Indra and the Thirty to tremble in battle." With these and many such words, Avindhya

1. 6.60; 67–68. 2. 6.80.

appeased the enraged Rāvaṇa, who followed his advice. The Night Stalker decided to march out himself, and he put on his sword and ordered his chariot readied.

Mārkaṇḍeya said:

274.1 Thereupon[1] the furious Ten-headed Rāvaṇa, whose beloved son had
been slain, mounted his chariot, which was adorned with gold and
gems, and rode out. Surrounded by ghastly Rākṣasas who bore all
kinds of weapons, he stormed at Rāma, shattering the leaders of
monkey herds. While he came rushing on angrily, Mainda, Nīla, Nala,
Angada, Hanūmān, and Jāmbavat surrounded him with their armies.
The leaders of monkey and bear packs annihilated Ten-headed
5 Rāvaṇa's army with trees before his very eyes. When[2] he saw his
army being mauled by the enemies the wizard Rāvaṇa, lord of the
Rākṣasas, displayed his magic. The hundreds and thousands of
Rākṣasas who had departed from their bodies were seen to return with
arrows, spears, and javelins. Rāma slew all the Rākṣasas with his
divine weapon. The overlord of the Rākṣasas once more resorted to
magic. Creating shapes of Rāma and Lakṣmaṇa, O Bhārata, Rāvaṇa
stormed at Rāma and Lakṣmaṇa. Upon reaching Rāma and Lakṣmaṇa
the Night Stalkers fell upon them, king, holding up their tall bows.
10 Sumitrā's son, scion of Ikṣvāku, on seeing the wizardry of the king
of the Rākṣasas, said to Rāma this mighty word, unperturbed: "Slay
the evil Rākṣasas who resemble you!" Then Rāma slew the Rākṣasas
who resembled him.

Thereupon,[3] on a chariot yoked with bay horses, bright as the son, Mātali, Indra's charioteer, came to Rāma on the battlefield.

Mātali said:

"This is the glorious chariot Jaitra, drawn by bay horses, of
Maghavan himself. With this noble chariot Śakra has slain Daityas and
Dānavas by the hundreds in battle, Kākutstha, tiger among men. On
this chariot, with me in attendance, you must hurry and kill Rāvaṇa
15 on the battlefield. Do not tarry!" When he heard this, he distrusted
the truth of Mātali's words. "It is a magic of the Rākṣasa." Vibhīṣaṇa
said to him, "This is not a magic of the evil-spirited Rāvaṇa, O tiger
among men. Therefore quickly mount the chariot of Indra, splendid
warrior." Joyously Kākutstha replied to Vibhīṣaṇa, "So I shall!" and
filled with ire he swiftly drove to Ten-headed Rāvaṇa on the chariot.
Routed by Rāvaṇa, the creatures screeched, and in heaven the celestial
lion roars roared to the beat of drums. The Night Stalker hurled at
Rāma a fearful spike like Indra's thunderbolt, as though it were the
20 upraised staff of Brahmā. Halfway, Rāma splintered the spike with

1. 6.83. 2. 6.87. 3. 6.90.

sharpened arrows. When he saw this rare feat, fear invaded Rāvaṇa.
Then the raging ten-headed fiend nimbly let loose sharp shafts at Rāma by the thousands and myriads, and all kinds of weapons, *bhuśuṇḍis*, spikes, cudgels, battle axes, javelins of many shapes, and hundred-killers with razor-sharp blades. When they saw the monstrous wizardry of Ten-headed Rākṣasa, all the monkeys fled in terror in all directions. Kākutstha took a superb arrow with fine feathers, fine head, and golden nock from his quiver and laid it on with the Brahmā spell.
25 This choice arrow Rāma enchanted with the Brahmā spell, and the Gods and Gandharvas led by Śakra rejoiced at the spectacle. Gods, Gandharvas, and Kiṃpuruṣas knew that the enemy Rākṣasa now had little life left, because of the invocation of the Brahmā spell.

Rāma[1] shot off the boundlessly powerful and dread arrow, which was to spell the death of Rāvaṇa, like the upraised staff of Brahmā. Enveloped in fiercely blazing fire, it set the chief of the Rākṣasas afire with chariot, horses, and charioteer. And the Gods, Gandharvas, and
30 Cāraṇas rejoiced, seeing Rāvaṇa killed by Rāma of unsullied deeds. The five elements departed from the lordly Rāvaṇa, for he was toppled in all worlds by the power of the Brahmā spell. The humors of his body, his flesh and blood burned with the Brahmā spell until they vanished; and no ashes were found.

Mārkaṇḍeya said:

275.1 After[2] slaying Rāvaṇa, the king of the Rākṣasas, the lowly enemy of the Gods, Rāma and Sumitrā's son were overjoyed. When the ten-headed fiend had been killed, the Gods led by the seers paid honor to the strong-armed hero with benedictions and blessings for victory. All the Gods praised Rāma of the lotus-leaf eyes, as did the Gandharvas and the celestials, with rains of flowers and words. When they had paid honor to Rāma, they went back whence they had come. All of space resembled one huge festival, O undefeated king.

5 Glorious Rāma, the lord victor of enemy cities, after the killing of Ten-headed Rāvaṇa, gave Laṅkā to Vibhīṣaṇa. Behind[3] Vibhīṣaṇa and Sītā, the ancient wise minister named Avindhya came out, and he said to the great-spirited Rāma, who was prey to distress, "Great-spirited one, receive your queen of chaste conduct, the daughter of Janaka." At these words the scion of Ikṣvāku dismounted from his superb chariot and gazed at Sītā, who was concealed by tears. As he was looking at Sītā of the lovely limbs standing on the wagon gaunt with grief, her body caked with dirt, her hair matted, wearing a black
10 robe, Rāma[4] suspected her of having been touched, and he said to Vaidehī, "Go, Vaidehī, you are free. I have done what I had to do. Once you found me as a husband, good woman, you were not to grow

1. 6.97. 2. 6.100. 3. 6.102. 4. 6.103.

old in a Rākṣasa's house—that is why I killed the Night Stalker. For
how would a man like me, who knows the decision of the Law,
maintain even for an instant a woman who had been in another
man's hands? Whether you are innocent or guilty, Maithilī, I can no
more enjoy you, no more than an oblation that has been licked by a
dog."

When[1] the young queen heard this gruesome word, she suddenly
15 fell down in grief, like a cut banana tree. The flush on her face that
had sprung from joy instantly vanished, like a breathed-on mist on
a mirror. All the monkeys as well as Lakṣmaṇa stood motionless when
they heard Rāma's words—they might have been dead. Thereupon,[2]
on a chariot, the pure-spirited God of the Four Faces, Grandfather,
creator of the world, appeared to Rāghava, as did Śakra, Fire, Wind,
Yama, Varuṇa, the lord of the Yakṣas, Bhagavat, and the spotless
seven seers. And King Daśaratha in a divine and luminous bodily
form, riding a precious and resplendent chariot that was yoked with
20 wild geese. And the entire sky crowded with Gods and Gandharvas
shone like the autumn sky dotted with stars. In[3] their midst Vaidehī
stood up, and the beautiful woman spoke this word to wide-chested
Rāma: "Prince, I am not angry with you, for I know the ways of
women and of men. Listen to my words. The wind of restless motion
that breathes in all creatures shall leave my spirit, if I have done
wrong! Fire, water, ether, earth, and wind shall leave my spirit, if I
25 have done wrong!" Thereupon[4] there spoke a Voice from the sky,
reverberating through all the quarters, holy, and gladdening the great-spirited monkeys.

The Wind said:

Rāghava,[5] O Rāghava, it is the truth! I am the wind of restless motion. Maithilī is innocent, king—reunite with your wife!

The Fire said:

I am the one that dwells within the body, scion of Raghu. Maithilī has not erred in the least, Kākutstha.

Varuṇa said:

The[6] juices in all creatures' bodies spring from me, Rāghava. Verily I tell you to take Maithilī back!

Brahmā said:

Son, for you to act here like this is not strange in you who obey the
Law of the royal seers and who walk the path of good conduct, good
30 man. Listen to these my words. You have brought down, hero, the
enemy of the Gods, Gandharvas, Snakes, Yakṣas, Dānavas, and the
great seers. Him, who had become, by my own grace, invincible to all
creatures. The evil-doer was ignored for some time for some reason.
Then the evil-spirited fiend abducted Sītā for his own death, and I

1. 6.104. 2. 6.105. 3. Cf. 6.104. 4. 6.106. 5. Omitted. 6. Omitted till vs. 35.

protected her by means of Nalakūbara's curse—he had once been told that if he sought the favors of any one woman who did not love him his body was sure to burst a hundredfold as a result. Have no doubt at all about this. Take her back, resplendent man. Like an Immortal yourself, you have accomplished a great feat.

Daśaratha said:

35 I[1] am pleased with you, my son. Hail to thee! I am your father Daśaratha. I give my permission—and rule the kingdom, best of men!

Rāma said:

I salute you, Indra among kings, if you are my begetter! I shall go to the lovely city of Ayodhyā at your behest.

Mārkaṇḍeya said:

Joyously, O overlord of men, his father said again, "Go and rule Ayodhyā, Rāma of the red-colored eyes!" Then Rāma bowed to the Gods and, saluted by his friends, was reunited with his wife, as great Indra with Paulomī. The enemy-burner thereupon gave a boon to Avindhya and bestowed wealth and honor on the Rākṣasī Trijaṭā.
40 Brahmā, amid the Gods headed by Śakra, said, "Son of Kausalyā! What of boons can I give you that you desire?" Rāma chose a life by the Law, victory over his foes, and[2] the revival of the monkeys that had been killed by the Rākṣasas. And at Brahmā's pronouncing "So be it," the monkeys regained consciousness and stood up, great king. Majestic Sītā gave a boon to Hanūmān: "Son, you shall live as long as Rāma's fame lasts. By my grace, celestial delicacies shall wait on
45 you, Hanūmān of the orange eyes!" Then, while they were looking on, those men of unsullied deeds, the Gods led by Śakra disappeared.

Śakra's charioteer gazed at Rāma reunited with Jānakī and in the midst of his friends and said, overjoyed, "You have removed the unhappiness of Gods, Gandharvas, and Yakṣas, of men, Asuras, and Snakes, you whose prowess is your truth. All the worlds with Gods, Asuras, and Gandharvas, Yakṣas, Rākṣasas, and Snakes shall tell of you as long as earth holds out." Having spoken he took leave of Rāma, first of swordsmen, and having paid honor drove off on that chariot luminous as the sun.

50 Preceded[3] by Sītā and accompanied by Sumitrā's son and all the monkeys headed by Sugrīva, he arranged for the protection of Lankā, following Vibhīṣaṇa, and once more crossed the domain of crocodiles by the causeway, on the resplendent sky-going chariot Puṣpaka that went where he pleased, a master surrounded by his chief councillors. Then on the same seashore where he, the king, had slept, the law-spirited man spent the night with all the monkeys. At the right time Rāghava assembled them and paid homage to them, then dismissed
55 them all with a largess of jewels. When the monkey chiefs, the cow-

1. 6.107. 2. 6.108. 3. 6.109.

tails, and the bears had gone, Rāma returned with Sugrīva to the
Kiṣkindhā. Followed[1] by Vibhīṣaṇa and accompanied by Sugrīva, he
showed Sītā the forest from the Puṣpaka chariot. And upon reaching
the Kiṣkindhā, Rāma, greatest of warriors, consecrated Angada, who
had done his deed, to Young King. Rāma went with them, and
Sumitrā's son by the same road to his own city, and when he reached
the city of Ayodhyā, the[2] lord of the realm dispatched Hanūmān as
his envoy to Bharata.
60 He[3] observed all the other's gestures and told him the good news:
then the son of the Wind returned, and Rāma went to Nandigrāma.
There[4] he found Bharata sitting on his seat behind Rāma's sandals, his
body caked with dirt, and wearing a bark shirt. And upon meeting
again with Bharata and Śatrughna, heroic Rāma and Lakṣmaṇa
rejoiced, O bull of the Bharatas. Bharata and Śatrughna, likewise, on
being reunited with their elder brother and seeing Vaidehī, attained to
great joy. Bharata transferred the kingdom, which had been his
honored trust, to his returned brother, in a spirit of supreme happiness.
65 Then[5] under the constellation of Viṣṇu and on an auspicious day,
Vasiṣṭha and Vāmadeva together consecrated the hero.

After his consecration he gave the good monkey Sugrīva, with his friends, and also Vibhīṣaṇa Paulastya leave to go home. He honored them with all manner of gems—they were pleased and full of joy—and, reflecting on his duty, he dismissed them, regretfully. Rāghava paid homage to the Puṣpaka chariot and gave it with pleasure to Vaiśravaṇa. Then, assisted by Gods and seers, he offered, along the bank of the River Gomatī, ten unimpeded Horse Sacrifices, at which three kinds of stipends were given.

Mārkaṇḍeya said:

276.1 Thus, strong-armed king, did Rāma of boundless puissance of yore
incur misfortune and live in the forest. Do not grieve, tiger among
men, you are a baron, enemy-burner, you are walking the road of
blazing resolve that relies on the prowess of your arms; for not the
slightest bit of guile is found in you. On that road even Indra with the
Gods and Asuras might well despair. The Thunderbolt-wielder killed
Vṛtra, the unassailable Namuci, and the Rākṣasī Dīrghajihvā by
5 banding together with the Maruts. All good things in this world are
with him who has companions—what does he not conquer in battle
who has Dhanaṃjaya as his brother? And this Bhīma of terrible
prowess, strong of the strong, and the youthful twins, the great archers
who are the sons of Mādrī? Why do you despair, enemy-burner, with
such companions? With these great, God-like bowmen as your
comrades, who would be able to vanquish the army of the

1. 6.111. 2. 6.113. 3. 6.114. 4. 6.115. 5. 6.116.

Thunderbolt-wielder and his band of Maruts, you too will vanquish all your enemies in battle, bull of the Bharatas!

Look at Kṛṣṇā Draupadī, who was abducted by the evil-spirited
Saindhava king, strong and drunk with power; but she was recovered
by your great-spirited brothers, who accomplished a difficult feat; and
10 King Jayadratha was vanquished and captured. Rāma recovered
Vaidehī without such companions, and only after he had killed the
ten-headed Rākṣasa of terrible prowess in battle. Apes were his allies
and black-faced bears, creatures of a different race, king—think that
over in your mind.

Therefore, tiger among the Kurus, do not grieve, bull of the Bharatas! For great-spirited men like you do not sorrow, enemy-burner.

Vaiśaṃpāyana said:

Having thus been consoled by the wise Mārkaṇḍeya, the king shed his grief. And again he spoke.

3(42.b) Sāvitrī

277–83 (B. 293–99; C. 16616–16917)
277 (293; 16616). Yudhiṣṭhira asks Mārkaṇḍeya whether any woman has ever been such a devoted wife as Draupadī (1). King Aśvapati of the Madras, being childless, offers with the sāvitrī *formula. After eighteen years the Goddess Sāvitrī appears and predicts he shall have a splendid daughter (1–15). She is born and named Sāvitrī; when she grows up, no man chooses her for his wife (20–30). Her father tells her to find a man on her own, and she departs on a pilgrimage (30–40).*
278 (294; 16658). Nārada is visiting Aśvapati when Sāvitrī returns: she has found her man in Satyavat, a Śālva prince, whose father Dyumatsena had gone blind and was then dethroned (1–10). Nārada exclaims that her choice is bad: though otherwise a paragon, Satyavat is flawed by imminent death (10–20). When her father demands that she find another husband, she insists on her choice; Nārada agrees, and the king acquiesces (20–30).
279 (295; 16691). Aśvapati visits with Dyumatsena and marries Sāvitrī to Satyavat (1–10). Sāvitrī doffs her finery and wears hermit's garb; she satisfies everyone (15–20).
280 (296; 16714). When the day of death nears,

Sāvitrī undertakes a three-day vow, standing up day and night, though her father-in-law remonstrates with her; upon its conclusion the brahmins bless her (1–15). Satyavat is about to go to the forest, and she insists on accompanying him; her father-in-law gives his permission (15–25). They go out together (25–30).
281 (297; 16757). While Satyavat is splitting wood, he weakens; Sāvitrī rests his head in her lap (1–5). Yama, the God of death, appears and draws out Satyavat's thumb-sized soul; when he leaves, Sāvitrī follows him (5–15). She pronounces formulas of wisdom, for which Yama grants her boons: eyesight and restoration for her father-in-law (20–30), sons for her father (30–35), sons for herself and Satyavat (35–40), and finally Satyavat's life (40–50). Yama sends Satyavat back with Sāvitrī, and she returns to the corpse (50–60). Satyavat wakes up, and Sāvitrī postpones explanations, for night has fallen and his parents must be worrying (60–70). Satyavat agrees: he is the sole support of his parents (70–90). They set out, she carrying his ax (90–105).
282 (298; 16858). Dyumatsena regains his eyesight (1). Worried, he and his wife look for Satyavat (1–5). The ascetics console him (10–20). The couple returns, and they, the parents, and the brahmins sit by the fire (20–25). Satyavat explains that he was taken ill and slept. Sāvitrī relates how she knew of Satyavat's imminent death and won over Yama, who gave her many boons. She is praised (25–30).
283 (299; 16903). Erstwhile ministers of Dyumatsena arrive and relate the death of his kingdom's usurper. Joyously he returns to his land with his family. All the boons come to pass (1–10). Draupadī, too, shall save her husband (15).

Yudhiṣṭhira said:

277.1 I do not so much grieve over myself or these brothers, great hermit, or even the rape of the kingdom, as over Drupada's daughter. When we were brought to grief by evil men at the dicing, we were saved by Kṛṣṇā, and now again she was abducted forcibly from the forest of Jayadratha. Has there ever been a woman, or has one been heard of, who was so devoted to her husband and great as Drupada's daughter?

Mārkaṇḍeya said:

Hear, King Yudhiṣṭhira, of the greatness of well-born women. All this was achieved by the Princess Sāvitrī.

In the land of the Madras there was a Law-spirited king steeped in the Law, brahminic, a ready refuge, true to his promises, master of his senses, a sacrificer and generous giver, competent, beloved by city folk and countrymen, a king named Aśvapati, who was intent on the well-being of all creatures. A patient man, true-spoken and in control of his senses, he was childless, and with advancing age he became much worried; and he undertook a severe vow to beget a child. At mealtimes he restricted his food, he was continent and subdued his senses, he offered oblations a hundred thousand times with the *sāvitrī* formula, O best of kings, and forewent his meal every sixth time. For eighteen years he lived with this life rule, and when the eighteenth year was full, Sāvitrī became contented. She showed herself to the king, O prince, arising from the *agnihotra* with much joy. And the boon-granting Goddess said to the king, "I am pleased with your continence, purity, restraint, and self-control, and with your whole-hearted devotion to me, O king. Aśvapati, king of the Madras, choose whatever boon you desire, but pay heed at all times to the Law."

Aśvapati said:

I undertook this effort to obtain a child, out of desire for the Law. May I have many sons, goddess, to prosper my lineage. If you are pleased with me, goddess, this I choose as my boon. For offspring, as the twice-born have told me, is the highest Law.

Sāvitrī said:

I knew before this of this intention of yours, O king, and I have spoken to Grandfather in your cause for sons. By the favor decreed to you on earth by the Self-existent, good man, a splendid girl shall soon be born to you. And you should make no reply at all to this, for I am pleased and say this to you on behalf of Grandfather.

Mārkaṇḍeya said:

The king acknowledged Sāvitrī's word: "So be it!" And once more he besought her: "May it happen soon." Sāvitrī disappeared, and the king went home. And he happily lived in his kingdom, ruling his subjects by the Law.

Some time went by, then the king, who was strict in his vows, planted a seed in his eldest queen who abode by the Law. The fruit waxed in the Mālava woman, who was the daughter of a king, bull of the Bharatas, as in the bright fortnight the moon waxes in the sky. When her time came, she gave birth to a lotus-eyed daughter, and happily the king performed the rites for her. The brahmins and her father gave her the name of Sāvitrī, for she had been given by Sāvitrī when she was pleased with the oblations he had offered with the *sāvitrī*. The princess grew up like Śrī embodied, and in time the girl became adolescent. When people saw the young woman with the fine waist and broad hips, like a golden statue, they thought, "A divine maiden has come to us!" But no man chose her with the eyes of lotus petals, blazing with splendor, for her splendor kept him away.

She fasted, bathed her head, approached the Gods, offered into the
fire ritually, had brahmins recite on the moon-phase day; then the
divine woman took the remaining flowers, went to her great-spirited
30 father, like Śrī incarnate, and saluted her father's feet. She first offered
the leftover flowers to him, and afterward the fair-hipped woman stood
at her father's side. Looking at his grownup daughter, beautiful as a
Goddess, yet not asked by suitors, the king grew sorrowful.

The king said:

Daughter, the time has come to marry you off, but no one is asking
me, Seek a husband for yourself with virtues that match yours. If you
wish a man, tell me about him; I shall inquire and give you away.
Choose whomever you want, for I have heard the brahmins recite this
35 from the Book of the Law—listen, my pretty, as I repeat it—"A father
who does not give away is reprehensible, reprehensible is the husband
who does not cohabit; reprehensible is the son who does not protect
his mother when her husband has died." These words you hear from
me, so hurry to find a husband and act lest I become reprehensible to
the deities.

Mārkaṇḍeya said:

Thus he spoke to his daughter, and he assigned old councillors to
her retinue and nudged her along: "Go now!" She saluted her father's
feet shyly but spiritedly, and having learned her father's orders she set
out unhesitatingly. Riding on a chariot amidst the ancient councillors,
40 she went to the lovely forests of austerities of royal seers. After saluting
the feet of the estimable elders, my son, she gradually traversed all the
woods. At every ford the princess gave freely to the chief twice-born
and went from place to place.

Mārkaṇḍeya said:

278.1 Meanwhile, the king of the Madras received a visit from Nārada, O Bhārata, and sat in the center of the assembly hall conversing. At that time Sāvitrī returned from her tour of all the fords and hermitages, and she entered her father's house with the councillors. Seeing her father seated with Nārada, the lovely woman lowered her head to the feet of both of them.

Nārada said:

Where has your daughter been, and from where has she returned? Why are you not marrying the young woman to a husband?

Aśvapati said:

5 I sent her out for that very purpose, and she has come back just now. Hear from her yourself whom she has chosen for her husband.

Mārkaṇḍeya said:

Prompted by her father with: "Speak in detail," the lovely woman
obeyed and, as fate would have it, said, "In the land of the Śālvas
there is a law-spirited baron and king who is famed as Dyumatsena.
Later in life he became blind. An old enemy on his border, seeing his
opportunity, took the wise king's realm, when he had lost his eyesight
and his son was still a child. Together with his wife, whose calf was
young, he departed for the forest and in the vast wilderness he
10 performed austerities, being noble in his vows. His son Satyavat, born
in the city and grown up in the forest of austerities, I have chosen in
my heart as the husband who suits me."

Nārada said:

Woe! Sāvitrī has done a great wrong, king, choosing the virtuous Satyavat in her ignorance! His father speaks the truth, his mother speaks the truth, therefore the brahmins gave him the name Satyavat. When he was a child, he loved horses and fashioned them out of clay and made paintings of them; therefore he is also called Citrāśva.

The king said:

Does the prince now have splendor and wisdom, is Satyavat patient and brave, and does his father find joy in him?

Nārada said:

15 He is splendid as Vivasvat, wise as Bṛhaspati, brave as great Indra,
patient as earth herself.

Aśvapati said:

Is Prince Satyavat generous and brahminic, is he handsome and noble, and of pleasing mien?

Nārada said:

In generosity, according to his ability, he is the equal of Rantideva
Sāṃkṛti, he is brahminic and true-spoken like Śibi Auśīnara. He is
noble as Yayāti, of an aspect as pleasing as the moon, and in beauty
Dyumatsena's sturdy son is like one of the Aśvins. He is self-controlled,
he is kind and brave, he is true, he is the master of his senses, he is
20 friendly, ungrudging, modest, and steady. In short, those who have
grown old in austerities and character always praise him for the
uprightness and fortitude that are his.

Aśvapati said:

My lord, you reply to me that he is rich in all virtues—now mention also his flaws, if indeed he has any.

Nārada said:

He has but one flaw. A year from today Satyavat's life will expire and he will abandon his body.

The king said:

Go, Sāvitrī! Go, my pretty, and choose another husband! He has one great flaw that overshadows his virtues. The venerable Nārada, who is honored by the Gods, tells me that in a year his life will run out and he will abandon his body!

Sāvitrī said:

25 Once does an inheritance befall, once is a daughter married off, once does a father say: "I will give her"—these three each occur but once. Long-lived or short-lived, virtuous or virtueless, I choose my husband once, and will not choose a second. Having made the decision with my mind, I am stating it with my speech, and shall accomplish it with my actions later. My mind is my authority.

Nārada said:

Best of men, your daughter Sāvitrī's mind is firmly made up. She can in no way be made to stray from this Law. No other man possesses the virtues that Satyavat has; therefore it looks correct to me for you to give your daughter away.

The king said:

30 The words you have spoken, my lord, are true and should not be doubted. I shall so do this, for you are my guru, my lord.

Nārada said:

May there be no impediment in the giving away of your daughter Sāvitrī. We shall finish now. Good luck to you all.

Mārkaṇḍeya said:

Having thus spoken, Nārada flew up to the sky and went to heaven. And the king had all preparations made for his daughter's marriage.

Mārkaṇḍeya said:

279.1 Wondering about the very purpose of his marrying off his daughter,
the king brought together all the necessaries for the wedding. On a
lucky lunar day he summoned all the brahmin elders, the sacrificial
priests, and his house priest and set out with his daughter. The king
betook himself to the holy wood and hermitage of Dyumatsena and
approached the royal seer with his brahmins on foot. There he saw
the lordly blind king seated on a cushion of *kuśa* grass by a *śāla* tree.
5 The king paid due homage to the royal seer and presented himself in
restrained words. The Law-wise king offered him the guest gift, a seat,
and a cow; and he said to the king, "Why have you come?" And the
other informed him fully of his intention and task regarding Satyavat.

Aśvapati said:

This is my lovely daughter, her name is Sāvitrī, royal seer. You who know the Law, take her from me according to the Law as your daughter-in-law.

Dyumatsena said:

> We have lost our domain and live in the woods
> As ascetics who strictly adhere to the Law.

How will your daughter, who does not deserve it,
Bear the hardships of life as a forest recluse?

Aśvapati said:

10 When my daughter knows as well as I do
That sorrow and happiness are and are not,
Such words do not suit a man like me—
I have come with conviction to you, O king.

Pray do not, out of friendship and affection, kill my hopes, do not deny me who have come here in a spirit of love. For in this alliance you are my peer and I am yours. Accept my girl as your daughter-in-law and Satyavat's wife.

Dyumatsena said:

Well before this have I wanted an alliance with you, but I hesitated, since I have been bereft of my kingdom. Then let this long-held wish be fulfilled for me today, for you are my wished-for guest.

Mārkaṇḍeya said:

15 Thereupon the two kings fetched all the brahmins who lived in the hermitage and had the wedding celebrated ceremonially. And after Aśvapati had given away his daughter with a suitable dowry, he returned to his palace most joyously. Satyavat too rejoiced at having obtained such a wife endowed with all virtues, and she was happy on having won the husband desired of her heart.

When her father had gone, she took off all her ornaments and put on bark and an ocher robe. With her attentions and virtues, her affection and restraint, and her seeing to all wants, she earned the contentment of all. Her mother-in-law she satisfied with the care of
20 her body and with all garments and such, and her father-in-law with divine worship and control of her tongue. Likewise she contented her husband with her pleasant speech, dexterity, and even tenor, as well as her private ministrations.

As these strict people were thus living together in their hermitage and performing austerities, some time passed by, Bhārata. But Sāvitrī, lying or standing, day and night, kept thinking of the words that Nārada had spoken.

Mārkaṇḍeya said:

280.1 Then, after a stretch of many days had gone by, the time came when Satyavat was to die, O king. Sāvitrī counted every day that went by, and Nārada's words kept turning in her mind. Knowing that he was to die on the fourth day, the radiant woman undertood a three-night vow and kept standing day and night. When the king heard of this painful restraint of the bride, he felt sorry, and he rose and said

5 soothingly to Sāvitrī, "The vow you have undertaken is too severe,
daughter of a king, for standing up for three nights is exceedingly
difficult."

Sāvitrī said:

Do not feel sorry, father, I shall finish the vow; for it is done with resolve, and resolve is the reason.

Dyumatsena said:

I am in no wise able to tell you to break your vow. One like me should properly tell you to finish it.

Mārkaṇḍeya said:

Having said this the great-minded Dyumatsena desisted; and Sāvitrī
stood upright as though she had become wood. That last night before
the day of her husband's death, bull of the Bharatas, went on by most
10 sorrowfully for Sāvitrī, who remained standing. "Today is the day,"
she thought, and she made a libation into the burning fire, performed
the morning rites when the sun had risen a mere four cubits. Then she
saluted all the brahmin elders and her mother-in-law and father-in-
law in succession, and stood subdued with folded hands. The holy
ascetics, who wished Sāvitrī well, all the inmates of the hermitage,
pronounced blessings for her never to be widowed. "So be it!" she
mused, sunk in thought, accepting all the words of the ascetics silently.
Suffering deeply, the princess waited for the time and the hour and
kept thinking on Nārada's words.

15 Her mother-in-law and father-in-law, O best of the Bharatas, then
said affectionately these words to the princess, who was standing
aside:

The parents-in-law said:

You have properly accomplished the vow as it is prescribed. It is now time to eat, then do the next thing.

Sāvitrī said:

I shall eat when the sun is down and I have fulfilled my wish. This is the intention and covenant I have conceived in my heart.

Mārkaṇḍeya said:

While Sāvitrī was thus having converse regarding her meal, Satyavat put an ax over his shoulder and started for the forest. Sāvitrī said to her husband, "Please do not go alone! I shall come with you, for I cannot bear to leave you."

Satyavat said:

20 You have never gone into the forest before, and the path is difficult,
my lovely. You are gaunt from your fast and vow—how will you
manage on foot?

Sāvitrī said:

I am not weak from my fast, and I do not feel fatigue. I have set my heart on going, please don't stop me!

Satyavat said:
If you have set your heart on going, I shall do what pleases you.
But first take leave of my parents, so no blame falls on me.
Mārkaṇḍeya said:
The woman of the great vows went to her mother-in-law and
father-in-law and said, "My husband is going to the forest to gather
fruit. I seek the lady's and my father-in-law's permission to go out with
25 him, for I cannot bear to be separated. Your son is starting out for his
parents' sake and the *agnihotra's*, and he cannot be stopped. He might
be stopped if he went to the forest for another reason. In close to a
year I have not ventured out of the hermitage, and I am most curious
to see the forest in flower."
Dyumatsena said:
From the day her father gave me Sāvitrī as a daughter-in-law I do
not recall her ever having made any sort of request. Let the bride have
her way then. But see to it, daughter, that you do not distract Satyavat
on the way.
Mārkaṇḍeya said:
With the permission of both the glorious woman went with her
30 husband, seemingly laughing but with burning heart. Wide-eyed she
looked at the lovely and colorful woods all about, which echoed with
the cries of peacocks. Gently Satyavat said to Sāvitrī, "Look at the pure
currents of these streams and the beautiful flowering trees!" And the
blameless woman kept watching her husband at all times, for,
remembering the hermit's words at the time, she thought him already
dead. She followed her husband, walking deftly, her heart cut in twain,
waiting for the hour.

Mārkaṇḍeya said:
281.1 Together with his wife the gallant man gathered fruit and filled his
strap with them; then he split logs of wood. While he was splitting the
wood, he broke out in a sweat and the exertion gave him a headache.
He went to his beloved wife and, weighed down with fatigue, said to
her, "I have got a headache from the exertion, and my body and heart
seem to be on fire. Sāvitrī of measured words, I feel as though I am
5 sick. My head feels as though it is pierced with spikes. I want to sleep,
my lovely, I don't have the strength to stand."
Sāvitrī came to him and embraced her husband. She sat down on
the ground and put his head in her lap. Thinking on Nārada's word,
the poor woman calculated the moment, hour, time of day, and the
day. In a little while she saw a person in a yellow robe and a turban,
a handsome man resplendent like the sun, smoothly black and red-
eyed. He had a noose in his hand and looked terrifying as he stood at
10 Satyavat's side and looked down on him. When she saw him she put

down her husband's head gently and rose up at once. She folded her hands and said piteously, with trembling heart, "I know that thou art a God, for thy form is not human. Tell me, if it pleases thee, who art thou, God, and what dost thou seek here?"

Yama said:

You are a devoted wife, Sāvitrī, and possess the power of austerities. Therefore I will reply to you—know that I am Yama, good woman. The life of your husband the Prince Satyavat has run out. I shall fetter him and take him along—that is what I seek to do.

Mārkaṇḍeya said:

Having said this, the blessed lord, the King of the Ancestors
proceeded to reveal his entire design exactly as a kindness to her:
15 "This man is possessed of the Law, beautiful, and a sea of virtues.
Therefore he does not deserve to be fetched by my familiars, hence I
have come myself."

Thereupon Yama forcibly drew from Satyavat's body a thumb-sized person, who was fettered with the noose and in his power. The body gave up its spirit, its breathing stopped, its sheen faded, and it became motionless and not pleasing to watch. Having tied him, Yama set out to the south, and Sāvitrī followed sorrowfully, this stately, devoted wife, perfected by her stressful vow.

Yama said:

Go, Sāvitrī, return! Perform his obsequies. You are acquitted of all debts to your husband. You have gone as far as you can go!

Sāvitrī said:

20 I too must go where my husband is led, or goes by himself—that is
the sempiternal Law. By the power of my austerities, my conduct toward my elders, my love for my husband, my vow, and by thy grace my course shall be unobstructed! The wise, who see the truth of the matter, say that he who walks the seven steps with one is his friend. This friendship I presuppose while I say something, listen.

> It is masters of their souls who practice
> The Law in the woods, and austerities;
> And knowing the Law they promulgate it—
> Hence the strict say the Law comes first.
>
> By the Law of the one as approved by the strict
> We all proceed on the course he has set.
> I don't want a second, I don't want a third—
> Hence the strict say the Law comes first.

Yama said:

25 Turn back, I am pleased with the words you speak
With vowel and consonant and fine reason.

Now choose you a boon, excepting his life,
I shall grant you any boon, woman sans blame.

Sāvitrī said:

My father-in-law lives a hermit's life,
Bereft of his sight and thrown from his throne.
By thy grace may the king regain his eyesight
And grow strong, ablaze like the fire or the sun.

Yama said:

I shall give this boon entire to you,
Just as you have said it, and so shall it be.
I see that the journey is tiring you,
Now go and return lest you get fatigued.

Sāvitrī said:

Why should I tire—I am near my husband,
For my course is sure wherever he goes;
My course will be where thou leadst, my lord,
O lord of the Gods, once more do thou listen.

With the strict a single encounter is praised
And friendship with them is higher still.
To meet a strict person is to have sure fruit;
Thence one should live in the midst of the strict.

Yama said:

30 The words that you speak are full of good counsel,
They are pleasing and add to the wisdom of sages.
Again excepting this Satyavat's life,
Choose, radiant woman, another boon!

Sāvitrī said:

My wise old father-in-law has been robbed
Of his own realm—may he regain it,
And may my guru not stray from the Law;
This I choose from you as my second boon.

Yama said:

He shall soon possess his kingdom again,
And the king shall never be lacking in Law.
Your wish is fulfilled, O child of a king,
Now go and return lest you get fatigued.

Sāvitrī said:

Thou subduest these creatures only by rule,
By the rule dost thou lead them, not by thy desire.

It is thus, God, that thou art famed as Yama.
Pray hear the words that I have to say.

Offering no threat to any creature by deed, mind, or speech, kindness,
35 and giving are the sempiternal Law of the strict. The world is mostly
like this: people are kind just as far as they can be, but the strict show
mercy even when their ill-wishers come.

Yama said:

The words that you speak are as satisfying
As water is to a thirsty man.
Again excepting this Satyavat's life,
Good woman, choose any boon you desire.

Sāvitrī said:

My father, the king of the land, is childless:
May he have a hundred sons, my brothers,
Who will insure that his line will last—
This boon I choose as my third from you.

Yama said:

Good woman, your father shall have a hundred
Of splendid sons to continue his line.
Your wish is fulfilled, O child of a king,
Return, you have come a long stretch of the road.

Sāvitrī said:

In my husband's presence it has not been far,
For my mind is rushing much farther still.
As thou goest thy course do thou listen again
To the ready words I shall speak to thee.

40 Thou art the majestic son of Vivasvat,
The wise call you therefore Vaivasvata.
The creatures please thee with Law and control,
And that, lord, makes thee the King of the Law.

Not even in oneself does one have so much trust as in the strict, therefore everyone wishes to show his love to the strict in particular. Trust, indeed, arises from one's friendship for all creatures; therefore people place trust in the strict particularly.

Yama said:

The words you have uttered here, beautiful woman,
I have not but from you heard their likes before.
I am pleased with them, therefore, excepting his life,
Choose you a fourth boon, then you must go.

Sāvitrī said:

May be born from my womb by Satyavat,
To the two of us to continue our line,
A hundred mighty and gallant sons:
This boon I choose as my fourth from you.

Yama said:

45 A hundred mighty and gallant sons
Shall be born, young woman, and give you delight.
But do not tire, O child of a king,
Return, you have gone a long stretch of the way.

Sāvitrī said:

The strict always abide by the Law,
The strict do not tremble, nor do they despair.
The meeting of strict with strict bears fruit,
From the strict the strict expect no danger.

With their truth do the strict give lead to the sun,
With their penance the strict uphold the earth.
The strict are the course of future and past,
They do not collapse in the midst of the strict.

Knowing that this is the eternal conduct that is practiced by the noble, the strict act in another's cause without expecting a return from it.

No favor is fruitless among the strict.
No profit, no honor will come to naught.
As this is forever the rule of the strict,
Therefore the strict are custodians.

Yama said:

50 Since every time you speak so well,
So pleasing, so meaningful of the Law,
My love for you is incomparable—
Choose you a compareless boon, strict woman!

Sāvitrī said:

You make no exception to your favor,
Pride-giver, as in the other boons!
I choose the boon that Satyavat live,
For I am as dead without my lord!

Deprived of my husband I wish no bliss,
Deprived of my husband I wish no heaven,
Deprived of my husband I wish no fortune,
Without my lord I will not live.

You have given the boon that a hundred sons
Will be born to me, yet you take my man.
I choose the boon that Satyavat live!
Your very own word shall now come true!

Mārkaṇḍeya said:

"So be it," said Yama Vaivasvata, and he loosened the nooses. Then
55 the king of the Law said to Sāvitrī with a joyous heart, "Look, good
woman, joy of your family, I have freed your husband. Take him with
you; he is healthy and shall succeed in his purposes. He shall attain
with you to a lifetime of four hundred years; and, after having offered
up sacrifices, he shall win fame in the world for his Law. Satyavat shall
beget on you a hundred sons, and they shall all be barons and kings
and have sons and grandsons. Your names shall forever be famous on
earth. Your father shall have a hundred sons by your mother Mālavī,
named the Mālavas, which, with their sons and grandsons, shall
continue forever. They shall be your baronial brothers, the likes of the
Thirty."

Having thus bestowed boons on her, the majestic King of the Law
60 turned Sāvitrī back and went to his own house. When Yama had
gone, Sāvitrī took hold of her husband and returned to the place where
her husband's corpse was lying. Seeing him there on the ground, she
approached her husband, embraced him, lifted his head in her lap, and
sat on the ground. Satyavat returned to consciousness, and he said to
Sāvitrī, looking at her lovingly again and again, as one who has
returned from a journey:

Satyavat said:

Why, I have slept a long time! Why did you not wake me up? And
where is that black person who dragged me from here?

Sāvitrī said:

Yes, you have slept a long time in my lap, bull among men. The
65 blessed lord Yama, the God who subdues the creatures, is gone. You
are rested now, my lord prince, and your sleep has gone. If you can,
stand up, see, night has fallen.

Mārkaṇḍeya said:

Having regained consciousness, Satyavat arose as from a pleasant
sleep, and looking in all directions at the woods, he said: "I went out
with you, my fine-waisted woman, to gather fruit. Then as I was
splitting wood I got a headache. And because of the pain in my head
I was unable to stand up anymore and fell asleep in your lap. All this
I remember, my lovely. I lost consciousness when I fell asleep in your
70 embrace, then I saw a terrible darkness and an august person. Tell me,
my pretty, if you know, whether it was a dream I saw, or was it real?

Sāvitrī said to him, "The night is spreading. Tomorrow I shall tell you everything as it happened, my prince. Stand up, stand up, hail to thee! You are an obedient son, so see your parents. The night has spread, and the sun is down. The rovers of the night are wandering here gleefully and making cruel noises, and the leaves are rustling from the animals that stalk the forest. Those fearfully barking jackals in the southwest are howling horribly, and they make my heart quaver."

Satyavat said:

75 The forest covered by dense darkness looks terrifying. You will not recognize the path and be unable to walk.

Sāvitrī said:

Here in this burned wood a dry tree is still burning and fire can be seen hither and yon, fanned by the wind. I shall bring fire from there and make it blaze high, here are these logs, don't worry. If you are unable to go—I see your head aches—and won't recognize the path in the darkness-covered forest, we'll go tomorrow morning, if you agree, when the forest is visible. We shall spend the night here, if you think so, prince sans blame.

Satyavat said:

80 My headache is gone and my limbs feel well. If you agree, I wish to
join father and mother. I have never before returned to the hermitage
out of time. Mother stops me at nightfall, and even in daytime my
parents worry when I go out. Father will be looking for me with the
hermitage-dwellers. I have often been reproved before by my much
worried father and mother: "You have come back late!" What state
will they be in over me now, I wonder! They must be very much
85 concerned, not seeing me. These old people love me very much. Once
when they were worried badly at night they told me with a flood of
tears, "Without you we will not live for an hour, little son. As long as
you live our life is assured, you are the crutch of two blind oldsters,
the dynasty rests on you. On you depend our ancestral oblation, our
fame, and our progeny." My old mother, my old father, whose crutch
they say I am, what state will they be in if they don't see me tonight!
I blame my sleep for causing my father and innocent mother to fear
90 for my life. And I am in danger, and doom is upon me, for neither can
I live without my father and mother! It is certain that at this very
hour my father, who has only the sight of knowledge, is questioning
with a perturbed mind each and every person in the hermitage. I don't
mind for myself as much as for my father, my lovely, and for my
mother, my very weak mother who has followed her husband. Now
they will be prey to the greatest worry over me. I live if they live, I
must support them, I must do what pleases them, that is what I live
for.

Mārkaṇḍeya said:

Having said this the Law-spirited and devoted son, who was
obedient to his parents, lifted his arms in grief and began to weep
95 aloud. And when Sāvitrī who walked in the Law saw her husband
thus, gaunt from grief, she wiped the tears from his eyes and said,
"If it is true that I have practiced austerities, if I have given, if I have
offered up, then this night shall be safe for my parents-in-law and my
husband. I do not recall that I have ever spoken a lie, even in jest—
by that truth my parents-in-law shall live today!"

Satyavat said:

I wish to see my parents. Come, Sāvitrī, don't tarry. If I find that anything untoward has happened to mother or father, I shall not live, fair-hipped wife, I swear it by the truth! If your mind is set on the Law, or if you wish me to live, or do me a kindness, then come to the hermitage.

Mārkaṇḍeya said:

100 Sāvitrī thereupon stood up, and the radiant woman gathered her
hair and made her husband rise, holding him by his arms. Satyavat
stood and wiped his body with his hand. He looked all about him and
his glance fell on the strap. Sāvitrī said, "Tomorrow you'll fetch the
fruit here. But I'll take this ax of yours for safety." She hung the strap
from a tree branch, took the ax, and joined her husband. The woman
of the lovely thighs put her husband's arm on her left shoulder, circled
his waist with her right arm, and went stepping deftly.

Satyavat said:

105 I am used to coming here, so I know the paths, timid girl. I can see
them by the moonlight that shines between the trees. Go by the same
path we came by this morning and gathered fruit, don't hesitate. And
at this *palāśa* grove, the path forks. Go by the northern path and make
haste. I am well, I am strong, and I want to see my parents.

Mārkaṇḍeya said:

And speaking thus he hastened on to the hermitage.

Mārkaṇḍeya said:

282.1 At this very time in the great forest Dyumatsena regained his
eyesight, and his soul was serene, and his eyes saw everything. He
went to all the hermitages with his wife Śaibyā, and he became
exceedingly concerned over his son. The couple made the rounds of all
the hermitages, rivers, woods, and lakes, and they searched all those
places. Whenever they heard a noise they looked up, thinking it was
5 their son, and rushed thither: "Satyavat is coming with Sāvitrī!" They
ran about like madmen, their bodies were sore from *kuśa* grass and
thorns, and their feet were split and rough and wounded and smeared
with blood. All the brahmins who lived in the hermitage came to

them, surrounded and comforted them, and they took them back to their own hermitage. The ancient ascetics stayed about him and his wife and soothed him with wondrous tales of previous kings. The two oldsters, calm now, began from sheer desire of seeing their son to recall stories of his boyhood, and they were most worried. Sick with concern, they repeated, lamenting, "Ah son, ah good bride, where are you, where are you?" and wept.

Suvarcas said:

10 As his wife Sāvitrī is endowed with austerity, self-control, and deportment, Satyavat must be alive!

Gautama said:

I have studied the *Vedas* with their branches, much austerity have I piled up, I am chaste as a boy, I have contented my elders and the fire, I have practiced all the vows religiously, fasted and lived on the wind, and I have done the deeds that promise health—and by virtue of that self-mortification I know all that has been designed. Learn you the truth from me—Satyavat is alive!

His pupil said:

The words that flow from my teacher's mouth can never be false, so Satyavat must be alive!

The seers said:

15 His wife Sāvitrī shows all the good signs that spell no widowhood, so Satyavat is alive!

Bhāradvāja said:

As his wife Sāvitrī is endowed with austerity, self-control, and deportment, Satyavat is alive!

Dālbhya said:

As your sight has returned, and as Sāvitrī has finished her vow without eating, Satyavat is alive!

Māṇḍavya said:

The way the animals and birds sound in the forbidden quarter and the way you act as a king, Satyavat is alive!

Dhaumya said:

As your son, whom the people love, is possessed of all virtues and shows signs of longevity, Satyavat is alive!

Mārkaṇḍeya said:

20 Thus did the true-spoken ascetics comfort him; and reflecting upon their various imports, the king stayed put. Then in a little while Sāvitrī returned with her husband Satyavat to the hermitage and entered happily.

The brahmins said:

Today we see you reunited with your son and restored in your eyesight, and all of us indeed inquire after your good fortune, king of the land! In your reunion with your son, in the spectacle of Sāvitrī, in the restoration of your eyesight you are blessed thrice with good fortune. Doubtless it has come out as we all said. And again and again we say, good fortune shall soon be yours!

Mārkaṇḍeya said:

25 All the brahmins then made the fire blaze up there and sat in
attendance with King Dyumatsena, O Pārtha. Śaibyā,* Satyavat, and Sāvitrī stood aside, but all of them gave them permission and they sat down with them happily. All the inmates of the forest, who were seated with the king, had their curiosity aroused, O Pārtha, and they questioned the king's son: "My lord, why did you and your wife not come home earlier? And why did you come in the dead of night? What kept you? Your father and mother were worried, and so were we, prince, and we know for good reason! Please tell us everything."

Satyavat said:

30 I went out together with Sāvitrī, with father's permission. Then,
while I was splitting logs in the forest, I got a headache. This much I know that I slept a long time because of the pain, and all that time I did not dream at all. Lest all of you worry more, I came back in the dead of night, that is the whole reason.

Gautama said:

Your father Dyumatsena's eyesight was restored all of a sudden. If
you do not know the reason, Sāvitrī must speak. Sāvitrī, I wish to hear
it, for you know the entire truth! I know you, Sāvitrī, you are like
35 Sāvitrī herself in splendid power. You know the reason behind it all,
therefore let the truth be told. If there is nothing secret in it for you,
do tell it to us!

Sāvitrī said:

You know it the way it is, and you have no ulterior intention. Nor
is anything a secret with me. Listen to the truth of it. The great-
spirited Nārada had presaged to me my husband's death. Today the
day came, therefore I did not leave his side. Yama himself came with
his familiars while he was asleep. He fettered him and led him to the
region the Ancestors inhabit. I praised the omnipresent God in truthful
40 speech, and he granted me five boons, hear which ones. His eyes and
his kingdom were the two boons for my father-in-law. For my father
I received a hundred sons, and another hundred sons for myself. My
husband Satyavat received a life of four hundred years. Indeed, it was
for the sake of my husband's life that I had performed a steadfast vow.
I have now told you completely the truth of how this great sorrow of
mine has ended in happiness.

The seers said:

The king of men's dynasty was mired
In a pool of darkness, beset by evils.

* = Satyavat's mother.

And you, good woman, blessed by the Law,
You, noble lady, have rescued it!

Mārkaṇḍeya said:

And then they honored and gave their praise
To the excellent woman, those seers assembled.
They graciously left the king and his son
And went happily home by propitious roads.

Mārkaṇḍeya said:

283.1 That night passed, the orb of the sun rose, and all the ascetics again
assembled after the morning rites. They did not tire of recounting
again and again to Dyumatsena the entire glory of Sāvitrī. Then, O
king, all the ministers arrived from the land of the Śālvas, and they
told the king had been slain by his own councillor. After learning that
the king, his companions, and relatives had been killed by his minister,
they informed Dyumatsena of what had happened and also of the fact
5 that the enemy's army had fled and that all the people were of one
mind concerning the king: "Whether sightless or seeing, he must be
the king!" "It is because of this decision," they continued, "that we
have been dispatched here, sire. The wagons have arrived, as has your
four-membered army. Set out, sire, hail to thee! Your triumph has
been proclaimed in the city. Take your seat, for many nights to come,
in your paternal and ancestral palace." Seeing that the king could see
and was of vigorous health, they prostrated themselves with their
heads, eyes wide-open in amazement.

Dyumatsena saluted the brahmin elders who lived in the hermitage.
10 All paid homage to him, and he set out for his city. Also Śaibyā
departed, in Sāvitrī's company, surrounded by an escort, and they rode
a resplendent, well-decked wagon that was pulled by men. The priests
joyously consecrated Dyumatsena, and anointed his great-spirited son
Young King. Over a long period of time Sāvitrī gave birth to a hundred
gallant and never-retreating sons, who increased her fame. And a
hundred most powerful brothers of hers were born to Aśvapati, king
of the Madras, by Mālavī.

Thus Sāvitrī by her toils saved them all—herself, her father and
mother, her mother-in-law and father-in-law, and her husband's entire
15 dynasty. Likewise the well-augured Draupadī, esteemed for her
character, shall rescue you all, just as the nobly-descended Sāvitrī!

Vaiśaṃpāyana said:

Thus did the great-spirited hermit pacify the Pāṇḍava. And the latter went on to live in the Kāmyaka, without sorrow or fever.

3(43) *The Robbing of the Earrings*

284–94 (B. 300–310; C. 16919–7221)
284 (300; 16919). At the beginning of the thirteenth year of the Pāṇḍavas' exile, Indra is about to beg Karṇa's earrings. The Sun God appears to Karṇa, his son, as a brahmin and warns him not to give away his earrings (1–20). He identifies himself as the sun. Karṇa replies that he shall have to give up his armor and earrings, if Indra comes begging, and thus he will earn fame (20–35).
285 (301; 16958). The sun repeats his warning: the gift will cost Karṇa his life; he speaks darkly of a secret (1–15).
286 (302; 16978). Karṇa assures him that he will defeat Arjuna (1–5). The sun implores him that if he has to give away his earrings, he should ask for an infallible spear in return (5–20).
287 (303; 16998). Janamejaya asks about the sun's secret (1). Once a brahmin appeared before Kuntibhoja and asked to be lodged and fed at his whim; the king assigns his daughter Pṛthā to his care, with strict instructions about how to serve a brahmin (1–25).
288 (304; 17207). Pṛthā, alias *Kuntī, agrees (1–10), and the king tells the brahmin so (10–15).*
289 (305; 17047). She serves the brahmin tirelessly for a year (1–10). The brahmin offers her a boon; when she declines, he gives her the power to conjure up any God (15). The brahmin departs contentedly (20).
290 (306; 17070). When Kuntī is in her menses, she conjures up the sun, who appears in person ready to serve her (1–10). Kuntī, afraid, tries to dismiss him, but he will not be the laughingstock of the Gods (10–20).
291 (307; 17097). Afraid of a curse, she gives in, on condition that she retain her virtue (1–10). The sun promises so; she will have a son born with armor and earrings (10–20). He lies with her and departs (20–25).
292 (308; 17126). After having hidden her pregnancy, she gives birth to Karṇa and floats him in a basket down the River Aśva, commending him to his father (1–20). The basket floats to the rivers Carmaṇvatī, Yamunā, and Ganges, as far as the town of Campā (20–25).
293 (309; 17153). The sūta *Adhiratha and his childless*

wife Rādhā retrieve the basket from the Ganges and happily adopt Karṇa (1–10), whom they name Vasuṣeṇa and Vṛṣa (15). Kuntī finds out about him (15). When he is grown, Adhiratha sends him to Hāstinapura, where he befriends Duryodhana and competes with Arjuna (15–20). Indra now appears before him (20).
294 (310; 17177). Indra demands his armor and earrings (1–15). Karṇa refuses (5–10). Indra insists and Karṇa gives in, on condition he receive the infallible spear (10–20). Indra agrees: the spear shall kill one enemy unfailingly (20–30). Karṇa promises to use the spear only in great danger (30). He cuts off his armor and earrings; the Pāṇḍavas rejoice (35–45). The Pāṇḍavas repair to Dvaitavana (40).

Janamejaya said:
284.1 Great brahmin, the words that Lomaśa spoke, when he at Indra's
behest had come to Pāṇḍu's son Yudhiṣṭhira, "When the left-handed
archer has returned here, I shall also take away that bitter fear of
yours that you never mention"—what was that great fear concerning
Karṇa, O first of the sages, and did the Law-spirited man indeed
mention it to no one?
Vaiśaṃpāyana said:
I shall tell that tale at your bidding, tiger among men, best of the
Bharatas, pray listen to my words.
5 When the twelfth year had passed and the thirteenth come, Śakra,
in order to do the Pāṇḍus a favor, prepared to go begging from Karṇa.
Knowing the design that the great Indra had on Karṇa's earrings, the
Sun God came to him, great king. The hero was lying on a costly bed
spread with covetable coverings, lying there confident, brahminic, and
true-spoken. The Sun God showed himself at night, at the end of a
dream, O Bhārata, Indra among kings, for he was filled with very great
compassion and love for his son. The Sun had become a handsome,
Veda-wise brahmin by his wizardry, and he said gently to Karṇa,
10 wishing him well, "Karṇa, you first of those who speak the truth,
listen to my words, son. I am speaking only for your own good,
strong-armed man, and out of friendship. Śakra will approach you in
the guise of a brahmin, Karṇa, seeking to rob you of your earrings in
order to help the Pāṇḍavas. All the world knows of your great custom
that whenever you are begged by the strict, you only give and do not
demand. For you cannot but give to the brahmins when they bid you,
son. Any possessions you have, so they say, you never refuse.
Knowing you to be thus, the Chastiser of Pāka himself will come, to

15 beg from you your earrings and armor. You must not give him the
earrings when he begs you. Appease him as far as you can, for that is
where your safety lies. When he speaks to you about your earrings,
son, you must stop him with many reasons, and many other kinds of
wealth, and do it again and again. Satisfy the Sacker of Cities, who
wants the earrings, with gems, women, pleasures, riches of many
kinds, and with many illustrations. Karṇa, if you give away your
beautiful inborn earrings, you will forfeit your life and fall in the power
of death. O giver of pride, you cannot be slain in battle by your
20 enemies, remember this word of mine. For your two jewels have arisen
from the Elixir, therefore you must guard them, Karṇa, if you want to
live!

Karṇa said:

Sir, who art thou that speakest to me thus, showing complete friendship? Tell me freely, my lord, who thou art that wearest a brahmin's guise?

The brahmin said:

I, son, am the thousand-rayed Sun, and I instruct you out of affection. Do as I say, for it is in your best interest.

Karṇa said:

Surely it is in my best interest that the Lord of the cows speaks to
me today, seeking my welfare! Listen to my reply, I propitiate thee,
granter of boons, and I speak with love: thou shouldst not keep me
25 from this my life rule, if thou holdst me dear. All the world knows of
this very vow of mine, Sun, that I most certainly will give my life
away to the brahmins. If Śakra comes to me in the guise of a brahmin,
to beg from me in order to favor the sons of Pāṇḍu, O thou most-high
of the Walkers of the Sky, I shall give him my earrings, best of the
Gods, and my superb armor, lest my fame vanish, which is renowned
in the three worlds. For to the likes of me, infamy that saves our lives
is not fitting, but fitting is a glorious death that the world approves.

30 I shall give Indra the earrings and the armor. If the Slayer of Vala
and Vṛtra approaches me as a beggar to ask for my earrings to help
out the sons of Pāṇḍu, it will redound to my fame in the world, and to
his infamy. For I choose fame on earth, Sun, if at the cost of my life.
The famous man attains to heaven, the inglorious man perishes. For
in the world fame gives life to a man like a mother, while infamy kills
life be the soul still alive. The Placer himself has chanted this ancient
verse, O Sun, lord of the world, of how fame is a man's very life.

In the world hereafter is fame
The highest estate of a man;
In this world fame if pure
Increases that man's life.

35 By giving away these inborn things I shall earn eternal fame, by
giving them as presents to the brahmins in the proper manner. By
offering up my body in war, by doing my difficult deed, or by
vanquishing my foes in the arena, I shall only harvest fame. By
granting safety in battle to the fearful who seek their lives, by setting
the old, the young, and the brahmins free from great danger, I shall
win supreme fame in the world, Slayer of Svarbhānu. Know that I
have vowed to protect my fame with my very life. By giving Maghavat
in his brahmin's guise this incomparable alms, I shall go, O God, the
highest course in the world!

The Sun said:

285.1 Karṇa, do not act against the interest of yourself, your friends, sons,
wives, father, and mother. Breathing creatures, O best of all that
breathe, desire to win glory without risking their lives, and their fame
is firm in heaven. But if you wish eternal fame at the price of your life,
it will disappear with your life, no doubt of that! They perform the
task of the living, your father, mother, sons, and any other relations in
this world, bull among men, as well as the kings, tiger among men,
5 they perform it with manly vigor, learn that from me. Only the fame
of a *living* man is good, illustrious Karṇa. What use is fame to a dead
person who has been reduced to ashes? A dead man does not know
fame—the living attain to fame. The fame of a dead mortal is like a
garland on a corpse.

I am telling you this out of a desire to help you, for you are my
devotee and I have to protect my devotees. And I know that this man
here is devoted to me with the strongest devotion, strong-armed
Karṇa. If devotion to me has arisen in you, then do as I say. There is
something superior within yourself, which has been created by a God,
hence am I speaking to you: act without hesitation. A secret of the
Gods you cannot know, bull among men, therefore I shall not tell you
10 the secret. You shall know it in time. I repeat to you again, Rādheya,
and take it to heart: do not give the earrings to the mendicant
Thunderbolt-wielder. With your bright earrings, lustrous man, you
shine like the spotless moon in the sky between the two stars of
Viśākha. Know that fame is good only for a living man. You must
refuse the Sacker of Cities the earrings, son. You can, with many
words couched in argument, dispel the king of the Gods' desire for the
earrings, prince sans blame. Remove this design of the Sacker of Cities,
Karṇa, with sweet and jeweled words whose purport is corroborated
15 by arguments. For you always rival the Left-handed Archer, tiger
among men, and the Left-handed Archer, champion in battle, competes
with you. But Arjuna cannot defeat you in a fight were Indra himself

his arrow, as long as you possess the earrings. Therefore do not give
your beautiful earrings to Śakra, if you desire to vanquish Arjuna in
an encounter, Karṇa!

Karṇa said:

286.1 Lord of the cows, of the very fierce rays, thou knowest that to no
other God am I as strongly devoted as to thee. Neither my wife, nor
my sons, nor my own self, nor my friends are as close to my devotion
as thou art, O Lord of the cows. Thou knowest, Spreader of Light, that
the great-spirited ones doubtlessly return love and loyalty to their
votaries and lovers. Considering that Karṇa loves thee as no other God
in heaven, thy lordship hath spoken to my well-being.

5 Once more I propitiate thee again and again, and beseech thee—my
reply is the same, Lord of the fierce rays, pray forgive thou me. I do
not fear death as I fear the lie—I have no hesitation to bestow on the
brahmins in particular and on all strict people my very life. Concerning
thy words to me about Phalguna Pāṇḍava, dispel the anxious grief of
thy heart, O God, Spreader of Light, about Arjun and myself. I shall
vanquish Arjuna in battle. Thou knowest too, O God, that I have a
great power of weapons that I have obtained from Jāmadagnya* and
the great-spirited Droṇa. Do permit me, best of the Gods, this vow of
mine: that I will give even my own life to the Thunderbolt-wielder, if
he comes begging!

The Sun said:

10 Son, if you want to give the bright earrings to the Thunderbolt-
wielder, you should talk to him, powerful man, to insure victory. You
will give the earrings to the God of the Hundred Sacrifices, because of
your vow; but as long as you wear the earrings, you are unslayable
by any creatures. The Killer of the Dānavas, who seeks to encompass
your destruction in battle at the hands of Arjuna, will try to steal the
earrings by begging, my calf. You should propitiate the Sacker of
Cities with many friendly words, and solicit the Lord of the Gods,
whose purpose is unfailing: "Give me a javelin that unfailingly will
eradicate my enemies, and I shall give you the earrings, God of the
15 Thousand Eyes, and my superb armor." Thus, under your vow, you
will give Śakra the earrings, and with the javelin you will kill your
enemies in battle, Karṇa. For the javelin of the king of the Gods will
return to your hand after not having failed to kill the foes a hundred
and a thousand times, strong-armed hero!

Vaiśaṃpāyana said:

Having thus spoken, the Thousand-rayed One suddenly disappeared.
When Karṇa had finished his morning prayers, he told his dream to

* = Rāma.

the Sun. Vṛṣan* related to him in sequence all that had happened, was
witnessed, and was said in the night between the two of them. Upon
hearing it, the venerable lord Sun, killer of Svarbhānu, said to Karṇa
20 with the semblance of a smile, "So be it then." Knowing now that it
was the truth, Rādheya, killer of enemy heroes, waited for Vāsava,**
desiring only that javelin.

Janamejaya said:
287.1 What was the secret that the hot-rayed Sun did not tell Karṇa?
What were the earrings like, and what the armor? Whence did the
earrings and armor come to him, great brahmin? This I wish to hear,
ascetic, tell it to me.

Vaiśaṃpāyana said:
Sire, I shall tell you Vibhāvasu's secret, and of what kind the
earrings were and the armor.

Sire, of yore a certain brahmin appeared before Kuntibhoja, a
brahmin of fierce luster, most luminous, wearing a beard, staff, and
5 hair tuft, handsome and flawlessly built, as though ablaze with
splendor. His skin was honey-colored, his words honeyed, and he wore
the jewels of austerities and Vedic study. The great ascetic said to King
Kuntibhoja, "I wish to beg a meal in your house, do not begrudge me.
Neither you nor your followers shall be false to me—thus will I dwell in
your house, if you agree, prince sans blame. I will come and go as I
please and no one shall slight me in bed and seat, O king."

King Kuntibhoja replied to him in pleasing words: "So shall it be and
10 more!" And again he said to him "Great brahmin, I have a glorious
daughter by the name of Pṛthā, a good girl of fine character and
conduct, modest and without pride. She shall wait on you with honor
and not slight you, and you shall be satisfied with her character and
conduct."

After having spoken thus to the brahmin and duly honored him, he
said to the wide-eyed Pṛthā, when she came in, "My calf, this lordly
brahmin wishes to live in my house, and I have promised him so,
saying confidently that you, my calf, know how to gratify a brahmin.
15 Therefore please do not belie my words in any way. This venerable
brahmin is an ascetic and strict in his studies. Whatever the mighty
man asks you must give him ungrudgingly. For brahmins are the
highest splendor, brahmins the highest austerity. It is because of the
salutations of the brahmins that the sun shines in the sky. The great
Asura Vātāpi, when he did not honor the ones so deserving of honor,
was killed by Brahmā's Staff, and so was Tālajangha. This is a great

* = Karṇa.
** = Indra.

burden that is put on you; you will always modestly seek to gratify
the brahmin.
"I know how from childhood you have been devoted to the
brahmins, joy of my life, to all of them as well as your elders and
20 relations, all the servants, friends, relatives, and mothers, and to
myself, in quite the proper manner and esteeming everyone. Not a
person here in this city and the palace is dissatisfied with you. With
your flawless beauty you behave correctly even to the serving folk.
Therefore I think you should be charged with this irascible brahmin.
You were made my daughter as a child, Pṛthā. You had been born the
beloved daughter of Śūra in the family of the Vṛṣṇis. Your father
himself at the time gave you to me out of affection when you were a
child. The sister of Vasudeva, you are the first of my daughters. And
now you are my daughter because he had promised me his first child.
25 "Born in such a family and raised in another, you have gone from
happiness to happiness, as from lotus pond to lotus pond. Lowborn
women especially, though somehow kept in check as children, usually
change for the worse afterward, my pretty. But birth in a royal house
and a wondrous beauty, O radiant Pṛthā, are both yours and in full
measure. Rid yourself of all pride, dissembling, and vainglory, radiant
girl. By pleasing the boon-granting brahmin you will be yoked with
well-being, Pṛthā. So, my beautiful and innocent girl, you shall
certainly obtain good things; but when the best of brahmins is
angered, my whole dynasty will burn down."

Kuntī said:

288.1 With all restraint I shall honor and attend on the brahmin, king,
just as you have promised, Indra of princes; and I do not speak a lie.
It is but my nature to honor the twice-born. To do what pleases you is
my greatest bliss. If the blessed lord comes in the evening, in the
morning, or at night, or in the middle of the night, he shall not be
angry with me. This will be my profit that by honoring the twice-born
at your behest, Indra of princes, I do what is beneficial, chief of men.
5 Rest assured, great king, the eminent brahmin will not be slighted
while he is living in your house, this I say to you as the truth. I shall
strive to do what pleases the brahmin and benefits you, prince sans
blame—let the fever of your mind abate. For lordly brahmins when
honored, O lord of the land, are able to save, and to kill in the opposite
case. With this knowledge I shall satisfy the good brahmin; you shall
not suffer grief from the brahmin on my account. For when brahmins
are insulted they bring down doom on kings, as Cyavana of yore on
10 Sukanyā's account. I shall wait on the great brahmin with the greatest
of self-control, just as you have told the brahmin, Indra among men!

The king said:

Yes, my good daughter, you must act unhesitatingly for my benefit, for the dynasty, and for yourself!

Vaiśaṃpāyana said:

Having thus spoken to the girl, glorious Kuntibhoja, who loved his
children, gave Pṛthā to the brahmin as his servant. "This is my young
daughter, brahmin. She has been reared in comfort. Do not brood in
your heart if she does anything wrong. Lordly brahmins usually are
never irascible to old people, children, and ascetics, even when they
15 are thwarted. When the error is very great, brahmins should practice
forgiveness. So then, best of brahmins, accept the homage she is able
and endeavors to give."

"So be it," said the brahmin; and the king in happy spirits gave him a house as white as a wild goose or a moonbeam. In his fire sanctuary he arranged for a beautiful stool for him, and gave him all the food and the like as fine. The princess cast aside all idleness and self-pride and devoted herself completely to the appeasement of the brahmin. Pṛthā, intent on her cleanliness, went to the brahmin who was so worthy of her services and tried to satisfy him like a God.

Vaiśaṃpāyana said:

289.1 So, great king, the girl of strict vows waited on the brahmin of strict
vows with a pure heart. Some time the brahmin would say, "I'll come
back in the morning," and then would come back in the evening or
the night, Indra of princes. And at all hours the girl would satisfy him
more and more with foodstuffs and shelter. Her hospitality to him with
food and the like, as well as attendance on bed and seat, increased by
5 the day, and was never wanting. In spite of his abuse, faultfinding, and
disagreeable speech, Pṛthā never did anything displeasing to the
brahmin, O king. He returned when the hour had passed, and often
not at all, and told her to serve him at times when food was hard to
come by. And Pṛthā would tell him that everything was ready, being
as well-disciplined as a pupil, or a son, or a sister. And by her efforts
according to his tastes the blameless girl kindled the affection of the
eminent brahmin. That best of the twice-born was satisfied with her
character and conduct, as she continued to wait on him assiduously.
10 Mornings and evenings her father used to question her, Bhārata,
"Daughter, is the brahmin well pleased with your service?" The
glorious maiden replied, "Completely!" And the great-minded
Kuntibhoja felt the greatest joy.

When a year had passed, and the greatest of the mumblers of spells had not observed any slight and had become fond of her, the brahmin became joyous of spirits, and he said to her, "I am completely pleased with your service, pretty girl. Choose a boon, my beautiful, such as men find hard to obtain, by which you shall surpass all women in glory!"

Kuntī said:

15 I have achieved everything already, greatest of the sages of the
Veda, if you and father are pleased with me. What will boons boot me,
brahmin?

The brahmin said:

If you wish no boon from me, my pretty and sweet-smiling girl, then accept this spell, to summon the celestials. Whichever God you call with this spell shall have to fall under your power, good woman. Whether willing or unwilling, that God is bound to be in your power and, controlled by your spell, to bow to your word like a servant.

Vaiśaṃpāyana said:

The innocent girl could not refuse that eminent brahmin a second
20 time, O king, out of fear for his curse. Thereupon the brahmin taught
the flawless maiden a series of spells that are revealed in the
Atharvaśiras. Having bestowed this, Indra of princes, he said to
Kuntibhoja, "I have dwelled joyfully in your house, king, and have
grown contented with your daughter who has obeyed me well and
honored me happily. Let us be done now!" he said and disappeared.
And when the king saw the brahmin disappear on the spot, he became
astonished and complimented Pṛthā.

Vaiśaṃpāyana said:

290.1 When that best of the twice-born had gone and some time had
passed, the maiden reflected upon the weakness or power of her canon
of spells. "What is this canon of spells like that the great-spirited seer
has given me? I shall very soon know its power!" While she was
pondering thus, she noticed that her period had happened, and the
young woman was ashamed having her flow while she still was a
spinster.

Then Pṛthā saw the thousand-rayed sun rise ablaze, and she was
5 not sated of the beauty of the sun enveloped by the dawn. Her eyesight
became divine, and she saw the God of divine aspect, accoutred with
armor and adorned with earrings. And a curiosity arose in her
concerning her spell, O lord of the people, and the radiant woman cast
forth a summons to the God. She rinsed her vital airs and called the
sun; and there he came, the Sun, hastening, O king. His complexion
was honey-yellow, his arms were large, his neck grooved like a conch
shell. He seemed to laugh, he wore upper arm bracelets, and appeared
to set fire to space. By his wizardry he had split himself in two, and
thus came there and went on shining in the sky. Then he spoke to
10 Kuntī coaxingly, and exceedingly sweetly, "I have come into your
power, good woman, by the force of your spell. What shall I do,

helplessly, queen? Speak, I shall accomplish it for you!"

Kuntī said:

Go back, my lord, whence thou hast come! Be gracious, my lord! I have summoned thee out of curiosity.

The Sun said:

Go I shall, as you tell me, small-waisted woman. But surely it is not
fitting to summon a God and send him away pointlessly! Your
intention, lovable girl, was to have a son by the sun, peerless in the
world for his prowess, and wearing armor and earrings. So woman
who strides like an elephant, give yourself to me, for I shall father a
15 son such as you desire. Or I shall go, good woman of the lovely smile,
without having lain with you, and I shall be angry and curse you, the
brahmin, and your father. On your account I shall set fire to them all,
no doubt of that, and to your foolish father who does not know of your
misconduct; and on that brahmin who gave you the spell without
knowing your character and behavior I shall heap extreme discipline.
All these Gods in heaven headed by Indra now see how I am deceived
by you, and they seem to be smiling, radiant woman—look at those
throngs of Gods, for you have divine eyesight: I gave it to you, so that
you could see me.

Vaiśaṃpāyana said:

20 And the princess saw the Thirty Gods,
All comfortable in their proper spheres,
And that mighty luminous God
Who gave forth light like the sun itself.

Upon seeing them the young woman, a goddess,
Grew bashful and fearful, and said to the Sun,
"Go, Lord of the cows, to thy own domain,
Your wooing spells grief to my maidenhood.

'My father and mother and other elders
Have the power to give this body away.
I shan't in this world infringe the Law—
To guard her body is a woman's glory.

"I summoned thee childishly, to learn the power of the spells; pray forgive me, my lord, I am only a child!"

Vaiśaṃpāyana said:

291.1 The headstrong girl spoke many a sweet word, but was unable to coax away the thousand-rayed Sun. When the maiden could not discourage the Dispeller of Darkness, she for a long time thought about a way out, O king, for fear of his curse: "How can I prevent that my innocent father, and the brahmin too, is cursed on my account by that angry Sun? The powers of fieriness and austerity, even though concealed, are not to be overreached foolishly, even if one is a child. Now I am sorely afraid, and sorely held by the hand—but how can I myself perpetrate the gift of myself, as it is forbidden?" Most fearful of the curse, she thought much in this manner and kept smiling, while her body was wrapped in confusion. Afraid for her relatives and fearing the curse, she spoke to the God in a voice unnerved by shame, O best of kings, lord of the people.

Kuntī said:

God, my father is alive, and my mother and other relatives. No such breach of the rules should occur while they are alive. If I lie with thee, God, against the rules, then the good name of my family in the world will perish on my account. But if thou thinkest this is the Law, O chief of the fiery ones, I shall do thy wish without being given away by my relatives. Having made the gift of myself, irresistible one, I shall remain virtuous—in thee are the Law, renown, fame, and life of the embodied!

The Sun said:

Neither your father, nor your mother and elders, sweet smiling girl of the beautiful hips, are capable—hail to thee! Listen to my word: a free girl is on earth called *kanyā*, from the root *kan*, my radiant, callipygous, fair-complexioned maiden, because she desires them all. You have perpetrated no lawlessness at all, beaming girl—how could *I* commit an Unlaw who have the well-being of the world at heart? All women are untrammeled, as are men, fair girl, this is the nature of people; anything different is known as perverse. Having lain with me you shall be a virgin again, and you shall have a strong-armed son of great renown.

Kuntī said:

If I receive a son from you, dispeller of all darkness, let him be ringed and armored, a hero of strong arms and great strength!

The Sun said:

Your strong-armed man child shall wear earrings and divine armor, and they both will be made of the Elixir, good woman.

Kuntī said:

If my son's earrings and superb armor will be made from the Elixir, then father him on me! I shall lie with thee, God, as my lord hath said, and may he have the gallantry, beauty, mettle, and prowess of thyself!

The Sun said:

Queen so excitable, Aditi herself gave me these earrings. I shall give them to him, timorous maiden, as well as this superb armor.

Pṛthā said:

I shall lie with thee blissfully, my Lord God, if my son will be as thou sayest, Lord of the cows!

Vaiśaṃpāyana said:

"So be it!" said the ranger of the skies, and he, the enemy of Svarbhānu, entered Kuntī in his yogic person, and he touched her to the navel. And the power of the Sun well-nigh unnerved the royal maiden, and she fell on her bed stupefied.

The Sun said:

25 I shall be done now, woman with the lovely buttocks. You shall
give birth to a son who shall be the first of all bearers of arms, and
you shall be a virgin.

Vaiśaṃpāyana said:

Bashfully the girl said to the Sun, "So be it," Indra among kings; and the Sun departed in all his splendor.

> When King Kunti's daughter had thus been promised
> At her bashful soliciting of the Sun,
> She fell on her blessed couch, and confusion
> Set in as she lay there, a broken creeper.
>
> And the Sun, confounding her with his splendor,
> With his wizardry entered and made her pregnant.
> But the day star did not despoil her at all,
> And the young woman again returned to her senses.

Vaiśaṃpāyana said:

292.1 Thereupon a child grew in Pṛthā, O king of the earth, as in the sky the
moon grows on the first day of the eleventh fortnight. Out of fear for her
relatives the young woman of the lovely hips hid her pregnancy while
she was carrying the child, and people did not find her out. But for her
nurse no other woman knew about the young girl who lived in the
maiden quarters and was clever at protecting herself. And in time the
fair, unmarried woman gave birth to a child as lustrous as an
5 Immortal by the grace of the God. He had a coat of mail tied on, and
sparkling golden earrings; and he was as orange-eyed and bull-
shouldered as his father. At the counsel of her nurse the radiant
maiden placed the child, as soon as it was born, in a basket that was
well-packed on all sides. And in that basket, comfortable, soft, sealed
with beeswax, and finely covered, she tearfully set her child afloat in
the River Aśva.

Though she knew that an unmarried girl is forbidden to bear a
child she lamented piteously, O Indra of kings, out of love for her son.
And as she cast off the basket in the water of the River Aśva, Kuntī
10 tearfully spoke these words, listen: "May you be safe from the
creatures of earth, atmosphere, and heaven, and from those that live
in the water, little son. May your pathways be auspicious, and not
adverse, and those who approach you, son, be without malice. May
King Varuṇa guard you in the water, the lord of the waters, and so in
the sky the wind that goes everywhere. May your shining father, best
of all lights, guard you everywhere, he who has given you to me, son,

by divine ordinance to be sure. The Ādityas, Vasus, Rudras, Sādhyas,
and All-the-Gods, the Maruts with Indra, and the Regions and their
15 Guardians, all celestials must protect you, in the smooth and in the
rough. I shall know you, even when abroad, by the armor that
betokens you.

"Fortunate is your begetter, son, the God Sun who shines wide, for
he will see you going down the river with his divine eye. Fortunate the
woman who will adopt you as her son, for you will drink thirstily at
her breast, son of a God. What dream will she have, the woman who
will adopt you who are as lustrous as the sun, wearing armor,
adorned with divine earrings, with long and wide lotus-like eyes, with
copper-red handpalms like red lotuses, and fine brow and handsome
20 locks? Fortunate they who will see you crawling on the floor, my son,
babbling away in sweet broken words and covered with dust.
Fortunate they who will see you in the bloom of your youth, like a
lion in full mane, born in the Himālayan wilderness!"

Thus did Pṛthā lament variously and pitifully as she floated the
basket on the water of the River Aśva, in the dead of night,
accompanied by her nurse, O king, weeping from her lotus eyes out of
grief over her son, yearning to see her man-child. After casting away
the basket, she reentered the royal palace, sick with sorrow and in fear
25 of awakening her father. From the River Aśva the basket floated into
the River Carmaṇvatī, from the Carmaṇvatī into the Yamunā, and
from the Yamunā into the Ganges. On the Ganges it came to the city
of Campā, which was the dwelling place of the Sūta. And in that
basket, carried on by the waves, the child wore its divine armor and
earrings that had sprung from the Elixir, the child and its ordained
destiny.

Vaiśaṃpāyana said:

293.1 At this very time a friend of Dhṛtarāṣṭra, a Sūta by the name of
Adhiratha, went with his wife to the Jāhnavī.* His wife, Rādhā by
name, was unequaled on earth in beauty, but the noble lady had not
found a son, though she had made special efforts to have children. She
happened to see the basket floating in the river with amulet ribbons
and adorned with a handle, and the waves of the Jāhnavī carried it
near her. Out of curiosity the radiant woman had the basket caught,
5 and told the Sūta Adhiratha about it. He reached out and lifted the
basket from the water, then he had it pried open with tools and saw
in it a little boy, bright like the morning sun, wearing golden armor
and with a face that was illumined by polished earrings.

The Sūta's and his wife's eyes widened with astonishment, and he
lifted the child on his lap and said to his wife, "For as long as I have

* = Ganges.

lived, this is indeed a miracle I behold, my timid and radiant wife! I
think this is the child of a God that has come to us. Surely the Gods
have given him as a son to me who am childless." With these words
10 he gave the son to Rādhā, O king, and Rādhā accepted the divine-
looking child duly as her son, this child of a God luminous as a lotus
cup and covered with fortune.

She nurtured him duly, and he grew up strong, and from then on
she had other sons of her own. Seeing that the child wore a costly
armor and golden earrings, the twice-born gave him the name of
Vasuṣeṇa. Thus the prince of boundless might came to be the son of a
Sūta known as Vasuṣeṇa and also Vṛṣa. The eldest son of the Sūta
grew up powerful of limb; Pṛthā found out about his wearing divine
15 armor through a spy. The Sūta Adhiratha, on seeing his son grown up
in time, dispatched him to the City of the Elephant. There he
approached Droṇa to learn archery, and the mighty man became
friendly with Duryodhana. He obtained the fourfold weaponry from
Droṇa, Kṛpa, and Rāma and became famed in this world as a superb
archer. Having allied himself with Dhṛtarāṣṭra's son and being hostile
to the Pārthas, he always hoped to do battle with the great-spirited
Phalguna. He always competed with Arjuna, O king of your people,
20 and Arjuna with him, from their first meeting onward. Yudhiṣṭhira,
seeing that Karṇa had earrings and was clad in armor, thought he
was invincible in war, and he was most unhappy.

When Karṇa, O Indra of kings, praised the shining sun at high
noon, standing in the water with folded hands, brahmins who wished
wealth used to approach him there, and at that point of time he could
not refuse the twice-born anything. Now Indra became a brahmin and
approached him: "Give me alms!" and Rādheya said, "You are
welcome."

Vaiśampāyana said:

294.1 When Vṛṣa saw the king of the Gods arrive disguised as a brahmin,
he bade him welcome. He did not know his intentions. "Can I give you
pretty women with golden throats, or villages with many cow-pens?"
said Adhiratha's son to the brahmin.

The brahmin said:

I do not want the gift of beautiful women with golden throats, or
other things that increase pleasure. Let them be given to those who
want for them. It is your inborn armor and earrings I want, man sans
blame. Cut them off and give them to me, if you are a man of your
5 word! Those I want you to give me at once, enemy-burner. That I
deem the greatest present of all!

Karṇa said:

I will give you land, women, cows, and rice for many years,

brahmin, but not my armor and earrings!

Vaiśaṃpāyana said:

Karṇa pleaded with the brahmin in these and various words, best of the Bharatas, but he chose no other boon. Though coaxed as much as he could, and honored according to the rules, the eminent brahmin desired no other boon. When the good brahmin chose nothing else,
10 Rādheya began to laugh and said, "My innate armor and earrings have sprung from the Elixir, therefore I cannot be killed anywhere in the worlds, and hence I will not give them away. Take from me my vast kingdom on earth, secure and without rivals, take it confidently, bull of the brahmins. If I am deprived of my earrings and my innate armor, I shall be vulnerable to my enemies, best of the twice-born!"

Vaiśaṃpāyana said:

When the blessed lord who is the Chastiser of Pāka did not choose another boon, Karṇa began to laugh and again said to him, "Lord God of Gods! I already knew who you were. And it would not be right for
15 me to give you a boon in the wrong spirit: for you are the lord of the God himself, so you should give *me* a boon, as you are the master of all other creatures, creator of creatures! If I am to give you, God, the earrings and armor, I shall become vulnerable, and you, O Śakra, laughable. Then take my earrings and superb armor from me, if you wish, Śakra, but as a barter; otherwise I will not give them."

Śakra said:

You had learned from the Sun that it was I who was coming—he told you all, no doubt of that! Very well, have what you wish, Karṇa. Except for my thunderbolt, choose what you wish.

Vaiśaṃpāyana said:

20 Karṇa thereupon joyously went up to Vāsava and, his desire fulfilled, chose the Never-failing Spear.

Karṇa said:

For the armor and the earrings, Vāsava, give me the Never-failing Spear, which kills masses of enemies on the battlefield.

Vaiśaṃpāyana said:

Vāsava reflected for a moment in his mind, O protector of the earth, and he said to Karṇa anent the Spear, "Give me the earrings and your inborn armor, Karṇa, and you will take the Spear from me on this condition. The Never-failing Spear when flung from my hands kills my enemies by the hundred when I am fighting the Daityas, and afterward
25 it returns to my hand. In your hand the Spear shall kill one powerful, thundering and sparkling enemy, but then, son of the Sūta, it shall return to me again!"

Karṇa said:

I want to kill but one enemy in a great battle, thundering and sparkling, of whom I stand in fear.

Indra said:

You shall kill one powerful and thunderous enemy in battle. But the one you want is protected by the great-spirited One whom the *Veda*-wise call the Boar, the unvanquished Hari, and the inconceivable Nārāyaṇa. He, Kṛṣṇa, protects him!

Karṇa said:

So let this supreme Never-failing Spear be mine for the slaying of
30 one hero, so that I may kill the fierce man! I shall strip off the earrings
and the armor and give them to you; and may I not look loathsome
with my body flayed.

Indra said:

You shall not look loathsome, Karṇa. Since you do not want to belie yourself, no wound shall show on your body. You shall once more have the skin color and splendor such as your father has, eloquent Karṇa! But if you unleash the Never-failing Spear absentmindedly, when other weapons are at hand, it shall fall upon yourself, without a doubt.

Karṇa said:

I shall fling Indra's spear only when I am in the greatest danger, just as you say, Śakra. This promise I make!

Vaiśaṃpāyana said:

35 Having accepted the flaming Spear, O lord of your people, he took
his sharp sword and flayed his entire body.

When the Gods and men and Dānavas
And the hosts of the Siddhas witnessed Karṇa
Flaying himself, they all roared forth,
For he moved no muscle in spite of the pain.

To the thundering sound of celestial drums
A divine rain of flowers fell from above
At the sight of Karṇa now flayed by his sword,
While that hero of men smiled time and again.

Having cut his armor loose from his body,
He gave it still wet to Vāsava;
He cut off his earrings and gave those too—
For his feat he is known as Vaikartana.

And Śakra laughed gleefully at his deception,
Which brought Karṇa renown in the world,
For he thought he had rescued the Pāṇḍavas;
And he flew thereupon back up to his heaven.

40 Having heard that Karṇa was robbed, the Kurus
All were dejected, their pride was broken;

And hearing the state that Karṇa was led to,
The Pāṇḍavas out in the forest rejoiced.

Janamejaya said:
But where were the Pāṇḍava heroes staying,
And whence did they hear the agreeable tidings?
When the twelfth year passed, what did they do?
Reveal, O my lord, all this to me.

Vaiśaṃpāyana said:
Having routed the Saindhava and regained Kṛṣṇā,
They left the Kāmyaka hermitage
With their priests, retainers, and chariots
After hearing the old feats of Gods and seers

In all their fullness from Mārkaṇḍeya,
And with all their cooks and kitchen masters
The heroes repaired to blissful Dvaita,
Having finished their full, dread stay in the forest.

3(44) The Drilling Woods

295–99 (B. 311–15; C. 17225–478)
295 (311; 17225). At Dvaitavana a brahmin, whose fire-drilling woods have been caught in a deer's antlers, asks Yudhiṣṭhira to retrieve them (1–10). The Paṇḍavas go in pursuit but do not find the deer (10–15).
296 (312; 17243). Yudhiṣṭhira tells Nakula to climb a tree and look for water (1–5). Nakula sees water birds and finds a lake with cranes; when he is about to drink, a voice warns him not to do so before he has answered questions. He pays no heed and collapses (5–10). Yudhiṣṭhira sends Sahadeva and the same happens (10–15). Arjuna follows, shoots arrows, and collapses (20–30), and finally Bhīma (30–35). Yudhiṣṭhira then goes himself (35–40).
297 (313; 17298). Yudhiṣṭhira finds his brothers and is puzzled (1–5). He plunges into the lake, and the voice warns him first to answer questions; Yudhiṣṭhira sees a Yakṣa, who repeats the warning (5–10). Yudhiṣṭhira agrees; the questions elicit proverbial responses (20–60). The Yakṣa allows him the life of one brother; Yudhiṣṭhira chooses Nakula's life, to the Yakṣa's astonishment

(65–70). The Yakṣa revives all the brothers (70).
298 (314; 17419). The Yakṣa reveals himself as Dharma and bestows a boon on Yudhiṣṭhira, who chooses the recovery of the brahmin's drilling woods (1–10). For his second boon he chooses that the Pāṇḍavas be not recognized during their thirteenth year of exile (10–20). For a third boon he chooses high moral character (20–25).
299 (319; 17450). Ready to leave the forest, Yudhiṣṭhira laments and Dhaumya comforts him: other heroes have gone into hiding before and triumphed later (1–15). Bhīma promises victory (20). The brahmins bless them and depart; the Pāṇḍavas journey a short distance and camp (25).

Janamejaya said:
295.1 After the Pāṇḍavas suffered dire distress when Kṛṣṇā had been
abducted, and had gained her back, what did they do?
Vaiśaṃpāyana said:
After they suffered dire distress when Kṛṣṇā had been abducted,
King Acyuta* and his brothers left Kāmyaka. Yudhiṣṭhira once more
went to lovely Dvaitavana by Mārkaṇḍeya's fetching hermitage where
the roots and fruit were sweet. The Pāṇḍavas all kept to a diet of fruit
and ate sparingly while they dwelled there with Kṛṣṇā, O Bhārata.
5 Living in Dvaitavana, King Yudhiṣṭhira, son of Kuntī, Bhīmasena,
Arjuna, and the twin sons of Mādrī, those Law-spirited enemy-burners
of strict vows, found when acting boldly in a brahmin's cause great
sorrow that ended in happiness.
While Ajātaśatru was sitting with his brothers in the forest, a
brahmin came running to him and said in anguish, "My gear with my
drilling woods was hanging from a tree, and it got caught in the
antlers of a deer that was rubbing against it. The big deer ran away
with it, king, dashing fast from the hermitage, leaping with great
10 speed. Follow its trail quickly and attack the big deer. Bring it back,
Pāṇḍavas, so my *agnihotra* is not spoiled!"
When Yudhiṣṭhira heard the brahmin's words, he was upset; and
the Kaunteya took his bow and rushed off with his brothers. All the
bowmen, bulls among men, girt themselves and hurried off in the
brahmin's cause and quickly pursued the deer. Shooting eared shafts,
reeds, and iron arrows, the warlike Pāṇḍavas yet did not hit the deer
that they saw close by. And while they were so busying themselves,
15 the deer disappeared. The mindful men no longer saw the deer, and

* = Yudhiṣṭhira.

they were tired and discouraged. In the depths of the forest the Pāṇḍavas sought shelter in the cool shade of a banyan tree and, their bodies sore with hunger and thirst, sat down together. While they were sitting there, Nakula said with vexation and impatience to his eldest brother, O chief of the Kurus,

> "The Law never lapses in this our house,
> Nor does laziness thwart our purposeful ends—
> Then why are we, who are peerless among
> All creatures, again in danger, O King?"

Yudhiṣṭhira said:
296.1 Misfortune has neither limit, condition, nor cause. The Law
distributes it here according to both good and bad.
Bhīma said:
The reason we are in danger is that I did not kill the usher who
brought Kṛṣṇā to the Hall like a servant!
Arjuna said:
The reason we are in danger is that I tolerated the harsh, bone-
piercing words that the *sūta's* son spoke!
Sahadeva said:
The reason we are in danger is that I did not kill Śakuni when he
had defeated you in the dicing game, Bhārata!
Vaiśaṃpāyana said:
5 King Yudhiṣṭhira said to Nakula, "Climb a tree, Mādreya, and look
in the ten directions. Look for water close by, or trees that grow near
water, for your brothers are tired, friend, and thirsty."
Nakula agreed, quickly climbed a tree, looked in all directions, and
said to his eldest brother, "I see plenty of trees that grow near water,
king, and I hear the screeching of cranes there is water here, no doubt
of that." Thereupon Kuntī's son Yudhiṣṭhira, steadfast in truth, said to
10 him, "Go, friend, and quickly fetch water to drink." Nakula agreed and
at his eldest brother's orders he rushed to the water, which he reached
shortly. He saw pure water surrounded by cranes, but when he
wanted to drink, he heard a voice from heaven: "Commit no violence,
friend. This is my old property. Answer my questions, Mādreya, then
you may drink and fetch." Nakula, who was very thirsty, did not heed
these words and drank the cool water. And having drunk he collapsed.
When Nakula was long returning, Kuntī's son Yudhiṣṭhira said to
15 his brother Sahadeva, heroic enemy-tamer, "Your brother is long,
Sahadeva, your senior brother. Go fetch your brother, and bring
water." Sahadeva agreed, went in the same direction, and saw his
brother collapsed on the ground. Burning with grief for his brother and
being sorely pressed by thirst, he ran to the water, and the voice said,

"Commit no violence, friend. This is my old property. Answer my questions if you please, then you may drink and fetch." Sahadeva, who was thirsty, did not heed these words, and drank the cool water. And having drunk he collapsed.

Then Kuntī's son Yudhiṣṭhira said to Vijaya, "Your brothers have been long gone, Terrifier, plower of your enemies. Go fetch them, hail to thee! and bring water." At these words Guḍākeśa took his bows and arrows and with sword drawn the sagacious man made for the lake. Then he of the white horses saw his tiger-like brothers fallen where they had gone to fetch water. The Kaunteya, a lion among men, struck by grief when he saw them as though asleep, raised his bow and looked into the forest. The left-handed archer saw no creature at all in the vast wilderness, and wearily he rushed to the water. As he did so the voice spoke from the sky, "Why did you come near? You cannot take this water by force. If you answer my questions, Kaunteya, then you shall drink and fetch the water, Bhārata!" Thus having been halted the Pārtha said, "Stop me where I can see you, so that you, pierced by my arrows, won't speak like this again!" The Pārtha pelted that entire region with enchanted arrows, displaying his skill at sound shooting. Discharging eared shafts, and iron arrows, O bull of the Bharatas, he showered the sky with many swarms of arrows.

The Yakṣa said:

What does this shooting profit you, Pārtha? Answer my questions and drink. If you do not answer you shall cease to be as soon as you drink!

Vaiśaṃpāyana said:

But after shooting off his never-failing arrows, Arjuna was so pressed by thirst that without paying heed to the questions he drank, and at once he collapsed.

Then Kuntī's son Yudhiṣṭhira said to Bhīmasena, "Nakula, Sahadeva, and the unvanquished Terrifier have now been gone for water a long time, and they are not coming back. Fetch them, Bhārata, hail to thee! and bring back water." Bhīmasena agreed and went to the same spot where his brothers, tigers among men, had been felled. Upon seeing them, and being sorely pressed by thirst, strong-armed Bhīma thought that it was the work of Yakṣas or Rākṣasas and reflected that he certainly would have to put up a fight. "But I shall first drink the water," and so the wolf-bellied Pārtha, bull among men, thirstily ran to the water.

The Yakṣa said:

Do not commit violence, friend. This is my old property. But answer my questions, Kaunteya, and you shall drink and fetch.

Vaiśaṃpāyana said:

At these words of the Yakṣa of boundless splendor, he did not pay heed, drank, and collapsed at once.

Thereupon Kuntī's son the king, bull among men, began pondering,
40 and the strong-armed man rose up with his mind on fire. He entered
the vast wilderness, whence all sound of people had gone. *Ruru* deer
frequented the woods, and bear and fowl, it was made beautiful by
dark and luminous trees, and it was buzzing with bees and birds as the
glorious man made his entrance. Walking in the forest the illustrious
prince set eyes upon that lake adorned with piles of gold, as though it
had been fashioned by Viśvakarman, on that lake covered with lotus
beds, *negundo* lilies, and reeds, with *ketakas*, *karavīras*, and *pippalas*. And
wearily he approached the lake and looked at it with amazement.

Vaiśaṃpāyana said:

297.1 There he saw his brothers, the likes of Śakra in weight, fallen like
the World Guardians when they are toppled at the end of the Eon. On
seeing Arjuna felled, with his bows and arrows scattered, and
Bhīmasena, and the twins, all motionless and lifeless, he shed tears of
grief and sighed long and hotly. In his mind he wondered, "Who has
felled the heroes? There is no mark of a weapon on them, nor is there
a sign of anyone else. Methinks it is some great being that has slain
my brothers. I must ponder this with my full mind—or after I have
5 drunk I shall find out. Well may it be that this is the work ordained
secretly by Duryodhana, and set afoot by the Gāndhāra prince of the
crooked mind as always. What hero would put his trust in that man of
evil mind and unmade spirit, for whom right and wrong are the same?
Or this may be the design of that evil spirit through hidden
henchmen!"

Thus the strong-armed prince thought in various ways. It occurred
to him that the water was not poisoned, as his brothers' faces were
healthy of color. "Who," he thought, "but Yama who finishes in Time
could best these superb men with the force of a flood one by one?"
10 With this conclusion he waded into the water; and as he plunged in
he heard from the sky—

The Yakṣa said:

A crane that lives on duckweed and fishes,
I have brought your brothers in the power of death.
You, son of a king, shall be the fifth
If you do not reply to the questions I ask!

Commit no violence, friend, this is my old property. But answer my
questions, Kaunteya, then drink and fetch!

Yudhiṣṭhira said:

I ask you, who are you, a God, the chief of the Rudras, the Vasus,
or the Maruts? This is not the doing of a Śakuni! Who in his splendor
has felled unto earth the four mountains Himālaya, Pariyātra,
15 Vindhya, and Malaya? First among the strong, a supremely great deed

have you accomplished, which neither Gods, nor Gandharvas, nor
Asuras, nor Rākṣasas would be able to do, a great miracle have you
wrought in a great battle. I do not know the task you have, I do not
fathom your intentions. Great curiosity has been aroused in me, and
terror has come over me. You who have brought anguish to my heart
and fever to my head, who, I ask you, are you who stand there?

The Yakṣa said:

I am a Yakṣa, hail to thee! I am no bird of the water. It is I who
felled all your august brothers!

Vaiśaṃpāyana said:

Upon hearing the ominous, rough-spoken words that the Yakṣa had
20 spoken, O king, he kept coming closer. And the bull of the Bharatas
saw standing on a dam an odd-eyed, big-bodied Yakṣa, tall as a palm,
fiery like fire and sun, unconquerable and mountainous, who was
chiding him powerfully in a voice as deep as a thunderclap.

The Yakṣa said:

I stopped these brothers of yours time and again, king, when they
tried to take water by force. Then I finished them off. This water is not
to be drunk by anyone here who wants to live, king. Pārtha, do not
commit violence! This is my old property. But answer my questions,
Kaunteya, and you may drink and fetch.

Yudhiṣṭhira said:

I do not at all covet your old property, Yakṣa, for strict people never
25 approve of such coveting. As a person himself gives an account of
himself, I shall answer your questions according to my lights, my lord.
Ask me!

The Yakṣa said:

What causes the sun to rise, and what are its companions? What
makes it set, and on what is it founded?

Yudhiṣṭhira said:

Brahman makes the sun rise, and the Gods are its companions. The
Law makes it set, and on truth is it founded.

The Yakṣa said:

By what does one become learned, by what does one attain to great
things, by what does one have a second, king, by what does one gain
insight?

Yudhiṣṭhira said:

By learning one becomes learned, by austerities one attains to great
things; one has a second in perseverance, one gains insight by
attending on one's elders.

The Yakṣa said:

30 What is the divine nature of the brahmins, what is their Law, like
that of the strict, what is their human nature, what is their vice as of
those without strictness?

Yudhiṣṭhira said:

Veda study is their divine nature, austerity their Law, as it is of the strict; mortality is their human nature, detraction their vice, as it is of those without strictness.

The Yakṣa said:

What is the human nature of the barons, what their Law, as it is of the strict? What is their human nature, what their vice, as it is of those without strictness?

Yudhiṣṭhira said:

Weaponry is their divine nature, sacrifice their Law, as it is of the strict; fear is their human nature, desertion their vice, as it is of those without strictness.

The Yakṣa said:

Which is the one sacrificial chant, which is the one sacrificial formula? What cuts down the sacrifice, what does the sacrifice not exceed?

Yudhiṣṭhira said:

35 Breath is the sacrificial chant, mind the sacrificial formula; speech alone cuts down the sacrifice, and the sacrifice does not exceed speech.

The Yakṣa said:

What is the best of the dropping, what is the best of the falling, what is the best of the standing, what is the best of the speaking?

Yudhiṣṭhira said:

Rain is the best of the dropping, seed the best of the falling, cows the best of the standing, a son the best of the speaking.

The Yakṣa said:

Who breathes, experiences the objects of the senses, is intelligent, honored in the world, and respected by all creatures—yet is not alive?

Yudhiṣṭhira said:

He who makes no offerings to the five, to wit Gods, guests, dependents, ancestors, and himself, may breathe but is not alive.

The Yakṣa said:

40 What has more weight than the earth, what is higher than heaven, what is faster than the wind, what more numerous than men?

Yudhiṣṭhira said:

The mother has more weight than the earth, the father is higher than heaven, the mind is faster than the wind, worries are more numerous than men.

The Yakṣa said:

What does not close the eyes when asleep, what does not stir when born, what has no heart, what grows by speeding along?

Yudhiṣṭhira said:

A fish does not close the eyes when asleep, an egg does not stir when born, a rock has no heart, a river grows by speeding along.

The Yakṣa said:

What is the friend of the traveler, what the friend at home, what the friend of the sick man, what the friend of the moribund?

Yudiṣṭhira said:

45 The caravan is the friend of the traveler, the wife is the friend at home, the physician is the friend of the sick man, charity the friend of the moribund.

The Yakṣa said:

What travels alone, what once born is born again, what is the cure for snow, what is the great acre?

Yudhiṣṭhira said:

The sun travels alone, the moon is reborn, fire is the cure of snow, the earth is the great acre.

The Yakṣa said:

What in a word makes the Law, what in a word is fame, what in a word leads to heaven, what in a word is happiness?

Yudhiṣṭhira said:

Ability in a word makes the Law, giving in a word is fame, truth in a word leads to heaven, character in a word is happiness.

The Yakṣa said:

50 What is the self of a man, what is the friend made by fate, what is the support of his life, what is his highest resort?

Yudhiṣṭhira said:

A son is the self of a man, a wife is the friend made by fate, the monsoon is the support of his life, charity is his highest resort.

The Yakṣa said:

What is the greatest of riches, what is the greatest of possessions, what is the greatest of boons, what is the greatest of comforts?

Yudhiṣṭhira said:

Ability is the greatest of riches, learning the greatest of possessions, health the greatest of boons, contentment the greatest of comforts.

The Yakṣa said:

What is the highest Law in the world, what Law always bears fruit, what does not grieve when tamed, what bond never comes loose?

Yudhiṣṭhira said:

55 Uncruelty is the highest Law, the Law of the *Veda* always bears fruit, the mind does not grieve when tamed, the bond of the good never comes loose.

The Yakṣa said:

Abandoning what does one become friendly, abandoning what does one not grieve, abandoning what does one become rich, abandoning what does one become happy?

Yudhiṣṭhira said:

Abandoning pride one becomes friendly, abandoning anger one

does not grieve, abandoning desire one does become rich, abandoning greed one becomes happy.

The Yakṣa said:

How is a man dead, how is a kingdom dead, how is a *śrāddha* dead, how is a sacrifice dead?

Yudhiṣṭhira said:

A poor man is dead, a kingless kingdom is dead, a *śrāddha* without a learned brahmin is dead, a sacrifice without payment is dead.

The Yakṣa said:

What is the right direction? What is called water? What is food, Pārtha, and what poison? Tell me the time for a *śrāddha*, then you may drink and fetch.

Yudhiṣṭhira said:

The strict are the right direction, space is water, the cow is food, a request is poison; and a brahmin is the right time for a *śrāddha*—or do you think otherwise, Yakṣa?

The Yakṣa said:

You have answered my questions correctly, enemy-burner! Now tell me, who is a man, and what man owns all riches?

Yudhiṣṭhira said:

The repute of a good deed touches heaven and earth; one is called a man as long as his repute lasts. And *he* possesses all riches to whom the pleasing and displeasing are the same, and happiness and unhappiness, past and future.

The Yakṣa said:

You have explained man and the baronial man of all riches. For that, one of your brothers shall live, whoever you please.

Yudhiṣṭhira said:

The dark one with the red eyes, shot up like a tall *śāla* tree, with the wide chest and the long arms, O Yakṣa, he shall live—Nakula!

The Yakṣa said:

You have Bhīmasena, you rely on Arjuna, then why, king, do you want their rival Nakula to live? You give up Bhīma, whose strength is the match of a myriad elephants, and want Nakula to live? People say you hold this Bhīmasena so dearly, then by what greater affection do you want his rival to live? All the Pāṇḍavas rely on the strength of Arjuna's arms, yet you abandon him and want Nakula to live?

Yudhiṣṭhira said:

Uncruelty is the highest of Laws, this I know as the final truth. And I will not be cruel, so, Yakṣa, Nakula shall live! "The king is by character always lawful." This do people know of me; and I shall not stray from my Law—Nakula shall live, Yakṣa! As Kuntī was, so was Mādrī; I allow no difference. I want the same for both my mothers—Nakula shall live, Yakṣa!

The Yakṣa said:

Uncruelty you hold superior to profit and pleasure: for that all your brothers shall live, Bharata bull!

Vaiśaṃpāyana said:

298.1 At that Yakṣa's word the Pāṇḍavas stood up, and the hunger and
thirst of all of them instantly disappeared.

Yudhiṣṭhira said:

I ask you, who are you, a God, who stands invincibly on one leg in
the lake? I do not think you are a Yakṣa. Are you one of the Vasus or
Rudras, or the chief of the Maruts, or the Thunderbolt-wielder, the
lord of the Thirty? For these brothers of mine can fight hundreds and
thousands, and I fail to perceive the manner in which they could be
5 brought down. I observe that their faculties have returned now that
they have been peaceably awakened—you are our friend, or are you
our father?

The Yakṣa said:

I am your begetter, son, the God Dharma, O man of mild prowess!
Know, Bull of the Bharatas, that I have come out of a desire to see
you. Fame, truth, self-control, purity, uprightness, modesty,
steadfastness, liberality, austerities, and chastity are my bodies.
Nonviolence, equanimity, tranquillity, austerity, purity, and
unenviousness—know that these are the doors to me. It is fortunate
that you are devoted to the five, and fortunate that you have
conquered the six states; two occur early, two in the middle, and two
10 at the end, leading to the world hereafter. I am Dharma, hail to thee!
and have come here to try you. I am pleased with your want of
cruelty. Prince sans blame, I shall grant you a boon. Choose a boon,
Indra of kings, for I shall grant it to you, blameless man. No mishap
befalls those men who are devoted to me!

Yudhiṣṭhira said:

May the fires of the brahmin whose drilling sticks that deer carried off not be disrupted! That shall be my first boon.

Dharma said:

I took the drilling woods of the brahmin in the guise of a deer, Lord Kaunteya, in order to test you.

Vaiśaṃpāyana said:

The blessed lord promised in answer, "I shall grant it! Choose another boon, hail to thee, God-like man."

Yudhiṣṭhira said:

15 The twelve years in the forest have passed, the thirteenth is at hand.
May people not recognize us wherever we dwell.

Vaiśaṃpāyana said:

The blessed lord promised in answer, "I grant it!" and once more

gave comfort to the Kaunteya, whose prowess was his truth. "Even though you may roam this earth in your own persons, no one in the three worlds will recognize you, Bhārata! By my grace you, scions of Kuru, shall live this thirteenth year hidden and unrecognized in the city of Virāṭa. Whatever appearance anyone of you fancies, that
20 appearance you all shall have according to your wish. Return these drilling woods to the brahmin, for I stole them in the guise of a deer in order to try you.

"Now choose a third boon, son, one incomparably great, for you have sprung from me, and Vidura partakes of a portion of me."

Yudhiṣṭhira said:

I have set eyes on your person, on you the everlasting God of Gods. I shall contentedly accept that boon, father, which you yourself will give me. May I conquer greed, and folly, and anger forever, my lord, and may my mind always be on charity, austerity, and truthfulness.

Dharma said:

25 By your very nature are you endowed with all virtues, Pāṇḍava. You are the King Dharma. Again you shall have what you ask.

Vaiśaṃpāyana said:

Having said this Dharma disappeared, the blessed lord who prospers the worlds; and the high-minded Pāṇḍavas slept peacefully together. Rested, the heroes all returned to the hermitage and gave the drilling woods to the austere brahmin.

> A self-controlled man, the master of his senses,
> Who recites the great story of the *Revival*
> *And Encounter* of father and son shall live
> For a hundred years with his sons and grandsons.
>
> And people who know this good tale will never
> Delight in lawlessness, nor in estranging
> Old friends, nor in theft or adultery,
> Nor in any ignoble way of life.

Vaiśaṃpāyana said:

299.1 When the Pāṇḍavas, whose prowess was their truth, had been dismissed by Dharma, and were about to embark upon a life of concealment in the thirteenth year, the sagacious men of strict vows seated themselves humbly; and the great-spirited and well-taught brothers spoke with folded hands to the ascetics who out of devotion for them had dwelled in the forest with them, in order to ask their leave to end the sojourn to which they had so avowedly held. "It is known to you entirely how we have been plundered of our kingdom and possessions in various ways by the deceitful Dhārtarāṣṭras. We now have lived in the forest, with much hardship, for twelve years, and during the remaining thirteenth year, the span of our life of concealment, shall remain hidden with equal hardship. Pray give us leave. Suyodhana of wicked soul, Karṇa and Saubala will, when they find us out, make trouble for our townsfolk and kinsmen and be committed in their efforts, for they are endlessly resentful of us. Shall it come to pass that we once more will live as kings in our royal domains in the company of brahmins?"

As he said this, the pure King Yudhiṣṭhira, the son of Dharma, felt so oppressed by sorrow and grief that he choked with tears and fainted.

All the brahmins and his brothers comforted him; and thereupon Dhaumya spoke these words of great import in reply to the king: "Sire, you are wise, controlled, true to your promises, and master of your senses, and such men do not lose their heads in any emergency. Even the great-spirited Gods in case of emergencies have often gone into hiding in various places to subdue their rivals. Indra went to the Niṣadhas, hid away in a hermitage on a mountain plateau, and accomplished the feat of subduing the power of his enemies. Viṣṇu, before he was to lie in Aditi's womb, lived for a long while in hiding, wearing a horse's head, to kill off the Daityas. You have heard how he who has the form of Brahman* assumed the shape of a dwarf and hid, and with his strides took the kingdom from Bali. You have heard, son, what the brahmin seer Aurva accomplished in the worlds while lying hidden in his mother's thigh. You have heard, Law-wise prince, what Hari accomplished when he entered and hid in Śakra's thunderbolt in order to subdue Vṛtra. You have heard what the Fire did for the Gods after entering the waters and staying concealed. Likewise Vivasvat of supreme splendor lived on earth in hiding and burned down all his enemies. Viṣṇu lived in Daśaratha's house,** and in disguise the God of terrible deeds killed Ten-headed Rāvaṇa in battle. Thus these great-spirited beings lived in hiding and vanquished their enemies in battle. So shall you triumph!"

Yudhiṣṭhira, gratefully comforted by these words of the Law-wise Dhaumya, no more wavered from the spirit of the *śāstras* and that of his own. Then the strong-armed and powerful Bhīmasena, strong of the strong, spoke to the king, raising his spirits: "Out of deference to you, great king, and in a spirit obedient to the Law, the Gāṇḍīva bowman has not burst into violence yet. I constantly keep Sahadeva and Nakula in check—these enemy-killers of terrible prowess are well capable of crushing the foes. We shall not desert whatever task you lay on us. You yourself must dispose it all, and we shall speedily vanquish the enemies!"

* = Viṣṇu.
** = as Rāma.

25 When Bhīmasena had spoken, the brahmins pronounced the most solemn benedictions, said farewell to the Bharatas, and went each to his own house. All the eminent *Veda*-wise ascetics and hermits spoke blessings according to the rules, hoping to see them again. Then the five sagacious Pāṇḍavas rose with Dhaumya; and taking Kṛṣṇā the heroes set out.

They journeyed the distance of a shout from that place for a reason, and on the morrow those tiger-like men, who stood ready to begin their life of concealment, sat down together in council; and they all knew different arts, were experts in counseling, and knew the time of peace and the time of war.

Notes

The Book of the Assembly Hall

2(20) The Building of the Assembly Hall

1.5. *Viśvakarman*, the architect of the Gods.

10. *Designs* seems in the context the best fitting translation of *abhiprāya*.

15. *The feats of the ancient Gods* (*pūrvadevacarita*, lit. of the "previous" Gods), viz., the Asuras, who are the "elder brothers of the Devas."

2(20.a) The Halls of the World Guardians

2.20. *Covenants*, namely to meet again.

3.1. *Vṛṣaparvan*, the old king of the Asuras, vid. *The Beginning, The Story of Yayāti, MBh.* 1 (7c), I:171 ff.

5. *Yauvanāśva*: Māndhātar, son of Yuvanāśva, an ancient *samrāj*; his story in *The Forest, The Story of Māndhātar*, 3(33)(e). ***Bhagīratha*: on his story vid. *Forest*, p. 427; he too was a *samrāj*.

10. *Not to set an example*: because they were unique. D.: "not declared in the *kalpasūtras*."

25. *Kiṃkaras*: lit. "servants"; as Rākṣasa equals Asura in the epic, it is possible to think of them as Maya's Persian guard.

30. *Some kings that came there*: notably Duryodhana, cf. below chap. 43 ff. ***Cakra birds*: cakravākas (*anas Casarcus*).

4.10. *Māṇḍavya-with-the-Stake*: for his story vid. *Beginning, MBh.* 1(6), I:134.

5.5. *Law, Profit, and Pleasure*: the three pursuits of men (*puruṣārtha*), covering all his lawful activities in life.

10. *Distributing them over time*: according to *Forest*, p. 288, Law should be pursued in the morning, Profit in the afternoon, Pleasure at night; Pleasure in the first period of life, Profit in the second, Law in the third. ***Six royal virtues*: D.: peace, war, conveyance, throne, enmity, and recourse. ***Seven means*: D.: flattery, bribery, alienation, punishment, disregards, witchcraft, magic tricks. ***The fourteen factors*: D.: elephants, horses, chariots, soldiers, weapons, allies, food, liquor, treasure, sentiments of amorousness, etc., harem; the *etc.* seems to cover heroism and awesomeness, the royal *rasas*. ***Eight trades*: D.

quotes *Kāmaṇḍaka Nīti* 5.77, which enumerates: plowing, commerce, fortification, damming, elephant training, digging, tax collecting, and settling of open land; D. gives as alternatives: eight royal occupations: hearing reports on the country's defense, on the income, and on the outgo; inspection of civil works (*paurakārya*); house-to-house inspection of bathing and dining conditions; inspection of horses, elephants, and arsenal; and horse training. ***Six officers*: the kingdom's seven *prakṛtis* minus the king himself; *Manu* 9.295: prince, minister, citadel, kingdom, treasury, punishment, and ally; but since our text obviously refers to persons, we might prefer D., who quotes: the officers in charge of the fort, executions, law and land; envoy; priest; and soothsayer—the "officer of the land" being the king himself.

20. *Capable of living*: in good health.

25. *Eighteen officers*: D. councillor, priest, army commander, Young King, doorkeeper, majordomo, herald, collector, manager (*saṃvidha?*), instructor, chief citizen, judge, administrator, council superintendent, mace bearer, overseer of fortifications. ***Fifteen*: probably the eighteen above minus councillor, priest, and Young King.

35. *Overbearing*: *ugrapratigrahitāram?*; D. *nityam ādānaśīlam*, "always in the habit of grasping."

45. *Threefold force*: elephant, horse, foot; D. strength of councillors, of retainers, and of allies.

50. *Four kinds of troops*: elephants, chariots, cavalry, and infantry; D., N.: troops of natives, retainers, allies, and forest tribes. ***Eight factors*: N.: chariots, elephants, horses, warriors, footmen, servants, spies, and principal inhabitants.

55. *Report your vice-induced outlays*: to show how much the king's dissipations have cost him.

65. *Pratika*: one *karṣāpana*, a weight of coins of varying value; the sense conveyed seems to be "a loan at 1 percent."

70. *Professions*: D.: husbandry, cattle-tending, commerce. ***Five officers*: the *pañcāyat*: but D.: the officers of the treasury, fortifications, countryside, punishment, and council. ***Old robbers*: hereditary dacoit tribes.

75. *Act like a Yama*: i.e., with severe justice. ***Eight-membered medicine*: treatment of intestinal ailments, infantile illnesses, planetary influences, thorns, fangs, discolored secretions, sores, and poison.

85. There appears to be no further information of the identity of a *puṇḍarīka* ("lotus") sacrifice; could it be a common *pūjā*? The next line seems to indicate this.

100. *Agnihotra*: a milk offering to the sun at dawn and dusk, the simplest of Vedic *śrauta* rites.

105. *Honey and butter*: probably a reference to the *madhuparka* (honey and milk) offered to brahmin guests, who by their consequent blessing of the king should keep his realm prosperous.

110. *City engineering*: *yantrasūtram nāgaram*. ***Brahmā's Staff*: D.: sorcery, that means *brahmadaṇḍa* in the sense of "punishment through *brahman*, i.e., spells."

6.5. *Smilingly*: D.: to reprove Yudhiṣṭhira's self-pride.

10. *The king of the ancestors*: Yama, who commands the south. ***Varuṇa* is the regent of the west. ***Indra*, of the east. ***Who dwells on Kailāsa*: Kubera, the regent of the north.

7.5. *Hrī, Kīrti, and Dyuti*: feminine personifications of modesty, fame, and splendor.

15. *Agnīṣoma*, etc.: deities to whom Soma oblations are offered.

20. *Stobhas*, i.e., the Sāmaveda. ***Mantras*, i.e., the *Ṛgveda*. ***Bṛhaspati and Śukra*: god-statesmen, of Devas and Asuras respectively.

25. *Puṣkaramālinī*: "lotus-garlanded."

8.25. *Who have a yogic body*, i.e., not their material body but one created with the power of their Yoga magic. ***Others who have bodies*, that means that the aforementioned classes of deceased ancestors are incorporeal. ***Śiṃśapa*: the sissoo tree, often associated with burning grounds. ***Palāśa*: *Butea Frondosa*. ***Kāśa*: the grass *Saccharum Spontaneum*. ***Kuśa*: the grass *Poa Cynosuroides*, used at sacrifices.

9.1. *Inside water*: Varuṇa being the god of the ocean.

5. *Vāruṇī*: his consort. ***Ādityas*: a group of gods, originally seven, headed by Varuṇa: Varuṇa, Mitra, Aryaman, Bhaga, Dakṣa, Aṃśa, and Savitar, to whom later other Gods are added, notably Viṣṇu, "the last and the greatest." ***Vasuki*, etc.: names of Snakes (*nāgas*) who are associated with water because they appear in great numbers during the rainy season.

10. *Kālakhañjas*: also known as a tribe of demons related to the Asuras of whom Varuṇa is the chief.

15. *Daityas and Dānavas*: synonyms of Asuras. ***Noose of the Law*: the weapon of Varuṇa. ***Kālindī*: the river Yamunā.

10.10. *Gandharvas*: here = Yakṣas.

15. *Śrī*: she being also the Goddess of wealth.

20. *Paśupati*: the god Śiva, who has a special relationship with Kubera; both live in the Himālaya. ***Slew Bhaganetra*: Bhaganetrahan/hara is an epithet of Śiva, interpreted as "robber of the eyes of Bhaga," for which *MBh.* 13, 175, provides the story. Is there more to it? Bhaganetra means also "with vaginas for eyes," reminiscent of Indra, "the God of the Hundred Eyes," which were originally vaginas covering his body as punishment for his lechery.

11.1. *Eon of the Gods*: the Kṛtayuga. **Āditya: the Sun God.

15. *Source-stuff and Evolute*: *prakṛti* and *vikāra*, which are cosmogonic causes in Sāṃkhya. ***Twenty-seven world guardians*: the 27 *nakṣatra* constellations of the lunar zodiac.

20. *Śukra*: the planet Venus; *Bṛhaspati*: Jupiter; *Budha*: Mercury; *Angāraka*: Mars; *Sanaiścara*: Saturn; *Rāhu*: the planet demon causing eclipses. ***Mantra*: Ṛgvedic verse; *Rathantara*: Sāmavedic melody. ***Double names*: e.g., *mitrāvaruṇau* "Mitra and Varuṇa." ***Books*: so? Text *parvāṇi*. ***Subordinate Vedas*: the *upavedas*, e.g., *dhanurveda*: archery; *gandharvaveda*: art of music. ***Sāvitrī*: the verse *RV.* 3.62.10, with which Vedic study begins.

25. *Sevenfold speech*: Māgadhī, Avanti, Prācya, Śauraseni, Ardhamāgadhī, Bāhlika, and Dakṣiṇātya; D.: Sanskrit, Prākrit, Paiśācī, Apabhraṃśa, profane (*laukika*), double entendre, and children's speech. ***Aditi*, etc., progenitrixes of Ādityas, Daityas, snakes, birds, Apsarās, Kālakeya demons, Devas, cows, and dogs; Gautamī is uncertain.

65. *They shall become*: it is unclear who the subjects are, I assume the Pāṇḍavas. ***Brahmin Rākṣasas*: Rākṣasas of brahmin rank who are out to obstruct brahmin rites.

2(21) The Council

12.1. *Ajātaśatru*, a regular name of Yudhiṣṭhira, lit., "He whose enemy has not yet been born."

10. *Varuṇa*: reminiscent of Varuṇa's high position in the Vedic pantheon. ***Six fires*: D. interprets these as fire rites: *agniṣṭoma*, *kṣatradhṛti*, *vyuṣṭi*, *dvirātrī*, *saptapeya*, and *saptadaśapeya* sacrifices.

20. *The anointing itself*: the unction (*abhiṣeka*) is the most important part of the consecration.

30. *Indrasena*: Yudhiṣṭhira's charioteer. ***His father's sister*: Kuntī.

13.1. *Have determined their lineage*, etc.: *krto'yam kulasaṃkalpaḥ kṣatriyaiḥ . . . nideśavāgbhih*; in other words, those barons have legitimized their dynasties by decree.

5. *Ila and Ikṣvāku*: founders of the solar and lunar dynasties respectively, the two official branches of the baronage, which here play no real role. ***Dynasties of Yayāti and the Bhojas*: the latter are the nonroyal descendants of Yayāti's first four sons; the descendants of his fifth son Pūru carry the dynasty; see *Beginning*, p. 191 ff. ***Double dispersion*: *dviguṇo* fits the context more meaningfully than (cr. ed.) *'tiguṇo*, since two parties are named: Yayāti's legitimate scions and the Bhojas. ***Honors their royalty*: the context appears to imply that such dynasts, though their *lakṣmī* is recognized, are not included among the 101. ***From birth*: so? *yonitaḥ*. But I do not see how *sāmrājya* is inheritable, unless one

invokes *Aitareya Brāhmaṇa* 8.14.2.3, where the presumably inheriting kings of the east are called *samrāj*. ***The mighty Śiśupāla*, etc.: D. wants to interpret this as: "being his marshal, has become King Śiśupala," which makes good sense too.

10. *(Bhagadatta) rules in the West*: but Arjuna conquers him in the North; below, p. 78.

15. *King of the Cedis*: but he is Śiśupala. Some conflation seems to have taken place between two of Kṛṣṇa's enemies, Śiśupala of Cedi and Vāsudeva of Puṇḍra. *Caturyu* appears only here as another name of Jarāsaṃdha; curiously another Caturyu occurs in the same chapter, below 20.

20. *Pāṇḍya*: a kingdom in South India. ***As his relations*: Kṛṣṇa's Vṛṣṇis belong to the Bhoja group.

25. *The other Pāñcālas*: the northern ones. ***Kaṃsa*: son of Ugrasena and cousin of Kṛṣṇa's mother Devakī.

43. *To his own city from Śūrasena*: *svapuram śūrasenānām*. Since Mathurā is in Śūrasena and Jarāsaṃdha obviously withdraws, so that the Vṛṣṇis can return to Mathurā, the only possible interpretation of the genitive is as an ablative; or we might simply adopt the reading *śūrasenebhyas* of a number of MSS.

45. *Kuśasthalī*: another name for Dvārakā/Dvāravatī.

52. *Mādhavītīrtha*: unknown otherwise. Since Mount Raivata is a *tīrtha*, it is preferable to take *mādhavītīrtham* as appositional to *girimukhyam*. The feminine *mādhavī* remains puzzling; perhaps we should accept the reading *mādhavaṃ tīrtham*, the *tīrtha* of the Mādhavas.

55. *The middle country*: here the region of Mathurā.

14.5. *From their release*: viz., of the captive kings.

15.11. *Determination*: *siddhiḥ*, which D. glosses *manobalam*.

15. *The saffron robe*: here pejorative as a symbol of undue resignation.

16.10. *Fasts and consecrations*: before a person is inaugurated for a sacrifice, he must fast.

15. *He would never offend him*: sc. by preferring one over the other.

17.5. *He became Jarāsaṃdha*: *saṃdha* is from *saṃdhi* "joint."

2(22) The Killing of Jarāsaṃdha

18.1. *Battle of breath*: endurance wrestling match.

25. *Suppressing works*, viz., the enemy's. ***Kālakūṭa*: name of a mountain of uncertain location, but in any case to the north. If we are to take the sequence literally (*krameṇaiva*), it is a circuitous route: first NE to Kālakūṭa, then S to cross the Gaṇḍakī. For them to cross the Śoṇa, a southern tributary of the Yamunā before crossing the Sadānīra, a northern tributary W of the Śoṇa, makes no sense; the order should be reversed. ***Sarayū*: river by the capital of Kosala. ***Carmaṇvatī*: a tributary of the Yamunā far SW of the Sarāyu. This part of the itinerary makes even less sense. ***Kurava*: must be the same as Kurabaka, the red amaranth tree.

19.1. *Stands guard over Girivraja*: i.e., the fortress nestles between these hills. ***Lodhra*: the *lodh* tree (*Symplocos Racemosa*).

5. *Priyāla*: the *piyāl* tree (*Buchanania Latifolia*).

15. *Had three bean stalks made into kettledrums*: *māṣanālās ca tisro bherīr akārayat*: I do not know how to picture this. D. *māsaśabdena dvādaśasaṃkhyā lakṣyate/vitastir anguṣṭham madhyame tālam dvadaśatālapramāṇa ity arthaḥ*, reading *tāla* for *nālā*. V., which reads *māṣanālāt*, explains the words as meaning the horns and neck of the bull, i.e., *ṛṣabha*. I prefer taking *ṛṣabha* as a proper name, perhaps of a vegetarian, bean-eating Jaina, which is at least more unusual than a bean-eating bull. But why Bṛhadratha should have killed a Jaina (or a bull) is still another riddle. ***The heroes broke in*: avoiding the main gate,

they breach the tower on the top of the *caitya*; I take *śṛnga* as "tower," because *purātana* "ancient" suggests it was manmade.

20. *Royal road*: the main street leading to the palace.

25. *Colorful robes*: *virāga* in the sense of "with various (red) colors"; D.: *vicitra*.

30. *His liferule*: it certainly demonstrates his piety.

35. *This much I know*: but in fact Snātakas do wear adornment (cf. Heesterman, "Samāvartana"), so perhaps we should take *snātaka* vow as "a vow to become a Snātaka," i.e., a young *brahmacārin*.

20.25. *Sahadeva*: Bṛhadratha's eldest son.

21.13. *Drove them off*: text *utsārya janam*; N. reads *utsāryajanam* as a *bahuvrīhi* compound, which seems preferable.

22.2. *Strangle him with his loincloth*: so? Text: *nāyaṃ pāpo mayā yuktaḥ syād anurodhitum/prāṇena . . . baddhavankṣaṇavāsasā*; I take *baddha*° as a *bahuvrīhi* to *mayā*.

25. *Vasu had obtained it*: the story in *Beginning*, *MBh.* 1(6), I:130 ff.

2(23) The Conquest of the World

23.1. *I have got a bow*: same line above 2.15.7.

15. *Śakala*: present Sialkot in Kashmir; the "islands" probably refer to Kashmir, which has many lakes. ***Prāgjyotiṣa*: Assam.

24.15. *Utsavasaṃketa tribes*: tribes that had a compact regarding festivals, i.e., sealing their compacts at specific feasts?

20. *Suhmas*: West Bengal. ***Coḷas*: they really belong in the South. ***Bahlikas*: in the Panjāb.

26.1. *Gaṇḍakī*: a river, tributary to the Ganges and constituting a boundary of Videha.

27.15. *Karṇa*: who had been made king of Anga; for the account see *Beginning*, *MBh.* 1(8) 127, I:281 ff.

20. *Pauṇḍras*: West Bengal. ***Vanga*: Bengal. ***Lauhitya*: the Brahmaputra.

28.5. *The mighty warrior vanquished*: the cr. ed. deletes the bracketed line, but some such reference is required to account for *tebhyaḥ*, "from them."

15. *Māhiṣmatī*: city in Avanti by the River Carmaṇvatī.

25. *Jātavedas*: attempt at etymology.

45. *Coḍras*: the Coḷas.

50. *Antioch and Rome*: see F. Edgerton, "Rome and (?) Antioch in the Mahābhārata," *J.A.O.S.*, 58.

29.1. *Conquered by Kṛṣṇa*: apparently a reference to the founding of Dvārakā; so the region stands for the West.

5. *Desert Country*: the desert of Sindh.

30. *Indrasena* is Yudhiṣṭhira's charioteer, Viśoka is Bhīma's. ***Satyavatī's son* is Kṛṣṇa Dvaipāyana. ***Brahmán*: the principal priest of the group belonging to the Atharvaveda; the office indicates that Kṛṣṇa belonged to the Angiras priesthood. ***Bull of the Dhanaṃjayas*: there occurs in the *Lāṭyayana śrautasūtra* (1.6.13) of the Sāmaveda an expert named Dhānaṃjayya, indicating that there was an old Samaveda family called Dhanaṃjaya. ***Yājñavalkya . . . adhvaryu*: a great sage known from earlier literature, notably the *Bṛhadāraṇyaka Upaniṣad*: he belonged to the White Yajurveda; the *adhvaryu* was the principal of the Yajurvedic group, responsible for the implementation of the actual rites. ***Paila*, known to the *Aśvālayana gṛhyasūtra* of the *Ṛgveda*, was a promulgator of the *Veda*; the *hotar* is the principal priest of the Ṛgvedic group. ***Shelters*: *śaraṇa* is often used for structures on the sacrificial terrain containing the fire hearths. ***Instructed Sahadeva*: who therefore acts as the *Somapravāka*, "proclaimer of the Soma sacrifice."

2(24) The Royal Consecration

31.15. *Middle Country*: the region of Mathurā.

20. *Sadasya*: name of one who is invited to sit with the sacrificer in the *sadas*, that area of the terrain where most of the priests sit.

32.5. *Saṃjaya*: the charioteer and confidant of Dhṛtarāṣṭra.

2(25) The Taking of the Guest Gift

33.10. *Partial incarnations*: see *Beginning*, *MBh.* 1(7.a), I:151 ff.

34.1. *Son of a river*: Bhīṣma, the son of the Ganges.

5. *Who is no king*: Indeed, Kṛṣṇa Vāsudeva is not called a *rājan*, and generally this is not a title used for the Vṛṣṇis, either because they were under the curse that Yayāti put on the Yādavas that they would be *bhojas*, not kings (*MBh.* 1.(7).79, I:192.) or because their form of government was not of the *rājya*, but *gaṇa* type.

10. *Once slew a king*: according to D. Kaṃsa, but he might well be Jarāsaṃdha.

35.20. *Unmanifest Cause and Sempiternal Doer*: *eṣa prakṛtir avyaktā kartā caiva sanātanaḥ*: that is to say, he is both the prakṛti, or material nature, and the soul active in it. ***Spirit*: *buddhi*; mind: *manas*; the Large One: *mahān*, often = *buddhi*, but here closer to *ahaṃkāra* (so D.). The series comprises the early eight prakṛtis (cf. my "Studies in Early Sāṃkhya 2: Ahaṃkāra," and "3: Sattva," *J.A.O.S.* 77(1957), and "The Large Atman," *History of Religions* 4(1964). ***Fourfold creation*: beings born alive, from eggs, from sweat (insects, etc.), and from plants.

36.1. *Put this foot of mine*: I shall humble him.

5. *Sunītha* here appears as another name of Śiśupāla.

10. *Commander of the army*: as he had been of King Jarāsaṃdha.

2(26) The Slaying of Śiśupāla

38.1. *Who live like a eunuch*: *tṛtīyāyāṃ prakṛtau*, lit., "in the third nature [= sex]," a reference to Bhīṣma's celibacy.

5. *The vulture*: the vulture-demoness Pūtanā. ***Aśva and Vṛṣabha*: the horse-shaped Keśin and the bull-shaped Ariṣṭa. **While a baby, Kṛṣṇa was left to sleep under a cart and he upended it with one kick. ***The mountain Govardhana*: Kṛṣṇa lifted that mountain to provide shelter for the rain-pelted cowherds.

15. *Cow-killer*: because he has killed the bull-shaped Ariṣṭa; *woman-killer*: because of the demoness Pūtanā. ***bhūlinga bird*: a bird that picks meat remnants from a lion's teeth, example of foolhardiness.

20. *Ambā who loved another*: see above, 1.96.47 ff. Ambā, however, was rejected by Śālva, the man she loved, and was reborn as Śikhaṇḍin, who was to cause Bhīṣma's death. ***The king did not seek*: this implies, no doubt insultingly, that not Bhīṣma but Vicitravīrya had released Ambā. ***Another had to beget offspring for you*: viz., Kṛṣṇa Dvaipāyana. ***Your celibacy is a lie*: i.e., hypocritical.

39.5. *Why did he not truthfully know*: if he had been omnipotent, he could have changed himself into a brahmin and have no cause to pretend.

10. *Mahāsena*: the war god Kārttikeya.

41.5. *For a Bhoja*: acc. to D. = Kaṃsa. ***Does not come by nature*: is hypocritical.

42.35. *Removal Ceremony*: the *avabṛtha* rite at the conclusion of the sacrifice, when the utensils are carried to a river and cast away, and the participants bathe.

2(27) The Dicing

The Dicing is complicated by the fact that of parts of it two versions appear side by side. The first one, at least the one that appears chronologically first, may be called the *simplicior*; the second, being more ornate, the *ornatior*. The *simplicior* comprises chaps. 43–45, ending with Dhṛtarāṣṭra's consent to the dicing and the building of a thousand-pillared hall; the *ornatior* comprises 46–51, also ending with Dhṛtarāṣṭra's consent and the building of the hall. The *ornatior* brings more color and drama to the story, but is otherwise completely parallel. Duryodhana's resentment before Śakuni is recast as his resentment before Dhṛtarāṣṭra, with massive descriptions of the magnificence of Yudhiṣṭhira's *rājasūya* added. As in the *simplicior*, Dhṛtarāṣṭra says he will seek advice from Vidura; in both versions Duryodhana protests. The transition between both versions is Dhṛtarāṣṭra's abrupt rescinding of his permission to dice (46).

Chaps. 52–59 show no divergence of versions, but chap. 60 once more has two varying accounts. First Duryodhana sends a *pratikāmin*, an usher, to fetch Draupadī; the usher goes and tells her that she has been gambled away. She sends the usher back with her famous question whether Yudhiṣṭhira had already gambled away himself before staking her. The usher once more returns to Draupadī.

Then suddenly Yudhiṣṭhira has an "acceptable messenger" at his disposal, whom he sends to Draupadī; she comes along meekly to the hall and stands before Dhṛtarāṣṭra (60.14–15). But in 60.16 she is still where she was in the woman's quarters. Duryodhana again dispatches the usher, who now (17) refuses to go, though in 60.3 he had no compunctions. Finally Duḥśāsana is sent.

Yudhiṣṭhira's sending his acceptable messenger, Draupadī's meek appearance before Dhṛtarāṣṭra, and her immediate translation back to where she was make no sense in the present context; nevertheless this *śloka* episode amidst *triṣṭubhs* may be the remnant of a simpler original. It is further possible to speculate that there was an usher version and a Duḥśāsana version, which have been blended.

43.5. *To save his face*: *ākāraṃ rakṣamāṇas*.

44.5. *Carry that hall*: *vahanti tāṃ sabhām*; I am not sure how to understand this.

45.20. *Vāṭadhāna*: a northwestern region south of the Indus. Were these brahmins not pure enough to rate admission, unless they paid more?

50. *Kali* was the God of gambling and discord.

55. *He went to Bhīṣma*: this incident is not followed up.

46.1. *The Bard said*: this bard can only be Ugraśravas, who is recounting to the hermits of the Naimiṣa Forest Vaiśaṃpāyana's account to Janamejaya. His unexpected appearance here is interesting. So, for that matter, is Janamejaya's, who asks only three questions in all of *The Assembly Hall*: at 2.28.16, here, and at the start of *The Sequel to the Dicing*. It is as though a new chapter begins after what might have been taken as a summary preamble.

47.5. The Govāsana and Dāsamīya brahmins clearly parallel the Vātadhāna ones of 45.20. ***Bharukaccha*: the modern Broach on the Arabian Sea.

10. *A jade vase*: *aśmasāramayaṃ bhāṇḍam*; *aśmasāra* ("essence of stone") is recorded as iron; but an "iron coffer" does not sound too munificent; a kind of precious stone seems to be meant.

25. *Romaśas*: could this name stand for the Romans? It is not inconceivable, given the fact that Rome is known to this Book; cf. above 2.28.50. One may note that a similar "suffix" is found in another borrowed name, the Pauliśa of the *Pauliśa-siddhānta*; apparently out of Paulus.

48.5. *Pipīlaka ants*: this is the only Indian reference in my knowledge to the fabled gold-digging ants of which Herodotus wrote (III.102): "There are found in this desert (viz., in northeastern Afghanistan) ants not as big as dogs but bigger than foxes . . . These ants make their dwellings underground, digging out the sand in the same manner as do the ants in Greece, to which they are very alike in shape, and the sand which they carry forth from the holes is full of gold." Note that this gold here is equally fabulous and ascribed to people who seem to be aborigines. ***Lohitya*: the River Brahmaputra.

10. *Daradas*: Dardic-speaking peoples of the NW. ***Bāhlīkas*: Bactrian. ***Kāśmīras*: people from Kashmir. ***Pahlavas*: Persians (cf. Persian *pahlaw*). ***Śakas*: Scythians.

15. *Vanga and Kalinga*: SE Bengal and Orissa. ***Tāmraliptakas and Puṇḍrakas*: people from southern and northern Bengal. ***Ḍukūla*: name of a plant with the fibers of which fine cloth is woven. ***Lotus-dotted*: Franklin Edgerton, in his introduction to *The Elephant Lore of the Hindus* (New Haven, 1931), quoting G. H. Evans, *Elephants and their diseases* (Rangoon, 1910), which was not available to me, writes as follows: "Evans . . . also mentions the good and bad points of elephants, chiefly on the basis of present-day beliefs in Burma. Of interest to us is the reference to "light-colored spots and blotches on the head and trunk," which are "pinkish in color," and are regarded as favorable marks. [G. P.] Sanderson (in *Thirteen Years among the Wild Beasts of India* [London, 1879]) also says that in India "if the face, base of trunk, and ears be blotched with cream-colored markings, the animal's value is enhanced thereby." It seems universally agreed among European observers that really "white" elephants do not exist, in spite of the traditional value attached to them, especially in Siam. ***Always rutting*: "rutting" is only an approximate rendering of the Sanskrit *matta*. The *matta* elephant, more generally known as the *must* elephant, is normally male and, more often than not, in the cold season undergoes a physiological change: its temporal glands swell and secrete an oily ichor. It becomes excited and at times dangerous (Edgerton, p. 29 ff., with quotations). Since this condition occurs only when the elephants are in good health, well taken care of, and underworked, the expression "rutting elephant" indicates one in the pink of health.

20. *Citraratha gave steeds*: are these the Gandharva horses he promised the Pāṇḍavas in *The Book of Citraratha* (1.158.45 ff.)?

30. *Siṃhalas*: Ceylonese.

35. *Blessing of the day*: *puṇyāhavācana*, a ceremony of good auspices.

49.1. *Concluding bath of the Upaniṣads*: for they constitute the *Vedānta*, the conclusion of the *Veda*. ***Wild cows*: *āraṇyāḥ* "belonging to the forest"; D.: "well-fed as though from the forest."

5. *Bāhlīka*: king of the Bāhlīkas. ***Sudakṣina*: king of the Kambojas. ***Sunītha*: Śiśupāla, the king of Cedi. ***The Magadhan*: Sahadeva of Magadha. ***Vasudāna*: king of Pāṃśu. ***Matsya*: Virāṭa, king of Matsya. ***Ekalavya*: the king of the humble Niṣādas, cf. *The Beginning* 1.123. ***Cekitāna*: a Vṛṣṇi chief.

15. *Dhṛṣṭadyumna*, etc.: the eight warriors who will survive the Bhārata war.

20. *Śambara's slayer*: Indra; but D. surprisingly = Kāma.

50.10. *You always say*: I am not sure I understand this: *bhaviṣyam artham ākhyāsi sadā tvaṃ kṛtyam ātmanaḥ* "you always call your own task a future matter"; D. for *bhaviṣyam*: *daivādhīnam*.

20. *Namuci*: an Asura.

51.1. *The dicing rug*: the carpet on which the dice were spread.

52.25. *Rohinī*: the constellation of Aldebaran (α, β, γ, δ, ε, Tauri). ***The four Pāṇḍavas that is*: implying that Yudhiṣṭhira had already been welcomed.

53.10. *The injunction is powerful*: *vidhi* is first of all the ritual injunction.

55.1. *Like a jackal*: 1.107.25 ff. ***Kāvya*: Uśanas Kāvya, who first laid down the prohibition against drinking liquor *MBh.* 1(7.c), I:179.

5. *This man*: Duryodhana is meant.

10. *Jambha*: an Asura killed by either Kṛṣṇa, Arjuna, or Indra. **This must, with Aesop 87, be one of the oldest mentions of the Goose That Laid the Golden Eggs.

56.6 A very difficult *triṣṭubh*. Every *pāda* appears to be a separate sentence. I take *arvākphalaḥ* of *a* as a bahuvrīhi to *ākarṣa*, "having downward fruit," i.e., resulting in downfall. In *pāda b*, *hṛdi prauḍho mantrapadaḥ samādhiḥ*, the only solution I see is to take *mantrapadaḥ* not as a nominative of *mantrapada*, but as a genitive of *mantrapad/pād*: "of him who steps according to council," this council being that of the *rājasūya*, cf. 2 (21) *The Book of the Council*. *Samādhi* in the sense of "attentiveness, absorbedness." The meaning of the sense is a warning: Yudhiṣṭhira, who, after council, has embarked on the *rājasūya*, is paying very close attention "in his heart," without letting on.

57.1. *Fratricide*: by Vidura's opposing Dhṛtarāṣṭra.

10. *If one has lit*: the idea is that of a forest fire: if one does not stay ahead of it, one dies.

20. At this point Vidura washes his hands of the matter, but remains in the hall, cf. 2.58.40.

58. *Whatever belongs to our color of people*: so? *yat kiṃcid anuvarṇānām* may possibly also mean "whatever [wealth] there is [of domestic animals] according to their different species."

15. *You are our elder and better*: I take this as sarcastic.

59.5. The bamboo fructifies after many years, then dies.

6–7. Repeated from 1.82.8 and 11.

8. For the history of the interpretation of this *triṣṭubh*, see Franklin Edgerton, "The Goat and the Knife," *J.A.O.S.* 59: 366 ff. It is found with variant in *Jātaka* 481: Some goat-thieves who lived in Benares having stolen a she-goat one night, determined to make a meal in the forest; to prevent her bleating they muffled her snout and tied her up in a bamboo clump. Next day, on their way to kill her, they forgot the chopper. "Now we'll kill the goat and cook her," said they; "bring the chopper here!" But nobody had one. "Without the chopper," said they, "we cannot eat the beast, even if we kill her: let her go! This is due to some merit of hers." So they let her go. Now it happened that a worker in bamboo, who had been there for a bundle of them, left a basket-maker's knife there hidden among the leaves, intending to use it when he came again. But the goat, thinking herself to be free, began playing about under the bamboo clump and, kicking with her hind legs, made the knife drop. The thieves heard the sound of the falling knife, and on coming to find out what it was, saw it, to their great delight; then they killed the goat and ate her flesh. The version of our verse, that the goat dug up the knife, seems to be the more current one; it is also found in the Greek version of Zenobius.

60.15. *In her one garment*: because she was in her menstrual period.

25. *You cannot take me*: because she was polluted and polluting.

30. *In this good man*: Dhṛtarāṣṭra.

61.5. *Sahadeva, bring the fire*: he is the keeper of the sacred fire of the Pāṇḍavas.

35. *She . . . is a whore*: this is one of the few occasions that Draupadī is berated for her polyandry.

62.25. *They must make King Dharma a liar*: the insistence with which the Pāṇḍavas, esp. Yudhiṣṭhira, are urged to speak out is intriguing and needs explaining. It is not only the question of Draupadī's status that is raised, but the King Dharma's very veracity is in question. For, if Yudhiṣṭhira were to confirm that he had *truthfully* staked himself, he had no right to stake Draupadī and his staking her was a *lie*. Yudhiṣṭhira cannot very well confirm that she was either won or not, for in either case he would have to confirm a lie: if she was won, he lied about his own stake, for he would still have been free to stake her; if she was not won, because he was no longer free, his staking her was the lie. Besides, the debate is riddled with other uncertainties, like can a slave have a wife of his own? and, can there be too much provocation for a passionate gambler?

63.1. *You are* his *now*: i.e., Duryodhana's.

10. *He exposed his left thigh*: while one might well think that the exposure of the thigh is a bowlderized version of the exposure of more private parts, there is no reason to. What Duryodhana is doing in showing Draupadī his left thigh is to invite her to sit on it as his wife. Compare *The Beginning* 1.92.9–10: "You embrace me while sitting on my right thigh, beautiful woman, that is the place to sit for children and daughters-in-law. The share of the mistress (= wife) is on the left." Of course, Indian art is replete with examples of wives sitting on their husbands' left thighs, from the donor couples of Bharhut and Sanchi onward; the posture is particularly prevalent in the iconography of Śiva and Pārvatī.

2(28) The Sequel to the Dicing

68.1. *Now the Wheel has begun*: i.e., the sovereignty.

10. *The Pārthas are eunuchs*: the idea is that when the Pāṇḍavas live in the forest they observe celibacy.

71.15. *Ruled by the Law of women*: in her menses.

Notes

The Book of the Forest

3(29) The Forest Teachings

1.40. *The hour that is both lovely and fearful*: dusk, when demoniac powers are strongest; cf. 1.158.5 ff.

2.10. It cannot be made out whether Sāṃkhya and Yoga are to be taken technically; there is little in Śaunaka's discourse to suggest this. The terms are probably used generally as in *The Bhagavadgītā*.

15. *Eight-membered*: if this refers to Yoga, the members are *yama* (restraints), *niyama* (constraints), *āsana* (posture), *prāṇāyāma* (breath control), *pratyāhāra* (sense withdrawal), *dhāraṇā* (retention of a thought), *dhyāna* (protracted meditation), *samādhi* (complete absorption). ***Janaka*, a king famous for his wisdom since his first appearances in *Śatapatha Brāhmaṇa* 11.3; 4; 6 ff., *Bṛhadāraṇyaka Upaniṣad* 3–5. It is not clear where Janaka's supposed discourse ends; fairly arbitrarily, I have it end at sloka 37.

50. *Do not cook for themselves*: ascetics.

55. *Vaiśvadeva offering*: of cooked food to Agni, Soma, Viśve Devāḥ, Dhanvantari, Kuhu, Anumati, Prajāpati, heaven, earth, and Agni Sviṣṭakṛt; *Manusmṛti* 3.84–86.

60. *Six senses*: the five and the coordinating sense (*manas*).

65. *Runaround*: viz. of transmigration (*saṃsāra*).

70. *Eightfold path*: this is of course contra the Buddhist path. ***The first four*: because they can be observed hypocritically, they do not by themselves lead to the supreme good. ***Ancestors' Journey*: the notion (e.g., *Chāndogya Upaniṣad* 5) that after death one can go two ways, the path of the ancestors (*pitṛyāna*), which leads back to transmigration, and the path of the Gods (*devayāna*), which leads to Brahman. ***Correct intention*: note how *samyak* is borrowed from the Buddhist formula.

75. *Copious serenity*: *śamaṃ puṣkalam*.

3.5. *Northern course*: when the sun rises progressively farther to the north, from winter to summer solstice. This creation account is a peculiar one. It appears to be based on a cosmogonic myth also reflected in *Chāndogya Up.* 6: the three rubrics are *tejas* (ChUp. = *tejas*), *rasa* (ChUp. = *āpas*), and *osadhiḥ* (ChUp. = *anna*). During winter, spring, and summer the sun with its *tejas* gathers the sky water; with the rainy season it enters (*niviśate*) the earth; in doing so it becomes in harvest the *kṣetra*, the cultivated fields with growing crops. The moon, as Lord of the Herbs, does a kind of repeat of this process: *tejas* into water into herbs.

10. *Offerings of flowers*: a kind of *pūjā* worship.

15. Sūrya, Pūṣan, Arka, Savitar, Ravi, and Gabhastimat are regular names of the sun. Aryaman, Bhaga, and Tvaṣṭar are *ādityas*, and the sun is the Āditya par excellence. **Aja: "unborn, original." ** Kāla, mṛtyu: time and therefore death. **Dhātar: creator. **Prabhākara: "Light-maker." **Pṛthivī–Vāyu: the elements. **Parāyaṇa: "last resort." **Soma–Angāraka: moon, Jupiter, Venus, Mercury, and Mars.

20. Indra: an Āditya. **Vivasvat–Sauri: names of sun and fire. **Śanaiścara: Saturn. **Brahmā–Rudra: the *trimūrti*. **Skanda: the son of fire. **Vaiśravaṇa: Kubera; the connection escapes me. **Yama: death. **Vaidyuta–Vedavāhana: sun as fire. **Kṛta–Kali: the four ages. **Sarvāmarāśraya: "refuge of all Immortals." **Kāla–Ṛtus: time and its measures. **Saṃvatsarakāra: "year-maker." **Vibhāvasu: sun. **Puruṣa–Viśvakarman: creative principles. **Tamonuda: sun. **Varuṇa, Sāgara: water deities. **Aṃśu: "ray." **Jīmūta: "cloud." **Jīvana: "enlivener." **Arihan: "enemy-killer."

25. Bhutāśraya–Sarvabhūtaniṣevita: lord of creatures. **Maṇi: "gem." **Suvarṇa: "gold." ***Bhūtādi*: creator. ***Kāmada and Varada*: granter of wishes. ***Sarvatomukha*: all-seeing. ***Jaya*: "victory." ***Viśāla*: "vast." ***Śīghraga*: "going fast." ***Prāṇadhāraṇa*: "sustainer of life." ***Dhanvantari*: divine physician. ***Dhūmaketu*: epithet of fire. ***Ādideva*: "first God." ***Āditya*: sun. ***Dvādaśātman*: "consisting in twelve [months]." ***Aravindākṣa*: "lotus-eyed." ***Pitar*: "father." ***Mātar*: "mother." ***Pitāmaha*: "grandfather." ***Svargadvārā*: "gate of heaven." ***Prajādvāra*: "gate to offspring." ***Mokṣadvāra*: "gate to release." ***Triviṣṭapa*: "protector of heaven." ***Dehakartar*: "sustainer of the body." ***Praśāntātman*: serene. ***Viśvātman*: "all-soul." ***Viśvatomukha*: all-seeing. ***Carācarātman*: "consisting of all that stands and moves." ***Śūkṣmātman*: "consisting of the subtle." ***Vapuṣānvita*: "endowed with beauty."

4.1. *Rose from the water*: the Ganges; cf. 3.3.10.

5.1. *Threefold goal*: Law, Profit, and Pleasure.

8.10. *Following the king's whim*: i.e., Duryodhana's, who has now in effect become king.

3(30) The Slaying of Kirmira

12.25. *Baka*: 1.145 ff.

30. *Hiḍimba*: 1.139 ff.

35. *The great Asura*: Vātāpi; see below, the story of *Agastya*.

45. *The brothers Vāli and Sugrīva*: *Rāmāyaṇa* 4.12; the "fortune" is the kingship of the monkeys.

55. *Whose temple glands had burst*: i.e., being in a *must* condition, see note to 2.48.15.

65. *Dvaita woods*: but they were heading for the Kāmyaka Forest according to 3.6.1.

3(31) The Mountain Man

13.10. *Puṣkara country*: the sacred site of Puṣkara (Pokkhar, Rajasthan). ***Vast Badarī*: the sacred site of Badrīnāth in the Himālayas. *Viśālā* "vast" is so regular an epithet of Badari that it has become a proper name, e.g., 3.140.10. ***Prabhāsa*: by Dvārakā.

3(31.a) The Razing of Saubha

15. Hell-on-earth: *narakaṃ bhaumam*, here apparently an Asura, "son of *bhūmi*, earth!" In 1.85.4 it is a description of the earth as site of transmigration.

20. *Turāyaṇa sacrifice*: according to *Kātyāyana Śrautasūtra* 24.7.1 a ritual of the *sattra* type. ***The son of Aditi*: i.e., one of the Ādityas. ***As a child*: this is a new element in the

development of the myth of the Three Strides of Viṣṇu, perhaps prefiguring the dwarf in the Vāmana *avatāra*, in which the three strides are reinterpreted.

25. *The Mauravas and the Pāśas*: so? *mauravāḥ pāśāḥ* also translates as "nooses made of *maurvī* fiber," if we take *maurava* for *maurva*, or "nooses of Muru, a demon"; no people called the Pāśa is further known. The context offers no help.

30. *You shall bring to the ocean*: this seems to refer to the migration of Kṛṣṇa's people from Mathurā to Dvārakā.

35. *While still a child*: probably the adventures of Kṛṣṇa's youth that are celebrated in *The Harivaṃśa* and later texts.

50. *Subject to the Law of women*: having her period.

60. *That makes her a wife*: play on *jāyā* "wife" and *jāyate* "he is born"; same statement *Manu* 9.8.

70. *Long ago*: the exile to Vāraṇāvata, 1.129 ff. ***The scoundral had poison dropped*: 1.119.35–40. ***At Pramāṇakoti*: 1.119.30.

75. *He had him bitten*: 1.119.35. ***Dealt his favourite charioteer*: 1.119.38; this repetition brings no clarity to the mysterious incident.

80. *He took the lady*: 1.136.15; note variants.

85. *Hiḍimba*: 1.139 ff.

95. *Heading for Ekacakrā*: 1.144.

100. *Baka*: 1.145 ff. ***Bridegroom Choice*: 1.174 ff.

14.5. *Vīrasena's son*: Nala; for his story see pp. 322 ff.; note how the optative does duty as conditional of the perfect, a usage not noted by Whitney 591 b.

15.1. *Saubha chariot*: which is simultaneously the sky-going city of Saubha.

10. *My brother, King Śiśupāla*: brother figuratively.

15. *To kill the Saubha*: i.e., the king of Saubha = Śālva.

16.1. *Śrautaśrava*: metronymic of Śiśupāla.

5. *Flame-throwers*: *bhuśuṇḍi*; fire seems to be involved with this war machine, cf. Hopkins: "Fire arms in the epic?"

10. *No liquor to be drunk*: the Vṛṣṇis were notorious tosspots.

20. *By well-paid troops*: *bhūridakṣiṇaiḥ*; but the use of *dakṣiṇā* in this context surprises.

17.1. *The four divisions*: foot, horse, chariot, elephant. ***Anthills*: because they might shelter snakes.

18.1. *Bali*: a demon who in the epic is embattled with Indra, but in later texts is killed by Viṣṇu in the dwarf incarnation.

21.5. *The kettledrum*: the war drum of the Vṛṣṇis; see 1.212.10.

22.20. *Like Yayāti tumbling down*: *MBh.* 1(7.c), I:171 ff. ***Like a planet*: the notion is that shooting stars are souls returning to transmigration.

23.40. *Subhadrā and Abhimanyu*: Kṛṣṇa's sister and nephew.

3.31 The Mountain Man (*continued*)

25.15. *Śāla tree*: (*shorea robusta*), a large timber tree with yellow blossoms; I follow hereafter the identification of flora in Appendix 5A of the *Vāmana Purāṇa*, ed. A. S. Gupta (Varanasi, 1968). ***Kadamba*: *anthocephalus indicus*. ***Sarja*: *vateria indica*. ***Arjuna*: *terminalia arjuna*; it derives its name from its small white flowers. ***Cakora*: a bird supposed to live on moonbeams.

20. *Bhogavatī*: according to N. = Sarasvatī. ***Cāraṇas, Siddhas*: semidivine beings.

26.5. *Rāma*: the hero of *The Rāmāyaṇa*.

27.6. *Bhṛgus*, etc.: names of brahmin lineages (*gotras*).

10. *Virocana's Asura son*: same reference in *MBh.* 12. 91.21, without further details.

31.10. *Cake oblations*: the New and Full Moon sacrifices. ***Desiderative*: rites not incumbent but undertaken to gain a specific desire.

15. *The Lotus Ceremony*: the *puṇḍarīka*. ***The Cow Ritual*: *gosava*, which I take as the *gavām-ayana* ritual.

32.1. *Heresy*: *nāstikya*.

35. *All this is*: *sarvam astīti*: "all this" is the orthodox faith (*āstikya*) in the necessity of the acts according to Dharma, and their efficacy in determining the conditions of one's future birth.

33.5. *Resurrection*: *utthāna*: I understand "resurrection" as the reappearance of the act as its fruit, the experiencing of which requires further action.

10. *Fate*: *diṣṭa* or *daiva*: that which has been assigned as a creature's lot by predetermination. ***Chance*: *haṭha*: lit., violence, viz., violent interference in the established pattern. ***Apostate*: *apasada*, lit., socially downward mobile, here used figuratively.

15. *That man's own doing*: *pauruṣam*. ***One's own act*: *svakarma*: *sva* here can hardly be reflexive of the subject, *dhātā*.

20. Here the role of the Placer seems to be that of the mediator between karman "act" and phala "fruit": he assigns man's lot according to his karman. ***The success of houses*: every house is the successful product of one among countless plans and actions.

30. *Chain*: *saṃtatiḥ*.

35. *They are as their worlds are*: what they are is evident from their circumstances. ***Manu*: reference is possibly to *Manu* 12, beginning. ***A rite of reparation*: to remove the obstruction.

40. *We have been rendered useless*: with this Draupadī returns full-circle to her starting point. The dialectic (see also Otto Strauss, "Ethischen Probleme aus dem Mahābhārata," *Giornale della Società Asiatica* 24(1911): 193 ff.) has moved through the following phases: Draupadī accuses Yudhiṣṭhira of being too forgiving (3.28); the limits of forgiveness exemplified (3.29). Yudhiṣṭhira expounds on the superiority of gentleness to anger; he will act with patience (3.30). Draupadī retorts that there is no free action at all: everything is predetermined by the Placer (3.31). Yudhiṣṭhira protests that this militates against the orthodox conception of act and fruit (3.32). Draupadī agrees to the extent that more factors are involved in an act, but that in any case it is imperative to act: Yudhiṣṭhira should do something (3.33).

45. *Godspeed*: *mangalam svasti*.

55. *My father once lodged*: to explain why Draupadī, a woman, should know so much.

34.5. *Bilva*: *aegle marmelos*.

10. *Sṛñjaya*: probably Dhrstadyumna, who in 5.47.37 is seen in the army of the Sṛñjayas, who were part of the Pāñcālas.

35.10. *The Five Rivers*: no doubt originally the Panjab; I conjecture that the expression harks back to early times when that part of India was all of the country of the Aryans, and came to stand figuratively for "the whole world."

15. *You'd have burned my hands*: 2.61.5. ***When we contracted*: viz., for the last game.

37.25. *The God whose companion is Nārāyaṇa*: viz., Nara.

38.15. *For gold coins*: *niṣkaiḥ*.

25. *Indra's Yoga*: *aindreṇa yogena*; this must be Vyāsa's spell, and the expression should perhaps be translated as "the Yoga that would lead to Indra."

39.25. *Pināka*: the name of Śiva's bow.

40.1. *Kāñcana*: lit., "golden," is descriptive of various trees; the comparison means that he was fair-colored.

35. *Who had given him the two quivers*: 1.216.

60. *The Bull-banner*: the bull is Śiva's emblem.

41.5. *Pāśupata*: belonging to Paśupati = Śiva.

42.10. *Airāvata*: Indra's elephant.

45.1. *Remarked by clouds and peacocks*: peacocks dance on hearing thunder.

25. *Destroyed the sons of Sagara*: below, the story of *Agastya*.

46.10. *Satisfied the Fire*: 1.214 ff.

20. *Sthāṇu of the eleven bodies*: because there are eleven Rudras.

47.15. *As Phalguna's charioteer*: there has been no talk of that yet, and there will not be until *MBh*. 5.7.

49. *Madhuparka*: a mixture of milk and honey offered to a guest.

3(32.b) Nala

52.5. *The World Guardians*: minus Kubera, that is.

56.6. *Bull-of-the-Cows*: a gambling term of uncertain meaning.

61.1. *Dhava*: *grislea tomentosa*. ***Tinduka*: *diospyros peregrina*. ***Inguda*: *terminalia catappa*. ***Kiṃśuka*: *butea monosperma*. ***Lodhra*: *symplocos racemosa*. ***Kāśmarī*: *gmelina arborea*. ***Plakṣa*: *ficus infectoria*. ***Udumbara*: *ficus glomerata*. ***Priyāla*: *buchanania latifolia*. ***Kharjūra*: *phoenix silvestris*. ***Haritaka*: *terminalia chebula*. ***Vibhītaka*: *terminalia bellerica*.

15. *King of the forest*: the tiger.

35. *Aśoka*: *saraca indica*. ***Bakula*: *mimusops elengi*. ***Puṃnāga*: *calophyllum inophyllum*.

45. *Vīrasena*: "who has an army of heroes."

85. *You will soon find*: it will take three years.

99. *The king of Dramiḍa*: i.e., of Tamilnad, South India; it is impossible to say what motivates the simile.

63.1. *Entering the center of the fire*: he had received the gift of being invulnerable to fire.

65.10. *Palāśa*: *butea monosperma*. **Love's Lust: Rati, the wife of the God of Love.

20. *Rohiṇī*: the constellation of Aldebaran.

69.10. *All ten curls*: *āvarta* appears to be a technical term; N. takes it as a bad mark, and construes *śuddha* with instrumental: "devoid of."

25. *Śālihotra*: apparently an ancient authority on horses.

70.30. *Kali quickly entered*: dicing was done with *vibhītaka* nuts.

71.10. *Like a eunuch*: i.e., not making undue demands on her?

76.15. *Engaged another charioteer*: for Vārṣṇeya would naturally stay with Nala.

78.1. *Jambūdvīpa*: the southern continent of which India is a part.

79.5. *Citraratha's park*: cf. 1.158.10.

10. *The many-handed Arjuna*: Arjuna Kārtavīrya, who had a thousand arms.

20. *He went north*: viz., at the Conquest of the World, see 2(23 ff.).

80.10. *A vow on behalf of his father*: perhaps in connection with his father Śaṃtanu's love for Satyavatī, cf. 1.94. Bhīṣma was the son of the Ganges. ***Gate of the Ganges*: Hardwār, where the Ganges enters the plains.

40. *Puṣkara*: present-day Pokkhar, Rajasthan. *N.B.* Hereunder *agniṣṭoma* will be translated "Land-of-the-Fire," *atirātra* "Overnight Sacrifice," *aśvamedha* "Horse Sacrifice," *rājasūya* "Royal Consecration," *vājapeya* "Horse Race Festival."

45. *The Grandfather*: there is the only temple in India dedicated to Brahmā.

50. *Kārttika*: October-November; the full moon is then near the Pleiades.

65. *Yayāti's Fall*: when Yayāti was cast out of heaven, 1(7.c), 1. ***Mahākāla*: in *Ujjayinī*; there was a famous Linga of Śiva. ***Bhadravaṭa*: near Ujjayinī.

70. *With Rantideva's leave*: this king made the Carmaṇvatī famous with his sacrifices. ***Arbuda*: Mount Ābū.

75. *Fruit of a thousand cattle*: when donated to brahmins. ***Prabhāsa*: by Dvārakā. ***Sarasvatī*: different from the regular one, which is farther north and runs dry in the desert; this is probably the Sarasvatī that runs into the Rann of Katch. Generally it can be expected that other sacred rivers and sites may borrow their names from the more famous ones.

80. *Seals marked with the stamp*: can these possibly be Indus Valley Civilization seals?

95. *Pañcanada*: the Panjab.

100. *Site of Bhīma*: probably Kapildhārā in Madhya Prades, where there is a footprint of Bhīma and a sanctuary.

105. *Caru oblation*: rice, barley, and pulse boiled in butter and milk and offered to the ancestors.

120. *Where the lotuses hide*: but Puṣkarāḥ may also stand for the sacred site of Puṣkara (often plural). ***Rabbits*: *śaśāyana* means "rabbit run."

130. *Confluence of the Sarasvatī*: still another Sarasvatī.

81.10. *Obtains that very reward*: viz., of ten Horse Sacrifices.

15. *Gaṇapati*: a chieftain of a group of familiars (*gaṇa*) of Siva.

20. *Lakes of Rāma*: see 1.2.

35. *Purity of body*: *kāyaśodhana* means "cleansing the body."

50. *Pull out dog's hairs*: this is the meaning of the name, but it does not explain much. ***Became human*: *mānuṣa* means "human."

65. *Countless gifts and prayers*: the names mean "what gifts" and "what prayers."

70. *Vaitaraṇī*: a river in Orissa.

80. *Dṛṣadvatī*: this must be other than the one in Kurukṣetra, for the Kauśikī is much farther east. ***Grief over his son*: nothing is further known; possibly there is conflation with the story of Vaṣiṣṭha, cf. 1.167. ***World of the sun*: *ahas* means "daytime," *sudina* "good day."

85. *Step of Viṣṇu*: because of the collocation of the dwarf, this must be the step with which Viṣṇu in this incarnation pushed King Bali into the netherworld.

100. *Saptasārasvata*: "[with the sanctity of] seven Sarasvatīs." ***The ascetic was overjoyed*: because he was no longer internally polluted with blood and had attained (no doubt by vegetarianism) the purity of a vegetable.

105. *Snow-white ashes*: which are even purer.

135. *Collected the four oceans*: i.e., the power of the four oceans is present there. ***A thousandfold*: *sahasra* means "a thousand."

145. *No reverses*: *anaraka* means "no hell."

155. *Jujube berries*: *badarī* is the jujube tree. ***Fasts one night*: *ekarātra* means "one-night period."

160. *Āditya*: here specifically "sun." ***An entrance to the Sārasvatas*: apparently a class of brahmins.

170. *Lotus-colored*: the lotus is Brahmā's seat. ***Acquire much gold*: probably we should interpret "acquire [the merit of a gift of] much gold."

175. *South of the Sarasvatī*: perhaps the directions should be reversed, for south of the Dṛṣadvatī and north of the Sarasvatī is the holy Naimiṣa Forest. ***Tarantuka, Arantuka,* and *Macakruka* are the gatekeeping Yakṣas. ***Samantapañcaka*: the area of the five Lakes of Rāma.

82.3. *Plakṣa*: name of a landmark banyan tree. ***Īśānādhyuṣita*: lit., "inhabited by the Lord = Śiva."

10. *Triśūlakhāta*: lit., "dug up with the Trident." ***She subsisted on vegetables*: *śāka* is "vegetable," the root *bhṛ* "to support."

15. *Your mouth shall be the universe*: cf. 3.186.20; it is a popular theme in the Kṛṣṇa story.

25. *Kanakhala*, a mountain range north of Kurukṣetra. ***A thousand ruddy cows*: *kapila* means "ruddy."

30. *Confluence of Ganges and Sarasvatī*: this must be another Sarasvatī, unless the mythical confluence at Prayāga is meant. ***Ṛṣikulya*: probably Ṛṣikeś in the Himālayas.

60. *He shines like the moon*: *vimala* means spotless. ***Rāma*: probably = *Paraśu-Rāma*.

65. *Benares*: the city is dedicated to Śiva.

70. *Gayā*: still an important tīrtha in U.P., especially devoted to ancestor worship; cf. L. P. Vidyarthi, *The Sacred Complex at Gaya* (New York, 1961). ***When the night has dawned*: in other words one should stay overnight.

75. *A ruddy cow*: *dhenu(kā)* means "milch cow."

80. *Who worships the sun*: Savitar is the sun god.

90. *Ahalyā*: she was Gautama's wife.

95. *Vināśana*: where the Sarasvatī vanishes.

105. *Śālagrāma*: "village of the *śāla* trees" on the River Gaṇḍakī.

110. *Recalling former births*: this is the meaning of *jātismara*.

83.1. *The rite of the Grandfather*: *pūjā* to Brahmā.

5. *He shines like the moon*: *viraja* means "dustless."

10. *Mount Mahendra*: in the Eastern Ghāṭs.

20. *Ford of the Maiden*: probably Kanyā Kumārī at Cape Comorin. ***Gokarṇa*: on the coast of Malabar.

25. *Gāyatrī*: *ṚV*. 3.62.10, with which Vedic instruction begins.

35. *Daṇḍaka Forest*: the site of Rāma's exile.

40–45. *Tungaka Forest*: the legend that the *Veda* was revived by Bhṛgu is remarkable.

65. *Cakracara*: lit. "wheel runner," a kind of semidivine being.

80. *Vāsuki*: king of Snakes; Bhogavatī is the Snakes' capital.

105. *King Mahābhiṣa*: he was reborn as Śaṃtanu: 1.91. The following are all names of famous kings and dynasty founders.

84.5. *Overwarriors*: *atiratha*; for their description see 5(57).

85.10. *It is called Prayāga*: *yāga* means sacrifice.

15. *Sadas*: area of the sacrifice where most priests sit.

86.10. *Land of the Pāṇḍyas*: extreme south of India.

87.1. *Priyangu*: *setaria italica*.

5. *Yayāti fell*: *MBh*. 1(7.d), I:195 ff.

10. *Vaikhānasas*: a class of ascetics.

89.10. *Viśvāvasu*: but above it was Citrasena.

90.5. *Dadhīca protected Indra*: Indra's thunderbolt was made from the other's bones.

91.25. *Mārgaśīrṣa*: the month November-December. ***Puṣya*: the constellation and lunar house of γ, δ, ϑ Cancri; it is the sixth nakṣatra.

93.10. *Saw his forebears hang*: the parallel with Jaratkāru is striking, *MBh*. 1(5), 41, I:103 ff.

3(33.a) Agastya

96. *Jarborn sage*: see introduction, p. 187 ff.

10. *Ikṣvāku*: i.e., a descendant of Iksvaku.

97.25. *Idhmavāha*: "firewood fetcher."

98.10. *Sāmans*: chants from the *Sāmaveda*.

99.15. *Fear-stricken Indra*: according to 5.10 ff. because he had violated a compact not to kill Vṛtra.

100.15. *Assuming the form of a boar*: the *varāha avatāra*.
20. *Man-lion*: the *nṛsiṃha avatāra*. ***In the form of a dwarf*: the *vāmana avatāra*.

101.10. *Suffered under Nahuṣa*: who oppressed brahmins; Nahuṣa was temporary king of the Gods when Indra had fled in fear after killing Vṛtra.

103.1. *Vāruṇi*: Agastya, who was the son of Mitra and Varuṇa.

104.2. *Each in a steaming pot*: the parallel with the birth of Dhṛtarāṣṭra's sons is striking (1.107.10 ff.).

106.10. *By their hooves*: *khureṣu*.
30. *He adopted the ocean*: "ocean" is *sāgara*, which can be interpreted as "son of Sagara."

107.5. *Love-their-youngs*: *putrapriyaiḥ*.

109.10. *The Ganges became triple*: flowing in heaven, atmosphere, and on earth.
15. *Adopted the Ganges as his daughter*: hence she is Bhāgīrathī.

3(33.b) Ṛśyaśṛnga

110.10. *A great lake*: but *mahāhrada* may also be a proper name.

111.10. *Parūṣaka*: berries of the grewia asiatica. ***dhanvana*: not identified.
15. *Tilaka*: *wendlandia exerta*.
20. *Cow and its calf*: Indians milked a cow with her calf present.

112.1. *What looked like cups*: necklace with big baubles.

114.5. *Rudra took the animal*: at the sacrifice of Dakṣa when he, though not invited, came to demand his share.
10. *Iṣṭi*: a cake offering.
20. *Rasātala*: a netherworld.

3(33.c) Kārtavirya

115.25. *Your mother's great son*: he will be Viśvāmitra.

116.1. *He wooed Reṇukā*: which may in part explain Rāma's martial nature, for through his mother he was part kṣatriya.
20. *Bear arrows*: so named either because of their shape or because they were used in hunting bear.

117.10. *Khāṇḍava-goers*: *khāṇḍavāyanāḥ*: attempt to etymologize the name (*khāṇḍa* "piece"); the original meaning is not certain, but it appears to be geographical.

118.10. *The altar of Ṛcīka's son*: this must be Rāma's altar described in 3.117.10.

119.15. *The kings of the east*: viz., at the Conquest of the World, 2.26. ***Who defeated the lords*: ib. 2.28. ***Defeated the kings of the West*: ib. 2.29.

120.1. *As Yayāti had in Śaibya*: viz., King Śibi, *MBh.* 1:87 f., 1:205 f.
15. *Aniruddha*: the son of Pradyumna.
20. *Abhimanyu*: Arjuna's son by Subhadrā.

121.5. *Seven rituals*: daily *agnihotra*; Full and New Moon Sacrifice (*darśapūrṇamāsa*), Seasonal Sacrifices (*cāturmāsyas*), Animal Sacrifice (*paśubandha*), Soma Sacrifice (*agniṣṭoma*), Royal Consecration (*rājasūya*), and Horse Race Festival (*vājapeya*).

3(33.d) Sukanyā

122.1. *Vīra posture*: *vīrasthānena*; this appears not to be an *āsana* but a stance; I have not been able to identify it.

124.10. *The Bhārgava drew the cup*: for the ritual of the *āśvina-graha-grahaṇa*, see W. Caland-V. Henry, *L'Agnistoma* (Paris 1906), §137.
15. *Mada*: "intoxication."

125.5. *With the drop*: *indunā*: i.e., with Soma.
10. *All the Puṣkaras*: i.e., all the *tīrthas*.

3(33.e) Māndhātar

126.25. *Me shall he suck*: *māṃ dhātā*.

3(33.f) Jantu

127.20. *When his caul is being offered*: the *vapā* ceremony, an important rite in the animal sacrifice.

129.1. *Iṣṭīkṛta*: not otherwise known; the word means "that which is made an offering."
5. *Śāmī*: *prosopis spicigera*; these seem to be familiar landmarks. ***The piśāca woman*: N. cites several interpretations; the likeliest is that by eating curds at Yugaṃdhara, etc., the brahmin woman had incurred guilt and that the *piśāca* woman is warning her not to stay longer than one night.
10–20. *Sārasvata sacrifices*: N.: with *sārasvata* brahmins.

130.5. *Camasa spring*: *camasodbheda*, where the Sarasvatī emerges again briefly. ***Vipaśā*: cf. 1.167.

3(33.h) Aṣṭāvakra

132.10. *By a sūta defeated*: as panegyrists and chroniclers the *sūtas* had their own tradition of erudition.

133.3. *Aṣṭāvakra said:* here he seems to address the gatekeeper.
5. *The Vedic Sarasvatī*: source of learning. ***One-syllabled*: the syllable *OM*, which sums up the variety of the *Veda*.
22. The year with six seasons, 12 months, 24 *pakṣas*, and 360 days.
23. Lightning and thunderbolt.
24. *Wind-driven one*: fire.

134.8. *Indra and Agni*: they are often mentioned together in the *Veda*, cf. J. Gonda, *Dual Deities* (*Transactions Amsterdam Academy* 1973).
9. *Thrice begotten by rite*: the *garbhādhāna* (conception), *puṃsavana* (son-bearing) and *jātakarman* (birth) rites. ***Three Vedas*: minus the Atharvaveda, which ideally should not be heard. ***Pressings*: there are three at the regular Soma sacrifice; the *adhvaryu* is the executive priest. ***Lights*: sun, moon, and stars.
10. *Stages of life*: *brahmacarya*, householding, forest retirement, and renunciation. ***Four make sacrifice*: the four Vedas or priests, belonging to the four Vedas. ***Cow is four-footed*: cow probably for speech: metrical utterance has four "feet" (*pādas*).
11. *Fires number five*: N.: *gārhapatya, dakṣiṇāgni, āhavanīya, sabhya*, and *āvasathya*. ***pankti*: a meter with five *pādas* of eight syllables. ***Rites*: *agnihotra, darśapūrṇamāsa, cāturmāsya*,

paśubandha, and *agniṣṭoma*. ***Five-tufted*: acc. to N. the Apsarās have five hair-tufts on their heads. ***Five holy rivers*: lit., the holy Panjāb.

12. *Laying-the-fire*: the *agnyādhāna* ceremony. ***Six seasons*: spring, summer, rains, autumn, winter, and dews. ***Senses*: the five and the *manas*. ***Sādyaskas*: name of six *ekāha* (one-day) rites with Soma bought that same day (*sadyas*).

14. *Śāna*: a weight, eight of which make up one *pala*. ***Sarvamedha*: the sacrifice of all possessions.

15. *Nine kindling verses*: the *sāmidhenī* stanzas at the New Moon sacrifice. ***Nine stages*: probably *puruṣa, prakṛti, buddhi, ahaṃkāra*, and the five elements. ***nine figures*: 1 through 9.

16. *Ten are the stages*: so? I presume a double sandhi *daśoktāḥ* for *daśā uktāḥ*; but the *diśas* "points of compass" of variant readings would fit more neatly. ***The irakas*, etc.: viz., the peoples Daśerakas, Daśadāśas, and Daśārnas.

17. *Eleven-day rite*: *ekādaśin*.

18. *A common rite*: any longer rite is a *sattra*.

20. *Ran for thirteen days*: I have no references. ***Aticchandases*: long meters with thirteen or more syllables to the *pāda*.

25. *Rescued the word*: the speech of the defeated brahmins who had fallen silent. ***Has your strength*: I read *śleṣmātakī-kṣīṇa-varcās* "you whose vigor has been drained by a phlegm disorder."

30. *Varuṇa* being the God of the sea.

35. *Ukthya*: for *uktha*, a type of Vedic recitation.

3(33.i) Yavakrīta

136.10. *The other's portent*: viz., the mountain range. ***With buffalo*: their role remains a mystery.

137.1. *The month of Mādhava*: spring.

10. *Who matched the other*: viz., Raibhya's daughter-in-law. ***His water bowl*: which he used to clean himself after evacuating.

3(33) The Tour of the Sacred Fords (*continued*)

140.1. *Suparṇas*: Garuḍas, semidivine birds.

141.25. *When the sun had cleared*: after the rains?

143.10. *The agnihotras*: the sacred fire (carried in a pot) and the utensils.

144.20. *My son Ghaṭotkaca*: Bhīma's son by the Rākṣasī Hiḍimbā: 1.143.

145.5. *By virtue of his own splendor*: in other words, without the help of the Rākṣasa.

10. *Vidhyādharas*: minor semidivine beings, rare in *The Mahābhārata* but popular in narrative literature.

146.5. *Saugandhika flower*: doubtless intended to be a rare if not mythical flower; the name ("redolent") expresses its fragrance. For a similar flower quest motif cf. 1.189.

20. *His father, the chill wind*: Vāyu's parentage seems to be recalled here to intimate Bhīma's coming encounter with Hanūmān, another son of the Wind.

55. *Indra pole*: a pole erected in honor of Indra and decorated like a maypole; cf. *MBh.* 1(6) 57, 1:130 ff.

75. *Humans and men*: the text is similarly pleonastic.

147.10. *Jumped the ocean*: the story in *Rāmāyaṇa* 5.1.

20. *The field of Kesarin*: i.e., Kesarin's wife.

25–30. All events described in *Rāmāyaṇa*, books 3 and 4.

35. *Rāmāyaṇa* 5 and 6.

148.15. *Single Veda*: not yet broken up into four. ***One and the same mantra*: not differentiated according to each Veda and Vedic school.

35. *Which will be shortly at hand*: after the *Mahābhārata* battle.

149.25. *Bṛhaspati and Uśanas*: supposedly authors of textbooks about practical life and politics.

150.15. *Perching on the flagstaff*: Arjuna's emblem is a monkey, which is identified with Hanūmān.

3(34) The Slaying of Jaṭāsura

154.35. *Baka and Hiḍimba*: for the stories see 1 (9) and (10), 1:294 ff.

50. *Vālin and Sugrīva*: rival apes in *Rāmāyaṇa*; for the *MBh.* version see below 3(42.a), p. 727 ff.

3(35) The War of the Yakṣas

155.15. *Vṛṣaparvan*: see introduction, p. 201.

25. *Vidyādharas*: semidivine aerial spirits, rare in the epic but popular in later narrative literature.

40. *Tinduka*: *dispyris peregrina.* ***Ajātaka*: not identified. ***Jīra*: *panicum miliaceum.* ***Likuca*: *artocarpas lacucha.* ***Moca*: *moringa pterygosperma.* ***Kharjūra*: *phoenix sylvestris.* ***pārāvata*: *diospyros embryopteris.* ***Campaka*: *michelia champaca.* ***Bilva*: *aegle marmelos.* ***Kapittha*: *feronia elephantum.* ***Kāśmarī*: *gmelina arborea.* ***Udumbara*: *ficus glomerata.* ***Aśvattha*: *ficus religiosa.* ***Vibhītaka*: *terminalia bellerica.* ***Inguda*: *terminalia catappa.* ***Bakula*: *mimusops elengi.*

45. *Puṃnāga*: *calophyllum inophyllum.* ***Saptaparṇa*: *alstonia scholaris.* ***Karṇikāra*: *erythrine variegata.* ***Kuṭaja*: *wrightia antidysenterica.* ***Śāla*: *shorea robusta.* ***Tamāla*: *garcinia morella.* ***Parijātaka*: *myctanthes arbortristis.* ***Kovidāra*: *bauhinia variegata.* ***Priyāla*: *buchanania latifolia.* ***Śālmalī*: *salmalia malabarica.* ***Kiṃśuka*: *butea monosperma.* ***Cakora*: *genus alectoris.* ***Priyavrata*: not identified. ***Cāṭaka*: *cuculus varius.*

45. *Cakravāka*: *anas casarca.* ***Karaṇḍava*: a kind of duck. ***Plava*: a waterbird. ***Peacocks*: it is a favorite theme of Indian love poetry that peacocks dance frenziedly at the onset of the monsoon.

55. *Sinduvāra*: *vitex negunda.* ***Kurubaka*: not identified. ***Tilaka*: *wendlandia exerta.*

60. *Śarabha*: a fabulous eight-legged inhabitant of the Himalayas.

85. *Kiṃpurusa, kiṃnara*: mythical creatures with human bodies and horse's heads.

156.25. *Naravāhana*: epithet of Kubera, so called because he has a man (*nara*) for his mount (*vāhana*).

157.20. *Khāṇḍava Forest*: for the story see *MBh.* 1(9), 1:412 ff.

50. *Fled to the south*: which is the region of death and demons.

158.15. *Krodhavaśa*: a band of Rākṣasas noted for their fury.

35. *Throne Puṣpaka*: in fact Kubera's chariot, which Rāma had recovered for him, see below 3.275.65, p. 759, *Rāmāyaṇa* 6.116.

159.10. *Alakas*: rare name for Yakṣas, probably deriving from the more common Alakā, the city of Kubera.

20. *Seven principal sacrifices*: probably, *agnihotra, darśapūrṇamāsa, cāturmāsya, agniṣṭoma, rājasūya, aśvemedha, vājapeya*, the principal rituals of the *śrauta* canon. ***Śaṃtanu*: the

reason this venerable king is introduced here must be the fact that Ārṣṭiṣeṇa is Devāpi, Śaṃtanu's brother, who took to the forest, leaving the succession to Hāstinapura to Śaṃtanu, *Bṛhaddevatā* 7.155 ff. Being a saint, Devāpi has survived for four generations.

160. *Sadas*: sacrificial site.

30. *Southern course*: when the sun rises progressively farther south between the summer and winter solstices.

161.5. *Kadamba*: a kind of goose.

162.10. I do not know what to do with cr. ed. *āpyāyata* ("caused to swell"), and read hesitantly *āghrāya tam* from the variants.

163.30. *Sthūṇākarṇa*: "stump-eared." ***Ayojāla*: "net of iron." ***Śaravarṣa*: "rain of arrows." ***Śarolbaṇa*: "fleece of arrows." ***Śaila*: "rocky." ***Aśmavarṣa*: "rain of stone."

164.30. *Nirṛti*: the Goddess of Death.

50. *Lore of the Gandharvas*: music and dance.

165.15. *Warrior gangs*: *yoddhavrātāni vikṛtasvarūpāni*; "with changed natures" probably indicates the special insignia they wore.

167.15. *Mādhava*: an epithet of Kṛṣṇa = Viṣṇu; the reference here is probably reminiscent of the myth that Viṣṇu entered Indra's thunderbolt to slay Vṛtra.

169.00. *Propelled by charms*: *astracodita-*; *astra* has the meaning both of "missile" and "incantation," which are not always easily distinguishable.

170.1. *Paulomas and Kālakeyas*: types of Rākṣasas.

35. *His head surrounded*: I do not know how to take *kṛtaśirsa* and read *vṛta-* instead.

40. *Hunter*: Śarva, a name of Śiva. ***Bhuruṇḍa*: an otherwise unknown animal.

55. *A City of Gandharvas*: idiom for a castle in the sky.

3(36) The Boa

174.5. *Jujube* tree: Badarī.

15. *Mount Yamunā*: possibly a reference to the mountain where the River Yamunā originates.

20. *Rohitaka*: *andersonia rohitaka*. ***Khādira*: *acacia catechu*. ***Śirīsa*: *acacia sirissa*. ***Pīlu*: not identified. ***Śamī*: *prosopis spicigera*.

176.10. *The royal seer Nahuṣa*: while Indra was in hiding because of guilt incurred by killing Vṛtra and Viśvakarman's son, the human Nahuṣa was made king of the Gods; he had himself carried by brahmins and was cursed by Agastya. The full story is found *MBh.* 5.9. ff. ***My benign heir*: I read *dāyādam* for *āyāntam*. ***The great chariot*: *vimāna*, also "palace." ***Capable or incapable*: *abhāvī bhāvī vā*: so?

177.25. *Ye yajāmahe*: the formula introducing the invocation (*yājyā*) that prompts the oblation. ***The sāvitrī formula*: this is not the usual *sāvitrī* (*tat savitur vareṇyam*, etc.), but the verse pronounced at the birth rite, quoted, e.g., *Śāṅkhāyana Gṛhyasūtra* 1.24.4. ***Manu*: the eponym of the *Manusmṛti* (where the verse is not found, however).

30. *No conduct*: viz., no identifiable class conduct.

178.10. The daily and principal rite: *nitye mahati ca*, sc. *karmaṇi*.

15. *Perception, Awareness, and Mind*: in this context the "awareness' (*buddhi*) is a person's consciousness, which has a specific "perception" (*jñāna* "cognition") through the "mind" (*manas*), which coordinates the impressions of the different sense organs.

25. *The Shock* (*utpāta*, elsewhere *kṣobha*) is the primordial contact between soul (*puruṣa*) and germinal matter (*prakṛti*) with which evolution starts so that the soul begins to act upon matter. ***Constituents*: the guṇas, *sattva*, *rajas*, and *tamas*, which determine the nature of all material things.

3(37) The Session with Mārkaṇḍeya

179.5. *Stokaka*: the bird *cāṭaka (cuculus varius)*.

10. *New enclosures*: i.e., boundaries for the now receding waters.

180.15. *The Law of the rustics*: fornication.

30. *Saubha*: for the story see above p. 254.

181.20. *Burn their bridges*: *bhinnasetavaḥ*.

25. *They who lack*: I read *'jñānadṛṣṭibhiḥ*.

183. *Śukra, Bṛhaspati*: here named because they are promulgators of treatises of policy.

184.5. *To the cities of God's city*: I take *puras* as acc. pl.

14. *Śrotriya*: a sacrificial priest. ***Throw the oblation away*: read *parāsiñcati*. ***I say*: *āha*: so?

15. *World of the cows*, apparently the world of the sun (cf. vs. 8) who is the Lord of Cows. **Wisdom of Gods: *prajñāṃ devīm*; vv. 11. *devi* and *daivīm*.

25. *Are worshiped*: *ījire*, middle for passive.

3(37.a) The Fish

186.1. *Four orders*: born alive, from an egg, from a plant, from sweat (insects).

25. *Any food*: not just pure food.

69. *Entire expanse*: I read *sarvam* for *sarve*.

85. *Śrīvatsa curl*: a peculiarly shaped curl of hair on Kṛṣṇa's chest.

187.10. *As Śeṣa*: the cosmic snake, cf. *MBh*. 1.32, 1:92 f. ***The form of a boar*: i.e., the *boar avatār*. ***Mare-headed fire*: the submarine fire. ***Brahmindom is my mouth, etc.*: imagery derived from *RV*. 1.90.

188.30. *Gifts in name only*: not properly performed and acceptable donations.

71. *Drought*: read *nirāvṛṣṭibhiḥ*.

73. *Without charges*: read *ācāryo 'panidhis*.

85. *Tiṣya*: the constellation of *Puṣya* (γ, δ and ϑ Cancri).

189.1. *Establishing, etc.*: as the antelope skins are symbolic of the brahmin and the weapons are symbolic of the baron, this means establishing the predominance of brahmindom and baronage.

5. *Heretical of late*: *sahapāsaṇḍāḥ*: I take it that the hermitages "with their heretics" are now reconverted to orthodoxy.

3(37.b) The Frog

The story in the original is for the most part in prose.

190.20. *Still intact*: *avighāṭitayā*: so?

25. *Atimukta*: *hiptage benghalensis*. ***Covered with a layer of stucco*: my reading of the story is that the king's minister was alarmed by his absorption in the woman, concluded that she was vulnerable to water, camouflaged a pond with stucco, enticed her into the park, and disposed of her.

3(37.c) Indradyumna

191.1. The story is entirely in prose. ***Mayhap*: note this function of *yadi* for *yadi syāt*.

10. *Akūpāra*: we have met with this tortoise earlier in The Churning of the Ocean, *MBh*. 1.16.5 ff., 1:73.

3(37.d) The Story of Dhundhumāra

195.1. *Śrāvasti*: a city well-known to the Buddhists, not far from Kapilavastu.

25. *The sons of Sagara*: for the story see above, p. 424 ff. ***Kumbhakarṇa*: a demon brother of Rāvaṇa in the Rāma story, see below, p. 750 ff.

3(37.e) The Devoted Wife

196.15. *Some hold the mother . . .*: the half-verse is clearly corrupt: cr. ed. *mātaram sāḍṛśīm tāta pitṛn anye ca manyate*, but the Annotations offer no justification or expression of bafflement. I render it according to context, picking up variants from the readings: *śreyasīm* for *sādṛśīm*, *manvate* for *manyate*.

197.25. *The fire of their fury*: I cannot identify the brahmins in question, but the juxtaposition of their cosmic ire and the Daṇḍaka Forest calls to mind the Viśvāmitra of *The Rāmāyaṇa*.

3(37.f) The Colloquy of the Brahmin and the Hunter

198.10. *Where you should not be standing*: the slaughterhouse is, of course, utterly polluting.

25. *Janaka here*: Janaka was a legendary learned king, ruling the land of Videha from his capital Mithilā: he has also been made the father of Sītā of *The Rāmāyaṇa*.

30. *I don't kill*: a curious, self-serving assertion, since the whole point of this colloquy appears to be that the cream of society, the brahmin, is lectured by the dregs, the hunter. The hunter is clearly being brahminized. ***A law-type person*: *dhārmikaḥ*.

35. *Stunted*: so? Cr. ed. *uruṇḍa*, with many variants.

45. *Not too clean*: read *mṛjāhīnāḥ*.

50. *Covers up the holes*: note this meaning for *vivṛṇoti*.

85. *Nonviolence . . . serenity*: the śloka is elliptic; supply: are the marks of the strict.

199.5. *King Śibi*: for his story see above, p. 470 ff. ***Rantideva*: a famous sacrificer of bloody offerings.

10. *Saudāsa*: for his story see *MBh*. 1.166 ff., 1:333 ff.

200.25. *Return to the Five*: sc. the five elements.

201.15. *Each in the series . . .*: a rather opaque way of saying that of the five elements ether has one quality (sound), wind two (that and touch), fire three (those and shape), water four (those and taste), earth five (those and smell).

20. *The Twenty-fourth*: borrowed from a different series: five elements, five properties, five senses, five bodily functions, mind, ego, *buddhi*, and soul.

202.10. *To be known as the Mark*: *lingagrāhyam*, i.e., the *linga* body, constituted by the higher mental faculties, breath and soul, which transmigrates.

15. *Ultimately rooted in knowledge*: in the sense that the "hindrance" (*kleśa*) is about the knowledge that it veils. ***Man is without . . .*: note the meaning of *jantu* here.

20. *Six constants*: the senses and mind.

203.15. Note that the five vital airs (*prāṇas*) are here considered the product of the interaction between the elements of fire and earth (= body). ***Samāna*: the vital air that distributes ingested matter over the entire body.

25. *The soul on the head*: the soul upon release escapes through the cranium.

30. *Knower-of-the-field*: *kṣetrajña*, i.e., the soul when embodied.

35. *Soul separate from himself*: *dṛṣṭvātmānaṃ nirātmānam*: *ātman* in *nirātman* in the sense of the phenomenal self.

3(37.g) Angiras

209.10. *The Fire Hymn*: it is impossible to make out which of the many hymns in the *Ṛgveda* is meant. ***Niścyavana*: "not falling." ***Vipāpa*: "without evil." ***Niṣkṛti*: "restoration."

15. *Svana*: "groan." ***Viśvajit*: "all-conquering."

20. *Upward-sharing*: *ūrdhvabhāj*; possibly because it rises from the bottom of the sea to burn its prey. ***Sviṣṭakṛt*: "making well-offered." ***Manyāti*: here associated with *manyu* "fury." ***Kāma*: "lust, love." ***Uktha*: a series of recitations; the first Uktha stands for *ukthya* oblation.

210.1. *Great utterances*: *mahāvyāhṛti*, invocations with *OṂ*, *bhūḥ*, *bhuvaḥ*, *svaḥ*. *mahaḥ*.

5. *Bṛhat, rathantara*: important sāmans from the *Sāmaveda*.

15. *Adhvaryu*: principal priest of the *Yajurveda*. ***Mitravinda*: "friend-finding" fire.

211. *The worship of Śiva*: it is at least remarkable to find Śiva and Śakti here collocated.

10. *Āgrayaṇa*: first-fruit offering. ***Niragraha*: "not failing to seize."

20. *Kapila*: he is indeed held to be the legendary founder of Sāṃkhya.

212. *Gṛhapati*: apparently the *gārhapatya* fire, the householder's fire in which the offerings are cooked.

5. *Atharvan*: = Angiras. **The fish reported on him: the story is from *Taittirīya Saṃhitā* 2.6.6.

20. *The Five Rivers*: namely those of the Panjāb.

213.1. *Kārtikeya*: I follow the spelling of the cr. ed.; the more correct form is *Kārttikeya*.

5. *Keśin*: "long-haired one," also a name of Śiva.

15. *Devasenā*: lit. "army of the Gods," *Daityasenā*: "army of the Daityas."

20. *Dākṣāyaṇī*: daughter of Dakṣa, here = Aditi, Indra's mother. ***Sister*: Diti, the mother of the Daityas?

25. *The hour of Rudra*: the first hour of the day. ***Oblations that had been offered*: viz., by the six seers of 3.210.1, cf. below, vs. 35.

40. *Āhavanīya*: the offering fire.

214.5. *The mothers*: the wives of the other seers.

10. *Reedstalks*: hence Kumāra is also known as born from a reed bed. ***Terrifying bands of ghosts*: *raudrair bhūtaganaiḥ*, also: Rudra's bands of ghosts.

15. *Skanda*: "spilling."

25. *Companions*: *pāriṣada*.

35. *On the fifth day*: because, acc. to vs. 15 ff., he had been complete in four days.

215.15. *Let all the Mothers attack*: viz., the demonesses that visit diseases on children.

20. *A goat-faced trader*: so? *Naigameyaś chāgavaktraḥ*.

216.1. *Airāvata*: Indra's elephant.

10. *Viśākha*: here etymologized from root *viś* "to enter"; the more likely meaning is "branched off."

218.5. *Born in six nights*: i.e., conceived in six.

25. *The Kṛttikās*: this is the first mention of the "Pleiades" (into which the six seers' wives are turned, see below); in fact, Svāhā placed the seed, vicariously prompted by the women, on Mount Śveta.

30. *The cock*: later the peacock in his emblem.

45. *The Sixth*: *ṣaṣṭhī*, which gave its name to Devasenā as Ṣaṣṭhī.

219.00. *The Goddess Abhijit*, etc.: the stellar picture is confusing but this is my reading of it. Abhijit, officially the star of the twentieth nakṣatra, is jealous of Rohiṇī, who was the star of the first nakṣatra. Abhijit performs austerities so that she may precede Rohiṇī as the first nakṣatra. Her exercise apparently was successful and created a vacancy in the series before Rohiṇī, which the Kṛttikās now occupy. But somehow Abhijit came back for she is still number twenty. I am not clear where Dhaniṣṭha comes in, the twenty-second nakṣatra. What this account of the nakṣastras does suggest is the memory of changes or additions made in the nakṣatra series.

10. *Vinatā*: the mother of Garuḍa, in whose guise Svāhā took the seed to Mount Śveta.

15. *Fabricated as the mothers*: i.e., the real natural mothers of their children. ***Progeny given away*: already given to others, the real mothers.

25. *Grasper*: i.e., a disease. ***Karañja*: *pomgania glaxbra.*

35. *Eighteen Graspers*: i.e., the nine "Mothers" and their diseases. ***Kadrū*: mother of the snakes.

45. *After an obeisance to Maheśvara* (= Śiva): i.e., in order to ward off the evil present in the account.

220.10. *Umā*: the wife of Rudra, now and ever since associated with Skanda's birth. ***Arka*: *calotropis gigantea.*

20. *Saṃtānaka*: the "spreading tree" in celestial flora. ***Karavīra*: *nerium indicum.* ***Japā*: Chinese rose tree.

221.1. *Bhadravaṭa*: ancient site of worship of Śiva as Paśupati, close to Ujjayinī. ***Pārvatī*: daughter of the mountain: first appearance of the name in the *MBh.*

10. *The gourd*: *kamaṇḍalu*, the begging bowl of Śiva in his mendicant form.

3(38) The Colloquy of Draupadī and Satyabhāmā

222.24. *I talk directly*: *atiraskṛtasaṃbhāṣā*: not via messengers.

40. *Eight thousand brahmins*, etc.: see above, p. 113.

50. *An ocean even Varuṇa could not manage*: the ocean is the source of treasures and Varuṇa is its king.

223.3. *Steady repute*: read *'viṣamā.*

3(39) The Cattle Expedition

226.1. *The eastern, etc., kings*: in other words, Duryodhana has taken over the Pāṇḍavas' conquests.

228.15. *Mistrust*: read *'viśrambhād.*

229.1. *Sadyaska sacrifice*: a one-day rite.

331.5. It is not clear what part of the chariot *triveṇu* (lit. three bamboos) describes.

10. *Priyadarśana*: lit. "of pleasing aspect," a royal title, also used by King Aśoka.

232.5. *Invincible Bhīma*: I read *aparājita.*

234.5. *Āgneya*: "fire-making."

15. *Sthūṇākarṇa*: lit. "stump-eared," as said of a cow; I cannot guess its function as weapon. ***Indrajāla*: "Indra's net." ***Saura*: "solar." ***Saumya*: "lunar."

234.25. *Of mean strength*: so? *Durbala*, usually "feeble."

236.5. *Karṇa came*: Karṇa had fled before Duryodhana's capture.

237.7. *Lest . . . be violated*: *parāmarśo mā bhaviṣyat*: note this use of the injunctive conditional.

239.20. *Kṛtyā*: lit. "magic."

241.25. *The greatest of sacrifices cannot be performed in your family*: this shows that the entire family is affected by the Royal Consecration of one of them.

30. *You must plow the ground*: as it happens in the *agnicayana* ritual. ***Vaiṣṇava*: Viṣṇu's, which may mean any ritual, since Viṣṇu is consistently identified with the sacrifice.

3(41) The Measure of Rice

245.30. *A measure of rice*: lit. *droṇa* "jar," a measure of about fifty pounds.

246.5. *Iṣṭīkṛta*: probably the *iṣṭi*, a cake oblation.

247.45. *Like spokes around an axle*: text *nemim*, which, however, means "wheel rim." My guess is a contamination between two similes: "like spokes stick to the rim," and "like spokes revolving around the axle."

3(42) The Abduction of Draupadī

249.5. *At home in the mountains*: the Kuṇindas were aborigines.

251.10. *Ruru, śambara*: kinds of deer, not further identified.

252.1. *Snorted*: read *visphūrjya*.
10. *Six virtues*: according to Nīlakaṇṭha: heroism, splendor, poise, dexterity, liberality, lordship, which are the "beautiful virtues" ascribed to Viṣṇu and their appropriateness here may be questioned.

253. *The lord of my life*: here is soul = heart.

255.25. *Handled*: so? *Talayukta*: possible "fitting his palm."
35. *There is no meat in this*: clearly a hunter's idiom.
40. *Duḥsālā*: the daughter of Dhṛtarāṣṭra, whom Jayadratha either had married or was about to marry.

3(42.a) Rāma

In order to allow the reader more easy comparisons between *The Story of Rāma* and *The Rāmāyaṇa*, I will depart from the usual style of the annotations and enter the correspondences at the foot of the page. References are to the Baroda edition; of the two figures given the first refers to the *kāṇḍa*, the second to the *adhyāya*.

259.40. *Called Rāvaṇa*: derived here from the root *ru*.

260.5. *On bears*: while mention is made on occasion of bears (*ṛkṣa*) the classification of monkeys is so preponderant that one might wonder whether these "bears" are not really a kind of monkey.

264.40. *One had two eyes*, etc.: this description also functions as proper name.
50. *A Rākṣasī named Trijaṭā*: lit. "with three hair-tufts."

265.20. *Who enjoy your pleasures*: if we read *bhadrasukha*; the variant *bhadramukha* "good friend" is much more likely.

266.45. *Long-seen*: *cīradṛṣṭa*: I do not know what this means here.

267.5. *Thirty-five*: *triṃśatpañca*: or "thirty, and five."
35. *Divine spells*: here *astra* clearly means "spell."

268.20. *With broken hearts*: read *saṃbhinnahṛdayāh*.
40. *Rāma had the upper hand*: *jayottaraḥ*.

271.15. *Presented as boons*: *dattavaraiḥ* for *varadattaiḥ*.

3(42.b) Sāvitrī

277.5. *Sāvitrī formula*: *RV.* 3.62.10 *tat savitur vareṇyaṃ bhargo devasya dhīmahi/dhiyo yo naḥ pracodayāt*, "We desire that covetable gift of the God Savitar, who must impel our thoughts," a famous verse.

15. *Make no reply*: the king might well be disappointed with the gift of just one child, and a daughter to boot.

20. *Mālava*: a region in northern India, presently Mālwā.

35. "*A father who*, etc.": cf. *Manusmṛti* 9.4.

278.15. *Set out to the south*: the region of death.

20. *The seven steps*: symbolic of the entire length of life's journey. ***I don't want a second*: viz., because the example of the conduct of one person, if approved by the strict, is a sufficient model.

40. *The creatures please*: I think *rañjitāḥ* has to be taken as active in meaning.

3(43) The Robbing of the Earrings

284.1. "*When the left-handed archer . . .*": cf. above, p. 404.

285.10. *Two stars of Viśākhā*: α and β Librae.

286.5. *I obtained from Jāmadagnya*: but via Droṇa, cf. *MBh.* 1.122.25 f., 1:269.

287.1. *A certain brahmin*: the account of 1.104 calls him Durvāsas: 1:240 f.

15. *Vātāpi*: see above, p. 412 ff.

288.5. *On Sukanyā's account*: see above, p. 457 ff.

289.20. *Atharvaśiras*: the name of an Upaniṣad.

290.20. *Their proper spheres*: lit. "hearths" (*dhiṣṇya*).

291.1. *Root kan*: "to enjoy"; according to this etymology *kanyā* would mean "an enjoyable woman."

3(44) The Drilling Woods

295.5. *Drilling wood*: fire for rites was drilled out of a log of soft wood with a hardwood stick.

296.1. *The usher*: see above, p. 141 ff.

40. *Ketaka*: *pandanus odoratissimus.* ***Vaṭa*: *ficus religiosus.*

298.5. *The five*: according to Nīlakaṇṭha the five qualities of the soul prerequisite for release. ***Six states*: Nīlakaṇṭha: hunger, thirst, grief, folly, fear, and death.

Concordance of Critical Edition and Bombay Edition

A complete Concordance of the critical edition and the Bombay edition of *The Mahābhārata* is found in vol. I, pp. 475–78. For the reader's convenience a partial concordance is entered hereunder of the critical and Bombay editions of *The Book of the Assembly Hall* and *The Book of the Forest.*

The concordance is of the chapters only. It is based on the marginal references marked B in the critical edition, and has been cross-checked with the *Concordanz* in Jacobi (1903). Since its purpose is principally to facilitate comparison with Sörensen, the "Roy" and Dutt translations, and other reference books that quote chapters by their number in B., the verse numbers of the Calcutta edition have not been collated: these numbers and their concordance with the verse numbers of the critical edition are only retrievable from the marginal figures marked C. in the critical edition, and, mostly, from the C. figures in my summaries.

Be it noted that the concordance, where it shows deletions [indicated by ( ), e.g., (22)], only shows deletions of chapters; it does not show the very numerous deletions of verses. For information on verse deletions the only recourse is the *apparatus* of the critical edition.

Critical Edition	Bombay
2. 1–10	1–10
11	11–12
12–16	13–17
17	18–19
18–22	20–24
23	25–26
24–42	27–45
	(46)
43–49	47–53
50	54–55

Critical Edition	Bombay
51	56–57
52	58
53	59–60
54–61	61–68
62	69–70
63–65	71–73
66	74–75
67–72	76–81
3. 1–3	1–3
4–44	3–43
45	44 (..)
	(45–46)
45	47
46	48–49
47–65	50–68
66–67	69
68–73	70–75
74–75	76
76–79	77–80
80	81–82
81–104	83–106
105–6	107
107–8	108–9
109–10	110
111–46	111–46
147	147–48
148–49	149–50
150	151–52

Critical Edition	Bombay
151–52	153–54
153	155
	(156)
154–60	157–63
161	164–65
162–63	166–67
164–65	168
166–79	169–82
180–81	183
182–89	184–91
190	192 (..)
	(193–98)
191	199 (..)
	(200)
192–202	201–11
203	212–13
204	214–22
213	223–24
214–19	225–30
220–21	231
	(232)
222–37	233–48
238	249–50
239–40	251–52
241	253–55
242–47	256–61
	(262–63)
248–299	264–315

*Index of Proper Names**

*Only the proper names occurring in the text of the translation are indexed; those occurring in the introductions, summaries, and notes are not.